Praise for *.NET Compact Framework Programming with C#*

"For nearly two decades, Paul Yao and David Durant have been acknowledged as experts on the Windows platform, so it's only natural that they would bring their experienced point of view to the .NET Compact Framework. With a unique combination of historical perspective and in-depth understanding of the subject matter, Yao and Durant take the reader through not only the technical guts of the Compact Framework but also the reasons behind the design decisions."

—*Joshua Trupin, Executive Editor,* MSDN Magazine

"Yao and Durant have written a book that, although it assumes no prior experience with the .NET Framework, serves both the rookie and advanced programmer equally well. This is definitely a rare quality among technical books and is certainly not an easy thing for an author to accomplish."

—*Doug Holland, Precision Objects*

"This is a very good hands-on book with plenty of sample code illustrating programming tasks and techniques, which any serious development effort for Windows CE or Pocket PC will require."

—*Bill Draper, Director of Software Development*

"This book serves as both a great reference and tutorial when building .NET Compact Framework applications. My only wish is that it had been available sooner."

—*Greg Hack, Senior Software Engineer, Allscripts Healthcare Solutions*

"Of the handful of books on Compact Framework, this book takes the cake. Paul Yao and David Durant's expertise with .NET Compact Framework is evident from their excellent and very insightful coverage of sections such as Building the User Interface, Managing Device Data, and Creating Graphical Output. The chapter discussing the topic of P/Invoke is unparalleled. After reviewing this book, I am certain that if there is one book that will help you understand .NET Compact Framework, this is the one."

—*Deepak Sharma, Senior Systems Specialist, Tata Infotech Ltd.*

"Yao and Durant's fresh, innovative, and in-depth look at the .NET Compact Framework gets developers up to speed using C# to develop robust and scaleable handheld software solutions. A definite must-read for mobile handheld developer enthusiasts!"

—*Andrew Krowczyk, Software Architect, Zurich North America*

.NET Compact Framework Programming with C#

Microsoft .NET Development Series

John Montgomery, *Series Advisor*
Don Box, *Series Advisor*
Martin Heller, *Series Editor*

The **Microsoft .NET Development Series** is supported and developed by the leaders and experts of Microsoft development technologies including Microsoft architects and DevelopMentor instructors. The books in this series provide a core resource of information and understanding every developer needs in order to write effective applications and managed code. Learn from the leaders how to maximize your use of the .NET Framework and its programming languages.

Titles in the Series

Brad Abrams, *.NET Framework Standard Library Annotated Reference Volume 1*, 0-321-15489-4

Keith Ballinger, *.NET Web Services: Architecture and Implementation*, 0-321-11359-4

Bob Beauchemin, Niels Berglund, Dan Sullivan, *A First Look at SQL Server 2005 for Developers*, 0-321-18059-3

Don Box with Chris Sells, *Essential .NET, Volume 1: The Common Language Runtime*, 0-201-73411-7

Mahesh Chand, *Graphics Programming with GDI+*, 0-321-16077-0

Anders Hejlsberg, Scott Wiltamuth, Peter Golde, *The C# Programming Language*, 0-321-15491-6

Alex Homer, Dave Sussman, Mark Fussell, *A First Look at ADO.NET and System.Xml v. 2.0*, 0-321-22839-1

Alex Homer, Dave Sussman, Rob Howard, *A First Look at ASP.NET v. 2.0*, 0-321-22896-0

James S. Miller and Susann Ragsdale, *The Common Language Infrastructure Annotated Standard*, 0-321-15493-2

Fritz Onion, *Essential ASP.NET with Examples in C#*, 0-201-76040-1

Fritz Onion, *Essential ASP.NET with Examples in Visual Basic .NET*, 0-201-76039-8

Ted Pattison and Dr. Joe Hummel, *Building Applications and Components with Visual Basic .NET*, 0-201-73495-8

Chris Sells, *Windows Forms Programming in C#*, 0-321-11620-8

Chris Sells and Justin Gehtland, *Windows Forms Programming in Visual Basic .NET*, 0-321-12519-3

Paul Vick, *The Visual Basic .NET Programming Language*, 0-321-16951-4

Damien Watkins, Mark Hammond, Brad Abrams, *Programming in the .NET Environment*, 0-201-77018-0

Shawn Wildermuth, *Pragmatic ADO.NET: Data Access for the Internet World*, 0-201-74568-2

Paul Yao and David Durant, *.NET Compact Framework Programming with C#*, 0-321-17403-8

Paul Yao and David Durant, *.NET Compact Framework Programming with Visual Basic .NET*, 0-321-17404-6

For more information go to www.awprofessional.com/msdotnetseries/

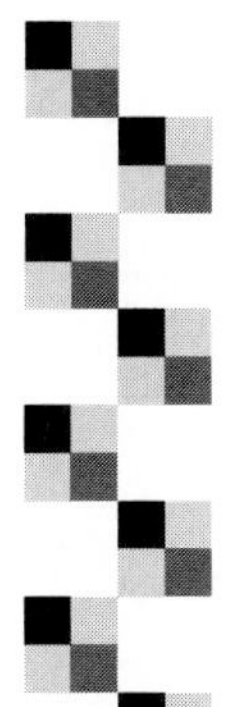

.NET Compact Framework Programming with C#

Paul Yao

David Durant

Addison-Wesley

Boston • San Francisco • New York • Toronto • Montreal
London • Munich • Paris • Madrid
Capetown • Sydney • Tokyo • Singapore • Mexico City

The publisher offers discounts on this book when ordered in quantity for bulk purchases and special sales. For more information, please contact:

U.S. Corporate and Government Sales
(800) 382-3419
corpsales@pearsontechgroup.com

For sales outside of the U.S., please contact:

International Sales
international@pearsoned.com

Visit Addison-Wesley on the Web:
www.awprofessional.com

Library of Congress Cataloging-in-Publication Data

Yao, Paul.
.NET compact framework programming with C# / Paul Yao, David Durant.
p. cm.—(Microsoft .NET development series)
Includes index.
ISBN 0-321-17403-8 (alk. paper)
1. C# (Computer program language) 2. Microsoft .NET Framework. I. Durant, David. II. Title. III. Series.

QA76.73.C154Y36 2004
005.13'3—dc22

2004002429

Pearson Education, Inc.
Rights and Contracts Department
75 Arlington Street, Suite 300
Boston, MA 02116
Fax: (617) 848-7047

Text printed on recycled and acid-free paper.

ISBN 0321174038
3 4 5 6 7 8 CRW 08 07 06
3rd Printing March 2006

For Rebecca: my wife, my partner, my best friend
— Paul

To John and Ruth Durant, whose love and courage
were an inspiration to their children
— David

Contents

Foreword

WELCOME, FUTURE SMART-DEVICE developer! Today we embark on an exciting journey. For the first time, mobile devices are impacting the lives of users in profound ways. Mobile devices have become an everyday ingredient in the lives of millions of people around the world, whether they are mobile employees working from the field or casual consumers playing the latest and greatest games. For example, my Pocket PC Phone Edition has more memory and processing power than the high-end PC I bought for a premium not even five years ago. I use my mobile device for everything from handling e-mail and browsing the Web to playing games, music, and videos. In many ways, it has replaced the heavy laptop I once lugged from meeting to meeting.

At the same time, the innovation in this space has driven the need for custom software development. With newer and more powerful devices comes the need for newer and more powerful software development tools. Driving this phenomenon—as always—is you, the software developer. To assist you, Microsoft is providing Visual Studio .NET and the .NET Compact Framework, the most capable development and runtime environments available, to enable you to make the most of opportunities with your customers, including mobile employees, casual consumers, and even the most uncompromisingly rabid device enthusiasts (our authors).

So why has mobile development become so important all of a sudden? Well, as any veteran developer can tell you, mobile development has been around for a long time. In fact, they often reminisce about the good old days of developing with eMbedded Visual Basic. (Hey, six months is a long time in the software industry!) The truth is that for the first time, several driving factors in the technology ecosystem have aligned to provide the solid foundation mobile-device developers need to gain true opportunities in the consumer and enterprise markets.

The first and most obvious factor driving this phenomenon is the introduction of Visual Studio .NET 2003 and the .NET Compact Framework. Combined, these tools provide a development powerhouse that enables you as a developer to take advantage of programming languages and skills you already know and use for developing desktop applications, including a rich subset of class libraries and the same secure, managed environment. You'll learn more about this in Part I, Foundations.

The next major factor is the Microprocessor Effect (also known as Moore's Law), which describes the regular doubling of the number of circuits in microprocessors. At present, circuit doubling occurs about every 18 months. In reality, the adoption of more processing power for mobile devices has exceeded the growth suggested by Moore's Law. But it hasn't been only increases in processing power that have exceeded predictions—increases in the capacity of other necessary components, such as memory and peripheral capabilities, have occurred as well.

The continued improvements in hardware capabilities coupled with the continued decrease in hardware costs have created an environment that has allowed for the proliferation of different types of mobile and embedded devices. Today, the .NET Compact Framework supports software development on the various generations of the Pocket PC, the Pocket PC Phone Edition, and the Microsoft Smartphone. It also provides great support for Windows CE–powered smart devices that run Windows CE .NET 4.1 and later.

All of this provides a great environment for developers to make the most of client-side development. You'll be able to rapidly design applications using the plethora of controls native to the .NET Compact Framework and create new controls, as you will learn about in Part II, Building the User Interface. The growth in device capacity means that mobile devices can have enough local storage to collect significant volumes of data, even when disconnected—a subject covered in this book in Part III,

Managing Device Data. The added horsepower also supports your ability to build stunning graphics, a topic that Paul and Dave address in Part IV, Creating Graphical Output.

Let us not forget, the .NET Compact Framework has native support for consuming Web Services, the industry standard for integrating applications across any platform. Through the detailed and extensive samples and discussions in this book, you will soon be an expert in building the most reliable, effective, data-driven, graphical applications; employing part-time and full-time connectivity; and using a variety of data storage solutions including SQL Server Windows CE Edition as well as integration with virtually any data source on the server.

Whether you are a seasoned Windows CE programmer, a developer familiar with using Visual Studio .NET and the .NET Framework, or someone totally new to both mobile development and .NET programming, this is the only book you will need. Whatever your background, this book provides the technical insights and coding samples you need to transfer your existing skills to the .NET Compact Framework.

This is truly an exciting time to be part of the mobile development industry. I would like to be among the first to welcome and congratulate you on joining the community of .NET mobile developers.

Happy coding!

Ed Kaim
Product Manager
Windows Developer Platform
Microsoft Corporation

Preface

WE FEEL PRETTY fortunate. During the past two decades, we have traveled the world teaching programmers what we know. The two of us have led many classes and together have taught thousands of smart, highly motivated software engineers, test engineers, and development managers. We enjoy working with the people who are inventing the future, and we enjoy being at the cutting edge of each successive wave of software development technology. We have learned much from the discussions we have had with these students. This book represents one way we can thank them for all their support.

We worked together on the first book published on the subject of Windows programming, *Programmer's Guide to Windows* (Sybex, 1987). Long out of print, in its day the book helped many programmers tackle the challenges presented by Windows version 1.01. That version of Windows came out in November 1985, and in those days developers typically worked on computers running MS-DOS with no hard drive, no network support, and no network servers to rely on.

Things have changed a lot during the 17 years since our first book came out. A pocket-sized computer now has more memory and CPU power than the typical desktop system of the 1980s. A typical desktop system has more raw computing power than a roomful of computers had back then. With this increase in capacity has come a dramatically improved set of development tools available to software developers: Online programming references, context-sensitive help, and graphical editors all help support the task of software development. Programmers can be more productive today thanks to all these tools.

With this increase in computing power and tool support has also come an increase in the complexity of programming interfaces. While the .NET initiative provides a new set of programming interfaces that are better organized than any other Microsoft has created, it is still very large and very intricate. Given enough time, most programmers can master these intricacies. But most programmers do not have enough time to learn about a new technology while also building new software, yet that is what their employers require of them.

Our primary mission is to support you, the software engineer, in saving time. In this book, we distill many years of research and sample code to give you the information you need in a way you can use. We do the same thing in our training classes, in our magazine articles, and in the talks we give at conferences. We concentrate our efforts on helping software engineers become more productive. Time saved in learning about software development issues can be focused on meeting the specific needs of the end users whom you are supporting (or, perhaps, on taking some time off between projects to recharge your mental and physical batteries).

What You Need to Use This Book

To make the most of what this book has to offer, you are going to need a few things, as described in the following subsections.

Hardware

Software developers have historically had the fastest and most capable computer systems they could get their hands on. Developing for smart devices like the Pocket PC and the Smartphone is no different. To get started, we recommend you have the following:

- Desktop system compatible with Microsoft Windows 2000 or Windows XP
- Minimum 128MB RAM (256MB recommended)

- Minimum 4GB hard drive (10GB recommended)
- Windows CE–powered device (Pocket PC, Pocket PC 2002, Pocket PC 2003, Smartphone 2003, or other Windows CE–powered device)

Strictly speaking, you do not need a Windows CE device because you can run your software on an emulator that runs on your development system. You will, however, eventually want to test your software on real devices, the same ones you expect your users to use. The emulator technology is very good—more than good, in fact. Today's emulators provide an excellent replication of the software on a device.[1] But the hardware and associated device drivers are not going to be the same on an actual device as on an emulator running on a PC. This is the major cause of differences between an emulator and an actual device. When we teach our Pocket PC programming classes, we always recommend to participants that a major portion of testing be done on devices.

While the focus of this book is on writing code, the reality of software development is that you spend a lot of time debugging your code. For that reason, you want to remove anything that slows down your debugging. We suggest you invest in a network connection between your development system and your smart-device system, which means you need the following:

- Network card (wired or wireless) for the desktop development system
- Network card (wired or wireless) for the Windows CE–powered device

1. Historically, not all emulators have provided high fidelity to device software. In particular, Windows CE 1.x and 2.x emulators were based on an older technology that was good but not great. The last emulator to use this older technology was the Pocket PC emulator that shipped with Microsoft eMbedded Visual C++ 3.0. All emulators for Visual Studio .NET 2003 use the newer emulation technology.

Software

The development tools can run on any supported version of Microsoft Windows. However, an emulator requires that you run on a 32-bit version of the operating system. This means you want one of the following:

- Microsoft Windows 2000 (with Service Pack 2 or later)
- Microsoft Windows XP Professional
- Microsoft Windows Server 2003

With the right operating system in place, you can then use the software development tools. The first item in the following list is required; the other items are "nice-to-have" tools.

- Microsoft Visual Studio .NET 2003 (required).
- (Optional) Microsoft eMbedded Visual C++ 3.0 (for Pocket PC and Pocket PC 2002).
- Microsoft eMbedded Visual C++ 4.0 (for Pocket PC 2003, Smartphone 2003, and later).
- P/Invoke Wizard, available from The Paul Yao Company, for help in creating declarations needed to call native code from the .NET Compact Framework. (Learn more about this tool and download a demo version from http://www.paulyao.com/pinvoke.)

The Latest Version of the .NET Compact Framework

As we were finishing this book, Microsoft made available Service Pack 2 of the .NET Compact Framework. Should you upgrade to this latest version (or whatever later version might be available by the time you read this)? We must say yes! This is a new technology, and the .NET Compact Framework team is still working on improvements and upgrades to make the library work better and faster. After shipping a new library, the .NET Compact Framework team members—like most development team members at Microsoft—take a weekend or two off, and then their reward for their hard work is that they get to start all over again, working to create something even better. It's a good thing that they like what they are doing—and that they are so good at it.

The Sample Code

You can download the code for this book from the following URL: http://www.paulyao.com/cfbook/code.

When you install the sample code directory tree from the Web site, you see four top-level directories.

- `..\CS` contains all the C# samples.
- `..\VB` contains all the Visual Basic .NET samples.
- `..\CPP` contains C/C++ samples.
- `..\Tools` contains binaries of useful tools.

Each of the .NET Compact Framework samples is available in two languages: C# and Visual Basic .NET. Some samples are written in C++, using the Windows API (also known as Win32).

Within the three samples directories (`..\CS`, `..\VB`, and `..\CPP`) you find a directory for each chapter. Within each chapter directory you find another set of directories for all the samples in that directory.

For example, one of the samples in Chapter 5 is named `FormEvents`. The C# version is at this location: `..\CS\Ch05_CreatingForms\FormEvents`. The Visual Basic .NET version is at this location: `..\VB\Ch05_CreatingForms\FormEvents`.

The Target Audience for This Book

We wrote this book to help programmers with the .NET Compact Framework. We assumed that no prior programming experience with Windows 95/98/2000/XP, with Windows CE, or with .NET was required. At the same time, if you have experience with programming for Windows on the desktop, with Windows CE, or with the .NET Framework, that experience will help you.

For Programmers Experienced with Windows CE

If you already have experience writing Windows CE programs, you might be wondering if you even need to use the .NET Compact Framework.

Whether you do or not depends on what tools you have been using and what type of work you expect to do.

If you have been using eMbedded Visual Basic (eVB) to write Windows CE programs, you are probably already aware that Microsoft plans to discontinue support for eVB. As of this writing, the Pocket PC 2003 supports eVB; that is the last platform to be supported. The .NET Compact Framework is a great replacement. It is well designed, and it provides Visual Basic programmers with support that puts them on a level playing field with C# programmers.

If you have been using the Microsoft Foundation Class (MFC) Library, the ActiveX Template Library (ATL), or the Windows Template Library (WTL), then the case for the .NET Compact Framework is still pretty good. Chapter 1 describes the .NET Compact Framework and its benefits. The new .NET programming paradigm provides many benefits for programmers who have worked with other frameworks. Getting involved with .NET Compact Framework programming is a great way to get into the world of .NET because the libraries are scaled back from the (sometimes) overwhelming number of classes and features found on the desktop .NET Framework. And there is an added bonus for making the move to the .NET Compact Framework: The fundamental elements of programming for the .NET Compact Framework programming are the same as the fundamental elements for all .NET-based technologies. So learning the .NET Compact Framework today will help you learn to build Web applications using ASP.NET, Windows Forms applications for the desktop, and managed-code stored procedures for Yukon (the code name for the next version of SQL Server).

If you have been using the core Windows API/Win32, then you might wonder whether to continue writing Win32 code or to jump into the .NET Compact Framework. For some things, including the following, you must continue using Win32.[2]

- Fastest executables
- Best real-time support

2. For a detailed discussion of these, see the following white paper on the Microsoft Web site: http://msdn.microsoft.com/library/en-us/dncenet/html/choose_api.asp.

- Source code portability between platforms
- Ability to wrap Component Object Model (COM) for access by .NET Compact Framework applications
- Ability to create device drivers
- Ability to create control panel applets
- Support for custom user interface skins
- Support for security extensions
- Ability to build Simple Object Access Protocol (SOAP) Web Service servers
- Support for Pocket PC shell extensions
- Ability to use existing Win32 code

For Programmers Experienced with the .NET Framework

If you are experienced with writing programs that use the .NET Framework, you are going to find much that is familiar. The C# and Visual Basic .NET languages, for one thing, use the same syntax for two very popular languages that are available for desktop .NET development. The fundamental data types that support interoperability between different languages on the desktop also play a core part of interoperability with smart-device programs.

One thing that may be surprising to desktop .NET Framework developers is the extent to which they might need to rely on P/Invoke support to call the underlying Win32 API functions that Windows CE supports. While the desktop .NET Framework provides an extensive set of classes that minimizes the need to call outside the framework, the .NET Compact Framework provides a reduced set of classes to meet the size constraints of mobile and embedded devices.

To help programmers move from the .NET Framework to the .NET Compact Framework, throughout the book we provide some detailed discussions of differences between the two frameworks. In the many workshops we have taught, we have observed the knowledge and skills of programmers who are experienced with the .NET Framework transfer quite readily to the .NET Compact Framework.

The primary challenge comes from an experience we refer to as "stubbing your toe"—tripping over a familiar desktop feature (whether a class, an enumeration, an attribute, or an operating system feature) that is not present on smart mobile devices. When this happens, you have found a limit on the support available in the .NET Compact Framework (or, perhaps, a limit on the support of the underlying Windows CE operating system). The attitude you take in dealing with such experiences will play a big role in determining how successful you are in .NET Compact Framework programming—and how enjoyable you will find it. We have observed that the programmers who excel with device development are the ones who are able to see in these limitations an enticing challenge and an opportunity to explore new ways to solve old problems.

We extend our very best wishes to you on your .NET Compact Framework development, whether for the Pocket PC, the Smartphone, or some other Windows CE–powered smart device. We look forward to seeing you in one of our workshops or at an industry conference, or trading comments with you online (contact us via e-mail at info@paulyao.com).

Paul Yao, Bellevue, Washington
David Durant, Goldendale, Washington
March 2004

Acknowledgments

ANY LARGE PROJECT—and a book is nothing if not a large project—takes a lot of time to do right. What makes it worthwhile is the support of the people you really care about.

Paul Yao wants to thank his dear wife, Rebecca, for her support and encouragement during the many months it took to work on this book. Paul also wants to acknowledge his son, Jasper, who provided the time and space necessary to work on the book and also the fun when Dad needed time off from writing and coding. Thanks also to Grandma Helen and Aunt Nancy for entertaining the troops while Paul was busy with the book.

David Durant would like to thank his wife, Betty, who endured it all while providing tranquility throughout.

Thanks also to the staff at The Paul Yao Company for believing in this project and helping to see it through to completion.

At Addison-Wesley, thanks are due to Martin Heller, who first contacted us about this project and believed in us enough to help push for the insanity of attempting to write two books as part of one writing project. Thank you, Martin; we owe you another lunch or two on Mulberry Street!

We also thank Stephane Thomas, the Acquisitions Editor for this project, for her work on getting approval for this project and for coordinating the many players that support the creation of a new manuscript. Thanks also to Stephane's assistant, Michael Mullen.

Also on the Addison-Wesley team, thanks are due to Julie Nahil and Kim Arney Mulcahy for their project management and support during the book's production to keep us on our tight schedule. Thank you also to Chrysta Meadowbrooke for laser-like precision during the copyediting process and helping us fine-tune our otherwise unreadable text.

At Microsoft, we got a lot of help and technical support. On the .NET Compact Framework team, thanks are due to Seth Demsey for prompt and friendly support for what probably seemed like an endless stream of questions. We also wish to thank Craig Neable, Jamie De Guerre, and Ben Albahari, who are also on the .NET Compact Framework team. In the SQL Server CE group, we thank Kevin Collins for help on the *MSDN Magazine* article, which serves as the foundation for Chapters 12 and 13. On the Visual Studio .NET team, thanks are due to Mark Cliggett, Benjamin Wulfe, and Ritchie Hughes.

A big word of thanks to the extended Windows CE core team, which has always been quick to provide help and support when we had questions, comments, or just needed someone to buy us a cup of coffee. Our thanks go to Todd Brix, Karen Carter, Jason Demeny, Mike Hall, Scott Horn, Jeana Jorgensen, Jay Loney, Mark Miller, Mark Mullen, Chip Schnarel, and Mike Thomson. Thanks also are due to the MVP program for the help they have provided in keeping us in touch with the inner workings of the Microsoft mother ship: Michael Fosmire and Anthony Russell.

We extend a special word of thanks to Robert Little on the Microsoft Word team for help with taming Word for Windows and for great answers and sample code to handle our many questions on macros, fields, and other word processing magic.

We thank Andy Harding of Intermec Corporation for his considerable contribution to the content of Chapter 11.

We also thank Kamel Patel for his tool that helped us convert C# code to Visual Basic .NET.[3]

Outside of Microsoft, thanks are due to the industry experts on Windows CE who have been so generous with their tips, insights, long-term prognostication, senses of humor, and errant puns. Thanks are due to Doug Boling, Ginny Caughey, Neil Cowburn, Nat Frampton, Bill Mar, Steve Maillet, Chris Muench, Michael Salamone, and Chris Tacke.

3. This tool is available at http://www.kamalpatel.net/ConvertCSharp2VB.aspx.

At Field Software, thanks are due to Tim Field for his help and support getting information about the PrinterCE development tool, which we discuss in Chapter 17.

Perhaps not many readers are aware of this, but one reason that Addison-Wesley books have such top-notch technical content is due to the extensive technical review each book receives prior to publication. This involves hiring experts on each subject to read chapters and to submit critiques to the authors. We found this a very valuable process, and we wish to thank the reviewers who participated in reviewing our book: Darrin Bishop, Bill Draper, Alex Feinman, Fabio Ferracchiata, Gerard Frantz, Greg Hack, Doug Holland, Andrew Krowczyk, Ivo Salmre, Jonathan Wells, and Michael Yuan.

In addition to the technical review of the text that Addison-Wesley conducted, we made all the chapters of the book available at The Paul Yao Company Web site while we were writing the book. We were inspired by Bruce Eckel, who pioneered the idea of open reviews for programmer books. We did this to solicit comments and suggestions and were very pleased with the response we got. Among the reviewers who participated in this effort, we would like to especially thank Richard Rosenheim for his many detailed comments. Thanks are also due to Andrew Byrne, Chris Craft, and Maarten Struys (eMVP) for the many suggestions they submitted to our book review Web site. The following reviewers also submitted comments and suggestions that provided us with useful insights into how we could make the text and code better: Henri Birecki, Lars Black, Jon Box, Steve Broadhead, Tim Chaffee, Christos Chorattides, Gayla R. Cocullo, Ray Collins, Mark Dale, Michael Drake-Brockman, Mehdy Draoui, Michelle Forren, David Andrew Giglio, Chris Howlett, Sasha Imamovich, Kris Luyten, Enio Ohmaye, Ian Payne, John Perkins, Bill Ritch, Gary Scheitlin, Ronald van der Putten, Tom Vande Stouwe, Asheesh Vashishtha, John Verbrugge, Paul Webster, David Welden, and Troy Wolbrink.

Thank are also due to the staff members at ISInc Training Centers of Sacramento, CA for their cooperation and support.

We wish to thank Sheri Wilson of ExecuServe secretarial service in Bellevue, Washington, whose deft translation of garbled dictation enabled Dave (who does not type anything but code) to be a coauthor of this book.

About the Authors

WITH MORE THAN thirty years of experience teaching complex programming technologies between them, Paul Yao and David Durant are uniquely qualified to explain the ins and outs of the .NET Compact Framework. This team wrote the first book published on the subject of Windows programming, *Programmer's Guide to Windows*, in 1987. This was the must-have book for programmers working on Windows 1.x.

Since that time, Paul and David have dedicated themselves to teaching programmers how to take advantage of just about every Microsoft technology there is, including Win32, Visual Basic, ASP, ASP.NET, ADO, ADO.NET, SQL Server, SQL Server CE, the .NET Framework, Windows CE, Pocket PC, Platform Builder, and even device drivers. This team has taught thousands of programmers, written dozens of magazine articles, and spoken at countless industry forums. In short, this team has pioneered every major technology from Microsoft.

Paul Yao is first and foremost a programmer. He has been writing code since his high school days, where he started working on an HP 2000E minicomputer at school. He learned enough to get a job at a timesharing company, where he worked on DEC 10 "mainframes" at the tender age of 13.

Paul is president of The Paul Yao Company (http://www.paulyao.com), which provides educational and consulting services on Microsoft Windows–based software technologies. He has written a total of seven Windows programming books and is a contributing editor to *MSDN Magazine*, writing regularly on topics of interest to developers. Paul speaks often at industry conferences, where he gets high marks for his ability to make complex topics understandable and fun. In his spare time, Paul writes code samples and software tools, and he is happiest when leading training seminars for his corporate clients.

Paul's hobbies include endurance sports and beagles. Currently, Paul is training for an Ironman-distance triathlon race in 2005. He lives in the Seattle, Washington, area with his wife, Becky, and son, Jasper.

David Durant is CEO of Durant Associates and lead author on *Programmer's Guide to Windows*. David began his computer science career in 1968 as a COBOL programmer. He was a presenter at both the first ORACLE users conference and the first Microsoft SQL Server users conference, and he taught Windows API programming at Microsoft University, where he received the Microsoft Award for Excellence. David was an early proponent of .NET and is a frequent contributor to industry journals and forums. He is often on the road leading seminars on .NET-based technologies for corporate clients worldwide.

David lives in Goldendale, Washington, with his wife, Betty. His primary hobby is visiting his grandchildren.

PART I
Foundations

1

.NET Compact Framework Architecture

The .NET Compact Framework is a programming interface and runtime library created at the nexus of two Microsoft technologies: (1) Windows CE, an operating system for mobile and embedded smart devices, and (2) .NET, Microsoft's reinvention of its programming interfaces and developer tools. This chapter covers key elements of Windows CE and key elements of .NET to show how they work together in version 1.0 of the .NET Compact Framework.

IN THE EARLY 1990S, Microsoft declared that two technologies were core to its long-term strategic plans: Win32 and COM. Microsoft created Win32, the 32-bit Windows Application Programming Interface (API),[1] as a successor to its then-dominant Win16 API. COM, Microsoft's architecture for building distributed components, was introduced as a way to snap together software components in a fashion analogous to the way that electronic integrated circuits are snapped together.

The Win32 API was created as an upgrade to the Win16 API, which provided the core programming interface for Windows version 1.x. The 16-bit interface was built for 16-bit processors, and had tight ties to MS-DOS (which was required for early versions of Windows). The Win16 API serves

1. An API is an interface that an operating system provides for the development of application software.

as the core programming interface for the following versions of Windows: Windows 1.x, 2.x, 3.x, Windows 95, Windows 98, and Windows Me.

The Win32 API was designed to provide a smooth migration from the Win16 API. The goal was to make it easy for a developer to take Win16 code and modify it to run under the Win32 API. The Win32 API is the primary programming interface for the following versions of Windows: Windows NT 3.1, Windows NT 3.5, Windows NT 4.0, Windows 2000, Windows XP, and Windows Server 2003. To further smooth the path between the two programming interfaces, Win32 support was added to the 16-bit versions of Windows, starting with Windows 3.1. This allows a single Win32 program to run on both 16-bit and 32-bit versions of Windows.

Microsoft shipped the first version of Windows CE in 1996, with the Win32 API at its core. Windows CE was designed to be a modular, configurable operating system that was optimized for mobile, battery-powered smart devices. Microsoft made it possible for developers to customize Windows CE for application-specific uses. In contrast, desktop versions of Windows have always shipped as a monolithic, noncustomizable set of libraries and applications. By contrast, a developer can configure Windows CE to include support for a display screen or to run in a headless configuration (with no display screen). In addition, Windows CE can be configured to use a standard keyboard, a custom keyboard, or no keyboard at all. Windows CE can also be configured to support a hard drive or not because the only required storage is a RAM-resident object store.

Windows CE is Microsoft's only operating system with Win32 as the primary API for both application development and device driver development.[2] In some respects, Windows CE was developed as a smaller, lightweight version of Microsoft's 32-bit operating systems—a kind of "Windows XP Lite." But Windows CE shares little if any code with the heavier desktop operating systems, having been written from scratch to address the

2. By contrast, other members of the Microsoft Windows operating system family use either VxDs (for Windows 95, Windows 98, and Windows Me) or a kernel-mode driver interface (for Windows NT, Windows 2000, Windows XP, and Windows Server 2003) that is decidedly not the Win32 API.

needs of hardware and software engineers working to develop mobile and embedded smart devices.

On Windows CE today, Win32 is still a valid option for application development. In some cases, Win32 provides the only way to accomplish some things. Real-time programming, for example, is best done in Win32 because unexpected delays can occur in the .NET Compact Framework runtime. Also, extensions to the operating system or to the operating system shell can be done only by using Win32 code. This includes control panel applets, items on the Pocket PC Today screen, device-side ActiveSync providers, and any kind of device driver.

COM provides the building blocks for a wide range of components. COM first supported compound documents with the *Object Linking and Embedding* (OLE) specification. OLE provides the ability to embed an object such as a spreadsheet or a bitmap into a container document, such as a word processing document. Microsoft renamed COM to *ActiveX* when Internet Explorer, with its support for ActiveX controls, was introduced. COM/ActiveX components allow third parties to add new components in the form of controls, plug-ins, and other kinds of extensions. COM can be used to build stand-alone components that have no user interface element but provide some type of useful service.

COM provides the glue for connecting components. As such, it addresses some critical development issues, including code reuse and programmer productivity. But COM is complex and quirky, requiring both developers and consumers of components to handle administrative chores that would be better handled if automated. For example, COM components must track connections to external clients with a reference count. Although simple in principle, COM programming in practice requires a serious investment of time and energy to master.

COM was designed to provide version control support through the use of interfaces and interface negotiation. The goal was to allow new versions of a program (or of the components used by a program) to be deployed without breaking existing programs. COM did not live up to this goal, and instead—for both COM components and regular Win32 software—the spread of incompatible components and the resulting broken software has come to be known as *DLL hell*. The .NET initiative addresses this problem for .NET programs through the use of strong naming, which provides built-in version control so that a program runs only with the libraries and components for which it was tested.

When the .NET initiative was announced in 2000, it heralded a replacement for both Win32 and COM. While Microsoft continues adding Win32 extensions to its various operating systems, Win32 is no longer the core programming interface. That role now falls to the .NET Framework on desktop versions of Windows and the .NET Compact Framework on mobile devices including Windows CE platforms such as the Pocket PC. And while support for COM continues,[3] the role of new software components is played by .NET assemblies and not by COM components.

The .NET Compact Framework brings the technologies of the .NET Framework to the mobile and embedded world of Windows CE. To better understand the dynamic of this mix, this chapter starts with a discussion of Windows CE. We next look at the broader scope of .NET as implemented in the .NET Framework with its support for Windows Forms, Web Forms, and Web Services. We conclude the chapter with a discussion of the .NET Compact Framework—what it is, how it works, and where it is going.

Windows CE Overview

As of this writing, the Pocket PC is the most successful Windows CE–powered device. As a result of that success, the .NET Compact Framework supports all versions of the Pocket PC, including the first two generations (the Pocket PC 2000 and the Pocket PC 2002), which are built on Windows CE 3.0. This is noteworthy because, except for the Pocket PC, all Windows CE–powered platforms must run Windows CE version 4.1 or later to support the .NET Compact Framework. (The third generation of Pocket PC, the Pocket PC 2003, runs Windows CE .NET, version 4.2.) It is worth noting that the .NET Compact Framework comes preinstalled on the Pocket

3. The .NET Framework supports COM with a feature referred to as *COM interop*. Version 1.0 of the .NET Compact Framework has no COM support; a future version will add COM interop support.

the Pocket PC 2003 in device ROM but must be manually installed for the Pocket PC and Pocket PC 2002 devices.

To many people, Pocket PC and Windows CE are one and the same. This is due, in part, to the use of the term *Pocket PC OS* to refer to the software that runs a Pocket PC. Some people seem to assume that the Pocket PC is running not Windows CE but some other operating system. However, that is not the case: the Pocket PC is built on the Windows CE operating system.

We are not being nitpicky; we just want to make sure that Pocket PC developers understand that some useful tools and technologies are sometimes labeled as being Windows CE compatible. If unaware of this common thread, a developer might miss something that might prove helpful. Understanding this common thread, a developer can start to see the wider impact that Windows CE has had—and will continue to have—and how it addresses the needs of embedded systems. Windows CE is the foundation for a wide range of other smart devices.

In the summer of 2003, Microsoft launched a marketing campaign with a new brand, Windows Mobile Devices, to tie the Pocket PC and the Smartphone together as mobile extensions to the Windows brand name. In August 2003, Microsoft made available a version of the .NET Compact Framework that is compatible with the Smartphone 2003. While the focus of this book is on the Pocket PC, we have no doubt that Smartphone support is going to be important to many software developers.

Beyond the Pocket PC and the Smartphone, many other smart devices are powered by Windows CE,[4] including barcode scanners from companies like Intermec, Psion Teklogix, and Symbol Technologies; smart displays from companies like ViewSonic and Philips; and automobile-based navigation and entertainment systems—running CE for Automotive—in cars from BMW (developed by Siemens VDO Automotive AG), Citroen, Fiat, Mitsubishi, Subaru, Toyota, and Volvo.

Because the Pocket PC and Windows CE are connected in the minds of so many, developers new to Windows CE often assume that a required

4. In some cases, vendors support both Pocket PC and non–Pocket PC smart devices. The underlying operating system for both types of devices is the same: Windows CE.

Pocket PC feature is also required for all Windows CE devices. But Windows CE is a highly configurable operating system, with hundreds of system components and device drivers to choose from. While many Windows CE–powered devices have display screens, headless configurations—such as network routers and set-top boxes—are also possible. Many Windows CE–powered smart devices run as mobile, battery-powered devices; but wall-powered, stationary smart devices are also possible, and Windows CE has been incorporated into automatic teller machines and computer printers. And while some Windows CE–powered devices rely solely on RAM with no rotating storage media, Windows CE supports Advanced Technology Attachment (ATA) drives and other installable file systems to extend available storage beyond what is available in the object store.[5]

We Wrote Our Sample Code for the Pocket PC

Because of the success of the Pocket PC, we wrote this book expecting that Pocket PC programmers would make up the majority of our readers. Most of our examples, in fact, are built for quarter-VGA portrait-mode display screens—the size and orientation that, until the present, has been standard on a Pocket PC.

For developers writing programs for devices other than the Pocket PC, our samples should run with few if any changes. The only thing required is that a platform be compatible with the .NET Compact Framework, installed either in ROM or at runtime into the object store.

Design Goals

When starting to look at any technology, it helps to know what the creators of the technology had in mind during their development process. We start, then, with a discussion of the design goals for Windows CE. We have found that each design goal has a real impact on what an application pro-

5. The object store is a RAM-based storage area with three elements: a file system, a registry, and the CE property databases. These are discussed in detail in Chapter 11.

grammer can do and that learning about these design goals helps programmers understand a wide range of choices made by the Windows CE development teams.

We learned about these design goals through discussions with the original Windows CE development team. These design goals still play an important role because they describe the requirements that subsequent development teams have followed as they enhanced and fine-tuned this operating system:

- Small
- Modular
- Portable
- Compatible
- Connected
- Real time

The following subsections discuss each of these design goals.

Small

The first design goal is also the most important: Windows CE was built to be small. The smallest Windows CE image is less than 500K—the tiny kernel that has no display screen and no device drivers. By itself, the tiny kernel image can support a file system, run processes, start threads, load dynamic link libraries (DLLs), and access memory. The tiny kernel does not support enough of the Win32 API to support the .NET Compact Framework but is certainly enough for simple devices like a dumb printer or a portable music player.

A more typical device image might occupy 5MB or 10MB of RAM—adequate to support a display screen and enough network protocols to run a Web browser. Devices such as the Pocket PC might have a 32MB (or larger) ROM image, consisting largely of application programs and optional device drivers.

This is not small by the standards of other embedded operating systems, which might have a minimum footprint even smaller than the tiny kernel. However, Windows CE does provide a feature-rich, configurable operating system. By way of comparison, consider the various desktop versions of Windows. Windows Me, for example, requires 100MB of disk space; Windows XP requires 500MB of disk space. In the Microsoft Windows family of operating systems, Windows CE is definitely the very small—and very flexible—sibling.

The emphasis on making Windows CE small was intended to reduce the required hardware, thereby making Windows CE a good fit for high-volume, low-cost consumer electronic devices. In that highly competitive market, development teams work hard to reduce costs by scaling back on the required hardware—the RAM, the ROM, the CPU, and the myriad components—because lower costs create a competitive advantage in the price-conscious world of consumer electronics.

The "small is good" mind-set for Windows CE mostly affects developers who come to Windows CE with Win32 or .NET Framework experience from desktop versions of Windows. Such programmers often "stub their toes," which occurs when programmers new to Windows CE start to get comfortable with whatever API they are using. Just when they think they have device-side programming figured out, they find they want to use an old familiar friend from the desktop that is not implemented under Windows CE. It might be a Win32 function call. It could be a .NET Framework namespace, class, property, method, or event. At first, these can be frustrating experiences that make you wonder what global conspiracy has deprived you of your favorite way to do some common task. In most cases, there is another way to accomplish what you need done. To make sense of the omission, it helps to remember that small is good and that Windows CE was built to be a small operating system.

Microsoft's .NET Compact Framework team followed this design goal. The first version of the .NET Compact Framework occupies less than 2MB.[6] This compares to the more than 30MB that the .NET Framework uses on desktop versions of Windows.

---

6. The actual size depends on the CPU and whether or not files are compressed. ROM-based files have the option of being compressed, and files in the RAM-based file system are always compressed with a fast-but-light compression algorithm that yields a 2:1 compression ratio.

Modular

Windows CE is modular, a quality that is necessary because Windows CE is configurable. Unlike desktop versions of Windows, which are developed and shipped as monolithic sets of files, Windows CE itself is made up of *modules* (programs as `.exe` files and libraries as `.dll` files), and some modules are made up of two or more *components* (each of which consists of Win32 functions or operating system features).

When a development team designs a new device, it uses a Microsoft tool called *Platform Builder.*[7] Platform Builder allows a third party to customize the operating system image by adding or removing various modules as needed for custom smart devices. Building a platform that needs File Open and File Save dialog boxes? There is a module for that. Need this display driver or that network driver? Platform Builder lets you fine-tune the elements of an operating system image so that you have just the set you need. Among available Platform Builder components is the .NET Compact Framework itself, which means that custom devices can include the .NET Compact Framework in their ROM[8] images. The Pocket PC 2003 platform, for example, includes the .NET Compact Framework as a built-in component.

In our training classes, we often get asked about the difference between a Pocket PC and a custom device built with Platform Builder. The short answer is that the core operating system is the same, so porting software between a Pocket PC and other Windows CE devices is very doable. For Win32 programs, the key issue is the available set of functions supported on each device. Assuming that two Windows CE–powered devices support the same set of Win32 functions, porting of Win32 or Microsoft Foundation Class (MFC) programs should require minimal effort. Compatibility problems are often the result of platform-specific assumptions that found their way into the source code, assuming a specific screen size, a specific CPU, a

---

7. For more details on Platform Builder, visit the Windows Embedded home page: http://www.microsoft.com/windows/embedded.

8. A device manufacturer might use ROM, although flash memory is often used. The benefit of flash memory is that field upgrades can often be accomplished without opening a device's physical case.

directory name for installable file systems, or another system state that should be queried at runtime, not hard-coded.

The Pocket PC and Platform Builder

The subject of the Pocket PC and Platform Builder often raises questions for smart-device developers. Can Platform Builder be used to create a custom image for a Pocket PC? Generally speaking, the answer is no. Only developers with a special Pocket PC–specific version of Platform Builder can create a custom Pocket PC operating system image. The security of Pocket PC devices is further ensured because the ability to install a new operating system image on a given platform normally requires special knowledge of that platform.

For developers targeting a specific smart device, the configurability of Windows CE means that the operating system image can be fine-tuned to include an exact set of desired features and functions. This quality is especially useful for developers of closed platforms (platforms that can be extended only by the original development team).

For other software developers, the configurability of Windows CE introduces some potential problems and risks. In particular, developers creating software for a wider range of Windows CE platforms need to think about what specific Win32 functions might be available on various platforms. This is important, for example, when developing a Win32 program, library, or development tool. Will the File Open dialog be present? What fonts will be available? What display screen will various devices have? How should you handle headless platforms?

To help address some of these issues, Microsoft defines a standard Software Development Kit (SDK) in Windows CE .NET 4.1 Platform Builder. This SDK provides a reference point as an aid for multiplatform development efforts. This standard should help promote the creation of tools that can run on a wide range of platforms. The standard SDK defines a platform that is roughly equal to a Pocket PC, although it is not exactly the same. It also provides a starting point for the creation of new platforms (most platform developers will probably fine-tune their platforms for the sets of libraries and functions required for specific platforms). A custom SDK can then be exported from Platform Builder to provide the platform-specific set of libraries and include files needed to build native executables for a given platform.

The configurability of Windows CE is something of a mixed blessing for Win32 programmers. With configurability comes the possibility that some platform might not support a feature or function that a given program needs. The Responding to Missing Libraries and Missing Functions sidebar describes what happens when a required library or function is not present.

Responding to Missing Libraries and Missing Functions

The response to a missing library or a missing function depends on whether the call is being made from a Win32 caller or a .NET Compact Framework caller. In native code, if a program references a missing DLL, the program cannot run. Instead, the user is presented with a message that the program or one of its components cannot be found.

If all required DLLs are present for a native caller but a referenced function is not present, the situation is handled differently. An exception occurs in response to the call to the missing function, but the exception is ignored unless a debugger is running (in which case the exception causes a break to the debugger).

The system is a bit more forgiving when a .NET Compact Framework caller is missing a library but less forgiving for missing functions. A .NET Compact Framework program can load even when a referenced module is missing. But when a call to a missing function is encountered in a .NET Compact Framework program, an exception is generated that—if left unhandled—causes the program to terminate.

For .NET Compact Framework programs, the potential problems caused by operating system configurability are much less of an issue. The problem does not entirely disappear because a minimum set of Win32 features must be present to support the .NET Compact Framework libraries.[9] Once that threshold has been crossed, however, this becomes less of an issue for .NET Compact Framework programmers. It remains an issue because .NET Compact Framework programs can make direct calls to native DLLs using Platform Invoke (P/Invoke), a subject we discuss in Chapter 4.

While Windows CE itself is highly configurable, the current version of .NET Compact Framework is not. This means that any platform that supports the .NET Compact Framework should be able to run any .NET Compact Framework program. For the present, then, programmers targeting the .NET Compact Framework can design and develop their software with a good idea of what the .NET Compact Framework itself can provide.

While the configuration of the .NET Compact Framework classes is static, there are differences in the coding practices based on the requirements of different devices. For example, programs on a Pocket PC run either as full-screen programs or as minimized programs. On other Windows CE–powered devices, multiple programs can appear simultaneously (similar to desktop versions of Windows). Another example can be seen with the Smartphone, which imposes limits on a program's menus. A top-level menu can have only two menu items, and only the right-side menu can have submenus. These restrictions are needed to maintain consistency in the user interface, which uses a pair of keys to access program menu items.

Portable

The major challenges to the success of any operating system include the availability of two critical categories of software: application programs and device drivers. Without a wide variety of software of each type, an operat-

9. For details on the required Windows CE components, see this white paper on the Microsoft Web site by Paul Yao: http://msdn.microsoft.com/library/en-us/dncenet/html/wincecompactfx.asp.

ing system has limited appeal. To help address this, Microsoft has worked hard to enhance the portability of existing software to Windows CE. The basic idea is to leverage the success of existing software—and software developers—in creating a successful Windows CE ecosystem.

The first step was to establish the Win32 API as the primary programming interface for both applications and device drivers. As we discuss earlier in this chapter, Win32 was positioned as the strategic API for all Windows operating systems since the API first shipped in 1992. That focus continues with Windows CE.

Other desktop programming interfaces have also been made available in Windows CE. This includes the MFC Library, which provides to C++ programmers an object-oriented layer on top of the Win32 API. It also includes the ActiveX Template Library (ATL), first created in support of lightweight ActiveX controls for Internet Explorer. It also included eMbedded Visual Basic, a lightweight version of the desktop Visual Basic environment. (Support for eMbedded Visual Basic ends with the Pocket PC 2003; for the future, eMbedded Visual Basic programmers will need to switch to the .NET Compact Framework or adopt a third-party tool such as that provided for NS-BASIC.[10])

To support the creation of new device drivers, Windows CE device drivers follow the desktop Windows NT/2K/XP driver model wherever possible. This is true for network (NDIS) drivers, as well as for display, printer, keyboard, and USB device drivers. The underlying implementation for all of these drivers is a simplified, lighter-weight version of what is found on the desktop. The inspiration and architecture are in desktop drivers, the better to encourage desktop driver writers to support a Windows CE–based device driver.

The Win32 API was designed as a portable programming interface, intended to provide *source-code portability* between different CPU platforms.[11] The goal, which has largely been achieved in Windows CE, is that

10. For details, see http://www.nsbasic.com.

11. The first operating system to host the Win32 API was Windows NT version 3.1, which was simultaneously developed for the MIPS R4000 processor and the Intel x86 family of processors. Subsequent versions ran on the DEC Alpha architecture and the PowerPC processor families.

a single body of source code can be rebuilt to run on different CPUs. Just about every Windows CE developer takes advantage of this design, sometimes without thinking about it. Consider a developer who builds software for a StrongARM-based Pocket PC. How might such a developer benefit from source-code portability? Obviously, if such a developer reused code from a desktop (or server) version of Microsoft Windows, that developer would be benefiting from source-code portability.

In addition, however, such a developer is likely to make use of an emulator for the Pocket PC that runs on x86-based development systems. The emulator runs the same software as on a Pocket PC in a window under Windows 2000 or Windows XP. A Pocket PC program running in the emulator is running native x86 instructions; when that same program is built to run on an actual Pocket PC, with its StrongARM (or XScale) processor, that same program would need to be rebuilt as a StrongARM executable.

The .NET Compact Framework takes the notion of portability one step further by supporting *binary portability* between different processor platforms. Once built, a single .NET Compact Framework (`.exe`) program runs unchanged under the .NET Compact Framework on any supported processor, including StrongARM, MIPS, SH3, SH4, and on x86 CPUs. In addition, that same executable also runs on desktop versions of Windows with version 1.1 of the .NET Framework.[12]

Several factors contribute to allowing this to happen. A .NET program gets compiled just like a C or C++ program, except that the resulting executable file is not the machine code of any specific CPU. Instead, the executable file uses a CPU-neutral machine-level language, the *Microsoft Intermediate Language* (MSIL)—sometimes known as the *Common Intermediate Language* (CIL). We discuss this language later in this chapter in our discussion of .NET.

A second factor allows a .NET Compact Framework program to run under the desktop .NET Framework. That factor, which we discuss next, is the compatibility between Windows CE programming interfaces and desktop programming interfaces.

12. .NET Compact Framework compatibility is not supported for version 1.0 of the .NET Framework.

Compatible

Portability makes it possible to move code from the desktop to Windows CE and between Windows CE devices built with different CPUs. Making the programming interfaces compatible means keeping the device-side interfaces as consistent as possible with the desktop interfaces. In doing so, the Windows CE team took the concept of portability one step further, making it as easy as possible to share code between desktop and smart devices.

In some cases, this involved matching features on the desktop with a comparable feature in Windows CE. Consider the file system. Both Windows CE and the desktop support a hierarchical file system with long names; the maximum file path in both environments is 260 characters. And both desktop and Windows CE use a hierarchical registry for system and application settings.

Compatibility is further enhanced by choices made for each of the various programming interfaces. While Windows CE supports fewer Win32 functions than the desktop does, those functions that are supported match the desktop equivalent as closely as possible. For example, the `CreateWindow` function on the desktop has the same number and type of parameters as that of the same function in Windows CE.

It seems obvious that new operating systems should maintain compatibility with the predecessors, but it has not always happened that way. For example, consider the OS/2 operating system, developed jointly by Microsoft and IBM as a successor to Windows. Presentation Manager, the GUI programming API, was "fixed" and "improved" compared with the Win16 API on which it had been based. But the resulting API was so different that the new API had lost all ties to the Win16 API it was meant to replace.

This was a problem because there was a large base of existing Win16 code and relatively little code for the Presentation Manager. Many developers found that porting Win16 code to the Presentation Manager required the same level of effort as porting the same program to other GUI systems such as Macintosh. To address this issue, Microsoft created a new programming interface, Win32, which had as its primary goal consistency and compatibility with the Win16 API. From this hard lesson came a greater understanding of the effort required to create an API upgrade path. Windows CE developers benefit from that experience and gain the advantage of easily porting Win32 software from the desktop.

A similar type of compatibility is found with the .NET Compact Framework. The .NET Compact Framework team worked hard to maintain consistency between the .NET Compact Framework and the .NET Framework. As we discuss later in this chapter, the .NET Compact Framework has many elements in common with the desktop version—a common set of namespaces, classes, properties, methods, and events.

Connected

Windows CE enables smart devices to be well connected—to other Windows CE devices, to both wired and wireless local area networks, and to the Internet. The Windows CE team has consistently added support for new connectivity options with each new release of the operating system. Windows CE–powered devices can connect to personal area networks (PANs), local area networks (LANs), and wide area networks (WANs).

A PAN describes the point-to-point connections that a Windows CE–powered smart device establishes in its direct proximity. Included as PAN devices are infrared (IrDA) ports and Bluetooth controllers. Using these technologies, two Windows CE devices can share data: from tiny bits of data such as calendar appointments and contact information up to entire files.

Most readers are familiar with LANs, which typically connect a group of client systems and server systems within the same building or the same floor of a building. Windows CE supports several types of LAN adapters, including Ethernet (802.3), Token Ring (802.5), and wireless Ethernet (802.11).

Windows CE also supports connections to broader WANs through a variety of devices and using a wide range of protocols. Windows CE supports the telephony API, which broadly speaking provides management of both incoming and outgoing telephone calls. Using the telephony API and a supported serial and/or modem driver, a Windows CE device can connect to the Internet using a dial-up connection through the plain-old telephone system (POTS). Dial-up networking supports both the Serial Line Internet Protocol (SLIP) and the Point-to-Point Protocol (PPP).

Security considerations are always paramount when communicating over the Internet. A Windows CE–powered smart device can establish a secure, private connection over the Internet to a distant corporate LAN using the Point-to-Point Tunneling Protocol (PPTP) to establish a secure Virtual Private Network (VPN). Among the other features that Windows CE provides for secure network communications are the Secure Socket Layer (SSL), support for the Cryptography API, Kerberos and NTLM authentication, and support for an IP firewall.

In general, when there is a client/server relationship, Windows CE and the .NET Compact Framework support the client side of the connection. For example, the .NET Compact Framework supports the creation of Web Service clients but not the creation of Web Service servers.[13]

The .NET Compact Framework supports many of the high-level network-oriented classes, just like the .NET Framework, including both Transmission Control Protocol (TCP) socket clients (the `TCPClient` class[14]) and User Datagram Protocol (UDP) socket clients (the `UDPClient` class[15]). An interesting omission—in both the .NET Compact Framework and the .NET Framework—is support for the RS232 serial port. Neither framework supports a direct connection to an RS232-driven device. Programs that need this support must bypass the frameworks and drill through to the underlying Win32 protocols. .NET Compact Framework programs can access Win32 libraries through P/Invoke (a subject we discuss in Chapter 4).

Real Time

The final design goal for Windows CE is support for the development of real-time systems. In the world of embedded programming, *real time* refers to the ability to perform some specific task—whether calculating a value, recording some input, or sending a command to some external device—within a specified time. Many systems require that a task (or a set of tasks)

13. Windows CE does, however, support the creation of Win32-based Web Service servers with version 2.0 of the SOAP toolkit.

14. Fully qualified name: `System.Net.Sockets.TcpClient`.

15. Fully qualified name: `System.Net.Sockets.UdpClient`.

be consistently and reliably performed, no matter how heavily loaded the system is.

Starting with Windows CE 3.0, the Windows CE team put in place a set of important features to support the development of real-time systems. Included among these features are support for 256 thread priorities (Window CE has always supported multithreaded programming) and support for nested interrupt requests. The Windows CE real-time support is defined in the documentation for Windows CE Platform Builder as follows:

- Guaranteed upper bounds on high-priority thread scheduling—only for the highest-priority thread among all the scheduled threads.
- Guaranteed upper bound on delay in executing high-priority interrupt service routines (ISRs). The kernel has a few places where interrupts are turned off for a short, bounded time.
- Fine control over the scheduler and how it schedules threads.

The world of real-time systems can be divided into two kinds: those with hard real-time requirements and those with soft real-time requirements. *Soft real-time requirements* allow for some of the deadlines to be missed some of the time with no serious consequences. *Hard real-time requirements* are those that cannot tolerate even a single late reply.

Consider a system that controls the movement of a robotic arm on a factory floor. Perhaps the arm must be moved out of the way so that the assembly line can move forward or so that other machinery can access the assembly line. If the failure to move the arm in a timely fashion results in damage to the arm, to the product, or to any part of an assembly line, this would be called a hard real-time requirement. (The assumption is that such a breakdown could stop an assembly line, with the resulting downtime and costs.)

While Windows CE provides good real-time support, the .NET Compact Framework is not the ideal programming interface for building real-time components. The reason is that various delays can occur at irregular intervals because of the requirements of the runtime engine. There is a delay, for example, when code is loaded and converted into native machine code by the execution-time just-in-time (JIT) compiler (which we discuss later in this chapter).

Managed Code versus Unmanaged Code

.NET Compact Framework code is sometimes referred to as *managed code*, but to an application programmer its most important feature is that the data—especially data cleanup—is managed by the runtime. The code is managed as well, though, because it is verified to make sure that bad memory pointers do not occur. This topic is covered in detail in Chapter 3.

Windows API code, by contrast, is sometimes referred to as *unmanaged code*. This is a .NET-centric way of looking at it, though, so we sometimes use different terms, including *native code* and *Win32 code*.

For a detailed discussion of the differences between managed code and unmanaged code, see Table 4.1 in Chapter 4.

Another delay occurs when the garbage collector is operating because all threads running in managed code are frozen. However, unmanaged-code threads are not. In this way, a .NET Compact Framework managed-code program can support a real-time thread.[16] But the real-time thread will most likely do its work in unmanaged code by calling into a Win32 DLL. These are, of course, only general guidelines. Given a fast CPU and a lightly loaded system, a thread running in managed code could provide sufficient response to provide the real-time support needed in a given system. For issues related to timing and performance, the approach taken by carpenters—"measure twice and cut once"—applies. The number of times you measure the required performance is likely to rise in direct proportion to the cost of missing a real-time deadline.

---

16. Maarten Struys and Michel Verhagen discuss this issue in an article available at this link: http://msdn.microsoft.com/library/en-us/dncenet/html/Real-Time_NETCF.asp.

Platforms and Platform Builder

In the world of Windows CE development, the term *platform* refers to a unique combination of hardware (CPU, memory, display screen, I/O devices) and software (operating system libraries, device drivers, and applications). The best way to understand the term is to consider some examples. Three Pocket PC platforms are well known: Pocket PC, Pocket PC 2002, and Pocket PC 2003. Among the mobile phone–enabled Windows CE platforms are the Pocket PC 2002 Phone Edition, and the Smartphone 2003.

Platform Builder, mentioned earlier, provides a wide range of elements needed to build a complete, working version of Windows CE, including application programs, DLLs, device drivers, fonts, and icons. Microsoft includes the .NET Compact Framework runtime with Platform Builder, so a custom Windows CE smart device can include the .NET Compact Framework runtime. It is an optional component, however, included at the discretion of the platform developer.

Some developers of .NET Compact Framework applications might need to develop device drivers to support their applications. Platform Builder also provides support for device driver developers, in the form of sample device drivers and documentation. As of this writing, device drivers must be written in C or C++ and use the Win32 API because there is no support for building device drivers in managed code.

Another reason why Platform Builder might be interesting to .NET Compact Framework developers is that Microsoft provides a significant portion of the Windows CE source code with Platform Builder. The source code, known as *Shared Source*, includes a significant portion of the Windows CE kernel, various server components, and various network and communications protocols. A small investment of time could yield a lot of understanding of various Windows CE components, including the Web server, Bluetooth support, display driver support, the scheduler, and the low-level memory manager. (This is only a small sample of the 1,400 source files—and millions of lines of source code—you can use to learn about the internals of Windows CE.)

You can develop application programs using Platform Builder. If you *only* want to develop applications, Platform Builder is overkill, and other tools are likely to be more appropriate. However, you may find it helpful to use Platform Builder for application programs that are part of a platform. For example, it might make sense to use Platform Builder to develop a configuration tool that every user of a given platform needs to use.

Generally, however, other tools are used to develop applications. We next discuss those tools, which ship with Microsoft's eMbedded Visual C++ product.

eMbedded Visual C++

Many .NET Compact Framework applications need both managed and unmanaged components. To this end, Microsoft provides two products with tools for developing Windows CE applications:

- eMbedded Visual C++ (eVC++) for native Win32 programs and DLLs
- Visual Studio .NET 2003 for .NET Compact Framework programs and shared libraries

The focus of the rest of this book is on the second product, Visual Studio .NET 2003, and the .NET Compact Framework. The first product has some useful features, though, so it is worth a brief note. Even if you never build Win32 programs or DLLs, there are several reasons to install eMbedded Visual C++.

eMbedded Visual C++ ships with an Integrated Development Environment (IDE) based on the same source code as the Visual C++ 6.0 IDE. So it lacks some of the refinements you might notice in Visual Studio .NET. What it does provide is the ability to create Win32, MFC, or ATL programs for Windows CE. You can build, download, and debug such programs to a remote Windows CE–powered device or to an emulator.

eMbedded Visual C++ supports a wide range of smart-device configurations. To configure the environment for a specific configuration, you install an SDK for the device in question. For example, there is an SDK for the Pocket PC 2002 and another one for the Pocket PC 2003 (the two are similar, though not exactly identical). Microsoft's tool for configuring custom Windows CE configurations, Platform Builder, generates the SDK to match whatever configuration has been selected for the operating system image. An SDK contains, among other things, a set of include files and linker libraries that are custom tailored for a specific platform. Application developers install a device-specific SDK after installing eMbedded Visual C++, which adds new options to the New Project Wizard, and to the WCE Configuration toolbar in the eMbedded Visual C++ IDE.

Tips for Using the eMbedded Visual C++ Emulator

The emulator lets you run Windows CE programs on a development workstation running Windows 2000 (Service Pack 2 required) or Windows XP. You cannot run the emulator on 16-bit versions of Windows because of the lack of Unicode support, which the emulator requires (Windows CE is a Unicode-only system).

When using the emulators with eMbedded Visual C++, be aware of the emulator version. Older emulators rely on the underlying operating system to simulate the behavior of Windows CE, and in many cases the behavior is quite different. Avoid using the emulator for the following devices: the Pocket PC, the Handheld PC, the HPC Professional, and the Palm-sized PC. These emulators ship with SDKs that are compatible with eMbedded Visual C++ 3.0.

Microsoft invested a lot of effort in creating an emulator that has a high degree of fidelity to Windows CE running on a device. Starting with the Pocket PC 2002, emulators are based on the newer technology. The emulators for the Smartphone and the Pocket PC 2003 use the newer technology, as does any emulator that is compatible with eMbedded Visual C++ 4.0.

Sometimes developers encounter problems getting the emulator to work properly. Here are some tips to help get the emulator going.

1. Make sure to install the latest service pack from eMbedded Visual C++ 4.0.
2. If your development system is not connected to a network, install the Microsoft loopback adapter.
3. With eMbedded Visual C++, you must log in to an account with Administrator privileges.

There are, in fact, two sets of emulators: one for eMbedded Visual C++ and another for Visual Studio .NET 2003. Each tool can work only with its own emulator. Sometimes this causes a minor inconvenience, such as when you want to run a .NET Compact Framework program and a Win32 library under the same emulator. Can this be done? Yes, but it requires some manual copying. Add the Win32 DLL to the Visual Studio .NET project, and run both on the Visual Studio .NET emulator.

In other cases, incompatibilities can cause one of the emulators to stop working altogether. Sometimes an emulator cannot start, or it can start but cannot receive a downloaded program. In other cases, a debug session to an emulator cannot start. To address this issue, we have had success by shutting down one (or both) emulators completely. To do this, shut down an emulator and select `Turn off Emulator` in the Shut Down dialog.

Remote Tools

eMbedded Visual C++ includes a set of tools that run on a desktop system and that display details about a connected Windows CE–powered device. Many of these tools are device-enabled versions of tools that ship with current or past versions of Visual Studio. Remote SPY++ and Remote Zoomin, for example, are adaptations of desktop tools.

Table 1.1 summarizes the available remote tools that ship with eVC++ 3.0 and eVC++ 4.0. Most tools are straightforward to use, but some require a bit more effort to understand how they work. The easiest way to start these programs is on the Tools menu in the IDE. The programs can run by themselves, but they are not placed on the Start menu by the eVC++ installation program. We include the name of the executable file in the table to help you create a shortcut for tools you use often. You can add to the Visual Studio .NET Tools menu a shortcut to any of these tools by selecting the Tools→External Tools... menu item.

Documentation

eMbedded Visual C++ provides documentation on Win32 functions as implemented in Windows CE. In some cases, this same information is available in the MSDN Library (the documentation set installed with

TABLE 1.1: Remote Tools in eVC++ 3.0 and eVC++ 4.0

Name in eVC++ Tools Menu	Executable File Name	Description	eVC++ 3	eVC++ 4
Remote SPY++	`cespy.exe`	Displays available windows and listens to window message traffic	Yes	Yes
Remote Registry Editor	`ceregedt.exe`	Allows you to view and edit device and desktop registry	Yes	Yes
Remote Heap Walker	`ceheapwk.exe`	Allows you to view available Win32 (`HeapAlloc`) heaps	Yes	Yes
Remote Process Viewer	`cepview.exe`	Allows you to view current system processes and details of each process, including the running threads and the modules (DLLs) running in each process; also allows you to terminate a process	Yes	Yes
Remote Zoomin	`cezoom.exe`	Displays a screen image for a target device (useful for writing documentation)	Yes	Yes
Remote File Viewer	`cefilevw.exe`	Allows you to browse a remote-device file system; supports copying files from a desktop system to a device or from a device to a desktop system	Yes	Yes

Name in eVC++ Tools Menu	Executable File Name	Description	eVC++ 3	eVC++ 4
Remote Call Profiler	`msic.exe`	Displays and analyzes program execution time	No	Yes
Remote Kernel Tracker	`kerneltracker.exe`	Allows you to observe the actions of the scheduler in passing control between threads (useful for analyzing deadlocks and other interthread synchronization problems)	No	Yes
Remote Performance Monitor	`ceperfmon.exe`	Collects statistics and displays graphical state for a wide range of system-level resources, including memory usage and network traffic (the Windows CE version of the desktop Performance Monitor)	No	Yes
Remote System Information	`cesysinfo.exe`	Displays static snapshot of system information for a device, such as model of CPU, available system memory, and system power state	No	Yes

Visual Studio .NET). In other cases, the eVC++ documentation provides details about device-specific functions that are not otherwise available (e.g., details about functions specific to the Pocket PC and also functions specific to the Smartphone).

This is particularly useful when you need to access a feature that is supported by the underlying operating system but is not supported by the .NET Compact Framework. Making such calls requires using the P/Invoke support of the .NET Compact Framework, which we discuss in detail in Chapter 4.

Obtaining eMbedded Visual C++

eMbedded Visual C++ is available at no cost. This is a bit unusual because Microsoft normally does not give away its development tools. However, to promote smart-device development, eMbedded Visual C++ is free. Make sure to download the correct version. For Windows CE 3.0 devices, download eMbedded Visual C++ 3.0; for Windows CE .NET 4.x devices, you need eMbedded Visual C++ 4.x. (Also be sure to download and install any service packs that might be available.)

What Is .NET?

From the moment Microsoft made its .NET initiative public, the question was "What is .NET?" The short answer is that .NET is a branding that covers all the different parts of a larger strategy. Another answer, from the Microsoft Web site, offers the following pithy explanation:

> Microsoft® .NET is a set of software technologies for connecting information, people, systems, and devices. This new generation of technology is based on Web Services—small building-block applications that can connect to each other as well as to other, larger applications over the Internet.[17]

This explanation focuses on the new features that .NET introduces: the network focus for .NET. Toward that end, it mentions one element of .NET, that is, Web Services. If you interpret this too literally, you risk missing the larger picture that .NET addresses. At this point, it should be clear that .NET is a large undertaking by a large company.

---

17. Quoted from http://www.microsoft.com/net/basics/, accessed in January 2004.

To put the .NET Compact Framework into perspective within the larger .NET picture, a more detailed description of .NET is required. Whether you spend your whole career developing .NET Compact Framework programs or whether you move on to desktop .NET development, an understanding of .NET is important because the effects of .NET will last for a decade or more. To get a good understanding of .NET, it helps to look at the following:

- Available .NET implementations
- The scale and scope of .NET
- Three .NET application classes
- Common programming elements

The following subsections discuss these topics.

Available .NET Implementations

At its heart, .NET is about a runtime that supports a certain set of features. Here is a list of implementations that provide something tangible for you to work with. Microsoft has created three public implementations of .NET, and there are at least two other efforts under way to create .NET runtimes.

- *The .NET Compact Framework* is Microsoft's runtime for Windows CE–powered platforms.
- *The .NET Framework* is Microsoft's runtime for desktop and server versions of Microsoft Windows. It is included with two shipping Microsoft operating systems: Windows XP Tablet Edition and Windows Server 2003. For other versions of Windows (Windows 98 and later), the .NET Framework can be installed using a downloadable installation file, `dotnetfx.exe`.
- *The Shared Source Common Language Infrastructure* (CLI) is the source code for some of the low-level support classes for the .NET Framework, as defined in the Common Language Infrastructure. Microsoft has released the source code to "Rotor," the code name

for an implementation of the CLI, in support of its submission to Ecma International[18] of this .NET technology as an Ecma International–approved standard. The Shared Source CLI can be downloaded from the Microsoft Web site and used as a resource to learn about the architecture and operation of the .NET runtime.

- *DotGNU* is the GNU project for building an open source implementation of the .NET Framework.
- *The Mono Project* is another open source project, from a company called Ximian, for creating an implementation of the .NET Framework.

The Scale and Scope of .NET

A complete answer to the question "What is .NET?" has proven elusive in part because the scale and scope of the .NET initiative contains so many elements. Remember the story about the group of blind men encountering an elephant? Each man experiences something different from the others: the broad flat surface is an ear; the skinny wavy object is the tail, and so forth. Each can discuss what he finds with the others, but none can agree on what exactly they have found because each encounters something different.

The Scale of .NET

The .NET initiative is a major technology initiative for Microsoft. Steve Ballmer, Microsoft's CEO, refers to .NET as a "bet-the-company" investment.[19] To put this into the perspective of Microsoft's (almost) thirty-year history, .NET is the third major initiative of this magnitude. The two previous efforts that had anywhere near the kind of impact that .NET promises were major direction changes for Microsoft. We refer here to the two operating systems that reshaped Microsoft and also had a major impact on the

---

18. A European association for standardizing information and communication systems. For details, visit the Web site at http://www.ecma-international.org.

19. Both Bill Gates and Steve Ballmer have used this term quite often. Steve Ballmer used this term at the launch of Visual Studio .NET on February 13, 2002, as noted on the Microsoft Web site at http://www.microsoft.com/presspass/exec/steve/2002/02-13vsnet.asp.

rest of the computer industry: MS-DOS and Microsoft Windows. Here is a brief summary of Microsoft's three major initiatives:

- 1981, the beginning of the MS-DOS era: character-based computing
- 1990, the beginning of the Windows era: GUI-based computing
- 2000, the beginning of the .NET era: network-centric computing

Microsoft was founded in 1975 to provide a BASIC interpreter for a new computer system, the MITS Altair. Because the company was founded to build a programmer tool, Microsoft has never lost sight of the importance of programmers in its long-term, strategic plans.[20]

In 1981, Microsoft acquired all rights to a character-based operating system from Seattle Computer Products, written by an employee named Tim Patterson. Microsoft licensed the operating system to IBM, and in August 1981 IBM started shipping the IBM PC. Microsoft subsequently licensed MS-DOS to the broader market for IBM-compatible computers. By doing this, Microsoft established itself as an operating system company and made its first major direction change: from a developer tool company to an operating system company.

In May 1990, Microsoft released Microsoft Windows 3.0, the version that achieved widespread success and established Microsoft Windows as the standard GUI for personal computers. This did not happen overnight; Microsoft started work on the first version of Windows in early 1983. Almost two years later, in November 1985, Microsoft shipped the first version of Windows.

There was a third operating system. In 1984, Microsoft embarked on a joint development agreement with IBM to develop OS/2. In those days, Microsoft was positioning OS/2 as the successor to Windows.[21] After the success of Windows 3.0, Microsoft dropped OS/2—an operating system in which Microsoft had made a sizable investment.

---

20. We omit some historic details in this discussion because this story is reported more completely elsewhere. Our purpose is to position the .NET initiative in the context of Microsoft's other major direction changes.

21. What eventually became known as Windows NT 3.1 had another, earlier name: OS/2 NT.

With Windows 3.0, Microsoft succeeded in making its second major direction change: from a character-based operating system company to a GUI-based operating system company. This change required many years of dedicated effort, in part because GUI systems are inherently more complex than character-based systems. Also, the competition was more intense for this second change, with operating system alternatives that included Apple's Lisa and Macintosh systems, GEM from Digital Research, DeskView from Quarterdeck, and TopView[22] from IBM.

In the grand scheme of things, .NET is significant because it represents only the third major direction change in Microsoft's history. Microsoft announced the .NET initiative in July 2000 at the Professional Developers Conference held in Orlando, Florida. .NET amounts to Microsoft's complete reinvention of its core software technologies, its software development tools, and ultimately all of its products. By contrast, the adoption of MS-DOS was simple: a group of engineers supported Microsoft's Original Equipment Manufacturer (OEM) customers. The total number of OEM customers for MS-DOS was under 100, a population that could be supported by the MS-DOS team itself. Windows required a much larger development team than MS-DOS did and also a larger support organization to assist the tens of thousands of software companies that built software for the operating system.

The .NET initiative involves[23] an even greater effort than what went into creating Windows, in large part because the .NET initiative involves recreating in three or four years a larger number of older technologies, some of which were developed over a decade or more. The driving force this time is not just a new user interface, one of the key features that Windows 3.0 provided. Instead, it involves redeploying these older technologies in a unified way that is ready to support the future of high-bandwidth, network-centric computing. You can get a sense for this by studying the three basic types of .NET applications: Windows Forms, Web Forms, and Web Services (which we'll discuss soon).

---

22. TopView added multitasking support to MS-DOS, which by itself is a single-tasking operating system. TopView did not, however, support GUI programming.

23. The effort is continuing as of this writing.

The Scope of .NET

.NET covers a very wide range of software technologies. Just how broad is the scope of .NET? Consider the following scenarios that involve programmers working with different aspects of .NET technology.

Web site developers are interested in ASP.NET, a set of services that support Web site creation. Like other Web server systems, ASP.NET runs on a Web server and interacts with Web browsers using HTML and some scripting language (JavaScript or VBScript). Older Web server systems (including Microsoft's own Active Server Pages, or ASP) freely mix HTML and script to create hard-to-read and hard-to-manage source files.

ASP.NET provides a host of improvements to the Web application development process. The most obvious is that the HTML is kept separate from the code, making each easier to work with and maintain. Another improvement is that ASP.NET programs are compiled code, with the same type system used by desktop and device-side Windows Forms programs. Also, the set of programming languages is much broader than just one or two scripting languages; all of the .NET-compatible languages are available for ASP.NET development. Those languages support a rich, object-oriented programming model, so Web developers can benefit from the encapsulation, inheritance, and polymorphism that other programmers have long enjoyed. Like other .NET programs, ASP.NET Web programs are compiled, which provides a performance improvement over interpreted script languages. And finally, proper debugging is supported for developers when they build Web programs using ASP.NET, something that Web developers have not had with earlier Web development tools.

Microsoft supports a Web browser interface for small-screen devices through *ASP.NET Mobile Controls*, an add-on to ASP.NET Web servers.[24] ASP.NET Mobile Controls allow a Web site to support a broad range of small-screen devices with a single set of Web pages. The Web pages themselves are stored in a generic XML format and then converted to support three

---

24. You can read about ASP.NET Mobile Controls in "Microsoft Mobile Internet Toolkit Lets Your Web Application Target Any Device Anywhere," written by Paul Yao and David Durant for the November 2002 issue of *MSDN Magazine*, available online at http://msdn.microsoft.com/msdnmag/issues/02/11/MMIT. This article refers to the controls by an outdated name, the Microsoft Mobile Internet Toolkit (MMIT).

markup languages that are common on small-screen devices: HTML 3.2, WAP/WML 1.0, and cHTML.

Consider another developer, this one building desktop database applications. This developer might want to create a GUI front end that interacts with a user and manages the interactions with a back-end SQL database. .NET offers this developer many things, but each is different from what the Web site developer works with. The developer creating desktop applications uses the Windows Forms portion of the .NET Framework to build the windows, menus, and dialog boxes that make up the user interface for a traditional Windows GUI application. He or she would probably use the ADO.NET classes to manipulate in-memory database tables and use the various data provider classes to move data to and from a database server.

A developer creating mobile database programs for a Pocket PC sees some of the same things as a desktop database programmer. The class hierarchy of the .NET Compact Framework was modeled after the class hierarchy of the Windows Forms classes in the desktop .NET Framework. The two frameworks are so similar, in fact, that code written for the .NET Compact Framework can run on the desktop[25] under version 1.1 of the desktop .NET Framework. The actual impact of this capability remains to be seen, given the many differences between desktop systems and Windows CE–powered systems.

A developer working in the mobile world of Pocket PCs must address issues that are unique to the world of mobile-device programming. As a mobile device, a Pocket PC is often disconnected from any desktop system and also from any network connection, either wired or wireless. Programmers working with Pocket PC databases may need to address two separate scenarios: (1) managing data when the device is disconnected, and (2) merging that data with an external database when the device is connected.[26]

---

25. The reverse is not true—that is, a desktop .NET program typically does not run on a mobile device.

26. Of course, a Pocket PC database can stand alone and not require synchronization with a central database, but the interesting real-world scenarios are the ones that push the limit—which in this case means having a distributed database and disconnected devices.

Both scenarios require addressing issues that are not typically part of the world of SQL programmers working on desktop or server systems. Mobile devices have less memory than desktop systems, and the disconnected nature of mobile devices requires some different thinking about databases and the synchronization of data between different data sets.

Part of .NET consists of elements that are common to all .NET programmers, which we address later in this chapter. Other parts of .NET provide specific support to solve problems that are important for some developers but are not very interesting to other developers.

Three .NET Application Classes

When you scratch the surface of .NET, you find three application classes: Windows Forms, Web Forms, and Web Services. The first two application classes differ from each other in the user interface and in the delivery mechanism for that user interface. Windows Forms applications run as stand-alone client applications, while Web Forms applications are run from within a Web browser. A Web service, on the other hand, has no user interface.[27] It describes, instead, a headless application that supports the other two types of application classes.

Windows Forms and Web Forms

A Windows Forms application is a traditional GUI application. Such an application might run as a stand-alone application, like a word processor, or it might run as the client portion of a networked client/server application. Windows Forms encompass the rich graphical and interactive elements traditionally associated with GUI systems. Figure 1.1 shows a desktop Windows Forms application with which every Windows user is familiar: the Windows Explorer.

A Web Forms application is an HTML/script application that appears in a Web browser. By definition, these are client/server applications, which require a live connection to a Web server to operate. Most of the computing work gets handled on the server side, and the client side involves displaying

---

27. We do not count the WSDL Web page as a user interface; it is at best a development and testing interface, not a user interface that interacts with nontechnical end users.

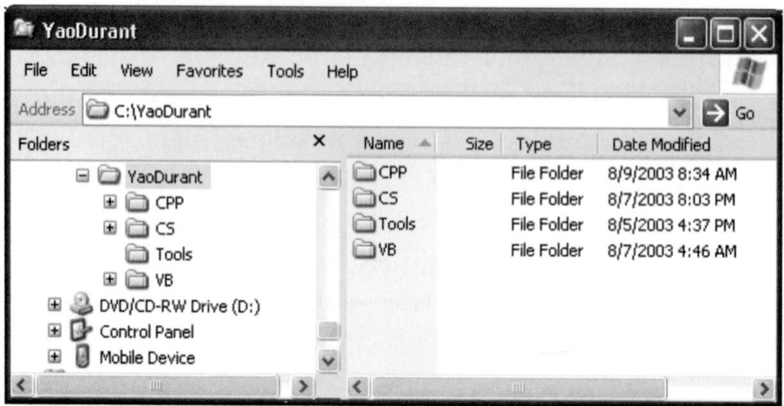

FIGURE 1.1: The Windows Explorer, an example of a Windows Forms application

HTML, navigating between Web pages, and handling data entry forms. Figure 1.2 shows an example of a Web Forms application running in Internet Explorer—the login page for a Web site we created for feedback from book reviewers.

To an end user, and to programmers when they first start to look at .NET, neither the Windows Forms nor the Web Forms seem to offer anything new. Nothing in the Windows Forms application in Figure 1.1 seems to be different from what was available prior to .NET. And, in fact, the Windows XP Explorer does not actually use the .NET Framework. All the same, it qualifies as a traditional GUI application, which is another term often used to describe Windows Forms applications.

The same can be said about the Web Forms application in Figure 1.2. To an end user it looks just like any other Web page.[28] The application displayed in the figure is, in fact, an ASP.NET application that was written using Visual Studio .NET and deployed to a Web server on which the .NET Framework had been installed. And yet for all these differences, it seems to present to the end user nothing that is new or revolutionary.

Based on what we have discussed so far, it would be easy to dismiss .NET as just a new name for the same old thing. To a software developer,

28. Astute readers may notice that the name of the page ends with `.aspx`, the only outward sign that a Web page is hosted by ASP.NET.

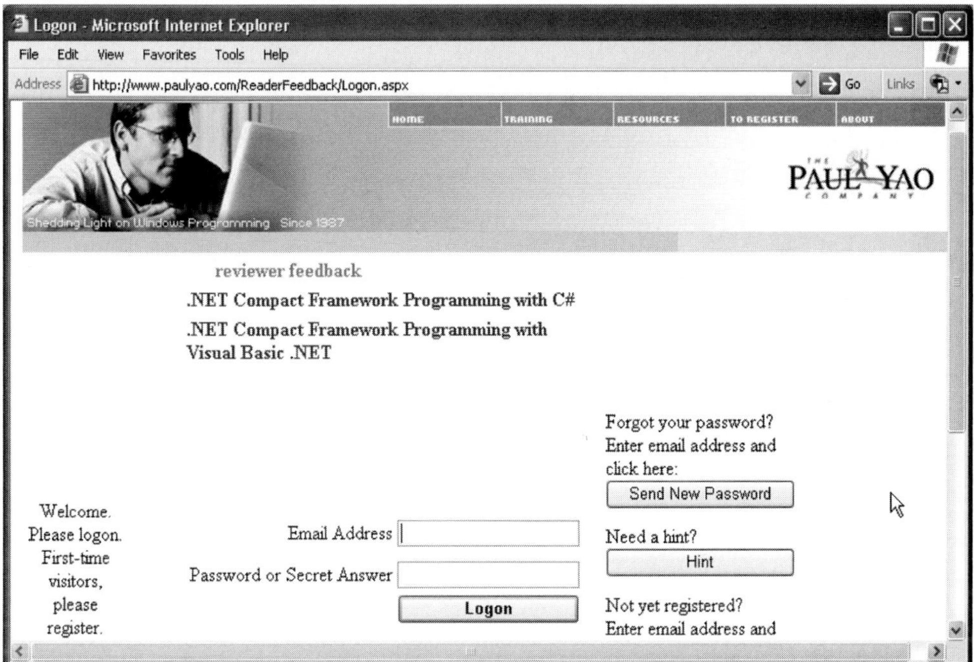

FIGURE 1.2: A sample Web Forms application

however, there are a huge number of very important differences. One is the third application class, Web Services, which we discuss next.

Web Services

The third class of .NET applications is Web Services (formerly known as *XML Web Services*). Web Services have no user interface but instead support the other two application classes by providing a standard mechanism for two computers to communicate with each other over a network.

This might not sound like anything new. After all, there have been network protocols as long as there have been networks. You transfer files with the FTP protocol, log into a command prompt with the TELNET protocol, attach to network printers and file servers with the SMB protocol, and browse Web pages with the HTTP protocol.

Web Services are built on a set of standard protocols, notably the *Simple Object Access Protocol* (SOAP). The purpose of this protocol is to support remote procedure calls (RPCs). Web Services provide the next generation for network-based client/server communications. Previous-generation technologies include Distributed COM (DCOM) from Microsoft, the industry standard DCE RPC protocol, and CORBA.

A wide range of large computer hardware and software companies are adopting Web Services as a standard. So while previous generations of RPC got bogged down in compatibility issues (COM versus CORBA comes to mind), Web Services are largely a platform-neutral RPC mechanism.

Why should application programmers care about Web Services? It is certainly possible for people to spend their whole programming careers building traditional GUI applications or building Web applications. You might find yourself in that situation—you do not build distributed, network-oriented applications. In the short term, that may remain the case. But Web Services are going to grow in importance.

One reason has to do with the growth in speed, reliability, and security of networks. The incredible advances in computer hardware have made the PC revolution possible. The rise of the Internet was made possible by these hardware advances and also by advances in computer communications technology. As digital communication continues to evolve, added speed and lower costs will contribute to making Web Services a key part of many new kinds of application software.

Another reason why Web Services will become important has to do with the growth and success of the World Wide Web. The World Wide Web is the most successful—and most visible—artifact of the computer industry. If you doubt this, start counting the number of URLs on consumer products; has any other computer artifact ever achieved this level of public awareness?

All large companies, government agencies, and nongovernmental organizations have made—and will continue to make for the foreseeable future—large investments in their Web sites. Web sites aggregate a huge amount of information, which gains value by being made public. A portion of this data is available in a human-readable form, HTML.

While HTML makes the data easy for people to read, HTML is difficult to access programmatically. Some programmers have built HTML-scraping tools to strip the HTML from data based in Web servers, but this is a fragile approach to accessing the data. For one thing, changes to a Web site break an HTML scraper. There are also legal issues to consider because Web site owners often own the copyrights to the contents of their Web sites.

One use for Web Services is to provide programmatic access to the huge collection of Web site data. Think back to the last two or three Web sites you browsed. Were you reading the *New York Times* online? Perhaps you were looking up a sports score or the weather in a city you are about to visit. If you live near a big city like Seattle, you might go online to check the traffic. In each of these cases, the data you searched for could have been made available programmatically. While using a search engine to find a piece of information is sometimes necessary (and, in fact, sometimes fun), any information that you regularly access is a candidate for accessing through a Web Services program.

While all Web browser HTML data is not yet available through a Web Service, as of this writing Web content from several large Web sites is available. Here is a partial list of Web sites and services that are externally accessible through Web Services.

- Amazon: Link third-party product inventory databases to the Amazon product database.
- eBay: Access auction information programmatically.
- Google: Submit Web site searches.
- MapPoint .NET: Use this Microsoft service for programmatic access to geographic data.

Common Programming Elements

The essence of .NET can be found in the new programming model that .NET introduces for Microsoft Windows. .NET provides a programming model that extends from small-screen mobile and embedded devices, through the personal computer—whether desktop, laptop, or tablet—on up to server-scale systems. .NET provides a unified way to develop many different kinds of software applications, including traditional GUI applications, applications accessible via Web-browsers, and back-end Web Service applications. The .NET initiative unifies software development across a wide range of device classes and incorporates a broad set of application types through the following common core elements:

- Well-designed programming interface
- Common Intermediate Language
- Common language runtime
- Common Language Specification
- Common type system
- Common Language Infrastructure

The following subsections consider each of these elements in turn.

Well-Designed Programming Interface

Back in the early 1980s, Microsoft's goal in creating Windows was simple: to make an easy-to-use GUI system. The goal never included making it easy to write code for the operating system. Quite to the contrary, it was just and proper that professional programmers bore the burden of taming the complexities of computers. The result was the various APIs behind Windows, first the 16-bit Win16 API followed by the 32-bit Win32 API. Because Win32 is the API for Windows CE, that is our focus here (although aside from some refinements and extensions, Win32 carries the same flaws as its 16-bit predecessor).

The Win32 API, while serviceable and necessary in many cases, has a number of design flaws, which Microsoft has addressed with the .NET initiative.

- Quirky API: Win32 has many inconsistencies, many poorly named functions, several functions with too many parameters, and many large, unwieldy data structures. (In many cases, some of the extra parameters are reserved and must be set to zero, and often the large data structures contain unused members.)
- Memory management: Application programs required to clean up system objects make the API prone to memory leaks.

- Low-level API: Sometimes called "the assembly language of Windows," the Win32 API often requires multiple steps to accomplish seemingly simple tasks.
- Procedure-oriented API: Win32 offers none of the benefits obtained from object-oriented languages.[29]

In fairness to the development team members who created Windows 1, they accomplished a lot in a short time and faced many obstacles. While creating a new GUI, they also were creating a new compiler, a new debugger, a new program loader, and a new memory manager. They worked on very slow computers (with 80286 and 80386 CPUs), with small storage devices (20MB was large in those days) and limited networking support. Given the obstacles they faced and what they accomplished, one wonders that they were able to deliver at all.

Once Windows started shipping, the Windows API acquired a momentum all its own. At the same time, programmers recognized that a better API was needed, and several efforts were put forth. One such effort was OS/2, a project staffed by many former Windows systems developers. However, as mentioned earlier, Microsoft abandoned OS/2 and its more refined programming interface. Other efforts to improve Windows programming include Visual Basic (which first shipped in 1992) and the MFC library for C++ programmers. Both provide improvements with fewer quirks than the native Windows API; neither completely replaces the Win32 API.

To programmers building software for Microsoft Windows, .NET represents a new programming interface that is a well-designed, feature-rich candidate for replacing Win32 programming. This interface is called the .NET Framework for desktop machines and the .NET Compact Framework for mobile and embedded devices. These frameworks follow a wonderfully consistent approach to exposing operating system services to programmers.

29. The first version of Windows predates the first PC-based C++ compiler by at least five years, so there were no object-oriented tools to support object-oriented development.

These frameworks are object-oriented. For example, everything in .NET is an object, derived from the `Object` base class.[30] In this object-oriented API, all support functions are contained in classes. Classes, in turn, are grouped by namespace. Namespaces are not new: C++, for example, has namespaces. But with .NET, namespaces are used to organize the system service classes, thereby providing a very visible and useful organization to operating system functions.

The structure and organization of the namespaces and classes help make the programming interface very *discoverable*, a term often applied to a well-designed user interface. If you know about one method or one class, it is easy to find other, related methods or classes. For example, when trying to figure out how to create graphical output, the `System.Drawing` namespace has everything you need. And when you find the `DrawString` method for drawing text, you soon find that other text drawing elements—fonts and brushes—are organized together in the same namespace. By contrast, a Win32 programmer sometimes searches long and hard to organize the functions needed for even the simplest operations.

While namespaces organize classes and code, container classes help programmers organize their data. Both the .NET Framework and the .NET Compact Framework make extensive use of the container classes in a wide range of settings, and this adds to the consistency and ease of use when writing code. For example, a window can contain other windows. A container of type `ControlCollection` exposes this containment relationship to the .NET code, which can access the collection using methods with names like `Add`, `Remove`, `Contains`, and `Clear`. The items in a listbox or a combobox are similarly available through a collection class, with a set of methods that have the same names: `Add`, `Remove`, `Contains`, and `Clear`. This type of consistency helps to make .NET a well-designed, easy-to-program API.

Common Intermediate Language

When you build a .NET program (`.exe`) file or a shared library (`.dll`) file, you create an executable file that outwardly is the same as Win32, MFC, or

30. We ignore for now the distinction between the lightweight value types and reference types.

compiled Visual Basic programs. This is known technically as a Win32 portable executable (PE) file.[31] Each PE file targets a specific instruction set. Some instruction sets are tied to a specific CPU family, which is true for the Intel x86, MIPS R4000, and Toshiba SH4 instruction sets.

One unique aspect of .NET executable files is that the executable files are written for an instruction set not tied to a specific CPU family. This is the Intermediate Language (IL) instruction set. It has other names, including *Microsoft Intermediate Language* (MSIL) and *Common Intermediate Language* (CIL), the name used in its submission as an Ecma International[32] standard.

Programmers sometimes express confusion about whether IL is interpreted or compiled. The concern usually involves program performance, because interpreted languages (like Smalltalk and some versions of BASIC) run slower than compiled languages. The sluggishness of an interpreted language occurs because most of the processing of source-level instructions occurs at runtime. An interpreted language is often easy to develop for, with a very interactive development environment that lets a programmer modify the code and continue running. However, the performance concerns have largely made interpreted languages useful for prototyping but not for production code. IL provides the portability of an interpreted language with speed benefits approaching those of a compiled language.

While using an IL interpreter is possible, all released implementations of .NET runtimes run by compiling IL to native instructions. The conversion from IL to native CPU instructions is done at runtime, on a per-function basis. Desktop versions of .NET allow for an entire IL executable to be converted to native instructions and added to the native image cache (using a tool called `ngen.exe`). This feature is not supported by the .NET Compact Framework, however, because a typical mobile device lacks the storage capacity for a native image cache.

IL is not the world's first portable instruction set, incidentally; there have been several before IL. For example, Java programs are often compiled to

---

31. The ASCII letters *PE* are the signature bytes in the Win32 header, visible in a hex dump of a `.exe` or `.dll` binary file.

32. See http://www.ecma-international.org.

create Java byte code executable files. At runtime, a Java Virtual Machine converts the portable instruction set to native machine instructions.

The conversion of portable instructions to native instructions is calling *JITting*[33] (the term used for both Java and .NET programs). With IL, JITting is done on a per-method basis on both the desktop and the .NET Compact Framework. By having this fine level of granularity, only the specific methods that are called get converted; methods that never get called are never JITted, saving both processing time and execution space.

Once a method has been converted from IL to native instructions, the native code version of the method stays in RAM. The collection of JITted native code is referred to as the *native image cache*. This means that the cost incurred for JITting can get amortized for methods that are called often. Native methods are not locked into memory; rather, the memory they occupy is subject to reclamation by the garbage collector just like unreachable data objects.

Windows CE 3.0, the First IL-Compatible Platform

Most programmers are unaware that Microsoft's first product with IL was Windows CE 3.0, under the name Common Executable Format (CEF). The Pocket PC supports converting IL to native CPU instructions. The Windows CE team adopted IL because it provided a portable, CPU-neutral language that allowed a single set of installation files to support a wide range of target CPUs.

There are other important differences between IL and CEF. One is that CEF provides install-time translation, not runtime JITting. The .NET runtime, on both desktops and smart devices, provides runtime JITting support.

33. *JIT* stands for "just-in-time," a term first used in product manufacturing to refer to last-minute delivery of required parts.

Common Language Runtime

The *common language runtime* refers to a set of services that support .NET executables. Among the services it provides are the loading of an executable into memory, the JITting of its IL to native instructions, and the allocating and freeing of objects.

The most commonly discussed task that the common language runtime handles is memory management, and in particular the reclaiming of unreachable objects known as *garbage collection*. The various .NET frameworks are not the first to implement this service: Smalltalk, Visual Basic, and Java all support garbage collection in one form or another.

.NET garbage collection is important because it represents the first automatic garbage collection that is compatible with many different programming languages. A program written in one language can call a component written in another language, and the two can freely share objects. This is possible because the two share a common memory allocator, as provided by the common language runtime. That memory is properly reclaimed as part of garbage collection, again provided by the common language runtime. We discuss garbage collection in more detail in Chapter 3.

Common Language Specification

The word *common*, which appears often in .NET terms, has many meanings, including "plain" and "ordinary." That is not what *common* means in .NET. A better word might be *standard* because these elements define a set of standards that allow a wide range of programming languages to interoperate with each other.

The *Common Language Specification* (CLS), in particular, refers to a set of standards created to promote interoperability between different programming languages. This is a very important architectural feature of the .NET initiative. It opens up the possibility that existing code libraries can more easily be made available as managed code libraries. It also allows programmers a wider range of programming languages instead of restricting them to just a few. In the world before .NET, the Win32 API was primarily available to C and C++ programs. Visual Basic programs were second-class citizens because aspects of Win32 and COM were difficult if not impossible to access from Visual Basic. As Microsoft shipped new versions of Visual Basic, the gap got narrower and narrower between what a C programmer and a Visual Basic programmer could do, but it never completely went away in unmanaged code. In the world of managed-code programming, however, that gap disappears.

In .NET, because it supports the CLS, Visual Basic .NET is a first-class citizen. It is fully the equal of other languages such as C#. .NET Compact Framework programmers, for example, can write programs and libraries in one of two languages: C# or Visual Basic .NET. Both languages use the same runtime (the common language runtime), and both support a common set of types (as defined in the common type system, discussed next). A library written in Visual Basic .NET can be called from a C# program and vice versa. The common standards used by .NET-compatible languages enable this interoperability.

Compilers Compatible with the .NET Compact Framework

As we were going to press, we learned of other compilers that are compatible with the .NET Compact Framework. These types of product introductions suggest the health of the .NET ecosystem—which can help all .NET programmers.

As of this writing, Borland is shipping tools that support managed-code development for the desktop .NET Framework in its C# Builder and in Delphi 8. Borland announced that a future version of C# Builder and Delphi will support the .NET Compact Framework.

An even larger set of programming languages is available on the desktop .NET Framework. The desktop version supports C# and Visual Basic .NET, just like the .NET Compact Framework. In addition, a .NET-compatible version of the C++ compiler supports a .NET-compatible mode known as *Managed C++*. At the initial .NET announcement, there was a demonstration of a .NET-compatible Web site that was written in COBOL. Other .NET languages we know of include Curriculum, Dyalog APL, Eiffel,

Forth, Fortran (Salford FTN95), Haskell, Java, J#, F#, JScript .NET, Mercury, Mondrian, Oberon, Oz, Pascal, Perl, RPG, Scheme, Smalltalk, and Standard ML.

Common Type System

The *common type system* (CTS), a fundamental building block for .NET programming, defines a standard set of types supported by all .NET-compatible compilers. The ability of .NET executables to freely interoperate between executables built from different languages relies on the common set of types defined by the CTS. We provide a more complete discussion of the CTS in Chapter 3.

Common Language Infrastructure

The *Common Language Infrastructure* (CLI) describes a subset of the .NET Framework that Microsoft submitted as a standard to ECMA. It does not include the Windows Forms classes, the Web Forms classes, or the Web Services classes. It does include enough of the low-level details to allow third parties to create .NET-compatible compilers, debuggers, and other tools. The CLI also includes the two items we just discussed, the CLS and the CTS.

Programmers who are eager to learn more about the CLI can find a set of Word files that spell out in detail the various elements. Those files are included with Visual Studio .NET 2003 and can be found in the program file directory in the `..\SDK\v1.1\Tool Developers Guide\docs` directory.

The .NET Compact Framework

Earlier in this chapter we focused on two key ingredients: the Windows CE operating system and Microsoft's .NET initiative. For the rest of this chapter, we explore what happens when these two are combined. The results are an important improvement in support for smart-device programming.

Design Goals

When the Microsoft team started to develop the .NET Compact Framework, various tools were already being used for applications on smart devices. eMbedded Visual C++ was the development tool of choice for creating Win32 and MFC-based software. Another development tool, eMbedded Visual Basic, was also being used to create smart-device applications. On the desktop, the development of the .NET Framework and its companion, Visual Studio .NET, was well under way and was planned for release before the .NET Compact Framework. The existing and soon-to-be-released tools were important because each would play a role in setting the expectations of the software development population targeted by the .NET Compact Framework team with its new framework. The .NET Compact Framework team made plans to address the perspectives of each group of developers.

Why Put .NET in Windows CE .NET?

The full name for the latest version of Windows CE is Windows CE .NET. People often ask us why .NET is included. The reason is simple: Microsoft sees Windows CE–powered devices—including, of course, the Pocket PC—as part of its larger .NET strategy. Using the .NET Compact Framework, programmers can build traditional GUI applications that consume the services of Web Service servers.

With two different browsers—Pocket Internet Explorer (PIE) and Generic Internet Explorer (GENIE)—Windows CE–powered devices can also run Web Forms applications. An add-on to the ASP.NET Web server, ASP.NET Mobile Controls, allows for server-side customizations to Web-based applications for small-screen devices.

The presence of .NET in the operating system name suggests to some people that perhaps Windows CE has been rewritten to run entirely in managed code, but that is not the case. A huge investment has already been made in building Win32 applications and device drivers. While Microsoft might someday embark on the ambitious project of rewriting Windows CE in this way, that has not been done for Windows CE .NET. Instead, this new version of Windows CE is an evolution from the previous version of the operating system, Windows CE 3.0.

Developers who had adopted eMbedded Visual Basic were expected to make up the largest group of .NET Compact Framework developers. Because of .NET Compact Framework's support for Visual Basic, easy-to-use development environment, and high level of portability, Microsoft decided to discontinue support for eMbedded Visual Basic. As of this writing, the Pocket PC 2003 is the last device for which the eMbedded Visual Basic runtime will ship. For this group of developers, the .NET Compact Framework team set out to provide a development experience that was as easy to use as eMbedded Visual Basic.

To address the needs of developers experienced with the desktop .NET Framework, the team members worked to maintain a high level of consistency with the existing framework. They knew that a Windows CE–based framework would not be as extensive as the .NET Framework. But they could make sure that the namespaces, classes, and other types found in the .NET Compact Framework had a high level of consistency with corresponding elements of the desktop framework.

The third group of developers consisted of those using C and C++ to develop Win32 and MFC applications with eMbedded Visual C++. The .NET Compact Framework team expected this to be the smallest of the groups to adopt the .NET Compact Framework. For those who did switch, the team wanted to allow the development of applications that had the power and speed approaching native Win32 applications. Toward that end, the team did a significant amount of performance tuning to help make the .NET Compact Framework attractive to this third and perhaps most demanding group of developers.

The .NET Compact Framework team adopted the following design goals for the .NET Compact Framework.

- Build on the benefits of the .NET Framework.
- Maintain consistency with the desktop version.
- Ensure that the framework runs well on mobile and embedded devices.
- Expose the richness of target platforms.
- Preserve the look and feel of platforms.
- Provide portability to other mobile operating systems.

The following subsections discuss each of these design goals.

Build on the Benefits of the .NET Framework

A relatively recent operating system, Windows CE has always borrowed heavily from existing desktop tools and technologies. Doing so has allowed Windows CE to benefit from existing code, existing tools, and existing programmer skills. The Win32 API, for example, was created for the desktop, but it became the centerpiece of Windows CE. And the various Pocket applications on the Pocket PC (such as Pocket Word, Pocket Excel, and Pocket Outlook) were created by porting from existing desktop applications.

All of the standard (common) elements of the desktop .NET Framework are also found in the .NET Compact Framework. Executable files use the CIL instruction set, which gets brought into memory and JITted into native machine instructions by the .NET Compact Framework's common language runtime. Memory gets reclaimed by automatic garbage collection, and most of the standards spelled out in the CLI are supported in the .NET Compact Framework. This includes the CTS as well as the CLS. While the framework is not as extensive as that on the desktop, the operation of the underlying runtime is identical.

Maintain Consistency with the Desktop Version

The second design goal of the .NET Compact Framework team was to maintain consistency with the experience found in the desktop version of the .NET Framework. Programmers experienced with desktop .NET Windows Forms applications will find many old friends in the .NET Compact Framework. Both share all of the same basic value types, most of the same namespaces, and many of the same classes.

The .NET Compact Framework development team worked hard to make the .NET Compact Framework consistent with its desktop counterpart. For one thing, the two frameworks share an identical structure. The names for .NET Compact Framework namespaces, for example, mirror existing desktop namespaces. In scaling back the Compact Framework to fit within a small, 2MB footprint, the team eliminated many of the desktop .NET Framework classes. Within the remaining classes, the team trimmed back available class members. Most .NET Compact Framework classes have fewer properties, methods, and events than their desktop counterparts.

You can get a sense for how consistent the two frameworks are by studying the online documentation. The high level of consistency allows a single documentation set to support both frameworks. As Figure 1.3 illustrates, class members with .NET Compact Framework support are labeled with the note "Supported by the .NET Compact Framework."

By maintaining a high level of consistency, the .NET Compact Framework team hoped to leverage the knowledge and programming skills of existing .NET programmers. Some things are immediately familiar to desktop .NET programmers because both frameworks support C# and Visual Basic .NET, share the same set of common types, and share many namespaces and classes. Many programmers who adopted the desktop .NET Framework quickly gain productive results with the .NET Compact Framework.

But because the .NET Compact Framework supports a significantly reduced feature set from the desktop .NET Framework, desktop programmers need to allow time to get comfortable with the .NET Compact Framework because many favorite desktop classes and class members are missing. Desktop programmers are likely to "stub their toes" a number of times before they get used to the reduced set of supported classes and supported class members provided by the .NET Compact Framework.

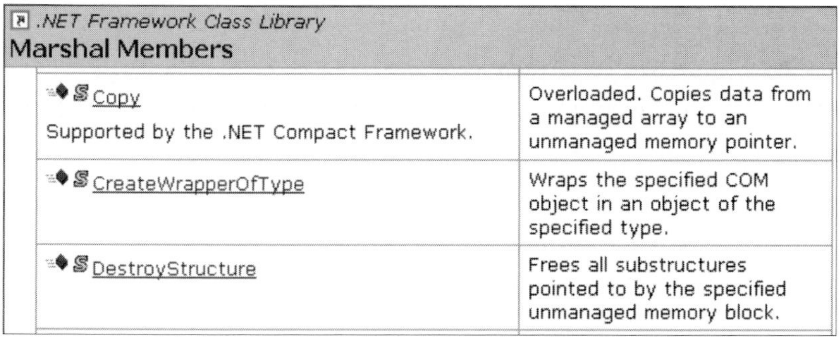

.NET Framework Class Library

Marshal Members

Copy Supported by the .NET Compact Framework.	Overloaded. Copies data from a managed array to an unmanaged memory pointer.
CreateWrapperOfType	Wraps the specified COM object in an object of the specified type.
DestroyStructure	Frees all substructures pointed to by the specified unmanaged memory block.

FIGURE 1.3: Online documentation that highlights .NET Compact Framework compatibility

While the move from the desktop to smart devices can be frustrating, the move going the other way is likely to be much less of a problem. Programmers who start their .NET career working with the .NET Compact Framework will move to the desktop .NET Framework quite easily. Because of the consistency between the desktop version and the .NET Compact Framework, and the fact that the desktop version is a true superset of the .NET Compact Framework, a .NET Compact Framework program can run unchanged on the desktop.[34]

Windows CE–specific extensions in the .NET Compact Framework are defined in namespaces other than those used in the desktop framework. For example, the `Microsoft.WindowsCE.Forms` namespace contains Windows CE–specific controls and structures. This namespace ships in the `Microsoft.WindowsCE.Forms.dll` library, which contains three elements: a `MessageWindow` class (for sending Win32 messages to managed code), the `Message` structure (for use with the `MessageWindow` class), and `InputPanel` (a wrapper class that can be used to manage the on-screen keyboard known as the Software Input Panel, or SIP). The SIP was first introduced with the original Pocket PC and is now supported on other Windows CE–powered smart devices, starting with Windows CE .NET 4.1.

The same tool used for desktop .NET development, Visual Studio .NET, is also used to build .NET Compact Framework applications. The Visual Studio .NET features that desktop programmers have come to rely on are available for .NET Compact Framework development, including IntelliSense, the Windows Forms Designer (with device-specific controls in a .NET Compact Framework–specific toolbox), the object browser, and an integrated debugger.

Ensure That the Framework Runs Well on Mobile and Embedded Devices

Another important .NET Compact Framework design goal was to make sure that it runs well on mobile and embedded devices. This meant addressing the two key challenges for any small device: size and speed.

34. This requires version 1.1 of the .NET Framework. A .NET Compact Framework program can run unchanged under the desktop .NET Framework provided that P/Invoke declarations referencing device-only libraries are not present.

Size is an issue because, at 25MB or greater, the desktop .NET Framework had to be scaled down to fit comfortably within the 32MB to 64MB of total storage space available on a typical mobile device like a Pocket PC or other Windows CE–powered device. Speed is an issue because even the fastest mobile and embedded CPUs are slower than the CPU in an average desktop system. To provide acceptable performance to users of fast desktop systems, the .NET Compact Framework team spent time tweaking the performance of the .NET Compact Framework.

At 2MB, the .NET Compact Framework has met the size goal. In working toward that goal, the .NET Compact Framework team took a page from the playbook of the Windows CE team: that is, if there were two or more ways to do the same operation, most got removed. On the desktop, the .NET Framework has the luxury of large hard drives and seemingly endless amounts of RAM. It can support, for example, several different ways to change the background color for most (but not all) controls. On the desktop, you can set the `BackColor` property, handle the `PaintBackground` event, or override the `OnPaintBackground` method. In the .NET Compact Framework, to save space, there is one way to change the color: override the `OnPaintBackground` method in a derived class. Some controls support the `BackColor` property—including `Form`, `Control`, `Panel`, `TabPage`, and `TextBox`—but most do not.

On its way to achieving the size goal, the .NET Compact Framework team left out desktop-centric features such as drag and drop, as well as large controls like the `RichTextBox` control. For each supported control, only the most basic functionality is supported. In particular, a focused subset of the properties, methods, and events (the *PMEs*, as the .NET Compact Framework team calls them) are supported in .NET Compact Framework controls. With all supported controls, the supported features are a subset of what is found on the equivalent control in the desktop .NET Framework. For developers who are moving from desktop .NET development, much of the effort required to learn about the .NET Compact Framework involves figuring out the exact subset of supported features. For example, programmers who are familiar with the `DataGrid` control on the desktop are sometimes surprised to find that the `DataGrid` control in the .NET Compact Framework is a read-only control and does not support editing.

To meet the performance goals, the .NET Compact Framework was benchmarked and tuned so that controls rely heavily on their Win32 counterparts. The Win32 controls reside in unmanaged code, and .NET Compact Framework code runs as managed code. There is a cost in crossing the boundary between managed and unmanaged code. The .NET Compact Framework team found that it could enhance the performance of the controls by allowing only a carefully controlled subset of Win32 messages to percolate as .NET events.

The .NET Compact Framework Provides CPU Independence

By meeting the goals for a framework with small size and good performance, the .NET Compact Framework team created a class library that is attractive to a wide range of application developers. For some developers, though, the most important feature is that .NET Compact Framework programs are CPU-independent.

Five different processor families have been validated to run Windows CE: ARM, MIPS, PowerPC, SH, and x86.[35] To build and ship native programs or libraries requires a large development and testing effort, especially when a target market needs support for several different processor families.

Things are much simpler with a .NET Compact Framework program or library. Instead of building and shipping five (or more) different versions, a single version can support all supported processors. (A single .NET Compact Framework program or library may require separate installation files, however, to accommodate CPU-specific setup programs.)

Expose the Richness of Target Platforms

The fourth design goal was to expose the richness of target platforms. In every case, the .NET Compact Framework relies on native controls to do

35. See http://www.microsoft.com/windows/embedded/ce.NET/evaluation/hardware/processors.asp.

the majority of the work. This has obvious benefits in terms of size and performance. It also provides a more authentic look and feel for .NET Compact Framework applications on each platform.

For example, the .NET Compact Framework `MainMenu` class provides the basic support for application menus. In a Pocket PC application, this menu appears—as in any other Pocket PC application—at the bottom of the window. On a non–Pocket PC Windows CE .NET device, that same .NET Compact Framework program displays its main menu at the top of the window like standard Windows CE .NET applications do. While the underlying Win32 menu implementations are different, the .NET Compact Framework conveniently hides this difference from developers through the .NET Compact Framework `MainMenu` and `MenuItem` classes.

Preserve the Look and Feel of Platforms

The fifth design goal was to preserve the look and feel of individual platforms. The challenge comes from subtle differences in the way the native controls are implemented. Many of these changes involve tiny, almost imperceptible differences—an extra pixel here, a deleted pixel there. Such differences are invisible when looking at two applications running on two different devices. But when two applications are running on the same device, such differences become readily apparent. The .NET Compact Framework team worked hard to make sure that the look and feel of different platforms was honored by the .NET Compact Framework. To a user, a .NET Compact Framework application is visually indistinguishable from non–Compact Framework applications.

Provide Portability to Other Mobile Operating Systems

The long-term vision for the .NET Compact Framework includes portability to other operating systems if and when it makes sense to do so. (After all, Windows CE is not the only available embedded operating system.) The first version of the .NET Compact Framework was built for Windows CE, but it was developed in a way that allows the .NET Compact Framework to be ported to other operating systems. For the present, however, Microsoft has not made public any plans to do such a port.

To facilitate its portability, all calls to the underlying operating system go through a single mapping layer called the Platform Adaptation Layer (PAL). The PAL happens to map very nicely to available Win32 API calls. The .NET Compact Framework could be ported to an operating system that did not support the Win32 API by providing a PAL that implemented features not provided by the underlying operating system.

While porting the .NET Compact Framework may be a long way in the future, the possibility of doing such a port did impact the design of today's .NET Compact Framework. This factor played a part in determining whether to include a class that had been defined in the desktop .NET Framework. The .NET Compact Framework does not support the Windows registry, for example, in part because other operating systems do not support a concept of a registry.

.NET Compact Framework Files

The .NET Compact Framework itself consists of a set of DLLs. A few are CPU-specific native-code libraries, but most of the supporting libraries are managed-code libraries. Table 1.2 summarizes the .NET Compact Framework modules, as installed by Visual Studio .NET 2003. Two of these modules, `ConManClient.exe` and `cmtnpt_tcpaccept.dll`, are used by Visual Studio .NET to communicate between a development workstation and a smart device.

One of these modules, `System.SR.dll`, contains a set of string resources to display the meaning of unhandled exceptions. When you are developing .NET Compact Framework software, this can help you identify unhandled exceptions in your code. The software you ship should catch all exceptions and handle them internally; you do not need to install the error message library on end-user systems. During development, though, it makes sense to add a reference to this library from Visual Studio .NET so you can see meaningful messages when an unhandled exception occurs.

The size of the standard .NET Compact Framework library components is around 2,383K. Adding the data providers for SQL Server and SQL Server 2000 Windows CE Edition (SQL Server CE), the size grows to just about 2.5MB. The actual on-device space required is significantly smaller than this because device storage adds a bit of compression that is fast but light, yielding a 2:1 compression on average.

TABLE 1.2: Compact Framework Modules

File Name	Description	Size (Kbytes)	Managed Code
cgacutil.exe	Compact global assembly cache utility, which adds a managed-code library to the global assembly cache to save device storage space. Base .NET Compact Framework libraries are installed in this way. This utility requires a file with an extension .gac and the name of the managed-code library (must be signed with strong names).	8	No
cmtnpt_tcpaccept.dll	Connection manager custom transport (helper for ConManClient.exe).	11	No
ConManClient.exe	Connection Manager Client, a device-side program that assists in connecting a device to Visual Studio .NET to support the downloading and debugging of managed-code modules.	36	No
Microsoft.VisualBasic.dll	Visual Basic–specific helpers, including constants (vbCr, vbCrLf) and built-in Visual Basic functions (Rnd, Mid, UCase, NPV), among others.	136	Yes
Microsoft.WindowsCE.Forms.dll	Windows CE–specific classes that support the Software Input Panel on a Pocket PC (a.k.a. InputPanel). These classes also support sending Win32 messages and creating window procedures to receive messages sent from unmanaged code.	11	Yes
mscoree.dll	Stub for mscoree1_0.dll.	13	No

continued

TABLE 1.2: Compact Framework Modules (continued)

File Name	Description	Size (Kbytes)	Managed Code
`mscoree1_0.dll`	Execution engine and Platform Adaptation Layer for .NET Compact Framework version 1.0.	461	No
`mscorlib.dll`	Low-level .NET support classes: data collections, file I/O, threads, application domains, object activator, garbage collector, globalization support, P/Invoke, text character set conversion (encoding and decoding), resources, standard system exceptions, definitions for common types, and basic types including `Object` and `ValueType`.	383	Yes
`netcfagl1_0.dll`	Native-code support for the user interface library, `System.Windows.Forms.dll`.	107	No
`System.Data.Common.dll`	Generic set of classes for accessing a data source.	106	Yes
`System.Data.dll`	Core support for the ADO.NET programming interface for in-memory database operations, primarily relational operations on in-memory tables, including support for view and joins.	394	Yes
`System.Data.SqlClient.dll`	(Optional) Data provider for remote, server-based databases for Microsoft SQL Server 7.0 or later.	145	Yes
`System.Data.SqlServerCe.dll`	(Optional) Data provider for local, device-based databases for Microsoft SQL Server 2000 Windows CE Edition.	121	Yes

File Name	Description	Size (Kbytes)	Managed Code
`System.dll`	Low-level .NET support for specialized collection classes, diagnostic helpers, low-level network connectivity classes including sockets, and regular expressions.	249	Yes
`System.Drawing.dll`	Classes that provide the `Graphics` object (the core drawing object) and drawing-support-objects including bitmaps, colors, fonts, pens, brushes, and icons.	38	Yes
`System.Net.IrDA.dll`	Infrared device support in the form of IrDA-compatible sockets and endpoint support.	11	Yes
`System.SR.dll`	(Optional) String resources for exceptions to help develop and debug applications.	91	Yes
`System.Web.Services.dll`	Support for creating SOAP-enabled Web Service clients.	94	Yes
`System.Windows.Forms.DataGrid.dll`	Data grid control and supporting classes.	38	Yes
`System.Windows.Forms.dll`	Core library for Windows Forms applications, including the `Application` object and user interface controls.	137	Yes
`System.Xml.dll`	XML schema and serialization support, along with XML reader and XML writer.	197	Yes

When you study the file system of a device with the .NET Compact Framework installed, you find all of the unmanaged modules in the `\windows` directory. No matter how hard you try, however, you do not find the managed modules listed in Table 1.2 anywhere on a device. A search for `System.dll`, for example, yields no results. What you *do* find is a file with the intriguing name of `GAC_System_v1_0_5000_0_cneutral_1.dll`.

"GAC" in the file name stands for *global assembly cache*, the name for the set of cached shared libraries. (In .NET, the term *assembly* refers to one or more modules—`.exe` or `.dll` files—that make up a logical unit.[36]) As on the desktop, the GAC in the .NET Compact Framework identifies a set of libraries that have been marked for sharing. When libraries are placed in the GAC, the loader performs some verification of the file's contents. The primary benefit of putting shared files in the GAC is the reduced storage required by keeping just one copy of a shared library. Most developers are probably not going to add libraries to the GAC, although knowing its purpose can help you understand the files you see for libraries in the GAC.

If you study the name of the GAC file, you see that the name contains the version number of the library (1.0.5000.0). The name also contains details about what culture the library targets. This library has a *neutral* culture, which means the library itself is not localized for any particular language or country. What we do not see in the file name is the key used to sign the library. The inclusion of these values—a version number, culture, and signing key—in addition to the friendly name of the library allows the common language runtime to uniquely identify each library.

Two additional, unseen elements are required for a library to be installed in the GAC: a public key and a digital signature. These last two items uniquely identify the developer of the library and also help verify that the contents of the library have not been tampered with or accidentally damaged in some fashion.

If you are just getting started with managed-code development, you should know about a utility that Microsoft ships with Visual Studio .NET.

36. We use the term *library* here because developers new to .NET are usually not familiar with the newer term *assembly*.

The name of the utility is `ildasm.exe`, which stands for IL Disassembly. This tool helps answer the question "What is inside a given managed module?" Figure 1.4 shows this tool in action, displaying an outline of the contents of the .NET Compact Framework's `system.dll` library.

Installing Shared Libraries in the Global Assembly Cache

You can add your own shared libraries to the system's GAC by creating a file with an extension of `.gac`. The file should be a text file with the full path of the library you want converted (for multiple libraries, put each library on a separate line). Copy that file, along with your libraries, to the `\windows` directory of a device. When the library is next loaded into memory, the loader creates the required GAC file for your library. Only signed libraries with strong names can be added to the GAC. Two example files are created by the .NET Compact Framework itself: `Microsoft .NET Compact Framework 1.0.gac` and `System.SR.ENU.gac`.

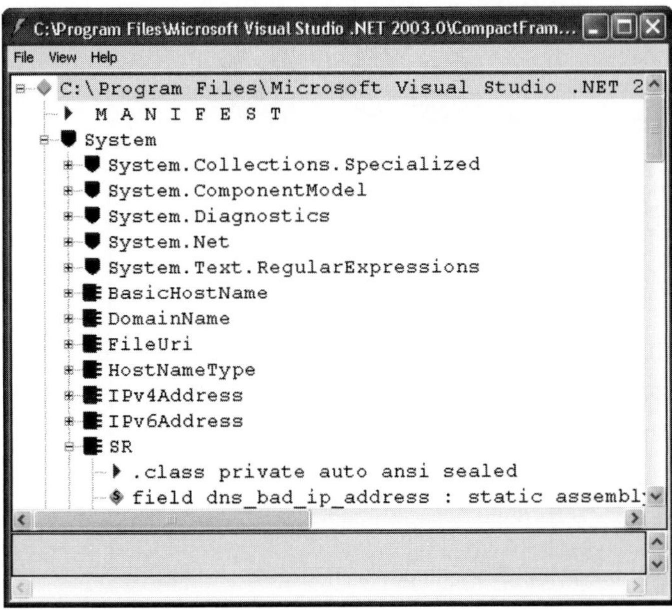

FIGURE 1.4: Contents of `system.dll` as shown in `ildasm.exe`

`ildasm.exe` provides a lot of details about managed-code libraries because managed-code modules contain all available type information encoded as metadata within the module file itself. You can find the namespaces and classes within a module, and within each class you can find the type information for each of the class members, including the names of both code and data (methods and fields). `ildasm.exe` disassembles a method to show the associated IL for the method. (To make it harder for competitors to reverse-engineer your code, obfuscator utilities jumble the metadata names in a managed-code module.)

A similar tool for unmanaged libraries is `depends.exe`, which also ships with Visual Studio .NET. This tool does not provide the same depth of information as `ildasm.exe` because much of the type information in unmanaged modules gets lost during the compile and link process. However, you can find the names of exported (public) functions, the names of libraries on which an unmanaged module depends, and the functions imported from the libraries. Figure 1.5 shows the output from this tool for one of the .NET Compact Framework's unmanaged libraries, `netcfagl1_0.dll`.

Programmers who have worked with the desktop .NET Framework can probably get a good idea about the .NET Compact Framework's capabili-

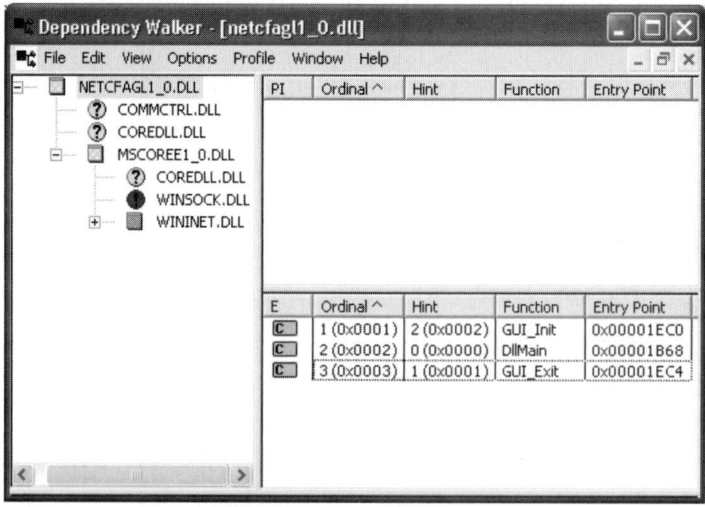

FIGURE 1.5: Output from `depends.exe` for an unmanaged library

ties and limitations just by poking around with these tools. In some cases, you have to use the tools to know exactly what is present. The online documentation also provides useful information, and as you browse through the various classes you may see the "Supported by the .NET Compact Framework" tag in quite a few places.

Hidden `ildasm.exe` Features

You can uncover some hidden `ildasm.exe` features by invoking the program with the `/adv` switch. Among these features is the ability to see statistics for a managed-code executable, such as the amount of space used for code, data, metadata, and so on. Using this feature, you can see that metadata takes up quite a bit of space—over 60% of the .NET Compact Framework's Windows Forms library, for example, consists of metadata. This helps explain in part why so many of the overloaded methods were pruned from the set available in the desktop framework.

While we recognize that some of our readers have experience with the desktop .NET Framework, we do not assume that most readers do. To help general readers start planning their smart-device development efforts, we turn our attention to a summary of what the .NET Compact Framework can—and cannot—do. We start on a positive note, with the capabilities of the .NET Compact Framework.

.NET Compact Framework Capabilities

The .NET Compact Framework was designed to be consistent with the desktop .NET Framework. Like it or not, the desktop version always seems to be lurking in the background, like a worried parent or a homeless puppy. A crude way to compare the frameworks is by number of files and disk space occupied. The .NET Compact Framework has 18 libraries (including optional ones) and occupies about 2.5MB. The .NET Framework version 1.1, by contrast, has 86 libraries and occupies about 40MB.

Supported Runtime Elements

So what can the .NET Compact Framework library do for us? First, the .NET Compact Framework implements most of the CLI, so the standard data types found on the desktop are also present for smart-device programming. At present, Microsoft supports two programming languages for the .NET Compact Framework: C# and Visual Basic .NET. This is quite a reduction from the 20 or more languages that support desktop .NET Framework. And yet, support for C# and Visual Basic .NET in the .NET Compact Framework shows that interoperability between languages is more than a promise; in the .NET Compact Framework, as on the desktop, we have direct evidence in the form of working, commercial-quality compilers that allow assemblies created in one language to freely interoperate with assemblies created in other languages.

The .NET Compact Framework supports an execution engine that provides JIT compilation of IL and that verifies the type safety of managed modules before loading them. The runtime for the .NET Compact Framework provides the same memory management as on the desktop, enabling memory allocation, heap management, and garbage collection of unreachable objects.

The .NET Compact Framework supports *application domains*, which is a kind of lightweight process. Multiple application domains can run in a single operating system process. On some operating systems, processes have high overhead, and the cost of context switching from one process to another is high. That certainly describes processes on desktop versions of Windows, and the application domains provide a lightweight alternative.

A process in Windows CE is already lightweight. As far as the CPU is concerned, all processes in Windows CE reside in a single process. So is there a benefit to using application domains in the .NET Compact Framework? The answer is yes. A side effect of having lightweight processes is that there is a fairly low limit to the number of processes that can be created on a Windows CE system. That limit is 32, and it is so tightly ingrained in the memory and process architecture of Windows CE that we usually call this a *hard limit*, by which we mean that this limit is unlikely to change in future versions of the operating system. The operating system itself uses a few of these processes, which leaves 24 or 25 available for application programs. A .NET Compact Framework programmer might use application domains to avoid using up all the available operating system processes for large, complex applications.

On the desktop, an unmanaged process can load the common language runtime into a process (using the `CorBindToRuntimeEx` function). This is how, for example, the managed code of ASP.NET Web Forms applications can be loaded into the unmanaged address space of the Internet Information Services (IIS) Web server process (`inetinfo.exe`). This feature is not supported in version 1.0 of the .NET Compact Framework.

The .NET Compact Framework runtime does support P/Invoke, the ability for managed code to call through to unmanaged code. There are some limitations in comparison to the desktop. One involves the complexity of the parameters that can be passed. Simple value types can be passed as parameters, as you might expect. Most reference types can also be passed as parameters, including strings, structures, and objects. But complex structures and complex objects—meaning those with embedded structures or embedded objects—cannot be marshaled automatically.[37] We discuss this subject in more detail in Chapter 4.

On the subject of interoperability, the .NET Compact Framework does not support COM interop. For the present, several approaches address this problem. One is to access COM/ActiveX components by creating an unmanaged wrapper around the component and then exporting a set of C-callable functions. This approach, though tedious, does allow use of existing components with a relatively small amount of effort in the form of this glue layer.

Another approach is to use the CFCOM interoperability layer offered by a company called Odyssey Software.[38] This software allows the use of ActiveX controls from .NET Compact Framework programs and the use of COM components from .NET Compact Framework programs.

While the .NET Compact Framework does not support COM interop, it might be said to be COM-aware because all .NET Compact Framework

---

37. The .NET Compact Framework, version 1.0, does not support the `MarshalAs` attribute. Complex objects can still be marshaled, using `IntPtr` and `static` (for Visual Basic programmers, `Shared`), members of the `System.Runtime.InteropServices.Marshal` class.

38. For details, visit http://www.odysseysoftware.com.

threads call `CoInitialize` and `CoUninitialize` so that you do not have to. Microsoft has publicly announced that additional support for COM will be provided in a future version of the .NET Compact Framework, although details about that support have not yet been made public.

Supported .NET Application Classes

Among the three .NET application classes, the .NET Compact Framework supports Windows Forms—traditional GUI applications. Support on both the desktop and in the .NET Compact Framework is provided by various classes in the `System.Windows.Forms` namespace. Of the 35 controls supported on the desktop, 28 are supported in the .NET Compact Framework. These controls are not supported in their entirety, however. To accommodate the size and performance constraints of mobile and embedded development, a subset of the desktop class members—the PMEs—is supported in the .NET Compact Framework.

The creation of Windows Forms applications is the subject of Part II of this book. We discuss the supported controls in Chapter 7, and in Chapter 9 we present a tool named `ControlPME` for testing each .NET Compact Framework control for supported PMEs. This tool is necessary because several .NET Compact Framework controls inherit unsupported members (this is also true of desktop controls but to a lesser extent).

Another .NET application class that the .NET Compact Framework supports is Web Services. A .NET Compact Framework program can create a Web Services client. For the present, the .NET Compact Framework supports providing the client side of Web Services, but the .NET Compact Framework does not support implementing a device-based Web Services server.

Native-code support for building Web Services is provided in Windows CE with version 2.0 of the SOAP[39] Toolkit. Does this make sense? It depends on how Windows CE is deployed. Windows CE can be configured to support a Web server, which provides a way for the outside world to communicate with the Windows CE system using industry-standard protocols like HTTP and HTML. We know of a Windows CE device that monitors certain physical properties of in-process chemical plants. These devices support a

39. *SOAP* stands for "Simple Object Access Protocol."

Web server that allows a chemical plant operator to monitor the status of many vats of chemicals from a Web browser. It takes a tiny leap of imagination to consider exposing that information in a programmable way—that is, through Web Services. As HTML, the information is available in human-readable form; as a Web Service, the information is available in machine-readable form.

The .NET Compact Framework has no support for Web Forms applications. As of this writing, this third application class can be implemented only on ASP.NET-compatible Web servers. The following operating systems can host a Web Forms–compatible Web server:

- Windows 2000 (Professional, Server, and Advanced Server)
- Windows XP Professional
- Windows Server 2003

As currently implemented, a Web Forms application is deployed on and run from a Web server system, not on a Web client system.

While the .NET Compact Framework does not support Web Forms applications, Windows CE devices—including Pocket PC—can certainly run as Web Forms clients. All that is required is a suitable Web browser. Windows CE supports two basic browsers. PIE is the smaller, lightweight browser that ships with Pocket PC. A more fully featured browser, GENIE, is a port of the desktop version of Internet Explorer. GENIE provides a Web browsing experience more like that found on the desktop.

Microsoft has created a set of ASP.NET controls to address small-screen Web browsers like Pocket PC. These controls, known as the ASP.NET Mobile Controls, support the creation of Web pages for three separate types of Web browsers: (1) HTML 3.2 (which includes the Pocket PC); (2) Compact HTML (cHTML), a lightweight version of HTML found on some devices; and (3) Wireless Markup Language/Wireless Application Protocol (WML/WAP), supported on mobile phones.

Using the ASP.NET Mobile Controls, an ASP.NET Web server can support a single set of Web pages, which can be correctly rendered for a wide range of browsers on a wide range of devices. While the ASP.NET Mobile Controls bridge the gap between markup languages on different mobile devices, they do not bridge the gap between mobile browsers and desktop browsers. In particular, to support both mobile and desktop browsers from a single set of Web pages, the pages must render only HTML 3.2 (and not HTML 4.0, which is the standard for desktop browsers). Thus, it is possible to create a single, common set of pages for both desktop and mobile browsers. But the ASP.NET Mobile Controls do not by themselves reformat existing Web pages to accommodate smaller screen sizes. In some cases, it might make sense to have two sets of Web pages: one for desktop browsers and another for mobile browsers.

Graphical Output

Windows CE has a pretty capable graphics engine, although it is nowhere near the extensive features provided by the drawing support of Microsoft Windows XP, or other desktop-based versions of Windows. What Windows CE does provide, though, is reasonably complete support for the three basic drawing families: text, raster, and vector.

TrueType fonts are supported for drawing text, although most smart devices do not have as many available fonts as desktops do. A typical Pocket PC, for example, ships with four fonts (one of which is a symbol font). And while Windows CE supports rotating TrueType fonts and also displaying the ClearType font technology, neither feature is exposed by version 1.0 of the .NET Compact Framework. In Chapter 16, we provide the basics of drawing text and also show how to drill through to the underlying libraries for some of the extra features.

For raster graphics—meaning bitmaps—the .NET Compact Framework is able to work with a wide range of raster file formats, including JPEG,[40] GIF,[41] PNG,[42] and of course the standard set of device-independent bitmap (DIB) formats. However, the .NET Compact Framework cannot rotate bit-

---

40. *JPEG* stands for "Joint Photographic Experts Group," the industry group that defined the standard file format. For more information, visit the Web site: http://www.jpeg.org.

41. *GIF* stands for "Graphics Interchange Format," a format commonly used to store images used in Web pages.

42. *PNG* stands for "Portable Network Graphics," a format created to store graphic images for use in Web pages.

maps because that support is not present in the underlying Windows CE drawing functions.

For vector graphics, the .NET Compact Framework can draw most of the same basic set of outlines and filled figures as on the desktop. Vector objects cannot be rotated, however, because once again the underlying Windows CE graphics support does not provide this.

The desktop .NET Framework supports a wide range of drawing coordinates. You can draw using pixel units, inches, millimeters, or printer's points. The .NET Compact Framework supports drawing only in pixels (except for font sizes, which are specified in printer's points). As with other limitations in graphics support, the .NET Compact Framework limitation on drawing coordinates is a direct result of what the underlying Windows CE drawing functions support.

We dedicate Part IV of this book to the subject of drawing. Programmers need to use drawing functions when displaying output directly in a form and also when creating custom controls.

Supported ADO.NET Elements

The largest portion of the .NET Compact Framework is consumed by the libraries that support ADO.NET, Microsoft's architecture for managing data from multiple data sources. Bill Vaughn, an author well known for his Visual Basic and ADO expertise, suggested to us that XDO might have been a more accurate name (for *XML Data Objects*) because XML serves as the underlying storage format. You get a hint of that from this quote, taken from an MSDN Library article: "In effect, the `DataSet` is an in-memory relational structure with built-in Extensible Markup Language (XML) support."[43]

The primary ADO.NET data management class is `DataSet`, which holds in-memory collections of one or more `DataTable` objects. A data table, in turn, is a collection of rows and columns. Tables in ADO.NET are structured according to a relational database model. Relationships between the `DataTable` objects are specified by creating `DataRelation` objects.

---

43. From ".NET Data Access Architecture Guide," by Alex Mackman, Chris Brooks, Steve Busby, and Ed Jezierski. Microsoft Corporation, October 2001. Available online at http://msdn.microsoft.com/library/default.asp?url=/library/en-us/dnbda/html/daag.asp.

ADO.NET does not have a built-in ad hoc query language, such as SQL. Instead, data gets read and written using members of objects created from the various ADO.NET classes.

A set of ADO.NET objects can be created from scratch, using various classes from the `System.Data` namespace. While the idea of creating an in-memory data table might seem like a lot of work, it can simplify the handling of data arrays. The `DataGrid` control, for one thing, provides an easy way to display such data. The data grid in the .NET Compact Framework supports data display but not data editing, unlike the desktop data grid, which supports both display and editing of data. We discuss the `DataGrid` control and binding a table to that control in Chapter 8.

The use of in-memory data tables forms the basis for a variety of .NET-based application software, including the ixio Smart Data Machine from ixio Corporation.[44] The architecture for this client/server system provides a way to encapsulate business logic in a manner analogous to the way that database management system software encapsulates the data management for applications. In the Smart Data Machine, the results returned by all transactions are of type `DataSet`. In the simplest cases, a data set contains one data table, which in turn has one row and one column: a simple scalar value. As dictated by the needs of individual transactions, data tables can contain multiple rows and/or columns, and data sets can contain multiple data tables. This approach provides a flexible mechanism for packaging client/server data in a simple, elegant manner.

A more traditional approach to using ADO.NET is to access a database that resides in more permanent storage. For this, ADO.NET requires the support of a data provider. A data provider is a kind of logical device driver for a database. Data providers enable connections to databases, the execution of database commands, and access to the results. The .NET Compact Framework ships with two data providers.

One data provider, `System.Data.SqlClient.dll`, supports using databases managed by SQL Server (version 7.0 or later) as the data source. SQL Server does not run on Windows CE but rather runs on desktop and server versions of Microsoft Windows. The use of SQL Server as a data

---

44. See http://www.ixio.com.

source requires a live network connection between the Windows CE system and the SQL Server system.

A second data provider, `System.Data.SqlServerCe.dll`, supports using local databases managed by SQL Server CE. This database runs on the Windows CE system itself, with database files stored in the Windows CE object store or on an installable file system. The only requirement for using this data source is that SQL Server CE be installed on the local Windows CE system. (A side note: SQL Server CE databases are not the same as Windows CE property databases, sometimes referred to as *CEDB databases*.)

The desktop .NET Framework supports two other data providers, which are not supported in the .NET Compact Framework as of this writing: the ODBC[45] data provider and the OLE DB[46] data provider. We discuss database programming in more detail in Chapters 12 and 13.

XML Support

An important data format for .NET programming is XML.[47] XML provides a standard way to create HTML-like custom tags. While HTML structures text and images for display in a Web browser, XML structures data for programmatic access. HTML, for example, is the format for Windows CE help files. XML, on the other hand, provides the format for storing data that can be shared between computers in a platform-neutral way.

There are many uses of XML in the computer industry today, including Microsoft's BizTalk Server, which provides an XML-based mechanism for exchanging documents (such as purchase orders and invoices) between companies. Microsoft SQL Server 2000 can use XML to send and receive data, which means any computer—whether running Microsoft Windows or not—can query and update a SQL Server–based database.

---

45. *ODBC* stands for "Open Database Connectivity."
46. *OLE DB* is the name for a database technology built on COM.
47. A very good summary of .NET support for XML appears in Aaron Skonnard's article, "XML in .NET: .NET Framework XML Classes and C# Offer Simple, Scalable Data Manipulation," *MSDN Magazine*, January 2001. Available online at http://msdn.microsoft.com/msdnmag/issues/01/01/xml/default.aspx.

There are myriad uses of XML within the .NET world. We mentioned one earlier: XML is used for ADO.NET data. Another well-known use of XML is within Web Services. SOAP, one of the underlying protocols for Web Services, is defined in terms of XML datagrams. An interesting feature of .NET support for Web Services is that while XML is used as the underlying format, the use of XML itself is buried within the Web Services support classes.

The extensibility of XML means that programmers can create custom tag dialects to suit a specific set of needs and structure the tags as needed. The ability to create custom tags introduces the need to validate an XML data set with a specific dialect. While the desktop .NET Framework supports both the document type definition (DTD) and the schema approach to validating XML—in the form of the `XMLValidatingReader` class—the .NET Compact Framework supports neither type of validation.

The .NET Compact Framework supports the XML Document Object Model (DOM), which allows an entire XML document to be read into memory and manipulated. Through its support of the `XMLDocument` class, the .NET Compact Framework supports traversing a RAM-resident XML hierarchy. Significantly, the .NET Compact Framework does not support the `XMLDataDocument` class, which loads an XML document into an ADO.NET data set. This additional support requires the presence of an XML schema to convert the XML document into the relational structure of ADO.NET. XML schemas, however, are not supported in the .NET Compact Framework.

The desktop .NET Framework provides XML document query support through various classes in the `System.Xml.XPath` namespace. On the desktop, you use these classes to step through a subset of nodes that match specific query criteria. However, the .NET Compact Framework supports none of the `XPath` features.

Strictly speaking, the .NET Framework and the .NET Compact Framework do not support the Simple API for XML (SAX). SAX was created before the .NET Framework as an alternative to the XML DOM. SAX provides a forward-reading, push-model "firehose" approach to parsing an XML document. .NET provides—both on the desktop and for the .NET Compact Framework—the pull-model `XmlTextReader` class. You use this class when searching an XML document for a specific value or attribute, when you do not want the memory overhead of reading an entire XML document into memory.

When working with XML documents, it sometimes becomes useful to convert an entire XML document from one set of tags to another. That is one of several services available with the eXtensible Stylesheet Language (XSL) and the associated XSL transformations. This type of transformation is commonly performed between a custom XML syntax and HTML (or another presentation markup language, like WML). On the desktop, this is done with the various classes of the `System.Xml.Xsl` namespace. The .NET Compact Framework does not support XSL transformations. The rationale for excluding this support is that XSL transformations are computationally expensive and are more likely to be done on a dedicated server than on a mobile or embedded device.

The .NET Compact Framework provides a basic set of XML services, which will meet the needs of most programmers. But not all the XML classes found on the desktop are present in the .NET Compact Framework. The effects of the "small is good" design goal for Windows CE are felt everywhere, and decisions that the increased code sizes were too high compared with the anticipated need for given features led to omissions from the desktop .NET Framework.

The Windows CE XML parser provides services not supported by the .NET Compact Framework. The XML parser under Windows CE is a componentized version of Microsoft's MSXML parser, version 3.0, Service Pack 1. This parser exposes its services as a set of COM interfaces, which means you must write a Win32 wrapper library to access the unmanaged XML parser. The unmanaged XML parser supports the following features that the .NET Compact Framework XML classes do not:

- DTD validation
- Schema validation
- XPath queries
- XSL transformations

Whether these feature are available to you depends on several factors: (1) whether your platform has been built to include the native XML parser and whether the specific configuration has the feature(s) you need, and (2) whether you are willing to write the required C++ native wrappers to work with your XML in native code.

.NET Compact Framework Limitations

The .NET Compact Framework is a smaller, simpler subset of the desktop .NET Framework. This discussion of missing features is by no means exhaustive but is instead meant to point out some of the features commonly used by desktop .NET programmers that do not appear in the .NET Compact Framework. In some cases, you can find support for missing capabilities in the unmanaged Win32 libraries, and a P/Invoke declaration may be all you need to access a required capability. In other cases, the lack of support may require you to redesign your software to accommodate the limitations inherent in a smaller, simpler platform.

The .NET Compact Framework does not support precompiling IL modules, and all IL-to-native conversion occurs at runtime as JITted code. Programmers familiar with the desktop .NET Framework might be familiar with a utility called `ngen.exe`, used to precompile modules and to manage the set of existing precompiled native images. Since the .NET Compact Framework does not support precompiling, there is no equivalent to `ngen.exe` in the .NET Compact Framework.

Web Services, which the .NET Compact Framework supports, are not the only kind of RPC mechanism in .NET. Another mechanism, .NET Remoting, is also supported on the desktop. .NET Remoting provides a lighter-weight mechanism than Web Services because it is largely driven by a low-level binary protocol. .NET Remoting is also more flexible than Web Services because an object can run locally on the same computer or remotely on a networked computer. It is not an industry-standard protocol, however, and because small is good in Windows CE, .NET Remoting is not supported in the .NET Compact Framework.

The underlying Windows CE libraries primarily[48] support the Unicode character set. Table 1.3 summarizes how various Microsoft operating sys-

48. We say "primarily" because a few of the network-oriented libraries, including the socket libraries and `wininet.dll`, are bimodal in supporting both ANSI and Unicode character sets.

TABLE 1.3: Character Sets Supported by Microsoft Operating Systems

Operating System	ANSI Support (Single-/Multi-byte Characters)	Wide Support (Unicode Characters)
Windows 98, Windows Me	Yes	No[a]
Windows NT, Windows 2000, Windows XP, Windows Server 2003	Yes	Yes
Windows CE .NET	No	Yes

a. With the Microsoft Unicode Library (MSUL), Unicode support is available.

tems support different character sets. The computer world is slowly making a transition to using Unicode characters. Windows CE supports only Unicode, but this just means that Win32 functions on Windows CE accept only Unicode characters. This is probably going to be an issue only when reading files that are not Unicode or when communicating with other computers with non-Unicode characters. (Most Web sites, for example, do not send Unicode characters.) In that case, you may need to convert between Unicode and other character sets. For such cases, the encoder and decoder classes from the `System.Text` class can provide you with conversion support.

The system registry is as important in Windows CE as on the desktop. But misuse of the registry has contributed to the complexity of software installation, software deinstallation, and software version control. This has led Microsoft to deemphasize the registry for .NET programs and recommend instead XML configuration (`*.config`) files. As part of this shift in emphasis, the .NET Compact Framework does not support the framework classes for accessing the registry. This omission supports the goal of making the .NET Compact Framework portable between platforms because no other embedded operating system supports a construct identical to the Windows registry.

The lack of registry support means that two classes, the `Registry` class and the `RegistryKey` class, are not supported by the .NET Compact Framework. If you need to use the registry, you can find a replacement class at the OpenNETCF Web site (see the sidebar). Another alternative is to call the native Win32 registry functions using P/Invoke wrappers, a subject we cover in Chapter 11.

Bridging the Gap: The OpenNETCF Web Site

To help bridge the gap between the .NET Compact Framework and the desktop .NET Framework, a group of pioneering software developers created the OpenNETCF Web site (http://www.OpenNETCF.org). As noted on its home page, this Web site was created "as an independent source for .NET Compact Framework development information working under the spirit of the open-source movement." Among the source code available on this site are a serial I/O library, registry library, notification library, and some wrappers for calling Windows API functions.

CONCLUSION

Microsoft has developed an implementation of the .NET Framework for the Pocket PC and Windows CE in the form of the .NET Compact Framework. The core features of both frameworks are identical: a common set of types that support interoperability between different computer languages, executable files with IL instructions that are JITted to native instructions at runtime, and automatic memory reclamation by the runtime.

On that core, the .NET Compact Framework supports a reduced subset of the namespaces found on the desktop, with an emphasis on building Windows Forms applications that store data using ADO.NET features and that communicate with the outside world using Web Services. The consistency between the two implementations is so strictly followed that .NET Compact Framework programs can run unchanged on the desktop under the .NET Framework version 1.1.

This completes our high-level look at the .NET Compact Framework. The remainder of this book focuses on the myriad details needed to write code that runs using the .NET Compact Framework on Pocket PC and Windows CE–powered smart devices. We begin this journey in the next chapter with a look at the code that goes into a .NET Compact Framework program.

2

What Is a .NET Compact Framework Program?

In the last chapter we looked at the .NET Compact Framework from a high-level, architectural perspective. This chapter answers the question "What is a .NET Compact Framework application?" by studying the details of a simple but complete .NET Compact Framework Windows application. Along the way, we introduce elements that are common to every .NET Compact Framework program, including forms, controls, classes, events, and event handlers. We also explain the relationship between the code generated for you by the Visual Studio .NET 2003 Windows Forms Designer and the code you must write yourself.

The Essence of a .NET Compact Framework Program

A .NET Compact Framework Windows program is a program built to use the .NET Compact Framework libraries. As discussed in Chapter 1, the .NET Compact Framework libraries run on the Win32 API support provided by the underlying Windows CE operating system. These same Win32 API services can be directly accessed from a .NET Compact Framework program, using the P/Invoke services of the .NET Compact Framework (see Chapter 4 for details on P/Invoke).

A .NET Compact Framework program can support any of several user interface paradigms. .NET Compact Framework programs can run headless—as an invisible process—with no user interface, as a console application,[1] or as a Windows application. Any of these might draw on one or more class libraries that you develop. While not denying the importance of headless and console-based user interfaces, the focus of this book is on building Windows applications—which means applications with a GUI. For the purposes of this book, then, we define a .NET Compact Framework program as a program with the following elements:

- Is built to use the .NET Compact Framework libraries
- Has a GUI
- Is defined entirely in accessible source code
- Has one or more classes derived from the `System.Windows.Forms.Form` class, one of which is instantiated at application startup as the application's main window

Let us take a look at each element of this definition.

Uses the .NET Compact Framework Libraries

As we discussed in Chapter 1, the .NET Compact Framework libraries are a set of DLLs. A small part of these are Win32 libraries, built with native, unmanaged code. Most of the .NET Compact Framework libraries are .NET managed libraries, and like managed applications these managed libraries are portable between different CPU architectures.

.NET Compact Framework programs require the presence of the .NET Compact Framework libraries, which can be either built into device ROM or installed into the RAM-based file system. Having the .NET Compact Framework in ROM is required for Pocket PC 2003 devices. For earlier Pocket PCs, the .NET Compact Framework has to be installed into the RAM file system. (Visual Studio .NET 2003 creates cabinet files, with the extension `.cab`, to set up .NET Compact Framework applications, but these `.cab` files do not include the .NET Compact Framework libraries. A separate set

1. Character-based applications rely on support from the underlying Windows CE operating system. Some platforms—most notably the Pocket PC family of platforms—do not support a character-based user interface.

of `.cab` files containing the runtime libraries is available with the .NET 2003 development environment.)

Has a Graphical User Interface

A .NET Compact Framework Windows application consists of forms and controls contained within those forms that execute in an event-driven GUI environment. The application presents information to the user, and the user responds by interacting with the forms and controls through the use of either mouse and keyboard or stylus, touch screen, and the on-screen Software Input Panel on supported devices.

An *event* is a predefined notification from an object that indicates something has happened that might be of interest to other objects (e.g., `textFirstName`'s text has changed, or button `cmdConnectToDatabase` has been tapped, or `connSQLCConnection`'s connection has successfully been opened). As we will see later in this chapter, any other object that holds a reference to the source object can sign up to receive events) from the source object. Whatever the source of an event, the destination is an *event handler*. Event handlers are class methods of the recipient. Their sole job is to watch for and respond to events.

If you have worked in any event-based programming environment, you will find that .NET Compact Framework event handlers have many familiar elements. When the paradigm of event-driven GUI programming was first introduced in the early 1980s—first on the Apple Macintosh in 1984 and then in Microsoft Windows 1.01 in 1985—it seemed arcane and difficult to comprehend. Since then, it has become the mainstream model for building interactive user interfaces. The basic model for all GUIs is the same; the differences are primarily in the syntax of function calls and in the details of the supported features.

Is Defined Entirely in Source Code

A .NET Compact Framework application consists entirely of code. When you draw forms and controls in the Visual Studio Designer, it does not create data definitions of these elements but instead generates code. So code defines forms and controls, code sets the properties of forms and controls, and code handles events. This is good news to programmers, who by the nature of their work are used to reading, writing, and—from time to time—debugging code.

Defining user interface objects entirely in code is different from the way environments like Visual Basic 6 operate. With Visual Basic 6, when a developer defines controls, they are generated by the development environment and hidden from the programmer. It is also different from what Win32 and MFC programmers are used to, where dialogs and menus are drawn in graphical editors but then stored away in the stale and often obscure format of resource (`.rc`) files. Even though you can view and even edit these text definitions, they are dead data, and they rely on hidden operating system code to bring them to life.

In the .NET Compact Framework environment, every change you make in the Designer causes code to be generated automatically for you. This code is not hidden from you; you can examine it and use it to learn all kinds of interesting things about .NET Compact Framework classes. To a certain extent, you can also modify this code.

Modifying Designer-Generated Code

Although you can modify Designer-generated code, in some cases such changes will be lost when the Designer regenerates the code. If you introduce errors into the code, you may even break the Designer.

Thus everything in a .NET Compact Framework application is defined within its source code, which has lead to the oft-quoted line, "You can write a .NET application in Notepad." However, almost no one does this because the Visual Studio .NET development environment is the much better tool for producing .NET Compact Framework Windows applications.

Has One or More Classes Derived from `System.Windows.Forms.Form`

A .NET Compact Framework application consists of one or more forms, each of which is created from a class derived from the `System.Win-`

dows.Forms.Form base class. Because each form is a class that derives from the Form base class, each form consists of PMEs. The PMEs supported by System.Windows.Forms.Form are the PMEs that exist within the forms that your application creates. .NET Compact Framework forms have a BackColor property because System.Windows.Forms.Form has a BackColor property. .NET Compact Framework forms do not have an Opacity property, however, because that property does not exist in System.Windows.Forms.Form. A complete list of supported PMEs for the System.Windows.Forms.Form class appears in Chapter 5.

One of these forms is the application's main window. When the application starts running, this main window appears to the user. It is the main door through which all the features of the program are made available.

Our definition is complete. It's time to enter the Visual Studio .NET application development environment and create a .NET Compact Framework Windows application.

Using Visual Studio .NET 2003

To create a new .NET Compact Framework application, start Visual Studio .NET 2003 and select the File→New→Project... menu item. The .NET development environment responds with the New Project dialog box (Figure 2.1).

All samples in this book are in C#, so select Visual C# Projects in the Project Type pane. Then select Smart Device Application in the Templates pane, and specify the application name and directory. When ready to proceed, click the OK button.

The next step in creating a .NET Compact Framework application is to specify the target platform and the project type to create. You can do this in the Smart Device Application Wizard (Figure 2.2), which appears after you click OK in the New Project dialog box. (For details on Windows CE platforms, see the discussion in Chapter 1. Note: The appearance of the wizard may vary from platform to platform.)

There are five possible project types that you can create in .NET Compact Framework; four of which are available for Pocket PC, and four for Windows CE, as summarized in Table 2.1.

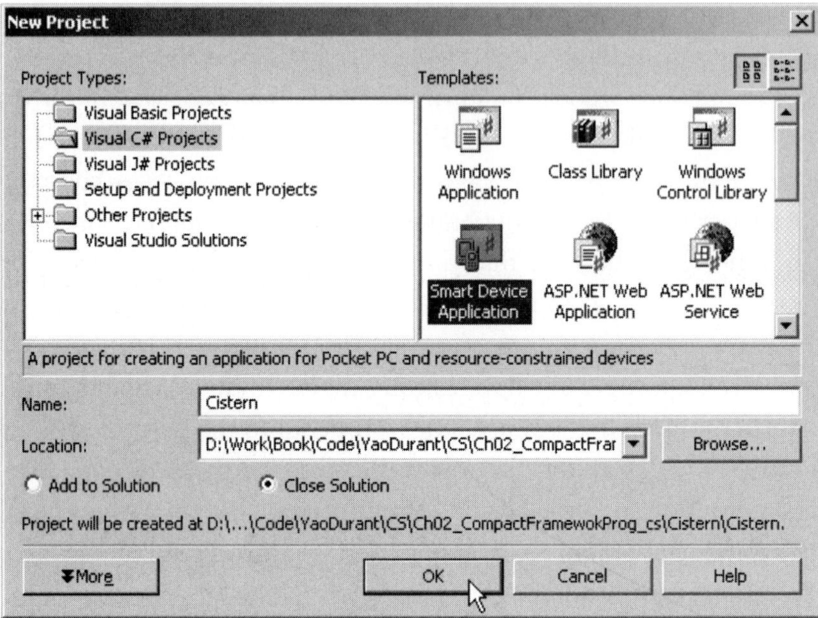

FIGURE 2.1: The New Project dialog box

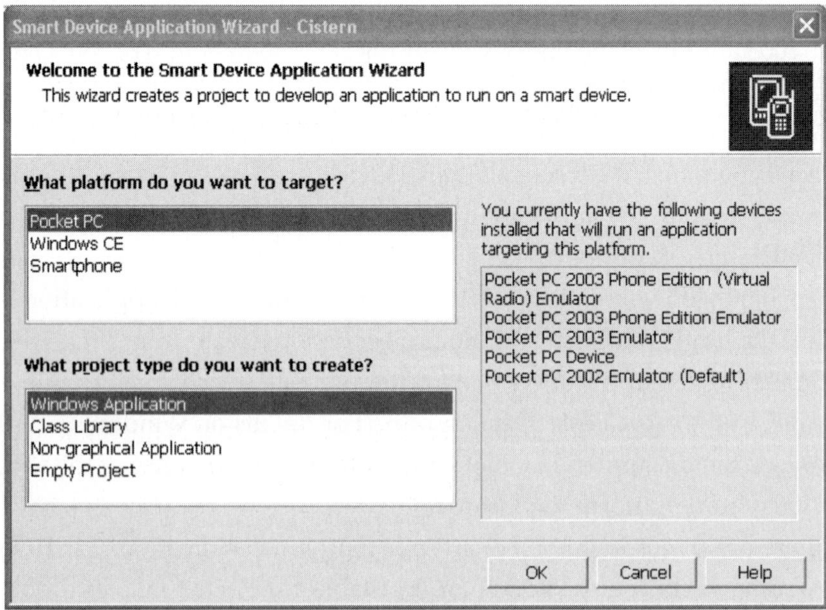

FIGURE 2.2: The Smart Device Application Wizard

TABLE 2.1: Project Types in the .NET Compact Framework

Project Type	Description
Windows Application	A GUI application that uses forms and controls to interact with the user
Class Library	A managed-code DLL
Non-graphical Application	An application with no user interface; not available on the Pocket PC
Console Application	An application with a character-based user interface; not available on the Pocket PC
Empty Project	A project file with no source files

In response to a request to create a Windows Application for the Pocket PC, the Smart Device Application Wizard generates all the files needed to support a .NET Compact Framework application and stores those files in the directory specified earlier. Visual Studio .NET next passes control to the Designer (Figure 2.3).

You now have a blank canvas on which you can begin shaping the elements of your masterpiece—a .NET Compact Framework Windows application. Although the Designer is not very interesting to look at, you nonetheless have a complete application consisting of one form and no controls. When we say "complete," we mean you can build the application without errors or warnings. (To build, select either Build Solution or Build <appname> from the Visual Studio .NET Build menu.)

The `Locked` Property

On the Pocket PC, forms are displayed full-screen. If you accidentally change the size of the form during design, the layout of the controls in the Designer might be different from the layout that will be displayed on a Pocket PC. To prevent this from happening, set the `Locked` property for forms to `true`.

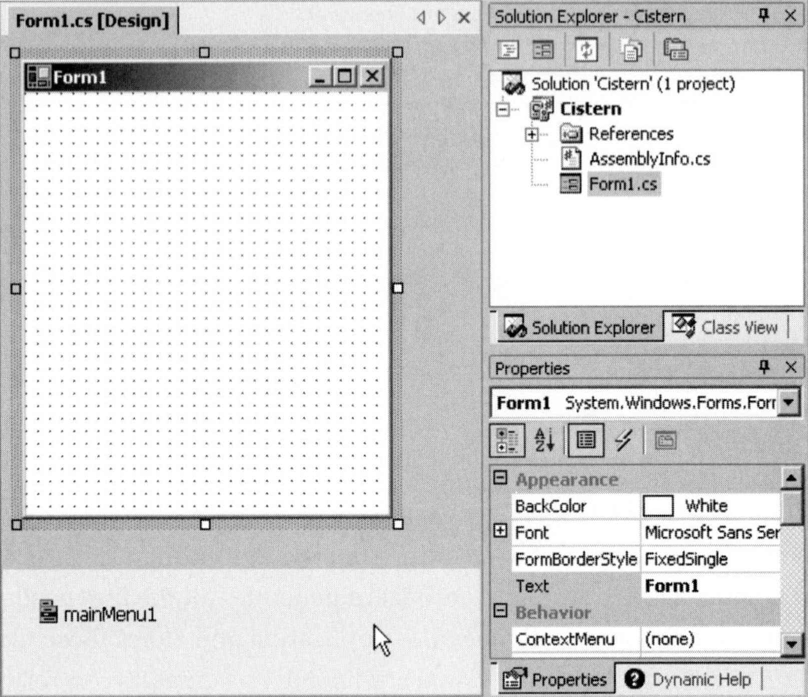

FIGURE 2.3: The Visual Studio .NET 2003 Designer

Once you build your program, you can run it—either on a connected Windows CE device or on the emulator—by selecting the Debug→Start Without Debugging command from Visual Studio .NET. This command causes a series of actions to occur.

1. As needed, save modified but unsaved source files.
2. As needed, build the application.
3. Connect to the target device or start and connect to the emulator.
4. As needed, download .NET Compact Framework libraries to the target device.
5. Copy (deploy) the program to the target device.
6. Start running the program.

Figure 2.4 shows the minimum program from Figure 2.3 running in the emulator. It is a complete application, but it does nothing. We enhance

FIGURE 2.4: A minimum program running in the emulator

this program later in this chapter, using the various features of Visual Studio .NET.

Before adding to the program, however, we need to mention an important step in the download process. Depending on how Visual Studio .NET is set up, you may have already seen the Deploy dialog box (Figure 2.5), which lets you pick where to deploy your program. You have two types of choices: a Pocket PC emulator or a Pocket PC device. (See the sidebar,

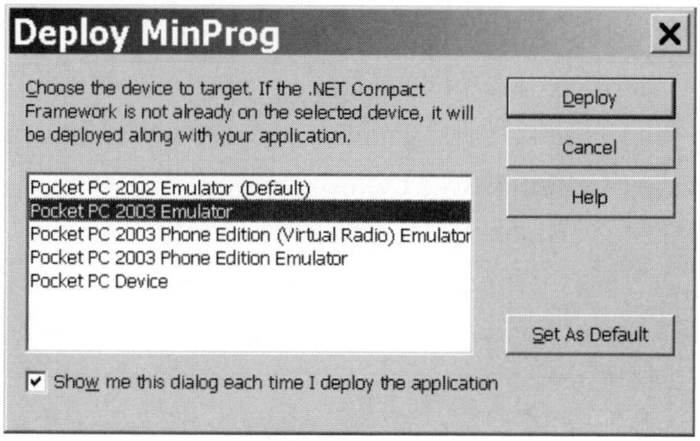

FIGURE 2.5: The Deploy dialog box

Emulator or Device?, for details on these choices.) To prevent this dialog from appearing, use the Tools→Options... property sheet and change the setting in the Device Tools options group on the General pane. You can then select your target device from the Device toolbar. (Toggle the display of this toolbar with the View→Toolbars→Device menu selection.)

Emulator or Device?

When we teach our Windows CE and .NET Compact Framework programming classes, students often ask about the trade-offs between testing software on an emulator versus on a device.

Microsoft has made significant improvements in its emulators over the years. Previously, in the Windows CE versions 1.x and 2.x SDKs, the emulator was a thin layer on top of the Windows NT libraries. In those days, you were never entirely sure how Windows CE would respond to a given function call. But that changed with Windows CE .NET (version 4.0 and later), when the new emulator was introduced. The new emulator consists of a Windows CE operating system image that runs in a virtual x86 emulation provided by Connectix Corporation of San Mateo, California. It consists of 100% Windows CE binaries built from Windows CE sources—just like what runs on the Pocket PC or any other Windows CE device.

The impact for software developers is that in the new emulator, code is running on the same software as on an actual device. The key benefit of the emulator is that you can test and debug when you do not have access to an actual Windows CE device. Downloading and testing on the emulator can sometimes be faster than downloading to a device—especially when a device is connected via serial connector or USB (which is what most docking cradles and ActiveSync cables use).

Whatever use you make of the emulator, you still must test your code on the same device that your users will use. While the emulator is good, there are still some important differences between an emulator and an actual device. The emulator is Intel x86 code, for example, and if your device is running a MIPS, SH3, or StrongARM processor, you might not uncover CPU-specific problems. Also, the emulator does not have the same hardware as an actual device.

The biggest obstacle to device-side testing and debugging is the time it takes to download via serial or USB connections. While Visual Studio .NET has a great source-level debugger, it is still very painful to debug over serial or USB connections. For that reason, we recommend that developers acquire a network card and use that for their device-side development. There is still some pain here—the setup can sometimes be fraught with difficulties.

Using the Development Environment

The development environment consists of a series of windows. The center window, which is normally the largest, can be toggled between the Design View of a form (shown earlier in Figure 2.3) and the Code View of a form (shown in Figure 2.6). When you are beginning to develop an application, there is relatively little code in the Code View window, but there is more code than you might think. We will examine that code soon. But for now we continue with our tour of the development environment.

On the left side there are two pop-out windows (windows that expand as the mouse passes over them): the Server Explorer and the Toolbox. The Server Explorer provides the developer with information about server resources, such as databases, and generates code for use in applications that access those resources. The Toolbox is the tool for adding controls to a form. As such, it is visible when Design View is selected but not when Code View is selected. Figure 2.7 shows the Toolbox being used to add a button to `Form1`.

The right side of the Visual Studio .NET IDE contains a variety of other windows. The Solution Explorer window displays the elements that make up the entire solution, such as the source file for each form. The Properties window displays the properties of the currently selected object, such as a control or form. Figure 2.8 shows the Properties window in the foreground, displaying the properties of a button from an upcoming sample application. The Class View window displays the class hierarchy of the application,

Form1.cs [Design]* **Form1.cs***

Cistern.Form1 | mainMenu1

```
using System;
using System.Drawing;
using System.Collections;
using System.Windows.Forms;
using System.Data;

namespace Cistern
{
    /// <summary>
    /// Summary description for Form1.
    /// </summary>
    public class Form1 : System.Windows.Forms.Form
    {
        private System.Windows.Forms.MainMenu mainMenu1;

        public Form1()
        {
            //
            // Required for Windows Form Designer support
            //
            InitializeComponent();

            //
```

FIGURE 2.6: The Code View window

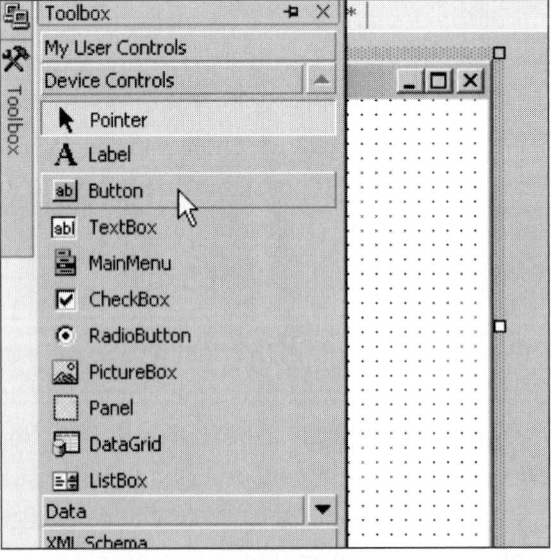

FIGURE 2.7: Using the Toolbox to add a button to `Form1`

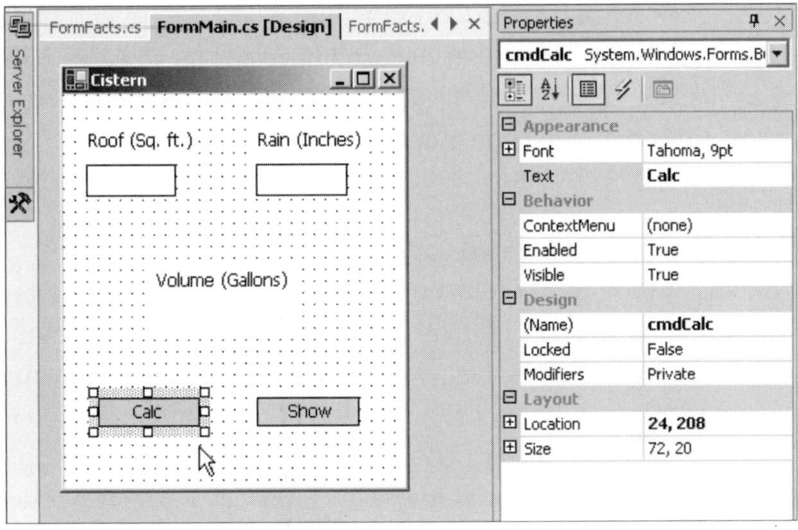

FIGURE 2.8: The Properties window

reminding us once more that a .NET application consists of objects. The last window, the Resource View window, displays the application's resources.

Visual Studio .NET gives you the option of modifying the arrangement of these windows to your personal taste. You can undock a window by grabbing its title bar and dragging it to a different location within the main window, or you can keep it docked but move it to a new location by using the same technique. You may have noticed that we did some window rearrangement between Figure 2.7 and Figure 2.8. The arrangement shown in Figure 2.7 required too much vertical scrolling when viewing the Properties window, so we moved the Properties window and docked it within the same window as the Solution Explorer window rather than beneath it. The set of tabs at the bottom of the window allows us to view one or the other, but not both at the same time.

Rearranging these windows is a little tricky because the behavior is very sensitive to the exact placement of the dropped window. If you have difficulty positioning the windows and they always seem to end up in the wrong location, you can return to the default arrangement by using the Tools→Options menu and selecting the Reset Window Layout button in the Environments group on the General pane.

We also often rearrange the Output window because we find that Auto Hide is the best choice. This causes the window to appear when we build but to hide as soon as we return the focus to the Code View window. Figure 2.9 shows how to set the Auto Hide property of the Output window.

Examining Designer-Generated Code

A set of tabs at the top of the main editing window allows you to move between Design View and Code View. You can also toggle between the two views by selecting one of the first two menu items in the View menu or by clicking on a button in the Toolbar at the top of the Solution Explorer window. To examine the Designer-generated code for the `Form1` example, we set our window to Code View, as it was in Figure 2.6. Each form is defined by a single code file, and because we have only one form, we have only one code file.

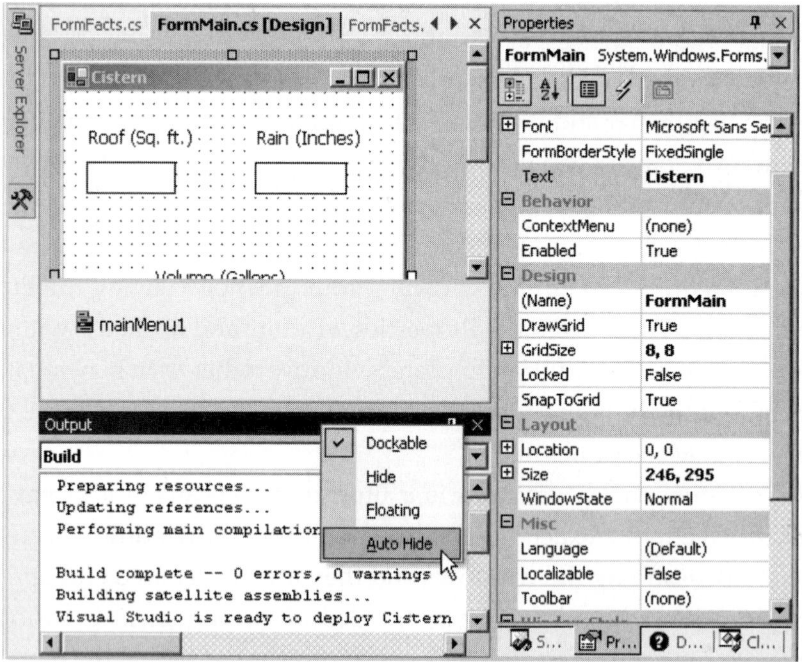

FIGURE 2.9: Turning on Auto Hide mode for the Output window

We proceed to examine the code that defines this form a few lines at a time, starting at the top and working down. Here is how the code begins.

```
using System;
using System.Drawing;
using System.Collections;
using System.Windows.Forms;
using System.Data;

namespace Cistern
{
   /// <summary>
   /// Summary description for Form1.
   /// </summary>
   public class Form1 : System.Windows.Forms.Form
   {
```

The first few lines of code specify namespaces that the Designer expects a typical form would use. (Namespaces are groupings of classes; see the related discussion later in this chapter.) The next line specifies the namespace of this form class. The final line from this block specifies that this form class is a new class, `Form1`, derived from `System.Windows.Forms.Form`.

The next line of code is the Designer-generated code for menus, which are always provided for smart-device applications.

```
private System.Windows.Forms.MainMenu mainMenu1;
```

Because menus are the subject of a later chapter (Chapter 9), we pass over this for now and move on.

We are now inside our class definition and can see that it consists of four routines, as shown in Listing 2.1: a constructor, `Form1`; a routine named `Dispose`; a routine named `InitializeComponent`; and the application entry point, `Main`.

LISTING 2.1: The Form Class Generated by the Designer

```
public Form1()
      {
         //
         // Required for Windows Form Designer support
         //
         InitializeComponent();
```

continues

continued

```
         //
         // TODO: Add any constructor code after
         //            InitializeComponent call
         //
      }
      /// <summary>
      /// Clean up any resources being used.
      /// </summary>
      protected override void Dispose( bool disposing )
      {
         base.Dispose( disposing );
      }
      #region Windows Form Designer generated code
      /// <summary>
      /// Required method for Designer support - do not modify
      /// the contents of this method with the code editor.
      /// </summary>
      private void InitializeComponent()
      {
         this.mainMenu1 = new System.Windows.Forms.MainMenu();
         //
         // FormMain
         //
         this.Menu = this.mainMenu1;
         this.Text = "Cistern";
      }
      #endregion

      /// <summary>
      /// The main entry point for the application.
      /// </summary>

      static void Main()
      {
         Application.Run(new Form1());
      }
   }
}
```

The first routine, `Form1`, is the form's default constructor. It calls the base class constructor and then calls the routine `InitializeComponent`, which we'll look at shortly. Then a comment tells us that any constructor code we write should be located after this call.

The second routine, `Dispose`, is roughly analogous to a destructor. Within this routine you should release all large nonshareable resources you have acquired on behalf of this form. This routine, which can be called from elsewhere in your application, is called by the garbage collector as the form is being destroyed. Like the constructor routine, this routine calls its base class equivalent to ensure that the standard disposing functionality is executed.

Within the third routine, `InitializeComponent`, the form creates and initializes its controls. The code is small in size because we currently have no controls, except the menu, on our form. As we add controls to our form, the amount of code increases and we can learn more from it.

The fourth routine, `Main`, is the starting point of the application. C# smart-device applications must have a *startup object* (in our case, `Form1`), and that object must have a `Main` method. The choice of startup object is specified by using the Project→Properties menu. If we added a second form to our application and then designated that form as the startup object, we would need to add a `Main` method to it.

When we look at the code for `Form1.Main`, we see that this application, like most .NET Compact Framework smart-device applications, begins by creating an instance of the startup object. It may seem odd that the code to create the form is located within the form itself, but remember that starting the execution of a program has always been a bootstrap process, and it still is. Because `Main` creates the startup object, it must execute before an instance of the startup object exists; and because `Main` is a member of the very class it is creating, it must be a class-specific, not instance-specific, method. Hence, it must be a `static` method.

Using Regions

Let us return to the `InitializeComponent` routine for a moment. This routine appears only because we expanded the line that begins with a pound sign and is located just above `InitializeComponent`, namely:

```
#region Windows Form Designer generated code
```

The expanded code is the block demarcated by the `#region` and `#endregion` directives.

The statement `Windows Form Designer generated code` is a little misleading, for all our code thus far has been generated by the Smart Device Application Wizard. The code in this region is the code that creates the form and the controls within that form. To a first-time .NET programmer this code is a little intimidating because it is full of warnings that hint at the bad things that will happen if you modify the code. Not modifying this code until you are an experienced .NET programmer is a good idea, but being intimidated by this code is not. The code contained in this region is an excellent learning tool for the beginning programmer, for in it you can see how controls are created, how they are positioned, and how event handling is defined—all things you may want your application to do at runtime. In other words, it is very similar to the code you can write yourself.

Because this code is complete and we will not be modifying it in the near future, and because we do not wish to look at it every time we scroll through the application code, we collapse this region back to its original single-line state.

In the same way that the Designer generates regions, you can also create them. The `#region` and `#endregion` keywords are directives that help support the outlining feature of the Visual Studio .NET editor. They are similar to open and close braces (`{` and `}`, respectively) in that they bound an area of code. They are different from most other keywords in that they are completely ignored by the compiler and have no impact on the generated IL code. If you have written and tested functionality in your application and you no longer need to view that part of the code on a regular basis, put it in a region, give the region a meaningful caption, and collapse the region.

Changing Form Classes and Form Files

Although the code for each form is contained in its own file, the Designer treats a form and its code file as separate entities. For instance, changing the name of the code file does not cause a matching change to the form name. To illustrate this here, we change the name of our form to `FormMain` and the file name to `FormMain.cs`. We change the file name by first selecting the file in the Solution Explorer window and then typing a new file name in the Properties window, as shown in Figure 2.10.

We change the form name in Design View by first selecting the form and then in the Properties window typing a new form name, as shown in Figure 2.11. When we return to Code View we notice that the name of the

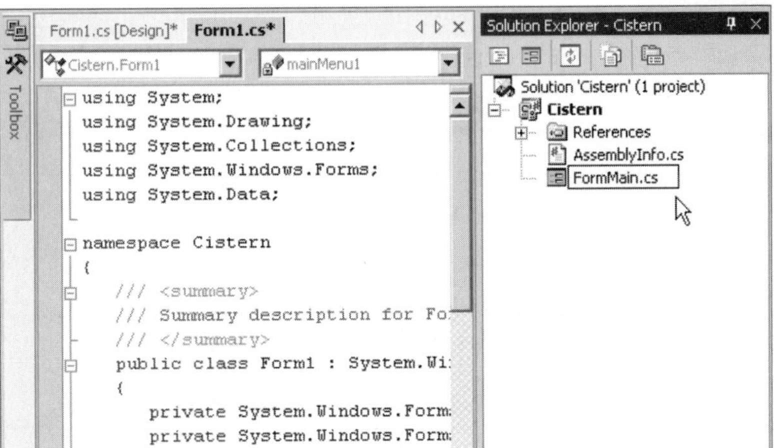

FIGURE 2.10: Changing the form's file name

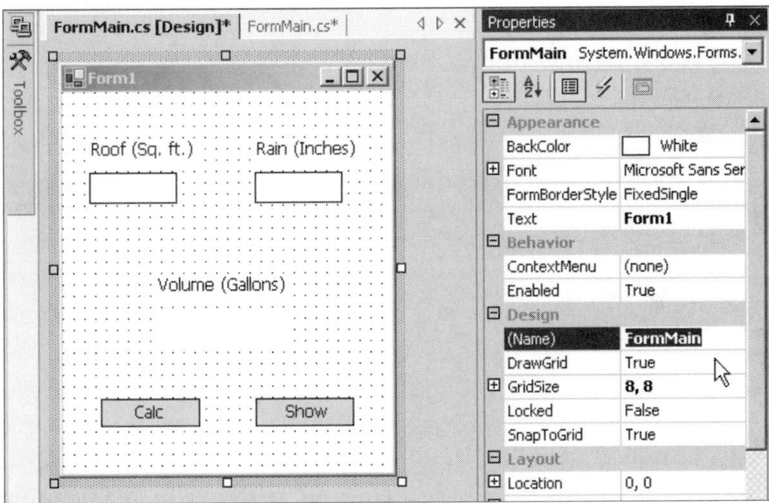

FIGURE 2.11: Changing the form's name

class has been changed by the Designer to match the name of the form, as shown in the following code excerpt.

```
namespace Cistern
{
   /// <summary>
   /// Summary description for Form1.
   /// </summary>
```

continues

continued

```
   public class FormMain : System.Windows.Forms.Form
   {
      :
      :
      :
   }
}
```

Not everything, however, is automatically changed when we change the form class name. For example, when we now attempt to run the application, the attempt fails, and we see the following error message:

```
The type or namespace name 'Form1' could not be found
(are you missing a using directive or an assembly reference?)
```

This error occurs because our newly renamed form is still the startup object for the application, it still contains a `Main` method, and that method still contains a line of code that creates an object of class `Form1`—a class that has been renamed to `FormMain`. We must modify the `Main` function to refer to `FormMain`, as shown here:

```
static void Main()
{
   Application.Run(new Cistern.FormMain());
}
```

With the startup object set, we can run the application. So changing the name of the startup form and its associated code file name is a two- or even three-step process.

We find that we almost always change the name of new objects we create in Visual Studio .NET. Generally speaking, it is the first thing we do when we create a new object. Fortunately, most other objects are not as fussy about being renamed as an application's main form—you just change the name in the Properties window and you are done. See the sidebar, Naming Standards in This Book, for details on the conventions we adopted for code found in this book.

Naming Standards in This Book

Having a standard for naming the elements of your programs—variables, classes, file names, and so on—and consistently using that standard can help make your code easier to read and therefore easier to maintain. Once written and deployed in a production setting, code may have a long maintenance life. Whether you are maintaining it or whether that job falls to others—perhaps engineers you hire after being promoted to manager—naming standards help make maintenance easier.

In this book, we adopt the Hungarian naming scheme for controls, properties, and fields (for details, see Appendix A). We have a convention of using `FormMain` for the name of the main form class and `FormMain.cs` (or `FormMain.vb` for the Visual Basic version) for the file that contains this class.

The `Cistern` Sample Program

During the remainder of this chapter, we demonstrate how to create a simple Windows application program. This application, named `Cistern`, calculates the amount of rainwater that runs off a roof during a storm or during the course of a year. We create this program in two steps. First we use the Designer to draw the user interface elements of our program, which results in new code generated for us, as mentioned earlier. The second step is to add code that builds on what the Designer created for us. This is the typical sequence you are likely to follow when developing .NET Compact Framework applications, except that real-world development tends to be iterative. Once your supporting code is written, you will likely continue to enhance your user interface. This is the primary reason for respecting the boundaries between your own code and the code that the Designer generates and maintains for you.

Step 1: Adding Controls Using the Designer

The first step in building a Windows application is laying out controls on a form. For this, we return to Design View and open the Toolbox by moving the mouse cursor over the Toolbox label so that the pop-out window appears (keep it open by clicking on the pushpin icon at the top of the Toolbox window). To create controls on the form, either double-click on controls in the Toolbox or drag controls from the Toolbox and drop them onto the form. Once a control is on the form, reposition it using either the mouse or the arrow keys. When positioning controls with the arrow keys, you can change the movement granularity to pixel granularity by simultaneously holding the Control key. Use the Shift key with the arrow keys to change the size of a control without changing its location. To change a control's properties, click on the control and make your desired changes in the Properties window, as shown in Figure 2.12.

We change the `Name` property of each control to follow the standards outlined in Appendix A and change the value of the `Text` property, as well as some others. When we are done adding controls and renaming them, we have the controls listed in Table 2.2. When we run the application, we get the results shown in Figure 2.13.

When we stop the application and return to Code View, we can view the code generated for us by the Designer—code that was generated as we

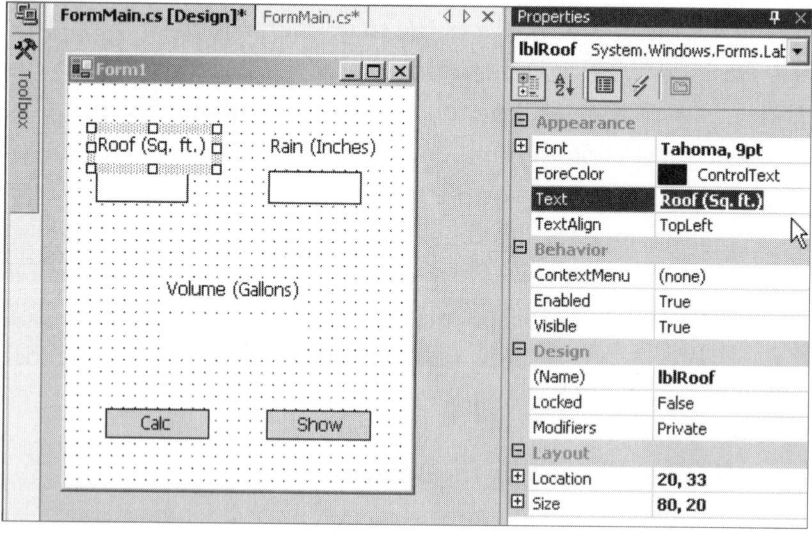

FIGURE 2.12: Changing control properties

TABLE 2.2: Control Names and Classes for the `Cistern` Program

Name	Class
lblRoof	Label
textRoof	TextBox
lblRain	Label
textRain	TextBox
lblAnswer	Label
lblAnswerHdr	Label
cmdCalc	Button
cmdFacts	Button

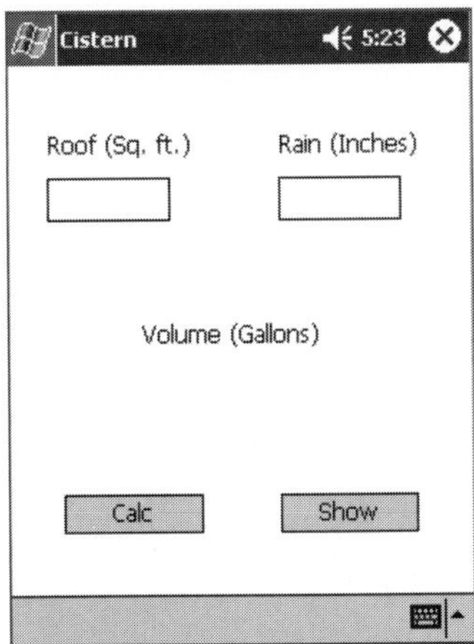

FIGURE 2.13: The `Cistern` application

added controls to the form and that was updated as we set the property values of those controls. Listing 2.2 shows this code.

LISTING 2.2: The Form Class After Controls Have Been Added

```
using System;
using System.Drawing;
using System.Collections;
```

continues

continued

```
using System.Windows.Forms;
using System.Data;

namespace Cistern
{
   /// <summary>
   /// Summary description for Form1.
   /// </summary>
   public class FormMain : System.Windows.Forms.Form
   {
      private System.Windows.Forms.TextBox textRoof;
      private System.Windows.Forms.TextBox textRain;
      private System.Windows.Forms.Button cmdCalc;
      private System.Windows.Forms.Button cmdFacts;
      private System.Windows.Forms.Label lblRoof;
      private System.Windows.Forms.Label lblRain;
      private System.Windows.Forms.Label lblAnswerHdr;
      private System.Windows.Forms.Label lblAnswer;
      private System.Windows.Forms.MainMenu mainMenu1;

      public FormMain()
      {
         //
         // Required for Windows Form Designer support
         //
         InitializeComponent();

         //
         // TODO: Add any constructor code after
         //             InitializeComponent call
         //
      }
      /// <summary>
      /// Clean up any resources being used.
      /// </summary>
      protected override void Dispose( bool disposing )
      {
         base.Dispose( disposing );
      }
      #region Windows Form Designer generated code
      /// <summary>
      /// Required method for Designer support - do not modify
      /// the contents of this method with the code editor.
      /// </summary>
      private void InitializeComponent()
      {
         this.mainMenu1 = new System.Windows.Forms.MainMenu();
         this.textRoof = new System.Windows.Forms.TextBox();
```

```
this.textRain = new System.Windows.Forms.TextBox();
this.cmdCalc = new System.Windows.Forms.Button();
this.cmdFacts = new System.Windows.Forms.Button();
this.lblRoof = new System.Windows.Forms.Label();
this.lblRain = new System.Windows.Forms.Label();
this.lblAnswerHdr = new System.Windows.Forms.Label();
this.lblAnswer = new System.Windows.Forms.Label();
//
// textRoof
//
this.textRoof.Location =
              new System.Drawing.Point(16, 48);
this.textRoof.Size =
              new System.Drawing.Size(64, 22);
this.textRoof.Text = "";
//
// textRain
//
this.textRain.Location =
              new System.Drawing.Point(136, 48);
this.textRain.Size =
              new System.Drawing.Size(64, 22);
this.textRain.Text = "";
//
// cmdCalc
//
this.cmdCalc.Location =
              new System.Drawing.Point(24, 208);
this.cmdCalc.Text = "Calc";
//
// cmdFacts
//
this.cmdFacts.Font =
              new System.Drawing.Font("Tahoma", 9F,
              System.Drawing.FontStyle.Regular);
this.cmdFacts.Location =
              new System.Drawing.Point(136, 208);
this.cmdFacts.Text = "Show";
//
// lblRoof
//
this.lblRoof.Location =
                  new System.Drawing.Point(16, 24);
this.lblRoof.Size = new System.Drawing.Size(80, 20);
this.lblRoof.Text = "Roof (Sq. ft.)";
//
// lblRain
//
```

continues

continued

```
         this.lblRain.Location =
                           new System.Drawing.Point(136, 24);
         this.lblRain.Size = new System.Drawing.Size(80, 20);
         this.lblRain.Text = "Rain (Inches)";
         //
         // lblAnswerHdr
         //
         this.lblAnswerHdr.Location =
                             new System.Drawing.Point(64, 120);
         this.lblAnswerHdr.Text = "Volume (Gallons)";
         //
         // lblAnswer
         //
         this.lblAnswer.Font =
                        new System.Drawing.Font("Tahoma", 9F,
                        System.Drawing.FontStyle.Bold);
         this.lblAnswer.Location =
                        new System.Drawing.Point(64, 144);
         //
         // FormMain
         //
         this.Controls.Add(this.lblAnswer);
         this.Controls.Add(this.lblAnswerHdr);
         this.Controls.Add(this.lblRain);
         this.Controls.Add(this.lblRoof);
         this.Controls.Add(this.cmdFacts);
         this.Controls.Add(this.cmdCalc);
         this.Controls.Add(this.textRain);
         this.Controls.Add(this.textRoof);
         this.Menu = this.mainMenu1;
         this.Text = "Cistern";

      }
      #endregion

      /// <summary>
      /// The main entry point for the application.
      /// </summary>

      static void Main()
      {
         Application.Run(new Cistern.FormMain());
      }
   }
}
```

Code Format

We added occasional blank lines or carriage returns to facilitate the display of code in printed form, so what you see in code listings in this book differs slightly from what you see in the Visual Studio .NET editor. The substance of the code, however, is the same. (Such changes disappear as soon as we do something in Design View that makes the Designer regenerate the code.)

The Designer creates the new code as we add each control to a form. When we look at the new code, including code outside the bounds of the region block, we see that the Designer does four things for each control:

1. Defines a variable to hold a reference to the control
2. Creates the control
3. Sets the control's properties
4. Adds the control to the form

This is the same code you would write if you wanted to create a control at runtime. There is nothing magical in the code generated by the Designer. It is simply code that we can examine, learn from, and use to extend the capabilities of our application.

In fact, not only does the Designer generate code from the design but the converse is also true: the Designer generates the design from the code. In other words, there is a two-way flow from Design View to Code View and back again. Every time you switch to Design View from Code View, the design is rebuilt.

You can demonstrate this quite easily. In the `Cistern` program, switch to Code View and search for each occurrence of `textRain`. As you find each one, remove it. Then switch back to Design View and notice that the `textRain` control has disappeared from the design. When you run the application, the startup form displays one `TextBox` control, not two. Stop the execution of the application, return to Code View, and use the Undo option of the Edit menu to restore the deleted code. Switch back to Design View and notice that the `textRain` control reappears on the form.

We think of the Designer as generating code from the design, but you can think of it the other way as well. What matters is the code. It does not matter which design-time tool you use (although currently you are limited to Visual Studio .NET anyway) as long as the code you generate can run using the .NET Compact Framework runtime libraries.

Step 2: Adding Code to the Program

Once we are done assembling the elements of the user interface, the next step is to add code to connect the user interface to the real work of the application. As we move forward, we enhance our `Cistern` application as follows.

1. Add a second form, `FormFacts`, to display basic water facts.
2. Display this form in response to user input.
3. Add a new class named `WaterMath` to perform the water volume calculations.
4. Use an object of this class to provide the functionality needed for the first form, `FormMain`.

We explore these enhancements in the following subsections.

Adding a New Form to an Application

To add a new form to our application, we select the Project→Add Windows Form… menu item. We name the new file `FormFacts.cs`, and Visual Studio .NET is kind enough to use our file name as the basis for the new form class it creates. To this form we add several `Label` controls to hold the information we want to display, and we set their `Text` properties accordingly. Figure 2.14 shows our form with multiple controls selected by pressing the mouse down in a vacant area of the form, sweeping it across the controls, and then releasing it in a vacant area on the opposite side of the form. The selected controls are being aligned through Format menu selections.

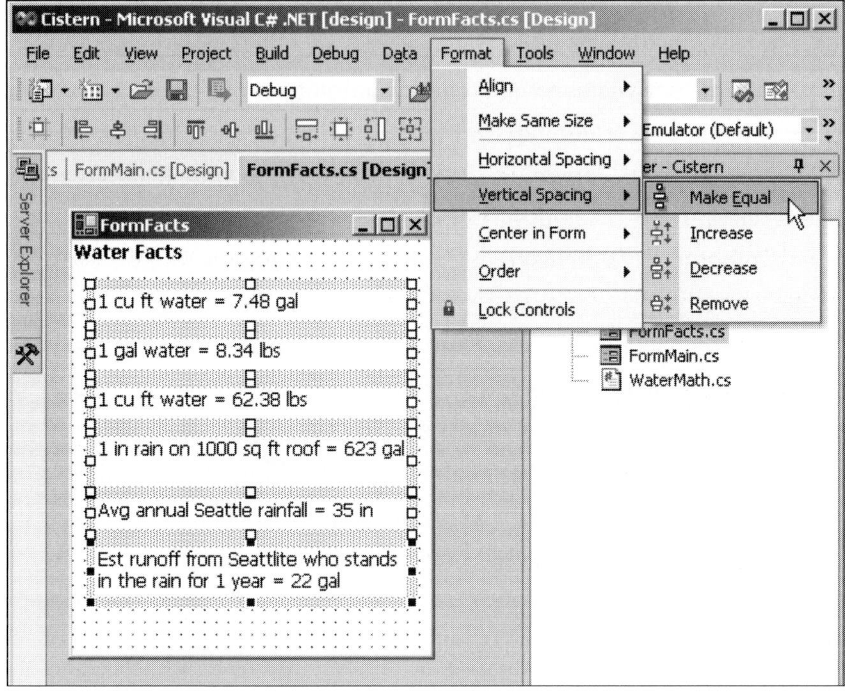

FIGURE 2.14: The `FormFacts` form in Design View

The Designer and Pocket PC Programs

If you are building .NET Compact Framework programs for a Pocket PC, there are two additional elements you ought to keep in mind: (1) the size of forms and (2) the `MinimizeBox` property in forms.

When you create a new form in the Designer, that form has a location of `(0, 0)` and a size of `(246, 302)`. Whatever changes you make to these values at design time, they are ignored at runtime because all forms are displayed in full-screen mode. For this reason, we suggest you leave the size alone to make sure that the location you specify for a control is visible. Better yet, set the `Locked` property to `true`; this prevents accidental changes to the form's size.

A second aspect of Pocket PC programs is that they always run and never shut down—at least as far as the user is concerned. Microsoft adopted this convention to match end users' expectations about how consumer electronic devices behave. Programs automatically save data that has changed and also remember the state when last viewed by a user. Think of a radio, which "remembers" the last station you were listening to and does not start up in a neutral, default state. This is a different model than what programmers are used to when creating software for personal computers.

The .NET Compact Framework supports this "always running" model by default. When you run a Windows application built with the .NET Compact Framework, that program continues to run even when you click on the Go Away box in the upper-right corner of a form. This is fine for shipping applications but a nuisance when you are in a cycle of building, downloading, and debugging .NET Compact Framework applications. The solution is to set the `MinimizeBox` property in the main form to `false`; this makes it easy to stop a running .NET Compact Framework program.

Adding controls at design time is just one way to place information on the form. There are at least two other common methods, one that is more flexible and one that uses fewer resources.

The most flexible method is to create and display the controls at runtime. We do this by writing code that is identical to the code just generated by the Designer. There are times when creating controls at runtime is a necessity. Perhaps your application does not know how much information must be processed (and, therefore, how many controls will be required) until after a user profile has been read or a database has been accessed. Or perhaps your form has some infrequently visited `tab` controls and wants to defer the creation of each `tab`'s constituent controls until they are needed. Creating controls at runtime and the related issues are covered extensively in Part II of this book.

The other option is to not use any controls at all. Instead, you can draw information directly on the form at runtime. By not having extra controls, you save the memory they consume and the processor slices used to create and update them. The drawback is that you must calculate the location of your information at runtime and you must do it in pixels. This capability is discussed in Part IV of this book.

We have chosen to use controls and to add them at design time so that, in this introductory chapter, programmers who are new to Visual Studio .NET will have as much exposure to the Designer as possible. Using the Designer enables us to produce our `FormFacts` form without writing any code. However, now we need to display the form, and that requires writing code—code that we cannot begin to write without first discussing events and event handling.

Understanding Events and Event Handlers

As mentioned earlier in this chapter, an *event* is a notification from an object (e.g., a form, a control) that something has happened. With controls, the event is usually an indication that the user has performed some action. All controls are capable of raising events, and different controls raise different events. If the user taps on a button, a `Click` event is raised; if the user enters a character into a `TextBox` control, the `TextChanged` event is raised; if the user taps on a `TextBox` control, the `Validating`, `Validated`, and `LostFocus` events might be raised for one `TextBox` while the `GotFocus` event would be raised for another `TextBox`.

To respond to a particular event, you must write an event handler for that event. The *event handler* is a method called by the .NET Compact Framework anytime the event is raised. One handler can handle one or more events for one or more controls; one event can cause one or more handlers to be called. A detailed discussion of events and event handlers is found in Chapter 7.

We need to write an event handler for the `Cistern` application to display our new form to users when they click on the `cmdFacts` button located in `FormMain`. In other words, the application must create the form in response to the `cmdFacts.Click` event. To begin writing our event handler, we return to Design View for `FormMain` and select the control whose event we wish to handle, in this case, the `cmdFacts` button. We proceed to the Properties window and click on the lightning bolt button in the window's toolbar, which results in the Properties window layout shown in Figure 2.15.

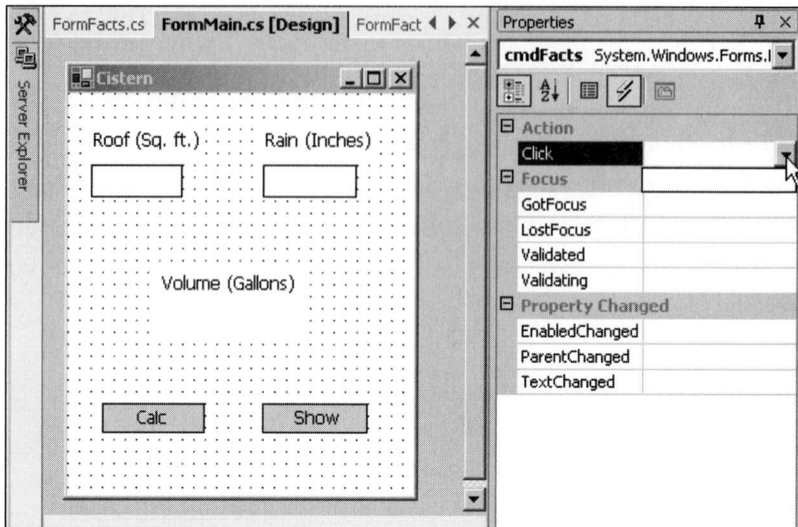

FIGURE 2.15: Specifying an event handler

The Properties window shows a list of every event that the selected control is capable of raising.[2] Beside each event is a drop-down list showing every routine that currently exists in the `FormMain` class that qualifies as a possible event handler for this event (i.e., methods that have the correct number of parameters with the correct data types). All the lists are currently empty, for although there are several routines in our `FormMain` class, none of them qualifies as an event handler. The lists are empty because we haven't yet written our first event handler.

To start writing code, we double-click in the Properties window on the event we wish to handle, in this case, the `Click` event. The Designer immediately generates two small sets of code, transitions to Code View, and places us within one of the generated code snippets. The code that we have been placed into is the event handler itself, shown here.

```
private void cmdFacts_Click(object sender, System.EventArgs e)
{

}
```

2. In some cases, the Designer omits events supported by some controls—an oversight in Visual Studio .NET 2003 that we hope will be fixed in a future version. We discuss supported events as we look at individual controls.

The other code that has been generated is one statement long and has been placed into the `Windows Form Designer generated code` region we saw earlier. This line, shown below, specifies that the code we are about to write (i.e., the routine named `cmdFacts_Click`) will be the `Click` event handler for the `cmdFacts` button. Whenever the user clicks on the `cmdFacts` button, the `cmdFacts_Click` routine will be called.

```
this.cmdFacts.Click += new System.EventHandler(this.cmdFacts_Click);
```

The name of an event handler has no special meaning; you can change it to any name you want, as long as you change it in both places. You cannot, however, change the parameters.

All event handlers will be passed exactly two parameters whenever the event is raised. The first parameter is a reference to the control that is raising the event, defined as a very generic `Object` and never as a `Control` or a specific control type such as `TextBox`.

The second parameter is an event argument object—that is, an object of type `System.EventArgs` (or a type derived from that type). The actual type of the second parameter depends on the event type and on the information that is being passed. For example, a `MouseMove` event provides mouse location information, while a `KeyPress` event provides keystroke information. The event argument type used by most events is `System.EventArgs`, which contains no event-specific information whatsoever. Thus, the event handler shown above knows only two things: what event is being raised and which control is raising it. That is enough for us to create and show a `FormFacts` form. Next, we write the form creation and display code that we place within this event handler.

Creating and Displaying a Second Form

The Designer-generated code shows many details of user interface programming, something that we can take advantage of. Because we must create and display our second form, it would be wise to look at the code that does the same for the startup form, which we have already seen and which is repeated on the next page.

```
static void Main()
{
   Application.Run(new Cistern.FormMain());
}
```

This code shows us what we must do to create our second form, namely, that we must create a new instance using our form's class. We cannot, for example, simple call the FormFacts.Show method. FormFacts, after all, is a class name, not an object variable name. This is different from some development environments, like Visual Basic 6, where, when you define a form at design time, you automatically get an instance of the form at runtime. In .NET, designing a form creates a class definition, but—aside from a main form—does not create an object with that class. To create an instance of our second form, we use the C# new operator, the same operator we use to create any other type of object.

There is an additional step required after we create our form because creating a form does not automatically make it visible. The startup form is automatically made visible only because the framework knows that it must be displayed as soon as it is created, for without it there would be no user interface at program startup. Subsequent forms are not automatically shown when created. We make a form visible by invoking its Show() method. We do both actions, creating and showing, by adding the following code. Note that most of the code is added to our event handler, but one line of code is external to the event handler.

```
// Variable to hold a reference to FormFacts.
private System.Windows.Forms.Form refFormFacts;
   :
   :
   :
private void cmdFacts_Click(object sender,
                            System.EventArgs e)
{
   // Create an instance of the form.
   this.refFormFacts = new FormFacts();

   // Show it.
   this.refFormFacts.Show();
}
```

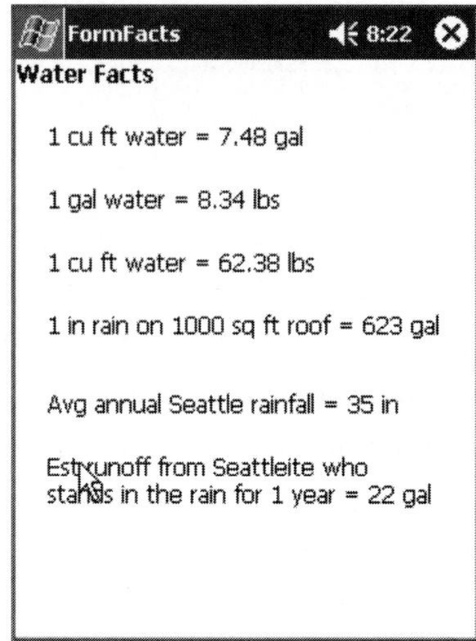

FIGURE 2.16: The completed `FormFacts` form

When the user taps on the `cmdFacts` button while the application is executing, the `FormFacts` form will display, overlaying the `FormMain` form, as shown in Figure 2.16. When the user clicks on the close button of this form, the form is removed from the screen, the form object is subsequently disposed by garbage collection, and the original form returns to view.

We are going to conclude our high-level tour of a .NET Compact Framework application by defining a new class and using it.

Adding Classes

Up to now in this chapter, we discussed creating various kinds of user interface objects, including forms and controls. While controls are obviously important for the development of .NET Compact Framework programs, you can also create other kinds of objects from your own, custom classes. Custom classes are important because they provide the locus of the domain-specific types that do the real work of a custom program. While you certainly can weave domain-specific processing, such as the calculation of runoff quantity, into user interface classes, should you? This practice is common, especially when creating sample code (like some in this book!) or when building quick and dirty prototypes.

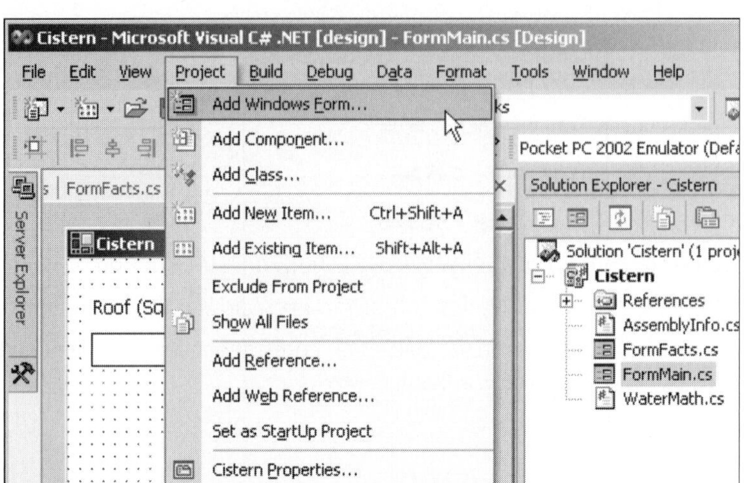

FIGURE 2.17: The Project menu

We recommend separating your user interface code from the business logic or application services that are the real work done by your programs. Such a separation helps make that code more portable, so that once deployed with the .NET Compact Framework, the code might later be deployed on an ASP.NET Web server or within an XML Web service. This separation also helps make code more reliable because simpler classes can be tested separately from the user interface.

Within Visual Studio .NET, the commands that allow you to create a new class are in the Project menu. As shown in Figure 2.17, several menu items start with the word *Add*. Most of these items summon the same dialog box—the Add New Item dialog box.[3] Of the available menu items, two seem to be equally correct for our purposes: Add Component and Add Class. This begs the question: "What is the difference between a component and other types of objects?" See the Component Classes and Object Classes sidebar for the answer.

3. We say "most" because the Add Existing Item... menu item summons another dialog box.

Component Classes and Object Classes

In the early 1990s, Microsoft announced that two technologies were core to the company's long-term strategy: the Win32 API and COM. Ten years later, it is interesting to note that Windows CE fully supports both technologies. As discussed in Chapter 1, Windows CE is built on a foundation of Win32 for both device drivers and application programs. And Windows CE supports the various execution contexts for a COM component: in-process, local, and remote (also known as DCOM).

Then along came the .NET initiative, which Microsoft announced in summer 2000. At that moment, .NET-based technologies became strategic, and COM became legacy. To support the large number of COM components created during the past decade, Microsoft created various hooks for calling out to COM components and for accepting calls from COM components. These various hooks are collectively referred to as *COM interop*.

Component classes—those derived from `System.ComponentModel.Component`—support the creation of COM objects in the .NET Framework. On the desktop-based .NET Framework, such objects support the passing of interface pointers to legacy COM objects, as well as the reference counting that is central to the proper operation of COM. In addition, components can marshal references; that is, such objects can communicate between applications and can participate in COM interoperability.

Because of size constraints, the .NET Compact Framework does not support COM interop, so the .NET Compact Framework implementation of the `System.ComponentModel.Component` class lacks the COM interop support of the desktop .NET Framework implementation. So what use does it serve in the .NET Compact Framework? In Chapter 1, we discussed .NET Compact Framework design goals, one of which is to maintain consistency with the desktop .NET Framework. So the .NET Compact Framework contains classes that exist in the desktop .NET Framework but are empty placeholders so that the .NET Compact Framework structure matches the structures of the .NET Framework. Several classes in both frameworks rely on the component class—most notably the base class for all windowing controls, `System.Windows.Forms.Control`.

When does it make sense to use `Component` versus `Object` as a base class? As we cover in Chapter 10, we use `Component` for custom controls that do not wrap around a Win32 window.[4] Basing our implementation on this class allows us to port our control more easily to the desktop should that be necessary. The presence of the `Component` class helps facilitate porting code that uses the class to a .NET Compact Framework implementation.

For the simplest, most basic type of object, we use `Object` as a base class. This is the base class for all classes, whether we explicitly request it or not. Reference types and value types all look to `Object` as their ultimate base class, as we explore more fully in Chapter 3.

Creating the `WaterMath` Classes

Because we wish to make our class as simple as possible, in this sample application we create a class derived from `System.Object` and not from `System.ComponentModel.Component`. To request this from Visual Studio .NET, we select the Project→Add Class... menu item. The code shown in Listing 2.3 is generated for us in its own source file.

LISTING 2.3: The Skeleton `WaterMath` Class

```
using System;

namespace Cistern
{
   /// <summary>
   /// Summary description for WaterMath.
   /// </summary>
   public class WaterMath
   {
      public WaterMath()
      {
```

4. The previously mentioned `Control` class is the best choice for custom controls that wrap around a window.

```
        //
        // TODO: Add constructor logic here
        //
      }
   }
}
```

Visual Studio .NET generates a separate file for our new class, which it does for all classes it creates, whether a form class or a custom class. We find this a good practice because it makes it easier to reuse classes—they are already separately packaged and so can be easily copied to a new directory with a new project. The physical separation of classes between files may promote better class design; the physical separation forces programmers to think of each class as separate and distinct from other classes. The Solution Explorer window, shown in Figure 2.18, contains the new file that has been added to our project.

Our application requires just one piece of functionality from this class: the ability to calculate rain runoff based on the size of a roof and the number of inches of rainfall. To provide this functionality, we write a method called `GetVolume`. This method returns the number of gallons of water that run off the roof as a result of the rain. Since users might want the value for the number of gallons of water per inch of rain as well as the number of

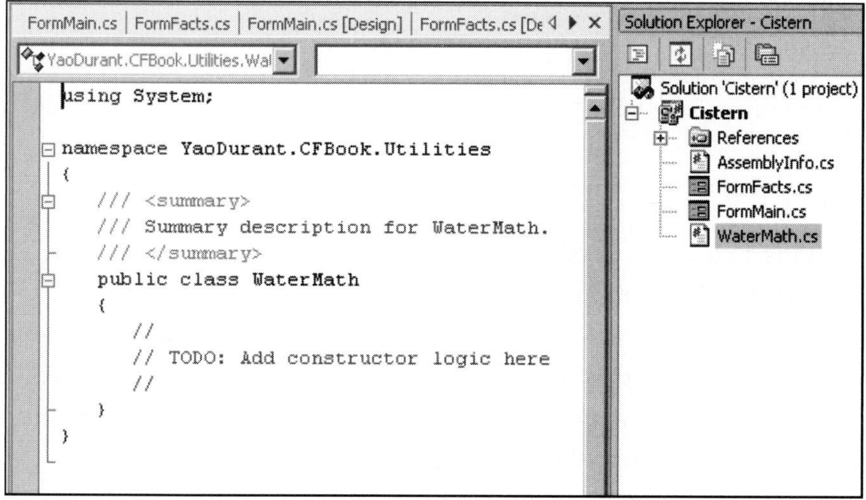

FIGURE 2.18: The `WaterMath.cs` file

gallons for any total amount of rainfall, we write two versions of our function. To put it another way, we engage in *function overloading*.

Overloading Functions

The first version of our function takes the roof size as a parameter and returns the runoff from one inch of rainfall. The second version accepts two parameters, roof size and rainfall, and returns the runoff from the specified amount of rainfall. Both versions are shown in Listing 2.4.

LISTING 2.4: The `GetVolume` Method Added to the `WaterMath` Class

```
public class WaterMath
{
    //  Constants
    private const double GALLONS_PER_FOOT = 7.48;
    private const int INCHES_PER_FOOT = 12;

    public int GetVolume( double dblSquareFeet )
    {
       //  This version of GetVolume
       //     assumes 1 inch of rain.
       return (int)(dblSquareFeet *
                    GALLONS_PER_FOOT / INCHES_PER_FOOT );
    }

    public int GetVolume( double dblSquareFeet,
                          int intInches )
    {
       //  This version of GetVolume
      //     accepts both roof size and rainfall.
      return (int)(dblSquareFeet * GALLONS_PER_FOOT *
                   intInches / INCHES_PER_FOOT);
   }
}
```

Having two versions of one function is called *function overloading*. This is characterized by the function having one name, one return value, and multiple sets of parameter types. Because our parameters differ in either the number of arguments or the argument data type, there is no possibility of ambiguity when the function is called. For instance, the following line of code is obviously calling the first version of `GetVolume`:

```
intGallons = GetVolume(2200);
```

while the next line calls the second version:

```
intGallons = GetVolume(2200, 35);
```

As you can see, distinct sets of parameters are required for proper function overloading.

Using the `WaterMath` Object

Now all we have to do is create and use one of these objects within our application. In the `Click` event of the `cmdCalc` button, we provide the requested information to the user. We extract the user-entered data from the two `TextBox` controls (`textRoof` and `textRain`), perform the calculation, and display the results in the `Label` control, `lblAnswer`.

We generate the skeleton of the `cmdCalc.Click` event handler in our `FormMain` class from the Designer by using the same technique we used for the `cmdFacts.Click` event handler. Within the event handler, we create an instance of our `WaterMath` object the same way we create any other object, with the `new` command. The skeleton that the Designer generates and the code that we add within that skeleton are shown below.

```
private void cmdCalc_Click(object sender, System.EventArgs e)
{
   //  Create a WaterMath object.
   Cistern.WaterMath wmCalc = new Cistern.WaterMath();

   //  Use it to calculate the runoff.
   lblAnswer.Text =
      wmCalc.GetVolume(
         double.Parse(textRoof.Text),
         int.Parse(textRain.Text) ).ToString();
}
```

Note the use of two complementary methods, `Parse` and `ToString`. The first converts a string to a specific data type, such as `double`; the second is the converse process, converting from a nonstring data type to a `string`.

This short, simple, straightforward code works correctly, but it does raise a question. Why must we create an instance of the object in order to do the calculation? After all, the runoff from a 2,000-square-foot roof during a two-inch rainfall is the same regardless of which instance of a WaterMath object was used to calculate that runoff. Let's look at this question from another perspective.

Defining and Using Static Methods

Consider the Integer class. It has a ToString method and a MinValue property. In most situations it would be pointless to invoke the ToString method without having a specific integer that you wanted converted to a string. It's obvious that invoking ToString is most applicable when you have a specific instance of an Integer object. Thus we often encounter this code:

```
strVariable = intVariable.ToString();
```

but seldom see this code:

```
strVariable = Integer.ToString();
```

On the other hand, the minimum value of an Integer object (–2,147,483,648) is the same regardless of the specific integer used to obtain it, so the following method call is meaningful.

```
intVariable = Integer.MinValue;
```

Think of MinValue as a property of the Integer class in general, and think of ToString as a method of a specific instance of an Integer object. Or think of the Main method of the startup form that we discussed earlier, mentioning that it had to be accessible even before an instance of the form was created. Properties and methods that do not require a specific instance of an object in order to provide meaningful results (such as MinValue, Main, and GetVolume) are referred to as *static* properties or methods and are denoted by the keyword static within their signatures. Thus we can modify our overloaded functions by adding the keyword static as shown here.

```
public static int GetVolume( double dblSquareFeet,
                             int intInches )
{
```

```
    //  This version of GetVolume
    //     accepts both roof size and rainfall.
    return (int)(dblSquareFeet * GALLONS_PER_FOOT *
                 intInches / INCHES_PER_FOOT);
}
```

This in turn enables us to simplify the code contained within the `cmdCalc` button's `Click` event handler by removing the object creation statement and changing the source of the `GetVolume` method to `WaterMath`, as shown here.

```
private void cmdCalc_Click(object sender,
                           System.EventArgs e)
{
    //  Calculate the runoff.
    lblAnswer.Text =
       Cistern.WaterMath.GetVolume(
          double.Parse(textRoof.Text),
          int.Parse(textRain.Text) ).ToString();
}
```

When we run the application using the values shown in Figure 2.19, we learn that approximately 48,000 gallons of water runs off a 2,200-square-foot Seattle roof during an average year.

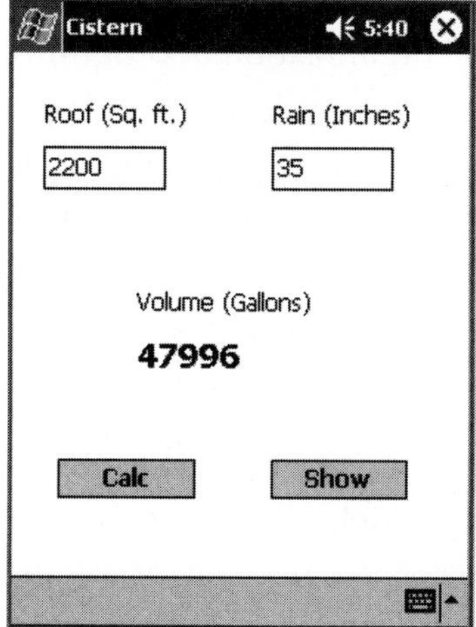

FIGURE 2.19: Annual Seattle rain runoff

With our code functionally complete, we can now take some time to organize it by adding a namespace.

Understanding Namespaces

As we discuss in Chapter 1, a key benefit of the .NET Framework is that it is a well-designed, structured programming interface. Part of the good design can be found in the consistency in naming conventions, data types, interoperability between languages, and placement of data elements into the various types of collections. The structure of the .NET Framework helps make its elements very *discoverable*—a term often used in the context of user interface design that applies equally well when discussing programming interface design. After all, if you cannot find a feature, it might as well not exist. The structure of the framework is supported through the use of namespaces.

A namespace provides a way to group related types together, so a namespace can be thought of as a collection of functionality. All code that you write becomes included into a namespace when compiled. The minimum size of a namespace is a class. More than one class can be combined into a single namespace, but a class can never be divided across multiple namespaces. Namespaces offer three benefits.

1. They provide internal organization of program logic.
2. They provide external organization of program logic, with logical groupings for use by other applications and developers.
3. They allow for the creation of duplicate class names for distinct classes that can be resolved unambiguously. For example, two separate `MathFunctions` classes can be used in the same application as long as they are in separate namespaces.

When you create a .NET Framework project in Visual Studio .NET, the name of the project is used by default as the name of the namespace. If you wish to change this namespace name, use the Project→Properties menu item to access the Property Pages dialog box and update the Default

Namespace field. If you wish to override the namespace name for one or more of your classes, change the `Namespace` keyword, as illustrated here.

```
namespace YaoDurant.CFBook.Utilities
{
   public class WaterMath
   {
      :
      :
      :
   }
}
```

A class is part of a namespace, not the other way around, so the namespace declaration must span the class definition. A namespace declaration cannot be placed inside a class definition.

Namespaces are a logical grouping that is hierarchical in structure. Consider the decisions that Microsoft made when spreading the .NET Compact Framework across namespaces. The common functionality required by most applications was placed in a namespace named `System`. Common database access functionality went into `System.Data`; functionality specific to SQL Server was placed in `System.Data.SQLClient`. It is you, the developer, who chooses the names of the namespaces and decides which classes belong in which namespaces.

Do not infer things from the names. `System.Data` is one namespace, not necessarily a subcomponent of a `System` namespace. `System.Data` is simply a name that is 11 characters long and contains a period as one of the middle characters.

The recommended convention for naming namespaces is to use a domain name (e.g., a company name) as the first portion of a namespace name, the major area of functionality as the middle section, and the specific functionality as the final portion, such as `Amalgamated.Accounting.Payables`.

Namespaces help you not only organize application functionality but also avoid conflict when duplicate class names are created within large projects and over projects that depend on third-party class libraries. Perhaps one day you will invent a better mousetrap; for example, you might create a ListBox class that everyone feels is the best ListBox ever developed. If you locate it within your JohnDoe.Commercial.WinControls namespace, other developers can set a reference to it and create a JohnDoe.Commercial.WinControls.ListBox control as well as a System.Windows.Forms.ListBox control, all within the same application. Through the use of a namespace you have organized your functionality for external use and you have ensured that the fully qualified name of your ListBox is unique throughout the world.

We do not have a better ListBox, but we do have the WaterMath class, with which we can illustrate the use of namespaces. We'll put WaterMath into its own namespace and then modify the class that uses it, FormMain, accordingly.

The code to put the WaterMath class into a separate namespace, YaoDurant.CFBook.Utilities, was shown in the previous code segment. Doing so changes the fully qualified name of the class from Cistern.WaterMath to YaoDurant.CFBook.Utilities.WaterMath, which means we must change the runoff calculation statement in FormMain as follows.

```
//  Calculate the runoff.
lblAnswer.Text =
   YaoDurant.CFBook.Utilities.WaterMath.GetVolume(
      double.Parse(textRoof.Text),
      int.Parse(textRain.Text) ).ToString();
```

Happily, we can get IntelliSense to help us as we code, as shown in Figure 2.20. (See the next subsection for more information on IntelliSense.)

You can reduce the amount of code and save yourself the trouble of extra typing by importing external namespaces—those defined outside your project—at the beginning of a source file or even at the beginning of a class definition. Consider the following line of code located at the start of FormFacts.cs:

```
Using System.Windows.Forms
```

It allows us when creating a new form or control to specify just the class name, such as Form, rather than having to specify the fully qualified name,

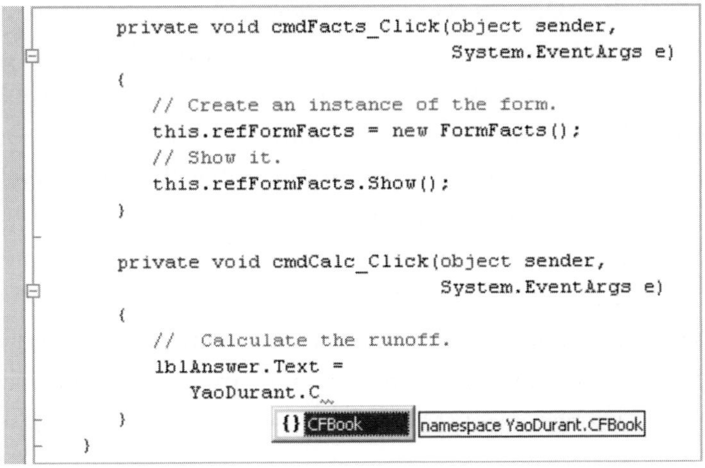

```
        private void cmdFacts_Click(object sender,
                                    System.EventArgs e)
        {
           // Create an instance of the form.
           this.refFormFacts = new FormFacts();
           // Show it.
           this.refFormFacts.Show();
        }

        private void cmdCalc_Click(object sender,
                                   System.EventArgs e)
        {
           //  Calculate the runoff.
           lblAnswer.Text =
              YaoDurant.C
        }          {} CFBook     namespace YaoDurant.CFBook
    }
```

FIGURE 2.20: IntelliSense namespace hint

namespace and all: `System.Windows.Forms.Form`. Thus our definition for the variable that will hold an instance of the form becomes:

```
// Variable to hold a reference to FormFacts.
private Form refFormFacts;
```

The more you work with .NET development, the more you work with namespaces. After a while you will begin to code your `using` statements as a first step in designing a class because you know that it helps you write tighter, cleaner, less cluttered code. And you begin to think about your own namespace organization at an early step in application design.

Using IntelliSense

IntelliSense is a code completion aid that has been around for some time now in both Microsoft and non-Microsoft products. Most .NET programmers are aware of it, yet we still see many of our students failing to take full advantage of it.

Most people are aware that IntelliSense provides a drop-down list whenever they key in a period while entering code, but many are unaware that they can continue to enter characters while the drop-down list is displayed and that it is advantageous to do so. Instead, they reach for the mouse the moment the drop-down list appears, costing themselves time and effort.

Consider a situation in which you are entering into the `FormMain` class some code that will set a `string` value into the form's `textRain` `TextBox` control, as shown here, but you cannot remember the name you gave the `TextBox` when you added it to the form.

```
this.textRain.Text = "44";
```

You know that with a form's class, the form itself is referred to by the keyword `this`, so you key in "`this`". And the drop-down list (in this case, a pop-up list because it is displayed just above the code being entered) appears. Having followed the naming conventions advocated in Appendix A, you narrow your choices by continuing to enter keystrokes, adding "`text`", which leaves you in the position shown in Figure 2.21.

Since the choice you want is now highlighted, you enter the character that will follow the highlighted word, in this case a period, and receive the next drop-down list, shown in Figure 2.22.

You key in a "t" and the `Text` property highlights, so once again you key in the character that will follow "`Text`", a space. You have now entered

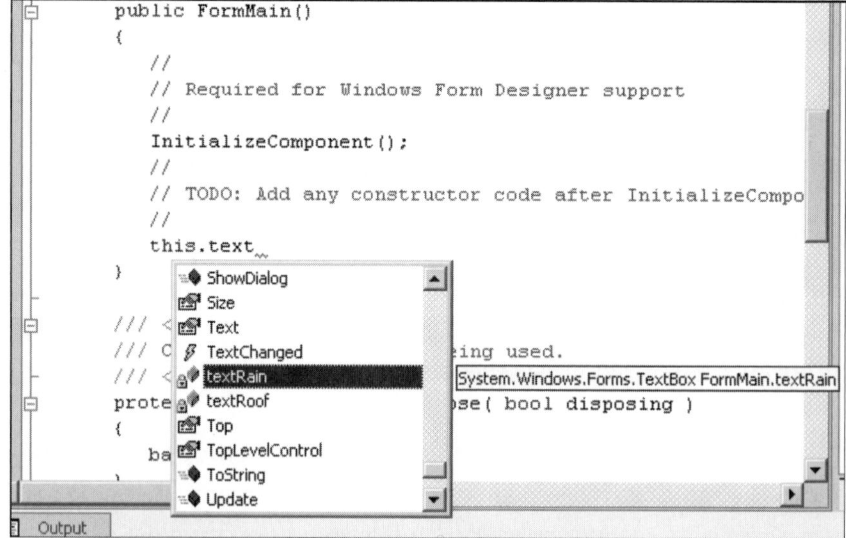
public FormMain()
{
//
// Required for Windows Form Designer support
//
InitializeComponent();
//
// TODO: Add any constructor code after InitializeCompo
//
this.text
}
ShowDialog
Size
Text
TextChanged
textRain
textRoof
Top
TopLevelControl
ToString
Update
System.Windows.Forms.TextBox FormMain.textRain
ing used.
se(bool disposing)
Output

FIGURE 2.21: IntelliSense positioned at the `TextBox` names

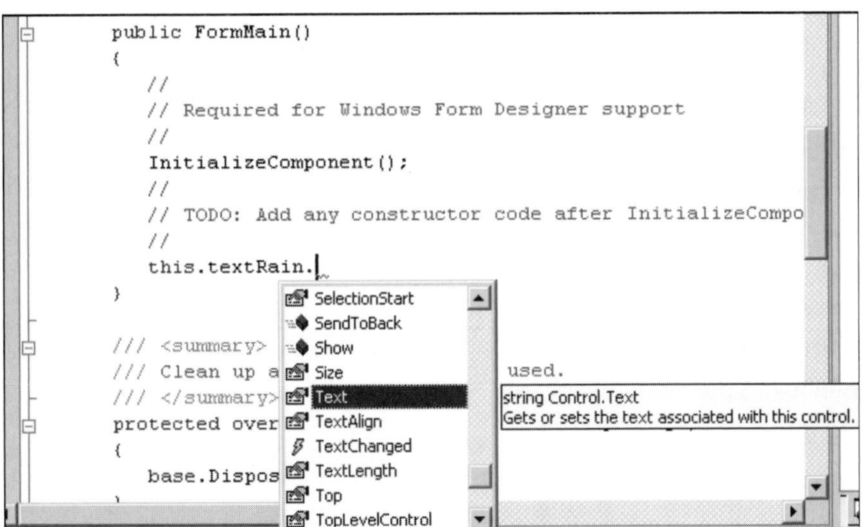
public FormMain()
{
//
// Required for Windows Form Designer support
//
InitializeComponent();
//
// TODO: Add any constructor code after InitializeCompo
//
this.textRain.
}
/// <summary>
/// Clean up a
/// </summary>
protected over
{
base.Dispos
SelectionStart
SendToBack
Show
Size
Text
TextAlign
TextChanged
TextLength
Top
TopLevelControl
used.
string Control.Text
Gets or sets the text associated with this control.

FIGURE 2.22: IntelliSense positioned at the `Text` property

"`this.textRain.Text`" in a dozen keystrokes even though you had forgotten the control name and knew only that the property name began with "t".

You can get to IntelliSense long before you get to the period: all you have to do is hit CTRL-space. When you do, a drop-down list appears, showing every possible valid word that will complete your entry. For instance, suppose you want to create a `WaterMath` object, that is, you want to write the line of code shown here (the `using` line is already in your class code), but you remember only that the class name begins with "`Water`".

```
using YaoDurant.CFBook.Utilities;
    :
    :
    :
  WaterMath wmABC = new WaterMath();
```

No problem, just key in "`wat`" and hit CTRL-space. Don't even worry about case sensitivity; CTRL-space is not case sensitive. Live like a Visual Basic .NET programmer for once in your life. In the situation of our sample application, "`WaterMath`" is the only possible word that begins with "`wat`", so no drop-down list is presented. Instead, because it is the only possibility, the word "`WaterMath`" is completed in the code for you.

So our first suggestion is this: Stay off the mouse and keep your hands on the keyboard until the word you want is highlighted, and then enter the character that follows that word. Our second suggestion is this: Use the CTRL-space key combination. And here's our third suggestion: Use Hungarian naming for objects and classes even if you prefer a different set of prefixes from those we present in Appendix A. If you know that all your `TextBox` names begin with "`text`", you can narrow the IntelliSense drop-down list to the available `TextBox` controls with just four keystrokes.

CONCLUSION

This chapter introduced the basics of using the Visual Studio .NET 2003 development environment to build .NET Compact Framework Windows programs. Such work typically begins with drawing the user interface elements with the help of the Designer, then writing code to support those objects. You can test and debug your programs by using the Pocket PC emulator, which is supplied with Visual Studio .NET, or by downloading and running your programs on an actual device. The emulator, which provides the convenience that no external hardware is required, is good for getting started with .NET Compact Framework development. Eventually you need to test your applications on real hardware, however, to duplicate the environment of your users and to make sure that you have addressed all potential issues prior to shipping your software.

This chapter also described how Visual Studio .NET supports creating your own classes. You saw how the .NET Compact Framework supports namespaces to help provide structure and organization to your software.

In the next chapter, we examine the .NET data types that are available as you write your code. These fundamental types are the building blocks for all data definition and data exchange in .NET Compact Framework.

3 The .NET Type System

This chapter provides a tour through the .NET types needed for .NET Compact Framework programming.

.NET PROGRAMMING PROVIDES a high level of interoperability between programming languages. By "interoperability" we mean that, more so than any other programming environment, the .NET model reduces differences between different programming languages. This gives developers greater freedom in selecting a programming language (assuming, of course, that a .NET-compatible compiler for a desired language is available). This high level of interoperability has never been achieved in traditional Windows programming, and Visual Basic programmers have often felt like second-class citizens.

Interoperability is achieved by a set of common standards. Among the .NET technologies that Microsoft submitted to Ecma International[1] was the Common Language Infrastructure (CLI). The CLI contains basic infrastructure elements of .NET but excludes the high-level Windows Forms and Web Forms classes. To interoperate with other .NET-compatible languages, a compiler must comply with the CLI. This chapter focuses on one of those standards: the common type system (CTS).

The .NET type system provides the foundation for a strongly typed, object-oriented programming environment. A programmer selects the most

1. Ecma International is a European standards body; see http://www.ecma-international.org.

appropriate type to represent the data item, in effect codifying the programmer's intent for how that data item should be used. Once the type is chosen, errors can be detected at both build time (by the compiler) and at runtime (by the runtime system). The .NET execution engine takes this one step further, supporting *verifiable code*, which relies on strong typing to ensure that the code does not access out-of-bounds memory.

An object-oriented approach organizes the raw material of software—meaning the code that runs and the data that is operated on—as *objects*. The content and behavior of an object are defined, in turn, by its type—that is, by its *class*. Programmers use classes to organize code and data. Using the terminology of .NET, we say that a *class* is a set of methods and fields, where a *method* is the most fundamental type of code, and a *field* is the most fundamental type of data.

This chapter reviews the elements of the .NET Framework type system that .NET Compact Framework programmers are likely to need. Our intent is not to teach C# programming—other books are better suited for that purpose. Nor is our intent to provide a complete discussion of the intricacies of .NET internals, a fascinating subject that is addressed in other, more specialized, books.[2]

Because this book focuses on C#, we expect readers to have learned C# programming from other sources. However, we do provide in this chapter some specific sidebars for C++ programmers and Visual Basic 6 programmers.

Using Type Information: Namespace References and Assembly References

To make use of a type that is defined in the .NET Compact Framework, you reference the location where that type is defined. A given type has a physical location and a logical location. The physical location is a file, typically with an extension of `.exe` or `.dll`. To use a type that is defined in a `.dll` file, you let the compiler know the file's location by providing an assembly

2. We recommend *Essential .NET, Volume 1: The Common Language Runtime* by Don Box with Chris Sells (Boston, MA: Addison-Wesley, 2003).

reference. Within your code, you specify the logical location of a type by providing a namespace.

We discussed namespaces in detail in Chapter 2, so we are not going to delve into that topic in great detail in this chapter. However, namespaces do provide a point of departure for the exploration of type information. As we discussed in Chapter 2, namespaces help organize the large number of types that are inevitable in a large, multifaceted programming environment. As such, a namespace provides part of a type's identity; it is the family name for a set of types.

For example, the `System.Drawing` namespace is the family of types used to create graphical output. Within that namespace are two sibling classes, `Brush` and `Pen`. The fully qualified names for these types are `System.Drawing.Brush` and `System.Drawing.Pen`. The fully qualified name gives these types a unique identity among the vast set of .NET-compatible types. In general, you probably will not want to use the fully qualified names for every class you refer to. In case of ambiguity, however, the fully qualified name provides a way to distinguish between similarly named classes, structures, interfaces, and other .NET types.

Namespace Contents

A namespace is the outermost organizing element of a type. Use of namespaces in your own program code is optional, but we recommend that you give some time and thought to how you wish to use them when organizing code libraries that other programmers are going to use. For class libraries, the convention is that the name of a namespace should also be the name of the DLL file. For example, in the .NET Compact Framework, the `System.Windows.Forms` namespace resides inside the `System.Windows.Forms.dll` file. In the sample code for this book, we use the `YaoDurant` namespace for shared libraries and for source files that we expect our readers are going to want to reuse.

Within a namespace, the most important kind of type that you can define is a class. Other kinds of type information can be included in a namespace, such as enumerations and structures. But after the namespace, the second most important organizing element in .NET programming is the class. You cannot define code or data directly in a namespace—you must put them in a class.

Within a class, code and data are defined using these two fundamental .NET types: *fields* and *methods*. The fragment in Listing 3.1 shows a field and a method defined in a class, which, in turn, resides in a namespace, `YaoDurant.Identity`.

LISTING 3.1: Four Fundamental Types: a Field, a Method, a Class, and a Namespace

```
namespace YaoDurant.Identity
{
   public class SimpleType
   {
      public int i;

      public int ReturnInteger()
      {
         return i;
      }

   } // class
} // namespace
```

The code in Listing 3.1 contains examples of four key elements of the .NET type system:

1. A namespace: `YaoDurant.Identity`
2. A class: `SimpleType`
3. A field: `i`
4. A method: `ReturnInteger`

The fully qualified name for the class is `YaoDurant.Identity.SimpleType`, and the fully qualified name for the method is `YaoDurant.Identity.SimpleType.ReturnInteger`. In the next subsection we discuss the `using` statement, which lets you reference a namespace to avoid having to use fully qualified names.

A program source file can have any number of namespaces. Namespaces help organize the various types that make up a program, serving as the general-purpose container for those types. The primary use of namespaces that most programmers encounter is within frameworks,[3] which use namespaces to organize the myriad number of types into manageable sets. Namespaces can hold any combination of the following types:

- Classes
- Interfaces
- Structures
- Enumerations
- Delegates

A namespace can also contain other namespaces, although namespaces are not considered a type. From an object-oriented programming perspective, classes are the preeminent type in a .NET program. A class is able to contain all other types, including other classes. Because namespaces are not a type, they cannot be contained in classes.

Accessing Namespaces

A fully qualified name provides an unambiguous way to identify a class, methods in a class, and static (or shared) fields. That is a good thing. When you look at the code generated for you by the Designer, you see a lot of fully qualified names. The Designer writes the code for you. It later reads the code when you decide to edit a form. In this context, a fully qualified name helps the Designer avoid confusion.

The disadvantage of fully qualified names is that they require a lot of typing. To avoid this extra effort, C# programmers indicate the namespaces they wish to use with a set of `using` statements. For example, if we had a separate source file, module, or assembly that needed to access the types in our namespace, we would eliminate the need for fully qualified names with a statement like the following:

```
using YaoDurant.Identity;
```

3. Meaning the .NET Framework, the .NET Compact Framework, and other frameworks that might be available.

Assembly versus Namespace

Close reading of the CLI reveals that an *assembly*, not a namespace, forms the outermost container of the .NET type system. One reason is that some CLI-compatible languages might not support namespaces. For most purposes, a namespace serves as the outermost container for everything in the .NET type system. There are times, however, when a namespace falls short of providing what we need.

A program sometimes needs to identify itself to the execution engine. There is no namespace class; instead, we use an object created from the `Assembly`[4] class. We use an `Assembly` object to access resources in a module, to load and run programs and shared libraries, and to query for type information.

By itself, a `using` statement hints at desired namespaces but does not indicate what actual module to use. For that, you must add a reference to a Visual Studio .NET project, a subject we discuss in the accompanying text.

On the desktop, an assembly can be created from two or more modules. The .NET Compact Framework does not support multimodule assembly, so every assembly has exactly one module associated with it.

When you create a new smart-device project in Visual Studio .NET, the Smart Device Application Wizard creates a set of `using` statements for you, as shown in Figure 3.1. These are not needed to build the code that has been generated for you because the Designer uses fully qualified names. Instead, these references tell the IDE about the namespaces needed to support IntelliSense.

Assembly References

An assembly reference provides the names of the shared libraries that a .NET program (or shared library) is going to use. While a namespace is a logical container for a set of classes (and other types), an assembly is a

4. Fully qualified name: `System.Reflection.Assembly`.

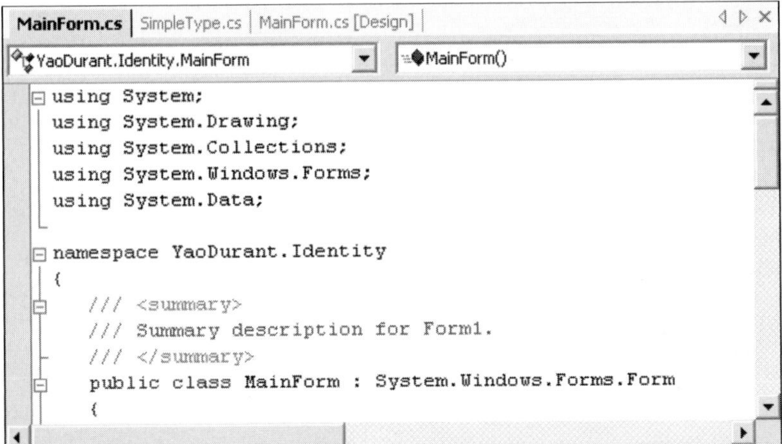

FIGURE 3.1: Set of `using` declarations created by the Smart Device Application Wizard

physical container—the name of one or more library files—that contains classes and other .NET types. A `using` statement provides a hint of the namespaces that might be required in an assembly but are purely optional; this convenient feature eliminates the need for fully qualified names for imported types.

An assembly reference, on the other hand, is not optional. Visual Studio .NET must know the names of the shared library that a program is going to access because it uses the library to extract the metadata required for type safety. It also provides a very secure type of version control by extracting the strong name of each assembly, which the loader will later use to verify a correct match before allowing a program to run.

When the Smart Device Application Wizard creates a project for you, it adds a set of assembly references to your project. Figure 3.2 shows an example of the default set provided in the Solution Explorer window. You add new assembly references by summoning the Add Reference dialog box. (From the Visual Studio menu, select Project→Add Reference..., or right-click on the Solution Explorer and select Add Reference....)

The minimum assembly reference required for all .NET programs is `mscorlib.dll`, a short name that stands for "Microsoft Core Library." As the name implies, this library holds the core elements for the .NET runtime system. This sounds like an important library to understand, so you might

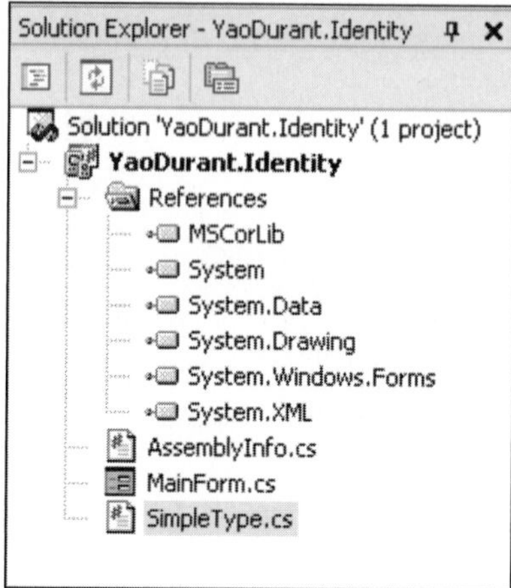

FIGURE 3.2: Assembly references created by the Smart Device Application Wizard

wonder how to explore it. One approach, which we mentioned in Chapter 1, is to use `ildasm.exe`—the IL disassembly tool. Another approach is to use the Object Browser in Visual Studio .NET. Figure 3.3 shows the Object Browser displaying the contents of `mscorlib.dll`. (Select the View→Object Browser menu item to summon the Object Browser.) The left side of the figure shows available namespaces and also classes in the `System.Threading` namespace. The right side shows details for the public members of the `Thread` class.

Standard Types

The CTS is the portion of the CLI that addresses how data types are defined and how they behave. The primary motivation for having a common type system—and the other elements of the CLI—is to promote interoperability between programming languages. The CTS is sometimes referred to as a *unified type system*. This term reflects the fact that two groups of types that are often split apart in some object-oriented environments are designed in a way that minimizes the differences. In the CTS, the two groups are called *value types* and *reference types*.

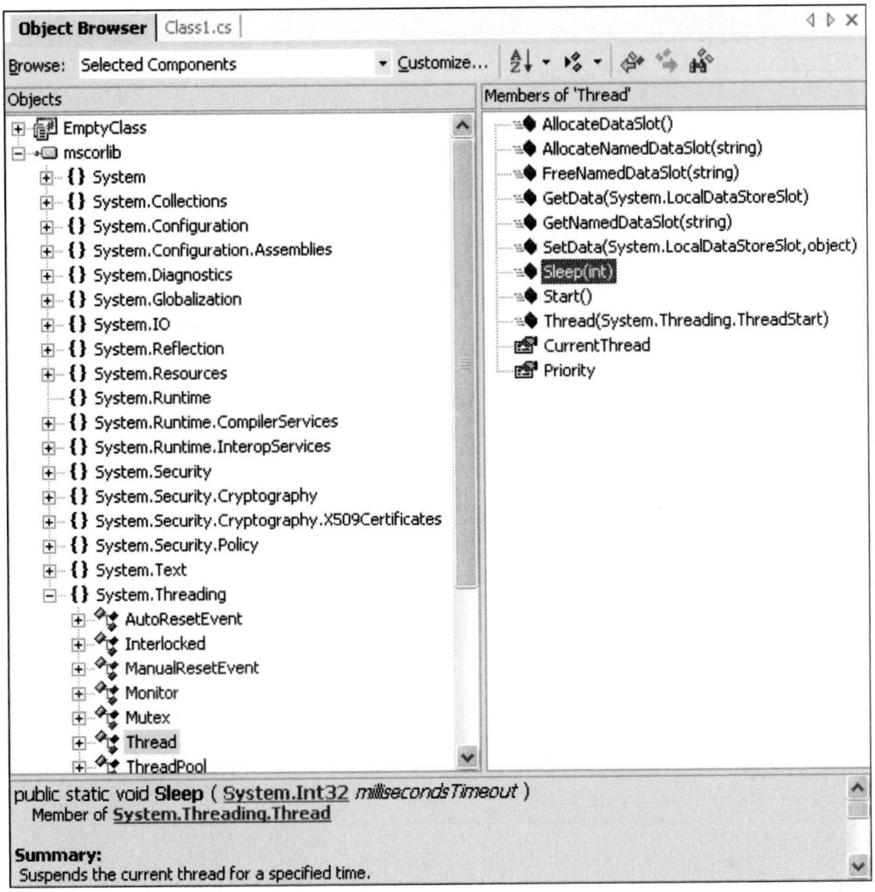

FIGURE 3.3: The Object Browser showing the contents of `mscorlib.dll`

Value Types

Value types are simple, low-overhead types intended to hold pure data. The CTS defines a core set of value types that all compilers must support to be able to interoperate with other .NET-compatible compilers. Value types are typically supported by language-specific keywords. Examples of value types include the following:

- Integers
- Floating-point numbers

- Data structures
- Enumerations

Value types are meant to be small and fast, avoiding the inevitable overhead of objects. When used as a local variable, a value type is allocated on the stack. When nested in an object, a value type is represented as a simple stream of bytes.

Take `Int32`, for example, the type that describes 4-byte signed integers. Such integers can be quickly loaded into 32-bit CPU registers and operated on. In the unified type system of .NET, the 4-byte signed integer is represented by the `System.Int32` class. Like other classes, there are methods for operating on 4-byte integers. We can, for example, call the `ToString` method to convert an integer to a string, as shown in Listing 3.2. As the code fragment shows, value types can have methods just like reference types.

LISTING 3.2: Converting an Integer to a String

```
int cCount = 10;
string strCount = cCount.ToString();
string strAnother = 10.ToString();
```

A value type can have other elements of objects, including fields. For example, the `Int32` class has two static fields, `MaxValue` and `MinValue`, which define the range of numbers supported by this class. (All numeric value types have similarly named static fields.)

Like all value types, the `System.Int32` class has a base class named `System.ValueType`. And that class, in turn, has a base class named `System.Object`. This is the same base class that all .NET types share, yet another aspect of the CTS.

Value types do have their limitations. While they are defined as .NET classes, they themselves are considered sealed classes. In other words, you cannot use `System.Int32` (or any other value-type class) as the base class for other types. Also, value-type variables must always contain a value and cannot be empty. By contrast, a reference type can have the value of `null`.

Integer and Floating-Point Value Types

Table 3.1 shows the basic set of built-in numeric value types in C#. Each data type in the table is defined in two ways—as a .NET type and as a language-specific alias. Which one should you use? It is probably a matter of personal taste because the language-specific alias gets converted by the compiler to the associated .NET type. We generally prefer language-specific aliases, and that is what you find in the sample code written for this book. For example, we use `int` instead of `System.Int32` or `Int32`, which makes our type definitions more consistent with the rest of our code. The C# compiler converts the language-specific alias into the corresponding .NET type.

TABLE 3.1: **Basic Set of Built-in Value Types**

.NET Type	Compatible with CLI?	Size (Bytes)	C# Alias
`System.Boolean`	Yes	1	`bool`
`System.Byte`	Yes	1	`byte`
`System.SByte`	No	1	`sbyte`
`System.Char`	Yes	2	`char`
`System.Int16`	Yes	2	`short`
`System.UInt16`	No	2	`ushort`
`System.Int32`	Yes	4	`int`
`System.UInt32`	No	4	`uint`
`System.IntPtr`	Yes	4	`N/A`
`System.Single`	Yes	4	`float`
`System.Int64`	Yes	8	`long`
`System.UInt64`	No	8	`ulong`
`System.Double`	Yes	8	`double`
`System.Decimal`	Yes	12	`decimal`

For C++ Programmers

Experienced Windows programmers who worked in C and C++ are likely to be uncomfortable at first with using native language types like `int` and `char` in Windows code. For many years, Microsoft recommended that Windows programmers use types like `LPSTR` and `LONG` in place of the equivalent C-types `char *` and `long`. The use of the uppercase types played a significant part in helping to make Win16 code portable to the Win32 API when the latter was introduced in the early 1990s.

The reasons for those recommendations had more to do with limitations of the C language than with anything inherently wrong with using built-in language types. For example, the implementer of a C compiler got to decide whether an `int` was 16, 32, or even 64 bits. (For a system software language like C, that choice arguably should be made on a system-specific basis.)

The language specification for C#, however, does not allow for that kind of flexibility. Instead, `int` is defined as a 32-bit signed integer equivalent to `System.Int32`, and `long` is defined as a 64-bit integer equivalent to `System.Int64`. There is no need for a portability layer with .NET programming languages because the CTS provides the standard. Changes, such as the addition of a 128-bit integer, will arrive as extensions and not revocations of the existing standard.

The second column of Table 3.1 indicates whether or not a type is compatible with the CLI. If you plan to build assemblies that provide full interoperability with all other .NET languages, use types that are compatible with CLI. Of the fourteen types listed in the table, only four are not CLI-compliant:

- `System.SByte`: signed 1-byte integer
- `System.UInt16`: unsigned 2-byte integer
- `System.UInt32`: unsigned 4-byte integer
- `System.UInt64`: unsigned 8-byte integer

By avoiding these types in C# code, you enable your shared assemblies to be called from Visual Basic programs (Visual Basic does not support these four types). You also gain compatibility with other CLI-compatible languages that may become available in the .NET Compact Framework.

You might notice in the online .NET documentation that built-in value types are referred to as *structures*. Figure 3.4 shows a portion of the MSDN Library table of contents, in which the `Int32` type is called `Int32 Structure`. You probably do not think of simple numeric types, such as 2-byte and 4-byte integers, as data structures. But in a world where everything is either a reference type (a class) or a value type (a structure), simple numeric types—as value types—fall into the category of structures.

Data Structures

As just mentioned, data structures within .NET are value types. The .NET Compact Framework includes support for a large number of data structures, most of which are used for the basic operation of the windowing and graphic systems. Table 3.2 summarizes some of the more commonly used structures in a .NET Compact Framework program.

> **For Visual Basic 6 Programmers**
>
> The Visual Basic 6 keyword, `Type`, for user-defined types, does not exist in Visual Basic .NET; Visual Basic .NET provides an alternative keyword, `Structure`, for user-defined types, and C# provides the `struct` keyword.

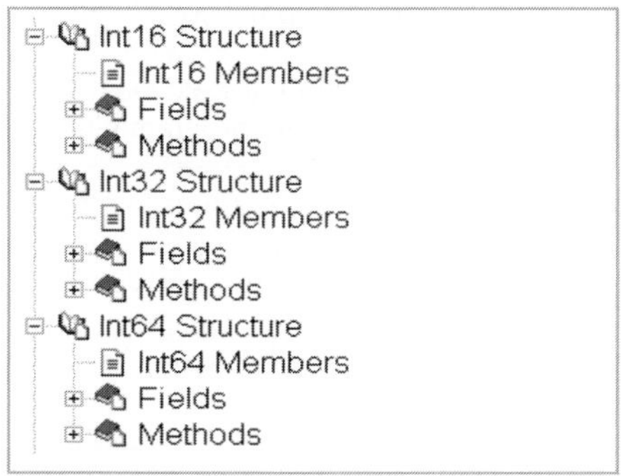

FIGURE 3.4: Example of value types referred to as structures in the MSDN Library

For C++ Programmers

A C++ programmer can think of a C# structure as similar to a C++ structure, with an important difference: While C++ allows a structure to behave like a class and vice versa, a C# structure is distinctly different from a C# class. The former is a value type, while the latter is a reference type. We discuss that difference later in this chapter.

TABLE 3.2: Common .NET Compact Framework Structures

Namespace	Class	Description
`System`	`DateTime`	A structure that stores date, time, or both date and time
`System.Drawing`	`Color`	A structure that stores color as RGB, a system color, or a named color
`System.Drawing`	`Point`	An (x,y) location with integer coordinates
`System.Drawing`	`Rectangle`	An area defined with integer coordinates as a pixel grid (a nonrotated rectangle with a top and a bottom, a left and a right)
`System.Drawing`	`RectangleF`	An area defined with floating-point coordinates as a pixel grid
`System.Drawing`	`Size`	A width and height pair for the size of a rectangle, with integer coordinates
`System.Drawing`	`SizeF`	A width and height pair for the size of a rectangle, with floating-point coordinates
`System`	`Guid`	A globally unique identifier, used in COM programming and network programming
`System`	`IntPtr`	A signed 32-bit wrapper for unmanaged code pointer and handles (a 64-bit wrapper on 64-bit platforms, although Windows CE—and therefore the .NET Compact Framework—runs only on 32-bit platforms)
`System`	`TimeSpan`	A structure that stores time duration

Reference Types

Reference types are the second major category of CTS types. Objects of reference types are accessed at runtime by using a reference, a pointer to the object itself. Examples of reference types include the following:

- Objects created from a class
- Objects encapsulating Win32 system objects (forms, controls, graphic objects, threads, mutexes, files, and so on)
- Arrays
- Strings
- Boxed value types

Just as there are built-in value types, there are also built-in reference types. These types form the foundation for the efficient operation of the type system. Our criteria for built-in reference types are that IL instructions create or require a type, a set that includes the following types:

- `System.Object`: the base type from which all other types are derived
- `System.String`: an immutable string class
- `System.Array`: a fixed-length array
- `System.Exception`: execution errors
- `System.IntPtr`: a pointer type

Note that there are three pointer types, but only `System.IntPtr` is exposed to the type system. Other pointers are used by the execution engine as references to instantiated objects.

Every object has a standard object header. The size of the object header[5] is 8 bytes, and the smallest possible object (an instance of type `Object`) is 12 bytes. We mention this simply to underscore that reference types take up a bit more space than value types do. Object headers contain references to class type information. A program can access this type information by using a set of services known as *reflection* which is available through classes in the

---

5. The header size is 8 bytes for two-integer fields in 32-bit systems. Object headers in 64-bit systems are 16 bytes.

`System.Reflection` namespace. In addition to the header, objects contain instance data: the public and private fields defined for the object's type.

Reference types have complete support for object-oriented programming. The most useful feature is *inheritance*, which lets you define new reference types from existing reference types. When defining a custom type that you expect to use as a base for other new types, the base type must be a class. Custom types that inherit from existing types, in turn, can inherit only from other reference types.

By contrast, inheritance is not supported for value types. Value types are said to be *sealed* because a value type cannot be used as a base type for other types. (A reference type can also be sealed, using the `sealed` keyword, which prevents that type from being used as the base type for new types.)

Objects of reference types are allocated on the runtime heap and so are subject to garbage collection. Objects without a live reference—either directly in a local variable or indirectly through another object—are called *unreachable objects*. When the garbage collector reclaims memory, it reclaims the memory occupied by unreachable objects. To make an object unreachable, set the value in all variables that reference the object to `null`:

```
object obj = new object();
obj = null;
```

Reference Types versus Value Types

When we teach our .NET programming classes, a common discussion topic involves the relative merits of reference types versus value types. Reference types are larger and more complex than value types. In terms of memory and processing time, then, reference types are more costly than value types. Is one better than the other?

This is an interesting question to ask in theory, but in practice both have their natural uses. Value types have less memory overhead, are of a fixed size, and are less extendable. By contrast, reference types are extendable via inheritance, can change size, are inexpensive to pass as parameters, can be shared between threads, and have built-in thread synchronization.

Garbage collection in the .NET runtime is sometimes referred to as *non-deterministic*. The cleanup of unreachable objects does not occur immediately, which is different than how other memory cleanup schemes work. In particular, the cleanup performed by ActiveX/COM objects is done deterministically, that is, when the reference count for a component reaches zero. In the .NET runtime, however, cleanup of unreachable objects is not likely to occur until later. How much later? As suggested by the name, there is no way to determine the timing of memory cleanup.

Declaration, Initialization, and Allocation

There are differences between value types and reference types. But a casual look at any .NET code makes those differences hard to detect because a common syntax works for both types of types. Both value-type variables and reference-type variables can be declared, initialized, and allocated with similar code. There is a real difference in the last step, however, namely in how the two types are allocated. Consider the code in Listing 3.3. This code defines two types that are identical in every way except that one is a value type and the other is a reference type.

LISTING 3.3: Comparing Value Types and Reference Types

```
// Structure -- a value type
struct PointStruct
{
   int X;
   int Y;
}

// Class - a reference type
class PointClass
{
   int X;
   int Y;
}

private void MyClick()
{
   PointStruct p1 = new PointStruct();
   PointClass  p2 = new PointClass();
}
```

The `MyClick` method declares a variable of each type, `p1` and `p2`. The use of `new` with both types implies that a new object is being created. There is similar code, but a different dynamic comes into play for each variable. Let's start with the value type, `p1`.

Value types do not require the use of `new` when a parameterless constructor is specified, which is the case in this code. On the other hand, if we had a constructor defined with parameters to pass, we would then use `new`. While optional, a parameterless constructor for a value type is benign.

The `p1` variable in our example is allocated on the stack. The compiler notices the use of a value type and includes space on the stack in the generated IL. At runtime, that space is automatically included as a variable on the stack.

On entry to the function, the contents of `p1` are initialized to zero. This is true for all types, including integer, floating-point, and decimal values. It is also true for reference-type variables, like `p2` in our example. All variables start in a known, defined state.

The use of `new` is required for reference types. On entry to the `MyClick` method, the local variable `p2` is initialized to zero. If we omit `new` and then use that variable to access a member, an exception is generated. Because an unhandled exception causes a program to terminate, we want to avoid using variables for null reference types.

When `new` is encountered for a reference-type variable, the memory allocator gets called to create space in the runtime heap. In addition, one or more constructors are called for the object starting with the constructor for `Object`, including constructors in all other inherited classes for our reference type.

Value Types and Reference Types as Parameters

Value types and reference types look the same when you are allocating them and accessing them, so sometimes you can ignore the distinction between them and let the compiler handle things. Aside from the need to use the `new` operator with reference types, the code that you write for dealing with both types is quite similar.

The difference between value types and reference types becomes important when you wish to pass a parameter to a method. Both value types and reference types can be passed as parameters, but the declarations are different for each. Value types can be either by-value parameters or by-reference parameters. Reference types can also be by-value parameters or by-reference parameters. The majority of the time, however, both value types and reference types are passed as by-value parameters.

Value Types as Parameters

Value types are allocated as bits local to the owner—on the stack for local variables and within the object instance data when a class field. As mentioned, value types can be passed either by value or by reference. Value types that are 32 bits and smaller are normally passed by value. Larger value types and structures containing value types are often passed by reference. When a value type is passed by value, a copy of the value is put on the stack. That value makes a one-way trip into the called function, and the local copy of that value is not affected.

When a value type is passed by reference, an implicit pointer is put on the stack. The called function uses that pointer to read the contents of the variable. The called function can also change the contents of the variable, which is why we sometimes say that a by-reference parameter makes a two-way trip—down to the called function, then back again with whatever changes the function has made. Listing 3.4 shows value types passed as by-value parameters and as by-reference parameters. Passing value parameters by reference is particularly useful when calling certain native Win32 functions, a topic we explore more fully in Chapter 4.

LISTING 3.4: By-Reference and By-Value Parameter Passing

```
private void ValueParameters()
{
   // Init to one
   int i1 = 1;
   int i2 = 1;

   // Function adds one to each
   Increment(i1, ref i2);

   // On return:
   //    i1 = 1
```

continues

continued

```
    //   i2 = 2
}

// i is a value type parameter passed by value
// pi is a value type parameter passed by reference
private void Increment(int i, ref int pi)
{
    i++;
    pi++;
}
```

Reference Types as Parameters

Reference types are allocated from the process heap. A reference-type variable contains a pointer that refers to the object. The terminology used can sometimes cause confusion. There are two types—reference types and value types—and two ways to pass parameters—by reference and by value. So you might expect that you pass reference types by reference and value types by value, right?

In fact, reference types are ordinarily passed as by-value parameters and not as by-reference parameters. The reason is that the value of a reference type is a pointer, and it is this value that is typically passed between functions. It is certainly possible to pass a reference type by reference, but it creates a pointer to a pointer. This is rarely done, but the capability exists for those few situations—such as in some calls to native code—when it may be necessary.

Strings

Strings get special treatment in the world of .NET programming. Special treatment makes sense because strings are costly in terms of memory consumed and also because strings are required to communicate with people. The .NET Compact Framework provides two main classes to support string operations: `System.String` and `System.Text.StringBuilder`.

To make optimal use of available memory, programmers working with string-intensive applications need to understand how these two classes work. The main difference involves the issue of immutability, a subject we explore later in this chapter.

For programmers writing software to be made available in different languages, strings add an additional level of complexity. A program written for Spanish-speaking users and English-speaking users must have two sets of strings for text to display to users, one for each language. The use of string resources allows programmers to separate strings from code, thus simplifying the task of preparing software for a multilingual end-user population.

Literal Strings

In the "good old days"[6] of Windows programming, we worried about literal strings. To reduce overhead, a programmer put redundant strings into global variables (or in a string table). As the Windows on the desktop got more RAM, fewer programmers worried about redundant strings.

With today's compilers, no one needs to worry about redundant literal strings because the C# compiler helps out by folding duplicate strings to reduce storage overhead. Listing 3.5 shows the `SayHello` method, in which `"Hello"` appears four times. The compiler reduces all four references to refer to a single string. In this way, an executable file is smaller than it might otherwise be.

LISTING 3.5: The `SayHello` Method

```
private void SayHello()
{
   string str1 = "Hello";
   StringBuilder sb1 = new StringBuilder("Hello");
   MessageBox.Show("Hello", "Hello");
}
```

At runtime, static strings are allocated from the heap like other types of objects. Allocation of such strings is handled in a JIT fashion, in the same way that the IL-to-native translation is handled. The runtime JIT compiler does not convert an entire module but rather converts individual methods

6. Some of you may remember the days when, knee-deep in snow, we walked uphill (both ways) to school. We allocated memory with a slide rule and drank from punch cards; we used scissors to cut and chewing gum to paste.

as they are called. Part of the JIT process involves allocating static strings that a specific method is going to need.

The JIT compiler works in a way that allows the garbage collector to remove unreachable strings and yet eliminates redundant strings. If a static string has already been allocated on the heap during the JITting of another method, the JIT compiler adds a new reference to the string but does not create a second copy of the string.

Literal strings are stored as UTF-16 (2 bytes per character) Unicode characters in an executable module. (Unicode is also the character set for strings in memory.) If you have many literal strings, you might consider storing those strings as resources. Strings stored as resources are stored in the smaller, more memory-efficient UTF-8 (1 byte per character) Unicode strings. We discuss the creation of string resources later in this chapter.

The `System.String` Class

A string is an array of characters. Most of the time, however, we do not want to deal with the fussiness of arrays. Instead, we want an easy way to display a message to a user or write an entry to a log file that we can read later. We get all these things in the `System.String` class, which provides a lightweight class useful for most string operations.

String Properties, Methods, and Operators

The `Length` property provides instant access to the number of characters in the string. An indexer (the `[n]` operator in C#) lets us treat the string as an array of characters when we need the benefits an array provides. Other member methods let us search a string, add or remove padding, or extract a substring. And best of all, the concatenation operator—the plus (+)—makes it easy to create a new string by joining two existing strings. Each of these is illustrated in Listing 3.6.

LISTING 3.6: Common String Operations

```
string str = "A literal string";
int cb = str.Length;
string strLength = "Length is " + cb.ToString();
string strFirst  = "First character is " + str[0].ToString();
```

```
MessageBox.Show("String is " + str + "\n" +
   strLength + "\n" +
   strFirst);
```

As mentioned, the `String` class has a concatenation operator, which makes it easy to combine two or more strings together. While this operator is very convenient, we suggest you use it sparingly and only when working with simple string operations. As we discuss shortly, the issue has to do with memory overhead caused by the fact that strings created from this class are immutable, which means that each string operation causes a new string to be allocated. When performing many string operations, it is more efficient to use the `StringBuilder` class.

For C++ Programmers

String operations in C++ are difficult and painful. C++ programmers who have worked primarily with the Win32 API celebrate when they start .NET programming because of the pain they have endured over the years. In particular, the `+` operator concatenates two strings. The `Length` property replaces the need to call the `strlen`[7] function to calculate a string length. Life, in short, gets easier.

Of course, some C++ programmers—such as programmers who regularly use class libraries like MFC—may yawn when they hear about the various string operators, because such class libraries typically have a string class that provides some of the same features as the `String` class in the .NET Compact Framework. For example, MFC programmers have the `CString` class. Visual Basic programmers, for their part, are equally unimpressed. Both come from a world where strings flow freely and are easy to allocate, concatenate, and work with.

We think the most interesting string method is a member of the `Object` class because every .NET type supports this method. We are referring to

7. Or the `wcslen` or `_tcslen` functions.

the `ToString` method, which creates a string that represents an object. The default behavior is to provide the object type, but some classes—notably the numeric classes—override this method to provide more useful results. Listing 3.6 shows examples of calling the `ToString` method for an integer and a character.

Value Type or Reference Type?

It is sometimes said that the `System.String` class is a reference type that gets treated like a value type. All other reference types require `new` for a new instance, but strings created from literal strings do not, as shown in the way `str` gets allocated in Listing 3.6. (However, you use `new` when creating strings from character arrays.) There is no other reference type that allows for the implicit creation of new objects in the manner supported for the `String` class.

Perhaps the one quality that makes strings seem like a value type is expressed best by the phrase "strings are immutable." In the system heap, a string is a read-only object. Once created, a string does not change. Every operation on a string causes a new string to be allocated, with no changes made to the original string.

Strings Are Immutable

Does this mean that you cannot change strings? Of course not! As a programmer it is your job to change things. The string class contains methods like `ToUpper` and `ToLower`, which change the case of a string. But each function leaves the original string unchanged, and what you get back is a transformed copy. You can change strings, but any operation on a string leaves the original string untouched. What happens to old strings?[8] They remain on the heap to be used by other references or to be garbage collected when they are unreachable.

Is there a good reason for making strings work this way? Yes, there are many good reasons, all centered around making strings lightweight and easy to work with. As immutable objects, strings can be passed as parameters and the caller knows that the original string cannot change.

---

8. For fans of American-style football: Old strings, like old quarterbacks, fade back and pass away.

Immutable (read-only) strings make multithreaded programming easier because two threads can use a common set of strings, and no extra care need be taken to coordinate the sharing of strings. By contrast, when a reference to a read/write object gets passed as a parameter or shared between two threads, there can be trouble. Sharing a read/write object requires strict rules to be followed; sharing read-only objects requires much less care.

The Other Side of Immutability

Strings behave more like integers than like other objects. There is one difference, though: Each operation on a `System.String` object creates a new item in the heap. By contrast, nothing gets created on the heap for integer operations.

The immutability of strings makes them easy to use, but the memory cost makes them a bad fit for extensive string processing. What do we mean by "extensive"? We mean processing involving any combination of many strings, large strings, or many string operations. For that kind of processing, the second string class is the one to use—the `StringBuilder` class.

The `System.Text.StringBuilder` Class

The `StringBuilder` class provides a memory- and processor-efficient way to create mutable strings for intensive string processing. For example, the P/Invoke Wizard tool created by The Paul Yao Company uses a string builder to read C/C++ function declarations and create equivalent managed-code declarations.

The `StringBuilder` class is not meant as a direct substitute for the regular `String` class. For one thing, the two classes do not have any kind of inheritance relationship. Instead, you pass regular strings into the various methods of the class and use the `StringBuilder`'s `ToString` method to retrieve the final results.

By itself, this class provides a good way to save memory. For optimal savings, however, you should set the size of the buffer (defined with the `Capacity` property) with enough characters to handle whatever strings you plan to work with. The default capacity is 16 characters, which is probably too small for all but the simplest operations. The `Capacity` property also defines the allocation granularity, so if you err you probably want to err on the high side.

String Resources

String resources provide an alternative to putting literal strings in your code. Literal strings can make it more difficult to build software for a multilingual end-user community. For non-Asian languages, literal strings occupy twice as much space as the same strings stored as resources. String resources are worth consideration, although their use does take a bit more effort than literal strings.

To create string resources, add an XML resource file to your project with the Visual Studio .NET menu item Project→Add New Item..., and pick Assembly Resource File from the available types. The extension for XML resource files is `.resx`. Figure 3.5 shows a set of strings we created (the second column) and the associated names (the first column), for which we are using single letters for simplicity.

Like everything in .NET, XML resources are strongly typed.[9] This is important to keep in mind because we access resources using a fully qualified name. As with code, a fully qualified name for a resource involves combining a namespace with a type name. The type name for the resource

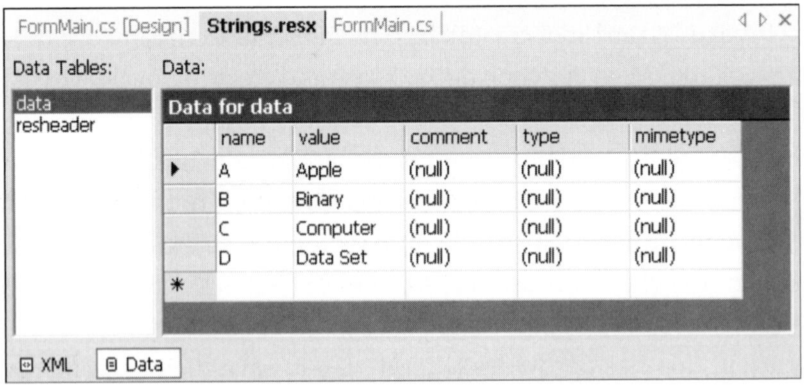

FIGURE 3.5: Creating string resources in Visual Studio .NET

9. We discuss untyped resources, also known as manifest resources, in Chapter 15 as part of the discussion of putting bitmap files into an assembly's resources.

in Figure 3.5 is the file name without the extension (`Strings`). The namespace is the default namespace for the project, which we can find in the project properties window. For our sample project, the default namespace is `StringResources`.

To access the strings in this string table, we create a resource manager object from the `ResourceManager`[10] class. The constructor for that object requires an identifier for the assembly object for our assembly, an object of type `Assembly`.[11] To access individual strings, we call the `GetString` method on the resource manager, specifying the string identifier. In our example, the string identifiers are the four letters for the four strings: `A`, `B`, `C`, and `D`. Listing 3.7 summarizes each of the steps needed to load the strings and display them when the form receives a `Paint` event. (This example manually writes the strings onto a form; a simpler alternative would be to assign the strings to the `Text` properties of labels.)

LISTING 3.7: Loading and Using String Resources

```
//...
using System.Resources;    // Needed for ResourceManager
using System.Reflection;   // Needed for Assembly
//...
namespace StringResources
{
   //...

      // Resource manager for our set of strings.
      ResourceManager resman;

      // The four strings we load
      string strA;
      string strB;
      string strC;
      string strD;

      private void
      FormMain_Load(object sender, System.EventArgs e)
      {
         // Create the resource manager.
```

continues

10. Fully qualified name: `System.Resources.ResourceManager`.
11. Fully qualified name: `System.Reflection.Assembly`.

continued

```
         Assembly assembly = this.GetType().Assembly;
         resman = new ResourceManager(
            "StringResources.Strings", assembly);

         // Load the strings.
         strA = resman.GetString("A");
         strB = resman.GetString("B");
         strC = resman.GetString("C");
         strD = resman.GetString("D");
      }

      private void
      FormMain_Paint(object sender, PaintEventArgs e)
      {
         float sinX = 10;
         float sinY = 10;
         SizeF szf;

         Brush brText = new SolidBrush(SystemColors.WindowText);
         szf = e.Graphics.MeasureString(strA, Font);

         e.Graphics.DrawString(strA, Font, brText, sinX, sinY);
         sinY = sinY + szf.Height;
         e.Graphics.DrawString(strB, Font, brText, sinX, sinY);
         sinY = sinY + szf.Height;
         e.Graphics.DrawString(strC, Font, brText, sinX, sinY);
         sinY = sinY + szf.Height;
         e.Graphics.DrawString(strD, Font, brText, sinX, sinY);
         sinY = sinY + szf.Height;
      }

//...
```

Type Conversion

In a strongly typed environment, type conversions play an important role in adding flexibility to the strict rules of the type system. Strong type checking is meant to help programmers, but it can be a hindrance. For example, integers can be used in arithmetic operations but must be converted to strings for display to users. Within .NET, a rich set of conversion features helps reduce the friction that sometimes occurs in a strongly typed system.

In some cases, conversion support is built into the language syntax. C# supports casting, and Visual Basic .NET has the `CType` function and the

DirectCast keyword to support type conversion. There are subtle differences between the conversions provided by each language. In converting a floating-point number to an integer, for example, C# truncates the remainder, while Visual Basic .NET rounds the remainder.

An additional set of conversion services is provided by various framework classes. In some cases, framework features duplicate existing language services. The Convert[12] class, for example, provides conversion from any built-in type to any other built-in type. (Like the Visual Basic .NET converters, this class rounds remainders instead of truncating them.)

An additional set of services provided by the framework enhances what is natively available in each language. For example, every numeric type supports a Parse method, which converts a string to a numeric value. Every .NET type supports a ToString method, which converts any object into a string. For most numeric types, the ToString method accepts a formatting string to provide a level of fine-tuning for the conversion.

Numeric Conversion

The rules for converting between numeric types are common sense. When no risk exists for losing information, conversion is automatic. These implicit conversions are referred to as *widening conversions*. Among integer types, for example, automatic conversion occurs from 1-byte integers to 2-byte integers (or larger), from 2-byte integers to 4-byte integers, and from 4-byte integers to 8-byte integers (see Table 3.1 for the built-in numeric types). These are illustrated by the code in Listing 3.8. With the floating-point types, implicit conversions are supported from the 4-byte to the 8-byte floating-point type (from float to double).

LISTING 3.8: Implicit Integer Conversions

```
byte byt;
short sh;
int  i;
long l;
byt = 1;
```

continues

12. Fully qualified name: System.Convert.

continued

```
sh = byt; // byte to short
i = sh;   // short to int
l = i;    // int to long
```

Explicit Conversion

Explicit conversion for numeric types is required for conversions that risk losing information. At build time, compiler errors notify you of conversions that require special attention. Often this type of conversion is required to squeeze data that happens to be stored in a wider format into smaller data structure definitions, or for method calls that lack sufficient overload methods to handle a variety of data types. In this situation, a programmer makes a judgment call about whether the range of expected values can cause an overflow. Listing 3.9 shows a set of explicit conversions for integer types.

LISTING 3.9: Explicit Integer Conversions

```
long l;
int  i;
short sh;
byte byt;

l = 0;
i = (int)l;       // long to int
sh = (short)i;    // int to short
byt = (byte)sh;   // short to byte
```

The Overflow Exception

The compiler requires explicit conversion for possible data loss, and the explicit conversion tells the compiler that you know about the problem and are not worried. But what happens if a value is outside the range for a target type? The code in Listing 3.10 contains just such a problem.

LISTING 3.10: Conversion with Data Loss Potential

```
long l = long.MaxValue;
int  i = (int)l;
```

By default, the C# compiler ignores this, and your program continues running without knowing that you have lost information. That is not a good situation. You can enable checking from the project property pages by

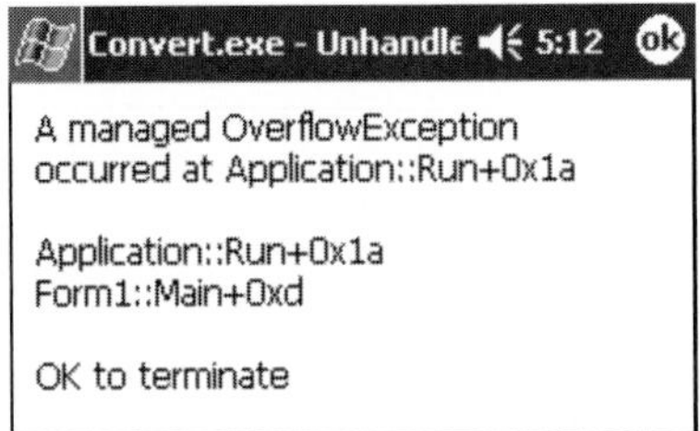
Convert.exe - Unhandle 5:12 ok
A managed OverflowException
occurred at Application::Run+0x1a
Application::Run+0x1a
Form1::Main+0xd
OK to terminate

FIGURE 3.6: Error message shown when unhandled overflow exceptions terminate a program

setting to `true` the code generation option titled Check for Arithmetic Overflow/Underflow.[13] When checking is enabled and the lines of code in Listing 3.10 execute, an overflow exception can occur. If an exception occurs and a program does not trap it, a serious problem is created. Unhandled exceptions cause a program to terminate, displaying to the user the lovely message shown in Figure 3.6. At a minimum, this is confusing and inconvenient to the user. In a worst-case scenario, it can cause loss of user data.

Handling Exceptions

Exceptions are a good thing—they notify your program that a problem was encountered. When exceptions occur, your program needs to handle them to avoid program termination and nasty messages.[14] This requires exception-handling syntax. Listing 3.11 shows one way to trap an overflow exception using the C# keywords `try` and `catch`.

LISTING 3.11: Handling an Overflow Exception

```
long l;
int  i;

try
{
   l = long.MaxValue;
   i = (int)l;
}
```

continues

13. The default in Visual Basic .NET is to always check for overflow/underflow.
14. It could be worse. Unhandled exceptions in low-level, kernel-mode components on desktop versions of Windows cause the dreaded "blue screen of death."

continued

```
catch(System.OverflowException ex)
{
   i = 0;
}
```

The syntax of exception handling is straightforward. Exception handling has many uses in .NET programming. If managed exceptions are new to you or if you have not worked with a similar exception-handling mechanism (like that of C++), it is well worth studying this syntax because it has many uses in .NET.

When an exception occurs, control is passed to the `catch` block. Within this block, we can find details of the exception through the properties of `ex`, an object of type `System.OverflowException`. We could, for example, read the `Message` property and write the details to a log file.[15]

The Cost of Exceptions

An exception is considered an abnormal condition that is rarely expected to occur. Exception handling provides a safety net for extraordinary circumstances. The cost of trapping and handling exceptions is higher than the cost of calling functions and returning from calls to functions. For that reason, when you design your program the goal should be to run with no exceptions occurring. Exception handling provides programmers with the ability to add greater reliability to their software but is not intended as the normal means for returning error conditions.

Converting Strings to Numbers

Each numeric class supports a static method named `Parse` for converting a string to a number. This conversion support is useful when reading a `TextBox` control for numeric values. The parsers are a bit fussy, though, and generate an exception when unexpected characters are found. When

15. Exception strings are available only if the `System.SR.dll` file is present.

parsing input from users, we always use an exception block and provide some kind of error reporting to the user. Listing 3.12 contains code that attempts to parse an integer from an input string.

No Support for String Parsing of Enumeration Values

In the desktop version of the .NET Framework, the `Enum.Parse` class converts a string to the equivalent numeric value in an enumeration. This method is not supported in the .NET Compact Framework.

LISTING 3.12: Converting a String to an Integer Using the `Int32.Parse` Method

```
bool bErrFormat = false;
string strInput = "123";
int iValue;
try
{
   iValue = int.Parse(strInput);
}
catch
{
   iValue = 0;
   bErrFormat = true;
}
```

String Conversion

Every object can be converted to a string because the base class for all types, `Object`, defines a `ToString` member method. So this method is available for all objects, but its usefulness depends on whether specific classes provide class-specific overrides.

The default `Object` implementation for the `ToString` method returns a string with an object's fully qualified type. For example, `System.Object` gets returned for instances of `Object` itself. And a string containing `System.Windows.Forms.Button` is returned for any button. In most cases, though, a programmer does not call this method looking for type information (there are other methods to call for type information).

The `ToString` method becomes useful only when a class overrides the default and provides a class-specific implementation. For example, the `StringBuilder` class defines a `ToString` method that returns the contents of its string buffer.

The most common use for the `ToString` method is to convert numeric types to strings. All value types—including `Point` and `Rectangle`—support the `ToString` method to simplify the creation of human-readable output. For many of the value classes, you can add formatting when you convert a number to a string.

Numeric Formatting

The `ToString` method for numeric classes supports an overload that takes a string parameter that defines how to format the number. Table 3.3 summarizes some of the different ways that an integer with a value of 10,000 can be formatted. Two of the formatting codes in this table can be used only for integers: `D` (for decimal) and `X` (for hexadecimal). All other codes

TABLE 3.3: **An Integer Formatted with Eight Formatting Codes**

Format Code	Description	Function Call	Output
`C`	Currency for current locale	`i.ToString("C")`	`$10,000.00`
`D`	Decimal (integer-only format)	`i.ToString("D")`	`10000`
`E`	Exponential	`i.ToString("E")`	`1.000000E+004`
`F`	Fixed-point	`i.ToString("F")`	`10000.00`
`G`	General	`i.ToString("G")`	`10000`
`N`	Number with locale-specific separators	`i.ToString("N")`	`10,000.00`
`P`	Percentage	`i.ToString("P")`	`1,000,000.00 %`
`X`	Hexadecimal (integer-only format)	`i.ToString("X")`	`2710`

are valid for any numeric type, floating-point or integer values. C programmers might recognize the similarity between this set of formatting codes and the set used with the `printf` function and other C-runtime functions. In fact, the numeric classes support a set of formatting codes that is much richer than what C programmers have used before; it comes closer to the level of formatting that a spreadsheet program like Microsoft Excel supports for numeric types.

Formatting codes hide any hint of the underlying type. For example, an integer type can be formatted with a decimal point and look identical to a similarly formatted floating-point number with the same value. So the number 10,000 when formatted as currency appears as `$10,000.00` (when the `locale` is `en-US`) whether the underlying type is `short`, `int`, `long`, `float`, `double`, or `decimal`.

Character Set Conversion

Unicode, the universal code page, is the main character set for the .NET Compact Framework. By this we mean that characters stored in `String` objects are stored as Unicode characters—the character set that Windows CE supports.

Although Unicode is meant to serve as a universal character set, it has not yet reached the point of universal acceptance and use. Until that time arrives, programmers will need to convert between Unicode and other character sets. To convert into Unicode, use the `Decoder`[16] class. To convert out of Unicode, use the `Encoder`[17] class. Chapter 11 shows how to convert while reading or writing to a stream.

Creating Formatted Strings

The `String` class has a static method named `Format`, which builds formatted strings. The code in Listing 3.13 calls this method twice. The results of both calls are the same, a string holding `Cost: $123.45 for 4 units`. The first call passes a decimal value and an integer; in the second call, the

16. Fully qualified name: `System.Text.Decoder`.

17. Fully qualified name: `System.Text.Encoder`.

decimal is formatted as a string using a locale-specific currency symbol. Notice how {0} and {1} serve as placeholders for the two values.

LISTING 3.13: Creating Formatted Strings Using the String.Format Method

```
decimal decCost = 123.45m;
int cUnits = 4;
string str;
string strCost;

str = String.Format("Cost: ${0} for {1} units. ",
   decCost, cUnits);
strCost = String.Format("Cost: {0} for {1} units. ",
   decCost.ToString("C"), cUnits);
```

The String.Format method supports five overloaded versions. Three of these methods are defined for one, two, and three input parameters. For more than three parameters, place them in an array and pass the array to a fourth version.

Each of the parameters is defined as the same type: a base object (Object). In our example, however, we use both value-type variables (an integer and a decimal) as well as reference-type variables (a string). How can this happen? This is handled through *boxing*, which the C# and Visual Basic .NET compilers automatically provide. We discuss this topic next.

Converting Values to Objects

When we pass a value-type variable to a method that expects an object, the compiler automatically converts the value-type variable into an object. In most cases, you are not aware that a conversion has taken place because it requires no extra effort on your part. This conversion is called *boxing*. While the code is simple, you ought to understand its implications on memory use.

The simplest case of boxing appears in Listing 3.14. When a value-type variable is assigned to an object-type variable, an object is allocated that is large enough to hold the value, and the contents of the value are copied to the newly created object. Once the boxing is complete, the original value (iValue in our example) and the object (obj) are completely independent of each other. In other words, obj does not reference iValue but instead references an object that has been allocated on the heap. (Another example of boxing appears in Listing 3.13, for the value types passed as parameters `String.Format`.)

LISTING 3.14: Boxing and Unboxing an Integer Value

```
int iValue = 1987;     // A value type.
object obj = iValue;   // Boxing
int iOut = (int)obj;   // Unboxing
```

Although we use a variable of type `Object`, that is not the type of a boxed value. The type is the same as the original boxed value. This can be verified by using the runtime type information functions: A call on an integer to the `GetType` method and then to the `ToString` method to the result—a call that looks like `iValue.GetType().ToString()`—produces the following string: `"System.Int32"`. This makes a lot of sense because it means that the recipient of a boxed value can find out what value type is in the box and then take appropriate steps to retrieve the value.

Boxing helps unify the type system so that value types can be treated as objects when convenient. To retrieve a boxed value, as shown in Listing 3.14, we copy the object variable to a variable of the original type. This is known as *unboxing*. When we unbox, we coerce the type of the outgoing object, which means we cast to explicitly specify the outgoing type. We cannot coerce an object to a type that does not match the value used to create the object. An attempt to unbox with a different type than the one used in boxing causes an exception of type `InvalidCastException` to be raised. Boxing puts a value into an object, and unboxing takes a value out of an object and copies it to a value-type variable.

The ability to convert value types to reference types helps unify the type system. While a value type is small and fast, there are things that a value type cannot do. By allowing a value type to become an object, the type system allows values to enjoy the full privileges of objects. But why have value types at all—why not use boxed value types instead? The answer is overhead. For example, a boxed integer consumes 16 bytes[18] to store 4 bytes of data.

18. This figure is the sum of 4 bytes for the object variable, 8 bytes for the object header, and then 4 bytes of actual data.

So what are the benefits of boxing? There are several.

- Values added to collections (array lists, queues, and so on) are automatically boxed.
- Values passed to `String.Format` are automatically boxed.
- Values can call virtual functions (such as the `ToString` method) by virtue of being boxed.
- A value type can implement an interface. A value must first be boxed to call interface functions.
- Multithreaded programs can synchronize on a boxed value (using the `lock` statement).

As we have shown, the strongly typed world of .NET Compact Framework programming provides a rich assortment of type conversion support. Just like the desktop .NET Framework, the .NET Compact Framework provides a rich set of features for converting from one numeric type to another, from a numeric type to a string, or from a string to a numeric value. Support for boxing and unboxing helps unify a type system that is otherwise divided into value types and reference types.

This discussion has prepared you to understand the fundamental elements of the .NET type system. Connecting this type information with the runtime behavior of instantiated objects requires us to take a step into the operation of the common language runtime, as implemented in the .NET Compact Framework. The road to making proper use of these types, in other words, requires us to delve into the subject of memory management.

Memory Management

A thorough understanding of memory management is necessary to appreciate the improvements that are provided by managed-code development. When most people hear the term *managed code*, they think about the automatic cleanup of allocated data. While that is an important part of the picture, memory is used for other things besides holding allocated data. Two other major uses of memory are to hold code and to hold metadata. The memory used by managed-code programs can be divided into three parts:

1. Metadata maps allocated by the class loader for each class
2. The JITted code pool allocated by the JIT compiler for each JITted method
3. Garbage collector pools (commonly referred to as "the heap") that provide instance data for each object allocated

The Scope of Managed Memory

When we teach .NET programming, we encounter a lot of confusion about the location of the heap where instance data gets allocated and the relationship between allocated memory and a program.

All of the memory allocated for a program resides in the context of an application domain.[19] When a program terminates, all of the allocated memory is automatically freed. This includes the memory for metadata maps, JITted code, and instance data.

Metadata Maps

Every .NET program and library file contains *metadata*, a dictionary of the types defined in a module.[20] At build time, a compiler creates metadata, which the execution engine uses at runtime. Metadata provides a rich snapshot of all the type information in the managed-code module. Every .NET type is defined in an executable module file as metadata.

---

19. As we discussed in Chapter 1, an operating system process can hold multiple application domains. By default, there is one application domain per operating system process.

20. By "module" we mean an application (`.exe`) file or a dynamic link library (`.dll`) file. Some programming environments use the term to refer to a source file.

Various utilities allow you to view metadata, including `ildasm.exe` and the Object Browser in Visual Studio .NET. Metadata can also be accessed programmatically using a feature of the .NET Compact Framework known as reflection.

At runtime, objects are instantiated by using type information, and code is verified for compatibility with the supported types. When a class is encountered in managed code, the loader creates an in-memory description of the class. Among its other elements are a method table for all of the methods defined in the class, including instance and static methods.[21] Once created, a metadata map for a class stays in memory until a program terminates.

The JITted code pool contains memory allocated by the JIT compiler, a subject we discuss next.

The JITted Code Pool

The biggest memory savings that managed code provides over native code is one that few programmers think about, yet its impact on overall memory use is profound. We are referring to the way that code gets loaded into memory. As we discussed in Chapter 1, an executable file containing managed code is compiled into the portable IL instruction set. When loaded into memory, IL instructions are converted into native machine instructions (JITted by the JIT compiler).

This represents a big improvement over the way code has traditionally been loaded for native modules under Microsoft Windows. Win32 programs and DLLs are staged as memory-mapped files. Portions of Win32 modules are brought into memory by memory faults when code, data, and resources are accessed. When a particular method gets called in native code, the page that contains the method gets loaded into memory. Except for the rarest of cases,[22] this approach brings more of the executable into

---

21. Box and Sells cover this topic in great detail in Chapter 6 of *Essential .NET, Volume 1* (Boston, MA: Addison-Wesley, 2003).

22. To be 100% memory efficient, a native-code method needs to meet two conditions: (1) The size must be exactly one page (1K or 4K, depending on the CPU), and (2) the method must start on a page boundary. If either of these conditions is not met, memory is wasted.

the file than is needed, strictly speaking. With a granularity of 4K pages on a typical system, it is almost certain that more memory is consumed in a Win32 module than by a comparable managed-code module. Managed heaps have a granularity of 4 bytes instead of the 4K used when loading elements from a native module.

As the execution engine converts IL to native machine instructions, each JITted method gets added to a RAM-resident collection known as the JITted code pool. When other methods do not provide sufficient free memory, the garbage collector flushes the JITted code pool. Because of the profoundly negative implications for system performance, this is used only as a last resort for memory reclamation.

The key design choice that saves system memory is this: Ensure that methods are JITted on an as-needed basis. Route all method calls through a method table that belongs to the class that contains the methods, including static methods, constructors, destructors, and properties as well as instance methods. When the method table is first created, every entry points to a *thunk*,[23] a tiny code stub that calls the loader for that method. Thunks have been supported by every version of Windows. The first time a method is called, the thunk routes the call to the JIT engine, which responds by loading the method from the executable file and creating the native code. The JIT engine then redirects the entry in the method's table to the newly generated code.

The *working set* of managed code loaded by the JIT engine is the set of methods that have actually been used. Once JITted, a method stays in memory in case it is needed again. Under severe memory pressure, however, the memory manager can purge the system of such methods to free memory for other uses. These purges can have a big (negative) impact on program performance, however, which is why the JITted code pool is the last place the memory manager looks when system memory is low.

The *granularity* of loading managed-code methods are single methods. When a method is first called, the IL code from the module (`.exe` or `.dll`)

---

23. While the term seems to have fallen out of favor with the advent of .NET, the implementers of the shared source CLI seem to like *thunk*—it appears more than 1,300 times in Rotor source code.

file is converted into native code, so that only the actual methods used by a program are JITted and loaded into memory.

By contrast, when native-code methods are loaded into memory, the granularity is set by the CPU as a virtual memory page (4K on a typical Pocket PC). It is likely that some memory waste occurs when loading native code into memory. The greatest benefits are probably in shared libraries that contain a large number of methods, of which a small number are called from any given program. The benefits are probably least evident with small programs, when all native code might be loaded with a few load operations.

JIT Caching and the Native Image Cache

The .NET Compact Framework's caching of JITted code is significantly simpler than that done on the desktop. With its greater storage capacity, the desktop maintains the native image cache as part of the global assembly cache. Programmers can add assemblies to the disk-bound portion of the native image cache on the desktop using a tool called `ngen.exe`. No such tool exists for the .NET Compact Framework because there is no native image cache stored in the file system.

Garbage Collector Pools

Garbage collection is the reclamation of memory[24] that has been allocated and used but is no longer needed. In the .NET Compact Framework, the portion of memory from which object instance data is allocated is referred to as the garbage collector pools. Many programming environments require a programmer to explicitly release resources. The various .NET frameworks provide automatic garbage collection for many different kinds of Windows applications (a subject we discussed in Chapter 1). The various .NET runtimes are not the first environment with automatic garbage col-

---

24. Other resources besides memory may need to be managed as well, including file handles and other operating system objects. For the purposes of this discussion, though, *memory* is a satisfactory term.

lection. Automatic garbage collection has been available for many years in Smalltalk, Visual Basic, and Java.

Win32 programmers have always needed to pay attention to manually cleaning up system objects they allocated. Two factors make the Win32 API prone to memory leaks: (1) the lack of automatic memory management and (2) the large number of functions that allocate memory. Memory leaks are not inevitable, but they require significant diligence on the part of programmers to prevent. Several third-party tools were created to help locate memory leaks. The Catching Windows CE Memory Leaks sidebar discusses a tool created for Windows CE developers.

Catching Windows CE Memory Leaks

Entrek of Seattle, Washington, provides a tool called CodeSnitch that detects memory leaks in code running on Windows CE systems. The tool can highlight the specific line of source code that allocated a leftover object. For details, visit http://www.entrek.com.

For programmers building COM/ActiveX components, the issue of memory cleanup has always centered on reference counts. The rule is simple: A component maintains a reference count; when a reference count reaches zero, a component destroys itself. In practice, an enormous amount of energy has been expended—both by component developers and by component users—getting components to shut down properly.

For .NET programmers, automatic garbage collection means better use of two scarce resources: programmer time and smart-device memory. Programmer time is saved because automatic garbage collection means rarely having to worry about object cleanup. System memory is saved because—compared with native Win32 executables—managed code is lazily allocated on as-needed basis, and managed data is systematically tracked so that unused memory can be effectively reclaimed.

Some of the data allocated by managed code is *not* subject to automatic garbage collection. Managed code, after all, can allocate both managed data and unmanaged data. It is this second category—unmanaged data, sometimes called native data—that a managed-code programmer must manually release because there is no automatic garbage collection of native data.

Garbage Collection and Data

In looking at the reclamation of memory occupied by data, we wish to address the broadest set of allocation issues for both managed code and native code. The reason is that .NET Compact Framework programmers are likely to need native operating system objects more often than desktop .NET programmers do. As we discussed in Chapter 1, the .NET Compact Framework has fewer features than the desktop .NET Framework. Managed code can allocate both managed data and unmanaged data. Native code, by contrast, is able to allocate only unmanaged data, not managed data. Table 3.4 summarizes the possible interactions between the two types of code and data.

Managed code can allocate managed data. Managed data lives on a restricted heap controlled by the execution engine. When managed objects are allocated from this heap, pointers provide the reference stored in a program's variables. But these pointers are implicit pointers and cannot be accessed like pointers in C (and other languages) for pointer arithmetic. Managed data can be moved by the memory manager without your code

TABLE 3.4: Possible Interactions between Code and Data

	Managed Data	Unmanaged Data
Managed Code	Allocate managed data with `new`; clean up by automatic garbage collection (in a few cases, a call to a `Close` method or a `Dispose` method is needed)	Allocate using P/Invoke to call native allocation functions; clean up by calling native clean up functions
Native Code	No support—cannot allocate managed data	Allocate by calling native functions; clean up by calling native cleanup functions

noticing that it has been moved. Finally, when no longer in use, managed data is subject to reclamation by automatic garbage collection.

Unmanaged data can be allocated either from managed code or from native code. The term *unmanaged* in this context means that the execution engine does not manage the memory. After a programmer writes code that allocates unmanaged data, that programmer must be sure to also write code to release the resources associated with the unmanaged data. When referring to what such code does, we use the term *manual memory management*, to parallel the automatic garbage collection provided by the runtime for managed data.

In this discussion of garbage collection, we start with a look at managed data: its allocation, management, and reclamation by the execution engine. We then turn our attention to unmanaged data and the native Win32 functions that allocate and free system objects.

Automatic Garbage Collection

One of the more convenient features of managed code is automatic garbage collection of managed data. Garbage collection is a relatively time-consuming process that the system postpones as long as possible. Normal allocation, by contrast, is very fast because the allocator does not use any kind of "best-fit" algorithm. Instead, new objects are always allocated next to the previously allocated object. If you have ever visited a large event where parking attendants direct incoming cars to the next free space, you have a good idea of how managed data is allocated. As each object is allocated, an entry is made into an *allocated object map*. This map plays a role in the first step of object cleanup, the mark and sweep phase.

Garbage collection is triggered when an allocation request causes the amount of allocated memory to exceed a certain threshold. The garbage collector starts by waiting for all managed-code threads to freeze at safe points. Threads running in native code—sometimes called *unmanaged threads*—are not frozen when the garbage collector is run, although any threads returning to managed code while the garbage collector is running are frozen.

Memory reclamation is performed in a stepwise fashion, from least to most painful as far as impact on system performance. When a step causes memory use to drop below the critical threshold, garbage collection ceases. There are three phases of garbage collection:

1. Mark and sweep
2. Compact the heap
3. Flush the JITted code pool

Garbage Collection in the .NET Framework and the .NET Compact Framework

The garbage collectors in the desktop version of the .NET Framework and in the .NET Compact Framework share a number of features. Most of the behavior described here applies equally to both.

One difference is that the desktop garbage collector makes its decisions about how it operates based on how long an object has been alive. Objects are grouped by generations, and the desktop supports three generations. In the .NET Framework, the value of the static `MaxGeneration` property in the `GC` class has a value of `2` (which means that three generations are supported: `0`, `1`, and `2`). By contrast, the .NET Compact Framework does not use this method of object aging, as indicated by the value `0` for the `MaxGeneration` property in the `GC` class.

The following subsections briefly discuss each of these phases in turn.

Phase 1: Mark and Sweep

During this first phase of garbage collection, the garbage collector searches for objects that are unreachable. The garbage collector knows how to find all memory allocated in managed code by walking the stack of all threads, looking for references to managed objects. Some objects refer to other objects, and this continues until every stack frame for every thread in a process (or, more accurately, within an application domain) has been taken into account. Objects referenced from static variables are reachable, as are objects referenced from local variables. In addition, object references nested in other objects, in arrays, and in collections are considered reachable.

Each object that can be reached, through either a direct or an indirect reference on the stack, is reachable data. Using the set of objects in the allocated object map as a starting point, the garbage collector identifies the reachable objects and removes them from this set. Any leftover objects are unreachable. They represent memory that is occupied but not used; the memory occupied by such objects is reclaimed by the garbage collector. If enough memory is reclaimed from unreachable objects, garbage collection stops. Otherwise, it continues to the next phase.

Phase 2: Compact the Heap

The second phase of garbage collection is to compact the heap. In this phase, reachable objects are moved to consolidate the space that is made available by freeing objects. This step is important because the managed-code allocator allocates only from the very end of the heap. By compacting the heap, the garbage collector can reclaim memory from unreachable objects that were not located at the end of the heap.

Phase 3: Flush the JITted Code Pool

When all else fails, the final step taken by the garbage collector is to free memory from the JITted code pool. The manner in which memory is chosen depends on the processor because each CPU has its own JIT engine. In the JIT compiler for the StrongARM processor, the CPU for Pocket PCs, a "least recently used" algorithm helps select which methods to discard.

Special Handling of Managed Data

A few special cases deserve discussion. Each causes a change to the garbage collector or to how the garbage collector deals with specific objects.

Calling the Garbage Collector

Portions of the garbage collector are exposed through the `GC`[25] class. By calling the `Collect` static method, for example, a program can request the

---

25. Fully qualified name: `System.GC`.

garbage collector to run through its first phase of operation to reclaim memory associated with unreachable objects. While it is not a good programming practice for programs to call the garbage collector, such calls can be used for testing and development purposes. For example, by forcing garbage collection, a program could get a truer sense of the memory required when another `GC` class method, `GetTotalMemory`, is called.

Calling the garbage collector is considered a poor practice because the garbage collector is part of the runtime's automatic memory management, and it has been tuned to operate when needed. In general, you want the garbage collector to run as infrequently as possible because all managed-code threads must be frozen prior to running the garbage collector, and this uses up precious CPU cycles (which on a mobile device can drain precious battery power). Making frequent manual calls to the garbage collector can cause performance problems for programs.

The `WM_HIBERNATE` Message

Windows CE has its own garbage collection–like mechanism that is part of the native, unmanaged code support libraries: the `WM_HIBERNATE` message. This message gets sent to all the top-level windows in the system when available system memory falls below a specific threshold (about 200K).

In spite of the name, this message has nothing to do with sleep (of either the operating system or applications), nor does it relate to power management. Instead, it has a single meaning: System memory is low. The requested response is to free whatever memory a program can afford to release. If available memory subsequently falls below 160K, the Pocket PC shell starts to send `WM_CLOSE` messages to top-level windows, asking them to close.

The first version of the .NET Compact Framework ignores the `WM_HIBERNATE` message[26] (a future version is expected to support it).

26. Our tests were performed with Compact Framework 1.0, Service Pack 2.

To detect this message, a .NET Compact Framework program needs to have a way to listen to the message traffic of a visible, top-level window. The `EventGrabber` sample in Chapter 9 can help with that because it lets you subclass any window and listen to the message traffic.

What do you do when you detect this message? To free managed memory, you can call the `GC.Collect` method. This reasonable choice may even reduce some of the memory pressure on the operating system. But unless the .NET Compact Framework shrinks the heap size (rather than freeing unused objects with reducing the size of the heap), calls to the garbage collector probably do not reduce the pressure on available system memory.

The best thing a .NET Compact Framework program can do is to free any native data that has been allocated. This will have a more direct impact on making more system resources available to Windows CE.

Figure 3.7 shows the output from one of this book's sample programs, `GCInfo`. This program calls various `GC` class members and also allocates and frees arrays of objects to demonstrate the effect of allocation on the memory used by a program. (This figure shows the maximum generations

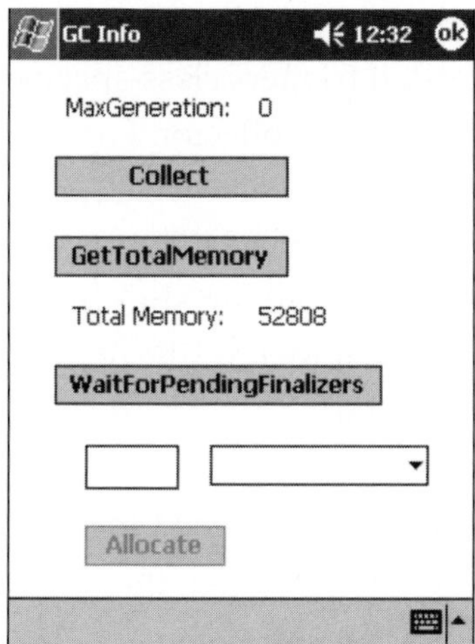

FIGURE 3.7: The `GCInfo` sample calls methods in the `GC` class.

supported by the garbage collector—the public property `MaxGeneration`—as zero, meaning that all objects are treated as the same age.)

Manual Cleanup Using the `Dispose` Method

As a general rule, automatic garbage collection works well, and programmers do not need to worry about the timing or manner by which objects are cleaned up. In a few cases, however, objects are wrappers for a resource that does require immediate cleanup. This might be a file that needs to be closed, a network connection that needs to be logged out, or an unmanaged library that needs to free some scarce resource. When that is the case, a single cleanup method is provided: `Dispose`.

In some cases, forgetting to call the `Dispose` method for an object can cause a program to crash because all instances of a critical resource are busy. This happens when you create a set of `Graphics` objects by calling the `CreateGraphics` method multiple times without calling the `Dispose` method. The documentation makes it clear that you must call the `Dispose` method when you are done drawing. The `Dispose` method frees the native device context wrapped within the `Graphics` class.

Some classes implement a `Close` method in addition to a `Dispose` method. Such is the case with a variety of data reading and writing classes with files, XML, and some database classes. For these classes, no call to the `Dispose` method is needed after a call to a `Close` method.

Incidentally, a `Dispose` method does not call the garbage collector, nor does this method free an object's memory. Instead, it triggers class-specific cleanup outside the normal work done by the garbage collector. For that reason, be sure to release references to objects after you call the `Dispose` function by setting the value of the reference to `null`. With a leftover reference, your code might accidentally try to use objects that are shut down but still reside in memory. Also, the leftover reference prevents the object's memory from being reclaimed by the garbage collector.

Implementing Class-Specific Cleanup Methods: `Dispose` and `Finalize`

When implementing a class that owns a nonmemory resource that must be cleaned up, you implement two methods: `Dispose` and `Finalize`. The first method, Dispose, provides the public method to be called from users of the class, as already discussed. For most cases, that is the only function called.

There is, however, a potential problem. The presence of Dispose suggests that cleanup is required. But what happens if that method does not get called? What happens to the resource? The architects of the .NET garbage collector asked themselves that question as well. One approach might have been for the system to detect that the Dispose method had not been called and to initiate the call itself. With that approach, however, the system has to second-guess both the class implementer and the class user.

Instead, we have the Finalize method, which provides a last-chance handler for cleanup right before the garbage collector frees memory. At first glance, the addition of a second method seems like overkill. After all, how much cleanup does an object need?

While one cleanup method might suffice in simpler cases, things change when several objects—each supporting a Dispose method—are aggregated. This more complex case best illustrates how a Dispose method differs from a Finalize method. When a Dispose method is called, an object responds by calling the Dispose methods of all nested objects to make sure that each has been called (in addition to cleanup that may be required with native objects). The Finalize method, on the other hand, never attempts to dispose managed objects (although it can clean up native objects).

Finalize methods are called only by the garbage collector and only when the garbage collector is iterating through a list of objects that are ready to be finalized. Within a Finalize method, any reference to objects that have been finalized results in an exception—a fatal error. So a Finalize method must leave alone any referenced objects, on the assumption that the garbage collector has—or will—take care of cleaning up other managed objects that need to be finalized.

A Finalize method is a last-chance cleanup method when a call to a Dispose method is required but has not been made. When a Dispose method is called, it can tell the garbage collector that the Finalize method does not need to be called. This is done with a static method in the GC class,

`SuppressFinalize`. And finally, the `ReRegisterForFinalize` method allows a class to add back to the finalize list an object that had previously been removed by a call to the `SuppressFinalize` method.

Use the `Finalize` Method or the Destructor?

The name of the finalizing method for all CLI-compatible languages is `Finalize`. This standard name is critical to support interoperability between languages.

However, the C# compiler defines a different syntax for the finalizing method. The syntax matches the syntax in C++ for class destructors, which is defined with a tilde (~) followed by the class name. While this appears to have a different name from the finalizing method in other languages, the actual method name in the IL code is `Finalize`.

The C# compiler adds two other elements: a `try-finally` block and a call to the `Finalize` method in the base class. Because these are the recommended elements for a finalizing method, the C# destructor syntax provides the cleanest and easiest way to implement a finalizing method in C#.

This syntax does pose a potential problem. A C++ programmer who is used to C++ destructor syntax in native code might think that the C# destructor syntax behaves in a similar fashion. It clearly does not, so C# programmers must be careful to avoid the *faux amis*[27] in the C# destructor syntax.

The presence of two cleanup methods adds a complication: A class might have redundant code. The suggested design pattern for manual object cleanup centralizes the cleanup work in a third method called by the other two methods. This third method, which by convention is called `Dispose`, differs from the first `Dispose` method in the number of parameters.

27. French for "false friends."

The original `Dispose` method has no parameters. The common `Dispose` method takes one parameter: a `bool` flag that indicates which of the first two methods is calling. A value of `true` indicates that a `Dispose` method is calling to dispose of an individual object; a value of `false` indicates that a `Finalize` method is calling, which means that the process is terminating[28] and the garbage collector is calling the `Finalize` method for all objects.

This difference is sometimes important. When our common `Dispose` method is called with a value of `true`, it means that a polite caller is advising us that we can clean up. At that point, we want to be sure to clean up any objects that can free up system resources, so that our program can continue to run efficiently and well. In particular, we need to call `Dispose` on any objects that are contained in our object (assuming those objects require a call to `Dispose`).

When the common `Dispose` method is called with a value of `false`, it means that the process is shutting down and the garbage collector is running down the list of objects that it knows about which need to have their `Finalize` methods called. The objects that are left around are the ones that are lost or forgotten, and as such the garbage collector tries to be as efficient as possible to allow the process to terminate quickly. What must be avoided is making a call to `Dispose` for any contained objects when the garbage collector is calling the `Finalize` methods. There are two reasons: first, because the garbage collector is already going to call all such objects; second, if we reference an object that has already been cleaned up, we risk causing an exception in our program.

Figure 3.8 shows `Disposer`, a sample program we wrote to demonstrate the operation of the `Dispose` and `Finalize` methods. The five buttons are labeled with five actions that affect the memory use and cleanup of an object.

- Create Object calls the object constructor.
- Dispose calls the object's `Dispose` method.

---

28. Or for a process with multiple application domains, that a given application domain is shutting down.

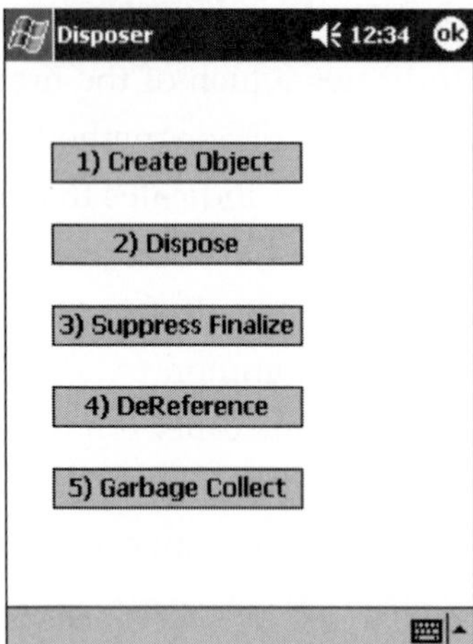

FIGURE 3.8: Disposer demonstrates the operation of the Dispose and Finalize methods.

- Suppress Finalize calls the `GC.SuppressFinalize` method on the object.
- DeReference sets the object reference to `null`.
- Garbage Collect calls the `GC.Collect` method.

Listing 3.15 shows the event handlers for the five buttons in the `Disposer` sample program. The `ResourceWrapper` class has four methods: a constructor, two `Dispose` methods, and a `Finalize` method. Each method displays a message box when called, to show the result of the action behind each of the buttons. Aside from the message boxes, this class should serve as a starting point for any resource wrapping class that you might wish to write.

LISTING 3.15: Event Handlers That Allocate and Free the `ResourceWrapper` Class

```
ResourceWrapper rw = null;

private void cmdCreate_Click(object sender, EventArgs e)
{
   rw = new ResourceWrapper();
}
```

```
private void cmdDispose_Click(object sender, EventArgs e)
{
   if(rw == null)
      MessageBox.Show("rw == null -> Exception! ");
   else
      rw.Dispose();
}

private void cmdSuppress_Click(object sender, EventArgs e)
{
   if(rw == null)
      MessageBox.Show("rw == null -> Exception! ");
   else
      GC.SuppressFinalize(rw);
}

private void cmdDereference_Click(object sender, EventArgs e)
{
   rw = null;
}

private void cmdCollect_Click(object sender, EventArgs e)
{
   GC.Collect();
}
```

You may need to change the code in Listing 3.15 to call the `Dispose` method for base classes that support a `Dispose` method. We commented out that call for our `ResourceWrapper` class because its base class, `Object`, does not have a `Dispose` method.

The `ResourceWrapper` class code shows, in addition to a constructor, the three standard cleanup methods. The declarations for these methods—two `Dispose` methods and one `Finalize` method—appear here.

```
public void Dispose()
protected void Dispose(bool bDisposing)
~<class_name>
```

Listing 3.16 shows the code for the `ResourceWrapper` class.

LISTING 3.16: The `ResourceWrapper` Class

```
// Simple resource wrapper class to demonstrate managed-code
// support for manual cleanup functions
```

continues

continued

```
//
public class ResourceWrapper : System.Object, IDisposable
{
   public ResourceWrapper()
   {
      MessageBox.Show("Constructor called");
   }
   ~ResourceWrapper()
   {
      MessageBox.Show("Finalize called");
      Dispose(false);
   }
   public void Dispose()
   {
      MessageBox.Show("Public Dispose called");
      Dispose(true);

      // Call Dispose when supported by base class.
      // base.Dispose();
   }

   protected void Dispose(bool bDisposing)
   {
      if (bDisposing)
         MessageBox.Show("Dispose(true) -- are disposing");
      else
         MessageBox.Show("Dispose(false) -- are finalizing");
   }
} // class ResourceWrapper
```

Weak References

Another special case involving the garbage collector are objects marked with weak references. Memory is a scarce resource and must be managed with care, yet some algorithms run faster when more memory is available. Weak references let you err on the side of using more memory to get better performance but still allow the garbage collector to reclaim that memory if such use causes a shortage of memory for other, more critical needs. For the sake of good performance, it is perhaps better to allow lower-priority data to be discarded than to force the garbage collector to discard code from the JITted code pool.

A weak reference provides a hint to the garbage collector that an object is easily replaceable. The garbage collector interprets as unreachable any object that is accessible only through a weak reference. The same is true for objects nested within an object that has a weak reference. Objects that are reachable *only* through weak references are subject to garbage collection. However, an object that has both a weak reference and a normal reference would not be subject to garbage collection.

Weak references are supported by the `WeakReference`[29] class. When you create a `WeakReference` object, you pass an object reference to a constructor. The object reference is available from the `WeakReference` object through the `Target` property. The Boolean `IsAlive` property returns `true` when the target still resides in memory. To access the contents of the object, copy the target to a regular variable, which then provides a strong reference to keep the object from being garbage-collected while you are using the object. You can find an example of using a weak reference in the `MainPlusOthers` sample presented in Chapter 5.

Manual Memory Management of Native Data

The garbage collector provides automatic reclamation for managed memory. Many managed classes are wrappers around native operating system objects and handle object cleanup. In some cases, the cleanup is automatic, while in other cases it is manual (or, at best, semiautomatic).

But when managed code calls native operating system functions to create native operating system objects, no automatic cleanup is provided for these objects. (That is why such objects are called *unmanaged* objects.) When your program does this, your program must provide manual cleanup—that is, manual garbage collection.

Programmers working in native code must keep track of all memory allocated. In some cases, allocation occurs with specific memory allocation functions (like `malloc`, `LocalAlloc`, `GlobalAlloc`, `HeapAlloc`, `VirtualAlloc`, or `MapViewofFile`). In other cases, memory allocation is a side effect of making certain operating system calls. The creation of a window, for example, causes memory to be allocated, as does the creation of various graphic drawing objects like pens, brushes, fonts, and bitmaps. Failure to

29. Fully qualified name: `System.WeakReference`.

properly track and clean up memory in native code causes memory leaks. It is possible for a memory leak to cause a program—or the operating system itself—to crash. Appendix D contains a table that summarizes the Windows CE system objects that are available through the Win32 API and the associated allocation and cleanup functions.

In most cases, .NET Compact Framework programmers do not need to allocate and free native operating system objects. Instead, it is better to rely on the .NET Compact Framework classes to deal with the details of managing such objects. This is particularly true for graphic objects, but it is also true for other types of objects. When available, we suggest you do as we do and use the managed-code equivalent for any native operating system object.

CONCLUSION

The .NET programming model provides a strongly typed, object-oriented environment in which a rich set of types are intelligently organized in a set of namespaces. In addition to being strongly typed, the .NET type system provides a unified model of lightweight value types and more capable medium-weight objects. A string in .NET is a reference type that acts like a value type, in part because a basic string (i.e., a `System.String` string) is immutable. A second string class, `StringBuilder`, supports complex string handling when a program must work with many strings, many operations, or large strings.

The importance of strings can be seen in the rich support for converting any object into a string with the `ToString` method. Numeric classes support a `Parse` method for converting strings back to numeric values. Value types can be converted to reference types through boxing and then converted back to value types by unboxing.

The .NET Compact Framework divides its memory into three areas. One memory area holds class metadata; once loaded, class metadata stays in memory. A second memory area is the JITted code pool, which holds methods that have been converted from IL to the native instruction set of the current CPU. The third memory area is made up of the garbage collector pools, which hold instance data for instantiated references-type objects.

The garbage collector reclaims memory from unreachable managed objects in a manner that is largely unseen. As we have shown, a program can call methods in the `GC` class to find the amount of memory being used and also to force the garbage collector to perform its mark and sweep operation. However, manually triggering the garbage collector is usually counterproductive in production applications.

Classes that wrap native resources can implement two different kinds of cleanup methods: a `Dispose` method and a `Finalize` method. To help managed-code programmers understand when native operating system resources need to be cleaned up, Appendix D provides a table of native objects and details on the functions for allocating and freeing those objects.

We prefer writing managed code over writing unmanaged code. However, there are times when it makes sense to write unmanaged code. In some cases, you would do this to access an operating system feature that is otherwise not supported in the .NET Compact Framework. More often, though, you would do this to access an existing DLL you have built, tested, and deployed. In the next chapter, we discuss in detail the support provided for calling native code from managed code: Platform Invoke.

4
Platform Invoke

In this chapter, we discuss Platform Invoke, a .NET feature for calling unmanaged libraries from managed code.

THIS CHAPTER COVERS Platform Invoke—also known as *P/Invoke*—a .NET feature for calling functions in unmanaged DLLs. Most of the time the .NET Compact Framework provides all the support you need to build programs. Sometimes, however, you will want to do something that the .NET Compact Framework does not support but that a function in a Win32 DLL can do.

To call a function in an unmanaged DLL from managed code, you create a *P/Invoke wrapper.* A P/Invoke wrapper is a .NET-compatible method declaration used to call a function in an unmanaged DLL. The syntax for creating P/Invoke wrappers is essentially identical to the syntax for creating managed method declarations, although one difference is that a P/Invoke wrapper does not include a function body—just the method name, return type, and parameter information. Also, a P/Invoke wrapper uses a `DllImport` attribute, which contains the details needed to locate the unmanaged DLL that contains the target function.

There are limitations on the parameters you can pass using P/Invoke, and we explore these limits in this chapter. In brief, acceptable parameters include value types, strings, structures created exclusively with value types, and arrays of value types. Unsupported parameters include arrays of strings, structures that contain any reference type (including strings, structures, arrays, unions, or any other kind of objects that is a reference type). Some workarounds for unsupported parameters are addressed in this chapter.

Programmers who have worked with the desktop .NET Framework might wonder how the .NET Compact Framework's support for P/Invoke compares with the support found on the desktop. A section later in this chapter, Comparing P/Invoke Support, provides insights into the differences.

Overview of P/Invoke

P/Invoke connects two different types of code: *managed code* and *unmanaged code*.[1] In other words, it provides a way for a .NET Compact Framework program to call native operating system functions. Before we dig into P/Invoke, we need to discuss some of the differences between managed code and unmanaged code. Table 4.1 summarizes the important differences.

Managed code is *portable code* because .NET executables can run on any platform that has the appropriate common language runtime, regardless of the CPU that is present. Managed code is also *safe code* because a broad set of features helps avoid problems that plague unmanaged code: implicit pointers and automatic memory management eliminate memory leaks, and array boundary protection prevents memory overwrites. We sometimes use the term *.NET code* because managed code relies directly on the programming interfaces provided within the .NET Compact Framework.

Unmanaged code is often referred to by various names. Each of these terms reflect a .NET-centric way of looking at unmanaged code and highlights some of the benefits of the common language runtime. To put unmanaged code into perspective, in Table 4.1 we present the related or implied managed-code concept next to each of the terms used for unmanaged code.

---

1. Experienced Windows programmers will see that P/Invoke is like two older Windows technologies: (1) the thunks that date back to Windows 1.x, and (2) the proxy/stub elements used in COM to marshal data between operating system processes and across a network in DCOM. Each represents a stateless layer to support a transition—a bridge—between two otherwise disconnected bodies of code. P/Invoke adopts the COM term *marshaling* to refer to the process of passing data into and receiving return parameters back from unmanaged libraries.

TABLE 4.1: **Comparison between Managed and Unmanaged Code**

Feature	Managed Code	Unmanaged Code
Aliases	Portable code Safe code .NET code C# code, Visual Basic .NET code	Native code Unsafe code Win32 code C code, C++ code
Supported languages	C#, Visual Basic .NET (in the .NET Compact Framework)	C, C++
`.exe/.dll` file format	Common Intermediate Language (CIL), a CPU-independent machine-level language converted to native machine instructions at runtime	Native machine language of the target processor, e.g., SH3, SH4, MIPS, StrongARM, XScale, x86
Memory management	Provided by the common language runtime as needed	Automatic cleanup of Win32 objects when a process terminates; otherwise, application (or driver) code responsible for cleaning up memory and Win32 objects
Safety checking	Yes	No
Array boundary protection	Yes	No
Support for pointers	Built-in implicit pointer support, but `unsafe` keyword required for explicit pointers; `Marshal`[a] class support for creation of pointers for passing to unmanaged code	Explicit pointers widely used

a. Fully qualified name: `System.Runtime.InteropServices.Marshal`.

Unmanaged code is sometimes called *native code* because the executable file format is not the portable IL that targets the services provided by the common language runtime but is instead the native machine instructions of, say, an SH3 or StrongARM processor. It is sometimes called *unsafe code* because it lacks the protection from memory leaks, bad pointers, and array overruns that is provided by the common language runtime. We sometimes call it *Win32 code* because such DLLs are often (but not always) built to directly use the Win32 API. The Win32 API provides the foundation for every version of Windows.

When to Use P/Invoke

Use P/Invoke to access features that are unavailable in managed code but are available in unmanaged code. In some cases, you can find desired features in your own unmanaged DLLs. In other cases, you can get the job done by calling the unmanaged Windows CE system libraries. In general, when there is a managed-code way to do something and an unmanaged-code way, we prefer to use the managed-code approach. We regard P/Invoke almost as a last resort, yet it is needed in several situations. As discussed in Chapter 1, an important design goal was to ensure that the .NET Compact Framework would run well—which means it has to have a small memory footprint. To achieve that, the development team cut back on available features compared to what you find in the desktop .NET Framework.

Table 4.2 summarizes some of the situations when you are likely to need P/Invoke, at least as implemented in version 1.0 of the .NET Compact Framework. We expect access to custom unmanaged DLLs to be the most common one. After all, application developers have been building, testing, and deploying countless unmanaged Win32 DLLs on Windows CE for many years. P/Invoke provides a way to tap into the value created in the large number of such libraries.

The other items listed in Table 4.2 are Win32 functions supported by Windows CE but not supported in the .NET Compact Framework itself. The CEFUN tool, available for free download from The Paul Yao Company,[2] summarizes the available Win32 functions that Windows CE supports. When run on a specific system, this utility provides a list of the functions that are present.

As of this writing, Microsoft has just started shipping the first version of the .NET Compact Framework (and, in fact, two updates in the form of service packs have already been made available). Plans are already under way

2. You can find this program at http://www.paulyao.com/resources/cefun.

TABLE 4.2: **Examples of When to Use P/Invoke for Win32 Features Not Supported in .NET**

Feature	Comments
ActiveSync	ActiveSync is a set of services for connecting a desktop PC with a Windows CE device (see Chapter 14). Most ActiveSync services are provided on the desktop itself, so getting .NET support for ActiveSync involves creating a set of P/Invoke wrappers for the desktop .NET Framework.[a]
Clipboard	A Windows Mobile device such as a Pocket PC supports a clipboard in the same way that desktop Windows does, allowing you to cut, copy, and paste data between applications. The underlying Win32 clipboard functions are supported in Windows CE, although the .NET Compact Framework does not have the same set of clipboard support that is found on the .NET Framework.
COM components	The .NET Compact Framework cannot directly call COM and ActiveX components—a feature that in the desktop .NET Framework is known as COM interop. To use your COM components, you must create a set of unmanaged functions that wrap the COM components. Another approach is to use the CFCOM interoperability layer from Odyssey Software.[b]
Common dialog boxes	Common dialog boxes provide prebuilt dialog boxes for opening and closing files, allowing a user to select a font or a color, and printing. The .NET Compact Framework supports the file open and save dialogs but not the font and color pickers. In such cases, direct calls to the underlying Win32 functions help fill this need.
Cryptography API	The Cryptography API provides encryption and decryption support to supplement the support provided in the `System.Security` namespace.
Custom controls	Custom controls implemented in unmanaged DLLs can be supported in .NET Compact Framework Windows Forms applications.
Custom, third-party unmanaged DLLs	P/Invoke support provides access to exported C-callable functions in a DLL. Such DLLs must be specifically built for Windows CE (or Pocket PC), and—unlike managed-code libraries—must be targeted toward the specific CPU on which the DLL is going to run. (DLLs built for the desktop need to be recompiled to run under Windows CE.)

continues

a. We provide a set of wrappers for RAPI functions. You can download that code from The Paul Yao Company Web site at http://www.paulyao.com/cfbook/code.

b. For details, visit the company's Web site at http://www.odysseysoftware.com.

TABLE 4.2: Examples of When to Use P/Invoke for Win32 Features Not Supported in .NET (continued)

Feature	Comments
Microsoft Message Queue (MSMQ)	MSMQ allows for asynchronous communication between different computers.
Point-to-point message queues	This interprocess communication feature, introduced in Windows CE .NET version 4.0, provides anonymous pipe support for interprocess or interthread communication.
Real-time threads	Windows CE provides great real-time support, with very consistent response times for the highest-priority thread in the system and for the highest-priority interrupt. When you have hard real-time requirements, the safest approach is to delegate that work to Win32 code. Unexpected delays can occur in managed code due to the time taken to convert IL to native machine instructions (IL JIT) or to collect garbage (all managed threads are blocked during memory cleanup; unmanaged P/Invoke threads run freely without blocking and block only on return to managed code if garbage collection is running).
Registry	In the desktop .NET Framework, reading and writing to the system registry are supported by the `Microsoft.Win32.Registry` class. But this class is not supported in the .NET Compact Framework. We show one alternative in Chapter 11.[c]
Running programs	Call the Win32 `CreateProcess` function to run a program.
Serial communication[d]	Microsoft considers communication with the RS-232 protocol as legacy (e.g., many PCs and laptops are shipping without traditional serial ports or printer ports). This is perhaps the reason that serial communication is not supported in either the .NET Compact Framework or the .NET Framework. Among smart devices, however, serial communication is very important because it is a low-cost, low-power, well-known standard. At the present, serial communication requires making native Win32 function calls or using a third-party library.
Shell functions	Some very useful Win32 functions have a prefix `SH`, which stands for "Shell." Some of the interesting ones include `SHGetSpecialFolderLocation`, `SHGetSpecialFolderPath`, and `SHBrowseForFolder` (Windows CE .NET 4.0 and later).

c. You can also find a managed-code solution at http://www.opennetcf.org.

d. You can find an article written by Chris Tacke that address serial communication using P/Invoke at this link: http://msdn.microsoft.com/mobility/default.aspx?pull=/library/en-us/dnnetcomp/html/pisapicf.asp.

Feature	Comments
Sounds	.NET Compact Framework does not support sounds, which are available with the Win32 `sndPlaySound` function.
Stream interface driver control codes	Windows CE uses stream interface drivers for system services such as a Web server (HTTPD), MSMQ, Universal Plug and Play (UPNP), and the Audio Compression Manager (ACM). This type of driver is also used for device drivers for some hardware, including the serial port, the infrared port, and various kinds of disk drives. Full access to these drivers requires the Win32 file I/O functions, including the `DeviceIoControl` function to send driver-specific control codes.

for new features in future versions. As features are added to the .NET Compact Framework, we plan to call the managed .NET Compact Framework class libraries instead of the equivalents in the unmanaged system libraries.

Why We Prefer .NET Compact Framework Classes over Win32 Functions

As a general rule, we prefer using the support provided in the .NET Compact Framework over calling Win32 functions. We have several reasons. First is that .NET Compact Framework functions get automatic memory management. By contrast when you call a Win32 function that creates a system object, you must eventually call the associated Win32 cleanup function. For example, if you create a bitmap by calling the Win32 `CreateDIBSection` function, you must later call the `DeleteObject` function to clean up the memory allocated for the bitmap. Win32 functions do not have automatic garbage collection like .NET functions do, so you must remember to take out the trash yourself or you cause memory leaks. A memory leak on a desktop or server system with 1GB of RAM is a bad thing because the system eventually slows down and crashes. A memory leak on a mobile or embedded system with 64MB of memory causes the same problem except that a crash is likely to occur sooner.

A second reason we prefer .NET functions is that their use enhances an application's portability. An application written today—for either the full .NET Framework or the .NET Compact Framework—is more portable when it has fewer dependencies on Win32 libraries. By this we mean that if the

.NET Framework becomes available on non-Windows platforms, programs without P/Invoke are more likely to be able to run without modification.[3]

Third, related to portability is the issue of trust and security. Code that uses P/Invoke is less trusted than code that does not—the part of the common language runtime that is responsible for security can look at CIL code and determine whether it is safe to run. When it cannot be verified to be safe, it is called *unsafe code*. Version 1.0 of the .NET Compact Framework does nothing to prevent unsafe code from running, although in certain scenarios (e.g., using code downloaded from a Web site) the desktop .NET Framework may prevent such code from running based on the security settings.

A fourth reason we prefer managed functions is because more work is required to call Win32 functions with P/Invoke. You have to create a function declaration as well as constants and data structures to support that function. In this chapter, we introduce a tool to help you do that, the P/Invoke Wizard, which considerably cuts down on the effort. Managed functions, by contrast, are immediately available by adding a reference to the Solution Explorer and the appropriate namespace reference (`using` in C# and `Imports` in Visual Basic).

Porting Unmanaged Code to Managed Code

We are big fans of managed code, but our enthusiasm has a limit. Programmers in our training classes often ask when to port unmanaged code to run as managed DLLs instead of using P/Invoke to access the unmanaged code. There is only one answer: "It depends."

If you have built and deployed an unmanaged DLL, you should use it. You have, after all, invested time and money in building and testing that DLL. Before porting it to a managed DLL, you have to make a business case that it makes sense to do so. When you have an unmanaged library that works, we suggest you use P/Invoke to access its services. By porting an unmanaged library to a .NET library, you have doubled your code maintenance without adding any real features.

3. We do not know of any plans for this to actually happen, but the high-tech industry changes quickly—who knows what tomorrow will bring?

There are, of course, reasons to port. First, libraries with large amounts of user interface code can benefit from being ported because running as a managed-code library can simplify interoperating with .NET Compact Framework–based user interface features. (You may, however, also lose some features because the .NET Compact Framework controls generally support fewer features than their Win32 counterparts.)

A second reason to port Win32 code to .NET is that debugging P/Invoke code can be difficult. Visual Studio .NET 2003 does not support debugging between managed and unmanaged code when dealing with .NET Compact Framework code (a feature that is supported for desktop code with the desktop .NET Framework). When a P/Invoke function call fails under the .NET Compact Framework, you get an error message in the form of a .NET exception with few details to help you identify the cause of the failure. To debug a native DLL, you must use the debugger that ships with the native development environment. For Windows CE 3.0, you use eMbedded Visual C++ version 3.0, and for Windows CE .NET 4.x, you use version 4.x of eMbedded Visual C++.

A third reason to port an unmanaged DLL to a managed DLL is to simplify the packaging and setup of your program, particularly when the software you deploy must run on systems with different CPUs with different instruction sets. For example, a single .NET program can run on all CPUs; a comparable unmanaged DLL needs a different executable file for each supported CPU.

Creating P/Invoke Declarations

A P/Invoke declaration—often referred to as a P/Invoke wrapper—follows the same rules for regular function declarations: They must be made within a class, have a return type, and have zero or more parameters. In addition, a P/Invoke wrapper needs these elements:

- The `DllImport` attribute
- The `static` keyword
- The `extern` keyword

P/Invoke Debugging Tip

If you are creating P/Invoke wrappers for a large number of DLL functions, it might be worth porting your library (or a portion of your library) to the desktop. When you have your P/Invoke code working on the desktop, you can then port the debugged code back to Windows CE and the .NET Compact Framework.

We suggest this approach because the debugger in Visual Studio .NET 2003 does not support stepping from managed code into unmanaged code for the .NET Compact Framework; this feature is supported only for the desktop .NET Framework. So if you find that you need debugger help while creating the P/Invoke declarations for a particular function, build a tiny Win32 DLL for the desktop containing that difficult function. You can then use the debugger to help you figure out the correct P/Invoke declarations to make your function work.

There are differences between the P/Invoke support on the desktop and in the .NET Compact Framework. For this technique to be effective, you have to make sure that you do not use a P/Invoke feature that does not exist in the .NET Compact Framework. In particular, avoid the `MarshalAs` attribute in your P/Invoke declarations. This declaration helps fine-tune the passing of parameters. For example, this attribute allows the passing of nested reference types. As of this writing, the .NET Compact Framework does not support this attribute, although this support could be added in a future version.

So port your trickier P/Invoke functions to a desktop DLL, do your debugging, then port the functions back. The desktop debugging support can save you time resolving managed-to-unmanaged coding problems. But be careful not to use desktop-only P/Invoke features.

To understand how these elements are used together to provide access to unmanaged DLL functions, it helps to look at some examples. Let's start with a simple P/Invoke declaration.

A Simple Function: MessageBox

A common example used for P/Invoke declarations is the MessageBox function, probably because it is a widely known function with relatively few parameters. That is where we are going to start, with a review of a basic MessageBox P/Invoke wrapper. We are then going to dig more deeply into the details of P/Invoke declarations.

The MessageBox function is declared in a Win32 include file, winuser.h, as follows:

```
// C++ Win32 declaration
int WINAPI MessageBoxW(HWND hWnd, LPCWSTR lpText,
    LPCWSTR lpCaption, UINT uType);
```

The W at the end of the function name in this code marks MessageBox as a Unicode function. With few exceptions,[4] all Win32 functions in Windows CE are implemented as Unicode functions—that is, all string parameters must be 16-bit (UTF-16) Unicode strings. You can either include or omit the W in a P/Invoke declaration because the runtime adds a W for you if it's not already there. Here are two valid declarations for the MessageBox function.

```
// Two C# MessageBox declarations -- one with 'W'...
[DllImport("coredll.dll"]
public static extern int
MessageBoxW(IntPtr hWnd, String lpText, String lpCaption,
   UInt32 uType);

// ...and one without 'W'
[DllImport("coredll.dll"]
public static extern int
MessageBox(IntPtr hWnd, String lpText, String lpCaption,
   UInt32 uType);
```

This declaration contains a reference to DllImport, which is worth discussing on several counts. From the perspective of .NET and C# programming, this is an example of an *attribute*. In C#, attributes always appear

4. The exceptions are for some network functions, for which both Unicode and multibyte functions are supported—for example, there is both an InternetOpenW and an InternetOpenA function in wininet.dll.

between square brackets ([and]) and allow you to fine-tune various .NET declarations. For example, the `WebMethod` attribute defines functions that are available through a Web Service. Like all other .NET objects, the `DllImport` attribute is defined in a class that resides in a namespace. To use this class, we reference the namespace with the following declaration:

```
using System.Runtime.InteropServices;
```

With the namespace declaration, we can call the `MessageBox` function as if it were a regular .NET method:

```
MessageBoxW(IntPtr.Zero, "Call to MessageBoxW", "Message", 0);

MessageBox(IntPtr.Zero, "Call to MessageBox", "Message", 0);
```

From the perspective of P/Invoke, the `DllImport` attribute identifies functions that reside in unmanaged libraries. An attribute declaration is a constructor for an object, and like other kinds of object constructors, an attribute constructor can accept parameters. A `DllImport` attribute is created from the `DllImportAttribute` class (by convention, all attribute classes have a suffix of `Attribute`). The `DllImport` attribute constructor takes a single parameter, a string that is the name of an unmanaged DLL.

As you begin to create P/Invoke declarations, you need to proceed slowly because the debugging support and error reporting is somewhat limited. You cannot, for example, use the Visual Studio .NET debugger to trace from .NET Compact Framework code into unmanaged code. An error causes an exception to be raised, which results in the display of a message like that shown in Figure 4.1. More often than not, this is the only error

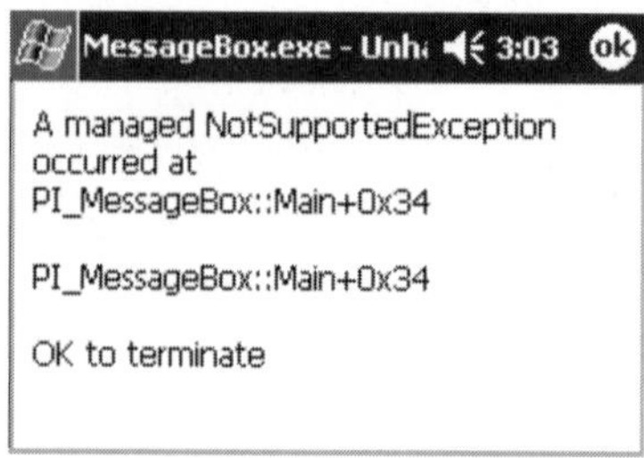

FIGURE 4.1: Example of an exception caused by a P/Invoke error

reporting you get when a problem is encountered in P/Invoke. If you look closely at the error message displayed, you get little information about why there was a problem—only that something is not supported.

Unmanaged Function Details

In C#, a function with the `DllImport` attribute must also have the `static` and `extern` keywords. The `static` keyword means that you can call the function anytime without having to create an instance of the class—this is the closest thing that C# has to a global function that C programmers are so used to. C++ programmers may recognize that the `static` keyword in a C# class function is similar to the same keyword in a C++ class. The `extern` keyword indicates that the actual implementation of a function is in another language besides C#.

The function we are calling, `MessageBox`, takes four parameters: (1) a window handle, (2) message text, (3) caption text, and (4) some flags. A close look at each of these will tell us more about how to pass parameters to this Win32 function.

```
// C++ Win32 declaration
int WINAPI MessageBoxW(HWND hWnd, LPCWSTR lpText,
    LPCWSTR lpCaption, UINT uType);
```

The first parameter, `HWND hWnd`, is a window handle that identifies a message box's parent window. When the message box is displayed, the parent window is disabled; when the user dismisses the message box, the parent is enabled and activated. While the Win32 API uses handles in many places, handles are not used in .NET, so we need an alternative type for a window handle; we define handles using `IntPtr`, a type provided for Win32 handles.[5] When there is no parent window, we pass a special value, `IntPtr.Zero`, which is the same as a Win32 null handle. Most of the time, `null` is an invalid value for a handle. But in a few cases, a null handle can be used. In a call to the `MessageBox` function, for example, a null handle means that the message box has no parent window.

5. An `IntPtr` is also used for pointers, as demonstrated in the `FindMemoryCard` example later in this chapter.

Some P/Invoke examples use regular integer types for handles, a technique that works but makes code less portable. Today all implementations of .NET are 32-bit implementations; there may someday be a 64-bit (or 128-bit) implementation. `IntPtr` is always the right size to hold handles (and pointers) for the platform on which a program is running, so its use helps make your code more portable. A second use of the `IntPtr` type is for unmanaged memory pointers, a feature that helps unravel some trickier problems encountered in calls to unmanaged code.

The second and third parameters, `LPCWSTR lpText` and `LPCWSTR lpCaption`, are strings. To an unmanaged function, these appear as string pointers. P/Invoke correctly passes simple string pointers like that shown in the call to the `MessageBox` function. However, P/Invoke has trouble handling strings embedded in structures, nested structures, and arrays. For each of these situations, P/Invoke needs help from the `IntPtr` type and members of the `Marshal`[6] class. We dig into just such an example later in this chapter.

The final parameter, `UINT uType`, is a bit-field flag parameter. This unsigned integer holds flags that indicate the buttons and icons to display in the message box. To fill in the proper bit values, you create .NET definitions for the Win32 flag values. (In a pinch, you can also hard-code constant values; however, this approach makes code harder to maintain, so we suggest you avoid that practice.) Here are the C++ definitions for the legal values to pass in the `uType` parameter, as defined in `winuser.h`:

```
#define MB_OK                          0x00000000L
#define MB_OKCANCEL                    0x00000001L
#define MB_ABORTRETRYIGNORE            0x00000002L
#define MB_YESNOCANCEL                 0x00000003L
#define MB_YESNO                       0x00000004L
#define MB_RETRYCANCEL                 0x00000005L
#define MB_ICONHAND                    0x00000010L
#define MB_ICONQUESTION                0x00000020L
#define MB_ICONEXCLAMATION             0x00000030L
#define MB_ICONASTERISK                0x00000040L
```

6. Fully qualified name: `System.Runtime.InteropServices.Marshal`.

When you need to define flags or constant values to call unmanaged functions, there are at least two approaches you can take. One approach is to define a set of constant values. A second approach is to define an enumeration. We show you both in Listing 4.1 so you can decide which you prefer, along with the associated declaration and call to the `MessageBox` function.

Which approach should you use? One benefit of the enumeration is that once defined in your code, it can be used by Visual Studio .NET to show the available options in a drop-down window as you type your code. This is very handy, and for this reason, we prefer enumerations.

LISTING 4.1: Two Approaches for a P/Invoke Wrapper for the `MessageBox` Function

```
// MessageBox.cs - Two ways to call Win32 MessageBox function
//
// Platform Invoke Sample.
// Code from _.NET Compact Framework Programming with C#_
// Authored by Paul Yao and David Durant.
//

using System;
using System.Runtime.InteropServices;

namespace PlatformInvoke
{
   class PI_MessageBox
   {
      public const string strApp = "MessageBox";

      // First approach - flags as integers
      [DllImport("coredll.dll")]
      public static extern Int32
      MessageBox(IntPtr hWnd, string lpText, string lpCaption,
         int uType);

      public const int MB_OK = 0x00000000;
      public const int MB_OKCANCEL = 0x00000001;
      public const int MB_ABORTRETRYIGNORE = 0x00000002;
      public const int MB_YESNOCANCEL = 0x00000003;
      public const int MB_YESNO = 0x00000004;
      public const int MB_RETRYCANCEL = 0x00000005;
      public const int MB_ICONHAND = 0x00000010;
      public const int MB_ICONQUESTION = 0x00000020;
      public const int MB_ICONEXCLAMATION = 0x00000030;
```

continues

continued

```
public const int MB_ICONASTERISK = 0x00000040;
public const int MB_ICONWARNING = MB_ICONEXCLAMATION;
public const int MB_ICONERROR = MB_ICONHAND;
public const int MB_ICONINFORMATION = MB_ICONASTERISK;
public const int MB_ICONSTOP = MB_ICONHAND;
public const int MB_DEFBUTTON1 = 0x00000000;
public const int MB_DEFBUTTON2 = 0x00000100;
public const int MB_DEFBUTTON3 = 0x00000200;
public const int MB_DEFBUTTON4 = 0x00000300;
public const int MB_APPLMODAL = 0x00000000;
public const int MB_SETFOREGROUND = 0x00010000;
public const int MB_TOPMOST = 0x00040000;

// Second approach - flag values in an enumeration
[DllImport("coredll.dll")]
public static extern Int32
MessageBoxW(IntPtr hWnd, string lpText, string lpCaption,
   MB uType);

public enum MB
{
   MB_OK = 0x00000000,
   MB_OKCANCEL = 0x00000001,
   MB_ABORTRETRYIGNORE = 0x00000002,
   MB_YESNOCANCEL = 0x00000003,
   MB_YESNO = 0x00000004,
   MB_RETRYCANCEL = 0x00000005,
   MB_ICONHAND = 0x00000010,
   MB_ICONQUESTION = 0x00000020,
   MB_ICONEXCLAMATION = 0x00000030,
   MB_ICONASTERISK = 0x00000040,
   MB_ICONWARNING = MB_ICONEXCLAMATION,
   MB_ICONERROR = MB_ICONHAND,
   MB_ICONINFORMATION = MB_ICONASTERISK,
   MB_ICONSTOP = MB_ICONHAND,
   MB_DEFBUTTON1 = 0x00000000,
   MB_DEFBUTTON2 = 0x00000100,
   MB_DEFBUTTON3 = 0x00000200,
   MB_DEFBUTTON4 = 0x00000300,
   MB_APPLMODAL = 0x00000000,
   MB_SETFOREGROUND = 0x00010000,
   MB_TOPMOST = 0x00040000
}

static void Main()
{
   // Flags defined as set of const values.
```

```
        MessageBox(IntPtr.Zero, "One way to define flags",
           strApp, MB_OK | MB_TOPMOST);

        // Flags defined as members of enum
        MessageBox(IntPtr.Zero, "Another way to define flags",
           strApp, MB.MB_OK | MB.MB_TOPMOST);
      }
   }
}
```

Function Return Values

As in managed code, unmanaged functions are not required to return a value. C# programmers specify a `void` return type, just as in C and C++.

An unmanaged function can return 32-bit and narrower integers. This means that you can return 1-byte integers, 2-byte integers, and 4-byte integers; 64-bit integers, however, cannot be used as return types. As far as using floating-point values goes, neither single nor double floating-point values can be used as the function's return value (although you can accomplish the same thing by passing a by-reference parameter). The C# types that can be used as return values are listed here[7]:

- `bool`
- `byte`
- `sbyte`
- `char`
- `short`
- `ushort`
- `int`
- `uint`
- `IntPtr` (a .NET type, with no C# alias)

When calling unmanaged code that returns a data pointer, you declare the function to return an `IntPtr` (which is a 32-bit integer). Once you get the `IntPtr` back from a called function, you next call various members of

7. This information also appears in Table 4.3 later in this chapter, which summarizes the use of managed types as parameters when calling unmanaged functions.

the Marshal class to copy the values to managed objects. You can find examples of using IntPtr and Marshal later in this chapter.

Getting Started: C-Style Function Declarations

To create a .NET-compatible P/Invoke declaration for an unmanaged function, you need a set of Win32 declarations: a function prototype, flag or constant values, and data structure definitions. Where do you get these declarations? There are two choices: the include files and the online documentation.

Microsoft defines the Win32 API in a set of include files. In the very beginning of Windows programming, all declarations were in a single file: windows.h. That file grew and grew until it had to be split into numerous smaller files—but windows.h is still a good starting point for finding which files are included (with very deep nesting of include files, it is easy to get confused). These include files are available in several different products, most notably with the Microsoft language compilers. Be aware that there are Windows CE–specific versions of the include files (and even platform-specific versions, so that the Pocket PC 2003 has a different set of include files from the Smartphone 2003). A simple solution is to get your hands on the SDK for your platform, which should have the include files you need.[8]

In a few cases, the include files do not have the best declarations, so we rely on the online documentation. Why? Because in some include files the parameters for function declarations do not include a sample parameter name, only the type information. If that were the case with the MessageBox function, the declaration might be as follows:

```
// C++ Win32 declaration
int WINAPI MessageBoxW(HWND, LPCWSTR, LPCWSTR, UINT);
```

---

8. Developers using Windows Mobile devices, including Pocket PC 2003 and Smartphone 2003, can find the SDK for these devices on the Web by browsing to http://www.pocketpc.com. Then follow the links for developers and then downloads.

Without the parameter names, it becomes harder to know the purpose of the middle two parameters. But when you know the parameter names are `lpText` and `lpCaption`, it makes it easier to guess the difference between these two parameters. That is the reason that we sometimes use the online documentation instead of the include files for some of the declarations we use for creating P/Invoke wrappers.

Setting up a P/Invoke call requires a lot of work—you need to create a P/Invoke wrapper for the function, and often you need to include definitions for flag values or other supporting constants. And for some function calls, you might also need to define one or more data structures. If you have only one or two declarations to deal with, it can be fun. If you have more than that, however, it can get boring very quickly. To find out how to access a tool that does the conversion automatically, read the sidebar about the P/Invoke Wizard.

P/Invoke Wizard

One of us created the P/Invoke Wizard out of necessity. Faced with the tedious task of converting 500 C-style declarations into both C# and into Visual Basic .NET, he decided he needed a tool to do the work for him. From that effort, the P/Invoke Wizard was born. The Paul Yao Company then started to sell the tool on its Web site, where it garnered a modest amount of interest. When we sent a copy of the tool to Mike Hall, a friend who works at Microsoft, Mike suggested we find a way to make it available to a wider audience. As a result of Mike's suggestion, a shareware version was created. You can download the tool from the company's Web site[9] and use it to explore the automatic creation of P/Invoke wrappers from C-language declarations.

9. To download the P/Invoke Wizard, visit http://www.paulyao.com/pinvoke.

The P/Invoke Wizard accepts C declarations for functions, enumerations, `#define` constant values, and data structures. You can type these declarations into the program's Edit window, open an include file when you have many wrappers to create, or paste from the clipboard. The tool returns a set of .NET-compatible declarations, in your choice of either C# or Visual Basic .NET. Figure 4.2 shows the Platform Invoke Wizard with Win32 declarations in the upper input window, and the resulting .NET-compatible P/Invoke declarations in the lower output window. For developers creating declarations for the desktop .NET Framework, the tool allows you to enable code generation for P/Invoke features that are not currently supported in the .NET Compact Framework.

The P/Invoke Wizard can open and convert a complete include file. You could, for example, open include files like `winbase.h`, `wingdi.h`, and `winuser.h`. This tool provides a quick and easy way to convert a large number of functions. We tested the P/Invoke Wizard on all the Win32 include (`*.h`) files. In addition, we have gotten feedback from users who have used the P/Invoke Wizard with include files from third-party DLLs.

The goal of the P/Invoke Wizard is to save time. We wanted to make it easy for programmers to handle the mind-numbing simple cases, which make up 99% of the work involved with creating P/Invoke declarations. This gives you more time to study and fix the other 1% that require refinement of the output generated by our wizard. You may need to handle some of the cases by hand because the P/Invoke Wizard is not a full-blown compiler, meaning it does not parse the full, rich syntax of the C and C++ programming languages. It can, however, handle declarations found within include files. We know that it works well with the Win32 include files because we used those files in our testing. It can read and create usable declarations for both desktop and Windows CE versions of `kernel32.h`, `gdi32.h`, `user32.h`, `toolhelp.h`, `rapi.h`, `advapi32.h`, and many of the other include files that make up the Win32 API.

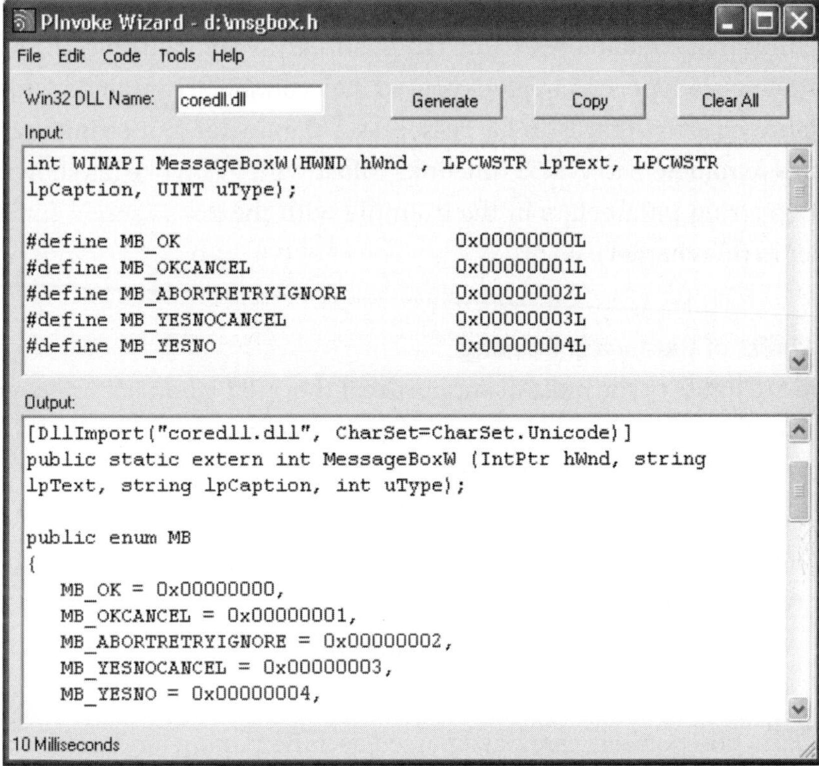

FIGURE 4.2: The P/Invoke Wizard converting the `MessageBox` function to C#

Supported P/Invoke Function Parameters

After you understand the basic P/Invoke syntax, the next step to using P/Invoke is to understand what parameter types can be passed. In his online series, "Working with C#," Eric Gunnerson of Microsoft writes that, "If the functions have simple interfaces, it's fairly easy to call them from a .NET language. As things get more complex, however, it's harder to use runtime interop."[10] This summarizes nicely our experience with P/Invoke.

---

10. Quoted from "Using Existing Code in C#," by Eric Gunnerson, July 14, 2002, accessed at http://msdn.microsoft.com/library/en-us/dncscol/html/csharp07152002.asp in January 2004. This article focuses on P/Invoke as implemented in the desktop .NET Framework. This article can provide good background, but some features that Eric discusses—like COM interop and marshaling attributes—are not supported in the .NET Compact Framework.

Simple data types—meaning value types—can be passed, as can strings, structures that contain only value types, and arrays of value types. Strings are a reference type, not a value type, so they cannot be contained within a structure or array that is to be passed as a parameter. But strings can be used as parameters to Win32 functions called with P/Invoke (as shown for the two string parameters in the example with the `MessageBox` function earlier in this chapter).

The Limits of Parameter Passing

There are limits to the built-in support that the .NET Compact Framework provides for parameters to an unmanaged function.

- Passing a variable number of parameters is not supported.
- Passing structures that contain strings, objects, arrays, other structures, or unions is not supported.
- Arrays of complex types are not supported.
- Arrays of strings are not supported.
- Function pointers cannot be passed as .NET parameters because calls to managed code from unmanaged code are not supported.[11]

Remember that our focus is on the .NET Compact Framework. In general, the desktop .NET Framework has richer support for P/Invoke than the .NET Compact Framework does. Given a bit of diligence, however, we have found that we can pass just about all data types to unmanaged code—it just takes more work in the .NET Compact Framework. The major limitation in .NET Compact Framework P/Invoke support involves code pointers—callback functions, interface functions, and class functions—that cannot be passed from managed code to unmanaged code in any meaningful way. Most other data pointers can be passed into (and, as appropriate,

---

11. On the desktop .NET Framework, however, function pointers to unmanaged code can be passed to unmanaged code. For an example, see Dino Esposito's article in the October 2002 edition of *MSDN Magazine,* "Windows Hooks in the .NET Framework," available at http://msdn.microsoft.com/msdnmag/issues/02/10/CuttingEdge/default.aspx.

back out of) managed code using a combination of the `IntPtr` data types and members of the `Marshal` class. The `FindMemoryCard` example later in this chapter shows how this is done.

Simple Data Types

Simple data types (value types that are 32 bits and smaller) can be passed as parameters. You can pass such values either by value or by reference. A by-value parameter makes a one-way trip into the called function, while by-reference parameters provide a pointer to the called method so that it can access the original input data (or the output buffer). Such parameters are either output parameters or input-output parameters that allow the data to take a round-trip into the called function, with any changes to the data returned to the caller.

Three Uses of Function Parameters

Function parameters are used in three ways: for input only, for output only, and for both input and output. To show the use of parameters, Microsoft has standard notation in its documentation. Input-only parameters are marked `[in]`; output-only parameters are marked `[out]`; and parameters used for both input and output—a rare usage—are marked `[in][out]`.

The movement of function parameters and return values over the boundary between managed code and unmanaged code is known as *marshaling*. There are specific limitations on what can be marshaled. Marshaling is easiest when managed and unmanaged representations of data are the same. This category includes most integer types: signed and unsigned 8-bit, 16-bit, and 32-bit integers. Simple types can be passed either by value or by reference. In C#, a by-reference parameter is marked with the `ref` keyword. The keyword is used in two different places: in the function definition and in function calls. When `ref` does not appear, a parameter is a by-value parameter.

Some types can be passed only by reference, including 64-bit integers, single-precision floating-point numbers, and double-precision floating-point numbers. The Win32 code you call must be written to receive a pointer to these types.

Then there are the value types for which there is no built-in marshaling support. `DateTime` and `Decimal` values fall into this category. These types—like all data types—can be marshaled, but extra work is required. Table 4.3 summarizes the .NET Compact Framework's built-in support for marshaling common .NET value types. Table 4.3 also shows whether a given type can be used for a valid return value. All 32-bit (4-byte) and narrower integers can be used as return values. If a data type cannot be used as a return value and if you need to receive data of that type from the called function, you might have to redefine your unmanaged-code function to retrieve the return value as a by-reference parameter.

Most items in Table 4.3 are self-explanatory and correspond to data types that exist across a wide range of programming environments. A few worth some extra mention are discussed further in the following subsections.

Boolean

Many Win32 functions return a Boolean value, as defined by the Win32 `BOOL` type. You might be tempted to use the .NET `boolean` type when building P/Invoke declarations because the names are the same. But you would not get the right results. You must instead use a signed (32-bit) integer, which matches the type used for the Win32 `BOOL` type. For example, the Win32 `IsWindow` function, which tells you whether a window handle is valid, is defined as follows:

```
BOOL IsWindow(HWND hWnd);
```

The equivalent P/Invoke declaration is:

```
[DllImport("coredll.dll")]
public static extern int IsWindow(IntPtr hWnd);
```

Signed versus Unsigned Integers

Table 4.3 lists both signed and unsigned integers. We recommend that you avoid using unsigned types when building P/Invoke declarations. The

TABLE 4.3: Built-in Support for Marshaling Common .NET Data Types

.NET Compact Frame-work Type	Size (Bytes)	C# Alias	Visual Basic Alias	Win32 by-Value Type	Win32 by-Reference Type	Valid as a Return Value?
Boolean	1	bool	Boolean	BYTE	BYTE *	Yes
Byte	1	byte	Byte	BYTE	BYTE *	Yes
SByte	1	sbyte	N/A	CHAR	CHAR *	Yes
Char	2	char	Char	WCHAR	WCHAR *	Yes
Int16	2	short	Short	SHORT	SHORT *	Yes
UInt16	2	ushort	N/A	UINT16	UINT16 *	Yes
Int32	4	int	Integer	INT32	INT32 *	Yes
UInt32	4	uint	N/A	UINT32	UINT32 *	Yes
IntPtr	4	N/A	N/A	HANDLE	HANDLE *	Yes
Single	4	float	Single	Not supported	FLOAT *	No
Int64	8	long	Long	Not supported	INT64 *	No
UInt64	8	ulong	N/A	Not supported	UINT64 *	No
Double	8	double	Double	Not supported	DOUBLE *	No
String	Varies	string	String	WCHAR *	Not supported	No
Decimal	12	decimal	Decimal	Not supported	Not supported	No

reason is that the CLI supports only signed integers (except for the 1-byte integer, in which case only the unsigned 1-byte integer is supported).

Visual Basic, for example, does not support unsigned integers. You may have noticed this fact from Table 4.3, which omits Visual Basic aliases for such aliases as `UInt32` and `UInt16`, among others, because such aliases do not exist. Avoiding unsigned integers helps promote interoperability between C# and Visual Basic programs. (For instance, you can create a C# library of P/Invoke declarations and use that library from a Visual Basic program!)

This sounds like a simple recommendation with an understandable benefit. Yet if you study the Win32 API, you will realize the impact of our recommendation. The Win32 API makes widespread use of unsigned integers. Many function definitions and data structures contain 16-bit unsigned integers (the Win32 `WORD` type) and 32-bit unsigned integers (the Win32 `DWORD` type) types. In other words, in making the move from a Win32 type to a CLI-compatible type, you may be forced to convert unsigned integers to signed integers. You may need to use the C# `unchecked` keyword to avoid overflow errors, as detailed in the sidebar on page 214.

The C# `long` Type

Programmers who are coming to C# programming with a background in C or C++ should note that a `long` in C# is different than a `long` in C/C++. In C#, `long` is a 64-bit integer, while `long` in C/C++ is a 32-bit integer. A 32-bit integer in C# is an `int`.

Passing Parameters by Value versus by Reference

An important part of every P/Invoke declaration involves deciding whether to pass a parameter by value or by reference. These terms are specific to .NET programming, but the underlying concepts are not new. The C programming language, which has been around since the late 1960s, supports both types of parameter passing. The following C function passes one by-value integer (`i`) and one by-reference integer (`pi`).

```
// C Code - passing parameters by-value and by-reference
int Add(int i, int * pi)
{
```

```
    return(i + *pi);
}
```

The preceding code is easily understood by a C programmer. What might be new to you—if you are new to C# programming—is how this translates into a valid P/Invoke interface. Here is what the P/Invoke Wizard creates for us.

```
// Add function w/ by-value & by-reference parameters
[DllImport("mydll.dll")]
public static extern Int32 Add(int i, ref int pi);
```

The new element is the keyword `ref`, which says that the function call should pass a pointer to the value. You also use this keyword in the function call.

```
int iFirst = 10;
int iSecond = 20;
int iThird = Add(iFirst, ref iSecond);
```

If you forget to use the `ref` keyword, the compiler complains at program build time. As in other cases, here the compiler's syntax checker is the best teacher a programmer could have.

An alternative to the `ref` keyword is an explicit pointer. We do not recommend this, but we mention it for the sake of completeness. The pointer syntax is identical to the pointer syntax that C and C++ programmers know.

```
// Add function with a pointer - requires unsafe keyword
[DllImport("PlaceHolder.dll")]
public static extern unsafe Int32 Add(Int32 i, Int32 * pi);
```

When you compare this declaration with the earlier one, you see two changes: (1) the addition of the `unsafe` keyword, and (2) the `*` in place of `ref`. A third difference, not visible in this code fragment, is best described by the error message generated by the compiler.

```
Unsafe code may only appear if compiling with /unsafe
```

In other words, the `unsafe` keyword requires the `/unsafe` compiler switch. The compiler will create an explicit pointer for you, but only if you are willing to mark your executable as unsafe. Better, we think, to use the implicit pointer created by the `ref` keyword than to use explicit pointers in your C# code.

The C# `unchecked` Keyword

In most cases, a signed integer in a P/Invoke declaration works just as well as an unsigned integer declaration. C# programmers run into trouble, however, when trying to assign values greater than `0x80000000` to a signed 32-bit integer. The reason? With signed integers, the high-order bit is used as the sign bit, which means that signed integers cannot hold the magnitude of values that unsigned integers can. Or, to put it another way, the range of signed integers includes both positive and negative numbers, but the range for unsigned integers is in positive numbers only. To account for this difference in the same number of bits, signed numbers cannot be any larger than 0x80000000—which accounts for the fact that numbers larger than this cause an overflow exception. For example, the compiler does not like the following line of code.

```
public const int E_FAIL = 0x80004005; // Compiler dislikes this!
```

The compiler can be placated by casting this value, but at runtime you get an exception complaining about an arithmetic overflow. The solution? Use the `unchecked` operator to tell the C# compiler not to check for overflows.

```
// Compiler is much happier with this:
public const int E_FAIL = unchecked((int)0x80004005);
```

Our recommendation makes life easier for Visual Basic programmers but adds a small complication for C# programmers. What is the impact on Visual Basic programmers? Visual Basic is not as fussy as C#, as demonstrated by the following Visual Basic statement, which causes neither compile-time errors nor runtime errors.

```
Public Const E_FAIL As Integer = &H80004005
```

Passing String Parameters by Value

An interesting aspect of strings is that they are passed by value and not by reference. For C and C++ programmers, this is a somewhat counterintuitive aspect of P/Invoke. A string object contains a pointer to a buffer that contains a character array. When you want to pass a pointer to other types, such as an integer, you make them by-reference parameters. From the .NET perspective, however, the value of the string is the pointer—and so we declare string parameters as by-value parameters. As we discuss later in this chapter, arrays passed as parameters are like strings in that they are also declared as by-value parameters.

On the subject of strings, you may have noticed two kinds of strings in Table 4.3: `String` and `StringBuilder`. As we discuss in Chapter 3, the `String` class is more efficient with a string that does not change (which Microsoft refers to as *immutable*), and the `StringBuilder` class is more efficient when performing a series of operations on a single string. For example, if you were going to concatenate many strings together, the `StringBuilder` class is likely to be more efficient. You could use the `String` class, but each operation would create a new string—potentially adding memory manager overhead.

As far as passing regular strings and `StringBuilder` strings as P/Invoke parameters, the .NET documentation suggests using the `String` class for one-way trips into managed code and using the `StringBuilder` class for two-way trips into unmanaged code and back again. In fact, either can be used for one-way or round-trip calls, but for two-way strings—that is, strings you send into managed code that may have been changed—the `StringBuilder` class is more efficient from the perspective of memory management.

Structures

Support for structures passed as parameters using P/Invoke wrappers plays an important role in letting you access operating system functions because the Win32 API contains definitions for over 2,000 structures. Many Win32 API functions require the use of pointers to structures as parameters.

The .NET Compact Framework's built-in support for passing structures to unmanaged code is considerably less capable than the desktop counterpart. P/Invoke in the .NET Compact Framework supports only structures that contain simple (32-bit or smaller) value types.

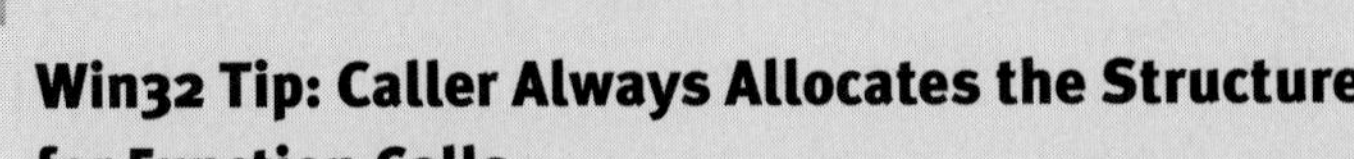

Win32 Tip: Caller Always Allocates the Structure for Function Calls

If you are new to Win32 programming, you should be aware that when passing a pointer to a structure to a Win32 function, the caller always[12] allocates the structure. In addition, many Win32 structures contain a field that you must initialize to the structure size (in bytes) before passing that structure to the Win32 function.

One useful Win32 function that accepts a structure is `CreateProcess`, which you call to start running a program. This function takes a pointer to the `PROCESS_INFORMATION` structure, which receives a pair of handles when a new process is created: a process handle and a thread handle. When creating a new process, you must disconnect both of these handles by calling the `CloseHandle` function to allow the system to properly clean up when the process terminates. Listing 4.2 shows a code fragment from the `Start` program, with the required P/Invoke declarations to create a new process. This program starts a new process when the user clicks on a button.

LISTING 4.2: Passing a Structure to a Win32 Unmanaged Function

```
static string strAppName = "Start";

[DllImport("coredll.dll")]
public static extern int
CreateProcess(string pszImageName, string pszCmdLine,
int Res1, int Res2, int Res3, CREATE_FLAG fdwCreate,
int Res4, int Res5, int Res6,
ref PROCESS_INFORMATION pProcInfo);

[DllImport("coredll.dll")]
public static extern int
CreateProcess(string pszImageName, int pszEmptyPath,
int Res1, int Res2, int Res3, CREATE_FLAG fdwCreate,
```

12. We say "always," but there are two or three exceptions. However, they are so rare that we are confident in recommending that you always allocate whatever structures are needed by Win32 functions that you may call.

```
int Res4, int Res5, int Res6,
ref PROCESS_INFORMATION pProcInfo);

[DllImport("coredll.dll")]
public static extern int CloseHandle(IntPtr hObject);

[DllImport("coredll.dll")]
public static extern int GetLastError();

public struct PROCESS_INFORMATION
{
   public IntPtr hProcess;
   public IntPtr hThread;
   public int dwProcessId;
   public int dwThreadId;
};

public enum CREATE_FLAG
{
   CREATE_SUSPENDED = 4,
   CREATE_NEW_CONSOLE = 0x10,
}

private void
cmdStart_Click(object sender, System.EventArgs e)
{
   string strPath = textPath.Text;
   PROCESS_INFORMATION pi = new PROCESS_INFORMATION();
   int bOk = CreateProcess(strPath, 0, 0, 0, 0, 0, 0, 0, 0,
   ref pi);
   if (bOk > 0)
   {
      CloseHandle(pi.hProcess);
      CloseHandle(pi.hThread);
   }
   else
   {
      MessageBox.Show("CreateProcess Failed", strAppName);
   }
}
```

The types that P/Invoke in the .NET Compact Framework *cannot* support in a structure include the following:

- Strings
- Arrays

- Nested structures
- Nested objects
- Other reference type

In some cases, you can get around these restrictions by defining a new structure that consists solely of simple data types. For example, you might flatten nested structures to create a single flat structure. In some cases, you can rewrite an unmanaged DLL to add new, P/Invoke-friendly functions. In most cases, however, you must move beyond the built-in P/Invoke support and do some "heavy lifting" using the `IntPtr` type and the `Marshal` class. The `FindMemoryCard` example, which appears later in this chapter, shows how to do that. For now, the `MemoryStatus` sample provides an example of passing a structure with simple data types.

Example: `MemoryStatus`

To pass a managed-code structure to unmanaged code, you declare the structure parameter as a by-reference parameter. An example of a function that takes a pointer to a structure as a parameter is the `GlobalMemoryStatus` function, a Win32 function that returns information about system memory. The declaration for this Win32 function takes the following form.

```
void GlobalMemoryStatus(LPMEMORYSTATUS lpBuffer);
```

Here is the equivalent P/Invoke declaration.

```
[DllImport("coredll.dll")]
public static extern
void GlobalMemoryStatus(ref MEMORYSTATUS lpBuffer);
```

The sole parameter has the type `LPMEMORYSTATUS`, a pointer to a `MEMORYSTATUS` structure. Both of these types—the structure and the pointer to the structure—are defined as follows.

```
typedef struct _MEMORYSTATUS {
DWORD dwLength;
DWORD dwMemoryLoad;
DWORD dwTotalPhys;
```

```
DWORD dwAvailPhys;
DWORD dwTotalPageFile;
DWORD dwAvailPageFile;
DWORD dwTotalVirtual;
DWORD dwAvailVirtual;
} MEMORYSTATUS, *LPMEMORYSTATUS;
```

This declaration defines a structure type named `MEMORYSTATUS` and a pointer type to that structure named `LPMEMORYSTATUS`.

Win32 Pointers and Hungarian Naming

Hungarian naming is a convention used through the definition of Win32 types, as well as by Win32 programmers when writing code. (We also use Hungarian naming in our .NET Compact Framework programming; for details, see Appendix A.) Among other things, Hungarian naming uses prefixes as reminders of type information. The `LP` prefix, for example, stands for "pointer." (It actually stands for "long pointer," a throwback to the days when Windows programmers used both long and short pointers on the segmented memory of early Intel x86 processors.)

The P/Invoke Wizard creates the following C# definition for the `MEMORYSTATUS` structure.

```
public struct MEMORYSTATUS
{
   public int dwLength;
   public int dwMemoryLoad;
   public int dwTotalPhys;
   public int dwAvailPhys;
   public int dwTotalPageFile;
   public int dwAvailPageFile;
   public int dwTotalVirtual;
   public int dwAvailVirtual;
};
```

The first element in this structure, `dwLength`, must be set to the size of the structure before the call to the `GlobalMemoryStatus` function.

After declaring this data structure, you then allocate and initialize the MEMORYSTATUS structure:

```
MEMORYSTATUS ms = new MEMORYSTATUS();
ms.dwLength = Marshal.SizeOf(ms);
```

As occurs so often for Win32 functions, we set a member of the structure—dwLength—to the size of the structure we are passing. To get the structure size, we rely on a static method in the Marshal[13] class: SizeOf. Once the dwLength field has been initialized, we can then call the GlobalMemoryStatus function. Listing 4.3 shows the complete source code for our .NET program that allocates the needed data structure, calls the Win32 function, and reports the results in a message box. An example of the output appears in Figure 4.3.

LISTING 4.3: Using P/Invoke in the MemoryStatus Function to Pass Structures That Contain Simple Types

```
// Program Name: MemoryStatus.exe
//
// File Name: MemoryStatus.cpp - Displays system memory status
// by calling a Win32 function and passing a pointer to a data
// structure.
//
// Code from _.NET Compact Framework Programming with C#_
// and _.NET Compact Framework Programming with Visual Basic .NET_
// Authored by Paul Yao and David Durant.
//

using System;
using System.Text;
using System.Runtime.InteropServices;
using System.Windows.Forms;

namespace MemoryStatus
{
   public class MemoryStatus
   {
      [DllImport("coredll.dll")]
      public static extern
      void GlobalMemoryStatus(ref MEMORYSTATUS lpBuffer);
```

13. Fully qualified name: System.Runtime.InteropServices.Marshal.

```
        public struct MEMORYSTATUS
        {
            public int dwLength;
            public int dwMemoryLoad;
            public int dwTotalPhys;
            public int dwAvailPhys;
            public int dwTotalPageFile;
            public int dwAvailPageFile;
            public int dwTotalVirtual;
            public int dwAvailVirtual;
        };
        const string CRLF = "\r\n";

        public static void Main()
        {
            MEMORYSTATUS ms = new MEMORYSTATUS();
            ms.dwLength = Marshal.SizeOf(ms);
            GlobalMemoryStatus(ref ms);

            string strAppName = "Memory Status";

            StringBuilder sbMessage = new StringBuilder();
            sbMessage.Append("Memory Load = ");
            sbMessage.Append(ms.dwMemoryLoad.ToString() + "%");
            sbMessage.Append(CRLF);
            sbMessage.Append("Total RAM = ");
            sbMessage.Append(ms.dwTotalPhys.ToString("#,##0"));
            sbMessage.Append(CRLF);
            sbMessage.Append("Avail RAM = ");
            sbMessage.Append(ms.dwAvailPhys.ToString("#,##0"));
            sbMessage.Append(CRLF);
            sbMessage.Append("Total Page = ");
            sbMessage.Append(ms.dwTotalPageFile.ToString("#,##0"));
            sbMessage.Append(CRLF);
            sbMessage.Append("Avail Page = ");
            sbMessage.Append(ms.dwAvailPageFile.ToString("#,##0"));
            sbMessage.Append(CRLF);
            sbMessage.Append("Total Virt = ");
            sbMessage.Append(ms.dwTotalVirtual.ToString("#,##0"));
            sbMessage.Append(CRLF);
            sbMessage.Append("Avail Virt = ");
            sbMessage.Append(ms.dwAvailVirtual.ToString("#,##0"));

            MessageBox.Show(sbMessage.ToString(), strAppName);
        }
    }
}
```

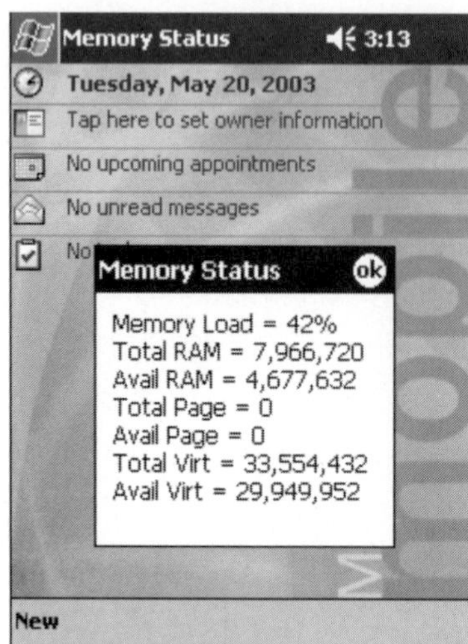

FIGURE 4.3: Results of a call to the `GlobalMemoryStatus` function

Type of Types versus Type of Parameters

As far as data types and parameter passing, there are two related but different concepts to keep straight. One concept deals with value type versus reference type. Another concept deals with passing by-value parameters versus passing by-reference parameters. The two topics are related (hence the similar names), but they are different.

Value types are often passed by value. This means that a complete copy gets put on the stack, and the called method can make any change without affecting the original. But be careful! Large structures passed by value involve a lot of copying. In such a case, it might make sense to pass the value type by reference.

Reference types are often passed by value as well. But what gets passed is a pointer to the object itself, not a copy of the object. Any change made by the called method is reflected in what the caller sees automatically. Reference types are very rarely passed by reference because that would mean passing a pointer to a pointer. Strings and arrays, which are both reference types, are normally by-value parameters.[14]

14. We say "normally" because it is possible to pass a string by reference, in which case there are two levels of indirection—a pointer to a pointer to the string. An array can also be passed by reference, which creates a pointer to a pointer to the array.

As we discussed earlier in this chapter, strings are a special case. When passed as parameters, they are more like value types—if the called method makes a change to the string, that value is not reflected in the caller's copy because strings are immutable. When passing a string to a method that might change the string, you may want to pass the string by reference instead of by value. This is one of the few uses of passing a reference type by reference.

The difference between value types and reference types becomes important when you wish to pass a parameter to a method. This is important whether or not the method resides in managed code. In other words, you must pay attention to this distinction whether you are creating a P/Invoke declaration to call a function in unmanaged code or writing a managed-code method. Both value types and reference types can be passed as parameters, but the declarations are different for each.

Value Types as Parameters

Value types are allocated on the stack (what C programmers call *local variables*). Value types that are 32 bits and smaller are normally passed by value. Larger value types and structures that contain value types are often passed by reference. When a value type is passed by value, a copy of the value is put on the stack. That value makes a one-way trip into the called function, and the local copy of that value is not affected.

When a value type is passed by reference, an implicit pointer is put on the stack. The called function uses that pointer to read the contents of the variable. The called function can also change the contents of a variable, which is why we sometimes say that a by-reference parameter makes a two-way trip—down to the called function, then back again with whatever changes the function has made. The example earlier in this chapter with the `GlobalMemoryStatus` function showed the use of a by-reference parameter to allow a Win32 function to fill in the contents of a `MEMORYSTATUS` structure.

Reference Types as Parameters

Reference types are allocated from the process heap. A reference-type variable contains a pointer that refers to the object. The presence of a pointer in a reference type creates a funny sort of paradox: In P/Invoke declarations, you pass a pointer to a reference type by declaring a by-value parameter. To illustrate this point, here is a different definition for the MEMORYSTATUS structure, using a class instead of a structure.

```
public class MEMORYSTATUS
{
   public int dwLength;
   public int dwMemoryLoad;
   public int dwTotalPhys;
   public int dwAvailPhys;
   public int dwTotalPageFile;
   public int dwAvailPageFile;
   public int dwTotalVirtual;
   public int dwAvailVirtual;
};
```

Declaring MEMORYSTATUS as a class makes it a reference type. To accommodate this object in calls to the GlobalMemoryStatus function, we change the P/Invoke declaration for the function.

```
[DllImport("coredll.dll")]
public static extern
void GlobalMemoryStatus(MEMORYSTATUS lpBuffer);
```

The change involves removing the ref keyword so that the parameter is now a by-value parameter. We must also remove that keyword when we call the function, as shown here.

```
MEMORYSTATUS ms = new MEMORYSTATUS();
ms.dwLength = Marshal.SizeOf(ms);
GlobalMemoryStatus(ms);
```

Arrays

P/Invoke support in the .NET Compact Framework seems to prefer simple data types, and that preference can also be seen with arrays. You can pass an array of simple data types as a P/Invoke parameter. Such an array can have one dimension, two dimensions, or more. You can also pass arrays of structures, as long as the structures contain only simple data types.

Arrays get passed by value and not by reference, which—as in the case with strings described earlier—is somewhat counterintuitive for some programmers. From the .NET perspective, however, arrays are inherently reference types, so it is the value—a pointer—that gets passed. The underlying unmanaged code sees a pointer to the first element of the array, and then it is up to the managed code to figure out what to do with that pointer. Table 4.4 summarizes the supported array types that can be passed to Win32 functions. The table shows that P/Invoke in the .NET Compact Framework supports passing arrays of all types of integers, but not for passing arrays of strings.

When dealing with character data, notice that there are several ways to pass an array of characters to unmanaged code. In the .NET Compact Framework, the `Char []` array can be used to pass an array of Unicode characters. An `SByte []` array can be used to pass non-Unicode characters (sometimes called ANSI, but more correctly referred to as single- and multibyte characters). A `String` implicitly contains a character array, and when we pass a string (which we pass by value), we are passing a pointer

TABLE 4.4: .NET Compact Framework P/Invoke Support for Arrays

.NET Compact Framework Type	Size (Bytes)	C# Alias	Visual Basic Alias	Win32 by-Value Type	Win32 by-Reference Type
`Byte []`	Varies	`byte []`	`Byte ()`	`BYTE *`	Not supported
`Char []`	Varies	`char []`	`Char ()`	`WCHAR *`	Not supported
`SByte []`	Varies	`sbyte []`	N/A	`CHAR *`	Not supported
`Int16 []`	Varies	`short []`	`Short ()`	`INT16 *`	Not supported
`UInt16 []`	Varies	`ushort []`	N/A	`UINT16 *`	Not supported
`Int32 []`	Varies	`int []`	`Integer ()`	`INT32 *`	Not supported
`UInt32 []`	Varies	`uint []`	N/A	`UINT32 *`	Not supported
`String`	Varies	`string`	`String`	`WCHAR *`	Not supported
`String`	Varies	`string []`	`string ()`	Not supported	Not supported

to an array of Unicode characters. While the .NET Compact Framework supports `string` parameters, there is no support for passing an array of strings as a parameter to an unmanaged function.

Example: Passing an Array of Integers

Consider the following C/C++ function, which accepts a pointer to an integer array, adds up the value of each of the integers, and returns this sum to the caller.

```
//----------------------------------------------------------------
// AddEmUp -- Adds up numbers in an integer array
//----------------------------------------------------------------
extern "C"
int __declspec(dllexport) __stdcall
AddEmUp(int * pi, int count)
{
    int i;
    int sum = 0;
    for (i = 0; i < count; i++)
    {
        sum = sum + pi[i];
    }

    return sum;
}
```

The .NET Compact Framework code to declare and call this function appears next.

```
[DllImport("intarray.dll")]
public static extern int AddEmUp(int [] pi, int count);

private void cmdAdd_Click(object sender, System.EventArgs e)
{
      int [] i = new int [] { 1, 2, 3};
      int c = AddEmUp(i, 3);

      MessageBox.Show("AddEmUp = " + c.ToString());
}
```

Just as we pass a string by value, we also pass an array by value. That value is, of course, a pointer to the array being passed. Because we pass a pointer, the parameter makes a two-way trip. Any changes made by the unmanaged code to the contents of the array are reflected in the contents of the array that appears to our managed code.

A Sample Program: `CallWin32`

Support for various data types as parameters might change in a future version of the .NET Compact Framework. For this reason, we wrote a program that calls a custom Win32 DLL with each of the parameters in Table 4.3 both by value and by reference. If a type is not supported, a message box appears to notify you of that fact. Figure 4.4 shows our program in action.

A portion of the source to the calling program, `CallWin32`, appears in Listing 4.4. A fragment of the C++ source code used to create the Win32 DLL appears in the next section in Listing 4.5. You can get the complete source code for both programs at the Web site for the book's code, http://www.paulyao.com/cfbook/code.

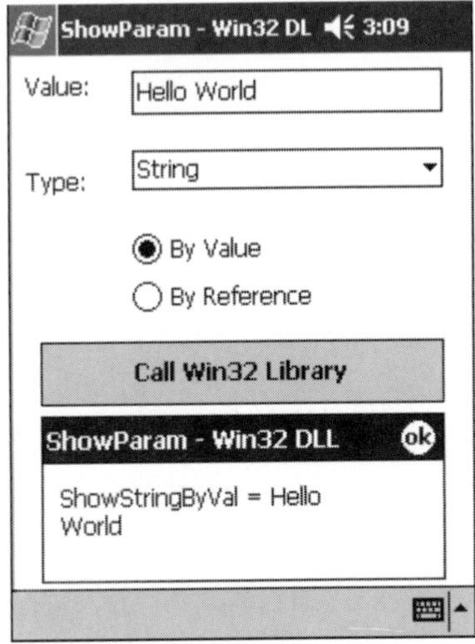

FIGURE 4.4: `CallWin32` **showing a string passed to** `ShowParam.dll`**, an unmanaged DLL**

LISTING 4.4: `CallWin32.cs` Code That Checks for Support in Calls by Reference and by Value

```
// CallWin32.cs - Declarations and functions to call
// Win32 functions in the Win32 library ShowParam.dll
//
// File Location: \YaoDurant\CS\PlatformInvoke\CallWin32
//
// Code from _.NET Compact Framework Programming with C#_
// Authored by Paul Yao and David Durant.
//
//
using System;
using System.Text;
using System.Windows.Forms;
using System.Runtime.InteropServices;

namespace CallWin32
{
   public class CallWin32
   {
      public const string DllName = "ShowParam.dll";

      [DllImport(DllName, CharSet=CharSet.Unicode)]
      public static extern void ShowBooleanByVal(Boolean b);
      [DllImport(DllName, CharSet=CharSet.Unicode)]
      public static extern void ShowBooleanByRef(ref Boolean b);
      [DllImport(DllName, CharSet=CharSet.Unicode)]
      public static extern void ShowByteByVal(Byte val);
      [DllImport(DllName, CharSet=CharSet.Unicode)]
      public static extern void ShowByteByRef(ref Byte val);
      [DllImport(DllName, CharSet=CharSet.Unicode)]
      public static extern void ShowSByteByVal(SByte val);
      [DllImport(DllName, CharSet=CharSet.Unicode)]
      public static extern void ShowSByteByRef(ref SByte val);
      [DllImport(DllName, CharSet=CharSet.Unicode)]
      public static extern void ShowInt16ByVal(Int16 val);
      [DllImport(DllName, CharSet=CharSet.Unicode)]
      public static extern void ShowInt16ByRef(ref Int16 val);
      [DllImport(DllName, CharSet=CharSet.Unicode)]
      public static extern void ShowUInt16ByVal(UInt16 val);
      [DllImport(DllName, CharSet=CharSet.Unicode)]
      public static extern void ShowUInt16ByRef(ref UInt16 val);
      [DllImport(DllName, CharSet=CharSet.Unicode)]
      public static extern void ShowInt32ByVal(Int32 val);
      [DllImport(DllName, CharSet=CharSet.Unicode)]
      public static extern void ShowInt32ByRef(ref Int32 val);
      [DllImport(DllName, CharSet=CharSet.Unicode)]
      public static extern void ShowUInt32ByVal(UInt32 val);
```

```
[DllImport(DllName, CharSet=CharSet.Unicode)]
public static extern void ShowUInt32ByRef(ref UInt32 val);
[DllImport(DllName, CharSet=CharSet.Unicode)]
public static extern void ShowInt64ByVal(Int64 val);
[DllImport(DllName, CharSet=CharSet.Unicode)]
public static extern void ShowInt64ByRef(ref Int64 val);
[DllImport(DllName, CharSet=CharSet.Unicode)]
public static extern void ShowUInt64ByVal(UInt64 val);
[DllImport(DllName, CharSet=CharSet.Unicode)]
public static extern void ShowUInt64ByRef(ref UInt64 val);
[DllImport(DllName, CharSet=CharSet.Unicode)]
public static extern void ShowSingleByVal(float val);
[DllImport(DllName, CharSet=CharSet.Unicode)]
public static extern void ShowSingleByRef(ref float val);
[DllImport(DllName, CharSet=CharSet.Unicode)]
public static extern void ShowDoubleByVal(Double val);
[DllImport(DllName, CharSet=CharSet.Unicode)]
public static extern void ShowDoubleByRef(ref Double val);
[DllImport(DllName, CharSet=CharSet.Unicode)]
public static extern void ShowCharByVal(Char val);
[DllImport(DllName, CharSet=CharSet.Unicode)]
public static extern void ShowCharByRef(ref Char val);
[DllImport(DllName, CharSet=CharSet.Unicode)]
public static extern void ShowStringByVal(String val);
[DllImport(DllName, CharSet=CharSet.Unicode)]
public static extern void ShowStringByRef(ref String val);
[DllImport(DllName, CharSet=CharSet.Unicode)]
public static extern
void ShowStringByVal(StringBuilder val);
[DllImport(DllName, CharSet=CharSet.Unicode)]
public static extern
void ShowStringByRef(ref StringBuilder val);

public static void
CallWin32Lib(String strVal, String strType, Boolean bByRef)
{
   //
   // User selection -- Boolean
   //
   if (strType == "Boolean")
   {
      Boolean b;
      if (strVal == "true") b = true;
      else if (strVal == "false") b = false;
      else
      {
         MessageBox.Show("Boolean needs true or false",
            frmMain.strApp);
```

continues

continued

```
                return;
            }
            if (bByRef)
            {
                ShowBooleanByRef(ref b);
            }
            else
            {
                ShowBooleanByVal(b);
            }
        }
        //
        // User selection -- Byte
        //
        else if (strType == "Byte")
        {
            Byte bytVal = Byte.Parse(strVal);
            if (bByRef)
            {
                ShowByteByRef(ref bytVal);
            }
            else
            {
                ShowByteByVal(bytVal);
            }
        }

        //...
        // Portion omitted from book text
        // ...

    }
  }
}
```

Writing Win32 Dynamic Link Libraries

Up to now, we have discussed how to write .NET code that calls Win32 code. But you might need to write a Win32 DLL that you can call using P/Invoke wrappers. This section covers the basics of how you can make this happen.

Development Tools

To create a Win32 DLL, you need the eMbedded Visual C++ development environment. This is available as a free download from the Microsoft Web site. You need this because Visual Studio .NET 2003 cannot build unmanaged executable files for Windows CE (although the same tool does a great job building unmanaged executables for desktop versions of Windows). Until we get an upgrade to Visual Studio .NET that can build unmanaged code for Windows CE, we must rely on eMbedded Visual C++ to build executable programs and DLLs.

Installing Unmanaged DLLs in Windows CE

Windows CE contains a large number of unmanaged DLLs, which you can access from the .NET Compact Framework by using P/Invoke. At times, you will want to call a DLL that is not already part of Windows CE. Whether you want to test a new DLL on a new smart device or test the DLL in the emulator, Visual Studio .NET can help. You can add an unmanaged DLL to a .NET Compact Framework project, and Visual Studio .NET can then copy the DLL to your smart device (or to the emulator). Here are the steps you follow to make this happen.

Open the Visual Studio .NET Solution Explorer. In the Solution Explorer, summon a pop-up menu with a right-click on the project name. Select the Add→Add Existing Item... menu item, and then browse the file system for your DLL file name. Visual Studio .NET makes a copy of your DLL to the project directory. When working with a DLL that is changing, we add a post-build entry in the eMbedded Visual C++ project to copy the target DLL to the Visual Studio .NET project directory. You can see an example of this post-build copying by opening the `ShowParam.dll` project from within the eMbedded Visual C++ development environment.

The eMbedded Visual C++ environment was created from Microsoft Visual Studio version 6.0. Programmers who are familiar with this older Microsoft development environment will find much that is familiar with the embedded tools. In the early days of Windows programming, you had a lot of work ahead of you when you wanted to build a DLL because the tools were geared toward creating applications. Today, the starting point for a DLL can be created and built with just a few mouse clicks. The challenge in creating DLLs today is in making sure you use the correct declarations for the functions you wish to define, and that is the focus of our discussion.

Declaring C++ Functions in a DLL

One challenge to writing your own unmanaged DLLs is that you can use two languages: C and C++. Each language has its issues, but to simplify things we are going to assume you are using C++. The compiler uses the file extension to determine what language you are using; an extension of `.c` means C language, and an extension of `.cpp` means C++. When porting older, C language source code, change the file name extension and rebuild to make your code conform to the declarations we describe here.

We should also mention that our focus here is on declaring public, exported DLL functions. By default, functions in a DLL are private. UNIX programmers may notice that this differs from how functions are handled in UNIX shared libraries, where all functions are public. In all versions of Windows, a function in a DLL is private unless it is exported. Only exported functions are visible to the outside world, which in the present context means the managed code of .NET Compact Framework applications and .NET Compact Framework DLLs.

The best way to understand the details of function declarations is to study an example. The following function, `ShowInt32ByVal`, was taken from the `ShowParam` example. It shows all of the elements needed to declare an exported C++ function in a DLL.

```
extern "C"  __declspec(dllexport)
void WINAPI ShowInt32ByVal(LONG val)
{
    WCHAR wch[128];
    wsprintf(wch, L"ShowInt32ByVal = %d", val);
    MessageBoxW(NULL, wch, pLibName, 0);
}
```

The `extern "C"` portion of the first line tells the C++ compiler to turn off *name mangling* (sometimes known as *name decorating*), which enables the overloading of function names in your C++ programs. While name mangling is helpful when writing C++ code called by other C++ code, it gets in the way of writing C++ code that can be called from managed code. The `ShowInt32ByVal` function, for example, is renamed to `?ShowInt32ByVal@@YAXJ@Z` without the `extern` declaration (underscoring why this is called *name mangling*).

The `__declspec(dllexport)` portion of the first line tells the C++ compiler to export a function. This is needed because by default all functions are private and hidden. Exporting a function makes it visible—and therefore callable—from outside the DLL.

The `WINAPI` declaration is also needed, but it hides an important element, the calling convention. The calling convention is important because if you use the wrong one, the function call is guaranteed to fail. It is a frustrating experience to spin your wheels trying to figure out why a function has failed, only to discover that you are using the wrong calling convention.

The calling convention describes how the compiler passes parameters between functions and also who cleans up the stack after a function call. In older Windows code, you sometimes see the `PASCAL` keyword as a reminder of the calling convention used in 16-bit Windows. (Some people thought this meant that Microsoft had implemented Windows in Pascal—an odd idea because Borland, an archrival to Microsoft, had the better Pascal compiler.) The two calling conventions that are interesting to Win32 programmers are represented by the declarations `CDECL` and `STDCALL` (portable aliases for the compiler's native `__cdecl` and `__stdcall` declarations).

Here is where the desktop and the device diverge. The standard for Win32 function calls on the desktop is the `STDCALL` calling convention, whereas on Windows CE the standard calling convention is `CDECL`. To allow for the creation of Win32 code that is portable between these two environments, Microsoft provides the `WINAPI` calling convention declaration. On the desktop, this is defined as `STDCALL`, and under Windows CE that declaration is defined as `CDECL`.

Listing 4.5 contains the source code for `ShowParam.cpp`, the DLL called in the CallWin32 sample presented earlier in this chapter.

LISTING 4.5: `ShowParam.cpp` Code That Displays Values Called by Reference and by Value

```
// ShowParam.cpp - Display various .NET data types both
// by reference and by value.
//
// File Location: \YaoDurant\CPP\PlatformInvoke\ShowParam
//
// Code from _.NET Compact Framework Programming with C#_
// Authored by Paul Yao and David Durant.
//

#include "stdafx.h"
#include "showparam.h"

LPWSTR pLibName = L"ShowParam - Win32 DLL";

BOOL APIENTRY
DllMain(HANDLE hModule,
         DWORD  ul_reason_for_call,
         LPVOID lpReserved)
{
    return TRUE;
}

//
// ShowBooleanByVal - Display Boolean value passed by value.
//
extern "C" __declspec(dllexport)
void WINAPI ShowBooleanByVal(BYTE val)
{
    WCHAR wch[128];
    wsprintf(wch, L"BoolByVal = %d", val);
    MessageBoxW(NULL, wch, pLibName, 0);
}

//
// ShowBooleanByRef - Display Boolean value passed by reference.
//
extern "C" __declspec(dllexport)
void WINAPI ShowBooleanByRef(BYTE * val)
{
    WCHAR wch[128];
    wsprintf(wch, L"BoolByRef = %d", *val);
    MessageBoxW(NULL, wch, pLibName, 0);
}

//
// ShowByteByVal - Display Byte value passed by value.
```

```
//
extern "C" __declspec(dllexport)
void WINAPI ShowByteByVal(BYTE val)
{
    WCHAR wch[128];
    wsprintf(wch, L"ShowByteByVal = %d", val);
    MessageBoxW(NULL, wch, pLibName, 0);
}

//
// ShowByteByRef - Display Byte value passed by reference.
//
extern "C" __declspec(dllexport)
void WINAPI ShowByteByRef(BYTE * val)
{
    WCHAR wch[128];
    wsprintf(wch, L"ShowByteByRef = %d", *val);
    MessageBoxW(NULL, wch, pLibName, 0);
}

// ...
// Portion omitted from book text
// ...
```

Manual P/Invoke Parameter Passing

As we have shown, the built-in support for calling into unmanaged code in the .NET Compact Framework is reasonable, but it has limits. You hit those limits when you deal with pointers to structures—especially when a structure contains reference types or arrays. You also hit those limits when you call functions that return linked lists, arrays of arbitrary size, or any of a dozen other cases.

To address these more complex parameter types, you need a more sophisticated way to pass parameters. These techniques require more work because you control specific details of how data gets sent to and retrieved from function calls that cross the managed/unmanaged boundary. There are two elements to these techniques: the `IntPtr` data type and the `Marshal` class.

Previously we have used `IntPtr` for handles, an artifact of the Win32 API used by the operating system as "magic" numbers to identify system objects. `IntPtr` provides another form of magic: holding unmanaged pointers. (You can hold pointers but not do pointer arithmetic; for that, a conversion to an integer type is required.) This data type is important, but not quite enough to bridge the gap between the managed and unmanaged worlds.

As mentioned, the other element needed is the `Marshal` class. This class contains a variety of static methods. Some of these methods copy data from managed data into unmanaged memory, while other methods create new managed objects from an unmanaged memory pointer. The `Marshal` class resides in the `System.Runtime.InteropServices` namespace, which is also the home of the `DllImport` attribute used to declare P/Invoke functions.

When digging into the low-level details of marshaling, a final item you must address is the direction of each parameter. As mentioned earlier in this chapter, the online documentation for the Win32 API describes three directional attributes: `[in]`, `[out]`, and both combined as `[in][out]`. Simple data types that are passed as parameters are almost always `[in]`-parameters: they get sent to and used by the called function. Parameters that pass a pointer can support any of these three directions, and you must pay careful attention when manually setting up marshaling.

We refer to built-in parameter marshaling as *automatic parameter marshaling* because almost all of the work is done for you. We refer to the more involved kind of parameter passing as *manual parameter marshaling*. (Automobile enthusiasts might notice a parallel between automatic transmission and manual transmission, although this distinction is probably lost on younger drivers who have never driven a manual transmission car or those lucky souls who never learned to drive, such as some residents of New York City whom we know!)

The `Marshal` Class

The `Marshal` class supports copying data from managed memory into unmanaged memory and from unmanaged memory to managed memory. If you study the online MSDN Library, you will see that the desktop .NET Framework supported methods in this class that allocate unmanaged memory and other methods that work with COM objects. None of the memory management or COM support methods are present in the .NET Compact Framework's implementation of `Marshal`. Table 4.5 summarizes the members of the `Marshal` class that are supported by the .NET Compact

TABLE 4.5: `Marshal` Class Members Supported by the .NET Compact Framework

`Marshal` Member	Description
Copy between Managed and Unmanaged	
`Copy`	Copies value-type arrays between managed and unmanaged memory. Supports CLI integer types, including 64-bit integers. Supports single- and double-precision floating-point numbers. Has 14 overloaded methods (7 copy to managed memory; 7 copy to unmanaged memory).
Copy to Unmanaged Memory	
`StructureToPtr`	Copies managed objects to unmanaged memory.
`WriteByte`	Writes 1 byte to unmanaged memory.
`WriteInt16`	Writes 2 bytes to unmanaged memory.
`WriteInt32`	Writes 4 bytes to unmanaged memory
Copy to Managed Memory	
`PtrToStringUni`	Creates a managed string from the contents of unmanaged memory.
`PtrToStructure`	Creates an object from the contents of unmanaged memory.
`ReadByte`	Reads 1 byte from unmanaged memory.
`ReadInt16`	Read 2 bytes from unmanaged memory.
`ReadInt32`	Read 4 bytes from unmanaged memory.
Informational	
`IsComObject`	Is hard-coded to return `false`.
`SizeOf`	Queries the unmanaged size of an object instance. Used to set structure size fields needed by some Win32 function calls.
`GetLastWin32Error`	Calls the `GetLastError` function to fetch Win32 error code.
`SystemDefaultCharSize`	Read-only field for the size of characters in the default character set. (Returns `2` in .NET Compact Framework.) For portability.

Framework: 13 method names (which have one or more overloaded versions) and 1 read-only field.

Some of the methods in the `Marshal` class let you write to unmanaged buffers, which you can then pass as parameters to unmanaged functions. Other methods from this class let you read values out of an unmanaged buffer into managed data objects. Both writing to and reading from buffers is important because the Win32 API (along with many other C-oriented APIs) makes extensive use of buffers to communicate from a caller to a called function.

This list does not include any functions for allocating unmanaged memory. The following memory allocation functions are described in the MSDN Library and supported in the desktop .NET Framework but are not supported in the .NET Compact Framework:

- `AllocHGlobal`
- `FreeHGlobal`
- `AllocCoTaskMem`
- `FreeCoTaskMem`

You need to have some unmanaged memory before you can read from or write to managed memory. Before digging into the `Marshal` class's memory copy methods, we need to see how a .NET Compact Framework programmer handles memory allocation.

Allocating Unmanaged Memory

We call it "unmanaged" memory because the runtime's garbage collector does not manage the memory. Instead, you must manage memory that you allocate, which means freeing the memory when you are done using it. Failure to free the memory causes a memory leak. When you get enough memory leaks, your program—or the operating system itself—could crash. You must take care to free any memory that you allocate. (For a summary of Win32 functions that allocate memory and the associated cleanup functions, see Appendix D.)

You are responsible for freeing any memory that you allocate, so you need to exercise a degree of discipline to get the job done right. When we write code that allocates memory, we always write the code that frees the memory immediately after writing the code that allocates it. We then check to make sure that we free the memory for every possible code path, not just the successful cases but also, more importantly, when an error condition occurs. This level of effort is required to avoid memory leaks, a major problem of the Win32 API (and a reason why the .NET initiative is so important; managed memory is managed automatically for you).

To allocate unmanaged memory in the .NET Compact Framework, you have to call the Win32 allocation functions. There are several functions to choose from, including the following:

- Private page allocator: `VirtualAlloc`, `VirtualFree`
- Shared page allocator: `MapViewOfFiles`
- Heap allocator: `HeapCreate`, `HeapAlloc`
- Local allocator: `LocalAlloc`, `LocalFree`
- COM allocator: `CoTaskMemAlloc`, `CoTaskMemFree`

Each memory type has an appropriate use, and you can choose an allocator by creating the corresponding P/Invoke declaration. We use the last two types—the local allocator and the COM allocator—to implement the four memory allocation functions defined in the `Marshal` class but not implemented by the .NET Compact Framework. We chose these functions to help port .NET code from the desktop to smart devices. Listing 4.6 contains the source code for the `YaoDurant.Allocator.Marshal` class, which implements the four allocation functions. We leave it up to you to fold this class into your own functions, or you can cut and paste the code as needed in your own projects.

LISTING 4.6: `Marshal.cs` Code That Provides Two Ways to Allocate Unmanaged Memory

```
using System;
using System.Data;
using System.Runtime.InteropServices;

namespace YaoDurant.Allocator
{
   /// <summary>
```

continues

continued

```
/// Summary description for Class1.
/// </summary>
public class Marshal
{
   public Marshal()
   {
      //
      // TODO: Add constructor logic here
      //
   }

   //-------------------------------------------------------------
   // Allocate / free COM memory
   //-------------------------------------------------------------
   [DllImport("ole32.dll")]
   public static extern IntPtr CoTaskMemAlloc(int cb);

   [DllImport("ole32.dll")]
   public static extern void CoTaskMemFree(IntPtr pv);


   public static IntPtr AllocCoTaskMem(int cb)
   {
      return CoTaskMemAlloc(cb);
   }
   public static void FreeCoTaskMem(IntPtr ptr)
   {
      CoTaskMemFree(ptr);
   }

   //-------------------------------------------------------------
   // Allocate / free regular heap memory
   //-------------------------------------------------------------
   [DllImport("coredll.dll")]
   public static extern IntPtr
   LocalAlloc(int fuFlags, int cbBytes);

   public const int LMEM_FIXED = 0x0000;
   public const int LMEM_ZEROINIT = 0x0040;

   public static IntPtr AllocHGlobal(int cb)
   {
      return LocalAlloc(LMEM_FIXED | LMEM_ZEROINIT, cb);
   }

   public static IntPtr AllocHGlobal(IntPtr cb)
   {
```

```
            return AllocHGlobal(cb.ToInt32());
        }

        [DllImport("coredll.dll")]
        public static extern IntPtr LocalFree(IntPtr hMem);

        public static void FreeHGlobal(IntPtr hglobal)
        {
            LocalFree(hglobal);
        }

    } // class
} // namespace
```

There are two allocator functions in Listing 4.6: one for regular heap memory (`AllocHGlobal`) and one for the COM shared component allocator function (`CoTaskMemAlloc`). In most cases, you use the regular heap allocator. The COM allocator allows one component to allocate some memory that another component frees.

Longtime fans of the Win32 API might wonder why we call the `LocalAlloc` function for the regular heap memory and not the `GlobalAlloc` function. These two functions were quite different in the age of the dinosaurs (meaning, of course, when 16-bit Windows ruled the world), but differences between these two sets of functions disappeared in the Win32 API. Because of this redundancy, the global allocator is not supported on Windows CE, leaving the local allocator as the lone survivor of the prehistoric allocators.

Copying to Unmanaged Memory

Many parameters to unmanaged functions are simple value types passed by value. Some value types are passed by reference. For both cases, the .NET Compact Framework's built-in P/Invoke support is sufficient. A by-reference value-type parameter causes a pointer to get sent to unmanaged code, but the .NET Compact Framework knows how to create these implicit pointers. The .NET Compact Framework can even handle many structures, as long as the structure contains only simple value types. Such structures are sent as by-value parameters, which causes a pointer to get sent to unmanaged code.[15] These are all the built-in cases where the .NET Compact Framework does all the work without the need to use `IntPtr` and `Marshal`.

When dealing with manual parameter passing, when the parameter direction is `[in]` or `[in][out]`, you must initialize the unmanaged memory by copying values to the memory before calling the target function. In this subsection, we talk about copying to unmanaged memory.

To get some data into unmanaged memory, you first allocate an unmanaged buffer and store the resulting pointer in an `IntPtr`. You next call a member of the `Marshal` class to copy the data to the buffer. Then you pass the pointer to the unmanaged function. The final step is to free the allocated memory.

By way of example, let us redefine the `MessageBox` function to accept an `IntPtr` for the caption (instead of `String` as in earlier examples). To keep things simple, we change one of the two `String` parameters, the caption:

```
// MessageBox with an IntPtr caption
[DllImport("coredll.dll")]
public static extern int
MessageBox(int hWnd, String lpText, IntPtr lpCaption,
   UInt32 uType);
```

Notice that the `IntPtr` parameter is a by-value parameter. The code to call this function in response to a button click appears in Listing 4.7.

LISTING 4.7: Calling the Unmanaged `MessageBox` Function

```
private void button1_Click(object sender, System.EventArgs e)
{
   // Create strings.
   string strCaption = "Caption";
   string strText = "Text";

   // Get count of characters in string.
   int cch = strCaption.Length;
```

15. Passing a structure by reference generates a pointer to a pointer; this is not used often, but it can be used, e.g., when an unmanaged function allocates the memory and returns an array of structures.

```
    // Create a character array from the string.
    char[] achCaption = new char[cch];
    strCaption.CopyTo(0, achCaption, 0, cch);

    // Allocate unmanaged buffer.
    IntPtr ipCaption = AllocHGlobal((cch+1) *
                       Marshal.SystemDefaultCharSize);

    if (! ipCaption.Equals(IntPtr.Zero))
    {
       // Copy the characters to the unmanaged buffer.
       Marshal.Copy(achCaption, 0, ipCaption, cch);

       MessageBox(IntPtr.Zero, strText, ipCaption, 0);

       FreeHGlobal(ipCaption);
    }
}
```

The code shows the four steps you always follow when using `IntPtr` and `Marshal` to send parameter data to an unmanaged function:

1. *Allocate the memory.* The memory allocation is performed by calling the `AllocHGlobal` function, which we wrote earlier to wrap the Win32 `LocalAlloc` memory allocator function.
2. *Copy data to that memory.* We copy the data to that memory by calling the `Marshal.Copy` method.
3. *Pass the pointer as a function parameter,* which in our example is the third parameter to the `MessageBox` function. Notice that we need a different P/Invoke declaration for the `MessageBox` function than we encountered before: one with an `IntPtr` as the third parameter.
4. *Free the memory,* which we do by calling the `FreeHGlobal` function, our wrapper for the `LocalFree` function.

We might need another step if the called function wrote any values to the buffer. The additional step—after step 3 and before step 4—would be to copy those values from the buffer to managed memory.

We do not need to do this to pass a string to an unmanaged function, of course. But this same approach works on any kind of array to handle manual parameter marshaling. A string, after all, is just an array of characters. In Windows CE, of course, that means an array of 2-byte Unicode characters.

Marshaling of the `String` Class

In the desktop .NET Framework, strings are marshaled automatically using a technique similar to the one shown here—memory is allocated and the string copied to that memory. By contrast, automatic string marshaling in the .NET Compact Framework involves no extra memory and no copying, so it is faster and uses less memory. In the .NET Compact Framework, unmanaged functions get a pointer to the managed string's internal memory.

Creating Objects from Unmanaged Memory

When you work with a manual parameter passing with a direction of `[in][out]` or `[out]`, the called function writes some data to unmanaged memory. To retrieve that data, you create a managed object from the unmanaged memory.

When calling a Win32 function that accepts a pointer as a parameter, the caller allocates the buffer.[16] This is a standard used in every part of the Win32 API. When we teach Windows programming classes, we notice that programmers new to Win32 often stumble over this issue. With practice, any programmer can master this style of function call.

When a returned structure contains only simple value types, the automatic P/Invoke support can copy values to a managed structure for you. You must manually create a managed object when the structure contains an array, a string, a pointer, or any other reference type. The `FindMemoryCard` example takes the memory returned from calls to unmanaged functions and shows how to use various static methods from the `Marshal` class to assemble a managed-code object.

---

16. Win32 function parameters with double indirection—a pointer to a pointer—involve the called function allocating the buffer. This is rare because normally the caller—not the called function—allocates the buffer. Two examples of a called function allocating a buffer are the RAPI functions `CeFindAllFiles` and `CeFindAllDatabases`, discussed in Chapter 14.

***Example:* `FindMemoryCard`**

As we discuss in Chapter 11, the primary storage area for every Windows CE system is the *object store*, which among other things contains a RAM-based file system. The file system has much in common with the file system of desktop Windows: a hierarchical structure consisting of directories and files, support for long file names, and the same maximum path size (260 characters). Because the object store is in volatile RAM, battery-operated smart devices normally have a backup battery to prevent catastrophic data loss.

To supplement the object store, many Windows CE devices have nonvolatile storage.[17] For example, Pocket PCs often have a slot for a Compact Flash memory card and/or a Secure Digital card (also known as a Multimedia Memory Card). Many of the Smartphones built on Microsoft Windows Mobile technology have a Secure Digital card slot. Other storage devices that can be attached to a Windows CE–powered device include hard drives, floppy diskette drives, and writable CD drives.

Unlike desktop Windows, which might have a C: drive and a D: drive, Windows CE does not use letters to distinguish file systems from each other. Instead, an installable file system gets installed as a directory in the file system's root directory. For example, we often encounter `\Storage Card` as the root directory for a Compact Flash storage card. You read and write directories and files on the storage device by including this root directory in the path strings that you pass to the various file access functions. Thus, to create a file named `data.dat` in the root directory of the previously named Compact Flash memory card, you create a file named `\Storage Card\data.dat`.

However, not all storage devices use the root `\Storage Card`. To determine whether any installed file systems exist and if so what name is the root, you call the following Win32 functions:

- `FindFirstFlashCard`
- `FindNextFlashCard`

---

17. This Windows CE feature is called *installable file systems* in the Platform Builder documentation and *mountable file system* in the Pocket PC documentation.

These functions fill a structure named WIN32_FIND_DATA, which, incidentally, is the same structure filled by the general-purpose Win32 file system enumeration functions, FindFirstFile and FindNextFile. The data structure is defined as follows.

```
typedef struct _WIN32_FIND_DATA {
DWORD dwFileAttributes;
FILETIME ftCreationTime;
FILETIME ftLastAccessTime;
FILETIME ftLastWriteTime;
DWORD nFileSizeHigh;
DWORD nFileSizeLow;
DWORD dwOID;
TCHAR cFileName[MAX_PATH];
} WIN32_FIND_DATA;
```

The WIN32_FIND_DATA structure contains four elements that make it impossible to use automatic parameter marshaling: the three FILETIME values and a character array. Our example calls each of the two Win32 functions using unmanaged memory that has been allocated with a call to the LocalAlloc function. A call is then made to a function that walks the unmanaged memory block, copying values to a structure that provides the managed-code equivalent to the unmanaged data structure, shown here.

```
public struct WIN32_FIND_DATA
{
   public int dwFileAttributes;
   public FILETIME ftCreationTime;
   public FILETIME ftLastAccessTime;
   public FILETIME ftLastWriteTime;
   public int nFileSizeHigh;
   public int nFileSizeLow;
   public int dwOID;
   public String cFileName;
};
```

For each element in this structure, the conversion function reads a value, then increments the pointer in preparation for reading the next value. The conversion function shown in Listing 4.8 assumes that the IntPtr parameter, pIn, has a pointer that points to unmanaged memory. It also assumes that the output is getting sent to an already instantiated managed object of type WIN32_FIND_DATA. Because we like reusing code, we wrote this function so that you could also use it when calling the generic Win32 file system enumeration functions (FindFirstFile and FindNextFile).

LISTING 4.8: Converting Unmanaged Data to a Managed Structure

```
private static void
CopyIntPtr_to_WIN32_FIND_DATA(IntPtr pIn,
   ref WIN32_FIND_DATA pffd)
{
   // Handy values for incrementing IntPtr pointer.
   int i = 0;
   int cbInt = Marshal.SizeOf(i);
   FILETIME ft = new FILETIME();
   int cbFT = Marshal.SizeOf(ft);

   // int dwFileAttributes
   pffd.dwFileAttributes = Marshal.ReadInt32(pIn);
   pIn = (IntPtr)((int)pIn + cbInt);

   // FILETIME ftCreationTime;
   Marshal.PtrToStructure(pIn, pffd.ftCreationTime);
   pIn = (IntPtr)((int)pIn + cbFT);

   // FILETIME ftLastAccessTime;
   Marshal.PtrToStructure(pIn, pffd.ftLastAccessTime);
   pIn = (IntPtr)((int)pIn + cbFT);

   // FILETIME ftLastWriteTime;
   Marshal.PtrToStructure(pIn, pffd.ftLastWriteTime);
   pIn = (IntPtr)((int)pIn + cbFT);

   // int nFileSizeHigh;
   pffd.nFileSizeHigh = Marshal.ReadInt32(pIn);
   pIn = (IntPtr)((int)pIn + cbInt);

   // int nFileSizeLow;
   pffd.nFileSizeLow = Marshal.ReadInt32(pIn);
   pIn = (IntPtr)((int)pIn + cbInt);

   // int dwOID;
   pffd.dwOID = Marshal.ReadInt32(pIn);
   pIn = (IntPtr)((int)pIn + cbInt);

   // String cFileName;
   pffd.cFileName = Marshal.PtrToStringUni(pIn);
}
```

Communicating between Unmanaged and Managed Code

P/Invoke supports one-way function calls, from managed code to unmanaged code. This is different from the support found in the .NET Framework, where callback functions are supported (see the upcoming section, Comparing P/Invoke Support, for more details). In this current section, we cover the available mechanisms you can use for communicating the other way—from unmanaged code to managed code.

The `MessageWindow` Class

The .NET Compact Framework team recognized the need for unmanaged code to call managed code. To address this need, the team added the `MessageWindow` class to the .NET Compact Framework. Incidentally, this is one of only five classes included in the .NET Compact Framework but not in the desktop .NET Framework.

If you have never programmed in the Win32 development environment, read the sidebar on `MessageWindow` to learn some beneficial background information related to the use of `MessageWindow` when communicating between unmanaged and managed code.

Because applications written in unmanaged code already use Windows messages for communication, Microsoft wanted the unmanaged-to-managed-code communication to use this known method. The `MessageWindow` class is a wrapper around an empty, invisible Win32 window. Like other Win32 windows, it has a window handle. Using that window handle, unmanaged code can transmit a message into managed code by using either the Win32 `PostMessage` or the Win32 `SendMessage` functions. The result of one of these calls by unmanaged code is the automatic invoking of a `MessageWindow` method, the `WndProc` method, in the managed code. Unmanaged code communicates using its familiar technique, Window messages; managed code communicates using its familiar technique, invocation of methods and access properties of an object.

Using the Win32 message delivery system provides a number of benefits. First, Win32 message delivery is flexible—it can be used when the sender and recipient are on the same thread, when they are on different threads in the same process, and when they are in different processes.

`MessageWindow` as a Win32-Style Class

Win32 programmers do not write code that handles events. Rather, they write *window procedures,* one for each window, that process messages. Whenever a user does something like clicking the mouse or pressing a key, a message is generated and, usually, placed in a queue. These are not MSMQ messages, and they are not placed in an MSMQ queue; this is a separate system message queue that is as old as Windows version 1.01 on the desktop.

When the Win32 messaging system determines that it is time for a message to be processed, the messaging system delivers the message to the appropriate window procedure, that is, the `WinProc` of that window. A message contains four pieces of information, which become parameters of the window procedure: the window handle, the type of message, 16 bits of additional information, and 32 bits of additional information.

Not only does the runtime generate messages but the application itself can also define and generate messages by calling the `SendMessage` and `PostMessage` Win32 functions. Because messages can be defined by applications, addressed to a window, and processed by the window procedure of that window, Win32 applications often use messages for communicating within an application or between applications. Messages can even be used for your choice of a synchronous or asynchronous interaction: a call to the `SendMessage` function causes an in-line call of the window procedure, while a call to the `PostMessage` function places the message in the queue for subsequent processing and returns immediately to the caller.

A second benefit of the Win32 message delivery mechanism is that it is guaranteed to be thread-safe. Threads are the unit of scheduling in Windows CE. When two threads share anything, care must be taken to share cooperatively. A failure to cooperate can result in deadlocks or random failures at random times. When the appropriate safeguards are in place to allow two or more threads to share things without conflict, we say that the resulting code is *thread-safe*. If two threads communicate using only Win32 messages, those two threads are guaranteed to be thread-safe with respect to each other.

You must use `MessageWindow` as a base class for a custom class; it will do you no good to create an instance of a `MessageWindow` object. This is because the `MessageWindow.WndProc` method is not an event handler—it is an already defined method. Therefore, you must override it to specify the message-handling functionality you want. Like a Win32 window procedure that gets passed four parameters (a window handle, a message value, and two parameter values—`wParam` and `lParam`), `MessageWindow.WndProc` is also passed these four parameters, but within a single structure that also contains a by-reference field for specifying a return value.

All calls to the `WndProc` method must be processed; that is, your derived function must call the base class function.

Here is a template for an overridden `WndProc` method.

```
protected override void WndProc(ref Message msg)
{
   switch(msg.Msg)
      {
         // Handle messages sent to this window.
      }

   // Send unhandled messages to the default handler.
   base.WndProc(ref msg);
}
```

A difference between this function and a Win32 window procedure is the parameters—a Win32 window procedure accepts four, while this function has one. That parameter is a reference to a `Message` structure that, as previously mentioned, has the four properties Win32 programmers expect to see, plus one they might not. Here are the five properties:

- `IntPtr HWnd`
- `int Msg`
- `IntPtr WParam`

- `IntPtr LParam`
- `IntPtr Result`

The four expected properties are `HWnd`, `Msg`, `WParam`, and `LParam`. The extra property, `Result`, is for holding the result value from handling a particular message—it is, in other words, the return value.

Table 4.6 shows the steps that must be taken in managed and unmanaged code at design time and at runtime to make this communication technique work.

Other Ways to Communicate between Unmanaged and Managed Code

`MessageWindow` is not the only way to communicate between unmanaged and managed code. Other ways include those listed here.

1. *Call and block*: Perhaps a good name for this approach would be the "bored messenger approach." The managed application calls into unmanaged code and waits for the unmanaged function to return something useful. For frequent calls or lengthy waits, a second thread is needed to avoid hanging the application's user interface. Users may get impatient and may shut down a nonresponsive application.
2. *Point-to-point message queue*: This operating system feature, introduced with Windows CE .NET (version 4.0), provides a service that in other operating systems is called an *anonymous pipe*. (For details, see the `CreateMsgQueue` function in the Win32 documentation.)
3. *Mutex*: A mutex is an operating system object for communicating between threads to enforce single-threaded access to some shared object. The .NET Compact Framework's `System.Threading.Mutex` class provides a wrapper around this object.
4. *Event*: An event is an operating system object that serves as an alarm clock to let one thread wake another thread. The .NET Compact Framework wraps two classes around events: `AutoResetEvent` and `ManualResetEvent`, both in the `System.Threading` namespace.

As you can see, there are quite a few ways that unmanaged code can communicate with managed code. Moving forward, Microsoft has announced

TABLE 4.6: **Steps for Communicating from Unmanaged Code to Managed Code Using the `MessageWindow` Class**

	In Managed Code	In Unmanaged Code
Overview	Derive a class from `MessageWindow`, overriding `WndProc` to respond to messages received from unmanaged code.	Send messages to window created in managed code using regular Win32 message delivery functions.
Initialization	(1) Create an instance of the `MessageWindow`-derived class.	(2) Define a global variable of type `HWND`. Write a startup routine to accept a window handle (of type `HWND`) as an input parameter.
	(3) Use P/Invoke to call the unmanaged-code startup routine mentioned in step 2, passing the object's `HWnd` property as the window handle input parameter.	(4) Receive and store the passed-in window handle.
Calling from unmanaged code to managed code	(6) The object's `WndProc` is now being called. Use the information passed in from unmanaged code and perform the necessary actions. Place a return value in the `Result` field of the parameter structure.	(5) Use the window handle received in step 4 to call a Win32 message delivery function, `SendMessage` or `PostMessage`.
		(7) Examine the contents of `Return` to determine if the call was successful.

that future versions are going to provide even richer support for bridging the gap between managed code and unmanaged code. Even when those new features and provided, the set listed in this section should still prove useful.

Comparing P/Invoke Support

If you are familiar with P/Invoke in the desktop .NET Framework, you need to be aware of differences in the .NET Compact Framework implementation. Some arise from the way that Windows CE itself works, so they are not so much limitations as they are accommodations for this operating system. Other differences reflect a cutback in the support provided by the .NET Compact Framework. It is worth mentioning that differences also arise from how the .NET Compact Framework itself is implemented.

Windows CE–Specific Differences

The first difference from desktop Windows involves character sets—Windows CE supports only Unicode. Windows XP and Windows 2000, on the other hand, support both the ANSI and Unicode character sets. Each Win32 function has two different versions (at least for the functions that take a character string), one for ANSI and a second for Unicode. The ANSI version has a suffix of `A`, and the Unicode version has a suffix of `W`. For example, `MessageBoxA` takes ANSI parameters, and `MessageBoxW` accepts Unicode parameters.

Windows CE is a Unicode-only operating system.[18] In recognition of that fact, the .NET Compact Framework support for P/Invoke supports only Unicode strings.

A second Windows CE–specific difference involves function-calling conventions. On Windows CE a single calling convention is supported: `CDECL`.

Limitations

There are four main differences between the desktop .NET Framework and the .NET Compact Framework that create limitations when working with the .NET Compact Framework, as described briefly in the following subsections.

No Support for COM Interop

The most significant differences from the desktop .NET Framework is that COM interop is not supported in the .NET Compact Framework. This means that if you have a COM component, you cannot directly call that component from .NET Compact Framework code. Aside from rewriting

---

18. To be precise, Windows CE is a predominantly Unicode operating system. Several of the networking functions—those implemented in `wininet.dll`, for example—have both ANSI and Unicode implementations. The Windows socket library is an ANSI-only library.

the component in managed code, one workaround is to write a set of C-callable wrapper functions around your COM component. This is the standard solution that Microsoft suggests for the present. It's worth noting that Microsoft has announced that a future version of the .NET Compact Framework is going to provide more COM interop support.

Another approach is to use the CFCOM interoperability layer from a company called Odyssey Software. This software allows the use of ActiveX controls from .NET Compact Framework programs and the use of COM components from .NET Compact Framework programs.[19]

No Support for Callback Functions

A second difference from the desktop is that P/Invoke in the .NET Compact Framework does not support callback functions.[20] Callback functions are fairly common in the Win32 API. They are used to enumerate objects like fonts (`EnumFonts`) and windows (`EnumWindows`) and support user interface programming as window procedures, dialog box procedures, property sheet procedures, and subclass procedures. Also, items in a `TreeView` control can be sorted by providing an application-specific callback function.

None of these features is directly accessible to a .NET Compact Framework application because callback functions are not supported. Instead you must implement the callback function in a Win32 library.

No Support for the `StructLayout` Attribute

A third difference from the desktop is that the .NET Compact Framework does not support the `StructLayout` attribute. This attribute has two basic uses in the desktop .NET Framework: forcing sequential layout of managed structures and supporting unions.

19. For details, visit the company's Web site at http://www.odysseysoftware.com.

20. Desktop .NET Framework programmers are often surprised to learn that the .NET Framework supports callbacks from unmanaged code to managed code. This is described very well in "Cutting Edge: Windows Hooks in the .NET Framework," an article by Dino Esposito that first appeared in the October 2002 edition of *MSDN Magazine*. This article is available at http://msdn.microsoft.com/msdnmag/issues/02/10/CuttingEdge.

Sequential layout of managed structures is required for the desktop .NET Framework because structures there are reorganized by the common language runtime to optimize memory use. In the .NET Compact Framework, however, all data structures are sequential—so one reason to have `StructLayout` is not even necessary in the .NET Compact Framework. In other words, this change does not matter in this instance.

However, the absence of `StructLayout` does involve the loss of something quite valuable when it comes to unions. A C/C++ union allows you to overlay several different data types in the same memory location. Unions are used in various places; the most well known is probably `VARIANT`—a single structure that holds many different data types for calls to COM Automation servers. Here is a fragment of the union from `VARIANT`.

```
typedef union
{
   unsigned char bVal;
   short iVal;
   long lVal;
   float fltVal;.
   double dblVal;
} VARIANT_FRAGMENT;
```

In the desktop .NET Framework, this could be supported with the following declaration.

```
[StructLayout(LayoutKind.Explicit)]
public struct VARIANT_FRAGMENT
{
   [FieldOffset(0)]public byte bVal;
   [FieldOffset(0)]public short iVal;
   [FieldOffset(0)]public int lVal;
   [FieldOffset(0)]public float fltVal;
   [FieldOffset(0)]public double dblVal;
}
```

This declaration is not valid in the .NET Compact Framework because it does not support the attributes used here—`StructLayout`, `LayoutKind`, and `FieldOffset`. You can get the same result by defining a set of data structures instead of just using one. The big challenge comes from adding extra bytes to match the extra bytes that are often added by a union.

In the example shown, any replacement structure must be as large as the largest element—meaning the 8 bytes required for the C++ `double` type. Here is some sample code to show how to do this for one of the elements in the union.

```
public struct VARIANT_FRAGMENT_BYTE
{
   public byte bVal;
   private byte Reserved1;
   private byte Reserved2;
   private byte Reserved3;
   private byte Reserved4;
   private byte Reserved5;
   private byte Reserved6;
   private byte Reserved7;
}
```

No Support for the `MarshalAs` Attribute

The fourth difference is that the .NET Compact Framework does not support the `MarshalAs` attribute. This attribute lets you specify how you want individual elements to be marshaled. This attribute can be applied to parameters in function definitions, to the return value from a function, and to the members of a data structure.

The lack of support for the `MarshalAs` attribute means that the .NET Compact Framework cannot support strings or other complex objects inside structures that are passed to Win32 functions.

.NET Compact Framework Implementation Details

The final set of differences from the Desktop Framework involves differences that arise from the .NET Compact Framework itself.

To reduce memory usage and allow the system to run faster, strings are marshaled without copying the strings. This means that unmanaged code is allowed to look at the memory inside managed objects. This is quite different from how string marshaling is handled in the desktop .NET Framework, where a copy is made of the string, and changes made in unmanaged code are not seen in managed code. Just the opposite is true in the .NET Compact Framework. Changes made to a string in unmanaged memory—

whether the wrapping managed object is a `String` or a `StringBuilder`—get reflected in the managed data object.

The second difference is that .NET Compact Framework objects have fewer Win32 handles than their desktop counterparts. Table 4.7 lists the desktop objects that contain handles and the .NET Compact Framework objects with handles. As the table shows, only three Win32 handles show up in the .NET Compact Framework—compared to more than a dozen on the desktop. The .NET Compact Framework adds support for `MessageWindow`, the control that creates an invisible window to allow Win32 messages to be sent from unmanaged code to managed code, as we demonstrated in an example earlier in this chapter.

TABLE 4.7: Win32 Handles in Framework Objects

Desktop .NET Framework	.NET Compact Framework
`Mutex.Handle`	`Mutex.Handle`
`AutoResetEvent.Handle`	`AutoResetEvent.Handle`
`ManualResetEvent.Handle`	`ManualResetEvent.Handle`
`Control.Handle`, `TextBox.Handle`, `Label.Handle`, and so on	
`Bitmap.GetHbitmap`	
`Font.ToHFont` method	
`Icon.Handle`	
`Graphics.GetHdc` method	
`Graphics.FromHwnd` method	
`Region.GetHrgn`	
(No .NET Framework equivalent)	`MessageWindow.HWnd`

CONCLUSION

Every programmer who builds a .NET Compact Framework program is going to need P/Invoke sooner or later, probably much more often than do programmers who use the .NET Framework on desktop versions of Windows. If you want to read or write registry values, you need P/Invoke. If you wish to access legacy Win32 DLLs, again you need P/Invoke. If you want to start a program, play a sound, or check for special folder names, you need P/Invoke to help you accomplish these tasks too.

For this reason, while the focus of this book is on using the .NET Compact Framework, when there are useful features in a native library, we do not hesitate to point these out. We assume that, like the programmers we teach in our programming classes, you need to get some job done within a reasonable time frame. As mentioned earlier, our first choice is always to use what the .NET Compact Framework has to offer. Failing that, P/Invoke is there to drill down to whatever legacy Win32 function or third-party DLL you may need to use.

The next part of this book, which includes Chapters 5 through 10, focuses on the elements needed to build the user interface of a .NET Compact Framework program. The .NET Compact Framework provides a set of controls that provide a lot of help in building that interface. Some controls are very familiar to programmers who have done even a small amount of GUI programming, including the `TextBox` control, the `Button` control, and the `ListBox` control. As with other parts of the .NET Compact Framework, the support provided is a subset of that found on the desktop .NET Framework.

Whatever controls you decide to use, you are going to place them in the one control that serves as the main container for groups of controls—the form. Creating and managing forms is the subject of the next chapter.

PART II
Building the User Interface

5

Creating Forms

In this chapter, we discuss forms, the basic element of a .NET Compact Framework GUI application, examining their unique characteristics and their role in providing the user interface.

What Are Forms?

.NET Compact Framework applications present information and receive input by displaying one or more forms to the user. These forms have a set of characteristics that make them unique among the object classes you encounter in .NET Compact Framework programming. These characteristics also make .NET Compact Framework forms somewhat different from desktop forms. What makes forms unique is that they:

- Are derived, directly or indirectly, from `System.Windows.Forms.Form`
- Support all inherited events
- Are displayed full-screen on a Pocket PC and are not resizable
- Can be displayed as modal or modeless forms
- Present Pocket PC users with a mechanism for closing or minimizing the form but not both
- Can be closed but not opened
- Are indestructible until they have been closed

- Are worthless after they have been closed
- Are owned by a thread

Because forms are displayed full-screen on a Pocket PC, the forms that comprise a .NET Compact Framework application relate to each other in the same manner that modal forms in a desktop application relate to each other. That is, a user who is interacting with one form cannot interact with other forms because the top-most form hides all other forms.

For this reason, .NET Compact Framework applications on a Pocket PC normally have a form that serves as the main entry point for an application. Additional forms can be used as dialog boxes, with obvious ways to summon the dialog box (e.g., via menu selection) and to dismiss the dialog box (e.g., with OK and/or Cancel buttons). These dialog boxes support the various functional areas of an application. For instance, an aircraft inspection application might have one form for ordering a replacement part and another form for displaying a picture of a correctly installed part so that inspectors can verify that the work under review was done correctly.

The main form serves as the home page through which the user navigates an application to access other forms in response to user input. You code these forms to either hide or dispose of themselves when dismissed by the user. If you choose to dispose of forms when they are not in use, you are saving resources—but at the cost of having to recreate the form when the user requests it. A hidden form can be displayed to the user in much less time than a form that must be recreated before it can be displayed.

On a Pocket PC, configuring a form as either a main program window or a dialog box is controlled by a single form property: the `MinimizeBox` property. When this property is set to `true`, a form operates as a main program window and displays a minimize box (a circle containing an "X") in the right side of the title bar. When `MinimizeBox` is set to `false`, a form operates as a dialog box and displays an OK box (a circle containing "ok"). The standard on a Pocket PC is that a program continues to run when the user clicks on the minimize box. During program development, and also for certain types of tools and utilities, it can make sense for a program to shut down when the user closes the program's main form.

The .NET Compact Framework was built to run on small-screen devices. This means that—with just a few exceptions—available space for forms is limited. An application must make optimal use of space-saving controls such as the main menu, context menus, toolbars, comboboxes, and tabbed controls.

Deriving Forms from the `Form` Class

Like everything else in .NET that is not a value type, forms are objects. Normally you derive forms directly from the `Form` class that is defined in the `System.Windows.Forms` namespace. This is the default derivation whenever you add a new form to the project. Listing 5.1 shows the code file that resulted when adding a form named `FormDemo` to a project.

LISTING 5.1: Code That Defines a New Form

```
using System;
using System.Drawing;
using System.Collections;
using System.ComponentModel;
using System.Windows.Forms;

namespace MainPlusOthers
{
   /// <summary>
   /// Summary description for FormDemo.
   /// </summary>
   public class FormDemo : System.Windows.Forms.Form
   {
            :
            :
```

The first few lines of code leave no doubt that you are defining an object class, one that inherits from `Form`.

Optionally, your form classes can be derived from other form classes, classes that were themselves derived from `Form`. For further discussion of deriving forms from other forms, see the Inheritance and Visual Inheritance section later in this chapter.

Properties, Methods, and Events

Because your forms are derived from the base class of `Form`, they inherit the properties, methods, and events (PMEs) of the `Form` class. The `Form` class itself obtains most of its PMEs through inheritance, with an inheritance chain that starts at `Object` and descends through the following classes: `MarshalByRefObject`, `Component`, `Control`, `ScrollableControl`, and `ContainerControl`.

Tables 5.1 through 5.3 list the properties, methods, and events, respectively, of the `Form` class. Those that are form-specific (i.e., defined within the `Form` class rather than inherited) are marked with an asterisk (*). For convenience we have broken them down into categories of our own choosing. Chapter 7 provides additional information about the `Control` class, which is the base class for all control classes that wrap around a native operating system window. The following subsections briefly discuss some specific PMEs.

Properties

Several of the properties are related to size and position, and you should leave them as they are. On the Pocket PC, forms are displayed full-screen. But if you accidentally change the size, the layout of controls in the Designer might not be the same as what the user will see on a Pocket PC. To ensure that you do not accidentally modify the size properties, use the `Lock Controls` option. Right-click on the form in Design View and select Lock Controls from the context menu.

The value of the form's `MinimizeBox` property determines whether the form displays a minimize box or a close box to the user. The impact of this choice is discussed in the Orphaned Forms section of this chapter.

The value of the form's `ControlBox` property determines whether the form displays a control box in the upper-left corner of the form. The presence of a control box allows the user to display the system menu.

The `DataBindings` collection is covered in Chapter 8.

The `DialogResult` property is most applicable to forms that are displayed as dialogs. This property is addressed in Chapter 9.

TABLE 5.1: Properties of the `Form` Class

Category	Property Name	Description	Pocket PC–Specific Comments
Ownership	`Parent`	Inherited from `Control` and is normally `null` because forms do not have a parent. When a form is a dialog box, however, its parent is the form that spawned the dialog (the parent is disabled).	For dialog boxes, do not set a parent.
	`Controls`	Contains the controls that reside on the form.	
	`TopLevelControl`	Inherited from `Control` and provides immediate access to the form that contains a set of controls.	
State	`Capture`	Indicates whether a form should grab all mouse/stylus input (Boolean property).	A form automatically sets the mouse capture for a `MouseDown` event and releases the mouse capture for a `MouseUp` event.
	`Enabled`	Indicates whether a form can receive keyboard and mouse input. When a form is disabled, all controls contained in the form are disabled (see Chapter 6).	
	`Focused`	Indicates whether keyboard input is directed to the form (Boolean property).	
	`Visible`	Indicates whether a form and its child controls are on the desktop and whether the top-level form appears on the task list (Boolean property).	

continues

Table 5.1: Properties of the `Form` Class (continued)

Category	Property Name	Description	Pocket PC–Specific Comments
State (continued)	`WindowState*`	Indicates whether a form is initially full-screen, i.e., maximized.	Forms always run full-screen on Pocket PCs, so this property is ignored.
Appearance	`BackColor`	Specifies the color used to draw the form surface.	
	`ControlBox*`	Causes the presence of a close button; when set to `false`, prevents the minimize box and the maximize box from appearing. When run on the desktop .NET Framework, this property controls whether a system menu appears. (The Windows CE user interface does not support a system menu.)	This property indicates whether a form has a close box or an OK button. (Pocket PC programs have no close button.)
	`FormBorderStyle*`	Specifies the type of border and whether a form is resizable. (.NET Compact Framework programs running under the desktop .NET Framework vary slightly from the same program running under CE.)	This property is ignored.
	`Icon*`	Appears only when running on the desktop .NET Framework. `Icon` sets an application icon from the Visual Studio project properties page.	This property is ignored on Pocket PC and Windows CE.
	`MaximizeBox*`	Determines whether the maximize box appears (requires `ControlBox` to be `true` for the box to appear).	This property is ignored.
	`MinimizeBox*`	Determines whether the minimize box appears (requires `ControlBox` to be `true` for the box to appear).	When `true`, the close box appears, which when clicked causes the form to hide and the program to continue running.

Category	Property Name	Description	Pocket PC–Specific Comments
Appearance (continued)			When `false`, the OK box appears, which when clicked causes the form to close and the program to terminate.
	`Text`	Specifies the text for a form's caption bar.	
Menus	`Menu*`	Specifies the form's main menu.	Access to the input panel (SIP) requires a menu or a toolbar. (There is no dedicated toolbar property, but toolbars are added to a form's controls collection.)
	`ContextMenu`	Specifies the form's context menu.	
Dialogs	`DialogResult*`	Contains the value to be returned by the `ShowDialog` method. Is set by the dialog box and received by the form that displayed the dialog box.	
Position and size	`Bottom`	Specifies the x-coordinate for the bottom of a window in the parent's client area or in-screen coordinates for top-level windows (read-only property).	
	`Bounds`	Creates a `Rectangle` equal to (`Left`, `Top`, `Right`, `Bottom`) coordinates in the parent's client area for contained controls and in-screen coordinates for top-level forms.	

continues

* Specific to the `Form` class.

Table 5.1: Properties of the `Form` Class (continued)

Category	Property Name	Description	Pocket PC–Specific Comments
Position and size (continued)	`ClientRectangle`	Creates a `Rectangle` equal to (`0`, `0`, `ClientSize.Width`, `ClientSize.Height`) (read-only property).	
	`ClientSize`	Equals `Size` minus nonclient elements.	
	`Height`	Specifies the form height (including nonclient elements).	
	`Left`	Specifies the y-axis location in parent (or in screen) coordinates.	
	`Location`	Specifies a `Point` equal to (`Left`, `Top`).	
	`Right`	Specifies the right coordinate (read-only property).	
	`Size`	Specifies a `Size` equal to (`Width`, `Height`).	
	`Top`	Specifies the x-axis location in parent (or in screen) coordinates.	
	`Width`	Specifies the form width (including nonclient elements).	
Data binding	`DataBindings`	Contains a collection of data-binding objects.	

Table 5.2: Methods of the Form Class

Category	Method Name	Description
Dialog box support	ShowDialog*	Displays a form as a dialog box, disabling the form's parent.
Drawing	CreateGraphics	Fetches a Graphic object for drawing on the surface of the form.
	Invalidate	Marks a portion of a form for lazy redrawing (through the Paint event).
	Refresh	Redraws a form and its controls immediately (like a call to Invalidate and Update on a form and on all contained controls).
	Update	Redraws invalid portions immediately.
Coordinate conversion	PointToClient	Converts a Point from screen coordinates to client coordinates.
	PointToScreen	Converts a Point from client coordinates to screen coordinates.
	Rectangle-ToClient	Converts a Rectangle from screen coordinates to client coordinates.
	Rectangle-ToScreen	Converts a Rectangle from client coordinates to screen coordinates.
Inherited type support	Equals	Checks a form for equality with another form.
	GetType	Returns System.Windows.Forms.Form.
	ToString	Returns a string with the fully qualified name of a form class.
Thread-safe access	Invoke	Calls a delegate in a form (or other Control-derived class) in a thread-safe manner. Thread-safe, by the way, does not mean the call must be made on a separate thread, a point of confusion with programmers new to Windows thread programming.

continues

* Specific to the Form class.

Table 5.2: Methods of the `Form` Class (continued)

Category	Method Name	Description
State	`Close*`	Requests that a form be closed.
	`Dispose`	Requests that resources associated with a form be reclaimed.
	`Focus`	Sets keyboard focus to a form.
	`Hide`	Makes the form and all its contained controls invisible.
	`Show`	Allows a form and all its contained controls to be visible.
Z-order	`BringToFront`	Moves a form to the top of the local-input z-order. The .NET Compact Framework does not support setting a form at the top of the global z-order; that requires calling the native `SetForegroundWindow` function.
	`SendToBack`	Moves a form to the bottom of the local-input z-order.

* Specific to the `Form` class.

Table 5.3: Events of the `Form` Class

Category	Event Name	Description
Activation state	`Activated*`	The form is becoming activated, which means it is the foreground top-level window in the system.
	`Deactivate*`	The form is losing activation because another top-level window is getting activated. The other window could be a message box or dialog created by the form or a window in another program.
Startup and shutdown	`Load*`	This one-time startup event occurs when a form loads into memory.
	`Closing*`	This request to close a form can be cancelled, otherwise the form closes.
	`Closed*`	This one-time shutdown event occurs when a form has been closed.

* Specific to the `Form` class.

Category	Event Name	Description
Startup and shutdown (continued)	`Disposed`	This event occurs when the `Dispose` method has finished processing.
Keyboard focus	`GotFocus`	The form has exclusive access to keyboard input.
	`LostFocus`	Exclusive keyboard access is with another window.
Keyboard input	`KeyDown`	A keyboard or SIP key has been pushed (hardware button event).
	`KeyPress`	Character input has been received.
	`KeyUp`	A keyboard or SIP key has been released (hardware button event).
Mouse input	`MouseDown`	The user has pushed down the mouse/stylus.
	`MouseMove`	The mouse/stylus has moved.
	`Click`	The user has pushed and released the mouse/stylus (this message arrives just prior to a `MouseUp` event).
	`MouseUp`	The user has released the mouse/stylus.
State change	`EnabledChanged`	The `Enabled` property has changed.
	`TextChanged`	The `Text` property has changed.
	`Paint`	The form is invalid; the form must redraw its display.
	`ParentChanged`	The `Parent` property has changed.
	`Resize`	Changes have been detected in size, location, or z-order.
Validation	`Validating`	Form validation is being requested.
	`Validated`	Validation was successfully accomplished.

In the current version of the .NET Compact Framework,[1] the `Icon` property is not used. This property accepts an icon created from a managed resource (in a `.resx` file). Such an icon can be loaded only as a managed `System.Drawing.Icon` object. However, the user interface shell of both Pocket PC and Windows CE devices requires a native (unmanaged) icon resource. Add a native icon to a program in the Property Pages dialog for a project by specifying the application icon.

The icon (`*.ico`) file format can accommodate more than one icon. When creating an icon for a .NET Compact Framework program, be sure that your icon supports two icons: a 16 × 16 image as well as a 32 × 32 image. The smaller image appears on the Start menu; the larger image appears in the Program window.

Methods

The `Show` and `Hide` methods are equivalent to setting the `Visible` property to `true` and `false`, respectively. Calling the `BringToFront` or `SendToBack` methods results in a form being placed at the top or bottom of the z-order, respectively.

The `Close` method is `Public`, while the `Dispose` method is `Protected`. Thus clients (and users) can "close" a form when done using it. Closing a form is the proper way to dispose of a form. The `Close` method is discussed in the Closing Forms subsection of this chapter.

Multithreading is addressed in the Multithreading subsection of this chapter. The drawing and coordinate conversion methods are discussed in Part IV.

Events

One of the themes of this book, covered most thoroughly in Chapter 7, is that Microsoft adopted a policy that "inherited does not mean supported" when developing the GUI objects of the .NET Compact Framework. Because of this policy, for example, you can write a handler for the `Click` event of a

---

1. Just before this book went to press, we tested this on the .NET Compact Framework, version 1.0, Service Pack 2.

TextBox control—code that IntelliSense can help you write, code that will compile cleanly, but code that is never executed. This is because the Click event of the TextBox class was "inherited but not supported." Fortunately, this policy was *not* adopted when implementing the Form class. All 17 form events that have been inherited have also been implemented. Code that you place in a handler for any of these events is going to be executed whenever the corresponding event occurs.

Two events have names that end in "ing": Closing and Validating. They are the only two that allow you to *cancel* the operation that raised the event, as indicated by their CancelEventArgs arguments parameter, shown here.

```
private void FormMain_Closing
    (object sender, System.ComponentModel.CancelEventArgs e)
{
        :
        :
}
```

Setting e.Cancel = true cancels the operation. For instance, it is common to cancel a close operation if unfinished work must be completed by the user before the form can close. When handling the Closing event in this situation, present a MessageBox to the user asking if they really meant to close the application. If he or she replies negatively, set e.Cancel = true. Similarly, the Validating event is often cancelled when a change made by a user causes the data to become unacceptable and must be corrected before further processing can occur. The two validation events are always caused by losing the focus, whether the focus is being lost to an object located outside the form or to a control within the form. See Chapter 7 for further discussion of the validation events.

An Event-Capturing Application

To illustrate the events that a form receives, we wrote a sample application, FormEvents, to handle every event by logging it into a list box and displaying the total count of events received in the form's title bar. Figure 5.1 shows the sample as it appears in the Designer of Visual Studio .NET.

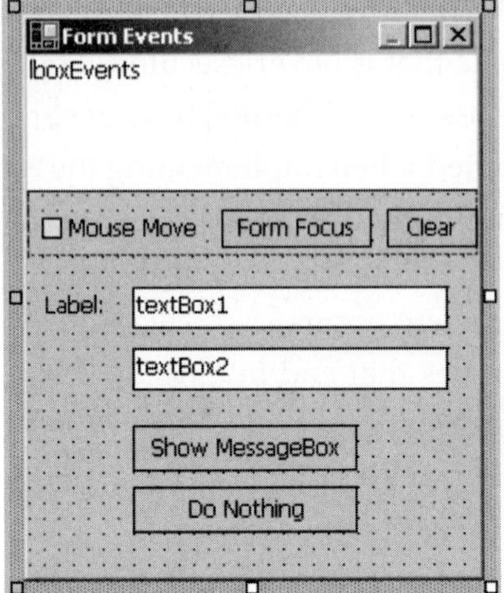

FIGURE 5.1: Form for recording form events

We added an event handler for each event. To receive IntelliSense help when writing event handlers, select the form (or the control for which you are adding an event handler), then in the Properties window click on the lightning bolt button, as shown in Figure 5.2. From here you can associate any already-written handler with an event by picking from a drop-down list, or you can start a new handler by double-clicking on the event name.

We added a small amount of code for each event handler, just enough to log the event and include any event details that might be of interest. A typical event handler in the application looks like the following code.

```
private void FormMain_MouseDown(object sender, MouseEventArgs e)
{
   string str = "FormMain_MouseDown (";
   str += e.X.ToString() + "," + e.Y.ToString();
   str += ")";
   AddItem(str);
}
```

Some additional code is added, namely (1) a property that not only maintains a count of the events received but also appends the count to the form's caption, (2) a Boolean field to indicate whether `MouseMove` events should be tracked, and (3) a routine that adds captured events into the `ListBox` and updates the event count, as shown in Listing 5.2.

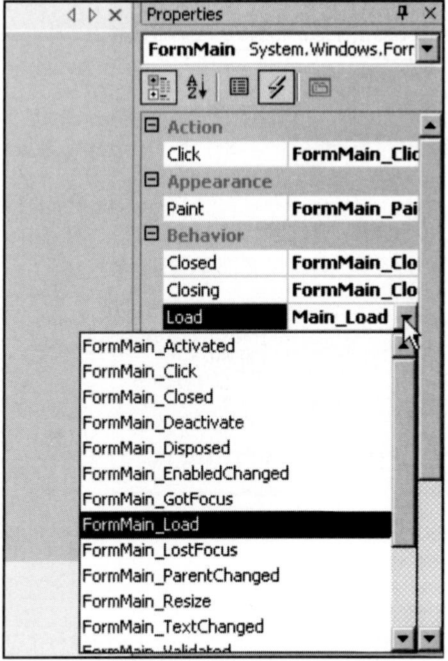

FIGURE 5.2: Adding an event handler

LISTING 5.2: Adding Additional Properties and a Method to a Form

```
private int m_cEvents;
private int cEvents
{
   get { return m_cEvents; }
   set
   {
      m_cEvents = value;
      Text = strAppName + " ("
                        + m_cEvents.ToString()
                        + ")";
   }
}
private bool bShowMouseMove = false;
   :
   :
private void AddItem(string strItem)
{
   lboxEvents.Items.Add(strItem);
   lboxEvents.SelectedIndex = cEvents;
   cEvents++;
}
```

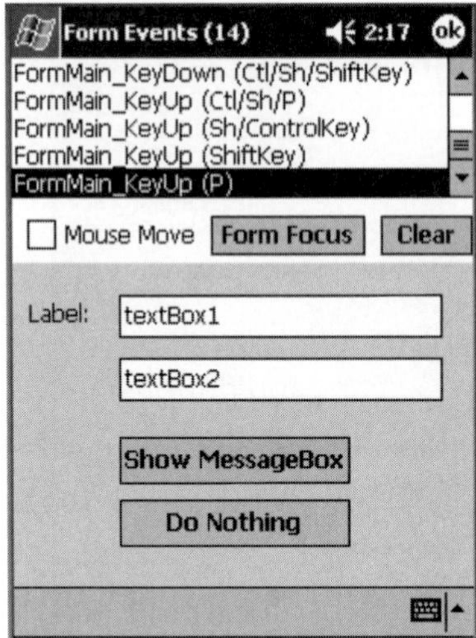

FIGURE 5.3: The `FormEvents` application at startup

We chose not to handle the `TextChanged` event because the program changes the form's caption on receipt of each event, which in turn generates the `TextChanged` event. An earlier version of the `FormEvents` program captured the `TextChanged` event and provided us with an infinite loop. Our sample spares you that entertainment.

When you run the program, as shown in Figure 5.3, you might notice that the form receives seven events as the application starts; three `Resize` events as it expands from a size of nothing to the full size of the display area and then gets squished to make room for the title bar at the top and the SIP bar at the bottom; plus `Activated`, `GotFocus`, `Load`, and `Paint` events.

Placing another window, such as a `MessageBox`, on top of the form causes the form to lose the focus and deactivate; removing that other window reverses the sequence. Any time a form loses the focus, even if the focus is merely shifting from the form itself to one of its contained controls, the two validation events fire.

Manipulating Forms

Forms exhibit some interesting behaviors as they are being created, displayed, and destroyed. Over the next few sections we'll look at these behaviors and at how you can control them to provide a pleasant user experience.

Creating Forms

Forms are created, like any other object, by invoking the `new` function, which in turn creates the form and calls the form's constructor. Creating a form does not cause it to be displayed to the user, but it does cause the form's contained controls (such as menus, toolbars, and buttons) to be created.

The Visual Studio .NET development environment generates the form's default constructor and something similar to a destructor, as well as the code to create and show your application's startup form. Listing 5.3 shows an example.

LISTING 5.3: Designer-Generated Code for the Form's Class

```
public FormMain()
{
   //
   // Required for Windows Form Designer support
   //
   InitializeComponent();

   //
   // TODO: Add any constructor code
   //       after InitializeComponent call.
   //
}
/// <summary>
/// Clean up any resources being used.
/// </summary>
protected override void Dispose( bool disposing )
{
   base.Dispose( disposing );
}
     :
     :
static void Main()
{
   Application.Run(new FormMain());
}
```

As you can see from Listing 5.3, forms have a default constructor into which you can add your own initialization code, but only after you have called the forms `InitializeComponent` routine. `InitializeComponent` initializes the form's properties and its contained controls. As you use the Designer to add more and more controls to your form, `InitializeComponent` becomes larger and larger.

You might be tempted to place your own custom initialization code into `InitializeComponent`. Resist this temptation. The Designer treats `InitializeComponent` as its own personal fiefdom and has a tendency to remove or reword code that you place there. Instead, write your own initialization routine and place a call to it directly after the following line in the form's constructor.

```
// Add any initialization after the InitializeComponent() call
```

A form class can have overloaded constructors. After all, you might want to specify the font or background color to be used by the form as you create it. This possibility of overloaded constructors is one reason why the Designer generates the separate `InitializeComponent` routine rather than simply embedding the code inside the default constructor. By placing component-initializing code in a separate routine, all constructors can initialize the form by calling two routines: `InitializeComponent` and the custom initialization routine you write for the form, if any.

The Designer for Visual Studio .NET 2003 omits two events that forms support: `Activated` and `Deactivate`. These events notify a form about a change in the user's attention. While the Designer does not support these events, IntelliSense does. Within the text editor, a handler for these events gets added when you type statements like these:

```
Activated +=
```

or

```
Deactivate +=
```

IntelliSense responds with a suggestion for completing the statement (`new EventHandler(Form1_Activated);`) along with the instruction "Press TAB to insert." The `InitializeComponent` routine is a very good place to associate form and control events with their handlers.

An alternative location for the form initialization code is in the form's `Load` event handler.[2] Because `Load` and `Closed` occur at opposite ends of a form's life cycle, it is common to place the creation of a resource in the `Load` event handler, and the removal of that resource in the `Closed` event handler. Aside from that, the two routines—the `Load` event handler and `InitializeComponent`—are identical in terms of suitability for initialization code.

Displaying Forms

Technically, your application does not display forms. Rather, it instructs the form to display itself. Forms have two methods for displaying themselves: `Show` and `ShowDialog`. When you call the `MyForm.ShowDialog` method, execution of the statements following the `ShowDialog` call does not occur until after the form has been shown, used, and closed. This is referred to as displaying the form *modally.* When you call the `MyForm.Show` method, the execution of the statements following the `Show` method proceeds even as the form is being displayed. This is known as a *modeless* display of the form.

You can designate the startup form for your .NET Compact Framework application in the Property Pages dialog (right-click on the project name in the Solution Explorer window), as shown in Figure 5.4.

The following line of code (shown in Listing 5.3), which starts the application and displays the form:

```
Application.Run(new FormMain());
```

is roughly equivalent to:

```
Dim frmMain As FormMain
frmMain = New FormMain
frmMain.ShowDialog()
```

This means that destroying the startup form terminates the application because closing `FormMain` allows the execution to reach the end of the

2. C++ programmers who prefer to minimize the amount of code contained in a C++ class constructor might be more comfortable with this approach.

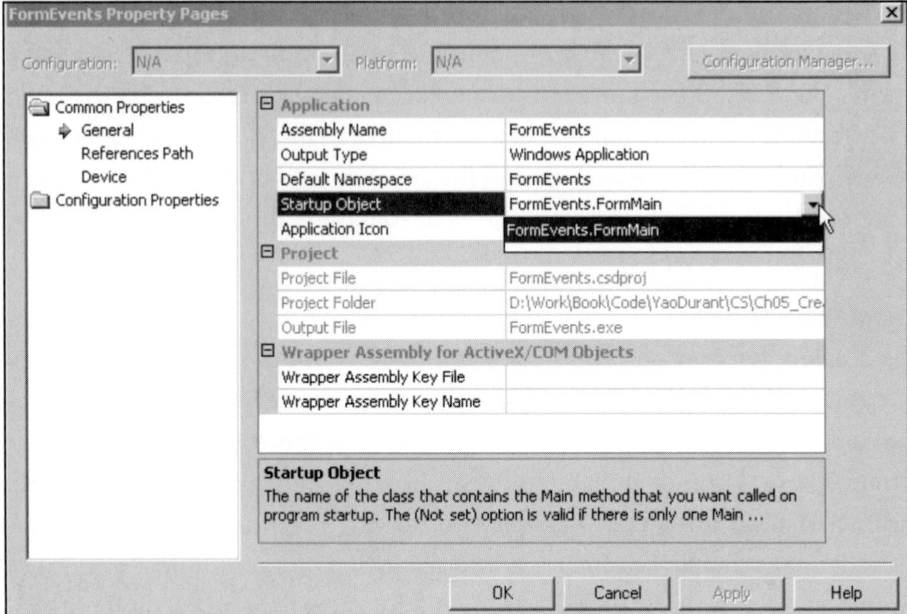

FIGURE 5.4: Setting the startup form

`Application.Run` method. This is different from some programming environments where, once a second form has been created, terminating the first form does not terminate the application. In environments where the application does not automatically terminate until all forms have been closed, you can adopt an "all forms are created equal" design policy. But in .NET Compact Framework, you need to adopt a "main form and other forms" design mentality. Think of the startup form as the anchor form, the one from which users begin their explorations of the application's other forms, always with the possibility of returning to the anchor form.

Closing Forms

Forms have a `Close` method, but they do not have an `Open` method. The `Close` method destroys most of the form's content, immediately freeing most of the memory that was consumed by the form. Figure 5.5 shows the command window of an application that is currently in break mode. The execution was halted just prior to closing a form, and the command window is displaying the contents of the form's `Text` property.

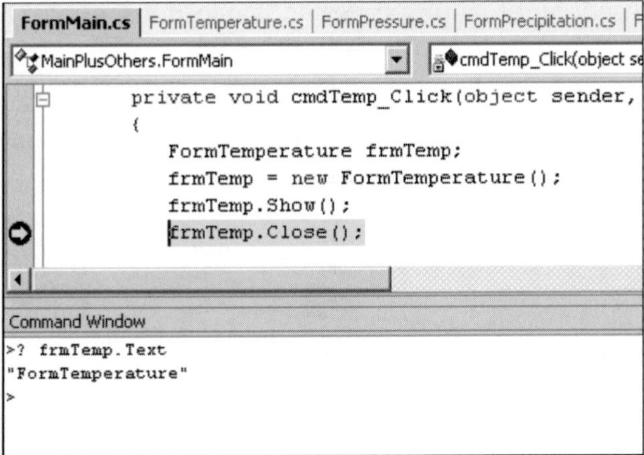

FIGURE 5.5: Contents before closing the form

Figure 5.6 shows the same command window after the form has been closed. After a form has closed, most of its properties are inaccessible, `null`, or default values.

Closing a form has an equal impact on the form's components. If you attempted to access the `Text` property of a control that was on the form, you would see the same error message shown in Figure 5.6.

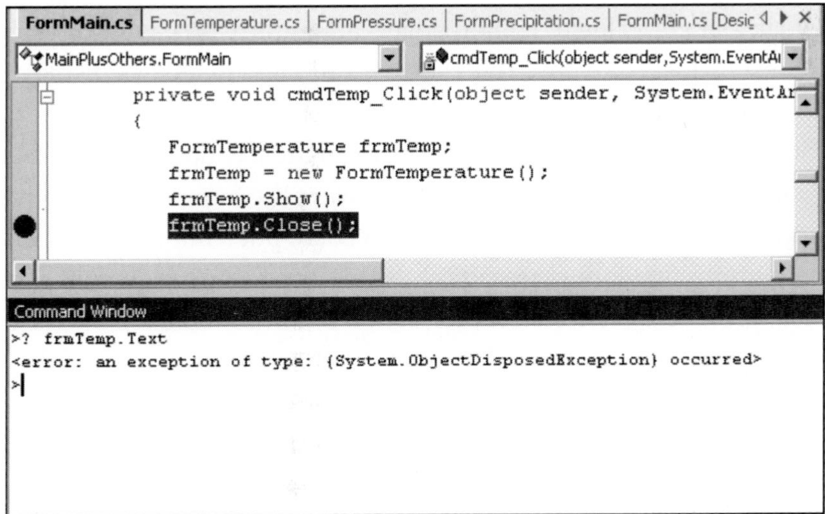

FIGURE 5.6: Contents after closing the form

After a form is closed, all of its properties and collections, except for a few private system properties (such as `m_hwn`) are gone.

Closing a form raises the form's `Closing` and `Closed` events but not the `Disposed` event. Once a form has been closed, it cannot be reopened. Your best policy then is to destroy all references and let the form be garbage collected.

Orphaned Forms

The memory occupied by a form does not get garbage collected until the form has been closed. Even if you set all form references to `null` or let them go out of scope, the form remains intact. This means that it is possible to create *orphaned forms*, forms that are unreachable and unclosed but whose memory cannot be reclaimed. You can neither use nor remove these forms. Always call a form's `Close` method before setting its references to `null` or allowing a form to go out of scope.

When .NET Compact Framework forms are displayed on a Pocket PC, a round icon appears in the upper-right corner of the screen. This icon can be either a close box or a minimize box. A close box has the word "ok" in it, as shown in Figure 5.3 earlier in this chapter; a minimize box has an "X" in it. Minimizing a form hides the form but does not close or destroy it. The choice of which box to show is determined by the form's `MinimizeBox` property value. The default value of `true` displays a minimize box, while a value of `false` results in a close box. The `ShowDialog` method always displays the form with a close box, regardless of the form's `MinimizeBox` value.

For forms other than the startup form you must choose whether to provide a minimize box or a close box. If you want the form to remain alive so that it can be quickly redisplayed when needed, put a minimize box on the form. If a form is seldom viewed by the user or requires minimal time to recreate, provide a close box, rather than a minimize box, for the form. In both cases, maintain a reference to any form that has not been closed.

To illustrate creating, displaying, and destroying forms, let's write an application that displays weather information. This example shows how to display weather data but does not demonstrate possible techniques for acquiring and accessing the data; these topics are subjects of Part III.

Pocket PCs and the `MinimizeBox` Property

During development on Pocket PC programs, we recommend setting your startup form's `MinimizeBox` property to `false`, which allows you to stop your program when you are ready to download and run an updated version. This is not the default setting of the Smart Device Wizard, so this is something you are likely to want to set when creating a new project.

When you ship a program for Pocket PC, we recommend that you set the startup form's `MinimizeBox` property to `true`. This is the standard for Pocket PC programs. A Pocket PC is more like a consumer electronic device than like a computer, so as much as possible you should follow patterns set by radios and clocks rather than patterns familiar from desktop computers.

Following this idea further, a program does not start or stop—it is always running. A user does not open files or save files; instead, any change is stored right away without asking the user "Are you sure?" A minimalist mind-set must guide the design of a Pocket PC program's user interface. To support that, a .NET Compact Framework program—like any other Pocket PC program—gets minimized instead of being shut down when the user has finished working with the program.

The Weather Sample Application

The application needs to display temperature, barometric pressure, and precipitation information to the user. It has a startup form plus a form for each of the three categories. We start with a new Smart Device Application project, rename the form to `FormMain`, designate it as the starting form, and add three more forms. In anticipation of a future requirement, we also add a class to our project, resulting in the solution shown in Figure 5.7, which we name `MainPlusOthers` to indicate the relationship between the forms.

We then proceed to write the event handlers for the three buttons on the form shown in Figure 5.7, and at first we get it *wrong*. That is, we write code

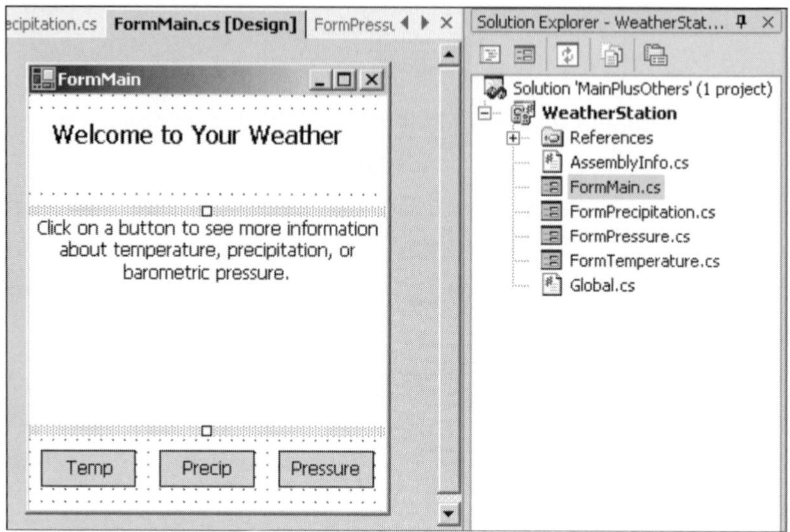

FIGURE 5.7: The `MainPlusOthers` solution

that will produce orphaned forms, which is easy to do. We do this by coding the `Click` event handler for the Pressure button as follows:

```
private void cmdPress_Click(object sender, System.EventArgs e)
{
   FormPressure frmPress = new FormPressure();
   frmPress.Show();
}
```

In this code the main form creates the `FormPressure` form, shows it, and loses the reference to it by letting it go out of scope. The application has no way to close this form, which would not be a problem if users had a way to do so, but they do not. We accepted the form's default `MinimizeBox` property of `true`, meaning users can minimize the `FormPressure` form but not close it.

When run, the application appears to work correctly. When the user clicks on the Pressure button, the `FormPressure` form appears, as shown in Figure 5.8.

When the user clicks on the minimize button, the form disappears and the startup form reappears. When the user again clicks on the Pressure

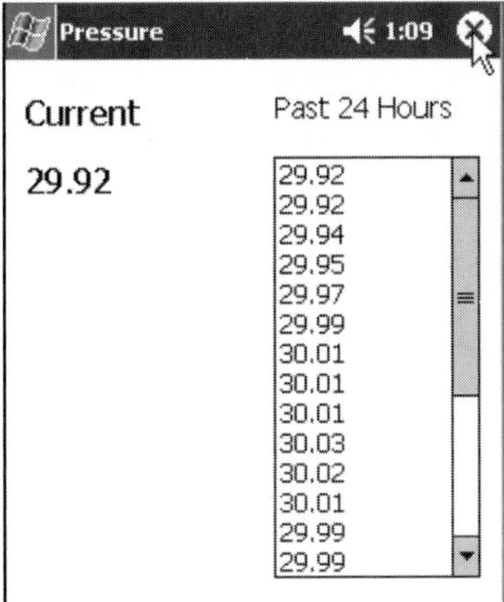

FIGURE 5.8: Minimizing the `FormPressure` form

button, the `FormPressure` form reappears; except, of course, it is not the original `FormPressure` form that appears. Rather, a newly created, second `FormPressure` form appears. The first `FormPressure` form is hidden, unreachable, unclosable, uncollectable—languishing in ether land, consuming resources, and waiting for the application to terminate.

You can verify this behavior by using `WeakReference` objects, which we have done with the `FormTemperature` form, as shown in the code that appears in Figure 5.9. (See Chapter 3 for a discussion of weak references.)

In this code, a `WeakReference` object is set to the first instance of the `FormTemperature` form, and the form's `Text` property is changed to make it distinguishable from the other instances. The weak reference is used to obtain a strong reference, which goes out of scope when the routine completes. Garbage collection is forced every time the routine executes.

We run the application and alternate between clicking the Temperature button on the startup form and then removing the `FormTemperature` form by clicking on its minimize box. After several iterations, we set a break point to stop the execution at the end of the routine and use the command window to determine whether the first instance of the form still exists, which it does. This confirms our statement that old instances of a form are not garbage collected even when no references to the form exist.

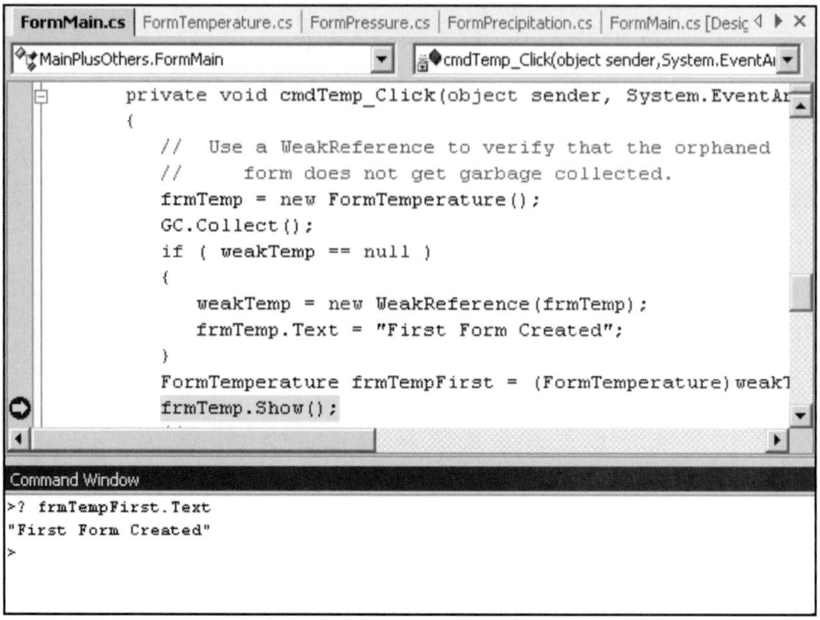

```
FormMain.cs | FormTemperature.cs | FormPressure.cs | FormPrecipitation.cs | FormMain.cs [Desig
MainPlusOthers.FormMain        cmdTemp_Click(object sender,System.EventA
        private void cmdTemp_Click(object sender, System.EventAr
        {
           //  Use a WeakReference to verify that the orphaned
           //     form does not get garbage collected.
           frmTemp = new FormTemperature();
           GC.Collect();
           if ( weakTemp == null )
           {
              weakTemp = new WeakReference(frmTemp);
              frmTemp.Text = "First Form Created";
           }
           FormTemperature frmTempFirst = (FormTemperature)weakT
           frmTemp.Show();
Command Window
>? frmTempFirst.Text
"First Form Created"
>
```

FIGURE 5.9: Weak reference to an orphaned form

We can solve the problem two ways: (1) by setting the `FormTemperature` form's `MinimizeBox` property to `false`, either at design time or in code, so that the form will be closed rather than minimized, or (2) by maintaining a reference to the hidden form so that we can redisplay it when needed. To do the latter we need to make the following changes in our application.

- Define `internal` variables to hold a reference to each form.
- Check to see whether an instance of the form already exists before creating a new one.
- Keep the default `MinimizeBox` property value of `true`.

We put our reference variables in the `Global` class we added to our application at the start of development. We make the contents that we add to the class `static` so that we can access them without creating an instance of the class, as shown in Listing 5.4.

LISTING 5.4: The `Global` Class

```
using System;

namespace MainPlusOthers
{
   /// <summary>
   /// Summary description for Global.
   /// </summary>
   public class Global
   {
      static internal FormTemperature frmTemperature;
      static internal FormPrecipitation frmPrecipitation;
      static internal FormPressure frmPressure;

      public Global()
      {
         //
         // TODO: Add constructor logic here
         //
      }
   }
}
```

Then we place the following code for displaying a form, such as `FormPrecipitation`, in `FormMain`.

```
private void cmdPrecip_Click(object sender,
                             System.EventArgs e)
{
   if ( Global.frmPrecipitation == null ) {
      Global.frmPrecipitation = new FormPrecipitation();
   }
   Global.frmPrecipitation.Show();
}
```

In your applications you must choose between closing and recreating the form versus hiding and redisplaying it, balancing the amount of memory available against the overhead of recreating the form. Regardless of the choice you make, always keep a reference to any minimized form so that you can later close it.

Tracking Forms

You might wonder why you have to explicitly keep references to forms. After all, many environments provide a built-in mechanism for enumerating the forms of an application. Such is not the case with .NET. To illustrate some generic code for tracking forms, let's modify the application we just created.

If your application permits multiple instances of the same form class, the code for tracking the forms is trivial. Just provide an accessible `ArrayList` to hold the references, such as the following:

```
static internal ArrayList arrForms = new ArrayList();
```

Then add the following code to each form's constructor:

```
Global.arrForms.Add(this);
```

And add the following code to each `Closed` event handler:

```
Global.RemoveForm(this);
```

In our case, we want only one instance of each form class, so we need to write a routine to check the array and create a form if an instance of the requested class does not exist, or to return a reference to the one that does exist. Writing this code will also allow us to illustrate determining a form's class from a reference. The routine is named `OpenForm`, but like many "open" routines in .NET, it opens something that exists or creates and opens the item if it does not exist. We also write a matching, trivial `RemoveForm` routine. Listing 5.5 shows the `FormsCollection` code.

LISTING 5.5: A Forms Collection for the Weather Application

```
using System;
using System.Collections;
using System.Windows.Forms;

namespace FormsCollection
{
   /// <summary>
   /// Summary description for Global.
   /// </summary>
   public class Global
   {
      public Global()
      {
         //
```

```
         // TODO: Add constructor logic here
         //
      }

      static internal ArrayList arrForms = new ArrayList();

      static internal Form OpenForm(Type typeForm)
      {
         //  Check to see if a form of the
         //     requested type already exists.
         foreach( Form frmLoop in arrForms )
         {
            if( frmLoop.GetType() == typeForm )
            {
               return frmLoop;
            }
         }

         //  if it does not exist, create it
         //     and add it to the collection.
         Form frmWork = null;
         if( typeForm ==
            Type.GetType("FormsCollection.FormTemperature") )
         {
            frmWork = new FormTemperature();
         }
         if( typeForm ==
            Type.GetType("FormsCollection.FormPressure") )
         {
            frmWork = new FormPressure();
         }
         if( typeForm ==
            Type.GetType("FormsCollection.FormPrecipitation") )
         {
            frmWork = new FormPrecipitation();
         }
         if( frmWork != null )
         {
            arrForms.Add(frmWork);
         }
         return frmWork;
      }

      static internal void RemoveForm( Form frmRemovee )
      {
         arrForms.Remove( frmRemovee );
      }

   }
}
```

The OpenForm routine takes a Type object as its only parameter, so OpenForm is called using code such as this:

```
Form frmX =
   Global.OpenForm(Type.GetType
         ("FormsCollection.FormTemperature"));
```

For the Temperature button's Click event handler, which only needs the reference in order to show the window and therefore does not need to declare a variable, we use this code:

```
Global.OpenForm(Type.GetType
    ("FormsCollection.FormTemperature")).Show();
```

The code for each form's Close event handler becomes this line:

```
Global.RemoveForm(this);
```

Maintaining your own forms collection requires a small amount of easily written code. It definitely can come in handy.

The Controls Collection

Unlike a forms collection, which we had to write ourselves, a form's Controls property is a collection implemented in .NET Compact Framework automatically. This collection allows you to iterate through all the child controls of a form. (See Chapter 7 for more information about the controls collection.) One of the benefits of the controls collection is that it helps you overcome the lack of ambient property support in the .NET Compact Framework.

The *ambient properties* are a group of properties common to forms and to many controls that appear within forms. Font is an example of such a property.

Support for ambient properties implies the ability of controls to automatically assume the ambient property values of their parent form. In such an environment, changing the form's font from Helvetica to Times New Roman causes the same font change to occur in the form's controls. Ambient properties are not supported in the .NET Compact Framework.

If you need to ripple form-level property changes down to the controls, you must override the property in your form class and iterate through a form's controls collection. You can receive IntelliSense help in overriding a form's property. Just enter "public override" and the drop-down list shown in Figure 5.10 will appear. Pick the property you want to override; IntelliSense will generate the skeleton code for you.

To the code that IntelliSense generates, we add four lines to iterate through the form's controls collection and to assign the form's new font to all its controls, as shown in Listing 5.6.

LISTING 5.6: Propagating the New Font to the Form's Controls

```
public override Font Font
{
   get
   {
      return base.Font;
   }
   set
   {
      base.Font = value;
      foreach( Control ctlX in this.Controls )
      {
         ctlX.Font = value;
      }
   }
}
```

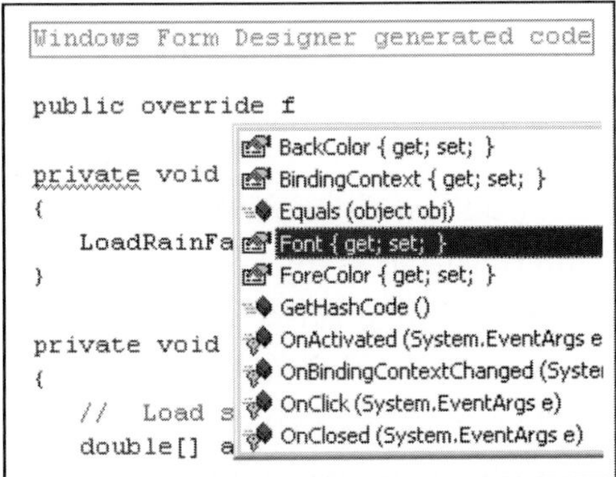

FIGURE 5.10: Overriding the `Font` property

Multithreading

Users want fast responses when interacting with your programs, so your programs' event handlers must execute quickly. There are times, however, when a user request cannot be handled quickly. Perhaps a program must download a large file from a network server, search a large database with complex search criteria, or perform a series of complex and involved calculations. In such cases, an event handler cannot execute quickly and also do the requested work. Thus an event handler might delegate the actual work to a separate thread. The primary benefit of this approach is that the event handler can return quickly to be ready to receive more user input.

To understand the benefit of threads, it helps to know about the relationship between threads and windows (after all, a form is a window). These two objects are part of a broader hierarchy of ownership that proceeds as follows. An operating system process contains one or more *application domains*. An application domain is associated with one or more threads, which are the unit of scheduling under Windows CE. Windows that are created are owned by the creating thread. All input to a window always goes through the message delivery mechanism associated with the thread that created the window. Such threads are sometimes referred to as *user interface threads*. To ensure that the system is responsive to user input, the best designs always perform a minimum of work in the user interface threads. Any big tasks are delegated to *background threads* (threads that have no window associated with them), which are therefore free to run without leaving users to wonder if a particular program has hung.

This is why your application should always create a separate thread to perform any time-consuming task. Doing so ensures that the form's main thread, the one used to create the form and its controls, is free to respond to user input.

Sometimes the creation of a window itself can take a long time, especially a window with a complex user interface and many controls. To provide maximum responsiveness to the user, it might make sense to display a simple form on one thread—like a login window—while the more complex form is being created on a separate thread. If you do this form creation using a separate thread, the user can continue to interact with the simpler form while the more complex form is being created. If the creation of that second form were not done on a separate thread, the user would receive no visible response from his or her input (such as tapping on a menu item) until the creation of the second form was completed.

Another approach you can take to improve the responsiveness of your program to user input is to simplify the number of controls on a form. In particular, you may wish to move some of the startup code from the `InitializeComponent` method to another location. This must be done with care because the Designer might get confused when required code is missing. By doing this, you can fine-tune the startup behavior of a form so that only a minimum of work is required—and a minimum of time is taken—before the form first appears. You can disable controls that are not initialized and perform the required initialization only when a user action indicates that the control is going to be used.

Very little code is needed to create a thread in our weather application. We continue to use the `OpenForm` function to create and open the form. But instead of creating a form and showing it when the user clicks on a button, the application creates a thread and allows the thread to create and show the form. The thread must use the `ShowDialog` method and show the form modally or the end of the thread procedure can be reached, terminating the thread and closing the form. Here is the procedure to create the form and display it modally:

```
private void CreateAndShowTemperature()
{
   Global.OpenForm(Type.GetType
      ("MultiThreaded.FormTemperature")).ShowDialog();
}
```

The code to create and start the thread that executes this procedure is:

```
private void cmdTemp_Click(object sender,
                           System.EventArgs e)
{
   Thread thrdTemperature;
   thrdTemperature =
      new Thread(new ThreadStart(CreateAndShowTemperature));
   thrdTemperature.Start();
}
```

Because we had already placed the code to create and open a form into an accessible function, it was easier to wrap that functionality inside a thread procedure.

Inheritance and Visual Inheritance

Every time you create a form, you inherit from an existing class, usually from `System.Windows.Forms.Form`. As you become more experienced with the .NET Compact Framework, you probably won't think much about it. But you can define a form by inheriting from any class that has `Form` somewhere in its inheritance chain. In other words, `Form` is simply the template from which your forms are derived. If you wish to develop a better template by deriving a new class from `Form`, you are welcome to do so.

For instance, our weather application has three very similar forms: `FormTemperature`, `FormPressure`, and `FormPrecipitation`. They all set their `MinimizeBox` properties when created, remove themselves from a collection when they are closed, and display three `Label` controls and one `ListBox` control to the user. Can we derive one base class that does all this and then derive our three form classes from this base class? Yes—this technique is familiar to desktop .NET Framework programmers, but getting the same results in the .NET Compact Framework takes a bit more work (and produces something less than the same results).

When you inherit from a base class, you are inheriting functionality; that is, you are inheriting code. But forms, although defined with code, are visual objects. If you add a new form to your project and then change the derivation to:

```
public class FormPrecipitation : WeatherGage.FormGage
```

you might expect the contents of the FormPrecipitation, as displayed in the Designer window, to look like `FormGage`. In other words, you might expect that the menus, toolbars, and controls that were defined in the `FormGage` class would appear in the Design View window, allowing you to add additional controls and code for your derived class. This display of a base class visual layout during the development of a derived class, called *visual inheritance*, is a feature of .NET on the desktop. Unfortunately, visual inheritance is not supported for .NET Compact Framework applications.

There are, however, some workarounds. In the .NET Compact Framework, when you modify your class definition statement, as shown in the previous line of code, your Design View window goes blank except for the following error message.

```
The designer could not be shown for this file because none of
the classes within it can be designed.  The designer inspected
the following classes in the file: FormTemperature --- The base
class 'WeatherGage.FormGage' could not be loaded.  Ensure
the assembly has been referenced or built if it is part of the
project.
```

If you are not concerned with the appearance of either the base class form or the derived form, and you wish only to add functionality, this loss of layout is an irritant but is not a showstopper. Perhaps you merely wish to connect to the appropriate database and display some data using the base class controls. Working with a blank screen in this case is not a major problem. As you write the code to load data into the `ListBox` control named `lboxPast`, you do not care exactly where the developer of the base class placed `lboxPast`.

If you are not concerned with the appearance of the base class but are concerned with the appearance of the derived class, there is yet another workaround. For instance, your base class might contain a menu, a toolbar, some custom properties and methods, but no other controls. In other words, the middle of the base form is a blank area on which you want to place controls and then write event handlers for those controls. This you can do, if you are willing to start designing from a blank form rather than from the base class form. That is, you can have the Designer present a blank form to you, one on which you can drag, drop, and position controls. You can write derived class code that references those controls, as well as the controls, properties, and methods of the base class. You just can't see the base class controls when laying out the derived form.

You make this happen by convincing the Designer that you are inheriting from `Form` while at the same time convincing IntelliSense and the compiler that you are inheriting from your base class. This is done with conditional compilation statements, as shown in the following code. You can use any word you want instead of `FORM_DESIGN` as long it is not already being used by the application.

```
#define FORM_DESIGN
      :
      :
#if (FORM_DESIGN)
   public class FormPrecipitation : System.Windows.Forms.Form
#else
   public class FormPrecipitation : WeatherGage.FormGage
#endif
```

The `#define` statement of the conditional constant must be defined at the very start of your form class code, prior to any `using` or `namespace` statements.

To see which predefined constants have been specified through the IDE, view the Configuration Properties | Build tab of the Property Pages dialog, shown in Figure 5.11.

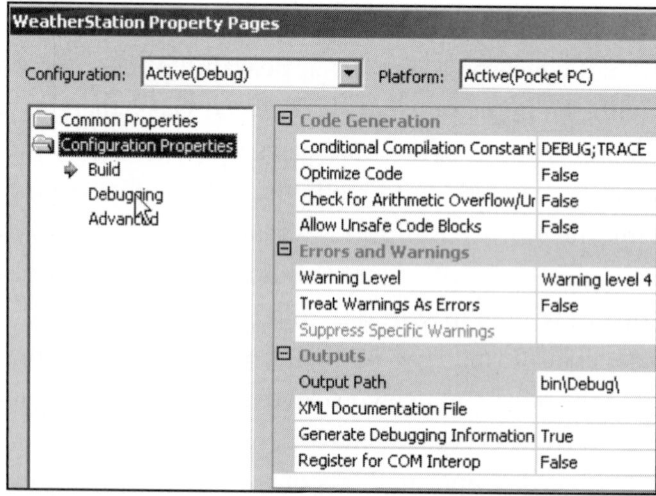

FIGURE 5.11: Setting the conditional constants

Start by adding a new Windows Form to your project. Switch to Code View for that form and change the inheritance specification of your form class to the code shown previously. Return to Design View and add the controls and menus you want. Use the Properties window to set their properties, just as you normally would. When you are finished with the layout of the controls, return to Code View.

When you return to Code View, comment out the `#define FORM_DESIGN` line before adding any code or doing a build. As long as that line is commented out, your form class is inheriting from your base class. If at any time you switch to Design View of your form and do not see a form for laying out your controls, take the following steps.

1. Close the Design View window.
2. Switch to Code View.
3. Uncomment the `#define FORM_DESIGN` line, if it is not already uncommented.
4. Reopen the Design View window.

For an example, we'll define a base class named `FormGage` that contains the common characteristics of our three data display forms, `FormTemperature`, `FormPressure`, and `FormPrecipitation`. We place this form in its own project named `WeatherGage`. Since `FormGage`'s controls must be accessible by the derived classes, we make them `protected`. Then we redefine the three data display forms, only this time we'll inherit from `FormGage` instead of `Form`.

The base class, `FormGage`, shown in Figure 5.12, contains four controls (plus some modifications to the property values for those controls) and code (not shown) to set the form's `MinimizeBox` property to `false` during load.

In our `WeatherStation` project, we delete our existing three forms and start their definition anew by adding three new forms, resulting in the solution shown in Figure 5.13. We also add a reference to the `WeatherGage` project.

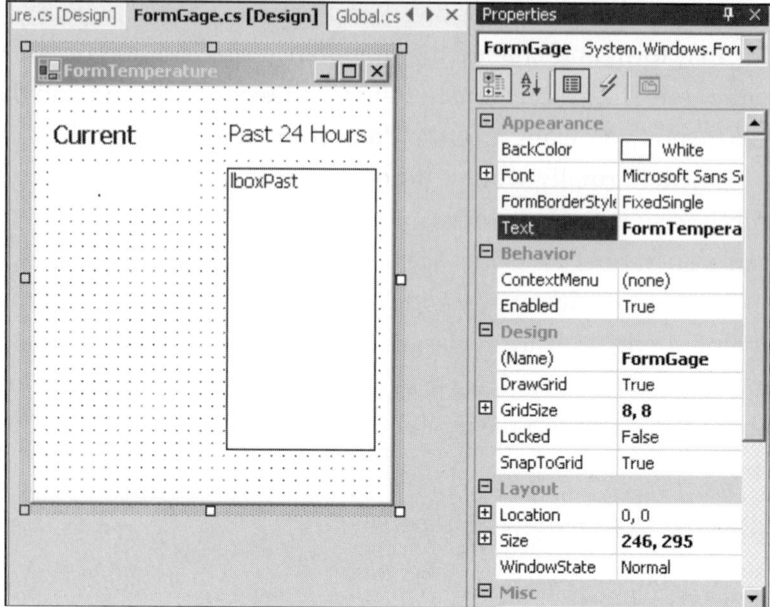

FIGURE 5.12: The `FormGage` base class form

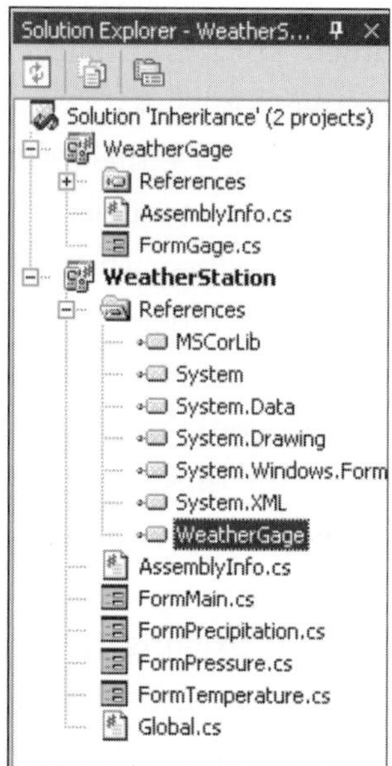

FIGURE 5.13: The solution with the `FormGage` base class added

For each form that inherits from `FormGage`, we modify the code generated by the Designer to include the conditional compilation code shown earlier and repeated here.

```
#define FORM_DESIGN
      :
      :
#if (FORM_DESIGN)
   public class FormPrecipitation : System.Windows.Forms.Form
#else
   public class FormPrecipitation : WeatherGage.FormGage
#endif
```

We want to add a button to the `FormTemperature` form that will let the user convert temperatures between Fahrenheit and Celsius. We return to Design View, drag a button from the toolbar, and drop it on the form, as shown in Figure 5.14.

When placing controls on a derived form, try to picture the base class layout in your mind as you position your derived class controls. Once the control is on the form, you can use the Properties window to set property values.

FIGURE 5.14: Placing a control on the derived form

Return to the code window and comment out the `#define FORM_DESIGN` line. Now you can add and compile code that references your newly added controls as well as the properties, methods, events, and components of the base class. In our application, for instance, the `FormTemperature` class needs code to load temperature data into the base class controls when being displayed, to remove its reference from the global array when being destroyed, and to have an event handler for the new button. Listing 5.7 shows the `FormTemperature` class.

LISTING 5.7: The Derived `FormTemperature` Class

```
#define FORM_DESIGN

using System;
using System.Drawing;
using System.Collections;
using System.ComponentModel;
using System.Windows.Forms;


namespace FormsCollection
{
   /// <summary>
   /// Summary description for FormTemperature.
   /// </summary>
   ///

#if (FORM_DESIGN)
   public class FormTemperature : System.Windows.Forms.Form
#else
   public class FormTemperature : WeatherGage.FormGage
#endif
   {
      private System.Windows.Forms.Button button1;

      public FormTemperature()
      {
         //
         // Required for Windows Form Designer support
         //
         InitializeComponent();

         //
         // TODO: Add any constructor code
         //       after InitializeComponent call
         //
      }
```

```
      /// <summary>
      /// Clean up any resources being used.
      /// </summary>
      protected override void Dispose( bool disposing )
      {
         base.Dispose( disposing );
      }

      #region Windows Form Designer generated code

      private void LoadTemperatures()
      {
         //  Load sample temperatures into controls.
         int[] intTemperatures  =
                 {  92, 92, 93, 93, 93, 93,
                    94, 94, 94, 95, 96, 96,
                    96, 96, 97, 97, 96, 96,
                    95, 95, 94, 94, 93, 93 };

         lblCurrent.Text = intTemperatures[0].ToString();
         foreach (int intTemp in intTemperatures)
            lboxPast.Items.Add(intTemp.ToString());
      }

      private void FormTemperature_Load(object sender,
                                        System.EventArgs e)

      {
         LoadTemperatures();
      }

      private void FormTemperature_Closed(object sender,
                                          System.EventArgs e)

      {
         Global.RemoveForm(this);
      }

   }
}
```

Figure 5.15 shows the `FormTemperature` form displayed to the user. Not too bad, considering that the placement of the Convert button was done on a blank form.

This technique is not as nice a solution as being able to see the base class layout in Design View during development, but it is an adequate workaround for most situations. With forms, as with any other object family, you can simplify things by placing common functionality in a base class and then deriving specific cases from that base class.

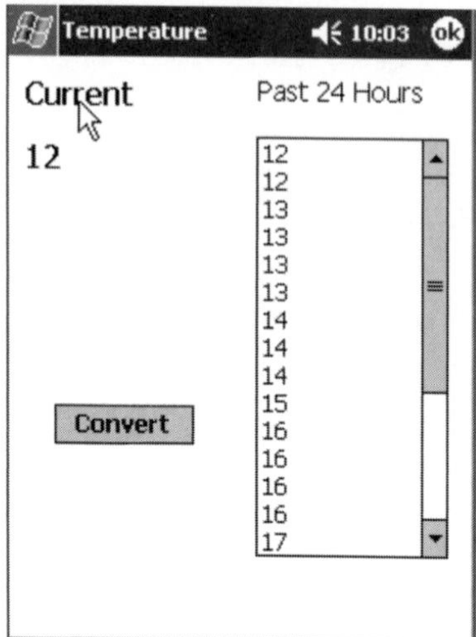

FIGURE 5.15: The derived `FormTemperature` form

If you must view the controls of both the base and derived classes as you are designing your form, you are out of luck. This functionality won't be available until visual inheritance is implemented in the .NET Compact Framework.

CONCLUSION

.NET Compact Framework forms are derived from the `Form` base class. They have some characteristics that you must become familiar with before you start developing applications. Each form is a derived class, with a base set of PMEs already defined. Customizing each form to meet its specific needs consists of defining additional PMEs and adding controls. Because the .NET Compact Framework is an environment of limited resources, you must decide whether to minimize or close forms that are not in use.

The use of multiple threads can make your forms appear faster to the user. Visual inheritance has not been implemented, but there are work-arounds for deriving forms from your own base classes.

In this chapter we looked at forms. In the next chapter, we look at how users can provide input to your forms.

6
Mouse and Keyboard Input

This chapter covers mouse and keyboard input and the smart-device equivalents. Mouses and keyboards are standard input devices on a desktop PC system, but no standard exists for smart-device input. There is, instead, a wide range of available input hardware, limited only by the imaginations of the platform development teams. Programmers who are new to smart-device programming need to adopt new approaches to thinking about user input when developing software for smart devices.

SOME SMART DEVICES have a mouse—or an equivalent, like the touch screen on the Pocket PC. Other devices have no pointing device; for example, the Smartphone has neither mouse nor touch screen. These differences in hardware mean that you will receive different types of input on each of these devices.

Some smart devices have a keyboard—or an equivalent. Some custom CE devices, for example, have a complete alphanumeric keyboard. Pocket PCs do not have a hardware keyboard, but the on-screen Software Input Panel (SIP) allows input of character data.[1] The keyboard on a Smartphone has a phone keypad plus a few command input keys. As these examples show, the available methods for getting character data vary widely.

---

1. You can connect external keyboards to various Pocket PCs, some from the device manufacturer and others from third parties. We wrote some of the text for this book, in fact, using an external keyboard with a Pocket PC.

We use the terms *mouse* and *keyboard* in this chapter to refer to any input device that provides the same type of input—pointing or character key input—as a desktop device.

Overview of Input

Most Windows CE–powered devices do not have the same input hardware found on desktop PCs. Consider a Pocket PC, which has a touch-sensitive screen for pointing and an on-screen SIP for character input. Some Pocket PCs have navigation keys, the equivalent of arrow keys (up, down, left, and right) found on desktop systems.

These are big differences that you ought to take into account in the design of your software. Otherwise, your software may disappoint your users and cause them to avoid using your software. To satisfy users, you must learn about their expectations, which are often based on their experiences using other software running on a particular smart device.

One way to understand your users is to become a user of the smart device you are targeting.[2] For example, if you plan to write software for a Pocket PC, you ought to acquire a Pocket PC and use it on a regular basis. If you plan to write software for a Smartphone, it is not enough that you have experience with other mobile phones. You must spend time using this particular breed of mobile phone to understand what users expect to find in the user interface and how they expect to navigate it.

Nothing can replace the experience of getting fully immersed in the rhythm and blues of a user interface paradigm. Just as you cannot truly experience music without listening to it, you cannot truly understand a user interface without spending a lot of time trying to accomplish many different real-world tasks while using that interface. You will likely feel frustrated at first as you try to accomplish tasks that you do easily in other

---

2. At Microsoft, using your own products is referred to as "eating your own dog food" (or sometimes just "dog fooding"). It is based on the idea—as expressed by Microsoft CEO Steve Ballmer—that the quality of dog food companies' products would naturally and inevitably improve if the employees of those companies consumed their own products. All Microsoft employees are encouraged to eat their own dog food, that is, to make extensive use of their own products.

environments, such as finding the system task list, setting the time, or viewing the contents of a directory in the file system.

You are equally likely to enjoy discovering those user interface elements that do more than just overcome the apparent limitations of a smart device and that instead highlight the available features of a smart device. A simple example of this can be found in the Solitaire program as implemented on the Smartphone (see Figure 6.1). On a desktop PC and on a Pocket PC, Solitaire is played by dragging and dropping cards by using the mouse[3] or stylus. The Smartphone has no explicit pointing device; the numeric keypad instead provides the means for selecting card locations. As highlighted by this example, clever use of numeric keys is often central to the design of the input to a Smartphone program.

To give you a sense of what we are talking about, here are some differences you may notice when you start using a Pocket PC. This is meant not as an exhaustive list but rather as a starting point to encourage you to

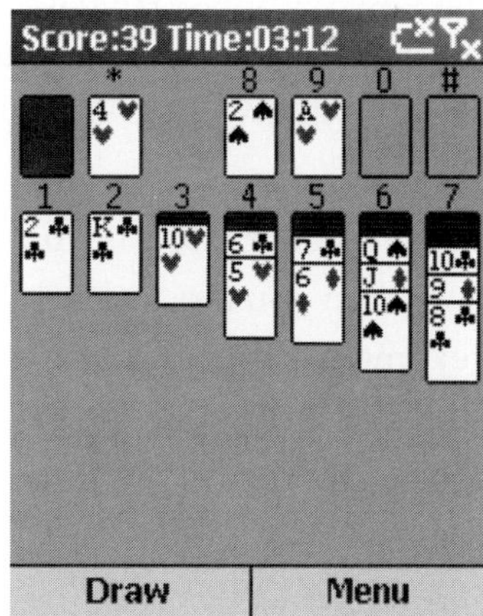

FIGURE 6.1: Solitaire on the Smartphone

3. On the desktop, it is possible—but painful—to play Solitaire by using the keyboard. This illustrates an old but now disregarded principle of Windows user interface design that recommends that mouse and keyboard input be equally supported for all input operations. This is but one element that separates good software on desktop PCs from great software. Newer software takes a more mouse-centric approach, workable until a mouse becomes unavailable or disabled.

spend the time getting to know whatever smart device you are targeting with your software.

- A Pocket PC has a small (240 × 320) screen (resolution is one-quarter the minimum VGA, 640 × 480, rotated by 90 degrees), full VGA, and also landscape orientation on new devices.
- The screen is covered by a touch-sensitive panel.
- Character input is accomplished by using the SIP.
- The SIP supports both handwriting recognition and an on-screen keyboard, two of several input methods. You can write your own input method window (a topic beyond the scope of this book).
- Pocket PC applications run full-screen.
- When you "close" most applications, they minimize (run in the background) instead of shutting down.
- The Pocket PC does not completely shut down when you turn the power off. Instead, the power switch toggles the Pocket PC between a fully on mode and a suspended mode. When a smart device is suspended, all applications in memory stay in memory but are asleep. This allows a Pocket PC—and many other Windows CE devices—to support "instant-on."
- Some Pocket PC applications make extensive use of context or pop-up menus, which appear when you tap and hold the stylus on a hot spot. Examples of context menus appear in these applications: Calendar, Contact List, and Pocket Excel.

Event-Driven Input

All GUI systems provide user input as events[4] because event-driven input works well for the type of interactive, user-driven approach that GUI systems are built to provide. The event-driven paradigm predates GUI systems; interactive simulators and computer games require such an approach.

---

4. This statement holds true for all GUI systems, from the first Apple Macintosh to the various members of the Microsoft Windows operating system, all UNIX and Linux-based GUIs, and both the .NET Framework and the .NET Compact Framework. They might have a different name—Win32 uses the term *message*—and the syntax for retrieving and handling the events may differ, but the general operation of all GUI systems is essentially the same.

These exceptions aside, before GUI systems were introduced most computer software was written to support batch-mode input (some readers may remember punch cards), screen-oriented forms data entry, and line-oriented input. With the introduction of GUI systems in the early 1980s, the event-driven paradigm entered the mainstream of computer programming.

Input events start life as electrical signals detected by hardware and transferred by a device driver into the operating system. The operating system stores this input in a FIFO[5] queue, which a program retrieves by reading the event queue. Some programming interfaces expose the event retrieval mechanism, while other interfaces hide it. The Win32 API exposes an input loop—sometimes called the *message loop* or *message pump*—which provides the event source.[6] By contrast, the message pump is hidden in MFC programs and Visual Basic 6 programs.

The .NET Compact Framework has a built-in, hidden message pump that lies buried in the `Application`[7] class. When the Visual Studio .NET New Project Wizard creates a C# program, the static `Run` method is called in wizard-provided code like the following.

```
/// <summary>
/// The main entry point for the application.
/// </summary>

static void Main()
{
   Application.Run(new Form1());
}
```

Another static method in the application class, `DoEvents`, polls the queue for events and delivers them to their respective targets. That method is equivalent to a standard message pump, which gets called to help flush messages from the message queue. As we discuss in Chapter 15, some multithreaded programs need to use this function to allow interthread access to controls (courtesy of the `Control.Invoke` method.)

5. *FIFO* stands for "first in, first out."

6. Win32 programmers will recognize the `GetMessage` function as the key function in that loop.

7. Fully qualified name: `System.Windows.Forms.Application`.

When an event enters the operating system queue, its journey is only half over. From the queue, the event must find its way to the correct window—a *form* or *control* in the terminology of the .NET Compact Framework—among the many windows in the system. Each window is owned by a thread, and that thread has a message pump responsible for retrieving the input for its windows. Each thread is owned by an operating system process. The second half of the journey gets complicated, in short, because the operating system supports multiple processes, multiple threads, and multiple windows. All the windows sit like baby birds in a nest, opening and closing their mouths, waiting for a mouthful from their mother. The choice of who gets fed is not arbitrary but depends on a very specific set of conditions.

In order for a .NET Compact Framework window—meaning a form or control—to get mouse or keyboard input, the following conditions are necessary (assuming that the associated class supports a given event).

- The window must be the foreground window (or a child of the foreground window).
- The window must be enabled (`Enabled` property is `true`).
- The window must be visible (`Visible` property is `true`).
- For keyboard input, the window must have the focus (call the `Focus` method to set focus to a window).
- For mouse input, the window must lie directly under the cursor or under the stylus (on systems without a cursor).

A few words on each item are in order.

The Foreground Window

The foreground window is the top-level window the user has chosen to work with. By "top-level" we mean a window without a parent. In general, each program has one top-level window. You should allow the user to select which top-level window to work with. This idea is so important that the .NET Compact Framework does not provide a way to force a window to the foreground. But the Win32 API does—the `SetForegroundWindow` function. You need this function when you have multiple forms in a program and you want to control which form is visible to the user. Here is the P/Invoke declaration for calling this Win32 function:

```
[DllImport("coredll.dll", CharSet=CharSet.Unicode)]
public static extern int SetForegroundWindow (IntPtr hWnd);
```

The `SetForegroundWindow` function takes one parameter, a window handle. In the desktop .NET Framework, that handle is provided as a property (`Handle`) of a control or form. The .NET Compact Framework does not provide this property, so we take another approach to get that value. We set the focus in managed code and then call the Win32 `GetFocus` function to query the focus window; the return value is a window handle. The following code fragment shows the declarations and function calls needed to set a form as the foreground window.

```
using System.Runtime.InteropServices;

// . . .

[DllImport("coredll.dll")]
public static extern IntPtr GetFocus();

[DllImport("coredll.dll", CharSet=CharSet.Unicode)]
public static extern int SetForegroundWindow(IntPtr hWnd);

private void timer1_Tick(object sender, System.EventArgs e)
{
   this.TopLevelControl.Focus();
   IntPtr hwnd = GetFocus();
   SetForegroundWindow(hwnd);
}
```

Enabled versus Disabled

To get mouse or keyboard input, a control must be enabled, meaning that its `Enabled` property must be `true`. All controls support this property, even controls that do not directly support mouse or keyboard events. This property influences three aspects of a control: mouse input, keyboard input, and control appearance.

Assuming that a control supports the events, the `Enabled` property acts like a switch. When enabled, a control can get mouse and keyboard events. A disabled control gets no input events.

A disabled control appears grayed, to notify the user that the control is not available. Figure 6.2 compares the appearance of various controls when enabled and disabled.

Visibility

To get mouse or keyboard input, a control must be visible—the `Visible` property must be `true`. Like many programming terms, the meaning of *visibility* does not map exactly to everyday usage. A control might not be visible to the user, but if the `Visible` property is `true`, the control has a presence within the user interface and so is able to get mouse or keyboard input. When this property is `false`, however, no amount of coaxing can cause the system to deliver either kind of input to a control.

Keyboard Input

Keyboard input arrives at the window that has the focus. The .NET Compact Framework supports a very small set of PMEs related to focus. The `Focused` property is a Boolean that lets you test whether a specific control has the focus or not. The `Focus` method lets you assign the focus to a specific control, which causes the focus to be taken away from whatever control previously had the focus. The two focus-related events are `GotFocus`,

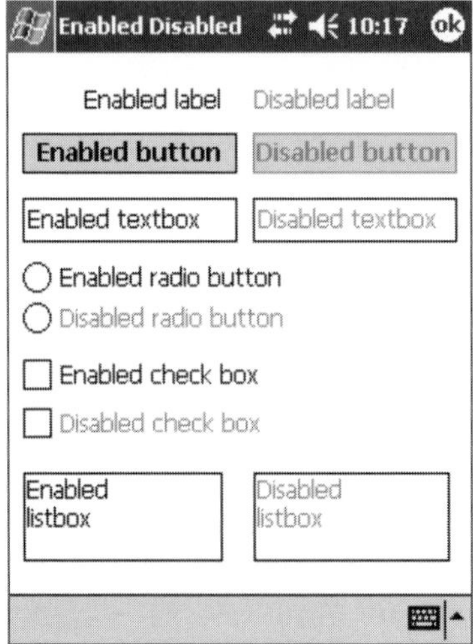

FIGURE 6.2: Enabled controls (black) compared with disabled controls (grayed out)

which tells a control that it is receiving the focus, and `LostFocus`, which tells a control that it is losing the focus. The two data validation events—`Validating` and `Validated`—are sent whenever a control loses the focus.

For controls that can receive keyboard input, a control with the focus gets keyboard input as a combination of three events: `KeyDown`, `KeyPress`, and `KeyUp`. The `KeyDown` and `KeyUp` events correspond to the user pushing and releasing a keyboard key (or its equivalent, a SIP key). These two events are useful for detecting keys that do not produce any printed output—such as the input from the arrow keys (left, up, right, and down), also generated when the user clicks the direction pad on a Pocket PC. (Many Pocket PCs have a rocker switch, which is treated as up arrow and down arrow input.)

The `KeyPress` event delivers alphanumeric keyboard input information, the character input information normally associated with printable characters. In a few cases, `KeyPress` events are generated for nonprintable keys including the enter, tab, and backspace keys.

To get a sense of the relationship between user input and the associated events, we wrote the `FormEvents` program (introduced in Chapter 5). Figure 6.3 shows the events generated by typing the letter "a". This program shows events as they are received by the program's form, and for that reason we set the focus to the form—by clicking the Form Focus button—prior

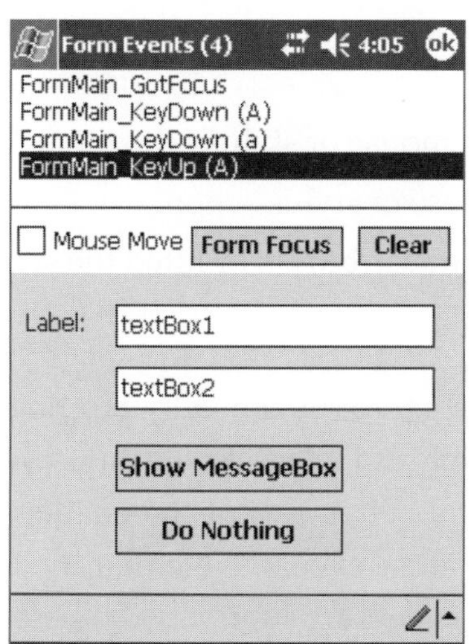

FIGURE 6.3: The `FormEvents` program showing the events generated by typing "a"

to typing the letter "a" on the SIP keyboard. That is why the first event shown is the `GotFocus` event. The events directly associated with typing "a" are the following.

- `KeyDown`: The user has pushed the A key (a virtual key, represented by the character code for the uppercase letter).
- `KeyPress`: The system generates the keyboard character "a" for program input.
- `KeyUp`: The user has released the A key (another virtual key).

The events associated with nonprintable input are simpler—the `KeyPress` event is omitted. When you push the up arrow, for example, you see the following set of events in the `FormEvents` program.

- `KeyDown`: The user has pushed the up arrow key.
- `KeyUp`: The user has released the up arrow key.

Mouse Input

Mouse input gets generated when the user either moves a mouse (for Windows CE devices that support a mouse) or touches a stylus to a touch-sensitive screen. Here are the basic sets of mouse events.

- `MouseDown`: The user has pushed the mouse button or has touched the stylus to the touch screen.
- `MouseMove`: The user has moved the mouse or stylus.
- `Click`: The user has finished the mouse or stylus action.
- `MouseUp`: The user has released the mouse button or lifted the stylus from the touch screen.

Figure 6.4 shows the events generated in `FormEvents` by tapping the screen of a Pocket PC (equivalent to clicking and releasing the mouse). You can experiment with this program to get a better idea of the relationship between user actions and the resulting mouse events. Note that the form itself is the gray area and that `MouseMove` events are suppressed unless you enable them with the check box labeled "Mouse Move."

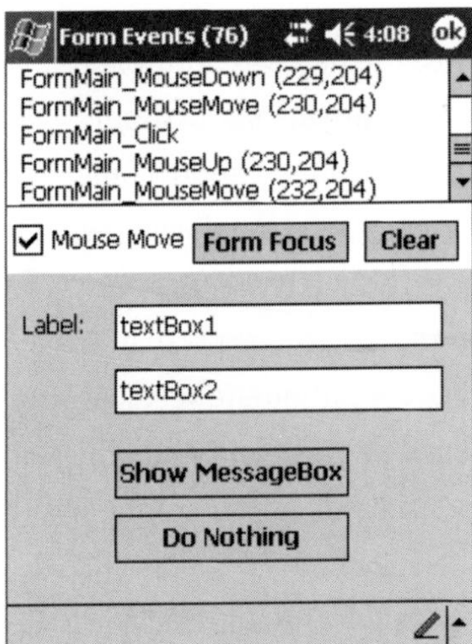

FIGURE 6.4: The `FormEvents` program showing the events generated by tapping and releasing on a touch screen

Windows CE Support for Win32 Input

The Win32 API is the core interface for Windows CE. The .NET Compact Framework itself is built on a foundation of Win32 libraries. You might wonder, then, how Win32 support on Windows CE compares with Win32 support on the desktop. Understanding this will help you know when you can accomplish some desired task by drilling through to the underlying Win32 functions and when such drilling would result in a dry well.

While many people use the term *subset* when they compare Win32 support on Windows CE with support on desktop versions of Windows, we prefer to say that Windows CE has "the greatest hits of the Win32 API." Windows CE provides the core features that are most popular with software developers.

The Win32 API on Windows CE supports the concept of global and local input states, just as you find on desktop versions of Windows. *Local input state* refers to the per-thread state of (a) the active window, (b) the window with the keyboard focus, and (c) the window with the mouse capture.[8] Although each operating system thread has its own private set of input states, the user sees only the input state of the foreground window (and its children). The only global input state value is the foreground window, which you set by calling the Win32 `SetForegroundWindow` function.

In general, the Win32 API on Windows CE operates the same way that it does on desktop versions of Windows. A hardware input queue receives mouse and keyboard input. That input gets passed to programs when they call the `GetMessage` function. Win32 messages can be passed around by calling `PostMessage` or `SendMessage`.

One difference is that Windows CE does not support hooks. On the desktop, hooks allow you to intercept Win32 messages. There are mouse hooks, keyboard hooks, get-message hooks, and send-message hooks. None, however, are supported on Windows CE.[9]

Windows CE does provide the ability to simulate keyboard and mouse events, which some Win32 programmers may recognize as the `keybd_event` and `mouse_event` functions. With these functions, your program can pretend to be the user and generate keyboard or mouse events.

Using Controls for Mouse and Keyboard Input

While the subject of this chapter is mouse and keyboard input, ironically our first recommendation is that you avoid handling mouse and keyboard input whenever possible. We recommend instead that you use a control, if you can find one that suits your purpose, because many controls do the work required to process the "raw" input made available by the mouse and keyboard. The .NET Compact Framework supports a nice set of controls that make it easy for you to retrieve many kinds of input. If you let a control do the work for you, you save time and effort. Our first recommen-

8. .NET Compact Framework controls that support mouse input always capture the mouse.

9. Or, more correctly, none are officially supported. The `SetWindowsHookEx` function does in fact exist on Windows CE, and it is rumored to support keyboard hooks. We have confirmed this rumor by getting a `WH_KEYBOARD_LL` hook to install and operate properly on a Pocket PC.

dation, then, is that you delegate your mouse and keyboard input to a control if a control can be found to do what you need.

Consider keyboard input. A user typing the letter "A", as mentioned earlier, generates three separate events.[10] `KeyDown`, `KeyPress`, and `KeyUp`. To accept keyboard input, you need to take this input and "cook it" to figure out what final text the user is entering. While it sounds simple, it sometimes is complicated by what a user can do while entering text—a user might hit the backspace key, use the arrow keys, or click with the mouse to change the input location. Converting raw mouse and keyboard input into the final "cooked" character string involves much work.

A `TextBox` control can do all of this work for you. Unless you have a special need to handle this input yourself, we suggest you simply create a `TextBox`. This built-in control, available in both single-line and multiline form, reduces the complexity of entering and editing text to just a few lines of code.

Mouse input arrives in an equally raw form, namely as a pair of x- and y-coordinates in a form or control. Suppose you wanted to display a list of items and allow the user to pick one. You certainly could do all the work involved with drawing the list, scrolling the list, and then selecting and deselecting items in the list. But a perfectly usable `ListBox` control can do all these things for you with a fraction of the effort. So unless you have a compelling reason to do all this work yourself, we suggest you save your energy for the truly new things you must build for your application.

Of course, in some situations the predefined controls do not provide exactly what you need. Sometimes you can fine-tune the operation of existing controls by subclassing a control class. In other cases, you may need to create a custom control and handle the mouse and keyboard yourself—a subject we cover in Chapter 10.

So how should you go about getting mouse and keyboard information? You will know you need to handle the raw input when you cannot find a control to do exactly what you need done. Controls are covered in detail in Chapter 7. Subsequent chapters provide details for the more widely used of the 30 controls in the .NET Compact Framework.

---

10. Events in .NET are identical to Win32 messages.

Control Support for Input Events

Table 6.1 summarizes the support each control provides for mouse and keyboard events inherited from the base `Control`[11] class. We created the original version of this table from conversations with the .NET Compact Framework development team. Because the support kept changing over time, we wrote a tool to provide a snapshot of support for inherited PMEs. You can review the output from this tool in Appendix B, which shows the support in the .NET Compact Framework version 1.0, Service Pack 2 (version 1.0.3316.0). You can download the tool we developed, which is named `ControlPME`, from the book's Web site.[12]

TABLE 6.1: Control Support for Mouse and Keyboard Input

Control	Keyboard	Focus	Mouse	Click
`Button`	Yes (SP2)[a, b]	Yes		Yes
`CheckBox`	Yes (SP2)[a, b]	Yes		Yes
`ComboBox`	Yes (SP2)[a, b]	Yes		
`ContextMenu`[c]				
`Control`	Yes	Yes	Yes	Yes
`DataGrid`	Yes	Yes	Yes	Yes
`DomainUpDown`	Yes (SP2)[a, b]	Yes		
`Form`	Yes	Yes	Yes	Yes
`HScrollBar`	Yes (SP2)[a, b]	Yes (SP1)[b, d]		
`ImageList`[c]				
`Label`	Yes (SP2)[a, b]	Yes (SP2)[a, b]	[e]	

11. Fully qualified name: `System.Windows.Forms.Control`.
12. See http://www.paulyao.com/cfbook/code.

Control	Keyboard	Focus	Mouse	Click
ListBox	Yes (SP2)[a, b]	Yes		
ListView	Yes (SP2)[a, b]	Yes		
MainMenu[c]				
MenuItem[c]				Yes
NumericUpDown	Yes (SP2)[a, b]	Yes (SP1)[b, d]		
Panel	Yes[b]	Yes	Yes[b]	Yes[b]
PictureBox	Yes[b]	Yes[b]	Yes[b]	Yes[b]
ProgressBar	Yes (SP2)[a, b]	Yes (SP1)[b, d]		
RadioButton	Yes (SP2)[a, b]	Yes		Yes
StatusBar	Yes (SP2)[a, b]	Yes (SP1)[b, d]		
TabControl	Yes (SP2)[a, b]	Yes		
TabPage	Yes (SP2)[a, b]	Yes	Yes (SP2)[a, b]	Yes (SP2)[a, b]
TextBox	Yes	Yes		
Timer[c]				
ToolBar				
ToolBarButton[c]				
TrackBar	Yes (SP2)[a, b]	Yes		
TreeView	Yes (SP2)[a, b]	Yes		
VScrollBar	Yes (SP2)[a, b]	Yes (SP1)[b, d]		

a. Service Pack 2 (available in December 2003) or later is required for this support.

b. The Designer in Visual Studio .NET 2003 omits mention of support for this event.

c. This control class derives from `Component`, so it cannot get raw mouse and keyboard input (that privilege is available only to controls derived from the `Control` class).

d. Service Pack 1 (available in August 2003) or later is required for this support.

e. Mouse events for a `Label` control are sent to the control's immediate parent.

The contents of this table require a bit of explanation. The first column lists controls. The second and third columns describe support for keyboard events. The fourth and fifth columns describe support for mouse events. A "Yes" in a column means a control supports that event or set of events. A few events were added with Service Pack 1, and those are identified in the table with "(SP1)" tags. Even more events were added with Service Pack 2, as identified by the "(SP2)" tag.

Let's take a closer look at the table and what it tells us about keyboard input first. The Keyboard column shows controls that receive keyboard input as `KeyDown`, `KeyPress`, and `KeyUp` events. The Focus column shows controls that can get the focus, as indicated by a control's ability to receive `GotFocus` and `LostFocus` events. On the desktop, the focus always means keyboard input, and the same is true in the .NET Compact Framework.

Starting with Service Pack 2, support for keyboard events for .NET Compact Framework controls is identical with support for controls on the desktop. The same is not true with support for mouse events, which .NET Compact Framework controls support only sparsely. The sidebar (Where Have All the Events Gone?) addresses this issue in detail. The short answer is that the .NET Compact Framework team boosted the performance and reduced overall runtime size by removing support for events that were not absolutely required.

Notice that a control that supports the focus event also supports keyboard events. (This was not always the case, however, prior to Service Pack 2.) The reason is that focus is associated with getting keyboard input—if a control supports one, it logically must support the other.

Related to the keyboard and focus events are the input validation events. The validation events are not listed in Table 6.1, but any control that supports the focus events also supports the input validation events. When a control loses the focus, it generates a `Validating` event. And then if input is accepted, another event—`Validated`—is generated. As we discuss in detail in Chapter 7, the validation events do not work the same way they do in the desktop. The validation events, incidentally, originate in managed code—and Win32 programmers may notice that the validation events have no equivalent in the Win32 API.

Where Have All the Events Gone?

Programmers who have built Windows Forms applications in the .NET Framework might ask themselves this question when they first look at the .NET Compact Framework. It becomes very clear that the .NET Compact Framework supports a significantly reduced subset of events from what is found in the .NET Framework. While support for keyboard events has been added to .NET Compact Framework controls to equal what is found on the desktop, the same is not true for mouse input.

Almost all .NET Framework controls can receive mouse events—from the lowly `Label` control up to every control that wraps a window (a `Timer` control, however, cannot get mouse events). By contrast, in the .NET Compact Framework only six controls can receive raw mouse input.

As we discussed in Chapter 1, an important design goal for the .NET Compact Framework was to run well. Among other things, this means being small and running fast. Smart devices have less memory, slower CPUs, and smaller screens than desktop (or laptop) systems. One reason for removing support for certain events was to make the size of the .NET Compact Framework smaller (it is less than 2MB, compared to more than 25MB for the .NET Framework).

Support for other events (such as mouse events) was limited to help .NET Compact Framework programs run faster. Most events are generated in unmanaged code, and there is a cost—a delay—in moving events from unmanaged code to managed code. Getting good performance required the .NET Compact Framework team to trim back the events that are allowed to bubble up into unmanaged code.

The Mouse column in Table 6.1 indicates whether a control can get the `MouseDown`, `MouseMove`, and `MouseUp` events. Unlike on the desktop .NET Framework, only a few—5 of 30 controls—support these events. The last column, `Click`, indicates whether a control can receive the `Click` event. Each control that gets the raw mouse events can also get `Click` events.

Four other controls also support the `Click` event. Unlike the other mouse events, the `Click` event does not report the mouse location; it indicates only that the user has tapped a user interface object. In many cases this is the only information needed for the control to do its work. With a menu item, for example, a `Click` event tells your program that the user has picked an item from a menu and that it is time for your program to respond by doing the work associated with that menu item.

Table 6.1 shows the extent to which controls are treated differently with regard to mouse and keyboard input. As mentioned, the omission of support in some cases enhances system performance and keeps the overall code size of the .NET Compact Framework libraries small. In other cases, a control does not get mouse or keyboard input because of the nature of the object itself. None of the controls derived from the `Component`[13] class support direct mouse or keyboard events (the `Click` event is supported for the `MenuItem` class, but not for the others):

- `ContextMenu`
- `ImageList`
- `MainMenu`
- `MenuItem`
- `Timer`
- `ToolBarButton`

All other controls derive from the `Control`[14] class (which itself derives from the `Component` class), and those controls do receive input of some type.

With regard to input events, differences between the two base classes are important. A control is a window to the underlying operating system, which means it can occupy pixels on the system display, it can get mouse or keyboard input, and it has all the other properties associated with a window. By contrast, a component is not a window. Menus and menu items, for example, are not windows in either the operating system or the .NET Compact Framework. So only `Control`-derived classes have any hope of

---

13. Fully qualified name: `System.ComponentModel.Component`.

14. Fully qualified name: `System.Windows.Forms.Control`.

getting events that are the result of Win32 messages; `Component`-derived classes get only events generated by the .NET Compact Framework—like `Click` with a menu item.

Input to `Label` Controls

One control class worth special mention is the `Label` class. This control receives neither mouse nor keyboard events. In this regard it is not special. What is odd is that mouse and `Click` events on a `Label` seem to pass through the `Label` to the `Label`'s parent. To the parent, which might be a form or a panel, the `Label` seems to ignore the event. No other control has this behavior. With all other controls, `Click` events are absorbed by the control and do not get sent to the control's parent. This is true both for controls that actually use the mouse click, like the `Button` and `TextBox` controls, as well as for controls that make no use of mouse clicks, such as the `StatusBar`.

A `Label` control cannot get mouse or keyboard events, but the `Label` class supports a property normally associated with mouse and keyboard events: `Enabled`. When this Boolean property is set to `true`, mouse clicks on the label get passed on to the `Label`'s parent; when set to `false`, no mouse clicks are passed to the parent. The `Label` control is one of the few controls that support different colors of text, as set by the `ForeColor` property. The text on a disabled `Label` control, however, is always grayed no matter what value has been set for the text color.

Determining a Control's Support for Specific Events

A theme of this book is that *inherited does not mean supported*, a phrase we first heard from Seth Demsey, a member of Microsoft's .NET Compact Framework team. This phrase describes the apparent contradiction between the PMEs supported by the `Control`[15] class and the PMEs supported by control classes derived from `Control`. Generally speaking, derived classes have more of everything than their base classes because

15. Fully qualified name: `System.Windows.Forms.Control`.

they inherit everything that the base class has. To meet speed and size requirements, however, .NET Compact Framework controls support a finely tuned subset of available PMEs, so a control may inherit the ability to receive an event from `Control`, and yet that control might never receive that event because the plumbing needed to deliver that event is not installed. The benefit of this situation is that .NET Compact Framework controls are fast and responsive.

When looking at mouse and keyboard input, this theme comes sharply into focus. The `Control` class supports all mouse and keyboard events; few derived classes have that same support. This may trouble programmers who have worked with the .NET Framework because it represents a departure from the way controls work on the desktop.

When working with .NET Compact Framework controls, you need to know which events a control supports. Table 6.1, along with Appendix B, provide the only accurate statement of current support that we know of.[16] Two other sources for this information are at least partially helpful.

The Designer in Visual Studio .NET 2003 displays a list of supported events for each control, as shown in Figure 6.5. To summon this list, click on the lightning bolt icon. The list is a good starting point for determining what events are supported, but it omits events that were added late in the development cycle or in a service pack. Table 6.1 provides a more accurate summary for the supported mouse and keyboard events for each .NET Compact Framework control. Incidentally, the Properties window list appears only when working with a C# program. A list of all inherited events is displayed for Visual Basic programmers at the top of the Code window, with no distinction between supported and unsupported events.

A second source of information about controls—and all other .NET Compact Framework classes—is provided by the Class Library Comparison Tool. This tool, written by Ben Albahari of Microsoft's .NET Compact

16. Microsoft's documentation teams face the huge challenge of getting all the details right prior to completing a product. By the time you read this, the company may have updated the documentation.

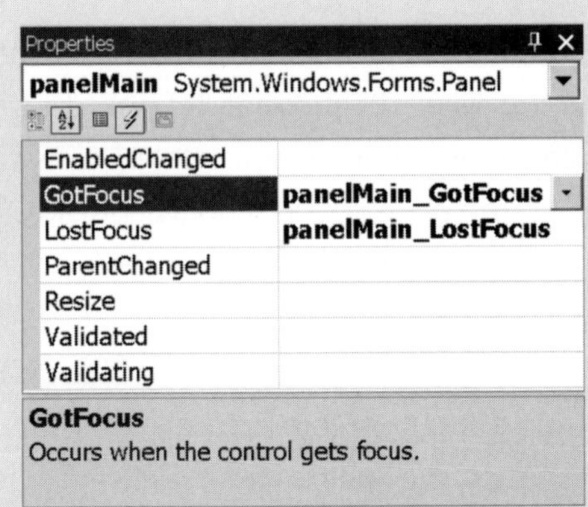

FIGURE 6.5: The Designer showing supported events for the `Panel` control

Framework team, compares .NET Compact Framework classes to .NET Framework classes. It does a good job of showing supported PMEs for controls. If you know the .NET Framework well, this tool will help you quickly learn whether your favorite class exists in the .NET Compact Framework.

The tool itself is a little hard to find but is well worth the effort. The tool is actually not a program but an XML data set with a filtering mechanism written in JavaScript. It is hard to find because it is buried in the MSDN Library for Visual Studio .NET 2003, with no way to directly search for it. A search for "Class Library Comparison Tool" yields no topics found.[17]

Here are two indirect ways to find this tool.

1. On the Index pane, enter "ASP.NET Mobile Designer". Display that page, and then click the blue up arrow to move to the previous topic. This succeeds because the Class Library Comparison Tool resides in the last topic in the previous section.
2. On the Index pane, enter "device projects" to locate the Smart Device Projects section. Synchronize the topic to the table of contents (use the Help→Sync Contents menu). Then browse to the last topic in the last section to find the Class Library Comparison Tool.

17. By the time you read this, the MSDN Library may have been updated to support this search.

Carets and Cursors

Both keyboard and mouse have user interface objects that show the current location for each type of input. A *caret* echoes the current keyboard input location, and a *cursor* echoes the current mouse location. These terms can be confusing because the term *cursor* refers to the keyboard pointer in character-based environments. In Windows (all versions, not just Windows CE), the cursor is the mouse pointer.

The caret is the only user interface object that blinks by itself. The .NET Compact Framework does not let you directly create a caret, although a `TextBox` control creates one for you. A caret appears in a `TextBox` when the following conditions are true.

- The parent (or the grandparent) of the `TextBox` is the foreground window.
- The `TextBox` has the focus.
- The length of the selection (the `SelectionLength` property) is `0`.

When these conditions are met, you can change the caret location by setting the `SelectionStart` property. Later in this chapter, we show you how to create a caret by calling the underlying Win32 caret creation functions.

The cursor echoes the mouse location, a fact that you know from your time spent as an end user of desktop versions of Windows. Some Windows CE devices support a mouse, but others—like the Pocket PC and the Smartphone—do not. On the Pocket PC, the stylus in the user's hand is the pointing device, and no cursor is needed to tell him or her where the stylus is pointing. So, in general, Pocket PC users do not see a cursor.

But cursors can sometimes be useful on a Pocket PC. For example, when an operation takes a long time, your program can alert the user to that fact by displaying an hourglass cursor. In other cases, a program can use a cursor to give the user feedback for some precise operation.[18] You might also notice that Pocket PC supports animated cursors. For example,

---

18. Pocket Word displays a cross-hair cursor for its drawing mode. You can access drawing mode by selecting the View→Drawing menu item.

in Pocket Outlook when you tap and hold, an animated ring of red dots dances around your stylus, followed by the display of a pop-up menu. The animated feedback for the tap and hold is built into the controls, but changing the cursor is not directly supported by the .NET Compact Framework. Because we feel they might be useful to programmers, we show how to accomplish this later in this chapter.

Programming for Mouse Input

Many situations may require you to write code to fetch mouse input. Perhaps you are writing a drawing program, which might use mouse input to track drawing coordinates as the user taps on the screen of a Pocket PC. Our first sample application, `DrawRectangles`, provides an example of doing just that. Or perhaps you need to create a custom control that lets the user select a location on a map (custom controls are covered in Chapter 10). In this section, we show you how to retrieve mouse events, how to draw in a control in response to mouse input, and how to change the mouse cursor.

Mouse Events

To get mouse input, you create an event handler for each event you wish to handle. Mouse (or touch-screen) input in the .NET Compact Framework generates the following possible events:[19]

- `MouseDown`
- `MouseMove`
- `MouseUp`
- `Click`

The first three of these mouse messages report the mouse location. .NET Compact Framework mouse coordinates are pixel coordinates, with the origin (0,0) located in the upper-left corner of a control. This coordinate

19. Programmers familiar with the .NET Framework may notice that the following events are not supported in the .NET Compact Framework: `MouseEnter`, `MouseHover`, `MouseLeave`, and `MouseWheel`.

system is the same as on desktop versions of Windows and Apple Macintosh and is therefore instantly familiar to programmers with experience on these systems.

Unlike the other three events, the `Click` event does not report mouse location. Instead, it notifies your program that a user has selected a control. The `Click` event itself is associated with the `MouseUp` event, which might seem odd to experienced GUI programmers because the `MouseDown` transition has traditionally been the primary mouse event in GUI programs. If you pay close attention when you interact with menu items and push buttons, you may notice that it is in fact the `MouseUp` transition that serves as the primary triggering event for several user interface actions.

Automatic Mouse Capture

.NET Compact Framework controls provide automatic mouse capture.[20] When a control gets a `MouseDown` event, all future mouse input is reserved for that control. This provides automatic support for something that Win32 and MFC programmers must request with a function call, a feature known as *mouse capture*. Once a .NET Compact Framework control captures the mouse, that control gets exclusive access to all mouse events up to and including a `MouseUp` event.

This is particularly useful when you are doing anything that involves handling both the `MouseDown` and the `MouseUp` events—such as drawing within a control or dragging an object. In such cases, automatic mouse capture guarantees that your control does not get left in an indeterminate state; you are guaranteed that every `MouseDown` event is eventually followed by a `MouseUp` event.

Mouse Event Handlers

To get mouse input, you need to create a mouse event handler for a control that supports mouse input. As mentioned earlier in this chapter, not all

---

20. This is also a feature of .NET Framework controls.

controls can receive mouse input, and in fact the .NET Compact Framework supports mouse events for only the following control classes:

- `Control`
- `DataGrid`
- `Form`
- `Panel`
- `PictureBox`
- `TabPage` (requires Service Pack 2)

Assuming you are using a control from this list, the Designer makes it easy for C# programmers to create mouse event handlers. Within the Designer, you select the control or form and push the yellow lightning bolt button in the Properties window. When you double-click an event name, the Designer creates the required event handler code for you.

In C#, there are two parts to event handler code. The first part is the event initialization code, which is ordinarily hidden in the Designer-generated `InitializeComponent` method. This code creates a new event handler object, which connects the user interface object to your event-handling function. Listing 6.1 shows four lines of code that initialize four mouse event handlers for a form.

LISTING 6.1: Adding Handlers for Mouse Events in C#

```
this.MouseDown +=
   new System.Windows.Forms.MouseEventHandler(
      this.FormMain_MouseDown);

this.MouseMove +=
   new System.Windows.Forms.MouseEventHandler(
      this.FormMain_MouseMove);

this.MouseUp +=
   new System.Windows.Forms.MouseEventHandler(
      this.FormMain_MouseUp);

this.Click += new System.EventHandler(this.FormMain_Click);
```

Each of these four event handlers refers to a function that gets called in response to an event. The Designer-generated code appears in Listing 6.2. (We have changed the format of this code to better fit the available space on a printed page; the code remains the same.)

LISTING 6.2: Four Mouse Event Handler Methods

```
private void
FormMain_MouseDown(object sender,
                   System.Windows.Forms.MouseEventArgs e)
{
}

private void
FormMain_MouseMove(object sender,
                   System.Windows.Forms.MouseEventArgs e)
{
}

private void
FormMain_MouseUp(object sender,
                 System.Windows.Forms.MouseEventArgs e)
{
}

private void
FormMain_Click(object sender,
               System.EventArgs e)
{
}
```

Three of the four mouse event handlers provide a `MouseEventArgs` parameter, which contains two integer values that report the mouse location in client-area coordinates: `X` and `Y`. The following code could be added to the `MouseDown`, `MouseMove`, or `MouseUp` event handlers to retrieve these coordinates and store them in a point.

```
Point ptMouse;

ptMouse.X = e.X;
ptMouse.Y = e.Y;
```

By contrast, the `Click` event does not report any location information. It tells us only that a pair of `MouseDown`/`MouseUp` events has occurred. In some cases, this is the only information you need to know; in fact, for some controls this is the only information that the .NET Compact Framework is willing to provide. The following controls support the `Click` event:

- `Button`
- `CheckBox`
- `Control`
- `DataGrid`
- `Form`
- `MenuItem`
- `Panel`
- `PictureBox`
- `RadioButton`

Incidentally, one control generates a class-specific click event, the `ButtonClick` event generated by the `ToolBar` control class when a user clicks on a button in the toolbar. This is different from the generic `Click` event; the `ButtonClick` event identifies the toolbar button that a user clicked.

The generic `Click` event is particularly useful for buttons and menu items, and you are most likely to use it for that purpose.

The next subsection presents a sample program that uses input from three of the four mouse events to draw rectangles. This program shows two different ways to echo mouse input to the user: (1) by echoing mouse coordinates as text, and (2) by drawing a stretchable rubber rectangle that allows a user to preview the location of new rectangles as each is drawn.

A Sample Program: `DrawRectangles`

Figure 6.6 shows our sample program, `DrawRectangles`, which draws rectangles in the program's main form. The program uses two pairs of x- and y-coordinates to draw these rectangles: one pair of coordinates is collected in response to a `MouseDown` event, and a second is collected in response to a `MouseUp` event. In between the `MouseDown` and `MouseUp` events, the program shows the user how the rectangle will look by drawing a rubber rectangle in response to `MouseMove` events. This program makes use of all the mouse input coordinates generated by the three mouse events.

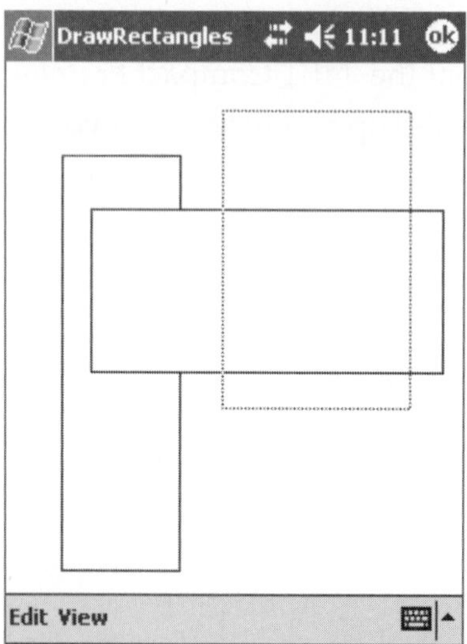

FIGURE 6.6: `DrawRectangles` **accepts mouse input to draw a set of rectangles.**

Drawing Stretchable Rubber Rectangles

Our program draws a series of rubber rectangles while the mouse is moving, although support for that is not found in the .NET Compact Framework itself.[21] Instead, we call a Win32 function, `DrawFocusRect`. We must also call four other functions to get this one to work as we wish. Because we felt this might be a generally useful feature, we have put this code into its own source file, `StretchRectangle.cs`, which appears in Listing 6.3.

LISTING 6.3: `StretchRectangle.cs` **Code That Supports Drawing Rubber Rectangles**

```
// Program Name: DrawRectangles.exe
//
// File Name: StretchRectangle.cs - StretchRectangle object draws
// and moves a stretchable rectangle.
//
// Code from _.NET Compact Framework Programming with C#_
// and _.NET Compact Framework Programming with Visual Basic .NET_
// Authored by Paul Yao and David Durant.
```

21. On the desktop, the .NET Framework has a class that can be used to get the same effect that we use here: the `System.Windows.Forms.ControlPaint` class. The static `DrawFocusRectangle` function can be used to draw a stretchable rectangle.

```
using System;
using System.Drawing;
using System.Windows.Forms;
using System.Runtime.InteropServices;

namespace DrawRectangles
{
   /// <summary>
   /// Summary description for StretchRectangle.
   /// </summary>
   public class StretchRectangle
   {
      // Declarations needed to draw stretchable rectangle.
      [DllImport("coredll.dll")]
      public static extern IntPtr GetDC (IntPtr hWnd);
      [DllImport("coredll.dll")]
      public static extern int DrawFocusRect (IntPtr hDC,
         ref RECT lprc);
      [DllImport("coredll.dll")]
      public static extern int ReleaseDC (IntPtr hWnd,
         IntPtr hDC);
      [DllImport("coredll.dll")]
      public static extern IntPtr GetFocus ();
      [DllImport("coredll.dll")]
      public static extern IntPtr SetFocus (IntPtr hWnd);

      public struct RECT
      {
         public int left;
         public int top;
         public int right;
         public int bottom;
      };

      private RECT m_rect;
      private Point m_ptAnchor = new Point(0,0);
      private Control m_ctrl;
      private bool m_bStretching = false;
      public StretchRectangle()
      {
      }
      public void Init(int x, int y, Control ctrl)
      {
         m_ptAnchor.X = x;
         m_ptAnchor.Y = y;
         m_ctrl = ctrl;
```

continues

continued

```
        m_rect.left = x;
        m_rect.top = y;
        m_rect.right = x;
        m_rect.bottom = y;

        m_bStretching = true;
    }

    public void Move(int x, int y)
    {
        if (!m_bStretching)
            return;

        // Remember window with focus.
        IntPtr hwndFocus = GetFocus();

        // Set focus to target window
        m_ctrl.Focus();
        IntPtr hwnd = GetFocus();

        // Get a DC from GDI
        IntPtr hdc = GetDC(hwnd);

        // Draw previous rectangle.
        DrawFocusRect(hdc, ref m_rect);

        if (x != -1 && y != -1)  // (-1,-1) means erase only
        {
            if (x > m_ptAnchor.X)
            {
                m_rect.left = m_ptAnchor.X;
                m_rect.right = x;
            }
            else
            {
                m_rect.left = x;
                m_rect.right = m_ptAnchor.X;
            }

            if (y > m_ptAnchor.Y)
            {
                m_rect.top = m_ptAnchor.Y;
                m_rect.bottom = y;
            }
            else
            {
                m_rect.top = y;
```

```
                m_rect.bottom = m_ptAnchor.Y;
            }

            // Expand rectangle to match new final rectangle.
            m_rect.right++;
            m_rect.bottom++;

            // Draw new rectangle.
            DrawFocusRect(hdc, ref m_rect);
        }

        // Clean up.
        ReleaseDC(hwnd, hdc);

        SetFocus(hwndFocus);
    }

    public void Done()
    {
        Move(-1, -1);
        m_bStretching = false;
    }
  }
}
```

The Win32 function we use, `DrawFocusRect`, was created to help draw the dotted rectangle that appears inside controls (such as buttons) when they have the focus. Some controls on the Pocket PC seem to use this function, but not as consistently as the controls on desktop versions of Windows. You can use this function when you create custom controls, as a way to highlight when a control has the focus (assuming you do not use a caret, which provides another way to echo keyboard input).

The trick to drawing a rubber rectangle is to continually draw and erase a sequence of rectangles in a way that does not damage the appearance of other objects that have been drawn in the window. The operation of the `DrawFocusRect` function requires a bit of explanation because when you study the code, you cannot tell the difference between where you draw a rectangle and where you erase a rectangle. This function uses a raster operator (or, to be precise, a ROP2 code) which makes the drawing occur as the equivalent of the Boolean NOT operator. (The XOR operator is the one actually used, probably because the original author of this function used mouse cursor code from display drivers—which use a pair of masks, one for an XOR operation and a second for an AND operation—as a model for one way to use raster operators.)

In simple terms, this means that you call this function once to draw a rectangle and a second time with the same coordinates to erase the previously drawn rectangle. Because of the use of the NOT operator, this function can cause a mark on just about any surface: it turns black pixels white and white pixels black. (The only limitation is that it cannot mark on 50% gray surfaces, which means surfaces drawn with an RGB of `128,128,128`.)

Collecting the Points

In one respect, this rectangle drawing is a bit odd; rectangles require four sets of points, not two. So how can we get away with drawing rectangles from just two corners? The answer is that we draw only unrotated rectangles, where each side is parallel to either the x-axis or the y-axis. The two points we collect define the opposite corners of the rectangle we wish to draw, just as a block of cells on a spreadsheet can be defined by identifying two diagonally opposite corner cells.

The rectangle drawing functions within the .NET Compact Framework itself support only unrotated rectangles. There are two such methods in the `System.Drawing` namespace, within the `Graphics` class: `DrawRectangle` and `FillRectangle`. This is, by the way, the only kind of rectangle drawing available on Windows CE, which does not support any kind of coordinate transformation. If we were willing to do a little bit of work, we could create rotated rectangles by using the `DrawPolygon` and `FillPolygon` methods. (We dig into .NET Compact Framework drawing in more detail in Part IV.)

We collect our points within an `ArrayList`, which we define as follows:

```
private ArrayList alRectangles = new ArrayList(50);
```

The chief benefit to using a collection class is that it grows as needed to accommodate additional rectangles. The actual collection of the drawing points is done with the help of three mouse event handler methods, shown in Listing 6.4.

LISTING 6.4: Three Mouse Event Handler Methods

```
private void
FormMain_MouseDown(object sender,
                   System.Windows.Forms.MouseEventArgs e)
{
   rectCurrent.X = e.X;
   rectCurrent.Y = e.Y;

   // Echo mouse coordinates to caption bar.
   if (mitemViewCoordinates.Checked)
      EchoCoordinates(e.X, e.Y);

   // Start stretchable rectangle drawing.
   stretch.Init(e.X, e.Y, (Control)this);
}

private void
FormMain_MouseMove(object sender,
                   System.Windows.Forms.MouseEventArgs e)
{
   // Move stretchable rectangle.
   stretch.Move(e.X, e.Y);

   // Echo mouse coordinates to caption bar.
   if (mitemViewCoordinates.Checked)
      EchoCoordinates(e.X, e.Y);
}
private void
FormMain_MouseUp(object sender,
                 System.Windows.Forms.MouseEventArgs e)
{
   int iTemp;
   int x = e.X;
   int y = e.Y;

   // End stretchable rectangle drawing.
   stretch.Done();

   // Echo mouse coordinates to caption bar.
   if (mitemViewCoordinates.Checked)
      EchoCoordinates(e.X, e.Y);

   // Make sure rectCurrent holds smaller X and Y values.
   if (rectCurrent.X > x)
   {
      iTemp = rectCurrent.X;
      rectCurrent.X = x;
      x = iTemp;
   }
```

continues

continued

```
    if (rectCurrent.Y > y)
    {
        iTemp = rectCurrent.Y;
        rectCurrent.Y = y;
        y = iTemp;
    }

    // Calculate rectangle width and height.
    rectCurrent.Width = x - rectCurrent.X + 1;
    rectCurrent.Height = y - rectCurrent.Y + 1;

    // Add rectangle to ArrayList.
    alRectangles.Add(rectCurrent);

    // Request Paint event.
    Invalidate(rectCurrent);
}
```

To collect the two points for drawing a rectangle, the input from only two events are needed: `MouseDown` and `MouseUp`. In our sample program, we store the coordinates for the first point in the rectangle structure named `rectCurrent` in the `MouseDown` event handler method. And then in the `MouseUp` event handler method, we retrieve the second point.

Once we have the two points, a few adjustments are needed. One is to make sure that the smaller of the two x and y values is used as the x and y for the rectangle coordinates. We need to do this because a rectangle is defined in terms of its location and its size; the location is defined in terms of an `(x,y)` pair in a `Point` structure. The size is defined in terms of a `(Height,Width)` pair in a `Size` structure. A negative size is not valid, so we juggle the pairs of coordinates to make sure we get a positive size value.

We also make an adjustment when we calculate the width and height. Notice that we subtract the two coordinates and then add `1` to the difference. This is needed because the width and height include the two endpoints, and simple subtraction excludes one point from the size. With these adjustments done, we are now ready to look at the code for drawing rectangles from the collected coordinate values.

Drawing the Rectangles

Once the points are collected in the array, it is a simple matter to draw them on receipt of a `Paint` event. Few .NET Compact Framework controls support the `Paint` event, but we are using a form, which does support the `Paint` event. Our program draws its rectangles by using the `Paint` event handler shown in Listing 6.5.

LISTING 6.5: The `Paint` Event Handler Method

```
private void
FormMain_Paint(object sender,
               System.Windows.Forms.PaintEventArgs e)
{
   Graphics g = e.Graphics;

   // Draw grid
   if (mitemViewGrid.Checked)
   {
      int cxWidth = this.Width;
      int cyHeight = this.Height;
      Pen penGray = new Pen(System.Drawing.Color.LightBlue);
      for (int x = 0; x < cxWidth; x += 10)
      {
         g.DrawLine(penGray, x, 0, x, cyHeight);
      }
      for (int y = 0; y < cyHeight; y += 10)
      {
         g.DrawLine(penGray, 0, y, cxWidth, y);
      }
   }

   // Draw rectangles.
   Pen penBlack = new Pen(System.Drawing.Color.Black);
   Brush brWhite = new SolidBrush(System.Drawing.Color.White);
   foreach (Rectangle rect in alRectangles)
   {
      g.FillRectangle(brWhite, rect);
      g.DrawRectangle(penBlack, rect);
   }
}
```

The rectangles themselves are drawn using code within the `foreach` loop at the end of Listing 6.5. For fun, we decided to add an option for drawing a grid in the background. That grid is selectable with a menu option. Figure 6.7 shows how the grid looks.

Mouse Debugging Tip: Echoing Mouse Coordinates as Text

When working with mouse input, you may encounter a problem—a mismatch between the coordinates you think you are getting and the results that are produced. Many factors might be causing this, from problems in your object design, to problems with the collection classes, to some other as yet unknown factor. This can be true for all types of programming, but it is particularly challenging with mouse events because they can race through the system and disappear so quickly. It can be hard to use a debugger to analyze some mouse event sequences because you need your hands to work the debugger, and that is difficult when one hand is trying to hold the mouse (or touch-screen stylus) at a particular location.

To help debug mouse input, we like to generate a stream of debugging data that we can then analyze at our leisure. One such method, which we implement in the `DrawRectangles` sample, is to echo mouse location in the caption bar of a window. Our program provides this as a feature that

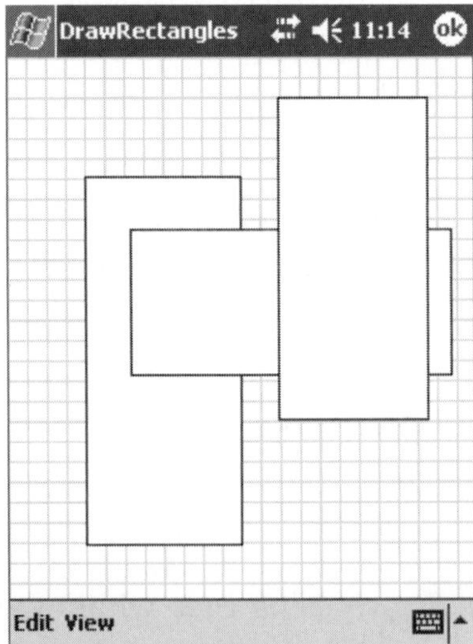

FIGURE 6.7: `DrawRectangles` with the background grid enabled

the user can enable from the View menu. Here is the function that each of our mouse event handlers calls when the user has enabled this feature:

```
private void
EchoCoordinates(int x, int y)
{
    this.Text = "Drawing (" + x.ToString() +
                "," + y.ToString() + ")";
}
```

This code is particularly helpful for dealing with `MouseMove` events, but of course it can also be helpful for debugging either `MouseDown` or `MouseUp` events. Each of our mouse event handlers has the following lines of code to call our coordinate echoing function:

```
// Echo mouse coordinates to caption bar.
if (mitemViewCoordinates.Checked)

   EchoCoordinates(e.X, e.Y);
```

About `Paint` Events

A key element in a GUI application is the graphical output. All GUI systems have a specific event reserved for creating graphical output. The Win32 API has the `WM_PAINT` message, MFC has the `CWnd::OnPaint` and `CView::OnDraw` handlers, and Visual Basic 6 has its `Paint` event. In all cases, the response is to redraw the contents of a window.

`Paint` events are caused by user actions—opening a file, drawing a rectangle, or dismissing a dialog box. In some cases, the operating system detects when a `Paint` event is needed, such as when user interface objects are opened or closed. In other cases, a program must request a `Paint` event when it detects that the contents of a window do not reflect internal program state.

Programmatically, there are two ways to request a `Paint` event, using two methods that are both in the `System.Windows.Forms.Control` class: `Invalidate` and `Update`. To understand the difference between the two, it helps to understand the theory behind how `Paint` events are handled by the operating system.

Relative to other operations that take place in a computer system, drawing on a display screen is slow. To enhance overall system performance, `Paint` events are assigned a low priority. All other system events—including mouse and keyboard input and system timers—have a higher priority than `Paint` events. To minimize screen redraw, the operating system collects all requests to redraw and generates the `Paint` event only when nothing else is happening in a program. A program generates a redraw request by calling the `Invalidate` method. One way to understand this function is to say that it puts a `Paint` request into the system event queue, so that redrawing is done at some later time. This is the most commonly used function and is the one used by our sample. In some cases, a program needs to force all `Paint` events to be handled—such as when you are taking a screenshot or when you need to make sure that all updates have been put in place. In that case, you call the second paint-related method, `Update`. This function does not define any new areas to redraw but flushes existing requests and puts them in effect.

One of the biggest challenges when building GUI programs is getting the `Paint` event handling to work exactly right. (This is a reason to use built-in controls; someone else has done that work for you.) When creating a `Paint` event handler, the goal is that graphical objects displayed in a window match the internal data objects held in program memory. When there is a mismatch, your program calls the `Invalidate` method and trusts your `Paint` event handler to do the rest. When program state changes and programmers forget to invalidate at the right time, a mismatch occurs between internal and external state. You might then be tempted to sprinkle calls to the `Invalidate` method throughout your program. You do not want to do this, however, because too many `Paint` requests create screen flicker that can annoy your users and create eye fatigue. The correct solution is to figure out exactly when to invalidate and to do so when needed.

Setting the Mouse Cursor with the `Cursor` Class

Support for mouse cursors—the user interface object that tracks mouse movement—varies on different smart devices. As mentioned earlier in this chapter, some smart devices have no pointing devices, others have touch screens, and still others have mouses. Smart devices with mouses support a wide range of mouse cursors.

A smart device without a mouse can still make use of a mouse cursor. Neither the Smartphone nor the Pocket PC has a mouse, for example, yet both provide partial support for a cursor. In particular, each supports one specific cursor, the wait cursor. .NET Compact Framework version 1.0 targets the Pocket PC, so the .NET Compact Framework itself supports only the wait cursor. The wait cursor gets displayed to let the user know that an operation may take some time and that the user should expect a bit of a wait.

In the context of .NET programming, two classes support mouse cursors:

- `System.Windows.Forms.Cursor`
- `System.Windows.Forms.Cursors`

Use the `Cursor` class to show, hide, or draw a cursor. This class also sets the current cursor. The `Cursors` (plural) class contains a collection of cursors for your use. On the desktop .NET Framework, each control can also have a default cursor (just as Win32 window classes can), but that is not true of the .NET Compact Framework.

Displaying the wait cursor in the .NET Compact Framework requires a single line of code:

```
// Display wait cursor.
Cursor.Current = Cursors.WaitCursor;
```

This code sets a property, which amounts to calling a function that wraps a data element. The function itself is nonblocking and immediately returns. Your program then does whatever work needs doing. Figure 6.8 shows the wait cursor on a Pocket PC, as demonstrated by our `WaitCursor` sample application.

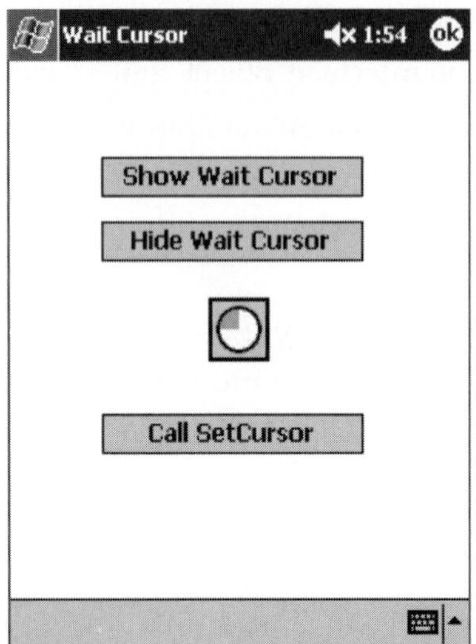

FIGURE 6.8: The Pocket PC wait cursor in the `WaitCursor` sample program

Until you hide the cursor, the user sees the wait cursor when your program is active. The cursor is part of the operating system's local input state so that one program can display a wait cursor while another program has another cursor or no cursor at all. When you switch away from a program that is displaying a wait cursor, the cursor disappears. When you switch back, the wait cursor reappears. To hide the wait cursor, set the cursor to the system's default cursor with the following code:

```
// Hide wait cursor.
Cursor.Current = Cursors.Default;
```

While the .NET Compact Framework supports one cursor, there are in fact two cursors defined in the `Cursors` class: wait and default. As shown in this code, the role of the default cursor is to allow us to turn off the wait cursor.

Setting the Mouse Cursor with Win32 Functions

When running a .NET Compact Framework program on smart devices that support more than one cursor, you can call Win32 cursor functions to access these additional system cursors. Our cursor sample application, `Wait-`

`Cursor`, shows and hides the wait cursor. It also shows how to call the Win32 functions for other system cursors. This method, taken from the sample, is the handler for the `Click` event on the Call SetCursor button. It lets you preview eight system cursors (see Listing 6.6).

Emulator Support for Mouse Input and Cursors with Pocket PC 2002 and Pocket PC 2003

In general, the emulator does a good job of representing how a program can be expected to behave on an actual device. There are limitations owing to various factors. Most limitations are based on the difference between the hardware of a development PC and a specific smart device.

Dealing with mouse input and mouse cursors for a Pocket PC is one example. To state the obvious, a Pocket PC has a touch screen, while a desktop PC has a mouse. A Pocket PC supports one cursor, while a desktop PC supports many. When running in the emulator, a Pocket PC program receives mouse input and has available cursors, unlike what such a program would see on an actual Pocket PC.

As far as mouse input goes, a mouse cannot jump very well, but a touch-screen stylus can. When running in the emulator, your program will get many more `MouseMove` events than the same program will encounter on an actual device. The simple act of moving the mouse over a control in the emulator causes a stream of `MouseMove` events, which occur on a Pocket PC only when the stylus is touching the screen. This difference means you must be sure to test mouse input code on an actual device. (As much as possible, you should test all your code on actual devices—but due to the difference in mouse input between an emulator and an actual device, you should allocate extra test time to address this area.)

The emulator relies on the desktop PC to show its cursors, so cursors in the emulator look different from cursors on an actual device. The wait cursor in the emulator, for example, is an hourglass that moves with the mouse. The wait cursor on a Pocket PC, as shown in Figure 6.8, is a spinning clock face.

LISTING 6.6: Displaying Available System Cursors

```
// ...
using System.Runtime.InteropServices;
// ...

[DllImport("coredll.dll", CharSet=CharSet.Unicode)]
public static extern IntPtr
LoadCursor (IntPtr hInstance, int iCursorID);

[DllImport("coredll.dll", CharSet=CharSet.Unicode)]
public static extern IntPtr SetCursor (IntPtr hCursor);

[DllImport("coredll.dll", CharSet=CharSet.Unicode)]
public static extern void Sleep (int dwMilliseconds);

public const int IDC_WAIT    = 32514;
public const int IDC_ARROW   = 32512;
public const int IDC_IBEAM   = 32513;
public const int IDC_CROSS   = 32515;
public const int IDC_UPARROW = 32516;
public const int IDC_NO      = 32648;
public const int IDC_HELP    = 32651;
public const int IDC_HAND    = 32649;

private void
cmdSetCursor_Click(object sender, System.EventArgs e)
{
   // Get button text.
   string strButtonText = cmdSetCursor.Text;

   // Create table of cursor IDs and names.
   Hashtable ht = new Hashtable();
   ht.Add(IDC_WAIT    , "IDC_WAIT");
   ht.Add(IDC_ARROW   , "IDC_ARROW");
   ht.Add(IDC_IBEAM   , "IDC_IBEAM");
   ht.Add(IDC_CROSS   , "IDC_CROSS");
   ht.Add(IDC_UPARROW, "IDC_UPARROW");
   ht.Add(IDC_NO      , "IDC_NO");
   ht.Add(IDC_HELP    , "IDC_HELP");
   ht.Add(IDC_HAND    , "IDC_HAND");

   foreach (object oKey in ht.Keys)
   {
       int iCursor = (int)oKey;
       SetCursor(LoadCursor(IntPtr.Zero,iCursor));
       cmdSetCursor.Text = (string)ht[oKey];

       Sleep(1000); // Pause for one second
   }
```

```
    // Display default cursor (no cursor for Pocket PC).
    Cursor.Current = Cursors.Default;
    cmdSetCursor.Text = strButtonText;
}
```

Our program adds the elements to a hash table and then enumerates the cursors from there. As each cursor is displayed, the cursor's name is displayed as the text for the `cmdSetCursor` button (the button otherwise labeled Call SetCursor). Our program needs a set of P/Invoke declarations to access the Win32 functions and to define the numeric ID for each cursor, as indicated in Listing 6.6. This set of declarations was created with the P/Invoke Wizard, which you can learn more about in Chapter 4.

Programming for Keyboard Input

The extent of your programming for keyboard input might be limited to fetching text from textboxes in your .NET Compact Framework programs. That is certainly the approach we prefer because we get all the support we could possibly want for entering and editing text, with very few lines of code. As mentioned earlier, only some .NET Compact Framework control classes support keyboard input:

- `Control`
- `DataGrid`
- `Form`
- `Panel`
- `PictureBox`
- `TextBox`

With all the time that you save by using a textbox to accept character input, you might decide to add some clever new features to your programs. Or you might find yourself doing Smartphone programming, which makes extensive use of the keyboard. Whatever your reason and whatever smart device you are working with, the following subsections cover the basics—plus a bit more—to help you take advantage of keyboard input to create brilliant .NET Compact Framework programs.

Sources of Keyboard Input

Keyboard input can come from four possible sources:

1. A device button
2. Input methods in the SIP
3. A key on a keyboard
4. From software using the Win32 `keybd_event` function

Let us look at each keyboard input source, starting with device buttons.

Device Buttons

By "device buttons" we mean hardware buttons like those on a Pocket PC. There are two sets of buttons on a Pocket PC: hot-key buttons and directional input buttons. In theory, you can use any button. When creating a special-purpose device—say, a Pocket PC to help track inventory in a retail store—it might make sense to assign all available buttons for application-specific needs. Or if we were to write a game, for example, we might take over all the buttons; the Game API (GAPI) library provides the C-callable `GXOpenInput` function to support us. For general-purpose programs, however, we prefer to use the directional input buttons.

Even if you do not use the hot-key buttons, you ought to know what they are. A typical Pocket PC has five hot keys to summon applications, with a default setting to record a message and to summon the various parts of Pocket Outlook: calendar, contact list, and task list. The user can modify these hot-key assignments through the Control Panel (Start→Settings). A program can programmatically assign itself a hot key by calling the Win32 `RegisterHotKey` function.

There are two sets of directional input buttons on Pocket PC 2002 and Pocket PC 2003 devices: an up/down rocker switch and a four-way directional rocker switch with an Action (or Enter) button. Taken together, this set of buttons can produce seven distinct types of input:

- Rocker up
- Rocker down

- Up
- Left
- Down
- Right
- Action/Enter

Software Input Panel

The SIP provides a set of input methods for entering character data. Figure 6.9 shows a list of the set of input methods as displayed by the Pocket PC 2003 emulator.

A U.S.-English Pocket PC 2003 comes with a minimum of three[22] input methods: the *Keyboard* (see Figure 6.10) with two different handwriting recognition engines, the *Block Recognizer* (see Figure 6.11), and the *Letter Recognizer* (see Figure 6.12). You could create your own custom input method by registering a COM component equipped with the required set of services, a subject beyond the scope of this book.[23]

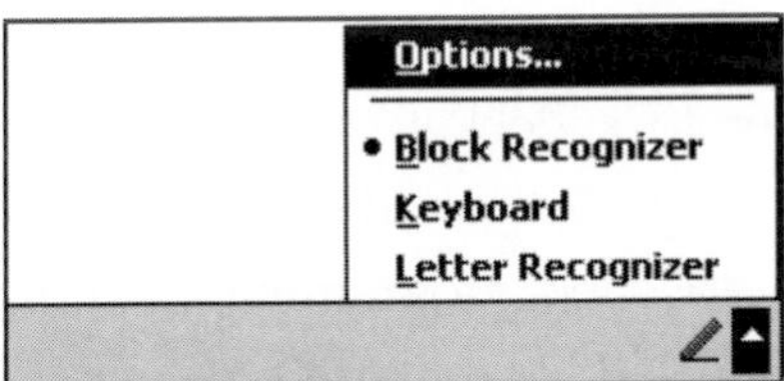

FIGURE 6.9: Three input methods supported by the Pocket PC 2003 Emulator

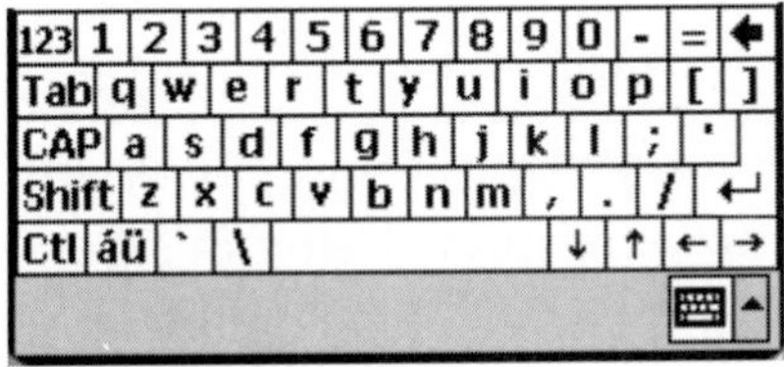

FIGURE 6.10: The Keyboard input method

22. A Pocket PC 2003 has at least three input methods, but more can be added in the ROM image by the device manufacturer or installed from other software.

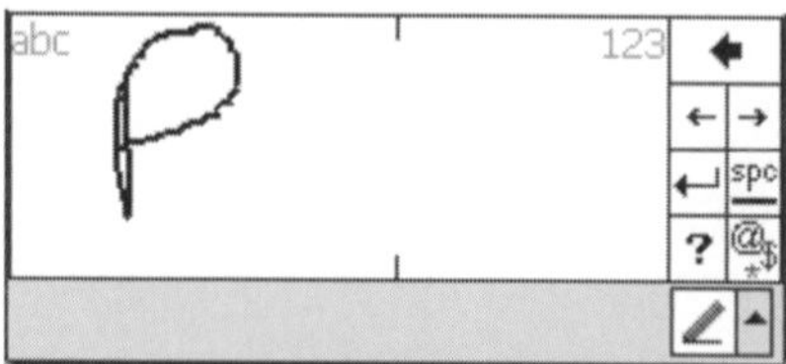

FIGURE 6.11: The Block Recognizer input method

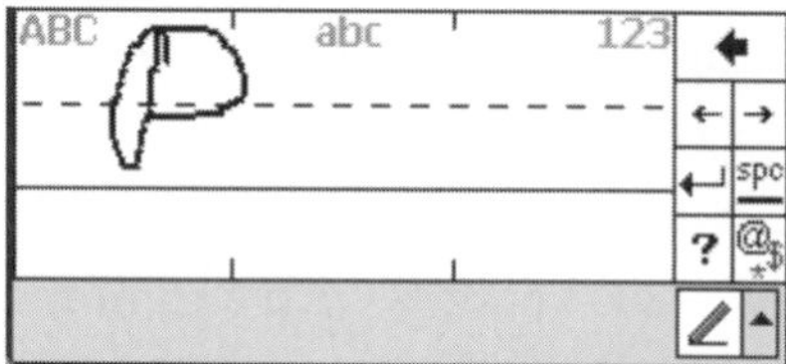

FIGURE 6.12: The Letter Recognizer input method

Users pick a preferred input method, then tap and click (or scrawl and scratch) to create character data. Your program sees only a sequence of keyboard events for the letters entered by the user. Your program does not know which input method was used, nor does it need to. It only needs to know that it received a sequence of keyboard events.[24]

One aspect of the SIP that does matter to a Pocket PC program is whether or not the SIP is displayed. The SIP can be opened or closed by a user, and these same actions can be accomplished programmatically in code. Your program can also request to be notified when a change occurs in the state of the SIP.

As we have said before, the .NET Compact Framework is a subset of the desktop .NET Framework. Sometimes, though, the .NET Compact Framework supports a feature not present on the desktop. The SIP is just such a feature, and the .NET Compact Framework has an `InputPanel` class, contained in the `Microsoft.WindowsCE.Forms` namespace. Using this class, your program can raise and lower the SIP, and you can also detect when

23. For details on creating a custom SIP, see Doug Boling's discussion of the topic in his book *Programming Microsoft Windows CE .NET* (Redmond, WA: Microsoft Press, 2003).

24. The Win32 function `GetMessageSource` can distinguish between SIP-entered keystrokes and hardware-entered keystrokes.

the SIP is opened and closed. (The `KeyInput` sample application, presented later in this chapter, shows how to receive these notifications in a .NET Compact Framework program.)

Keyboards

While the SIP provides a nice way to enter short amounts of data, lengthy input requires a real keyboard. Some Windows CE devices have built-in keyboards, and optional add-on keyboards are available for other devices like Pocket PCs. Add-on keyboards include foldable full-size keyboards, as well as tiny "button boards" that resemble the keyboards on some instant messaging devices.

One of us makes extensive use of an add-on keyboard for taking notes during meetings and even for writing large projects (including some of the chapters in this book, written while camped out at a local coffee shop). The lightweight, small form and long battery life make this a great word processing system for use on an airplane.

If you write software for the Pocket PC market, you might want to think about how an external keyboard can affect the potential market for your software. For example, when designing the database for a Pocket PC–based program, you might decide to store text notes with the data. With a SIP, a user might type just one or two lines. With a keyboard, a user might type two or three pages of data. Make sure that your program allows a user to enter long comments and that you do not impose arbitrary limits on your users.

The Win32 `keybd_event` Function

Windows CE allows any program to generate keyboard events by calling the `keybd_event` function.[25] This function, incidentally, is also supported on desktop versions of Windows. There was a time when it seemed that the most popular software was to capture and replay keyboard input. In those days, the developers of that type of software had to be a little sneaky in getting their utilities to work; some captured the low-level keyboard interrupt, and others installed hooks in the operating system. (We heard a story about two utilities that would fight for control over the keyboard, by deinstalling

---

25. A similar function for mouse input, `mouse_event`, is also supported.

themselves and reinstalling themselves every ten seconds or so to make sure that they were the first keyboard handler called.)

Windows CE does not support the mechanism for recording keystrokes—that is what keyboard hooks are for. If you have recorded keystrokes, you can call the `keybd_event` function to play back those keystrokes. You can also call this function to generate entirely new keyboard events. The `Sleep` program, presented later in this chapter, shows how to use this function to push the power switch, putting the system into a suspended state.

Keyboard Events

Handling keyboard input starts with paying attention to the following core keyboard events.

- `KeyDown`: A key (or SIP button) has been pushed.
- `KeyPress`: Character input has been detected.
- `KeyUp`: A key (or SIP button) has been released.

Most of the rest of this chapter covers how to handle these important events. Because these events occur in the context of other events, we start by discussing the other events that affect keyboard input.

Focus Events

Keyboard input can arrive only when a control has focus, so the focus events play an important role by setting the context in which keyboard input can occur. Here are the focus events:

- `GotFocus`: The control owns the system focus.
- `LostFocus`: The system focus is passing to another control.

A control must gain the focus to get any keyboard input, so the `GotFocus` event is a good time to handle whatever initialization might be needed in a control before keyboard input occurs. Before another control gains access to keyboard input—that is, before another control gets the focus—the `LostFocus` event notifies the focus owner of the end of keyboard input. This event is useful for handling whatever cleanup might be required. One user interface object directly related to the focus is a caret. Later in this chapter, we present the `Caret` sample program, which creates a caret when a control gets the focus, then hides and destroys the caret when the focus is lost.

Activation Events

Because Windows CE is a multiprocess operating system, a control may lose focus when another program starts running. For example, a user might switch away from our program to look up a phone number in a contact list, or a reminder might appear to announce an upcoming appointment by displaying a pop-up window. In both cases, control passes to another program. When the user switches control back to our program, we assign focus to the control that last had the focus. This, incidentally, is an easily overlooked test case, which programmers and test engineers would do well to address. It seems that when we focus on writing a program, we may forget to test how that program operates in the multitasking environment of real-world usage.

There are actually two parts to this problem, and the .NET Compact Framework solution is neither obvious nor always easy. The goal is this: When our program becomes active again, we set focus to the control that had the focus when our program was interrupted. To do this, we need to remember the control that had the focus when our program became inactive. The challenge for the second part is that a .NET Compact Framework program does not know when the program is becoming inactive.[26]

Win32 programmers solve both parts of this problem with the `WM_ACTIVATE` message, an event not supported in the .NET Compact Framework. To remember what control last had the focus, a program must set up a variable and watch each and every focus event. As each control gains focus—that is, as each control receives the `GotFocus` event—the variable stores a reference to that control. Later, when a program becomes inactive and then active again, the main form on a Pocket PC receives the following events.

- `Resize`: The form is becoming active.
- `GotFocus`: The form is getting focus.

26. The `Activated` and `Deactivate` events are supported, but these events do not appear in the Designer's list of supported events. To use these event, you must manually create event handlers.

Our program can respond to either of these events to set focus to the control that should have the focus. It might seem strange that the `Resize` notification triggers program activation. Here is one way to think about this event: As the form becomes active, it changes from having no size to having a size. (However, a form does not get a `Resize` event when the form becomes inactive.)

Another set of events related to keyboard input are the input validation events. The .NET Compact Framework supports the following data validation events when a control loses the focus.

- `Validating`: This event queries whether control contents are correct.
- `Validated`: This event notifies that control contents are correct.

The first event, `Validating`, essentially asks this question: "Are the control's contents valid?" It assumes that the answer is "yes." If all event handlers agree, then a second event, `Validated`, is sent. You can give a "no" answer to the validating question by setting a Boolean value in the event handler. The following code declares the control's contents invalid when the length of the text in the control is `0`.

```
private void
textFirstName_Validating(object sender,
   System.ComponentModel.CancelEventArgs e)
{
   if (textFirstName.Text.Length == 0)
   {
      statusMain.Text = "Please enter first name";
      textFirstName.Focus();
      e.Cancel = true;
   }
}
```

As a result of setting the `Cancel` flag to `true`, the second validating event—`Validated`—is not triggered, but nothing else happens. We force the focus back to the input control, which prevents the user from doing anything except dismissing the form.

Keyboard Event Sequences

In theory, event-driven programming allows events to arrive in any order. Object-oriented programming theory similarly suggests that class methods be written to be as free as possible from hidden assumptions about any order for calling the methods. These are good design goals; following them makes better event-driven programs and better object-oriented code.

For Desktop .NET Framework Programmers

Unlike the .NET Framework, the .NET Compact Framework does not force the focus to return to an invalid control. Also, the `CausesValidation` property is not supported in the .NET Compact Framework. In both environments, be careful not to force the focus to a control because it prevents users from canceling a dialog (or quitting an application). In this respect, the .NET Compact Framework is more forgiving because a dialog can be dismissed even when the focus is forced to an invalid control.

That said, there are a few predictable sequences in the world of event-driven programming. For example, we have seen that mouse events occur in a specific order: `MouseDown`, `MouseMove`, and `MouseUp`. Keyboard events also occur in a standard set of sequences. This is described in the following subsections.

Printable Character Keys. When the user types a printable character, say, a lowercase "a", this event sequence occurs.

- `KeyDown`: The A key has been pushed.
- `KeyPress`: The "a" character input has been detected.
- `KeyUp`: The A key has been released.

An uppercase character involves more events.

- `KeyDown`: The Shift key has been pushed.
- `KeyDown`: The A key has been pushed.
- `KeyPress`: The "A" character input has been detected.
- `KeyUp`: The A key has been released.
- `KeyUp`: The Shift key has been released.

We refer to the KeyPress event as the printable character event, but some keys that you might not associate with printable characters generate a KeyPress event, including the keys listed in Table 6.2.

Nonprintable Keys. The sequence of events is slightly different for nonprintable keys. When the user types an up arrow key, this sequence of events occurs.

- KeyDown: The up key has been pushed.
- KeyUp: The up key has been released.

These are the only events you see when the user types any of the various modifier keys: Shift, Alt, or Control. Table 6.3 shows some of the keyboard keys that make up the set of nonprintable keys.

Pocket PC Device Buttons. As we mentioned in Chapter 1, the Pocket PC has evolved over time. First there was the Palm-sized PC, which gave rise to the Pocket PC, which led to the Pocket PC 2002. The third generation is the Pocket PC 2003. When Compaq Computer (now part of HP) released its first iPaq-branded Pocket PC, the company introduced to the market a four-way rocker switch and action key.[27] Now many Pocket PCs—starting

TABLE 6.2: Keyboard Keys with a KeyPress Event for Nonprintable Characters

Keyboard Key	System.Windows.Forms.Keys Value
Tab	Tab
Control + <any key>	Varies, depending on which key was struck
Backspace	Back
Enter	Enter
Action key	Enter

27. When one of us saw his first iPaq at an industry event, he recognized this innovation in the product category. It was so new that Compaq salespeople at the trade show booth did not know how to use the rocker switch and action key.

TABLE 6.3: Keyboard Keys without a `KeyPress` Event for Nonprintable Characters

Keyboard Key	`System.Windows.Forms.Keys` Value
Shift	`Tab`
Control	`Control`
Alt	`Back`
Cap/Caps lock	`CapsLock`
Left	`Enter`
Right	`Right`
Up	`Up`
Down	`Down`

with the Pocket PC 2002—feature a standard four-state button. Figure 6.13 shows an image of the emulator, highlighting the various Pocket PC device buttons. It should be noted that not all Pocket PCs have a two-way rocker switch like the one shown in the figure.

The buttons on a Pocket PC generate a hybrid event sequence that makes it appear to your program as if the user has pushed two (or more) keyboard keys. For example, the following sequence of events occurs when the left side of the four-way rocker button is pushed and released.

- `KeyDown`: The left key has been pushed.
- `KeyDown`: The F21 key has been pushed.
- `KeyUp`: The left key has been released.
- `KeyUp`: The F21 key has been released.

Two sets of `KeyDown`/`KeyUp` events are generated each time one of these buttons is pushed and released (and three sets are generated for the action key, as shown in Figure 6.14). Table 6.4 summarizes the key values associated with each Pocket PC button.

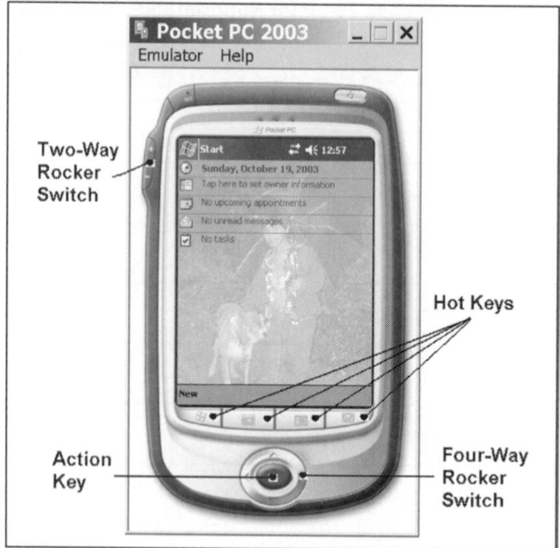

FIGURE 6.13: Pocket PC 2003 emulator showing Pocket PC device buttons

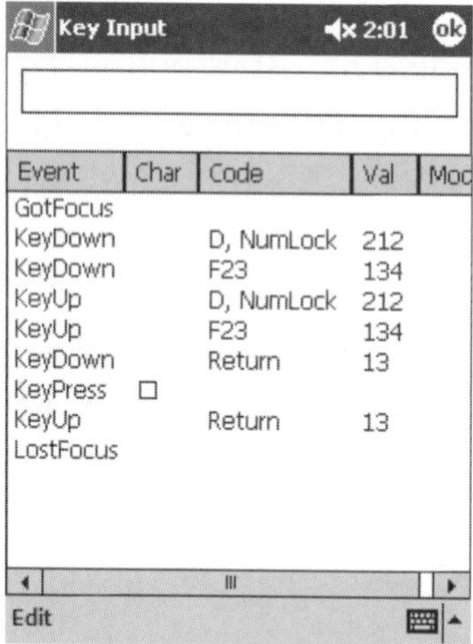

FIGURE 6.14: Events generated by pushing the action key

Whether these details are important to you depends on how you want to use the buttons. If you just want directional keys, then the rocker button and the four-way switch can be handled identically. We provide a sample program later in this chapter, named `KeyState`, which shows how to know which of these two buttons generated the keyboard events.

TABLE 6.4: Mapping Pocket PC Buttons to Key Code Values

Pocket PC Device Button	`System.Windows.Forms.Keys` Value
Two-way rocker up	`Up, F20`
Two-way rocker down	`Down, F20`
Four-way rocker left	`Left, F21`
Four-way rocker up	`Up, F21`
Four-way rocker right	`Right, F21`
Four-way rocker down	`Down, F21`
Action key[a]	`NumLock, F23, Enter`

a. The action key generates the most complex sequence of any button; see Figure 6.14.

Device Buttons in the Pocket PC 2002 and Pocket PC 2003 Emulators

There is a discrepancy between the key values generated on an actual device compared with the key values generated in the emulator. Identical sets of events are generated for the four-way rocker switch on both emulator and actual devices. Where there is disagreement is in the events generated for the two-way rocker switch. In particular, the emulator's two-way rocker switch generates a key value of `F21`. On devices, the two-way rocker switch generates a key value of `F20`. The discrepancy, in brief, is that the emulator generates a key value of `F21` for both the two-way rocker switch and the four-way rocker switch, while on actual devices `F20` is seen for the two-way rocker and `F21` for the four-way rocker.

Keyboard Event Handlers

Listing 6.7 shows empty event handler methods for the three core keyboard events.

LISTING 6.7: Empty Event Handler Methods for Keyboard Events

```
private void
FormMain_KeyDown(object sender,
                System.Windows.Forms.KeyEventArgs e)
{
}

private void
FormMain_KeyPress(object sender,
                System.Windows.Forms.KeyPressEventArgs e)
{
}

private void
FormMain_KeyUp(object sender,
              System.Windows.Forms.KeyEventArgs e)
{
}
```

The `KeyDown` and `KeyUp` events both receive the same event argument, a `KeyEventArgs` object, which contains eight members. As shown in the following list, four of the members describe the state of the modifier keys (Alt, Control, and Shift), three contain various types of keyboard key information, and one holds a flag to indicate whether a keyboard event was handled.

- `Alt` is a Boolean for whether the Alt key was pressed.
- `Control` is a Boolean for whether the Control key was pressed.
- `Shift` is a Boolean for whether the Shift key was pressed.
- `Modifiers` is a flag field for the Alt, Control, and Shift keys.
- `KeyCode` is a simple key value that holds a single value from the `Keys` enumeration (or, more completely, the `System.Windows.Forms.Keys` enumeration).
- `KeyData` is a complete key value, combining key code and modifiers information.
- `KeyValue` is a numeric scan code, as generated by the keyboard hardware itself. For example, the key values for uppercase "A" and lowercase "a" are the same, `65`.
- `Handled` is a Boolean for whether the key event was handled.

The `KeyPress` event—the printable (actually, semiprintable) character event—arrives with its arguments packed in a `KeyPressEventArgs` object, which contains the following members.

- `Handled` is a Boolean for whether the key was handled.
- `KeyChar` is the associated Unicode character for the key combination.

The remainder of this chapter presents a set of keyboard sample applications to help bring keyboard input to life and to provide you with sample code to use in your own programming projects.

The Unicode Character Set

The character set used by Windows CE is Unicode, a standard created by a consortium of hardware and software companies. Unicode solves a problem that has long troubled anyone who sells software in multiple languages. Put simply, before Unicode was introduced, there were too many character sets. The Unicode standard provides a single, standard character set that incorporates all of the characters needed for written business communication using modern languages.

Before Unicode, every language had its own character set to reflect language-specific characters, including characters with diacritical marks (like the "ü" in "München") and punctuation. The challenge was made even greater because some languages had multiple character sets.

A second problem was that certain Asian languages—Chinese, Japanese, and Korean—use many more characters than, say, English. While U.S. English uses fewer than 128 characters, written Chinese needs thousands of characters. This difference creates a problem because the English version of software would use an 8-bit character set, while Chinese required a 16-bit character set. Some character sets combined both 8-bit characters and 16-bit characters, a practice that changes string-handling rules. For example, how do you count the number of characters when some characters are 1 byte and others are 2 bytes? The Unicode standards address these problems by providing a single, unified set of code points, making it easier to create global software. A common set of string functions works across all languages.

All Windows CE functions require Unicode strings, so all .NET Compact Framework strings are Unicode strings. This creates a problem when your program reads non-Unicode files and needs to create .NET Compact Framework objects to hold those strings. You can convert between Unicode and other character sets by using the `Encoder` and `Decoder` classes, located in the `System.Text` namespace.

A Sample Program: `KeyInput`

Our first sample keyboard program, `KeyInput`, is both a tool and a sample. It is a tool because by running it you can study details of keyboard events. As you type, characters are displayed in a textbox while details of each keyboard event are echoed in the `ListView` control. This program is a sample because its source code serves as an example of useful .NET Compact Framework programming techniques, such as responding to SIP events and subclassing .NET Compact Framework controls.

`KeyInput` has three visible controls and one invisible control. The visible controls are a textbox, a list view, and a menu. The invisible control is an input panel created from the `InputPanel` class.[28] This Windows CE–specific class lets you raise and lower the SIP. It also generates events when the SIP is raised and lowered, to allow a program to adjust the location or size of controls to adapt to the change.

Figure 6.15 shows the output created by `KeyInput` when the user types the word "Hi" in the textbox. Notice that two `KeyDown` events are needed to create an uppercase "H", first the Shift key and then the H key. The system delivers a `KeyPress` event to report when a printable character has

28. Fully qualified name: `Microsoft.WindowsCE.Forms.InputPanel`.

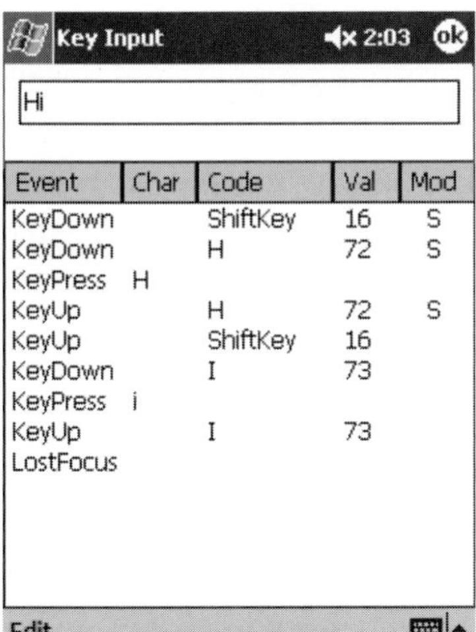

FIGURE 6.15: The `KeyInput` program echoing keyboard event details

actually been generated. The textbox itself only needs to pay attention to the `KeyPress` event and can ignore both the `KeyDown` event and the `KeyUp` event that were also generated.

Responding to SIP Changes by Using the `InputPanel` Control

The `ListView` control handles the details of managing the event list. When the list grows longer than the available screen space allows, the control displays a scroll bar on the right side to let the user know that some of its contents are not visible. In general, this control does most of the work required to be useful.

The `ListView` control does not respond to changes in the SIP. When the user displays the SIP to access the various character input methods, the `ListView` control gets covered. The contents of the control are hidden, as is the scroll bar that might otherwise allow the user to move hidden items into view.

The .NET Compact Framework provides the `InputPanel` control, which lets users access the basic features of the SIP. This control is very simple to use. In the Designer, we drag and drop an `InputPanel` from the Toolbox onto our form (or onto the icon panel at the bottom of the Designer window). The InputPanel control supports one property and one event.

- Enabled is a read/write Boolean property that reads or sets the status of the SIP. When this property's value is true, the SIP is open, and when false, the SIP is closed.
- EnabledChanged is the event that fires when the SIP opens or closes.

Once we add the InputPanel control to our program, we change its name to sipMain. Listing 6.8 shows the event handler method for the EnabledChanged event in our sample program. When this event handler is called, it changes the size of the ListView control (named lviewOutput)—shrinking the ListView when the SIP is opened and enlarging the ListView when the SIP is hidden.

LISTING 6.8: EnabledChanged Event Handler Method for the Input Panel

```
private void
sipMain_EnabledChanged(object sender, System.EventArgs e)
{
        // SIP is open
   if (sipMain.Enabled)
   {
      // Adjust list view height to make room for SIP.
      lviewOutput.Height = this.Height -
         lviewOutput.Top -
         sipMain.Bounds.Height
         + 1;
   }
   else // SIP is closed
   {
      // Adjust scroll bar height to form height.
      lviewOutput.Height = this.Height -
         lviewOutput.Top
         + 1;
   }
}
```

Subclassing versus Event Handlers

KeyInput subclasses a TextBox control to trap keyboard events as they occur. This is admittedly overkill because you can get event information just by defining an event handler (with much less code). But subclassing is such a useful technique that we decided it would be worthwhile to provide this code sample, even though in this context its use is probably not warranted.

Subclassing lets you create a new class from an existing class. Our new class, `TextEventSpy`, gathers details about specific events but does not change the behavior of the underlying `TextBox` control. With minor changes to our code, we could create very different kinds of text entry controls. We could create, for example, a numeric textbox, an uppercase-only textbox, or a telephone number textbox.

So when does it make sense to use event handlers, and when does it make sense to subclass? You will use event handlers to be notified of events without necessarily changing the underlying behavior of a control. By subclassing, on the other hand, you control the flow of events from the system to a control. You can ignore events, send modified events, convert a single event into multiple events, or make whatever other changes you need in the way that events get delivered to a subclassed control class.

Subclassing a `TextBox` *Control*

The act of subclassing the `TextBox` control class is the same as subclassing any class. The basic syntax of C#, an object-oriented language, makes subclassing a clean and easy process. We create the `TextEventSpy` class from the `TextBox` class by using the following declaration for the new class:

```
public class TextEventSpy : System.Windows.Forms.TextBox
{
// class definition
}
```

While the basic syntax is simple, what makes it possible is a well-designed and well-defined class that behaves in a predictable and logical fashion. If we did not know how `TextBox` worked, we would not be able to modify its operation. If it were poorly designed, we might have trouble getting our new class to work properly.

Our new class inherits everything that was in the base class. But we can change only parts of what we inherit. In particular, we can replace methods marked as replaceable. In C# terms, methods defined with the `virtual` keyword can be overridden. When we decide to replace a virtual function, we must use the `override` keyword in our version of the method. In the `TextBox` class (as with all control classes), we can override only event-related methods (methods whose names start with `On`, as in `OnKeyDown`). Table 6.5 shows the events supported by the `TextBox` class and the names of the virtual methods we can replace.

Subclassing and the Windows Forms Designer

In Visual Studio .NET 2003, the Windows Forms Designer does not recognize .NET Compact Framework controls defined by subclassing. This can create problems if you plan to refine your program's user interface over time because the Designer knows about only the built-in classes and whatever other classes are created as formal custom controls (a subject we cover in Chapter 10). Programmers who have worked with the .NET Framework may find this particularly annoying because the Designer easily recognizes derived classes for desktop applications.

One solution is to create a full-blown custom control, which can then get full support from the Designer. If you are creating a control that many other people will use, that is probably your best approach. A little extra

TABLE 6.5: Events and Virtual Methods in the `TextBox` Class

Event	Event Handler Method
`KeyDown`	`OnKeyDown`
`KeyPress`	`OnKeyPress`
`KeyUp`	`OnKeyUp`
`EnabledChanged`	`OnEnabledChanged`
`GotFocus`	`OnGotFocus`
`LostFocus`	`OnLostFocus`
`ParentChanged`	`OnParentChanged`
`TextChanged`	`OnTextChanged`

work on your part will make your control more acceptable to the programmers who use your control.

Another solution, appropriate when subclassing a control for one-time use, is to let the Designer work with the built-in control and substitute your own control at runtime. We take this approach for this sample, which declares two controls: one a built-in `TextBox` and the other for our derived class:

```
private System.Windows.Forms.TextBox textInput;
private TextEventSpy textspy;
```

Within the constructor for the form, after we call `InitializeComponent` (which creates all the other controls), we substitute our new control for the old control, then delete the old control as follows:

```
// Put our TextBox (TextEventSpy) in place of
// default TextBox.
textspy = new TextEventSpy((Control)this, m_deleNewEvent);
textspy.Location = textInput.Location;
textspy.Size = textInput.Size;
textspy.Text = textInput.Text;
this.Controls.Add(textspy);
this.Controls.Remove(textInput);
```

In setting the new control's properties, we borrowed code from our program's Designer-generated region. By using that code as a reference point, we are sure to take into account all the properties and event handlers defined within the Designer.

Identifying Methods to Override

How do you know which methods are candidates for replacing? The documentation is not very helpful. One approach is to override a function and rely on compiler errors to see which functions cannot be overridden. This approach, which we refer to as "throwing mud against a wall"[29] is not a good use of time.

29. ". . . and hoping that some sticks"—in other words, a trial-and-error approach.

A better approach is to use the `ildasm.exe` tool that ships with Visual Studio .NET. This tool can let you see very quickly which functions can be overridden. You can either look at functions one at a time or dump an entire DLL and study the dump for hints about which methods are virtual. Figure 6.16 shows a disassembly of the `OnPaint` method in the `Control` class. The presence of the `virtual` keyword in the function declaration (the end of the first line) marks the `OnPaint` method as replaceable.

To replace an event handler, define a function in the new class with the same name and the same function signature. To make it clear that we wish to replace an existing method, C# requires the `override` keyword in the method declaration, as shown in this replacement for the `OnKeyDown` handler:

```
protected override void
OnKeyDown(KeyEventArgs e)
{
   base.OnKeyDown(e);
}
```

When called, this empty handler calls `OnKeyDown` in the base class, represented in this code by the C# `base` keyword. When we subclass a .NET control, we start with a set of do-nothing functions like this, to make sure that we have the basic syntax correct. Once that is in place, we are ready to fine-tune the handler. Listing 6.9 shows the complete listing for our `TextEventSpy` class.

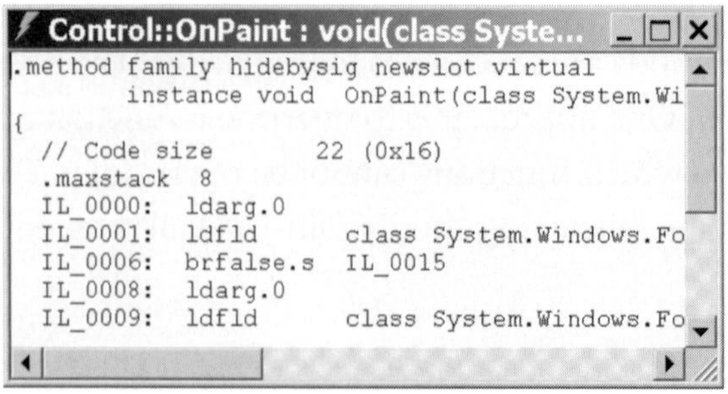

```
Control::OnPaint : void(class Syste...
.method family hidebysig newslot virtual
        instance void  OnPaint(class System.Wi
{
  // Code size       22 (0x16)
  .maxstack  8
  IL_0000:  ldarg.0
  IL_0001:  ldfld      class System.Windows.Fo
  IL_0006:  brfalse.s  IL_0015
  IL_0008:  ldarg.0
  IL_0009:  ldfld      class System.Windows.Fo
```

FIGURE 6.16: `ildasm.exe` displaying details about the `Control::OnPaint` method

LISTING 6.9: Subclassing a TextBox Control

```
using System;
using System.Collections;
using System.Windows.Forms;

namespace KeyInput
{
   /// <summary>
   /// Summary description for TextEventSpy.
   /// </summary>
   public enum EventType
   {
      Event_KeyDown,
      Event_KeyPress,
      Event_KeyUp,
      Event_GotFocus,
      Event_LostFocus
   }

   // Buffer for passing event info to form.
   public struct KeyEventItem
   {
      public EventType etype;
      public KeyEventArgs eUpDown;
      public KeyPressEventArgs ePress;
   }

   /// <summary>
   /// Summary description for TextEventSpy.
   /// </summary>
   public class TextEventSpy : System.Windows.Forms.TextBox
   {
      private KeyEventItem m_kei = new KeyEventItem();
      private Control m_ctrlInvokeTarget; // Interthread control
      // Interthread delegate
      private EventHandler m_deleCallback;

      public KeyEventItem kei
      {
         get { return m_kei; }
      }

      public TextEventSpy(Control ctrl, EventHandler dele)
      {
         //
         // TODO: Add constructor logic here
         //
```

continues

continued

```
        m_ctrlInvokeTarget = ctrl;  // Who to call.
        m_deleCallback = dele;     // How to call.
    }

    protected override void
    OnKeyDown(KeyEventArgs e)
    {
        // Add new event info to list.
        m_kei.etype = EventType.Event_KeyDown;
        m_kei.eUpDown = e;

        // Trigger 'new event' notification
        m_ctrlInvokeTarget.Invoke(m_deleCallback);

        base.OnKeyDown(e);
    }

    protected override void
    OnKeyPress(KeyPressEventArgs e)
    {
        // Add new event info to list.
        m_kei.etype = EventType.Event_KeyPress;
        m_kei.ePress = e;

        // Trigger 'new event' notification
        m_ctrlInvokeTarget.Invoke(m_deleCallback);

        base.OnKeyPress(e);
    }

    protected override void
    OnKeyUp(KeyEventArgs e)
    {
        // Add new event info to list.
        m_kei.etype = EventType.Event_KeyUp;
        m_kei.eUpDown = e;

        // Trigger 'new event' notification
        m_ctrlInvokeTarget.Invoke(m_deleCallback);

        base.OnKeyUp(e);
    }

    protected override void
    OnGotFocus(EventArgs e)
    {
        // Add new event info to list.
```

```
            m_kei.etype = EventType.Event_GotFocus;

            // Trigger 'new event' notification
            m_ctrlInvokeTarget.Invoke(m_deleCallback);

            base.OnGotFocus(e);
        }

        protected override void
        OnLostFocus(EventArgs e)
        {
            // Add new event info to list.
            m_kei.etype = EventType.Event_LostFocus;

            // Trigger 'new event' notification
            m_ctrlInvokeTarget.Invoke(m_deleCallback);

            base.OnLostFocus(e);
        }

    }
}
```

A Sample Program: `KeyState`

Programmers who build .NET Compact Framework programs for a Pocket PC may want to read input from the device buttons, meaning the two-way rocker switch and the four-way rocker switch. As mentioned earlier in this chapter, the Pocket PC sends two pairs of down/up messages for these buttons (and three pairs for the action key). Table 6.6 summarizes the key code values for the various `KeyDown` and `KeyUp` events (this information was presented earlier in Table 6.4 and is repeated here for convenience).

What makes these buttons different from keyboard buttons is that there are two (or three) `Down` events for each push and two or three `Up` events for each release. So the following sequence of events occurs when the rocker button is pushed in the up direction.

- `KeyDown`: The up key has been pushed.
- `KeyDown`: The F20 key has been pushed.
- `KeyUp`: The up key has been released.
- `KeyUp`: The F20 key has been released.

TABLE 6.6: Mapping Pocket PC Buttons to Key Code Values

Pocket PC Device Button	`System.Windows.Forms.Keys` Value
Two-way rocker up	`Up, F20`
Two-way rocker down	`Down, F20`
Four-way rocker left	`Left, F21`
Four-way rocker up	`Up, F21`
Four-way rocker right	`Right, F21`
Four-way rocker down	`Down, F21`
Action key[a]	`NumLock, F23, Enter`

a. The action key generates the most complex sequence of any button; see Figure 6.14.

If you only want to watch for `Up` or `Down` events, your task is an easy one. And if you only want to watch for F20 or F21 events, that also is easy. What is not so easy is distinguishing between a rocker switch `Up` and a four-way switch `Up`, or between a rocker switch `Down` and a four-way switch `Down`. The information provided for each event tells only half the story. Figure 6.17 shows the output from our `KeyState` program when the user clicks the up button on the four-way switch.

`KeyState` relies on a Win32 function, `GetAsyncKeyState`, to tell the difference between two-way rocker button input and four-way rocker button input. This function takes a single parameter: a virtual key code. In Win32, virtual key codes are named with symbols that have a prefix of `VK_` (e.g., `VK_F21`, `VK_UP`, `VK_DOWN`, and so on). When a specified key is down, this function returns a value less than zero. The Windows virtual key codes appear in .NET within the `Keys`[30] enumeration, so that our P/Invoke declaration for calling the `GetAsyncKeyState` function is as follows:

```
[DllImport("coredll.dll", CharSet=CharSet.Unicode)]
public static extern short GetAsyncKeyState (Keys vKey);
```

30. Fully qualified name: `System.Windows.Forms.Keys`.

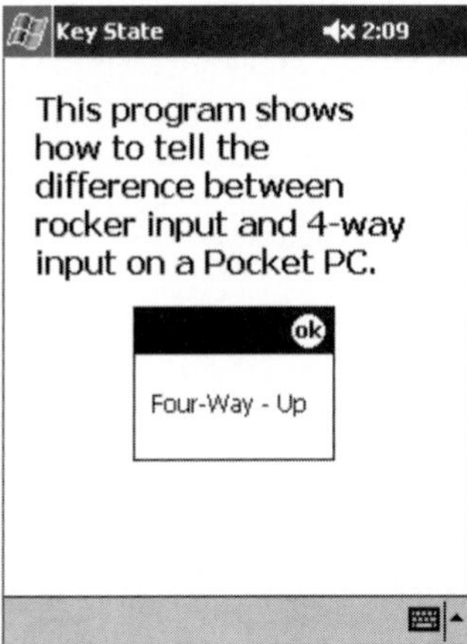

Figure 6.17: The `KeyState` program distinguishing between rocker and four-way button input

We can call this function to check whether the `F21` key is pressed by using a statement like this:

```
if (GetAsyncKeyState(Keys.F21) < 0)
{  /* F21 is pressed */ }
```

Or we can check whether the up key is pressed by using this statement:

```
if (GetAsyncKeyState(Keys.Up) < 0)
{ /* Up key is pressed */ }
```

Listing 6.10 shows an event handler method that can distinguish between two kinds of up and down button clicks.

Listing 6.10: Detecting Input from Pocket PC Input Buttons

```
private void
FormMain_KeyDown(object sender,
                 System.Windows.Forms.KeyEventArgs e)
{
   // Detecting F20 / F21
   if (e.KeyCode == Keys.F21)
   {
      if (GetAsyncKeyState(Keys.Up) < 0)
```

continues

continued

```
        {
            MessageBox.Show("Four-Way - Up");
        }

        if (GetAsyncKeyState(Keys.Down) < 0)
        {
            MessageBox.Show("Four-Way - Down");
        }
    }

    if (e.KeyCode == Keys.F20)
    {
        if (GetAsyncKeyState(Keys.Up) < 0)
        {
            MessageBox.Show("Rocker - Up");
        }

        if (GetAsyncKeyState(Keys.Down) < 0)
        {
            MessageBox.Show("Rocker - Down");
        }
    }

    // Detect Action key
    if (e.KeyCode == Keys.F23)
    {
        MessageBox.Show("Action key");
    }
} // FormMain_KeyDown
```

A Sample Program: `Caret`

A caret is a keyboard pointer. It is the only user interface object that blinks by itself, and it is familiar to anyone who has entered text in a Windows-based text editor or word processor. Because carets are keyboard pointers, we create a caret when a window gets the focus and destroy the caret when the window loses the focus. This describes how a program that wants to use a caret must operate because it describes what every version of Windows—from the desktop version 1.01 up to and including Windows XP, along with every version of Windows CE—expects. It all boils down to a simple assumption: Only one caret can be visible at any moment. The operating system creates one timer that makes the caret blink. If two windows try to have a caret at the same time, the last one to create the caret always wins.

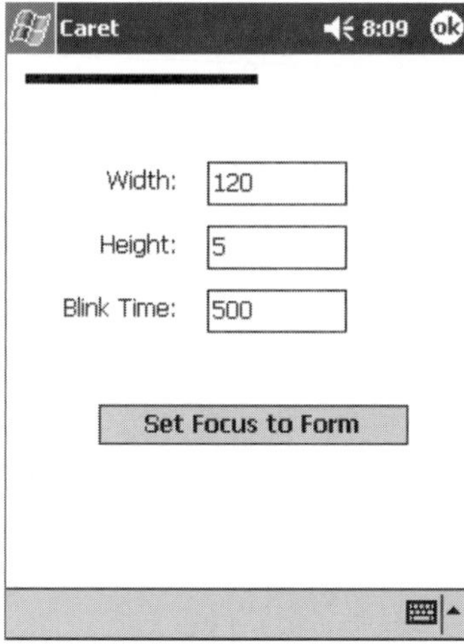

FIGURE 6.18: The `Caret` program displaying a large horizontal caret

The .NET Compact Framework refers to carets only in a `TextBox` control and otherwise lacks support for carets. (The same is true for the desktop .NET Framework.) But carets are useful. With the help of a few P/Invoke calls to the Win32 API, you can create and control carets in any .NET Compact Framework window. Figure 6.18 shows our sample application, `Caret`, which displays a caret in the program's main form, lets you modify the various attributes of a caret, and also lets you move the caret around the form in response to either mouse or keyboard input.

Listing 6.11 shows the declarations we use to access the Win32 caret functions from the .NET Compact Framework.

LISTING 6.11: P/Invoke Declarations for Win32 Caret Functions

```
//..
using System.Runtime.InteropServices;
//..
[DllImport("coredll.dll", CharSet=CharSet.Unicode)]
public static extern int
CreateCaret (IntPtr hWnd, IntPtr hBitmap, int nWidth,
int nHeight);

[DllImport("coredll.dll", CharSet=CharSet.Unicode)]
public static extern int SetCaretPos (int X, int Y);
```

continues

continued

```
[DllImport("coredll.dll", CharSet=CharSet.Unicode)]
public static extern int ShowCaret (IntPtr hWnd);

[DllImport("coredll.dll", CharSet=CharSet.Unicode)]
public static extern int HideCaret (IntPtr hWnd);

[DllImport("coredll.dll", CharSet=CharSet.Unicode)]
public static extern int DestroyCaret ();

[DllImport("coredll.dll", CharSet=CharSet.Unicode)]
public static extern int
GetCaretPos (ref System.Drawing.Point lpPoint);

[DllImport("coredll.dll", CharSet=CharSet.Unicode)]
public static extern int GetCaretBlinkTime ();

[DllImport("coredll.dll", CharSet=CharSet.Unicode)]
public static extern int SetCaretBlinkTime (int uMSeconds);

[DllImport("coredll.dll", CharSet=CharSet.Unicode)]
public static extern IntPtr GetFocus ();
```

Creating and Destroying a Caret

Since the caret is tied to the focus, the two most interesting events are the `GotFocus` and `LostFocus` events. Listing 6.12 presents the event handler methods for these two events. On receipt of the keyboard focus, our program creates a caret, moves it to the desired location, and makes it visible. When the focus is lost, our program hides the caret and then destroys it.

LISTING 6.12: Focus Event Handler Methods for Managing a Caret

```
private void
FormMain_GotFocus(object sender, System.EventArgs e)
{
   int cxWidth;
   int cyHeight;
   int msBlinkTime;
   try
   {
      cxWidth = int.Parse(textWidth.Text);
   }
   catch
   {
      cxWidth = 2;
      textWidth.Text = "2";
```

```
    }
    try
    {
       cyHeight = int.Parse(textHeight.Text);
    }
    catch
    {
       cyHeight = 20;
       textHeight.Text = "20";
    }
    try
    {
       msBlinkTime = int.Parse(textBlinkTime.Text);
    }
    catch
    {
       msBlinkTime = GetCaretBlinkTime();
       textBlinkTime.Text = msBlinkTime.ToString();
    }

    IntPtr hwnd = GetFocus();
    CreateCaret(hwnd, IntPtr.Zero,  cxWidth, cyHeight);
    SetCaretPos(10, 10);
    SetCaretBlinkTime(msBlinkTime);
    ShowCaret(hwnd);
}

private void
FormMain_LostFocus(object sender, System.EventArgs e)
{
    IntPtr hwnd = GetFocus();
    HideCaret(hwnd);
    DestroyCaret();
}
```

Moving a Caret

The other interesting thing to do involves moving the caret, which we do in response to mouse input as shown in Listing 6.13.

LISTING 6.13: Moving the Caret from Mouse/Stylus Input

```
private void
FormMain_MouseDown(object sender,
                   System.Windows.Forms.MouseEventArgs e)
{
   SetCaretPos(e.X, e.Y);
}
```

Listing 6.14 shows how we move the mouse in response to input from a keyboard (and also from a Pocket PC device button).

LISTING 6.14: Moving the Caret from Keyboard/SIP Input

```
private void
FormMain_KeyDown(object sender,
                 System.Windows.Forms.KeyEventArgs e)
{
   Point ptCaret = new Point();
   GetCaretPos(ref ptCaret);

   switch (e.KeyCode)
   {
      case Keys.Left:
         ptCaret.X -= 10;
         break;
      case Keys.Right:
         ptCaret.X += 10;
         break;
      case Keys.Up:
         ptCaret.Y -= 10;
         break;
      case Keys.Down:
         ptCaret.Y += 10;
         break;
   }

   // Make sure that caret stays in the window.
   if (ptCaret.X < 0) ptCaret.X = 0;
   if (ptCaret.Y < 0) ptCaret.Y = 0;

   int cxCaretWidth = int.Parse(textWidth.Text);
   int cyCaretHeight = int.Parse(textHeight.Text);

   if ((ptCaret.X +  cxCaretWidth) > this.Width)
      ptCaret.X = this.Width - cxCaretWidth;
   if ((ptCaret.Y + cyCaretHeight) > this.Height)
      ptCaret.Y = this.Height - cyCaretHeight;

   // Move caret to new position.
   SetCaretPos(ptCaret.X, ptCaret.Y);

} // FormMain_KeyDown
```

A Sample Program: `Sleep`

The final sample application in this chapter lets you simulate the push of the power-off button using the Win32 `keybd_button` function. When the power-off button is pushed on a Pocket PC, it does not actually turn off the power. Instead, it puts the device into a power-saving sleep state. Not every Windows CE device responds this way to the power-off button, but Pocket PCs and Smartphones do. (The Pocket PC emulator, however, ignores this button, so at least one feature of our sample program requires you to have an actual device.)

Figure 6.19 shows the `Sleep` program and three timer values. The Battery timer defines the wait (in seconds) for putting the device to sleep when on battery power. The External timer defines the wait when a smart device has an external power source, such as when a device is plugged into a wall charger. The Snooze timer defines the wait after a device has awoken because of a user-defined wake-up event, such as what the calendar program does when it delivers an appointment reminder.

Our `Sleep` program uses the P/Invoke declarations shown in Listing 6.15.

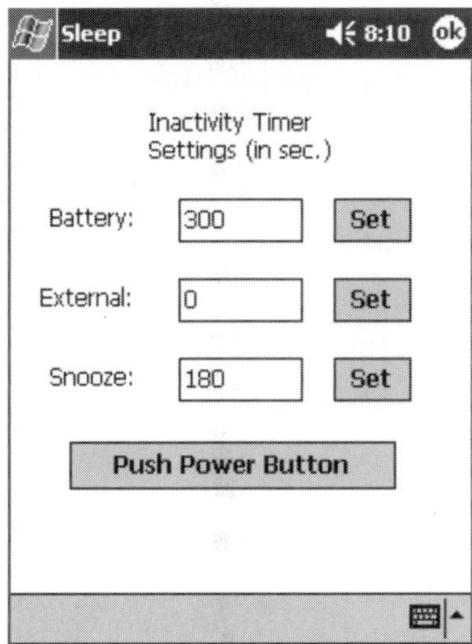

FIGURE 6.19: The `Sleep` program showing system timers

LISTING 6.15: P/Invoke Declarations for the `Sleep` Sample Program

```
using System.Runtime.InteropServices;
//...
[DllImport("coredll.dll", CharSet=CharSet.Unicode)]
public static extern void
keybd_event (byte bVk, byte bScan, int dwFlags, int dwExtraInfo);

public const int VK_OFF = 0xDF;

[DllImport("coredll.dll", CharSet=CharSet.Unicode)]
public static extern int
SystemParametersInfo (int uiAction, int uiParam,
   ref int piParam, int fWinIni);

[DllImport("coredll.dll", CharSet=CharSet.Unicode)]
public static extern int
SystemParametersInfo (int uiAction, int uiParam,
   int iReserved, int fWinIni);

public const int SPI_SETBATTERYIDLETIMEOUT = 251;
public const int SPI_GETBATTERYIDLETIMEOUT = 252;
public const int SPI_SETEXTERNALIDLETIMEOUT = 253;
public const int SPI_GETEXTERNALIDLETIMEOUT = 254;
public const int SPI_SETWAKEUPIDLETIMEOUT = 255;
public const int SPI_GETWAKEUPIDLETIMEOUT = 256;
public const int SPIF_UPDATEINIFILE = 0x0001;
public const int SPIF_SENDCHANGE = 0x0002;
```

Pushing the Power Button

In general, the `keybd_event` function can use the virtual key definitions found in the `Keys`[31] enumeration. However, we did not use a value from that enumeration; instead, we defined our own `VK_OFF` constant. The reason is that the corresponding `Keys` value, `Keys.Oem8`, did not contribute to the readability of the code. (It does, however, suggest a great question for you to ask your programmer friends the next time you play ".NET Compact Framework trivia.") Here is the `Click` event handler that puts the device to sleep when the user clicks on the button labeled Push Power Button:

```
private void
cmdSleepButton_Click(object sender, System.EventArgs e)
{
   keybd_event(VK_OFF, 0, 0, 0);
}
```

31. Fully qualified name: `System.Windows.Forms.Keys`.

Reading and Writing System Timeout Values

We read system timer settings and update those settings by using the following Win32 function: `SystemParametersInfo`. This function lets us access a wide range of system values, not just system timer settings. We create two declarations for this function because the function works differently depending on whether you are reading a value or writing a value. Here is the version we use to read a value.

```
[DllImport("coredll.dll", CharSet=CharSet.Unicode)]
public static extern int
SystemParametersInfo (int uiAction, int uiParam,
   ref int piParam, int fWinIni);
```

The function detects that we want to read a value by checking for a non-`null` pointer in the third parameter. Notice how the third parameter is a by-reference parameter. Here is how to read the battery timeout setting and put the value in the correct `TextBox` control.

```
int iValue = 0;
SystemParametersInfo(SPI_GETBATTERYIDLETIMEOUT, 0, ref iValue, 0);
textBattery.Text = iValue.ToString();
```

To change a setting, we call the same function but with a `null` pointer in the third parameter. Because pointer use is discouraged in .NET programs, we pick the next best thing: an `IntPtr` that has a special value explicitly defined for passing zero pointers: `IntPtr.Zero`. We need a second function declaration to call our function this way, as shown here.

```
[DllImport("coredll.dll", CharSet=CharSet.Unicode)]
public static extern int
SystemParametersInfo (int uiAction, int uiParam,
   IntPtr iReserved, int fWinIni);
```

When we call this function, we must be careful to set the third parameter to zero. Whenever that is the case for P/Invoke functions, we have a convention of giving the parameter a name like `Reserved` (or `Res1`, `Res2`, and so on for multiple reserved parameters). We set the battery timeout value when the user clicks the appropriate button, as shown in Listing 6.16.

LISTING 6.16: Setting the Battery Idle Timeout Value

```
private void
cmdSetBatteryTimeout_Click(object sender,
                           System.EventArgs e)
{
   try
   {
      int iValue = int.Parse(textBattery.Text);
      if (iValue < 0)
         throw(new Exception());
      SystemParametersInfo(SPI_SETBATTERYIDLETIMEOUT, iValue,
         IntPtr.Zero, SPIF_UPDATEINIFILE | SPIF_SENDCHANGE);
}
   catch
   {
      MessageBox.Show("Invalid timeout value entered. ",
         strAppName);
   }
}
```

The most noteworthy part of this code is not the call that sets the value but rather the exception handling (the `try`, `throw`, and `catch` statements). We use these statements to recover when the user enters non-numeric values in a textbox. The statement that actually triggers an exception is the call to the static `int.Parse` method, which attempts to convert the string value into an integer. Without the `try` ... `catch` handler, a non-numeric value in the battery timeout textbox would cause our program to crash. With the handler, our program can display a semi-friendly message to the user and continue running.

CONCLUSION

Among the various ways that a user can create input to your program, the most basic and fundamental are represented as mouse and keyboard input. You will probably use a .NET Compact Framework control to retrieve input, assuming that one of the supported controls does what you need to have done. Failing that, you will need to handle user input yourself. This chapter provided the basic elements needed to understand and handle mouse and keyboard input. In addition to discussing the basics of mouse and keyboard input, this chapter also dug into the handling of mouse cursors and the keyboard caret. In some cases the .NET Compact Framework provides what you need; in other cases, as we have shown, some assistance from P/Invoke declarations helps you access the support provided by the underlying Win32 functions.

This chapter's discussion of mouse and keyboard input provides a foundation for the coverage in other chapters of the various types of .NET Compact Framework controls. Chapters 7, 8, and 9 provide more details on specific controls. Not surprisingly, mouse and keyboard input plays a role in most of these controls. Most of the time, individual controls handle the low-level details of managing events and input data, and for such cases the mouse and keyboard input discussed here is mainly background information.

You need to understand the details of mouse and keyboard input when you want to capture input that is different from how standard controls handle input. In such cases, you are likely to consider creating a custom control. As discussed in Chapter 10, a custom control might make only minor changes to an existing control—such as modifying a `TextBox` control to display a date. Or you might want to develop a completely new type of control to handle a unique type of data. Whatever the requirement, the details of mouse and keyboard input that we provided in this chapter should serve you well.

In Chapter 7, we take a detailed look at the supported controls in the .NET Compact Framework. These controls serve as the core elements in the user interface for a typical .NET Compact Framework program.

7
Inside Controls

In this chapter, we discuss controls (the objects of the GUI) and then use five of them to develop a sample application.

What Are Controls?

What is a .NET Compact Framework control? In a nutshell, it is an object, it has a visible interface, and it was derived by Microsoft from a control that exists in the desktop .NET Framework. These characteristics have determined what the .NET Compact Framework controls are and what they can do for us.

Visible Objects

Because controls are objects, they provide a valuable service in a nice, neat package. And because they are objects, they expose their functionality through PMEs. Understanding the PMEs that are available for a control and the interrelationships between them is the key to successful .NET Compact Framework programming.

All control classes derive either directly or indirectly from one of two base classes: `Component` and `Control`. Like other objects, controls have code (the class methods) and data (the class properties). A control owner manipulates a control by calling the class methods and further manages it by reading and writing the control's properties.

Consider the `TextBox` control. Among its other properties, the `TextBox` control has a `Multiline` property (a `boolean` to select single-line or multiline operation) and a `Text` property (to access the text being displayed and edited). Among its various methods, some modify the visible state—`Show` and `Hide`—and others modify the z-order—`BringToFront` and `SendToBack`. Properties and methods provide two ways to connect to and manipulate a control, but they are not the only means available. Events and the ability to respond to events represent a very important part of the work of controls.

One way that controls differ from most other types of objects is that they are more likely to raise events. `Timer` controls, for example, issue a `Tick` event when the desired time span has passed. A `TextBox` control sends a `TextChanged` event when its contents change. `Button` controls send `Click` events when tapped. The fact that controls are visible and are the provider of the GUI means that they are constantly receiving taps and clicks and keystrokes from the user, events that the control must pass on to the application. Events and their handlers are a central theme of this chapter.

The events raised by the control can either be ignored or processed by the application. You write the code, called *handlers*, to process each event you are interested in. You tie the code to the event by adding a *delegate*, the .NET equivalent of a function pointer, to the event's list of handlers, as shown in the following code fragment. This code specifies that the function named `txtTaskComments_TextChanged` should be called whenever the `txtTaskComment`'s `TextChanged` event is raised.

```
this.txtTaskComments.TextChanged +=
   new System.EventHandler(this.txtTaskComments_TextChanged);
```

Because controls are objects, they can be extended and they can be inherited from, allowing us to expand the capabilities of existing controls or to write our own new control classes. These two capabilities are the subject of Chapter 10 and are not discussed in this chapter. In this chapter we focus instead on the controls that the .NET Compact Framework provides.

Descended from the Desktop .NET Framework

Because controls have descended from the desktop .NET Framework and have, by necessity, lost some capability in that descent, they are both familiar to programmers with .NET Framework experience and occasionally alien to these same programmers. This evolutionary history serves as a good starting point for this chapter; understanding how .NET Compact Framework controls came to be helps you understand what they can do for you.

Microsoft created the .NET Compact Framework controls by porting the desktop controls implemented in the .NET Framework (what we call the desktop .NET Framework) with the following design goals in mind.

- Build on the benefits of the .NET Framework.
- Maintain consistency with the desktop version.
- Ensure that the framework runs well on mobile and embedded devices.
- Expose the richness of target platforms.
- Preserve the look and feel of platforms.
- Provide portability to other mobile operating systems.

We discussed these design goals more fully in Chapter 1, and we mention them here, some with further elaboration, to help put the subject of .NET Compact Framework controls in perspective.

Maintain Consistency with the Desktop Version

The .NET Compact Framework controls are implemented in the same namespace as the desktop .NET Framework control, `System.Windows.Forms`. In the .NET Compact Framework, this namespace contains a strict subset of the classes and controls found on its desktop counterpart. For example, the desktop .NET Framework supports 35 controls; the 30 controls in the .NET Compact Framework `System.Windows.Forms` namespace are a subset of these. Table 7.1 presents a list of all supported .NET Compact Framework controls.

And just as the .NET Compact Framework controls are a subset of their desktop counterparts, so too are the PMEs supported by .NET Compact Framework controls a strict subset of the PMEs supported by the desktop .NET Framework. For example, the number of "core" events (those supported by all controls) was pared down from 17 in the desktop .NET

TABLE 7.1: .NET Control Classes Supported in the .NET Compact Framework Version 1.0

Control	Control Category	Covered in This Book
`Button`	Single-item	Chapter 7
`CheckBox`	Single-item	Chapter 7
`ComboBox`	Multi-item	Chapter 7
`ContextMenu`	Command input	Chapter 9
`Control`	Ultimate parent	Chapter 7
`DataGrid`	Multi-item	Chapter 8
`DomainUpDown`	Multi-item	
`Form`	Ultimate parent	Chapter 5
`ImageList`	Background	Chapter 9
`Label`	Single-item	Chapter 7
`ListBox`	Multi-item	Chapter 7
`ListView`	Multi-item	
`MainMenu`	Command input	Chapter 9
`MenuItem`	Command input	Chapter 9
`NumericUpDown`	Visual numeric value	
`Panel`	Container control	Chapter 7
`PictureBox`	Single-item	
`ProgressBar`	Visual numeric value	
`RadioButton`	Single-item	Chapter 7
`HScrollBar`	Visual numeric value	
`VScrollBar`	Visual numeric value	
`StatusBar`	Single item	

Control	Control Category	Covered in This Book
`StatusBar`	Single item	
`TabControl`	Container control	
`TabPage`	Container control	
`TextBox`	Single-item	Chapter 7
`Timer`	Background	
`ToolBar`	Command input	Chapter 9
`ToolBarButton`	Command input	Chapter 9
`TrackBar`	Visual numeric value	
`TreeView`	Multi-item	

Framework controls to just 7 in the .NET Compact Framework controls: `Disposed`, `ParentChanged`, `Validated`, `Validating`, `EnabledChanged`, `GotFocus`, and `LostFocus`.

Ensure That the Framework Runs Well on Mobile and Embedded Devices

One of the oldest and most sacrosanct goals of Windows CE is to be small. The 25MB of RAM (or more) of the desktop .NET Framework would not work well on devices that might have a total of only 32MB, so the .NET Compact Framework team set out with a goal of creating a system that would occupy less than 1MB. They managed to get the system to occupy less than 2MB—an important accomplishment that makes the .NET Compact Framework a good Windows CE citizen. On its way to achieving the size goal, the .NET Compact Framework team left out desktop-centric features such as drag-and-drop ability, large controls like the `RichTextBox`, and owner draw controls. Also, in working toward the goal, the .NET Compact Framework team took a page from the playbook of the Windows CE team. Namely, if there are two or more ways to do the same operation, all are removed but one. Hence, there are significantly fewer overloaded method calls in the .NET Compact Framework than in the desktop .NET Framework.

To run well also means having good performance—not appearing sluggish to the user and not taking too long to do common operations. To meet the performance goals, the .NET Compact Framework was benchmarked and tuned so that controls rely heavily on their Win32 counterparts. The Win32 controls reside in unmanaged code, and .NET Compact Framework code runs as managed code. There is a cost in crossing the boundary between managed and unmanaged code. The .NET Compact Framework team found that it could enhance the controls' performance by allowing only a carefully controlled subset of Win32 messages to percolate as .NET events.

If you are an experienced Windows programmer—whether with the desktop .NET Framework, Win32, MFC, or C#—you will find that the .NET Compact Framework controls support a significantly reduced set of events (or messages) from what you are used to working with. To give you an idea of how significant, consider the `System.Windows.Forms.TextBox` control—commonly called just `TextBox`—which wraps the Win32 `EDIT` control. On the desktop .NET Framework, 66 events are supported. In the .NET Compact Framework, only 11 events are supported. As an example of how drastic this change is, none of the native Microsoft controls supports the `Paint` event. This means that you cannot draw your own control by simply overriding the `OnPaint` method as you can in the desktop .NET Framework. The underlying Win32 controls support the `Paint` event, but the .NET Compact Framework team decided, for performance reasons, that the `Paint` event would not be included in the subset of Win32 messages that cross process boundaries and become .NET events.

Expose the Richness of Target Platforms

For almost every control, the .NET Compact Framework relies on a native control to do most of the work. (The one exception is the `DataGrid` control, which has been implemented entirely in managed code.) This has obvious benefits in size and performance. It also provides a more authentic look and feel for .NET Compact Framework applications on each platform.

For example, the .NET Compact Framework `MainMenu` class provides the basic support for application menus. In a Pocket PC application, this menu appears at the bottom of a window, as in any other Pocket PC application. But on other Windows CE .NET devices, that same .NET Compact Framework program displays its main menu at the top of the window like a standard Windows CE .NET application. While the underlying Win32 menu implementations on each platform are different, the .NET Compact Framework hides this from the developer in its `MainMenu` and `MenuItem` classes.

Preserve the Look and Feel of Platforms

The .NET Compact Framework team found that each platform has subtle differences in how the Win32 controls are used. For example, some Windows CE platforms support custom skins—an enhancement that lets a platform implementer customize the user interface of all running programs. A platform might have round buttons instead of square ones or windows with a 3D look or a flat look. The .NET Compact Framework adapts itself to support all of these differences.

On some platforms (e.g., the Pocket PC), the difference from a standard Windows CE user interface is more subtle. Such differences might appear only when two applications, one .NET and one not, are running on the same device. For such cases, the .NET Compact Framework team worked hard so that .NET Compact Framework applications blend in with other kinds of applications.

Documentation, Development, and Confusion

Microsoft has done a lot to leverage the work on the desktop .NET Framework when building the .NET Compact Framework. For one thing, the .NET Compact Framework code was derived from the desktop .NET Framework. Also, both frameworks share a common development environment—Visual Studio .NET 2003. To make the differences between the two frameworks clear, the documentation for the .NET Compact Framework piggybacks on the desktop .NET Framework documentation. In general, these are all good things.

There are, however, a few shortcomings; once you understand them, the impact on your development can be minimized. Both the documentation and the development environment are at times unclear about which capabilities are in the .NET Compact Framework and which capabilities are

TABLE 7.2: Summary of Documentation Accuracy

	Documentation	Designer	IntelliSense
Properties	Correct	Correct	Correct
Methods	Correct	N/A	Incorrect
Events	Missing	Mostly correct	Incorrect

not. When we say "capabilities," we mean the PMEs supported by each control. Table 7.2 illustrates the "state of accuracy" of the documentation, the Designer's Properties window, and IntelliSense. Usually, supported properties are correctly represented everywhere. To get accurate information on supported methods, however, you must rely on the online documentation—not on the information reported by IntelliSense in the editor window. And finally, the supported events that you see listed by the Designer (in the Properties window) are mostly correct. We have found a few omissions—events that are supported by a control even though the Designer does not report them—which we discuss in detail as we address individual controls.

Categories of Controls

Someone once said, "The world is divided into two kinds of people: those who divide the world into two kinds of people and those who do not." Instead of two types, however, we divide the .NET Compact Framework control classes into seven categories. This is our own set of categories, not one from the Microsoft documentation. This categorization enables us to bring some organization to the subject of controls. It also allows us to look at the PMEs that are common to each group of controls and to the PMEs that are common to all controls. In the following subsections, we briefly describe the categories we use.

The Ultimate Parent Controls

- `Form`
- `Control`

The first category contains just two controls: `Form` and `Control`. This is because, depending on how you define the word *parent*, `Form` and `Control` are the parents of every other control.

If *parent* means "container," then `Form` is the parent of all controls. That is, every control is visually contained within a `Form` (or within another control, like `Panel`, that itself is contained by a `Form`). This container class serves as both the main window in every .NET Compact Framework application and also as the main window for all dialog boxes. As we discussed in Chapter 2, when we cover our minimum .NET Compact Framework program, the Visual Studio .NET New Project Wizard creates a new class—derived from `Form`—for you.

If *parent* means "base class"—another common use of the word *parent*—then our other parent control, `Control`, is the parent of (almost) all the other control classes. All control classes are derived, either directly or indirectly, from this base class. Even our ultimate container, `Form`, is derived from `Control`. (We say "almost" because a few controls—`Timer`, `ImageList`, `MainMenu`, `MenuItem`, and `ContextMenu`—are derived from `Component` and not from `Control`. All controls that wrap a Win32 window are derived from `Control`.)

In their roles as container and base class for all other controls, `Form` and `Control` are important. They also play an important role in helping programmers understand all other controls because these two classes have the most complete set of PMEs of any .NET Compact Framework control.

One of the most confusing aspects of .NET Compact Framework controls is that the base control class, `Control`, has more PMEs than any other control class. This is confusing because base classes are supposed to be the simpler, less evolved types. A major theme of this chapter is that *inherited does not mean supported* (see the related sidebar). This is the description that Seth Demsey, a member of Microsoft's .NET Compact Framework team, gave us to describe the state of .NET Compact Framework controls.

The Container Controls

- `Panel`
- `TabControl`
- `TabPage`

Inherited Does Not Mean Supported

All of the PMEs of .NET Compact Framework controls are implemented as class methods. The base control class, `Control`, supports a broad range of PMEs. Other classes are derived from `Control` and so inherit all these PMEs. In many cases, however, the underlying implementation does not actually implement the inherited PMEs.

Consider the `BackColor` property, which is defined in `Control`. This property is inherited by the `Label` control, and you can write code that reads and writes this property. However, none of the changes you make to this property change the background color of labels as they appear to users. In other words, the `BackColor` property is *inherited but not supported*. What makes this confusing is that you can write code that references this property, and you can then build and run that code and see no error messages. It is only at runtime that you discover that this property is not supported, when you see that a `Label`'s background color does not change.

As another example, consider the `CreateGraphics` method—defined in `Control`, inherited by all controls, but supported by none of them. If we believe what IntelliSense tells us, this is a legal method to call. You only discover that this method is not supported at runtime—when you call the method and get a "Not Supported" exception.

To meet the strict size and performance goals for the .NET Compact Framework, the internal wiring for unsupported PMEs was omitted for some controls. To help you understand and use them, we will provide details on all the supported PMEs for each of the controls in the .NET Compact Framework.

Container controls are controls that hold other controls. They have no GUI capability of their own but instead rely on the contained controls to do all the real work. The primary reason for placing controls into a container is so that you can show them, hide them, and move them as a unit.

Container controls all receive mouse events (which is how touch-screen input arrives on devices like the Pocket PC), unlike all the other control categories, which do not receive raw mouse input. For other controls, mouse messages are translated into control-specific events, such as a `Click` event, or produce a side effect, such as gaining or losing the focus. In other cases, mouse events are ignored altogether by .NET Compact Framework controls.

The Single-Item Controls

- `Button`
- `Checkbox`
- `Label`
- `PictureBox`
- `RadioButton`
- `StatusBar`
- `TextBox`

Single-item controls display and usually accept a single piece of information. They have a `Text` property to hold the value, and they also receive a `TextChanged` event when the value of that item changes. For instance, if the user is entering text into a `TextBox` control, each newly added character causes the `TextChanged` event to fire.

All single-item controls support a feature known as *data binding*. This feature lets you connect user interface objects to data objects. When such a connection has been established, any change in the user interface causes an automatic update to the object in memory—and vice versa. Data binding helps automate something that GUI programmers from the dawn of time have had to handle manually, and it can make your coding work much simpler. All single-item controls use the same technique for data binding, a technique called *simple data binding* (see Chapters 8 and 12 for detailed information on data binding).

The Multi-Item Controls

- `ComboBox`
- `DataGrid`

- `DomainUpDown`
- `ListBox`
- `ListView`
- `TreeView`

Multi-item controls display a list or array and allow the user to select an item from the list. Each control class allows you to access the displayed data using a container—either an array or a list—that is made available as a property of the control. Such controls let you access the underlying data in an object-oriented way. For all controls—except the `DataGrid`—the actual data lives in an underlying Win32 control.

Control Data and Program Performance

It is always a good practice to separate the user interface from the business logic, and this is certainly true in .NET Compact Framework applications. If you do not separate your program's processing of data from the display of that data, you may encounter performance problems. One of us was working on a text-processing tool and used a `TextBox` to hold the text being processed. As the text size grew, the tool got slower and slower. The simple fix was to copy the data out of the control, process it, and then copy the data back to the control. The same principle applies to any control that holds a large amount of data, such as these multi-item controls.

Except for the `DataGrid` control, each multi-item control allows you to create an initial item list at program build time. The Visual Studio .NET Designer lets you create this collection of items from the Properties window. (For the `TreeView` control, the collection is called `Nodes` and has a hierarchical structure instead of the flat structure in the `Items` collection of the other controls.) This ability to set the initial value for these controls can make your life a bit easier, because—unless the initial values are not known until runtime—the Designer creates the required code for you. If you do need to make changes at runtime, the code created by the Designer can give you a good head start at learning how to access the collections.

To help connect your program's data to the data of these controls at runtime, the multi-item controls support data binding. As we discuss in Chapter 8, the technique for data binding to multi-item controls is different from that of single-item controls. Multi-item controls use *complex data binding*, which is, paradoxically, simpler to program.

The Command Input Controls

- `ContextMenu`
- `MainMenu`
- `MenuItem`
- `ToolBar`
- `ToolBarButton`

Command input controls allow the user to specify that a desired action be executed, usually by tapping directly on the control. Each has a `Text` property to describe the action and three Boolean properties—`Visible`, `Enabled`, and `Checked`—to indicate the control's state. The control receives a `Click` event when selected by a user. We cover command input controls in more detail in Chapter 9.

The Visual Numeric Value Controls

- `NumericUpDown`
- `ProgressBar`
- `HScrollBar` and `VScrollBar`
- `TrackBar`

This set of controls provides a visual indication of a numeric value. Each has `Maximum` and `Minimum` properties to indicate the range and a `Value` property for the current value. Each also has properties such as `Increment`, `Step`, `LargeChange`, and `SmallChange` to indicate the amount by which the `Value` should change during user input.

The Background Controls

- `Timer`
- `ImageList`

Background controls have no graphical interface, are never visible to the user, and can be contained only within a form, never within a container control.

`Timer` controls raise `Tick` events at regular intervals, specified in milliseconds in the `Interval` property. This property is an `int` (`Int32`) type, so the acceptable range is from 1 millisecond to `Int32.MaxValue`, or roughly 23 days. Once started, a timer continues to raise the `Tick` event for as long as its `Enabled` property is `true`, which makes it like an alarm clock. Once set, it goes off every `Interval` milliseconds. Shut the alarm off by setting `Enabled` to false. `Timer` events have a low priority. If the user taps on a `TextBox` at the same time that a timer raises an event, all events (such as `GotFocus`, `LostFocus`, `Validating`, and `Validated`) raised as a result of the tap get processed before the `Tick` event gets delivered. If the power is off, the `Tick` event does not cause a Windows CE device to wake from its slumber state—rather, it gets delivered when the power comes back on. Windows CE does support a power-on timer in `CeRunAppAtEvent`, a Win32 function.

The `ImageList` control is used to hold an array of images, most commonly in support of toolbar buttons. Like other controls, you can set the startup values—a list of images—in the Visual Studio .NET Designer. Visual Studio .NET supports a wide range of file types, including bitmaps, JPEG, GIF, PNG, icons, and Windows metafiles. All of these types are supported in the desktop .NET Framework, but not all are supported in the .NET Compact Framework. Metafiles, for example, are not supported in the .NET Compact Framework. In the .NET Compact Framework, support for some formats—like JPEG, GIF, and PNG—depends on the presence of the `imgdecmp.dll` library in Windows CE (Pocket PC has this library, but some custom Windows CE platforms might not). The graphic type supported everywhere is the humble bitmap. We discuss the `ImageList` control more fully in Chapter 9.

Properties, Methods, and Events

To a great extent, a control's supported PMEs define the control. They define what it knows, what it can do, and what it can react to. We begin our discussion with a look at the core PMEs, the ones that are common to all—or almost all—controls. We start with events because almost all code execution in a .NET Compact Framework application occurs as the result of an event being raised and handled. We then move on to properties, and finally discuss methods. We then divide the controls into categories and examine the PMEs common to each category.

If your most recent programming experience is not with an object-oriented environment, you will see much that is new. It takes time o get used to the fact that everything in .NET is an object. For example, the C# `int` type is a synonym for the .NET native data type `System.Int32` derived from `System.ValueType`, which in turn is derived from `Object`. All properties are objects, and all return values from method calls are themselves objects. In general, this makes the work of programming a bit easier because in most cases the objects are "smart" and do the right thing for us. This allows a style of programming in which we connect many different elements together—all connected by the dot operator (`.`). Sooner or later, you will encounter code like this somewhat exaggerated example:

```
txtLength.Text =
   txtReason.Text.Split(' ').Length.ToString();
```

We are constantly working with properties or objects that are themselves properties of objects that were returned to us from a function call. It is just the nature of the .NET style of object-oriented programming.

The Core Events

Events are a notification by a control that something potentially interesting has happened. As you build your application, you can respond to—or ignore—any event. To respond to an event, you write code to process the event. The code is called an *event handler,* and it is called every time the control raises the event. Listing 7.1 shows an example of an event handler.

LISTING 7.1: A `TextChanged` Event Handler

```
this.txtOne.TextChanged += new
      System.EventHandler(this.txtSomeData_TextChanged);
this.txtTwo.TextChanged += new
      System.EventHandler(this.txtSomeData_TextChanged);
this.txtThree.TextChanged += new
      System.EventHandler(this.txtSomeData_TextChanged);

        :
        :
        :

private void txtSomeData_TextChanged(
                 object sender,
                 System.EventArgs e)
{
//  If the text contains the word "money",
//     make the text green.
   TextBox txtThis = (TextBox)sender;
   if( txtThis.Text.ToLower().IndexOf("money") != -1 )
   {
      txtThis.ForeColor = System.Drawing.Color.Green;
   }
   else
   {
      txtThis.ForeColor = System.Drawing.Color.Black;
   }
}
```

This particular event handler handles the `TextChanged` event for three `TextBox` controls, changing the foreground color of the text to green whenever the text contains the word *money*.

You can give event handlers any name you want, and one event handler can handle the same event for different controls or different events for the same or different controls. A single event can be handled by more than one handler. So you have considerable flexibility when designing your application structure.

All event handlers are always passed just two parameters. The first parameter is a reference to the control that is raising the event. It is always defined as `object`, never as a specific type of control. If we wish to treat it as a specific type of object, we must typecast it, as shown in Listing 7.1. This allows us to receive IntelliSense help when writing the code and provides for stronger type checking when the code is running. As long as we are casting down the inheritance chain, we can use either

```
TextBox txtThis = (TextBox)sender;
```

or

```
TextBox txtThis = sender as TextBox;
```

The second parameter is an event arguments object. The specific object type differs from one event type to another, depending on the information that needs to be passed from the .NET Compact Framework to the application. The most commonly used event argument type is `System.EventArgs`, which contains no event-related information. Events with event-specific information use a different event arguments class. For example, the `MouseUp` event passes a `System.Windows.Forms.MouseEventArgs` object containing the x- and y-coordinates of the mouse. (As you might expect, `MouseEventArgs` is derived from `EventArgs`.)

To reiterate, `System.EventArgs` contains no event-specific information. In Listing 7.1, all we know is that the `Text` property of a `TextBox` has changed. There is nothing in `System.EventArgs` to tell us what the old text was, or what time it is, or what happened to cause the text to change. Since `System.EventArgs` is the event arguments parameter passed to most event handlers, the only information available to most event handlers is which control raised the event and what event was raised.

Let us examine the core events of the .NET Compact Framework—the most common events you will encounter in your .NET Compact Framework programming. Most (if not all) controls generate these events, shown in Table 7.3. The following subsections discuss these core events in more detail.

The `Disposed` Event

As shown in Table 7.3, the `Disposed` event is common to all controls. All controls are objects, and objects can be destroyed, which in turn means that they can be disposed of. Before we discuss the `Disposed` event, some background information is in order to clarify the meaning of two terms: *dispose* and a related term, *finalize*.

TABLE 7.3: Core Events in the .NET Compact Framework Control Classes

Class	Disposed	Parent-Changed	Validating and Validated	Enabled-Changed	GotFocus and LostFocus
`Button`	X	X	X	X	X
`CheckBox`	X	X	X	X	X
`ComboBox`	X	X	X	X	X
`ContextMenu`	X				
`Control`	X	X	X	X	X
`DomainUpDown`	X	X	X	X	X
`Form`	X	X	X	X	X
`ImageList`	X				
`Label`	X	X	X	X	
`ListBox`	X	X	X	X	X
`ListView`	X	X	X	X	X
`MainMenu`	X				
`MenuItem`	X				
`NumericUpDown`	X	X	X	X	X
`Panel`	X	X	X	X	X
`PictureBox`	X	X	X		
`ProgressBar`	X	X	X		
`RadioButton`	X	X	X	X	X
`HScrollBar`	X	X	X	X	
`VScrollBar`	X	X	X	X	
`StatusBar`	X	X	X		

Class	Disposed	Parent-Changed	Validating and Validated	Enabled-Changed	GotFocus and LostFocus
TabControl	X	X	X	X	X
TabPage	X	X	X	X	X
TextBox	X	X	X	X	X
Timer	X				
ToolBar	X	X			
ToolBarButton	X				
TrackBar	X	X	X	X	X
TreeView	X	X	X	X	X

Events and Win32 Messages

Win32 programmers are used to messages with names like `WM_CREATE` and `WM_PAINT`, and some .NET events are a repackaging of those messages. For example, the `EnabledChanged` event is triggered by the `WM_ENABLE` message, and the `GotFocus` and `LostFocus` events are triggered by the `WM_SETFOCUS` and `WM_KILLFOCUS` messages.

Other events have no equivalent Win32 message and instead are extra features that the .NET Compact Framework obtains from the desktop .NET Framework. Whatever the source, experienced GUI programmers should have no trouble learning new events and adopting them to their proper use.

In .NET—for both the .NET Compact Framework and the desktop .NET Framework—the process of reclaiming the memory occupied by objects on the heap is called *garbage collection*. Garbage collection occurs as needed, which means that some time passes between when an object is no longer used (i.e., when no piece of code references the object) and when the memory used by the object is reclaimed. The technical term for this is *nondeterministic garbage collection.*

The base class of all objects, `Object`, has a `Finalize` method. When the garbage collector gets around to destroying an object, it notifies the object that it is doing so by calling the object's `Finalize` method. This gives the object an opportunity to close and release any resources it might be holding. However, if an object holds nonshareable resources such as a database connection or resources written in unmanaged code, it is sometimes advantageous to release those resources as soon as possible, rather than waiting for garbage collection to take place. Under such circumstances, an application can call the object's `Dispose` method, another method that all classes inherit from `Object`. Unlike the `Finalize` method (which only the garbage collector can call), applications can call the `Dispose` method to notify the object that the application is finished using the object and to request the object to release any resources it is currently holding.

When Do You Need to Call the `Dispose` Method of a Control?

In general, you do not need to call the `Dispose` method when working with .NET Compact Framework controls, for controls do not hold nonshareable resources or unmanaged resources within their properties. In addition, closing a form will dispose of all the controls on that form anyway.

If you wish to remove a control from your application, you can just set all references to that control to `null`, without first calling its `Dispose` method. Omitting the call to the `Dispose` method will normally result in better performance.

However, if you do not wish to track all the references to the control, and if you wish to remove the control from the application without closing its form, and if your testing shows that performance is not a problem—call the `Dispose` method. This situation is most common when you have created a control at runtime, added it to the form, and then wish to remove it. Calling the `Dispose` method guarantees that it will be removed.

The Disposed event is raised as one of the last steps in the processing of the Dispose method. By the time the control receives the Disposed event, the cleaning process is just about complete. To see this, place a break point at the start of a method that handles the Disposed event, and then start the application running under the debugger. When the application hits that break point, inspect the object being disposed from the Command window, as shown in Figure 7.1.

At that time, most of the properties are so far gone that accessing them causes an exception, and properties that still exist are normally empty. A simple handler for a Disposed event, in this case the disposing of a TextBox, is shown here.

```
private void txtTaskName_Disposed(
                    object sender,
                    System.EventArgs e)
{
   ((TextBox)sender).Text = string.Empty;
}
```

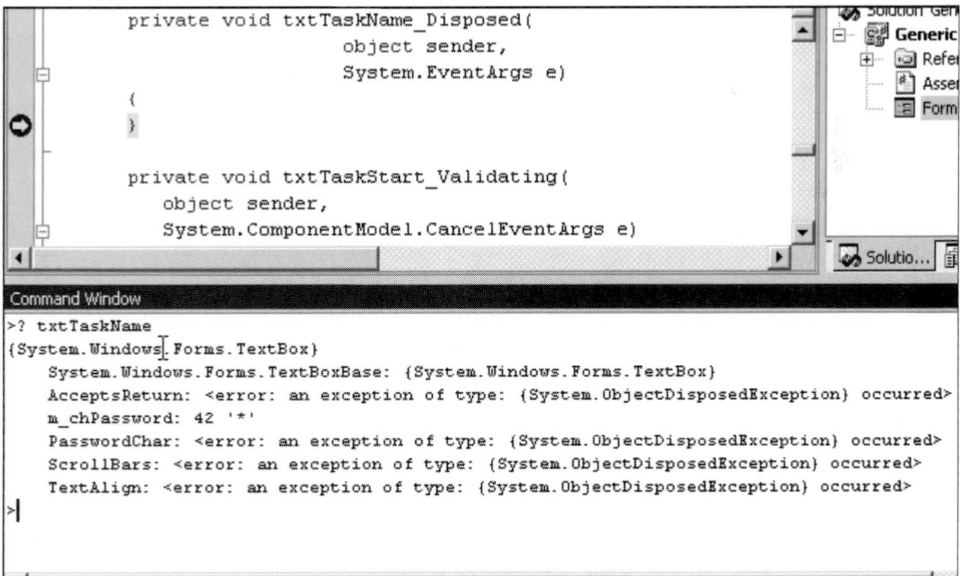

FIGURE 7.1: The state of a disposed object

We mentioned earlier that `System.EventArgs` contains no event-specific information. Therefore, within this handler code, all we know is that the object referenced by `sender` is being disposed, and nothing more. We respond by setting the `Text` property to an empty string. Note how we typecast `sender` to `TextBox`. We must do this because `Object` does not have a `Text` property.

If this event handler were handling the `Disposed` event for more than one type of control, we would need to typecast `sender` to `Control` because `Text` is a property of `Control`, a property that is inherited by all derived controls.

So the `Disposed` event is very much an after-the-fact event. When you receive it, it is telling you that the control is gone.

The Debugger and Viewing Control Properties

As we mention elsewhere in this book, we are big fans of using an interactive debugger. It provides the best way to look inside your program, to learn about system operation, to debug new code, and to learn about the operation of old code.

When learning about control properties, the debugger can be especially helpful. When you are not sure which property contains the value or values you need, it is often a simple matter of creating a control with the Designer, tracing into your code, and then examining the properties—in a watch window—to see how the properties expose the capabilities and features of each control.

The `ParentChanged` Event

The `ParentChanged` event informs the event handler that a control has moved to a new parent. Perhaps the control has been moved from one `TabPage` control to a different `TabPage` control, or maybe the control has been moved from a `Panel` onto a form. As you can see from Table 7.3, six controls do not support this event: `ContextMenu`, `ImageList`, `MainMenu`, `MenuItem`, `Timer`, and `ToolBarButton`. These controls are either not visible or it does not make sense to change their parents. Only controls that can be contained in a parent other than the form can raise a `ParentChanged` event. Like the `Disposed` event, the `ParentChanged` event is an after-the-fact event that provides no additional information. It simply tells you that a control has been moved to a different parent container. In the following code, we respond to this notification by setting the control's font to its new parent's font.

```
private void txtTaskName_ParentChanged (
                  object sender,
                  System.EventArgs e)
{
   txtTaskName.Font = txtTaskName.Parent.Font;
}
```

The `Validating` and `Validated` Events

`Validating` and `Validated` allow an application to check the contents of a control to make sure some input criteria are met. The `Validating` event gets sent first. Its event handler examines the contents of the control—and perhaps other controls for multicontrol validation—and sets a flag if the contents are valid. When the contents are determined to be valid, the second event, `Validated`, gets triggered. The handler for the second event lowers the drawbridge to allow the good data to pass. When the time comes to take an action—either dismiss a form, dismiss a dialog, or trigger some external event—you must first check to see that all required validation has been handled. If not, you report an error to the user and ask him or her to try again.

Comparing .NET Compact Framework Validation with Desktop .NET Framework Validation

The `Validating` and `Validated` events are more alike in behavior in the .NET Compact Framework than in the desktop .NET Framework. In particular, in the .NET Compact Framework an event handler cannot prevent the change of focus and thus cannot force the user to enter valid data in one field before moving to the next field. These events are raised by a control that is in the process of losing the focus, allowing the application to check the control's contents to see if the user has made an error while entering data. The `Validating` event is raised first with a `System.ComponentModel.CancelEventArgs` parameter, which contains a `Cancel` property. In the desktop .NET Framework, setting the `Cancel` property to `true` prevents transfer of the focus, keeping the focus within the control being validated. That is, the event handler can force a user to enter data that meets input criteria.

This is, of course, a potentially dangerous capability, for a user may get frustrated and simply click the Cancel button. But as long as the event handler continues to cancel the transfer of the focus, the focus remains in the control being edited, and clicking on any other control—even a Cancel button—has no effect.

For this reason, the desktop .NET Framework provides a property that allows a control to say, in effect, "If the focus is coming to me, do not send a `Validating` event to the control that is losing the focus." This property is typically applied to Cancel buttons. The `CausesValidation` property of a control sets this condition. When this property is set to `true`, it prevents the control losing the focus from receiving the `Validating` and `Validated` events. So, buttons that must function no matter the state of the data normally have their `CausesValidation` property set to `true` at design time.

The .NET Compact Framework does not support the `CausesValidation` property. Therefore, to ensure that users cannot be trapped in a control, setting the `CancelEventArgs.Cancel` property to `true` in the .NET Compact Framework does not suppress the transfer of focus. What it does suppress is the raising of the `Validated` event that normally follows the `Validating` event. So the `Validating` event says, "The user is leaving a field, perform any checking that may be required." For invalid data, set the `Cancel` property to `true`. The `Validated` event says, "The data in the field meets the criteria for correct data." When the `Validated` event has been raised, you know the data is valid and therefore is ready for processing.

In Listing 7.2, the `Validating` event handlers check each field for a valid date, turning light pink the fields that contain invalid dates. The `Validated` event handler, knowing that the dates are valid, calculates the time interval between the two dates and displays the duration in a message box.

LISTING 7.2: The `TextBox` Validation Event Handlers

```
this.txtTaskStart.Validating += new
   System.ComponentModel.CancelEventHandler
      (this.txtTaskStart_Validating);
this.txtTaskStart.Validated += new
   System.EventHandler
      (this.txtTaskDates_Validated);
this.txtTaskEnd.Validating += new
   System.ComponentModel.CancelEventHandler
      (this.txtTaskEnd_Validating);
this.txtTaskEnd.Validated += new
   System.EventHandler
      (this.txtTaskDates_Validated);

     :
     :
     :

private void txtTaskStart_Validating(
   object sender,
   System.ComponentModel.CancelEventArgs e)
{
   //  If the date entered is after today,
   //     make the background light pink.
   TextBox txtSender = (TextBox)sender;
   if ( Convert.ToDateTime(txtSender.Text) >
      DateTime.Today )
   {
      txtSender.BackColor = Color.LightPink;
   }
}

private void txtTaskEnd_Validating(
   object sender,
   System.ComponentModel.CancelEventArgs e)
{
   //  If the date entered is before today,
   //     make the background light pink.
   TextBox txtSender = (TextBox)sender;
```

continues

continued

```
    if ( Convert.ToDateTime(txtSender.Text) <
       DateTime.Today )
    {
       txtSender.BackColor = Color.LightPink;
    }
}

private void txtTaskDates_Validated(object sender,
                                    System.EventArgs e)
{
    //  display the duration.
    if( txtTaskStart.Text != String.Empty
       &&  txtTaskEnd.Text != String.Empty )
    {
    MessageBox.Show
       ("Days allotted for this task:  "
       + (Convert.ToDateTime(txtTaskEnd.Text).Subtract
         (Convert.ToDateTime(txtTaskStart.Text)
       ).ToString()));
    }
}
```

Could we have placed all the validating code into a single event handler? Probably. Are there times when we would want to use separate events? Yes, and this is one of them. Our editing requirements are different for the start and end dates, but the "after edit" action is the same for both; thus we have three functions to perform. Spreading the three functional requirements over three separate event handlers is the best design.

The `EnabledChanged` Event

The `EnabledChanged` event notifies the application that a control's `Enabled` property has toggled between `true` and `false`. A control that has been disabled cannot get mouse or keyboard input. When disabled, most controls change their appearance to let the user know that they are no longer accessible. Here is a template for an `EnabledChanged` handler.

```
private void txtTaskName_EnabledChanged(
                              object sender,
                              System.EventArgs e)
{
```

```
    if( txtTaskName.Enabled )
    {
        // Control has been enabled.
    }
    else
    {
        // Control has been disabled.
    }

}
```

The GotFocus and LostFocus Events

The GotFocus event informs the application that a control is now designated as the recipient of keyboard input—whether that input is from a hardware keyboard or, as is often the case with a Pocket PC, from the SIP keyboard. The LostFocus event informs the application that the control has stopped receiving keyboard input. Only controls that can receive keyboard input support these events. For example, the Label event, whose only job is to show a line of text, does not support the focus events. And a Timer control, which triggers the passage of time, also does not get focus events. Neither of these controls, after all, have anything to do with keyboard input. Here is an empty handler for a GotFocus event; a LostFocus event handler would be identical in structure.

```
private void txtTaskName_GotFocus(object sender,
                                  System.EventArgs e)
{
    // Control has just received the focus.
}
```

> This completes our look at the seven events that almost all controls receive. As we move on to the subject of properties, you may notice a relationship between some properties and events—namely, that setting some properties may raise related events, thus ensuring that a control (and any handler that you have set up) is always aware of the control's current state.

The Core Properties

Properties are inherently easier to understand than events because properties are a control's public data members. Table 7.4 lists the core properties, by which we mean the properties supported by almost all controls. A cursory look at the available properties shows that most describe the location of a control. Because controls must always be contained within a container, "location" means the control's location within its parent (i.e., container) control.

Just as with controls we divide supported properties into categories. There are four categories of control properties: (1) parent/child properties, (2) positional properties, (3) data-binding properties, and (4) control state properties. The following subsections discuss these categories.

The Parent/Child Properties

- `Controls`
- `Parent`
- `TopLevelControl`

TABLE 7.4: Core Properties Supported in the .NET Compact Framework

`BindingContext`	`Left`
`Bottom`	`Location`
`Bounds`	`Parent`
`ClientRectangle`	`Right`
`ClientSize`	`Size`
`ContextMenu`	`Top`
`Controls`	`TopLevelControl`
`DataBindings`	`Visible`
`Enabled`	`Width`
`Height`	

The `Parent` and `Controls` properties relate to the parent/child relationship between a control and its container. The `Parent` property is a reference to the container control that holds the control. Every control must have a parent, even if that parent is the form itself, so every control class has a `Parent` property. Because a control can be contained within only one other control at any point in time, modifying the `Parent` property of a control causes the control to move from one container to another. That change triggers the `ParentChanged` event.

The `TopLevelControl` property identifies the outermost control that is the outermost container control for all other controls—always a `Form` or `Form`-derived control. Whether this is the parent of a control, the grandparent, or the great-great-great-grandparent, this property makes it easy to quickly find the top of a family tree.

The `Controls` property is a collection of references, one reference for each control contained within this control. This collection includes first-level children only. Thus, if a `Form` control contains a `Panel` control that in turn contains a `TextBox` control, the `Panel` is in the `Controls` collection of the `Form`, and the `TextBox` is in the `Controls` collection of the `Panel`. Put another way, each container knows about its children but not about its grandchildren.

All controls, including container controls and all other types of controls, have a `Controls` property. If you think about it, this seems an odd design choice. A control such as a `TextBox` does not normally contain other controls. But it is beneficial for all controls, even those that do not hold other controls, to have a `Controls` collection. This consistency helps you write code that traverses a hierarchy of controls without writing a lot of special case code. To see why, examine the following code. This code is a recursive routine that iterates through all the controls on a form. The simplicity of this code is possible only because every control has a `Controls` collection. If any control lacked this property, we would need additional code to test for the presence of a `Controls` collection.

```
private void AccessAllControls( Control paramControl )
{
   foreach( Control childControl in paramControl.Controls )
```

continues

continued

```
    {
        //   Do something to this control.
        childControl.BackColor = Color.NavajoWhite;
        //   Recursively access all its children.
        AccessAllControls(childControl);
    }
}
```

To process all controls on any form, we call this routine and pass a reference to the top of the control hierarchy, as shown here.

```
AccessAllControls(this);
```

Like any collection in .NET, you access and maintain the `Controls` collection through a standard set of `Add`, `Clear`, `Remove`, and `RemoveAt` methods. For instance, the following code removes all controls from `panelABC` located in the top half of the panel.

```
foreach( Control childControl in panelABC.Controls )
{
    if(childControl.Top >
        panelABC.ClientRectangle.Height / 2 )
    {
        panelABC.Controls.Remove(childControl);
    }
}
```

The following line moves the `TextBox` control named `textTaskName` from one container to another.

```
textTaskName.Parent = panelABC;
```

The location of a child within the parent's `Controls` collection has no influence on its location within the parent's client area; that is determined by the child's `Bounds` and `Visible` properties. Adding, moving, or removing a child from a parent does not alter these position-related properties. If you want the child control to be in a different position in the new parent than in the old parent, you will need to modify the positional properties of the child control accordingly.

In a world where resources, especially screen resources, are scarce, container controls allow you to modularize your application's interface in a manner that lets a user navigate—which on a Pocket PC means to tap—quickly from one area of the interface to another. We look next at the available properties related to the location of controls.

The Positional Properties

- `Left`
- `Top`
- `Width`
- `Height`
- `Location`
- `Size`
- `Bounds`
- `Right`
- `Bottom`
- `ClientRectangle`
- `ClientSize`

The list above may seem long, but most of the properties in the list provide convenient alternatives for the first four—`Left`, `Top`, `Width`, and `Height`—which form the basic set. For instance, `Left` and `Top` are combined into a `Point` structure in the `Location` property. To place a control along the left side of a form and halfway down, we would write the following line of code.

```
textABC.Location = New Point(0, this.ClientSize.Height / 2);
```

Similarly, `Width` and `Height` are combined into `Size`. And all four of the basic set are combined into `Bounds`. If we had two controls, only one of which was going to be visible at any one time, and we wanted to colocate them, we would write the following line of code.

```
bttnXYZ.Bounds = bttnABC.Bounds;
```

The read-only properties `Right` and `Bottom` are defined as `Left` plus `Width` and `Top` plus `Height`, respectively.

The `ClientRectangle` and `ClientSize` properties measure the area in a control available for use by the control, excluding borders and scroll bars. `ClientRectangle` is a `Rectangle` structure with four values: `Left`, `Top`, `Right`, and `Bottom`. For a `ClientRectangle`, the values of two of these properties—`Left` and `Top`—are always `0`. The `ClientSize` property provides the exact same information, but as a `Size` structure containing `Width` and `Height` members. Because `Left` and `Top` are always `0` for a `ClientRectangle`, `Right` and `Bottom` always equal `Width` and `Height`, respectively.

The Data-Binding Properties

- `BindingContext`
- `DataBindings`

These two properties support data binding, a method of connecting a control to an external data object. A change to the control causes an automatic update to the data object and vice versa. We cover this subject more fully in Chapters 8 and 12.

The Control State Properties

- `Enabled`
- `Visible`

For controls with a user interface, the `Enabled` property allows or disables mouse (or touch-screen) input and keyboard (or SIP) input. Controls change their appearance when disabled. For example, the text of a disabled push button appears grayed. An application can then enable the button—say, when an item is selected from a list—to allow a user to push it.

For controls without a user interface, setting `Enabled` to `false` prevents the control from functioning; that is, it stops the control's ability to receive input and to raise events. Disabling a `Timer` control, for example, prevents it from raising `Tick` events.

For Win32 Programmers

Win32 programmers may recognize the `Visible` property as being the same as the `WS_VISIBLE` style bit. Setting and clearing this property produces the same effect as calling the Win32 `ShowWindow` function.

The `Visible` property simply indicates whether the control should be displayed. It does not really indicate visibility; a control whose `Visible` property is set to `true` but whose location is outside the client area of its parent does not display. Also, a control cannot be visible unless its parents—including all parents up to the root form—have their `Visible` properties set to `true`.

In general, the core control properties are fairly straightforward. These are not the only properties supported by controls, but they are the ones common to almost all controls. As we study each control later in this chapter and in subsequent chapter, we provide a more detailed look at the properties supported by each type of control.

The Core Methods

Table 7.5 lists the methods supported by most controls.

TABLE 7.5: Core Methods Supported in .NET Compact Framework Controls

`BringToFront`	`PointToScreen`
`Dispose`	`RectangleToClient`
`Hide`	`RectangleToScreen`
`Invoke`	`SendToBack`
`PointToClient`	`Show`

As for the core properties, we divide the core control methods into several categories, which are briefly summarized in the following subsections.

Thread-Safe Function Calls

- `Invoke`

The `Invoke` method is important when you have more than one thread in a .NET Compact Framework program. It is the only thread-safe method supported by controls and so provides the basic means by which code running in one thread can access controls running in another thread.

Object Cleanup

- `Dispose`

We discussed the `Dispose` method earlier in this chapter when we discussed the `Disposed` event. Calling the `Dispose` method informs an object that it is no longer needed and that it is scheduled for future reclamation by the garbage collector. When you implement your own classes, you may wish to implement this method to support the reclamation of nonmemory resources. A call to this method tells a class that it should release whatever hold it has on any external resource (especially unmanaged Win32 resources).

Coordinate Conversion

- `PointToClient`
- `PointToScreen`
- `RectangleToClient`
- `RectangleToScreen`

These methods convert values between client and screen coordinate systems. The difference between these two coordinate systems is the location of the origin—that is, the (0,0) pixel. Client coordinates put the origin at the upper-left corner of a control's client area, while screen coordinates put the origin at the upper-left corner of the screen itself. This conversion is needed in a few situations when a particular user interface object requires screen coordinates instead of client coordinates, such as with a context menu.

Z-Ordering

- `BringToFront`
- `SendToBack`
- `Form.Controls.SetChildIndex`

The x- and y-axes refer to the two-dimensional coordinate system of the display screen. The z-axis is the coordinate system that is perpendicular to the display screen. The z-order has to do with how controls are layered one on top of the other. Call these methods to move a control to the top layer (`BringToFront`), to send a control to the bottom layer (`SendToBack`), or to position it relative to its sibling controls (`Form.Controls.SetChildIndex`).

Local and Global Input State

The z-order of a control describes its position relative to its sibling controls. There is also a z-order relationship between container controls, so that two forms—say, an application's main window and a dialog box—can be moved such that one is visible while the other is hidden.

The z-order is one of several properties that are part of the *local input state*. The other properties are keyboard focus, mouse capture, and window activation. All of these properties are local to the thread that created the controls.

At any moment in time, only one thread in the system can have its local input state visible to the user. What the user sees is described as the *global input state*. The .NET Compact Framework does not supply a way to modify the global input state. A call to a Win32 function, `SetForegroundWindow`, is instead required, which in turn requires a P/Invoke call. (Making P/Invoke calls is covered in Chapter 4.) Assume that your source file has the following declaration.

```
using System.Runtime.InteropServices;
```

You then need to declare two Win32 functions, as shown here.

```
[DllImport("coredll.dll")]
public static extern IntPtr GetFocus();

[DllImport("coredll.dll")]
public static extern Int32 SetForegroundWindow(IntPtr hWnd);
```

At that point, you can make a form be the foreground form by setting the focus to the form and calling the two declared Win32 functions, as shown here.

```
this.TopLevelControl.Focus();
SetForegroundWindow(GetFocus());
```

Visibility

- `Hide`
- `Show`

These methods set and clear the `Visible` property, which we discussed earlier. A user can see only controls whose `Visible` properties are set to `true`. To be seen by a user, a control must also not be covered by other controls or forms (i.e., it must be at the top of the z-order) and must also be positioned in a visible portion of its parent (and not scrolled out of view).

These core methods provide a set that almost all controls support. Taken together, the core properties, core methods, and core events provide the starting point for manipulating .NET Compact Framework controls. But this is just the beginning of the story. The really interesting part involves the PMEs that each control implements.

Working with Control Type Information

The soul of any object-oriented framework is the type system and the resulting types that serve as the building blocks for software development. (We discussed .NET Compact Framework types in detail in Chapter 3.) The nature of working with .NET Compact Framework controls requires some additional details because sometimes you need to override an object's type or to query an object's type. In particular, you sometimes need to do operations like the following:

- Typecasting to change a generic type (such as `Object` or `Control`) to a more specific type
- Comparing control references to see whether two references are really the same object
- Checking a control's type

The following subsections briefly discuss these situations.

Typecasting Controls

In our discussion of event handlers, we said that the type of the object that generated the event was provided as `System.Object` and that this did not tell us much about the sender. A benefit of this approach is that any object can be the source of an event; however, to access the actual object we must typecast the sender to something more specific.

Consider a `Validated` event handler that might want to set the background color of a `TextBox` control to the default background color when valid data has been entered (assume that the `Validating` handler set the color to red for invalid values). We cast the sender to a specific object type so that we can access its individual properties and methods, as we have done in previous examples and as we do again here for emphasis.

```
private void txtTaskDates_Validated(object sender,
                                    System.EventArgs e)
{
   TextBox txtSender = (TextBox)sender;
   txtSender.BackColor = SystemColors.Window;
}
```

Comparing Two Control References

Sometimes in an event handler we need to check whether an event was sent from a specific control. Perhaps, for example, we need to perform a task only when the specific control is the one referenced by our `txtTaskEnd` field, so we need to determine whether `sender` is `txtTaskEnd`. To do so, use the `==` comparison operator, as shown here.

```
private void txtTaskDates_Validated(object sender,
                                    System.EventArgs e)
{
   if( sender == txtTaskEnd )
   {
      :
      :
   }
}
```

Checking a Control's Type

Finally, there are times when we wish to check not the identity of the sender but the type. To test for the data type of a control, use the C# `is` operator, as shown here.

```
if( sender is System.Windows.Forms.TextBox )
{
   :
   :
}
```

The wonder of the type system is that we can create generic code with iterators and event handlers that ignore the underlying types. Treating everything as an `Object` simplifies our code and the interfaces to our code. But that same type system is then able to provide type-specific support—either through casting or by explicitly querying about an object's type—when that information can help us. The code we have just seen illustrates how the type system supports these three common tasks with .NET Compact Framework controls.

Five Commonly Used Controls

In this chapter we focus on eight controls: `Panel`, `Label`, `TextBox`, `ListBox`, `ComboBox`, `Button`, `RadioButton`, and `CheckBox`. These controls are commonly used both on the desktop and for smart-device programming, which is why we discuss them here. `ListBox` and `ComboBox` are so closely related that we discuss them as one. `Button` is one of three controls derived from the `ButtonBase` class. The other two, `RadioButton` and `CheckBox`, are covered later in this chapter.

The `DataGrid` control is introduced in Chapter 8, while some additional controls of specific interest to .NET Compact Framework programmers are covered in Chapter 9.

But for now, the ones mentioned above will give us a good start and enable us to develop a sample application.

The complete list of PMEs available to the five controls is shown in Tables 7.6, 7.7, and 7.8. We present the summary of supported PMEs because they are critical to working with controls, and we have yet to find a complete and accurate statement of the supported PMEs anywhere else.

Events are the primary method used by controls to communicate with your program. Events also represent the way that users communicate—through a control—with your program. Properties and methods, on the other hand, provide the means by which your program responds.

Programmers who have worked with the desktop .NET Framework are always surprised to see the difference between the PMEs supported on the desktop compared to what they find in the .NET Compact Framework—at least, that is the reaction we see from programmers who attend our training classes. The reduction in supported PMEs helps significantly reduce the overall size of the .NET Compact Framework binaries when compared to the comparable binaries for the .NET Framework. This reduction often means that many familiar PMEs either are not supported or do not behave in exactly the same way as they do on the desktop. Often there is another way to accomplish what you want done, but in some cases you must get along without a feature—or write all the code to support that feature yourself. To get an idea of the difference between the number of PMEs, consider that the list of design-time `Label` properties in the .NET Compact

TABLE 7.6: Support for Properties Inherited from `Control`

	`Button`	`Label`	`ListBox`	`TextBox`	`Panel`
Links to Other Controls					
`Controls`	X	X	X	X	X
`ContextMenu`	X	X	X	X	X
`Parent`	X	X	X	X	X
`TopLevelControl`	X	X	X	X	X
Positional					
`Bottom`	X	X	X	X	X
`Bounds`	X	X	X	X	X
`ClientRectangle`	X	X	X	X	X
`ClientSize`	X	X	X	X	X
`Height`	X	X	X	X	X
`Left`	X	X	X	X	X
`Location`	X	X	X	X	X
`Right`	X	X	X	X	X
`Size`	X	X	X	X	X
`Top`	X	X	X	X	X
`Width`	X	X	X	X	X
Data Binding					
`BindingContext`	X	X	X	X	X
`DataBindings`	X	X	X	X	X
Control State					
`Capture`					
`Enabled`	X	X	X	X	X

	Button	Label	ListBox	TextBox	Panel
Focused	X		X	X	
Visible	X	X	X	X	X
Control Appearance					
BackColor				X	X
Font	X	X	X	X	
ForeColor		X		X	
Text	X	X	X	X	X

Framework, shown in Figure 7.2, is one-third as long as its desktop counterpart. This control class has 34 properties on the desktop, but just 12 in the .NET Compact Framework.

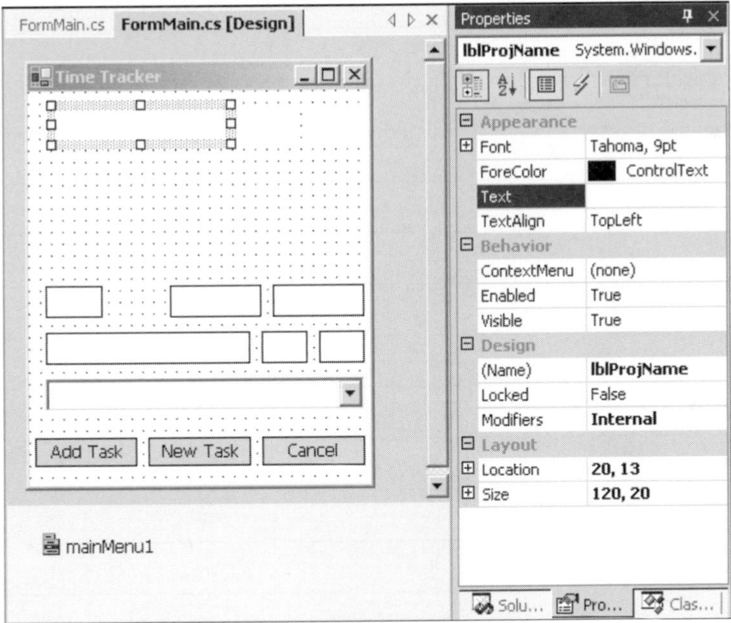

FIGURE 7.2: The design-time properties of a `Label` control

TABLE 7.7: Support for Methods Inherited from `Control`

	`Button`	`Label`	`ListBox`	`TextBox`	`Panel`
Thread-Safe					
`Invoke`	X	X	X	X	X
Object Support					
`Dispose`	X	X	X	X	X
`Equals`	X	X	X	X	X
`GetHashCode`	X	X	X	X	X
`GetType`	X	X	X	X	X
`ToString`	X	X	X	X	X
Coordinate Conversion					
`PointToClient`	X	X	X	X	X
`PointToScreen`	X	X	X	X	X
`RectangleToClient`	X	X	X	X	X
`RectangleToScreen`	X	X	X	X	X
Z-Ordering					
`BringToFront`	X	X	X	X	X
`SendToBack`	X	X	X	X	X
Visibility					
`Hide`	X	X	X	X	X
`Show`	X	X	X	X	X
Drawing					
`CreateGraphics`					
`Invalidate`	X	X	X	X	X
`Refresh`					
`Update`		X			
Control State					
`Focus`	X		X	X	X

TABLE 7.8: Support for Events Inherited from `Control`

	`Button`	`Label`	`ListBox`	`TextBox`	`Panel`
Garbage Collection and Validation					
`Disposed`	X	X	X	X	X
`Validated`	X	X	X	X	X
`Validating`	X	X	X	X	X
Focus Changes					
`GotFocus`	X		X	X	X
`LostFocus`	X		X	X	X
Control Property Changes					
`EnabledChanged`	X	X[a]	X	X	X
`ParentChanged`	X	X	X	X	X
`Resize`					X
`TextChanged`	X	X		X	
Keyboard Input					
`KeyDown`				X	X[a]
`KeyPress`				X	X[a]
`KeyUp`				X	X[a]
Mouse Input					
`Click`	X				X[a]
`MouseDown`					X[a]
`MouseMove`					X[a]
`MouseUp`					X[a]
Drawing					
`Paint`					

a. The Designer omits mention of support for this event.

Although the list of supported PMEs is relatively short, we expect you will find—as we have—that this is a very workable set. For programmers who have worked on the desktop .NET Framework, the primary challenge is getting comfortable with the fact that some old favorites from the desktop are not supported in the .NET Compact Framework.

A Sample Program: `TimeTracker`

The `TimeTracker` sample application helps track time spent on projects. There are many such applications available in the mobile environment today, and it is not our intention to reinvent the wheel or even to produce the ultimate mousetrap. Rather, the very fact that this application is so common makes it ideal for illustrating problems and solutions for the mobile environment.

Our database for this sample program consists of projects, each of which has a number of tasks. There is a desktop version of our application and a mobile-device version. The desktop version is not shown in this chapter because we want to concentrate on the mobile version. The desktop version does have the capability to maintain all information about all projects and all tasks. The mobile version is a more limited version, allowing users to download information about a particular project (including all its tasks), browse through those tasks, modify information about a task, and add new tasks, but not modify information about the project in general. Figure 7.3 shows the application shortly after startup, displaying information about the "Assemble Woobletogles" task of the .NET CF Book project.

Writing the Code

Without further ado, let us begin programming our sample application. Every C# .NET program starts with a set of `using` statements, which establish the namespaces to be used (see Chapter 2 for details). In our application, we begin by declaring the following namespaces.

```
using System;
using System.Drawing;
using System.Collections;
using System.Windows.Forms;
using System.Data;
```

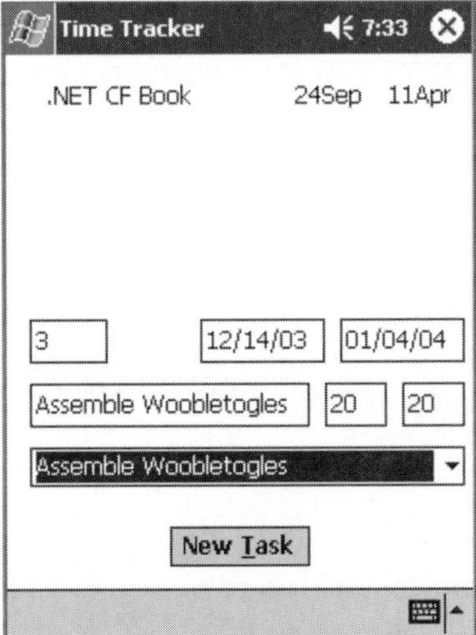

FIGURE 7.3: The `TimeTracker` application

Because we have not yet reached the chapters on data storage and databases, here we simulate a database using first a `Structure`, and then using an `ArrayList` object. First we define a structure to hold project information.

```
private struct Project
{
   public string strProjNo;
   public string strProjName;
   public DateTime dateProjStart;
   public DateTime dateProjEnd;
   public int ctProjTasks;
   public string strProjComments;
}
```

Then we define a structure to hold task information.

```
private struct Task
{
   private string strTaskIdent;
   private string strTaskName;
   public DateTime dateTaskStart;
   public DateTime dateTaskEnd;
   public int durTaskEstimated;  //  In hours;
   public int durTaskActual;     //  In hours;
   public string strTaskComments;
}
```

A Comment on Workarounds for Desktop Programmers

In this chapter we occasionally present situations where some functionality that desktop .NET programmers would normally use to accomplish a certain task is not available in the .NET Compact Framework. Often we use code at that point to illustrate how to achieve the same functionality using the .NET Compact Framework controls—in other words, a workaround. We do this for three reasons:

1. To provide more detail on the differences between a .NET Compact Framework control and its desktop counterpart
2. To show that a small amount of fairly simple code can usually provide the familiar desktop functionality, illustrating (we hope) that these reductions in functionality are not show stoppers
3. To encourage readers to visit Chapter 10 to see how existing controls can be extended to provide added functionality

We do not encourage using workarounds as a standard practice. If the functionality of your application can be achieved through a user interface comprised entirely of .NET Compact Framework controls, that is the best way to do it. If not, then the second-best way to provide the user interface is to incorporate your workaround into a custom control.

If you are moving from the desktop to .NET Compact Framework and you encounter some "missing" functionality, ask yourself if it really is missing. Maybe it's not missing; maybe it's just not applicable in the mobile environment.

An important part of object-oriented programming is that objects can be initialized within a custom constructor, which makes it easier to create a new instance of an object. For this reason, we add a custom constructor for each of our structures. Listing 7.3 shows our complete project structure.

LISTING 7.3: The Structure of a Project

```
private struct Project
{
   public string  strProjNo;
   public string  strProjName;
   public DateTime dateProjStart;
   public DateTime dateProjEnd;
   public int ctProjTasks;
   public string  strProjComments;

   public Project( string  strNo,  string  strName,
                   DateTime dateStart,  DateTime dateEnd,
                   int ctTasks,  string  strComments)
   {
      strProjNo = strNo;
      strProjName = strName;
      dateProjStart = dateStart;
      dateProjEnd = dateEnd;
      ctProjTasks = ctTasks;
      strProjComments = strComments;
   }
}
```

When we add a constructor, our task structure appears as shown in Listing 7.4.

LISTING 7.4: The Structure of a Task

```
private struct Task
{
   private string  strTaskIdent;
   private string  strTaskName;
   public DateTime dateTaskStart;
   public DateTime dateTaskEnd;
   public int durTaskEstimated;  //  In hours;
   public int durTaskActual;     //  In hours;
   public string  strTaskComments;

   public Task( string strNo, string strName,
                DateTime dateStart,  DateTime dateEnd,
                int durEstimated,  int durActual,
                string  strComments)
   {
      strTaskIdent = strNo;
      strTaskName = strName;
```

continues

continued

```
        dateTaskStart = dateStart;
        dateTaskEnd = dateEnd;
        durTaskEstimated = durEstimated;
        durTaskActual = durActual;
        strTaskComments = strComments;
    }
}
```

Because this is a lot of code in terms of line count and because we don't want to have to scroll through it while looking for other things, we'll put it in a region so that we can collapse the region and forget it. The following line of code creates a region for the project and task structures.

```
+ #region " Database Structure Simulated "
```

Although they spend most of their time hidden, you can view either structure by hovering your mouse over the region (a nice feature available courtesy of IntelliSense), as well as by expanding it.

Our application allows the user to access only one project at a time, so a single instance of the project data structure is all that is needed to hold project information. But we need an `ArrayList` of task data structures to hold the task information, not only because a project can have more than one task but also because we need the ability to add tasks to a project. (An `Array` object has a fixed length and does not allow new entries to be added, while an `ArrayList` object does allow new entries to be added.)

To complete our database code, we write a routine to simulate reading a database and loading the project data from that database into our structures. Listing 7.5 shows this `LoadProject` routine, which is called at application startup.

LISTING 7.5: The Method to Load a Project and Its Tasks

```
private bool LoadProject(  int ProjectID )
{
   //  Simulate having retrieved project data
   //     from a database.  Here, we use our
   //     Project and Task data structures to
   //     hold the data.
```

```
   theProject.strProjNo = "1";
   theProject.strProjName = ".NET CF Book";
   theProject.dateProjStart = DateTime.Today.AddDays(-100);
   theProject.dateProjEnd = DateTime.Today.AddDays(100);

   alTasks.Add(new Task("0",
      "Create Blueprints",
      DateTime.Today.AddDays(-17), DateTime.Today.AddDays(22),
      120, 60, ""));
   alTasks.Add(new Task("1",
      "Build Franistans",
      DateTime.Today.AddDays(-11),
      DateTime.Today.AddDays(0),
      35, 30, ""));
   alTasks.Add(new Task("2",
      "Build Widgets",
      DateTime.Today.AddDays(-4),
      DateTime.Today.AddDays(44),
      400, 45, ""));
   alTasks.Add(new Task("3",
      "Assemble Woobletogles",
      DateTime.Today.AddDays(-19),
      DateTime.Today.AddDays(2),
      20, 20, ""));
   alTasks.Add(new Task("4",
      "Weld Mainwareing",
      DateTime.Today.AddDays(-100),
      DateTime.Today.AddDays(50),
      20, 6, ""));
   return true;
}
```

With our data structures in place, we can begin laying out the elements of our program's user interface.

The Application Interface

As shown in Figure 7.3, our application displays project information across the top of the form, with the currently selected task displayed underneath. Under the task fields is the drop-down list of tasks, which allows the user to scroll through the tasks of the project one at a time. Along the bottom is the button for adding a new task.

We put the drop-down list below the task fields rather than above because the lower area of the form is where the SIP appears, and we would prefer that it overlay the drop-down list rather than the fields that are receiving the keyboard input.

One of us is a fan of doing graphical layout via drag and drop from the toolbox, while the other is a "double-click on the Toolbox icon and then use the arrow keys to position the control" person. Regardless of which technique you prefer, the results are the same. And the results are in the code generated by the Designer, code that provides us with some insight into control creation and placement.

If this is your first experience with .NET, this Designer-generated code is a bit intimidating. After all, it begins with a comment that warns you against modifying this code. As we mentioned in Chapter 2, not modifying the code (unless you really know what you are doing) is a good idea. But being intimidated by this code is not a good idea. You can gain many insights into .NET programming by studying this code. This Designer-generated code shows you how controls are generated, positioned, and added to a form, as well as how events and event handlers are linked together. These are all things you may want to do yourself in your applications, and in fact these are things that we do in this chapter and throughout the rest of the book. So we suggest that you take the time to read this Designer-generated code as a resource so you can learn more about what the Designer does and how you can adopt its tricks for your own uses.

Because this code is quite repetitious and because aspects of it were covered in Chapter 2, we examine only a small sample here, the code that was generated for the `txtTaskName` `TextBox`, for it is very similar to code that we use later in this chapter to create a control at runtime.

```
internal System.Windows.Forms.TextBox txtTaskName;

this.txtTaskName = new System.Windows.Forms.TextBox();

this.txtTaskName.Location = new System.Drawing.Point(12, 165);
this.txtTaskName.Size = new System.Drawing.Size(144, 22);
this.txtTaskName.Text = "";

this.Controls.Add(this.txtTaskName);
```

There are three steps required to produce the desired control at the desired location. This is true regardless of whether you are writing the code or whether the Designer is generating it for you.

1. Create the control.
2. Set the positioning properties.
3. Add the control to the form's `Controls` collection.

Even the Designer has to generate object-oriented code. You can see from the previous code fragment that the `Size` and `Location` properties are objects. Thus, neither the Designer nor you can write code like the following line.

```
this.txtTaskName.Location = (5,7); ' This does not work
```

Instead, because `Location` is a `Point`, you must designate a new `Location` by creating a new `Point`, as shown here.

```
this.txtTaskName.Location = new System.Drawing.Point(8, 168);
```

Variable Naming

In the example, the `TextBox` control is named `txtTaskName`, a style of variable naming known as *Hungarian notation*. The essence of this approach is the use of a prefix (such as `txt`) to add type information to a variable name. We like Hungarian notation because, when you know the basic set of prefixes, it helps make code easier to read. We like it so much that in Appendix A we have defined a set of tags for many of the commonly used types encountered in .NET programming.

Coding Event Handlers

All GUI applications, including .NET Compact Framework applications, execute by reacting to events. So we begin building our program by writing our event handlers. We know from earlier in this chapter that this means writing two pieces of code: the event handler itself and the code that ties the handler to the event.

```
this.txtOne.TextChanged += new
      System.EventHandler(this.txtSomeData_TextChanged);
```

The Designer will generate this code and the skeleton of the event handler for you. Just select the control or the form in Design View, go to the Properties window, and click on the lightning bolt button. This will display a list of the events that the control supports, as shown in Figure 7.4. For each event, a drop-down list of the handlers you have already coded that could handle the event is displayed. You can either chose an existing event/handler combination from the list or double-click on an event to have the skeleton of a new handler generated for you. When you double-click on an event, the code shown above will be written for you, and you will be positioned within the Code View window inside the event handler skeleton.

We start our coding with the form's `Load` event handler. In general, this event provides the best opportunity for handling most initialization for forms or controls on a form. In our program, we respond to the `Load` event by setting up the various buttons (we get the form ready by hiding some

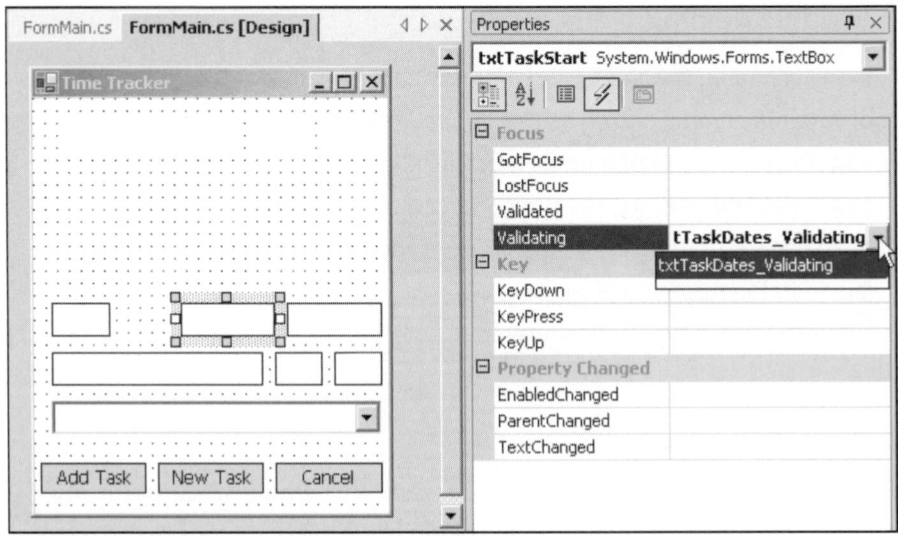

FIGURE 7.4: Choosing the event to handle

controls) and call the LoadProject routine mentioned earlier. Listing 7.6 shows the code for our load handler and a function it calls.

LISTING 7.6: Initializing Controls During the Form Load Event

```
private void FormMain_Load(object sender, System.EventArgs e)
{
   //  set the initial state of the controls.
   InitControlState();

   //  Load and display a project.
   if ( LoadProject(42) )
   {
      DisplayProject();
   }
   else
   {
      this.Close();
   }
}
   :
   :
   :
private void InitControlState() {
   //  Hide the Add button directly under the New button.
   cmdAddTask.Visible = false;
   cmdAddTask.Bounds = cmdNewTask.Bounds;
   //  Hide the cancel button
   cmdCancel.Visible = false;
}
```

You might wonder why we hide buttons; in particular, why not just set the Visible property of the various buttons at design time? The answer is that it is easier to maintain and modify a single block of initialization code than to search through the Designer's Properties window for each control, looking for the values that need to be set. This is especially true if you consider one of the lines of code shown earlier, the one that sets the Bounds property to colocate two buttons. It is easier and more flexible to write one line of code than to set four design-time property values. For instance, if we set the location properties in the Designer and then later changed the property values for cmdAddTask, we would need to remember to change the same properties for cmdNewTask.

Another important reason is that setting properties in the Designer does not reduce code size, nor does it make your program run faster. Code must be written to initialize all nondefault properties. Whether you write it or the Designer writes it has no impact on the code's size and speed.

Having handled the form's `Load` event, we need to make the individual controls work for us, beginning with the labels.

The `Label` Control

The `Label` control is the control for display text. Table 7.9 summarizes the PMEs that are unique to the `Label` control. In general, labels are not overly complicated controls. But there are a few unique qualities worth knowing. For example, a `Label` control is transparent to mouse events. That is, any click that occurs on a label passes through to the form (or panel) underneath the label. Programmers who are used to having "clickable" labels, such as can be found in desktop .NET Framework programs, have to find another way to get that same support in the .NET Compact Framework.

A `Label` control receives neither mouse nor keyboard input, and yet `Label` controls support a property that is normally associated with mouse and keyboard input: `Enabled`. When we say "supports," we mean that something interesting—and also useful—happens when we modify that property. When enabled, most other controls are able to receive mouse and/or keyboard input; when disabled, most other controls do not receive mouse and keyboard input. Most controls, including `Label` controls, change their appearance when disabled. For example, the text on disabled buttons and disabled labels appears grayed and italicized. Because labels

TABLE 7.9: PMEs Specific to the `Label` Control

Element	Description
Properties	`TextAlign`: Specifies left, right, or center alignment
Methods	None
Events	None

are one of the few controls that support the foreground (text) color property, this change can be useful to let a user know when a feature is available and when it is unavailable.

Display, Yes; Update, No

`Label` controls display text, but they do not allow the user to modify the text; specifically, `Label` controls cannot receive keyboard events like `TextBox` controls can. Because of this simplicity, there are few label-specific PMEs.

Even though the user cannot change a label's text, a program can modify the text by modifying the label's `Text` property. The text change, in turn, raises the `TextChanged` event. As you will see, our application responds to this event to visually highlight overdue projects.

To do this, we write a `TextChanged` event handler for `lbldateProjEnd`, the label that displays the project end date. If the scheduled end date has already passed (i.e., if the scheduled end date is earlier than the current date), we change the color of the `Label` control's text to red. While you might prefer to change the background color to red, `Label` controls do not support the background color property. In the next section, Transparency, we will emulate the background color property, but for now the `ForeColor` property is the one we must use. The event-handling code is shown here.

```
private void lblProjEnd_TextChanged(object sender,
                                    System.EventArgs e)
{
   //  If this project is due or
   //      overdue, use red ink.
   SetBkColor(lblProjEnd,Color.Red);
   if( (DateTime)lblProjEnd.Text < DateTime.Today )
   {
      lblProjEnd.ForeColor = Color.Red;
   }
}
```

Transparency

Although `Label` controls do not have many properties, they do have a characteristic that other controls do not have: transparency. They are transparent both to the eye of the user and to the click of the mouse. We will discuss transparency in that sequence.

Earlier, when we said that labels did not have a background color, we did not mean "labels do not have a BackColor property" but instead that this property is not supported in the .NET Compact Framework. Because Label controls are transparent, the background color of the parent control becomes the background color of the Label control. We can take advantage of that fact to give our Label control the equivalent of a background color property by placing it with a Panel control and setting the background color of the Panel.

What we need is a function that takes two input parameters: a reference to a Label control and a background color. This function will then make the specified color the apparent background color of the Label. More specifically, it will create a Panel control, colocate the Panel with the Label, put the Label in the Panel, and set the panel's BackColor property to the requested color.

This subroutine might be called several times with various colors, and thus the Label might already be contained within a Panel. We would want to use that existing Panel, not create a new one. Or the desired background color might be that of the form, in which case the application should place the Label on the form and destroy the Panel. As the label moves in and out of the form, we must position it correctly; within the Panel the Label is always located at (0,0), but within the form it is hardly ever at (0,0).

In the end, we dodge the aforementioned obstacles and write the code shown in Listing 7.7.

LISTING 7.7: A Method for Giving a Label a Background Color

```
private void SetBkColor(Label lblTarget,  Color colorBack)
{
   //  If the desired background color is the background
   //     color of this form, remove the label from the
   //     panel and dispose of the panel.
   if ( colorBack.Equals(this.BackColor) )
   {
      if (lblTarget.Parent.Equals(this) )
      {
      }
      else
      {
         Panel panelBackColor = (Panel)(lblTarget.Parent);
         lblTarget.Bounds = panelBackColor.Bounds;
```

```
         lblTarget.Parent = this;
         panelBackColor.Dispose();
      }
   }
   else
   {
      //  If the desired background color is not the
      //     background color of this form, then if the
      //     label is already inside a panel, set the
      //     background color of that panel.  If not,
      //     create a panel, position it, put the label
      //     in it, and set the background color.
      if ( lblTarget.Parent.Equals(this) )
      {
         Panel panelBackColor = new Panel();
         panelBackColor.BackColor = colorBack;
         this.Controls.Add(panelBackColor);
         panelBackColor.Visible = true;
         panelBackColor.Bounds = lblTarget.Bounds;
         lblTarget.Location = new Point(0, 0);
         panelBackColor.Controls.Add(lblTarget);
      }
      else
      {
         ((Panel)(lblTarget.Parent)).BackColor = colorBack;
      }
   }
}
```

Although it is a subroutine, not a property, this code does let us emulate the unsupported background color property of a `Label` control. In Chapter 10, you will learn how to define your own `Label` control, one that could have a background color property.

To implement our background color feature, we modify our `lbldate-ProjEnd_TextChanged` event handler as shown in the following code, deleting the code that used the `Label` control's `ForeColor` property to indicate an overdue date and replacing it with our `SetBkColor` subroutine.

```
   private void lblProjEnd_TextChanged(object sender,
                                       System.EventArgs e)
{
   //  If this project is due or
   //      overdue, use red ink.
   SetBkColor(lblProjEnd,Color.Red);
}
```

With these changes, we obtain the result shown in Figure 7.5.

As we mentioned earlier, not only are labels visually transparent, they are also transparent to the click of the mouse. It is true that labels do not receive `MouseDown` and `MouseUp` events. But the control behind the label, the parent control, does receive the mouse events. It is as if the mouse click just passed through the label and went right on down to the container control. Once again this is something we can take advantage of, making our application react appropriately whenever the user taps or clicks on a `Label` control.

To illustrate with an example that is not part of our application, we'll write a `MouseUp` event handler for a `Panel` that checks the location of the tap against the `Bounds` of the controls contained within the `Panel` to determine which `Label` control was tapped on. Then the code calls a subroutine, passing it the reference to the `Label` control. This subroutine becomes, for all practical purposes, the `MouseUp` event handler for the `Label` control. Listing 7.8 shows the code for both of these subroutines: the real `MouseUp` handler (that of the `Panel`) and the pseudo handler (that of the `Label` control).

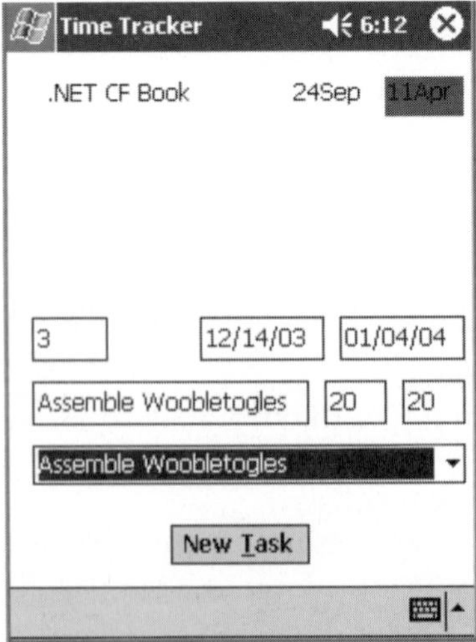

FIGURE 7.5: Project end date with background highlighted

LISTING 7.8: Determining Which Label Control Was Clicked

```
#region Windows Form Designer generated code
/// <summary>
/// Required method for Designer support - do not modify
/// the contents of this method with the code editor.
/// </summary>
private void InitializeComponent()
{
             :
             :
             :
   //
   // Added by YaoDurant
   //
   this.panelABC.MouseUp +=
      new MouseEventHandler(panelABC_MouseUp);
}
#endregion

private void panelABC_MouseUp( object sender,
                               MouseEventArgs e )
{
   //  Determine which label control, if any, was
   //     the intended target of the mouse hit.
   foreach( Control childControl in panelABC.Controls )
   {
      if( childControl.Bounds.Contains(e.X, e.Y) )
      {
         if( childControl is System.Windows.Forms.Label )
         {
            label_MouseUp(childControl as Label);
         }
      }
   }
}

private void label_MouseUp(Label lblSender)
{
   //
   //  lblSender, you have just been clicked upon.
   //  do something.
   //
   MessageBox.Show("You tapped " + lblSender.Text);
}
```

Figure 7.6 shows the result of the user clicking on the "First Name" label.

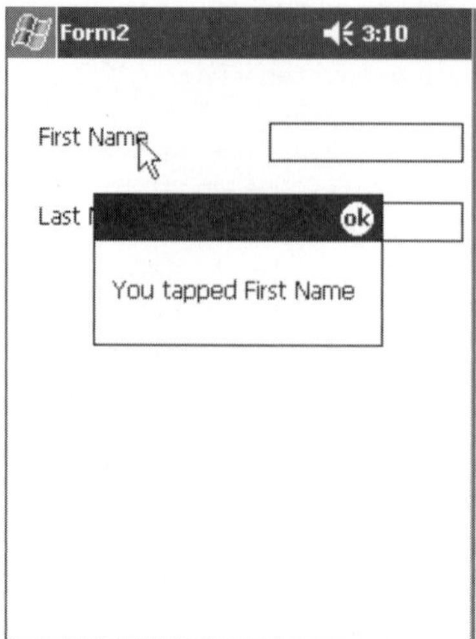

FIGURE 7.6: Clicking on the "First Name" label

Even with this transparency characteristic, labels are an easy control to work with. They have a minimal number of PMEs. You put text in the label, and the user reads the text. Let us move on to a slightly more complex control, the `TextBox`.

The `TextBox` Control

We used `Label` controls to display project information because our mobile application does not allow the user to modify that information. Since our application does allow the user to modify task information, we must use `TextBox` controls for the display and update of task data.

Table 7.10 shows the PMEs (beyond the core PMEs) supported by the `TextBox` control.

Display, Yes; Input, Yes

Because a `TextBox` control allows the user to change the text, this control class supports more PMEs than does the `Label` class. These PMEs relate to the selecting and changing of text: events such as `Validating`, methods such as `SelectAll`, and properties such as `ForeColor`.

TABLE 7.10: PMEs Specific to the TextBox Control

Element	Description
Properties	AcceptsReturn: Specifies whether the TextBox control accepts new lines, or whether the enter key causes the Click event to be raised by the default button AcceptsTab: Specifies whether the tab key advances to the next control or is accepted by the current control as input MaxLength: Sets a limit on the number of characters allowed Modified: Specifies whether the contents have been changed Multiline: Specifies whether the control is single-line or multiline PasswordChar: Sets the character used to mask input of passwords ReadOnly: Specifies whether the text is read-only ScrollBars: Specifies whether multiline TextBox controls should have scroll bars SelectedText: Contains the currently selected text SelectionLength: Sets the length of the selection SelectionStart: Sets the starting point of the selection TextAlign: Specifies left, center, or right aligned TextLength: Sets the length of text in the TextBox control WordWrap: Specifies whether multiline TextBox controls should have auto word wrapping
Methods	ScrollToCaret: Scrolls the contents to the current caret position Select: Selects text in the control SelectAll: Selects all text in the control
Events	None

Our application uses TextBox controls to display and update task information for the task currently selected in the drop-down ComboBox control. Whenever the user selects a new task, the application must respond by displaying new information in the TextBox controls. To do this we write a routine, named LoadTaskFields, which will take an index into the task ArrayList as the lone input parameter and load the fields of that task into the TextBox controls. For those fields that are not of data type string, we use the data type's ToString method to convert the value to a string. Listing 7.9 shows LoadTaskFields; the code that calls this routine will be covered in the discussion of ListBox and ComboBox controls.

LISTING 7.9: Loading the Fields of the Selected Task into TextBox Controls

```
private void LoadTaskFields( int intTaskNo)
{
   //  Load the fields for the specified
   //     task into the text boxes.  If
   //     intTaskNo is out of range, clear
   //     the textboxes.
   if ( intTaskNo >= 0 && intTaskNo < alTasks.Count )
   {
      //  Create a variable of a specific type
      //     so that we can do early binding.
      Task refTask = (Task)alTasks[intTaskNo];
      txtTaskNo.Text = refTask.strTaskIdent;
      txtTaskName.Text = refTask.strTaskName;
      txtTaskStart.Text =
         refTask.dateTaskStart.ToString("MM/dd/yy");
      txtTaskEnd.Text =
         refTask.dateTaskEnd.ToString("MM/dd/yy");
      txtTaskEstimated.Text =
         refTask.durTaskEstimated.ToString();
      txtTaskActual.Text =
         refTask.durTaskActual.ToString();
   }
   else
   {
      txtTaskNo.Text = string.Empty;
      txtTaskName.Text = string.Empty;
      txtTaskStart.Text = string.Empty;
      txtTaskEnd.Text = string.Empty;
      txtTaskEstimated.Text = string.Empty;
      txtTaskActual.Text = string.Empty;
   }
}
```

Note that the LoadTaskFields procedure checks to make sure that the index is within the Bounds property of the ArrayList, which is always a good thing to do. But it has an additional benefit for us that a SelectedIndex value of -1, meaning that no item has been selected, results in the TextBox fields being cleared. This is something we will take advantage of later when we provide the user with the ability to enter a new task.

We now have the ability to display a task; we still need a way for the user to indicate which task should be displayed. For that we'll use a ComboBox control.

The ListBox and ComboBox Controls

ListBox controls and ComboBox controls differ from each other in appearance, but they are so similar in functionality that we will use the terms ListBox and ComboBox interchangeably throughout this chapter. What we say in reference to one type of control applies to the other. Both allow the user to select from a list of possible choices; neither allows the user to directly enter text. For many developers coming to the .NET Compact Framework from other Windows environments, the lack of direct entry of text is a surprising limitation. Later in this chapter, as we are developing our RegisterMembers application, we introduce a workaround for this limitation; for now we limit ourselves to the inherent functionality of ListBox and ComboBox controls.

The real difference between ListBox and ComboBox controls is in their appearance, not their functionality. The visual difference lies in the fact that the height of a ListBox is determined by its Bounds property, while a ComboBox is one element tall, showing its full list only on demand, as illustrated in Figure 7.7.

ListBox and ComboBox controls share the same PMEs, which are listed in Table 7.11. The three PMEs that relate to data binding—DataSource, DisplayMember, and ValueMember—are covered in Chapter 8.

The List in ListBox Controls

A ListBox control is just that, a list inside a visible box. The key thing is to understand the "list" in a ListBox control. The list in a ListBox control is an ArrayList of objects and is not limited to a list of strings. Almost any class of object can be placed into this list as long as it has at least one displayable property. In addition to the one property that can be used as the display property, a second property of the object in the list can be chosen to be the identifier property.

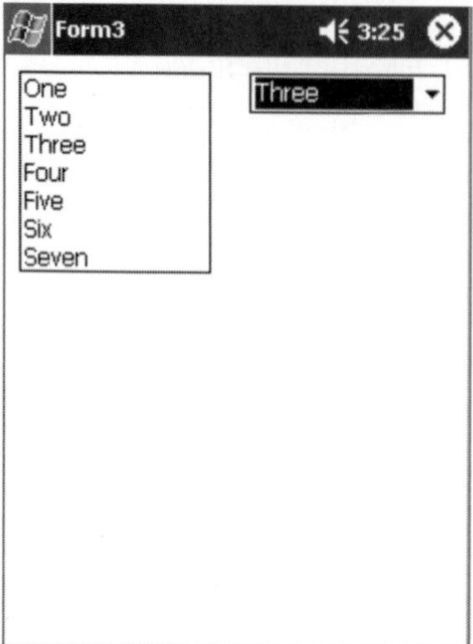

FIGURE 7.7: The visual difference between `ListBox` and `ComboBox` controls

TABLE 7.11: PMEs Specific to the `ListBox` and `ComboBox` Controls

Element	Description
Properties	`DataSource`: Used with data-binding property `DisplayMember`: Used with data-binding property `Items`: Sets the collection of elements in the list `SelectedIndex`: Specifies the index of the currently selected item `SelectedItem`: Indicates the currently selected item `SelectedValue`: Holds the value of the selected item `TopIndex`: Specifies the index of the first visible item `ValueMember`: Used with data binding property
Methods	`GetItemText`: Gets the text of the specified item
Events	`SelectedIndexChanged`: Indicates that a different item in the list is now the selected item `SelectedValueChanged`: Indicates that the value of the selected item has changed

The names of these two properties of the object in the list are themselves properties of the ListBox: the DisplayMember property and the ValueMember property. Using database terminology, the ValueMember property is equivalent to the primary key of the list, and the DisplayMember property is the equivalent of a descriptive attribute. Because property names are always strings, the DisplayMember and ValueMember properties of the ListBox are string properties.

In our application, we use a ComboBox control to display the list of project tasks, and we do so by building a list of task names within the ComboBox. In Chapter 8, we extend this and bind the entire ArrayList of tasks to the ComboBox.

Because the user, or the executing program itself, can select an entry in the list, ListBox controls have a SelectedIndex property, a SelectedItem property, and a SelectedValue property. The SelectedIndex property is a zero-based integer. The SelectedItem property is the selected object in the list, be it as simple as our string or as complex as a System.Data.DataRow. The SelectedValue property is the value of the ValueMember property of the SelectedItem. Therefore, it also might be of any data type.

The Text property of a ComboBox control deserves special mention here. The Text property is the text value of the selected item. Retrieving the Text property of a ComboBox control returns the selected item as a text value, as in the following line of code.

```
strName = lbxNames.Text;
```

Setting the Text property, however, does not change the text value of the selected item; rather, it will set the SelectedIndex property to the item whose text value is equal to the Text property, if any. Thus, the following line of code will find the next "John Doe" entry in the list and select it. It will not change the value of the current item.

```
lbxNames.Text = "John Doe";
```

When the user completes the selection about to be made in Figure 7.8, two properties in the ComboBox control will change: SelectedIndex will

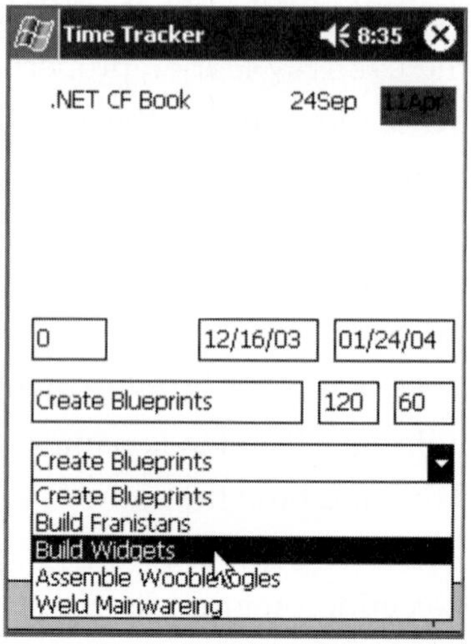

FIGURE 7.8: Selecting from the ComboBox control

have a value of 2 (remember, it is a zero-based list), and SelectedItem will have a value of "Build Widgets".

Because a ListBox list is zero-based, a SelectedIndex value of 0 means that the first element is selected. A SelectedIndex value of -1, on the other hand, means that no element is selected. Whenever the user or the program changes the value of the SelectedIndex property, a SelectedIndexChanged event is fired. Without a doubt, this is the most commonly handled event for ListBox and ComboBox controls because it notifies your program that the user has picked a new item from the list. Your program might respond by changing values displayed in other controls or by enabling (or disabling) other controls to reflect the new program state.

Using the ComboBox Control in the Sample Application

An important part of working with either kind of list control is initializing the contents of the list. You can add items to a list at design time, by clicking the Items property in the Designer. Or you can add items at runtime. The code for each is the same; the difference is whether you type item values at design time or write the code yourself for runtime initialization.

In our sample application, we initialize our ComboBox control with a list of project task names in the DisplayProject routine (this same routine initializes labels with project information). Once we have the list loaded, we set the SelectedItem property to the first item in the list and then set the focus to the ListBox control so that our program is ready to scroll through the task list. Listing 7.10 shows the code for the DisplayProject routine.

LISTING 7.10: A Method to Display a Project in the Form

```
private void DisplayProject()
{
   //  Load Proj data into the labels.
   lblProjName.Text = theProject.strProjName;
   lblProjStart.Text =
      theProject.dateProjStart.ToString("ddMMM");
   lblProjEnd.Text =
      theProject.dateProjEnd.ToString("ddMMM");

   //  Load the tasks into the drop-down ComboBox.
   foreach( Task theTask in alTasks )
   {
      cboxTasks.Items.Add(theTask.strTaskName);
   }

   //  Start with the first task as
   //     the currently selected task.
   cboxTasks.SelectedIndex = 0;

   //  Set the focus to the tasks ComboBox.
   cboxTasks.Focus();
}
```

Whenever the user selects a task from the ComboBox control, we load information about that task into our TextBox controls by calling the LoadTaskFields routine (introduced earlier during our discussion of TextBox controls). This is the only thing we do in response to a SelectedIndexChanged event. Since both the ComboBox's list and the task ArrayList are zero-based, we use the index found in the SelectedIndex property as the index into the ArrayList. This makes our event handler the simple routine shown here.

```
private void cboxTasks_SelectedIndexChanged(
   object sender,
   System.EventArgs e)
{
   LoadTaskFields(cboxTasks.SelectedIndex);
}
```

We have reached the point in our application where users can view a project and scroll through its individual tasks. Our next step is to provide the ability to add new tasks and to modify existing tasks, which leads us to the subject of buttons.

The `Button` Control

Buttons are a common user interface object of all GUI environments, and that is certainly true with the GUI environments that support the .NET Compact Framework. You have seen buttons, clicked or tapped on buttons, and no doubt expect something to happen each time you push a button. So, whether or not you have ever written code to deal with buttons, you would expect that you would get told when a click or tap occurs. .NET Compact Framework buttons will not disappoint you, then, because when a user clicks or taps on a button, you get an event—the `Click` event—which is the most commonly handled event for buttons.

Table 7.12 shows the PMEs (in addition to the core PMEs) that relate to the `Button` control.

Triggering Actions

Our application needs a way for the user to create a new task, which we provide in the form of a button labeled New. An important principle of good user interface design is to allow users to change their minds. For example, when a user starts to create a new task, we need to provide him or

TABLE 7.12: PMEs Specific to the `Button` Control

Element	Description
Properties	`DialogResult`: Specifies the value returned to the parent when the button is clicked (see Chapter 9)
Methods	None
Events	None

her a way to not create the task after all. Perhaps a phone call interrupted the work, or the user remembered a need to check with someone before creating the task.

For this reason, in our application, there are two possible ways to end the task creation process, both implemented with buttons. One possibility is that the user completes the entry of the information and wishes to store a task in the database, and for this we provide an Add button in the GUI. Another possibility is that the user wishes to cancel the operation and not store a new task in the database, and for this we provide a Cancel button.

The `New` action and the `Add` action are mutually exclusive because only one is applicable at any point in time. To make this clear to the user, we show only one of these two buttons, depending on the program state. But how should we go about implementing this in code? We might have one button and change its text to either `"New"` or `"Add"`, then respond to the `Click` event based on the button text. That would certainly provide a workable solution. Instead, we implement two separate buttons at the same location but make only one visible at a time. We take this approach to show how to arrange and manipulate controls, ignoring for now whether this is the optimal approach.

The following code colocates the New button and the Add button and sets the appropriate visibility for both buttons. This routine, named `InitControlState`, is called from the form's `Load` event.

```
private void InitControlState()
{
   //  Hide the Add button directly under the New button.
   cmdAddTask.Visible = false;
   cmdAddTask.Bounds = cmdNewTask.Bounds;
   //  Hide the Cancel button.
   cmdCancel.Visible = false;
}
```

Not only are we adding more controls at design time but we also need to create a control at runtime. That in turn means we must write code at design time to handle events for the control we will not create until runtime. No problem—if the Designer can do it, we can do it.

Adding a Control at Runtime

As you probably have noticed, our application, being very simple up to this point, has an adequate amount of screen space to display the information it needs to display. But a more complex application might not have enough space and might need to create, show, hide, and dispose of controls at runtime. Our application has now reached the point where we need to create a control at runtime: a large multiline TextBox control into which users can enter comments about the tasks they are adding to their projects. Our application must create this control, add it to the form, position it, make it visible, bring it to the top z-order, add an event handler for its TextChanged event, and subsequently dispose of the control.

The application must handle the TextChanged event for this control because there is a company policy that says, "Verbose comments are to be discouraged." (We should be so lucky.) When the comment becomes overly long, the background color of the TextBox control must change to red. The code for this is very simple.

```
private void txtTaskComments_TextChanged(object sender,
                                         EventArgs e )
{
   txtTaskComments.BackColor =
      (txtTaskComments.Text.Length > 30) ?
      Color.Red : Color.White;
}
```

It is important to remember that, in .NET, naming a subroutine ABC_TextChanged does not cause it to handle TextChanged events. We must establish that relationship elsewhere in the program, after we have created the TextBox control.

Also, the TextChanged event fires with every keystroke, so the background color will change back to white as soon as the user has deleted the excess characters.

Handling the Click Event for the New Button

Our application must provide functionality that begins with the user clicking on the New button, the results in the task fields being cleared, the new multiline TextBox control created and displayed, the buttons rearranged, and the ComboBox control being hidden. Our code causes the result shown in Figure 7.9.

We hide the ComboBox control so that the user does not accidentally select a task while entering a task, which would erase the new task information from the TextBox controls.

The routine that does all this, the New button's event handler, first saves the index of the currently selected task so that it can reposition back to the previous task if the user cancels his or her entry. The code to do so is shown here.

```
//  The index number of the previous task.  We will
//     need to know it in case the user cancels out
//     during task creation.
private int ixTaskPrev;
   :
   :
   :
private void cmdNewTask_Click(object sender,
                              System.EventArgs e)
{
   //  Save the index number of the previous task.  We will
   //     need to know it in case the user cancels out
   //     during task creation.
   ixTaskPrev = cboxTasks.SelectedIndex;
```

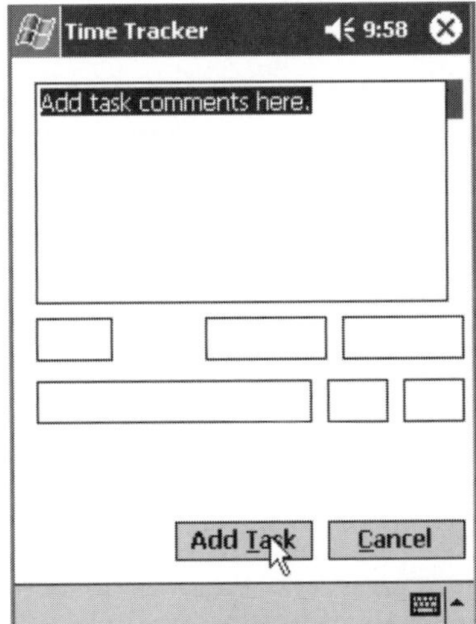

FIGURE 7.9: Displaying the comments TextBox control

Next the `SelectedIndex` property of the `ComboBox` control is set to `-1`.

```
//  Deselect the current task from the drop-down
//      ComboBox.  This will also cause the
//      SelectedIndexChanged event to fire,
//      which will cause the task fields to clear.
cboxTasks.SelectedIndex = -1;
```

Because we are setting `SelectedIndex` to `-1`, the `ComboBox` control's `SelectedIndexChanged` event will fire. This in turn causes our `LoadTaskFields` procedure to be called with a parameter of `-1`, which clears out the `TextBox` controls, preparing them for user input of the new task.

Next we create and show the multiline `TextBox` control into which the user can enter comments regarding the new task. We create the control using the same code that the Designer generated when creating our other `TextBox` controls, and we save the reference to it in a variable, as shown here.

```
//  A reference to a control to be created later
private TextBox txtTaskComments;
                 :
                 :
                 :
   txtTaskComments = new TextBox();
```

We then set the `Multiline` property like this.

```
txtTaskComments.Multiline = true;
```

For illustrative purposes we want this control to be large enough that it overlays other controls. It is a common practice to position controls relative to other controls, especially when creating them at runtime. In our application it is essential that we position our new control based on the location of other controls because we want the multiline `TextBox` control to start at the top of the project fields and extend down until it is just above the top of the task fields. We align it on the left with the other task fields, and we give it the same amount of clearance on the right-hand side as on the left-hand side, as shown here.

```
txtTaskComments.Left = txtTaskNo.Left;
txtTaskComments.Top = lblProjName.Top;
txtTaskComments.Width = this.Width - (2 * txtTaskComments.Left);
```

```
txtTaskComments.Height =
    (txtTaskNo.Top - txtTaskComments.Top) -
    (txtTaskNo.Height / 3);
```

In setting the size and location of a control, you have at least three options. You can set individual properties one at a time (as shown above), you can set the `Location` and `Size` properties, or you can set the `Bounds` property, as shown in the following line.

```
txtTaskComments.Bounds = New Rectangle(44, 92, 18, 18);
```

Because we don't have enough space in our form for a label above or to the left of this control, and because we have considerable space inside the control, we place user instructions inside the control. We select the text of those instructions so that they are highlighted when the control receives the focus and so that they will be removed as the user begins to enter the comments. Here are the two lines of code that do this.

```
txtTaskComments.Text = "Add task comments here.";
txtTaskComments.SelectAll();
```

We add the `TextBox` control to the form with the following code.

```
this.Controls.Add(txtTaskComments);
```

This is an important step because if you create a control but do not add it to a form, the control does not appear where the user can see it. This is an easy mistake to make and can result in lost time spent debugging what is a pretty simple problem. When in doubt about creating controls dynamically, compare your code with the code created by the Designer.

You can create a control, set its properties, and invoke its methods without having added it to the container's `Controls` collection. This last step allows the user to see your control. The `TextBox` control's properties that we have discussed up to now can be set at any time. As we next show, some properties must be set after a control is added to a form in order for those properties to take effect.

We move the `TextBox` control on top of all other controls in the form, that is, we put it at the top of the z-order. This ensures that the `TextBox` control overlays all other controls located in the same part of the screen. We also set the focus to the control to highlight the instructions and to tell the system to send keyboard input to our `TextBox` control. We accomplish this with the following two lines of code.

```
txtTaskComments.BringToFront();
txtTaskComments.Focus();
```

When you create a new control, you need to enable any event handlers that you wish to have respond to events generated by that control. We use the following code to tie the control's `TextChanged` event to the code that will process that event.

```
this.txtTaskComments.TextChanged +=
   new System.EventHandler(
      this.txtTaskComments_TextChanged);
```

As discussed earlier, we show and hide buttons so that the user knows what options are available.

```
cmdAddTask.Visible = true;
cmdCancel.Visible = true;
cmdNewTask.Visible = false;
```

Bringing all of this together, Listing 7.11 presents our complete code to handle a `Click` event for our New button.

LISTING 7.11: The New Button `Click` Event Handler

```
private void cmdNewTask_Click(object sender,
                              System.EventArgs e)
{
   //  Save the index number of the previous task.  We will
   //     need to know it in case the user cancels out
   //     during task creation.
   ixTaskPrev = cboxTasks.SelectedIndex;

   //  Deselect the current task from the drop-down
   //     ComboBox.  This will also cause the
   //     SelectedIndexChanged event to fire,
   //     which will cause the task fields to clear.
   cboxTasks.SelectedIndex = -1;
   cboxTasks.SelectedIndex = -1;
```

```
   //  Create and display a multiline TextBox
   //     for the user to enter comments.
   txtTaskComments = new TextBox();
   txtTaskComments.Multiline = true;

   //  Locate it relative to other
   //     controls on the form.
   txtTaskComments.Left = txtTaskNo.Left;
   txtTaskComments.Top = lblProjName.Top;
   txtTaskComments.Width =
      this.Width - (2 * txtTaskComments.Left);
   txtTaskComments.Height =
      (txtTaskNo.Top - txtTaskComments.Top) -
      (txtTaskNo.Height / 3);

   //  Enter and select some text.
   txtTaskComments.Text = "Add task comments here.";
   txtTaskComments.SelectAll();

   //  Add the control to the form.
   this.Controls.Add(txtTaskComments);

   //  Bring it to the z-axis top and
   //     set the focus into it.
   txtTaskComments.BringToFront();
   txtTaskComments.Focus();

   //  Associate the TextChanged event handler
   //     that we have written for this
   //     control with this control.
   this.txtTaskComments.TextChanged +=
      new System.EventHandler(
         this.txtTaskComments_TextChanged);

   //  Hide self and show Add and Cancel.
   cmdAddTask.Visible = true;
   cmdCancel.Visible = true;
   cmdNewTask.Visible = false;
}
```

We next take a close look at the event handlers for the Add and Cancel buttons, starting with the Add button.

Handling the `Click` Event for the Add Button

When the user clicks on the Add button, our program adds a new task to the `ArrayList` of task structures. That item then becomes the current task, so we make the new task the currently selected one by setting the index in the `SelectedItem` property of the `ListBox` control that contains the tasks. Because the user is done entering text, we destroy the `TextBox` control we created when the user clicked the New button. We also set visibility for our various buttons as appropriate for the program state. Listing 7.12 shows the code.

LISTING 7.12: The Add Button `Click` Event Handler

```
private void cmdAddTask_Click(object sender, System.EventArgs e)
{
   //  Add the task to the Tasks array list.
   alTasks.Add(new Task(
      txtTaskNo.Text,
      txtTaskName.Text,
      Convert.ToDateTime(txtTaskStart.Text),
      Convert.ToDateTime(txtTaskEnd.Text),
      Convert.ToInt32(txtTaskEstimated.Text),
      Convert.ToInt32(txtTaskActual.Text),
      txtTaskComments.Text));

   //  Select the added task.
   cboxTasks.SelectedIndex = alTasks.Count - 1;

   //  Destroy the comments TextBox.
   txtTaskComments.Dispose();
   txtTaskComments = null;

   //  Hide Add and Cancel and show New.
   cmdAddTask.Visible = false;
   cmdCancel.Visible = false;
   cmdNewTask.Visible = true;

   //  Set the focus to the Tasks ComboBox.
   cboxTasks.Focus();
}
```

Let us now turn our attention to the Cancel button and the event handler that we create to allow users to change their minds and safely interrupt the process of adding a new task.

Handling the `Click` Event for the Cancel Button

When the user clicks on the Cancel button, our program responds by undoing the actions we performed to allow entry of a new task. We reset the

ComboBox control so that its current item is the one that was selected when the user clicked on the Add button. Aside from adding new entries to the database, the cleanup for the Cancel button is similar to the cleanup for the Add button, so we could borrow the last seven lines of code from the cmdAddTask_Click routine. Instead, we create a new subroutine that gets called from the Click event handler for both buttons. The Cancel button's Click event handler and this new subroutine are shown in Listing 7.13.

LISTING 7.13: The Cancel Button Click Event Handler

```
private void cmdCancel_Click(object sender,
                             System.EventArgs e)
 {
    //  Clean up the form and reselect the old task.
    AfterNewTaskCleanup(ixTaskPrev);
 }
    :
    :
    :
 private void AfterNewTaskCleanup(int ixTask)
 {
    //  Destroy the comments TextBox.
    txtTaskComments.Dispose();
    txtTaskComments = null;

   //  Hide Add and Cancel and show New.
   cmdAddTask.Visible = false;
   cmdCancel.Visible = false;
   cmdNewTask.Visible = true;

   //  Select the specified task.
   cboxTasks.SelectedIndex = ixTask;

   //  Set the focus to the Tasks ComboBox.
   cboxTasks.Focus();
}
```

This concludes our discussion of buttons. Like most GUI applications, our program spends much of its time waiting for button clicks. But when Click events do happen, we call methods and set properties. Some of these actions cause other events to occur, to which we respond by invoking other methods and setting other properties. This is the typical life cycle for any GUI program and certainly for .NET Compact Framework

Windows programs. Along the way, our program rearranged the screen, created controls on-the-fly, accepted input from the user, and stored that input in our database.

It could have been easier. In fact, as you will see, we wrote more code than we needed to, for we did not use *data binding*, an important and sometimes misunderstood capability of the .NET Framework that connects user interface objects to data objects. In general, we prefer showing the best way to do things from the start. We want to save you time and not disappoint you later by saying, "Oh, by the way, there's a better technique." We made an exception in this case because, while data binding is the best way to do much of what we have done in this sample program, data binding is a potentially complex subject. Our focus in this chapter has been on introducing the basics of these controls. The subject of data binding is so important that it has a chapter of its own: Chapter 8.

This brings us to the end of our tasks application but not to the end of our chapter. Two variations on buttons[1]—radio buttons and check boxes—do not fit into our `TimeTracker` sample program, but they are important and need to be discussed. So in the next section, we introduce a new sample program to help demonstrate these two control classes.

The `RadioButton` and `CheckBox` Controls

Radio buttons and check boxes are familiar objects to users of GUI systems. Radio buttons appear in groups and allow mutually exclusive selection. Check boxes let a user toggle the program state between true/false, yes/no (and optionally a third "maybe" state). These objects are so familiar to users that you can build a .NET Compact Framework program that uses radio buttons and check boxes and trust that little explanation is required for how to use these controls. Programming these controls is generally simple, with any complications arising more from user interface design and interfield dependencies than from any intrinsic complexity of the controls themselves.

---

1. We say that these are variations on buttons because a single Win32 window class, `button`, provides the underlying support for these three .NET Compact Framework classes: `Button`, `CheckBox`, and `RadioButton`.

A Sample Program: `RegisterMembers`

Our sample program has a data collection form, similar to one that a club or community group might use to register new members. The business requirement for this program is that all members fall into one of three categories: Adult, Child, and Associate. The type of information we collect varies depending on the member type. For instance, all types of members have an ID number and a name. Adult and Associate members need to have address information entered, while Child members do not (the assumption being that a Child member lives with an Adult member). A Child member is the only type whose date of birth must be entered. Both Child and Associate members must be connected to a specific Adult member; that is, they must have a sponsor. Address information includes street, city, state/province ("SP"), and postal code ("PC"). Figure 7.10 shows the complete set of input fields displayed in the Designer window.

Three radio buttons appear along the top of this form for the type of member. As a user chooses the member type, our program hides the fields

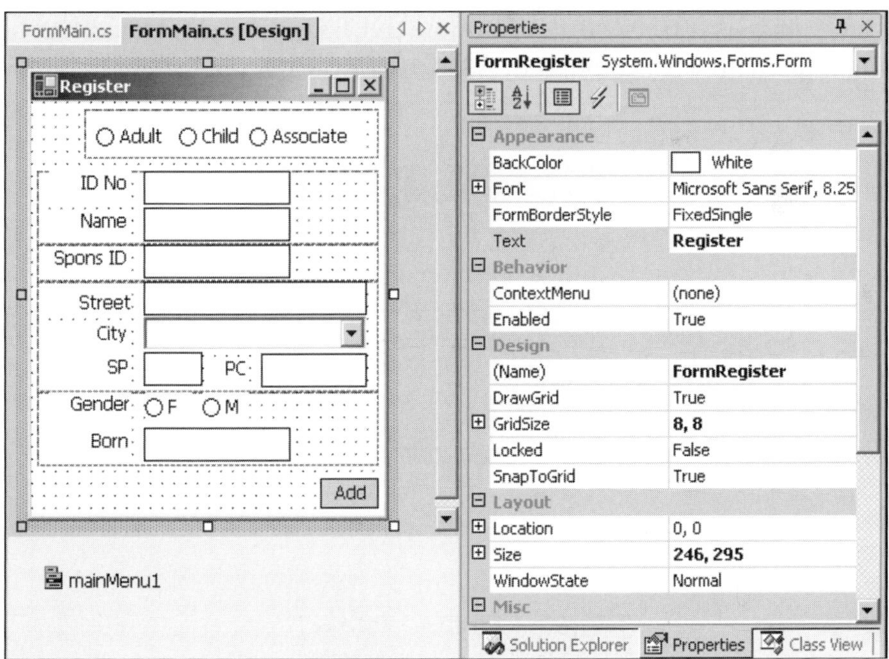

FIGURE 7.10: The registration input fields

that are inappropriate to that member type and shifts the remaining fields together to eliminate empty space from the form. The resulting layout for entering Child member information is shown in Figure 7.11.

Using Radio Buttons

Radio buttons are simple. A radio button has two possible states, either checked or not checked, as indicated by the `Checked` property. Radio buttons receive two button-specific events: one to indicate a change in the `Checked` property, and the other when a user has clicked on the button (regardless of whether the click causes a state change).

Radio buttons are mutually exclusive. At most, one `RadioButton` control within a group of `RadioButton` controls can be checked at any one time. The user's selection of one radio button causes the .NET Compact Framework to deselect the others. It is possible for the application itself to unselect all buttons within a group, by setting all `Checked` properties to `false`, but it is not possible for the user to do so.

Radio buttons work together as a group. You define a group by placing them together in a container control, either a form or some other container control such as a panel. If you come to .NET Compact Framework programming with a background of ASP.NET programming, you may notice

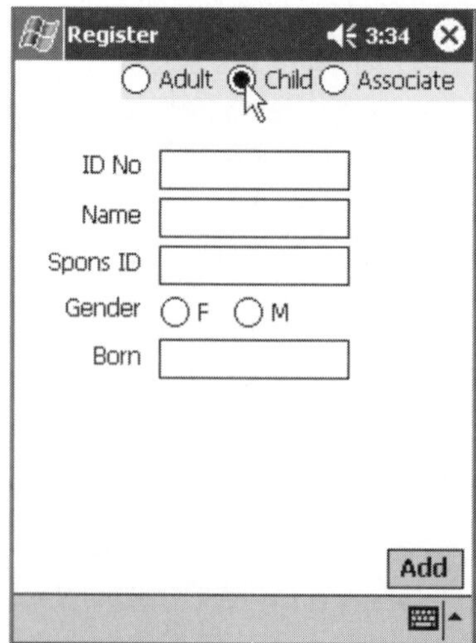

FIGURE 7.11: Enrolling a Child member

that this grouping technique is different from how Web-based radio buttons are grouped, which is based on the `GroupName` property of the radio buttons. Radio buttons in the .NET Compact Framework, on the other hand, are grouped based on location, not on any control property.

Radio buttons are normally used in one of two ways. The first is similar to the regular buttons we saw earlier in this chapter. The user taps on the button and expects some action to occur. This is the case for our type-of-member buttons. The user taps on one and expects to see the input fields rearrange themselves. In this situation the application responds to the `Click` event and so needs a `Click` event handler.

The second usage—similar to textboxes—involve radio buttons for data entry. As an illustration of this second type of usage, our program has a set of radio buttons that indicates whether the member is male or female. Typical of this usage, the `Click` event is ignored; instead, the value of the `Checked` property gets collected along with all the other values being entered in response to some later event, which in our sample program will be the Add button's `Click` event.

Building `RegisterMembers`

With this background information behind us, let us get to work on our program. We begin by writing code that arranges the data entry fields, which includes a `Panel` control that contains three `RadioButton` controls, plus an Add button. Because all the address-related fields need to be hidden whenever the member type is Child, we place them in a `Panel` control so we can show and hide them as a group with a single line of code, which allows us to easily get the data entry form shown in Figure 7.11.

Once again we use code, not design, to arrange the controls on the form, a decision that is just a matter of personal preference. As we mentioned earlier in this book, design-time layout is usually easier, runtime layout is more flexible, and performance is the same regardless of whether the Designer wrote the code or you wrote it. We write a routine that will right-justify the `RadioButton` controls within their container `Panel` and then place the `Panel` in the upper-right corner of the screen. We call this routine during the form's `Load` event. The code appears in Listing 7.14; the resulting screen layout can be viewed in Figure 7.11, shown earlier.

LISTING 7.14: A Method for Positioning Radio Buttons within the `Panel`

```
private void PositionOptionButtons()
{
//  Place the option buttons in a line along the
//     top of the form, right justified.
   panelMemberType.BackColor = Color.Bisque;
   panelMemberType.Height = optAdult.Height;
   panelMemberType.Width = optAdult.Width
                         + optAssociate.Width
                         + optChild.Width;
   panelMemberType.Location =
      new Point(this.ClientRectangle.Width -
                     panelMemberType.Width, 0);
   optAssociate.Location =
      new Point(panelMemberType.ClientRectangle.Width -
                     optAssociate.Width, 0);
   optChild.Location =
      new Point(optAssociate.Left - optChild.Width, 0);
   optAdult.Location =
      new Point(optChild.Left - optAdult.Width, 0);
}
```

For our first group of radio buttons, the three that collect the member type, we are interested in the `CheckedChanged` event. We handle this event for all three radio buttons with a single event handler. This handler is shown in Listing 7.15.

LISTING 7.15: The Radio Button `CheckedChanged` Event Handler

```
private void optAny_CheckedChanged(object sender,
                                   System.EventArgs e)
{
   //  Hide what you do not need,
   //     show what you do need.
   panelSponsor.Visible =
         optAssociate.Checked || optChild.Checked;
   panelAddress.Visible =
         optAdult.Checked || optAssociate.Checked;
   panelChild.Visible = optChild.Checked;

   //  Position panels.
   int topNext = panelWho.Bottom;
   if (panelSponsor.Visible )
   {
      panelSponsor.Top = topNext;
      topNext = panelSponsor.Bottom;
```

```
   }
   if (panelAddress.Visible )
   {
      panelAddress.Top = topNext;
      topNext = panelAddress.Bottom;
   }
   if (panelChild.Visible )
   {
      panelChild.Top = topNext;
      topNext = panelChild.Bottom;
   }
}
```

The other group of radio buttons in our application is the pair that indicates whether the applicant is male or female. Our policy is that gender is an optional field; the user is not required to select either button, which gives us three possibilities for the field's value: male, female, or blank. The code to capture the user's choice and place it in the `genderMember` variable is located in the Add button's `Click` event handler, shown here.

```
private void cmdAdd_Click(object sender, System.EventArgs e)
{
   //  Code to register a member goes here.
   //        :
   //        :
   genderMember =
      optFemale.Checked ? "F" :
         optMale.Checked ? "M" : "X";
   //        :
   //        :
   ClearInputFields(this);
}
```

Our `RegisterMembers` program shows two ways to use radio buttons: an action-oriented approach and a data-oriented approach. Both are typical of Windows Forms applications on the desktop and on mobile devices. For an action-oriented radio button, a program monitors the `CheckedChanged` event; for a data-oriented radio button, a program queries the `Checked` property as the need arises.

We mentioned earlier that `RadioButton` controls have a second event they can handle, the `Click` event. It is raised any time the user clicks or taps on a radio button. The `Click` event is raised after the `CheckedChanged` event, so the `Checked` property of the target button is already set to `true`. When handling this event, you cannot know the state of the button prior to the `Click` event. For this reason, a `Click` event is of limited value to a `RadioButton` control and is not handled as frequently as the `CheckedChanged` event.

Using Check Boxes

The last variation on the buttons is the `CheckBox` class, which is very similar to the `RadioButton` class. Both classes have a `Checked` property. One difference is that grouping is not important to `CheckBox` controls. Any check box can be checked or unchecked by the user regardless of its location without impacting the state of any other check box. As with radio buttons, it is up to the application to react to the `CheckedChanged` and `Click` events or to subsequently examine the `Checked` property of the `CheckBox` control to determine its current state.

So, like all .NET Compact Framework controls, the button's simplicity is both an asset (reducing the time it takes to implement functionality) and a liability (limiting what that functionality can be). In a nutshell, buttons are excellent for displaying limited choices to the user, especially in a stylus-oriented world.

Improving `RegisterMembers`

We would like to improve our `RegisterMembers` application by minimizing the amount of typing users must do, especially because they may be registering members in situations where no keyboard is available and the SIP must be used. We can reduce the need for keyboard input by replacing some `TextBox` controls with `ComboBox` controls, for new members are likely to come from the same geographic area as the existing members. The same cities, states, and postal codes will appear again and again. By loading the most common of these into `ComboBox` controls, we allow users to pick from a list and thus reduce the required amount of keyboard input. It provides some improvement, but the `ComboBox` control provided by the .NET Compact Framework comes up a little short.

Question: When is a `ComboBox` not a `ComboBox`?

Answer: When it is a .NET Compact Framework `ComboBox`.

We say this because a complete `ComboBox` control, such as the one found in the desktop .NET Framework, allows the user to pick from a list or enter free text directly into a combobox. In fact, the word *combobox* was derived from "a *comb*ination text*box* and list*box*." But the .NET Compact Framework `ComboBox` control only allows users to pick from the list. This limitation was not a problem in the `TimeTracker` sample application in which we first used `ComboBox` controls earlier in this chapter. In that program, the user selected a task from the list or entered information about a new task into a set of `TextBox` controls, with no need to enter a single field of text in lieu of a `ComboBox` choice.

But in the `RegisterMembers` application, there is a need for direct text entry. Although we can load the most common choices, we cannot load all possible choices. We must give our users both capabilities: to select from a list and to enter text directly. In the `RegisterMembers` application we provide these capabilities by using both a `ComboBox` control and a `TextBox` control, colocating them, and displaying one at time. When the application starts, the `ComboBox` is the visible control, and it has an entry for the user to choose free-form text entry, as shown in Figure 7.12.

If the user chooses free-form text entry, the `TextBox` control replaces the `ComboBox` control on the form; that is, the `ComboBox` is hidden and the `TextBox` is displayed, as shown in Figure 7.13.

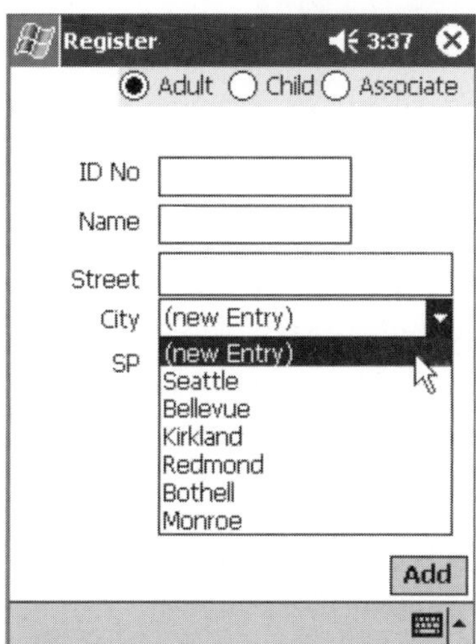

FIGURE 7.12: The `ComboBox` control for cities

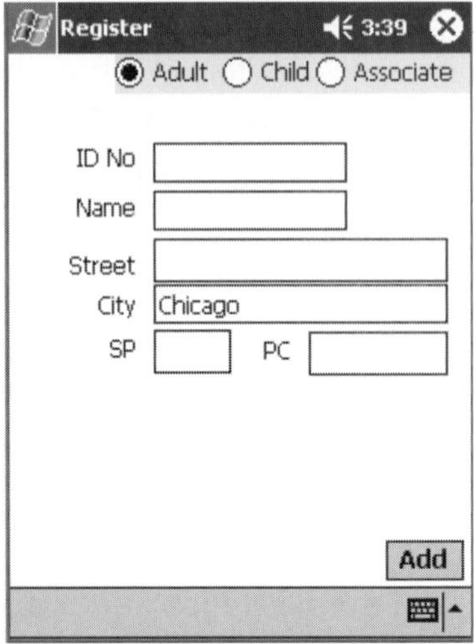

FIGURE 7.13: Entering a new city with the `TextBox` control

When the user has finished entering text, the entry is added to the `ComboBox` control's drop-down list, that entry becomes the `ComboBox`'s `SelectedItem`, and the `ComboBox` reappears, as shown in Figure 7.14.

In this chapter we do not go into the subject of determining which cities, states, and postal codes should be preloaded, nor how we obtain them. You

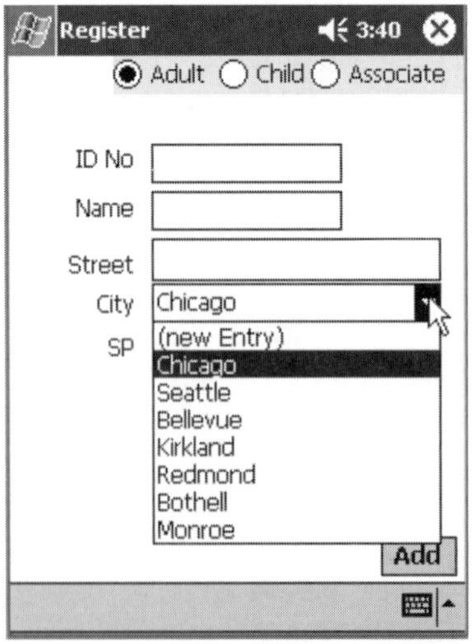

FIGURE 7.14: The cities `ComboBox` control after entry of a new city

might assume for now that they were downloaded by some other means, such as by using ActiveSync. Also, for brevity's sake, we show the code for the city field only, but the same solution applies to the state/province and postal code fields as well.

This added capability is easy to program if we know the answer to one question: How do you know when a user is finished entering data into a textbox? The `Validated` event lets us know. After all, the `Validated` event fires as the user is leaving a field but after the `Validating` event has fired and the data has been edited. Therefore, it is in response to the `Validated` event that we process the city name the user keyed in.

Our enhancement to the application, therefore, requires us to provide functionality for three events: the form's `Load` event, during which the option for free-form text entry must be added to the `ComboBox` control's drop-down list; the `ComboBox`'s `SelectedIndexChanged` event; and the `TextBox` control's `Validated` event. Listing 7.16 shows the code for all three.

LISTING 7.16: The Form's `Load` Event Handler

```
private void FormRegister_Load(object sender,
                               EventArgs e)
{
   //  Clear the input fields.
   ClearInputFields(this);

   //  Place the option buttons in a line along the
   //     top of the form, right justified.
   PositionOptionButtons();

   //  Colocate the city ComboBox and
   //     its associated TextBox.
   textCity.Bounds = cboxCity.Bounds;

   //  Add the "(New Entry)" item to the top of the list.
   //  Select it.
   //  Show the ComboBox.
   cboxCity.Items.Insert(0, "(New Entry)");
   cboxCity.SelectedIndex = 0;
   cboxCity.BringToFront();

   //  Default to an Adult entry.
   this.optAdult.Checked = true;
}
```

continues

continued

```
private void cboxCity_SelectedIndexChanged(object sender,
                                            EventArgs e)
{
   //  if ( the user requested free-form test entry
   if ( cboxCity.SelectedIndex == 0 )
   {
   //  Clear the TextBox.
   //  Show it.
      //  Give it the focus.
      textCity.Text = string .Empty;
      textCity.BringToFront();
      textCity.Focus();
   }
}


private void textCity_Validated(object sender,
                                EventArgs e)
{
   //  The user has completed the data entry
   //     and that data has passed all edits.
   if ( textCity.Text.Trim() != string.Empty )
   {
      //  Add the entry to the ComboBox drop-down list.
      //  Select it.
      //  Show the ComboBox.
      cboxCity.Items.Insert(1, textCity.Text);
      cboxCity.SelectedIndex = 1;
   }
   cboxCity.BringToFront();
}
```

It's simple code, it does the job, and it executes when we want it to. Actually, it executes more often than we want it to, but it does so with no side effects. During the form's `Load` event, we add an entry to the `ComboBox` control. As we mentioned earlier in this chapter, this causes the `ComboBox`'s `SelectedIndex` property to change, which causes the `SelectedIndexChanged` event to fire. Our event handler reacts to this by replacing the `ComboBox` with the empty `TextBox` for user input. Fortunately, two lines later our `Load` event handler replaces the `TextBox` with the `ComboBox`, which causes the `TextBox` to lose the focus (a control that is not visible cannot have the focus), which causes the `Validated` event to fire. Wisely, our event handler checks for and does not add empty strings, so no harm is done.

A solid understanding of what causes events to fire and the sequence in which they occur is essential when designing, coding, and debugging .NET Compact Framework applications.

CONCLUSION

The eight control classes gave us sufficient PMEs, especially for handling text and initiating user requests, for us to be able to produce our applications with a relatively small amount of code. Even in situations where control functionality available in other Windows environments was not available, we were able to provide workarounds.

The biggest limitation of these classes is that they are, by design, string-oriented. There is no date-oriented `TextBox` class that edits user input, automatically detecting invalid dates for us; no task-oriented `ProgressBar` class with properties `StartDate`, `EndDate`, `CurrentDate`, and `PercentComplete` that are evaluated to produce a meaningful graphic.

So as we move forward in this book, we look at the other control classes available to us in the .NET Compact Framework, at extending the capabilities of existing control classes, and at developing our own control classes.

The 30 predefined controls that come with .NET provide an excellent starting set of functionality; the eight that we looked at in this chapter are oriented toward text and action. They provide visual boxes that encapsulate functionality by providing PMEs. We produce our application by invoking the methods and setting the properties in reaction to the events. The more we understand these PMEs, the tighter, faster, more maintainable, and more enjoyable our programs will be.

8
Data Binding to Controls

In this chapter, we examine data binding, the ability to associate non-GUI objects that hold and maintain data with the controls that present and receive that data.

Data Binding

Most controls, especially single-item and list-based controls, display and accept data. Most data, when it is not being displayed or modified within a control, is kept in a database. And we're using the term *database* quite loosely here—loosely enough to include anything from an `ArrayList` to a SQL Server database. Because the data is kept in a database and because we need to display and modify it through the use of controls, we need a simple, consistent, property-oriented technique for moving data between our database and our controls. Data binding provides the ability to tie a control to a source of data, simplifying the movement of data within a data-centric application. Data binding specifically was developed to facilitate the movement of data between the business tier and the presentation tier of a traditional three-tiered application, as shown in Figure 8.1.

We cannot actually go directly from a database to and from a control, but we can go from an object containing the data to and from a control. The data object might be an `ArrayList` (such as our `ArrayList` of project task structures used in the `TimeTracker` sample application in Chapter 7), or it might be a database-specific object (such as a `System.Data.DataView`

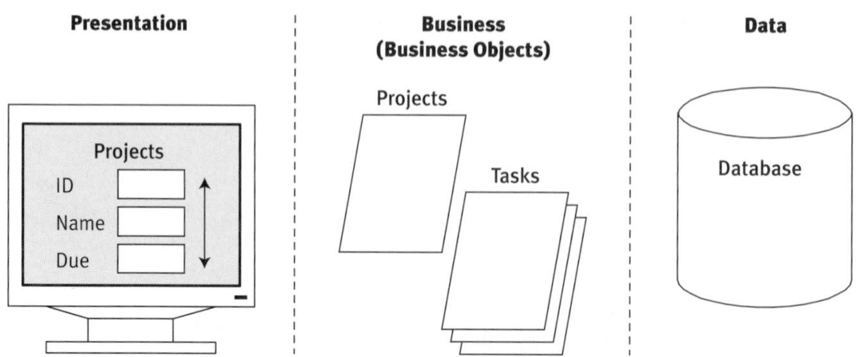

FIGURE 8.1: Application tiers

object, which looks much like a relational database table). One benefit of data objects is that they provide the presentation layer an independence from the database layer. A `DataTable`, for instance, has the same PMEs regardless of the database product that persists the data. Thus your presentation layer code remains the same whether your database is SQL Server CE or a homegrown collection of files.

Data binding is a two-way relationship. Any change in the data object's data will be reflected in the control and vice versa. This eliminates the need to reload the control whenever the data in the data object changes. It also means that any bindable control can be used to update the data object. Even controls that do not accept user input of data (such as the `Label`, `DataGrid`, and `ListBox`/`ComboBox` controls) provide for programmatic update of their properties, for example, as in `myLabel.Text = "ABC"`. Data binding ensures that this change occurs in the bound data object as it occurs in the control.

All visible controls are bindable, but some are better suited to data binding than others. Controls that are typically used with data binding include the `Label`, `TextBox`, `ComboBox`, `ListBox`, and `DataGrid` controls. The `DataGrid` control, the only control written entirely in managed code, was specifically developed for use with data binding. Figure 8.2 shows the project data that was introduced in Chapter 7 being displayed in a `DataGrid` control without any styling applied. We discuss the `DataGrid` control in more detail later in this chapter.

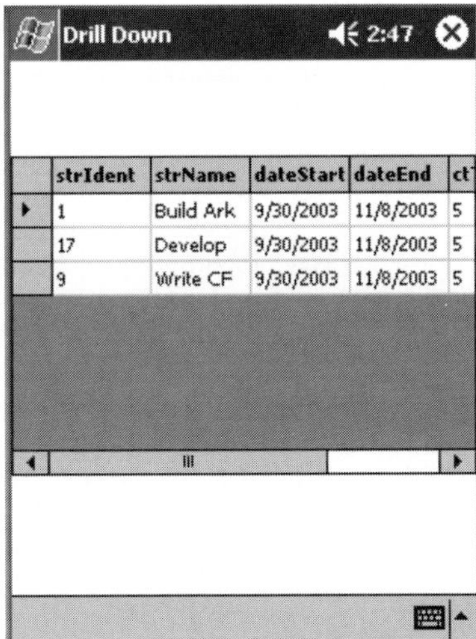

FIGURE 8.2: Project data displayed in a `DataGrid` control

Because the subject of this chapter is data binding, we are only interested here in the movement of data between the data objects and the controls. The subject of moving data between the data objects and the underlying databases is covered in Part III. And because data binding is such an important part of that movement, we will revisit the subject of data binding in Chapter 12, when we cover binding controls to `System.Data` objects. Because of the capabilities of `System.Data` objects, we cover row position and hierarchical relationships in greater detail there than here. In many respects, this chapter could be called "Data Binding," while Chapter 12 could be called "Son of Data Binding," among other things.

Data-Bindable Controls

Controls differ in their data-binding capabilities and in the method used to do the data binding. Some controls can display more data than others, some accept user input while others are only for display, and some can take advantage of *complex data binding* while others require *simple data binding*.

Consider the `System.Data.DataTable` object, shown in Figure 8.3, which holds the project data mentioned earlier. A `DataGrid` control can display the entire table, while `ListBox` and `ComboBox` controls can display

Projects

strIdent	strName	dateStart	dateEnd	ctTask
1	Build Ark	3/2/2003	4/10/2003	5
17	Load Supplies	3/2/2003	4/10/2003	5
9	Load Animals	3/2/2003	4/10/2003	5

FIGURE 8.3: A `DataTable` object that contains project information

only a single column from the table, and single-valued controls such as `TextBox` and `Label` controls can display only a single data element.

Figure 8.4 shows a `ComboBox` control displaying one column of information from a bound `DataTable` object of project data, while the `TextBox` controls display data elements of the currently selected project.

Controls that can display an entire table, or at least a column of that table, use a mechanism called *complex data binding*, which involves the control's `DataSource` property. Controls that can display only a single data element require *simple data binding*, which is done through the `Bindings-`

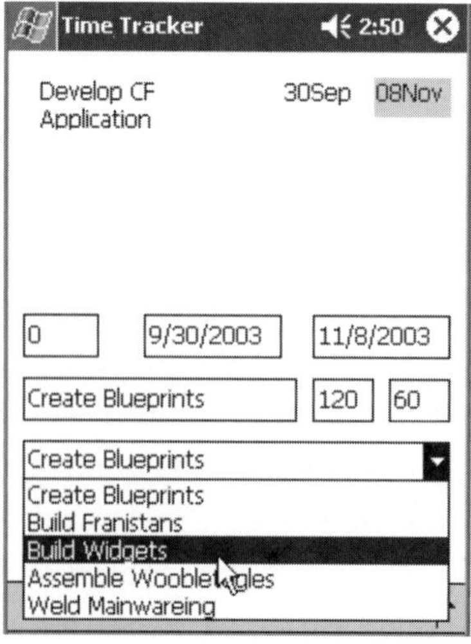

FIGURE 8.4: Different controls bound to the same data

Collection property of the control. The terms are slightly confusing because, from a developer's point of view, complex binding is usually the easier of the two to program. All objects that inherit from the Control base class have a BindingsCollection property, but only objects that can display a list or a table, such as DataGrid, ListBox, or ComboBox controls, have a DataSource property.

Not only are there inevitable limitations to the data-binding capability of each control class, there are also limitations on the data objects that can be bound to those controls in the .NET Compact Framework.

Data-Bindable Objects

As we mentioned earlier, data objects hold data but have no ability to display that data, so the control must display the data. The .NET Compact Framework limits bindable data objects to those data objects that have a *tabular* data structure. Having a tabular data structure means that every item in the data object must have the same structure as every other item in that data object. An ArrayList of Project structures qualifies as tabular because every item in it is an item of Project structure data type. The same would be true for the ArrayList of Tasks introduced in Chapter 7, for every item is an item of Task structure data type. If you had only one ArrayList object and had added both Project and Task structures to it, it would not be tabular and it would not be usable for data binding within the .NET Compact Framework environment.

This requirement for tabular structure eliminates certain System.Data objects. For instance, a System.Data.DataTable and a System.Data.DataView are bindable objects because of their tabular structures. However, the System.Data.DataSet object is *not* bindable in the .NET Compact Framework environment. This object can contain multiple DataTable objects, tables that can be related to each other through the use of keys. Figure 8.5 shows a diagram of a DataSet object that contains two DataTable objects. Because the DataSet object is hierarchical in structure rather than tabular, it cannot be bound to any control in the .NET Compact Framework environment. Either DataTable object or any DataView object based on those tables could be bound to a control, but the entire DataSet object could not be.

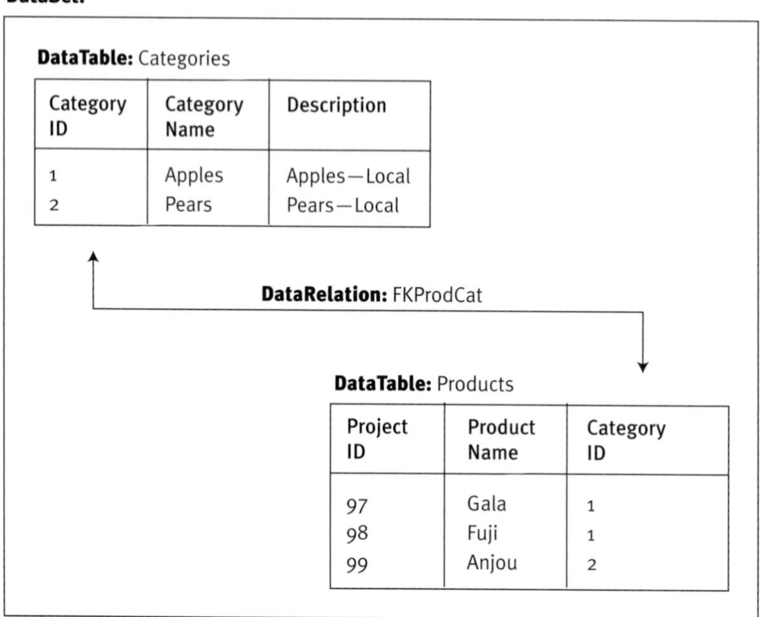

DataSet:
DataTable: Categories
Category ID
Category Name
Description
1
2
Apples
Pears
Apples—Local
Pears—Local
DataRelation: FKProdCat
DataTable: Products
Project ID
Product Name
Category ID
97
98
99
Gala
Fuji
Anjou
1
1
2

FIGURE 8.5: A `DataSet` object that contains two `DataTable` objects

Also eliminated from data binding in the .NET Compact Framework because of their hierarchical nature are objects from the `System.XML` namespace, such as `XMLDocument` and `XMLDataDocument` objects.

To be bindable, a data object must expose its columns as *public properties,* not merely as fields. This is something to keep in mind when you define your own data structures and object classes. The `Task` structure shown in Listing 8.1 could not be used in data binding because its data is exposed as fields, not as properties.

LISTING 8.1: An Unbindable Version of the Task Structure

```
private struct Task
{
   public string  strTaskIdent;
   public string  strTaskName;
   public Date dateTaskStart;
   public Date dateTaskEnd;
```

```
   public int durTaskEstimated;
   public int durTaskActual;
   public string  strTaskComments;
   public void Task( string  strNo,  string  strName,
                     Date dateStart,  Date dateEnd,
                     int durEstimated,  int durActual,
                     string  strComments)
   {
      strTaskIdent = strNo;
      strTaskName = strName;
      dateTaskStart = dateStart;
      dateTaskEnd = dateEnd;
      durTaskEstimated = durEstimated;
      durTaskActual = durActual;
      strTaskComments = strComments;
   }
}
```

To make the `Task` structure usable for data binding, we must modify it to expose its data as public properties, as shown in Listing 8.2.

Listing 8.2: A Bindable Version of the Task Structure

```
public struct Task
{
   private string  m_strIdent;
   private string  m_strProjIdent;
   private string  m_strName;
   private DateTime m_dateStart;
   private DateTime m_dateEnd;
   private int m_durEstimated;
   private int m_durActual;
   private string  m_strComments;

   public string  strIdent
   {
      get
      {
         return m_strIdent;
      }
      set
      {
         m_strIdent = value;
      }
   }
```

continues

continued

```
public string  strProjIdent
{
   get
   {
      return m_strProjIdent;
   }
   set
   {
      m_strProjIdent = value;
   }
}
public string  strName
{
   get
   {
      return m_strName;
   }
   set
   {
      m_strName = value;
   }
}
public DateTime dateStart
{
   get
   {
      return m_dateStart;
   }
   set
   {
      m_dateStart = value;
   }
}
public DateTime dateEnd
{
   get
   {
      return m_dateEnd;
   }
   set
   {
      m_dateEnd = value;
   }
}
public int durEstimated
{
   get
```

```
        {
           return m_durEstimated;
        }
         set
         {
            m_durEstimated = value;
         }
      }
      public int durActual
      {
         get
         {
            return m_durActual;
         }
         set
         {
            m_durActual = value;
         }
      }
      public string  strComments
      {
         get
         {
            return m_strComments;
         }
         set
         {
            m_strComments = value;
         }
      }

      public Task( string  strIdent,
                   string  strProjIdent,
                   string  strName,
                   DateTime dateStart,  DateTime dateEnd,
                   int durEstimated,  int durActual,
                   string  strComments)
      {
         m_strIdent = strIdent;
         m_strProjIdent = strProjIdent;
         m_strName = strName;
         m_dateStart = dateStart;
         m_dateEnd = dateEnd;
         m_durEstimated = durEstimated;
         m_durActual = durActual;
         m_strComments = strComments;
      }
}
```

It is a lot of code in terms of line count, but not much in terms of mental challenge or object code size.

Throughout this chapter we need to illustrate data binding, and to be complete we need to bind to an `ArrayList` during some of the examples and to a `System.Data` object such as a `DataTable` for other examples. Normally a `DataTable` object is created by executing a `SELECT` statement against a database, but because programming a database is the subject of Part III, we'll bypass this step and instead create and load a `DataTable` object from scratch.

More specifically, we create a `Projects` `DataTable` object and a `Tasks` `DataTable` object and load each from the corresponding `ArrayList` objects we used in Chapter 7. We also write four routines to retrieve project or task data as either an `ArrayList` or a `DataTable`. We add a class named `UtilData` to our project and place this code within it. This class will provide data for the sample applications of this chapter. The `UtilData` class code is located in the `BindDataTableToDataGrid` project.[1]

With the `UtilData` class available to provide data, we're ready to start binding that data, beginning with complex data binding.

Complex Data Binding

We mentioned earlier that both single-item controls, such as `TextBox`, and multi-item controls, such as `ListBox`, can be the recipients of data binding. Because single-item controls are inherently simpler than multi-item controls, you might think that data binding to a single-item control would be easier than data binding to a multi-item control. In fact, just the opposite is true. This is because a bindable data object must contain a tabular array of data, and multi-item controls are designed to display arrays of data. There is a natural match between a data object and a multi-item control.

Table 8.1 lists the controls that support complex data binding; Table 8.2 shows the control properties used with complex data binding. (Note: The

---

1. You can download all the projects mentioned in this chapter from http://www.paulyao.com/cfbook/code. Follow the instructions listed on the Web site.

TABLE 8.1: Controls That Support Complex Data Binding

Control	Remarks
ComboBox	
DataGrid	Displays the entire data object
ListBox	

TABLE 8.2: Control Properties Used with Complex Data Binding

Property	Definition	Remarks
DataSource	The data object	Required
DisplayMember	The data object property (column) to be displayed	Optional for DataGrid
ValueMember	The property of the data objected to be used as the row identifier	Optional; the primary key column of the data object
SelectedIndex	The index of the currently selected item	Zero based
SelectedItem	The data object item that maps to the currently selected item	Equals DataObject[Control.SelectedIndex]
SelectedValue	The ValueMember value of the currently selected item	

SelectedItem and SelectedValue properties are used to extract data object data after the binding has been completed. They are not used to perform the binding.)

Of the three controls listed in Table 8.1, two, ListBox and ComboBox, were introduced in Chapter 7. We'll begin our coverage of complex data binding with these two already familiar controls and then complete the subject when we discuss the DataGrid control later in this chapter.

Using Complex Data Binding with ListBox and ComboBox Controls

Something we said earlier bears repeating here: A ListBox/ComboBox is a list of objects, not simply a one-dimensional list of strings, even though we see only one field in a ListBox/ComboBox. But each ListBox/ComboBox item can be thought of as containing three fields: the display field, the key field, and the indexer field.

To illustrate complex data binding, we'll modify the TimeTracker application from Chapter 7 (a screenshot of which appears in Figure 8.4 earlier in this chapter) to use complex data binding of the Tasks structure with the ComboBox control. Later, when we cover simple data binding, we'll further modify the application to data bind the TextBox controls. The completed application is located in the BindArrayListToControls project.

To data bind to our ComboBox, we set three of the properties listed in Table 8.2: one to identify the data source, one to identify which property of the data source is to be displayed, and one to identify which property of the data source is the primary key field.

```
//  Bind the drop-down ComboBox to the Tasks ArrayList.
cboxTasks.DataSource = alTasks;
cboxTasks.DisplayMember = "strName";
cboxTasks.ValueMember = "strIdent";
```

This code replaces the code shown next, which iterated through the ArrayList of tasks and loaded the ComboBox programmatically.

```
//  Load Proj data into the ComboBox.
foreach( Task theTask in theTasks )
{
   cboxTasks.Items.Add(theTask.strTaskName);
}
```

When we look at the two code snippets there does not seem to be much benefit to using the former instead of the latter. Both appear to be about the same size and difficulty. But using data binding gives you added benefits. You can use the control's SelectedValue and SelectedIndex properties to access the selected item in the data object, or you can pass the SelectedValue property to a database routine that requires a primary key as input.

And, most importantly, changes made to the data in the control will be reflected in the data object and vice versa. So complex data binding is really just the opposite of what its name implies—it is simple. But, as we mentioned, it is available only with the multi-item controls listed in Table 8.1. For other controls, you must use simple data binding.

Simple Data Binding

All controls support simple data binding because it is built into the `Control` base class, but it is usually used with controls that display a single value, such as a `TextBox` control. For this reason simple data binding is a bit more involved than complex data binding. When we bind to a single-item control, we are binding a single data element of the data object to a single valued property of the control, such as the `Text` property. To identify a single data element within a tabular array of data, we need to specify three pieces of information: the identity of the object, which column, and which row.

Because we are binding that data element to a single valued property of the control, we need to specify two more pieces of information: a reference to the control and the name of the property. Thus simple data binding requires five pieces of information.

Like the information needed for complex data binding, the information required for simple data binding is stored in properties of the control being bound to. In the case of complex data binding, the information is stored in the control's `BindingsCollection` property.

The `BindingsCollection` Property

Each entry in the `BindingsCollection` property is an object of type `Binding` and contains the information necessary to bind one data element of the source data object to one property of the control. Table 8.3 lists the binding-specific PMEs of a `Binding` object.

The following code shows how to bind a column of a data source to a property of a control. In this case the data object has already been bound to the `ComboBox` control named `cboxTasks`. The data object column whose

TABLE 8.3: The PMEs of a `Binding` Object

PME	Definition	Remarks
Properties		
`BindingManagerBase`	The object that manages all bindings for this column of this data source	Normally only one binding per data source column
`Control`	The control	
`PropertyName`	The control's bound property	
`DataSource`	The data object	
`BindingMemberInfo`	The data object's bound column	
`IsBinding`	The property that indicates whether this binding is active	
Events		
`Format`	The event raised as the data element is moved from the data object to the control	Allows the application to format incoming data
`Parse`	The event raised as the data element is moved from the control to the data object	Allows the application to unformat the outgoing data, converting it to the data type required by the bound data object

name is specified by `strColumnName` is being bound to the `Text` property of the `txtTarget` `TextBox` control.

```
txtTarget.DataBindings.Add("Text",
                           cboxTasks.DataSource,
                           strColumnName);
```

When we look at this code, it seems to cover only four of the five pieces of information mentioned earlier. We specified the identity of the control as part of the method call, so that's one piece. Three more pieces of information were specified as parameters of the method call: the control's property, a reference to the data object, and the name of a column in the data object. So, we're short one piece of information. How do we specify which row contains the data element to be bound to? The answer is, we don't.

We are dependent on the source data object being able to keep track of the "current" row. In database terminology, this means that the source object needs a *cursoring* capability. That capability does not exist in an ArrayList object. Although our Task structure's ArrayList has an indexer method to allow us to access any row, it does not have a property that tracks which row we are currently accessing.

However, we can still bind our TextBox controls to our Task structure's ArrayList. We simply do it through the ComboBox control, for the ComboBox does have a cursor capability, and we have already bound our ArrayList to the ComboBox. The SelectedItemIndex property is the ComboBox control's cursor. So once we have bound our ArrayList to our ComboBox, we can then bind that ArrayList, through the ComboBox, to our TextBox controls, one binding for each TextBox. The following code performs one of these bindings.

```
txtTaskActual.DataBindings.Add(
   "Text", cboxTasks.DataSource, "durTaskActual" );
```

Once we have done this, the durTaskActual value of the currently selected row will be bound to the Text property of the txtTaskActual TextBox control. As the user selects a new item from the ComboBox, the TextBox controls will automatically update, displaying the fields of the newly selected project. Any change in the value of a TextBox control's Text property, whether by user input or by programmed update, will update the data object; and any change in the data element of the data object will update the TextBox control's Text property, a change that will immediately be visible to the user.

Note that we bind our TextBox controls to the DataSource property of the ComboBox, not the ComboBox itself. That means we bind our TextBox controls to our Task structure's ArrayList. Our only reason for using the

ComboBox in the binding is the fact that the ComboBox, not the ArrayList, is capable of maintaining the knowledge of the current row.

If the data column that we wished to bind to, txtTaskActual.Text, were already known to the ComboBox, such as the ComboBox's ValueMember property, we could write the data-binding statement as shown here.

```
txtTaskActual.DataBindings.Add(
  "Text", cboxTasks.DataSource, cboxTasks.ValueMember );
```

Either variation is acceptable because the third parameter requires that we specify a string that contains the name of the data object column, and the ComboBox's ValueMember and DisplayMember are string properties that identify columns of the bound data object.

In Chapter 12, when we revisit data binding and work with data objects that do not have a concept of *current row*, we will go deeper into the subject of how to programmatically position bound controls to a specific row.

Because data binding results in the movement of data between the not-visible data object and the visible control, you may need to transform the data as it is being moved; that is, you may need to *format* or *parse* the data.

Formatting and Parsing

Simple data binding causes data to flow between a data object and a property of a control. This is no problem if the data element, like the Text property, is a string. But durTaskActual is not a string; it is an integer, just as dateTaskStart is not a string but a date. What if we need to format this data as it moves from the data object into the control? In fact, we do need to format date fields, for we intend to save screen space by removing the time component before displaying the date. No 12/12/2003 11:45:30:001 dates for us.

We solve the problem of when and how to format bound data by responding to events. What you add to the BindingsCollection of a control is a Binding object, and Binding objects raise events. They raise a Format event as they are moving data into the target control, and they raise a Parse event as they are moving data back into the data object.

We need to handle the Format event in our application so that we can strip off the time component from our two date fields. We do not need to handle the Parse event because our formatted string, such as 02/05/2004, will convert back to a date without a problem. We never had an interest in the time portion anyway, so losing it is not a problem.

To simplify things, we write a short routine to do the data binding and formatting for each field, passing it a reference to the target TextBox and the target property name (which is always Text in our application) as parameters. We name our routine BindToTextbox. We also write an event handler, named Date_Format, for the Format event and use AddHandler to tie it to the Binding object's Format event. Listing 8.3 shows these two routines.

LISTING 8.3: The Generic Binding Routine and Format Event Handler

```
private void BindToTextbox( TextBox txtTarget,
                            string  strColumnName)
{
   //  Bind the TextBox to a column of the drop-down
   //     ComboBox's DataSource (the Tasks ArrayList).
   txtTarget.DataBindings.Add("Text",
                              cboxTasks.DataSource,
                              strColumnName);
   //  Specify an event handler for formatting those
   //     fields that are datatype DateTime.
   if( txtTarget == txtTaskStart ||
       txtTarget == txtTaskEnd )
   {
      txtTarget.DataBindings[0].Format +=
         new ConvertEventHandler(this.Date_Format);
   }
}

private void Date_Format( object sender,
                          ConvertEventArgs e)
{
   //  Format each date as it is moved by data binding
   //     from the ArrayList into a TextBox.
   e.value = e.Value.ToString("d");
}
```

Life, or at least coding, is made a little easier by the fact that each TextBox has only one property, Text, that uses binding. Thus each TextBox has only one Binding object in its DataBindings collection, and we can access that Binding object as DataBindings(0).

Then we write a routine to do all the binding (the binding to the ComboBox and to each TextBox), as shown in Listing 8.4.

LISTING 8.4: Binding Tasks to a ComboBox and Several TextBox Controls

```
private void BindTasksToControls()
{
   // Bind the drop-down ComboBox to the Tasks ArrayList.
   cboxTasks.DataSource = alTasks;
   cboxTasks.DisplayMember = "strName";
   cboxTasks.ValueMember = "strIdent";

   // Bind each TextBox to a column of the drop-down
   //    ComboBox's DataSource (the Tasks ArrayList).
   BindToTextbox(txtTaskNo, "strIdent");
   BindToTextbox(txtTaskName, "strName");
   BindToTextbox(txtTaskStart, "dateStart");
   BindToTextbox(txtTaskEnd, "dateEnd");
   BindToTextbox(txtTaskActual, "durActual");
   BindToTextbox(txtTaskEstimated, "durEstimated");
}
```

And while we're on a roll, we write a routine to unbind everything and to clear out our TextBox controls. We need to unbind and then rebind while we are adding new tasks to our data object, and having a routine to do each will help. We make it easier to write this unbinding routine by adding a Panel control to our form at design time and then placing the six TextBox controls that hold task information into that Panel control. With that done, Listing 8.5 shows our unbinding routine.

LISTING 8.5: Unbinding the Tasks from the TextBox and ComboBox Controls

```
private void UnbindTasksFromControls()
{
   // Iterate through all the controls in the TaskFields
   //    Panel, unbind them, and clear them.
   foreach( Control theControl in panelTaskFields.Controls )
   {
      theControl.DataBindings.Clear();
      theControl.Text = string.Empty;
   }

   // Unbind the ComboBox.
   cboxTasks.DataSource = null;
}
```

That's the new data-binding code. What about the old code from Chapter 7? What can we remove? For starters, we can delete the `SelectedIndexChanged` handler and the `LoadTaskFields` routine it called. The only reason we handled the `SelectionChanged` event was to keep the `TextBox` controls in synch with the `ComboBox`, something that is now done for us by data binding.

Do we gain anything? Yes, we have made huge gains. Before data binding, our application allowed users to view and add tasks but not to update them. Now users can update tasks without requiring any extra code on our part. Updating is built into data binding. In our new version of the application, as the user modifies the contents of a bound `TextBox`, the matching data element in the data object is updated.

So, simple data binding, which is inherited from the `Control` base class, is implemented by specifying a control and its target property, plus a data object that supports cursoring and its source property. It is available for you to use with all controls, and it uses the same PMEs regardless of the control's class.

We have just finished using simple data binding with control classes that were introduced in an earlier chapter. Now it's time to formally introduce a new control, the `DataGrid`, and apply both simple and complex data binding to it.

The `DataGrid` Control

The purpose of the `DataGrid` control is to display tabular data from a data object, as shown in Figure 8.6.

As of this writing, the `DataGrid` is the only .NET Compact Framework control written entirely in managed code and, therefore, the only .NET Compact Framework control written from the ground up. It is, as advertisers would say, "All new." It even has its own namespace, `System.Windows.Forms.DataGrid`, which you reference at the start of a program that uses the `DataGrid` control.

Tables 8.4 through 8.6 list the PMEs of the base `Control` object class that are supported by the `DataGrid` control, while Table 8.7 lists the `DataGrid`-specific PMEs.

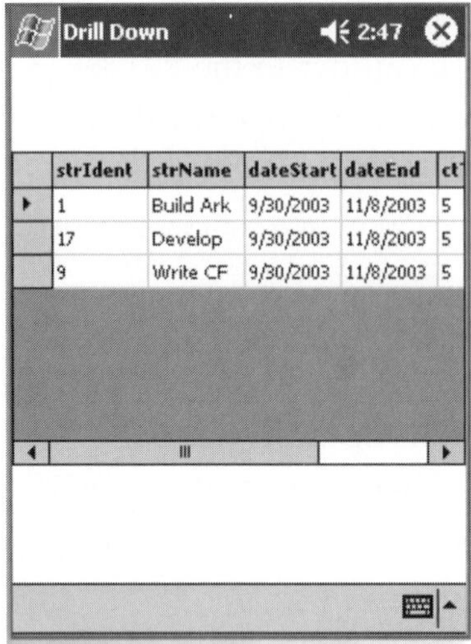

FIGURE 8.6: A `DataGrid` control displaying a `DataTable` object

TABLE 8.4: Support for Properties Inherited from `Control`

	`DataGrid`
Links to Other Controls	
`Controls`	X
`ContextMenu`	X
`Parent`	X
`TopLevelControl`	X
Positional	
`Bottom`	X
`Bounds`	X
`ClientRectangle`	X
`ClientSize`	X

	DataGrid
Height	X
Left	X
Location	X
Right	X
Size	X
Top	X
Width	X
Data Binding	
BindingContext	X
DataBindings	X
DataSource	X
Control State	
Capture	
Enabled	X
Focused	X
Visible	X
Control Appearance	
BackColor	X
Font	X
ForeColor	X
Text	X

TABLE 8.5: Support for Methods Inherited from `Control`

	`DataGrid`
Thread-Safe	
`Invoke`	X
Object Support	
`Dispose`	X
`Equals`	
`GetHashCode`	
`GetType`	X
`ToString`	
Coordinate Conversion	
`PointToClient`	X
`PointToScreen`	X
`RectangleToClient`	X
`RectangleToScreen`	X
Z-Ordering	
`BringToFront`	X
`SendToBack`	X
Visibility	
`Hide`	X
`Show`	X
Drawing	
`CreateGraphics`	
`Invalidate`	X
`Refresh`	
`Update`	
Control State	
`Focus`	X

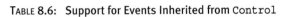

TABLE 8.6: Support for Events Inherited from `Control`

	`DataGrid`
Garbage Collection and Validation	
`Disposed`	X
`Validated`	X
`Validating`	X
Focus Changes	
`GotFocus`	X
`LostFocus`	X
Control Property Changes	
`EnabledChanged`	X
`ParentChanged`	X
`Resize`	X
`TextChanged`	X
Keyboard Input	
`KeyDown`	X
`KeyPress`	X
`KeyUp`	X
Mouse Input	
`Click`	X
`MouseDown`	X
`MouseMove`	X
`MouseUp`	X
Drawing	
`Paint`	X

TABLE 8.7: PMEs Specific to the DataGrid Control

Properties	
ColumnHeadersVisible	RowHeadersVisible
CurrentCell	SelectionBackColor
CurrentRowIndex	SelectionForeColor
FirstVisibleColumn	TableStyles
GridLineColor	VisibleColumnCount
HeaderBackColor	VisibleRowCount
HeaderForeColor	
Methods	**Events**
GetCellBounds	CurrentCellChanged
HitTest	
UnSelect	

Using Complex Data Binding with the DataGrid Control

As we've mentioned, the purpose of the DataGrid control is to display tabular data from a data object, and the easiest way to do it is to bind a data object containing the data to the DataGrid control. For instance, if our application displayed a DataGrid control named dgridDisplay and also used our UtilData class to load a DataTable named dtabProjects, the following code would bind the DataTable to the DataGrid, resulting in the output shown earlier in Figure 8.6.

```
dgridDisplay.DataSource = dtabProjects;
```

In this case the data binding was very easy. We had to set only one property of the DataGrid control to achieve the binding and display the data.

However, in the code just shown, we deferred all decisions about the appearance of that data to the DataGrid control. In a typical application this would not be the case; you might want to display column titles that were different from the column names of the underlying data object, or not display some of the columns, or alter the left-to-right sequence of the columns, or make some of the columns wider than others. So, with the `DataGrid` control, the binding was easy, but styling the display is going to require some additional code. It will not be the same code or even the same technique used to format and parse the simple binding example we just presented.

Styling the Display of Data in a `DataGrid` Control

To control the display of data in a `DataGrid`, you control the transformation of that data from the data object into the `DataGrid`. That is, you map columns of the data object to `DataGrid` columns, specifying additional information about each mapping. Each column mapping is referred to as a `DataGridColumnStyle` and is itself an object. The complete set of `DataGridColumnStyle` objects used to map all columns of one data object to the `DataGrid` is a collection that is a property of a `DataGridTableStyle` object. A `DataGridTableStyle` object consists of some individual properties plus a collection of `DataGridColumnStyle` objects, which taken together define the appearance of one data object to the `DataGrid` control. Table 8.8 lists the binding-specific PMEs of the `DataGridTableStyle` object; Table 8.9 lists the `DataGridColumnStyle` PMEs. As you have found elsewhere in the .NET Compact Framework, both sets of PMEs are much shorter than their desktop .NET Framework counterparts. Here the lists consist solely of properties.

You may need to provide more than one `DataGridTableStyle` object for a single `DataGrid`, for you may be planning to bind first one data object to the `DataGrid` and then a different data object to the `DataGrid` later in the

TABLE 8.8: PMEs for the `DataGridTableStyle` Object

PME	Definition
`MappingName`	The name of the data object
`GridColumnStyles`	The `GridColumnStyles` collection

TABLE 8.9: PMEs for the `DataGridColumnStyle` Object

PME	Definition
`MappingName`	The data object column name
`HeaderText`	The text to be displayed in the `DataGrid` column header
`NullText`	The text to be displayed in `DataGrid` cells in lieu of nulls
`Width`	The width, in pixels, of the `DataGrid` column

application. Perhaps you first display information about projects within the `DataGrid` and then, as a result of user input, display the selected project's required tasks in the grid. We do this in the next example, which displays project information as shown in Figure 8.7.

Figure 8.8 shows the same `DataGrid` now displaying the tasks required for that project.

You are not required to supply a new `DataGridTableStyle` object each time you change the binding from one data object to another. Instead, you can define the `DataGridTableStyle` object for each data object in advance

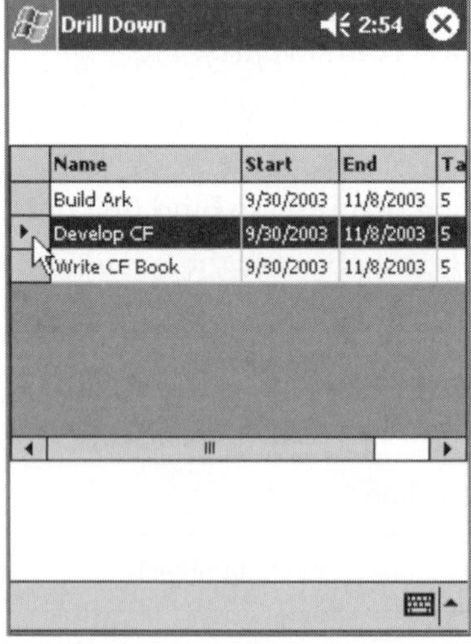

FIGURE 8.7: A `DataGrid` control with the projects table bound to it

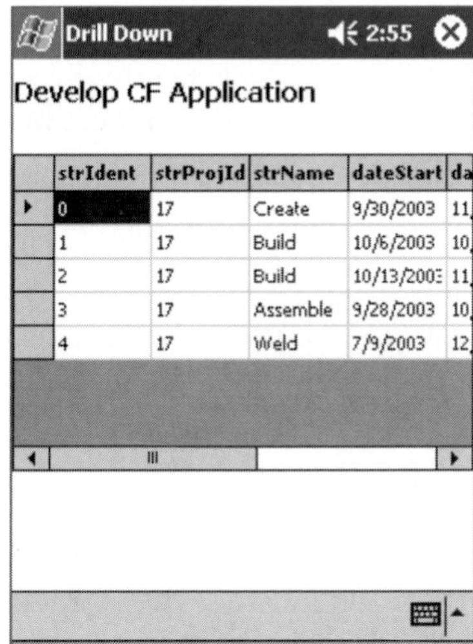

FIGURE 8.8: A `DataGrid` control with a `DataView` of the tasks table bound to it

and then add all the `DataGridTableStyle` objects to the `DataGrid` control's `TableStyles` collection at the start of the application. When the application assigns a new data object to the `DataGrid` control's `DataSource` property, the `DataGridTableStyle` object for the new data object is invoked. Thus a `DataGrid` control has a `TableStyles` collection, and each `TableStyle` includes a `GridColumnStyles` collection.

`DataTable` objects have a large number of PMEs, most of which are related to the transfer of data between a `DataTable` and a database. Once again, because this chapter covers transferring data between a data object and a bound control, we will not cover those properties in this chapter, deferring them until Part III. However, two `DataTable` properties are applicable to creating styles for data binding. The first is the `TableName` property, which is the property of the `DataTable` object that serves to identify it. Each instance of a `DataTable` object has its own name, which can be specified as the table is created, as the following code shows.

```
dtabProjects = new DataTable("Projects");
```

Within a `DataTable` object, the columns also have names. Both the table name and the column names are needed when styling the display of

DataTable data in a DataGrid control. As was shown in Tables 8.8 and 8.9, they are themselves properties of the DataGridTableStyle and DataGridColumnStyle objects. The TableName property of the data object becomes the MappingName property of the DataGridTableStyle object, and the column names become the MappingName properties of the DataGridColumnStyle objects.

This requirement that the data objects must have a TableName property in order for their display to be styled is one of the reasons why a DataTable rather than an ArrayList will be used for the remainder of this chapter. An ArrayList can be bound to the DataGrid, as was shown in earlier code, but it cannot be styled because the ArrayList class does not have a TableName property.

Creating Table and Column Styles

Table styles and their associated column styles can be defined at either design time or runtime. It's a little easier to understand them if you build them at design time, but you give yourself more flexibility when you build them at runtime. For this reason, we'll build our first one at design time and then later write the code to create it at runtime.

First, let's look at our data object, decide how we want it to appear within the DataGrid, and then create the styles needed to achieve this appearance. We will use the projects DataTable, whose display before styling appears in Figure 8.7, as our data object.

We decide that we do *not* want to display the identity column, duration completed, duration estimated, or comments. We want our DataGrid column sequence to be project name, start date, end date, and task count. For a preview of the end result, see Figure 8.13 later in this chapter.

To define our styles, we use Visual Studio .NET. We begin by selecting our DataGrid in the Designer window and then choosing the TableStyles collection in the Properties window, as shown in Figure 8.9.

This results in the display of the DataGridTableStyle collection dialog box. Within this dialog box we click on the Add button and are presented with the information shown in Figure 8.10.

We can name the DataGridTableStyle object anything we want; we name ours dgtsProjects. We must give the MappingName property the

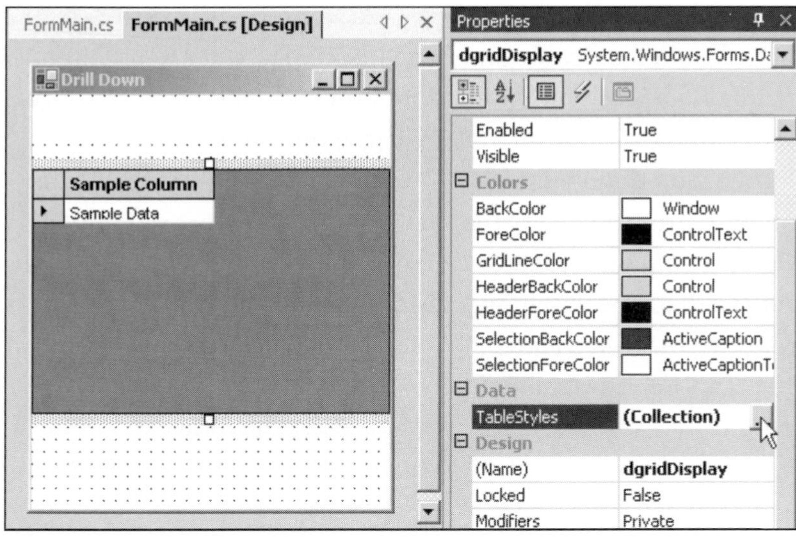

FIGURE 8.9: Choosing the `TableStyles` collection

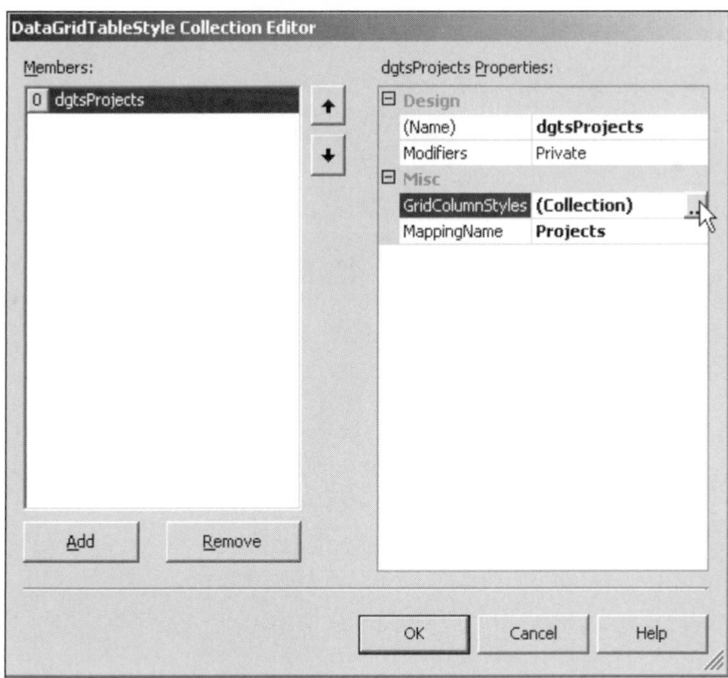

FIGURE 8.10: Adding a table style

value of the `DataTable` object's `TableName` property, which is `Projects`. Then we click on the GridColumnStyles button to add a new column style.

Once again we are presented with a new dialog box, and once again we click on the Add button and are presented with a `DataGridColumnStyle` collection dialog, which allows us to enter information mapping a column of our data object to the first column of the `DataGrid`. We enter a name for our column style object, decide what we want the column header within the `DataGrid` to say, and specify the data object's column name, in this case, `strName`. We leave the `NullText` specification unchanged and double the `Width` from the default of 50 pixels to 100 pixels. Then we add this column style to our `DataGridTableStyle`, as shown in Figure 8.11.

We repeat this step for each data object column we wish to display in the `DataGrid`. Then we return to the `DataGridTableStyle` collection dialog box and add the `TableStyle` to the `DataGrid`. Now all that remains is

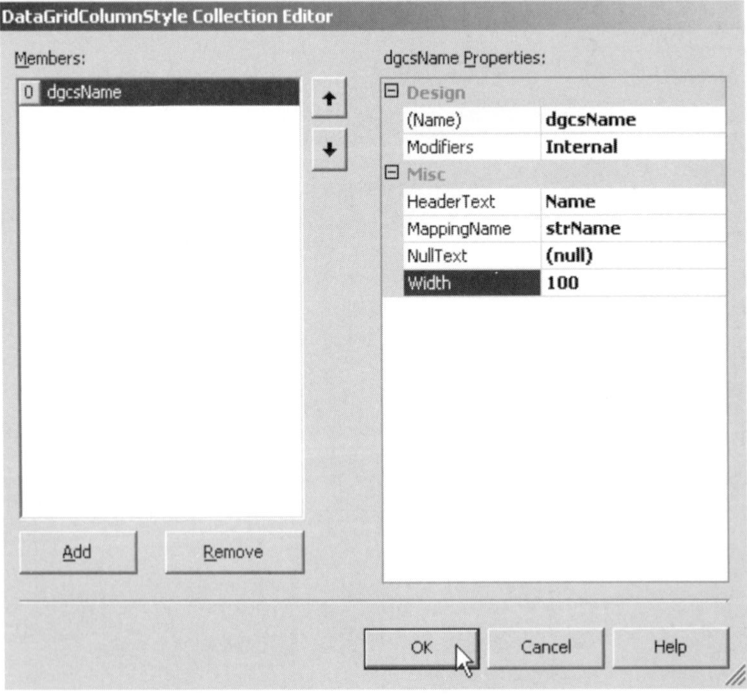

FIGURE 8.11: Entering `DataGridColumnStyle` properties

to write the following code to bind our `DataTable` to the `DataGrid` and place it within the form's `Load` event.

```
dgridProjects.DataSource = dpProjects.GetProjectsDT();
```

When we run the application, we get the more refined result that appears later in this chapter in Figure 8.13, which is the result we wanted.

Creating Styles at Runtime

We could have built the `DataGridTableStyle` object that we just created in the Designer by writing code instead, and there are some benefits in doing this. It is usually easier to modify code than to modify a design, and it's almost always easier to produce a second `DataGridTableStyle` object by modifying the code of a previous creation rather than by repeating the entire design-time style creation process. Design time is nice, but it's not very reusable.

Listing 8.6 shows the code to create a `DataGridTableStyle` object that is identical to the one we just created at design time.

LISTING 8.6: Creating `DataGrid` Table and Column Styles

```
internal static void AddCustomDataTableStyle
                              (
                                 DataGrid dgridTarget,
                                 string  strTable
                              )
{
   DataGridTableStyle dgtsStyle;
   DataGridTextBoxColumn dgtsColumn;

   switch (strTable)
   {
      case "Projects":
         //  Define a Style for the Projects
         //     DataTable or ArrayList to be used by
         //     the DataGrid when displaying projects.

         dgtsStyle = new DataGridTableStyle();
         //  Specify that it is to be applied whenever
         //     a data object named Projects is assigned
         //     to the DataGrid's DataSource property.
         dgtsStyle.MappingName = "Projects";
```

continues

continued

```
         //  Add columns.
         //  Specify:
         //     Column/field name
         //     Column header
         //     Column width in pixels

         dgtsColumn = new DataGridTextBoxColumn();
         dgtsColumn.MappingName = "strName";
         dgtsColumn.HeaderText = "Name";
         dgtsColumn.Width = 100;
         dgtsStyle.GridColumnStyles.Add(dgtsColumn);

         dgtsColumn = new DataGridTextBoxColumn();
         dgtsColumn.MappingName = "dateStart";
         dgtsColumn.HeaderText = "Start";
         dgtsColumn.Width = 50;
         dgtsStyle.GridColumnStyles.Add(dgtsColumn);

         dgtsColumn = new DataGridTextBoxColumn();
         dgtsColumn.MappingName = "dateEnd";
         dgtsColumn.HeaderText = "End";
         dgtsColumn.Width = 50;
         dgtsStyle.GridColumnStyles.Add(dgtsColumn);

         dgtsColumn = new DataGridTextBoxColumn();
         dgtsColumn.MappingName = "ctTasks";
         dgtsColumn.HeaderText = "Tasks";
         dgtsColumn.Width = 50;
         dgtsStyle.GridColumnStyles.Add(dgtsColumn);

         //  Add the style to the DataGrid.
         dgridTarget.TableStyles.Add(dgtsStyle);

         break;
      case "Tasks":
         break;
      default:
         break;
   }
}
```

To modularize our application, we add a class named `UtilGUI` and place the code from Listing 8.6 within that class. This code is located in the `BindToDataGridStyled` project.

Now that we have the ability to present the data from our data object to our user, let's examine how we handle the user's reaction to this data. That is, let's look at the events raised by the `DataGrid` control and at how to obtain the information we need to respond to those events.

Responding to User Input

When it comes to data binding, the `DataGrid` control is the most capable and the most complex. We saw an indication of this when we did styling, and we see it again as we respond to the events raised by the `DataGrid` in response to user input.

The `DataGrid` control is a read-only control. Although users can designate a current cell by tapping with the stylus, they cannot then enter data into that cell. So, reacting to user input may involve drilling down further into the selected item, or it may require presenting an input control to the user followed by updating the data.

A `DataGrid` control displays cells of data to the user. The surface area of the `DataGrid` control is broken down into regions of different types. These types are listed in the `DataGrid.HitTestType` enumeration defined in the `System.Windows.Forms.DataGrid` namespace and are shown, in brief, in Table 8.10. A more detailed listing can be found in the online help under `DataGrid.HitTestType`.

TABLE 8.10: Types of Regions of the `DataGrid` Control

Type	Location
0	Empty area of the `DataGrid` control
1	Data cell
2	Column header
4	Row header
8	Column resize
16	Row resize

As shown in Table 8.10, data cells are type 1 cells. The cells located just above the data columns, where the column titles appear, are type 2 cells. The cells just to the left of each row are type 4 cells. The thin dividing line between each column heading is type 8, while the line between rows is type 16. Any other area of the `DataGrid` control is type 0.

As mentioned in the previous paragraph, the `HitTestType` of all data cells is 1, which maps to an enumeration name of `Cell`. In addition, the data type of all data cells is `System.String`. Regardless of the data type of the underlying bound data object column, the contents of a `DataGrid` cell is always a string.

The data cells, being a two-dimensional, zero-based array, are numbered beginning at the upper-left with cell (0,0). At any point in time at most one data cell is the current cell. The user designates the current cell by tapping with the stylus or by using the tab or arrow keys.

When a user taps on a data cell, that data cell becomes the current cell, which the `DataGrid` control indicates by highlighting the cell's background. If the user taps on a row header, the `DataGrid` control highlights the entire row. Even with an entire row highlighted, only one cell is the current cell—the cell whose row number is the same as the highlighted row and whose column number is the same as the previously selected current cell. Thus, if the current cell is cell (2,1)—row 2, column 1—and a user taps the row header of row 0, then cell (0,1) becomes the new current cell.

Sometimes it is not the current cell but the cell located under the mouse that is of interest to your application. This is the case not only when the user is tapping on a data cell but also when the user is tapping elsewhere within the `DataGrid` control, such as within a row header.

The `DataGrid` control's `HitTest` method, which takes `DataGrid` coordinates as input and returns a `HitTest` object, is used to determine the cell type, row number, and column number of the cell located under the mouse. Table 8.11 lists the PMEs of the `HitTest` object.

Once the row and column numbers are known, the `Item` property can retrieve that actual data value from the cell. This is illustrated in Listing 8.7, which reacts to a `MouseMove` event by obtaining the row, column, type, and value information for the cell that is under the mouse and displaying that information in the `lblDatum` set of labels.

TABLE 8.11: PMEs of the `HitTest` Object

PME	Definition	Remarks
`Type`	Cell type	`DataGrid.HitTestType`
`Column`	Column number	
`Row`	Row number	
`Nowhere`	Location of type 0	Static method

LISTING 8.7: Displaying `HitTest` Information

```
private void Grid_MouseMove(object sender,
                            MouseEventArgs e)
{
   //  Store the DataGrid object for early binding.
   DataGrid dgridSender = (DataGrid)sender;

   //  Use the DataGrid's HitTest method to get the
   //     HitTest object for this mouse location.
   DataGrid.HitTestInfo httstInfo;
   httstInfo = dgridSender.HitTest(e.X, e.Y);

   //  Display HitTest properties in the labels.
   lblDatumType.Text = httstInfo.Type.ToString();
   lblDatumRow.Text = httstInfo.Row.ToString();
   lblDatumColumn.Text = httstInfo.Column.ToString();
}
```

So when responding to mouse events, the application can always determine whether the event is occurring within a data cell or within a particular area of the `DataGrid` control located outside of the data cells.

A more difficult task is to trace a cell of the `DataGrid` control back to the data element of the underlying data object. You might never need to do this, for data binding ties each cell of the `DataGrid` control to a data element of the bound data object for you. To change a value in the data object, all you need to do is programmatically change the corresponding value in the `DataGrid`; you do not need to directly access the data object yourself. Perhaps, however, you need to know the column name or data type of the data element bound to a particular DataGrid cell before you do the update. This will be the case in an in-place editing sample application later in this chapter, for it must check the data object column name to ensure that a certain column is not being updated. So, in case you ever need direct access into the data object bound to a DataGrid control, the technique for doing so is explained here.

To access fields of the data object, you will need to reverse-engineer the mapping you established earlier between the DataGrid control and the data object. Because the .NET Compact Framework DataGrid control does not support sorting, there will be a one-to-one relationship between the rows of the DataGrid control and the rows of the data object; row 4 in the DataGrid control will be row 4 in the data object, row 0 in the DataGrid control will be row 0 in the data object.

But the same is not true for columns. Columns of the data object can appear in any sequence within the DataGrid control, or they can be absent. Therefore, you must access the current DataGridTableStyle object to determine which data object column maps to which DataGrid column. The current DataGridTableStyle object will be the one whose MappingName property equals the TableName property of the DataGrid control's DataSource property. Then iterate through the GridColumnStyle collection of the TableStyles object. The GridColumnStyle objects will be in the same sequence as the DataGrid columns, and for each column style the MappingName property will contain the name of the data object column.

You can see why we recommend letting data binding do the work for you.

Table 8.12 lists the paths to follow to obtain information about a DataGrid control and its bound object when responding to the CurrentCellChanged event or to mouse events.

To illustrate Table 8.12, we will write a sample application. This application is located in the DisplayBindingInfo project.

The application will react to CurrentCellChanged events and MouseMove events by displaying information about the current cell and the cell located beneath the mouse. This information includes the cell type, row number, and column number of the cell; the contents of the cell; the column

TABLE 8.12: Obtaining `DataGrid` and Bound `DataTable` Information

Reference Number	Datum	Path (Where `e` is the `MouseEventArgs` Parameter)
1	Cell under mouse: cell type	`DataGrid.HitTest(e.X,e.Y).Type`
2	Cell under mouse: row number	`DataGrid.HitTest(e.X,e.Y).Row`
3	Cell under mouse: column number	`DataGrid.HitTest(e.X,e.Y).Column`
4	Current cell: cell type	Always 1
5	Current cell: row number	`DataGrid.CurrentCell.RowNumber`
6	Current cell: column number	`DataGrid.CurrentCell.ColumnNumber`
7	Data value of cell located at row X, column Y	`DataGrid[X,Y]`
8	Bounds of cell located at row X, column Y	`DataGrid.GetCellBounds(X,Y)`
9	`TableName` of bound data object	`DataGrid.DataSource.TableName`
10	`TableStyle` used with bound data object	`TableStyle` object whose `MappingName` property equals #9
11	Data object row number of `DataGrid` row number X	`X`
12	Data object column name of `DataGrid` column number Y	`MappingName` property value of `GridColumnStyles[Y]` of #10
13	Data object column number of `DataGrid` column number Y	Column number of #12
14	Data object data element that maps to `DataGrid` row X, column Y	Value of `DataTable.Rows[X][#11]`
15	Data type of data object data element that maps to `DataGrid` row X, column Y	`GetType` method of #14

name, value, and data type of the bound field in the underlying DataTable; and the primary key value of the current row. This information is necessary to determine not only the cell in question but also to access the corresponding data element within the bound DataTable.

Normally we do not respond to MouseMove events in our sample applications because most applications must run in a nonmouse environment. In this application, however, we use the MouseMove event rather than the MouseDown or MouseUp events because the information displayed is applicable to any mouse event, and responding to MouseMove events produces a more animated display.

We use both simple and complex data binding with the DataGrid control in this application. The reason for using complex data binding is obvious—as in past applications, it is the mechanism through which the project information is displayed within the DataGrid. The reason for using simple data binding with the DataGrid control is less obvious but potentially just as beneficial.

Using Simple Data Binding with the DataGrid Control

As with the previous sample application, we have chosen *not* to display the Project Identity field, strIdent, in the DataGrid control. But if the user requests a drill-down operation, desiring additional information about the current row, we need to know the identity value of that row; that is, we need to know the project's primary key value even though it is not displayed in the DataGrid control. It would be ideal if this value were stored in a property of the DataGrid control, but it isn't.

However, we can use simple data binding to achieve this by taking advantage of the fact that a DataGrid control's Text property is normally unused. We can use it to hold the primary key value by binding the DataGrid control's Text property to the primary key column of the data object, in this example, strIdent, as shown in the following code.

```
dgridProjects.DataBindings.Add(
                 "Text",
                 dgridProjects.DataSource,
                 "strIdent");
```

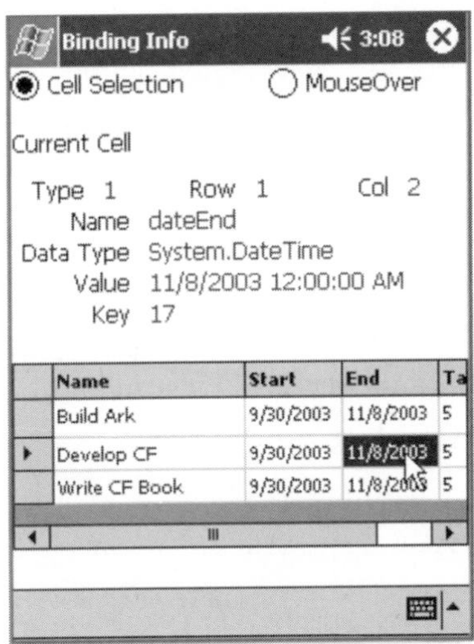

FIGURE 8.12: Displaying cell information

Having the primary key value of the current row available in the `Text` property is very useful when working with databases because data retrieval routines often require a primary key value as an input parameter.

Accessing `DataGrid` Information

When we run the application (whose code is presented in this subsection, beginning with Listing 8.8 and ending with Listing 8.12) and request to see information based on the `CurrentCellChanged` event, we obtain the output shown in Figure 8.12. Note that the Name and Data Type fields refer to the data object, not the `DataGrid` control, and that the Key field displays the selected cell's primary key value, also from the data object.

We begin our application with some namespace declarations, followed by Designer-generated code, some of which we have removed for the sake of compactness in Listing 8.8.

LISTING 8.8: The Start of the Hit Testing Program

```
using System;
using System.Drawing;
using System.Windows.Forms;
```

continues

continued

```
using System.Data;
using YaoDurant.Data;
using YaoDurant.GUI;

namespace DisplayBindingInfo
{
   public class FormMain : System.Windows.Forms.Form
   {
      internal System.Windows.Forms.Panel panelChoice;
      internal System.Windows.Forms.RadioButton optMouseOver;
               :
               :
               :
      internal System.Windows.Forms.Label lblDatumEvent;
      private System.Windows.Forms.DataGrid dgridProjects;
      private System.Windows.Forms.MainMenu mainMenu1;

      public FormMain()
      {
         InitializeComponent();
      }

      protected override void Dispose( bool disposing )
      {
         base.Dispose( disposing );
      }
      #region Windows Form Designer generated code

      static void Main()
      {
         Application.Run(new FormMain());
      }
```

Next comes the form's `Load` event handler (shown in Listing 8.9), which loads, binds, and styles the data using the utility routines we mentioned earlier.

LISTING 8.9: The Load Event Handler

```
      private void FormMain_Load(object sender, EventArgs e)
      {
         YaoDurant.Data.UtilData utilData = new UtilData();
         YaoDurant.GUI.UtilGUI utilGUI = new UtilGUI();

         //  Make the Project table the DataSource.
         //  Make the strIdent field of the currently
```

```
      //     select row the Text property of the DataGrid
      //     control.
      dgridProjects.DataSource = utilData.GetProjectsDT();
      dgridProjects.DataBindings.Clear();
      dgridProjects.DataBindings.Add(
                        "Text",
                        dgridProjects.DataSource,
                        "strIdent");

      //  Use a utility routine to style the
      //     layout of Projects in the DataGrid.
      UtilGUI.AddCustomDataTableStyle(dgridProjects,
                                    "Projects");
   }
```

The application handles `MouseMove` events by using the `sender`, `DataSource`, `HitTest`, and `TableStyle` objects to obtain information about the cell under the mouse and its bound data element, as shown in Listing 8.10.

LISTING 8.10: Performing Hit Testing as the Mouse Is Moving

```
   private void dgridProjects_MouseMove(object sender,
                                        MouseEventArgs e)
   {
      //  If the user is not interested in
      //     this event, do not handle it.
      if (! optMouseOver.Checked )
      {
         return;
      }

      //  Tell the user what information is being shown.
      lblDatumEvent.Text = "Cell Under Mouse";

      //  Store the DataGrid object for early binding.
      DataGrid dgridSender = (DataGrid)sender;

      //  Store the DataGrid's DataSource object.
      DataTable dtabDataSource =
         (DataTable)dgridSender.DataSource;

      //  Use the DataSource name to retrieve
      //     and store the current TableStyle.
      DataGridTableStyle dgtsCurrent =
         dgridSender.TableStyles[dtabDataSource.TableName];
```

continues

continued

```
// Use the DataGrid's HitTest method to get the
//     HitTest object for this mouse location.
DataGrid.HitTestInfo httstInfo;
httstInfo = dgridSender.HitTest(e.X, e.Y);

// Clear the labels that are meaningful only
//     if the mouse is over a data cell.
lblDatumName.Text = string.Empty;
lblDatumValue.Text = string.Empty;
lblDatumDataType.Text = string.Empty;

// Display HitTest properties in the labels.
lblDatumType.Text = httstInfo.Type.ToString();
lblDatumRow.Text = httstInfo.Row.ToString();
lblDatumColumn.Text = httstInfo.Column.ToString();

// If the mouse is positioned over a data column...
if (httstInfo.Column != -1 )
{
   // Obtain the DataSource's column name from
   //     the ColumnStyles collection of the
   //     current TableStyle.
   string strColumnName =
      dgtsCurrent.GridColumnStyles[httstInfo.Column].
         MappingName;
   lblDatumName.Text = strColumnName;

   // Obtain the DataSource column's data type.
   lblDatumDataType.Text =
      dtabDataSource.Rows[0][strColumnName].
         GetType().ToString();

   // If the mouse is positioned over a data cell...
   if (httstInfo.Row != -1 )
   {
      //          EITHER

      // Obtain and display the cell value from
      //     the underlying DataSource object.
      lblDatumValue.Text =
         dtabDataSource.Rows[httstInfo.Row]
                              [strColumnName].ToString();

      //             OR

      // Obtain and display the cell value from
      //     the DataGrid itself.
```

```
            lblDatumValue.Text =
               dgridSender[httstInfo.Row,
                           httstInfo.Column].ToString();
         }
      }
   }
```

The `CurrentCellChanged` event handler is similar, except that it uses the `CurrentCell` object rather than obtaining a `HitTest` object to determine the appropriate cell. Listing 8.11 shows the code.

LISTING 8.11: Obtaining Information about the New Current Cell

```
private void dgridProjects_CurrentCellChanged(
                                        object sender,
                                        EventArgs e)
{
   //  If the user is not interested in
   //      this event, do not handle it.
   if (! optCellSelection.Checked )
   {
      return;
   }

   //  Tell the user what information is being shown.
   lblDatumEvent.Text = "Current Cell";

   //  Store the DataGrid object for early binding.
   DataGrid dgridSender = (DataGrid)sender;

   //  Store the DataGrid's DataSource object.
   DataTable dtabDataSource =
      (DataTable)dgridSender.DataSource;

   //  Use the DataSource name to retrieve
   //      and store the current TableStyle.
   DataGridTableStyle dgtsCurrent =
      dgridSender.TableStyles[dtabDataSource.TableName];

   DataGridCell cellCurr = dgridSender.CurrentCell;

   //  Display CurrentCell properties in the labels.
   lblDatumType.Text = "1";
   lblDatumRow.Text = cellCurr.RowNumber.ToString();
   lblDatumColumn.Text = cellCurr.ColumnNumber.ToString();
```

continues

continued

```
      //  Obtain the DataSource's column name from
      //      the ColumnStyles collection of the
      //      current TableStyle.
      string  strColumnName =
         dgtsCurrent.GridColumnStyles[cellCurr.ColumnNumber].
            MappingName;
      lblDatumName.Text = strColumnName;

      //  Obtain the DataSource column's data type.
      lblDatumDataType.Text =
         dtabDataSource.Rows[0][strColumnName].
            GetType().ToString();

      //            EITHER

      //  Obtain and display the cell value from
      //      the underlying DataSource object.
      lblDatumValue.Text =
         dtabDataSource.Rows[cellCurr.RowNumber]
                             [strColumnName].ToString();

      //               OR

      //  Obtain and display the cell value from
      //      the DataGrid itself.
      lblDatumValue.Text =
         dgridSender[cellCurr.RowNumber,
                     cellCurr.ColumnNumber].ToString();

      //  Display the primary key of the row, based on
      //      the DataBindings entry that was added
      //      during the Load event.
      lblDatumKey.Text = dgridSender.Text;
   }
```

The final routine in the application, as shown in Listing 8.12, responds to the user's request to switch from `CurrentCell` mode to `MouseMove` mode.

LISTING 8.12: Changing Modes

```
   private void optAny_CheckedChanged(object sender,
                                      EventArgs e)
   {
      //  Clear the Labels.
      this.lblDatumEvent.Text = string.Empty;
      this.lblDatumType.Text = string.Empty;
      this.lblDatumRow.Text = string.Empty;
```

```
            this.lblDatumColumn.Text = string.Empty;
            this.lblDatumName.Text = string.Empty;
            this.lblDatumValue.Text = string.Empty;
            this.lblDatumKey.Text = string.Empty;
            this.lblDatumDataType.Text = string.Empty;
            this.lblHdrKey.Visible = optCellSelection.Checked;
        }
    }
}
```

Now that we know how to obtain the necessary information to react to user input, we'll write two applications that use this information. Each application will address a common challenge associated with the `DataGrid` control. The first application will provide *drill-down* capability, while the second application will perform *in-place editing*.

Providing Drill-Down Capability

Our drill-down application (located in the `DrillDownSameForm` project) presents project information within the `DataGrid` control, similar to the previous application. When the user taps within a row header, thus selecting a particular project, the application presents a context menu allowing the user to request that the application drill down into the selected project, as shown in Figure 8.13.

The application drills down into the project by replacing the information in the `DataGrid` control with a list of the tasks required for the selected project, as shown in Figure 8.14. The application also displays the name of the selected project in a table located above the `DataGrid` control.

The initial display of project information within the `DataGrid` control uses the same database simulation routine and `DataGrid` styling routine we used in the previous application. We use a context menu to allow the user to make selections, but we do not comment here on the context menu code because context menus are the subject of Chapter 9. For our current purposes, the context menu is simply the mechanism that allows the user to request a drill-down operation.

Because the routine that drills down into the selected project requires the project's primary key as an input parameter, we once again use both simple and complex data binding.

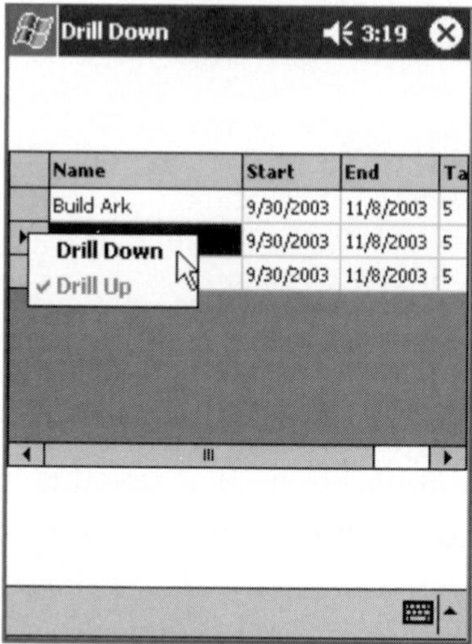

FIGURE 8.13: Context menu for requesting the application to drill down into a project

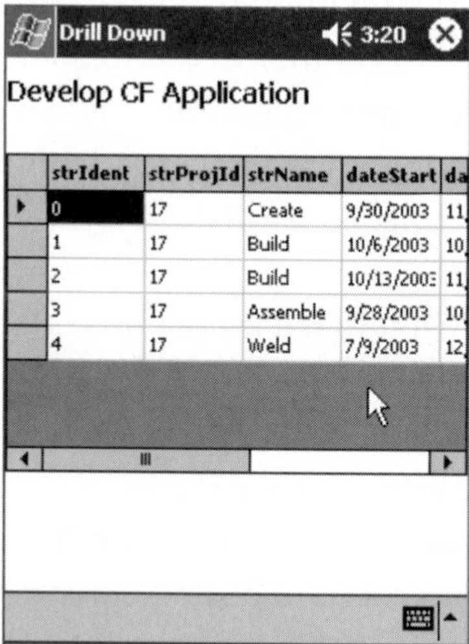

FIGURE 8.14: Response to the drill-down request

The complete drill-down application is presented in Listings 8.13 through 8.15. We begin our application with five reference variables to hold information we will need during the course of the application plus two to hold context menu entries, as shown in Listing 8.13.

LISTING 8.13: The Start of the Drill-Down Program

```
using System;
using System.Drawing;
using System.Collections;
using System.Windows.Forms;
using System.Data;
using YaoDurant.Data;
using YaoDurant.GUI;

namespace DrillDownSameForm
{
   public class FormMain : System.Windows.Forms.Form
   {
      internal System.Windows.Forms.Label lblProjectName;
      private System.Windows.Forms.DataGrid dgridDisplay;
      private System.Windows.Forms.ContextMenu cmenuDrill;
      private System.Windows.Forms.MainMenu mainMenu1;

      public FormMain()
      {
         InitializeComponent();
      }
      protected override void Dispose( bool disposing )
      {
         base.Dispose( disposing );
      }
      #region Windows Form Designer generated code

      static void Main()
      {
         Application.Run(new FormMain());
      }

      //  A reference to the DataSet
      private DataSet dsetTimeTracker;
      //  A reference to the Projects DataTable
      private DataTable dtabProjects;
      //  A reference to the Tasks DataTable
      private DataTable dtabTasks;

      //  Two context menu items
      private MenuItem mitemDrillDown = new MenuItem();
      private MenuItem mitemDrillUp = new MenuItem();
```

The reference variables are followed by our `FormLoad` event handler, which performs the data binding and styling, as shown in Listing 8.14.

LISTING 8.14: The Form's Load Event Handler

```
private void FormMain_Load(object sender, EventArgs e)
{
   // Create utility objects.
   YaoDurant.Data.UtilData utilData = new UtilData();
   YaoDurant.GUI.UtilGUI utilGUI = new UtilGUI();

   //  Set references to data objects.
   dsetTimeTracker = utilData.GetProjectsDataSet();
   dtabProjects = dsetTimeTracker.Tables["Projects"];
   dtabTasks = dsetTimeTracker.Tables["Tasks"];

   //  Make the Projects table the DataSource.
   //  Make the strIdent field of the currently
   //     selected row the Text property of the DataGrid
   //     control.
   dgridDisplay.DataSource = dtabProjects;
   dgridDisplay.DataBindings.Clear();
   dgridDisplay.DataBindings.Add(
      "Text",
      dgridDisplay.DataSource,
      "strIdent");

   //  Use a utility routine to style the
   //     layout of Projects in the DataGrid.
   UtilGUI.AddCustomDataTableStyle(dgridDisplay,
      "Projects");

   //  Initialize the context menu.
   InitContextMenu();
}
```

When the user taps within the `DataGrid` control, we need to determine whether the tap is within a row header, and if so, we need to present the context menu that allows the user to request a drill-down operation, as shown below.

```
private void dgridDisplay_MouseUp(object sender,
                                  MouseEventArgs e)
{
//  If the user has clicked in a row header,
//     display the context menu.
   if (dgridDisplay.HitTest(e.X, e.Y).Type ==
       DataGrid.HitTestType.RowHeader )
   {
```

```
        dgridDisplay.ContextMenu.Show(
                                  dgridDisplay,
                                  new Point(e.X, e.Y));
      }
   }
```

When the user requests a drill-down operation, we call the DrillDown routine, passing it the identity value of the selected row.

```
private void mitemDrillDown_Click(object sender,
                                  EventArgs e)
{
   // The Text property of the DataGrid has been bound
   //    to the strIdent column of the DataSource row.
   //    So, the identity of the selected project will
   //    be in the Text property.
   DrillDown(dgridDisplay.Text);
}
```

Note how much simpler this code is because of the simple data binding that we established during the Load event, a binding that causes the row's primary key value to be bound to the Text property of the DataGrid control.

The DrillDown routine, which replaces the information in the DataGrid control with the list of required tasks for the chosen project, is shown next. It uses a DataView of the Tasks DataTable, which it limits to just the tasks of the selected project by setting the DataView's Filter property, and then binds the DataView to the DataGrid. The DataView class is covered in greater detail in Chapter 12.

```
private void DrillDown(string  strProjIdent)
{
   // Note which project is being displayed.
   lblProjectName.Text =
      dtabProjects.Rows[
         dgridDisplay.CurrentCell.RowNumber]["strName"].
            ToString();

   // Create a view of the Tasks table.
   DataView  dviewProjectTasks = new DataView(dtabTasks);

   // Set it to display only strProjIdent tasks.
```

continues

continued

```
      dviewProjectTasks.RowFilter =
                "strProjIdent = '" + strProjIdent + "'";

      // Bind it to the DataGrid control.
      dgridDisplay.DataSource = dviewProjectTasks;
   }
```

If the user requests a drill-up operation, the code is even simpler, for all that is needed is to clear the `Label` control and to rebind the project table to the `DataGrid`, as shown in the following code.

```
   private void DrillUp() {
      // Bind the Projects DataTable to the DataGrid control.
      dgridDisplay.DataSource = dtabProjects;

      // Clear the project name display.
      lblProjectName.Text = string.Empty;
   }
```

Two other routines, in support of the context menu, are needed to complete our program. The first one initializes the context menu by adding the two possible choices to it.

```
   private void InitContextMenu()
   {
      // Add "Drill Down" and "Drill Up" entries
      //    to the context menu.
      cmenuDrill.MenuItems.Clear();

      mitemDrillDown.Text = "Drill Down";
      mitemDrillDown.Click +=
         new EventHandler(mitemDrillDown_Click);
      cmenuDrill.MenuItems.Add(mitemDrillDown);

      mitemDrillUp.Text = "Drill Up";
      mitemDrillUp.Click +=
         new EventHandler(mitemDrillUp_Click);
      cmenuDrill.MenuItems.Add(mitemDrillUp);
   }
```

The second routine enables and disables the context menu items so that the user cannot select Drill Down when already down or Drill Up when already up. Listing 8.15 shows the end of the program.

LISTING 8.15: The End of the Drill-Down Program

```
      private void cmenuDrill_Popup(object sender, EventArgs e)
      {
      //  If already "Up", the user can only go "Down",
      //     and vice versa.
         if ( dgridDisplay.DataSource == dtabProjects )
         {
            mitemDrillDown.Enabled = true;
            mitemDrillDown.Checked = false;
         } else {
            mitemDrillDown.Enabled = false;
            mitemDrillDown.Checked = true;
         }
         mitemDrillUp.Enabled = ! mitemDrillDown.Enabled;
         mitemDrillUp.Checked = ! mitemDrillDown.Checked;
      }
   }
}
```

So, by understanding how to perform a hit test to determine the mouse location within a DataGrid control, by knowing how to obtain information about the current cell, and by making full use of both simple and complex data binding, we can provide drill-down capability to the application with a minimum amount of code.

Let's move on to address the other user input challenge associated with the DataGrid control: in-place editing.

Providing In-Place Editing Capability

A .NET Compact Framework DataGrid control is used for display only. Unlike its desktop counterpart, it does not provide any data modification capability to the user. To overcome the display-only limitation of the DataGrid control, you must provide the data modification capability yourself.

Your application must take two steps to provide in-place editing for a DataGrid control.

1. Present a control capable of accepting input, such as a TextBox, preferably with the text already highlighted, whenever the user indicates that they wish to modify the contents of the CurrentCell.

2. Provide a mechanism for the user to indicate that they have completed, or are canceling the update. If an update was requested, move the contents of the input control into the `CurrentCell`. If appropriate, hide the input control.

Here are some things to keep in mind as you design your in-place editing functionality.

- You could respond to an update request in a manner similar to Microsoft Excel by permanently displaying a `TextBox` control above the grid. Alternatively, you could choose to temporarily display the `TextBox` control directly over the current cell for the duration of the data entry.
- If you choose to display the input control only while the update is in progress, it will be difficult to automate the edit, update, and cancel steps. That is, it's tricky to make the input control automatically appear with highlighted text as the user taps, tabs, or arrows into a new current cell. It's also hard to update the old current cell as the user moves into a new current cell while the old current cell is being edited.
- You will not need to update the underlying data object because data binding will do that for you as you update the `DataGrid` control.

Because of the complexity involved in doing the "automated" in-place editing, consider providing a manual capability in which the user explicitly requests editing, updating, and canceling. Figure 8.15 shows an application that uses the manual method, with Edit, Update, and Cancel buttons. Once you have a working version of manual in-place editing in your application, you can consider upgrading to automated in-place editing.

In the remainder of this chapter we look at providing manual in-place updating first and then address the challenges of automating it. We begin by writing an application to do the manual variation.

In this application (located in the `DisplayBindingInfo` project and shown in Listings 8.16 through 8.19), we use the collocation technique, plac-

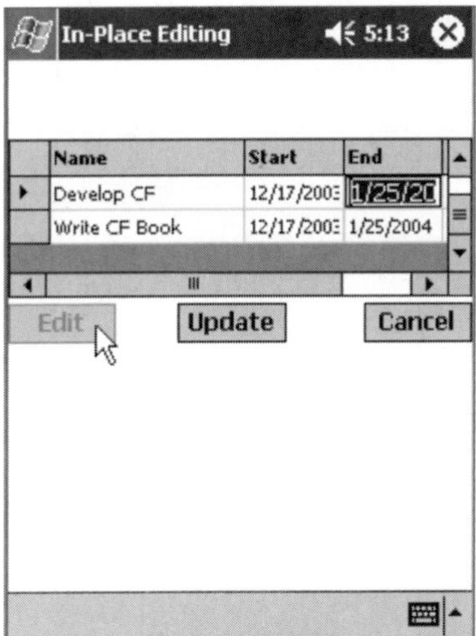

FIGURE 8.15: Manual in-place editing

ing our input control over the current cell while the editing is in progress, as shown in Figure 8.15, and removing it when the update or cancel operation is complete. This emphasizes the in-place aspect of the editing and gives you some experience using the location properties of the `CurrentCell` object.

You already know how to do everything that needs to be done. In Chapter 7 you saw how to create, position, show, and hide a `TextBox` control. Table 8.12 earlier in this chapter listed the methods for obtaining the bounds of the `CurrentCell` object and accessing its value. All we need to do now is put this information to work and write our manual in-place editing application.

The application displays the `DataGrid` control and three `Command` buttons: Edit, Update, and Cancel. The buttons allow users to indicate what they want done. However, because the Task Count field represents the number of required tasks associated with this project, it is a nonupdatable field; we must prevent users from attempting to update this field. The application does this by checking the column name in the bound data object. If users attempt to update a field of the Tasks column, they are presented with a message box informing them it is a nonupdatable field.

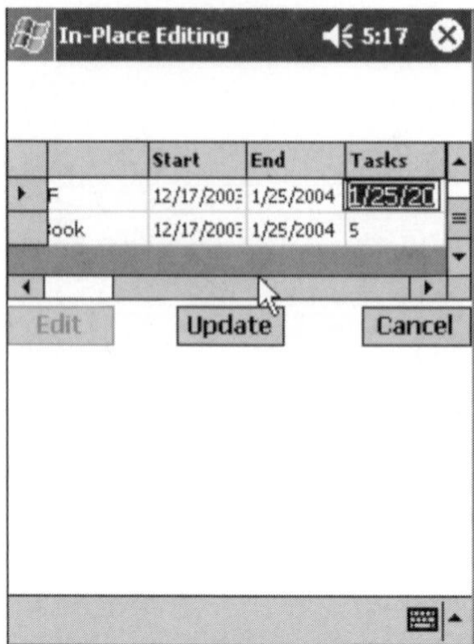

FIGURE 8.16: The `TextBox` control no longer colocated with the `CurrentCell` object

As expected, we use the same database simulation routines and `DataGrid` styling routine for obtaining and displaying information that we have used in the previous applications of this chapter.

When the application starts, the user is presented with a `DataGrid` control that displays project information. After the user has selected a specific cell and then clicked on the Edit button, the form presents the edit control, located on top of the current cell, as shown in Figure 8.15.

We should mention here that although the `TextBox` control is colocated with the `CurrentCell` object, they are not tied together. This will become obvious to the user if he or she now scrolls the `DataGrid` control. The cells of the `DataGrid` will move, but the `TextBox` will not, resulting in the display shown in Figure 8.16.

We begin our application code by declaring a variable that will hold a reference to the input `TextBox` control, as shown in Listing 8.16.

LISTING 8.16: The Start of the Manual In-Place Editing Program

```
using System;
using System.Drawing;
using System.Collections;
```

```
using System.Windows.Forms;
using System.Data;
using YaoDurant.Data;
using YaoDurant.GUI;

namespace InPlaceEditManual
{
   public class FormMain : System.Windows.Forms.Form
   {
      internal System.Windows.Forms.Label Label1;
      internal System.Windows.Forms.Panel Panel1;
      internal System.Windows.Forms.Button cmdCancel;
      internal System.Windows.Forms.Button cmdUpdate;
      internal System.Windows.Forms.Button cmdEdit;
      private System.Windows.Forms.DataGrid dgrdProjects;
      private System.Windows.Forms.MainMenu mainMenu1;

      public FormMain()
      {
         InitializeComponent();
      }
      protected override void Dispose( bool disposing )
      {
         base.Dispose( disposing );
      }
      #region Windows Form Designer generated code

      static void Main()
      {
         Application.Run(new FormMain());
      }

      //  A TextBox control to be used for in-place editing
      private TextBox textEdit;
```

In the form's `Load` event we bind the `Projects DataTable` to the `DataGrid` control and then apply the styling. Then we create our `TextBox` control and add it to the `DataGrid`'s controls collection. We want the `TextBox` to be contained within the `DataGrid`, not the form, because we want to position the `TextBox` using `DataGrid` coordinates and we want to ensure that when the `DataGrid` is not visible, the `TextBox` also is not visible. Finally, we set the application state to "Not Editing." Listing 8.17 shows the code.

LISTING 8.17: The Form's Load Event Handler

```
private void FormMain_Load(object sender, EventArgs e)
{
   //  Make the Projects table the DataSource.
   YaoDurant.Data.UtilData  utilData = new UtilData();
   dgrdProjects.DataSource = utilData.GetProjectsDT();

   //  Use a utility routine to style the
   //      layout of Projects in the DataGrid.
   UtilGUI.AddCustomDataTableStyle(dgrdProjects,
                                   "Projects");

   //  Create the TextBox to be used with in-place
   //      editing and add it to the DataGrid control.
   textEdit = new TextBox();
   textEdit.Visible = false;
   this.dgrdProjects.Controls.Add(textEdit);

   //  Set the form's GUI state to "Not Editing."
   this.SetEditingState(false);
```

As shown in Listing 8.18, when the user taps on the Edit button, we check to see if he or she is attempting to edit the read-only `ctTasks` field. If so, we display a message box informing the user that the field cannot be edited; otherwise, we position the `TextBox` control within the bounds of the `CurrentCell` object, load the contents of the `CurrentCell` into the `TextBox`, highlight the `TextBox`, show it, set the focus to it, and set the application state to "Editing."

LISTING 8.18: Initiating Editing by Displaying the `TextBox` Control

```
private void cmdEdit_Click(object sender, EventArgs e)
{
   //  Check the DataSource column's name;
   //      if it is ctTasks, do not update.
   DataGridCell cellCurr = dgrdProjects.CurrentCell;
   if ( dgrdProjects.TableStyles["Projects"].
            GridColumnStyles[cellCurr.ColumnNumber].
               MappingName == "ctTasks" )
   {
      MessageBox.Show("Count of tasks only changes as" +
                      " the result of adding / removing" +
                      " a task.");
      return;
   }
```

```
    //  Position textEdit for in-place editing.
    textEdit.Bounds = dgrdProjects.GetCellBounds(
                            cellCurr.RowNumber,
                            cellCurr.ColumnNumber);

    //  Load the CurrentCell's value into textEdit.
    textEdit.Text = dgrdProjects[
                      cellCurr.RowNumber,
                      cellCurr.ColumnNumber].ToString();

    //  Highlight the text.
    textEdit.SelectAll();

    //  Show textEdit and set the focus to it.
    textEdit.Visible = true;
    textEdit.Focus();

    //  Set the form's GUI state to "Editing."
    this.SetEditingState(true);
}
```

When the user clicks the Update button, we set the contents of the `CurrentCell` object to `textEdit.Text` and set the application state to "Not Editing." Data binding automatically updates the bound data object's data element for us.

```
private void cmdUpdate_Click(object sender, EventArgs e)
{
    //  Move the contents of textEdit
    //      into the CurrentCell.
    dgrdProjects[dgrdProjects.CurrentCell.RowNumber,
                 dgrdProjects.CurrentCell.ColumnNumber] =
                 textEdit.Text;

    //  Set the form's GUI state to "Not Editing."
    this.SetEditingState(false);
}
```

When the user taps on the Cancel button, we simply set the editing state to "Not Editing," as shown here.

```
private void cmdCancel_Click(object sender, EventArgs e)
{
    //  Set the form's GUI state to "Not Editing."
    this.SetEditingState(false);
}
```

Finally, Listing 8.19 shows the routine to toggle the application state between "Editing" and "Not Editing."

LISTING 8.19: The End of the Manual In-Place Editing Program

```
      private void SetEditingState( bool boolInProcess)
      {
         textEdit.Visible = boolInProcess;
         cmdEdit.Enabled = !boolInProcess;
         cmdCancel.Enabled = boolInProcess;
         cmdUpdate.Enabled = boolInProcess;
      }
   }
}
```

So by understanding the properties of the DataGrid control, the CurrentCell object, the styling objects, the data object, and data binding itself, we're able to compensate for the display-only nature of the DataGrid control and provide a data-updating mechanism to the user.

Now let's raise the bar one notch and see what problems we encounter when we try to automate our in-place editing capability (i.e., so the input control automatically appears, with highlighted text, as the user taps, tabs, or arrows into a new current cell; and so the cell being edited automatically updates as the user taps a different cell).

Providing Automated In-Place Editing Capability

For reasons we are about to cover, providing in-place editing capability for a DataGrid control is more complicated than you might expect. Thus, we keep our functional specification as simple as possible.

1. When a cell becomes the CurrentCell object, the colocated TextBox control with highlighted text must appear.
2. The user can cancel the current edit by hitting the escape key when entering text into the TextBox control or by tapping in the row header of the current row and choosing Cancel from the pop-up menu that appears, as shown in Figure 8.17 a little later in this chapter. In either case, the cell will *not* be updated, and the TextBox control will be removed.

3. The user can commit the current update by hitting the enter key when entering text into the `TextBox` control or by tapping in the row header of the current row and choosing Update from the pop-up menu that appears. In either case, the cell will be updated and the `TextBox` will be removed.
4. If the user taps on a new cell while editing the current cell, the old cell being edited will be updated and the edit process will begin at the new cell.

Note: You cannot display a context menu as the result of a tap on the `TextBox` control because `TextBox` controls do not receive mouse messages.

To automate your in-place editing capability, you need to know which events to react to and the sequence in which those events occur. You also need to know that one of those events will occur in the wrong sequence.

When the user taps on a data cell that is not the `CurrentCell` object, the following sequence occurs.

1. The `MouseDown` event is raised.
2. The `DataGrid` control's `CurrentCell` property is set to the new current cell.
3. The `CurrentCellChanged` event is raised.
4. The `Click` event is raised.
5. The `MouseUp` event is raised.

When you automate the presentation of the input control to the user, the correct event to react to is the `CurrentCellChanged` event. This event tells you that the user has selected a new cell, which in turn tells you that you should display the input control for modifying the contents of the cell.

This event sequence doesn't look like a problem, but it is. It is a problem because the `CurrentCellChanged` event is caused by the mouse coming down, not by the mouse coming up. This is different from most other generic mouse-driven events. For example, the `Button.Click`, `ComboBox.SelectedIndexChanged`, and `TextBox.Validating` events are triggered by the mouse coming up, thus assuring you that there will be no subsequent mouse-related activity after you handle the event. This is not the case with the DataGrid control's CurrentCellChanged event.

If the user taps on a cell and you respond to the resulting CurrentCellChanged event by displaying a TextBox control containing highlighted text, that text is not going to remain highlighted for long—the user is about to release the mouse button and the MouseUp event is about to occur. Because your input TextBox control is now located where the mouse is, it will receive the MouseUp-related events, one of which will cause it to unhighlight the text and reposition the text cursor. This is not the behavior you are trying to present to the user.

You might decide to wait until the MouseUp event occurs and then present the TextBox control. That solution will not work because the MouseUp event might never occur; the user might have reached the new CurrentCell object by tabbing or using an arrow key. So, in the CurrentCellChanged event handler you need to know whether the current cell is changing because of mouse activity. In the .NET Compact Framework, you cannot interrogate the status of a mouse except during a mouse event, so you must respond to three mouse-related events: MouseDown, to note whether editing should begin when the CurrentCellChanged event occurs or be delayed until the MouseUp event arrives; CurrentCellChanged; and MouseUp.

If you are editing the CurrentCell object and the user taps on a different cell, the challenge becomes even greater because now you need to close out the editing of the old cell and initiate the editing of the new cell. As we discussed in Chapter 7, the TextBox control's Validating event tells you that the entering of data into the old cell is finished. The problem is that, as we have seen, the CurrentCellChanged event occurs as the mouse comes down, while the Validating event is caused by the mouse coming up. Thus, the event that tells you to close out the old cell arrives after the event that tells you to begin editing the new cell. This means that when you react to the Validating and Validated events, the CurrentCell object has already changed from the cell you need to update to the cell you are going to edit. Therefore, you must save the identity of the CurrentCell object as you begin the editing process so that you will update the correct cell.

But updating a cell makes it the `CurrentCell` object. So now you not only must store the identity of the old `CurrentCell` as you began the edit process but also must store and restore the identity of the new `CurrentCell` as you perform the update.

All of this is why we tried to keep our functional specifications simple. The resulting application (located in the `InPlaceEditAuto` project) is shown in Figure 8.17.

As always, we'll use the same database simulation routines and `DataGrid` styling routine for obtaining and displaying information that we have used in the previous applications of this chapter.

Because we understood the meaning and sequence of the events that we must handle, our code is as small and simple as we can make it. Not as small and simple as the previous application, but considering the issues related to automating the editing process, this code is quite reasonable. The complete automatic in-place editing application is presented in Listings 8.20 through 8.27.

We begin by declaring the necessary variables, as shown in Listing 8.20.

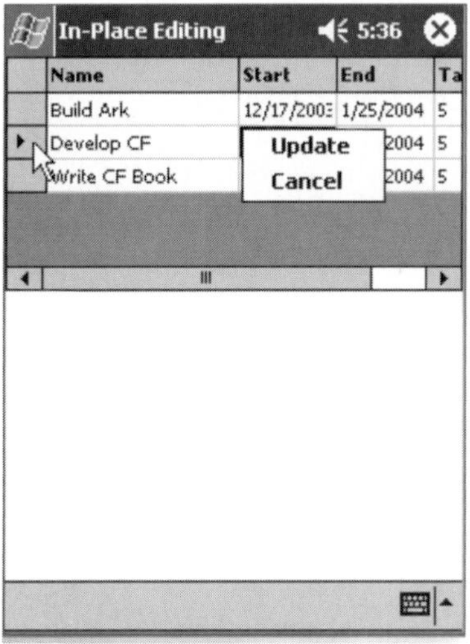

FIGURE 8.17: Committing an update

LISTING 8.20: The Start of the Automatic In-Place Editing Program

```
using System;
using System.Drawing;
using System.Collections;
using System.Windows.Forms;
using System.Data;
using System.ComponentModel;
using YaoDurant.Data;
using YaoDurant.GUI;


namespace InPlaceEditAuto
{
   public class FormMain : System.Windows.Forms.Form
   {
      private System.Windows.Forms.MainMenu mainMenu1;
      private System.Windows.Forms.ContextMenu cmenuEdit;
      private System.Windows.Forms.DataGrid dgrdProjects;

      public FormMain()
      {
         InitializeComponent();
      }

      protected override void Dispose( bool disposing )
      {
         base.Dispose( disposing );
      }
      #region Windows Form Designer generated code

      static void Main()
      {
         Application.Run(new FormMain());
      }


      //  A TextBox control to be used for in-place editing
      private TextBox textEdit;

      private MenuItem mitemUpdate = new MenuItem();
      private MenuItem mitemCancel = new MenuItem();

      //  The DataGrid's CurrentCell.  We must save it
      //     because a new CurrentCell may be assigned
      //     before we are finished with the old one.
      private DataGridCell CurrentCell;

      //  These fields are used to determine when
```

```
//     in-place editing should begin.
private bool boolMouseDriven;
private bool boolDoEdit;

//  This field is to track whether the update
//     should be completed or cancelled.
private bool boolCancelUpdate;
```

As in the previous version of the application, in the form's `Load` event we bind the `Projects DataTable` to the `DataGrid` control and then apply the styling. Then we create our `TextBox` control and add it to the `DataGrid`'s controls collection. We want the `TextBox` to be contained within the `DataGrid`, not within the form, because we want to position the `TextBox` using `DataGrid` coordinates and we want to ensure that when the `DataGrid` is not visible, the `TextBox` also is not visible. We also build the context menu at this time. Listing 8.21 shows the code.

LISTING 8.21: The Form's Load Event Handler

```
private void FormMain_Load(object sender, EventArgs e)
{
   //  Make the Projects table the DataSource.
   YaoDurant.Data.UtilData  utilData = new UtilData();
   dgrdProjects.DataSource = utilData.GetProjectsDT();

   //  Use a utility routine to style the
   //     layout of Projects in the DataGrid.
   UtilGUI.AddCustomDataTableStyle(dgrdProjects,
      "Projects");

   //  Create the TextBox to be used with in-place
   //     editing and add it to the DataGrid control.
   textEdit = new TextBox();
   textEdit.Visible = false;
   this.dgrdProjects.Controls.Add(textEdit);

   //  Initialize the Update/Cancel context menu.
   this.InitContextMenu();

   //  The default is:  Do the update.
   this.boolCancelUpdate = false;
}
```

In the MouseDown event handler, shown in Listing 8.22, we decide whether the context menu should be displayed and also note that mouse activity is in process.

LISTING 8.22: The MouseDown Event Handler

```
private void dgrdProjects_MouseDown(object sender,
                                    MouseEventArgs e)
{
   //  If editing is in progress
   if( textEdit.Visible && e.Button == MouseButtons.Right )
   {
      //  If the user tapped in the row header of the row
      //     being edited, display the Update/Cancel
      //     context menu to the user.
      if( dgrdProjects.HitTest(e.X, e.Y).Type ==
          DataGrid.HitTestType.RowHeader
      &&  dgrdProjects.HitTest(e.X, e.Y).Row ==
          dgrdProjects.CurrentRowIndex )
      {
         cmenuEdit.Show(textEdit, new Point(0, 0));
      }
   }

   //  When the user taps on a data cell or a row
   //     header, the current cell will change.
   //     Our CurrentCellChanged event will need to
   //     know that this was caused by a mouse tap,
   //     rather than by a tab or programmatically.
   boolMouseDriven =
      ( (dgrdProjects.HitTest(e.X, e.Y).Type ==
         DataGrid.HitTestType.Cell)
      ||
        (dgrdProjects.HitTest(e.X, e.Y).Type ==
         DataGrid.HitTestType.RowHeader) );
}
```

In the CurrentCellChanged event handler, shown in Listing 8.23, we decide whether to begin the editing process or to defer it until the ButtonUp event arrives.

LISTING 8.23: The CurrentCellChanged Event Handler

```
private void dgrdProjects_CurrentCellChanged(object sender,
                                             EventArgs e)
{
```

```
      // If this is a mouse-caused event, we must wait
      //    for the Click and MouseUp events to complete
      //    before displaying the edit TextBox.  If not
      //    caused by a mouse, we can display the edit TextBox
      //    after this message has completed processing.
      if ( boolMouseDriven )
      {
         boolDoEdit = true;
      }
      else
      {
         this.InitEdit();
      }
      boolMouseDriven = false;
   }
```

In the `MouseUp` event handler, we begin the editing process, if needed.

```
   private void dgrdProjects_MouseUp(object sender,
                                     MouseEventArgs e)
   {
      //  If editing has been requested, we need
      //     to display textEdit to the user.
      if ( boolDoEdit )
      {
         this.InitEdit();
      }
   }
```

In the event handlers related to the two methods we gave the user for committing and canceling the edit, we note whether *commit* or *cancel* was requested and then hide the edit `TextBox` control, which will result in the `TextBox`'s `Validating` event being fired. Listing 8.24 shows the code.

LISTING 8.24: The Context Menu's `MenuItem_Click` Event Handler

```
   private void MenuItem_Click(object sender,
                               EventArgs e)
   {
      //  Note which was requested.
      //  Hide the edit TextBox.
      this.boolCancelUpdate = (sender == mitemCancel);
      textEdit.Visible = false;
   }
```

continues

continued

```
private void textEdit_KeyUp(object sender,
   KeyEventArgs e)
{
   //  Check to see if the keystroke was enter or escape.
   switch (e.KeyCode)
   {
      case Keys.Enter:
         this.boolCancelUpdate = true;
         textEdit.Visible = false;
         break;
      case Keys.Escape:
         this.boolCancelUpdate = false;
         textEdit.Visible = false;
         break;
      default:
         break;
   }
}
```

When the `Validating` event arrives, we check to see whether we should update or cancel and proceed accordingly.

```
private void textEdit_Validating(object sender,
                                 CancelEventArgs e)
{
   //  To cancel or not to cancel,
   //     that is the question.
   e.Cancel = boolCancelUpdate;
   boolCancelUpdate = false;
}
```

Because of what we did when handling the `Validating` event, the `Validated` event will fire only if the update should be done. Performing the update consists of saving the identity of the new `CurrentCell` object, updating the old `CurrentCell`, and restoring the new `CurrentCell`, as shown in Listing 8.25.

LISTING 8.25: The `TextBox` Control's `Validated` Event Handler

```
private void textEdit_Validated(object sender,
   EventArgs e)
{
   //  Do the update.
   //  Two issues must be addressed here.  The cell
```

```
      //      we need to update might no longer be
      //      the CurrentCell; and modifying the contents of
      //      a cell makes it the CurrentCell.  Therefore,
      //      we need to save the identity of the CurrentCell
      //      at the start, update the cell whose identity
      //      was saved during InitEdit, then restore the
      //      identity of the CurrentCell.
      //  Save the identity of the CurrentCell.
      DataGridCell CurrentCell = dgrdProjects.CurrentCell;

      //  Move the contents of textEdit into the
      //      "correct" CurrentCell.
      dgrdProjects[this.CurrentCell.RowNumber,
         this.CurrentCell.ColumnNumber] =
         textEdit.Text;

      //  Restore the identity of the CurrentCell.
      dgrdProjects.CurrentCell = CurrentCell;
   }
```

Our routine to initiate the editing process locates the edit `TextBox` control over the `CurrentCell` object, places the `CurrentCell` contents into the `TextBox`, highlights the text, gives it the focus, and notes the identity of the cell being edited. Listing 8.26 shows the code.

LISTING 8.26: The Method for Initializing the Editing Process

```
   internal void InitEdit()
   {
      //  Add the event handlers.
      textEdit.KeyUp += new KeyEventHandler(textEdit_KeyUp);
      textEdit.Validating +=
         new System.ComponentModel.CancelEventHandler
            (textEdit_Validating);
      textEdit.Validated +=
         new EventHandler(textEdit_Validated);

      //  Position textEdit for in-place editing.
      DataGridCell cellCurr = dgrdProjects.CurrentCell;
      textEdit.Bounds = dgrdProjects.GetCellBounds(
         cellCurr.RowNumber,
         cellCurr.ColumnNumber);
      textEdit.Text = dgrdProjects[cellCurr.RowNumber,
                                   cellCurr.ColumnNumber].
                                             ToString();
      textEdit.SelectAll();
```

continues

continued

```
            textEdit.Visible = true;
            textEdit.Focus();

            //  Save the CurrentCell.  We must save it because,
            //     if the user terminates the edit by tapping on
            //     a different cell, a new CurrentCell will be
            //     assigned before we are finished with the old
            //     one.
            this.CurrentCell = dgrdProjects.CurrentCell;

            //  Set the form's GUI state to "Editing."
            boolDoEdit = false;
         }
```

Finally, Listing 8.27 shows the routine to build the context menu.

LISTING 8.27: The End of the Automatic In-Place Editing Program

```
         private void InitContextMenu()
         {
            //  Add "Update" and "Cancel" entries
            //     to the context menu.
            mitemUpdate.Text = "Update";
            mitemUpdate.Click += new EventHandler(MenuItem_Click);
            mitemCancel.Text = "Cancel";
            mitemCancel.Click += new EventHandler(MenuItem_Click);

            cmenuEdit.MenuItems.Clear();
            cmenuEdit.MenuItems.Add(mitemUpdate);
            cmenuEdit.MenuItems.Add(mitemCancel);
         }

      }
   }
```

Figure 8.18 shows our application after the user tapped on the Name column of the third row, entered "A New Project," and then tapped on the Name column of the first row.

So, having made some good decisions about which events to handle and with an understanding of the cause and sequence of those events, we were able to overcome several challenges and provide an automated in-place editing application using a `DataGrid` control. We can only dream

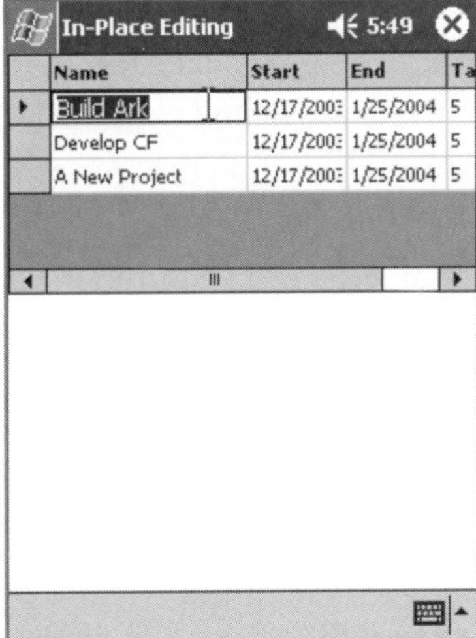

FIGURE 8.18: Moving to a new cell

about how many fewer event handlers and how much less code we would have needed if the `CurrentCellChanged` event had been triggered by the mouse button's coming up and had arrived after the `Validated` event.

The challenge of automated in-place editing is definitely the last challenge we are going to attempt in this chapter, for it completes our coverage of data binding, from complex data binding with `ListBox` and `TextBox` controls to simple data binding with any control to both methods of binding with the `DataGrid` control.

CONCLUSION

Data binding provides a consistent PME-oriented mechanism for staging information that has been retrieved from a database in standard data objects and then associating those objects with the controls used to present that data to the user. It is a bidirectional process, allowing the changes made within the controls to propagate back to the data objects. In Part III we will see how to complete the journey, moving the data between the data object and the database of choice.

Controls vary in their data-binding capability. All are capable of simple data binding through the `Bindings` collection derived from the `Control` base class. Additionally, the list-oriented controls, `ListBox` and `ComboBox`, can take advantage of complex binding through the `DataSource` property. The control developed specifically for binding to a data object, the `DataGrid`, is the most capable and the most complex; it provides for tabular displaying, styling, scrolling, and tracking of the current cell. It is the only .NET Compact Framework control written in managed code.

9

Inside More Controls

This chapter examines more .NET Compact Framework controls and other elements that are useful for creating .NET Compact Framework programs, including menus, toolbars, and dialog boxes. This chapter also introduces `ControlPME`, a tool that detects support for PMEs in the standard .NET Compact Framework controls.

Detecting Support for Properties, Methods, and Events

Visual Studio .NET provides many features that help programmers create, debug, and deploy .NET Compact Framework programs. Woven into these features is knowledge of many aspects of programming: syntax checking helps tag errors even before you build; automatic code generation provides a starting point for your code; and IntelliSense shows available namespaces, classes, and other type information to simplify your code development.

And yet support for .NET Compact Framework controls is incomplete. In Chapter 7, we introduced the expression "Inherited does not mean supported." To minimize code size and maximize performance, some of the PMEs that controls inherit from the `Control` class[1] are not supported by every control. We provide details of the support as we discuss each control, but that support may change in a future version of the .NET Compact Framework. In addition, because of space constraints, this book does not cover all of the .NET Compact Framework controls.

1. Fully qualified name: `Windows.Systems.Forms.Control`.

We asked ourselves how to solve these problems, and the answer was immediately evident: We needed to create a tool to dynamically determine what each control supports. We wrote a .NET Compact Framework program, `ControlPME`,[2] to test controls for support of the various PMEs inherited from the `Control` class.

A Tool: `ControlPME`

`ControlPME` makes a series of calls to test all of the PMEs that each .NET Compact Framework control[3] inherits from the `Control` class. Based on the runtime evidence it collects, `ControlPME` indicates which PMEs are supported and which ones are not supported. Figure 9.1 shows sample output for the `Label` class. This tool verifies that the `Label` class does not support the `Click` event or the `MouseDown` event. Several other events are shown to be supported, however, including the `EnabledChanged`, `Got-`

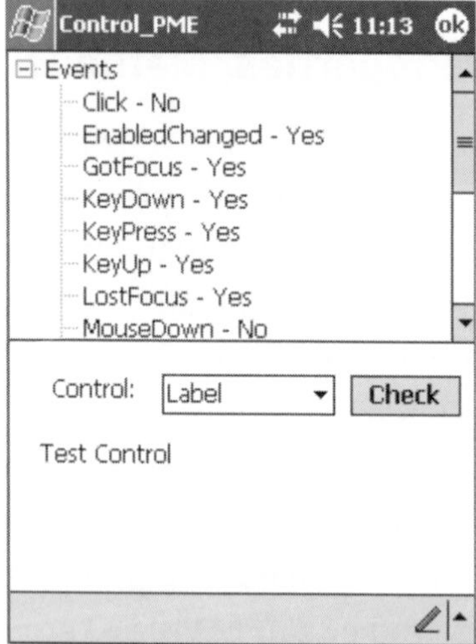

FIGURE 9.1: `ControlPME` showing results for the `Label` control in the .NET Compact Framework

2. This tool is available online with the book's source code at http://www.paulyao.com/cfbook/code.

3. This tool tests only controls derived from the `System.Windows.Forms.Control` class, not the controls derived from `System.ComponentModel.Component` (such as the `Timer` control).

`Focus`, and `LostFocus` events. You can find a copy of this tool in the tools directory, `\YaoDurant\Tools`, with the source code available on the Web site for this book.

A few minutes with `ControlPME` reveals many interesting aspects of .NET Compact Framework controls. In particular, it should save you time by showing what support you can expect to receive for a given control class. For example, this tool shows that only three controls support all of the events inherited from the `Control` base class: the `DataGrid`, `Panel`, and `PictureBox` controls. `ControlPME` also shows that only one control class supports the `CreateGraphics` method, namely, the `DataGrid` control.

.NET Compact Framework Controls in a Desktop .NET Framework Program

As we discussed in Chapter 1, a core design goal for the .NET Compact Framework is consistency with the desktop .NET Framework. One of the benefits of this approach is that a .NET Compact Framework program can run as a desktop .NET Framework program.[4] Figure 9.2 shows our PME tracking tool running as a desktop .NET Framework program.

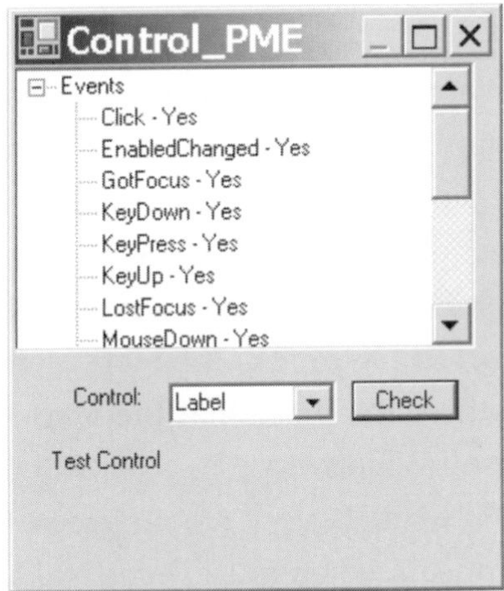

FIGURE 9.2: `ControlPME` showing results for the `Label` control in the desktop .NET Framework

---

4. Running a .NET Compact Framework program on desktop versions of Windows requires version 1.1 of the .NET Framework.

If you compare the output of our tool when running under Windows CE (Figure 9.1) with the same output running on Windows XP (Figure 9.2), you see that the desktop .NET Framework does in fact treat a .NET Compact Framework program as if it were a desktop .NET Framework program. When our tool runs on the desktop, its tests are performed on desktop controls. The desktop `Label` control, for example, supports all of the events. The .NET Compact Framework `Label` control, on the other hand, supports fewer than half of the events it inherits.

Menus

Windows CE supports three types of menus:[5]

- The Start menu
- Program menus
- Context menus

The following subsections discuss these menus.

The Start Menu

The Start menu holds a list of programs that a user can start running with a mouse click (or a stylus tap). The Start menu sits in one of two places, depending on the type of smart device. On a Pocket PC, the Start menu rests in the upper-left corner of the screen (see Figure 9.3).

On non–Pocket PC devices, the Start menu resides in the lower-left corner of the screen. As shown in Figure 9.4, the Start menu on this class of smart devices appears in the same place that the Start menu appears on desktop versions of Microsoft Windows.

On a Smartphone 2003, with its very small screen typical of mobile phones, the Start menu appears when a user requests a list of programs (see Figure 9.5).

5. The Pocket PC adds a fourth type of menu, the New menu, on the Today screen. The .NET Compact Framework does not support this menu type. Adding an item to the New menu requires an in-process COM DLL that supports a specific set of COM interfaces.

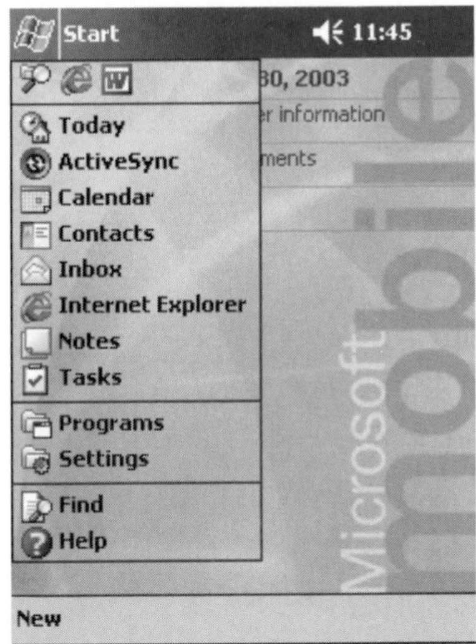

FIGURE 9.3: The Start menu for a Pocket PC drops down from the top of the screen.

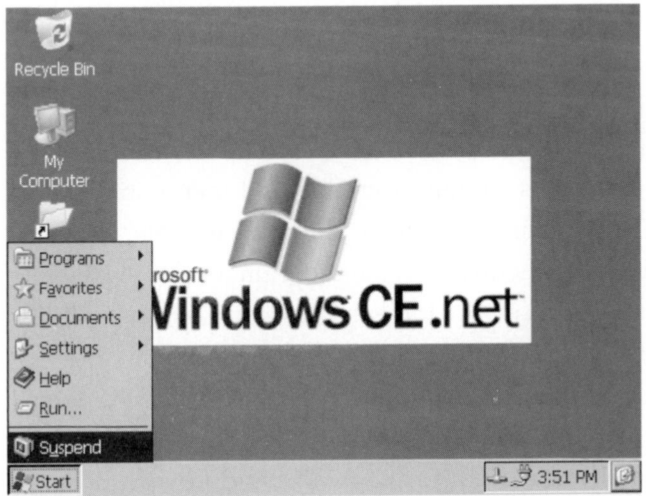

FIGURE 9.4: The Start menu for non–Pocket PC systems starts at the bottom and pops up.

The single biggest difference between the user interface of a Pocket PC and the user interface of other Windows CE systems is in the arrangement of the Start menu and of program menus. The Pocket PC has the Start menu at the top of the screen and program menus at the bottom. This is exactly opposite from what is found on other Windows CE devices, which

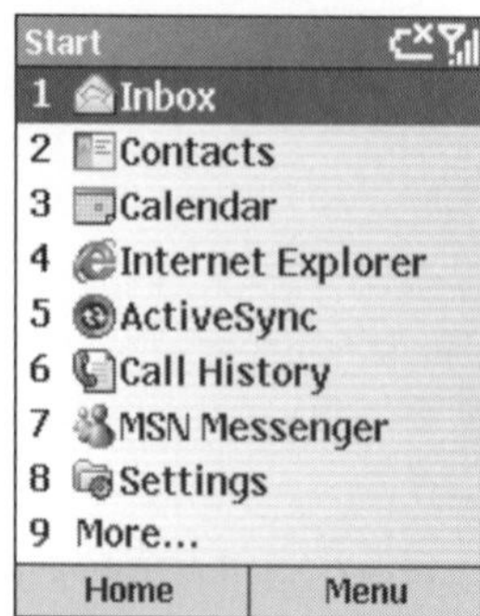

FIGURE 9.5: The Start menu for a Smartphone 2003

have the Start menu at the bottom of the screen and program menus at the top of program windows.

Incidentally, this difference arises from a fundamental design choice that was made for the Pocket PC: It was designed with a stylus-oriented user interface. Consider program menus on the Pocket PC. A user can pick items from program menus without his or her hand obstructing the view of the display screen. That would not be possible with the program menu at the top of the screen.

Of course, when a user picks an item from the Start menu on a Pocket PC, the user's hand covers the display screen. Is that acceptable? Yes, it is. The Start menu is used less frequently than the program menus. And when the user does summon the Start menu, it means he or she is done with the current program and ready to look at a different program.

This is a departure from other Windows CE–powered devices, which are expected to have a user interface more similar to that on desktop versions of Windows, namely, oriented toward mouse and keyboard input. When designing a .NET Compact Framework program, you need to know which type of user interface to target because a mouse-oriented user interface operates differently from a stylus-oriented one.

The .NET Compact Framework has no programmatic support for the Start menu, although a .NET Compact Framework program can be added to the Start menu in the same way that any other program can be added. You do this by copying a program file (or a link to a program file) to a special system directory, `\Windows\Start Menu`.

The .NET Compact Framework supports the other two types of menus: program menus and context menus. We discuss these next.

Program Menus

A program menu is associated with a program's main window. As we mentioned in the previous subsection, program menus sometimes appear at the top of a window and sometimes at the bottom, depending on the device. The system's Start menu is sometimes at the top of the screen and sometimes at the bottom. Figures 9.6 and 9.7 show a program menu for a Pocket PC and a program menu for non–Pocket PC systems, respectively.

Menus are in some ways similar to other types of controls. Like other controls, you lay out menus in Visual Studio .NET with the Designer, adding new menu items and menu item separators within a menu. Like other controls, menu items generate events. Your code that responds to the selection of a menu item does so by handling the `Click` event.

Menus are also different from other controls. All other types of controls are represented by a single object with a single object identifier. A menu, on the other hand, is a container for a set of menu items. The menu itself,

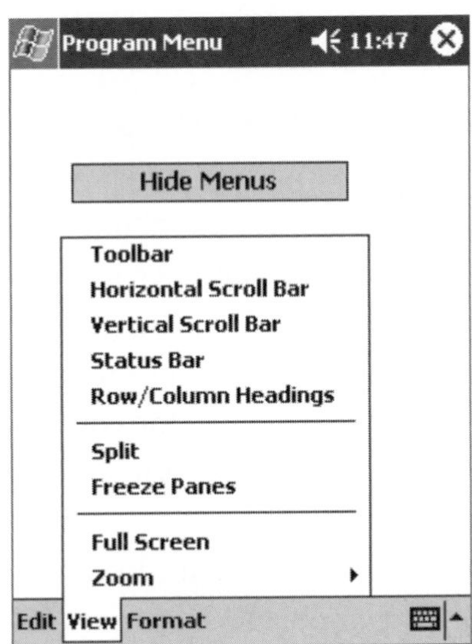

FIGURE 9.6: Program menus on a Pocket PC sit at the bottom of the screen next to the SIP.

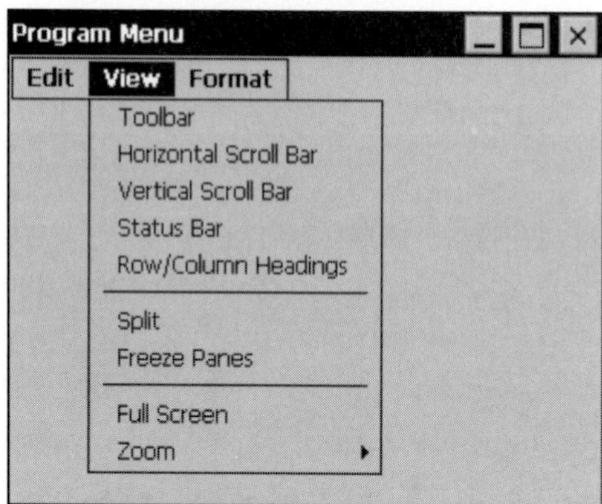

FIGURE 9.7: Program menus on non–Pocket PC systems sit at the top of the program window.

along with each menu item within the menu, is an object—each with its own object identifier.

Menus differ in other ways from other types of controls. Controls like a `TextBox` or a `Label` must live on a form, so with most controls you create them by dragging them from the Toolbox onto a form. You can add several `MainMenu` controls to a form, but only one is active at any time. This gives you the option of having a completely different set of menu items, depending on the state of your program.

The Designer lets you define additional menus that are initially not associated with any form. This flexibility allows you to create multiple menus for a program and to modify the current menu as the program state changes. Switching from one menu to another involves setting the `Menu` property for the desired form.

To be visible to the user, a program menu must be associated with a form. While a menu needs a form to appear, the converse is not true—that is, a form does not need a menu. When a form's `Menu` property is set to `null`, no menu appears in the form.

On a Pocket PC, a form without a menu does not display the SIP. A Pocket PC form without a program menu runs in full-screen mode, as shown in Figure 9.8. In this mode, the SIP is not available. The SIP, it turns out, needs a menu—even an empty menu will do—to appear. (The SIP also

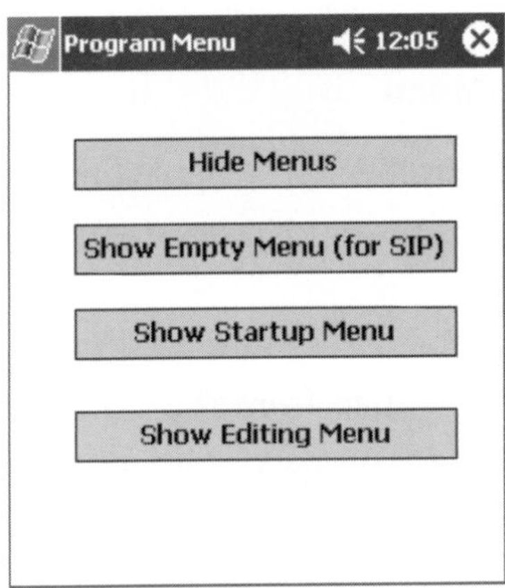

FIGURE 9.8: A Pocket PC form without a menu runs in full-screen mode.

appears when a toolbar—even an empty toolbar—is connected to a form; we discuss toolbars later in this chapter.)

A menu can contain one or more items, and each item can have one of two states: `Checked` and `Enabled`. The `Checked` state indicates whether a checkmark appears next to a menu item. This is useful for letting a user see the current state of some program setting. The `Enabled` state indicates whether the menu is available for use. A disabled menu item appears in grayed text in the same way that a disabled control appears grayed to let a user know that it is not currently active. Figure 9.9 shows five menu items: one enabled, one disabled, one checked, and another not checked. The fifth menu item is a menu separator.

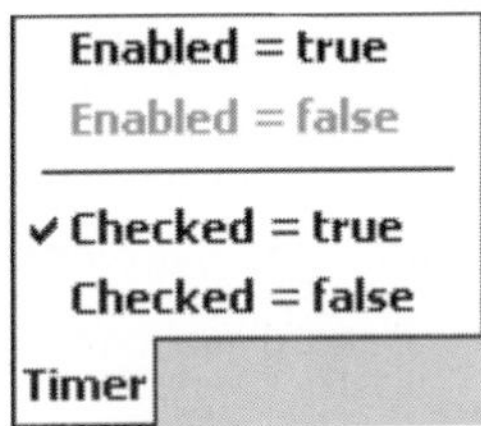

FIGURE 9.9: Various states for menu items

Adding Separators to a Menu

When creating a menu, type a hyphen (-) as the text for a menu item to create a menu separator.

You set a menu item's initial state from the Designer and, like other object properties, get and set these properties in your code in response to changing conditions. For example, the following code toggles the check state for a menu item named `mitemShowName`.

```
mitemShowName.Checked = !mitemShowName.Checked;
```

Program menus are supported by two .NET Compact Framework classes: `MainMenu` and `MenuItem`. You use the Designer to build whatever menu structure makes sense for your program. You programmatically alter the contents of a menu (e.g., adding or removing menu items, changing the state of menu items) as your needs dictate. The code generated by the Designer provides a good starting point for understanding the basic operation of each type of control. This is especially true for menus and menu items.

Menus and menu items represent one portion of a program where we find Hungarian naming (see Appendix A) to be particularly useful. Whether you adopt our naming convention or not, a consistent naming scheme for menu items is particularly valuable when you have multiple menu items.

Renaming Menu Items to Programmer-Friendly Names

The Designer assigns names to each control it creates. The naming scheme is very consistent, but the resulting names are not programmer-friendly. Three new menu items might be named `menuItem3`, `menuItem4`, and `menuItem5`.

We recommend that you rename controls to something easy to remember *immediately* after creating *any* control. This is important because the Designer uses the control name itself as part of the event handler methods it creates. So for a menu item named `menuItem3`, the Designer creates a method named `menuItem3_Click` for a `Click` event handler method. You can rename a control at any time from within the Designer, but doing so after method names have been created for you can cause inconsistencies because existing method are not renamed when a control is renamed.[6]

We use the prefix `mitem` for menu items, and to that prefix we add a more descriptive name for the specific menu item. For the Edit→Copy menu item, for example, we use a name like `mitemEditCopy`. We use the prefix `menu` for `MainMenu` objects and then add a descriptive name to help distinguish the different menus from each other. Our sample program uses the following Hungarian names for the three main menus: `menuEmpty`, `menuStartup`, and `menuEdit`.

A Sample Program: `ProgramMenu`

The sample application, `ProgramMenu`, shows the effect of setting different program menus when running on a Pocket PC. This program has four different buttons, which put the program into one of four different states.

- The Hide Menus button: The main form's `Menu` property is set to `null`. As shown in Figure 9.8, this causes the main form of a Pocket PC program to display in full-screen mode, hiding the SIP.

6. You can rename controls in a .NET Compact Framework program (or controls in a desktop .NET Framework program), and everything continues to work fine. However, if you rename a control in an ASP.NET application after you have written some code, you may break any forms handling code because the Designer does not fix changes to control IDs in the associated HTML. The best practice, which works whatever kind of program you are working on, is to rename a control immediately after creating it and not change the name after that.

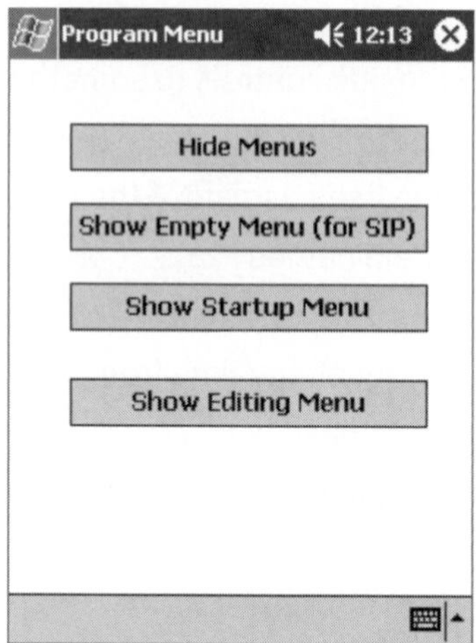

FIGURE 9.10: `ProgramMenu` **application with an empty menu to make the SIP available**

- The Show Empty Menu (for SIP) button: The main form's `Menu` property is set to a valid menu that contains no menu items. As shown in Figure 9.10, this makes the SIP available in a Pocket PC program.
- The Show Startup Menu button: The main form's `Menu` property is set to one menu, as might appear at program startup. With a menu present, the SIP is available on Pocket PC programs.
- The Show Editing Menu button: The main form's `Menu` property is set to a second menu, containing menu items that might contain editing commands (see Figure 9.6). The SIP is available on Pocket PC programs.

Each of the four buttons in the `ProgramMenu` sample application have a `Click` event handler method. These four methods are shown in Listing 9.1. The actual work that is done in each of these cases is to set the value of the `Menu` property for the program's main form.

LISTING 9.1: Setting the `Menu` Property to Set the Current Program Menu

```
private void
cmdHideMenus_Click(object sender, System.EventArgs e)
{
   this.Menu = null;
}
```

```
private void
cmdShowStartupMenu_Click(object sender,
System.EventArgs e)
{
   this.Menu = menuStartup;
}

private void
cmdShowEditMenu_Click(object sender,
System.EventArgs e)
{
   this.Menu = menuEdit;
}

private void
cmdEmptyMenu_Click(object sender,
System.EventArgs e)
{
   this.Menu = menuEmpty;
}
```

A program's main menu is always attached to a program's main form. This is an important menu for a program because it is always available to the user. It provides the backbone of a program's available commands. Programs can also make use of another type of menu to supplement the commands available in the program menu. A context menu can be associated with a form or with a control. We address this topic next.

Context Menus

A context menu can appear anywhere in a program and is not tied to a program's main menu. Context menus are sometimes called *pop-up menus* because they can pop up anywhere; the location of a context menu is based on where the user is pointing. In fact, it is the pointing—whether by mouse or by stylus—that normally defines the context for which context menus are named.[7]

The user action to summon a context menu depends on the pointing device. On a stylus-based, touch-screen device like a Pocket PC, a "tap-and-hold"

7. Pointing normally defines the context for a context menu, but a keyboard interface for context menus exists; most PC keyboards have a context-menu key. This is not, however, a standard key for Windows CE devices.

operation is required (the Tablet PC[8] uses the same action). This action is foreign to first-time Pocket PC users, yet it is an integral part of operating most of the built-in Pocket PC programs. This action is so important that the cold-boot process for a Pocket PC includes a practice session with the tap-and-hold action.

You create context menus in the Designer in the same way you create a program menu. The Toolbox contains a `ContextMenu` object, which you drag and drop onto the Designer's icon area. Like a program menu, a context menu can contain any combination of menu items, menu separators,[9] and submenus. You can create as many context menus as you wish.

Once you create a context menu, you associate that menu with one or more controls. All .NET Compact Framework control classes support context menus, including `Label` controls, `TextBox` controls, and even `Form` and `Panel` controls. At any moment, a control can have only one context menu associated with it. However, you can programmatically create a different assignment—or even assign a control to have no context menu.

Once a context menu is assigned to a control, your work is done because the context menu appears automatically when summoned by the user. You can also summon a context menu programmatically by calling the context menu's `Show` method. Context menus, like program menus, are one of the simplest user interface objects in the .NET Compact Framework.

A Sample Program: `TextBoxClipboard`

This sample program creates a context menu for a textbox. The context menu, shown in Figure 9.11, has the usual menu items you associate with the clipboard: cut, copy, and paste. The .NET Compact Framework itself has no support for clipboard operations, but the underlying Win32 edit control does. We rely on this underlying support to enable the clipboard for our sample program.

---

8. A Tablet PC has a stylus for a pointer, but the stylus activates a subscreen digitizer because the screen of a Tablet PC is not pressure-sensitive. Tablet PCs run an enhanced version of Windows XP Professional, not Windows CE.

9. In version 1.0 of the .NET Compact Framework, a Visual Basic .NET program cannot have a separator in a context menu. The presence of a separator raises a runtime exception.

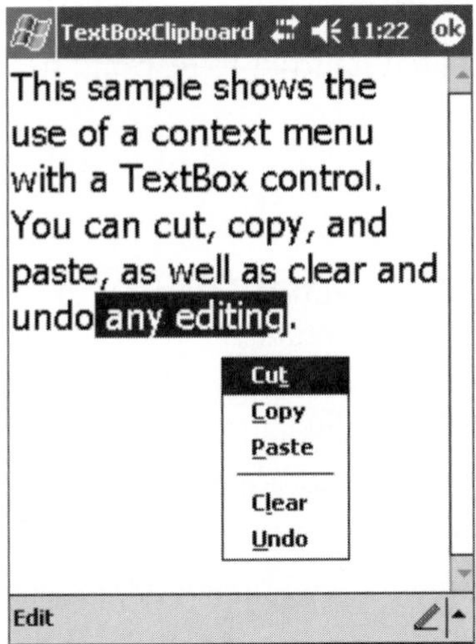

FIGURE 9.11: `TextBoxClipboard` application displaying the clipboard context menu

Our sample program demonstrates three programming techniques:

1. Handling a context menu
2. Using P/Invoke calls for clipboard support in a `TextBox` control
3. Implementing an event grabber (Win32) DLL that fine-tunes the behavior of a `TextBox` control so that the text stays selected when the context menu appears (see Figure 9.11)

The first two techniques are fairly straightforward and are covered in the following two subsections. The third technique is a bit more involved and requires a bit more explanation to make use of it; for that reason, we discuss it in the next section of this chapter.

The Context Menu

The Designer makes quick work of creating a context menu. After a drag-and-drop operation to move a new context menu to the Designer icon area, we create six menu items (the sixth being a separator). We rename each menu item so that the object name reflects the menu command, giving us a set of objects with names like `mitemCut`, `mitemCopy`, and so on. With a few mouse clicks, we create an event handler to respond to the `Click` event for each menu item.

> **Choosing the Correct Native-Code Library for `TextBoxClipboard`**
>
> When you run this sample application, make sure to use the correct version of the native-code library `YaoDurantControls.dll`. We provide two versions with our sample code. The `ARM_YaoDurantControls.dll` file was built for the StrongARM/XScale family of CPUs. The `X86_YaoDurantControls.dll` file was built to run in the emulator on an x86 (IA32) family of processors. Make sure that `YaoDurantControls.dll` contains the version that matches the CPU of your target system.

Our sample also has an Edit menu with the same items found in our context menu. This is not required, but it can be helpful for users unfamiliar with context menus. The tap-and-hold action, after all, is a recent addition to the available user actions in the Windows GUI. The Designer allows us to double-up on the event handlers; for example, the Edit→Copy command and the Copy command on the context menu both get handled by the same event handler.

Clipboard Support in a `TextBox` Control

The .NET Compact Framework does not support the clipboard; that support does exist, however, in the underlying Windows CE system libraries. So we must rely on P/Invoke to drill through to the Win32 clipboard support. There are at least two ways to get clipboard support with a `TextBox` control.

The generic approach involves doing all the work ourselves, with the help of the Win32 clipboard functions. These functions, which have names like `OpenClipboard` and `GetClipboardData`, provide the greatest flexibility in accessing all the features and all the data formats supported by the clipboard. That flexibility comes at a cost, however, in terms of extra work and extra function calls.

Thanks to the native Win32 control on which the `TextBox` control relies, a simpler approach is available. The control underlying the .NET Compact Framework `TextBox` is the Win32 `Edit` control, and it has built-in clipboard support. We access this support by sending messages to the control: `WM_CUT`, `WM_COPY`, and `WM_PASTE`.

To send Win32 messages to a control, we first need the window handle for the control. The easiest way to get a window handle is to set the focus to the control by calling the `Focus` method. We then call the Win32 `GetFocus` function, which returns the window handle for the `TextBox` control. We send the actual message by calling the `SendMessage` method of the `MessageWindow` class.[10] Listing 9.2 shows the basic approach to sending clipboard messages.

LISTING 9.2: Sending Clipboard Messages to the `Edit` Control

```
private EventGrabberWindow m_emw;    // Gets grabbed msgs
private EventGrabber m_eg;           // Event grabber
private Microsoft.WindowsCE.Forms.Message m_msg;

// Event-grabber flags
public const int EVENT_KEYDOWN = 0x0001;
public const int EVENT_KEYPRESS = 0x0002;
public const int EVENT_KEYUP = 0x0004;
public const int EVENT_MOUSEDOWN = 0x0008;
public const int EVENT_MOUSEMOVE = 0x0010;
public const int EVENT_MOUSEUP = 0x0020;

// Clipboard messages
public const int WM_CUT = 0x0300;
public const int WM_COPY = 0x0301;
public const int WM_PASTE = 0x0302;
public const int WM_CLEAR = 0x0303;
public const int WM_UNDO = 0x0304;

// P/Invoke declaration
[DllImport("coredll.dll", CharSet=CharSet.Unicode)]
public static extern IntPtr GetFocus();
```

continues

10. Fully qualified name: `Microsoft.WindowsCE.Forms.MessageWindow`.

continued

```
private void FormMain_Load(
   object sender,
   System.EventArgs e)
{
   // TextBox origin is (-1,-1).
   // Adjust TextBox size to available screen space.
   // Add *two* to hide right and bottom borders.
   textEditor.Width = this.Width + 2;
   SetEditorHeight();

   // Set focus to TextBox window.
   textEditor.Focus();

   // Fetch window handle of TextBox.
   IntPtr hwndEditor = GetFocus();

   // Create message structure for sending Win32 messages.
   m_msg = Message.Create(hwndEditor, 0, IntPtr.Zero,
      IntPtr.Zero);

   // MessageWindow-derived object receives MouseDown.
   m_emw = new EventGrabberWindow(textEditor, hwndEditor);

   // Event grabber sends MouseDown event.
   m_eg = new EventGrabber(hwndEditor, m_emw,
      EVENT_MOUSEDOWN );
}

private void FormMain_Closed(
   object sender,
   System.EventArgs e)
{
   // Clean up event grabber.
   m_eg.Dispose();
}

private void SetEditorHeight()
{
   if (sipMain.Enabled)
      textEditor.Height = sipMain.VisibleDesktop.Height + 2;
   else
      textEditor.Height = this.Height + 2;
}

private void sipMain_EnabledChanged(
   object sender,
   System.EventArgs e)
```

```
{
   SetEditorHeight();
}

private void mitemCut_Click(
   object sender,
   System.EventArgs e)
{
   m_msg.Msg = WM_CUT; // WM_CUT does not work...

   // ...and yet Copy and Clear work, so we do that instead.
   m_msg.Msg = WM_COPY;
   MessageWindow.SendMessage(ref m_msg);
   m_msg.Msg = WM_CLEAR;
   MessageWindow.SendMessage(ref m_msg);
}

private void mitemCopy_Click(
object sender,
System.EventArgs e)
{
   m_msg.Msg = WM_COPY;
   MessageWindow.SendMessage(ref m_msg);
}

private void mitemPaste_Click(
   object sender,
   System.EventArgs e)
{
   m_msg.Msg = WM_PASTE;
   MessageWindow.SendMessage(ref m_msg);
}

private void mitemClear_Click(
   object sender,
   System.EventArgs e)
{
   m_msg.Msg = WM_CLEAR;
   MessageWindow.SendMessage(ref m_msg);
}

private void mitemUndo_Click(
   object sender,
   System.EventArgs e)
{
   m_msg.Msg = WM_UNDO;
   MessageWindow.SendMessage(ref m_msg);
}
```

Support for the context menu is built into the `TextBox` control, as it is for other .NET Compact Framework controls. If the `TextBox` control has a context menu assigned to it, a tap-and-hold operation summons a context menu. The built-in support for context menus is what makes them so attractive in the first place. On a Pocket PC, a ring of red dots appears around where the tap occurs to let the user know that a context menu is coming.

As we started to implement the context menu clipboard support for the `TextBox` control, we noticed something odd. Before its context menu appears, a `TextBox` control deselects any text that has been selected. This is not a problem for menu items that do not rely on the selected text. But two of the three standard clipboard operations—cut and copy—operate on selected text. Without selected text, our clipboard support is limited to the paste operation.

The specific problem is that—between the Win32 `Edit` control and the .NET Compact Framework `TextBox` control—the `MouseDown` event (the Win32 `WM_LBUTTONDOWN` messages) always hides the current text selection. To prevent this from happening, we must grab the event before it can be processed, as described in the next section. An additional requirement is that we must not break any other operation of the `TextBox` control nor cause any performance problems.

Problem Fixed with Service Pack 2!

As this book was going to press, we tested our code with the latest version of the .NET Compact Framework, version 1, Service Pack 2. We discovered that the problem described here—the hiding of text selection in a `TextBox` control—has been fixed in Service Pack 2. Needless to say, we are delighted with this development and know our readers will be as well. In practical terms, this means that you do not need to use the event grabber (discussed in the Grabbing Events section) to enable clipboard support for a `TextBox` control if you know that your users are going to be running this version (or later) of the .NET Compact Framework.

But event grabbing is still a useful technique. It allows a Compact Framework program to get access to events that are supported in the underlying Win32 control but not supported in the .NET Compact Framework control. As mentioned in Chapter 7, Microsoft restricted the flow of events in the interest of great performance for .NET Compact Framework controls. Event grabbing lets you override this restriction when you need access to an otherwise unsupported event.

Grabbing Events

In Chapter 7, we discussed how .NET Compact Framework controls support a subset of the PMEs of their counterparts in the desktop .NET Framework. The primary reasons—code size and system performance—are two very compelling concerns. It is hard to argue that these are not important issues because smart devices have a fraction of the memory of desktop systems, and the CPUs in smart devices are slower than those found in desktop systems.

Yet sometimes you'll find (as we did when creating the context menu for the `TextBox` control) that you need just one more feature. In our case, we needed the `MouseDown` event for a `TextBox` control to prevent the control's selection state from changing. One of our friends on the Microsoft Visual Studio .NET team, Mark Cliggett, once remarked that everyone has just three features they would like to have added to the .NET Compact Framework from the desktop, but each person seems to want a different set of features from every other person.

No doubt you will someday need to fetch events that a given control does not support in managed code. When that happens, you must write a native-code library to do the work for you. We wrote our event-grabber code to be as portable as possible to support other events and other controls. We expect you can use our code as a starting point for whatever event and whatever control you need to upgrade.

Our event grabber resides in a native-code library, `YaoDurantControls.dll`. We have a managed-code class, `EventGrabber`, which wraps around the native DLL. The technique we use to grab events is called *subclassing*, a very old technique well known by Win32 programmers. The technique works because each window is associated with one function, known as a *window procedure*, to handle that window's messages. Subclassing works by providing an alternative function—called a *subclass procedure*—which we substitute as the handler for a given window's messages.

The magic of a subclass procedure is that it calls the original window procedure most of the time but has the ability to listen into and modify the calls made to that window procedure. The subclass procedure in our event grabber calls into managed code—via a message to a `MessageWindow`-derived helper—to report on messages of interest. A decision is made in managed code whether or not to send the message to the original window procedure. For best performance, only a small number of messages should be trapped by an event grabber. If you write an event grabber that is "too grabby" (one that grabs too many messages and sends them into managed code), you risk causing performance problems for your program. Listing 9.3 shows the managed-code class that wraps our Win32 subclassing library.

LISTING 9.3: The `EventGrabber` Class

```
// YaoDurant.Controls.EventGrabber.cs - Wrapper class for
// control event-grabber support provided by
// YaoDurantControls.dll
//
// Code from _.NET Compact Framework Programming with C#_
// and _.NET Compact Framework Programming with Visual Basic .NET_
// Authored by Paul Yao and David Durant.
//

using System;
using System.Windows.Forms;
using System.Runtime.InteropServices;
using Microsoft.WindowsCE.Forms;

namespace YaoDurant.Controls
{
   /// <summary>
   /// EventGrabber - managed-code wrapper around a generic
```

```
/// event grabber for .NET Compact Framework programs. Note
/// that this requires an unmanaged-code DLL to work
/// correctly: YaoDurant.Controls.dll.
/// </summary>
public class EventGrabber : IDisposable
{
   private IntPtr m_hwndTarget;
   public EventGrabber(
      IntPtr hwndCtrl,  // Window handle of control
      MessageWindow mw, // A MessageWindow-derived object
      int fEvents)      // Which events to trap
   {
      // We keep a private copy of the window handle.
      m_hwndTarget = hwndCtrl;
      CreateEventGrabber(hwndCtrl, mw.Hwnd);
      SetEventFlags(hwndCtrl, fEvents);
   }

   ~EventGrabber()
   {
      Dispose(false);
   }

   // Required IDisposable method
   public void Dispose()
   {
      Dispose(true);
      GC.SuppressFinalize(this);
   }

   protected virtual void Dispose(bool bExplicit)
   {
      // Explicit call to Dispose from program?
      if (bExplicit)
      {
         // Unhook handler from our program.
         DisposeEventGrabber(m_hwndTarget);
      }
   }

   //------------------------------------------------------
   // Methods implemented in YaoDurantControls.dll
   //------------------------------------------------------
   [DllImport("YaoDurantControls.dll")]
   public static extern int CreateEventGrabber(
      IntPtr hwndControl,
      IntPtr hwndDispatch);
   [DllImport("YaoDurantControls.dll")]
```

continues

continued

```
      public static extern int DisposeEventGrabber(
         IntPtr hwndControl);
      [DllImport("YaoDurantControls.dll")]
      public static extern int SetEventFlags(
         IntPtr hwndControl,
         int flags);
      [DllImport("YaoDurantControls.dll")]
      public static extern int GetEventFlags(
         IntPtr hwndControl);
   } // class
} // namespace
```

The managed-code side of the event grabber is fairly short: it has startup code and shutdown code. The event-grabber startup code is the class constructor, the method named `EventGrabber`. This method receives three parameters: the window handle of the control to subclass (`hwndCtrl`), a reference to a `MessageWindow`-derived object containing the window handle of a managed-code helper window that receives notifications sent from the subclass procedure (`mw`), and a set of flags that identify the messages to trap (`fEvents`). The constructor calls two functions in the Win32 library, `YaoDurantControls.dll`. The first of these functions, `CreateEventGrabber`, creates an instance of a C++ object in the Win32 library. The second function, `SetEventFlags`, lets the subclass procedure know which events are interesting. The flags are defined as follows for the sample program.

```
// Event-grabber flags
public const int EVENT_KEYDOWN = 0x0001;
public const int EVENT_KEYPRESS = 0x0002;
public const int EVENT_KEYUP = 0x0004;
public const int EVENT_MOUSEDOWN = 0x0008;
public const int EVENT_MOUSEMOVE = 0x0010;
public const int EVENT_MOUSEUP = 0x0020;
```

The cleanup code involves one function in the Win32 library and three managed-code methods. The Win32 library function, `DisposeEventGrabber`, disconnects the subclass procedure. This is important because failing to do so can cause shutdown problems for the program. What might seem odd is that there are three cleanup methods:

- The manual cleanup method (`Dispose` with no parameters)
- The automatic cleanup method (the finalize method, `~EventGrabber`)
- The common cleanup method called by the other two (`Dispose` with one parameter)

Are all three needed?

Yes. The `EventGrabber` class wraps a Win32 resource—a subclass procedure—that must be cleaned up. This class demonstrates the standard pattern for such classes. As we discussed in Chapter 3, in the discussion of the garbage collector, the manual cleanup method (`Dispose` with no parameters) allows application code to clean up after itself. But if an application fails to do so, the automatic cleanup method (the finalize method) gets called to make sure that proper cleanup occurs. Strictly speaking, the common cleanup method is not required. But it represents a common design pattern that centralizes the cleanup work in a single method.

Subclassing to Intercept Win32 Messages

Subclassing a window allows complete control over all messages sent to a window. A subclass procedure can handle intercepted messages (a.k.a. "events") in any of several different ways, including the following.

- Deliver a message unchanged to the original window procedure.
- Process the message without sending it to the original window procedure.
- Modify the message and then deliver the modified message to the original window procedure.
- Discard the message.

Among these techniques, the first is the most important: Deliver the message to the original target window procedure. Why? As much as possible, we want to leave a control unchanged, and that means letting messages get handled without changing them. We change only a few messages—for example, in our case we are interested in only a single Win32 message: `WM_LBUTTONDOWN`.

We tried to make our implementation as generic as possible to minimize the amount of work it would take to adapt it to other circumstances. For example, although we are interested in only one message, we added some extra code to show how to intercept multiple messages from a managed-code control. As built, our message grabber is set up for three mouse messages and three keyboard events. It would be a simple matter to extend our event grabber to handle a wider range of events should that be necessary. We also set up the event grabber to support multiple controls simultaneously, with different messages filtered for each control. Listing 9.4 shows the C++ code for the subclass procedures. Listing 9.5 contains the C++ code for a helper class that maintains a linked list of event grabbers. The third key file from this project is the include file, `YaoDurantControls.h`, which appears in Listing 9.6.

There is one limitation to subclassing. You can subclass a .NET Compact Framework control only if the control has a window inside it. Some control classes—such as the `Timer` class[11]—do not have a window and so cannot be subclassed. The controls that you can subclass are the ones derived from the `Control` class[12]; other controls, like the `Timer` class, derive instead from the `Component` class.[13]

LISTING 9.4: The Subclass Procedure for Grabbing Events

```
//--------------------------------------------------------------
// YaoDurantControls.cpp : Supports event-grabber functions,
// which allow a .NET Compact Framework control to receive Win32
// messages.
//
// Code from _.NET Compact Framework Programming with C#_
// and _.NET Compact Framework Programming with Visual Basic .NET_
// Authored by Paul Yao and David Durant.
//
//--------------------------------------------------------------

#include "stdafx.h"
#include "YaoDurantControls.h"
```

11. Fully qualified name: `System.Windows.Forms.Timer`.
12. Fully qualified name: `System.Windows.Forms.Control`.
13. Fully qualified name: `System.ComponentModel.Component`.

```
//--------------------------------------------------------------
// Static data
//--------------------------------------------------------------
EventGrabberList * m_peglist = NULL;  // List of event handlers

HWND m_hwndLast;           // Cache - last window handle
LPEVENTGRABBER m_pegLast; // Cache - last event grabber

//--------------------------------------------------------------
//--------------------------------------------------------------
BOOL APIENTRY DllMain(
   HANDLE hModule,
   DWORD  dwReason,
   LPVOID lpReserved)
{
   switch (dwReason)
   {
      case DLL_PROCESS_ATTACH:
      case DLL_THREAD_ATTACH:
      case DLL_THREAD_DETACH:
      case DLL_PROCESS_DETACH:
         break;
   }
   return TRUE;
}


//--------------------------------------------------------------
// GetEventGrabber - find grabber from window handle
//--------------------------------------------------------------
__inline LPEVENTGRABBER GetEventGrabber(
   HWND hwndControl)
{
   if (hwndControl == m_hwndLast)
      return m_pegLast;
   else
   {
      if (m_peglist == NULL)
         return (LPEVENTGRABBER)NULL;
      m_hwndLast = hwndControl;
      m_pegLast = m_peglist->FindEventGrabber(hwndControl);
      return m_pegLast;
   }
}

//--------------------------------------------------------------
// Helper - the subclass procedure
//--------------------------------------------------------------
```

continues

continued

```
LRESULT WINAPI
ControlSubclassProc(
    HWND hwnd,
    UINT msg,
    WPARAM wParam,
    LPARAM lParam)
{
   LPEVENTGRABBER lpeg = GetEventGrabber(hwnd);
   BOOL bGrabIt = FALSE;
   BOOL bSendIt = TRUE;
   switch(msg)
   {
      case WM_KEYDOWN:
         if (lpeg->fEvents & EVENT_KEYDOWN)
            bGrabIt = TRUE;
         break;
      case WM_CHAR:
         if (lpeg->fEvents & EVENT_KEYPRESS)
            bGrabIt = TRUE;
         break;
      case WM_KEYUP:
         if (lpeg->fEvents & EVENT_KEYUP)
            bGrabIt = TRUE;
         break;
      case WM_LBUTTONDOWN:
         if (lpeg->fEvents & EVENT_MOUSEDOWN)
            bGrabIt = TRUE;
         break;
      case WM_MOUSEMOVE:
         if (lpeg->fEvents & EVENT_MOUSEMOVE)
            bGrabIt = TRUE;
         break;
      case WM_LBUTTONUP:
         if (lpeg->fEvents & EVENT_MOUSEUP)
            bGrabIt = TRUE;
         break;
   } // switch

   // If flag is set, send messages to MessageWindow
   // window in .NET Compact Framework program to deliver details
   // about message.
   if (bGrabIt)
   {
      int iResult =
      SendMessage(lpeg->hwndGrabber, msg, wParam, lParam);

      // Returns whether to send it to original handler.
```

```
      if (iResult == 0)
         bSendIt = FALSE;
   }

   // Pass on to original caller.
   if (bSendIt)
      CallWindowProc(lpeg->lpfn, hwnd, msg, wParam, lParam);

   return 0L;
} // ControlSubclassProc

//----------------------------------------------------------------
// Helper - search for window
//----------------------------------------------------------------
BOOL WINAPI IsOnWindowList(
   HWND hwndControl)
{
   LPEVENTGRABBER lpeg = GetEventGrabber(hwndControl);
   return (lpeg != NULL);
}

//----------------------------------------------------------------
// Helper - install subclass procedure
//----------------------------------------------------------------
BOOL WINAPI
SubclassControlWindow(
   HWND hwndControl,
   HWND hwndGrabber)
{
   if (m_peglist == (EventGrabberList *)NULL)
      m_peglist = new EventGrabberList();    {
   }

   WNDPROC lpfn;
   lpfn = (WNDPROC)GetWindowLong(hwndControl, GWL_WNDPROC);
   SetWindowLong(hwndControl, GWL_WNDPROC, (LONG)ControlSubclassProc);

   m_peglist->AddEventGrabber(hwndControl, hwndGrabber, 0, lpfn);
   return TRUE;
}

//----------------------------------------------------------------
// Helper - uninstall subclass procedure
//----------------------------------------------------------------
BOOL FreeSubclassControlWindow(
   HWND hwndControl)
{
   LPEVENTGRABBER lpeg = GetEventGrabber(hwndControl);
```

continues

continued

```
    if (lpeg == NULL)
        return FALSE;

    // Reset window procedure to original control window procedure
    WNDPROC lpfn = lpeg->lpfn;
    SetWindowLong(hwndControl, GWL_WNDPROC, (LONG)lpfn);

    // Remove item from our list.
    return m_peglist->RemoveEventGrabber(hwndControl);
}

//-------------------------------------------------------------
// Create event grabber.
//-------------------------------------------------------------
extern "C" int
CreateEventGrabber(
    HWND hwndControl,
    HWND hwndGrabber)
{
    // Check that window handles are valid.
    if (!IsWindow(hwndControl) || !IsWindow(hwndGrabber))
        return 0;

    // Check whether we already subclassed this window.
    if (IsOnWindowList(hwndControl))
        return 0;

    return (SubclassControlWindow(hwndControl, hwndGrabber));
}

//-------------------------------------------------------------
// Remove subclass procedure for a specified window.
//-------------------------------------------------------------
extern "C" int DisposeEventGrabber(
    HWND hwndControl)
{
    return (FreeSubclassControlWindow(hwndControl));
}

//-------------------------------------------------------------
// Specify which events to handle.
//-------------------------------------------------------------
extern "C" int SetEventFlags(HWND hwndControl, int flags)
{
    // Check whether window has been subclassed.
    LPEVENTGRABBER lpeg = GetEventGrabber(hwndControl);
    if (lpeg == NULL)
        return FALSE;
```

```
   lpeg->fEvents = flags;

   return TRUE;
}

//----------------------------------------------------------------
// Query which events are being handled.
//----------------------------------------------------------------
extern "C" int GetEventFlags(HWND hwndControl)
{
   // Check whether window has been subclassed.
   LPEVENTGRABBER lpeg = GetEventGrabber(hwndControl);
   if (lpeg == NULL)
      return -1;

   return lpeg->fEvents;
}
```

LISTING 9.5: The Container Class for a Linked List of Event Grabbers

```
//----------------------------------------------------------------
// EventGrabber.cpp : Maintains grabber linked list
//
// Code from _.NET Compact Framework Programming with C#_
// and _.NET Compact Framework Programming with Visual Basic .NET_
// (c) Copyright 2004 Paul Yao and David Durant.
// All rights reserved.
//----------------------------------------------------------------
#include "stdafx.h"
#include "YaoDurantControls.h"

EventGrabberList::EventGrabberList()
{
   m_pegHead = NULL;
   m_pegTail = NULL;
}

//-------------------------------------------------------------
// Add new handler for control.
//-------------------------------------------------------------
BOOL EventGrabberList::AddEventGrabber(
   HWND hwndCtrl,
   HWND hwndGrabber,
   int flags,
   WNDPROC lpfn)
{
```

continues

continued

```
    // Allocate memory for event grabber.
    LPEVENTGRABBER peg;
    peg = (LPEVENTGRABBER)malloc(sizeof(EVENTGRABBER));
    if (peg == NULL)
        return FALSE;

    peg->hwndControl = hwndCtrl;
    peg->hwndGrabber = hwndGrabber;
    peg->fEvents = flags;
    peg->lpfn = lpfn;

    // First time called?
    if (m_pegHead == NULL && m_pegTail == NULL)
    {
        m_pegHead = peg;
        m_pegTail = peg;
        peg->pPrev = NULL;
        peg->pNext = NULL;
    }
    else
    {
        // Last becomes second to last.
        m_pegTail->pNext = peg;

        // Last becomes our previous item.
        peg->pPrev = m_pegTail;

        // New item is now last item.
        m_pegTail = peg;
        peg->pNext = NULL;
    }

    return TRUE;
} // AddEventGrabber()

//-------------------------------------------------------------
// Find handler for control.
//-------------------------------------------------------------
LPEVENTGRABBER WINAPI
EventGrabberList::FindEventGrabber(HWND hwnd)
{
    LPEVENTGRABBER peg;
    for (peg = m_pegHead;
         peg != NULL;
         peg = peg->pNext)
    {
        if (peg->hwndControl == hwnd)
            return peg;
    }
```

```
   return peg;
} // FindEventGrabber()

//------------------------------------------------------------
// Find first grabber in list (cleanup helper).
//------------------------------------------------------------
LPEVENTGRABBER WINAPI EventGrabberList::FindFirstEventGrabber()
{
   return m_pegHead;
} // FindFirstEventGrabber

//------------------------------------------------------------
// Remove grabber for control.
//------------------------------------------------------------
BOOL WINAPI EventGrabberList::RemoveEventGrabber(HWND hwnd)
{
   LPEVENTGRABBER peg = FindEventGrabber(hwnd);
   if (peg == NULL)
      return FALSE;

   // Clean up singleton entry on list.
   if (peg->pPrev == NULL && peg->pNext == NULL)
   {
      m_pegHead = NULL;
      m_pegTail = NULL;
   }
   else
   {
      // Fix up pointer to previous grabber.
      if (peg->pPrev == NULL)
      {
         // Previous item is now head of list.
         m_pegHead = peg->pNext;
      }
      else
      {
         // Previous item gets our next pointer.
         peg->pPrev->pNext = peg->pNext;
      }
      // Fix up pointer to next grabber.
      if (peg->pNext == NULL)
      {
         m_pegTail = peg->pPrev;
      }
      else
      {
         // Next item gets our previous pointer.
         peg->pNext->pPrev = peg->pPrev;
```

continues

continued

```
        }
    }

    // Free memory for grabber.
    free(peg);

    return TRUE;
} // RemoveEventGrabber
```

LISTING 9.6: The Include File for the Subclass DLL

```
//-----------------------------------------------------------------
// YaoDurantControls.h : Key definitions for event grabber
//
// Code from _.NET Compact Framework Programming with C#_
// and _.NET Compact Framework Programming with Visual Basic .NET_
// (c) Copyright 2004 Paul Yao and David Durant.
// All rights reserved.
//-----------------------------------------------------------------

extern "C" int CreateEventGrabber(
   HWND hwndControl,
   HWND hwndGrabber);
extern "C" int DisposeEventGrabber(
   HWND hwndControl);
extern "C" int SetEventFlags(
   HWND hwndControl,
   int flags);
extern "C" int GetEventFlags(
   HWND hwndControl);

//-----------------------------------------------------------------
// Bit-wise flags for the desired event
//-----------------------------------------------------------------
#define EVENT_KEYDOWN    0x0001
#define EVENT_KEYPRESS   0x0002
#define EVENT_KEYUP      0x0004
#define EVENT_MOUSEDOWN  0x0008
#define EVENT_MOUSEMOVE  0x0010
#define EVENT_MOUSEUP    0x0020

//-----------------------------------------------------------------
// Structure holding event-grabber details
//-----------------------------------------------------------------
typedef struct __EVENTGRABBER
{
```

```
    HWND hwndControl;   // Handle to CF control
    HWND hwndGrabber;   // Handle to MessageWindow -- dispatcher
    int  fEvents;       // Events to handle
    WNDPROC lpfn;       // Original window procedure
    struct __EVENTGRABBER * pPrev; // Previous item in list
    struct __EVENTGRABBER * pNext; // Next item in list
} EVENTGRABBER, *LPEVENTGRABBER;

//----------------------------------------------------------------
// C++ wrapper class for event-grabber list
//----------------------------------------------------------------
class EventGrabberList
{
private:
    LPEVENTGRABBER m_pegHead;
    LPEVENTGRABBER m_pegTail;
public:
    EventGrabberList();
    BOOL AddEventGrabber(HWND hwndCtrl, HWND hwndGrabber,
        int flags, WNDPROC lpfn);
    LPEVENTGRABBER WINAPI FindEventGrabber(HWND hwnd);
    LPEVENTGRABBER WINAPI FindFirstEventGrabber();
    BOOL WINAPI RemoveEventGrabber(HWND hwnd);
};
```

Getting Messages into Managed Code by Using the `MessageWindow` Class

The use of subclassing allows us to detect the `WM_LBUTTONDOWN` message in unmanaged code. But detecting that message is just half the work we need done. The other half involves triggering some piece of managed code to display a context menu for a tap-and-hold operation but allowing messages to go to the original control when the user taps without holding.

We deliver the message into managed code with the help of the `MessageWindow` control,[14] which was included in the .NET Compact Framework to help in this exact circumstance (it doesn't appear in the desktop .NET Framework). The `MessageWindow` control provides the only way for native code to initiate calls into managed code. It has no user interface and in fact does not even appear in the Designer Toolbox.

14. Fully qualified name: `Microsoft.WindowsCE.Forms.MessageWindow`.

We use the `MessageWindow` class as the base class for our own new class, which is required to use this class to receive messages in the message handler function, `WndProc`. This function gets called when new messages arrive, packed into a `Message` structure.[15] The new class we define, `EventGrabberWindow`, appears in Listing 9.7.

LISTING 9.7: The `EventGrabberWindow` Class

```
//-------------------------------------------------------------
// MessageWindow-derived class to support grabbing the
// WM_LBUTTONDOWN message (or MouseDown event) from the
// TextBox control.
//-------------------------------------------------------------
class EventGrabberWindow : MessageWindow
{
   private Control m_ctrlTarget;
   private IntPtr m_hwndTarget;
   public EventGrabberWindow(
      Control ctrlTarget,
      IntPtr hwndTarget)
   {
      m_ctrlTarget = ctrlTarget;
      m_hwndTarget = hwndTarget;
   }

   // Message values
   public const int WM_MOUSEMOVE = 0x0200;
   public const int WM_LBUTTONDOWN = 0x0201;
   public const int WM_LBUTTONUP = 0x0202;
   public const int WM_KEYDOWN = 0x0100;
   public const int WM_KEYUP = 0x0101;
   public const int WM_CHAR = 0x0102;

   // Start -- SHRecognizeGesture declarations
   [DllImport("AygShell.dll", CharSet=CharSet.Unicode)]
   public static extern int SHRecognizeGesture(
      ref SHRGINFO shrg);
   public struct SHRGINFO
   {
      public int cbSize;
      public IntPtr hwndClient;
      public System.Drawing.Point ptDown;
      public int dwFlags;
   };
```

15. Fully qualified name: `Microsoft.WindowsCE.Forms.Message`.

```
public const int GN_CONTEXTMENU = 1000;
public const int SHRG_RETURNCMD = 0x00000001;
// End -- SHRecognizeGesture declarations

protected override void WndProc(
   ref Microsoft.WindowsCE.Forms.Message msg)
{
   switch (msg.Msg)
   {
      case WM_MOUSEMOVE:
         break;

      case WM_LBUTTONDOWN:
         int xyBundle = (int)msg.LParam;
         int x = xyBundle & 0xffff;
         int y = (xyBundle >> 16);

         SHRGINFO    shinfo;
         shinfo = new SHRGINFO();
         shinfo.cbSize = Marshal.SizeOf(shinfo);
         shinfo.hwndClient = m_hwndTarget;
         shinfo.ptDown.X = x;
         shinfo.ptDown.Y = y;
         shinfo.dwFlags = SHRG_RETURNCMD;

         if (SHRecognizeGesture(ref shinfo) == GN_CONTEXTMENU)
         {
            Point pt = new Point(x,y);
            Point pt2 = m_ctrlTarget.PointToScreen(pt);
            m_ctrlTarget.ContextMenu.Show(m_ctrlTarget, pt2);

            // We handle event.
            // Do not pass to original wndproc.
            msg.Result = IntPtr.Zero;
         }
         else
         {
            // Tell handler to send to original wndproc.
            msg.Result = (IntPtr)1;
         }
         break;

      case WM_LBUTTONUP:
         break;

      case WM_KEYDOWN:
         break;
```

continues

continued

```
         case WM_KEYUP:
            break;

         case WM_CHAR:
            break;
      } // switch
   } // WndProc
} // EventMessageWindow class
```

The essential parts of a message are the following values:

- `HWnd`: a Win32 window handle that identifies the target window
- `Msg`: an integer value that identifies the message type (e.g., `WM_LBUTTONDOWN`)
- `LParam`: a 32-bit value with additional message-specific information
- `WParam`: another 32-bit value with additional message-specific information

The event grabber responds to one event, the `WM_LBUTTONDOWN` message. On receipt of that message, we call the `SHRecognizeGesture` function. This function resides in a native-code library named `AYGSHELL.DLL`. This library was first introduced in the Pocket PC, although starting with Windows CE version 4.2, this library is available on non–Pocket PC devices.

The `SHRecognizeGesture` function tells us whether the user wants to display a context menu (i.e., whether the user is performing a tap-and-hold operation). A nice feature of this function is that it handles all the messy details that would otherwise be required, such as setting a timer and trolling for other messages.

On return from this function, our event grabber can do one of two things. If the user wants to see the context menu, our event grabber displays the one associated with the single control it knows about. If the user does not want to see a context menu, our event grabber does not display one.

As each button-down event gets trapped, our event-grabber code reports to the caller about whether the button-down event should get passed to the original window. This value gets passed in the message structure's `Result` field. The value that we write in that field gets returned to the subclass procedure in the native-code event grabber. The subclass procedure uses the return value to determine whether to send the event to the control's regular window procedure (`Result = 1`), or whether to consider the message handled and to discard the message (`Result = 0`). It is odd to put a return value into a structure instead of simply returning it. This is no doubt because the message structure itself resides in unmanaged memory, and several extra steps are needed to return control from this managed-code function to the unmanaged code that called it. To avoid losing the return value, then, it gets put in a safe place—back to the message structure that the unmanaged caller originally allocated.

The `ToolBar` and `ImageList` Controls

We next look at the role of toolbars in the user interface of a .NET Compact Framework program. The addition of a `ToolBar` control lets you enhance a program menu with graphical images. Without a `ToolBar` control, a program menu is limited to displaying text.

While a `ToolBar` control lets you add graphical images to your program, there is nothing inherently graphical about a `ToolBar` control. A `ToolBar` control serves instead as a container for a set of controls that *are* inherently graphical: toolbar buttons. What makes a toolbar button graphical is a bitmap associated with the button. The buttons on the toolbar appear to the right of the program menus, as shown in Figure 9.12.

In the context of menus and toolbars, Windows CE supports a feature not available on desktop Windows: the ability to merge toolbar buttons and program menu items. Items in a toolbar do not appear on a separate vertical band on a device display screen; instead they appear as part of the program menu itself. As implemented in the .NET Compact Framework, a program can have only a single toolbar—by which we mean a single program menu with a single set of toolbar buttons on the menu. To someone familiar with the multi-toolbar look and feel that appears in many desktop application programs, the user interface of a Pocket PC program can look sparse. This approach makes sense, however, because most devices have small screens, and merging menus and toolbars makes for more effective use of available screen space.

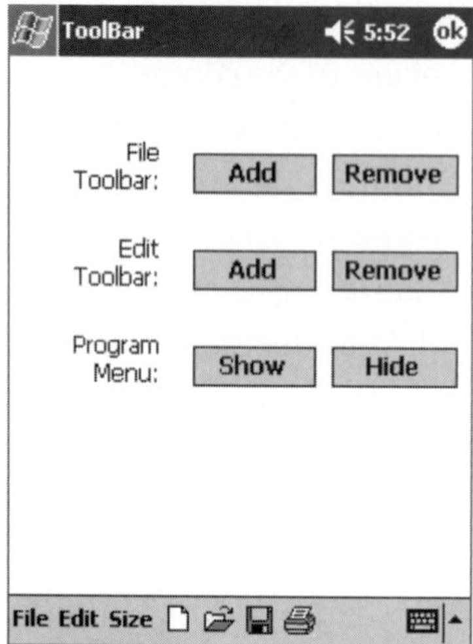

FIGURE 9.12: `ToolBar` **controls add graphical images to program menus.**

The Relationship of Toolbars to the SIP

On a Pocket PC, a form can display the SIP (the `InputPanel`) only when either a toolbar or a menu (or both) are connected to the form. Even a toolbar with no buttons (or a main menu with no menu items) is sufficient to cause the SIP to be visible. As an alternative, a form runs full-screen when the form has neither toolbar nor menu attached to it—that is, when the form's `Menu` property is set to `null` and when the form's control collection (the `Controls` property) does not include a toolbar.

While menus and toolbars are visually merged, each is supported by a different set of .NET Framework classes. As we discussed earlier in this chapter, the `MainMenu` and `MenuItem` classes provide the program menu. `ToolBar` controls, on the other hand, are supported by the `ToolBar` class. Each `ToolBar` control manages a set of toolbar buttons provided by the `ToolBarButton` class. Each button displays a bitmap, and the set of bitmaps for a toolbar's buttons are kept in an `ImageList` control.

Except in the simplest of cases, developing a user interface is an iterative process. Due to user feedback, changing requirements, and scheduling constraints, a user interface changes as a program moves from prototype to final shipping version. Changes require flexibility, and flexibility is what the .NET Framework classes provide when dealing with the various toolbar support classes. In other words, you can develop your images first or your toolbar first—it is up to you.

In this discussion, we start with the `ToolBar` control. Following that, we discuss the `ImageList` control.

Toolbars

A toolbar is a control. Like many other controls, a `ToolBar` control is derived from the `Control` class and so inherits a set of PMEs. The inherited PMEs supported by the .NET Compact Framework toolbars are summarized in Table 9.1.

The most important toolbar event is a toolbar-specific event, `ButtonClick`. This event is not inherited from a base class but rather is defined specifically for the `ToolBar` class. The `ButtonClick` event signals that the user has tapped the stylus (or clicked the mouse) on a toolbar button. The response is similar to the response for the selection of a menu item or for a click on a `Button` control. In other words, the user has requested an action, and that action should start right away. In some ways, then, toolbar buttons are sometimes like elevator buttons—the user expects a response when he or she pushes the button.

Toolbar buttons and `Button` controls are not exactly the same, of course. One difference is where each type of button can be placed: `Button` controls can go on forms and on panels; toolbar buttons can go only on toolbars. Another difference arises because there are four different styles of toolbar buttons: push button, toggle button (like a check box), separator (like a menu separator), and drop-down button (like a push button and a pop-up menu).

`Button` controls and toolbar buttons also differ in the relationship between the buttons and the event handler code. A `Button` control is a stand-alone control, so each button generates a `Click` event to the button's dedicated `Click` event handler. Toolbar buttons, on the other hand, are all part of a `ToolBar` control, and all events for a given toolbar get sent to the `ButtonClick` event handler for the toolbar, not for each button. On receipt

TABLE 9.1: ToolBar Support for Inherited PMEs

Properties	Supported	Methods	Supported	Events	Supported
BackColor	No	BringToFront	Yes	Click	No
ForeColor	No	CreateGraphics	No	EnabledChanged	Yes
Focused	No	Focus	Yes	GotFocus	No
Enabled	Yes	Hide	Yes	KeyDown	No
Visible	No	Invalidate	Yes	KeyPress	No
TopLevelControl	Yes	Invoke	Yes	KeyUp	No
Text	No	Refresh	Yes	LostFocus	No
		Show	Yes	MouseDown	No
		Update	Yes	MouseMove	No
				MouseUp	No
				Paint	No
				ParentChanged	Yes
				Resize	No
				TextChanged	Yes
				Validated	No
				Validating	No

of the `ButtonClick` event, if the toolbar has more than one button, the handler has to determine which button was touched.

The handler for the `ButtonClick` event gets a `ToolBarButtonClickEventArgs` object, `e`, which contains a property named `Button`. To determine which button was clicked, you compare `e.Button` to each toolbar button to determine which was clicked. Listing 9.8 presents an example taken from this chapter's `ToolBar` sample application code.

LISTING 9.8: Determining Which `ToolBar` Button Was Clicked

```
private void tbarFile_ButtonClick(
   object sender,
   System.Windows.Forms.ToolBarButtonClickEventArgs e)
{
   string strButtonName = string.Empty;
   if (e.Button == tbbNew)
   {
      strButtonName = "tbbNew";
   }
   else if (e.Button ==  tbbOpen)
   {
      strButtonName = "tbbOpen";
   }
   else if (e.Button == tbbSave)
   {
      strButtonName = "tbbSave";
   }
   else if (e.Button == tbbPrint)
   {
      strButtonName = "tbbPrint";
   }

   MessageBox.Show("User clicked " + strButtonName +
   " toolbar button. ");
}
```

Two properties of a toolbar are noteworthy:

- `Buttons`: a collection of toolbar buttons
- `ImageList`: a collection of images for use by the toolbar buttons

When you create a toolbar in the Designer, you can dynamically add toolbar buttons by using the ToolBarButton Collection Editor. This tool, which

Tiptoe around the Toolbar

In version 1.0 of the .NET Compact Framework, a toolbar generates a "not supported" exception at some unexpected times. Here are two tips to help prevent you from stumbling into these exceptions.

1. Do not add a second toolbar to a form. A form supports only one toolbar, so before connecting a toolbar to a form, remove any toolbar currently connected to the form.
2. On a Pocket PC, only forms can hold toolbars. Do not add toolbars to panels on a Pocket PC. (On non–Pocket PC platforms, on the other hand, panels *can* hold toolbars.)

appears in Figure 9.13, provides a single place for defining the set of buttons that go on a toolbar. We discuss these next.

Toolbar Buttons

You create toolbar buttons by using the editor shown in Figure 9.13. As with all .NET Compact Framework objects, we rename each button to

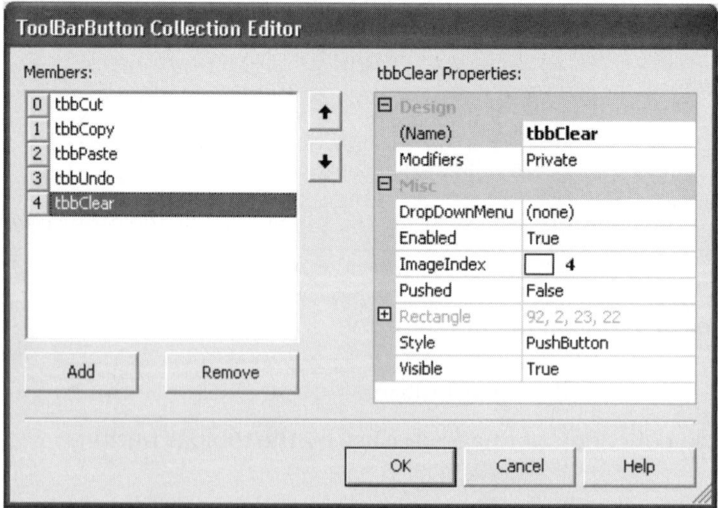

FIGURE 9.13: The ToolBarButton Collection Editor

reflect its role in our program. Using the Hungarian prefix `tbb`, the names of toolbar buttons that we use for clipboard commands are as follows: `tbbCut`, `tbbCopy`, and `tbbPaste`.

There are four types of toolbar buttons, which you select by setting the value of the `Style` property to one of the following values:

- `PushButton`: behaves like a `Button` control in that a click requests an action
- `ToggleButton`: behaves like a two-state `CheckBox` control and is either pushed or not (`Pushed = true` or `Pushed = false`)
- `Separator`: provides visual separation between groups of toolbar buttons
- `DropDownButton`: two objects in one: a button (for requesting an action) and an arrow (for summoning a context menu)

Except for the separator, all styles of toolbar buttons generate a `ButtonClick` event when the user taps (or clicks) on the button. You handle this event in the same way that you handle the `Click` event for other types of controls.

A drop-down button is actually two user interface objects in one. One part is a push button, and the other part is a button with an arrow drawn on it. The push button generates the `ButtonClick` event when tapped. The arrow button, however, does not generate any events. Instead, when clicked, the arrow summons a context menu. At this point, the context menu behaves like any context menu—when a menu item is selected, a `Click` event is generated.

A toolbar button is graphical because it has a bitmap. Unlike other user interface objects, a toolbar button does not have a `Text` property[16] associated with it—so you cannot assign a text label to a toolbar button. Toolbar buttons get their bitmaps from a specialized control that has only one job: organizing bitmaps for other user interface objects. That control, which is required for adding bitmaps to toolbar buttons, is the `ImageList` control.

---

16. The online documentation lists a `Text` property for the `ToolBarButton` class, but that property is not supported in version 1.0 of the .NET Compact Framework.

Toolbar Button Size

An important issue to consider is the size of toolbar buttons. All buttons on a given toolbar are the same size, and that size is determined by the image size of the associated `ImageList` control. The exact behavior depends on whether your device is a Pocket PC or a non–Pocket PC device.

Pocket PC program menus and toolbars are fixed in size, with a height of 24 pixels. The standard size for Pocket PC toolbar button images is 16 × 16, although 18 × 18 images also look pretty reasonable. With images taller than 18 pixels, the image—or the button wrapped around the image—expands so the bottom disappears.

On non–Pocket PC devices, the toolbar height grows to accommodate the height of toolbar buttons. The height of toolbar buttons, in turn, is a function of the height of the bitmaps in the associated `ImageList` control. Unlike a Pocket PC, however, the program menu does not change in response to changes to the size of toolbar buttons.

The difference in the behavior between Pocket PC and non–Pocket PC toolbars is a direct result of the underlying implementation. On a Pocket PC, the toolbar itself is part of the program menu. On other smart devices, the toolbar is a separate object from the program menu.

`ImageList` Controls and Images

The `ImageList` control is one of the few controls with no user interface because it inherits from the `Control` class rather than the `Component` class. So the available PMEs for an `ImageList` control are different from those of other controls whose roles center more on the user interface.

An `ImageList` control serves as a container for bitmaps. Once you load the bitmaps into an `ImageList` control, you access them with a zero-based index. A nice feature of the `ImageList` control is that the control stretches each bitmap to conform to a standard size. You set the requested size by setting the control's `ImageSize` property. Whatever the size of incoming bitmaps, the control stretches outgoing images to the width and height as set in the `ImageSize` property.

Three control types use the `ImageList` control: `ToolBar`, `TreeView`, and `ListView`. You create an `ImageList` control in the Designer, using the Image Collection Editor (see Figure 9.14), which lets you point to the target bitmap files. The bitmaps that you decide to use are then bound to your program as resources and automatically loaded into the `ImageList` control at program startup.

At design time, if you click on the Add button, a File Open dialog box appears to help you pick image files. The Image Collection Editor can read seven types of image files, including bitmaps, GIFs, JPEGs, icons, and metafile files. Whatever the format of the image file you select, the Image Collection Editor converts that image into a format that is compatible with the `Bitmap` class[17] in the .NET Compact Framework. (For details on bitmaps and raster graphics, see Chapter 15.)

Image files can be large, which can create problems on smart devices that have a small amount of storage space. Some formats are compressed and other formats are uncompressed. So what format should you use? No one format works best all the time, so you may need to run your own tests.

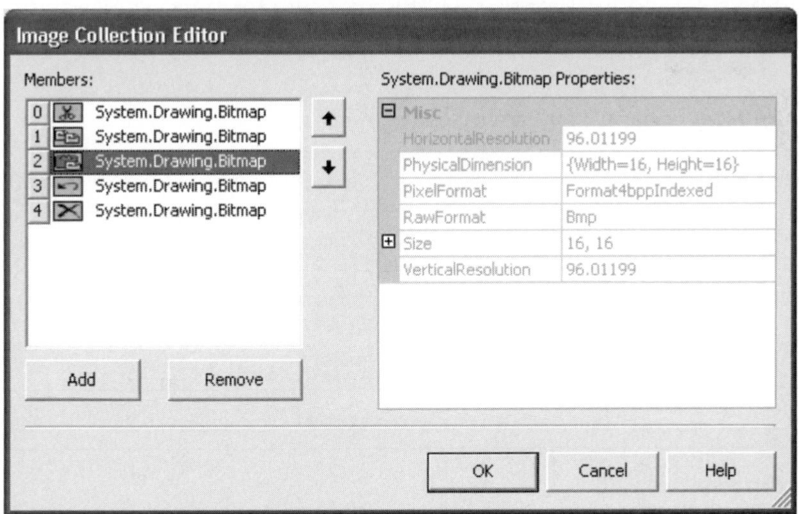

FIGURE 9.14: The Image Collection Editor

---

17. Fully qualified name: `System.Drawing.Bitmap`.

Table 9.2 shows the results, sorted by size, of a simple test we ran for seven images types.

For this test, we created a set of 16 × 16 image files using Microsoft Paint. Each image was a single color, black. These seven file types can be divided into two basic types: uncompressed images and compressed images.

The four uncompressed image types are the ones with a file extension of `.bmp`: 1 bit per pixel (bpp), 4bpp, 8bpp, and 24bpp. These are Device-independent bitmaps (DIBs). As the name suggests, the purpose of the DIB file formats is to provide some device independence to raster data. This means that color information is stored in a standard format: as a set of RGB values. There is a color table for three of the formats (1bpp, 4bpp, and 8bpp). A 24bpp bitmap does not have a color table; instead, each pixel consists of its own RGB triplet.

The presence of the color table makes the 8bpp bitmap file larger than the 24bpp bitmap file. The size of the color table is variable, though, and another image editor could probably store an 8bpp image in a smaller space than the size shown in Table 9.2.

The other three files—PNG, JPEG, and GIF—are the compressed file formats. The JPEG file format was created to compress photographs and should be reserved for that use. That leaves two formats—PNG and GIF—

TABLE 9.2: Size Comparison for Different Image Formats

Image Format	File Extension	Size (in Bytes)
Monochrome bitmap (1bpp)	`*.bmp`	126
Portable Network Graphics (PNG)	`*.png`	149
16-color bitmap (4bpp)	`*.bmp`	246
JPEG	`*.jpg`	631
True color bitmap (24bpp)	`*.bmp`	822
GIF	`*.gif`	832
256-color bitmap (8bpp)	`*.bmp`	1,334

for other types of simple images. As you begin to experiment with different types of images, you may notice that sizes of compressed formats vary with how well the compression algorithm can manage the contents of a particular image.

Where to Get Images?

A common problem is where to get image files. One answer is that you can draw your own. There are several tools available to help, including a bitmap editor in Visual Studio .NET. Or, you can use Microsoft Paint (`mspaint.exe`) or any of several third-party bitmap editing tools.

Another source of image files is the set that ships with Visual Studio .NET. For details, check the end-user license agreement and the list of redistributable files (`redist.txt`). The list that ships with the first two versions of Visual Studio .NET (version 2002 and 2003) is a shorter version than what shipped with previous versions of the compiler, and in particular it does not include any graphic files. Our sources at Microsoft assure us, however, that the graphic files are meant to be redistributed and that a more comprehensive list is being created and should be available in future compiler versions or from the Microsoft Web site.

The graphic files—bitmaps, icons, cursors, and metafiles—are located in the Visual Studio .NET install directory under the `Common7\Graphics` subdirectory.

A Sample Program: `ToolBar`

Our sample application, `ToolBar`, has two toolbars and one program menu. To show the relationship between these three user interface objects, there are buttons that allow you to show or hide each of the items independently. The program also lets you set the size for the toolbar buttons. Figure 9.12 earlier in this chapter shows this sample with a visible program menu and 16 × 16 images on the toolbar with File menu commands. Figure 9.15 shows the

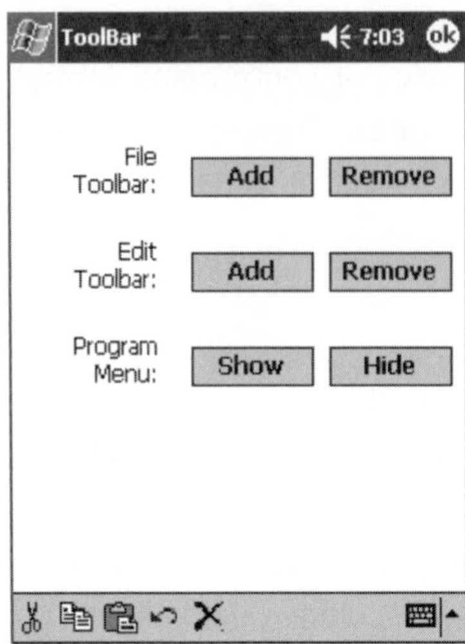

FIGURE 9.15: `ToolBar` application with images on the Edit command toolbar

`ToolBar` program with no program menu and 18 × 18 images on the Edit command toolbar.

A toolbar holds a collection of buttons, but toolbar buttons are not like regular buttons. The reason is that the toolbar buttons are all part of a single control. A regular button, by contrast, is itself a stand-alone control. While each regular button can have its own set of event handler methods, all of the buttons on a toolbar share a single set of event handler methods. This is not a major complication, but it does represent a difference worth noting. The event-handling code for our toolbar sample program appears in upcoming Listing 9.9.

Our sample has two different toolbars, although—as noted earlier—on a Pocket PC only a single toolbar can be displayed at a time. The `ButtonClick` event handler method for all of the buttons on the Edit toolbar is the method named `tbarEdit_ButtonClick`. And when the File toolbar is enabled, all of its buttons send their `Click` events to the method named `tbarFile_ButtonClick`.

On a Pocket PC, if you add a toolbar to a form that already has a toolbar attached, an exception is generated. If you do not capture the exception (using the C# `try ... catch` syntax), this exception crashes your program. Our sample program does not check for the presence of a toolbar when one of the two Add buttons is clicked; nor does it catch an exception. We set this up so you could see the effect of adding a second toolbar in the safe, controlled world of a sample program.

To change from one toolbar to another on a form, you must explicitly remove the first toolbar from the form's control collection (accessible through the form's `Controls` property) before adding the new toolbar. To remove a toolbar, call the `Controls.Remove` method with a reference to the toolbar to remove. To add a new toolbar, call the `Controls.Add` method.

While two calls are needed to change a form's toolbar, to change from one menu to another is a one-step process: just change the form's `Menu` property. This is yet another example of the difference between a form's menu and a form's toolbar. While these two user interface objects are visually linked, they are programmatically very different from each other.

Listing 9.9 presents the event-handling code for our sample program.

LISTING 9.9: Toolbar Event Handling

```
// Remember currently selected toolbar.
private System.Windows.Forms.ToolBar m_tbarCurrent;

private void FormMain_Load(
   object sender,
   System.EventArgs e)
{
   // Disconnect both toolbars, so we always know which
   // toolbar we start with (can change this inadvertently
   // in the Designer).
   this.Controls.Remove(tbarEdit);
   this.Controls.Remove(tbarFile);

   m_tbarCurrent = tbarFile;
   this.Controls.Add(m_tbarCurrent);
}

private void cmdAdd1_Click(
   object sender,
   System.EventArgs e)
{
   Controls.Add(tbarFile);
   m_tbarCurrent = tbarFile;
}

private void cmdRemove1_Click(
```

continues

continued

```
    object sender,
    System.EventArgs e)
{
    Controls.Remove(tbarFile);
    if (m_tbarCurrent == tbarFile)
        m_tbarCurrent = null;
}

private void cmdAdd2_Click(
    object sender,
    System.EventArgs e)
{
    Controls.Add(tbarEdit);
    m_tbarCurrent = tbarEdit;
}

private void cmdRemove2_Click(
    object sender,
    System.EventArgs e)
{
    Controls.Remove(tbarEdit);
    if (m_tbarCurrent == tbarEdit)
        m_tbarCurrent = null;
}

private void cmdShowMenu_Click(
    object sender,
    System.EventArgs e)
{
    this.Menu = menuMain;
}

private void cmdHideMenu_Click(
    object sender,
    System.EventArgs e)
{
    this.Menu = null;
}

private void ResetImageListSize(
    int cxWidth,
    int cyHeight)
{
    this.ilistEdit.ImageSize =
        new System.Drawing.Size(cxWidth, cyHeight);
    this.ilistFile.ImageSize =
        new System.Drawing.Size(cxWidth, cyHeight);
```

```
    if (m_tbarCurrent != null)
    {
        this.Controls.Remove(m_tbarCurrent);
        this.Controls.Add(m_tbarCurrent);
    }
}

private void ToggleMenuCheckMark(
    MenuItem mitemSender)
{
    // Clear checkmark from all other menu items.
    int citems = menuSizePopup.MenuItems.Count;
    for (int i = 0; i < citems; i++)
    {
        menuSizePopup.MenuItems[i].Checked = false;
    }

    // Set checkmark on requested menu item.
    mitemSender.Checked = true;
}

private void mitem12x12_Click(
    object sender, System.EventArgs e)
{
    ResetImageListSize(12,12);
    ToggleMenuCheckMark((MenuItem)sender);
}

private void mitem12x20_Click(
    object sender, System.EventArgs e)
{
    ResetImageListSize(12,20);
    ToggleMenuCheckMark((MenuItem)sender);
}

private void mitem14x14_Click(
    object sender, System.EventArgs e)
{
    ResetImageListSize(14,14);
    ToggleMenuCheckMark((MenuItem)sender);
}

private void mitem14x20_Click(
    object sender, System.EventArgs e)
{
    ResetImageListSize(14,20);
    ToggleMenuCheckMark((MenuItem)sender);
}
```

continues

continued

```
private void mitem16x16_Click(
   object sender, System.EventArgs e)
{
   ResetImageListSize(16,16);
   ToggleMenuCheckMark((MenuItem)sender);
}

private void mitem16x20_Click(
   object sender, System.EventArgs e)
{
   ResetImageListSize(16,20);
   ToggleMenuCheckMark((MenuItem)sender);
}

private void mitem18x18_Click(
   object sender, System.EventArgs e)
{
   ResetImageListSize(18,18);
   ToggleMenuCheckMark((MenuItem)sender);
}

private void mitem18x20_Click(
   object sender, System.EventArgs e)
{
   ResetImageListSize(18,20);
   ToggleMenuCheckMark((MenuItem)sender);
}

private void mitem20x20_Click(
   object sender, System.EventArgs e)
{
   ResetImageListSize(20,20);
   ToggleMenuCheckMark((MenuItem)sender);
}

private void mitem24x24_Click(
   object sender, System.EventArgs e)
{
   ResetImageListSize(24,24);
   ToggleMenuCheckMark((MenuItem)sender);
}

private void mitem32x32_Click(
   object sender, System.EventArgs e)
{
   ResetImageListSize(32,32);
   ToggleMenuCheckMark((MenuItem)sender);
}
```

```
private void tbarFile_ButtonClick(
   object sender,
   System.Windows.Forms.ToolBarButtonClickEventArgs e)
{
   string strButtonName = string.Empty;
   if (e.Button == tbbNew)
   {
      strButtonName = "tbbNew";
   }
   else if (e.Button ==  tbbOpen)
   {
      strButtonName = "tbbOpen";
   }
   else if (e.Button == tbbSave)
   {
      strButtonName = "tbbSave";
   }
   else if (e.Button == tbbPrint)
   {
      strButtonName = "tbbPrint";
   }

   MessageBox.Show("User clicked " + strButtonName +
   " toolbar button. ");
}

private void tbarEdit_ButtonClick(
   object sender,
   System.Windows.Forms.ToolBarButtonClickEventArgs e)
{
   string strButtonName = string.Empty;
   if (e.Button == tbbCut)
   {
      strButtonName = "tbbCut";
   }
   else if (e.Button ==  tbbCopy)
   {
      strButtonName = "tbbCopy";
   }
   else if (e.Button == tbbPaste)
   {
      strButtonName = "tbbPaste";
   }
   else if (e.Button == tbbUndo)
   {
      strButtonName = "tbbUndo";
   }
```

continues

continued

```
    else if (e.Button == tbbClear)
    {
        strButtonName = "tbbClear";
    }

    MessageBox.Show("User clicked " + strButtonName +
        " toolbar button. ");
}
```

Dialog Boxes

Dialog boxes are container windows that play a very specific role in a program's user interface. That role might be to display some status, collect input from a user, or—as often occurs—to both display status and collect input. When that task is accomplished, the user dismisses the dialog box and the dialog box disappears. A typical dialog box, then, is a short-term visitor whose appearance and disappearance are controlled by the user.

The most common way to summon a dialog box is with a user action, typically a menu selection. Following a long-standing design guideline for Windows visual interfaces, each menu item that summons a dialog box has a trailing ellipsis (...) after its name in the menu, which serves as a visual clue to the user that the menu has a dialog box to back it up. In some cases, a dialog box might appear when the user clicks on a button, and once again a trailing ellipsis in the text of the button lets the user know what to expect.

Programs use dialog boxes for a wide range of tasks, such as getting the name of a file to save, specifying the name of a file to open, setting colors, and setting other program settings. A dialog box is built using standard controls and typically has an OK button. If the dialog box can perform any kind of irreversible action, it contains a Cancel button to allow the user to gracefully back away from that action.

One might argue that another use exists for dialog boxes, namely, to serve as the main window of a program. In that case, however, we would not use the term *dialog box* because we reserve that term for secondary windows that support the work of another, main form. We use the terms *main window* and *main form* for a window that in other respects may look and behave like a dialog box. We addressed dialog-box-like main windows in Chapter 5, and that is certainly a valid approach to building a user interface. In this section, however, our focus is on the container windows that play a supporting role in a program's user interface.

Built-in Dialog Boxes

The .NET Compact Framework provides two built-in dialog boxes to handle file-open and file-save operations. In general, it is easier to use a built-in dialog box than to create your own from scratch. Also, by using the built-in dialog boxes, you ensure that your program is able to take advantage of any improvements Microsoft makes to those dialog boxes in the future. In a matter of a few minutes, you can create good-looking results with a minimum of effort. Figure 9.16 shows the built-in File Save dialog box as it appears on a Pocket PC.

In addition to the two File dialog boxes provided by the .NET Compact Framework, Windows CE itself has several built-in dialog boxes. These are not supported directly by version 1.0 of the .NET Compact Framework. However, you can access the built-in dialog boxes through P/Invoke

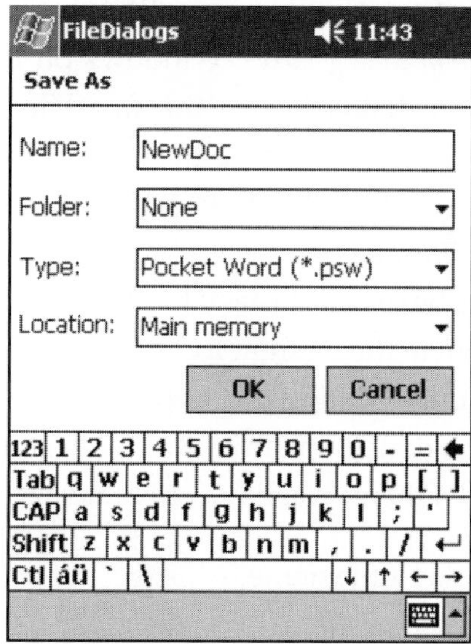

FIGURE 9.16: The File Save dialog box

declarations. Here is a list of some of the built-in dialog boxes available on some Windows CE systems:

- Color common dialog box: discussed in Chapter 16
- Document list dialog box: a Pocket PC–specific dialog box that provides a full-screen alternative to the File Open dialog box; used by both Pocket Excel and Pocket Word; requires P/Invoke wrappers for the Win32 functions defined in the `doclist.h` C++ header file
- Folder name browser dialog box, provided by the Win32 `SHBrowseForFolder` function: duplicates a popular user interface object from desktop Windows; not available on Pocket PC platforms
- Network user interface (`NETUI`) dialog boxes (various): built into the `NETUI` component to support network login as well as network configuration operations
- Page Setup dialog box: discussed in Chapter 17
- Print dialog box: discussed in Chapter 17
- Telephone configuration dialog boxes (various): provided by Telephony API (TAPI) service providers

Two built-in dialog boxes are available from the Toolbox in the Designer, the File Open and File Save dialog boxes. Both are part of a set of dialog boxes known as *common dialog boxes*. Windows on the desktop supports eight types of common dialog boxes: the two File dialog boxes, a font picker, a color picker, two Print dialog boxes, and two text search dialog boxes. Of the five of these that Windows CE supports, two are supported by the .NET Compact Framework.

The two File dialog boxes are so easy to use that you can set up most of what you need for them in the Designer. Once set up, a single line of code is all you need to make either dialog box appear. To set up a File dialog box, you start by dragging a dialog box from the Toolbox, which you then drop onto the Designer. From there, you have only four properties to set up:

- `FileName`: the default file name.
- `Filter`: a string containing pairs of file name descriptions and wildcard values, separated by the `|` character (e.g., `Bitmap Files (*.bmp)|*.bmp|All Files (*.*) | *.*`).

- `FilterIndex`: a one-based index for the initial file filter.
- `InitialDirectory`: the starting path. On a Pocket PC, the File Open and File Save dialog boxes can only view files inside (or files nested in folders below) the `\My Documents` folder.

Once these properties are set up, you make the dialog box appear by calling the `ShowDialog` method, which takes no parameters but returns one of the values from the `DialogResult` enumeration. When the user clicks the OK button, the `ShowDialog` method returns `DialogResult.OK`; otherwise, the return value is `DialogResult.Cancel`. The following code summons a File Open dialog box named `dlgFileOpen` and displays a message box if the user clicks the OK button.

```
DialogResult dlgres =
dlgFileOpen.ShowDialog();
if (dlgres == DialogResult.OK)
{
   MessageBox.Show("File Name is " + dlgFileOpen.FileName);
}
```

Program Performance and the File Dialog Boxes

When you drag and drop either of the two File dialog boxes onto a form, either the `OpenFileDialog` or the `SaveFileDialog`, the Designer generates code that creates the requested File dialog object when the form is loaded into memory. For small programs, this is probably not a major issue. As a program grows, however, you may notice that the load time for the form does take longer and longer.

When performance-tuning a .NET Compact Framework program for faster startup time, you want to eliminate all noncritical startup activities. In such a situation, you might move the File dialog creation code out of the `InitializeComponent` function and create the dialog object only at the moment when you need it.

A Sample Program: FileDialogs

The File Open and File Save dialog boxes get a lot done with a minimal amount of effort on your part. Listing 9.10 shows the `Click` event-handling code for the four standard File menu items: New, Open, Save, and Save As.

LISTING 9.10: Event Handlers from the FileDialogs Program

```
private string m_strAppName = "FileDialogs";

// mitemFileNew_Click - Handler for File->New menu item
private void mitemFileNew_Click(
   object sender,
   System.EventArgs e)
{
   textFileName.Text = "NewDoc";
   textFilter.Text = "Pocket Word (*.psw)|*.psw|" +
      "Pocket Excel (*.pxt)|*.pxt|" +
      "Text Files (*.txt)|*.txt|" +
      "All Files (*.*)|*.*";
   nudFilterIndex.Value = 1;
   textInitialDir.Text = @"\My Documents";

   MessageBox.Show("Resetting fields. ", m_strAppName);
}

// mitemFileOpen_Click - Handler for File->Open menu item
private void mitemFileOpen_Click(
   object sender,
   System.EventArgs e)
{
   // Read current settings from controls.
   dlgFileOpen.FileName = textFileName.Text;
   dlgFileOpen.Filter = textFilter.Text;
   int i = (int)nudFilterIndex.Value;
   dlgFileOpen.FilterIndex = i;
   dlgFileOpen.InitialDirectory = textInitialDir.Text;

   string strResult;

   DialogResult dres =
   dlgFileOpen.ShowDialog();
   if (dres == DialogResult.OK)
   {
      strResult = "User clicked ok.\n" +
         "Filename: " + dlgFileOpen.FileName;

      // Copy file name to our file name control.
      textFileName.Text = dlgFileOpen.FileName;
```

```
    }
    else
    {
        strResult = "User clicked Cancel. ";
    }

    MessageBox.Show(strResult, m_strAppName);
}

// mitemFileSave_Click - Handler for File->Save menu item
private void mitemFileSave_Click(
    object sender,
    System.EventArgs e)
{
    MessageBox.Show("File saved. ", m_strAppName);
}

// mitemFileSaveAs_Click - Handler for File->Save As menu item
private void mitemFileSaveAs_Click(
    object sender,
    System.EventArgs e)
{
    // Read current settings from controls.
    dlgFileSave.FileName = textFileName.Text;
    dlgFileSave.Filter = textFilter.Text;
    int i = (int)nudFilterIndex.Value;
    dlgFileSave.FilterIndex = i;
    dlgFileSave.InitialDirectory = textInitialDir.Text;

    string strResult;

    DialogResult dres =
        dlgFileSave.ShowDialog();
    if (dres == DialogResult.OK)
    {
        strResult = "User clicked ok.\n" +
            "Filename: " + dlgFileSave.FileName;

        // Copy file name to our file name control.
        textFileName.Text = dlgFileSave.FileName;
    }
    else
    {
        strResult = "User clicked Cancel. ";
    }

    MessageBox.Show(strResult, m_strAppName);
}
```

Creating Custom Dialog Boxes

During much of the time you spend building a program's user interface, you're likely to be creating custom dialog boxes or custom controls. A program normally has one main window and several dialog boxes, in the same way that a theatrical play has one lead character and a host of supporting characters. Pocket Word, for example, has one editing window and ten dialog boxes. We discuss custom dialog boxes in the remainder of this chapter. Custom controls are the subject of Chapter 10.

We create custom dialog boxes by using the `Form` class,[18] which is the same class used for a program's main window. At some level, then, a custom dialog box shares common elements with a program's main window. A dialog box and a main window, for example, have a common set of PMEs. The same Designer used for the main window also serves to lay out the elements of dialog boxes; a common set of controls can be used on for both dialog boxes and main windows. In short, everything you already know about the `Form` class, about the Designer, and about controls helps you when you go to create dialog boxes.

There are, however, important differences. Although both are built from the same raw material, a main window stays present as long as a program is running, while dialog boxes enter briefly, do their work, and then exit. And although either type of window can have a menu and a toolbar, their use is typically reserved for a program's main window; to do otherwise risks confusing users. Also, when creating dialog boxes for a Pocket PC, there are additional issues, which we address in the next subsection.

Designing Pocket PC Dialog Boxes

On the inside, running the multitasking Windows CE operating system, a Pocket PC is a multitasking, multiprocess, multithreaded computer. On the outside, though, its small screen means that only one program at a time is visible to a user. All of a program's top-level windows—the main window and every dialog box—run in full-screen mode. Over time, a set of best practices has been adopted that help users navigate through the various full-screen windows and dialog boxes.

---

18. Fully qualified name: `System.Windows.Forms.Form`.

First, every top-level window in a program displays the same text caption. For example, each of the ten dialog boxes in Pocket Word display the caption "Pocket Word," which is also the caption displayed by the program's New Document window and the Edit window. In .NET Compact Framework terms, this means that the `Text` caption for each of these top-level windows is set to the same value. Figure 9.17 shows the Find dialog box from Pocket Word, and the caption—which appears at the top of the screen next to the Start menu icon—is "Pocket Word."

The second element of many dialog boxes in Pocket PC programs is the dialog box's name just below the caption bar. This is different from what you find in dialogs on desktop Windows and for dialogs in other Windows CE devices, in which the caption bar holds the name of a dialog box. Because a Pocket PC program uses the caption bar just for the program name, the task of displaying the dialog box name moves into the *subcaption area*. If you study a few dialog boxes from Pocket PC programs, you will notice that this subcaption area has two elements: (1) the text in blue letters and (2) a line. In our sample programs, we create this effect in response to the `Paint` event by drawing these two elements ourselves.

The third element of a Pocket PC dialog box is the SIP, which of course sits in the bottom-right corner of a Pocket PC screen. A Pocket PC program

FIGURE 9.17: The Find dialog box used by Pocket Word

controls the raising and lowering of the SIP for a dialog box through the .NET Compact Framework's `InputPanel` class, just as you would do for a regular form. As the state of the SIP changes state, events are generated to notify you when the SIP is raised or lowered. (We discussed the SIP more fully in Chapter 6.)

When the SIP keyboard is hidden, only a keyboard button and a context-menu arrow are visible (see Figure 9.17). However, one other important—and entirely invisible—part is needed to make the SIP keyboard button appear: an empty menu (an empty toolbar works just as well). When a dialog box has a textbox, you also want to add an empty menu to make the SIP available to the user.

On the other hand, you might want to disable the SIP and hide the SIP button. Is that possible? Yes. You can create a full-screen dialog box in a .NET Compact Framework program by setting the form's `Menu` property to `null` (and also by not adding a toolbar to the form). Figure 9.18 shows a dialog box from the `DialogBoxes` sample application, with no SIP button on the screen.

A full-screen dialog box has some extra pixels, which can be used for one or two additional controls on a dialog box. This option makes sense in

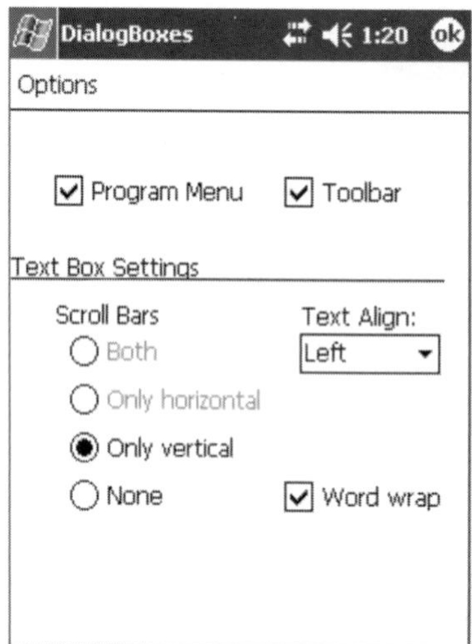

FIGURE 9.18: The Options dialog box from the `DialogBoxes` sample program

two circumstances. One is when your program's active window does not have a textbox, which is the case with the dialog shown in Figure 9.18. A second situation is when an external keyboard is connected to the system. Several makers of Pocket PCs also sell external keyboards (both full-size and tiny-button keyboards are available). Third-party vendors also make and sell these kinds of add-ons (e.g., the Targus keyboard, which one of the authors uses extensively).

Programming Custom Dialog Boxes

When you create a new dialog box in a .NET Compact Framework program, you start by creating a new form. There are several ways you can do this in Visual Studio .NET. Here is one: Select the menu item Project→Add Windows Forms..., and the Add New Item dialog box appears with a request for the name of the source file for your new form.

The new source file has the starting source code for a new class that, like the main form of our sample programs, is derived from the base `Form` class. Like other classes, a dialog box class can have private data members for its own internal uses.

In addition to the private data members, a dialog box class typically also has public data members—either properties or fields. The public data provides a communication channel with the outside world. The initialization of a dialog box involves initializing these data members, then summoning the dialog box with a call to the `ShowDialog` method. This is a blocking call, which does not return until the user has dismissed the dialog box. On return from the call, the public data members contain new values, new preferences, new options, or new settings. The caller uses these public data members to retrieve the results retrieved by the dialog box.

A dialog box class also handles events. At a minimum, the following two events must be handled:

- `Load`: reads the incoming settings and initializes the state of the dialog box controls
- `Closed`: reads the state of the dialog box controls and updates the public data elements

In addition to these two events, a dialog box class might handle any of a wide range of events from the controls within the dialog box. In general, controls are very self-sufficient and can do a lot of work with little outside intervention.

Where the dialog box class may get involved, however, is in the job of coordinating the work of two or more controls. Quite often you see dialog boxes where an action in one control causes some effect in other controls. Consider the File Open dialog, for example. When the user types in a wildcard for the file name—say, `*.abc`—an update occurs in the control displaying the list of files to open, to show the names of files that match the new file specification. This seems automatic and natural to the user, but there is nothing automatic about it. That update occurs because the dialog box responds to a particular event from one control and triggers a response in another control.

Fixing a Pocket PC Task List Problem

As we have been saying, dialog boxes in the .NET Compact Framework are just like forms. Most of the time this is a good thing; a common programming model simplifies a programmer's job. In one respect, however, this similarity creates a problem: A new dialog box gets added to the system task list, which normally includes only the main window of each program.

On a Pocket PC, the task list is called the Running Program List (see Figure 9.19). It is available through the Memory icon in the Pocket PC Settings window. Summon this list with this sequence of user actions.

1. Click on the Start icon.
2. Select Settings.
3. Select the System tab.
4. Select the Memory icon.
5. Select the Running Programs tab.

What is commonly called the task list is really a list of top-level windows. The list itself contains the text of every top-level window. The problem with .NET Compact Framework dialog boxes is that each dialog box shows up on the task list next to the program's main window.

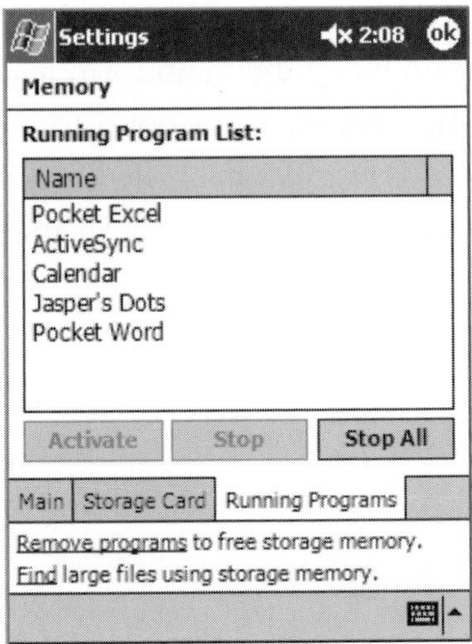

FIGURE 9.19: The Running Program List in a Pocket PC

Is this really a problem? If so, is there a reasonable solution? In studying this problem, we think the severity depends on the platform you are targeting. There is a potential for user confusion on a Pocket PC, less so on non–Pocket PC platforms. We have suggestions for some solutions, and our `DialogBoxes` sample program illustrates an approach that seems to work for the Pocket PC.

What problems does this create on a Pocket PC? In the most common case, there is no problem. By "most common case" we mean the case in which a user summons a dialog box, uses it, and then dismisses it. If, however, a user switches to another program while the dialog box is up, there can be confusion in returning to the correct window. If the user returns by way of the system task list (the Running Program List on a Pocket PC), that user will encounter two windows for the program. And because the caption is the same for the main window and all dialog windows (on a Pocket PC, at least; see the Pocket Word dialog in Figure 9.17), the user does not know which window to return to.

Things work perfectly, however, for users who return to the program through the Start menu or whatever means they had previously used to start the program. So the likelihood of this problem occurring is very low. Yet for the cost of a few lines of code the problem goes away completely.

The basic solution is for the dialog box to hide the main form when the dialog box first appears and then make the main form reappear when the dialog box goes away.[19] The two events to respond to are the `Load` and `Closed` events. Listing 9.11 shows fragments of the two event handlers in question and assumes that somewhere—probably in the constructor for the dialog box class—we have received a reference to the main window (`m_formParent` in this example).

LISTING 9.11: Hiding and Displaying the Dialog's Parent Form

```
/// Dlg_Load - Initialize dialog box controls.
private void Dlg_Load(
   object sender,
   System.EventArgs e)
{
   // Hide parent on load to prevent double task list
   // entries on a Pocket PC.
   m_formParent.Visible = false;

   // ... portions removed
}

/// Dlg_Closed - Copy values from dialog
/// controls to associated public fields.
private void Dlg_Closed(
   object sender,
   System.EventArgs e)
{
   // Make parent window visible when closing.
   m_formParent.Visible = true;

   // ... portions removed
}
```

On non–Pocket PC systems, the problem is less confusing. When a .NET Compact Framework dialog box appears, there are two entries on the system task bar: one for the main window and the other for the dialog box. This does not match the behavior of non–.NET Compact Framework programs, but it does not seem to have the same potential for confusion as on a Pocket PC.

19. We tried to assign the main window as the parent of the dialog box, but the dialog box became disabled and unable to accept any user input.

A Sample Program: `DialogBoxes`

This sample application, `DialogBoxes`, supports two dialog boxes that allow users to control various textbox settings and also various program settings, including whether to display a program menu or a toolbox. Figure 9.18 (earlier in this chapter) shows the Options dialog box, which appears when the user selects the Tools→Options... menu item. A second dialog box, shown in Figure 9.20, appears when the user selects the Edit→Font... menu item. This dialog box allows the user to select the font to use in the textbox.

Creating the Options Dialog Box

Dialog boxes are normally created when a user makes a menu selection. Here are the basic steps for creating a dialog box.

1. Create an instance of a dialog object (`DlgToolsOptions` for the Options dialog box).
2. Set an initial value for data members of the dialog object.
3. Summon the dialog box by calling the `ShowDialog` method, which blocks until the dialog box is dismissed.
4. When the `ShowDialog` method returns `DialogResult.Cancel`, ignore the return value.
5. When the `ShowDialog` method returns `DialogResult.OK`, fetch the dialog object data members that hold desired output values.

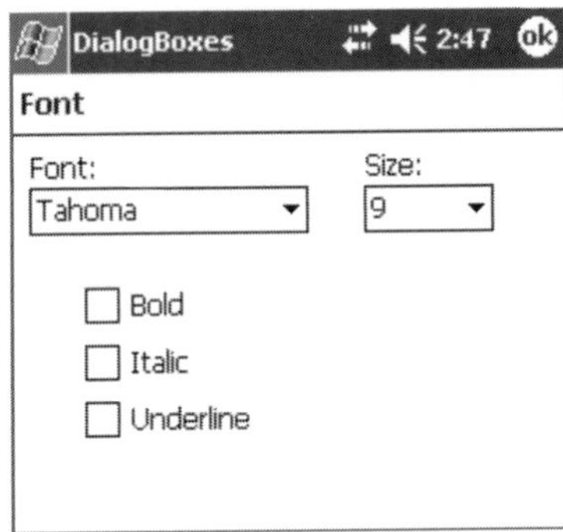

FIGURE 9.20: The Font dialog box from the `DialogBoxes` program

Listing 9.12 shows a `Click` event handler for a menu item named `mitem-ToolsOptions`.

LISTING 9.12: Displaying and Responding to the Options Dialog Box

```
/// mitemToolsOptions -- Respond to menu selection
/// Tools->Options....
private void mitemToolsOptions_Click(
   object sender,
   System.EventArgs e)
{
   DlgToolsOptions dlg = new DlgToolsOptions(this);

   // Get flag for whether toolbar is being displayed.
   bool bHasTB = this.Controls.Contains(tbarCommands);

   // Initialize input values to dialog box.
   dlg.sbScrollBars = textInput.ScrollBars;
   dlg.bProgramMenu = (this.Menu != null);
   dlg.bToolbar = bHasTB;
   dlg.haTextAlign = textInput.TextAlign;
   dlg.bWordWrap = textInput.WordWrap;

   // Summon dialog box.
   if (dlg.ShowDialog() != DialogResult.OK)
      return;

   // Hide textbox to minimize redrawing time.
   textInput.Visible = false;

   // Modify settings based on user input.
   textInput.ScrollBars = dlg.sbScrollBars;
   this.Menu = (dlg.bProgramMenu) ? menuMain : null;

   // Do we need to add toolbar?
   // (Adding a toolbar twice causes an
   //  exception, so we have to be careful.)
   if(dlg.bToolbar && (!bHasTB))
      this.Controls.Add(tbarCommands);

   // Do we need to remove toolbar?
   // (Okay to remove a toolbar twice -- we
   //  do the following to parallel the add code.)
   if (bHasTB && (!dlg.bToolbar))
      this.Controls.Remove(tbarCommands);

   // Update text alignment.
   textInput.TextAlign = dlg.haTextAlign;
```

```
    // Update word-wrap setting.
    textInput.WordWrap = dlg.bWordWrap;

    // Make textbox visible again.
    textInput.Visible = true;

} // mitemToolsOptions_Click
```

Controlling the Options Dialog Box

While inside the call to the `ShowDialog` method, a program's main window is disabled and so does not receive any mouse or keyboard events. (Other types of events, such as the `Timer` event, can be received.) When the dialog box appears to the user, the dialog box class handles all incoming events. In our sample program, we provide event-handling code for the following form-specific events:

- `Load`: sets the initial state of controls from the contents of public data members
- `Closed`: gets the current state of controls and copies it to public data members
- `Paint`: draws the Options subcaption and separator line

Most of the code in a dialog box is straightforward and unremarkable. This is good news because everything you know about forms and controls applies to dialog boxes.

Listing 9.13 shows a portion of the event-handling code for one of the two dialog box classes in our sample application, the `DlgToolsOptions` class.

LISTING 9.13: A Portion of the Event-Handling Code for the Options Dialog Box

```
// Our private data
private Control m_formParent;  // main form.

// Public fields for initial and updated values
public ScrollBars sbScrollBars;
public bool bProgramMenu;
public bool bToolbar;
public HorizontalAlignment haTextAlign;
public bool bWordWrap;
```

continues

continued

```
enum Align
{
   Left = 0,
   Center,
   Right
}

public DlgToolsOptions(Control ctrlParent)
{
   //
   // Required for Windows Form Designer support
   //
   InitializeComponent();

   // Remember parent to help later in cleanup.
   m_formParent = ctrlParent;

   // Set default values.
   sbScrollBars = ScrollBars.None;
   bProgramMenu = true;
   bToolbar = true;
   haTextAlign = HorizontalAlignment.Left;
   bWordWrap = false;
}

/// DlgToolsOptions_Load - Initialize dialog box controls.
private void DlgToolsOptions_Load(
   object sender,
   System.EventArgs e)
{
   // Hide parent when opening dialog.
   m_formParent.Visible = false;

   // Initialize scroll bar settings.
   switch(sbScrollBars)
   {
      case ScrollBars.Both:
         optBothScroll.Checked = true;
         break;
      case ScrollBars.Horizontal:
         optHorzScroll.Checked = true;
         break;
      case ScrollBars.Vertical:
         optVertScroll.Checked = true;
         break;
      case ScrollBars.None:
         optNoScroll.Checked = true;
         break;
   }
```

```
    // Initialize program menu and toolbar settings.
    chkProgMenu.Checked = bProgramMenu;
    chkToolbar.Checked = bToolbar;

    // Set text alignment.
    if (haTextAlign == HorizontalAlignment.Left)
       comboTextAlign.SelectedIndex = (int)Align.Left;
    else if (haTextAlign == HorizontalAlignment.Center)
       comboTextAlign.SelectedIndex = (int)Align.Center;
    else
       comboTextAlign.SelectedIndex = (int)Align.Right;

    // Set word wrap.
    chkWordWrap.Checked = bWordWrap;

    // Initialize constraints.
    UpdateTextAlignConstraints();
    UpdateWordWrapConstraints();
}

/// DlgToolsOptions_Closed - Copy values from dialog
/// controls to associated public fields.
private void DlgToolsOptions_Closed(
    object sender,
    System.EventArgs e)
{
    // Make parent visible when closing dialog box.
    m_formParent.Visible = true;

    // Update scroll bar setting.
    if (optBothScroll.Checked)
       sbScrollBars = ScrollBars.Both;
    else if (optVertScroll.Checked)
       sbScrollBars = ScrollBars.Vertical;
    else if (optHorzScroll.Checked)
       sbScrollBars = ScrollBars.Horizontal;
    else
       sbScrollBars = ScrollBars.None;

    // Update program menu and toolbar settings.
    bProgramMenu = chkProgMenu.Checked;
    bToolbar = chkToolbar.Checked;

    // Update text alignment setting.
    Align iSel = (Align)comboTextAlign.SelectedIndex;
    if (iSel == Align.Left)
       haTextAlign = HorizontalAlignment.Left;
    else if (iSel == Align.Center)
       haTextAlign = HorizontalAlignment.Center;
```

continues

continued

```
   else
      haTextAlign = HorizontalAlignment.Right;

   // Update word wrap setting.
   bWordWrap = chkWordWrap.Checked;
}

/// DlgToolsOptions_Paint - Handle Paint event for dialog,
/// which means draw a line and post name of dialog.
private void DlgToolsOptions_Paint(
   object sender,
   System.Windows.Forms.PaintEventArgs e)
{
   Graphics g = e.Graphics;

   Brush brText = new SolidBrush(SystemColors.ActiveCaption);
   g.DrawString("Options", Font, brText, 5, 5);

   Pen penBlack = new Pen(Color.Black);
   g.DrawLine(penBlack, 0, 25, 240, 25);
}

/// UpdateTextAlignConstraints -- When text alignment
/// changes, update word wrap setting to reflect
/// behavior of actual textbox.
private void UpdateTextAlignConstraints()
{
   // Alignment center or right --
   // turn word wrap *on* and disable.
   if (comboTextAlign.SelectedIndex != (int)Align.Left)
   {
      chkWordWrap.Checked = true;
      chkWordWrap.Enabled = false;
   }
   else
   {
      // Alignment left --
      // enable word wrap.
      chkWordWrap.Enabled = true;
   }
}

/// UpdateWordWrapConstraints -- When word wrap
/// changes, update scroll bar settings to reflect
/// actual behavior of textbox.
private void UpdateWordWrapConstraints()
{
   if (chkWordWrap.Checked)
```

```
   {
      if (optBothScroll.Checked)
      {
         optBothScroll.Checked = false;
         optVertScroll.Checked = true;
      }
      else if (optHorzScroll.Checked)
      {
         optHorzScroll.Checked = false;
         optNoScroll.Checked = true;
      }
      optBothScroll.Enabled = false;
      optHorzScroll.Enabled = false;
   }
   else
   {
      optBothScroll.Enabled = true;
      optHorzScroll.Enabled = true;
   }
}

/// comboTextAlign_SelectedIndexChanged - Handle change to
/// text alignment value.
private void comboTextAlign_SelectedIndexChanged(
   object sender,
   System.EventArgs e)
{
   UpdateTextAlignConstraints();
}

/// chkWordWrap_CheckStateChanged - Handle change to
/// word wrap check box.
private void chkWordWrap_CheckStateChanged(
   object sender,
   System.EventArgs e)
{
   UpdateWordWrapConstraints();
}
```

This Options dialog box shows the typical elements that make up a .NET Compact Framework dialog box class. Two event handler methods provide the startup and shutdown handling: `DlgToolsOptions_Load` and `DlgToolsOptions_Closed`. In general, dialog boxes do not draw on their surface; that work is left to the controls. In the case of a Pocket PC dialog, however, we handle the `Paint` event—in the `Paint` handler method `DlgToolsOptions_Paint`—to provide the standard look and feel that users expect for Pocket PC programs. Many of the other methods shown in Listing 9.13 support the startup or shutdown of the dialog.

While we have suggested that the dialog code is unremarkable, this is not a short piece of code. That is certainly the feedback we get when we present the topic of dialog boxes in our programming classes. The `DlgOptions.cs` source file, for example, is around 350 lines (about half of which appears in Listing 9.13).

The trickiest part of writing code to support a dialog box is figuring out which control-specific events need to be handled. In our dialog box, two such events are handled: the `SelectedIndexChanged` event for the `TextAlign` combobox and the `CheckStateChanged` event for the `WordWrap` checkbox. These two events are used to trigger changes in other controls, to change the valid options available to the user. As we mentioned earlier in this chapter, the proper handling of events like these creates a unified look and feel for an application. Some examples might help underscore why this is so.

In our Options dialog box, the `TextAlign` combobox allows the user to select the alignment in the `TextBox`. Possible settings include `Left`, `Center`, and `Right`. The importance of this setting is that it affects the operation of another `TextBox` property, namely, whether or not word wrap is supported. The reason is that word wrap operates only for left-aligned text, not for the other two alignments. To make this clear to the user, our Options dialog box disables the `WordWrap` checkbox when alignment is not set to `Left`.

Our dialog box must also handle another dependency, namely, that between word wrap and available scroll bars. When word wrap is enabled, vertical scroll bars can be selected, but horizontal scroll bars cannot. The reason is that when text is word wrapped, all words fit into a single column, and horizontal scrolling—and therefore horizontal scroll bars—become unnecessary. We show this fact to the user by disabling some of the scroll bar settings when word wrap is enabled.

The purpose of handling control-specific events is to provide consistency between available program settings and discernable, reasonable changes in program state. Such customizations take time and are the hallmark of well-written GUI programs. Users appreciate such programs because they are consistent with user expectations and because they behave predictably. Such are the types of programs our users enjoy using; and such are the types of programs we think our readers ought to aspire to create.

CONCLUSION

This chapter discussed the controls that help create the command input structure for a .NET Compact Framework program. Users depend on a variety of menus as the most common tool for command input, and this chapter covered standard program menus and context menus. Another common element in a program's command structure is the toolbar, which on small-screen Windows CE–powered devices adds graphical buttons to the program menu. The chapter concluded with a discussion of dialog boxes—windows that have the same basic infrastructure as the main window in a program but that typically spend less actual time on the user's screen.

This chapter also introduced a new way to look at the PMEs that each control supports. We showed you the `ControlPME` tool, which provides an interactive way to test each .NET Compact Framework control for supported PMEs. We showed that this program can also run under the desktop .NET Framework version 1.1, where it can be used to verify some of the differences between desktop controls and .NET Compact Framework controls.

We also introduced and demonstrated the technique of *grabbing events*, which involves subclassing a Win32 control underlying a .NET Compact Framework control to gain access to events that are not otherwise available. We wholeheartedly support Microsoft's goal of making the .NET Compact Framework small and fast, which is the primary reason that access to events is limited. Our event-grabbing technique shows how to reach down into the well of Win32 and bring up a bucket of messages when you find that you absolutely must have an event to accomplish an important task. In our case, we added clipboard support for a `TextBox` control and needed to prevent the selected text from becoming deselected.

Given the overall usefulness and widespread familiarity of the clipboard, we felt the messiness of event grabbing was well worth the results.

In the next chapter, we continue our exploration of programming user interfaces for the .NET Compact Framework with a topic that is central to user interface programming. That topic is, of course, the creation of custom .NET Compact Framework controls, along with the incorporation of those controls into the Designer's Toolbox.

10
Building Custom Controls

In this chapter, we describe how to develop custom controls, including extending existing controls, building composite controls, and creating controls that provide their own rendering. Coverage includes adding animation to custom controls, creating controls for multithreaded applications, and incorporating your custom controls into the Windows Forms Designer Toolbox in Visual Studio .NET. We also present key background information, discuss design issues, and demonstrate recommended coding practices.

Custom Controls

The .NET Compact Framework provides you with a variety of features for creating applications. Included among these features are the controls in the Toolbox. Sometimes the functionality of the built-in controls is not quite enough—almost, but not quite, providing the functionality that you need. In such cases, you can create a custom control to fill the gap. Here are some examples of when you might want to create a custom control.

- You want a `TextBox` control, but one that accepts and displays only dates that lie within a user-specified range.
- You have placed a set of controls on a form to display name and address information and you want to use this set of controls in several other applications.

- You need to accept mouse or keyboard input in a nonstandard way, perhaps to use mouse input to draw a picture or keyboard input to navigate the display of some data.
- You wish to display application-specific information, such as the current state of a game or bar graph that represents the progress of a project.

The .NET Compact Framework handles all of these situations by letting you extend the capability of existing controls. Because all .NET controls, from the universal `Control` base class to its most complex derivation, are object classes, all of them can be extended through inheritance. The key benefit of this is that you can reuse existing objects as if they were black boxes. There is no need to read and analyze other programmers' code in order to add functionality. In development environments where you must understand other people's code, the effort required to extend the application grows linearly (or worse) as the code size grows.

An Opinion: Work versus Results

We find that inheritance provides a good trade-off between effort and results; that is, the work required to add functionality seems to be directly proportional to the amount of functionality. In contrast, environments like Visual Basic 6 allowed you to add functionality very easily until you bumped into a wall, at which point producing additional functionality required great effort because you had to climb over that wall. In .NET the walls are fewer and lower, and the effort seems to us to be roughly proportional to the amount of functionality produced.

You can extend existing controls in three ways.

1. You can derive from an existing control. An existing object, such as a `TextBox` control, does most but not all of what you need. You wish to extend the functionality of this existing object to handle your special case (e.g., a `TextBox` control that accepts and displays only dates).

2. You can create composite controls. The functionality that you want is not found in a single existing control but can be achieved by combining several controls. You wish to package these controls into a single custom control, such as a name and address control, for use in one or more applications.
3. You can create new controls. You need a control that handles input in a unique way, or you need a control that is graphically unique—that is, one that displays information in a manner not provided by any existing .NET Compact Framework control, such as a control that displays the current state of a game.

This chapter provides examples of each approach to creating custom controls. Whatever approach you take, all have this in common: A custom control is always defined as a new class. As such, success in creating .NET Compact Framework custom controls requires you to understand the existing controls and the base classes on which they are built. This is particularly important if you have experience building custom controls for the desktop .NET Framework because the .NET Compact Framework controls are different from their desktop counterparts. In some cases, as we discussed in Chapter 7, the .NET Compact Framework control is a slimmed-down version of what you find on the desktop; in other cases, such as the `DataGrid` control, the .NET Compact Framework control is quite different, having been written from scratch in managed code. In general, .NET Compact Framework controls are more lightweight versions of their desktop .NET Framework counterparts.

Controls as Objects

A key design element of the .NET programming model is its object-oriented nature. Controls—whether built-in or custom—are objects. Because objects are created from[1] classes, to create a custom control you must define a new class.

1. Or "instantiated," in the lingo of object-oriented programming.

Packaging Custom Controls

You have two choices when packaging a custom control: inside a .NET Compact Framework program file (`.exe`) or in a shared class library (`.dll`). Assuming that you have the original source code, you can package any custom control within your program file by adding the source files to your program's Visual Studio .NET project.

One of the benefits of putting a custom control into a DLL is that the control can be shared with other developers. In addition, you must put a custom control into a DLL if you wish to add it to the Visual Studio .NET Toolbox (details of which appear in this chapter).

However, there is more to creating a custom control than simply defining a new class. In this section, we provide some design recommendations for custom control classes and then examine the core elements that custom controls typically provide: the PMEs.

Design Recommendations

The path to success in creating a custom control involves understanding the basic elements of the existing built-in controls. These controls contain many examples of good practices and also show some patterns that programmers expect to find in controls. (We assume that a custom control created by one programmer will be used—or maintained—by another programmer.)

Most Controls Are Wrappers around Native Windows Classes

As we mentioned in Chapter 7, most .NET Compact Framework controls are wrappers around controls that are part of the underlying Win32 layer of Windows CE. Most of the work of the control is done in unmanaged code, and this factor contributes to the relatively small size of the .NET Compact Framework runtime. Many events (a.k.a. "messages") received and processed by the Win32 control are not sent into managed code, which is why only a subset of the defined events are available in managed code.

This factor contributes to the snappy performance of the .NET Compact Framework user interface.

Because the .NET Compact Framework relies on Win32 controls, you can as well. And so, one way to create a custom control is to create a managed-code wrapper around a Win32 control. This chapter does not include an example of this recommendation, but because there has been a substantial amount of Win32 code written for Windows CE, this technique is worth mentioning as one possible implementation choice.

Some controls—such as the `DataGrid`—are implemented entirely in managed code. So, another way to create a custom control is to implement it entirely in managed code. If you choose to do that, one question you may ask yourself is this: What base class should I start with? That is the topic of the next subsection.

The Possible Base Classes for Your Custom Control

The first step in creating a custom control involves picking a base class. We see four choices for a .NET Compact Framework programmer. We list these choices here, from most to least preferred—meaning from least to most work required to create a working control.

1. An existing control class: The most common custom control is one that changes the behavior of an existing control in a very small way. If you want a control that behaves similar to a `TextBox` control, inherit from the `TextBox` class and proceed. No point reinventing the wheel.
2. `System.Windows.Forms.Control`: Use this base class for custom controls that stand alone on a form alongside other controls. In other words, this base class wraps around a Win32 window that has a presence on the user's display and that receives mouse and keyboard events.
3. `System.ComponentModel.Component`: Use this base class for controls that do not wrap around a Win32 window. In other words, use this as a base class for objects that do not have a user interface or that supplement the user interface of another control. This is the base class

used by the following .NET Compact Framework control classes: `Timer`, `Menu`, `ImageList`, `ToolBarButton`, and `ColumnHeader` (used by the `ListView` control).

4. `Object`: The ultimate base class for all .NET Compact Framework classes is `Object`. This class could be used for a .NET Compact Framework control as an alternative to `Component`. The advantage of the `Object` class is that it provides the lightest class and therefore the least overhead. But such a class would not port well to the desktop .NET Framework, where `Component` would be a better choice.

The Foundation of All Controls Are PMEs

As we discussed in Chapter 7, the operation of all controls is defined by the supported set of PMEs. For this reason, new control classes extend the functionality of existing control classes by adding new PMEs and overriding existing PMEs.

For example, the code in Listing 10.1 defines a custom `TextBox` control that

- Is twice as wide as the normal `TextBox` control
- Highlights its text when it receives the focus
- Stores its text as uppercase letters
- Provides a method to return the text as lowercase letters

We present an explanation of the code throughout this chapter; it appears here as a general illustration of adding and overriding PMEs.

LISTING 10.1: A Custom `TextBox` Control That Inherits from the Built-in `TextBox` Class

```
using System;
using System.Windows.Forms;
namespace YaoDurant.Gui
{
   public class TextBoxPlus : TextBox
   {
      // Constructor
      public TextBoxPlus()
      {
```

```
            this.Width *= 2;
        }

        // Overridden method
        protected override void OnGotFocus(EventArgs e)
        {
            base.OnGotFocus(e);
            this.SelectAll();
        }

        // Overridden property
        public override string Text
        {
            get
            {
                return base.Text;
            }
            set
            {
                value = value.ToUpper();
                base.Text = value;
            }
        }

        // Original method
        public string ToStringLower()
        {
            return this.Text.ToLower();
        }
    }
}
```

"Inherited Does Not Mean Supported"

As we mentioned in Chapter 7, both the online help and Visual Studio .NET IntelliSense imply that certain events are supported when, in fact, those events are not. A portion of the online help page that displays PMEs for the `TextBox` class, shown in Figure 10.1, is an example. The page includes a list of protected `OnXXX` methods, several of which are designated as being "Supported by the .NET Compact Framework." While they may be supported by some part of the .NET Compact Framework, not all of them are actually implemented. The catch phrase for this, which comes from Seth Demsey (a member of Microsoft's .NET Compact Framework team) is that "inherited does not mean supported." For further discussion of this subject, see the

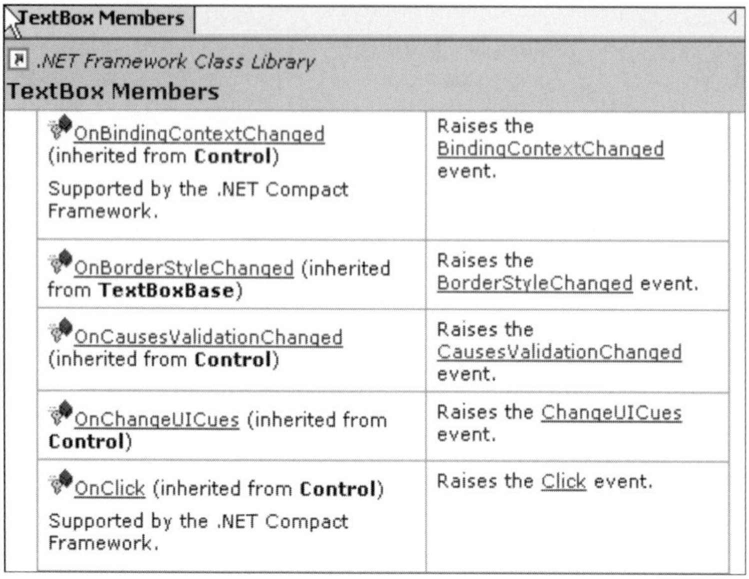

TextBox Members

.NET Framework Class Library

TextBox Members

OnBindingContextChanged (inherited from **Control**) Supported by the .NET Compact Framework.	Raises the BindingContextChanged event.
OnBorderStyleChanged (inherited from **TextBoxBase**)	Raises the BorderStyleChanged event.
OnCausesValidationChanged (inherited from **Control**)	Raises the CausesValidationChanged event.
OnChangeUICues (inherited from **Control**)	Raises the ChangeUICues event.
OnClick (inherited from **Control**) Supported by the .NET Compact Framework.	Raises the Click event.

FIGURE 10.1: Online help page for the `TextBox` class

Inherited Does Not Mean Supported sidebar in the Ultimate Parent Controls subsection of Chapter 7.

The nature of an object-oriented interface is that a member of a base class cannot be erased. To achieve the best performance and smallest possible footprint, the .NET Compact Framework team did not install the plumbing necessary to support all of the PMEs for all of the controls. Most controls rely on the underlying Win32 control, after all, and the cost of sending all events from unmanaged code to managed code caused significant slowing of the performance of these controls. Thus, many of the "Supported by the .NET Compact Framework" overridable `OnXXX` methods have been inherited but not implemented. If an inherited method is not implemented in the .NET Compact Framework, the runtime will never call it. Hence, even if you override the method, the runtime still will not call it when handling user interface events.

Consider the following three `TextBox` `OnXXX` methods mentioned in the online help: `OnGotFocus`, `OnClick`, and `OnBorderStyleChanged`. The first two are designated as "Supported by the .NET Compact Framework," but only `OnGotFocus` has actually been implemented; `OnClick` has been inherited but not implemented. Thus the three methods fall into the following separate categories:

- `OnBorderStyleChanged`: not supported
- `OnClick`: supported; inherited but not implemented
- `OnGotFocus`: supported; inherited and implemented

Because `OnClick` is designated as "Supported by the .NET Compact Framework," IntelliSense helps write the overriding `OnClick` method (see Figure 10.2), and no compilation error will occur during the build. However, the overriding `OnClick` method will never be executed because the method simply is not called by the .NET runtime.

There is no way to determine from the information provided by IntelliSense, the online help, or the resulting IL code (examined by using the `ildasm.exe` tool, even if you proceed beyond the interface definition and read the actual IL code itself) which of the inheritable methods, those designated as "Supported by the .NET Compact Framework," are actually implemented.

Consider Using Context Menus in Custom Controls

A context menu is connected to a control and appears in response to a tap-and-hold operation (on Pocket PCs) or a right mouse click (on systems

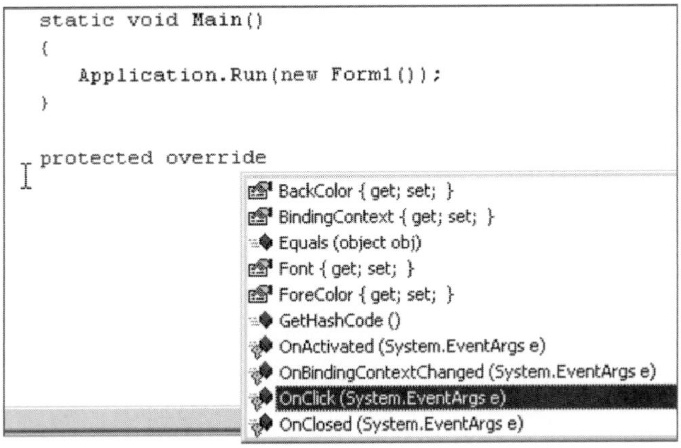

```
static void Main()
{
   Application.Run(new Form1());
}

protected override
```


FIGURE 10.2: IntelliSense drop-down list for overrides

equipped with a mouse). Context menus are self-contained menus in that they stand alone from a program's main menu and from the menus of other controls. In a DLL, a context menu resides in the DLL and gets deployed with the control. It is easier to create and handle a context menu at design time than to write code to alter a program's main menu at runtime. (The main menu cannot be accessed during the design of a control.) Context menus can be used for user input and also to display information to the user without having to alter the control's main display area.

The Methods for Testing Controls

When you create a custom control that you plan to deploy in a DLL, you run into a problem testing that control because DLLs cannot be run by themselves. We address this issue in two ways.

First, during the initial development of the control, we create the control in a regular program project. This gives us an easy way to test the control—just build and run.

Second, when we deploy the control in a DLL, which is needed to put the control in the Visual Studio .NET Toolbox, we use a Visual Studio .NET solution with two projects, as shown in Figure 10.3. One project holds the custom object/control classes, which creates the control's DLL. The second

FIGURE 10.3: Custom control and test projects in one solution

project is for an application that creates and tests the custom control as deployed in the shared library. In the example shown in Figure 10.3, the solution has been named `WaterTemp`, while two projects have been named `WaterTempControl` and `WaterTempTest`, respectively.

About Properties and Methods

From the outside of a control, properties and methods look quite different. A property, after all, appears to be a data member. A method, on the other hand, is a function (or subroutine) that can accept parameters and can have a return value. Inside a control, however, aside from the differences in syntax, properties and methods are quite similar. (Chapter 3 reviews the syntax for defining properties.) Because of this similarity, we discuss properties and methods together.

Properties Are Executable Code and Can Be Overridden Just Like Methods

A property is executable code, so everything you know about .NET methods also applies to properties. A property can have one or two methods, more properly referred to as *accessors*: a `get` method, which returns the current value, and a `set` method, which changes the current value. Either or both of these methods can be overridden (we illustrate this with the `Text` property in Listing 10.1). Throughout this chapter, we use the standard .NET terminology to refer to these methods, commenting on a property's `get` accessor or its `set` accessor.

Overriding a Method or Property to Replace the Base Class Method

When inheriting from another class, you can override existing methods or properties by defining a replacement whose signature is exactly the same as the original—same name, same return type, and same parameters. Use of the `override` keyword causes the compiler to verify that a method of identical signature exists in the base class; absence of the `override` keyword causes the compiler to verify that a matching base class method does not exist.

Using the example from Listing 10.1, code within the class that references the `Text` property, such as:

```
this.Text = "ABC";
```

executes the `get` accessor of the `Text` property of the derived class shown above, as does any code located outside the class, such as an the following:

```
MyCustomTextbox.Text = "ABC";
```

The methods and properties of existing .NET controls have been defined such that their scope modifiers and data types cannot be changed by overriding them. Nor can parameters be introduced or removed during an override. In Listing 10.2, all but one of the method overrides cause build errors when added to a .NET Compact Framework class.

LISTING 10.2: Correct and Incorrect Overriding of a Method

```
// Error - Cannot change accessibility
//            of public methods to private
private override string ToString()
{
   return "XXX";
}

// Error - Cannot change return type of overridden method
public override DateTime ToString()
{
   return DateTime.Today;
}

// Error - Cannot change parameter list for overridden method
public override string ToString(string strX)
{
   return "XXX";
}

// Okay - this is the only acceptable override
public override string ToString()
{
   // Call the base class method
   return base.ToString();
}
```

You Can Supplement a Method or Property Instead of Replacing It

As the previous example shows, when you replace a method or property, the signature of the new version must be identical to the original. In some cases, however, you do not want to replace a method or property. For example, you might want to add a new version of an existing method or property that accepts a different set of parameters or has a different return value.

You notify the compiler that you are supplementing but not replacing an existing method or property with the `new` keyword. If you forget this keyword, the compiler issues an error to notify you that the name you have chosen for your method or property already exists. Suppress this message by adding the `new` keyword (or use the `override` keyword to hide the existing item).

Using this approach, you can effectively change the return type of a method by providing a version that accepts the same number and type of parameters, but with a different return value. The following code effectively changes the return type of `ToString` from `string` to `DateTime`.

```
public new DateTime ToString()
{
   return DateTime.Today;
}
```

A Private Version of a Method or Property "Shadows" the Base Class Method

While you cannot override a method or property and make it disappear, it is possible to define a new method or property that differs from the base class method or property only in terms of its visibility.

The following code, if added to the `TextBoxPlus` class defined in Listing 10.1, results in two versions of `ToString`: one visible from within the class and one visible from outside the class.

```
   private new string ToString()
   {
      return "Hi Mom";
   }
```

A call from within the class calls this method and receives `"Hi Mom"` as the return value. A call from outside the class calls the base class `ToString` method.

This is correct .NET syntax, but from a design perspective we suggest you avoid creating new methods or properties like this. If the method or property you wish to create does not exist in the base class, you define your "new" version without using the `new` keyword (as shown in Listing 10.1); if it does exist in the base class, you probably want to override it, not create a new version of it. Using the `new` keyword can make your code hard to understand and hard to use and can cause confusion about which method is actually getting called. We point out this `new` keyword capability to show you that it does exist and to help you avoid accidentally creating a new method when you would be better off overriding an existing one.

To Extend a Method, Call the Base Class Method

When creating a new class, often you want only to make minor changes to the base class while still using most of the base class functionality. To access base class PMEs from within your derived class, use the `base` keyword, which defines the scope of a method call or property access to the base class instead of the current class.

In the following code snippet, the `OnLostFocus` method calls `base.OnLostFocus` to ensure that the base class event handling (i.e., raising the `Validating`, `Validated`, and `LostFocus` events) is performed.

```
// Overridden method
protected override void OnLostFocus(EventArgs e)
{
   this.Text = this.Text.ToUpper();
   base.OnLostFocus(e);
}
```

Hardware Input Bypasses Property Accessors

Various events—such as mouse and keyboard events—change the state of a control. In some cases, there is a property associated with the state. The property accessors are not called when the underlying state changes, which can sometimes cause confusion. For example, as a user enters text into a .NET Compact Framework `TextBox` control,[2] the `Text` property changes, but the `Text` property's `set` accessor is not called. Properties are meant to wrap around programmatic access to a control and are not intended to act as a fortress around a control's state.

2. The same behavior is observed in the desktop .NET Framework `TextBox` control.

About Events

As we discussed earlier, all GUI programming is based on event-driven programming. All controls generate events. An event notifies the outside world that something of interest has occurred to a control. When you implement a custom control, you must pay attention to events in the same way that you must pay attention to properties and methods.

You Cannot Override Events, but You Can Override the Methods That Raise Events

Unlike properties and methods, events are not overridden per se. Instead, every overridable event has a corresponding protected method that contains the code that raises the event. By convention, this method is named `OnXXX`, where `XXX` is the name of the event, such as `OnClick`. Calling the method causes the event to be raised. For instance, when the user taps on a `TextBox` control that does not have the focus, the .NET runtime calls the `TextBox`'s `OnGotFocus` method. Code within the method raises the `GotFocus` event.

The `OnXXX` event methods have a scope of protected, not public, which means that code outside the class cannot call the method. For example, a form can receive and respond to a `TextBox` control's `GotFocus` event, but it cannot call the `TextBox`'s `OnGotFocus` method. You can, however, call a protected method from a class that inherits from the base class—a technique that allows the new class to rely on the base class for doing most of the work.

When you override a protected method such as `OnLostFocus` in a new class, you receive help from IntelliSense in the Visual Studio .NET editor window. Just typing the words `protected override` triggers IntelliSense to display a list of the base class methods, as shown earlier in Figure 10.2. Highlight your choice, either by entering letters or by using the arrow key, and then hit the space key. IntelliSense generates the code shown here for you.

```
protected override void OnLostFocus(EventArgs e)
{
   base.OnLostFocus (e);
}
```

Custom Control Classes Can Either Respond to Events or Override the Base Event Handler

An alternative to overriding the event handler (`OnXXX`) method is to handle the event within the object class. For instance, the code in Listing 10.3, if added to the `TextBoxPlus` class defined in Listing 10.1, is called when the control loses focus, to deliver the `Validating` event. Event handlers like this one are called in the order in which they are added to the event handler collection. Each handler in the list gets called, and the last one to be called gets the final word in determining whether a valid value has been entered because it will be the last one to set the `e.Cancel` property value.

LISTING 10.3: Handling the `Validating` Event within a Custom Class

```
this.Validating += new CancelEventHandler(this.this_Validating);

    :
    :
    :

private void this_Validating(object sender,
                             CancelEventArgs e)
{
   // Ensure that the Text property is 25 words or fewer
   if( this.Text.Split(' ').GetLength(0) > 25 )
   {
      e.Cancel = true;
      throw(new ArgumentException("Must be <= 25 words."));
   }
}
```

When writing code to handle one of your own events, you can receive help from IntelliSense. At the location in your code where you wish to associate the event with its handler, usually the class constructor, enter the word `this` followed by a period. IntelliSense then displays a list of the events for the class, including those derived from the base class, as shown in Figure 10.4.

Highlight the one you want, and then enter + =. When you hit the tab key, IntelliSense generates the code shown here.

```
this.TextChanged +=new EventHandler(TaskStatus_TextChanged);
```

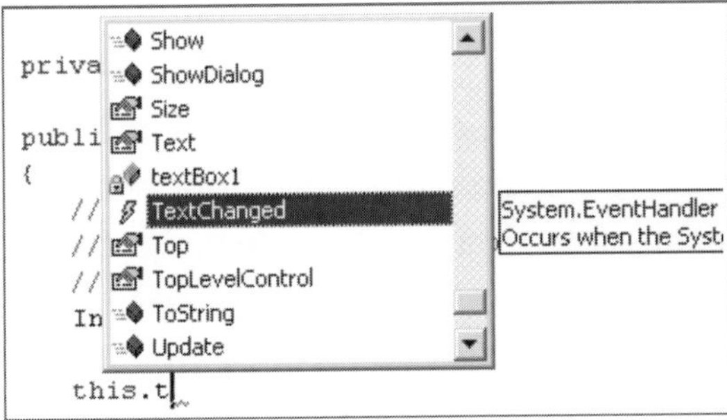

FIGURE 10.4: IntelliSense drop-down list for adding handlers

This code expects that you are using a default event delegate, and it also suggests a name for your handler. Based on the generated code, IntelliSense anticipates that your handler will look like this:

```
private void TaskStatus_TextChanged(object sender,
                                    System.EventArgs e)
{
   // Event handler code here
}
```

You can use a different handler name by changing the name in both places where the name appears. If your event handler will receive a different event argument class than the default, such as `CancelEventArgs` rather than `EventArgs`, both the signature of your handler and also the line of code in which the handler is being associated with the event will reflect this. For instance, if your handler signature looked like this:

```
private void TaskStatus_Validating(
   object sender,
   System.ComponentModel.CancelEventArgs e)
{
   // Event handler code here
}
```

then the code that associated the event with the handler would look lik this:

```
this.TaskStatus.Validating +=
   new CancelEventHandler(this.TaskStatus_Validating);
```

Although adding an event handler is always our first choice, because it is quick and easy, it does not give you the complete control over the distribution of events that you can achieve by overriding the `OnXXX` event handler method. Code that executes within an `OnXXX` override method can prevent the bubbling up of the event to the code in the client object by simply *not* calling the base class `OnXXX` method. Thus code in an `OnLostFocus` override method can prevent a `LostFocus` event from being raised in the form. The code of the client form could still contain a `LostFocus` event handler for the control, but this code would not be called if the control's `OnLostFocus` method did not call `Base.OnLostFocus`.

The `OnLostFocus` Method Raises Three Events: `Validating`, `Validated`, and `LostFocus`

In the desktop .NET Framework, `Validating`, `Validated`, and `LostFocus` events are each raised by different methods. In the .NET Compact Framework, all of these events are raised by the `OnLostFocus` event-dispatching method. This can be verified by examining the .NET Compact Framework `System.Windows.Forms.dll` file using the `ildasm.exe` tool, as shown in Figure 10.5. (The binary files for all of the .NET Compact Framework libraries reside in the Visual Studio .NET 2003 directory tree, normally `Program Files\Microsoft Visual Studio .NET 2003\CompactFrameworkSDK\v1.0.5000\Windows CE`.) The entry for `TextBox` contains no entries for `OnXXX` methods or for the corresponding events, and neither does `TextBoxBase`. The entries are at the next higher level of the inheritance chain, `Control`. Opening the `OnLostFocus` method reveals the IL code, showing the invoking of the three events (as shown in the top-level window in Figure 10.5). `OnLostFocus` is the only .NET Compact Framework `OnXXX` method that raises more than one event.

So, with this background information in mind, we can begin to develop custom controls.

Deriving Custom Controls from an Existing .NET Control

We begin our discussion of creating custom controls by starting with the first option we mentioned earlier, extending an existing control, which is

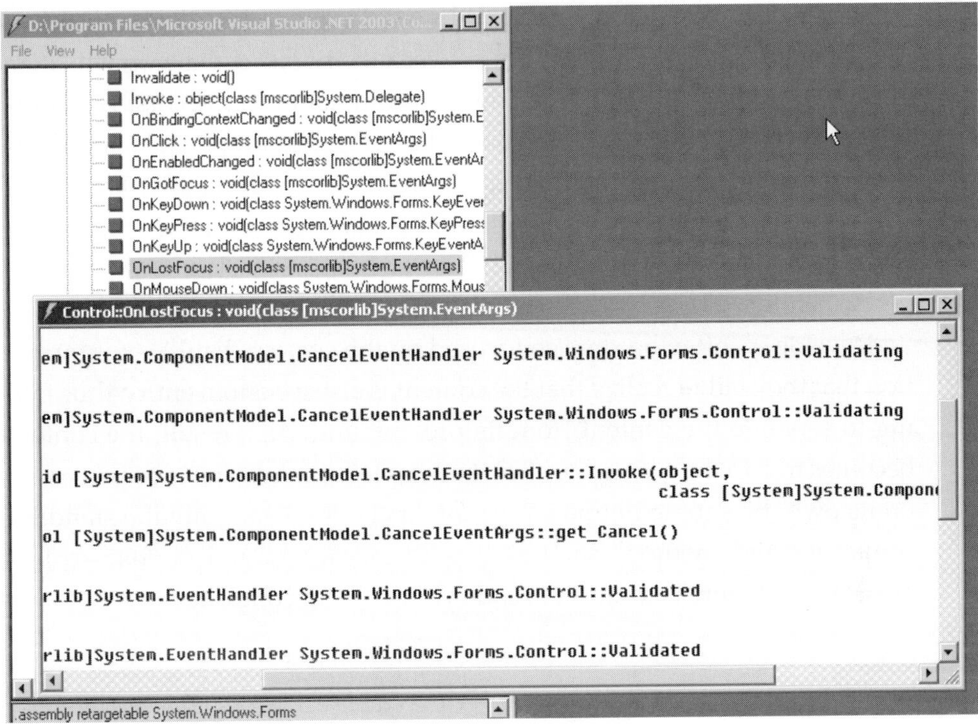

FIGURE 10.5: Viewing the `Control` class's OnLostFocus method in `ildasm.exe`

usually the easiest of the three to do. Later in this chapter we address composite controls and then new controls.

In this section, we use two examples of deriving from existing controls because we want to illustrate two common scenarios related to extending the functionality of existing .NET Compact Framework control classes. The code for these two applications is presented throughout this chapter and can be found on the Web site in the `DateAndStatusControls` project and the `WaterTempControl` project, respectively.[3]

The first example is a custom `TextBox` control for displaying dates, which we name `DateBox`; the second example is a custom `TextBox` control for displaying water temperatures, which we name `WaterTemp`. They sound

3. You can download the projects mentioned in this chapter from http://www.paulyao.com/cfbook/code. Follow the instructions listed on the Web site.

so similar that you might wonder, "Why two? Why not one?" The answer is that there is a significant difference between the two, one that you will often encounter when authoring your own custom controls. The first control is easier to code because the data type of the `DateTime` property, including its formatting and parsing capabilities, is already defined in .NET. This is not true for water temperature. Our second custom control is not displaying integers, it is displaying a special class of integer—a class that we must define before we begin to code the custom control that will display it.

Developers often become so focused on the custom display of information that they fail to realize that the content is also a custom entity, thus failing to separate the content from its presentation. As a result, the content becomes tied to the custom control that displays it and cannot be processed on its own. Be sure to define your content classes (especially the standard properties and methods such as `ToString`, `Parse`, and `CompareTo`) as appropriate before beginning to code your custom controls.

The `DateBox` Control Example

In our first example, the `DateBox` control, we extend the standard `TextBox` class to

- Limit the input to include only valid dates
- Allow the user to specify maximum and minimum dates
- Allow the user to specify a desired display format
- Change the background color whenever the date is beyond the acceptable range

This control reflects three typical customization needs: (1) to constrain an existing property (`Text` is to be restricted to `DateTime`), (2) to provide a self-contained menu, and (3) to customize the control's appearance (background color has a special meaning).

We begin our multiproject solution by creating an empty solution and then adding two projects to that solution. It's easiest to add the testing project first and the custom object project second because the first project

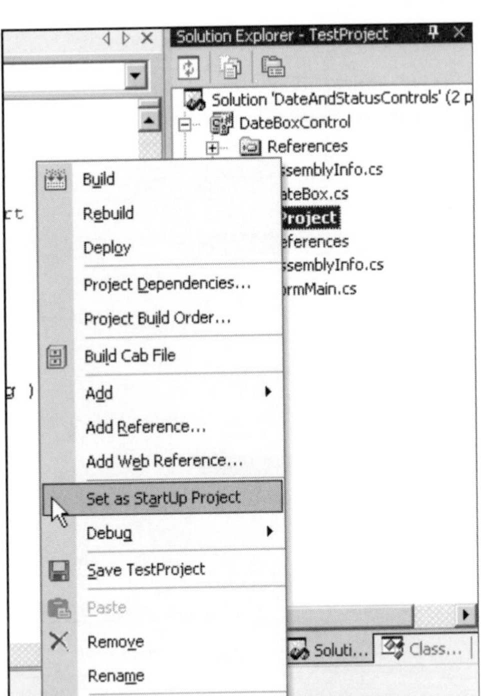

FIGURE 10.6: Setting the startup project

added is the one that will be run whenever we execute the Start Debugging selection from the menu. If we decided to add the projects in a different sequence, we could always right-click on the test project name within the Solution Explorer window and designate it as the startup project, as shown in Figure 10.6.

Once we have our empty solution, we add the testing project via the File→Add Project→New Project menu selection, specifying Smart Device Application and then Windows Application. As always, we rename our form to `FormMain`.

Adding a custom control project is similar to adding the testing project with one slight difference. When the Smart Device Application Wizard dialog appears, we select Class Library, not Windows Application, as shown in Figure 10.7.

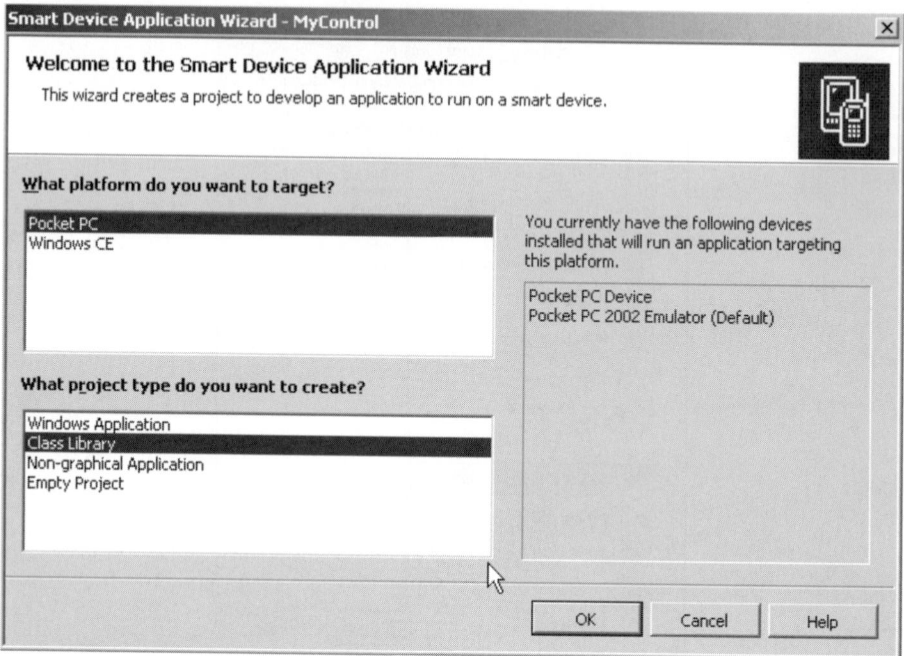

FIGURE 10.7: Specifying a class library project

New Project Wizard Guideline

You might be tempted to choose Control Library rather than Smart Device Application as the project template for a custom control class library. It certainly sounds like the correct choice, but it is not. Only the Smart Device Application template generates .NET Compact Framework code; all other templates generate code for the desktop .NET Framework.

Once again, if we inadvertently make the wrong choice, we can always fix it. To do so, we right-click on the project name in the Solution Explorer window and select Property, then change the project type as shown in Figure 10.8.

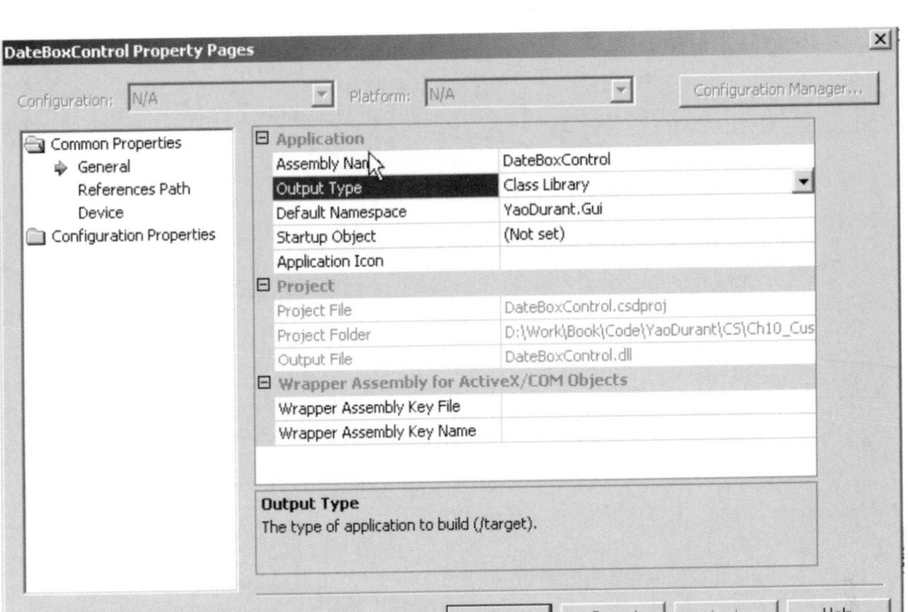

FIGURE 10.8: Changing the project's type

Design Decision #1: Exposing Custom Control Content

We begin the definition of the `DateBox` class by deciding which `TextBox` properties and methods we need to override and which properties and methods we need to add. The first design decision we must make is this: How do we expose the date to our users, both to the human users who enter a date into our `DateBox` control and to client code that sets and gets the `Date` property? You must make this type of decision anytime you are authoring a custom control that constrains the value that can be assigned to a base class property. In our case, we need to restrict `TextBox.Text` to `System.DateTime` data.

Realistically, we have five choices, summarized in Table 10.1.

Option 1 is certainly a valid option, but, in our opinion, most developers would expect a control that displays only dates to have a public `Date` property and would expect a control that has a `Text` property to accept any valid string. So we decide against option 1.

TABLE 10.1: **Design Alternatives for Exposing the Contents of a Custom Control**

Option	Description	Implementation
1	Use the existing `Text` property.	Override the `Text` property with one that checks for a valid date.
2	Change the `Text` property data type to `DateTime`.	Override the `Text` property with a new `Text` property of data type `DateTime`.
3	Replace the `Text` property with a `Date` property.	This option cannot be done. (See discussion in the text.)
4	Add a `Date` property.	Provide a public `Date` property. Write code to synchronize the `Text` and `Date` properties.
5	Add a `Date` property, and make the `Text` property read-only.	Provide a public `Date` property. Have the `Text` property's `get` accessor return the `Date` property as a string.

We reject option 2 because it also is confusing to users. Everyone expects `Text` to be a string. That's the way it is in the `Object` class and in all .NET-derived classes, and that's the way we like it.

We reject option 3 because it cannot be done. Even if we shadow the `Text` property with the following code, the `Text` property is still visible to clients.

```
public new string Text
{
   get
   {
      return base.Text;
   }
   set
   {
      value = value.ToUpper();
      base.Text = value;
   }
}
```

It is the base class `Text` property accessor that clients see, but they still see it. You cannot make a public property or method disappear when inheriting from a base class. This is a deliberate design feature of Object Implementation. It ensures the author of a base class that any property or method that he or she publicly exposes will always be available to users of any object classes derived from the original base class.

Option 4 is a valid option; a control that displays only dates should have a public `Date` property.

Option 5 is a valid choice for the same reason. And, because input is available through the `Date` property, making the `Text` property read-only does not cause a problem.

Option 5 would be the easier option to code, and we would probably choose option 5 for a real-world application. Implementing option 4, however, will allow us to encounter some additional issues that we wish to cover in this book. Therefore, we chose to implement option 4 for our `DateBox` control example, which leads to our next design decision.

Design Decision #2: Where to Validate/Filter Incoming Data

The `Date` and `Text` properties must be kept in sync, which means that we must override the `Text` property. But we know from an earlier discussion in this chapter that the overriding `Text` property's `set` accessor will *not* be called when the user enters a value into the `DateBox` control, making it more difficult to keep the two properties in sync.

There are several ways we can detect that the user has modified the contents of the textbox. We can react to the changing of individual characters within the display area by monitoring the `TextChanged` event or wait for all characters to be entered by monitoring the `LostFocus` event or one of the `Validation` events. We choose the `Validating` and `Validated` events as the appropriate indication of change, especially because we wish to edit the text after the user has entered it, not while he or she is entering it (e.g., is "14-J" an invalid date or a half-completed valid date?).

Unfortunately, the two validation methods fall into the "inherited but not implemented" category. Thus, if we overrode the `OnValidating` and `OnValidated` protected methods, our code would never be executed. Because we do want to avail ourselves of the `Validating` event's `CancelEventArgs.Cancel` property for indicating an invalid value, we'll handle the control's `Validating` event rather than overriding the `OnLostFocus` method.

As we mentioned earlier in this chapter, hardware input bypasses property accessors, so in our handling of the `Validating` event, we set the `Text` property. This kills two birds with one stone; setting the `Text` property serves as our validation because it fails if the text is not a valid `DateTime` value. If the text is a valid `DateTime` value, we have successfully called our overriding `Text` property accessor, something that the user's entry of the text did not cause.

In summary, we need to take the following actions. First, we add the following new properties:

- `Date`: the actual `DateTime` value being displayed by the control
- `Format`: the desired display format
- `MaxDate`: the maximum allowable date
- `MinDate`: the minimum allowable date
- Context menu properties: sufficient additional properties to create the context menu shown in Figure 10.9

Then we override the following current property:

- `Text`: to synchronize with the `Date` property

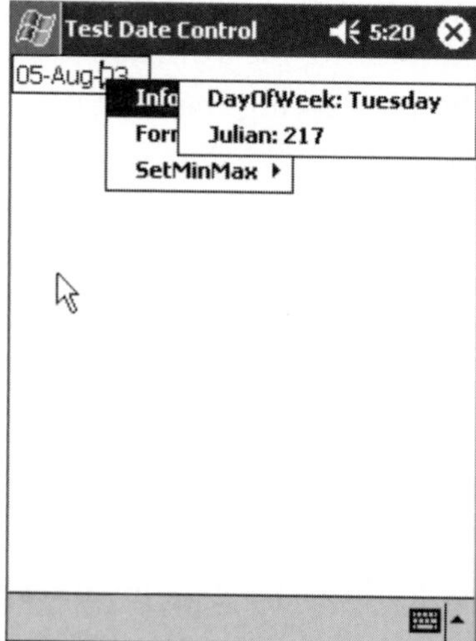

FIGURE 10.9: The `DateBox` control's context

Finally we handle the following event:

- `Validating`: to set the `Date` property; with an empty string interpreted to mean "today"

With the design completed, albeit somewhat casually, we can begin coding.

The `DateBox` *Code*

Because `TextBox` is a class and because we want to create something that derives from `TextBox`, we switch to the `DateBox` control project and select New Class from the Project menu. The skeleton file generated by this action will be our code file, so we no longer need the code file originally generated for us when we added the project. We delete that file, as shown in Figure 10.10.

We begin the coding of a custom control the same way we begin the coding of any class: by setting the references, the `using` statements, the namespace name, and the class name. For this project, we add some needed

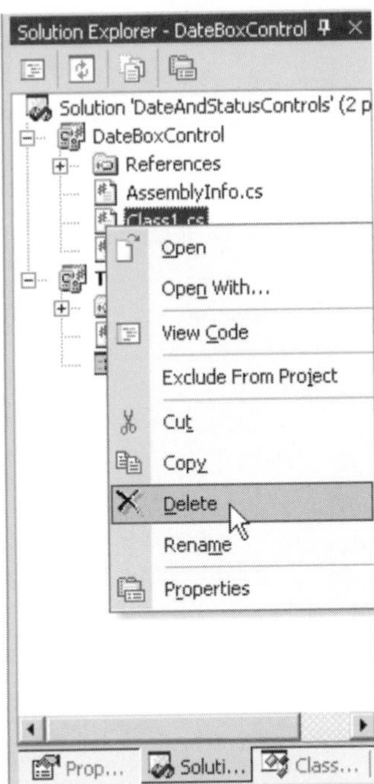

FIGURE 10.10: Deleting the default code

.NET namespaces to the references list in the Solution Explorer and add the required `using` statements to our code. Then we change our namespace name to the name we use for all derived controls throughout this book, `YaoDurant.Gui`. Finally, we rename our class name to `DateBox` and specify that we are deriving it from `TextBox`.

We continue by defining some private strings needed for the control's context menu. We use one string array for each menu or submenu contained within the context menu. We specify the strings ourselves for all the arrays except one because the string array of possible date formats can be obtained from the `DateTime` data type itself. We also define some private enumerators that will make it easier to reference the menu selections within our code. The resulting code is shown in Listing 10.4.

LISTING 10.4: The Beginning of `DateBox.cs`

```
using System;
using System.ComponentModel;
using System.Drawing;
using System.Windows.Forms;

namespace YaoDurant.Gui
{
   /// <summary>
   /// Summary description for DateBox
   /// </summary>
   public class DateBox : TextBox
   {

      // Menu Text strings
      string[] astrMenu = {"Info", "Format", "SetMinMax"};
      string[] astrInfo= {"DayOfWeek: ", "Julian: "};
      string[] astrFormat = new string[7];
      string[] astrMinMax =
                        {"Set minimum date","Set maximum date"};

      // SubMenu index values
      private enum MenuItemIndex
      {
         miiInfo, miiFormat, miiMinMax
      }
      private enum MinMaxIndex
      {
         miiMin, miiMax
      }
```

Next we define four new properties and one overridden property, starting with the `Date` property. The reasoning behind the five properties is discussed here; the code for each is shown in interspersed listings.

The `Date` Property. We use a private variable to hold the actual value and a public property that we expose to our clients. The `get` accessor merely returns the private variable. The `set` accessor stores the value into the private variable, sets the `Text` property to the selected format of the date, and sets the background color to indicate whether the date is inside the minimum/maximum range.

Because setting the `Date` property causes the `Text` property to be set and vice versa, we must include code to prevent an infinite loop when either property is set. An infinite loop is always a possibility whenever one property sets another property, which is always a possibility whenever one property "customizes" another property.

We also have to add some code to the `Date` property because of a side issue. The `DateBox` control will allow users to specify the maximum and minimum acceptable dates. The `DateBox` control itself is used to do this. The user puts the `DateBox` control into minimum/maximum entry mode by selecting SetMinMax from the context menu (Listing 10.11 later in this chapter shows the code for handling this event). The `DateBox` control responds by setting its background color to gray to indicate that it is in minimum/maximum entry mode rather than normal date entry mode. The user enters the new minimum or maximum date into the `DateBox` control and then uses the context menu to indicate that the entry is completed. Therefore, whenever the code within the `Date` property executes, it must differentiate between the entry of an actual date versus the entry of a minimum/maximum date.

We use three private properties to maintain information during the setting of a minimum/maximum date: two that indicate whether the minimum or maximum date is being entered, if either, and one to hold the current date, which must be restored after a minimum or maximum date has been entered. Listing 10.5 shows the code.

LISTING 10.5: The `Date` Property in the `DateBox` Custom Control

```
// Date
//    The date contained and displayed in this control
private DateTime m_Date = DateTime.Today;
public DateTime Date
{
   get { return m_Date; }
   set
   {
      // If the user has been inputting the Min or Max
      //    date, then store it in the appropriate
      //    property and restore the actual date.

      if( m_MinChanging )
      {
         m_MinValue = value;
         m_MinChanging = false;
         return;
      }
      if( m_MaxChanging )
      {
         m_MaxValue = value;
         m_MaxChanging = false;
         return;
      }

      // Set the private date.
      m_Date = value;

      // Set the Text property.
      this.Text = m_Date.GetDateTimeFormats('d')[m_Format];

      // Set the background color to indicate whether
      //    the date is within the user-specified range
      //    or not.
      this.BackColor = Color.White;
      if( ! (m_MinValue <= m_Date && m_Date <= m_MaxValue))
      {
         this.BackColor = Color.LightPink;
      }
   }
}
```

The `Text` Property. We must override the default `Text` property because our `Text` and `Date` properties must be kept in sync; they are really two representations of the same data. As with the `Date` property, we must avoid an infinite loop when doing this. We validate the `Text` property's value by assigning it to the `Date` property, as shown in Listing 10.6. If the `Date` property cannot be set to the `Text` property's value, then the user entered an invalid date and we throw an argument exception.

LISTING 10.6: The `Text` Property in the `DateBox` Custom Control

```
// Text
public override string Text
{
   get
   {
      return base.Text;
   }
   set
   {
      try
      {
         // There is no such thing as an "empty" date.
         //    An empty string means "today."
         if( value == String.Empty )
         {
            value = DateTime.Today.ToShortDateString();
         }

         // To prevent an infinite loop...
         // If this code is being called because the Date
         //    property is being set, do not set
         //    the Date property.  Else, set the Date
         //    to keep it in sync with the Text property.
         if( boolSettingDate )
         {
            base.Text = value;
         }
         else
         {
            this.Date = Convert.ToDateTime(value);
         }
      }
      catch
      {
         // Unable to convert value to DateTime.
         // (Highly unlikely that "base.Text = value;"
         //    would cause the exception.)
         throw new
            System.ArgumentException("Not a valid date");
```

continues

continued

```
            }
            finally
            {
            }
        }
    }
```

The `MinValue` and `MaxValue` Properties. The `MinValue` and `MaxValue` properties are self-explanatory and are presented in Listing 10.7 without comment.

LISTING 10.7: The `MinValue` and `MaxValue` Properties in the `DateBox` Custom Control

```
// Min and Max dates
private bool m_MinChanging;
private bool m_MaxChanging;

private DateTime m_MinValue = DateTime.MinValue;
public DateTime MinValue
{
   get { return m_MinValue; }
   set
   {
      m_MinValue = value;
   }
}

private DateTime m_MaxValue = DateTime.MaxValue;
public DateTime MaxValue
{
   get { return m_MaxValue; }
   set
   {
      m_MaxValue = value;
   }
}
```

The `Format` Property. We also need a property for tracking the desired format. Conveniently, the `DateTime` data type provides us with the list of possible formats through its `GetDateTimeFormats` method. Our `Format` property is merely an index into this list and is therefore an `Integer` property. The only code needed for this property is the code shown in Listing 10.8, which ensures our display is updated whenever the format is changed.

LISTING 10.8: The `Format` Property in the `DateBox` Custom Control

```
// Format
//    An index into the GetDateTimeFormats('d') array.
private int m_Format;
public int Format
{
   get { return m_Format; }
   set
   {
      // Set the format.
      m_Format = value;

      // Force it to take effect.
      this.Date = this.Date;
   }
}
```

Five properties down; we have a constructor, an event handler, and some context menu code still to go.

The Default Constructor. Next we will add some initialization code to the default constructor. Whenever a `DateBox` control is created, it will initialize the `Date`, `Format`, and `Width` properties; create the context menu; and define the `Validating` event handler delegate, as shown in Listing 10.9.

LISTING 10.9: The Default Constructor for the `DateBox` Class

```
public DateBox()
{
   // Initialize Date and Format.
   this.Date = DateTime.Today;
   this.Format = 6;

   //  Place the first seven of all possible DateTime
   //     formats into the astrFormat array.
   Array.Copy(
      DateTime.Today.GetDateTimeFormats(), 0,
      astrFormat, 0, 7);

   // Set the initial size.
   this.Width = (int)this.Font.Size * 8;

   // Create the context menu.
   this.ContextMenu = this.BuildContextMenu();
```

continues

continued

```
      // Handle own Validating/Validated events.
      // Note -- Cannot override OnValidated as it is
      //    "inherited but not implemented" in the
      //    .NET Compact Framework.
      this.Validating +=
         new CancelEventHandler(this.this_Validating);
   }
```

The* `Validating` *Event Handler. The `Validating` event handler will validate text by assigning it to the overridden `Text` property. If the assignment fails, the date is invalid. If the date is invalid, the `DateBox` control will set its background color to red and set the `Cancel` property of the event argument to `true`, as shown in Listing 10.10.

LISTING 10.10: The `Validating` Event Handler for the `DateBox` Class

```
   private void this_Validating(object sender,
                                CancelEventArgs e)
   {
      // Ensure that the Text property contains a date
      //    and that the date lies within the MinDate
      //    to MaxDate range.
      // If test fails, set background color to red and
      //    set the EventArg's Cancel property to true
      //    to indicate that validation failed.
      try
      {
         this.Text = this.Text;
      }
      catch
      {
         this.BackColor = Color.Red;
         e.Cancel = true;
      }
      finally
      {
      }
   }
```

The Context Menu Routines. Finally, we add four utility routines related to our context menu and the choices it presents.

We need one utility routine, named `BuildContextMenu`, to build the context menu from our string arrays.

We also need to write event handlers for each of the menu selections. The informational menu items, DayOfWeek and Julian, depend on the `Date` property value and must be filled in as the menu is being shown to the user. Thus we must handle the context menu's `PopUp` event.

When the user makes a selection from the Format menu, our `mnuFormat_Click` handler is called. It determines the index of the string array item that matches the selected item and sets the `Format` property to it.

When the user indicates a desire to set the maximum or minimum date, our `mnuMinMax_Click` handler is called. This handler saves some state information (including the current date), empties out the display area, makes the background color light gray, and sets the focus to itself.

Listing 10.11 shows these context menu routines.

LISTING 10.11: The Context Menu Routines for the `DateBox` Class

```
private ContextMenu BuildContextMenu()
{
   // Build the context menu for this class.
   MenuItem miWork;
   MenuItem miWork2;
   ContextMenu cmenuThis = new ContextMenu();

   // Submenu - GeneralInfo
   //    Menu items for this submenu do not need a
   //    handler, they are just informational entries
   //    (such as the day of week) that are completed
   //    as the context menu is being presented.
   miWork = new MenuItem();
   miWork.Text = astrMenu[0];

   miWork.MenuItems.Add(new MenuItem());
   miWork.MenuItems.Add(new MenuItem());
   cmenuThis.MenuItems.Add(miWork);

   // Submenu - Formats
   //    Use GetDateTimeFormats('d') to
   //    get the possible formats.
   miWork = new MenuItem();
   miWork.Text = astrMenu[1];
   foreach(string dateFormat in astrFormat)
   {
      miWork2 = new MenuItem();
      miWork2.Text = dateFormat;
```

continues

continued

```
         miWork2.Click +=
            new System.EventHandler(this.mnuFormat_Click);
         miWork.MenuItems.Add(miWork2);
      }
      cmenuThis.MenuItems.Add(miWork);

      // Submenu - MinMax
      miWork = new MenuItem();
      miWork.Text = astrMenu[2];

      miWork2 = new MenuItem();
      miWork2.Text = astrMinMax[0];
      miWork2.Click +=
         new System.EventHandler(this.mnuMinMax_Click);
      miWork.MenuItems.Add(miWork2);

      miWork2 = new MenuItem();
      miWork2.Text = astrMinMax[1];
      miWork2.Click +=
         new System.EventHandler(this.mnuMinMax_Click);
      miWork.MenuItems.Add(miWork2);
      cmenuThis.MenuItems.Add(miWork);

      // Some entries are dynamic.  Need to handle
      //    the Popup event for this context menu.
      cmenuThis.Popup +=
         new EventHandler(ContextMenu_Popup);

      // Done
      return cmenuThis;
   }


   private void ContextMenu_Popup(object sender, EventArgs e)
   {
      // Fill in the "Info" submenu menu items.
      MenuItem miWork =
         this.ContextMenu.MenuItems
         [(int)MenuItemIndex.miiInfo];
      miWork.MenuItems[0].Text =
         "DayOfWeek: " + this.m_Date.DayOfWeek;
      miWork.MenuItems[1].Text =
         "Julian: " + this.m_Date.DayOfYear;
   }
```

```
      private void mnuFormat_Click(object sender, System.EventArgs e)
      {
         // The Format property of this control is an index
         //    into the array of formats, astrFormat.  The
         //    user has selected the format string from the
         //    context menu; we must find that string within
         //    the array and set the property to the string's
         //    index within the array.
         this.Format =
            Array.IndexOf(astrFormat,
            ((MenuItem)sender).Text, 0,
            astrFormat.GetLength(0)-1);
      }


      private void mnuMinMax_Click(object sender,
         System.EventArgs e)
      {
         // To set the Min or Max allowable date, the user
         //    must use this control to do so.  Therefore,
         //    we must save the current date and set a
         //    switch to indicate that we are in "MinMax
         //    change" mode.
         // Once the user has completed specifying the
         //    Min or Max date, we will set the MinMax
         //    Date and restore the original date.  This
         //    will be done in the Date property.

         switch( Array.IndexOf( astrMinMax,
                                ((MenuItem)sender).Text,
                                0,
                                astrMinMax.GetLength(0)-1) )
         {
            case (int)MinMaxIndex.miiMin:
               m_MinChanging = true;
               break;
            case (int)MinMaxIndex.miiMax:
               m_MaxChanging = true;
               break;
         }
         this.BackColor = Color.LightSlateGray;
         this.Text = string.Empty;
         this.Focus();
      }

   }
}
```

This completes the code for our `DateBox` control, fully meeting the design goals we set earlier. Now we just have to test and debug the control.

Testing the `DateBox` Control

To test, we switch over to the test project. First we set a reference to our control project by going to the Solution Explorer window, right-clicking on the References line, and selecting Add Reference, which brings up the dialog box shown in Figure 10.11. Then we select the Projects tab because the object to be referenced is located in another project of this solution—in our case, the `DateBoxControl` project.

> **Suggestion about Setting References**
>
> When you set a reference, you are setting a reference to an assembly, not to a project. That is, you are setting a reference to the compiled output of the project, not to the source code of the project. When setting a project reference, always rebuild the referenced project immediately prior to setting the reference. That way you will be setting the reference to the compiled version of the project that matches the source-code version.

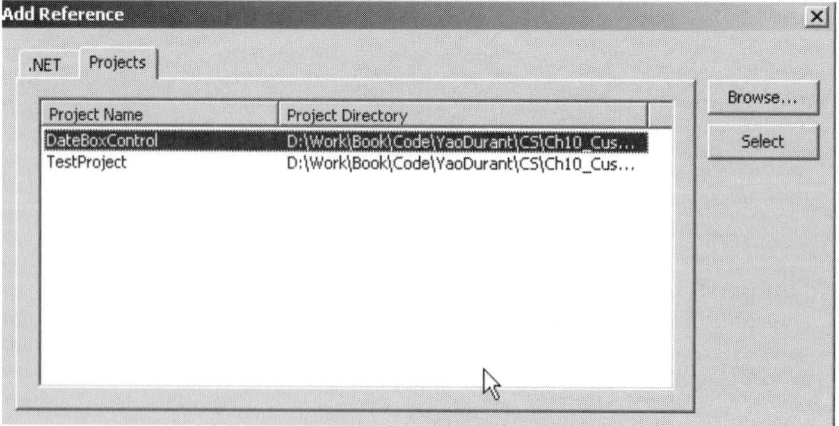

FIGURE 10.11: Adding a project reference

Later in this chapter, we show how to add a custom control to the Visual Studio .NET Toolbox. But for now, because we cannot add our custom control to our form from the toolbar, we just write code to create the control and add it to the form's `Controls` collection, as shown here.

```
public class FormMain : System.Windows.Forms.Form
{
   private YaoDurant.Gui.DateBox dboxTest;
            :
            :
            :
   private void FormMain_Load(object sender,
                              System.EventArgs e)
   {
      dboxTest = new YaoDurant.Gui.DateBox();
      this.Controls.Add(dboxTest);
            :
            :
            :
```

Then we run the solution and test our control, mostly by stepping through the context menu choices, shown earlier in Figure 10.9, and by manually changing the date, as shown in Figure 10.12. Our `DateBox` control works, fulfilling the functional specifications of our design.

FIGURE 10.12: Changing the date in the `DateBox` Control

The success of our custom control is directly related to our earlier design decisions.

- We provided a `Date` property and channeled all change of content through that property; `Validating` "calls" `Text`, `Text` "calls" `Date`.
- We provided a context menu for runtime customization and for displaying information to the user.
- We used the `DateBox` control itself for the entry of minimum and maximum dates rather than displaying any additional input dialogs.

To quote an old programming law: "There is no substitute for good design."

The `WaterTemp` Object Example

For our second example, we extend a standard .NET `TextBox` control to add the following capabilities:

- Display water temperature
- Allow the user to specify the unit of measure, such as Fahrenheit, Celsius, or Kelvin
- Change the background color to indicate whether the temperature represents ice, water, or steam
- Reject temperatures that are below absolute zero

To keep things simple, we dispense with a context menu; we've already shown one in the `DateBox` example.

Both this example and the previous example are similar and typical in that they enable users to edit input, allow users to specify information and limitations about the data, and adjust the displays based on the value of the data. But, as we mentioned earlier, there is also a significant difference between the two examples; this is why both are included in this chapter.

More Design Decisions

In the `DateBox` example, we did not need to separate the presentation from the functionality because the necessary functionality is already contained in the `DateTime` data type. But in this example we do need to add functionality, namely, a new data type, that will be independent of the object(s) used to display this data type. We will achieve this separation by creating two new classes, one that defines a `WaterTemp` data type plus one that derives from `TextBox` and displays `WaterTemp` values.

You can think of this as defining an underlying data type or you can think of it as defining a custom class. In .NET they are the same. By now you have probably noticed that .NET data types have methods and properties, such as `Integer.MinValue` and `DateTime.GetDateTimeFormats`, just as objects do. So whether we call it "defining our own data type" or "defining a custom class" makes no difference. What is important is that by defining a `WaterTemp` data type, we are separating the functionality of our underlying object, the water temperature, from the presentation of that object.

We begin by designing the `WaterTemp` data type, using the .NET data types as a guideline:

- Consists of an `Integer` temperature and a `String` unit of measure
- Can be defined by a `String`, such as `"100C"` or `"-22 F"`
- Has an overloaded constructor that can accept the initial temperature as a `String` parameter
- Provides a `ToString` method for translating a temperature to a string
- Provides a `Convert` method for changing the temperature from one unit of measure to another
- Provides `CompareTo` and `Clone` methods
- Throws an exception when set to a temperature lower than absolute zero

This still leaves us with one more design decision, one that seems unimportant and irrelevant but actually has major consequences: Do we want `WaterTemp` objects to be immutable? That is, should a `WaterTemp` object have methods that allow clients to change the content of the object? Our answer is "Yes" to the first, and therefore "No" to the second for the following reason.

We are defining a data type that will be used as a property of a control. If the client container of that control can modify the contents of a control property without the control being aware that the contents have changed, the control will be unable to update its display to reflect the change and will be unable to notify its client that a change has occurred. To illustrate this, consider the `String` data type, the `TextBox.Text` property, and the relationship between them.

Strings are immutable—they cannot be changed. That is one of the first things that anyone who attends .NET training learns. Thus you can invoke any string method, such as `ToUpper`, without modifying the string used to invoke the method. `ToUpper`, for instance, returns a new string; it does not modify the current string. Thus, the following line of code does not modify the `Text` property of the `TextBox` named `txtDemo`.

```
txtDemo.Text.ToUpper();
```

Instead, to change the `Text` property to all uppercase letters, you must code as follows.

```
txtDemo.Text = txtDemo.Text.ToUpper();
```

Your code cannot change the string that is in the `Text` property; it can only replace the old string with a new string. In other words, it must access the `Text` property's `set` accessor code to change the `Text` property's value. It cannot make the `Text` property change itself. Thus, by placing logic in the `set` accessor, the author of the `TextBox` class can guarantee that a `TextBox` will update its display and raise a `TextChanged` event whenever your code modifies its `Text` property, something that would not be possible if the `ToUpper` method modified an existing string rather than creating a new string.

And because the `Text` property is first defined in the `Control` base class, not in `TextBox`, the benefit of having immutable strings as the `Text` property data type propagates to all `Control`-derived classes.

So, we will make `WaterType` an immutable class. We recommend that you do the same for all of your classes that you intend to treat as custom data types (see the Creating Well-Behaved Properties sidebar).

Creating Well-Behaved Properties

One part of creating a custom control involves defining properties. By themselves, properties are easy to understand: You wrap code around some data value, and that code must be executed to either read or write that value.

To make this work reliably, we suggest that you limit the types you use for properties to immutable types. Why? If a property is not immutable, the value of the property can be changed without the control itself knowing that something has changed.

Immutatble types, such as the value types, require an existing value to be replaced by a new value; they do not provide methods that allow an instance to modify its own value. One reference type, `String`, is also immutable. Any of these make reasonable properties. By limiting your properties to immutable types, you ensure that your custom control is aware of any changes to its state. The code for the property can then trigger the appropriate data validation, screen update, and flag setting that might be needed to trigger later database or data file updates.

In some cases, a custom control might have to expose a mutable type—an object that wraps some data that can change: an array, a queue, or any more complex object. There are several workable solutions.

One approach is to create a collection class as a property. The `ListBox` class, for example, uses this approach in the form of its `Items` property. In this case, the collection class (`ListBox.ObjectCollection`) triggers the containing `ListBox` when changes occur.

Another approach involves defining a set of events that the contained class can use to notify the container (the custom control) that a change has taken place. This approach allows the data container class to be reused by several custom controls.

Whatever approach you take, one thing is certain: Well-behaved properties, like guests at someone's house, let the host know when there is a change that affects the host.

The `WaterTemp` Object

With the `WaterTemp` data type now defined, again somewhat casually, we can proceed with coding. As in the previous example, we begin with an empty solution and then add the test project and the custom data type project.

In the custom data type project, from the Project menu, we choose the Add Class menu selection to create a custom object class (as shown in Figure 10.13). Then we set the references, specify the external namespaces, and set our namespace name and class name.

Moving on to the definition of our properties, we add some private strings to hold error messages, plus two public read-only properties: one for holding the temperature and one for holding the unit of measure.

Next come the constructors: one that takes no parameters and one that takes a string, such as `"32 F"`. The constructor is the most complex method in the `WaterTemp` class, for it must do all of the following:

- Generate a temperature of zero degrees Kelvin if an empty string is specified
- Accept positive and negative temperatures
- Allow for embedded spaces between the temperature and the unit of measure
- Allow for uppercase and lowercase units of measure
- Default to Kelvin if no unit of measure is specified
- Raise an exception if an incorrectly formatted string (such as `"88X"` or `"1 2"`) is specified
- Raise an exception if the temperature is below zero degrees Kelvin

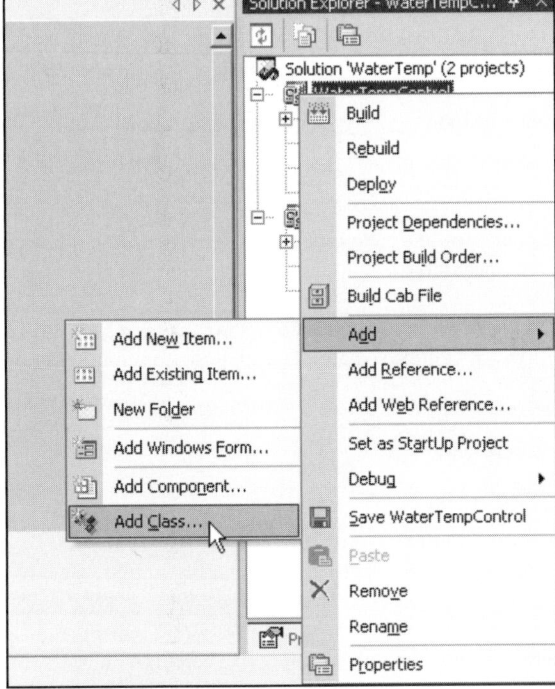

FIGURE 10.13: Adding a new class

The Meaning of "Ok"

Fonts can be confusing. In the code of this application, "0k" is zero degrees Kelvin, not the name of the corral where the gunfight occurred and not the American expression meaning "All is well."

The `Convert` method is very straightforward, consisting of integer arithmetic, the formulas for which can be obtained from a variety of existing Web sites. Note that, in keeping with our decision regarding immutability, it returns a new `WaterTemp` object rather than modifying the current one.

The `CompareTo` method is straightforward; the `ToString` method is trivial, as is the `Clone` method.

Listing 10.12 shows the code for the `WaterTemp` class.

Listing 10.12: The WaterTemp Data Type Class

```
using System;
using System.Text;

namespace YaoDurant.Types
{
   /// <summary>
   /// Summary description for WaterTemp
   ///   Consists of integer temperature and a one-character-long
   ///      unit of measure: K (Kelvin), F (Fahrenheit), or
   ///      C (Celsius).
   ///   Has an overloaded constructor that accepts a string.
   ///   Has ToString, CompareTo, Clone, and Convert methods.
   /// </summary>

   public class WaterTemp
   {
      private string strError;
      private string strerrFormat =
         "Argument is not a valid water temperature.  Must " +
         "be a positive integer followed by 'C', 'F', or 'K'.";
      private string strerrUofM =
         "Argument is not a valid unit of measure.  " +
         "Must be 'C', 'F', or 'K'.";
      private string strerrTemp =
         "Temperature must be greater than absolute 0.";

      private int m_Temperature;
      public int Temperature
      {
         get { return m_Temperature; }
      }

      private string m_UnitOfMeasure;
      public string UnitOfMeasure
      {
         get { return m_UnitOfMeasure; }
      }

      public WaterTemp()
      {
         InitializeWaterTemp(string.Empty);
      }

      public WaterTemp( string strTemp )
      {
         InitializeWaterTemp(strTemp);
      }
```

```
private void InitializeWaterTemp( string strTemp )
{
   // Convert a string, e.g., " -44 c ", to a
   //    temperature and a unit of measure.

   // An empty string produces a cold WaterTemp!
   if( strTemp == string.Empty )
   {
      strTemp = "0k";
   }

   // The last character, optional, is the unit of
   //    measure.  Everything else is the temperature.
   strError = strerrFormat;
   try
   {
      // Split the input string on 'K', 'C', or 'F'.
      string[] strarrTemp;
      strTemp = strTemp.Trim().ToUpper();
      strarrTemp = strTemp.Split("KCF".ToCharArray());

      // Store the temperature portion.  (If any letter
      //    other than K, C, or F was specified as the
      //    unit of measure, it will be in strarrTemp[0]
      //    and will cause an exception here.)
      this.m_Temperature =
         System.Convert.ToInt32(strarrTemp[0]);

      // The unit of measure, if any, is the last character.
      // The default unit of measure is 'K' (Kelvin).
      this.m_UnitOfMeasure =
         strarrTemp.Length == 2 ?
         strTemp.Substring(strTemp.Length-1,1) : "K";

      strError = strerrTemp;
      // Temperature cannot be below 0 Kelvin.
      // (Do not use Convert here.  Fahrenheit precision
      //    will be lost when converting to/from Kelvin.)
      strError = "Temperature cannot be below 0 Kelvin.";
      if( (m_UnitOfMeasure == "K" && m_Temperature < 0)
         ||(m_UnitOfMeasure == "C" && m_Temperature < -273)
         ||(m_UnitOfMeasure == "F" && m_Temperature < -460)
         )
      {
         throw new ArgumentException(strError);
      }
   }
   catch
```

continues

continued

```
        {
            throw new ArgumentException(strError);
        }
        finally
        {
        }
    }

    public WaterTemp Convert( string strUofM )
    {
        strUofM = strUofM.ToUpper();
        int intTemp = m_Temperature;

        switch( strUofM )
        {
            case "K":
            switch( m_UnitOfMeasure )
            {
                case "F":
                    intTemp =
                        (((intTemp + 40) * 5) / 9) - 40;
                    intTemp += 273;
                    break;
                case "C":
                    intTemp += 273;
                    break;
            }
                break;
            case "C":
            switch( m_UnitOfMeasure )
            {
                case "K":
                    intTemp -= 273;
                    break;
                case "F":
                    intTemp =
                        (((intTemp + 40) * 5) / 9) - 40;
                    break;
            }
                break;
            case "F":
            switch( m_UnitOfMeasure )
            {
                case "K":
                    intTemp -= 273;
                    intTemp =
                        (((intTemp + 40) * 9) / 5) - 40;
                    break;
```

```
            case "C":
               intTemp =
                  (((intTemp + 40) * 9) / 5) - 40;
               break;
         }
            break;
         default:
            throw new ArgumentException(strerrUofM);
      }

      return new WaterTemp(intTemp.ToString() + strUofM);
   }

   public int CompareTo(WaterTemp wtTarget)
   {
      // If this and the target are the
      //    same unit of measure, compare temperatures.
      // Otherwise, convert this to the
      //    other's unit of measure and compare temperatures.
      if( this.UnitOfMeasure == wtTarget.UnitOfMeasure  )
      {
         return
            m_Temperature.CompareTo(wtTarget.Temperature);
      }
      else
      {
         return
            m_Temperature.CompareTo(
               wtTarget.Convert(m_UnitOfMeasure).Temperature);
      }
   }

   public override string ToString()
   {
      return m_Temperature.ToString() + m_UnitOfMeasure;
   }

   public WaterTemp Clone()
   {
      return new WaterTemp(this.ToString());
   }

  }
}
```

That completes the immutable `WaterTemp` data type.

The `WaterBox` *Object*

Having defined a temperature data type class makes the definition of the water temperature `TextBox` object extremely simple. All we need is to take an ordinary `TextBox` control and add water. (Just kidding.) Actually, all we need to do is take an ordinary `TextBox` control and add a `WaterTemp` property. Plus, we'll have our `TextBox` set its background color to something representative of the state of the water: blue for ice, white for water, and red for steam (assuming standard atmospheric pressure).

The lessons learned from our `DateBox` control example apply to this control too. When two properties represent the same data, we channel all activity through the most restrictive one (in this case, the `WaterTemp` property). So we use the same logic as before: `Validating` sets `Text`, `Text` sets `WaterTemp`.

To create the custom control that will display `WaterTemp` data, return to the Project menu of the `WaterTempControl` project and add a new class. Make changes similar to those we made in the custom `DateBox` example presented earlier in this chapter regarding references, `using` statements, the namespace name, the class name, and the base class, as shown in the upcoming listing. Note that we include our own namespace, `YaoDurant.Types`, as well as the .NET namespaces, for we will be creating and manipulating `YaoDurant.Types.WaterTemp` objects.

As was the case with the `DateBox` custom control, we need to have an underlying property, in this case the `WaterTemp` property instead of the `Date` property, and we need to keep this property in sync with the `Text` property. Once again, keeping the two in sync means overriding the `Text` property and handling the `Validating` event.

We also need two constructors so that the client code can create a `WaterBox` object with or without specifying an initial temperature.

Thus, much of the `WaterBox` code, which is shown in Listing 10.13, is similar to the `DateBox` code.

LISTING 10.13: The `WaterBox` Custom Control Class

```
using System;
using System.ComponentModel;
using System.Drawing;
```

```
using System.Windows.Forms;
using YaoDurant.Types;

namespace YaoDurant.Gui
{
   /// <summary>
   /// Summary description for WaterBox.
   /// </summary>
   public class WaterBox : TextBox
   {

      // WaterTemp
      //    The WaterTemp contained and displayed
      //       in this control
      private bool boolSettingTemperature;
      private WaterTemp m_Temperature;
      public WaterTemp Temperature
      {
         get { return m_Temperature; }
         set
         {
            // Set the private Temperature.
            m_Temperature = value;

            // Set the Text property.
            boolSettingTemperature = true;
            this.Text = m_Temperature.ToString();
            boolSettingTemperature = false;

            // Set the background color to
            //    indicate ice, water, or steam.
            this.BackColor = Color.White;
            if( m_Temperature.CompareTo(new WaterTemp("0c")) == -1)
            {
               this.BackColor = Color.LightSteelBlue;
            }
            if( m_Temperature.CompareTo(new WaterTemp("100c")) == 1)
            {
               this.BackColor = Color.LightPink;
            }
         }
      }


      // Text
      public override string Text
      {
         get
         {
            return base.Text;
```

continues

continued

```
        }
        set
        {
           try
           {
              // There is no such thing as an "empty"
              //    Temperature.  If there is no value for
              //    Temperature, treat it as zero degrees
              //    Kelvin.
              if( value == String.Empty )
              {
                 value = "0k";
              }

              // To prevent an infinite loop...
              // If this accessor is being called because
              //    the Temperature property is being set,
              //    do not set the Temperature property.
              //    Else, set the Temperature to keep it
              //    in sync with the Text property.
              if( boolSettingTemperature )
              {
                 base.Text = value;
              }
              else
              {
                 this.Temperature = new WaterTemp(value);
              }
           }
           catch
           {
              // Unable to convert value to WaterTemp.
              // (Highly unlikely that "base.Text = value;"
              //    would cause the exception.)
              throw new
                 System.ArgumentException(
                               "Not a valid temperature");
           }
           finally
           {
           }
        }
     }


     public WaterBox()
     {
        // Initialize Temperature.
        this.Temperature = new WaterTemp("0k");
```

```
         // Initialize the remainder of this control.
         InitializeWaterBox();
      }

      public WaterBox(string strTemp)
      {
         // Initialize Temperature.
         this.Temperature = new WaterTemp(strTemp);

         // Initialize the remainder of this control.
         InitializeWaterBox();
      }

      private void InitializeWaterBox()
      {
         // Handle own Validating events.
         // Note -- Cannot override OnValidated as it is
         //    "inherited but not implemented" in the
         //    .NET Compact Framework.
         this.Validating +=
            new CancelEventHandler(this.this_Validating);
      }

      private void this_Validating(object sender,
                                   CancelEventArgs e)
      {
         // Ensure that the Text property contains a Temperature.
         // If not, set the background color to red and set the
         //    EventArg's Cancel property to true to indicate
         //    that validation failed.
         try
         {
            this.Text = this.Text;
         }
         catch
         {
            this.BackColor = Color.Red;
            e.Cancel = true;
         }
         finally
         {
         }
      }
      #endregion
   }
}
```

This completes our `WaterBox` definition.

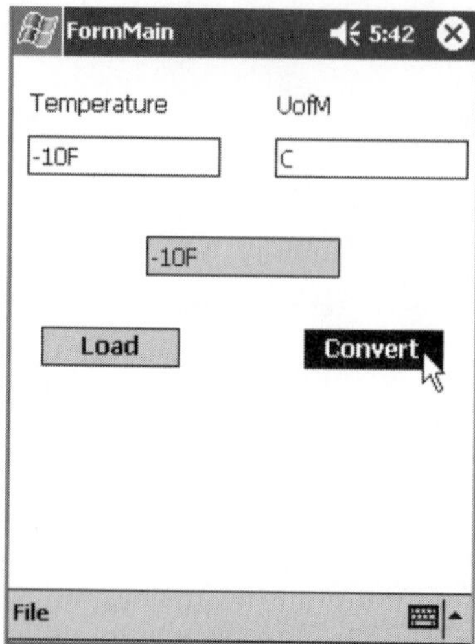

FIGURE 10.14: The `WaterTemp` test program

With both the data type and the custom control defined, we can proceed to the test project. Once again, from within the test project, we set a reference to the custom objects project and add code to the form that will create an instance of the custom control and display it on the form. We'll also add a few other controls for use in testing the constructors and the `Convert` method. Listing 10.14 shows this code, and Figure 10.14 shows the results of running it.

LISTING 10.14: The `WaterBox` Testing Form

```
private void FormMain_Load(object sender, System.EventArgs e)
{
   wbTest = new YaoDurant.Gui.WaterBox("44f");
   wbTest.Location =
      new Point( (this.Width/2) - (wbTest.Width/2),
                 txtTemp.Bottom + 30);
   wbTest.Parent = this;
   wbTest.Focus();
}

private void cmdLoad_Click(object sender,
                          System.EventArgs e)
{
```

```
        wbTest.Temperature =
            new WaterTemp(txtTemp.Text + txtUofM.Text);
    }

    private void cmdConvert_Click(object sender,
                                System.EventArgs e)
    {
        wbTest.Temperature =
            wbTest.Temperature.Convert(txtUofM.Text);
    }
```

So you have now completed two examples of extending the capabilities of an existing control class: one in which you only needed to enhance the display and user interface capabilities, and one in which you provided some encapsulated functionality that was independent of the user interface. Along the way, we covered the following topics:

- How to separate functionality from presentation
- How to constrain existing properties
- How to use context menus
- What benefits we obtain from using immutable object classes as properties
- What differences exist between the `new` and `override` keywords
- When to call the base class method

So, now that you have created two custom controls by extending a control class, let's look at another way to create a custom control.

Creating Composite Controls

Another approach to creating controls is to combine several controls to create a single, new control where each of the controls works together. A well-known example of this is the `ComboBox` control. As its name implies, this control combines a `ListBox` with one other control—either a static text `Label` or a `TextBox`.

A Clarification of Terminology

Composite controls are controls that you author yourself and to which you add already-defined control classes, such as `Label` and `TextBox`, to provide some or all of the functionality of the composite control. They are similar in concept to two other types of controls: user controls, which apply to ASP.NET programming, and container controls, which are .NET controls such as the `Panel` control whose primary purpose is to be containers for other controls.

For further discussion of this subject, consult the Visual Studio .NET online help. Use the Index tab to search for "composite controls" and then choose "Composite Controls ASP.NET Mobile Controls."

For our next example, then, we create a custom control not by extending other controls but by containing other controls. Figure 10.15 shows the control we create, the `TaskStatus` control.

This control displays information about the status of a task by providing the start date, the end date, the estimated number of person-days that

FIGURE 10.15: The `TaskStatus` custom control

will be needed, and the actual number of person-days expended thus far. The information is displayed in four controls, two `DateBox` controls and two `TextBox` controls, which are contained within the parent control. Packaging the functionality of several constituent controls into a single custom control is a common requirement and a fairly easy thing to do.

As you design any composite control, you need to keep in mind that the PMEs of the constituent controls are exposed to the composite control but not to the application that uses the composite control. As you author a custom composite control, you can access the constituent controls just as if you had placed them on a form. But developers who use your control do not have access to them unless you expressly provide it. Developers see your control as just that—a single control. Developers can access the content of the constituent controls only for the elements you expose as public properties or methods of your control. Part of your work in creating the control, then, consists of deciding what to hide from the outside world and what to share.

The `TaskStatus` Control Example

We dive right in to our composite control example without further preliminaries because the creation of composite controls can be accomplished with a straightforward development process. We first add a new project to the existing solution, the solution that already contains the `DateBoxControl` project. We name the new project `TaskStatusControl`.

As usual, we then set references, `using` statements, the namespace name, and the class name. Because the `TaskStatus` control will contain `DateBox` controls and because the `DateBox` project is in the current solution, we set a project reference to the `DateBox` project. If the `DateBox` project were not the current solution, we would need a reference to the `DateBox` assembly file. To ensure that the source code and IL code are in sync, we rebuild the `DateBox` project just prior to setting the reference.

We move on to defining the properties of the `TaskStatus` control. Because the control will contain four other controls (two `DateBox` controls and two `TextBox` controls), we must define private variables to hold those controls. We expose the values that will be displayed in those controls as public properties. We also need a default constructor to create and position the contained controls during instantiation.

Listing 10.15 shows the resulting code for our `TaskStatus` control. This code can be found in the `DateAndStatusControls` project on the Web site.

LISTING 10.15: The `TaskStatus` Composite Control

```
using System;
using System.Windows.Forms;
using System.Drawing;
using YaoDurant.Gui;

namespace YaoDurant.Gui
{
   /// <summary>
   /// Summary description for TaskStatus
   /// </summary>

   public class TaskStatus : System.Windows.Forms.Control
      {

      // The contained controls
      private DateBox tskdtBegin, tskdtEnd;
      private TextBox txtEstimated, txtActual;

      // Their four values
      public DateTime dateBegin
      {
         get { return tskdtBegin.Date; }
         set { tskdtBegin.Date = value; }
      }
      public DateTime dateEnd
      {
         get { return tskdtEnd.Date; }
         set { tskdtEnd.Date = value; }
      }
      public int durEstimated
      {
         get { return Convert.ToInt32(txtEstimated.Text); }
         set { txtEstimated.Text = value.ToString(); }
      }
      public int durActual
      {
         get { return Convert.ToInt32(txtActual.Text); }
         set { txtActual.Text = value.ToString(); }
      }


      public TaskStatus()
      {
```

```
            // Create two DateBox controls and two TextBox controls
            tskdtBegin = new DateBox();
            tskdtBegin.Parent = this;
            tskdtEnd = new DateBox();
            tskdtEnd.Parent = this;
            txtEstimated = new TextBox();
            txtEstimated.Parent = this;
            txtEstimated.Width = tskdtBegin.Width / 2;
            txtActual = new TextBox();
            txtActual.Parent = this;
            txtActual.Width = tskdtBegin.Width / 2;

            // Position them from left to right to fill this.
            int PrevRight = 0;
            foreach( Control cntlX in this.Controls )
            {
               cntlX.Left = PrevRight;
               PrevRight += cntlX.Width;
               cntlX.Visible = true;
            }
            this.Height = tskdtEnd.Height;
            this.Width = PrevRight + (this.Height / 3);
         }
      }
   }
```

We must cover one more aspect of composite control programming before we can be finished: programming the relationships between the controls.

Programming for the Relationship between Components

We have finished programming for the individual component controls that make up our composite control. For example, we wrote a `Validating` event handler for the `DateBox` controls to ensure that the user entered only valid dates into a `DateBox` control. But we have not yet addressed the issue of programming for the relationship between our component controls. For instance, as the application now stands, it is possible for a user to enter an ending date that is prior to the starting date.

We need to write code that does not allow this to happen. Thus, we need to add code to the `TaskStatus` class. As always, the first question is: "Into what event handler(s) should this code be placed?" Because we wish to validate user-entered data, the answer is: "In the `Validating` event handler of both DateBox controls." We will be reacting to events raised by the component DateBox controls, so we must include the WithEvents modifier when declaring the reference variables for these controls.

A Validating event handler takes two parameters: an object (sender) and a System.ComponentModel.CancelEventArgs. Because we need to handle a change in either DateBox control identically, we use the same handler for both DateBox controls' Validating events. We add a using statement to reference System.ComponentModel at the start of the program, and we name our handler Dates_Validating, as shown here.

```
using System.ComponentModel;
             :
             :

private void Dates_Validating(object sender,
                              CancelEventArgs e)
{
}
```

We tie the Validating event of our two controls to our handler as we create them.

```
// Create two DateBox controls.
tskdtBegin = new DateBox();
tskdtBegin.Parent = this;
tskdtBegin.Validating +=
   new CancelEventHandler(this.Dates_Validating);
tskdtEnd = new DateBox();
tskdtEnd.Parent = this;
tskdtEnd.Validating +=
   new CancelEventHandler(this.Dates_Validating);
```

We handle the event by comparing the start date with the end date. If the relationship is not valid, we notify the user and set the CancelEventArgs Cancel property to true, as shown in Listing 10.16.

LISTING 10.16: Relating the Start and End Dates

```
// Convert the two date textbox's Text
//    property values into dates.
DateTime dtBegin =
            System.Convert.ToDateTime(tskdtBegin.Text);
```

```
DateTime dtEnd =
            System.Convert.ToDateTime(tskdtEnd.Text);

// Start date must be prior to end date.
if( dtEnd < dtBegin )
{
MessageBox.Show(
   "Start date must be prior to end date.",
   "Error",
   MessageBoxButtons.OK,
   MessageBoxIcon.Exclamation,
   MessageBoxDefaultButton.Button1);
e.Cancel = true;
}
```

Writing this code for this event handler might give you a feeling of either déjà vu or confusion—or both. After all, we already wrote code to handle the `Validating` event raised by a `DateBox` control. But that was in the `DateBox` class, where we were checking to ensure that a valid date was entered into the individual `DateBox` control. Now we are in the `TaskStatus` class, and we are checking the value of a date entered into one of our component `DateBox` controls against the date in the other `DateBox` control.

As the user completes the entry of a date into a `DateBox` control, one `Validating` event will be raised and both event handlers will be called. The `DateBox` class's handler will be called first; the `TaskStatus` class's handler will be called second. The same instance of the `EventArgs` parameter will be used for both calls. If the first handler executed sets the `Cancel` property to `true`, the calling of handlers will still continue, and the second handler will be able to determine that the previous hander considered the data to be invalid. We need to take advantage of this here because there is no point in comparing an invalid date against another date, especially because doing so would raise an exception. So we check to see if the `DateBox` control itself approved the date before we compare it to the other date, as shown in the code below, which we place at the start of the `Validating` event handler.

```
if( e.Cancel != true )
{
      :
      :
}
```

Listing 10.17 shows the now complete `Validating` event handler.

LISTING 10.17: The `Validating` Event Handler for the `DateBox` Controls

```
private void Dates_Validating(object sender,
                              CancelEventArgs e)
{
   // If the DateBox's validation routine determined
   //    that the date is invalid, do not compare it
   //    to the other date.  (There is only "bad" data,
   //    there is no "even worse" data.)
   if( e.Cancel != true )
   {
      // Convert the two date textbox's Text
      //    property values into dates.
      DateTime dtBegin =
                  System.Convert.ToDateTime(tskdtBegin.Text);
      DateTime dtEnd =
                  System.Convert.ToDateTime(tskdtEnd.Text);

      // Start date must be prior to end date.
      if( dtEnd < dtBegin )
      {
      MessageBox.Show(
         "Start date must be prior to end date.",
         "Error",
         MessageBoxButtons.OK,
         MessageBoxIcon.Exclamation,
         MessageBoxDefaultButton.Button1);
      e.Cancel = true;
      }
   }
}
```

So, you can establish relationships between your contained controls by reacting to the events raised by those controls. Doing so requires that the contained control's reference variable be defined as `WithEvents`. When you handle the event of a contained control, its own event handler has already executed. In the case of a `Validating` event, the previous handler may have determined that the data is invalid. Your handler will execute even if a previous handler has declared the data invalid and should check for that condition.

We test our completed `TaskStatus` control the same way we tested our `DateBox` control—by adding a test project to our solution, creating an instance of the control during the form's initialization, and adding it to the form's `Controls` collection.

> Custom composite controls are easy to define because the constituent controls are there to do most of the work for you. Composite controls allow you to package the functionality of several existing controls, plus some custom functionality, into a single custom control that you and other developers can use.

Creating New Controls

The third, and final, variation on custom controls that we examine is new controls created from scratch—or, at least, from the foundation that the `Control`[4] class provides. As the author of a new control, you override the `OnPaint` method and optionally the `OnPaintBackground` method and make the Graphic Device Interface (GDI) calls necessary to present text and graphics to users.

Design Tips

Before we get into the details of coding, we start with a review of some design tips that will help you create custom controls.

Custom Controls Support More Events Than Built-in Controls

As we discussed in Chapter 7, the built-in controls get a subset of all possible events. The .NET Compact Framework relies heavily on the underlying Win32 implementation of each control and, to provide the best overall performance, does not allow all events to bubble up from unmanaged code to the managed-code layer.

Because the .NET Compact Framework team wanted to provide the opportunity for programs to get the broadest set of events when they need them, the `Control` class supports all events that have been defined; that is,

4. Fully qualified name: `System.Windows.Forms.Control`.

everything that is inherited has been implemented. Derive a custom control from the `Control` class, for example, to get a complete set of mouse and keyboard events, as well as the `Paint` event (which we discuss in more detail next).

You Can Override the Drawing Only for Controls Directly Derived from `Control`

This is a .NET Compact Framework limitation. The desktop environment allows custom controls derived from `Label`, `TextBox`, and so on to override the `OnPaint` method and do their own drawing. But in the .NET Compact Framework, if you want to create a custom control in which the derived control does the drawing, your custom control class must inherit directly from `Control`.

The reason is that the `OnPaint` method is not supported for most .NET Compact Framework controls. This is an example of the "inherited does not mean supported" concept we discussed in Chapter 7. So although you can add a handler for the `Paint` event for a `Button` or `TextBox` control, that event handler will never be called in the .NET Compact Framework.

The `Paint` event *is* supported for a few .NET Compact Framework controls, for example, the `Form` control, which means you can create a custom application with custom graphics without creating a custom control. The `Paint` event is also supported for the `Control` class and for any custom class[5] you derive from this class. The `Paint` event is also apparently supported for the `Panel` control, although the Designer excludes the `Paint` event on the list of supported `Panel` control events. You must manually create the event handler, but when you do, the handler is called and you can draw in the `Panel` control.

A Redrawing Can Be Requested by the Runtime or Initiated by the Application

The GUI environment generates a `Paint` event to let a control know that its contents need to be redrawn. The application (or the control itself) can force a redrawing whenever it feels that the image is out of sync with the

---

5. Strangely, however, the built-in classes that derive from `Control` do not support the `Paint` event.

state of the application. Your program requests redrawing by calling the control's `Invalidate` method.[6] This is the only correct way to request the redrawing of any control (including forms and panels).

Within the runtime, the call to the `Invalidate` method causes a `Paint` event, and the runtime responds by calling a control's `OnPaint` procedure to request that the control redraw itself. This can happen in several situations, such as when a control acquires pixels that it did not previously own, when resizing a control, when showing a previously hidden control, and when removing an overlaying window.

Drawing in a Custom Control

In a custom control, the control itself is responsible for drawing whatever needs to appear in its display area. We cover the details of creating graphical output more fully in Part IV of this book.

Providing Our Own Display for the `TaskStatus` Control

With the background information out of the way, let's apply that knowledge by enhancing the `TaskStatus` class we developed in the `TaskStatus` Control Example subsection to provide an alternate display format. This alternate format provides the same information as the earlier format but presents it as a horizontal bar graph, with the right and left sides representing the start and end dates, respectively, a small triangle representing the current date, the bar representing the amount of the project that has actually been completed, and the background color (green or red) indicating whether the project is ahead of or behind schedule. The user can toggle the display mode of the `TaskStatus` control by clicking on it.

The enhanced control design will include the following items:

- A property that indicates the current display mode of the control (text mode or graphic mode)
- Four brushes for the possible bar and background colors

---

6. Win32 programmers recognize this as the surrogate for the Win32 `InvalidateRect` function. MFC programmers recognize this as the replacement for the `CWnd::Invalidate` method.

- An override of the `OnClick` method that will toggle the display mode
- An override of the `OnPaint` method that will draw the bar graph

We add the property definition code immediately after the four properties we already created (see Listing 10.15 earlier). When authoring the display mode property we must remember that changing the display mode must make the constituent controls disappear or reappear. Listing 10.18 presents the code for our new properties.

LISTING 10.18: The Additional Properties of the `TaskStatus` Class

```
// The current display mode: text or graphic
private enum Modes { modeText, modeGraphic }
private Modes m_Mode;
private Modes Mode
{
   get { return m_Mode; }
   set
   {
      // Set the mode.
      m_Mode = value;

      // Child controls are used only when in modeText.
      foreach( Control cntlX in this.Controls )
         cntlX.Visible = (m_Mode==Modes.modeText);          {
      }

      // State has changed; redraw this.
      this.Invalidate();
   }
}

// Brushes for filling
private SolidBrush brushRed =
   new SolidBrush(Color.Red);
private SolidBrush brushGray =
   new SolidBrush(Color.LightSlateGray);
private SolidBrush brushGreen =
   new SolidBrush(Color.Green);
private SolidBrush brushBlack =
   new SolidBrush(Color.Black);
```

We need to initialize the display mode during construction, and we'll use a background color of gray (gray just seemed to be the most attractive background color for both text mode and graphic mode). We do this by adding the following code to the constructor:

```
// Set background color to light gray.
this.BackColor = Color.LightSlateGray;

// Set the mode.
this.m_Mode = Modes.modeText;
```

The code for toggling the display mode whenever the user clicks on our control is very simple, for all it needs to do is change the display mode property. The code for the overridden `OnClick` method is shown here.

```
protected override void OnClick(EventArgs e)
{
   // Call the base class method.
   base.OnClick(e);

   // Swap modes.
   switch( this.Mode )
   {
      case Modes.modeText:
         { this.Mode = Modes.modeGraphic; break; }
      case Modes.modeGraphic:
         { this.Mode = Modes.modeText; break; }
   }
}
```

Drawing our own bar graph requires overriding the `OnPaint` method because the control has no idea how to draw our graph. First, we call the base class `OnPaint` method to ensure that the background is erased. If the control is in text mode, we're done—the display of information will be done by the contained controls. But if the control is in graphic mode, it needs to draw the bar graph.

You may have worked in a graphics environment that supports *anisotropic mapping*, which allows graphic output to be done in whatever arbitrary coordinates are convenient. The .NET Compact Framework does not support anisotropic mapping or any of the other mapping modes you may be used to using. The only available coordinate system is—pixels! Because anisotropic mapping is not available, we must do some integer arithmetic to provide our own coordinate system. Once we do that, we can draw the bar that represents project progress and the triangle that represents the current date, then choose the color that represents the status of the project. The code that does this, by overriding the `OnPaint` method, is shown in Listing 10.19.

LISTING 10.19: The Drawing Routine of the `TaskStatus` Class

```
protected override void OnPaint(PaintEventArgs e)
{
   // Call the base class method.
   base.OnPaint(e);

   switch( this.Mode )
   {
      case Modes.modeText:
      {
         // In text mode, the contained controls
         //    do all the work.
         break;
      }
      case Modes.modeGraphic:
      {
         // The client rectangle represents the time
         //    from task start to task end.  Draw a
         //    rectangle from the left that represents
         //    the percentage of task completion.  Draw
         //    a small triangle to mark today, relative
         //    to task start/end.
         // If the triangle is located to the right of
         //    the rectangle, the project is behind
         //    schedule; color the rectangle red.  If
         //    the triangle is located within the
         //    rectangle, the project is ahead of
         //    schedule; color it green.

         // Calculate coordinates.
         int daysStartToEnd =
            dateEnd.Subtract(this.dateBegin).Days;
         int daysStartToNow =
            DateTime.Today.Subtract(this.dateBegin).Days;
         Rectangle rectX = this.ClientRectangle;
         int xposToday =
            (rectX.Width*daysStartToNow) / daysStartToEnd;
         int xposComplete =
            (rectX.Width * durActual) / 100;
         int yposAll = this.Height / 2;
         Point[] arrptTriangle =
            {
              new Point(xposToday-(yposAll/2), 0)
```

```
            , new Point(xposToday, yposAll)
            , new Point(xposToday+(yposAll/2), 0) };

         // Draw rectangle.
         rectX.Width = xposComplete;
         e.Graphics.FillRectangle(
            (xposToday <= xposComplete) ?
                                 brushGreen : brushRed,
            rectX);

         // Draw triangle.
         e.Graphics.FillPolygon(brushBlack, arrptTriangle);

         break;
      }
   }
}
```

That completes the code for our enhanced `TaskStatus` control.

> In summary, a few properties, some initialization, and two overridden methods were all we required to create the `TaskStatus` control. Mostly, we let the other classes, `TextBox` and `DateBox`, do the work for us. When that was not enough and we needed a custom graphic, we overrode the `Control` class's `OnPaint` method.

Adding Animation to a Custom Control

Writing custom controls with static output can take you a long way, and most of the time that is all you need. There are cases, however, when it makes sense to animate a control. When the underlying data is changing rapidly, you may need to animate it. Or when you want to underscore visually the sequences involved in some change, then animation provides the only way to do that. And whether or not you need to add animation per se, animation puts a stress on the system—so a successful case study in animation can teach lessons that apply even outside the graphic animation case. Finally, creating a visually interesting program is just plain fun. This is perhaps the most important reason that GUI programming has flourished during the past few decades.

The Game of Life

For our animation example, we implement a program that is a bit more complex than our previous examples. We write a program to run the John Horton Conway game called Life. For further information on the game of Life, see the sidebar.

A Brief History and Definition of the Game of Life

The game of Life was invented by John Horton Conway in the late 1960s and became popular when featured in a *Scientific American* article written by Martin Gardner.

It is not a game in the traditional sense. You do not compete against the computer or against another person. In fact, other than choosing a starting pattern, you have no influence at all. It is a "game" in which any pattern produces a new pattern, the next generation, according to a very simple set of rules.

Conway devised the game for his students to illustrate the difficulty of predicting the future, even when the rules are simple and all the inputs are known. It is certainly "lifelike" in that small changes can have a great impact, long-term results are hard to predict, and symmetrically flawed patterns grow better than symmetrically perfect ones.

A pattern is a checkerboard grid consisting of live cells and dead cells. Each cell touches eight other cells: the cells above, below, left, and right plus the four corner cells. The following rules are used for calculating the next generation.

- Any live cell that is touched by two or three live cells remains alive.
- Any dead cell that is touched by three live cells becomes alive.
- All other cells die.

For example, the pattern consisting of three horizontal live cells, XXX, will become three vertical live cells in the next generation because the left and right cells die (each is a live cell touched by only one live cell), the center cell remains alive (live cell touched by two live cells), and the top center and bottom center cells become alive (dead cell touched by three live cells).

This new vertical string of three live cells will then revert to the original horizontal pattern in its next generation. Thus, XXX is a "steady-state" pattern, toggling between horizontal and vertical forever.

Some patterns are completely static, such as a 2 × 2 square of live cells.

The pattern shown in Figure 10.16, called a Glider pattern, will glide diagonally across the grid, moving one unit of distance every four generations.

Most patterns become steady-state in a few generations, excluding any Glider patterns that they have spun off toward infinity. But some last a surprisingly long time. There is one five-cell pattern that lives for more than 1,000 generations.

Perhaps the most amazing pattern is the Glider Pump pattern, shown in Figure 10.17, which a *Scientific American* reader submitted shortly after

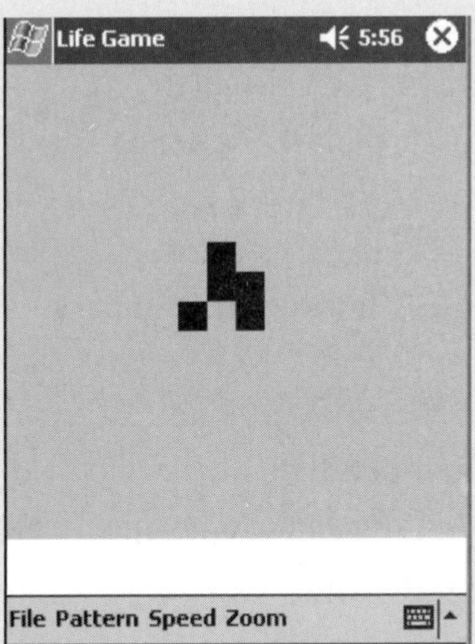

FIGURE 10.16: The Glider pattern

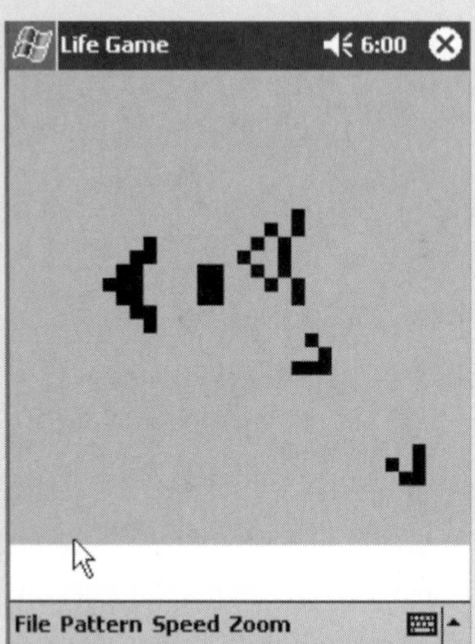

FIGURE 10.17: The Glider Pump pattern

the initial article appeared. It is that great rarity, a pattern that never reaches a static state, pumping out gliders forever.

Asymmetrical patterns live longer than symmetrical ones. The Flawed Vertical Line pattern shown in Figure 10.18 will live far longer than an unflawed vertical line of the same length.

Compare the Self-Fixing Checkerboard pattern shown in Figure 10.19 with the Self-Destructive Checkerboard pattern shown in Figure 10.20. The former will quickly “reject” the extra cell located at the center and become a steady-state pattern, while the latter is unable to do the same, slowly disintegrating until every cell has disappeared. Conway likened this latter pair to a study of cancer. In one case a foreign cell is introduced into a stable pattern at a symmetrical point and is immediately rejected by the pattern. In the other, the foreign cell is introduced at an asymmetrical location, and it proceeds to slowly eat the pattern alive.

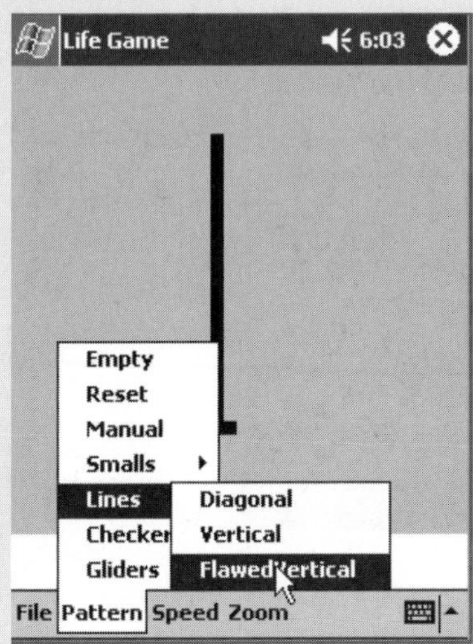

FIGURE 10.18: The Flawed Vertical Line pattern

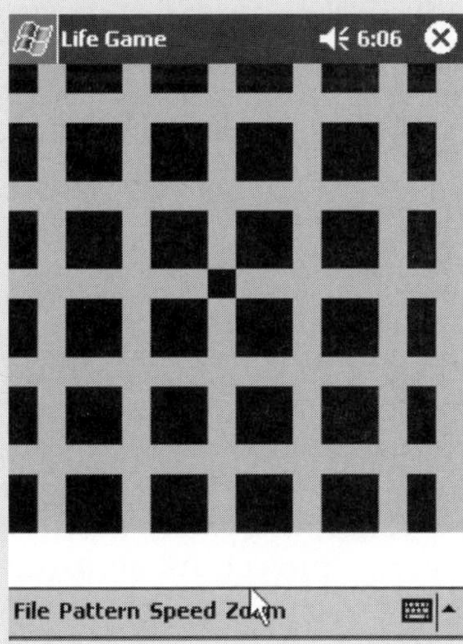

FIGURE 10.19: The Self-Fixing Checkerboard pattern

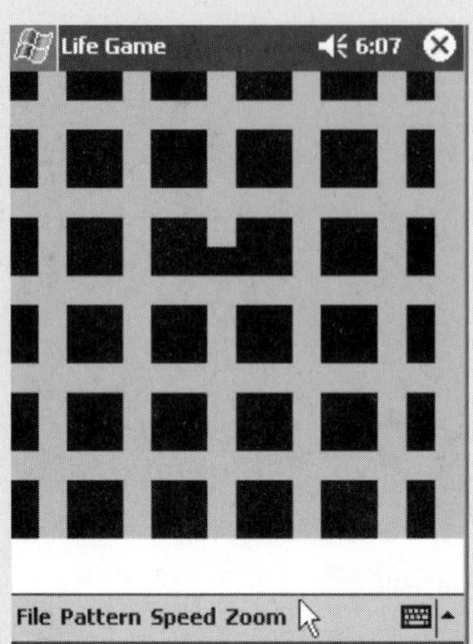

FIGURE 10.20: The Self-Destructive Checkerboard pattern

Interestingly, neither Conway nor Gardner knew how to program a computer. Conway did all his initial development on paper. The article was the first *Scientific American* article to receive wide response from programmers, who were a small and arcane group in those days. The magazine was stunned that anyone could, or would, write a computer program to calculate generations.

We present the game of Life in this book primarily as a fun application and as a self-study item. We do not go into it in detail, nor do we show all of the code. Instead we concentrate on an aspect of custom control development that we have not yet encountered: animation. The entire application can be found in the `LifeGame` project. As an extra bonus, we also include the version for the desktop .NET Framework.

As we mention in the sidebar, the game is not a game in the usual sense of the word—the user does not compete against another user or the computer. It is a cellular automation application, something that was quite popular a generation ago. The science of cellular automation is still used today, for applications as diverse as weather prediction and medical research. In our application, the user produces a starting pattern by selecting from the menu or by tapping on the screen, as shown in Figure 10.21. Once the initial pattern has been specified, the user starts the application running by selecting Start from the File menu. At any time the user can increase or decrease the run speed and can zoom in or out via menu selections. The game runs until it reaches a steady state or the user halts it.

`LifeGame` is a sufficiently complicated application that we need to do some good object-oriented design at the start. We begin as always by separating the functionality that must occur in the background from the presentation of that functionality. Obviously we will need a `Form` class, and it certainly looks like there is no .NET Compact Framework control that could be used for the display, so we will need a custom control. These two classes will cover the presentation aspect of our application.

This leaves us with the task of breaking the game itself down into object classes. The design that we chose is certainly not the only one that would work, but it is based on the experience that one of us has had in writing this application in multiple languages and development environments ever since the article first appeared.

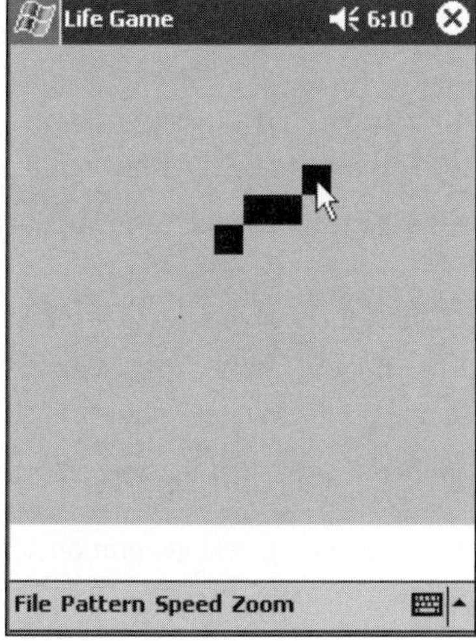

FIGURE 10.21: Building a pattern by tapping

The game itself is an object, each generation is an object, and each row is an object. It's advantageous to make each generation an object because generations must be compared against each other to determine whether the game has reached a static state. It's advantageous to make each row an object because performance optimization involves comparing rows against neighboring rows of the same generation and against the same row of the previous generation.

Breaking things down further, we come up with the class definitions outlined in Table 10.2. Examine the source code in the `LifeGame` project to learn more about other aspects of the code not related specifically to animation (the only subject we cover in the rest of this discussion).

TABLE 10.2: Classes for the Game of Life

Class	What It Does
`FormMain`	Extends `Form`
	Creates and maintains the menu
	Creates and displays the `LifeControl`
	Provides a delegate that can be called when the calculation of the next generation is complete
	Provides a delegate that can be called when the game has reached a steady state
`LifeControl`	Extends `Control`
	Draws the current generation when requested
	Optimizes drawing performance and appearance by minimizing the number of drawing calls
	Does not allow the background to be erased from one generation to the next
	Does not draw cells that have not changed state
	Draws contiguous cells of the same color with one drawing call
`LifeRow`	Calculates a row of the next generation
	Sets cells from an array
	Toggles a cell

Class	What It Does
`LifeMain`	Maintains a set of predefined patterns Maintains four generations (enough to detect a steady-state pattern) Maintains the run speed by suspending the main thread between generations Starts and stops the game Notifies the client when the calculation of the next generation is complete Notifies the client when the game has reached a steady state Reuses a generation object as it ages out, rather than creating a new generation object
`LifeGeneration`	Maintains an array of rows Initializes a generation Calculates the next generation Compares one generation to another Sets a generation equal to a predefined pattern

Providing Consistent Speed and Minimal Flicker

Animated controls must display a sequence of images to the user as rapidly and consistently as possible, much as a motion picture projector does; and they must do so with minimal flicker.

Consistent speed is achieved by having a thread that continuously draws and sleeps, draws and sleeps. This is usually achieved with a `Timer` control or by a call to `Thread.Sleep` at the completion of the drawing. Since the object that is generating the data for the images is usually not the control that is displaying the images, a custom event or callback is used to indicate that the next image is ready to be drawn. (The `LifeGame` application uses a call to `Thread.Sleep` and a callback named `NextGenReady` to control its display speed, as shown in Listing 10.20, excerpted from `FormMain.cs`.)

LISTING 10.20: Handling the Event That Shows the Next Generation Has Been Calculated

```
   //   Specify the delegate function to be notified
   //      when a new generation has been calculated.
   refLifeMain.NextGenReady +=
   new LifeMain.deleNextGenReady( LifeMain_NextGenReady );
                  :
                  :
                  :
private void LifeMain_NextGenReady( object sender, EventArgs e )
{
   // Place a reference to the current and previous
   //    generations into properties of the control.
   //    Then have the control draw the current
   //    generation.
   this.facadeLifeGame.refCurr = refLifeMain.genCurr;
   this.facadeLifeGame.refPrev = refLifeMain.genPrev;
   this.facadeLifeGame.Invalidate();
   Application.DoEvents();
}
```

The continuous flow of generations is done through a simple loop, shown in this code from `LifeMain.cs`.

```
boolRun = true;
while (boolRun)
{
   CalcNextGen();
   boolPaintAll = false;
   OnNextGenReady();
   boolPaintAll = true;
   Thread.Sleep( (int)RunSpeed );
}
```

Flicker occurs when the color of one or more pixels changes more than once during the drawing of a single image. In the `LifeGame` application, this means never changing the color of a cell from live to dead and back to live when drawing the next generation. Preventing flickering, therefore, includes preventing the normal erasing of a control's background when drawing each image. If the `LifeGame` screen went blank between each generation, it would be very disconcerting to the user.

The code for doing this, excerpted from the `LifeControl` custom control, is shown in Listing 10.21. The override of the `OnPaintBackground` routine is necessary to prevent erasing the background between generations. The override routine does nothing; most importantly, it does *not* call the base class `OnPaintBackground` routine. A global switch used within the application indicates whether the background should be erased. Menu event handlers, for instance, set this switch to `true` because the image of the menu must be removed from the screen after the menu selection has been made.

LISTING 10.21: Overriding the `OnPaint` Event

```
protected override void OnPaint(PaintEventArgs pe)
{
   // If requested, erase the background.
   if( LifeMain.boolPaintAll )
      pe.Graphics.FillRectangle
         (new SolidBrush(this.BackColor),
          pe.ClipRectangle);

   // Draw the current generation.
   //   The previous generation is included for optimization
   //   purposes only (draw only what has changed).
   if( refCurr != null )
   {
      this.DrawGeneration(refCurr, refPrev, pe.Graphics);
   }
}

protected override void OnPaintBackground
                           (PaintEventArgs pe)
{
   // Do NOT call the base class routine.
   //    This control erases the background
   //    from within the Paint
   //    event.
}
```

Preventing flickering also requires a disciplined drawing routine, one that never changes a pixel's color twice during a single execution. The `LifeGame` application achieves this by drawing only those cells whose values have changed since the previous generation. The code for doing it, also taken from the `LifeControl` custom control's class code, is shown in Listing 10.22. It consists of comparisons, integer arithmetic, and GDI calls that seem to go on forever. Reading it in detail would probably not be the high point of your life. We recommend skimming it lightly to get the gist. But note that, like all drawing routines, it requires the `Graphics` object from the `PaintEventArgs` parameter than was passed to the `OnPaint` method.

LISTING 10.22: The Drawing Routine for a Generation

```
// Draw the current generation.
internal void DrawGeneration(
   LifeGeneration genCurr,
   LifeGeneration genPrev,
   Graphics graphLifeGame)
   {
   // Calculate the range of rows to display.
   int displayLo =
      genCurr.middle - ((LifeMain.noofDisplay-1)/2);
   int displayHi =
      displayLo + (LifeMain.noofDisplay-1);

   // For each of those rows:
   for (int j = displayLo; j <= displayHi; j++)
   {
      // Only draw the row if necessary.
      if( LifeMain.boolPaintAll == true
         || genCurr.countGeneration <= 1
         || genCurr.Rows[j].CompareTo(genPrev.Rows[j])
            != 0 )
      {
         this.DrawRow(genCurr.Rows[j],
                      genPrev.Rows[j],
                      j,
                      graphLifeGame);
      }
   }
}

// Draw the current row.
internal void DrawRow(
   LifeRow rowCurr,
   LifeRow rowPrev,
   int ixRow,
   Graphics graphLifeGame)
{
   // Calculate the range of rows to display.
   int displaySpan = LifeMain.noofDisplay;
   int displayLo = rowCurr.middle - ((displaySpan-1)/2) ;
   int displayHi = displayLo + (displaySpan-1);
```

```
// Drawing tools
int xUnit =
   (int)(this.ClientRectangle.Width / displaySpan);
int yUnit =
   (int)(this.ClientRectangle.Height / displaySpan);
SolidBrush brshLive = new SolidBrush(Color.Black);
SolidBrush brshDead = new SolidBrush(Color.Tan);

// This routine attempts to optimize the
//    drawing of rows.  Rows are drawn
//    using FillRect.  The three primary
//    optimizations are:
// 1.   Do not erase the background.
// 2.   Draw contiguous cells of the same
//      state (color) in a single FillRect
//      call.
// 3.   Do not call FillRect if the rectangle
//      specified is already the correct
//      color, that is, if there is no
//      change in the range of cells since
//      the previous generation.

int ixStart = displayLo  // The left cell of the rect.
   , ixEnd = displayHi   // The right cell of the rect.
   , j = displayLo;      // The current cell.
byte byteCurrent = rowCurr.cellsRow[displayLo];

// Force the last cell of a row to end a rectangle.
byte cellTemp = rowCurr.cellsRow[displayHi];
rowCurr.cellsRow[displayHi] = 2;

// Scan from the end of the previous rectangle until
//    a change in cell value occurs, indicating the
//    need for a new rectangle.
for (j = displayLo; j <= displayHi; j++)
{
   if (rowCurr.cellsRow[j] != byteCurrent)
   {
      // Note the end of the rectangle.
      ixEnd = j-1;

      // Call FillRect only if necessary.
      if ( LifeMain.boolPaintAll
         || rowCurr.CompareTo(rowPrev,
                              ixStart,
                              ixEnd) != 0 )
      {
```

continues

continued

```
                graphLifeGame.FillRectangle(
                    byteCurrent == 1 ? brshLive : brshDead,
                    (ixStart-displayLo)*xUnit,
                    (ixRow-displayLo)*yUnit,
                    ((ixEnd-ixStart)+1)*xUnit,
                    1*yUnit);
            }

            // Note the start of the next rectangle.
            ixStart = j;
            // Note the value of the new rectangle's
            //    starting cell.
            byteCurrent = rowCurr.cellsRow[j];
        }
    }

    // Restore the last cell to its original value.
    rowCurr.cellsRow[displayHi] = cellTemp;
}
```

Object Reuse

Another guideline of .NET Compact Framework programming in general and animation programming in specific is *object reuse*. For repetitive activity to run smoothly in a limited resource environment, object creation, disposition, and finalization must be kept to a minimum. Existing objects should be reused, rather than new ones created, whenever possible.

When we wrote the desktop .NET Framework version of `LifeGame`, using the design specified earlier, it ran well except for one flaw. The animation speed was better than expected; new generations replaced old generations on the screen as rapidly as frames in a motion picture. But every few seconds the application froze for a moment. When we examined our code, we realized that each generation was creating a new generation object to hold its pattern, and each generation object consisted of 512 row objects. As each new generation object was created, its reference was assigned to a variable, overlaying the reference that was already in the variable. As the old reference was destroyed, the old generation object, and its 512 row objects, became "unreachable" and, thus, eligible for garbage collection.

With 512 + 1 objects per generation, 20 generations per second—after a while that's a lot of objects. The periodic freeze occurred when the garbage collector in essence said, "You are running low on managed memory. Let me remove a few thousand objects for you." Once we modified our code to reuse generation objects as they aged out of the life cycle, reducing the total number of generation objects created during the life of the application to 5, the periodic freeze went away.

An alternative solution here would have been calling the `GC.Collect` method at the completion of each generation. If the number of objects to be collected is relatively small, the pause between generations will be imperceptible. This would be one of rare cases where calling the `GC.Collect` method is justified.

> This section offered a brief discussion of animation, but it hit the highlights: Maintain a consistent speed, minimize flicker, control the erasing of the background, minimize the number of GDI calls that must be made, and reuse objects whenever possible.
>
> Now, let's look at another aspect of custom control development—developing for the multithreaded environment.

Authoring Custom Controls for the Multithreaded Environment

Controls present information to and receive information from the user. It is essential to the success of your application that your controls be as quick and responsive in doing this as possible. When the user taps on a control, he or she expects a rapid response to that tap. If the control must wait for an existing task to complete before it can respond to the user's input, the user will not be happy.

The responsiveness of a control is based on the intrinsic behavior of the control. A control that draws complex objects is going to be slow. A control that displays the results of complex calculations must take the time to perform those calculations.

At some point, however, a custom control might have to ask for help. In particular, at some point a control might need a second thread to do large or complex tasks for it. For example, a control that displays the results from downloading some large object from a network must wait for the download to be complete. To stay responsive to the user, such a control might spawn an additional thread to handle the actual work of downloading.

Two threads working together can achieve very good responsiveness while also making the best use of the system CPU—and other hardware—to do the actual work needed. But to work together, two threads must follow certain rules, in the same way that two people who share any resource must act in a coordinated way. The members of a family might share a car, but conflicts are inevitable without agreement on who gets to use the car and when. Two coworkers might share a specialized piece of test equipment, a work area, or a telephone. Some rules are needed, or conflict occurs.

When two threads attempt to work together, some of the rules are established by the operating system. When dealing with controls, only a single control method—`Invoke`—is truly thread-safe.

Our purpose is not to delve into the details of multithreaded programming, a subject that we revisit in Chapter 14. Instead, we address the issue of custom controls and how they can be made to operate well in the context of multiple threads.

A Control's Main Thread and Its Service Threads

All controls are associated with a particular thread, the thread that created the control. From the perspective of a control, it has a single thread used for processing inputs to that control. The thread that was used to execute the `new` command that created the control is the thread that is used by the runtime to call the control's event handlers; most often this is the application's main thread. For the remainder of this chapter, we refer to this thread as the *control's thread*. This thread is responsible for synchronizing the inputs that a thread receives. (A typical program has a single thread that supports all user input.)

To ensure prompt response to user input, a separate thread should be used to perform long tasks, such as gathering data from a database or accessing a Web service. A separate thread is also typically used to connect to any external, asynchronous hardware—such as a barcode scanner, a network card, or any other input device that requires continual attention to operate properly. For the remainder of the chapter, we refer to these threads as *service threads*. The creation of separate threads for background processing leaves the control's thread free to respond to user input. It also increases the amount of input that a control will receive, for the control will receive input both from the user and from the service threads. Because the control's thread must synchronize the receiving of input, *the control's thread should be used for passing data between itself and the service threads.*

Using the control's thread to pass data from the control's thread to the service threads is simple to do and, ironically, usually not needed. It's the passing of data back from the service thread to the control's thread, using the control's thread to do so, that is the tricky part.

The first step in solving the problem of passing data between threads, using the control's thread for passing the data in both directions, is to create a thread wrapper object. Because service threads are created to perform specific functions (e.g., retrieving vendor information from a database), the best way to harness them is to define a wrapper object that performs the specific function and have the wrapper object create and run the thread.

Once this is done, using the control's thread to pass information from the control's thread to the service thread is easily achieved by passing a reference to an object containing the data as an overloaded constructor parameter of the wrapper object.

Passing data back by using the control's thread is, as we said, a little trickier. The service thread, not the control's thread, is the thread running when the need to pass the data arises. This means that the service thread must induce a context switch from itself to the control's thread. .NET provides one method for doing this: the `Invoke` method of the `Control` base class. This method allows a service thread to wake up a control and start it running on the control's thread. It exists specifically to provide for correct synchronization of control input and the resulting promptness of user input response.

You might think that three techniques would be available to you for passing data from the service thread to the control's thread.

1. Have the service thread raise an event.
2. Have the service thread call a public method of the custom control.
3. Have the service thread call a callback routine provided by the custom control.

But in reality you have only two options, one of which is usually preferred. Option 1 on this list is eliminated simply because the processing of an event is done by the thread that raises the event, and in our situation that thread is the service thread, not the control's thread.

Options 2 and 3 on the list are both possible, but both are constrained by a limitation of the .NET Compact Framework. Unlike the desktop .NET Framework, the .NET Compact Framework supports only one version of the `Invoke` method, namely:

```
public object Invoke( Delegate );
```

and only one type of delegate, namely:

```
private void methodXXX(object sender, System.EventArgs e)
```

Therefore, options 2 and 3 on the list are both possible, but only if the control's public method/callback is defined with the signature shown in this code. Using a callback gives the control developer more flexibility because it does not require the service thread to use (or know the name of) a prespecified method. Therefore, we recommend using option 3.

Because neither of the delegate parameters can hold the data being passed from the service thread to the control's thread (`sender` is the service thread wrapper object, and `System.EventArgs` does not contain any properties into which data can be placed), an object that will hold the data must be created and a reference to it must be shared between the threads. And because the control's thread must synchronize the receiving of data, possibly from many service threads, it should create the container object that will hold the data. The ideal container object to use is a `System.Collections.Queue` object because it can hold objects of any class, and its "first in, first out" nature makes it easy for the control's thread to extract the data in the correct sequence.

So, the control must create a `Queue` object whose reference will be passed to the service threads and must provide a callback method delegate that can be invoked by the service threads. The overloaded constructor of the thread wrapper class should have three parameters: a reference to the calling control (so the wrapper will know who to call), the delegate to the callback (so the wrapper will know what to call), and a reference to the queue (so the wrapper will know where to place the data).

A Clarification of the Word *Queue*

A `Queue` object—meaning here a `System.Collections.Queue` object—is not the same thing as a message queue object. A `System.Collections.Queue` object is a collection class that belongs to the same family of objects as `ArrayList` and `Dictionary` objects.

Because several server threads might attempt to access the queue at the same time, each thread must obtain a lock on the queue before placing data in it. This is done by obtaining a lock on the object whose reference is in the queue's `SyncRoot` property, as shown here, rather than a lock on the `Queue` object itself.

```
lock(queueX.SyncRoot) { queueX.Enqueue(dsetData); }
```

The control's callback method should extract all the data from the queue each time it is called and should never assume that a specific amount of data will be in the queue at the time of execution. To understand why, consider the following situation.

- `controlX` will create and run two service threads, `threadA` and `threadB`, each of which will create a `DataSet` object, place it in the queue, and invoke the callback. It is impossible to predict the execution sequence of unsynchronized operations, such as those of `threadA` and `threadB`, but the following is a possible scenario.
- `controlX` creates and starts `threadA`, giving it a lower priority and passing it a reference to the queue and a delegate to the callback.
- `controlX` creates and starts `threadB`, giving it a lower priority and passing it a reference to the queue and a delegate to the callback.

- `threadA` builds a `DataSet` object, places it in the queue, and is swapped off the processor.
- `threadB` builds a `DataSet` object (taking less time to do so than `threadA` did), places it in the queue, and invokes the callback.

The Role of the `DataSet` Object

Here we use `DataSet` objects only to illustrate a scenario. A detailed understanding of them is not necessary at this time. We cover `DataSet` objects in Part III.

At this point, there are two `DataSet` objects in the queue and the callback routine has begun to execute. If the callback routine removes only one `DataSet` object from the queue each time it is called, then this invocation by `threadB` will remove only the `DataSet` object placed in the queue by `threadA`. If `threadA` now terminates, `threadB`'s `DataSet` object will never be removed from the queue.

The Multithread Example

With the background out of the way, let's see if we can incorporate our own recommendations into an application. We'll create a custom control that creates a thread to retrieve data from a simulated database and then displays that data to the users. Our application will be somewhat three-tiered in that it consists of three classes: the form, the custom control, and the thread wrapper object. We'll use only one project and define all three classes within it, as shown in Figure 10.22. The code for this can be found in the `MultiThreaded` project on the Web site.

The Testing Form

The form comes first and is the easiest to define, containing an instance of the custom control and a button to initiate the processing. Figure 10.23 shows the runtime form itself, and Listing 10.23 presents the relevant parts of its code.

FIGURE 10.22: One project, three classes

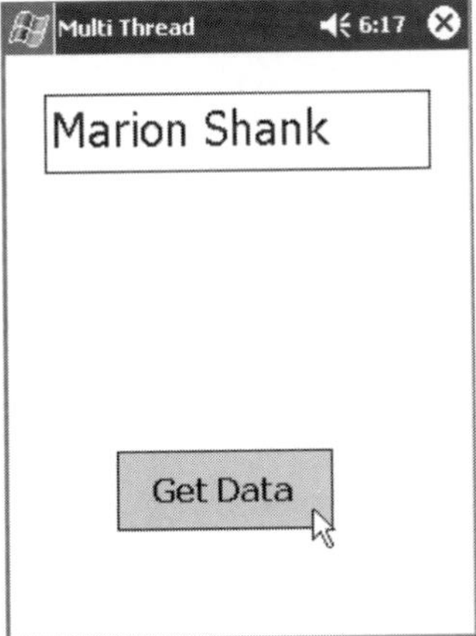

FIGURE 10.23: The multithreaded testing form

Why Marion Shank?

The individual referenced in the sample program, Marion Shank, is the late father-in-law of one of us. He is the only person we have ever known whose given name, street name, and town name were the same: Marion Shank lived on Marion Avenue in Marion, Ohio. A great guy with an easy mailing address.

LISTING 10.23: The Code for the Multithreaded Testing Form

```
using System;
using System.Collections;
using System.Drawing;
using System.Windows.Forms;
using YaoDurant.Gui;

namespace MultiThreadedCS
{

   public class FormMain : System.Windows.Forms.Form
   {
      private System.Windows.Forms.Button cmdGetData;
      private YaoDurant.Gui.MultiThreadBox mtbPerson;

   #region Unmodified Generated Code
   #endregion

   #region Windows Form Designer generated code
   #endregion

      private void FormMain_Load(object sender, System.EventArgs e)
      {
         mtbPerson = new MultiThreadBox();
         InitializeTheControl(mtbPerson);
      }

      private void cmdGetData_Click(object sender, System.EventArgs e)
      {
         mtbPerson.RequestData();
      }

   #region Cosmetic Utility Routine
   #endregion
   }
}
```

What you do not see in this code is the `Unmodified Generated Code` region, which contains the default `Main`, `Constructor`, and `Dispose` routines. Code in the `Windows Form Designer generated code` region is also unmodified. The `InitializeTheControl` routine, which is the only occupant of the `Cosmetic Utility Routine` region, positions the custom control on the form and scales its font size.

What you can see in Listing 10.23 is that the form's `Load` event creates an instance of the custom control and that the button's `Click` event calls the control's `RequestData` method.

The Custom Control

The custom control's code is shown, in segments, in this subsection. Some of the comments that appear in the source code have been removed because they are covered by the content of this chapter. The control itself is derived from `TextBox`.

The `using` statements, namespace name, and class name are shown here.

```
using System;
using System.Drawing;
using System.Collections;
using System.Windows.Forms;
using System.Data;
using System.Threading;
using System.ComponentModel;
using MultiThreadedCS;

namespace YaoDurant.Gui
{

   public class MultiThreadBox : TextBox
   {
```

The variables that hold the queue and the delegate, and the default constructor that initializes them, appear next.

```
      private Queue qPassData;
      private EventHandler deleReceiveData;

      public MultiThreadBox()
      {
         // Create a System.Collections.Queue object to be used by
         //    the service threads to pass data back to the
         //    this control.
         qPassData = new Queue();

         // The delegate to the form's method that will be
         //    invoked by the service threads
         deleReceiveData = new EventHandler(this.ReceiveData);
      }
```

Then comes the routine called by the button's `Click` event to begin the asynchronous gathering of data. As you can see, this routine creates the thread wrapper object, passing it a reference to this control, a delegate to the callback, and a reference to the `Queue` object.

```
public void RequestData()
{
   // Create a GetDataWrapper object.  The object will
   //    create and start a thread.  The thread will get
   //    a DataSet, place it into qPassData, and then
   //    invoke ReceiveData via a delegate.
   GetDataWrapper refGetData =
      new GetDataWrapper( this,
                          deleReceiveData,
                          qPassData );
}
```

The callback routine, which iterates through the `Queue` object, extracting all the data and displaying it to the user, is shown here.

```
private void ReceiveData(object s, System.EventArgs e)
{
   // Retrieve the DataSet that was placed into qPassData
   //    by the service thread and display it in controls.
   DataSet dsetPerson;
   IEnumerator queueEnumerator = qPassData.GetEnumerator();

   // Enumerate through all the
   //    DataSets that are in the queue.
   while( queueEnumerator.MoveNext() )
   {
      dsetPerson = (DataSet)(queueEnumerator.Current);
      // Move the DataSet contents into the Text property.
      this.Text = dsetPerson.Tables[0].Rows[0]
                                 ["FirstName"].ToString()
               + " "
               + dsetPerson.Tables[0].Rows[0]
                                 ["LastName"].ToString();
   }
}
```

That's it for the `MultiThreadBox` custom control class, except to close out the class and namespace definitions with the following two lines.

```
   }
}
```

This leaves only the thread wrapper class, `GetDataWrapper`. The code for this class is shown in Listing 10.24. When instantiated, it saves the three parameters that were passed to it during construction (reference to the control, callback delegate, and reference to the queue). Then it creates and starts a thread to do the actual processing. This thread's thread procedure simulates database retrieval by creating a `DataSet` object from scratch and placing it in the queue. Having placed the data in the queue, it invokes the callback.

LISTING 10.24: The `GetDataWrapper` Thread Wrapper Class

```
using System;
using System.Windows.Forms;
using System.Collections;
using System.Data;
using System.Threading;

namespace MultiThreadedCS
{
   /// <summary>
   /// Summary description for GetDataWrapper
   /// </summary>

   public class GetDataWrapper
   {
      // Data passed in the constructor
      //    by the caller is stored here.
      private Control formCaller;
      private EventHandler deleCallback;
      private Queue queueArgs;

      // The class's thread
      private Thread thrdGetData;

      // The caller can request that the thread terminate.
      bool TerminateRequestReceived = false;


      // The only constructor, which takes three parameters
      public GetDataWrapper
         (
         // Location of delegate; could
         //    be a control or a form
         Control formCaller,
```

continues

continued

```
      // The delegate to invoke after the data has
      //    been gathered
      EventHandler deleCallback,

      // The Queue object to use for passing data
      Queue queueArgs;
      )
   {
      // Save the input parameters.
      this.formCaller = formCaller;
      this.deleCallback = deleCallback;
      this.queueArgs = queueArgs;

      // Create and start the thread.
      thrdGetData = new Thread(new ThreadStart( ThreadProc ));
      thrdGetData.Start();
   }


   // The thread proc.
   private void ThreadProc()
   {
      // Simulate contacting a Web Service and receiving
      //    a returned DataSet object.  In this example,
      //    we'll simply create and load the DataSet here.
      // The DataSet will contain one DataTable, which will
      //    contain one row that holds a person's
      //    first name and last name.
      DataTable dtblPerson = new DataTable("Person");

      dtblPerson.Columns.Add
         ("FirstName", Type.GetType("System.String"));
      dtblPerson.Columns.Add
         ("LastName", Type.GetType("System.String"));
      dtblPerson.Rows.Add
         (new System.String[2] {"Marion","Shank"});

      DataSet dsetPerson = new DataSet("Person");
      dsetPerson.Tables.Add(dtblPerson);

      // The .NET Compact Framework has no Thread.Stop, or
      //    comparable, method.  We stop by reaching the
      //    end of the ThreadProc ASAP.
      if( ! TerminateRequestReceived )
      {
         // Place the data into the queue.
         lock(this.queueArgs.SyncRoot)
```

```
            {
               this.queueArgs.Enqueue(dsetPerson);
            }
            // Invoke the callback.
            this.formCaller.Invoke(this.deleCallback);
         }
      }


      // A termination routine
      private void Stop()
      {
         TerminateRequestReceived = true;
      }
   }
}
```

So, with a good understanding of multithreading concepts and by following the recommended procedures, you can write .NET Compact Framework applications that asynchronously execute tasks to provide a more responsive user interface.

Adding a Custom Control to the Visual Studio .NET Toolbox

Now we come to what can be the most difficult step of all: adding a custom control to the Visual Studio .NET Toolbox. Before you can do this, however, you must overcome some obstacles.

Obstacles to Putting Custom Controls in the Toolbox

You have designed, authored, and tested a custom control, and it is brilliant. You have packaged it with its own class library DLL to make it available to you, to your coworkers, and perhaps also to your company's customers. You would like to display your control in the Visual Studio .NET Toolbox, so that it can be dragged from the Toolbox and dropped on a form. So what keeps your custom control from being displayed in the Visual Studio .NET Toolbox?

A .NET Compact Framework Control Cannot Be Added to the Toolbox

You have authored a custom control that is a .NET Compact Framework control. But Visual Studio .NET is not a .NET Compact Framework application—it is instead a desktop application that uses the desktop .NET Framework. Only desktop controls can be placed in the Toolbox. Therefore, to put a control in the Toolbox, you must create a desktop control that matches your .NET Compact Framework custom control as closely as possible.

You Are Developing a Desktop Control That Is Different from a Normal Desktop Control

The desktop control that you have developed and want to add to the Toolbox represents a .NET Compact Framework control. Visual Studio .NET needs to know this because it must limit what it provides to you at design time to match the capabilities of the .NET Compact Framework runtime. You can notify Visual Studio .NET about this situation through a set of special references. Specifically, you reference a set of libraries that are themselves compatible with the desktop .NET Framework but that expose only those namespaces, classes, and types that are compatible with the .NET Compact Framework.

You See Build Errors

When building your custom control, you referred to two versions of some classes—one version is the desktop .NET Framework version, the other version is the .NET Compact Framework version. By default, Visual Studio .NET warns you that you have references set to more than one version of the same object classes. These errors can be suppressed by setting a project property, which will be illustrated later in this chapter.

Testing Design-Time Controls Takes a Bit More Effort

First, design-time controls must reside in a special directory so that Visual Studio .NET can locate them. This design-time assembly must reference the location of the assembly of the runtime version of your control, which also must be in a specific directory. To test the design-time version of your control, you must copy the design-time and runtime class library (`.dll`) files to system directories. This copying must be done between completion of the build and commencement of the test.

Second, Visual Studio .NET must be shut down if a previous version of your control is already in the Toolbox. You cannot overwrite the design-time class library while Visual Studio .NET is using it because Visual Studio .NET locks the `.dll` files of controls that are in the Toolbox. If you try to overwrite the library, the file copy fails with the following error message:

```
The process cannot access the file because it is being used
by another process.
```

So you cannot just change your source code and hit F5 (or CTRL+F5) to test. As you change the custom control runtime file, you must add some extra steps to your development process: Shut down Visual Studio .NET, copy the necessary file(s), and restart Visual Studio .NET.

Freeze Version Numbers during Testing

Visual Studio .NET expects the version number of the design-time control in the Toolbox to remain constant during testing. When a control is added to the Toolbox, Visual Studio .NET sets an internal reference to the design-time version, including the version number. And the design-time version of the control references the runtime version, including the version number as part of this reference. Any change to either the design-time or runtime version number during testing causes problems.

One or Two Sets of Source Files?

To add a custom control to the Toolbox, you must create a second desktop-compatible custom control, as we noted earlier. One question to consider is whether to use a single set of source files to create both controls or whether to have a second set of source files for the Toolbox version. Both approaches can be made to work, and the difference is largely a matter of personal taste.

The benefit of having one set of source files is that you put all your code in one place and separate the design-time code from the runtime code by using conditional compilation. The disadvantage of one set of source files is that Visual Studio .NET does not make it easy to share a single source file between two projects.

The benefit of having two sets of source files is that each project is simpler to set up and simpler to work with. The disadvantages are the duplication of code and the extra effort required to keep the two sets of source files in sync.

The choice is yours. In spite of what you may see in various custom control examples, you can be sure that the source file for the design-time version and the runtime version do not have to be the same.

Developing a Design-Time Custom Control

Before you start work on the design-time control, we suggest you create and thoroughly test the runtime version of the custom control. This allows you to understand the scope of the runtime control—the PMEs—without worrying about how these appear at design time. This is important because design-time development is complicated by a more difficult build process and by the need to be compatible with both the desktop .NET Framework and the .NET Compact Framework.

The Setup Process for a Design-Time Control Project

Here is our recommended procedure for setting up a project for a design-time version of a custom control; we walk through these steps in an upcoming example.

1. Modify the `AssemblyInfo` file of the runtime control to set a fixed version number.
2. Create a new project. In the New Project Wizard, select a desktop control library. We find it helpful to have the new project share the same solution as the runtime control.
3. Modify the assembly of the design-time control, including the following tasks.
   - Freeze the version number by setting the same version number in both the runtime version and the design-time version of your custom control.
   - Set the project references to the .NET Compact Framework design-time assemblies.

4. Suppress potential "Duplicate Definition" errors from the project's Properties window (suppress warning number 1595; see Figure 10.25 later in this discussion).
5. Delete the default skeleton source files from the design-time project and attach to the existing runtime source files (by selecting Add Existing Item).
6. Remove existing references and set the project references to the `*.CF.*` assemblies. These assemblies, which have names like `System.CF.dll`, contain only elements defined in the .NET Compact Framework. These assemblies can run under Visual Studio .NET because they are compatible with the desktop .NET Framework.
7. Add a reference to the runtime control.
8. Create a batch command file that shuts down Visual Studio .NET, copies the design-time files to the correct Visual Studio .NET directory, then starts Visual Studio .NET running. (To overwrite an assembly that Visual Studio .NET itself uses, you must first terminate Visual Studio .NET.)

The Development Process for a Design-Time Control Project

Once you have set up a project, as defined in the eight steps in the previous subsection, follow the development process outlined here.

1. Modify the source code and build.
2. Close Visual Studio .NET.
3. Run the command file (created in setup step 8).
4. When Visual Studio .NET reopens, test your changes.

With these steps accomplished, we are ready to create a design-time version of our `DateBox` control.

An Example of Setting Up a Project with the `DateBox` Custom Control

Because we have developed and tested our `DateBox` runtime control (presented earlier in the chapter), we are ready to begin. We follow the eight-step process for setting up a design-time control project.

The first step is to modify the assembly files for the runtime version of the control. For that, we open the assembly file, `AssemblyInfo.cs`, and change the `AssemblyVersion` value as shown here:

```
[assembly: AssemblyVersion("1.0.1.0")]
```

It does not matter what version number we use as long as we replace the default value, which contained an asterisk, with a specific value. If we leave the asterisk in, every build produces a new version number, which would likely cause the runtime control to be different from the design-time control. That's all we need to do in to our runtime version.

The second step is to add the design-time control project to our solution. Because the design-time version of our custom control is a desktop control, we choose Windows Control Library (not Smart Device Application) as our project template in the New Project Wizard, as shown in Figure 10.24. We name this project `DateBoxDesign`.

Step 3 is to modify the assembly information file of the design-time control. We start by setting the same version number that we set in our run-

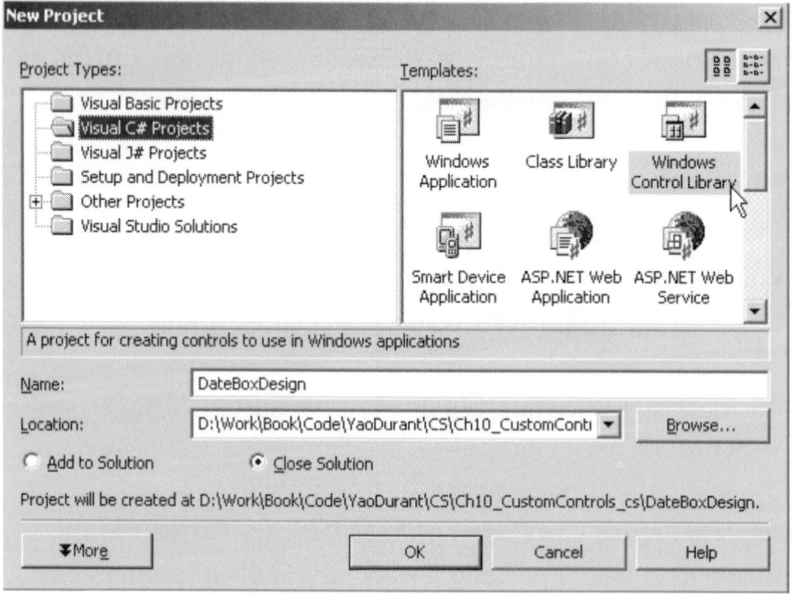

FIGURE 10.24: Adding a Designer control project

time project. We then make another change to the assembly of the design-time version. First, we add an assembly directive to associate the runtime version of our control with this design-time version. This association must specify the strong name of the runtime control's assembly, including assembly name, version number, culture, and public key if applicable. In our runtime project we specified neither a culture nor a public key, so our design-time assembly directive looks like this, and we place it directly under our version number directive.

```
[assembly: AssemblyVersion("1.0.1.0")]
[assembly: System.CF.Design.RuntimeAssembly(
                               "DateBoxControl,
                                Version=1.0.1.0,
                                Culture=neutral,
                                PublicKeyToken=null")]
```

Step 4 is to suppress potential "Duplicate Definition" warning messages. We do this, as shown in Figure 10.25, with the following steps.

a. Summon the project property page (select the Project→<project-name> Properties... menu item).
b. Click the Configuration Properties folder and the Build item.
c. Select the Suppress Specific Warnings item.
d. Enter a value of `1595`.

Step 5 is to add the source files from the runtime control to the design-time control project. We start by deleting the file that contains the skeleton code from our project. We add the existing runtime control's source code file, from the runtime project, to the design-time project by using the following menu item: Project→Add Existing Item..., which brings up the dialog box shown in Figure 10.26.

Step 6 is to add references to the required `*.CF.*` assemblies. The assemblies that we need to reference are located in the `Windows CE\Designer` directory of the .NET Compact Framework installation directory, which is part of the Visual Studio .NET 2003 installation directory. Once we locate the

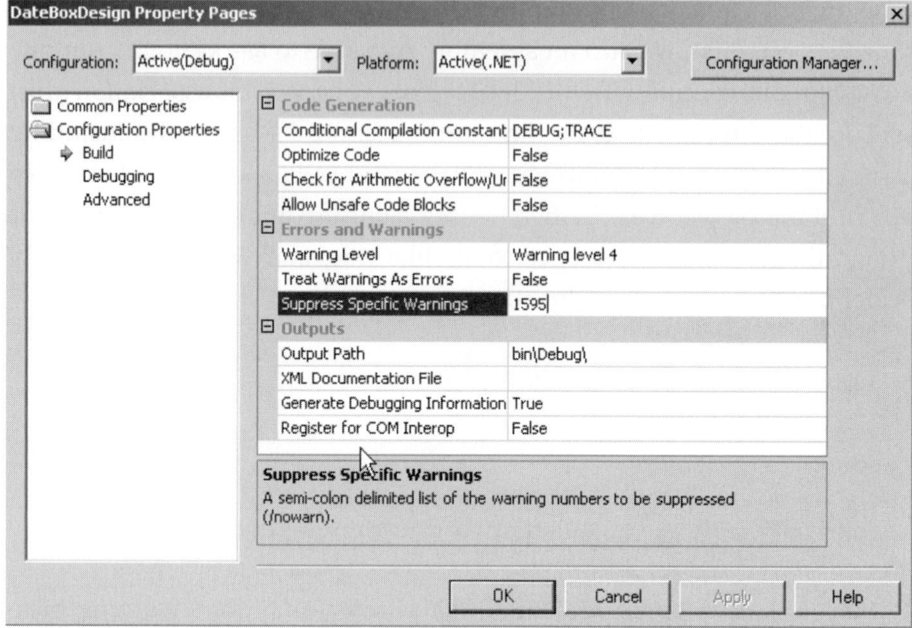

FIGURE 10.25: Suppressing the "Duplicate Definition" warnings

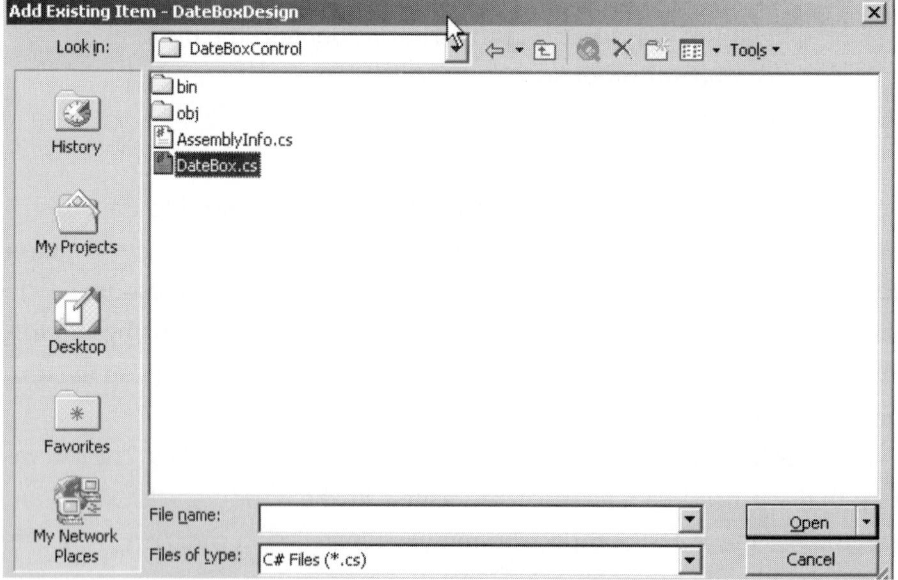

FIGURE 10.26: Adding runtime code to the design-time project

directory that contains Visual Studio .NET, we browse to `\CompactFrameworkSDK\v1.0.5000\Windows CE\Designer`. When we add the new references, we first remove the existing references to the desktop .NET assemblies `System.Windows.Forms` and `System.Drawing` that were set when the project was added to the solution. Using the Browse button on the Add Reference's dialog box, we add the following assemblies as references to our project, as shown in Figure 10.27:

- `System.CF.Design`
- `System.CF.Windows.Forms`
- `System.CF.Drawing`

Step 7 is to add a reference to the existing runtime control, as shown in Figure 10.28. We need to do this because the design-time control needs to reference the runtime control.

The eighth and final step for the setup process is to create a batch command file that copies the design-time library to a special Visual Studio .NET directory. The batch file we use is shown here. Note that the lines wrap to

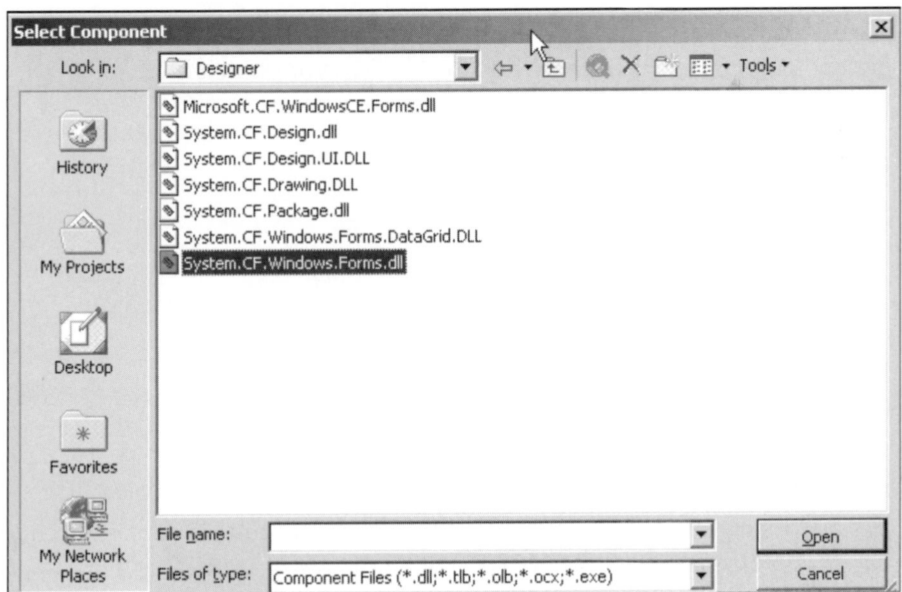

FIGURE 10.27: Setting Designer references

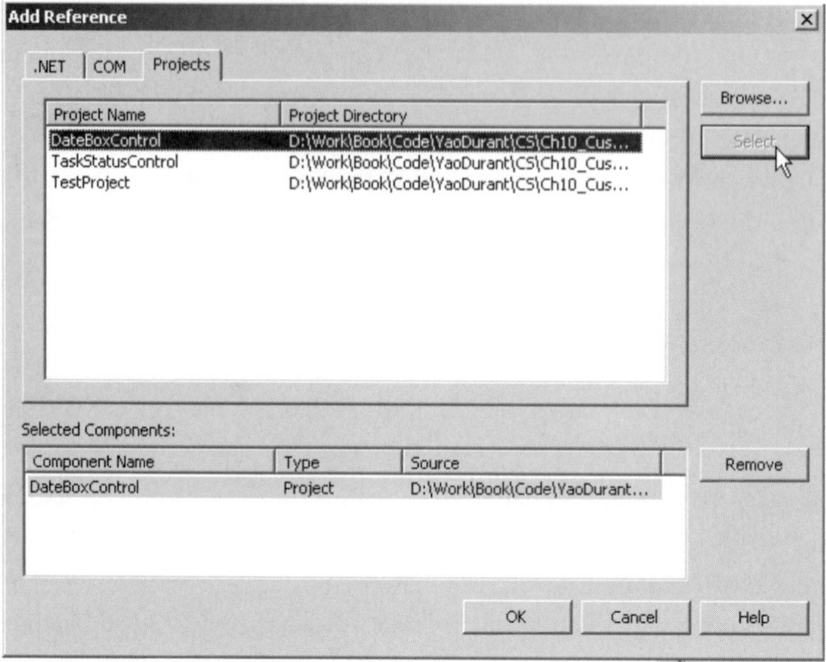

FIGURE 10.28: Referencing the runtime project

allow them to be displayed in printed form; do not wrap these five commands (`cls`, `copy`, `copy`, `pause`, and `devenv`) in your batch file.

```
cls
Copy DateBoxDesign\Bin\Debug\DateBoxDesign.dll
      "\Program Files\Microsoft Visual Studio .NET 2003
       \CompactFrameworkSDK\v1.0.5000\Windows CE\Designer"
Copy DateBoxControl\Bin\Debug\DateBoxControl.dll
      "\Program Files\Microsoft Visual Studio .NET 2003
       \CompactFrameworkSDK\v1.0.5000\Windows CE"
pause
"\Program Files\Microsoft Visual Studio .NET 2003
      \Common7\IDE\devenv.exe"
      DateAndStatusControls.sln
```

When run, this batch file copies the two assembly files to the correct directories and then pauses so we can verify the success of the file copies. Then it starts Visual Studio .NET and loads our project so that we can add our control to the Toolbox if it is not already there (or do further testing if it is).

As you can see from the command file shown above, before adding a control to the Toolbox the design-time file must be located in the `Windows CE\Designer` directory of the .NET Compact Framework installation directory, normally `Program Files\Microsoft Visual Studio .NET 2003\CompactFrameworkSDK\v1.0.5000\Windows CE\Designer`. The runtime assembly must be located one level higher, in the `Windows CE` directory. (Note that we named our runtime control project `DateBox-Control` and named our design-time control project `DateBoxDesign`.)

Building and Installing the Design-Time `DateBox` Control

We start our coding of the design-time control without using any conditional compilation statements because we want our design-time control to be as identical to our runtime version as possible. Our current solution now contains three projects: the runtime control, the design-time control, and the test application. We rebuild it, checking the Output window to verify success, and then close Visual Studio .NET. We run our command prompt file from within a .NET command prompt window, verify that the files copied successfully, and start up Visual Studio .NET again.

Now it is time to add our design-time control to the Toolbox. We first add a new tab to our Toolbox by right-clicking in an empty area of the Toolbox and choosing Add Tab, which we name My User Controls.

We right-click in an empty area of My User Controls and chose Add/Remove Items. In the Customize Toolbox dialog, we click the Browse button and browse to the location of our designer control, `Program Files\Microsoft Visual Studio .NET 2003\CompactFrameworkSDK\v1.0.5000\Windows CE\Designer`, the directory specified in our command file. We find `DateBoxDesign` in the list, select it (as shown in Figure 10.29), click Open, and then click OK for the remaining dialog boxes.

When we are done, the control is sitting in the Toolbox, as shown in Figure 10.30.

With our design-time control in the Toolbox, we test it by dragging and dropping an instance of it onto a form. It appears on the form as shown in Figure 10.31, and we can move or resize it.

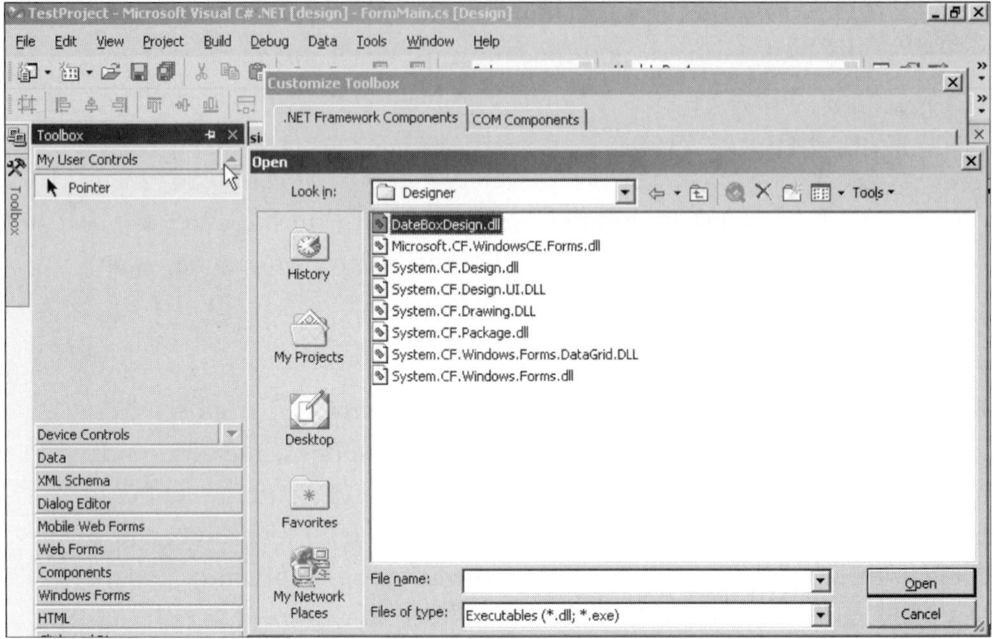

FIGURE 10.29: Adding the Designer control to the Toolbox

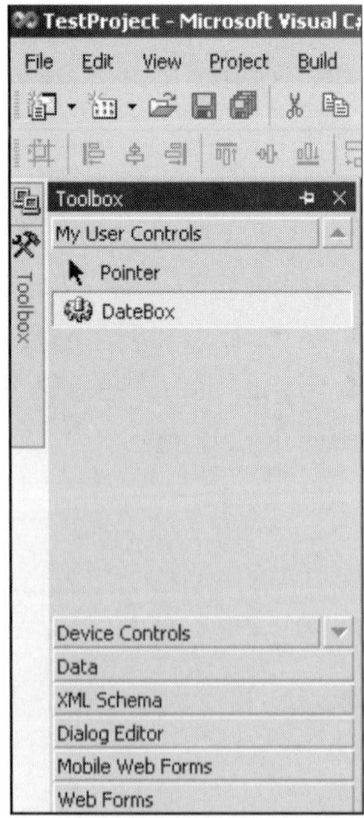

FIGURE 10.30: The Toolbox with the Designer control added

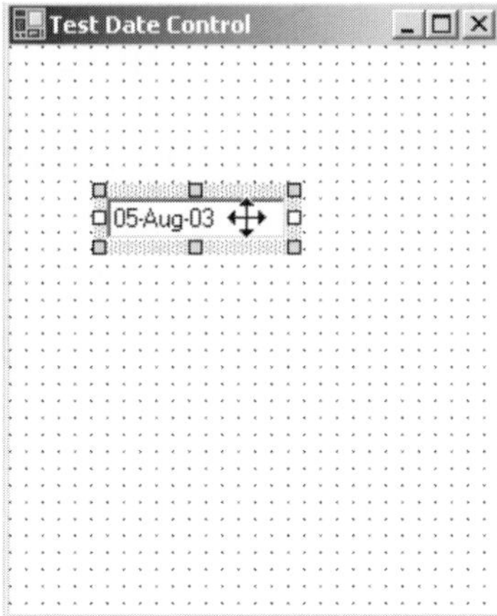

FIGURE 10.31: The custom control added to the form

When we look in the Properties window, we see the properties that were inherited from `TextBox`, such as `Name`, plus the properties that we created, such as `Date`, all of which we can change through the Properties window, as shown in Figure 10.32.

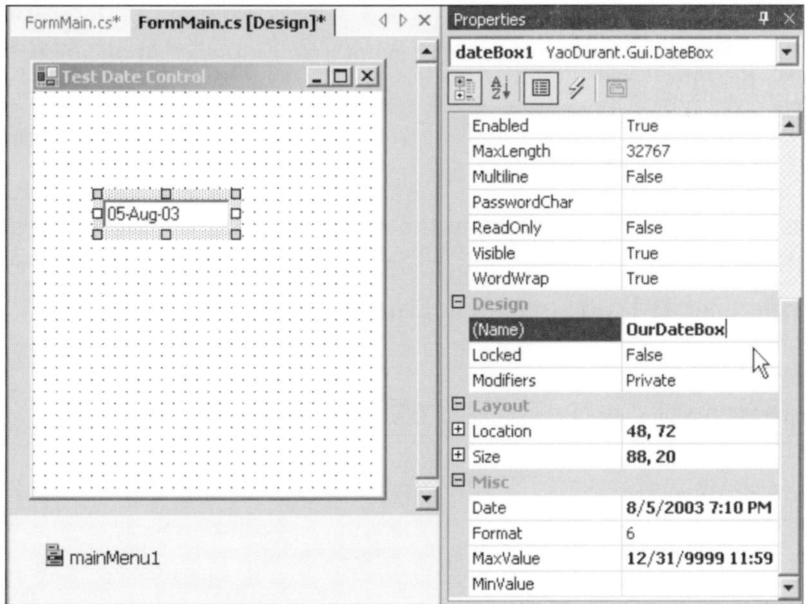

FIGURE 10.32: The custom control properties

Troubleshooting Tips

There are many steps involved in this process, any of which can easily go wrong. If you are unable to add the control to the Toolbox, or if it is added but disabled, check the following list for possible causes. If the control is added to the Toolbox and your next test results in an immediate "Missing Method" exception, the problem is usually one of the first four items in this list.

- The project was rebuilt, but the `.dll` files were not copied.
- The `.dll` files did not get copied to the correct directories.
- The name/version number specified in the design-time `AssemblyInfo.cs` file does not match the name/version number of the file copied to the runtime directory.
- The control was already in the Toolbox, and the name/version number of the file copied to the design-time directory is different from the name/version number of the file added to the Toolbox. (You need to remove the old version from the Toolbox and then add the new version.)
- The runtime control, rather than the design-time control, was added to the Toolbox.
- The active window in your solution is not a Smart Device Application form window.

This detection of properties by the Designer is also evident when we open the code for the form on which we placed the control and expand the Designer-generated code, shown in Listing 10.25.

LISTING 10.25: Designer-Generated Code for Our Custom Control

```
//
// dateBox1
//
this.dateBox1.BackColor = System.Drawing.Color.White;
this.dateBox1.Date =
     new System.DateTime(2003, 6, 11, 21, 27, 15, 593);
```

```
this.dateBox1.Location =
     new System.Drawing.Point(168, 80);
this.dateBox1.Format = 6;
this.dateBox1.MaxValue =
     new System.DateTime(9999, 12, 31, 23, 59, 59, 999);
this.dateBox1.MinValue =
     new System.DateTime(((long)(0)));
this.dateBox1.Size =
     new System.Drawing.Size(64, 20);
this.dateBox1.Text = "6/11/2003";
```

Setting Default Property Values

Because the constructor of our `DateBox` control initializes the `Format`, `MaxDate`, `MinDate`, `Date`, and therefore `Text` properties, five of the lines of code generated by the Designer are redundant. They exist because the Designer compared the initial property values of the control that it created when we did our drag-and-drop operation with the default values for those properties. Because we have not yet defined any default property values, code was generated for all our properties. We can prevent some but not all of the redundant lines of code by defining default values for some properties of our design-time `TextBox` control.

For instance, our constructor initialized the `Format` property to `6`. We can prevent the `this.dateBox1.Format = 6;` line of code from being generated by adding a `DefaultValue` attribute to our design-time control's `Format` property, as shown here.

```
[DefaultValue(6)]
public int Format
{
   get { return m_Format; }
   set
   {
      :  :  :
   }
}
```

Not all our properties lend themselves to a default value definition because a default value must be defined as a constant, and some values—the `Date` property, for instance—do not get initialized as constants. (The `Date` property is initialized by the control's constructor to `DateTime.Today`, which is not a constant.) Nor are `DateTime.MinDate` and `DateTime.MaxDate` considered constants when defining default values. In fact, we were not able to get `0`, `(long)0`, or `1/1/0001 00:00:00:0000` to work as the default value. They were all accepted as constants, but their use did not suppress the Designer-generated code.

> Creating a design-time version of a control and adding it to the Visual Studio .NET Toolbox requires that you create a special version of a control. The special version must have several unique elements to allow it to safely straddle the world of desktop-based and smart-device-based .NET runtimes.

CONCLUSION

Custom controls let you extend the functionality of existing controls. In this object-oriented environment, you create new types by inheriting from existing types. You can extend an existing control class, such as `TextBox` or `Button`, by using the respective class as the base class for the new custom control class. An important issue, which we addressed in this chapter, is selecting the appropriate base class to inherit from. To create a totally new type of control, you use the `Control` class when the desired control is to appear as a window on a form. Otherwise, you can choose between `Object` and `Component` as a base class—the latter being more in tune with common practices in the desktop .NET Framework.

This chapter discussed three approaches to creating custom controls. One approach is to extend the capabilities of an existing control to fine-tune its behavior and appearance. A second approach involves developing a composite control, which is a composite of two or more other controls. A third approach is to create a wholly new type of control, with a completely unique appearance and behavior.

This chapter also presented three techniques to help you create more robust and usable custom controls. We discussed developing custom controls in the multithreaded environment and using the `Invoke` method as the only thread-safe method for interthread calling of a control. We also explored animation techniques for smooth drawing of dynamic controls. And finally, we discussed techniques for adding a custom control to the Visual Studio .NET Toolbox, which requires the creation of a specialized desktop-compatible version of a .NET Compact Framework control.

PART III
Managing Device Data

11

Storage

In this chapter we examine the .NET Compact Framework's capabilities for accessing local storage, concentrating on file I/O and registry access.

Smart-Device Data Storage

Storage is an area where Windows CE–powered devices and desktop systems differ significantly. On desktop machines the primary storage media is disk, while on Windows CE–powered systems the primary storage media is RAM. Windows CE can support rotating magnetic storage media, but this is the exception rather than the rule.[1] Battery-powered mobile devices in particular, such as Pocket PCs, are not suited to support power-hungry rotating media. Thus, Windows CE storage centers on using RAM instead of disk, and mobile-device storage tends to be fast but small. Windows CE–powered devices use a combination of ROM and RAM. Most Pocket PCs support removable storage, primarily in the form of Compact Flash cards or Secure Digital media.

Another difference from desktop systems is that a Windows CE operating system image resides in nonvolatile media. This might be ROM, or it could be flash memory.[2] The ROM contains operating system components, applications, device drivers, and other supporting files needed for device

1. One exception is the IBM Microdrive; it uses rotating media in a Compact Flash form factor.

2. The HP Web site uses the term "Flash ROM" for the flash memory used in iPaq Pocket PCs. The benefit of flash memory is that it enables field upgrades.

operation. Microsoft provides the Platform Builder tool that third parties use to create specific operating system images. While Microsoft provides guidelines for what a Pocket PC or Smartphone device should include, the actual content is determined by the device manufacturer that creates the actual operating system image. This is why smart devices from different manufacturers sometimes have a slightly different set of applications and device drivers.

In spite of these differences in the physical media, there are many common features at a higher level of abstraction. Both device and desktop storage support a hierarchical file system. And both device and desktop storage support a hierarchical registry.

The Object Store

On a Windows CE–powered device, RAM is divided into two portions: program memory and the object store. *Program memory* serves the purpose that most desktop programmers associate with memory—providing the space for code to load and run and the space for data to be allocated, used, and reclaimed.

The *object store* serves as the primary storage area for Windows CE. The object store contains three things: a file system, the system registry, and CE property databases. The .NET Compact Framework has built-in support for file I/O but not for the registry or property databases. To use the registry and CE property databases, a program calls native functions using P/Invoke.

The maximum allowable size for the object store is 256MB. This maximum size is exactly one-half the total RAM that Windows CE can support, which is 512MB.[3] The maximum size for individual files in the object store is 32MB. RAM not used for the object store is available for use as program memory.

This chapter covers two of the three types of objects in the object store. We cover the use of .NET Compact Framework classes to access the file system directories and files. In addition, we cover using P/Invoke to access native functions to access the system registry. We do not cover Windows CE property databases aside from the description in the related sidebar.

3. That is factory-installed memory. Windows CE does not support adding additional RAM.

Windows CE Property Databases

Most Windows CE features are ported from desktop Windows. However, certain features were created to serve a need not met by existing desktop technologies. Windows CE property databases are one of those technologies.

Property databases provide a simple, low-overhead mechanism for storing record-based data. A property database provides, in essence, a very flexible flat-file manager. A fairly simple set of C-callable functions are provided to create records. The names of the functions reflect the Windows CE–centric nature of these functions; each has a prefix of `Ce`. Included among the property database functions are `CeCreateDatabaseEx` to create a new database, `CeOpenDatabaseEx` to open an existing database, `CeSeekDatabaseEx` to search for a record, `CeReadRecordPropsEx` to read a record, and `CeWriteRecordProps` to write a record.

The .NET Compact Framework does not support accessing CE property databases, except through P/Invoke wrappers for these functions. We do not cover that topic in this book. If you need to access CE property databases from a .NET Compact Framework program, you have two choices. One is to first write a set of Win32 functions that do all the main database work and then write a set of custom wrapper functions to pass your database records up to your managed code.

A second choice involves writing P/Invoke wrappers for direct calls to the CE property database functions. The P/Invoke Wizard described in Chapter 4 can help. We created a set of wrappers for a related set of functions, the desktop Remote API (RAPI) functions. As described in Chapter 14, RAPI functions allow a desktop program to access the object store of a Windows CE device using ActiveSync. We used our wrappers to create the sample programs we wrote for Chapter 14; the complete source code for the wrappers are available online at the book's Web site.

You can use these same wrappers within a .NET Compact Framework program because RAPI functions are identical to device-side functions. In fact, the functions are so similar that this often causes confusion for developers. There is, for example, a RAPI function named `CeCreateDataBaseEx` that can be used to remotely create a database. There is also a device-based function named `CeCreateDataBaseEx` that does the same thing. Each of the two functions takes the same number and type of parameters. So the P/Invoke wrappers we wrote for the RAPI functions can also be used from within your .NET Compact Framework program to run on a device.

System Power States

RAM is volatile and requires a power source to maintain its integrity. Device manufacturers normally provide a backup battery, whose sole function is keeping the object store intact when the main battery is drained. When the main battery is too low for safe operation to continue, a warning message appears briefly, and then the device enters a power-critical state. At that point, the device can start up only when the main battery is replaced or recharged.

When both main battery and backup battery are removed, the contents of RAM—the object store and program memory—are lost. When battery power is again available to the device, a *cold boot* is run by a bootloader in ROM. Among its other tasks, the bootloader initializes the object store to its startup state.

A Pocket PC has a power switch, but turning off a device is different from turning off a desktop system. On a Pocket PC, the RAM remains powered, which maintains the viability of the object store and the program memory. For this reason, applications are not shut down but wait in a frozen, hibernating state. After waking a Pocket PC, the user encounters a device in the same state as when the device was turned off. The instant-on support makes Windows CE suited for consumer devices.

Most Pocket PCs also have a reset switch, which can be necessary when a device gets hung. This switch causes a *warm boot*; it resets program memory but leaves the object store intact.[4]

---

4. You can find more details about power management in "Power Management Features of Windows CE .NET," an article written by Paul Yao, at http://msdn.microsoft.com/library/en-us/dncenet/html/power_management_features.asp.

Installable File Systems

In addition to the RAM-based object store, Windows CE supports *installable file systems*, which provide nonvolatile data storage. The most common storage devices are two forms of flash memory, Compact Flash and Secure Digital. The IBM Microdrive provides a rotating hard drive packaged in the form factor of a Type II Compact Flash card, originally available in 340MB and 1GB storage capacities. In December 2002, Hitachi bought IBM's Microdrive division; a year later, Hitachi started to ship 2GB and 4GB drives.

A maximum of 256 installable file systems can be made available on a single Pocket PC 2003 or Windows CE .NET 4.1 or later device (the limit is 10 on Windows CE 3.0 devices such as the Pocket PC and Pocket PC 2002). Many installable file systems are FAT-based, including FAT12, FAT16, and FAT32; the legacy of MS-DOS/Windows lives on.

Files in an installable file system have a maximum size of 4GB, considerably more than the 32MB maximum for object store files. On a Pocket PC, a storage card file system might appear in the `\Storage Card` directory. At present, however, there are no standard names. Because this is a localizable name, you should avoid hard-coding directory names.

Pocket PC programmers can address this issue with a pair of native Win32 API functions: `FindFirstFlashCard` and `FindNextFlashCard` enumerate installed file systems. (See the `FindMemoryCard` sample application in Chapter 4 for an example of calling these functions.)

Thus, the files accessible to your application can be located in ROM, RAM, or the additional devices mentioned earlier. They can be part of the native Windows CE file system or an installable file system.

The Windows CE File System

The Windows CE file system provides a unified view of all available storage devices, including the following:

- Files and directories from the operating system image (ROM-based)
- Files and directories in the object store (RAM-based)
- Files and directories on installable file systems

The Windows CE Platform Builder documentation describes this as "seamless integration" of each of these different file systems.

The architects of Windows CE simplified the file system structure from the legacy MS-DOS/Windows disk storage architecture. They eliminated drive letters so that Windows CE uses a simpler single-tree file system hierarchy. Instead of 26 possible starting points, there is only one: the root directory (\).

Because Windows CE does not support a "current directory" for a process, you must fully qualify all path names in your application. Aside from these differences, the file system directory structure has similarities to desktop file systems: a hierarchical file system with support for long file names. The maximum file path on Windows CE, as on desktop file systems, is 260 characters.

The Windows CE file system does support memory-mapped files, thus providing a mechanism for interprocess memory sharing. However, the .NET Compact Framework does not support memory-mapped files. Chapter 4 provided details on accessing native Windows CE functionality.

ROM-Based Files

Files located in ROM reside in the `\windows` directory and are read-only by definition. Many have the `system` or `hidden` attribute or both. At system boot time, the object store is initialized with whatever directories may be required. At that time, ROM-based files can be mapped to other directories besides the `\windows` directory.

Platform Builder packages the Windows CE operating system as a ROM image, compressing some of these files and leaving others uncompressed, as determined by the platform developer. Uncompressed ROM files run in place, in what is called an eXecute In Place (XIP) region. An advantage of XIP regions is that ROM images can be mapped directly into virtual memory, allowing system files to be available without using precious program memory. On the downside, some ROM is slower than RAM, so code running in ROM may execute a little slower than code located elsewhere.

The `\windows` folder can also include files from the RAM-based object store. You can copy files and even overwrite some of the ROM-based files that are in the `\windows` folder. Of course, the file system does not actually copy to or overwrite ROM files, but it does note when you have a newer version of a ROM file in RAM and uses the newer version whenever the file is requested.

Another difference between Windows CE–powered systems and desktop systems is that Windows CE does not support a `PATH` environment variable that determines in what order to search directories when resolving requests to locate programs or shared libraries. Here is the hard-coded search sequence:

- The absolute path (when specified)
- The `.exe` launch directory (when searching for libraries)
- The `\windows` directory
- ROM DLL files

While there is no `PATH` variable, starting with Windows CE 4.1 there is support for a registry key that provides a search path: `HKEY_LOCAL_MACHINE\Loader`, with the `SystemPath` property. The best resource for details on this subject is the Win32 documentation for Windows CE, specifically the remarks that accompany the Win32 `LoadLibrary` function.

RAM-Based Files

At system boot time, the amount of RAM available for the object store is specified during platform creation. Users can modify this value on some platforms (including the Pocket PC) by using the *Memory* tab of the Control Panel. This change can also be made programmatically through the native `SetSystemMemoryDivision` Windows CE functions. (A companion function, `GetSystemMemoryDivision`, lets you query the current setting.) These functions are available to application programs but, as of this writing, are documented only in Platform Builder.

Because the object store has a limited size, a compression algorithm is applied to data in the object store. It is a simple, fast algorithm that achieves approximately 2:1 compression. The maximum size of a single object store file is 32MB. The maximum size of a CE property database (also located in the object store) is 16MB.

On the Pocket PC, user files are meant to be stored in a directory named `My Documents`. This is the only directory available through the system-provided File Open and File Save dialog boxes, although a user can see the contents of other directories by using the File Explorer application.

This completes our introduction to storage. You now know that there a unified view of a physically diverse file system and that there is a RAM-based object store, which contains a file system, a registry, and CE property databases. The focus for the remainder of this chapter is file I/O and registry access.

File I/O

In the .NET Framework—and, for that matter, in the desktop .NET Framework—file I/O and the objects used for handling file I/O can be broken into three general categories:

1. Manipulating files, which includes creating, deleting, discovering, and copying files and maintaining attributes. Table 11.1 in the `File` and `Directory` Classes subsection lists the file manipulation classes.
2. Reading and writing bytes to and from a file (i.e., performing low-level file I/O). Byte-level I/O is performed through `Stream` objects, which are shown in Table 11.2 in the Byte-Level I/O subsection.
3. Reading and writing at a higher level, such as the transfer of value data types, Unicode characters, strings, and lines of text. Table 11.3 in the Higher-Level I/O subsection presents these higher-level I/O objects.

Version 1.0 of the .NET Compact Framework does not support the higher-level serialization classes, which convert objects to a flattened, serialized format and then back again into objects. Included among these serialization classes are the following:

- `BinaryFormatter`[5]
- `SoapFormatter`[6]
- `XmlSerializer`[7]

The `File` and `Directory` Classes

The `File` and `Directory` classes provide for the creation and maintenance of files and directories. They are not used to do the actual I/O, although they can be used to create the objects that are. For instance, `File.AppendText` returns a `StreamWriter` object that can be used to add characters to a file.

TABLE 11.1: File Manipulation Classes

Implementation Class	Description	Available Static Methods

`Directory`	Manipulates directories	`CreateDirectory`
		`Delete`
		`Exists`
		`Move`
		`Get/SetCreationTime`
		`Get/SetCurrentDirectory`
		`GetDirectories`
		`GetFiles`

`File`	Manipulates files	`Create`
		`CreateText`
		`Copy`
		`Move`
		`Delete`
		`Exists`
		`Open`
		`OpenRead`
		`OpenText`
		`OpenWrite`
		`GetAttributes`
		`SetAttributes`

5. Fully qualified name: `System.Runtime.Serialization.Formatters.Binary.BinaryFormatter`.
6. Fully qualified name: `System.Runtime.Serialization.Formatters.Soap.SoapFormatter`.
7. Fully qualified name: `System.XmlSerialization.XmlSerializer`.

The `Directory` and `File` classes consist entirely of static methods. Instead of creating instances of objects, you invoke static methods through a class reference, as shown in the following code.

```
using System.IO;
//...
if (! Directory.Exists(strDirName) )
{
   Directory.CreateDirectory(strDirName);
}
Directory.SetCurrentDirectory(strDirName);

if (! File.Exists(strFileName) )
{
   File.Create(strFileName).Close();
}
```

To do the actual I/O you need an I/O object, either a low-level I/O object or one of the higher-level objects that are built on the low-level ones.

Byte-Level I/O

While you use the `File` and `Directory` classes entirely through static methods, the objects used to perform the I/O must be instantiated. The low-level I/O objects, shown in Table 11.2, enable you to read and write arrays of bytes to and from a variety of endpoints in a consistent fashion.

The `Stream` objects transfer `bytes` to and from a storage medium, such as a file or a network socket. Since a byte is the most basic unit of data transfer, the `Stream` objects provide a basic data transfer capability, independent of the specific storage media. These byte-level I/O classes are also the building blocks for the higher-level file I/O classes.

The abstract base `Stream` class defines the interface—the properties and methods—for transferring bytes to and from a data source. This base class itself has no concept of the source or destination but defines the basic capabilities of stream I/O, which is to read, to write, to seek, and to close. The real work gets done in the classes derived from `Stream`, such as `FileStream`, which incorporate the capabilities of a specific type of storage media. Thus, you use the same properties and methods to write bytes to a file as you do to write bytes to a network socket. The implementation

TABLE 11.2: Byte-Level I/O Classes (Streams)

Interface (Abstract Base) Class	Implementation Class	Description	Major PMEs

`Stream`	N/A	Abstract base class; defines reading/writing bytes to a source	`Read`
			`Write`
			`Seek`
			`Close`
			`CanSeek`

`Stream`	`FileStream`	Reads/writes bytes to a file	See above
`Stream`	`NetworkStream`	Reads/writes bytes to a network socket	See above
`Stream`	`MemoryStream`	Reads/writes bytes to memory	See above

of the underlying class is different for each media type, but the interface is identical.

The `Stream`-derived classes provide access via a common interface for byte-oriented access to a variety of storage media. That's nice if you are working with bytes, but what if you want to read and write Unicode characters (the default Windows CE character set) which has two bytes per character? Perhaps you want to read and write integers, floating-point values, or strings in their native mode. Or maybe you want to work at an even higher level of abstraction, such as reading and writing lines of text.

Higher-Level I/O

The .NET Compact Framework supports some of the higher-level I/O .NET classes. Various reader and writer classes, summarized in Table 11.3, deliver a higher level of abstraction by providing data-specific functionality for any stream regardless of its actual storage media. They do this by wrapping themselves around one of the `Stream` objects that were shown in Table 11.2.

TABLE 11.3: Data-Specific I/O Classes (Higher-Level Readers/Writers)

Interface (Abstract Base) Class	Implementation Class	Description	Key Methods

`TextReader`	N/A	Abstract base class; defines the interface for reading bytes as characters, strings, or lines	`Read`
			`ReadLine`
			`ReadBlock`
			`ReadToEnd`
			`Close`

`TextReader`	`StreamReader` `StringReader`	Reads characters and strings from a stream (`StreamReader`) or from a string (`StringReader`)	See above

`TextWriter`	N/A	Abstract base class; defines the interface for writing bytes as characters, strings, or lines	`Close`
			`Flush`
			`Write`
			`WriteLine`

`TextWriter`	`StreamWriter` `StringWriter`	Writes characters and strings to a stream (`StreamWriter`) or to a string (`String-Writer`)	See above

N/A	`BinaryReader`	Reads value data types from a stream	`Close`
			`Read`
			`ReadBoolean`
			`ReadByte`
			`ReadChar`
			`ReadInt16`
			`ReadInt32`
			`ReadString`
			`ReadSingle`
			`ReadDouble`

N/A	`BinaryWriter`	Writes value data types to a stream	`Close`
			`Flush`
			`Seek`
			`Write`

Interface (Abstract Base) Class	Implementation Class	Description	Key Methods
N/A	XmlReader	Reads XML from a stream	Close MoveToAttribute MoveToElement Read ReadAttributeValue ReadElementString ReadInnerXML Skip
N/A	XmlWriter	Writes XML to a stream	Close WriteNode WriteStartAttribute WriteAttributeString WriteEndAttribute WriteStartElement WriteElementString WriteEndElement

The data-specific I/O classes use a `Stream` object to do the underlying I/O. This `Stream` object can be provided as a constructor parameter, or it may be created by the constructor, as needed.

The `XmlReader` class is the base class for three derived classes: `XmlNodeReader`, `XmlTextReader`, and `XmlValidatingReader`. The `XmlWriter` class is the base class for the `XmlTextWriter` derived class.

The `BinaryWriter` class's `Write` method has 18 overloads (essentially one for each value data type), each capable of outputting the binary image of that data type. Reading the data by using a `BinaryReader` object, however, requires that you specify a data type–specific routine, such as `ReadSingle`, for each value that you wish to read, or that you use its generic `Read` method and then decipher the input bytes yourself. We think it is much easier to use the type-specific methods for reading.

Thus, if you want to write the fields of a structure to a file, you can use a `BinaryWriter` object to do so. You first create a `FileStream` object and then create a `BinaryWriter` object, specifying the `FileStream` object as an input parameter. The `BinaryWriter` is then used to output the contents of the structure to the file, as shown in Listing 11.1. To read the data back in, create a `BinaryReader` object and use the appropriate type-specific reading methods, as we illustrate later in this chapter for the sample application.

Or, if you felt that XML was the appropriate storage format for your data, you could use the XML I/O classes to persist your data in an XML file, as we will also do later in this chapter.

LISTING 11.1: Using a `BinaryWriter` Object

```
using System;
using System.Text;
using System.IO;
         :
         :
      private struct ourFontInfo
      {
         public string  strName;
         public float sglSize;
         public int intStyle;
      }

      ourFontInfo fiNotepadCE;
         :
         :
   '  Place data in the fields.
         :
         :
   '  Open a writer for the file.
         BinaryWriter bwrtFile =
            new BinaryWriter(
            new FileStream(strFileName,
                           FileMode.OpenOrCreate,
                           FileAccess.Write,
                           FileShare.None),
            encodeFile);

   '  Write the three fields to the file.
         bwrtFile.Write(textInput.Font.Name);
         bwrtFile.Write(textInput.Font.Size);
         bwrtFile.Write(unchecked((int)textInput.Font.Style));
         bwrtFile.Close();
```

Reader and writer objects wrap themselves around a `Stream` object and can provide their functionality only through their contained `Stream` object. In Listing 11.1, to write the same structure to a socket instead of to a file, you would create a `NetworkStream` object instead of a `FileStream` object. All other code would remain the same.

Encoding and Decoding Data

As data is being transferred, it can also be encoded or decoded. Encoding converts data from Unicode to another character set. Among supported character set conversions, applied as the bytes are being transferred between the storage media and the stream, are 7-bit ASCII, 8-bit Unicode (UTF-8), Simplified Chinese, and Japanese shift-jis. Decoding converts characters from these character sets into Unicode.

Encoding is done by members of the `System.Text.Encoding` class. Pick the encoding you want and specify it as a constructor parameter of the reader or writer object. The encoding properties of reader and writer objects cannot be changed after the object has been created. Table 11.4 shows the common properties and methods of the `Encoding` class, and Table 11.5 shows several of the more common encodings.

The reader and writer objects determine how the data is to be streamed; the stream type determines the stream destination. This mix-and-match capability for marrying data-oriented functionality with different types of endpoints highlights the flexibility of .NET file I/O. It allows you to transfer a variety of data types, in a variety of encodings, to a variety of storage media while using (mostly) the same methods for any combination.

Using the I/O Classes

Having introduced the I/O classes, we now proceed to using them. For our example program, we create a .NET Compact Framework version of Notepad, shown in Figure 11.1, building on elements introduced in Chapter 9. The sample allows a user to read, write, and edit the contents of text files, just like Notepad on desktop systems, and to save and restore the application settings to a file. Writing the content of the Notepad involves the use of a `TextWriter` object; while we first save the settings with a `BinaryWriter` object and a custom `Structure` object, then later with an `XmlTextWriter`

TABLE 11.4: The Encoding Class

Properties and Methods	Description
`Convert`	Converts a byte array from one encoding to another
`GetEncoding`	Gets the object that does the encoding for a specified code page or encoding name, e.g., `GetEncoding(1252)` or `GetEncoding("GB18030")` (see Table 11.5)
`Default`	Gets the object that does default (Utf7) encoding
`ASCII`	Gets the object that does ASCII encoding
`Unicode`	Gets the object that does Unicode encoding
`BigEndianUnicode`	Gets the object that does big-endian encoding
`UTF7`	Gets the object that does Utf7 encoding
`UTF8`	Gets the object that does Utf8 encoding

TABLE 11.5: Common Encodings

Code Page	Name
932	"Japanese shift-jis"
1200	"UTF-16LE", "utf-16", "ucs-2", "unicode", or "ISO-10646-UCS-2"
1201	"UTF-16BE" or "unicodeFFFE"
1252	"windows-1252"
65000	"utf-7", "csUnicode11UTF7", "unicode-1-1-utf-7", "unicode-2-0-utf-7", "x-unicode-1-1-utf-7", or "x-unicode-2-0-utf-7"
65001	"utf-8", "unicode-1-1-utf-8", "unicode-2-0-utf-8", "x-unicode-1-1-utf-8", or "x-unicode-2-0-utf-8"
20127	"us-ascii", "us", "ascii", "ANSI_X3.4-1968", "ANSI_X3.4-1986", "cp367", "csASCII", "IBM367", "iso-ir-6", "ISO646-US", or "ISO_646.irv:1991"
54936	"GB18030"

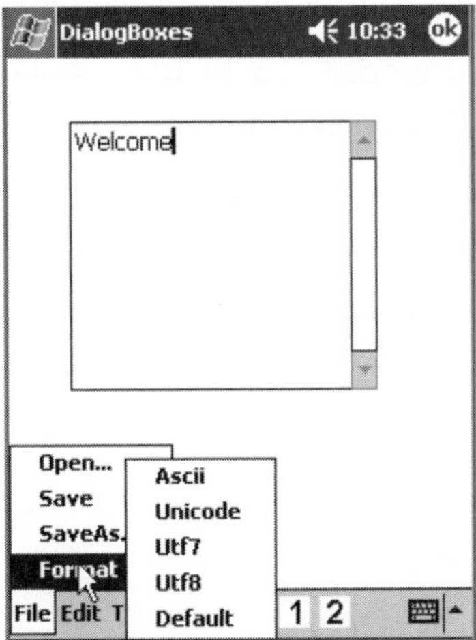

FIGURE 11.1: The sample application, a .NET Compact Framework version of Notepad

object. The code for the initial version of this application is presented in Listings 11.2 through 11.10 and can be found on the book's Web site in the `Storage` project. Subsequent enhancements to the application are presented in Listings 11.11 through 11.23.

Because `OpenFileDialog` and `SaveFileDialog` dialogs display only files and directories located under the `My Documents` directory, we use `My Documents\YaoDurant\NotepadCE` as the directory for all file I/O performed by this application.

We use the IDE to define the menu shown in Figure 11.1 and then write the code to handle the various selections. As always, we make sure that the necessary namespaces have been specified and that our directory path is defined, as illustrated in Listing 11.2.

LISTING 11.2: The Start of the `Storage` Program

```
Using System
Using System.Text              '  StringBuilder
Using System.Drawing           '  FontStyle
Using System.Windows.Forms     '  DialogResult
Using System.IO                '  Directories, files, streams
                   :
                   :
    private string  strDirName = @"My Documents\NotepadCE";
```

The selections on the Encoding Choices menu can all be handled by one routine that sets a `Form` variable named `encodeFile` to the requested encoding. This routine is shown in Listing 11.3. Also shown in Listing 11.3 is the code to initialize the `encodeFile` variable.

LISTING 11.3: Handling the Encoding Choices

```
private Encoding encodeFile = Encoding.Default;
                    :
                    :
                    :
private void mitemFFFormat_Click(object sender,
                                 EventArgs e)
{
   //  Set this.encodeFile to the selected encoding.

   this.encodeFile = Encoding.Default;
   if ( ((MenuItem)sender) == mitemFFAscii )
   {
      this.encodeFile = Encoding.ASCII;
   }
   if ( ((MenuItem)sender) == mitemFFUnicode )
   {
      this.encodeFile = Encoding.Unicode;
   }
   if ( ((MenuItem)sender) == mitemFFUtf8 )
   {
      this.encodeFile = Encoding.UTF8;
   }
   if ( ((MenuItem)sender) == mitemFFUtf7 )
   {
      this.encodeFile = Encoding.UTF7;
   }
}
```

Because the content of the Notepad is really the content of the multiline `TextBox` control that overlays most of the form, reading and writing the content means transferring the `TextBox` control's `Text` property to and from the file.

Text File I/O

When the user selects Open from the File menu, the application creates a `System.Windows.Forms OpenFileDialog` object (if one has not already been created), sets its initial `Directory` and `Filter` properties, and presents the dialog to the user. After the user has either canceled the dialog or specified the desired file, the application saves the file name for future reference, creates a `FileStream` object for the requested file, and uses it plus the requested encoding to create a `StreamReader` object. Using the `StreamReader` object, the application reads the entire contents of the file into the multiline `TextBox` control and then closes the file. Listing 11.4 shows the code.

LISTING 11.4: Handling the Request for File Open

```
private void mitemFileOpen_Click(object sender,
                                 EventArgs e)
{
   //  Create an OpenFileDialog if necessary.
   if ( fdlgOpen == null )
      { fdlgOpen = new OpenFileDialog(); }
   fdlgOpen.InitialDirectory = "NotepadCE";
   fdlgOpen.Filter =
      "dat files (*.dat)|*.dat|" +
      "txt files (*.txt)|*.txt|" +
      "All files (*.*)|*.*";

   //  Show it.
   switch (fdlgOpen.ShowDialog())
   {
      //  Check the user's response.
      case DialogResult.OK:

         //  Save the file name.
         strCurrentFile = fdlgOpen.FileName;

         //  Open, read, and close the file.
         StreamReader srdrFile =
            new StreamReader(
               new FileStream(strCurrentFile,
                              FileMode.Open),
               this.encodeFile);
            this.textInput.Text = srdrFile.ReadToEnd();
            srdrFile.Close();
         break;

      default:
         break;
   }
}
```

The File menu's Save handler checks to see if there is a current file name. If there is not, it calls the SaveAs handler to complete the process. Once the file name has been specified, the process is almost identical to the Open process; a `FileStream` object is created and used to create a `StreamWriter` object that writes the contents of the `Text` property to the file. Listing 11.5 shows the code.

LISTING 11.5: Handling the Request for File Save

```
private void mitemFileSave_Click(object sender,
                                 EventArgs e)
{
   //  If the user has not yet specified
   //     a file name, do SaveAs.
   //  Else,
   //     open, write, and close the file.
   if ( strCurrentFile == string.Empty )
   {
      mitemFileSaveAs_Click(sender, e);
   }
   else
   {
      //  If the file does not exist,
      //     create it.
      if (! File.Exists(strCurrentFile) )
      {
         File.Create(strCurrentFile).Close();
      }

      //  Create Writer.
      StreamWriter swrtFile =
         new StreamWriter(
            new FileStream(strCurrentFile,
                           FileMode.Truncate),
            this.encodeFile);

      //  Write the file.
      swrtFile.Write(this.textInput.Text);

      //  Close the file.
      swrtFile.Close();
   }
}
```

The SaveAs handler presents a `SaveFileDialog` object to the user. If the user enters a file name, the handler stores the file name into the Form variable and then calls the Save handler to complete the process, as shown in Listing 11.6.

LISTING 11.6: Handling the Request for File Save As

```
private void mitemFileSaveAs_Click(object sender,
                                   EventArgs e)
{
   //  Get the file name from the user.
   if ( fdlgSave == null )
   {
      fdlgSave = new SaveFileDialog();
   }

   switch (fdlgSave.ShowDialog())
   {
      case DialogResult.OK:
         //  Save the file name.
         strCurrentFile = fdlgSave.FileName;
         //  Save the file.
         mitemFileSave_Click(sender, e);
         break;
      default:
         break;
   }
}
```

So transferring the text content of our Notepad to and from a file is a matter of using a reader or writer object wrapped around a `Stream` object to specify the file, designate the encoding, and transfer the text.

Binary File I/O

For the second enhancement, to allow saving and restoring the application's settings to a file, we use reader and writer objects that can handle more than just text—some of our settings are the value types `System.Single` and `System.Int32`, as well as `System.String`. For handling this variety, `BinaryReader` and `BinaryWriter` objects are the best choice because they were designed to read and write value data types.

In the mobile world where time and space are limited, reading and writing data in binary format is often advantageous. Binary format saves space because integers, singles, doubles, and so on normally require less space in their value-typed formats than they do as text characters. For example, 1.234567E12 requires 4 bytes of storage as a `System.Single` but 22 bytes (11 × 2) as a `System.String`. Binary format also saves time because the data does not need to be converted to and from `String`, nor does it need to be encoded.

Additionally, desktop programmers may find they are more likely to use binary file I/O in the .NET Compact Framework than on the desktop because .NET's binary serialization classes have not been ported to the .NET Compact Framework. Binary file I/O then becomes a mechanism for "rolling your own" serialization of property values to a file.

To keep things simple, in our example we save and restore only our font settings (`Name`, `Size`, and `Style`). Later in this chapter, we modify the application to use the registry instead of a file for program settings.

Several settings, such as `Font.Style`, are customized integers. That is, although their definition is derived from `Integer`, they are not truly a value data type. Some have the `FlagsAttribute` attribute set. Because the `BinaryReader` and `BinaryWriter` classes are designed to work with value data types, you must cast these derived integers to an integer, and because of the `FlagsAttribute` you will need to use an `unchecked` cast to do it.

Writing Binary Data

Listing 11.7 shows the code for saving the font settings to a file in binary format.

LISTING 11.7: Saving Data in Binary Format to a File

```
private void SaveSettingsToFile()
{
   //  Create the directory if it does not
   //     already exist, and make it the
   //     current directory.
   if (! Directory.Exists(strDirName) )
   {
      Directory.CreateDirectory(strDirName);
   }
   Directory.SetCurrentDirectory(strDirName);
```

```
    //  Create the file if it does not
    //     already exist.
    if (! File.Exists(strFileName) )
    {
       File.Create(strFileName).Close();
    }

    //  Create a BinaryWriter (wrapped around a
    //     FileStream wrapped around the file)
    //     for output using the user-specified
    //     encoding.
    BinaryWriter bwrtFile =
       new BinaryWriter(
       new FileStream(strFileName,
                      FileMode.OpenOrCreate,
                      FileAccess.Write,
                      FileShare.None),
       encodeFile);

    //  Write the three fields, each of a
    //     different data type.
    //  Close the file.
    bwrtFile.Write(textInput.Font.Name);
    bwrtFile.Write(textInput.Font.Size);
    bwrtFile.Write(unchecked((int)textInput.Font.Style));
    bwrtFile.Close();
}
```

The `SaveSettingsToFile` routine is passed the directory and file names, plus the desired encoding. It begins by using the `Directory` and `File` classes to create the directory and the file, if they do not already exist. This code is technically superfluous, for a `Stream` object will soon be created and one of its constructor parameters specifies "open or create." We include the superfluous code to illustrate the following points.

- The `Directory` and `File` static methods are used without instantiating an object.
- Using the `File` class to create a file also opens the file. A `Stream` object cannot be created for an already open file. Therefore, if you use the `File` class to create a file that you plan to subsequently access with a `Stream` object, you must close the file after you create it.

Once the file has been created and closed, the application creates a `BinaryWriter` object wrapped around a `Stream` object for the file. Opening a

BinaryWriter object is identical to opening the StreamWriter object we used earlier in this chapter, as we showed earlier in Listing 11.5. We specify an encoding because one of the fields that we write is a string field. The encoding parameter, which defaults to UTF-8, is applied to all strings. Once the file is opened and the BinaryWriter created, we simply write each field individually and then close the file. Each of the three Write statements calls a different overload of the function, outputting a string, a single-precision floating-point number, and an integer.

Reading Binary Data

Reading binary data is a little trickier than writing it. When writing data, you do not have to pay much attention to data types of individual fields because all the methods for writing data in the BinaryWriter class are named Write. You leave it up to the compiler to find the correct overloaded method.

When reading data, however, you must pay closer attention to data type because the BinaryReader class has 18 different methods, with the expected type as part of the method name. For example, you call ReadInt32 to read a 32-bit integer and ReadDouble to read a double-precision floating-point number. Although not an overwhelming amount of effort, it is a bit more than required when writing the binary data.

The code for our sample program that reads the application settings from a binary file appears in Listing 11.8. As illustrated in the calls to the ReadString, ReadSingle, and ReadInt32 methods, you must pay attention to the expected data types, and the expected sequence, to read binary files.

LISTING 11.8: Reading Binary Data from a File

```
private void ReadSettingsFromFile()
{

   //  Make the directory the current directory.
   Directory.SetCurrentDirectory(strDirName);

   //  Create a BinaryReader (wrapped around a
   //      FileStream wrapped around the file)
   //      for input using the user-specified
   //      encoding.
   BinaryReader brdrFile =
```

```
        new BinaryReader(
           new FileStream(strFileName,
                          FileMode.OpenOrCreate,
                          FileAccess.Read,
                          FileShare.None),
           encodeFile);

     //  Read the three fields and create the font.
     //  Close the file.
     textInput.Font =
        new Font(brdrFile.ReadString(),
                 brdrFile.ReadSingle(),
                 (FontStyle)brdrFile.ReadInt32());
     brdrFile.Close();

  }
```

Binary I/O and Structures

You can make your I/O code easier to maintain by getting into the habit of organizing related fields into structures and coding structure-specific methods that handle the I/O. When your data is in a structure, it is easy to remember that adding and removing fields from the structure requires a corresponding modification to the I/O routines; it is also easier to specify the correct data types in the read routine if the write routine and the field definitions are located in the same section of code as the read routine.

We create such a structure for our font fields; Listing 11.9 shows that code. The structure contains the fields, a write routine, and a matching read routine.

LISTING 11.9: The Font Settings Structure

```
private string  strDirName = @"My Documents\NotepadCE";
private string  strFileName = "Settings.dat";
                :
                :
//  A structure containing font information and
//     the routines to write/restore that information
//     to/from a file.
private struct ourFontInfo
{
   public string strName;
   public float sglSize;
   public FontStyle fsStyle;
```

continues

continued

```
public void WriteToFile(string  strDirName,
                        string  strFileName,
                        Encoding encodeFile)
{
   //  Create the directory if it does not
   //     already exist, and make it the
   //     current directory.
   if (! Directory.Exists(strDirName) )
   {
      Directory.CreateDirectory(strDirName);
   }
   Directory.SetCurrentDirectory(strDirName);

   //  Create the file if it does not
   //     already exist.
   if (! File.Exists(strFileName) )
   {
      File.Create(strFileName).Close();
   }

   //  Create a BinaryWriter (wrapped around a
   //     FileStream wrapped around the file)
   //     for output using the user-specified
   //     encoding.
   BinaryWriter bwrtFile =
               new BinaryWriter(
                  new FileStream(
                           strFileName,
                           FileMode.OpenOrCreate,
                           FileAccess.Write,
                           FileShare.None),
               encodeFile);

   //  Write the three fields, each of a
   //     different data type.
   //  Close the file.
   bwrtFile.Write(this.strName);
   bwrtFile.Write(this.sglSize);
   bwrtFile.Write((int)this.fsStyle);
   bwrtFile.Close();
}

public void ReadFromFile(string  strDirName,
                         string  strFileName,
                         Encoding encodeFile)
{
```

```
        //  Set the current directory.
        Directory.SetCurrentDirectory(strDirName);

        //  Create a BinaryReader (wrapped around a
        //     FileStream wrapped around the file)
        //     for input using the user-specified
        //     encoding.
        BinaryReader brdrFile =
                       new BinaryReader(
                          new FileStream(
                                   strFileName,
                                   FileMode.OpenOrCreate,
                                   FileAccess.Read,
                                   FileShare.None),
                       encodeFile);

        //  Read the three fields.
        //  Close the file.
        try
        {
           this.strName = brdrFile.ReadString();
           this.sglSize = brdrFile.ReadSingle();
           this.fsStyle = (FontStyle)brdrFile.ReadInt32();
        }
        catch
        {
           this.strName = "Tahoma";
           this.sglSize = 9;
           this.fsStyle = FontStyle.Regular;
        }
        finally
        {
           brdrFile.Close();
        }
     }
  }
```

The presence of this structure allows the application to save the font settings using the code shown in Listing 11.10, a much simpler routine than the version shown earlier in Listing 11.7. The structure would also allow for an equal simplification of the restore routine, ensuring that the processes of saving and restoring the value type fields are always synchronized.

LISTING 11.10: Using the Structure to Save the Settings

```
private void SaveSettingsToFile()
{
   //  Create an ourFontInfo structure, load it from
   //     TextInput's font, and have the structure save
   //     its contents to the file.

   ourFontInfo fiFont;
   fiFont.strName = textInput.Font.Name;
   fiFont.sglSize = textInput.Font.Size;
   fiFont.intStyle = textInput.Font.Style;
   fiFont.WriteToFile(strDirName,
                      strFileName,
                      Encoding.Default);
}
```

This is a good demonstration of a central principle of object-oriented programming: encapsulation. We push the messy details of reading and writing the data into the data structure so that once we get it working we can ignore that relatively low-level code. Then users of this structure call the higher-level methods and the work gets done. The simplified code in Listing 11.10 is ample justification for our recommendation that you associate reading and writing methods with structures and classes that must be transferred to streams.

XML File I/O

Another option for saving settings is to save them in an XML file. XML is a text-based format for the exchange of information, standardized by the World Wide Web Consortium. Although XML requires a large number of bytes for the amount of data it carries, its text-based format makes it readable by both people and machines, and its standardization makes it portable across a variety of platforms. For small amounts of data, such as our font settings, it is an excellent format.

XML stores data within elements, which can be nested within other elements, as shown in the XML text listed here.

```
<?xml version="1.0" encoding="us-ascii"?>
<NotepadCe>
   <Font>
      <Name>Microsoft Sans Serif</Name>
```

```
        <Size>8.25</Size>
        <Style>0</Style>
    </Font>
    <Textbox>
        <ScrollBars>0</ScrollBars>
        <TextAlign>0</TextAlign>
        <WordWrap>true</WordWrap>
    </Textbox>
</NotepadCe>
```

An element can contain values, such as `Microsoft Sans Serif` and `8.25`, either in the body of the element or in its attributes. In our application we avoid the use of attributes and keep things simple by writing our settings values as element data rather than as attribute values.

To read and write XML we use an `XmlTextReader` object and an `XmlTextWriter` object. The `XmlTextReader` object uses a `TextReader` object to do the actual I/O (and similarly for the `XmlTextWriter`) while providing us with XML-specific functionality, such as writing the opening tag of an element or setting the number of spaces to be used for indentation.

As we did with binary I/O, we define a structure to hold the necessary settings and give it the ability to read from and write to a file by coding a read method and a write method within the structure itself. The structure will group the settings into two categories: those that are font settings and those that are settings of the multiline `TextBox` control, as shown in the previous XML code.

We begin by defining the element names and a field to hold a reference to the multiline `TextBox` control. Because we are saving the settings of this `TextBox` control's font, not the form's font, we do not need a separate variable for the font. We provide an overloaded constructor so that the reference to the multiline `TextBox` control can be specified as the structure is created. Listing 11.11 shows the code.

LISTING 11.11: The Start of the Structure for Saving Settings

```
public struct ourFormInfoXML
{
    //  Field names
    private const string strNotepadCE = "NotepadCe";
    private const string strFont = "Font";
```

continues

continued

```
   private const string strName = "Name";
   private const string strSize = "Size";
   private const string strStyle = "Style";
   private const string strTextbox = "Textbox";
   private const string strScrollBars = "ScrollBars";
   private const string strTextAlign = "TextAlign";
   private const string strWordWrap = "WordWrap";

   //  The TextBox whose settings are to be saved
   private TextBox textThis;

   //  Constructor
   public ourFormInfoXML(TextBox textThis)
   {
      //  Store reference to the TextBox.
      this.textThis = textThis;
   }
```

The routine to save the settings creates an `XmlTextWriter` object and sets it for an indentation size of three spaces, as shown in Listing 11.12.

LISTING 11.12: The Start of the Structure's Routine for Saving Settings

```
   public void WriteToFile(
      string strDirName,
      string strXMLFileName,
      Encoding encodeFile)
   {

      //  Ensure the directory and file exist.
      if( ! Directory.Exists(strDirName) )
      {
         Directory.CreateDirectory(strDirName);
      }

      Directory.SetCurrentDirectory(strDirName);
      if( ! File.Exists(strXMLFileName) )
      {
         File.Create(strXMLFileName).Close();
      }

      //  Create the XmlTextWriter.
      XmlTextWriter xmlwrtFontInfo =
         new XmlTextWriter(strXMLFileName, encodeFile);
```

```
//  Set indentation.
xmlwrtFontInfo.Formatting = Formatting.Indented;
xmlwrtFontInfo.Indentation = 3;
```

Then the routine begins the output of the XML document and writes the opening tag of the `NotepadCE` element (`<NotepadCE>`).

```
//  Begin the document and root element.
xmlwrtFontInfo.WriteStartDocument();
xmlwrtFontInfo.WriteStartElement(strNotepadCE);
```

Next the routine writes the opening tag of the `Font` element, followed by the three elements that contain data, followed by the closing tag of the `Font` element, as shown in Listing 11.13. Because the three elements that contain data do not have any child elements nested within them, they can be written with a single method call. We have chosen to write the values as strings solely to make the resulting file as readable as possible.

LISTING 11.13: Writing the Font's `Name`, `Size`, and `Style` Properties to the XML File

```
//  Begin the Font element,
//     write the three data elements
//     (Name, Size, Style), and
//     end the Font element.
xmlwrtFontInfo.WriteStartElement(strFont);
xmlwrtFontInfo.WriteElementString(
   strName, this.textThis.Font.Name);
xmlwrtFontInfo.WriteElementString(
   strSize,
   XmlConvert.ToString(this.textThis.Font.Size));
xmlwrtFontInfo.WriteElementString(
   strStyle,
   XmlConvert.ToString(
      unchecked((int)this.textThis.Font.Style)));
xmlwrtFontInfo.WriteEndElement();
```

In the same way, the `Textbox` element and its three nested elements are written, as shown in Listing 11.14.

LISTING 11.14: Writing Three of the `TextBox` Control's Properties to the XML File

```
      //  Begin the Textbox element,
      //     write the three data elements (ScrollBars,
      //     WordWrap, TextAlign), and
      //     end the Textbox element.
      xmlwrtFontInfo.WriteStartElement(strTextbox);
      xmlwrtFontInfo.WriteElementString(
            strScrollBars,
            XmlConvert.ToString(
               unchecked((int)textThis.ScrollBars)));
      xmlwrtFontInfo.WriteElementString(
            strTextAlign,
            XmlConvert.ToString(
               unchecked((int)textThis.TextAlign)));
      xmlwrtFontInfo.WriteElementString(
            strWordWrap,
            XmlConvert.ToString(textThis.WordWrap));
      xmlwrtFontInfo.WriteEndElement();
```

Finally, the `NotepadCE` element's closing tag is written, the buffer is flushed, and the file is closed.

```
      //  End the root element, end the document,
      //     and flush and close the file.
      xmlwrtFontInfo.WriteEndElement();
      xmlwrtFontInfo.WriteEndDocument();
      xmlwrtFontInfo.Flush();
      xmlwrtFontInfo.Close();
   }
```

The read routine used to restore the file is similar in the way that it opens and closes the file, but it is different in the way that it processes the file—it uses a read loop and extracts the nodes it is interested in as they are retrieved.

Listing 11.15 shows the opening code.

LISTING 11.15: The Start of the Routine for Reading Values from the XML File

```
   public void ReadFromFile(
      string strDirName,
      string strXMLFileName,
      Encoding encodeFile)
```

```
{
    //  Temp fields to hold values as they are read
    string tempName = string.Empty;
    float tempSize = 0.0F;
    int tempStyle = 0;
    bool tempWordWrap = false;
    int tempScrollBars = 0;
    int tempTextAlign = 0;

    //  Set the current directory.
    Directory.SetCurrentDirectory(strDirName);

    //  Create the XmlTextReader.
    XmlTextReader xmlrdrFontInfo =
       new XmlTextReader(strXMLFileName);
    xmlrdrFontInfo.WhitespaceHandling =
                                  WhitespaceHandling.None;
```

The routine then uses the `MoveToContent` method to step over any element(s) at the start of the file that do not contain data. The `MoveToContent` method can be used at any time in the processing of an XML file. It will bypass elements such as comments and processing instructions (elements that often appear at the start of an XML file).

```
//  Skip over nondata stuff at start of file.
xmlrdrFontInfo.MoveToContent();
```

The main processing loop reads each element, checking the element name to see if it is one we are interested in. More correctly, the loop reads each node. Thus, after the routine has read the value from the `Style` element, the file is positioned at the closing tag of the `Font` element. The next read will position the file at the opening tag of the `Textbox` element, and the next read will position it at the opening tag of the `ScrollBars` element, where `ReadElementString` can be used to extract the value. This loop is shown in Listing 11.16.

One advantage of using XML over binary file I/O is that we can alter the sequence in which we write the settings values without needing to recode our read routine.

LISTING 11.16: The Main Processing Loop for Reading Values from the XML File

```
// Read each node, looking for the data. If it
//    is a node we are interested in, read
//    the value.
//    Note:  ReadElementString will move to the
//    next node when done.  Do NOT call
//    ReadElementString and Read, or you will
//    advance the file two nodes instead of
//    one node.
while( ! xmlrdrFontInfo.EOF )
{
   switch( xmlrdrFontInfo.Name )
   {
      case strName:
         tempName =
            xmlrdrFontInfo.ReadElementString();
         break;
      case strSize:
         tempSize =
            float.Parse(
               xmlrdrFontInfo.ReadElementString());
         break;
      case strStyle:
         tempStyle =
            int.Parse(
               xmlrdrFontInfo.ReadElementString());
         break;

      case strScrollBars:
         tempScrollBars =
            int.Parse(
               xmlrdrFontInfo.ReadElementString());
         break;
      case strWordWrap:
         tempWordWrap =
            bool.Parse(
               xmlrdrFontInfo.ReadElementString());
         break;
      case strTextAlign:
         tempTextAlign =
            int.Parse(
               xmlrdrFontInfo.ReadElementString());
         break;
      default:
         xmlrdrFontInfo.Read();
         break;
   }
}
```

Finally, the file is closed and the values are applied to the multiline `TextBox` control.

```
         //  Close the XmlTextReader.
         xmlrdrFontInfo.Close();

         //  Restore the settings that were just read.
         this.textThis.Font = new
            Font(tempName, tempSize, (FontStyle)tempStyle);
         this.textThis.ScrollBars =
            (ScrollBars)tempScrollBars;
         this.textThis.WordWrap = tempWordWrap;
         this.textThis.TextAlign =
            (HorizontalAlignment)tempTextAlign;
      }
   }
```

To use our structure to save the settings, we create an instance of it and invoke its `WriteToFile` method, as shown here.

```
ourFormInfoXML fiForm = new ourFormInfoXML(textInput);
fiForm.WriteToFile(
   strDirName, strXMLFileName, Encoding.Default);
```

Restoring the settings becomes a matter of invoking our structure's `ReadFromFile` method.

```
ourFormInfoXML fiForm = new ourFormInfoXML(textInput);
fiForm.ReadFromFile(
   strDirName, strXMLFileName, Encoding.Default);
```

When we run and test the application, it produces a file that contains the XML text we listed at the start of this subsection.

This completes a very introductory look at XML. We narrowed our scope to sequential reading and writing of just elements and their values. But even with this narrow scope we saved and restored our information in a file format that was readable and portable.

The key points of .NET Compact Framework file I/O are summarized here.

1. Use static methods in the `Directory` and `File` classes for creating, copying, deleting, existence testing, and maintaining attributes of files and directories.
2. To read and write to a file, use a `FileStream` object wrapped inside the appropriate reader or writer object.
3. Chose an encoding prior to creating the `Stream` object.
4. Add read and write member functions to structures and classes to encapsulate data transfer between memory and files.

Once you have determined the type of data you need to read and write (such as binary, text, or XML), choose the appropriate object class for that data type, and you're on your way.

Registry Access

Accessing the registry and accessing files are different in two fundamental ways. First, when accessing the registry, you are setting or querying one named data element at a time. Second, object classes for accessing the registry are not supported in the .NET Compact Framework. Therefore, you must access the registry with P/Invoke calls to the registry API functions located in `coredll.dll`. (See Chapter 4 for more information on P/Invoke.)

The Windows CE registry is located in the object store as a hierarchical set of nodes, called *keys*, and data values. Keys can contain other keys and data values. Three root-level keys exist—`HKEY_CLASSES_ROOT`, `HKEY_CURRENT_USER`, and `HKEY_LOCAL_MACHINE`—fewer than the number of root keys in desktop versions of Windows. Keys are defined by text names. Three basic data types are supported: integers, strings, and binary arrays. Data values are described by their name, value, and type.

If you have not worked with registry functions before, you can get a good idea of the basic layout of the registry with a registry editing tool. One such tool, `regedit.exe`, ships with each 32-bit version of Microsoft Windows. Run this tool by typing its name into the Run dialog box. Another registry tool, the Remote Registry Editor, lets you view the registry of Windows CE devices. This second tool ships with the Embedded Visual Tools.

Opening a Registry Key

To access data in the registry, you must obtain a handle to the desired registry key and then use that handle to open the key. Once the key has been opened, you can read and write data to and from the registry. When opening a key, you can specify that the key be created if it does not already exist. So querying and setting data to and from the registry is similar to file I/O in that a tree-structured hierarchy is used and data is read from and written to specific locations within that structure.

Windows CE registry functions are located in a native library named `coredll.dll`. For each registry function you wish to call, you need a P/Invoke function declaration with a `DllImport` attribute like the one shown here.

```
[DllImport("coredll.dll")]
public static extern int
RegOpenKeyEx(IntPtr hKey,
             string lpSubKey,
             int ulOptions,
             int samDesired,
             ref IntPtr phkResult);
```

You can use this function to open a registry key. This P/Invoke declaration supports the native function `RegOpenKeyEx`, whose C/C++ function definition is shown here.

```
LONG RegOpenKeyEx(HKEY hKey,
                  LPCWSTR lpSubKey,
                  DWORD ulOptions,
                  REGSAM samDesired,
                  PHKEY phkResult );
```

Finally, you need a `using` statement to reference the `System.Runtime.InteropServices` namespace, as shown here.

```
using System.Runtime.InteropServices;
```

The Need for P/Invoke Wrappers

A P/Invoke declaration allows managed code to call an unmanaged library function. The declaration must specify data types that map to the native API data types and a type for the return value that maps to the unmanaged function's return type. We briefly discuss how to do this in this chapter (Chapter 4 presented more detail). The best solution, however, is not to write your own wrappers but to find ones that have already been written. For this, you have several choices.

One choice comes from Chapter 14. Among the samples for that chapter is a project named `YaoDurant.Win32.Rapi`, which has a source file `rapi.cs`. This file contains P/Invoke declarations for desktop functions that use ActiveSync to access the object store. Those declarations are identical to what you need to access device-side registry functions from the .NET Compact Framework.

A second choice is the smaller set of registry-only functions in `winregce.cs`. This file is included on the Web site in the `Storage` project that we have been using throughout this chapter and are about to enhance with registry access. (The Chapter 14 sample project just mentioned was written for the desktop .NET Framework.)

A third alternative is available from a source not associated with this book. If you are looking for registry code compatible with the desktop .NET Framework's registry classes, visit http://www.opennetcf.org. This Web site advertises itself as a "central repository for open source projects specifically targeting the .NET Compact Framework." We have met some of the people involved with this Web site and wish to pass along their URL, as it may be of benefit to you.

If you decide to write your own P/Invoke declarations, see Chapter 4 for discussion of the P/Invoke Wizard and P/Invoke techniques that can help you.

Mapping Registry Types to Managed Types

To use P/Invoke declarations for registry access, you must start by understanding the available registry types and how those types match to managed types. The registry supports a minimal set of types, sufficient for defining settings for programs, device drivers, and the operating system itself. When you write values to the registry, you specify the input type to the registry write function (`RegSetValueEx`). When you read values from the registry, the registry read function (`RegQueryValueEx`) informs you of the type of data it returns. In this context, data type is not related to the managed-code types. Instead, a set of flags with the prefix `REG_` are defined as part of the registry programming interface. Table 11.6 maps the .NET types to their corresponding registry data types.

As shown in the table, the registry supports three basic data types: integers (`REG_DWORD`), strings (`REG_SZ` and `REG_MULTI_SZ`), and binary arrays (`REG_BINARY`). The registry itself supports two kinds of strings: single strings and multiple strings. A multiple string (`REG_MULTI_SZ`) allows a system setting to support multiple values. For example, a single network adapter can have multiple IP addresses. In this case, a multiple string contains several IP addresses, separated from each other by a single zero byte. The entire string itself is terminated with a double zero byte.

For single strings, we list two .NET types. In the strictest sense of .NET type compatibility, one type can be used only for input (`String`), while the other can be used for either input or output (`StringBuilder`). This is how

TABLE 11.6: Translation of Common .NET Data Types to Unmanaged Registry Types

.NET Type	Registry Type	C# Alias	Visual Basic Alias
`Byte (array)`	`REG_BINARY`	`byte []`	`Byte ()`
`Char (array)`	`REG_MULTI_SZ`	`char []`	`Char ()`
`Int32`	`REG_DWORD`	`int`	`Integer`
`String`	`REG_SZ`	`string`	`String`
`StringBuilder`	`REG_SZ`	N/A	N/A

things are done on the desktop. In the .NET Compact Framework, where a few corners have been cut, we notice that `String` is acceptable as an output parameter as well as an input parameter in calls into unmanaged code. However, we tend to use `StringBuilder` for output parameters in calls into unmanaged code because a future version of the .NET Compact Framework might enforce more of the desktop-like behavior.

Support for byte arrays (`REG_BINARY`) is really a catchall for storing arbitrary types of arbitrary size in the registry. You could, for example, read or write a structure of arbitrary size[8] into a binary registry entry. While Table 11.6 indicates that the associated .NET type is a byte array, you can create P/Invoke declarations that allow you to use whatever type you need.

Unmanaged code routines that are passed strings expect to be passed two parameters: a pointer to the string itself and an indication of the string's length. For input strings, this is the actual length of the string; for output strings it is the maximum number of bytes, including the `null` terminator, that the native routine can place into the `StringBuilder` object. The following subsections illustrate calling a native-code function, `RegQueryValueEx`, to retrieve a value from the registry.

Opening and Accessing Registry Keys

Before we can read or write anything to the registry, we first must open a registry key. We mentioned the `RegOpenKeyEx` function earlier, which opens an existing key without creating a new one. However, we find it more convenient to create and open a key with a single function. The `RegCreateKeyEx` function does just that—it opens an existing key or creates a key if the key does not exist.

Listing 11.17 shows the code needed to read a value from the registry. It calls three native registry functions (defined as static functions in a utility class, `WinRegCE`, in our sample program):

- `RegCreateKeyEx`: opens a registry node, returning the key to that node
- `RegQueryValueEx`: reads the value of the opened registry node
- `RegCloseKey`: closes the registry node

---

8. The maximum limit on the size of individual registry entries is 4K.

Listing 11.17: Reading a Value from the Registry

```
private const int cbMAX = 255;
private IntPtr hkeyHive = new
   IntPtr(unchecked((int)WinRegCE.HKEY.HKEY_LOCAL_MACHINE));
private string strYDKey = @"SOFTWARE\YaoDurant";
               :
               :
   //  Open HKEY_LOCAL_MACHINE\SOFTWARE\YaoDurant\...
   //      and place its handle in hkeyCurrent.
   intReturn =
      WinRegCE.RegCreateKeyEx(hkeyHive,
                              strYDKey + @"\" + strKeyName,
                              0, string.Empty, 0, 0,
                              IntPtr.Zero,
                              ref hkeyCurrent,
                              ref regdispResult);
   if ( intReturn != 0 ) { return false; }

   //  Create fields to hold the output.
   StringBuilder  sbValue = new StringBuilder(cbMAX);
   int cbValue = cbMAX;

   //  Read the value from the registry into sbValue.
   WinRegCE.REGTYPE rtType = 0;
   intReturn =
      WinRegCE.RegQueryValueEx(hkeyCurrent, strValueName,
                               0, ref rtType,
                               sbValue, ref cbValue);
   if ( intReturn != 0 ) { return false; }

   //  Close the key.
   intReturn = WinRegCE.RegCloseKey(hkeyCurrent);
   if ( intReturn != 0 ) { return false; }

   //  Set the string into the output parameter.
   strValue = sbValue.ToString();
         //    :
         //    :
```

When the native API method writes the string into the `StringBuilder` object, it will write the bytes (including the `null` terminator, if any) into the `StringBuilder`. The presence of the `null` terminator in the string is the reason why the received string may appear to be missing its terminating quotation mark when you view the `StringBuilder` object in the debugger. The `StringBuilder` object's `ToString` method removes the terminating `null` character as it extracts the string.

Reading Registry Values

Once a registry node has been opened, the associated key can be used to read and write values. A single function, `RegQueryValueEx`, supports reading registry values. The native-code signature for that function appears here.

```
LONG RegQueryValueEx(HKEY hKey,
                     LPCWSTR lpValueName,
                     LPDWORD lpReserved,
                     LPDWORD lpType,
                     LPBYTE  lpData,
                     LPDWORD lpcbData );
```

Note the following points about this code.

- The `hKey` parameter is a registry handle that identifies the registry node to access, as returned by a call to `RegCreateKeyEx` or `RegOpenKeyEx`.
- The `lpValueName` parameter is the name of the data value being retrieved (corresponding to the right column in the registry editor).
- The `lpReserved` parameter is reserved and should be set to `0`.
- The `lpType` parameter is an `[out]` (output-only) parameter. On return from the function call, the variable referenced by this parameter contains the registry type (`REG_` flag) for the value being queried.
- The `lpData` parameter identifies the location where the actual value is to be written.
- The `lpcbData` parameter is a pointer to an integer field. Before calling this function, you set the size (in bytes) for the output buffer. On return, this value holds the actual number of bytes received.

The matching P/Invoke function declaration (taken from our `WinRegCE` class) is as follows.

```
[DllImport("coredll.dll")]
public static extern int
RegQueryValueEx(IntPtr hKey,
                string lpValueName,
                int Res1,
                ref REGTYPE lpType,
                StringBuilder strData,
                ref int lpcbData);
```

This declaration is suitable for retrieving a string (`REG_SZ`) value from the registry. Note that for the fifth parameter, the `StringBuilder` is a reference type that we pass as a by-value parameter. The native function expects this parameter to be a pointer to the location where the data is to be placed. And, as we discussed in Chapter 3, the impact of passing the reference variable by value is that a pointer to the string buffer contained within the `StringBuilder` object is passed to the native function (reference variables are always passed as pointers).

We do the opposite when reading integers (`REG_DWORD`) from the registry. We define the integer parameters, which would normally be passed as values, as by-reference parameters (using the C# `ref` keyword), causing them to be passed as pointers rather than as values. Once again, this ensures that the native function receives a pointer to the location where the data must be placed.

Writing Registry Values

The native function that writes values to the registry is `RegSetValueEx`. The P/Invoke declaration for this function is as follows.

```
[DllImport("coredll.dll")]
public static extern int
RegSetValueEx(IntPtr hKey,
              string lpValueName,
              int Res1,
              REGTYPE dwType,
              string strData,
              int cbData);
```

Note the following points about this code.

- The `hKey` parameter is a registry handle that identifies the registry node to access, as returned by a call to `RegCreateKeyEx` or `RegOpenKeyEx`.
- The `lpValueName` parameter is the name of the data value being retrieved (corresponding to the right column in the registry editor).
- The `Res1` parameter is reserved and should be set to `0`.
- The `dwType` parameter identifies the registry type (`REG_` flag) for the value being set. Supported values include `REG_SZ` for a singleton

string, `REG_MULTI_SZ` for a multiple string, `REG_DWORD` for an integer, and `REG_BINARY` for an arbitrary binary block (which can be up to 4K in size). Our sample program defines the `REGTYPE` enumeration for this set of flags.

- The `strData` parameter is a pointer to the new value to be written to the registry. As defined, this function accepts a string (which means that `dwType` must be `REG_SZ`). In the next subsection, we discuss the use of function overloading to define a set of registry reading and writing methods.
- The `cbData` parameter identifies the size of the input buffer in bytes.

The version of `RegSetValueEx` shown here writes strings to the registry. When calling the operating system function from native code, a C programmer casts the fifth parameter (`strData`) to match the type of data being supplied. This is harder to do with strongly-typed .NET compilers. There is a better way: function overloading, which we discuss next.

Using Function Overloading for Registry Access

The native registry functions are defined in the C programming language, which does not support function overloading.[9] The standard way that C programmers read and write different types using a single function is by *casting*, a type conversion technique that is fast but not very safe.

In object-oriented programming languages like C# and Visual Basic .NET, function overloading provides a type-safe way to define different sets of input parameters for a group functions that have the same name. We can use this feature for P/Invoke declarations, provided that the types we declare are compatible with the type defined in the native function. Listing 11.18 shows four P/Invoke declarations for two native registry functions. There are two overloads for `RegQueryValueEx`: one to retrieve a

9. The C++ language, on the other hand, does support function overloading. However, C++ function signatures are incompatible with .NET function names and cannot be accessed by using P/Invoke declarations.

string and one to retrieve an integer; and there are two similar overloads for RegSetValueEx.

LISTING 11.18: Overloaded Wrappers for Two Registry Functions

```
//  System.StringBuilder version
[DllImport("coredll.dll")]
public static extern int
RegQueryValueEx(IntPtr hKey, string lpValueName,
                int Res1, ref REGTYPE lpType,
                StringBuilder strData,
                ref int lpcbData);

//  System.Int32 version
[DllImport("coredll.dll")]
public static extern int
RegQueryValueEx(IntPtr hKey, string lpValueName,
                int Res1, ref REGTYPE lpType,
                ref int piData, ref int lpcbData);

//  System.String version
[DllImport("coredll.dll")]
public static extern int
RegSetValueEx(IntPtr hKey, string lpValueName,
              int Res1, REGTYPE dwType,
              string strData, int cbData);

//  System.Int32 version
[DllImport("coredll.dll")]
public static extern int
RegSetValueEx(IntPtr hKey, string lpValueName,
              int Res1, REGTYPE dwType,
              ref int piData, int cbData);
```

Our project has a file named winregce.cs, which contains P/Invoke wrapper declarations for native registry functions. The RegQueryValueEx overloaded methods shown in Listing 11.18 were taken from this file.

Using Registry Utility Classes

A P/Invoke function declaration contains no code but is used to map parameters and return values between managed code and unmanaged functions. We sometimes find it helps to write managed-code utility classes to handle tedious housekeeping chores. Such functions might calculate required length parameters, initialize strings, or obtain registry key handles before calling a native function.

In our `Storage` sample application, we implement a registry utility class named `UtilRegistry`, which we place in a file named `utilregistry.cs`. Listing 11.19 shows the code for the `UtilRegistry` class in its entirety. We do not comment on the entire contents of this file because it is long, but we do comment on certain routines that provide solutions to common challenges that must be addressed when accessing the registry.

LISTING 11.19: A Registry Utility Class That Calls Native Registry Functions

```
using System;
using System.Runtime.InteropServices;    //  SizeOf
using System.Text;                       //  StringBuilder
using YaoDurant.Win32;                   //  Registry access

//  UtilRegistry:
//     A utility class for reading and writing data to the
//        HKEY.HKEY_LOCAL_MACHINE\SOFTWARE\YaoDurant node
//        of the registry

public class UtilRegistry
{
   private IntPtr hkeyHive =
      new IntPtr(unchecked(
                  (int)WinRegCE.HKEY.HKEY_LOCAL_MACHINE));
   private string  strYDKey = @"SOFTWARE\YaoDurant";
   private WinRegCE.REGTYPE iType;
   private IntPtr hkeyCurrent;
   private int intReturn, cbData;
   private WinRegCE.REGDISP regdispResult;
   private const int cbMAX = 255;


   //  Delete a registry key.
   public bool DeleteKey( string  strKeyName )
   {

      intReturn =
         WinRegCE.RegDeleteKey(hkeyHive,
         strYDKey + @"\" + strKeyName);
      if ( intReturn != 0 )
      {
         return false;
      }
      return true;
   }
```

```
// Read a System.String from the registry.
public bool GetValue(string strKeyName,
                     string strValueName,
                     ref string strValue)
{
   // Open HKEY_LOCAL_MACHINE\SOFTWARE\YaoDurant\...
   //    and place its handle in hkeyCurrent.
   intReturn =
      WinRegCE.RegCreateKeyEx(hkeyHive,
                              strYDKey + @"\" + strKeyName,
                              0, string.Empty, 0, 0,
                              IntPtr.Zero,
                              ref hkeyCurrent,
                              ref regdispResult);
   if ( intReturn != 0 ) { return false; }

   // Create fields to hold the output.
   StringBuilder sbValue = new StringBuilder(cbMAX);
   int cbValue = cbMAX;

   // Read the value from the registry into sbValue.
   WinRegCE.REGTYPE rtType = 0;
   intReturn =
      WinRegCE.RegQueryValueEx(hkeyCurrent, strValueName,
                               0, ref rtType,
                               sbValue, ref cbValue);
   if ( intReturn != 0 ) { return false; }

   // Close the key.
   intReturn = WinRegCE.RegCloseKey(hkeyCurrent);
   if ( intReturn != 0 ) { return false; }

   // Set the string into the output parameter.
   strValue = sbValue.ToString();

   return true;
}


// Read a System.Int32 from the registry.
public bool GetValue(string strKeyName,
   string strValueName,
   ref int intValue )
{
   // Open HKEY_LOCAL_MACHINE\SOFTWARE\YaoDurant\...
   //    and place its handle in hkeyCurrent.
```

continues

continued

```
      intReturn =
         WinRegCE.RegCreateKeyEx(hkeyHive,
                                 strYDKey + @"\" + strKeyName,
                                 0, string.Empty, 0, 0,
                                 IntPtr.Zero,
                                 ref hkeyCurrent,
                                 ref regdispResult);
      if ( intReturn != 0 ) { return false; }

      //  Retrieve the value into intValue.  For platform
      //     independence, use Marshal.SizeOf(intValue),
      //     not "4", to specify the size in bytes of
      //     a System.Int32.
      int cbValue = Marshal.SizeOf(intValue);
      WinRegCE.REGTYPE rtType = 0;
      intReturn =
         WinRegCE.RegQueryValueEx(hkeyCurrent, strValueName,
                                  0, ref rtType,
                                  ref intValue, ref cbValue);
      if ( intReturn != 0 ) { return false; }

      //  Close the key.
      intReturn = WinRegCE.RegCloseKey(hkeyCurrent);
      if ( intReturn != 0 ) { return false; }

      return true;
   }


   //  Read a System.Bool from the registry.
   public bool GetValue(string  strKeyName,
                        string  strValueName,
                        ref bool boolValue)
   {
      //  Use the integer version of GetValue to get the value
      //     from the registry, then convert it to a Boolean.
      int intValue =0;
      bool boolReturn =
         GetValue(strKeyName, strValueName, ref intValue);
      if (boolReturn)
      {
         boolValue = Convert.ToBoolean(intValue);
      }

      return boolReturn;
   }
```

```
// Write a System.String  to the registry.
public bool SetValue(string  strKeyName,
                     string  strValueName,
                     string  strValue)
{
   // Open HKEY_LOCAL_MACHINE\SOFTWARE\YaoDurant\...
   intReturn =
      WinRegCE.RegCreateKeyEx(hkeyHive,
                              strYDKey + @"\" + strKeyName,
                              0, string.Empty, 0, 0,
                              IntPtr.Zero,
                              ref hkeyCurrent,
                              ref regdispResult);
   if ( intReturn != 0 ) { return false; }

   // Store strValue under the name strValueName.
   intReturn =
      WinRegCE.RegSetValueEx(hkeyCurrent, strValueName,
                             0, WinRegCE.REGTYPE.REG_SZ,
                             strValue,
                             strValue.Length * 2 + 1);
   if ( intReturn != 0 ) { return false; }

   // Close the key.
   intReturn = WinRegCE.RegCloseKey(hkeyCurrent);
   if ( intReturn != 0 ) { return false; }

   return true;
}


// Write a System.Int32 to the registry.
public bool SetValue( string  strKeyName,
                      string  strValueName,
                      int intValue )
{
   // Open HKEY_LOCAL_MACHINE\SOFTWARE\YaoDurant\...
   intReturn =
      WinRegCE.RegCreateKeyEx(hkeyHive,
                              strYDKey + @"\" + strKeyName,
                              0, string.Empty, 0, 0,
                              IntPtr.Zero,
                              ref hkeyCurrent,
                              ref regdispResult);
   if ( intReturn != 0 ) { return false; }

   // Store intValue under the name strValueName. For
   //    platform independence, use Marshal.SizeOf(intValue),
```

continues

continued

```
      //     not "4", to specify the size in bytes of a
      //     System.Int32.
      intReturn =
         WinRegCE.RegSetValueEx(hkeyCurrent,
                                strValueName,
                                0, 0,
                                ref intValue,
                                Marshal.SizeOf(intValue));
      if ( intReturn != 0 ) { return false; }

      //  Close the key.
      intReturn = WinRegCE.RegCloseKey(hkeyCurrent);
      if ( intReturn != 0 ) { return false; }

      return true;
   }


   //  Write a System.Bool to the registry.
   public bool SetValue(string  strKeyName,
                        string  strValueName,
                        bool boolValue)
   {

      //  Cast the value as a Boolean, then use the integer
      //     version of SetValue to set the value into the
      //     registry.

      //  There is no Convert.ToInteger method.  For platform
      //     independence, we cast to the smallest integer,
      //     which will always implicitly and successfully cast
      //     to Int.
      return SetValue(strKeyName,
                      strValueName,
                      Convert.ToInt16(boolValue));
   }
}
```

The `SetValue` and `GetValue` methods create keys, if they do not already exist, and then make the `RegSetValueEx` and `RegQueryValueEx` calls to save and restore values. The class stores values wherever the client specifies, but always within the `SOFTWARE\YaoDurant` key in the `HKEY_LOCAL_MACHINE` hive.

Updating the Storage Sample Application to Use the Registry

To illustrate accessing the registry, we modify our sample application to save and restore settings to the registry rather than to a file. We have a head start with our wrapper functions and our utility class already written. In the updated version of our sample application, we create an object of type UtilRegistry and define a set of strings that we use for the registry key name and the various registry values, as shown in Listing 11.20.

LISTING 11.20: Declarations for Registry Access

```
//  Variables for registry access
UtilRegistry  urNotepad = new UtilRegistry();

string  strNotepadCE = "NotepadCe";
string  strFont = "Font";
string  strName = "Name";
string  strSize = "Size";
string  strStyle = "Style";
string  strOptions = "Options";
string  strMenu = "Menu";
string  strToolBar = "ToolBar";
string  strScrollBars = "ScrollBars";
string  strTextAlign = "TextAlign";
string  strWordWrap = "WordWrap";
```

The request to save the settings, shown in Listing 11.21, is handled by calling to the various overloaded versions of the SetValue method, once for each registry value we wish to save.

LISTING 11.21: Saving Settings to the Registry

```
private void mitemSettingsSave_Click(object sender,
                                     EventArgs e)
{
   //    Use the UtilRegistry object to save the
   //       font settings.
   //    UtilRegistry has three overloads for
   //       SetValue: string, integer, and boolean.
   //    Font Size and Style are data types that
   //       derive from integer; they have to
   //       be converted to integer for this call.
   //    Font.Style data type, because it has
```

continues

continued

```
        //      the [Flags] attribute, requires an
        //      unchecked conversion.
        urNotepad.SetValue(
           strNotepadCE + @"\" + strFont,
           strName,
           textInput.Font.Name);
        urNotepad.SetValue(
           strNotepadCE + @"\" + strFont,
           strSize,
           Convert.ToInt32(textInput.Font.Size));
        urNotepad.SetValue(
           strNotepadCE + @"\" + strFont,
           strStyle,
           unchecked((System.Int32)textInput.Font.Style));

        //    Use the UtilRegistry object to save the
        //      Textbox settings, three of which are
        //      boolean, two of which are [Flags]
        //      attributed unsigned integers.
        urNotepad.SetValue(
           strNotepadCE + @"\" + strOptions,
           strMenu,
           this.Menu == this.menuMain);
        urNotepad.SetValue(
           strNotepadCE + @"\" + strOptions,
           strToolBar,
           this.Controls.Contains(tbarCommands));
        urNotepad.SetValue(
           strNotepadCE + @"\" + strOptions,
           strScrollBars,
           unchecked((System.Int32)textInput.ScrollBars));
        urNotepad.SetValue(strNotepadCE + @"\" + strOptions,
           strTextAlign,
           unchecked((System.Int32)textInput.TextAlign));
        urNotepad.SetValue(strNotepadCE + @"\" + strOptions,
           strWordWrap,
           textInput.WordWrap);
     }
```

To restore the settings, we reverse the process by which we saved the settings, calling the `GetValue` method for each value we wish to retrieve, as shown in Listing 11.22.

LISTING 11.22: Restoring Settings from the Registry

```
private void mitemSettingsRestore_Click(object sender,
                                        EventArgs e)
{
   //  Read Font information, if any, from the registry.
   //  Create a font from that information, or use default
   //     values if no information is in the registry.
   //  Set textInput.Font = that font.
   string  strFontName;
   int intFontSize;
   int intFontStyle;

   strFontName = "Tahoma";
   urNotepad.GetValue(strNotepadCE + @"\" + strFont,
                      strName,
                      ref strFontName);

   intFontSize = 9;
   urNotepad.GetValue(strNotepadCE + @"\" + strFont,
                      strSize,
                      ref intFontSize);

   intFontStyle = (int)FontStyle.Regular;
   urNotepad.GetValue(strNotepadCE + @"\" + strFont,
                      strStyle,
                      ref intFontStyle);
      textInput.Font =
         new Font(strFontName,
                  intFontSize,
                  (FontStyle)intFontStyle);

   //  Read Option information, if any, from the registry.
   //  Set the properties from that information, or use
   //     default values if no info is in the registry.
   bool boolTemp;
   int intTemp;

   //  .Menu is either menuMain or null.
   boolTemp = true;
   urNotepad.GetValue(strNotepadCE + @"\" + strOptions,
                      strMenu,
                      ref boolTemp);
   this.Menu = boolTemp ? this.menuMain : null;

   //  .Controls either contains
   //     tbarCommands or it doesn't.
```

continues

continued

```
      boolTemp = true;
      urNotepad.GetValue(strNotepadCE + @"\" + strOptions,
                         strToolBar,
                         ref boolTemp);
      if ( boolTemp )
      {
         if (! this.Controls.Contains(this.tbarCommands) )
         {
            this.Controls.Add(this.tbarCommands);
         }
      }
      else
      {
         if ( this.Controls.Contains(this.tbarCommands) )
         {
            this.Controls.Remove(this.tbarCommands);
         }
      }

      //  .ScrollBars
      intTemp = (int)ScrollBars.Both;
      urNotepad.GetValue(strNotepadCE + @"\" + strOptions,
                         strScrollBars,
                         ref intTemp);
         textInput.ScrollBars = (ScrollBars)intTemp;

      //  .TextAlign
      intTemp = (int)HorizontalAlignment.Left;
      urNotepad.GetValue(strNotepadCE + @"\" + strOptions,
                         strTextAlign,
                         ref intTemp);
         textInput.TextAlign = (HorizontalAlignment)intTemp;

      //  .WordWrap
      boolTemp = true;
      urNotepad.GetValue(strNotepadCE + @"\" + strOptions,
                         strWordWrap,
                         ref boolTemp);
         textInput.WordWrap = boolTemp;
   }
```

The last selection that the user can make from the Settings menu is the Init Settings selection. The application handles this by deleting the registry key (which removes all its content, subkeys, and data) and then calling the Restore Settings handler. That handler, shown in Listing 11.22, restores default values for any missing settings. Because all the settings are now missing from the registry, a complete set of default values will be set. The code appears in Listing 11.23.

LISTING 11.23: Initializing the Settings

```
private void mitemSettingsInit_Click(object sender,
                                     EventArgs e)
{
   //    Initialize the settings by deleting the
   //       registry key where they are stored and
   //       then restoring from the nonexistent
   //       key to reinstate all default values.
   urNotepad.DeleteKey(strNotepadCE);
   mitemSettingsRestore_Click(this, EventArgs.Empty);
}
```

That completes our discussion on using the registry. As with file I/O, we could have modularized and solidified our code by defining a custom structure and placing the fields and routines within it.

The key to success when doing registry access comes from having the right set of P/Invoke function declarations, writing a utility class that reflects the needs of your application, and then using them.

CONCLUSION

This chapter covered .NET Compact Framework programming to support two types of local storage: the file system and the registry.

Many of the desktop .NET file I/O classes have been ported to the .NET Compact Framework. The most important ones are the `Directory` and `File` classes, which are used for file manipulation. Also available are the various `Stream` classes, which are used for byte-level I/O to a variety of stream types. Finally, the various reader and writer classes provide higher-level I/O to and from streams.

The desktop .NET Framework classes for registry access are not available in version 1.0 of the .NET Compact Framework. To access the registry, we use P/Invoke declarations and rely on the native Win32 registry functions. Function overloading of native functions is a good idea because it adds type safety and ease of use to otherwise tricky pointer handling. Access to the registry can be simplified by writing a utility class that does necessary housework before calling the native registry functions.

Applications that save and restore a known set of values can benefit from packaging those values in a structure (or a class), regardless of where the values are being stored.

The next few chapters continue along the theme of storage by looking at storing and retrieving information from databases with the support found in the .NET Compact Framework.

12

ADO.NET Programming

This chapter introduces ADO.NET, a set of .NET Compact Framework classes used for database programming in managed code. Like its counterpart on the desktop, the ADO.NET classes in the .NET Compact Framework provide a convenient, flexible model for operating on memory-resident databases. Three options are presented for the persistent storage of ADO.NET data sets: XML files, Microsoft SQL Server CE databases on a Windows CE device, and Microsoft SQL Server databases (version 7.0 or 2000) on a desktop or server version of SQL Server.

A .NET COMPACT FRAMEWORK program that manages a significant volume of data is probably going to use the ADO.NET classes to manage that data. ADO.NET provides managed-code support for table-based memory-resident data (in other words, a memory-resident database) and for the transfer of that data to and from a persistent data store, such as a SQL Server database or an XML file. Some of the ADO.NET classes provide the ability to create the memory-resident database and to programmatically manipulate the data in its data tables. Other classes provide the ability to move data between the memory-resident database and various data sources.

Central to the design of the memory-resident database classes is the independence of these classes from any particular database product or storage format. This means that an ADO.NET table might be constructed with data from two or more data sources plus some application-generated data.

Conversely, the classes that transfer data between the memory-resident database and a data source are specific to the data source. For example, there is one set of these classes for use with SQL Server CE databases and a different set (with similar names and nearly identical PMEs) for use with SQL Server 2000 databases. These classes, therefore, are referred to as the *data provider classes*.

Table 12.1 summarizes all of the persistent data storage options available to .NET Compact Framework programmers, including ADO.NET. As indicated in this table, ADO.NET supports three different storage types. Two storage types reside in the file system of a Windows CE–powered device: SQL Server CE databases and XML files. These are appropriate for a mobile device, such as a Pocket PC or Smartphone, which needs to run in a self-contained, disconnected mode. Additionally, using the SQL Server 2000

TABLE 12.1: Persistent Storage Options Available on Windows CE–Powered Devices

Type of Storage	Managed API	Native API
SQL Server CE database	ADO.NET with SQL Server CE Data Provider	ADOCE OLEDBCE
SQL Server 2000 (and above) database	ADO.NET with SQL Server Data Provider	ADOCE OLEDBCE
Other databases	ADO.NET with database-specific provider	ADOCE OLEDBCE
XML files	ADO.NET	DOM provided by `msxml.dll`
Raw data files	`System.IO` classes (see Chapter 11)	Win32 API file access functions
CE property databases	N/A	Windows CE–specific Win32 API functions including `CeCreateDataBaseEx` and others
System registry	N/A	Win32 API functions required (see Chapter 11)

data provider, a .NET Compact Framework program can directly access a third type of storage on a connected server, a SQL Server 2000 database. This requires a live network connection between the Windows CE client system and a server running SQL Server 2000.

Supported ADO.NET Data Providers

As of this writing, we know of several ADO.NET data providers that are available for the .NET Compact Framework: Microsoft SQL Server CE, Microsoft SQL Server (version 7.0 and 2000), IBM's DB2 and DB Everyplace, SyBase SQL (through iAnywhere), and Pocket Access (available from In The Hand, http://www.inthehand.com).

The following data providers are available for the desktop .NET Framework, but as of this writing they are not available for .NET Compact Framework programs: OLE DB, ODBC, Oracle, and MySQL.

As we implied in the opening part of this discussion, there are two layers of ADO.NET classes. One layer provides memory-resident database programming support, and its classes are not tied to a specific database or file format. Instead, the classes operate on in-memory objects that model relational data tables.

A second layer of classes, the data provider classes, provide the connection between in-memory objects and physical databases that reside in permanent storage. Alternatively, you can choose not to use a formal database and instead allow the ADO.NET classes to store your data in XML files in the Windows CE file system.

We expect that many databases on Windows CE–powered devices will need to be synchronized with databases on desktop and server systems. Table 12.2 summarizes the available options for synchronizing data with desktop and server systems. Two of these techniques are appropriate for synchronizing a device-based SQL Server CE database with a SQL Server 2000 database: Merge Replication and Remote Data Access (RDA). We discuss these in detail in Chapter 13.

Table 12.2: Data Synchronization Options on Windows CE–Powered Devices

Synchronization Technique	Description
Merge Replication	A publish-and-subscribe model for moving data between a SQL Server CE database and a SQL Server 2000 database. See Chapter 13 for more detail.
Remote Data Access (RDA)	A SQL-driven mechanism for moving data between a SQL Server CE database and a SQL Server 6.5, SQL Server 7, or SQL Server 2000 database. See Chapter 13 for more detail.
Web Services	A general-purpose RPC mechanism for support and document delivery, supported by the desktop .NET Framework and the .NET Compact Framework. Web Services are built on SOAP, an XML-based industry standard remoting protocol.
ActiveSync	A general-purpose mechanism for synchronizing desktop and smart-device data. ActiveSync relies on service providers, which currently must be implemented in native DLLs that export a specific set of COM interfaces. Both desktop and device-side service providers are supported. SQL Server CE does not use ActiveSync for any of its synchronization. However, ActiveSync does support synchronizing a Pocket Access (`.cdb`) file with a desktop Microsoft Access (`.mdb`) file. Pocket Access is a discontinued product, but third-party support[a] exists for the Pocket Access file format (in the form of an ADO.NET-compatible data provider), and third-party development tools are also available.
Remote API (RAPI)	Part of the ActiveSync support libraries. The RAPI routines provide a general-purpose mechanism for accessing the object store and installable file systems of a smart device from an ActiveSync-connected desktop system. This mechanism can be used to install or back up anything on a Windows CE device. However, RAPI has no specific ADO.NET support or support for SQL databases. RAPI is described in detail in Chapter 14.

a. For details on the ADOCE .NET Wrapper available from In The Hand, visit http://www.inthehand.com.

Examining ADO.NET

ADO.NET is a set of classes for accessing and managing in-memory data. These classes provide the primary means for bringing data from a database into a managed-code program. The ADO.NET classes provide in-memory data support in a variety of environments for a wide range of application types, including desktop Windows Forms applications, Web Forms applications, Web Services, and mobile-device applications. In fact, a good way to access a database that does not yet have a .NET Compact Framework provider is to wrap access to that database in a Web Service. (Web Services are covered later in this chapter.)

The ADO.NET classes were designed to work with data that is drawn from a variety of sources or, in the terminology of ADO.NET, from a variety of *data providers*. Whatever the source of the data, the ADO.NET classes allow data to be managed and presented in a standard fashion. As mentioned earlier, to make this happen, one layer of the ADO.NET classes is *provider-specific*, meaning those classes are capable of working with only one data provider, such as the `SqlCeConnection` class, which can only connect to a SQL Server CE database, or the `SqlCommand` class, which can only submit a SQL statement to a SQL Server database.

The other layer contains *provider-independent* memory-resident database classes, such as the `DataSet`, `DataTable`, and `DataView` classes. The data contained within these classes has been converted to the ADO.NET data types, and the structure of the data supported by these classes is independent of the database engine that provides the data. Thus an ADO.NET data set may contain data tables with data drawn from multiple sources. For example, a data set could contain some tables that have been read from a Microsoft SQL Server CE database and other tables read from a Microsoft SQL Server 2000 database.

The ADO.NET memory-resident database classes treat data as provider-agnostic, meaning there is no easy way—and, hopefully, no need—to determine which data came from what data source. You can even build and populate data sets and data tables from scratch without reference to a particular database. Additionally, data sets can read and write their data to XML files without the need for any provider-specific software.

A Layered Approach

Because of the capabilities of the ADO.NET classes, you can use either a two-layer approach or a three-layer approach to data management; that is, you can use a memory-resident database to hold your data, or you can bypass the memory-resident database and move the data directly from the data source to its final destination.

Limitations of ADO.NET in the .NET Compact Framework

Strongly typed data sets are not supported in the current version of the .NET Compact Framework. Strongly typed data sets are bound to the schema of a database, which means you can use database field names instead of column indexes. Early binding makes it easier to write, read, and maintain code. This capability may become available in future versions of the .NET Compact Framework, but it is not available in the current version.

However, before we lament this limitation too much, keep the following in mind: While strongly typed data sets are a nice ease-of-use feature, they are simply a set of strongly typed classes built on top of the untyped ADO.NET data sets. Strongly typed data sets do not provide a performance improvement over untyped data sets; in fact, because they are a layer built on top of untyped data sets, they execute more slowly than untyped data sets.

In a two-layer approach, you submit SQL queries to the database and retrieve the data into program variables and control properties. You then build SQL statements to make the user-requested changes to the data and submit them to the database (see Figure 12.1). This is often referred to as the *connected approach* because the application must be connected to the database while transferring data. Do not confuse this meaning of the term *connected* with being connected to a network. Throughout this chapter, when we use the term *connected*, we mean connected to the data source, such as a SQL Server or SQL Server CE database.

In a three-layer approach, you bring the data into a memory-resident data set, perhaps manipulate the data as it resides in the data set, and then bind some or all the data to controls on your form. Changes made by the user to the data in the form are automatically propagated back to the data set; class methods then propagate changes from the data set to the database (see Figure 12.2). This is often referred to as the *disconnected approach*, meaning that the application is not connected to the database while it is accessing the data in the data set.

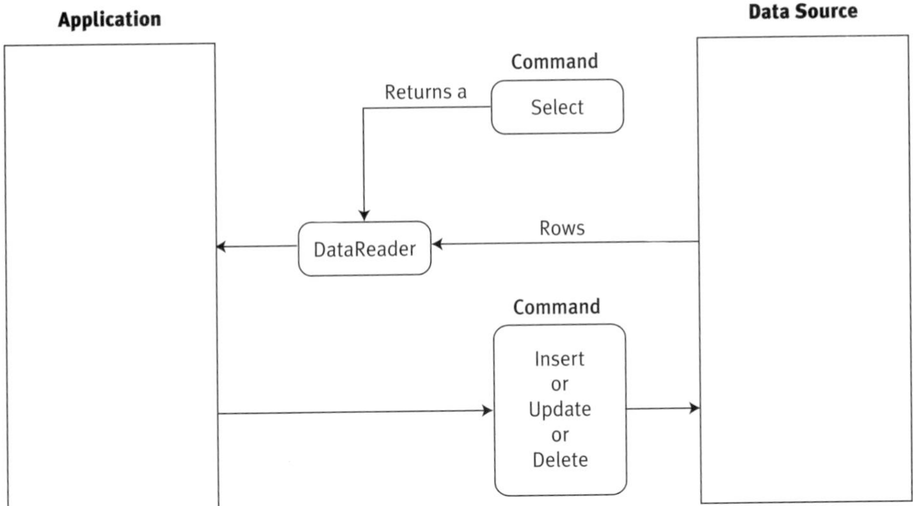

FIGURE 12.1: A two-layer (connected) approach

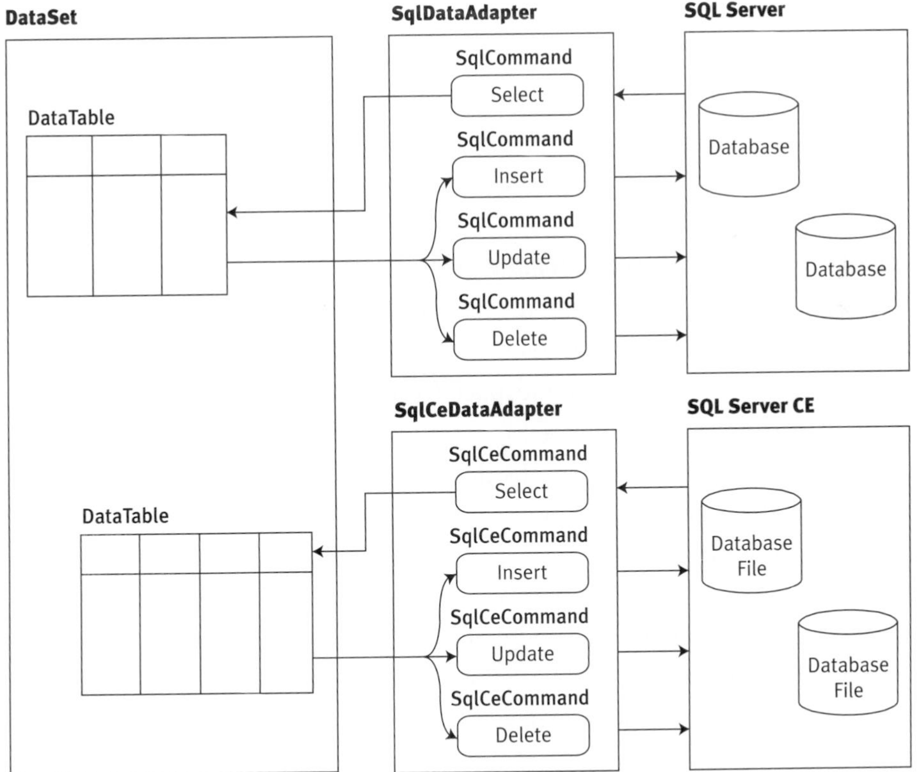

FIGURE 12.2: A three-layer (disconnected) approach

The ADO.NET Classes

Table 12.3 presents an overview of the classes you can use to access SQL Server CE databases. We discuss many of these classes in detail later in this chapter. They fall into four general categories:

1. File system classes
2. Provider-specific ADO.NET classes
3. Provider-independent ADO.NET classes
4. Data-bindable control classes

We discussed the file system classes in detail in Chapter 11, and we covered controls used for data binding in Chapter 8.

Note that SQL Server permits multiple open connections but only one open data reader per connection, while SQL Server CE is just the opposite, permitting only one open connection but allowing multiple open readers on that connection.

Also note that .NET Compact Framework multi-item controls do not permit users to enter data. As we mentioned in Chapter 8, the `DataGrid` control is for display only, and the `ComboBox` control does not permit direct entry of a value, allowing the user to select only from the list.

Namespace References and Assembly References

The SQL Server CE–specific ADO.NET classes are located in the `System.Data.SqlServerCe` namespace. There is a similar set of classes in the `System.Data.SqlClient` namespace for use when accessing SQL Server. Other namespaces hold classes for accessing data via Oracle, OLE DB, ODBC, and other providers on the desktop and, if supported, on a device.

Because the classes are located in specific namespaces, you must set some references in your project before writing any code. You need to set a reference to the `System.Data.SqlServerCe` namespace because it holds the classes you must use to access a SQL Server CE database; and you need to set a reference to the `System.Data.SqlClient` namespace when accessing SQL Server. You also need to set a reference to the `System.Data.Common` namespace because it contains private classes used by the data adapter class.

TABLE 12.3: Classes for Accessing, Maintaining, and Displaying Data

Category	Class	Purpose and Comments
File system classes[a]	`Directory`	To create, delete, move, and detect directories.
	`File`	To create, delete, move, copy, and detect files.
Provider-specific classes for SQL Server CE[b] and SQL Server[c]	`SqlCeEngine`	To create and compact a SQL Server CE database.
	`SqlCeConnection`, `SqlConnection`	To open a connection to a database. Only one open connection per SQL Server CE database at a time.
	`SqlCeCommand`, `SqlCommand`	To submit a SQL statement to the database. Contains the connection object.
	`SqlCeDataReader`, `SqlDataReader`	To retrieve the rows returned by a command. Can only be created by the command's `ExecuteReader` method. Only one open data reader per SQL Server connection at a time.
	`SqlCeDataAdapter`, `SqlDataAdapter`	To move data between a database and a `DataTable`. Contains up to four (`SELECT`, `INSERT`, `UPDATE`, and `DELETE`) command objects.
	`SqlCeCommandBuilder`, `SqlCommandBuilder`	To reverse-engineer a simple `SELECT` statement to create the `INSERT`, `UPDATE`, and `DELETE` statements used by an adapter to move modified data from a `DataTable` back to the database.
Provider-independent ADO.NET classes[d]	`DataSet`	To provide a memory-resident database. Contains the provider-independent classes listed below.
	`DataTable`	To provide a memory-resident table.

continues

a. In the `System.IO` namespace.

b. In the `System.Data.SqlServerCe` namespace.

c. In the `System.Data.SqlClient` namespace.

d. In the `System.Data` namespace.

TABLE 12.3: Classes for Accessing, Maintaining, and Displaying Data (continued)

Category	Class	Purpose and Comments
Provider-independent ADO.NET classes[d] (continued)	DataRow	To provide a row within a DataTable object. Contains the data. Has methods to access other rows in other tables based on DataRelation objects, such as the GetChildRows method.
	DataView	To sort and filter the rows of a DataTable object. Primarily for use with data binding.
	DataRelation	To specify the parent/child relationship between two DataTable objects.
	UniqueConstraint	To constrain a DataTable object.
	ForeignKeyConstraint	To constrain two DataTable objects.
Data-binding support classes[e]	Multi-item controls: DataGrid, ListBox, ComboBox	To display one or all columns of a DataTable or DataView object (when data bound). Cannot be updated.
	Single-item controls: TextBox, Label, RadioButton, CheckBox, Button, etc.	To display one column of one row of a DataTable or DataView object (when data bound). Automatically propagates data changes back to the bound DataTable. A CurrencyManager object (see below) manages row positioning and data updating.
	DataBindings collection	To specify data binding between a DataTable or DataView object and the single-item control; is a property of a single-item control.
	BindingContext	To contain a collection of CurrencyManager objects; is a property of a form. Used by the form to manage all data binding of all contained controls. Created by the .NET runtime.

d. In the System.Data namespace.

e. In the System.Windows.Forms namespace.

Category	Class	Purpose and Comments
Data-binding support classes[e] (continued)	CurrencyManager	To manage the automatic updating of bound DataTable objects. Can be used to override the automatic updating of bound DataTable objects by canceling the update or forcing the immediate execution of the update. Contains a read-write indexer property that identifies the "current" row of the bound DataTable or DataView. Created by the .NET runtime. Can be obtained by calling the form's BindingContext(DataTable/DataView name) indexer property.

e. In the System.Windows.Forms namespace.

And, finally, you need a reference to the System.Data namespace because it contains the provider-independent classes listed in Table 12.3. Therefore, among the namespace references and the assembly reference you may need are those listed in Table 12.4.

Functionality: Super Sets and Subsets

The minimum set of provider-specific classes, methods, properties, and events that must be supported by a provider has been specified by Microsoft and is the same for all providers. As you move between SQL Server CE and

TABLE 12.4: Commonly Used Namespaces for Data Access

Namespace	Located in Assembly
System.Data	System.Data.dll
System.Data.Common	System.Data.Common.dll
System.Data.SqlServerCe	System.Data.SqlServerCe.dll
System.Data.SqlClient	System.Data.SqlClient.dll

SQL Server 2000, you use the same properties and methods to access the data regardless of provider. For example, we're about to use the `SqlCeDataReader` class, which has a `NextResult` method. The `SqlDataReader` class and the `OleDbDataReader` class also have this same method, as does the `AdoceDataReader` class in the Pocket Access data provider from In The Hand. They must all have the `NextResult` method because the standard requires it.

The advantage of this standards-driven approach is that the same code can be used to access data from a variety of providers, yet the underlying classes can be optimized to take advantage of the capabilities of the individual data provider. The disadvantage of this approach, especially for SQL Server CE programmers, is that functionality that is inappropriate for SQL Server CE exists in our classes simply because it may be appropriate for SQL Server or Oracle or some other data provider and therefore has been included as part of the standard.

Continuing with our example, the `SqlCeDataReader` class's `NextResult` method provides for the processing of commands that contain multiple `SELECT` statements. But the SQL Server CE database does not support multiple `SELECT` commands. For this reason, the `NextResult` method is not supported and so is completely inappropriate when accessing a SQL Server CE database.

Thus, learning the object model in the `System.Data.SqlServerCe` namespace requires more than just learning the properties and methods—it also involves learning which of those properties and methods are appropriate for SQL Server CE (or whatever ADO.NET data provider you choose to use). One of the goals of this chapter is to focus on the classes, methods, and properties that are important for some typical processing scenarios in SQL Server CE.

Just as the SQL Server CE syntax is a subset of that found in SQL Server, ADO.NET for Windows CE is also a subset of the desktop version. For instance, only three of the eight overloads for the `DataSet.ReadXml` method are implemented. In general, however, ADO.NET for Windows CE has most of the functionality that the desktop version has, and you should not feel constrained.

ADO.NET Error Handling

Before diving into SQL Server CE programming in general, we take a moment to examine error handling. In the .NET Compact Framework, ADO.NET error handling uses the standard `try...catch...finally` technique used in any .NET application. If an error occurs, a `SqlCeException` is thrown. There is only one `SqlCeClient` exception class, `SqlCeException`, not one derived class for each possible error or category of error. Because SQL Server CE is written in unmanaged (native) code, it is written for the world of error numbers and `HResults`, not exceptions. Thus each error represented by a `SqlCeException` contains its own error information.

The `SqlCeException` class has an `Errors` collection property, consisting of one or more `SqlCeErrors` (each containing the `Source`, `Message`, `NativeError`, and `HResult` properties, which are also properties of the `SqlCeException` class) plus three string parameters and three numeric parameters. In the `SqlCeException` class properties, `Source`, `NativeError`, and `HResult` are equal to the properties of the same name of `SqlCeException.Errors[0]`, while `Message` is equal to `String.Empty`. The `SqlCeException` class also has an `InnerException` property, which is often empty. So, your best plan when handling a SQL Server CE exception is to examine its `Errors` collection. For instance, if a `SELECT` statement contains a misspelled column name, you receive the following information via the `SqlCeException.Errors[0]` object:

`Source`: Microsoft SQL Server 2000 Windows CE Edition.

`Message`: The column name is not valid.

`NativeError`: 25503.

`HResult`: -214721900.

`ErrorParameters[0]`: Empty.

`ErrorParameters[1]`: [The name of the misspelled column.]

`ErrorParameters[2]`: Empty.

`NumericErrorParameters[0]`: 0.

`NumericErrorParameters[1]`: 0.

`NumericErrorParameters[2]`: 0.

You should always use error handling. If nothing else, error handling allows your application to present the most meaningful message possible to the user and to exit gracefully, as shown in the following code.

```
private string  strConn = "Data Source=" +
                          @"My Documents\ourProduceCo.sdf";
             :
             :
SqlCeEngine dbEngine = new SqlCeEngine();
dbEngine.LocalConnectionString = strConn;
             :
             :
try
{
   dbEngine.CreateDatabase();
}
catch( SqlCeException exSQL )
{
   MessageBox.Show("Unable to create database at " +
                   dbEngine.LocalConnectionString +
                   ". Reason:  " +
                   exSQL.Errors[0].Message );
}
```

We mention error handling because it is a necessary part of production code. Without it, your code is brittle to the touch of all but the most casual user. With it, your code becomes robust enough to withstand the most brutal attack. That said, you may notice that our sample code in this book has only a minimal amount of error handling (and sometimes none at all). We do this to keep the focus on the subject at hand and to help make the sample programs easier to understand.

Utility Routines

In any programming environment it is advantageous to have a set of utility routines for performing generic tasks. This is certainly true in the ADO.NET environment, where data is repetitively moved from one tier to another or converted from one format to another. For instance, several ADO.NET methods return an array of data rows, arrays that you might like to convert into a data table so you could bind it to a control. This "convert from row array to data table" task is a good candidate for being handled by a generic routine. We have written some generic routines for use in this chapter and placed them in the `UtilData` class located in the `UtilData` project at the book's Web site, http://www.paulyao.com/cfbook/code.

Working with Data Sets

The ADO.NET `DataSet` class lies at the center of the three-tiered approach and at the heart of this chapter. Understanding the `DataSet` class and its contained objects is a key to successful data management in managed code. Let's recap what we have already said about data sets (including Table 12.3).

- A `DataSet` object is a memory-resident database.
- A `DataSet` object can contain multiple `DataTable` objects.
- `DataTable` objects can have constraints defined for them (e.g., `primary key`, `foreign key`, and `unique`).
- Parent/child relationships can be specified between the `DataTable` objects of a `DataSet` object.
- A `DataTable` object contains an instance of a `DataView` object, which sorts and filters the rows of the `DataTable`.

Remember that the `DataSet` class and associated classes are located in the `System.Data` namespace and therefore are not provider-specific. That is, a single `DataSet` object can be used to hold the data regardless of the provider from which the data was obtained and regardless of the environment in which it is being used. The `DataSet` class is used today in Web Services, Web applications, and Windows applications, as well as mobile applications.

DataSet objects provide four major benefits for the mobile application developer.

1. They can contain data from a variety of remote data sources.
2. They function while disconnected from those data sources.
3. They can persist their data locally as XML files through their ReadXml/WriteXml methods.
4. They display their data through data binding.

Although DataSet objects do not have all the functionality of SQL Server CE (see the DataSet Class Limitations sidebar), their capability to retrieve, disconnect, data bind, persist locally, reconnect, and update remotely is ideal for lightweight remote applications that do not need the full functionality of SQL Server CE. Additionally, if the application does require SQL Server CE, DataSet objects are still the best way to display the data to the user and to persist all of the data (or subsets of it) as XML files.

DataSet Class Limitations

DataSet objects do not have an ad hoc query capability. Instead, the data in a DataSet object is accessed programmatically, not through a SELECT statement. Properties and methods of the data objects are used to access the data. Thus you access all rows of a data table by iterating through its Rows collection with a For Each statement; you access all the rows of a data table that meet a certain criteria through the table's Select method; and you access the rows of a relationship by using the parent row's GetChildRows method.

Creating and Accessing DataSet, DataTable, and DataView Objects

Creating a DataSet object is easy: You simply "new" it, with the option of specifying a name, as follows:

```
dsetDB = new DataSet("AnyName");
```

Within a `DataSet` object, you can create a `DataTable` object and populate it from scratch, as shown in Listing 12.1.

LISTING 12.1: Building a `DataTable` Object from Scratch

```
private void CreateTable() {
     //  Create an empty table.
     DataTable  dtabCustomers = new DataTable("Customers");

     //  Create three columns.
     DataColumn  dcolID = new DataColumn("ID");
     dcolID.DataType = typeof(int);
     dcolID.AutoIncrement = true;
     dcolID.AutoIncrementSeed = 1;
     dcolID.AutoIncrementStep = 1;

     DataColumn  dcolName = new DataColumn("Name");
     dcolName.DataType = typeof(string );

     DataColumn  dcolAddress = new DataColumn("Address");
     dcolAddress.DataType = typeof(string );

     //  Add the columns to the table.
     dtabCustomers.Columns.Add(dcolID);
     dtabCustomers.Columns.Add(dcolName);
     dtabCustomers.Columns.Add(dcolAddress);

     //  Add a primary key constraint.
     dtabCustomers.Constraints.Add("PKCust", dcolID, true);

     //  Add two rows to the table
     DataRow drowCust;
     drowCust = dtabCustomers.NewRow();
     drowCust["Name"] = "Amalgamated United";
     drowCust["Address"] = "PO Box 123, 98765";
     dtabCustomers.Rows.Add(drowCust);
     drowCust = dtabCustomers.NewRow();
     drowCust["Name"] = "United Amalgamated";
     drowCust["Address"] = "PO Box 987, 12345";
     dtabCustomers.Rows.Add(drowCust);
     }
  }
```

However, the most common way to create and populate a data table is to execute a `SELECT` statement against a database and place the results into a `DataTable` object. These `SELECT` statements can be as simple as

SELECT * FROM Products or as complex as a multitable join with an aggregate function and grouping. Different data tables in the same data set can be drawn from different databases. We cover the details of moving data between a data set and a database in the Microsoft SQL Server CE and Microsoft SQL Server sections later in this chapter. For now, we are only interested in accessing the data as it resides in the data set and in the movement of data between the data set and the user.

Understanding Data Tables

A data table consists of a collection of columns and a collection of rows. DataRow objects are a collection of Items, which are the fields of the row. To access a value in a data table you must specify the row number and column identifier (either column name or number), as shown in the following code, which sets the CategoryName column of the second row in the dtabCategories data table to Muzzy.

```
dtabCategories.Rows[1]["CategoryName"] = "Muzzy";
```

You can also use the DataTable class's Select method to access rows by value. The following code returns the array of rows whose CategoryName is Widgets.

```
dsetDB.Tables["Categories"].Select("CategoryName = 'Widgets'");
```

To save the reference to the first row in the array, you would code the following line. (Remember that arrays are zero-based; the first row of this array is row 0.)

```
drowX = dsetDB.Tables["Categories"].Select(
        "CategoryName = 'Widgets'")[0];
```

Accessing columns by name makes your code more readable, but the code will execute faster if you access columns by index value rather than by name. A good performance strategy is to look up the row index value for the name once and thereafter access the column by index value.

We often think of a data table as a two-dimensional object, but we should think of it as a three-dimensional object. Each data element (i.e., each field) in a data table can have up to four values, referred to as *versions*: `Current`, `Original`, `Proposed`, and `Default`.

Having four possible values for each field does not necessarily make the data table four times as large because values exist only when necessary. The `Default` version, for instance, applies at the column level, not the individual field level. There is at most one `Default` value per column, not one for each field.

In addition to multiple possible field versions, individual rows have a status value, such as `Unchanged`, `Modified`, `Added`, or `Deleted`. Understanding the meaning of the versions and status codes, and the relationship between them, is essential when programming for data sets.

To illustrate this, we focus on two field versions, `Original` and `Current`, and two row statuses, `Unchanged` and `Modified`.

When new rows are added to a data table, the `Original` and `Current` values are equal to each other and the status is set to `Unchanged`. When field values change in a data table—either because of changes done by your code or from user actions on a data-bound control—the new value becomes the `Current` value, the old value remains the `Original` value, and the state is set to `Modified`.

At some point in the execution of the program, you decide that you have "completed" your changes, that new values are no longer "new." That is, you want the `Original` value thrown away and replaced with the `Current` value, and you want the row status set back to `Unchanged`. Normally this desire to "shuffle" versions and statuses occurs because you have pushed the changes back to the underlying database, but it could occur for a variety of other reasons as well.

You accomplish this synchronization of versions and changing of states by calling the `DataRow` class's `AcceptChanges` method. The `DataSet` and `DataTable` classes also have `AcceptChanges` methods, which operate by cascading the `AcceptChanges` call down to the individual rows. Never call the `AcceptChanges` method just prior to updating the database. The class used for transferring data from a data table to the database, the data adapter class, examines the rows' status first. Data in rows that have their status marked as `Unchanged` do not cause updates to the database. (See The `SqlCeDataAdapter` Class subsection later in this chapter.)

Having mentioned the Current, Original, and Default versions of a data row, we need to say a word about the fourth version, the Proposed version. The Proposed version is used to provide transaction commit and rollback capabilities and exists only during the life of a transaction.

Working with Data Rows

As mentioned earlier, data rows contain the actual data, which can be accessed or modified by specifying the row and the column within the row. Columns can be specified by either name or index.

Data rows have methods for accessing other rows based on data relations that have been defined in the data set. Two of the most common methods are GetChildRows and GetParentRow. For example, the code in Listing 12.2 creates a relationship between the Categories and Products tables and then retrieves an array of all rows containing all products in the Widgets category, assuming that the dsetDB data set already contains the Categories and Products tables.

LISTING 12.2: Creating and Using a DataRelation Object

```
//  Define the relationship
//     between Products and Categories data tables.

dsetDB.Relations.Add(
   "FKProdCat",
   .Tables["Categories"].Columns["CategoryID"],
   .Tables["Products"].Columns["CategoryID"],
   true);

//  Select the Widgets row in the Categories data table.
//    Use it to retrieve all Widgets rows from the
//    Products data table.

dsetDB.Tables["Categories"].
   Select("CategoryName = 'Widgets'")[0].
      GetChildRows("FKProdCat");
End With
```

Introducing Data Views

A data view is always a view of a single data table, and it provides only two capabilities: sorting and filtering rows. A DataView object cannot be used to do joins, evaluate aggregate functions, or filter out columns. It is not intended to behave like a SQL Server view. Its purpose, instead, has to do with data binding.

Every data table has a `DefaultView` property. When this property is first accessed, the `DataView` object is created, and its `Filter` and `Sort` properties are set to `String.empty`. So its contents are, on first access, identical to the table's contents. Thereafter, you can set the `Filter` and `Sort` properties to anything you want.

Having discussed the `DataSet` object and its contained objects, it's time to cover moving data between the data set and the presentation tier—in other words, *data binding*.

Data Binding

Data binding is the ability to associate an object that holds data with a control that displays and updates that data. We covered the subject in Chapter 8, but now we need to apply it to the `DataTable` and `DataView` classes specifically. The following list summarizes what we covered in Chapter 8.

- The `DataGrid` control can display the entire contents of a bound data object.
- Binding to a `DataGrid` control is done by setting its `DataSource` property.
- Unlike the desktop `DataGrid` control, the .NET Compact Framework version is read-only. We presented a workaround for this limitation in Chapter 8.
- The `ListBox` and `ComboBox` controls can display one column of a `DataTable`/`DataView` and can use one other column for an identifying key.
- Binding to a `ListBox` or `ComboBox` control is done by setting its `DataSource`, `DisplayMember`, and `ValueMember` properties.
- Unlike the desktop `ComboBox` control, the .NET Compact Framework version is read-only. That is, the user can select from the list of choices but cannot enter text into the `ComboBox` control.

- Single-item controls, such as the `TextBox`, `Label`, `RadioButton`, and `CheckBox`, can bind to a single data element of a data object.
- Binding to a single-item control is done by adding entries to its `DataBindings` collection.
- The `DataBindings` collection specifies the column to be bound to but not the row. A "current" row of a `DataTable`/`DataView` is always used for binding.
- Data binding is a two-way street. Changes to data made in the control are automatically pushed back to the bound data table.

To lead into our upcoming discussion of data binding, we add the following information to our list.

- Every `DataTable` object has an associated `DataView` object that can be used for data binding. Additional views can be created for each table, but one view is always present once the table has been created.
- `DataTable` objects do not really have a "current" row. Instead, the `DataTable`'s `CurrencyManager` object, located within the form's `BindingContext` property, must be used to position the `DataTable` to a row.

We begin by writing a very simple application to illustrate the benefits and issues of data binding. We use a very simple SQL Server CE database to populate the data set. The tables in the data set are the `Categories` and `Products` tables; the relationship between them has been defined within the data set by adding a `DataRelation` object named `FKProdCat` to the data set. Once the data set has been populated, we use data binding to display the information in the tables to the user. The focus here is on the binding of data between the data set and the controls, not on the movement of data between the data set and the database. The latter is covered in detail later in this chapter when we discuss accessing SQL Server CE and SQL Server databases.

The application, located in the `DataBinding` project on the book's Web site,[1] consists of two forms. The first form, shown in Figure 12.3, consists of

1. You can download the projects mentioned in this chapter from http://www.paulyao.com/cfbook/code. Follow the instructions listed on the Web site.

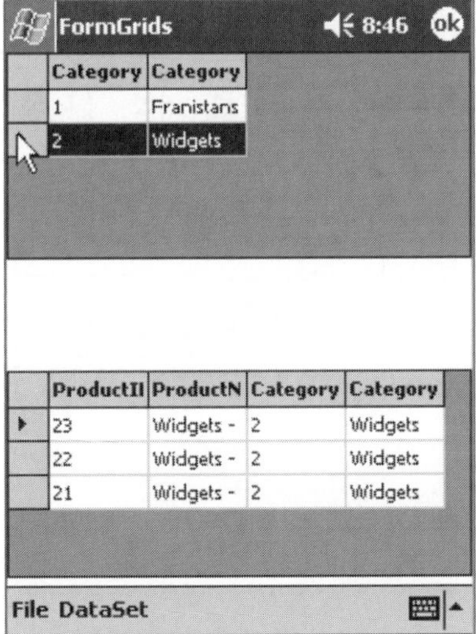

FIGURE 12.3: The parent/child form

two `DataGrid` controls, one for displaying the `Categories` rows and one for displaying the `Products` rows of whichever `Category` the user selects. In other words, we want to reflect the parent/child relationship between categories and products on the form.

The second form, shown in Figure 12.4, displays one product at a time in `TextBox` controls and provides the user with a variety of ways to specify the desired product. It also allows the user to update the product information.

The two forms are not related in a business sense; we are simply using one to illustrate multi-item data binding and the other to illustrate single-item data binding.

The first form is the simpler to program, as we shall see, for it binds data tables to multi-item controls.

Binding to Multi-Item Controls

The form shown in Figure 12.3 declares a private variable to hold the data set named `dsetDB`; creates a new data set, storing the reference in `dsetDB`; and loads `dsetDB` with data from the SQL Server CE database. At this point, we have a data set that contains two data tables and the relationship between them.

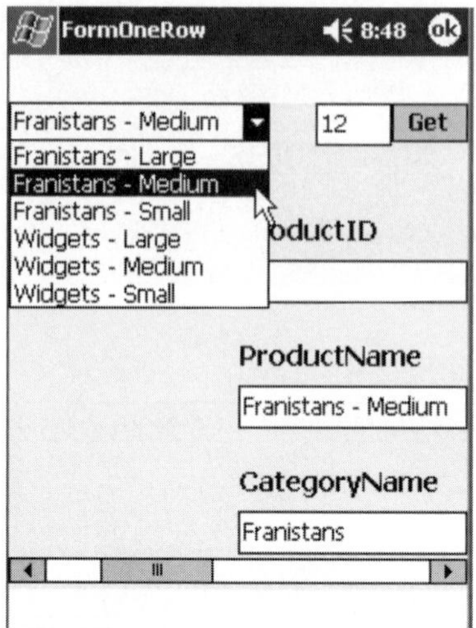

FIGURE 12.4: The single-item form

To reflect that relationship on the form, we bind the upper `DataGrid` control to the `Categories` data table so that the entire table is displayed within the `DataGrid` control. We bind the lower `DataGrid` control to the default view of the `Products` table because we can easily update the view whenever the user selects a new category. Here is the data-binding code.

```
private void mitemDisplayDS_Click(object sender, EventArgs e)
{
   //  Display the Categories and Products tables
   //     in the parent and child DataGrids.
   dgridParent.DataSource =
      dsetDB.Tables["Categories"];
   dgridChild.DataSource =
      dsetDB.Tables["Products"].DefaultView;
}
```

Whenever the user selects a new category, the application reacts to the `CurrentCellChanged` event by setting the row filter for the `Products` view to select only products of that category, as shown in this code.

```
private void dgridParent_CurrentCellChanged(object sender, EventArgs e)
{
   DataTable dtabParent = (DataTable)dgridParent.DataSource;
   DataView dviewChild = (DataView)dgridChild.DataSource;
```

```
    dviewChild.RowFilter =
        "CategoryID = " +
        dtabParent.Rows[dgridParent.CurrentRowIndex]["CategoryID"];
}
```

Thus, the `DataView` class is the key piece in reflecting the parent/child relationship to the user.

Binding to Single-Item Controls

When asked to display the second form, shown in Figure 12.4, the first form stores a reference to the data set in an `Internal` variable so that the second form can retrieve it and then displays the second form. The second form displays one product row at a time, using `Label` and `TextBox` controls. This makes it inherently more complex than the first form. Binding to single-item controls is more difficult than binding to multi-item controls for three reasons.

1. The user must be given a mechanism to specify which product should be displayed.
2. The `TextBox` controls must display the specified row.
3. The `TextBox` controls can be used to update data as well as display it.

Data binding to single-valued controls, such as `TextBox` controls, requires some additional design decisions. Making good decisions requires an understanding of data-binding internals. So let's look at the following decisions that must be made and the impacts of each.

1. How does the user designate which row is to be displayed?
   a. *By matching binding.* Bind the data object to a multi-item control, such as a `ComboBox` or `DataGrid`, as well as to the single-item controls, such as the `Label` and `TextBox` controls. The user selects the desired row from the multi-item control.
   b. *By indexing.* Provide a scroll bar or some other position control. The user indicates the relative position of the desired row within the data object. The application positions to that row.

   c. *By search key.* Provide a textbox. The user enters a value. The application searches the data object for the row containing the entered value.

2. How should that row be assigned to the control?
   a. *By current row.* The application designates the desired row as the current row of the data object.
   b. *By data view.* The application binds the single-item controls to the data table's `DefaultView` object and then sets the view's `Filter` property to limit the view to just the desired row.
3. When should the data table be updated with the values from the single-item controls?[2]
   a. *When the user moves to a new field?* No. It is not necessary to update the data object if the user is continuing to modify other fields of the same row; wait until the user moves to a new row.
   b. *When the user positions to a new row?* No. Data binding will automatically update the old row values whenever the user moves to a new row.
   c. *When the user indicates that he or she is finished with the edit (e.g., by using a Cancel or Update button or by closing the form)?* Yes. You need to use the data table's `CurrencyManager` object to complete or cancel the update of the current row if the user exits the operation without moving to a new row.

The following subsections discuss these three decisions in more detail.

Designating the Row to Be Displayed

Figure 12.5 shows the single-item form providing all three methods mentioned previously for designating which row to display. We use this form to cover the issues being addressed here. It's not the most beautiful form we ever designed, but it does illustrate the functionality we want to cover.

---

2. The question of when and how the data should be propagated from the data table down to the database is covered later in the Microsoft SQL Server CE and Microsoft SQL Server sections of this chapter.

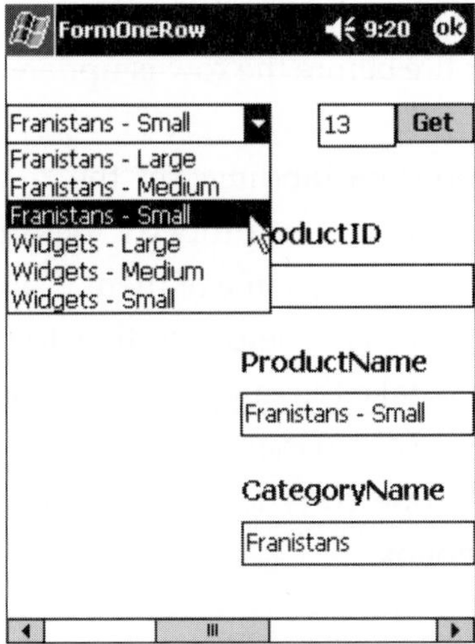

FIGURE 12.5: Three ways to designate which row to display

Matching Binding. Of the three designation methods, the easiest to program is matching binding. Once you bind the single-item controls and the multi-item controls to the same data object, you no longer have to decide how to assign the row to the single-item controls because the user's selection is automatically reflected in the single-item controls. In our example, the binding is done in the form's `Load` event handler, as shown here.

```
//  Bind the ComboBox with the Product names.
comboProductIDs.DisplayMember = strPKDesc;
comboProductIDs.ValueMember = strPKName;
comboProductIDs.DataSource = dtabProducts;
comboProductIDs.SelectedIndex = 0;

//  Bind the DataTable's columns to the textboxes.
textProductID.DataBindings.Add
   ("Text", dtabProducts, strPKName);
textProductName.DataBindings.Add
   ("Text", dtabProducts, strPKDesc);
textCategoryName.DataBindings.Add
   ("Text", dtabProducts, strFKDesc);
```

When the user taps on an entry in the combobox, that row is displayed in the textboxes. If the user enters new values in the textboxes, those values are updated to the data set as soon as the user selects a new row; and the validation events for the textbox fire before the row is updated. What more could we want?

When writing the code to do data binding, set the `DisplayMember` property prior to setting the `DataSource` property. Setting the `DataSource` property causes things to happen, some of them visible to the user. Therefore, you want everything in place before setting the `DataSource` property. To illustrate this, you can take the sample code shown on the previous page and reposition the two calls so that the `DataSource` property is set prior to the `DisplayMember` property. When you run the code you may notice a slight flicker in the combobox.

Indexing. Indexing is easy to implement, but not as easy as matching binding. And although indexing is easy, it is not obvious. When the user positions the scroll bar to a value of *n*, the application knows that it needs to make row *n* the current row of the data table. Unfortunately, data tables do not have a current row property because the concept of a current row is meaningful only within data binding. To maintain a current row context when not data bound would be wasted overhead.

Because data binding involves controls and because controls reside within forms, the `Form` class assumes the responsibility for managing the bindings and for maintaining the concept of the current row. When the first binding in the previous code excerpt that involved the `dtabProducts` data table executed, the form created an instance of the `BindingContext` class for managing `dtabProducts` bindings. As the subsequent binding code executed, that object was updated with information about the additional bindings.

When the user tapped on the *n*th entry in the combobox, the form reacted to the combobox's `SelectedIndexChanged` event by noting that the combobox was bound to `dtabProducts` and that the textboxes were also bound to `dtabProducts`. So the form notified the textboxes to obtain their `Text` property values from row *n* of the data table, and it updated the binding context object for `dtabProducts` to have a `Position` property value of `n`.

To control the current row of a bound data table and thus control which row is displayed in the textboxes, you need to tap into the form's binding management capability. Specifically, you need to obtain the `CurrencyManager` object for the data table (or data view) and set its `Position` property's value to `n`. The `CurrencyManager` object for a data object is contained in the default collection within a form's `BindingContext` object. In our application this means handling the scroll bar's `ValueChanged` event as shown in the following line of code (assuming the scroll bar is named `hsbRows` and its minimum and maximum values are 0 and the number of rows in the data object minus 1, respectively).

```
this.BindingContext[dtabProducts].Position = hsbRows.Value;
```

This causes the textboxes to update their `Text` property values with the values from the row of the `dtabProducts` table indicated by `hsbRows.Value`.

It seems like we are saying that indexing implies assigning controls according to the current row. Instead, you might wonder what's wrong with binding the textboxes to `dtabProducts.DefaultView`, rather than to the data table itself, and then reacting to the scroll bar's `ValueChanged` event by setting the view's `Filter` property with the primary key of the *n*th row, as shown here.

```
dtabProducts.DefaultView.RowFilter =
        "ProductID = " +
        dtabProducts.Rows[hsbRows.Value]["ProductID"];
```

Now the textboxes are bound to a view that contains only one row, which is the row they display, and the concept of current row becomes meaningless.

You can do it this way, and it works fine until you try to update the fields by entering new values into the textboxes. When you enter data into the textboxes and then reposition the scroll bar thumb, two things go wrong. First, tapping in the scroll bar does not cause the textbox to lose focus, and thus the validation events do not fire. Second, you do not move from one row to another row within the bound view; instead, you replace the contents of the bound view with new contents, and thus the values in the underlying data table are not updated.

So, although indexing does not necessarily imply assigning controls by current row, we recommend doing it that way whenever you choose to use indexing. And as you just saw, you can implement that choice in one line of code.

Search Key. The third method to use when designating the desired row has the user enter a search value, which fits nicely with the indexing option because both are value-based rather than position-based techniques. The single-item controls can be bound to the data table's default view, as shown in the following code.

```
//  Bind the DataTable's columns to the textboxes.
textProductID.DataBindings.Add
   ("Text", dtabProducts, strPKName);
textProductName.DataBindings.Add
   ("Text", dtabProducts, strPKDesc);
textCategoryName.DataBindings.Add
   ("Text", dtabProducts, strFKDesc);
```

Then the controls can be positioned to the requested row by extracting the user-entered key value and specifying it when setting the default view's `Filter` property.

```
dtabProducts.DefaultView.RowFilter =
   "ProductID = " + textGet.Text;
```

Because `ProductID` is the primary key, this limits the view to at most one row.

Using data views to assign the row to the textboxes in this situation does not lead to the data-set updating problems that option had when used in conjunction with a scroll bar. When the user begins to enter a new key value after entering new field values in the old row, the focus does shift, the validation events are called, and the underlying data table is updated.

Conversely, assigning rows according to the current row, which is position based rather than value based, does not fit well with having users designate rows by search keys. No single property or method of the `DataTable`, `DataView`, or `DataRow` classes translates a primary key value into a row number. If you need this type of translation, you need to write your own routine to provide it.

Assigning the Controls to a Row

Because, as we have just seen, this subject is so tightly tied to the issue of designating the row to be displayed, we have already covered it. We summarize with these points.

- If the user is designating the desired row by selecting from a multi-item control bound to the same data object as the single-item controls, do nothing.
- If the user is designating the desired row by entering an index value, bind your single-item controls to the data table, obtain the binding context for the data table from the form, and set the `Position` property to the index value.
- If the user is designating the desired row by entering a search value, bind your single-item controls to the data table's default view, and use the `Filter` property to accept only rows that contain the search value.

Updating the Bound Data Table

We said earlier that data binding is a two-way street: Changes made in the control propagate back to the data set. However, bound controls do not update the underlying row until they are repositioned to a new row. Normally you want this behavior because the row is probably out of sync with itself as its individual fields are being entered and updated, and it is best to wait for the automatic update that occurs when the user moves to a new row.

It is always possible for the user to complete the editing of a row and not move to a new row. If the user positions to a row, makes a change to the contents through a bound control, and then closes the form, the change the user made is not persisted—it is lost. This is because the application never repositioned to a new row after the change was made, and therefore, the data table was not modified.

This is why forms tend to have specific Update and Cancel buttons on them and why we handle not only the `Click` events of those buttons but also the form's `Closing` and `Deactivate` events. To programmatically complete or cancel an update (i.e., to force or prevent the transfer of data from the single-item controls to the data table), use the `CurrencyManager` object's `EndCurrentEdit` or `CancelCurrentEdit` method, respectively. This is the same `CurrencyManager` object used earlier in this chapter to specify the current row of a data object. For instance, the following code reacts to the form's `Closing` event by completing the edit of the current row, thus causing the data in the controls to propagate to the row.

```
using System.ComponentModel;
   :
   :
   private void FormUpdate_Closing(object sender,
                                    CancelEventArgs e)
   {
      //  Force the current modification to complete.
      this.BindingContext[dtabCategories].EndCurrentEdit ();
   }
```

The `CurrencyManager` object has both an `EndCurrentEdit` method to force the update to occur and a `CancelCurrentEdit` method to prevent the update from occurring, as well as the `Position` property that is used to specify the current row.

So, the key points to consider when using data binding to update data-set data is how to let the user position the controls to a specific row and how to prevent lost or unintended updates to that row.

This concludes our discussion of moving data between the data set and the presentation layer. For the rest of this chapter we examine moving data between the data set and persistent storage.

Reading and Writing a Data Set as XML

A database is not the only source for or destination of data-set data. XML files can also be the storage media for the data. Unlike database access, which requires a separate provider-specific class to perform the transfer, XML file I/O is done by the `DataSet` class itself. After all, an XML file is a text file of information in a standard format; therefore, access to it is provided in a standard manner by derived classes of the `Stream` class.

The `DataSet` class has four methods for performing XML file I/O:

1. `WriteXml`: writes the contents of a data set as XML to a file
2. `WriteXmlSchema`: writes the structure of the data set as an XML schema to a file

3. `ReadXml`: reads the contents of an XML file into a data set
4. `ReadXmlSchema`: reads the contents of an XML schema file and builds the data set structure from it

The XML schema is translated to and from `Constraint` and `DataRelation` objects in the data set, as well as the `DataTable` objects. Unlike relational data, which is flat in structure, XML is hierarchical. The `DataRelation` classes are the mechanism for expressing the hierarchy within the data set. For instance, the following code, which we used earlier in Listing 12.2, creates a `DataRelation` object that specifies the parent/child relationship between the `Categories` and `Products` tables.

```
//  Add relation to the DataSet.
dsetDB.Relations.Add(
   "FKProdCat",
   dsetDB.Tables["Categories"].Columns["CategoryID"],
   dsetDB.Tables["Products"].Columns["CategoryID"],
   true);
```

This relationship has been in our data set ever since we first built the data set. If we now execute the `WriteXml` method, as shown in the following code excerpt, and then view the contents of the file, we can see the generated XML (see Figure 12.6).

```
//  The XML file
private string strXMLFile =
                        @"My Documents\ourProduceCo.xml";
          :
          :
private void mitemWriteXml_Click(object sender,
                                 EventArgs e)
{
   dsetDB.WriteXml(strXMLFile);
}
```

The XML shown in Figure 12.6 not only contains the data but also reflects the relationship between the tables; the first category element is the first entry in the file, and it contains the product elements for all its products, then the next category element, and within it all its product elements, and so on. The need to display nested relationships in this manner is the reason why the `DataRelation` class has a `Nested` property.

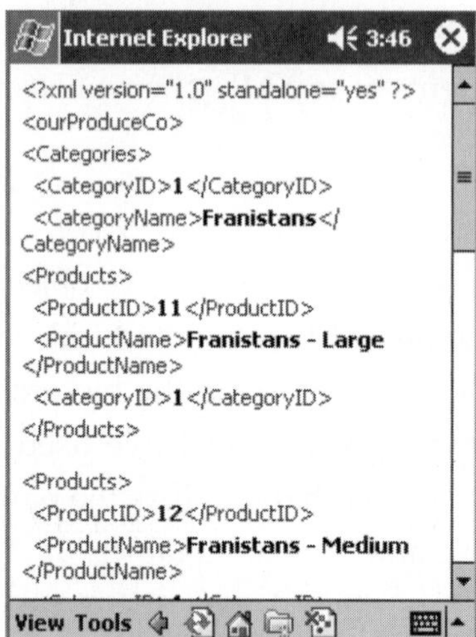

FIGURE 12.6: The XML generated by executing the `WriteXml` method

When we added the `FKProdCat` data relationship to our data set in the code shown earlier, we added it with a `Nested` property value of `false`. To ensure that your XML and XML schema reflect the hierarchical nature of your data set, set the `Nested` property of your data relationships to `true`, as shown here.

```
//  Make each relationship a nested relationship
foreach( DataRelation drelForXML in dsetDB.Relations )
{
   drelForXML.Nested = true;
}
```

Or, for a single data relationship, use the following code.

```
//  Make the FKProdCat relationship nested.
dsetDB.Relations["FKProdCat"].Nested = true;
```

It is also possible to obtain nested XML by having matching primary keys and foreign keys defined on the respective data tables, but nested relationships are usually easier to work with because all the information about the relationship is contained within a single `DataRelation` object rather than being spread across two constraint objects.

Thus, .NET Compact Framework data sets give you a convenient way to convert relational data to and from XML format. This, in turn, gives you a way to save data-set data that your application has captured to a file without incurring the overhead of using a database to do so.

Microsoft SQL Server CE

A variety of databases are available for mobile devices, but the one we use throughout these chapters is SQL Server 2000 Windows CE Edition, a slimmed-down version of Microsoft's desktop database, SQL Server 2000 (in the interest of brevity, we refer to the CE version as "SQL Server CE"). It is the mobile database of choice for .NET Compact Framework programming because it is fully supported in the .NET Compact Framework runtime environment and the .NET Compact Framework development environment.

Most applications written for SQL Server CE have two primary database tasks:

1. Manipulating the data while disconnected
2. Transferring the data to SQL Server when the device is connected to the desktop machine

The first database task involves using the generic ADO.NET classes, which we discussed earlier in this chapter, and the provider-specific classes, which we discuss shortly. For programmers who have worked with ADO.NET on desktop systems, all of the generic classes on the .NET Compact Framework implementation of ADO.NET are very familiar.

The second major database task, the transfer of data between SQL Server and SQL Server CE, involves not only the participating database engines but also Microsoft Internet Information Services (IIS). There are two different mechanisms available to help with this: Merge Replication and Remote Data Access (RDA). These two topics are the subject of Chapter 13.

Accessing SQL Server CE Databases from Native Code

ADO.NET classes are available only in managed code. But you do not need managed code to access the data in a SQL Server CE database. Two separate native APIs are available for manipulating the data in a SQL Server CE database. One involves a COM object (ADOCE), and the other is an API (OLEDBCE). These components match up with their desktop counterparts, ADO and OLE DB.

SQL Server CE Files

Each SQL Server CE database is stored as a single file on your CE device. The recommended naming convention for the file extension is `.sdf`, and the name of the file is the name of the database. Thus, you open a connection to `mydb.sdf`, not to `mydb`. You may associate a password with the database and also encrypt the physical file using 128-bit RSA encryption. Because each database is one file, it is visible in the File Explorer. Figure 12.7 shows a database file selected in the File Explorer.

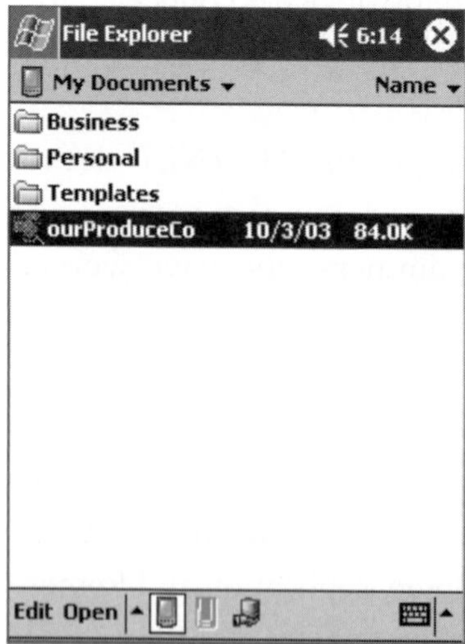

FIGURE 12.7: A database file viewed in the File Explorer

Because SQL Server CE databases are files in the Windows CE file system, they can be accessed using the `File` and `Directory` classes that we discussed in Chapter 11. For example, you can copy a database file, delete a database file, or test for the existence of a specifically named database file. Your ability to operate on database files is subject to the same restrictions as other files in the file system; for example, you can delete a database file only if the file is not currently in use.

SQL Server CE reclaims space within a database file only when you ask it to; it's not a capability available through the data manipulation language, nor is it provided as a background process. To reclaim space within a SQL Server CE database, you must use the `Compact` method of the `SqlCeEngine`[3] class.

SQL Server CE Syntax

SQL Server CE programming is simpler than SQL Server programming because the SQL language supported by SQL Server CE is a subset of the SQL available with SQL Server. For example, because a SQL Server CE database is a single-user database whose security is controlled by a file password, there is no need for `GRANT`, `DENY`, and `REVOKE` statements.

Also missing are SQL Server's Transact SQL extensions: no stored procedures, triggers, multistatement batches, or `DECLARE`, `SET`, `IF`, or `WHILE` statements. Even some standard SQL had to be left out; for example, views are not supported. Not all the SQL Server data types could be included, but most of the missing ones can be converted to ones that do exist. For example, Windows CE itself supports only Unicode, and so Unicode is the only character data type (`nchar`, `nvarchar`, `ntext`).

What SQL Server CE does provide is support for tables, indexes, defaults, and referential integrity. It also has the ability to add, modify, and delete rows in those tables using standard SQL Data Manipulation Language (DML). Therefore, your application can manipulate data in SQL Server CE by connecting to the database file and submitting `INSERT`, `UPDATE`, and `DELETE` statements to the database. You can write these DML

3. Fully qualified name: `System.Data.SqlServerCe.SqlCeEngine`.

statements yourself, or you can have ADO.NET write them for you as one step in the synchronizing of data-set updates to the database. Also, the SQL syntax uses single quotes to delineate literals, which is very convenient when you are quoting that SQL within your code—it eliminates the need to quote quotes.

Your SQL Server CE–based application may be more elementary than what you've come to expect from a typical SQL Server application, but it should provide enough functionality to be useful in mobile situations. The lack of the complete Transact SQL syntax is an inevitable limitation given the available memory of a typical Windows CE–powered device. Yet in spite of this size limitation, SQL Server CE provides a more than adequate set of SQL commands for just about any Windows CE–based application you are likely to need.

Tables 12.5 and 12.6 list what functionality in SQL Server is unsupported and supported, respectively, in SQL Server CE.

TABLE 12.5: **Unsupported SQL Server Functionality in SQL Server CE**

Functionality	Comments
DCL[a] `GRANT`, `REVOKE`, `DENY`	These are not needed in a single-user database.
DDL[b] Views, triggers, stored procedures, user-defined functions, user-defined data types	Most of these are SQL Server Transact SQL extensions to the ANSI functionality. This is logic that could reside on the SQL Server. It must be coded into the application when using SQL Server CE.
DML[c] `IF-ELSE`, `WHILE`, `DECLARE`, `SET`	Most of these are SQL Server Transact SQL extensions to the ANSI functionality.
`INFORMATION_SCHEMA TABLES`	This is replaced by `MSysObjects` and `MSysConstrains` tables.

a. Data Control Language.

b. Data Definition Language.

c. Data Manipulation Language.

TABLE 12.6: **Supported SQL Server Functionality in SQL Server CE**

Functionality	Comments
DDL Databases, tables, data types, indexes, constraints	Only Unicode character types are supported.
DML `SELECT`, `INSERT`, `UPDATE`, `DELETE`	
Functions `Aggregate`, `Math`, `DateTime`, `String`, `System`	
Transactions	The transaction isolation level is always `READ COMMITTED`. The limit on nesting is 5. Exclusive lock granularity is table level and is held for the duration of the transaction. Single-phase commit is the only commit type allowed.

ANSI Standard SQL

The specification for the SQL syntax is a standard established by an American National Standards Institute (ANSI) Standards Committee. Both SQL Server and SQL Server CE are highly compliant with the ANSI 92 standard. SQL Server 2000 has some options for choosing between ANSI compliance and compliance with older versions of SQL Server. These options are not supported in SQL Server CE; ANSI compliance is the only choice in SQL Server CE.

SQL Server CE is a little fussier about syntax than SQL Server. Having a smaller footprint means having less code that can "deduce" what you meant. Thus the following SQL, which is missing the comma between the last column definition and the constraint definition that is required by the

ANSI 92 specification, executes as intended in SQL Server 2000 but produces a syntax error in SQL Server CE.

```
CREATE TABLE Products
          ( ProductID integer not null primary key
          , ProductName nchar(20) not null
          , CategoryID integer not null
            CONSTRAINT FKProductCategory foreign key (CategoryID)
                                references Categories(CategoryID)
           )
```

Constraints

There are two primary constraints for databases: primary key and foreign key. The primary key constraint specifies the column or columns of a table in which duplicate values are prohibited and a non-null value is required. The product ID in a product table and the order number in an order table are both examples of primary keys. Foreign keys are values that exist as primary keys elsewhere in the database. For instance, the customer number column in an order table is an example of a foreign key because its value must exist in the customer table also.

Column names can be aliased within a `SELECT` statement. These aliases propagate into the data objects and onto the bound controls by default. Thus the following `SELECT` statement, used to fill a `DataTable` object bound to a `DataGrid` control, would provide the results shown in Figure 12.8.

```
SELECT P.ProductID as ID
     , P.ProductName as Name
     , C.CategoryName as Category
  FROM Products P
  JOIN Categories C on C.CategoryID = P.CategoryID
```

The primary reason to use column aliases is to provide column names for calculated columns and literals or to resolve ambiguous names; it is not

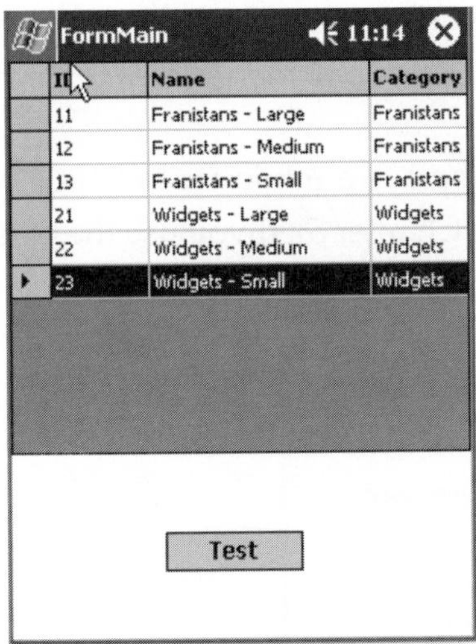

FIGURE 12.8: A `DataGrid` control with aliased column names

the preferred way to specify a column title of a `DataGrid` column. Rather, using the `DataGridColumnStyle` object, covered in Chapter 8, is the preferred way to set `DataGrid` column names because it is independent of the underlying `SELECT` statement.

SQL Server CE Query Analyzer

The primary utility tool for viewing and querying a SQL Server CE database is the SQL Server CE Query Analyzer. Like its counterpart for SQL Server 2000, the SQL Server CE Query Analyzer provides a convenient way to create and submit ad hoc queries.

The installation of the SQL Server CE Query Analyzer depends on the development environment onto which SQL Server CE is installed. When you install SQL Server CE, the SQL Server CE Query Analyzer is not installed by default on a device. Once the Query Analyzer (as we'll call the CE version for brevity in the rest of this discussion) is installed on the device, you can run the executable file, `Isqlw20.exe`, directly from the Start menu or from the directory in which it is installed. Clicking on a database file from within the File Explorer also opens the Query Analyzer.

The Query Analyzer allows you to see structural information about the database (as shown in Figure 12.9) and submit queries to that database (as shown in Figure 12.10).

The Query Analyzer form displays a minimize box, not a close box (a topic we discussed more fully in Chapter 5). If you use the Query Analyzer

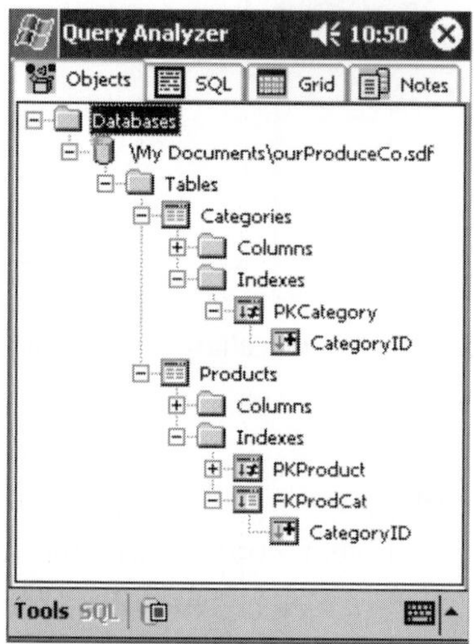

FIGURE 12.9: SQL Server CE Query Analyzer, Objects tab

FIGURE 12.10: SQL Server CE Query Analyzer, SQL tab

to examine your database and then click on the minimize box, the Query Analyzer disappears but does not close, nor does it close the database it is displaying. Any other application that tries to access the database cannot do so until you either close the database connection in the Query Analyzer (in the Objects tab, click on the tree node with the database name and then click the Stop button on the toolbar) or close the Query Analyzer itself (select Tools→Exit).

To help explain the ADO.NET classes, in this chapter we create a series of sample applications. We begin with database creation and table and index creation; then we explore retrieving, displaying, and updating data using the two-tier approach; and finally we discuss the three-tier approach of creating and using data sets and data binding.

Creating a SQL Server CE Database

Our first sample application for accessing SQL Server CE is located in the `CreateDatabase` project for this chapter on the Web site. Shown in Figure 12.11, our application is used to create and populate a database.

To create a SQL Server CE database, we use the `Engine` class located in the `System.Data.SqlServerCe` namespace. Because each SQL Server CE database is a single file, all that we need to tell the `Engine` object is the path

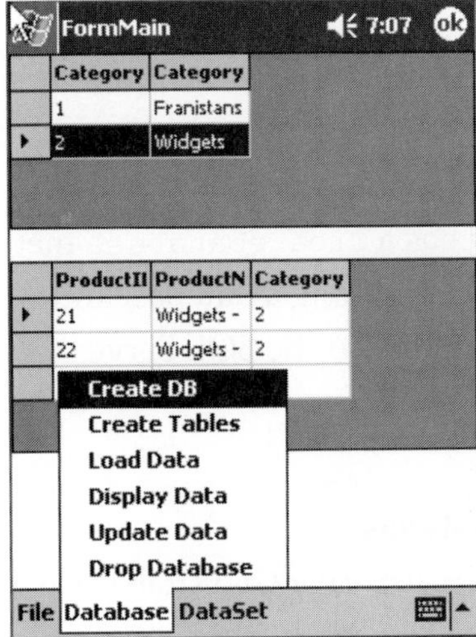

FIGURE 12.11: The `CreateDatabase` program

and name of that file. We can do this either in the `Engine` class constructor or by setting the object's `LocalConnectionString` property. In either case we must specify the file name prior to executing the `CreateDatabase` method of the `Engine` class because this method does not take any parameters.

Thus, the code to create a SQL Server CE database looks like Listing 12.3.

LISTING 12.3: Creating a SQL Server CE Database

```
private string  strFile = @"My Documents\ourProduceCo.sdf";
private string  strConn = "Data Source=" +
                          @"My Documents\ourProduceCo.sdf";


private void mitemCreateDB_Click(object sender, EventArgs e)
{
   if ( File.Exists(strFile) ) { File.Delete(strFile); }

   SqlCeEngine dbEngine = new SqlCeEngine();
   dbEngine.LocalConnectionString = strConn;
   try
   {
      dbEngine.CreateDatabase();
   }
   catch( SqlCeException exSQL )
   {
      MessageBox.Show("Unable to create database at " +
                      strFile +
                      ". Reason:  " +
                      exSQL.Errors[0].Message );
   }
}
```

Although the `Engine` class has a `CreateDatabase` method, it does not have a `DropDatabase` method. Dropping a database must be done by submitting a `DROP DATABASE` statement to the SQL Server CE database or by using the `File` class to delete the file.

Populating a SQL Server CE Database

Now that we have created our SQL Server CE Database, we can populate it with tables, indexes, and data. You might think that we use the `Engine` class to do this, but we do not. The `Engine` class operates only on an entire database, not on the individual components within the database, such as tables. In Chapter 13 we look at populating a SQL Server CE database from a connected SQL Server database, but in this chapter we focus on creating and maintaining the database. Therefore, to populate our SQL Server CE database, we use standard SQL DDL statements, such as `CREATE TABLE` and `CREATE INDEX`, and the standard SQL DML language statements `INSERT`, `UPDATE`, and `DELETE`.

Submitting SQL statements to a database requires two classes, one to open the connection and one to submit the statement.

The `SqlCeConnection` and `SqlCeCommand` Classes

The `SqlCeConnection` class opens a connection to a database and thus needs the name of the database file. The `SqlCeCommand` class submits one SQL statement at a time to the database using an `Execute` method and needs to know the connection object to use and the SQL statement to be submitted. The `SqlCeConnection` object and the DML statement are properties of the `SqlCeCommand` object. They must be set and the connection must be opened before the command's `Execute` method can be called. There are three possible `Execute` methods, summarized in Table 12.7.

Listing 12.4 shows the code for creating two simple tables.

TABLE 12.7: The `Execute` Methods of the `SqlCeCommand` Class

Method	Function
`ExecuteNonQuery`	Executes a SQL statement that returns no rows, such as `INSERT` or `CREATE`
`ExecuteScalar`	Executes a SQL statement that returns just one value, such as `SELECT SUM(Value) FROM Orders WHERE CustomerID = "ABCD"`
`ExecuteReader`	Executes a SQL statement that returns multiple columns or multiple rows

LISTING 12.4: Creating Two Tables

```
private void mitemCreateTables_Click(object sender, EventArgs e)
{
   SqlCeConnection  connDB = new SqlCeConnection();
   SqlCeCommand  cmndDB = new SqlCeCommand();

   connDB.ConnectionString = strConn;
   connDB.Open();

   cmndDB.Connection = connDB;

   cmndDB.CommandText =
      " CREATE TABLE Categories " +
      "  ( CategoryID integer not null " +
      "         CONSTRAINT PKCategories PRIMARY KEY " +
      "  , CategoryName nchar(20) not null " +
      "  )";
   cmndDB.ExecuteNonQuery();

   cmndDB.CommandText =
      " CREATE TABLE Products " +
      "  ( ProductID integer not null " +
      "         CONSTRAINT PKProducts PRIMARY KEY " +
      "  , ProductName nchar(20) not null " +
      "  , CategoryID integer not null " +
      "  , CONSTRAINT FKProdCat " +
      "       foreign key (CategoryID) " +
      "       references Categories(CategoryID) " +
      "  )";
   cmndDB.ExecuteNonQuery();

   connDB.Close();
}
```

SQL Server CE automatically creates indexes for the three constraints specified in Listing 12.4. You need to submit `CREATE INDEX` statements only for indexes that are not covered by constraints.

Listing 12.5 shows the code for inserting rows into the tables.

LISTING 12.5: Adding Rows to Tables

```
private void mitemLoadData_Click(object sender, EventArgs e)
{
   SqlCeConnection  connDB = new SqlCeConnection();
   SqlCeCommand  cmndDB = new SqlCeCommand();
```

```
    connDB.ConnectionString = strConn;
    connDB.Open();

    cmndDB.Connection = connDB;
    cmndDB.CommandText =
       " INSERT Categories " +
       "   (CategoryID, CategoryName)" +
       "   VALUES (1, 'Franistans' )";
    cmndDB.ExecuteNonQuery();
    cmndDB.CommandText =
       " INSERT Categories " +
       "   (CategoryID, CategoryName)" +
       "   VALUES (2, 'Widgets' )";
    cmndDB.ExecuteNonQuery();

    cmndDB.CommandText =
       " INSERT Products " +
       "   (ProductID, ProductName, CategoryID)" +
       "   VALUES (11, 'Franistans - Large', 1 )";
    cmndDB.ExecuteNonQuery();
    cmndDB.CommandText =
       " INSERT Products " +
       "   (ProductID, ProductName, CategoryID)" +
       "   VALUES (12, 'Franistans - Medium', 1 )";
    cmndDB.ExecuteNonQuery();
    cmndDB.CommandText =
       " INSERT Products " +
       "   (ProductID, ProductName, CategoryID)" +
       "   VALUES (13, 'Franistans - Small', 1 )";
    cmndDB.ExecuteNonQuery();
    cmndDB.CommandText =
       " INSERT Products " +
       "   (ProductID, ProductName, CategoryID)" +
       "   VALUES (21, 'Widgets - Large', 2 )";
    cmndDB.ExecuteNonQuery();
    cmndDB.CommandText =
       " INSERT Products " +
       "   (ProductID, ProductName, CategoryID)" +
       "   VALUES (22, 'Widgets - Medium', 2 )";
    cmndDB.ExecuteNonQuery();
    cmndDB.CommandText =
       " INSERT Products " +
       "   (ProductID, ProductName, CategoryID)" +
       "   VALUES (23, 'Widgets - Small', 2 )";
    cmndDB.ExecuteNonQuery();

    connDB.Close();
}
```

Because no data is returned by the SQL statements in Listing 12.5, we use the `ExecuteNonQuery` method.

So, two classes, a few methods and properties, some standard SQL, and we have a populated database. Granted, it is a very simple database, but we would use the same classes, properties, and methods to produce a more complex one.

Retrieving and Displaying Data

Now that we have populated our SQL Server CE Database with some data, we'll look at how to display that data to the user. We start with the two-tier approach, which uses the `SqlCeDataReader` class, and then move on to the three-tiered approach based on the `DataSet` class.

The `SqlCeDataReader` Class

The `SqlCeDataReader` class allows your program to access the rows returned by a SQL query. It provides read-only, forward-only access to one row at a time. Once positioned at a row, you use methods of the `DataReader` class to access the information located in the individual fields of that row. Many of these methods tend to be very data specific, and those whose names begin with the word `Get` treat the fields as a zero-based array of data. Thus, if the underlying `SELECT` statement were `SELECT ProductID, ProductName FROM Products`, the call to retrieve the `ProductID` field (field 0) from the `DataReader` object's current row would be one of the following lines of code.

```
intVar = drdrDataReader.GetInt32(0);

//  or the slightly less efficient

intVar = drdrDataReader.GetValue(0);

//  or

intVar = drdrDataReader.Item["ProductID"];
```

Similarly, the call to retrieve the `ProductName` field would be one of the following lines of code.

```
strVar = drdrDataReader.GetString(1);

// or

strVar = drdrDataReader.GetValue(1);

// or

strVar = drdrDataReader.Item["ProductName"];
```

You cannot create a `DataReader` object directly; you must use the `SqlCeCommand` object's `ExecuteReader` method to create the `DataReader` object. When first created, the `DataReader` object is open but not yet positioned at a row. You have two ways to position it to a row.

The first is to use the `DataReader` object's `Read` method to move sequentially through the rows. The second is to use the `DataReader` object's `Seek` method to position to a specific row. The `Seek` method requires the following conditions.

- The underlying database table is indexed.
- Additional properties of the `SqlCeCommand` object are set before executing the `ExecuteReader` method.
- The index name and key value(s) are specified in the call to the `Seek` method.
- The call to the `Seek` method is followed by a call to the `Read` method.

The advantage of using the `Seek` method is performance. In fact, performance is the very reason why the .NET Compact Framework development team added the `Seek` method to the product beginning with version 1.1. Using the `Seek` method is almost always faster than using the `WHERE` clause of a `SELECT` statement for locating specific rows. The disadvantage is that the `Seek` method provides access to only one table at a time, and knowledge of the index is required. The former means that you cannot combine the `Seek` method with the joining of two or more tables; the latter goes against the very grain of relational database theory. Of course, many programmers have gone against the grain when it was the faster way to go.

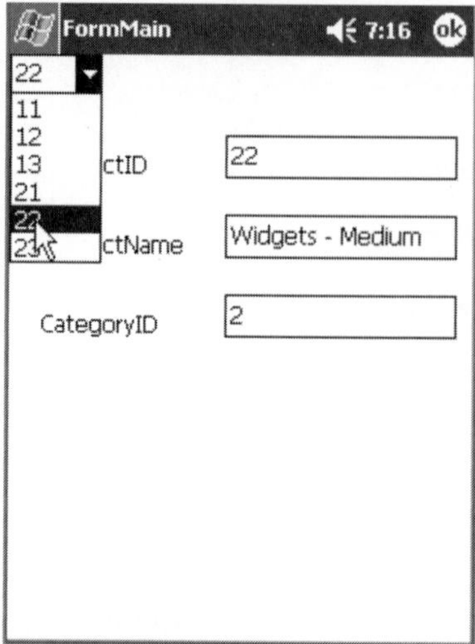

FIGURE 12.12: The `DataReader` program

To illustrate both the `Read` and `Seek` methods, the following sample application, shown in Figure 12.12 and located in the `DataReader` project on the Web site, loads a `ComboBox` control with product key values. When the user clicks on the `ComboBox` control, the fields of the selected product are displayed in the `TextBox` controls.

Listing 12.6 shows the code for this application.

LISTING 12.6: Source Code for the `DataReader` Program

```
using System;
using System.IO;
using System.Drawing;
using System.Collections;
using System.Windows.Forms;
using System.Data;
using System.Data.Common;
using System.Data.SqlServerCe;

namespace DataReader
{
   /// <summary>
   /// Summary description for FormMain
   /// </summary>
   public class FormMain : System.Windows.Forms.Form
   {
```

```
internal System.Windows.Forms.Label lblCategoryName;
internal System.Windows.Forms.Label lblProductName;
internal System.Windows.Forms.Label lblProductID;
internal System.Windows.Forms.TextBox textCategoryName;
internal System.Windows.Forms.TextBox textProductName;
internal System.Windows.Forms.TextBox textProductID;
internal System.Windows.Forms.ComboBox comboKeys;

public FormMain()
  {
    //
    // Required for Windows Form Designer support
    //
    InitializeComponent();
 }
 /// <summary>
 /// Clean up any resources being used.
 /// </summary>
 protected override void Dispose( bool disposing )
 {
    base.Dispose( disposing );
 }
 #region Windows Form Designer generated code


 /// <summary>
 /// The main entry point for the application
 /// </summary>

 static void Main()
 {
    Application.Run(new FormMain());
 }


 //  File path and name
 private string  strFile = @"My Documents\ourProduceCo.sdf";

 //  Connection string
 private string  strConn = "Data Source=" +
                           @"My Documents\ourProduceCo.sdf";

 //  Select product keys.
 private string strGetProductIDs =
    " SELECT ProductID " +       "   FROM Products ";

 //  Select one product, joined with its category.
 private string strGetOneProduct =
    " SELECT ProductID, ProductName, CategoryName " +
    "   FROM Products P " +
```

continues

continued

```
        "   JOIN Categories C on C.CategoryID = P.CategoryID " +
        "  WHERE P.ProductID = ";

    //  Used to bypass the SelectIndexChanged event
    //     during the loading of the ComboBox
    private bool boolLoading = true;


    private void FormMain_Load(object sender, EventArgs e)
    {
       //  Display a close box.
       this.MinimizeBox = false;

       //  Let the form present itself.
       Application.DoEvents();

       //  Ensure that the database exists.
       if (! File.Exists(strFile) )
       {
          MessageBox.Show(
             "Database not found.  Run the CreateDatabase " +
             "program for this chapter first.  Then run " +
             "this program.");
       }

       //  Load product keys into the ComboBox
       //     and select the first one.
       LoadProductIDs();
       comboKeys.SelectedIndex = 0;
    }

    private void comboKeys_SelectedIndexChanged(object sender,
                                                EventArgs e)
    {
       //  A product key has been selected; retrieve
       //     and display the corresponding product.
       if (! boolLoading )
       {
          LoadOneProduct((int)comboKeys.SelectedItem);
       }
    }

    private void textProductName_Validated(object sender,
                                           EventArgs e)
    {
       //  Update this product row in the database.
       UpdateSelectedRow(int.Parse(textProductID.Text),
                         textProductName.Text);
    }
```

```
private void LoadProductIDs()
{
   //  Clear the ComboBox.
   comboKeys.Items.Clear();

   //  A connection, a command, and a reader
   SqlCeConnection connDB =
      new SqlCeConnection(strConn);
   SqlCeCommand cmndDB =
      new SqlCeCommand(strGetProductIDs, connDB);
   SqlCeDataReader drdrDB;

   //  Open the connection.
   connDB.Open();

   //  Submit the SQL statement and receive
   //      the SqlCeReader for the results set.
   drdrDB = cmndDB.ExecuteReader();

   //  Read each row.  Add the contents of its
   //      only column as an entry in the ComboBox.
   //      Close the reader when done.
   while ( drdrDB.Read() )
   {
      comboKeys.Items.Add(drdrDB["ProductID"]);
   }
   drdrDB.Close();

   //  Close the connection.
   connDB.Close();

   //  Start responding to ComboBox's
   //      SelectedIndexChanged events.
   this.boolLoading = false;
}

private void LoadOneProduct( int intProductID)
{
   //  A connection, a command, and a reader
   SqlCeConnection  connDB = new SqlCeConnection(strConn);
   SqlCommand  cmndDB = new SqlCommand(strSQL,connDB);
   SqlCeDataReader drdrDB;

   //  Open the connection.
   connDB.Open();

   //  Set the Command object to retrieve
   //      rows from one table via one index.
   //  Then retrieve the reader.
   cmndDB.Connection = connDB;
```

continues

continued

```
    cmndDB.CommandType = CommandType.TableDirect;
    cmndDB.CommandText = "Products";
    cmndDB.IndexName = "PKProducts";
    drdrDB = cmndDB.ExecuteReader();

    //  Retrieve the first (only) row from the
    //     Products table that has the ProductID
    //     that was selected in the ComboBox.
    //  Load the fields into the form's controls.
    //  Close the reader.
    drdrDB.Seek(DbSeekOptions.FirstEqual, intProductID);
       if( drdrDB.Read() )
       {
          LoadControlsFromRow(drdrDB);
       }
    drdrDB.Close();

    //  Close the connection.
    connDB.Close();
 }


 private void LoadControlsFromRow( SqlCeDataReader drdrDB)
 {
    //  Transfer the column titles and the field
    //     contents of the current row from the
    //     reader to the form's controls.
    lblProductID.Text = drdrDB.GetName(0);
    textProductID.Text = drdrDB.GetValue(0).ToString();
    lblProductName.Text = drdrDB.GetName(1);
    textProductName.Text = drdrDB.GetValue(1).ToString();
    lblCategoryName.Text = drdrDB.GetName(2);
    textCategoryName.Text = drdrDB.GetValue(2).ToString();
 }

 private void UpdateSelectedRow(int intProductID,
                                string strProductName)
 {
    //  A connection and a command
    SqlCeConnection connDB = new SqlCeConnection(strConn);
    SqlCeCommand cmndDB = new SqlCeCommand();

    //  Open the connection.
    connDB.Open();

    //  Update the product name for the selected product.
    cmndDB.Connection = connDB;
```

```
            cmndDB.CommandText =
               " UPDATE Products " +
               " SET ProductName = " + "'" + strProductName + "'" +
               " WHERE ProductID = " + intProductID;
            cmndDB.ExecuteNonQuery();

            //  Close the connection.
            connDB.Close();
        }
    }
}
```

The LoadProductIDs routine submits a SELECT statement and uses a DataReader object to process all the rows retrieved by that SELECT statement. Note that the properties of the SqlCeCommand object must be initialized before a DataReader object can be created. Because the reader is not positioned to the first row when created, the Read method must be called at the start of the iterative loop, not at the end of the loop. In general, this makes for cleaner code and is a definite improvement over past ADO classes.

The LoadOneProduct routine uses the Seek method followed by the Read method to retrieve a single row from the database. Note also that a call to the Read method must follow the call to the Seek method. Without this call to the Read method, no row would be in the reader. Although there would be no row in the reader if the Read method call were missing, no exception would be raised. From ADO.NET's point of view, nothing has gone wrong; you simply have an empty reader.

As you can see from the output shown earlier in Figure 12.12, all the columns came from the Products table, a built-in limitation of the Seek method. Listing 12.7 shows an alternative version of the LoadOneProduct method. It uses a WHERE clause rather than a Seek method index to specify the desired product. As the output in Figure 12.13 shows, this alternative version of the LoadOneProduct method can gather fields from more than one table, resulting in the more informative CategoryName field associated with each product, rather than the less informative CategoryID field. However, as mentioned earlier, this version of the method executes more slowly.

LISTING 12.7: An Alternative Version of the `LoadOneProduct` Method

```
private void LoadOneProduct( int intProductID)
{
   // Append the desired ProductID to the SELECT statement.
    string strSQL = strGetOneProduct + intProductID;

   // A connection, a command, and a reader
   SqlCeConnection connDB = new SqlCeConnection(strConn);
   SqlCommand cmndDB = new SqlCommand(strSQL,connDB);
   SqlCeDataReader drdrDB;

   // Open the connection.
   connDB.Open();

   // Submit the SQL statement and receive
   //     the SqlCeReader for the one-row
   //     results set.
   drdrDB = cmndDB.ExecuteReader();

   // Read the first (only) row.
   //     Display it. Close the reader.
   if ( drdrDB.Read() )
   {
      LoadControlsFromRow(drdrDB);
   }
   drdrDB.Close();

   // Close the connection.
   connDB.Close();
}
```

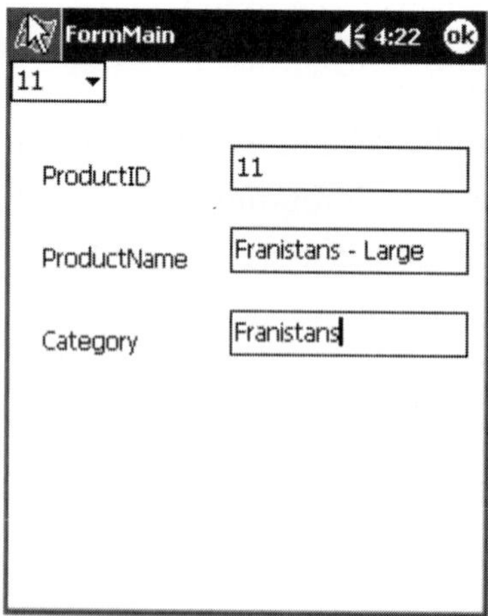

FIGURE 12.13: The output from a join using the alternative `LoadOneProduct` method

We mentioned earlier that the DataReader object returned from the ExecuteReader method is not yet positioned to the first row. But it is already open, and it is your responsibility to close it. Unlike the desktop DataReader objects, which live in the multiuser environment, the SqlCeDataReader object was written for the mobile-device world. This means that you can have multiple readers open on the same connection at one time. This is a somewhat necessary capability, given that you are allowed only one open SqlCeConnection object per database at a time.

The current row of a DataReader object and a DataRow object are not the same thing. A DataRow is an object unto itself, while the current row of a DataReader is not. As we saw, we access the contents of the current row of a DataReader object by using methods and properties of the DataReader itself.

Updating a SQL Server CE Database

Now that we have presented data to the user, we'll continue by allowing the user to modify that data and submit those modifications to the database. We've already presented an example of this when we first populated our database. So the code you are about to see is very similar to code you have already seen.

The application that allows the user to change the product name does so by reacting to the textProductName.Validated event as shown here.

```
private void textProductName_Validated(object sender, EventArgs e)
{
   //  Update this product row in the database.
   UpdateSelectedRow(int.Parse(textProductID.Text), textProductName.Text);
}
```

The called routine updates the product row as shown in Listing 12.8.

LISTING 12.8: The UpdateSelectedRow Method

```
private void UpdateSelectedRow(int intProductID,
                               string strProductName)
{
   //  A connection and a command
   SqlCeConnection connDB = new SqlCeConnection(strConn);
   SqlCeCommand cmndDB = new SqlCeCommand();
```

continues

continued

```
    //  Open the connection.
    connDB.Open();

    //  Update the product name for the selected product.
    cmndDB.Connection = connDB;
    cmndDB.CommandText =
       " UPDATE Products " +
       " SET ProductName = " + "'" + strProductName + "'" +
       " WHERE ProductID = " + intProductID;
    cmndDB.ExecuteNonQuery();

    //  Close the connection.
    connDB.Close();
}
```

If the application allowed more than one field to be updated, we would set a "needs updating" flag within the `Validated` event handler of each field and react to the `ComboBox` control's `SelectedIndexChanged` event and the form's `Close` event by doing the update at that point, if needed.

If this application is the only application accessing a database, it does not need to open and close the connection each time a query is submitted to the database. In that situation, we could move the `Open` and `Close` calls into the form's `Load` and `Closed` events, respectively.

You have now seen how to use the `SqlCeConnection`, `SqlCeCommand`, and `SqlCeDataReader` classes to retrieve data from a SQL Server CE database, present that data to the user in controls on the form, accept changes from the user, and submit those changes back to the database. And that, in turn, completes our coverage of SQL Server CE in the two-tiered application.

The `SqlCeDataAdapter` Class

It is time to address the three-tiered approach, the approach that has you move data between your SQL Server CE database and a data set. You cannot do that without using and understanding the `SqlCeDataAdapter` class, the primary means for moving data between a database and a data set.

Using a `SqlCeDataAdapter` Object to Retrieve Data

Just as the `SqlCeCommand` class has a property that holds the `SqlCeConnection` object to be used, the `SqlCeDataAdapter` class has a `Select-`

Command property that holds the SqlCeCommand object to be used to retrieve the data. The SqlCeDataAdapter class also holds three other command properties, all optional, for inserting database records (InsertCommand), updating database records (UpdateCommand), and deleting database records (DeleteCommand).

It also has the Fill method, which is used to connect to the database, execute the SELECT command, create the data table if necessary, and place the selected rows into the data table. Thus, the following code creates a data table named Categories in a previously created data set named dsetDB, connects to the ourProduceCo database, submits the SELECT statement, and places the returned rows into the Categories table.

```
SqlCeDataAdapter daptDB =
      new SqlCeDataAdapter(
         "SELECT * FROM Categories",
         "Data Source=My Documents\ourProduceCo.sdf");
daptDB.Fill(dsetDB, "Categories");
```

When you look at the code, it seems that only one object, the SqlCeDataAdapter object, is being created, for there is only one new function call. Actually, four objects are created; one is then disposed, and the remaining three are kept. The overloaded constructor shown here created a connection object and a command object from the parameters we provided, as well as creating the data adapter object. A reference to that command object is now stored in the adapter's SelectCommand property, and a reference to the connection object is now stored in the command object's Connection property. A fourth object, a data reader object, was created, used to retrieve the rows, and was then closed and disposed.

The second parameter of the Fill method is the name to be given to the new data table in the data set. This name is completely unrelated to any table name in the underlying database. It may be the same name as a database table name, but no inherent relationship is assumed based on the choice of name.

The Fill method leaves the connection object in the state in which the method found the object. If the connection is open at the time the method is called, then the connection is left open. If the connection is closed at the time the method is called, the `Fill` method opens the connection, retrieves the rows, places them into the data table, and closes the connection.

The `Fill` method creates a new data table if one of the same name does not already exist. If the data table does exist, primary key values are used to determine whether each incoming row should create a new row or update an existing row.

At this point it's reasonable to ask, "Why is a separate object needed to move the data between the database and the data set? Why can't the data table just 'pull' the rows in, similar to the way an ADO `Recordset` object pulls data into itself by using its `Open` method?"

A data table cannot load itself because it is provider-independent. That is, the `DataSet` and `DataTable` classes have no knowledge of SQL Server, Pocket Access, or SQL Server CE. They do not know how to perform such tasks as translating the underlying data types into .NET data types or obtaining schema definitions from the underlying data source. We need a provider-specific class to act as the middleware. When the database is SQL Server CE, `SqlCeDataAdapter` is that class.

Although not mandatory, it is a good practice to have a separate instance of `SqlCeDataAdapter` for each data table instance. If your application uses the `SqlCeDataAdapter` class to update the database, having a separate `SqlCeDataAdapter` object for each table is highly recommended.

Using a `SqlCeDataAdapter` Object to Update a Database

Remember that the `SqlCeDataAdapter` object lies between the `DataSet` object and the underlying database. The `SqlCeDataAdapter` object is used to pull the data from the database and place it into the data table, and it can be used to push any changes made to the data in the data table back to the database. Just as a `SqlCeDataAdapter` object has a `SelectCommand` property, it also has `InsertCommand`, `UpdateCommand`, and `DeleteCommand` properties, each holding a `SqlCeCommand` object. These commands are used to push changes made to the data tables back to the database. They are called by the `SqlCeDataAdapter` object's `Update` method. You can call them directly, but normally you let the `Update` method do it for you.

Coming up with the parameterized SQL statements for these command objects may be very simple or quite difficult. It all depends on the complexity of the `SELECT` statement in the `SelectCommand` property. The `SqlCeDataAdapter` object can build the `InsertCommand`, `UpdateCommand`, and `DeleteCommand` command objects for you if you give it some help (which is provided by the `SqlCeCommandBuilder` class) and if all of the following conditions are true.

- The `SelectCommand` property's `SELECT` statement accesses just one database table.
- The table being accessed has a primary key or unique constraint.
- The columns that make up that constraint are in the `SELECT` clause of the `SELECT` statement.
- Each data element in the output of the `SELECT` statement can be traced back to a single data element in the database (no literals, aggregates, or functions).

If your `SELECT` statement meets these criteria, and if you have created a `SqlCeCommandBuilder` object and associated it with the `SqlCeDataAdapter` object prior to calling the `SqlCeDataAdapter` object's `Update` method, the `SqlCeCommandBuilder` object builds the `Insert`, `Update`, and `Delete` command objects for you.

To illustrate this, we add a simple form to our project for updating category information, as shown in Figure 12.14.

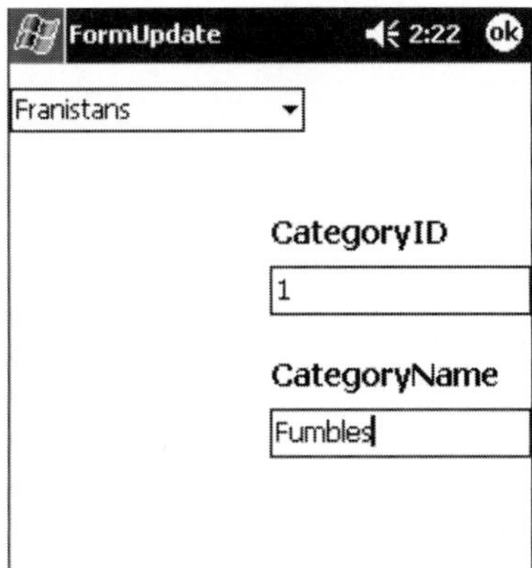

FIGURE 12.14: The category modification form

Listing 12.9 shows the code for this form. Most of it is familiar, consisting of creating and loading the data set and binding to the controls. New concepts in the code are the creation of the `SqlCeCommandBuilder` object in the `Load` event handler and the update-specific code in the `Closing` event handler.

LISTING 12.9: The Category Modification Form Class

```
using System;
using System.Data;
using System.Data.Common;
using System.Data.SqlServerCe;
using System.Drawing;
using System.Collections;
using System.ComponentModel;
using System.Windows.Forms;

namespace CreateDatabase
{
   /// <summary>
   /// Summary description for FormUpdate
   /// </summary>
   public class FormUpdate : System.Windows.Forms.Form
   {
      internal System.Windows.Forms.Panel panelCategory;
      internal System.Windows.Forms.ComboBox comboCategoryIDs;
      internal System.Windows.Forms.TextBox textCategoryName;
      internal System.Windows.Forms.Label lblCategoryName;
      internal System.Windows.Forms.TextBox textCategoryID;
      internal System.Windows.Forms.Label lblCategoryID;

      public FormUpdate()
      {
         InitializeComponent();
      }

      protected override void Dispose( bool disposing )
      {
         base.Dispose( disposing );
      }

      #region Windows Form Designer generated code

      //  Connection string
      private string  strConn =
         "Data Source=" + @"My Documents\ourProduceCo.sdf";
```

```
//  The data set, adapter, table
private DataSet dsetDB;
private SqlCeDataAdapter daptCategories;
private DataTable dtabCategories;

private bool boolLoading = true;


private void FormUpdate_Load(object sender, EventArgs e)
   //  Present a close box.      {
   this.MinimizeBox = false;

   //  Create the data set.
   dsetDB = new DataSet("Produce");

   //  Create the data adapter.
   daptCategories = new
      SqlCeDataAdapter("SELECT CategoryID, CategoryName " +
                       "  FROM Categories",
      strConn);

   //  Create the command builder for the adapter.
   SqlCeCommandBuilder cbldCategories =
      new SqlCeCommandBuilder(daptCategories);

   //  Create and fill the data table, and
   //     save a reference to it.
   daptCategories.Fill(dsetDB, "Categories");
   dtabCategories = dsetDB.Tables["Categories"];

   //  Bind the combobox with the category names.
   comboCategoryIDs.DataSource = dtabCategories;
   comboCategoryIDs.DisplayMember = "CategoryName";
   comboCategoryIDs.ValueMember = "CategoryID";
   comboCategoryIDs.SelectedIndex = 0;

   //  Load labels with data table column names.
   lblCategoryID.Text = "CategoryID";
   lblCategoryName.Text = "CategoryName";

   //  Bind the data table's columns to the textboxes.
   textCategoryID.DataBindings.Add
      ("Text", dtabCategories, "CategoryID");
   textCategoryName.DataBindings.Add
      ("Text", dtabCategories, "CategoryName");

   //  Give the panel some tone.
   panelCategory.BackColor = Color.Beige;
```

continues

continued

```
         // Loading is finished.
         boolLoading = false;
         comboCategoryIDs.SelectedIndex = 0;
      }

      private void textCategoryName_Validated(object sender,
                                              EventArgs e)
      {
         // Force the current modification to complete.
         this.BindingContext[dtabCategories].EndCurrentEdit();
      }

      private void FormUpdate_Closing(object sender,
                                      CancelEventArgs e)
      {
         // Force the current modification to complete.
         this.BindingContext[dtabCategories].EndCurrentEdit();

         // Push data set changes back to the database.
         daptCategories.Update(dsetDB, "Categories");
      }
   }
}
```

Regardless of whether you are letting the `SqlCeCommandBuilder` object build the adapter's three modification commands or building them programmatically yourself, calling the `SqlCeDataAdapter` object's `Update` method pushes changes that have been made in the data set back to the database. The `Update` method does this by examining the row status of each of the rows of the data table and then executing the `Insert`, `Update`, or `Delete` commands as necessary.

As we mentioned earlier, never call the `DataTable` object's `AcceptChanges` method just prior to calling the `SqlCeDataAdapter` object's `Update` method. The `AcceptChanges` method sets all row statuses to `Unchanged`, which means that the `Update` method would find no rows to update.

Unlike the adapter class for use with SQL Server 2000, the `SqlCeDataAdapter` object does not detect conflicts when updating a database. Conflict detection prevents an application from modifying data that has been modified by some other application since the first application read the data. This ensures users that they are updating data whose values are still the values being presented to the user. In a multiuser environment, conflict detection is a very beneficial guardian; in the single-user world, it is a lot of overhead. If the user runs two applications to update the same data at the same time, the `SqlCeDataAdapter` object quite rightly lets the user trash his or her own updates if the user chooses to do so.

Even though you use an adapter to bring data into a data set, using it to push changes back to the database is always optional. You can always write your own DML statements and place them into the `CommandText` properties of the adapter's command objects. As we mentioned, if the `SELECT` statement is sufficiently complex, the `SqlCeCommandBuilder` object cannot generate the `Insert`, `Update`, and `Delete` statements; you have to write them yourself.

You might want to write those statements yourself for additional control or application documentation reasons. Your application can always create a connection and a command object and use the command object's `ExecuteNonQuery` method to submit an update to a database. And, for reasons we will explain in the upcoming Microsoft SQL Server section, you are more likely to provide your own updating when connected to SQL Server rather than to SQL Server CE. But first we examine one last aspect of SQL Server CE programming: obtaining information about a database's schema.

Querying Schema Information

In an environment where data is being collected from a variety of sources and stored in your data tables, knowing the schema of that data can be very important. Historically, database engines have always provided a method for querying information about a database schema, such as the names of the tables, the names and data types of the columns, and the names and included columns of the primary keys and foreign keys.

The database engines all did this differently, mainly because their internal storage mechanisms for holding this information varied from engine to engine. To improve cross-engine compatibility, the ANSI Standards Committee introduced a standard syntax for querying schema information, known as the `INFORMATION_SCHEMA` views. For instance, using this syntax you can query the database for a list of table names by submitting the following query.

```
SELECT TABLE_NAME
  FROM Information_Schema.TABLES
 WHERE TABLE_TYPE = 'TABLE'
```

SQL Server CE schema querying capability differs significantly from that of SQL Server and from the ANSI standard. This is necessary to maintain the smaller footprint of SQL Server CE. Many of the ANSI standard tables related to constraints have been removed and replaced by a single table that is more appropriate for a single-user database: the `MSysConstraints` table. For instance, the following ANSI standard query obtains foreign key information when submitted to SQL Server; but it yields a syntax error when submitted to SQL Server CE.

```
--***
--***  SQL Server version
--***
SELECT C.CONSTRAINT_NAME
     , PK.TABLE_NAME
     , PK.COLUMN_NAME
     , FK.TABLE_NAME
     , FK.COLUMN_NAME
  FROM Information_Schema.REFERENTIAL_CONSTRAINTS C
  JOIN Information_Schema.CONSTRAINT_COLUMN_USAGE PK
    ON PK.CONSTRAINT_NAME = C.UNIQUE_CONSTRAINT_NAME
  JOIN Information_Schema.CONSTRAINT_COLUMN_USAGE FK
    ON FK.CONSTRAINT_NAME = C.CONSTRAINT_NAME
```

Instead, the following query must be used with SQL Server CE to obtain foreign key information.

```
--***
--***  SQL Server CE version
--***
SELECT C.CONSTRAINT_NAME
     , C.REFERENCED_TABLE_NAME
     , C.REFERENCED_COLUMN_NAME
     , C.TABLE_NAME
     , C.CONSTRAINT_COLUMN_NAME
  FROM MSysConstraints C
  WHERE C.CONSTRAINT_TYPE = 1
```

In the world of SQL Server CE, schema queries are very useful tools. As we discuss in Chapter 13, the data in your SQL Server CE database may have been imported from a connected database such as SQL Server. You may need to ascertain schema information after the data has been received. Additionally, as you move data from your SQL Server CE database into a data set, you may wish to reproduce the database schema, such as constraints and relationships, into the dataset.

As an example of querying schema information, the `UtilData` class located in the `UtilData` project on the Web site has a shared method, `BuildDataSet`, that does the following:

- Creates a data set
- Finds all the tables in a specified SQL Server CE database
- Uploads them to the data set
- Finds all the constraints in the specified SQL Server CE database
- Creates the corresponding relations and constraints in the data set
- Returns the data set

Listing 12.10 presents the code.

LISTING 12.10: Building a Data Set from a Database

```
public static DataSet BuildDataSet( string  strDB )
{
   DataSet dsetWork;

   if (! File.Exists(strDB) ) { return(null) ; }

   string  strConn = "Data Source=" + strDB;
   SqlCeConnection connDB;
   connDB = new SqlCeConnection(strConn);
   connDB.Open();

   dsetWork = new DataSet("ourProduceCo");

   SqlCeDataReader drdrTableNames;
   drdrTableNames = GetTableNames(connDB);
   while ( drdrTableNames.Read() )
   {
```

continues

continued

```
      LoadTable(dsetWork,
               connDB,
               drdrTableNames.GetString(0));
   }
   drdrTableNames.Close();

   LoadRelationships(dsetWork, connDB);

   connDB.Close();

   return dsetWork;
}


// ****************************************************//
//
//     GENERIC ROUTINES
//

public static SqlCeDataReader GetTableNames
                              ( SqlCeConnection connDB )
{
      SqlCeCommand  cmndDB =
         new SqlCeCommand(strGetTableNames, connDB);
      return cmndDB.ExecuteReader();
}

public static void LoadTable (DataSet dsetDB,
                              SqlCeConnection connDB,
                              string  strTable)
{
   SqlCeCommand cmndDB =
      new SqlCeCommand(strGetTableRows + strTable, connDB);
   SqlCeDataAdapter daptProducts =
      new SqlCeDataAdapter(cmndDB);
   daptProducts.Fill(dsetDB, strTable);
}

public static SqlCeDataReader GetRelationships
                              ( SqlCeConnection connDB )
{
   SqlCeCommand cmndDB =
      new SqlCeCommand(strGetRelationships, connDB);
   return cmndDB.ExecuteReader();
}
```

```
public static void LoadRelationships(
                                DataSet dsetDB,
                                SqlCeConnection connDB)
{
//  Retrieve foreign key information from the
//     database.  For each foreign key, create
//     a relationship in the data set.

//  Create the GetRelationships command object.
SqlCeCommand cmndDB =
   new SqlCeCommand(strGetRelationships, connDB);

//  Execute GetRelationships.
SqlCeDataReader drdrRelationships;
drdrRelationships = cmndDB.ExecuteReader();
string  strRelation;
DataColumn dcolParent, dcolChild;

while ( drdrRelationships.Read() )
{
   //  For each foreign key in the database
   //  Extract and convert name, parent, child info.
   strRelation =
      drdrRelationships.GetString(0);
   dcolParent =
      dsetDB.Tables[drdrRelationships.GetString(1)]
            .Columns[drdrRelationships.GetString(2)];
   dcolChild =
      dsetDB.Tables[drdrRelationships.GetString(3)]
            .Columns[drdrRelationships.GetString(4)];

      //  Add the relation to the data set.
      dsetDB.Relations.Add
                  (strRelation, dcolParent, dcolChild);
   }
   drdrRelationships.Close();

   //  Make each relationship a nested relationship.
   foreach( DataRelation drelForXML in dsetDB.Relations )
   {
      drelForXML.Nested = true;
   }
}
```

The `SqlServerCe` namespace contains the classes for accessing a Microsoft SQL Server CE database. You need a connection and a command object, plus either a `SqlCeDataReader` or a `SqlCeDataAdapter` object. The data reader lets you retrieve rows into your application one at a time, forward only. The data set is a memory-resident database that allows for programmatic access to data from a SQL Server CE database and from other sources. It provides data binding and automatic updating.

Interestingly, all of these points are as true for Microsoft SQL Server as they are for Microsoft SQL Server CE. But programming for one is not exactly the same as programming for the other, as we are about to see.

Microsoft SQL Server

If, as we said earlier, there are a variety of databases available for mobile devices, then there is an even greater variety of databases available for desktop machines and servers. Of these, Microsoft SQL Server was designed with built-in support for .NET Compact Framework applications—it provides synchronization of data between a SQL Server database and a SQL Server CE database (the subject of Chapter 13). The .NET Compact Framework also provides applications with access to SQL Server databases through the provider-specific classes that run on Windows CE devices. Just as there are `SqlCeConnection`, `SqlCeCommand`, and other classes in the .NET Compact Framework for accessing SQL Server CE, there are also `SqlConnection`, `SqlCommand`, and other classes available for accessing SQL Server.

The Microsoft SQL Server provider-specific ADO.NET classes are located in the `System.Data.SqlClient` namespace. Because the provider-specific classes adhere to a common specification, accessing SQL Server from your application is similar to accessing SQL Server CE: You open connections, submit commands, process returned rows with a data reader, and transfer data to and from a data set by using a data adapter. The text within the `ConnectionString` and `CommandText` properties may be more complex when accessing SQL Server, but the properties and methods of the classes are predominately the same.

Earlier in this chapter we introduced SQL Server CE. It is not our intent to present the same level of detail for SQL Server. SQL Server is a far more complex product, one that does not run on a device and one that has already been covered in innumerable books and other sources. Instead, here we cover some of the differences between SQL Server CE and SQL Server 2000 that you might encounter while using the .NET Compact Framework's ADO.NET classes.

We begin by recapping some statements regarding the differences between SQL Server and SQL Server CE as they relate to accessing each from your application.

- Connecting to a SQL Server database is more complicated than connecting to a SQL Server CE database.
  - A network connection to the server must exist.
  - One server can host multiple SQL Servers.
  - One SQL Server can contain many databases.
  - SQL Server provides for detailed user access security.
- The syntax is more complete in SQL Server than in SQL Server CE.
  - Views, triggers, functions, and stored procedures are supported.
  - `GRANT`, `REVOKE`, and `DENY` statements are supported, along with system stored procedures for maintaining user access rights.
  - The ANSI standard `INFORMATION_SCHEMA` views are supported.
- Data integrity is more rigorous in SQL Server than in SQL Server CE.
  - Triggers and stored procedures provide for additional server-side data checking that cannot be overridden by the application.
  - User access permissions can be granted at the table and stored procedure levels.
- Stored procedures are supported in SQL Server, but not in SQL Server CE.
  - Parameterized application functionality can be defined on the server and invoked from the client.
  - The `SQLCommand` class contains built-in support for stored procedures.

- Some `System.Data.SqlServerCe` classes, properties, methods, and events are not available in `System.Data.SqlClient`.
  - No `Engine` class exists. Instead, databases must be created by submitting DDL statements.
  - The data reader's `Seek` method is not supported.
- The relationship between a connection and a data reader is different.
  - SQL Server allows multiple open connections but only one open reader per open connection.
  - SQL Server CE allows only one open connection but multiple open readers per open connection.
- Concurrency is handled differently.
  - SQL Server provides concurrency protection.
  - SQL Server CE does not provide concurrency protection.
- More things can go wrong in SQL Server.
  - The need for a remote connection, the granularity of user access security, and the server-side data integrity capabilities all increase the possibility that your application's request can fail and an exception will be raised. (This is a client-side judgment. From SQL Server's point of view, access security and data integrity constraints don't cause things to go wrong, they prevent things from going wrong.)

Despite the major differences between the two products, accessing each from your application is remarkably similar. We hope this emerges from the upcoming discussion of the subject.

We begin with connecting to the database. We use the same sample applications we used when discussing SQL Server CE programming in the previous section of this chapter; we merely change them to access SQL Server's Northwind database, the sample database that is created whenever SQL Server is installed.

Once we have set an assembly reference to the `System.Data.SqlClient.dll` module and optionally added the matching `using` statement shown here, we are ready to create a connection object and open a connection to a SQL Server database.

```
using System.Data.SqlClient;
```

Connecting to SQL Server

We use essentially the same connection class to connect to a SQL Server database as we used to connect to a SQL Server CE database, although the connection classes reside in different namespaces and have slightly different names. (In SQL Server CE, we connect using the `SqlCeConnection`[4] class, whereas with SQL Server we use the `SqlConnection`[5] class.) But both classes adhere to the same Microsoft specification for provider-specific classes, so the PMEs are the same.

The code shown in Listing 12.11 is the code for the `DataReader` application that we originally wrote for SQL Server CE and have now modified for SQL Server. We introduced the `DataReader` application in Figure 12.12 and Listing 12.6 earlier in this chapter. For convenience, in Figure 12.15 we again show the main screen of the `DataReader` program.

As shown in Listing 12.11, we modified the original code to access SQL Server. We did so by changing the statement in which the connection string is defined, by changing `SqlCe` to `Sql`, and by setting a reference to the SQL Server client namespace rather than to the SQL Server CE client namespace.

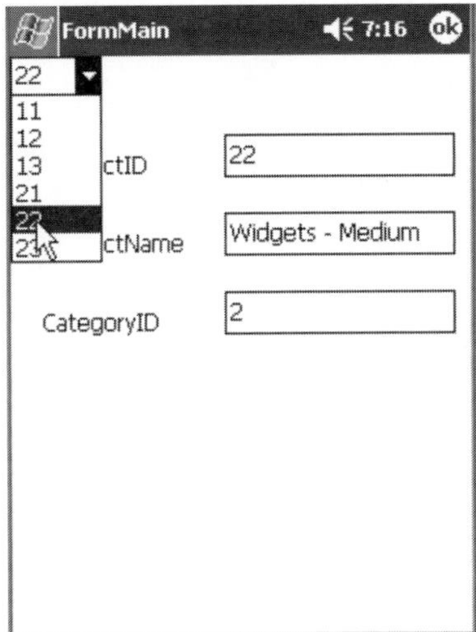

FIGURE 12.15: The `DataReader` program (repeated)

4. Fully qualified name: `System.Data.SqlServerCe.SqlCeConnection`.
5. Fully qualified name: `System.Data.SqlClient.SqlConnection`.

Because the `Seek` method is not supported by the `SqlDataReader` class, we use the version of the `LoadOneProduct` method that we showed earlier in Listing 12.7.

LISTING 12.11: Using a `DataReader` Object with SQL Server

```
using System;
using System.Windows.Forms;
using System.Data;
using System.Data.SqlClient;

namespace DataReader
{
   /// <summary>
   /// Summary description for FormMain
   /// </summary>
   public class FormMain : System.Windows.Forms.Form
   {
      #region Assorted Generated Code

      #region Windows Form Designer generated code


      //  Connection string
      private string  strConn =
         "data source=OurServer;" +
         "initial catalog=Northwind;" +
         "user id=DeliveryDriver;" +
         "pwd=DD;" +
         "workstation id=OurDevice;" +
         "packet size=4096;" +
         "persist security info=False;";

      //  Select product keys.
      private string strGetProductIDs =
         " SELECT ProductID FROM Products ";

      //  Select one product, joined with its category.
      private string strGetOneProduct =
         " SELECT ProductID, ProductName, CategoryName " +
         "   FROM Products P " +
         "   JOIN Categories C on C.CategoryID = P.CategoryID " +
         "  WHERE P.ProductID = ";

      //  Used to bypass the SelectIndexChanged event
      //     during the loading of the ComboBox
      private bool boolLoading = true;
```

```
private void FormMain_Load(object sender, EventArgs e)
{
   //  Display a close box.
   this.MinimizeBox = false;

   //  Let the form present itself.
   Application.DoEvents();

   //  Load product keys into the ComboBox
   //     and select the first one.
   LoadProductIDs();
   comboKeys.SelectedIndex = 0;
}


private void comboKeys_SelectedIndexChanged(object sender,
                                            EventArgs e)
{
   //  A product key has been selected; retrieve
   //     and display the corresponding product.
   if (! boolLoading )
   {
      LoadOneProduct((int)comboKeys.SelectedItem);
   }
}


private void textProductName_Validated(object sender,
                                       EventArgs e)
{
   //  Update this product row in the database.
   UpdateSelectedRow(int.Parse(textProductID.Text),
                     textProductName.Text);
}


private void LoadProductIDs()
{
   //  Clear the ComboBox.
   comboKeys.Items.Clear();

   //  A connection, a command, and a reader
   SqlConnection connDB =
      new SqlConnection(strConn);
   SqlCommand cmndDB =
      new SqlCommand(strGetProductIDs, connDB);
   SqlDataReader drdrDB;

   try
   {
```

continues

continued

```
        //  Open the connection.
        connDB.Open();

        //  Submit the SQL statement and receive
        //      the SqlReader for the results set.
        drdrDB = cmndDB.ExecuteReader();

        //  Read each row.  Add the contents of its
        //      only column as an entry in the ComboBox.
        while ( drdrDB.Read() )
        {
           comboKeys.Items.Add(drdrDB["ProductID"]);
        }

        //  Close the reader.
        drdrDB.Close();
     }
     catch( SqlException exSQL )
     {
        foreach( SqlError errSQL in exSQL.Errors )
        {
           MessageBox.Show(errSQL.Message);
        }
     }
     finally
     {
        //  Close the connection.
        connDB.Close();

        //  Start responding to the ComboBox's
        //      SelectedIndexChanged events.
        this.boolLoading = false;
     }
  }


  private void LoadOneProduct( int intProductID )
  {
     //  Append the param ProductID to the SELECT statement.
     string  strSQL = strGetOneProduct + intProductID;

     //  A connection, a command, and a reader
     SqlConnection  connDB = new SqlConnection(strConn);
     SqlCommand  cmndDB = new SqlCommand(strSQL,connDB);
     SqlDataReader drdrDB;

     //  Open the connection.
     connDB.Open();
```

```
    //  Submit the SQL statement and receive
    //      the SqlReader for the one-row
    //      results set.
    drdrDB = cmndDB.ExecuteReader();

    //  Read the first (only) row.
    //      Display it.  Close the reader.
    if ( drdrDB.Read() )
    {
       LoadControlsFromRow(drdrDB);
    }
    drdrDB.Close();

    //  Close the connection.
    connDB.Close();
}


private void LoadControlsFromRow( SqlDataReader drdrDB )
{
    //  Transfer the column titles and the field
    //      contents of the current row from the
    //      reader to the form's controls.
    lblProductID.Text = drdrDB.GetName(0);
    textProductID.Text = drdrDB.GetValue(0).ToString();
    lblProductName.Text = drdrDB.GetName(1);
    textProductName.Text = drdrDB.GetValue(1).ToString();
    lblCategoryName.Text = drdrDB.GetName(2);
    textCategoryName.Text = drdrDB.GetValue(2).ToString();
}


private void UpdateSelectedRow(int intProductID,
                               string strProductName)
{
    //  A connection and a command
    SqlConnection connDB = new SqlConnection(strConn);
    SqlCommand cmndDB = new SqlCommand();

    //  Open the connection.
    connDB.Open();

    //  Update the product name for the selected product.
    cmndDB.Connection = connDB;
    cmndDB.CommandText =
       " UPDATE Products " +
       " SET ProductName = " + "'" + strProductName + "'" +
       " WHERE ProductID = " + intProductID;
```

continues

continued

```
            cmndDB.ExecuteNonQuery();

            //  Close the connection.
            connDB.Close();
         }
      }
   }
```

The one statement that we changed to effect the transition from SQL Server CE to SQL Server is shown here in its modified form.

```
//  Connection string
private string  strConn =
   "data source=OurServer;" +
   "initial catalog=Northwind;" +
   "user id=DeliveryDriver;" +
   "pwd=DD;" +
   "workstation id=OurDevice;" +
   "packet size=4096;" +
   "persist security info=False;";
```

As you can see from the connection string, a SQL Server connection is more complex than its SQL Server CE counterpart, which was:

```
private string  strConn = "Data Source=" +
                          @"My Documents\ourProduceCo.sdf";
```

In the new version, we specify the server name, database name, SQL Server user name and password, and some other information. We did not code this ourselves—we got Visual Studio .NET to do it for us, and we recommend that you do the same.

To obtain this assistance, your development environment must be able to connect to your development server. Open a new Windows Application project rather than a Smart Device Application project. In a Windows Application project, the entries under the Toolbox's Data tab are enabled and you can drag and drop them onto the form. Figure 12.16 shows a connection object being dropped on the form.

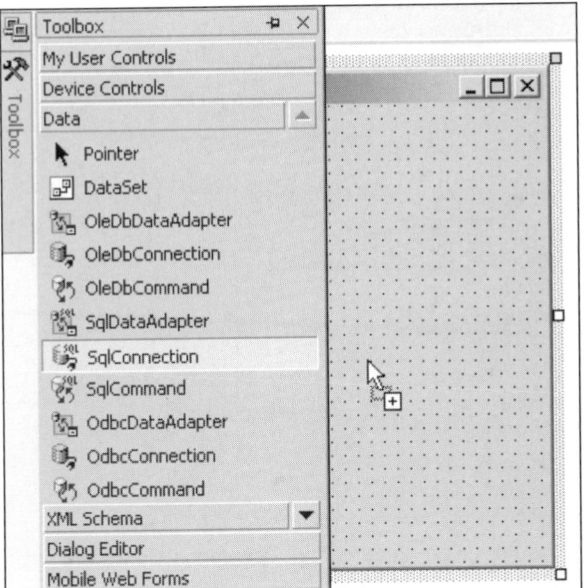

FIGURE 12.16: Dragging and dropping a connection object

When dropped, a connection object does not appear in the form itself but rather in the blank area beneath the form. Once the connection object is there, you can select it and access its properties. One of your choices in the connection string drop-down list is <New Connection…> (see Figure 12.17). Choosing this item produces the dialog box shown in Figure 12.18.

Once you enter your information and dismiss the dialog box, the generated connection string appears in the Properties window. From there, you can cut and paste the connection string into your .NET Compact Framework program.

Creating Command Objects

Once you have the connection object, you can move on to creating a command object. As you can see from the code, there is very little difference between the `SqlCommand` class and the `SqlCeCommand` class. Nor is there much difference between the two data reader classes. The only change that we had to make in the program is caused by the absence of the `Seek` method in the `SqlDataReader` class.

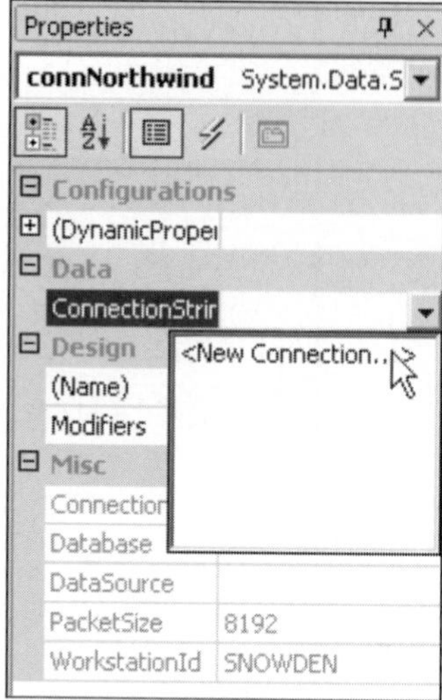

FIGURE 12.17: Requesting a new connection string

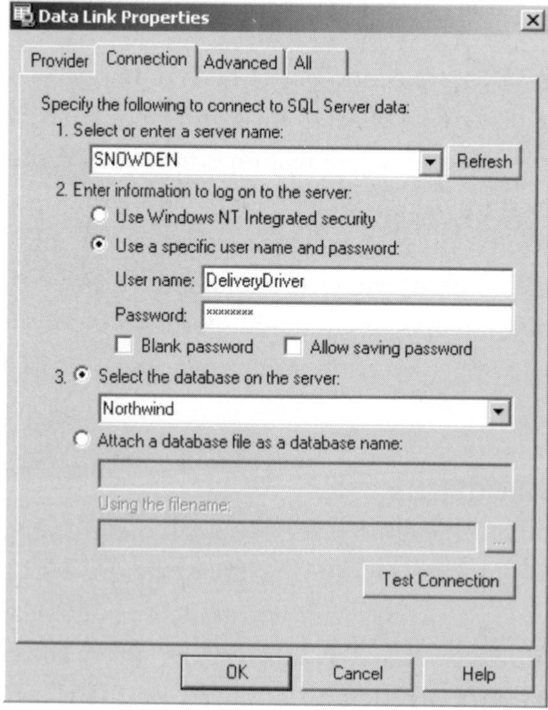

FIGURE 12.18: Specifying connection information

Although there is very little difference between the two command classes, there can be a great difference in how you use them. This is because SQL Server has stored procedures and SQL Server CE does not, and access to the stored procedures is provided only through the `SqlCommand` class.

Using SQL Server Stored Procedures

A stored procedure is a procedure that is written in SQL, stored in a SQL Server database, and executable by a client program. It can have input and output parameters and returns an integer value. A stored procedure can be as simple as a single `SELECT` statement or as complex as a multitable update with parameter checking and error handling. Stored procedures encapsulate functionality on the server side.

One benefit of stored procedures is that they execute much faster than the same logic would in a submitted batch of SQL statements. With a stored procedure, the database engine performs query analysis and optimization and caches the compiled query optimization plan when the stored procedure is first created. On subsequent executions of the stored procedure, the database engine can bypass the analysis, optimization, and compilation. To execute a submitted batch of SQL statements, on the other hand, the entire process must be performed each time a batch is submitted.

Listing 12.12 shows a stored procedure that updates name and price information for a specified product. We use this stored procedure, named `procModifyProductInfo`, during this discussion. It is not the most efficient code ever written, but it is straightforward and readable, and it adheres to the SQL Server convention that successfully executed procedures should return `0`.

LISTING 12.12: The `procModifyProductInfo` Stored Procedure

```
CREATE PROCEDURE procModifyProductInfo
   @ProductID int = null,
   @ProductName nvarchar(40) = null,
   @UnitPrice money = null
AS
BEGIN
   IF @ProductID is null
   BEGIN
```

continues

continued

```
        RAISERROR('Product ID not supplied.',10,1)
        RETURN 1
    END

    IF not exists (SELECT *
                   FROM Products
                  WHERE ProductID = @ProductID)
    BEGIN
        RAISERROR('Product ID not on file.',10,1)
        RETURN 1
    END

    BEGIN TRANSACTION

    IF @ProductName is not null
        UPDATE Products
            SET ProductName = @ProductName
            WHERE ProductID = @ProductID
    IF @@ERROR <> 0
    BEGIN
        ROLLBACK TRANSACTION
        RAISERROR('Unable to update Products table.',10,1)
        RETURN 1
    END

    IF @UnitPrice is not null
        UPDATE Products
            SET UnitPrice = @UnitPrice
            WHERE ProductID = @ProductID
    IF @@ERROR <> 0
    BEGIN
        ROLLBACK TRANSACTION
        RAISERROR('Unable to update Products table.',10,1)
        RETURN 1
    END

    COMMIT TRANSACTION
    RETURN 0
END
```

Client programs execute the stored procedure by submitting the following SQL statement, for example, to the SQL Server. The sample statement shown here changes the name and price of product 18 to "Carnavon Tigers" and $987.65, respectively.

```
EXEC procModifyProductInfo 18, 'Carnavon Tigers', 987.65
```

To submit this SQL statement to the server, your application could set the statement into the `CommandText` property of a command object and then call the `ExecuteNoResults` method. But there is a better way, one that makes it easier to repetitively reexecute the same procedure with new parameter values each time and to access the return value. In your application, perform the following steps.

1. Create the connection and command objects.
2. Set the command object's `CommandType` property to `CommandType.StoredProcedure`.
3. Set the command object's `CommandText` property to the name of the stored procedure.
4. To the command object's `Parameters` collection, add parameter objects for each parameter and for the return value.
5. Set the input value for each parameter.
6. Use the appropriate `Execute` method to cause the execution of the procedure at the server.
7. Repeat steps 5 and 6 for each execution of the store procedure.

Step 4 is the most difficult of these steps. Once again, if your development environment can connect to a development SQL Server, Visual Studio .NET can generate the code for you, with some help from you in the form of a few drag-and-drop operations, as follows.

Once you have created a stored procedure on the development server, open a Windows Application project in Visual Studio .NET and navigate the Server Explorer window to your development SQL Server. Expand the server until you have reached the stored procedure; then drag and drop the stored procedure onto the form, as shown in Figure 12.19.

The resulting command object is added below the form, where you can select it and view its properties. When viewing the properties, you may note that the command object has a `Parameters` collection that displays itself graphically as shown in Figure 12.20.

Getting back to our example, we do not want the graphical representation of the command; instead, we want the underlying code. So we set a

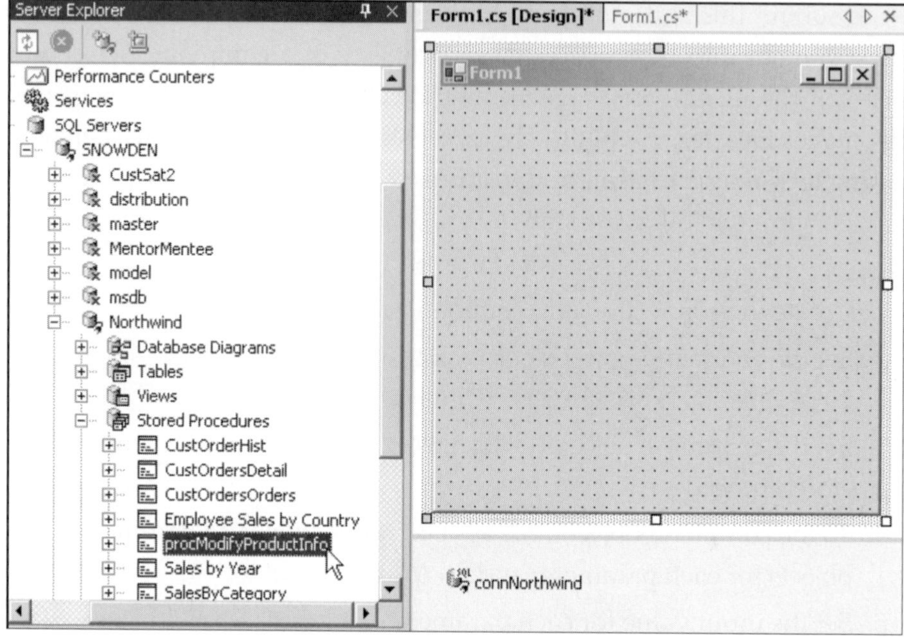

FIGURE 12.19: Adding a stored procedure command to a project

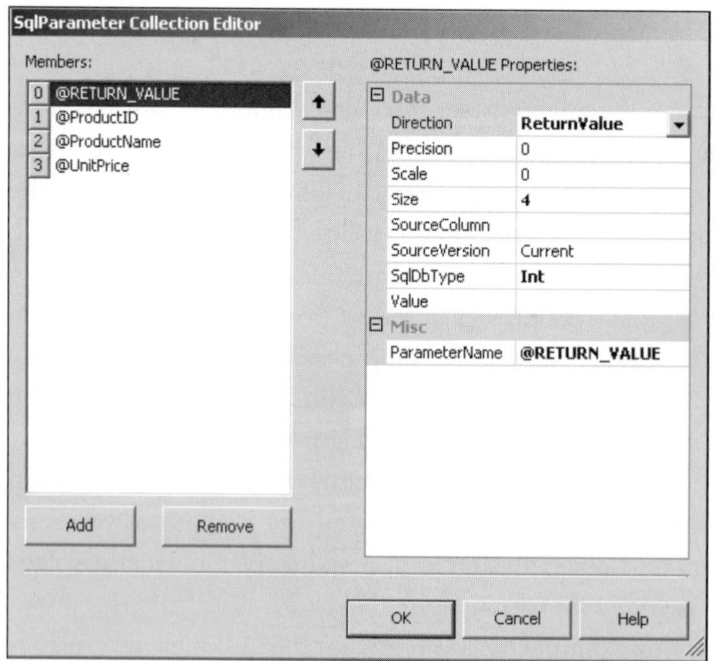

FIGURE 12.20: Graphic representation of a `Parameters` collection

few final properties for the command object in the Properties window, such as the name (in this case cmndDB) and the connection, and then switch to Code View and expand the Windows Form Designer generated code region. As we proceed through the code, we come upon the generated code for our command, shown in Listing 12.13.

LISTING 12.13: Designer-Generated Code to Create a Command Object

```
SqlCommand cmndDB = new SqlCommand();
        :
        :
//
// cmndDB
//
this.cmndDB.CommandText = "ModifyProductInfo";
this.cmndDB.CommandType = CommandType.StoredProcedure;
this.cmndDB.Connection = this.connNorthwind;
this.cmndDB.Parameters.Add(
   new SqlClient.SqlParameter(
      "@RETURN_VALUE", SqlDbType.Int, 4,
      ParameterDirection.ReturnValue, false,
      ((System.Byte)(0)), ((System.Byte)(0)),
      "", DataRowVersion.Current, null));
this.cmndDB.Parameters.Add(
   new SqlClient.SqlParameter(
      "@ProductID", SqlDbType.Int, 4));
this.cmndDB.Parameters.Add(
   new SqlClient.SqlParameter(
      "@ProductName", SqlDbType.NVarChar, 40));
this.cmndDB.Parameters.Add(
   new SqlClient.SqlParameter(
      "@UnitPrice", SqlDbType.Money, 4));
```

This is exactly what we want and exactly what we did not want to write. So we cut and paste this code to move it from the Windows Application project into our Smart Device Application project, pasting it into the UpdateSelectedRow routine. We remove some of the code that was in the previous version of our application, change all occurrences of SqlCe to Sql, and add code to move values from the controls into the parameters and to execute the command. Along the way we remove a few superfluous references to this and add some minimal error handling. Listing 12.14 shows the resulting code.

LISTING 12.14: Stored Procedure Version of the `UpdateSelectedRow` Routine

```
private void UpdateSelectedRow(int intProductID,
                               string strProductName)
{
   //  A connection and a command
   SqlConnection connDB = new SqlConnection(strConn);
   SqlCommand cmndDB = new SqlCommand();

   try
   {
      //  Open the connection.
      connDB.Open();

      //  Initialize the command (including
      //    creating the parameters).
      cmndDB.CommandText = "procModifyProductInfo";
      cmndDB.CommandType = CommandType.StoredProcedure;
      cmndDB.Connection = connDB;
      cmndDB.Parameters.Add(
         new SqlParameter(
         "@RETURN_VALUE", SqlDbType.Int, 4,
         ParameterDirection.ReturnValue, false,
         ((System.Byte)(0)), ((System.Byte)(0)),
         "", DataRowVersion.Current, null));
      cmndDB.Parameters.Add(
         new SqlParameter(
         "@ProductID", SqlDbType.Int, 4));
      cmndDB.Parameters.Add(
         new SqlParameter(
         "@ProductName", SqlDbType.NVarChar, 40));
      cmndDB.Parameters.Add(
         new SqlParameter(
         "@UnitPrice", SqlDbType.Money, 4));

      //  Assign values to the parameters.
      cmndDB.Parameters["@ProductID"].Value =
         int.Parse(comboKeys.SelectedItem.ToString());
      cmndDB.Parameters["@ProductName"].Value =
         textProductName.Text;
      cmndDB.Parameters["@UnitPrice"].Value = 123.45;

      //  Execute the stored procedure.
      cmndDB.ExecuteNonQuery();

      //  Check the SQL Server return value.
      if((int)cmndDB.Parameters["@RETURN_VALUE"].Value != 0)
      {
         MessageBox.Show(
```

```
            "You should have already caught a SqlException."
            );
      }
   }

   catch( SqlException exSQL )
   {
      foreach( SqlError errSQL in exSQL.Errors )
      {
         MessageBox.Show(errSQL.Message);
      }
   }

   finally
   {
      //  Close the connection.
      connDB.Close();
   }
}
```

We placed all the code in one routine to make it more readable. In reality, we would move any code that needed to be executed only once, such as initializing the command and creating the parameters, into a separate routine. What would remain is the code that had to be executed every time, such as assigning values to the parameters, executing the procedure, and examining the return value.

Using Stored Procedures with `DataSet` Objects

Stored procedures can be specified in the `CommandText` property of the command objects that reside within a data adapter, that is, the `SELECT`, `INSERT`, `UPDATE`, and `DELETE` commands. The command builder object, used earlier in this chapter to generate commands for the data adapter, does not generate commands that use stored procedures. If you want the adapter to use stored procedures, you must create the commands yourself.

The purpose of the data adapter is to move data between the database and the data set, and stored procedures are an excellent way to retrieve and update data (sometimes the only way, as when the updating requirements are very complex or access to the database is channeled through stored procedures for security reasons). Thus it is beneficial to know how to use command objects based on stored procedures with the data adapter.

Using a stored procedure in a `SELECT` command is quite simple; any command object based on a stored procedure that consists of a single `SELECT` statement can be used as the data adapter's `SelectCommand` property. As long as you have permission to execute the procedure and set the parameter values before calling the adapter's `Fill` method, the procedure can be used to select the rows that are then loaded into the receiving data table.

Using a command object based on a stored procedure for the adapter's `INSERT`, `UPDATE`, and `DELETE` commands requires an additional piece of information and an extra step. The extra information is required during the creation of each parameter because the value of each parameter must now come from a field in the data table whose data is being updated to the server. Because the data adapter updates one row at a time, the values from each row are loaded into the parameters, the procedure is executed, and then the process continues with the next row. You must specify which column goes with which parameter.

The extra step comes from the fact that the values assigned to the parameters come from the "new" version of the row, which is what you would expect and want. But the parameter(s) that comprise the primary key of the row, which are the values to be used to specify the database row(s) to be updated, must come from the "old" version of the rows. Because primary key values should not be modified, this is, hopefully, a moot point. However, you need to specify it just in case.

For example, earlier in this chapter we added a form to our `DataReader` sample program that allows a user to change data in bound controls. The changes in the bound control data are automatically propagated to the underlying data table. We discussed the added code necessary for the data adapter to propagate the changes from the data table back to the database. This form was shown earlier in Figure 12.14; for convenience, we repeat it here in Figure 12.21.

Now we create a very simple stored procedure, shown in Listing 12.15, that modifies the category name for a given category ID.

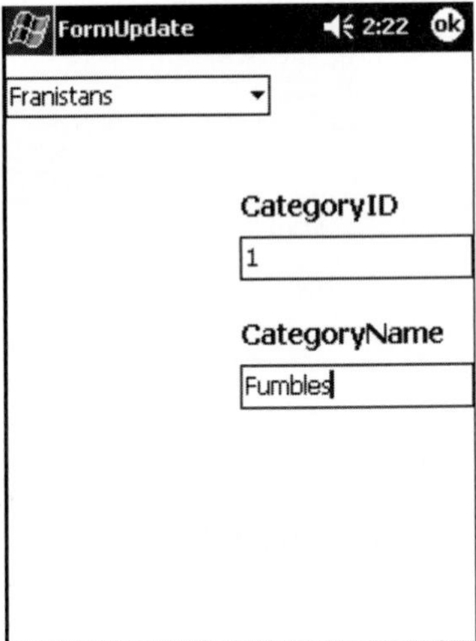

FIGURE 12.21: The category modification form (repeated)

LISTING 12.15: The Stored Procedure for Category Modification

```
CREATE PROCEDURE procModifyCategoryInfo
   @CategoryID int = null,
   @CategoryName nvarchar(40) = null
AS
BEGIN
   IF @CategoryID is null
   BEGIN
      RAISERROR('Category ID not supplied.',10,1)
      RETURN 1
   END

   IF not exists (SELECT *
                   FROM Categories
                  WHERE CategoryID = @CategoryID)
   BEGIN
      RAISERROR('Category ID not on file.',10,1)
      RETURN 1
   END

   BEGIN TRANSACTION

   IF @CategoryName is not null
      UPDATE Categories
         SET CategoryName = @CategoryName
```

continues

continued

```
        WHERE CategoryID = @CategoryID
   IF @@ERROR <> 0
   BEGIN
      ROLLBACK TRANSACTION
      RAISERROR('Unable to update Categories table.',10,1)
      RETURN 1
   END

   COMMIT TRANSACTION
   RETURN 0
END
```

This procedure requires two parameters: the category ID of the category to be updated and the new name to be given to that category. Both of these values must come from the rows of the data table.

The code that builds the `UpdateCommand` object for use by the data adapter is shown in Listing 12.16. This code must execute before the `Update` method executes; it can execute either before or after the `Fill` method executes.

LISTING 12.16: Building a Command Object That Uses a Stored Procedure

```
//  Initialize the command (including
//     creating the parameters).
SqlCommand cmndDB = new SqlCommand();
cmndDB.CommandText = "procModifyCategoryInfo";
cmndDB.CommandType = CommandType.StoredProcedure;
cmndDB.Connection =
   daptCategories.SelectCommand.Connection;

cmndDB.Parameters.Add(
   new SqlParameter(
   "@RETURN_VALUE", SqlDbType.Int, 4,
   ParameterDirection.ReturnValue, false,
   ((System.Byte)(0)), ((System.Byte)(0)),
   "", DataRowVersion.Current, null));

cmndDB.Parameters.Add(
   new SqlParameter(
   "@CategoryID", SqlDbType.Int, 4, "CategoryID"));

cmndDB.Parameters.Add(
   new SqlParameter(
   "@CategoryName", SqlDbType.NVarChar, 40, "CategoryName"));

cmndDB.Parameters["@CategoryID"].SourceVersion =
   DataRowVersion.Original;
```

In the next-to-last statement in this code, the fourth parameter specifies the column of the data table with the value for the `"@CategoryName"` command object parameter.

The last statement in Listing 12.16 specifies that the primary key value should be the value that was loaded into the data table from the database, not any new value that is now in the data table.

We have discussed the remaining code before; most of it was generated in a Windows Application project with a drag-and-drop operation.

Using stored procedures in a command object provides you a number of benefits. First, it frees you from the details of the SQL code (especially if someone else writes the stored procedure for you). Second, it provides for a more efficient execution of code on the server side. A third benefit, which we demonstrate in this chapter, is that the presence of a stored procedure makes it easy to set up repetitive execution of the same command while varying the parameters with each execution.

As each stored procedure executes, your program receives the stored procedure's return value, which your program can use to decide whether the procedure executed successfully or not. Procedure-based command objects are helpful whether they are being used by a data adapter to move data between the database and ADO.NET objects or by your application to operate directly on a database without the involvement of ADO.NET classes.

`DataSet` Objects and Concurrency

Unlike SQL Server CE, SQL Server provides *concurrency protection*; that is, if data within a row of a data table is modified on the server (probably by some other user) after the `Fill` method has executed and before the `Update` method executes, the update of that row fails. After the `Update` method has completed, your application can determine which rows did not successfully update and retrieve their new values from the database. There is no automatic response for this situation. Your application must decide whether to resubmit its values, submit revised values, notify the user, forget it, and so on.

SQL Server Books Online contains information on *optimistic concurrency*, which is the concurrency model used by the data adapter. The Visual Studio

.NET Combined Help Collection contains information about the `SqlDataAdapter.Update` method, including the sequence in which rows are updated and the result of a concurrency collision. There is no need for us to repeat here what is well covered in the SQL Server documentation, but you do need to be aware that SQL Server rejects updates because of overlapping modification of the data. This is different from the simpler model used by the SQL Server CE database engine, where the last updater wins.

> Programming with ADO.NET for Microsoft SQL Server is similar to programming for Microsoft SQL Server CE. The namespaces are different and the class names are different, but their PMEs are mostly the same. The major differences are caused by the different capabilities of the two engines, not by the classes themselves. Connectivity, security, stored procedures, advanced data integrity, concurrency, and differences in schema definition combine to make programming for SQL Server different from programming for SQL Server CE.

Web Services

Every day millions of people around the world access Web pages in search of information. Many of these pages contain executable code that gathers the information, formats it into text-based HTML, and returns it to the browser. And for almost as long as people have been doing this, application developers have been asking, "If I can do this, why can't my application do it, and do it in an object-oriented way?" That is, "Why can't my application post a request for information to a Web page and receive the response from that page by creating objects and invoking their methods and then, like HTML, send and receive the request/response by using a text-based format so that the process can be platform-independent?"

Out of the desire for platform-independent, standards-based, Web-based exchange of data came Web Services. Out of the desire for an object-oriented invoking of these Web Services came the Visual Studio .NET development tools we are about to discuss.

XML, XSD, and SOAP

The World Wide Web Consortium publishes a format standard for text-based data exchange. This standard specifies both a format for exchanging data (XML) and a format for specifying the schema of that data (XSD). Web Services use these formats to send and receive data. Figure 12.22 shows an XML document containing catalog and product information. Figure 12.23 shows the schema (which is itself XML) for the XML document shown in Figure 12.22.

For the sender and the receiver to be able to transmit the data not just as XML but in an object-oriented fashion (i.e., sending the data as input parameters, output parameters, and return values of class methods), some additional information must be added into each XML transmission. This additional information is formatted in SOAP.

Microsoft defines a Web Service as "A URL addressable set of functionality that is exposed over a network to serve as a building block for creating distributed applications."[6] That is, a Web Service is a Web site, and at that

FIGURE 12.22: An XML document

6. Microsoft Official Curriculum Course #2524, *Developing XML Web Services Using Microsoft ASP.NET.*

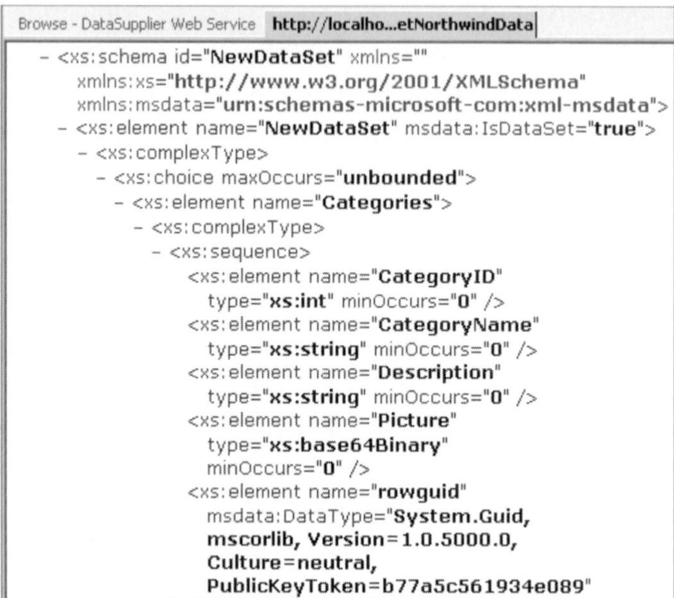

FIGURE 12.23: The XSD schema for the document in Figure 12.22

Web site are `.asmx` pages containing class definitions of objects that can be instantiated and accessed via the Internet. From the perspective of a .NET Compact Framework client, the client instantiates objects of those classes and then sets properties and invokes methods. Visual Studio .NET generates the code that substitutes the transmissions of the SOAP messages between the client and the Web site for the method calls you write. As the application developer, you code instantiations of objects and invocations of methods; as an executing assembly, your application posts XML to a URL.

To illustrate the relationship between what you code and what is transmitted, let's write a Web Service application. Our intent in this book is not to make you a Web Services developer, but we are going to develop a simple Web Service here to illustrate some basic concepts. Understanding the basic development of a Web Service will help you write your client applications. Our Web application will consist of two Web Services, `Primes` and `DataSupplier`. The first supplies prime numbers, the second supplies data sets. `Primes` is typical of services that do a large amount of processing to generate a small amount of data. `DataSupplier` is just the opposite, generating a large amount of data from a small amount of processing.

A Web Service Application

To create a Web Service, we start a new project in the IDE and choose ASP.NET Web Service, as shown in Figure 12.24.

Creating the project creates a Web site. This site is created at the location we specified in the New Project dialog box. It cannot reside on a device, nor can the project be a Smart Device Application project. A Web Service cannot run on a mobile device because, currently, the lack of a fixed IP address for a device and the processing power and regular availability required by a Web Service preclude this. The clients of Web Services run on mobile devices.

The project is created with one Web Service page already in place, `WebForm1.asmx`. Each `.asmx` page, referred to as a *service*, can have one or more classes defined within it, and one application can have as many pages as it needs. When we open the generated sample code from `WebForm1`, shown in

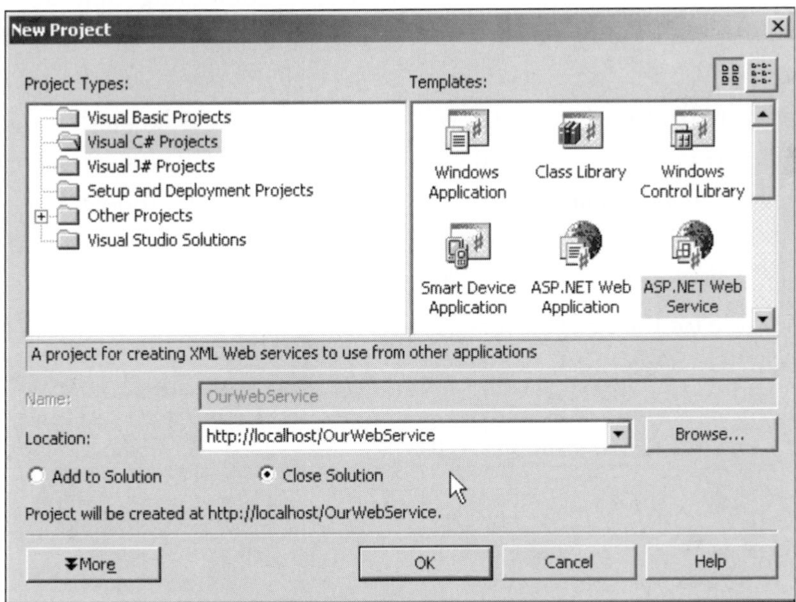

FIGURE 12.24: Creating a new Web Service

Listing 12.17, we see a single class with just one method defined but commented out.

Listing 12.17: A Web Method

```
      // WEB SERVICE EXAMPLE
      // The HelloWorld() example service
      //    returns the string Hello World
      // Uncomment the following lines then
      //    save and build the project
      // To test this Web Service, press F5

//      [WebMethod]
//     public string HelloWorld()
//     {
//         return "Hello World";
//     }
```

This method is made visible to clients by adding the `WebMethod` attribute. Simply making a method public is not enough to make it accessible to the client. Any method that does not have the `WebMethod` attribute can be invoked from within the class or assembly but not from a client.

For our first service, `Primes`, we choose something that dovetails nicely with the inherent strengths and avoids one of the common weaknesses of a Web Service. Specifically, the service involves complex processing and a small amount of data exchange. The service is located in a `.asmx` page named `Primes.asmx` that we add to the project. The `Primes` service implements just one class, `Primes`, which has just one method, `GetFloorPrime`, which returns the largest prime number less than or equal to a given number.

The code for the `Primes` service, that is, all the code on the `.asmx` page, is shown in Listing 12.18.

Listing 12.18: The `Primes` Web Service Class

```
using System;
using System.Collections;
using System.ComponentModel;
using System.Data;
using System.Diagnostics;
using System.Web;
```

```
using System.Web.Services;

namespace WSService
{
   /// <summary>
   /// Summary description for Primes
   /// </summary>
   public class Primes : System.Web.Services.WebService
   {
      public Primes()
      {
         //CODEGEN: This call is required
         //   by the ASP.NET Web Services
      InitializeComponent();
      }

      #region Component Designer generated code

      [WebMethod] public int GetFloorPrime( int Target )
      {
         if( Target <= 1 )
         {
            return 1;
         }
         if( Target == 2 )
         {
            return 2;
         }
         int k = Target - (Target % 2 == 0 ? 1 : 0);
         for( int j=k; j>=1; j-=2 )
         {
            if( IsPrime(j) )
            {
               return j;
            }
         }
         return 1;
      }

      private bool IsPrime( int Candidate)
      {
         for( int j=3; j<=Candidate - 1; j+=2 )
         {
            if( Candidate % j == 0 )
            {
               return false;
            }
            if( j * j >= Candidate )
```

continues

continued

```
                {
                    break;
                }
            }
            return true;
        }
    }
}
```

We can test this page the same way we test any Web page that is under development, by right-clicking on the page and selecting View in Browser from the context menu. When we do, the image shown in Figure 12.25 appears in the browser.

It might seem strange that anything shows in the browser. After all, our page has no visible interface; it is just a collection of object classes. But some of the `System.Web.Services` classes, via reflection, generate WSDL, the language for describing the class's interface over the network (see the Web

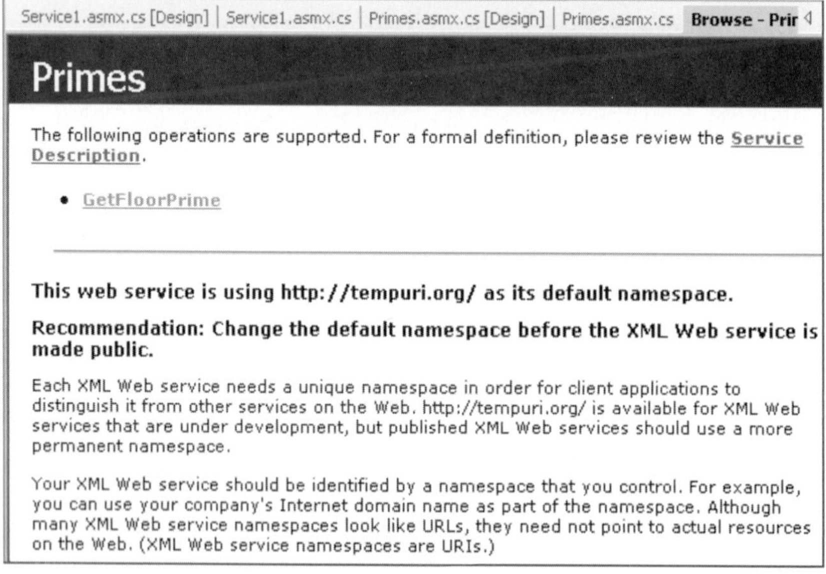

FIGURE 12.25: The `Primes` Web Service page in the browser

Services Description Language sidebar). Thus, the complete signature of the `Primes` class has just been delivered to the browser for display, in what is called the *help page* for the Web Service, as shown in Figure 12.25. The help page was generated by code in the Web Service that itself was generated by Visual Studio .NET. When a Web Service is being authored using Visual Studio .NET, code is generated that returns a help page whenever the `.asmx` page accessed without any query string parameters being provided.

For instance, accessing the following URL causes the help page to be delivered as the response: http://www.OurServer.com/WSService/Primes.asmx. The same URL with the attached query string shown here, http://www.OurServer.com/WSService/Primes.asmx?op=GetFloorPrime, indicates that the `GetFloorPrime` Web method of the service was to be invoked.

Web Services Description Language

The Web Services Description Language (WSDL) is an XML-based language that Web Services use to define the requests they will accept and the responses they will return. From the perspective of a .NET Compact Framework programmer, the most important information in the WSDL is the signatures of the classes. Thus the WSDL received from a Web Service will tell the client the names of the classes and the names and data types of the public properties, methods, parameters, return values, and so on. In other words, the WSDL relays all the information necessary for a client program to create an instance of a class at the Web Service and to invoke the class's methods and properties.

Because the browser now has all the necessary information to generate and send the SOAP messages that represent the method calls, we can test the page's class methods, as shown in Figure 12.26.

The test page also shows the SOAP message that will be sent and received by a method call, in this case `GetFloorPrime`, as shown in Figure 12.27.

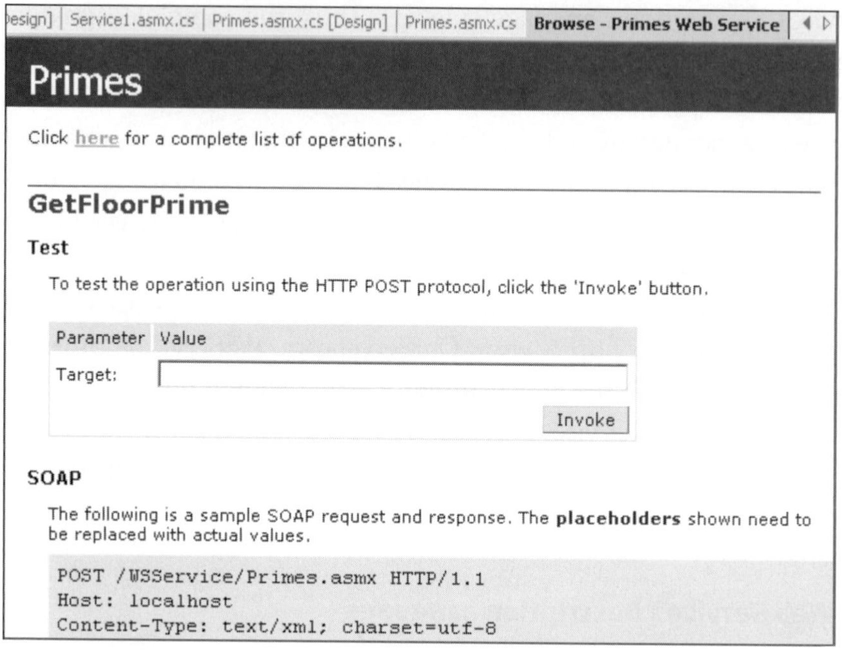

esign] | Service1.asmx.cs | Primes.asmx.cs [Design] | Primes.asmx.cs | **Browse - Primes Web Service**

Primes

Click here for a complete list of operations.

GetFloorPrime

Test

To test the operation using the HTTP POST protocol, click the 'Invoke' button.

Parameter	Value
Target:	
	Invoke

SOAP

The following is a sample SOAP request and response. The **placeholders** shown need to be replaced with actual values.

```
POST /WSService/Primes.asmx HTTP/1.1
Host: localhost
Content-Type: text/xml; charset=utf-8
```

FIGURE 12.26: Testing the Web Service page's `Primes` class in the browser

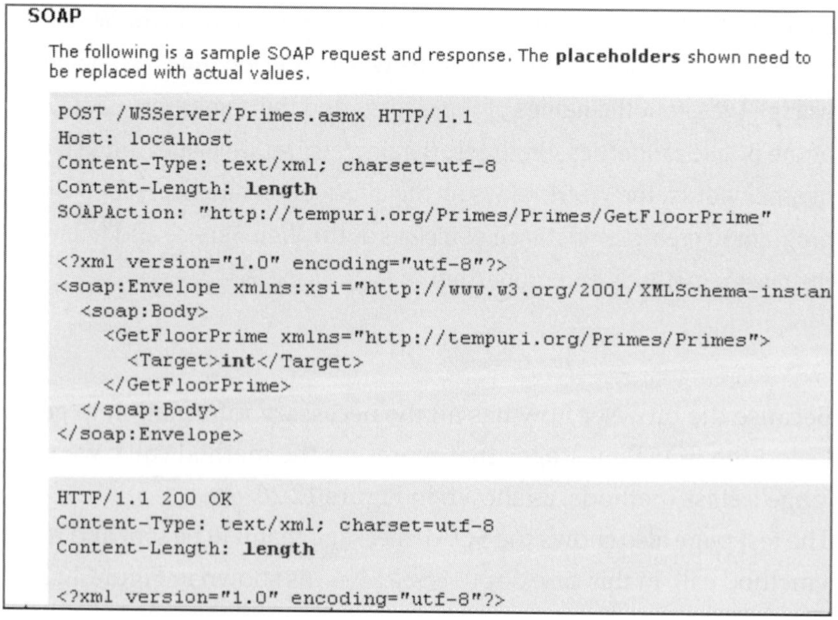

SOAP

The following is a sample SOAP request and response. The **placeholders** shown need to be replaced with actual values.

```
POST /WSServer/Primes.asmx HTTP/1.1
Host: localhost
Content-Type: text/xml; charset=utf-8
Content-Length: length
SOAPAction: "http://tempuri.org/Primes/Primes/GetFloorPrime"

<?xml version="1.0" encoding="utf-8"?>
<soap:Envelope xmlns:xsi="http://www.w3.org/2001/XMLSchema-instan
  <soap:Body>
    <GetFloorPrime xmlns="http://tempuri.org/Primes/Primes">
      <Target>int</Target>
    </GetFloorPrime>
  </soap:Body>
</soap:Envelope>
```

```
HTTP/1.1 200 OK
Content-Type: text/xml; charset=utf-8
Content-Length: length

<?xml version="1.0" encoding="utf-8"?>
```

FIGURE 12.27: The structure of a SOAP message request

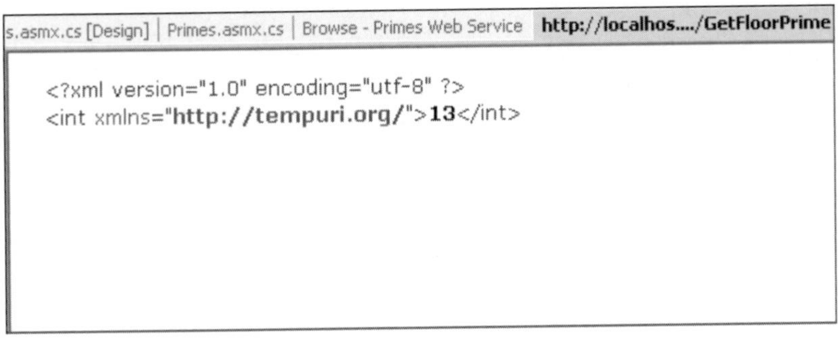

s.asmx.cs [Design] | Primes.asmx.cs | Browse - Primes Web Service | http://localhos..../GetFloorPrime

```
<?xml version="1.0" encoding="utf-8" ?>
<int xmlns="http://tempuri.org/">13</int>
```

FIGURE 12.28: The SOAP message returned by the `GetFloorPrime` method call

We test the `Primes` service by asking for the largest prime less than 16. Figure 12.28 shows us the SOAP message returned by the service. Buried within it is "13," the return value from the `GetFloorPrime` method call.

Next we add another Web Service page, named `DataSupplier`, to our project and code our second service. This one also has just one class and one method. The method does very little processing and returns a data set that was built when the application first started. This is a common practice for Web Services because they often need to bring data into memory, hold it in memory for a period of time, and make it available to clients during that time. The code for this service is shown in Listing 12.19.

LISTING 12.19: The `DataSupplier` Web Service Class

```
using System;
using System.Collections;
using System.ComponentModel;
using System.Data;
using System.Diagnostics;
using System.Web;
using System.Web.Services;

namespace WSService
{
   /// <summary>
   /// Summary description for DataSupplier
   /// </summary>
   public class DataSupplier : System.Web.Services.WebService
   {
      public DataSupplier()
```

continues

continued

```
        {
           //CODEGEN: This call is required
           //         by the ASP.NET Web Services
           InitializeComponent();
        }

        #region Component Designer generated code

        [WebMethod] public DataSet GetNorthwindData()
        {
           return Global.dsetDB;
        }
     }
}
```

The code that creates the data set is in the global area of the Web Service, `Global.asax`. It uses the ADO.NET classes we have already covered, including `System.Data` and `System.Data.SqlClient`, to create the data set and load the `Categories` and `Products` tables from the Northwind database into the data set. Much of the code was generated by dragging the two tables from the Server Explorer window onto the `Global.asax` designer. Listing 12.20 shows the code for the `.asax` page.

LISTING 12.20: The `Global.asax` Web Service Page

```
using System;
using System.Data;
using System.Data.SqlClient;
using System.Collections;
using System.ComponentModel;
using System.Web;
using System.Web.SessionState;

namespace WSService
{
   /// <summary>
   /// Summary description for Global
   /// </summary>
   public class Global : System.Web.HttpApplication
   {
      /// <summary>
      /// Required designer variable
      /// </summary>
      private System.ComponentModel.IContainer components = null;
```

```
public Global()
{
   InitializeComponent();
}

internal
   System.Data.SqlClient.SqlDataAdapter daptCategories;
internal
   System.Data.SqlClient.SqlCommand SqlSelectCommand1;
internal
   System.Data.SqlClient.SqlConnection connNorthwind;
internal
   System.Data.SqlClient.SqlCommand SqlSelectCommand2;
internal
   System.Data.SqlClient.SqlDataAdapter daptProducts;

public static DataSet dsetDB;

protected void Application_Start(Object sender,
                                 EventArgs e)
{
   dsetDB = new DataSet();
   LoadDataSet(dsetDB);
}

protected void Session_Start(Object sender, EventArgs e)
{

}

protected void Application_BeginRequest(Object sender,
                                        EventArgs e)
{

}

protected void Application_EndRequest(Object sender,
                                      EventArgs e)
{

}

protected void Application_AuthenticateRequest(
                                        Object sender,
                                        EventArgs e)
{

}
```

continues

continued

```
      protected void Application_Error(Object sender,
                                       EventArgs e)
      {

      }

      protected void Session_End(Object sender, EventArgs e)
      {

      }

      protected void Application_End(Object sender, EventArgs e)
      {

      }

      private void LoadDataSet( DataSet dsetDB)
      {
         daptCategories.Fill(dsetDB, "Categories");
         daptProducts.Fill(dsetDB, "Products");
         dsetDB.Relations.Add(
            "FKProdCAt",
            dsetDB.Tables["Categories"].Columns["CategoryID"],
            dsetDB.Tables["Products"].Columns["CategoryID"],
            true);
      }

      #region Web Form Designer generated code
   }
}
```

We test this service by viewing it in the browser just as we did the previous service. This is very easy to do because the `DataSupplier` service's only method requires no parameters. That method returns a data set. More correctly, it returns the SOAP message representation of a data set, which is identical to the XML persistence format that `DataSet.WriteXml` produces.

Figure 12.29 shows the output of our test invocation of the `GetNorthwindData` method. As you can tell from the size of the scroll bar thumb, it is a lot of bytes—far more bytes that SQL Server's own format, which is used by the `SqlClient` classes and by the synchronization classes we encounter in Chapter 13.

```
  <?xml version="1.0" encoding="utf-8" ?>
- <DataSet xmlns="http://tempuri.org/">
  - <xs:schema id="NewDataSet" xmlns=""
      xmlns:xs="http://www.w3.org/2001/XMLSchema"
      xmlns:msdata="urn:schemas-microsoft-com:xml-msdata">
    - <xs:element name="NewDataSet" msdata:IsDataSet="true">
      - <xs:complexType>
        - <xs:choice maxOccurs="unbounded">
          - <xs:element name="Categories">
            - <xs:complexType>
              - <xs:sequence>
                  <xs:element name="CategoryID" type="xs:int"
                    minOccurs="0" />
                  <xs:element name="CategoryName"
                    type="xs:string" minOccurs="0" />
                  <xs:element name="Description" type="xs:string"
                    minOccurs="0" />
                  <xs:element name="Picture"
                    type="xs:base64Binary" minOccurs="0" />
                  <xs:element name="rowguid"
                    msdata:DataType="System.Guid, mscorlib,
                    Version=1.0.5000.0, Culture=neutral,
```


FIGURE 12.29: The SOAP message representation of a data set

Figure 12.29 gives you an insight into the two downsides of XML: it is verbose and not secure. Actually, it is the transport that is not secure. XML is no less secure than HTML, and most of us have allowed our credit card information to be transmitted via that protocol. The key is to use a secure transport protocol, that is, HTTPS (Secure Sockets Layer) instead of HTTP. HTTPS won't solve the verbosity problem, but it will address the security issue.

There are enormous upsides to Web Services. The platform independence they provide, the use of the Internet as the transmission mechanism, the adherence to developing standards, the presence of an independent standards committee, and the ease of client program development all make a strong case for using Web Services, especially if the clients are requesting small amounts of data from within a secure networking environment.

A Web Services Client Application

To illustrate the ease of developing Web Service client programs in Visual Studio .NET, we develop a client application for our two Web Services. The application consists of two forms, one for calling the `Primes` service and one for calling the `DataSupplier` service, as shown in Figures 12.30 and 12.31, respectively.

We open a new Smart Device application, add our two forms, and place the controls on them. We are ready to start writing code.

But writing code works best when we have IntelliSense help, and that means having the class definitions available while we code. The compiler

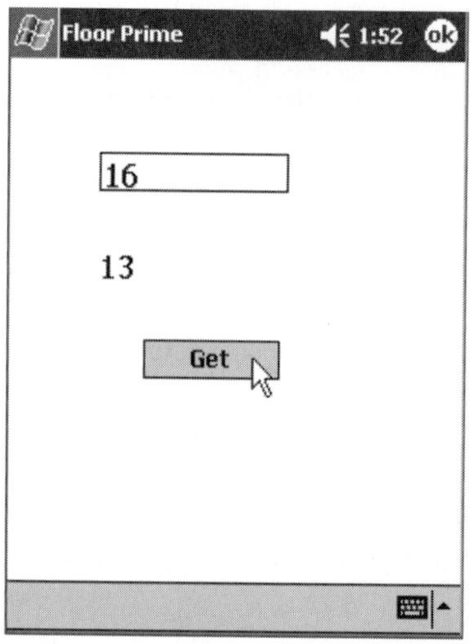

FIGURE 12.30: Using the `Primes` service

FormData 1:53

	Category	Category	Descripti	Picture	ro
▸	1	Beverages	Soft	System.By	40
	2	new	Sweet	System.By	b0
	3	Confectior	Desserts,	System.By	1f
	4	Dairy	Cheeses	System.By	b7
	5	Grains/Cer	Breads,	System.By	38
	6	Meat/Poull	Prepared	System.By	47
	7	Produce	Dried fruit	System.By	1a
	8	Seafood	Seaweed	System.By	21
	9	Beer/Wine	Beer and	(null)	62

FIGURE 12.31: Using the `DataSupplier` service

also needs those definitions because it must perform type checking during compilation. The place to get those class definitions is from the WSDL that the `.asmx` pages emit. Just as the browser took full advantage of the WSDL to provide us with a test environment, Visual Studio .NET uses the WSDL to provide us with a development environment. Throughout this book we have been getting class information by setting references to assemblies. Now we will get our class information by setting our reference to the `.asmx` page. Either way we are setting a reference to an object that provides interface definition information for a class.

In our Solution Explorer window, we right-click on References and select Add Reference from the context menu, receiving the dialog box shown in Figure 12.32.

We enter the URL of our Web Service page, as shown in the figure, and click the Add Reference button, producing a reference entry. We want to

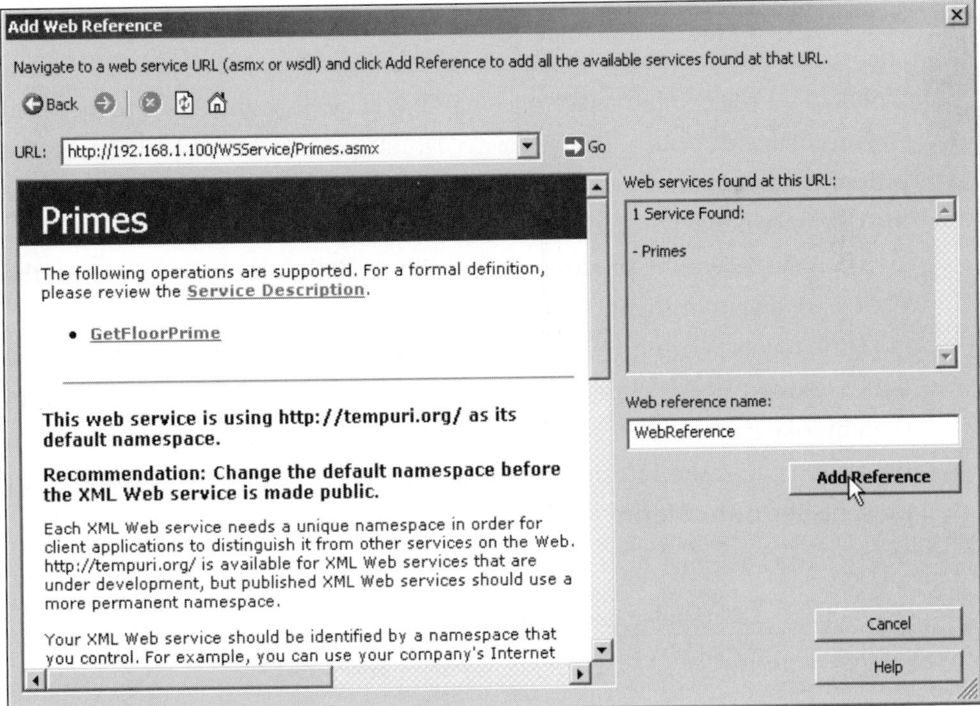

FIGURE 12.32: The Add Web Reference dialog box

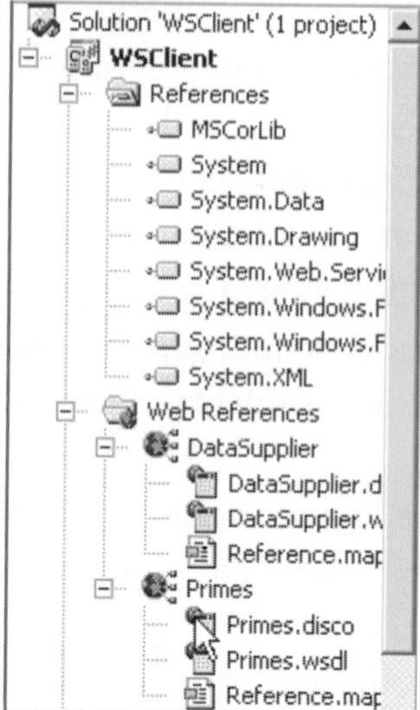

FIGURE 12.33: The renamed reference entry

rename the reference, which is a good practice in general. Think of the reference name as if it were the namespace name of the Web Service class because, when you write code, the reference name will be the namespace name. That is, you create a new `ReferenceName.ClassName` object in order to access the properties and methods of that Web Service class. In our example, we change the reference name to `Primes`, as shown in Figure 12.33.

Then we repeat the process for the other Web Service page located at the `WSServer` site, naming it `DataSupplier`.

This makes writing the code quite simple. For our first form, the one that uses the `Primes` class, we create an instance of the `Primes` object and then invoke its `GetFloorPrime` method. The input value is obtained from the textbox, and the returned value is displayed in the label. Listing 12.21 presents the code; Figure 12.30 shows the results.

LISTING 12.21: Calling the `Primes` Client

```
private void cmdGet_Click(object sender, EventArgs e)
{
   Primes.Primes  refPrimes = new Primes.Primes();
```

```
      lblFloorPrime.Text =
         refPrimes.GetFloorPrime(
            int.Parse(txtTarget.Text)).ToString();
}
```

We have already seen how much SOAP text had to be transmitted to submit the one integer to the service and receive back the one prime.

Our second form creates an instance of the `DataSupplier` class and retrieves the data set by calling its `GetNorthwindData` method. The `Categories` table from the data set is assigned to the data grid's `DataSource` property. The code, shown in Listing 12.22, is even simpler than that for the first form, but the number of bytes transferred between client and server is much greater, as we already know. Figure 12.31 shows the results.

LISTING 12.22: Calling the `DataSupplier` Client

```
private void FormData_Load(object sender, EventArgs e)
{
   DataSupplier.DataSupplier  refDataSupplier =
         new DataSupplier.DataSupplier();
   dgridNorthwind.DataSource =
      refDataSupplier.GetNorthwindData().Tables["Categories"];
}
```

So in this section we have seen the good and the bad of Web Services. If you need to make available functionality that requires small exchanges of data, Web Services are a good candidate. If you are planning to regularly exchange large data sets with a server machine, Web Services are a bad candidate; the SQL Server Merge Replication and Remote Data Access techniques covered in the next chapter might be a better choice.

CONCLUSION

We have now completed our coverage of ADO.NET programming. We started with the memory-resident database that is the data set and its contained objects and continued with a discussion of SQL Server CE databases and SQL Server databases. We moved through the various techniques for retrieving, presenting, and updating the information in those databases, emphasizing both the two-tier and the three-tier approaches. Finally, we looked at Web Services as a way to retrieve data, including entire data sets, from a remote server.

But it is the rare mobile application that lives in a vacuum. More common are applications that depend on data from the outside world—and the outside world is changing rapidly. In the next chapter we examine how to transfer data between your mobile application and SQL Server.

13
Synchronizing Mobile Data[1]

In the last chapter, we covered managing and displaying data on the device using ADO.NET and SQL Server CE. In this chapter, we expand outward to retrieve that data from a desktop SQL Server and to post it back to the desktop after it has been modified on the device.

THREE THINGS MAKE up the core of a typical SQL Server CE application scenario: a Windows CE device, some data to be stored, and a user who is most likely—though not necessarily—mobile. While scaled down from its desktop and server counterpart, SQL Server CE supports a very capable database engine that can easily support a single stand-alone database.

In addition, the SQL Server CE database engine has built-in support for sharing data between a locally stored database and a remote SQL Server 2000 (or later) database. This support, and how you can use it to move data between a SQL Server CE database and a SQL Server 2000 database, is the subject of this chapter.

By itself, SQL Server CE is a single-user database engine. But it can participate in schemes to share a central database with other users through the support of the server-side database engine, SQL Server 2000. For example, a company might equip each member of its sales force with a Windows CE

1. Some material in this chapter first appeared in an article we wrote, "SQL Server CE: New Version Lets You Store and Update Data on Handheld Devices," *MSDN Magazine*, 16(6), June 2001. Available at http://msdn.microsoft.com/msdnmag in the Back Issue Archive. Reprinted with permission of *MSDN Magazine*.

device. When a salesperson is visiting customers, a SQL Server CE database could operate as a stand-alone database engine. When a salesperson comes back to the office (or dials into the central system via modem or remote Internet connection), the device-based database can share updates with the central database while also receiving updates back from the central server. Two elements are central to these types of scenarios: a central data store maintained by a SQL Server database and a transport mechanism for moving the data between the Windows CE device and the SQL Server database.

In this chapter we look at the .NET Compact Framework capabilities for moving, modifying, and synchronizing data between a SQL Server 2000 database on a desktop machine and a SQL Server CE database on a device.

Terminology: SQL Server CE and SQL Server

For the remainder of this chapter, we use "SQL Server CE" to designate SQL Server 2000 Windows CE Edition. Unless otherwise noted, we use "SQL Server" to refer to the versions of SQL Server that run on Windows NT and Windows 2000. (SQL Server 6.5 and SQL Server 7.0 have some limitations when interfacing with devices. These limitations will be mentioned as they are encountered in this chapter.)

Understanding Remote Data Applications

.NET Compact Framework applications that access common data stored in a desktop SQL Server are characterized by the four capabilities, two methods, and one connectivity mechanism that the .NET Compact Framework provides and by an overwhelming desire to avoid errors rather than handle them.

The .NET Compact Framework provides the following four capabilities for synchronizing mobile data with a SQL Server 2000 (or later) database:

1. Retrieve data from a SQL Server database into a SQL Server CE database on a device
2. Add to, remove, or modify that data at the device *and have SQL Server CE track those changes*

3. Have SQL Server CE submit the changed data to the SQL Server and receive any exceptions resulting from failed updates on the server
4. Submit SQL statements directly from the .NET Compact Framework application to a SQL Server database

Activities 1, 2, and 3 are related; activity 4 is independent of the other three. We covered one method that supports activity 4, the ADO.NET provider classes for SQL Server, in Chapter 12; we cover a second method in this chapter.

An application that synchronizes data between SQL Server and SQL Server CE does so by retrieving data from SQL Server, accepting data from the user, having SQL Server CE determine what data needs to be sent back to SQL Server, and having SQL Server CE send that data. Two software components, introduced in this chapter, provide the support for this: the SQL Server CE Client Agent and the SQL Server CE Server Agent. The SQL Server CE Client Agent component running on the device (in conjunction with the SQL Server CE Server Agent and the SQL Server engine running at the server) retrieves data from SQL Server and subsequently determines which user-entered data represents changes to the original and propagates those changes back to SQL Server.

The .NET Compact Framework, when combined with Windows CE and SQL Server, provides two methods for performing this data transfer: (1) Remote Data Access (RDA), which provides all four capabilities listed previously and connects the SQL Server versions 2000, 7.0, and 6.5, and (2) Merge Replication, which does not support method 4, direct submission of SQL statements, and connects only with SQL Server 2000 (or later versions of SQL Server).

Regardless of the method used, the connection between SQL Server CE and the desktop SQL Server is established using Internet-standard protocols. The server side of the connection requires that you configure a Web site and install the SQL Server CE Server Agent component at that Web site. That component sends and receives data via HTTP, translates the data into SQL Server commands, connects to the SQL Server, submits the commands, and returns the results to SQL Server CE on the device.

The device side of the connection can be established using any of several methods, provided that the end result is a TCP/IP connection to the Web site that hosts the connection to the central database. For example, a device could be connected to a desktop system using ActiveSync 3.5, which has built-in support for providing network access to a connected device. With earlier versions of ActiveSync, SQL Server CE provides its own bridging through a component called SQL Server CE Relay. A device can also connect to a server using a dedicated wired or wireless network card. A connection can be accomplished using a modem for servers that are visible through the Internet or a modem with a Virtual Private Network connection for servers that are protected behind a network firewall.

Throughout this book we have talked about handling errors. But in the remote data environment, it is always best to avoid errors rather than handle them. In a sense you cannot handle them because "what SQL Server 2000 says, goes." If SQL Server 2000 rejects your changes, you must undo those changes in the SQL Server CE database or resynchronize with SQL Server 2000 and notify the user. When this happens, you need to make new changes to the data—ones that can be accepted by the server—and resubmit those changes. We address the topic of avoiding synchronization errors later in this chapter, in the Using Good Design to Avoid Synchronization Failures subsection.

RDA and Merge Replication

Two separate mechanisms are provided to move data and schema between SQL Server CE and SQL Server: RDA and Merge Replication. Both are used in conjunction with a Web server based on Microsoft's Web server technology, Internet Information Services (IIS). The complex part of any SQL Server CE application is the transfer of data between SQL Server CE and SQL Server, especially if you have never used replication in your development or developed IIS-based applications.

One of the design benefits of RDA and Merge Replication is that they move both data and schemas. This transfer of data and schemas can be as broad as an entire database or as narrow as a subset of a table. This control of schemas resides on the SQL Server and in most cases eliminates the need for explicit data definition statements in SQL Server CE applications altogether.

The primary benefits of RDA are its smaller footprint on the device and somewhat faster speed due to the reduced functionality and tracking. The key disadvantages of RDA are that it requires more code, both ADO.NET code as well as SQL code; provides little support for handling conflicts; and is not an established database interface, being used only in SQL Server CE.

Merge Replication, on the other hand, can be set up by a database administrator, requires very little code, and allows for the establishment of database update rules, including rules for conflict resolution when synchronizing new data into an existing SQL Server 2000 database. While RDA is supported for all versions of SQL Server, Merge Replication requires SQL Server 2000. Table 13.1 summarizes the data replication support provided for different versions of SQL Server.

IIS Connectivity

The SQL Server CE team chose to use IIS as its primary conduit for several reasons. A very important segment of the user base consists of mobile users, so the connectivity options needed to be as widespread as possible. By building SQL Server CE around HTTP connectivity—wherever users can gain access to an Internet connection to browse the Web—they can also connect to their SQL Server home world. In addition to its widespread availability, an IIS connection also provides authentication and authorization so that a user's data can get through a corporate firewall. And finally, IIS provides the ability to encrypt data when using a certificate (i.e., HTTPS access) so private data can remain private.

When data is transmitted between SQL Server CE and SQL Server, it is automatically compressed for its trip between the CE device and the HTTP

TABLE 13.1: SQL Server Data Replication Support

SQL Server Version	Remote Data Access	Merge Replication
SQL Server 6.5	X	
SQL Server 7.0	X	
SQL Server 2000	X	X

site. In one benchmark, using the Northwind database, the data was compressed to approximately one-eighth of its original size.

While compression is always enabled, encryption is not. However, you can enable encryption of the data being transferred between SQL Server CE and the IIS Server by using the standard encryption capability of IIS. This encryption is entirely transparent to the two database engines.

ActiveSync and SQL Server CE

No discussion of connectivity to a Windows CE device would be complete without some mention of ActiveSync. ActiveSync describes a mechanism for moving data between a Windows workstation and a Windows CE device. For example, ActiveSync is the primary mechanism for moving e-mail messages, appointments, task lists, and contact information between a Windows CE device and a desktop. It's important to be aware that SQL Server CE does *not* use ActiveSync for the transmission of data. But when installing SQL Server CE on a device like a Pocket PC or a Handheld PC, ActiveSync must be present to assist in this operation.

Database Connectivity

While IIS is used for data transmission, SQL Server CE components are used at both ends of the transmission for database connectivity. SQL Server CE has two components used for this: SQL Server CE Client Agent runs on the device, and SQL Server CE Server Agent runs on the desktop. Thus, five components are involved in the transfer of data between SQL Server and SQL Server CE (see Figure 13.1):

- On the device:
  - SQL Server CE
  - SQL Server CE Client Agent
- On the server(s):
  - SQL Server CE Server Agent
  - IIS Server
  - SQL Server

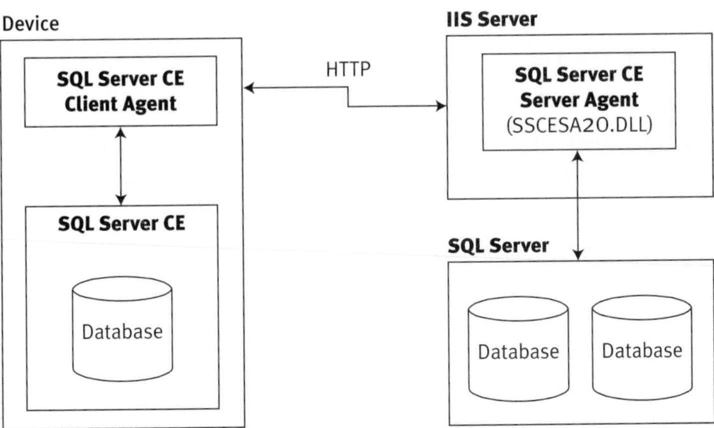

FIGURE 13.1: The five components of remote data connectivity

The three server-side components can be deployed with some amount of flexibility. In particular, IIS and SQL Server 2000 can be deployed either on the same server system or on separate machines. The SQL Server CE Server Agent component, however, must be deployed on the same system with IIS.

The SQL Server CE Client Agent is a device-side component that tracks changes made to data on the device and, when instructed to do so, submits them to the SQL Server CE Server Agent. Note that the track-change support for SQL Server CE is not the same as the track-change support for ADO.NET data sets.

The SQL Server CE Server Agent is a server-side component that receives changes from the client agent and connects to the SQL Server 2000 database on behalf of the device. The Server Agent combines three different roles within one component:

1. As an ISAPI[2] extension DLL to a Web server running Microsoft's IIS
2. As part of a URL (i.e., its name), which provides the means by which the Client Agent and the Server Agent are able to find each other
3. As a SQL Server client program because it connects to and interacts with a SQL Server 2000 database

2. *ISAPI* stands for Internet Server Applications Programming Interface, a mechanism for extending the functionality of IIS.

Because it is an ISAPI extension DLL, the SQL Server CE Server Agent must be copied to a Web site and also registered with that Web site. Because the name of the Server Agent is part of a URL, you need to specify that URL in your application. Because it is a SQL Server client program, you may need to provide SQL Server logon information in your application. And because the transfer of data to and from SQL Server is done via IIS, your request must pass through both IIS security and SQL Server security. All of this impacts how you configure the components on the server side.

Enabling ISAPI Extensions

As part of the effort to improve security, version 6.0 of IIS has a different set of default settings from previous versions. This version, which ships with Windows Server 2003, starts up with ISAPI extensions disabled. For the SQL Server CE Server Agent to operate properly, you must enable these extensions. This is done from a logon account with administrator privileges through the server's Administrative Tools. Open IIS and open the Web Service Extensions node.

During this chapter we cover how to install and configure the various components required to synchronize mobile data. In this chapter we do not intend to make you an IIS administrator or a SQL Server administrator. Instead, the intent of this chapter is to provide you with enough information that you can set up a development environment on your desktop machine at work or at home.

It might seem strange that you need to install SQL Server CE server-side components to run the sample applications for this chapter but did not need to do any SQL CE install for Chapter 12. You do not need to install SQL Server CE for local data access because SQL Server CE is automatically installed on a device along with an application whenever an application contains a reference to the `System.Data.SqlServerCe.dll` assembly. But SQL Server CE Server Agent is not automatically installed on your IIS Web server system. You or an administrator must do that installation. We cover that topic next.

Installing Remote Data Connectivity

People familiar with IIS recognize that the device-to-IIS connection can be made in Anonymous, Basic Authentication, or Integrated Windows Authentication mode; people familiar with SQL Server 2000 know that the IIS-to-SQL-Server connection can be made in Windows Authentication or SQL Server Authentication mode. All this results in a connectivity/security chain that involves your SQL Server CE application, the network, the operating system, IIS, NTFS, SQL Server, and, in the case of Merge Replication, a shared directory.

Creating the Virtual Directory

As we stated, three security contexts exposed by IIS can be used with SQL Server CE (Anonymous, Basic, and Integrated). Of the three, Integrated is the most restrictive when using SQL Server CE because it requires having IIS and SQL Server on the same machine. This is because NTLM does not support proxying security credentials through machines. Kerberos Authentication does support this in Windows 2000, but support for Kerberos is not available on Windows CE devices. As with any Web-based application, if you use Basic Authentication, it is recommended that you also use SSL (i.e., Web connections should use HTTPS instead of HTTP as the transfer protocol) to prevent the user name and password from being deciphered between the device and the IIS box.

Before you begin to code the application, you have to address a number of standard Web development issues. You must decide the following: Where will the ISAPI extension `.dll` file be located? Where will the SQL Server be located? Will there be a firewall or proxy server between them? What operating system user should the Server Agent execute as? How do you ensure that that operating system user is a valid SQL Server login? Should there be multiple sites, each with its own security? Or should there be just one site, one connection point for all the applications?

These questions include the typical setup procedures for doing any Web-based application that also has back-end database support (setting up a virtual directory, installing the server-side components in the virtual directory, choosing the authentication modes for the virtual directory, assigning user rights, and setting up the necessary security and access rights for gaining access to SQL Server). It is not our intent to repeat the details for doing this that can be found in the SQL Server CE Books Online. Rather, we'll take a high-level look at the SQL Server CE application to IIS to SQL Server chain.

Fortunately, SQL Server CE provides a tool for creating and configuring the Web server to be accessed by client devices. That means you must install the server-side component of SQL Server CE and then use it to install the IIS site(s). Books Online refers to this as "Installing SQL Server CE," but it is really installing the server-side components of SQL Server CE.

If you are doing your initial development in a single-machine environment at work or at home, and if you have already installed Visual Studio .NET on your machine, then you already have the SQL Server CE Server Agent on that machine. It is not yet installed, but it is present on your system. To install it, go to the Visual Studio install folder, which is by default `\Program Files\Microsoft Visual Studio .NET 2003\CompactFrameworkSDK\vN.N.N` (where `N.N.N` is the actual version number). In the `Windows CE` subdirectory you can find the self-extracting zip file `sqlce20sql2ksp2.exe`. (The name of the file denotes the SQL Server 2000 service pack that must be installed for this version to work correctly.) Run it to install the SQL Server CE Server Agent and some tools.

If you do not have Visual Studio .NET installed, you can install the SQL Server CE Client Agent from a CD copy of SQL Server CE. On the CD of SQL Server CE that came with our MSDN subscription, for instance, `setup.exe` is located at `\ENGLISH\SQLCE11`.

Regardless of how you install SQL Server CE on the server machine, the `\Program Files\Microsoft SQL Server CE 2.0\Server` directory will contain a file named `sscesa20.dll`. This file is the SQL Server CE Server Agent. It is shown in Figure 13.2, along with the Start menu entry that was added by the installation of SQL Server CE.

But installing the Server Agent does not yet mean that you can transfer data between the device and the desktop. Because this transfer is done via the Internet, you must establish one or more sites on your IIS machine for use by SQL Server CE. Into each site you must install the `sscesa20.dll` file, and you must set the appropriate permissions for that site.

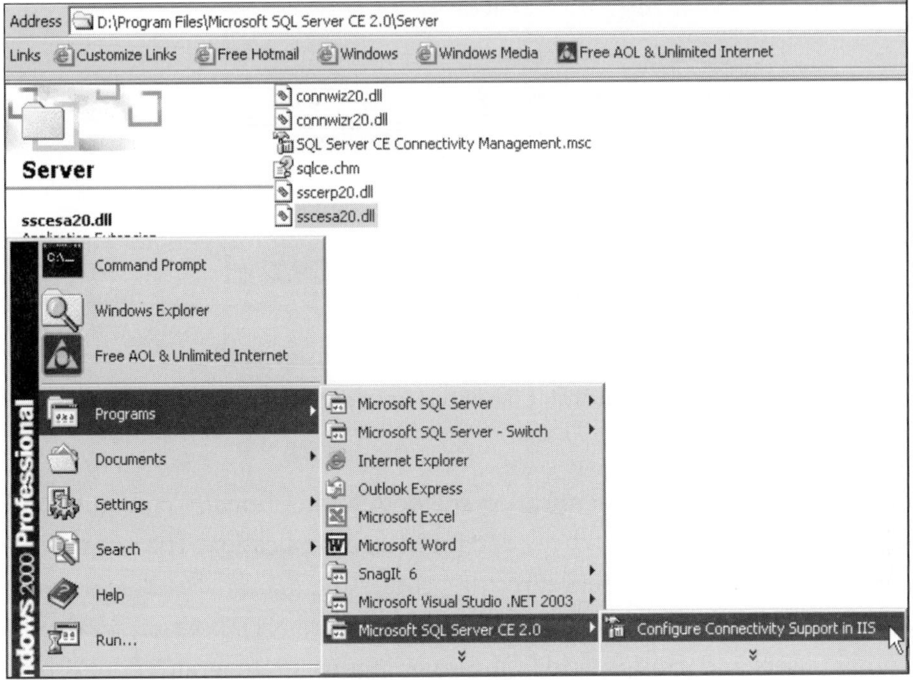

FIGURE 13.2: After server-side installation of SQL Server CE

The program that helps you do this, the SQL Server Connectivity Management program, is reached from the Start menu entry shown in Figure 13.2. This management application allows you to reach the Virtual Directory Creation Wizard, which helps you configure the site. To configure a new site from the SQL Server Connectivity Management program, select Microsoft SQL Server CE in the left-hand panel and click on Create a Virtual Directory in the right-hand panel, as shown in Figure 13.3. To modify an existing directory configuration, select the directory from the right-hand panel.

The wizard walks you through five self-explanatory dialog boxes.[3] Through the wizard you specify the name and location of the virtual

3. We placed screenshots of them in Appendix C in the Virtual Directory Creation Wizard section because the figures require several pages and would interrupt the flow of the chapter if shown here. But we do want to make them available for readers who are visually oriented and who learn by seeing.

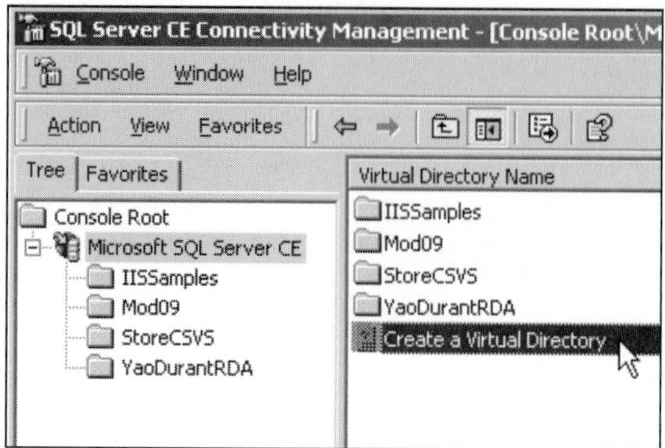

FIGURE 13.3: Launching the Virtual Directory Creation Wizard

directory, choose the authentication method, and optionally configure and share the snapshots directory needed for Merge Replication. The wizard creates the Web site and virtual directory, copies the `sscesa20.dll` file to it, and registers `sscesa20.dll`. It does not configure NTFS permissions, add domain users and groups, add SQL Server logons, or generate code. You or an appropriate administrator must perform those tasks after analyzing the needs of the site.

For instance, the need to provide read-only access to public data usually results in:

- A site that allows anonymous access
- A SQL Server logon for the `IUSR_MachineName` user
- A SQL Server that allows SQL Server logon authentication
- Application code that does not specify any of the change-tracking options

Authenticated access to corporate data might be accomplished with:

- A site that uses Integrated Windows Authentication and SSL
- A new SQL Server logons group

When you have finished configuring a Web site, you can test it by opening your browser and navigating to http://<server name>/<virtual

directory name>/sscesa20.dll, as shown in Figure 13.4. If you receive the response shown in the figure, your site installation was successful.

If you specified a security model that required authentication and if you were not currently logged on when you navigated to the site, you were asked to enter your user name and password. Whatever URL provides access to the server agent is the URL to specify in your application code. Whatever user name and password you specified to log on is the user name and password to specify in your application code.

If you are unable to browse to the site from your device, try browsing from the server machine, using `localhost` as the server name. If this local access attempt fails, the problem lies in the Web server configuration. Return to the SQL Server Connectivity Management program and check the properties and spellings of your configuration.

If local access succeeds, the problem lies in configuring your device. From your device, try to browse to a known site, such as http://www.microsoft.com. If that fails, you have a general network connectivity problem. If it succeeds, the problem lies in connecting your device specifically to your server.

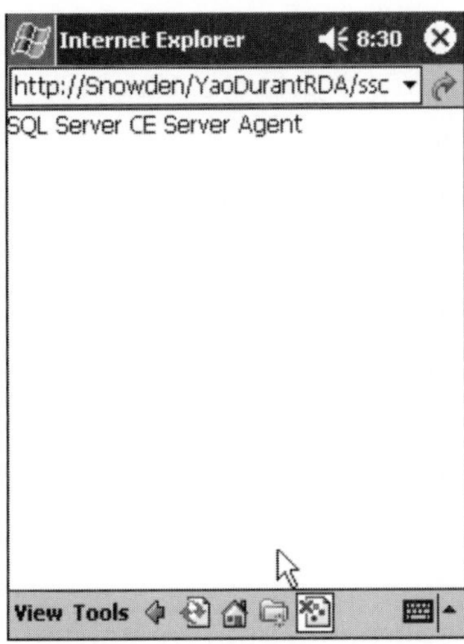

FIGURE 13.4: Configuration test showing successful site installation

Configuring Additional Components

The IIS authentication configuration that you specify determines the user name that SQL Server CE Server Agent uses when it connects to SQL Server and when it accesses the shared directory required by Merge Replication. This user must be able to log onto SQL Server and to access the directory, which in turn must be shared. Your application is ready to connect when you have accomplished all of the following tasks.

- All operating system users and groups, if any, have been added.
- All SQL Server logons and groups have been added.
- The directory has been shared.
- Share permissions have been granted.

Using RDA

Once you have completed configuring the components, you can develop and test your RDA and Merge Replication applications. We begin with RDA, the easier to administer but less capable of the two.

RDA Capabilities and Overhead

RDA enables a SQL Server CE application to:

- Retrieve data and schemas from a SQL Server database into a SQL Server CE database on a device
- Add to, remove, or modify that data at the device and have SQL Server CE track those changes
- Have SQL Server CE submit the changed data to the SQL Server database and receive any exceptions resulting from failed updates on the server
- Submit SQL statements directly from the .NET Compact Framework application to a SQL Server database

RDA is simpler than Merge Replication, but it requires that you write more code, both C# code and SQL code. It also requires that you use an

ADO.NET class that was not needed in Chapter 12 when we accessed a SQL Server database: the `SqlCeRemoteDataAccess` class.

RDA uses a concurrency model that the online documentation calls *Optimistic Concurrency.* The meaning of Optimistic Concurrency in RDA is different from the meaning known by many veteran SQL Server programmers. In RDA, Optimistic Concurrency means the following activities take place.

1. Pull data from the server to the device.
2. Modify the data on the device.
3. Submit data changes to the server.
4. Make changes even if the data on the server has been modified since it was pulled to the device.

So, you need to adopt a new mind-set if you are used to Optimistic Concurrency meaning the following.

1. Retrieve data into the application.
2. Modify data within the application.
3. Submit data changes to the server.
4. Changes are *not* made if the data on the server has been modified since it was read by the application.

For instance, the following RDA scenario causes one update to overlay another.

08:00	Client A pulls data from the server.
08:00	Client B pulls data from the server.
12:00	Client A updates row X on device A.
12:00	Client B updates row X on device B.
18:00	Client A pushes updates to the server.
19:00	Client B pushes updates to the server.

Client B's update overlays Client A's update. No warning, error, exception, or conflict occurs.

The following change to the scenario causes B's update to fail.

12:00 Client A deletes row X.

In the new scenario, there is no row X on the server at 19:00, and B's update fails. When this failure occurs, RDA logs the failure in the local database. It is up to the client application to make whatever changes to local data that it feels is appropriate and to notify the user of the failure.

Programming for RDA

The primary ADO.NET class for RDA programming is `SqlCeRemoteDataAccess`. This class has three methods, corresponding to the three capabilities mentioned earlier (`SubmitSQL`, `Pull`, and `Push`) plus additional methods inherited from its base classes. It also has a set of properties for providing connection information. Table 13.2 lists the main methods and properties of the `SqlCeRemoteDataAccess` class.

TABLE 13.2: Methods and Properties of the `SqlCeRemoteDataAccess` Class

Name	Comment
Methods	
`Pull`	Submits a `SELECT` statement to a SQL Server 2000 database. Creates a table and indexes in a SQL Server CE database to hold the selected data. Retrieves the selected rows and inserts them into the table. Initiates tracking of changes made to the selected data.
`Push`	Submits changes made to previously pulled data back to the SQL Server 2000. Receives errors from the SQL Server 2000 and stores them in an application-specified error table.
`SubmitSQL`	Submits SQL statements to a SQL Server 2000.

Name	Comment
Properties	
`InternetLogon`	Internet user name.
`InternetPassword`	Internet user password.
`InternetProxyLogon`	Proxy user name.
`InternetProxyPassword`	Proxy password.
`InternetProxyServer`	Proxy server name.
`InternetURL`	URL of the `sscesa20.dll` file at a Web site (i.e., the virtual directory specified in the Virtual Directory Alias and Content Folder dialog box of the Virtual Directory Creation Wizard; see Appendix C).
`LocalConnectionString`	Connection string for the SQL Server CE database.

Pulling Data

The `Pull` method submits a SQL `SELECT` statement to the SQL Server for processing. The method creates the table to hold the returned rows; that table must not already exist. Some of the information the `Pull` method needs is specified by setting properties before invoking the method; some is supplied through the parameters, which are shown in Table 13.3.

For example, the code shown in Listing 13.1 pulls information from the Northwind `Categories` table and stores it in a newly created table that is also to be named `Categories`. Listings 13.1 through 13.5 show the code, which can be found in the `RDA` project at the Web site.

LISTING 13.1: An RDA Pull

```
//  The database file
private string  strDBFile = @"My Documents\Northwind.sdf";

//  The local connection string
```

continues

continued

```
private string  strConnLocal =
        "Data Source=" + @"My Documents\Northwind.sdf";

//  The remote connection string
private string strConnRemote = "Provider=sqloledb; "
                             + "Data Source=Snowden; "
                             + "Initial Catalog=Northwind; "
                             + "Integrated Security=SSPI;";

//  The URL
private string strURL =
        "http://207.202.168.30/YaoDurantRDA/sscesa20.dll";


private void mitemPull_Click(object sender, EventArgs e)
{
//  Create an RDA object.
SqlCeRemoteDataAccess  rdaNW = new SqlCeRemoteDataAccess();

try
{
   //  Have RDA:
   //     Create local tables named Categories and
   //        ErrorCategories.
   //     Connect to the remote server and submit the
   //        SELECT statement.
   //     Place the results in the local Categories table.
   rdaNW.LocalConnectionString = strConnLocal;
   rdaNW.InternetUrl = strURL;
   rdaNW.InternetLogin = "";
   rdaNW.InternetPassword = "";
   rdaNW.Pull("Categories",
              "SELECT CategoryID, CategoryName " +
              "  FROM Categories",
              strConnRemote,
              RdaTrackOption.TrackingOnWithIndexes,
              "ErrorCategories");
}
catch(SqlCeException exSQL)
{
   HandleSQLException(exSQL);
}
finally
{
   rdaNW.Dispose();
}
```

TABLE 13.3: Parameters of the `Pull` Method

Parameter	Comment
`localTableName`	Name of the SQL Server CE table to be created to receive the output of the `SELECT` statement.
`sqlSelectString`	The `SELECT` statement.
`oledbConnectionString`	The connection string used to access the SQL Server 2000 database.
`trackOptions`	An enumerated indicator specifying whether changes to the data in the table should be tracked so that they can be subsequently pushed back to the SQL Server 2000. Also specifies whether indexes should be created on the local table.
`errorTable`	The name of a table to be created in the local database that holds errors returned by subsequent pushes.

Fixing the `IDENTITY` Property

When you pull a table from SQL Server down to your device using RDA, the schema of that table is brought with the data so that the table can be created on the device. That schema might be incorrect regarding the `IDENTITY` property. If the SQL Server table has an `IDENTITY` property column, the new SQL Server CE table also has that column designated as an `IDENTITY` property column, but its seed and increment are always set to `(1,1)`. You must initially correct them to the values you want, as shown in Listing 13.2.

LISTING 13.2: Setting the `IDENTITY` Property Column's Seed Value

```
//  The IDENTITY property seed value of the new table
//      is at 1, even after the retrieved rows have
//      been added to the table.  "Fix" it.
SqlCeConnection connLocal = new SqlCeConnection(strConnLocal);
connLocal.Open();

SqlCeCommand  cmndLocal = new SqlCeCommand();
int intMaxCategoryID;
try
{
   cmndLocal.Connection = connLocal;
```

continues

continued

```
    //  Retrieve the highest CategoryID in the table.
    cmndLocal.CommandText =
       "SELECT max(CategoryID) FROM Categories";
    string strMaxCategoryID =
       cmndLocal.ExecuteScalar().ToString();
    intMaxCategoryID = int.Parse(strMaxCategoryID);

    //  Set the seed one higher.
    cmndLocal.CommandText =
       "ALTER TABLE Categories " +
       "ALTER COLUMN CategoryID IDENTITY (" +
       (intMaxCategoryID + 1).ToString() + ",1)";
    cmndLocal.ExecuteNonQuery();
}
catch( SqlCeException exSQL )
{
    HandleSQLException(exSQL);
}
finally
{
    connLocal.Close();
}
```

Be aware that that the auto-generated `CategoryID` value of any rows that you insert into the local `Categories` table is always overridden with a new value when those rows are pushed to the host server.

Viewing the Pulled Schema

If you use RDA to retrieve data from the desktop and you plan to propagate local changes to that data back to the desktop server, you must specify one of the change-tracking enumerations in the fourth parameter when you pull the data.

Two of the tracking options also specify that indexes are to be created on the local table. The `TrackingOnWithIndexes` option adds yet one more index to your table. Do your own performance testing to determine whether your application benefits from the indexes. Using either tracking option adds the two extra columns shown in Figure 13.5 to your database. Using the `TrackingOnWithIndexes` option adds the extra index also shown in Figure 13.5.

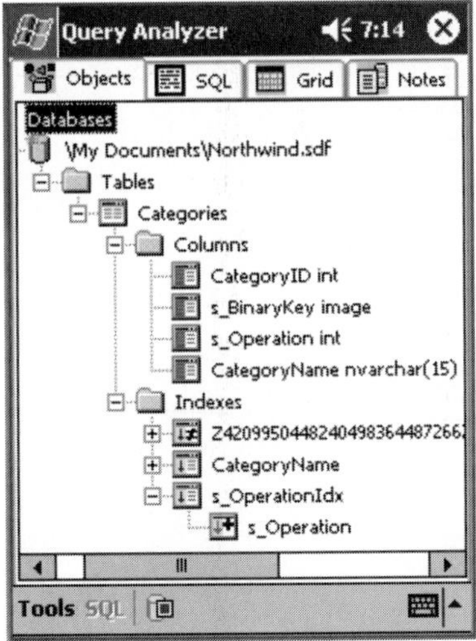

FIGURE 13.5: A table pulled with tracking and indexes

Modifying Pulled Data Locally

The connection to SQL Server 2000 is open only while the data is being pulled. When the data has been transferred to the SQL Server CE data table, the SQL Server 2000 connection is closed. Once you have pulled the data and, if necessary, altered the `IDENTITY` property, you can modify the data locally using the techniques covered in Chapter 12 and illustrated in Listing 13.3.

LISTING 13.3: Modifying Pulled Data at the Device

```
private void mitemUpdate_Click(object sender, EventArgs e)
{
   SqlCeConnection  connLocal =
      new SqlCeConnection(strConnLocal);
   connLocal.Open();

   SqlCeCommand  cmndLocal = new SqlCeCommand();
   try
   {
      cmndLocal.Connection = connLocal;
      cmndLocal.CommandText =
                     "UPDATE Categories " +
```

continues

continued

```
                     "    SET CategoryName = 'new Name'   " +
                     " WHERE CategoryID = 2";
      cmndLocal.ExecuteNonQuery();

      cmndLocal.CommandText =
         "DELETE Categories WHERE CategoryID = 3";
      cmndLocal.ExecuteNonQuery();

      cmndLocal.CommandText =
         "INSERT Categories (CategoryName) " +
         "         VALUES ('new Category I') ";
      cmndLocal.ExecuteNonQuery();
   }
   catch( SqlCeException exSQL )
   {
      HandleSQLException(exSQL);
   }
   finally
   {
      cmndLocal.Dispose();
      connLocal.Close();
   }
}
```

Figure 13.6 shows the `Categories` data after modification. The row for `CategoryID = 3` has been deleted, the row for `CategoryID = 2` has been modified, and a new row with `CategoryID = 10` has been added.

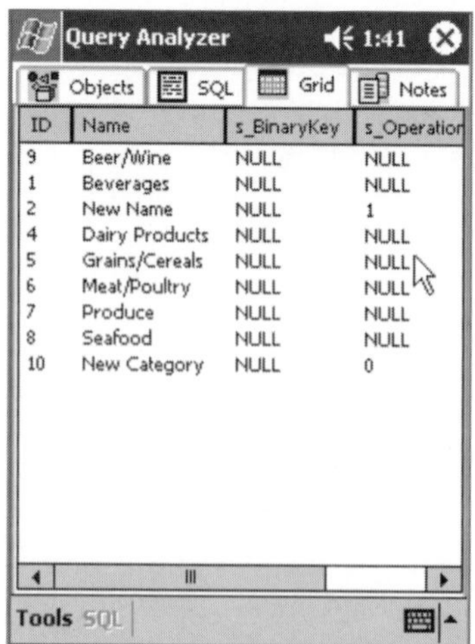

FIGURE 13.6: The `Categories` table after updates

The inserted and modified rows are marked in the s_Operation column; the deleted row is represented in the MSysRDATombstone table.

Pushing Data

To propagate the table's changes back to the desktop SQL Server, you use the Push method of the SqlCeRemoteDataAccess class. This is shown in Listing 13.4.

LISTING 13.4: An RDA Push

```
private void mitemPush_Click(object sender, EventArgs e)
{
   //  Create an RDA object.
   SqlCeRemoteDataAccess  rdaNW =
      new SqlCeRemoteDataAccess();
   try
   {
      //  Have RDA:
      //     Create local tables named Categories and
      //        ErrorCategories.
      //     Connect to the remote server and submit
      //        the changes.
      rdaNW.LocalConnectionString = strConnLocal;
      rdaNW.InternetUrl = strURL;
      rdaNW.InternetLogin = "";
      rdaNW.InternetPassword = "";
      rdaNW.Push("Categories", strConnRemote);
   }
   catch( SqlCeException exSQL )
   {
      HandleSQLException(exSQL);
   }
   finally
   {
      rdaNW.Dispose();
   }
}
```

After the Push method completes, you can detect the rows that failed to update at the server due to concurrency conflicts by accessing the local table that was specified as a Pull method parameter. In our case this was the ErrorCategories table, shown on the next page in the code snippet extracted from Listing 13.1.

```
rdaNW.Pull("Categories",
          "SELECT CategoryID, CategoryName " +
          "  FROM Categories",
          strConnRemote,
          RdaTrackOption.TrackingOnWithIndexes,
          "ErrorCategories");
```

Figure 13.7 shows the contents of the `Categories` table that we pulled to the local database.

When we push the changes back to the SQL Server database, using the code in Listing 13.4, the following activities happen.

1. The modified row from our local database is modified on the server.
2. The deleted row in our local database fails to delete because of a foreign key violation; there are some `Confections` products in the remote database, so the category cannot be deleted.
3. The inserted row from our local database fails to insert because a `CategoryId = 10` row already exists in the remote database. Perhaps some other user added this row; perhaps we added it with a `SubmitSQL` method call.

This can be verified by viewing the contents of the `Categories` table on the server after the push has completed, as shown in Figure 13.8.

When the `Push` method executed, it raised the exception shown in Figure 13.9. As a result of the exception, the rows shown in Figure 13.10 were added to the SQL Server CE `ErrorCategories` table.

	CategoryID	CategoryName	Description	Picture
▶	1	Beverages	Soft drinks, coffee:	<Binary>
	2	Condiments	Sweet and savory :	<Binary>
	3	Confections	Desserts, candies,	<Binary>
	4	Dairy Products	Cheeses	<Binary>
	5	Grains/Cereals	Breads, crackers, p	<Binary>
	6	Meat/Poultry	Prepared meats	<Binary>
	7	Produce	Dried fruit and bea	<Binary>
	8	Seafood	Seaweed and fish	<Binary>
	9	Beer/Wine	Beer and Wine	<Binary>
*				

FIGURE 13.7: Remote data before the push

CategoryID	CategoryName	Description	Picture
1	Beverages	Soft drinks, coffees	<Binary>
2	New Name	Sweet and savory :	<Binary>
3	Confections	Desserts, candies,	<Binary>
4	Dairy Products	Cheeses	<Binary>
5	Grains/Cereals	Breads, crackers, p	<Binary>
6	Meat/Poultry	Prepared meats	<Binary>
7	Produce	Dried fruit and bea	<Binary>
8	Seafood	Seaweed and fish	<Binary>
9	Beer/Wine	Beer and Wine	<Binary>
10	New Category II	From SubmitSQL	<Binary>

FIGURE 13.8: Remote data after the push

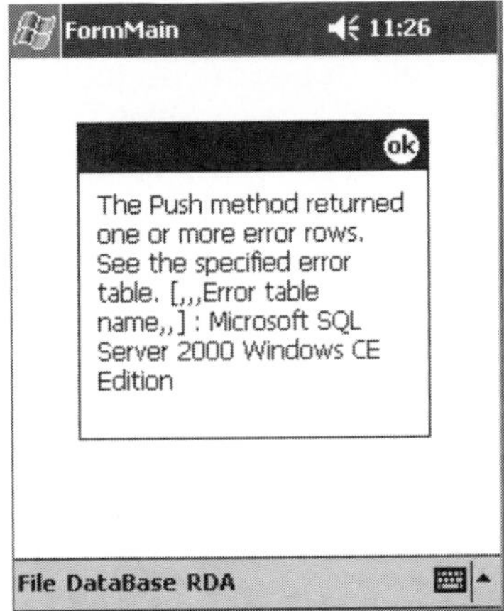

FIGURE 13.9: The `Push` method error message

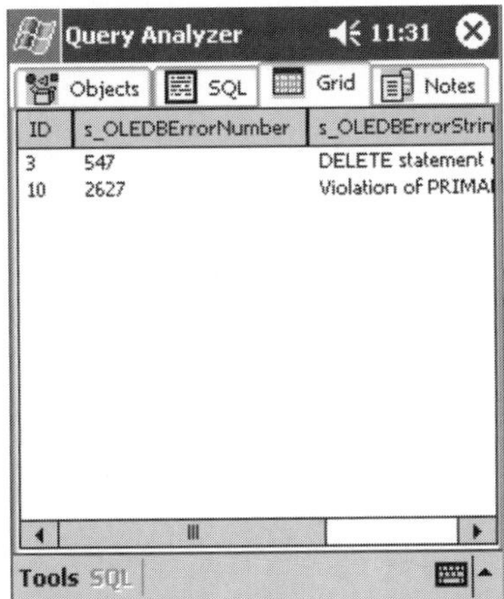

FIGURE 13.10: The `ErrorCategories` table after the push

There is no automatic conflict resolution in RDA. You must examine the failed rows placed in the error table and decide what changes to make to the data on your device as a result of the failed server updates.

The `SubmitSQL` Method

The `SubmitSQL` method is pretty self-explanatory. It bypasses the SQL Server CE database completely and simply submits a SQL statement to the SQL Server for processing. This method is used for submitting updates to the server. (If you submit a `SELECT` statement, no exception will be thrown, but you will not accomplish anything.) For example, Listing 13.5 shows the code used to insert a row into the remote `Categories` table; in fact, it was one of the rows that caused our subsequent push to fail.

LISTING 13.5: Executing the `SubmitSQL` Method

```
private void mitemSubmitSQL_Click(object sender, EventArgs e)
{
   //  Create an RDA object.
   SqlCeRemoteDataAccess  rdaNW = new SqlCeRemoteDataAccess();
   try
   {
      //  Have RDA:
      //     Create local tables named Categories and
      //        ErrorCategories.
      //     Connect to the remote server and submit
      //        the changes.
      rdaNW.LocalConnectionString = strConnLocal;
      rdaNW.InternetUrl = strURL;
      rdaNW.InternetLogin = "";
      rdaNW.InternetPassword = "";
      rdaNW.SubmitSql(
         "INSERT Categories (CategoryName, Description)" +
            "VALUES ('New Category II', 'From SubmitSQL')",
         strConnRemote);
   }
   catch( SqlCeException exSQL )
   {
      HandleSQLException(exSQL);
   }
   finally
   {
      rdaNW.Dispose();
   }
}
```

As is the case with the `Push` and `Pull` methods, the `SubmitSQL` method requires that you set property values with the information appropriate to your Web site configuration and that you correctly code your SQL statements. Once you have done that, transferring the data is a matter of a single method call.

As we are about to see, this emphasis on providing connection information through property values and the need to understand database technology continues into Merge Replication. But when you understand how your application connects to the server and how to request data from the server, you will be able to transfer data with even less code than RDA requires.

Using Merge Replication

If you have worked with replication, you know that prior planning and design are important. First-time replicators often think that having the same data in two places and needing to keep that data in sync is an easy task. But consider just two examples of the unexpected complexity involved in replication.

1. SQL Server provides a capability called *triggers*; a change in `TableX` automatically causes a change to occur in `TableY`. But SQL Server CE does not support triggers. If `TableX` and `TableY` are replicated down to a SQL Server CE database, a change in `TableX` does not cause an automatic change to `TableY`. Thus the same statement executed on the "same" table, `TableX`, produces different results, and the tables no longer are in sync.
2. If you replicate a table that has a foreign key, you need to replicate the primary key table as well to validate the rows inserted into the foreign key table. Perhaps you wish to replicate only some of the rows in the foreign key table, say, only the rows for delivery route West92. You want to replicate only those rows from the primary key table (the `Products` table) that are relevant to delivery route West92. But delivery route code probably is not a column in the `Products`

table, so how do you specify which `Products` table rows should be replicated? (As we see later in this chapter, it can be accomplished by publishing all the tables involved in enforced relationships or by adding a horizontal filter that extends outward to include related rows from other tables.)

At first, such considerations may make you wish for the perceived simplicity of RDA. But after you examine some key differences between Merge Replication and RDA, you will realize that Merge Replication is quite attractive. Merge Replication requires less code than RDA. Merge Replication provides the ability to have the server control much of the application logic, instead of having the logic distributed to the device. For example, Ranged Identity columns and dynamic horizontal partitions are two key areas where the logic resides on the server and not on the device. This can substantially reduce the amount of code on the device and allow application maintenance to be performed on the server rather than on the device.

Any replication schema must be well planned and well designed, including the ones you plan to use with your SQL Server CE applications. Therefore, we take a moment to review the basic concepts of SQL Server's Merge Replication and then follow up with a detailed examination of design considerations.

In Merge Replication, as it is used with a SQL Server CE application, the SQL Server is referred to as the *publisher* with one or more defined publications on one or more databases, and the SQL Server CE databases are referred to as the *subscribers*. Publications are made up of a defined set of tables, columns, and filters. These chosen tables are referred to as the *articles of a publication*; and the definition of a subset, such as "only `columnA`, `columnB`, `columnC` of `TableX`" or "only those rows of `TableY` where route code equals `'West92'`" are referred to as *filters*. Filters allow you to replicate a vertical subset of a table (such as the first example in the previous sentence) or replicate a horizontal subset of table (such as the second example) or both. They also can be dynamic, such as "only rows in the `Orders` table where `EmployeeID` equals the employee ID of the user performing the synchronization."

With this flexibility in publication design comes the need to ensure that changes made to this subset of the data residing on the device will synchronize correctly when propagated back to the server.

Using Good Design to Avoid Synchronization Failures

Most mobile applications that have a Merge Replication component consist of three repetitively executed steps.

1. Subscribe to a publication located at the server and synchronize the data to the device.
2. Make updates to that data as it resides on the device.
3. Synchronize with the server to submit the changes made locally back to the server database.

All mobile application designers hope that step 3 succeeds so that modifications are applied at the server without errors and that those modifications do not overwrite any modifications made by other users. Many mobile application designers end up wondering why step 3 failed. The purpose of this subsection is to explain why publication design decisions can cause synchronization failures and to provide a blueprint on how to avoid those failures.

A mobile application that uses Merge Replication for the transfer of data between SQL Server and SQL Server CE does so by subscribing to a publication that resides on the server. Since SQL Server CE provides only for anonymous subscriptions, the entire publication must be subscribed to. But mobile applications usually do not want to work with large amounts of data; rather, they want just the data that applies to the subject at hand and to the user of the device. They almost always want less than the entire server database. This means that almost all publications are defined as subsets of the database and, therefore, that all mobile applications work with a subset of the database.

Working with a subset of data always creates the possibility of data integrity problems occurring in the subset that will not be detected until the data is synchronized with the full set of data residing at the server. For example, the Northwind database that comes with SQL Server contains two tables that are related by a foreign key constraint: `Products`, which contains the foreign key, and `Categories`, which contains the primary key. Now suppose that you define a publication that includes the `Products` table but not the `Categories` table. When you synchronize, the `Products` table is brought to the device. That table has a `CategoryID` column both on the server and on the device. At the server, the list of possible values that can be entered into that column is known; by definition it is the list of values in the `Categories` table's primary key column. But on the device, that list is not known. The local application cannot insert rows into the `Products` table or update the `CategoryID` field in rows that are already there because the application does not know what values will be accepted or rejected when the data is synchronized to the server.

Not all developers understand that each decision made during the design of the publication results in a specific and definable limitation that must be placed on the application for local data modifications to synchronize successfully at the server. As we look at publication design decisions and the resulting restrictions that those decisions place on your local application, let us be clear about something: The design of a publication does not place automatic restrictions on your application; rather, it creates situations that force you to design limitations into your application as you develop it.

To illustrate this "choice and impact" world in which you must develop applications based on Merge Replication, we develop a sample publication and mobile application design. For our server database, we pick the Northwind database. Our Merge Replication–based mobile application synchronizes order data for one employee with the Northwind database. In the publication definition, a row filter specifies that only order information for the employee who is performing the synchronization should be delivered to the device. Our definition of "order information" is illustrated by the SQL Server data diagram in Figure 13.11. Thus our publication includes the employee row, all orders related to that employee, all customers and order details connected to those orders, and all products for the order details. We included only those columns we determined to be essential to our application.

Our publication (and therefore the data delivered to the device) is a four-way subset of the host database; it contains some of the tables, some of the columns, some of the rows, and some of the constraints of the North-

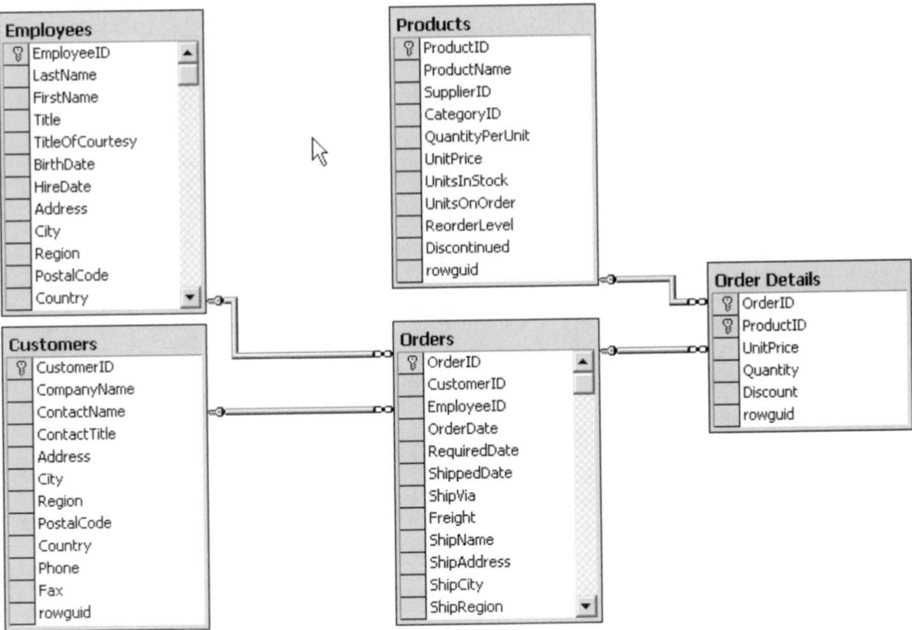

FIGURE 13.11: Tables to be included in the sample publication

wind database. Each of these reductions in content places limitations on the modifications that the application can make to that data on the device.

For the sake of illustration, the employee named Nancy Davolio is performing the synchronization, unless otherwise stated.

Table 13.4 relates publication design decisions with their impacts on the application.

Many of the restrictions in Table 13.4 sound like nothing more than common sense, but they are grounded on the basic principles of relational algebra. These restrictions are not arbitrary or optional; they cannot be circumvented by clever application code or expensive hardware. Common sense is not always common. When you are involved in a design-time discussion, it's nice to know that your recommendations are based on solid ground, especially when those of others are not.

Having studied the restrictions that will be placed on our application by our publication, we decide that the restrictions are acceptable. It is time now to configure the publication.

Table 13.4: Impacts of Publication Design

Type of Subset	Impact on Local Application	Example
Not all columns of a table are included.	We cannot insert rows unless the database at the server contains default value definitions or permits nulls for the missing columns. Deleting rows will result in the loss of unknown information.	The sample application should not add new customers or delete existing customers.
Not all rows of a table are included.	Inserted rows must adhere to the row filter specified by the publication.	The sample application should not add a new employee or any orders for that new employee. The new rows would successfully update to the server, but they would disappear from the device during the next synchronization because they would not be Nancy Davolio's data.
A table that has a foreign key is included, but the table containing the matching primary key is not.	New rows cannot be inserted into the table, nor can the foreign key column be updated.	The sample application should not insert rows into the `Products` table or update its `CategoryID` column because the domain of allowable values is not known.
A table that has a primary key column is included, but the table with the corresponding foreign key column is not.	The primary key column cannot be updated (which isn't allowed anyway). Rows cannot be deleted from the table.	The sample application should not delete a customer because that customer may have data in the `CustomerCustomerDemo` table on the server.

Type of Subset	Impact on Local Application	Example
Some rows are not unique to a specific synchronization (i.e., they will be propagated to more than one device). This is an inevitable result of a many-to-many relationship, such as employees and customers. For instance, a customer might have placed orders with several employees.	The table whose rows can synchronize to more than one device cannot be updated unless ownership of rows and columns can be assigned to a single subscriber. Rows cannot be deleted from the table. Updating the row on more than one device will result in conflicts during synchronization. The last update synchronized will be the winner.	The sample application should not update customer information. (However, if the customer table had a `ResponsibleEmployee` foreign key column, the sample application could permit only that employee to make modifications.)
A column that has the `IDENTITY` property is included in the publication.	SQL Server's Ranged Identity capability must be specified in the publication definition. The application should not try to solve this problem.	If, for example, an `Identity` column were added to the `Orders` table on the server, then Ranged Identity would assign a range of possible identity values to each subscriber, ensuring that two devices did not give different orders the same identifying number.
Derived (calculated) columns are included in the publication definition.	These columns normally should not be updated. Their values are derived from other values in the database. They can be updated only if all their source values are included in the publication.	The sample application should not recalculate `Product.UnitsInStock` based on subscriber activity. Any such updates would reflect only the activity of the local user. During synchronization, each subscriber's value would overwrite the previous subscriber's value. All values would be wrong; the last subscriber's value would persist and propagate.
A recursive relationship on a table with a row filter specified is included in the publication.	The table will not synchronize to the device.	When Nancy Davolio synchronizes, her row is the only employee row brought to the device. In the `ReportsTo` column of that table is the employee ID of her manager. The foreign key constraint mandates that her manager's row be on the device before her row can be inserted. But her manager's row is not on her device because it was filtered out by the publication.

Configuring Merge Replication

We have completed the necessary steps that lead up to configuring Merge Replication, as summarized here.

1. The configuration of an IIS site (covered earlier in this chapter) is complete.
2. The necessary domain users and groups have been added.
3. The necessary SQL Server logins and users have been added.
   a. All Northwind employees have been added as SQL Server logins. (An alternative scenario would have been to add them as domain groups and users and use Windows Authentication, but we wanted to keep the focus on SQL Server, not on domain management.)
   b. The logins have been added as users of the Northwind database and given the necessary permissions.
4. The publication has been designed but not implemented.
   a. It consists of the tables and columns shown earlier in Figure 13.11.
   b. It contains a dynamic filter to limit the data to that which is appropriate for the user executing the synchronization.

We are ready to define our publication. Fortunately, SQL Server's Enterprise Manager console snap-in has the Create Publication Wizard to help us. We run it by selecting <Server Name>→Databases→Northwind→Publications in Enterprise Manager's Tree window, right-clicking on it, and choosing New Publication from the pop-up menu. After working through about 20 dialog boxes, including the specification of dynamic filters and expanded (join) filters, we have defined our publication.[4]

If we need to modify the definition of our publication once we have completed the Create Publication Wizard, we can do so by right-clicking on the publication name in Enterprise Manager's Tree window and selecting Properties. When we make changes to a publication, we need to resynchronize all

4. Once again, because such a long chain of figures requires several pages, we have placed the screenshots in Appendix C in the Create Publication Wizard section. For the benefit of those readers who like to follow the flow from design to finished product, we show the dialog boxes in the order in which they appear.

devices. Additionally, some selections cannot be changed, requiring that we delete the publication and create a new one with the desired selections. As always, having a solid publication design before beginning development is most important.

Once we have completed the publication, we are two-thirds of the way home. Configuring our Internet connectivity was the first third, defining our publication was the second third, and writing the .NET Compact Framework application that does synchronizations and modifies data is the final third.

Programming for Merge Replication

Programming a .NET Compact Framework application to work with Merge Replication consists of using the `SqlCeReplication` class located in the `System.Data.SqlServerCe` namespace to initially subscribe to a publication and to periodically synchronize with that publication. Between synchronizations, the application updates the data in the SQL Server CE database using the classes and techniques covered in the Microsoft SQL Server CE section of Chapter 12.

Our sample application will subscribe to the publication we just created, synchronize the data to the device, modify the data on the device, and resynchronize to transmit the modifications back to the server and to receive new data (other user's modifications) from the server. Along the way we use some utility routines to view the schema created by the subscription and the data delivered by the synchronization. The application is predominately menu driven, with a single `DataGrid` control for displaying information. Figure 13.12 shows the application. The code for this application is shown in Listings 13.6 through 13.9 and can be found in the `Repl` project at the Web site.

The code begins with the same references we used in Chapter 12.

```
using System;
using System.IO;
using System.Windows.Forms;
using System.Data;
using System.Data.Common;
using System.Data.SqlServerCe;
```

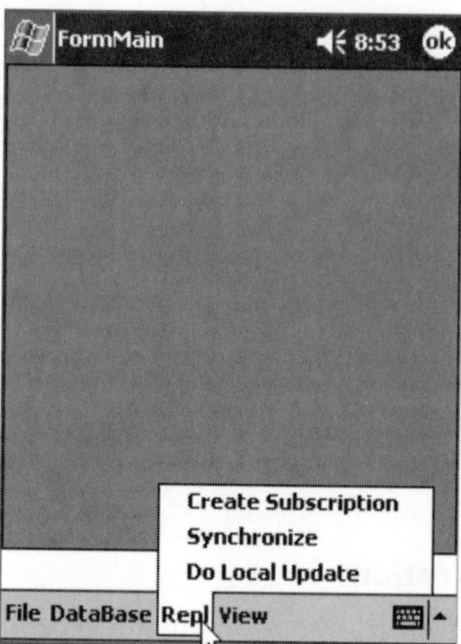

FIGURE 13.12: The Merge Replication sample application

The `FormMain` class begins with some generated code followed by the local connection information and the remote connection information. The remote information defines the connection to the Web site but not the SQL Server connection string. That string will be built by the `sscesa20.dll` code from parameters that will be passed in the `AddSubscription` and `Synchronize` calls, parameters that are declared in Listing 13.6.

LISTING 13.6: Declaring Connection Parameters

```
/// <summary>
/// Summary description for Form1
/// </summary>
public class FormMain : System.Windows.Forms.Form
{
   internal System.Windows.Forms.MainMenu MenuMain;
   internal System.Windows.Forms.MenuItem mitemFile;
         :
         :
   private System.Windows.Forms.DataGrid dgridOutput;

   public FormMain()
   {
      //
      // Required for Windows Form Designer support
      //
```

```
      InitializeComponent();
   }
   /// <summary>
   /// Clean up any resources being used.
   /// </summary>
   protected override void Dispose( bool disposing )
   {
      base.Dispose( disposing );
   }

   #region Windows Form Designer generated code

   /// <summary>
   /// The main entry point for the application
   /// </summary>

   static void Main()
   {
      Application.Run(new FormMain());
   }

   //  The database file
   private string  strDBFile = @"My Documents\Northwind.sdf";

   //  The local connection string
   private string  strConnLocal =
      "Data Source=" + @"My Documents\Northwind.sdf";

   //  The URL
   private string strURL =
      "http://207.202.168.30/YaoDurantRDA/sscesa20.dll";
```

Subscribing to a Publication

A .NET Compact Framework application needs to subscribe to a publication only once. Doing so causes information about the subscription to be stored at the server. Thereafter, each time the application attempts to synchronize, the server verifies that the subscription does exist, that the publication has not be modified or recreated since the previous subscription, and that valid credentials are being presented by the application.

To subscribe, the application must create a `SqlCeReplication` object, set its properties, invoke its `AddSubscription` method, and dispose of it, as shown in Listing 13.7. Subscribing does not cause data or schemas to be transmitted to the device.

LISTING 13.7: Subscribing to a Publication

```
private void mitemCreateSubscription_Click(object sender,
                                           EventArgs e)
{
   SqlCeReplication  replNW = new SqlCeReplication();
   try
   {
      replNW.ExchangeType = ExchangeType.BiDirectional;
      replNW.InternetUrl = strURL;
      replNW.InternetLogin = "";
      replNW.InternetPassword = "";
      replNW.Publisher = "SNOWDEN";
      replNW.PublisherDatabase = "Northwind";
      replNW.Publication = "EmployeeOrderInfo";
      replNW.PublisherSecurityMode =
         SecurityType.DBAuthentication;
      replNW.PublisherLogin = "Davolio";
      replNW.PublisherPassword = "Nancy";
      replNW.Subscriber = "YaoDurant";
      replNW.SubscriberConnectionString = strConnLocal;

      replNW.AddSubscription(AddOption.CreateDatabase);
   }
   catch( SqlCeException exSQL )
   {
      HandleSQLException(exSQL);
   }
   finally
   {
      replNW.Dispose();
   }
}
```

The properties whose names begin with `Pub` are used by the `sscesa20.dll` file at the `strUrl` location to connect to the specified server, find the database, and subscribe to the publication. Because we specified SQL Server Authentication, both at the server and here in our code, we must specify a publisher login and password. That login will be used by `sscesa20.dll` as it subscribes to the publication on the application's behalf; that is, it will subscribe as `"Davolio"`. `"Davolio"`, in turn, will become the `user_name` value that the publication filter uses. Thus, information about Nancy Davolio's orders will be synchronized to the device.

Synchronizing the Data

Once we have subscribed to a publication and once the snapshot agent for that publication has run at least once, we can synchronize with the publication, resulting in the two-way exchange of data between the server and the device.

Listing 13.8 shows the code. It is identical to the subscription code in Listing 13.7 except that the `Synchronize` method is called instead of the `AddSubscription` method.

LISTING 13.8: Synchronizing the Device with the Remote Server

```
private void mitemSynchronize_Click(object sender,
                              System.EventArgs e)
{
   SqlCeReplication  replNW = new SqlCeReplication();
   try
   {
      replNW.ExchangeType = ExchangeType.BiDirectional;
      replNW.InternetUrl = strURL;
      replNW.InternetLogin = "";
      replNW.InternetPassword = "";
      replNW.Publisher = "SNOWDEN";
      replNW.PublisherDatabase = "Northwind";
      replNW.Publication = "EmployeeOrderInfo";
      replNW.PublisherSecurityMode =
         SecurityType.DBAuthentication;
      replNW.PublisherLogin = "Davolio";
      replNW.PublisherPassword = "Nancy";
      replNW.Subscriber = "YaoDurant";
      replNW.SubscriberConnectionString = strConnLocal;

      replNW.Synchronize();
   }
   catch( SqlCeException exSQL )
   {
      HandleSQLException(exSQL);
   }
   finally
   {
      replNW.Dispose();
   }
}
```

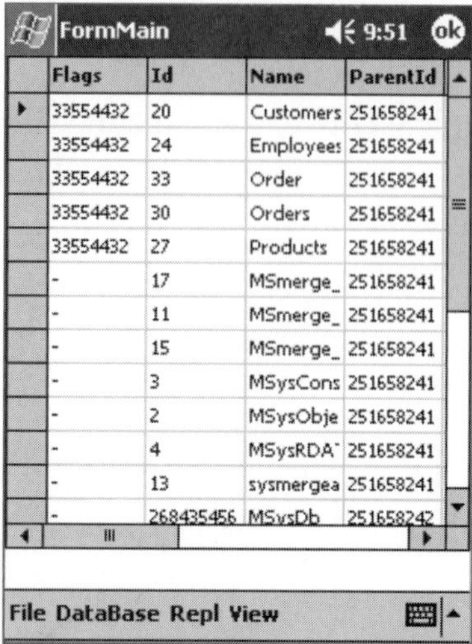

FIGURE 13.13: Objects after synchronization

Synchronization brings new data and schemas, if necessary, to the device and closes the connection to the server. Because we have not previously synchronized, there is no data already on our device that came from the remote server and therefore no data that will be returned to the server during this synchronization.

Our sample application has methods that select all rows from `msysObjects` and `msysConstraints` and display the results in the `DataGrid` control. Figures 13.13 and 13.14 show the information presented by these routines, respectively. We can see that both tables and constraints have been propagated from the server to the device.

Modifying the Data at the Device

Once the data is on our device, we can add, update, and delete as covered in Chapter 12 and in accordance with the restrictions described in Table 13.4 earlier in this chapter. Listing 13.9 shows a simple example.

LISTING 13.9: Updating the Data Locally

```
private void mitemLocalUpdate_Click(object sender,
                                     System.EventArgs e)
{
```

```
      SqlCeConnection  connLocal =
         new SqlCeConnection(strConnLocal);
      connLocal.Open();

      SqlCeCommand  cmndLocal = new SqlCeCommand();
      try {
         cmndLocal.Connection = connLocal;
         cmndLocal.CommandText =
            "INSERT \"Order Details\" " +
            " (OrderID, ProductID, UnitPrice, " +
            "  Quantity, Discount) " +
            " VALUES (10258, 1, 19.95, 44, 0.0)";
         cmndLocal.ExecuteNonQuery();
      }
      catch( SqlCeException exSQL )
      {
         HandleSQLException(exSQL);
      }
      finally
      {
         cmndLocal.Dispose();
         connLocal.Close();
      }
   }
```

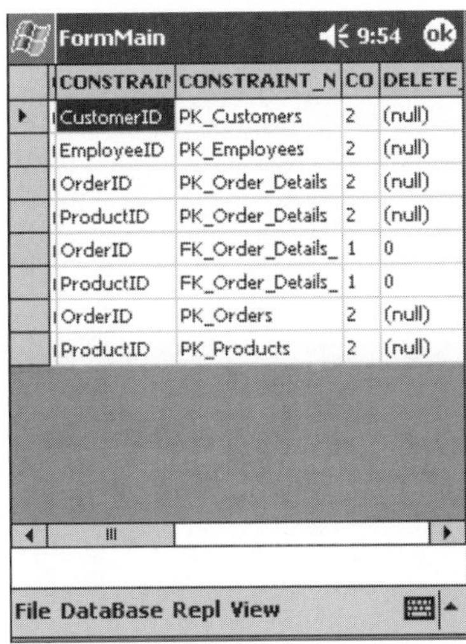

FIGURE 13.14: Constraints after synchronization

After executing this statement, we examine the order details table on the device to verify that the row is there, as shown in Figure 13.15.

When we synchronize again, we use Enterprise Manager to view the row on the server (see Figure 13.16), thus verifying that it was received.

ProductII	UnitPrice	Quantity	Discount
1	19.95	44	0
2	15.2	50	0.2
5	17	65	0.2
32	25.6	6	0.2
36	15.2	30	0
43	36.8	25	0
24	3.6	12	0.05
59	44	6	0.05
1	14.4	45	0.2
40	14.7	40	0.2
53	26.2	36	0.2
20	64.8	20	0
18	50	12	0

FIGURE 13.15: Order detail row added for Merge Replication

OrderID	ProductID	UnitPrice	Quantity
10257	27	35.1	25
10257	39	14.4	6
10257	77	10.4	15
10258	1	19.95	44
10258	2	15.2	50
10258	5	17	65
10258	32	25.6	6
10259	21	8	10
10259	37	20.8	1
10260	41	7.7	16
10260	57	15.6	50
10260	62	39.4	15
10260	70	12	21
10261	21	8	20

FIGURE 13.16: Order detail row viewed at the server

This completes the walkthrough of our sample application. During it, we subscribed, synchronized, modified data, and resynchronized—the steps that every Merge Replication application must perform.

A Merge Replication application requires a small amount of code to subscribe and synchronize because it is drawing on components defined outside of the program, mainly the virtual directory configuration and the publication definition. Good planning and design of these outside components is essential for success.

Choosing between Merge Replication and RDA

An important design issue that you have to address when you start to think about using SQL Server CE involves selecting which of the two connectivity solutions to use. If you must work with older versions of SQL Server (versions 6.5 and 7.0), the choice is easy: You must use RDA because Merge Replication is not supported. With SQL Server 2000, however, you can use either method.

The biggest difference is that Merge Replication lets you specify the relationship between the desktop data and the Windows CE data declaratively, through the definition publications, while RDA requires that you write SQL code to define the data to be transferred. Thus, with Merge Replication, the central data store controls data movement, while RDA allows the Windows CE devices to run the show.

Initially, this might make RDA seem the better choice. You just code a `SELECT` statement, use the `Pull` method, and, voilà, SQL Server CE creates a table and transfers the selected data into the table. No need to bother with the administrative effort of setting up replication.

For a simple or "one-time" application, this might be true. But for a major application, Merge Replication probably is the way to go. Merge Replication provides capabilities that are not matched in RDA (e.g., conflict resolution, Ranged Identity columns, and dynamic partitions). These declarative capabilities, which are not built into RDA, are extremely difficult to hand-code into an RDA application. The deeper you go into enterprise application development, the more you need Merge Replication. Although a good replication scenario requires up-front thought, planning, and design, the resulting reduction in code necessary to complete the application makes it worth the effort in the development of full-scale applications.

CONCLUSION

Developers who are experienced with building SQL applications on the Windows desktop will find much that is familiar with SQL Server 2000 Windows CE Edition. That is, you have a host of old standbys like the SQL database statements, as well as the ADOCE and the OLEDB CE programming interfaces to work with. What is new is the connectivity model that SQL Server CE provides for the merging of mobile data into a central data store.

Developers who have built Web-based applications will also find much that is familiar here. SQL Server CE provides a high-powered, client-oriented database engine that lets you coordinate the movement of data between mobile, sometimes connected, devices and a central data store. And, of course, it also can run as a stand-alone database quite nicely.

14

The Remote API

Chapter 13 discussed various options for connecting mobile systems to desktop and server systems, and Chapter 12 ended with a discussion of Web Services. This chapter covers the Remote API (RAPI), another option for making the device-to-desktop connection for devices that are connected using ActiveSync.

THIS CHAPTER DISCUSSES RAPI, an extension to the Win32 API on desktop versions of Microsoft Windows. The RAPI functions provide a mechanism for code running on the desktop to access Windows CE–powered devices that are connected to the desktop via ActiveSync. Most of the RAPI functions involve accessing the object store of a connected device, although a host of other functions provide some interesting ways to access a Windows CE system from a desktop system. Because RAPI depends on ActiveSync, it makes sense to start this chapter with an exploration of ActiveSync.

What Is ActiveSync?

ActiveSync is a desktop-oriented set of services for connecting a Windows CE device to a desktop system running any recent version of Microsoft Windows (Microsoft Windows 98 or later). ActiveSync connections serve the following purposes:

- Moving data from a device to a desktop system
- Moving data from a desktop system to a device

- Installing applications
- Uninstalling applications
- Allowing a device to access a network by using the desktop computer's network card and ActiveSync's Pass Through support

ActiveSync Pass Through

When ActiveSync 3.5 or later is on the desktop, a docked Pocket PC 2002 has access to ActiveSync Pass Through. Andreas Sjöström, of Business Anyplace[1] in Sweden, wrote an article on this subject on Microsoft's Pocket PC site, which you can read at http://www.microsoft.com/mobile/developer/technicalarticles/passthrough.asp. From a development point of view, Andreas makes two key points about which protocols Pass Through supports and which ones it does not.

In brief, Pass Through supports HTTP, HTTPS, IMAP, and POP3. It does not support UDP, ICMP, or PPTP.

Kenny Goers suggests that FTP works well in the Pass Through layer as well. Kenny is a developer at Magenic[2] and the moderator of the Yahoo Group where one of us likes to hang out and offer friendly advice and the occasional bad pun. For details on the list, browse to http://groups.yahoo.com/group/windowsce-dev.

ActiveSync itself is installed on desktop systems, not on Windows CE devices. Devices like the Pocket PC come packaged with a docking cradle that acts as a battery charger and also provides the physical connection between a device and a serial or USB connection. When a device is put into its docking cradle, ActiveSync wakes up and establishes a connection.

When you purchase a Pocket PC or other Windows CE–based device, you normally also find a CD containing ActiveSync for installation on your

1. See http://www.businessanyplace.net.
2. See http://www.magenic.com.

desktop system. ActiveSync is also available for download from the Microsoft Web site,[3] and you can use it to create connections to custom Windows CE–based devices as well.

When a password has been established on a Windows CE device, ActiveSync asks for a password before allowing access to a device. Windows CE devices support two kinds of passwords: a simple four-digit number and a longer alphanumeric value. Users set the password in the Windows CE Control Panel.

ActiveSync treats Pocket PCs and other Windows CE–powered devices as remote peripherals. This approach to Windows CE devices is very different from the one we've used in other chapters in this book. For this reason, most of the code in this chapter runs on the desktop and not on a device. Two sample programs run on a device, but these are downloaded and run from a desktop program. Table 14.1 summarizes this chapter's sample programs.

Partners and Guests

When a device connects to a desktop, ActiveSync determines whether the desktop and the device have an established partnership. If so, ActiveSync performs a set of synchronization tasks. If there is no partnership, the user can establish a partnership or connect as a guest. Full synchronization services are available only to partner devices and not to guests.

Both partner and guest devices can do the following:

- Manually transfer files between the desktop and the device using the desktop Windows Explorer.
- Add or remove (i.e., install or uninstall) programs.
- Back up and restore device data.
- Connect to an intranet or the Internet using ActiveSync Pass Through.

3. You can download ActiveSync from http://www.microsoft.com/windowsmobile/resources/downloads/pocketpc/activesync35.mspx.

TABLE 14.1: ActiveSync Sample Programs in This Chapter

Name	Description
RapiStartup	A simple RAPI program with startup and shutdown and no threads
FindPrograms	A program that searches the device file system for *.exe files by using the CeFindFirstFile and CeFindNextFile approach
FindProgramsFaster	A faster program search sample using CeFindAllFiles
FindProgramsOnConnect	The FindProgramsFaster program with IDCC-Man connect detection, used to search for program files automatically when a connection is detected
RegShowStartup	A program that queries the device registry to show programs and DLLs that are automatically started at CE system cold boot
ShowDatabases	A program that queries the device for mounted property database volumes and property databases
YaoDurant.Win32.Rapi	A library that contains P/Invoke wrappers for rapi.dll
SimpleBlockModeInvoke	A C++ DLL that calls the Win32 API to demonstrate block mode calls to CeRapiInvoke (with the online samples, located in the CPP source tree)
CallDeviceDll	A test program that calls SimpleBlockMode-Invoke.dll

Devices with partnerships can perform the following additional tasks:

- Synchronize files. Files that have been selected as files to synchronize get copied from the device to the desktop or from the desktop to the device, depending on which was more recently modified.
- Synchronize databases. When a partner device connects to a desktop system, ActiveSync runs all active database synchronizations. There

are several built-in database synchronization objects, including one for the Pocket Outlook calendar, contact list, inbox, and task list. Applications can also install custom database synchronization objects.

A device can establish a local connection to a desktop system by using any of several mechanisms: via USB port, serial port, infrared (IrDA) port, or Bluetooth. Once a partnership has been established between a device and a desktop, remote connections can be established using your choice of dial-up modem, a hard-wired network connection, or a wireless Wi-Fi network connection.

ActiveSync Limitations

Before digging into ActiveSync, we ought to point out its limitations.

- ActiveSync supports only one active connection at a time.
- ActiveSync cannot access the Windows CE emulator.
- ActiveSync does not synchronize between devices.
- ActiveSync does not synchronize with servers.

Only One Active Connection

A given Windows CE device can have a partnership with at most two different desktop systems. Desktop systems, on the other hand, can have partnerships with an unlimited number of devices. ActiveSync itself, however, can handle only one device connection at a time. Windows handles multitasking, but ActiveSync does not.

This makes ActiveSync suitable for some scenarios and inappropriate for others. ActiveSync works well when there is a one-to-one mapping between devices and desktops. ActiveSync does not work as well with a many-to-one relationship between devices and desktop systems. For example, if you have a large number of devices that leave in the morning and come back in the evening, ActiveSync is probably not your best choice. This is why Microsoft SQL Server CE, a database that runs on Windows CE, does not use ActiveSync for its device-to-database connectivity.

Because it does not rely on ActiveSync, SQL Server CE allows multiple Windows CE devices to simultaneously synchronize with a single central database server.

No Emulator Support

The lack of emulator support means that to build and run ActiveSync applications, you must have an actual Windows CE device. If you plan to spend any time working on ActiveSync code, we suggest you make the investment in a network card for your Windows CE device. The reason is simple: Network hardware is relatively inexpensive, and it allows for much faster development and debugging. In fact, this suggestion is not limited to just ActiveSync development; we recommend using network hardware for all your device-side development and testing. Network downloading and debugging—whether by wired network or wireless—is just plain faster than serial or USB port connections.

ActiveSync and the Emulator

Microsoft has made available a tool called Emulator ActiveSync Connection Tool. According to the Microsoft Web site, this tool "allows ActiveSync to connect to your Emulator session from Visual Studio .NET 2003." The tool is available with a package of tools known as the Windows Mobile Developer Power Toys, a free download available from the Microsoft Web site.[4]

No Synchronization between Devices

ActiveSync is not a general-purpose synchronization mechanism. It is specifically designed to connect devices with desktops running Microsoft Windows 98 and later. Supported versions of Microsoft Windows include Windows 98, Windows Me, Windows NT (Service Pack 6), Windows 2000, Windows XP, and the Windows 2003 Server.

---

4. To access these tools, set your browser to http://www.pocketpc.com (an alias that points into the Microsoft Web site), then navigate to Downloads and Developers.

ActiveSync Backup and Restore

While ActiveSync does not provide support for synchronizing between devices, it does allow you to back up the object store from one device and restore it to another Windows CE device. The end result is two identical devices. For users of Windows CE–based devices, this ability to back up and restore can help safeguard against data loss when a device is lost or damaged.

No Synchronization with Servers

ActiveSync does not synchronize Windows CE devices with servers. However, some server-side systems do communicate with Windows CE–powered devices. These are summarized in the Connecting Devices to Servers sidebar. Those server-side systems do not use ActiveSync but rather support direct connections to devices through TCP/IP.

Connecting Devices to Servers

Microsoft's commitment to mobile and embedded devices can be seen in the energy devoted to create and enhance Windows CE, which first shipped in 1996. Version 4.1 started shipping in summer 2002. In recent years, Microsoft has started adding Windows CE device support to its various server-side products.

SQL Server 2000 Windows CE Edition. Known also as SQL Server CE, this is a single-user, stand-alone database engine for Windows CE devices. SQL Server CE supports two mechanisms for connecting to servers and synchronizing device data with server data—Merge Replication and RDA. The connection between a Windows CE device and a SQL Server database is not through ActiveSync but instead is an HTTP-based connection.

The typical scenario for a SQL Server CE user is a salesperson with a Pocket PC and a mobile phone (or the two combined, as in the Pocket PC 2002 Phone Edition). The user can remotely synchronize the mobile database with the central office database. Between sales calls, the mobile SQL Server CE database can connect, via the mobile phone network, to the central server to both upload orders and download status information. For details, see "SQL Server CE: New Version Lets You Store and Update Data on Handheld Devices," an article we wrote for the June 2001 edition of *MSDN Magazine*. This article is available online at http://msdn.microsoft.com/msdnmag/issues/01/06/sqlce/default.aspx.

ASP.NET Mobile Controls. The ASP.NET Mobile Controls, previously known as Microsoft Mobile Internet Toolkit, supports Web-based applications for mobile and handheld devices. It allows developers to add mobile-device support to ASP.NET-based Web sites. A separate set of controls is needed because devices such as PDAs and cell phones have smaller displays than desktop systems. Devices often have browsers that support simpler markup language than what is found in desktop browsers. ASP.NET Mobile Controls support all of these differences. As of this writing, these controls support four markup languages: HTML 3.2, Compact HTML (cHTML), Wireless Markup Language (WML), and XHTML. For details, see our article "Microsoft Mobile Internet Toolkit Lets Your Web Application Target Any Device Anywhere," from the November 2002 edition of *MSDN Magazine*. This article is available online at http://msdn.microsoft.com/msdnmag/issues/02/11/MMIT/default.aspx.

Mobile Information Server. Microsoft created the Mobile Information Server (MIS) to allow device-to-server connectivity for Exchange Server, Microsoft's e-mail server system. MIS allows remote access from a Pocket PC or other supported Windows CE device to data that a user might access from the desktop using Microsoft Outlook. A device user can log in and remotely access e-mail, task lists, contact lists, and calendars. Details are available at http://www.microsoft.com/miserver.

Systems Management Server. Another Microsoft server-side system called Systems Management Server (SMS) allows for centralized control of downloading and installing software. As of this writing, Microsoft has made available a beta version of an add-on called Device Management Feature Pack for SMS 2003.[5] This feature pack makes available hardware inventory, software inventory, and software distribution, among its other features. For deployment of a large number of devices, SMS 2003 promises to make life easier for corporate IT departments.

ActiveSync Compared with Web Services

Because ActiveSync and Web Services both support desktop-to-device connectivity, you might at this point wonder how they compare. Both provide RPC support; however, ActiveSync is a more specialized form of RPC, while Web Services provide a more general type of RPC.

ActiveSync differs from Web Services in that the locus of control for a Web Service is at the client—it is, after all, the device that calls the Web Service. With ActiveSync, on the other hand, control is located on the desktop because that is where your code primarily runs.

ActiveSync is a desktop-oriented programming interface that provides a very simple RPC mechanism for accessing the object store of a Windows CE device. Use it when your usage scenario involves having a home base for a roaming device. The home base—the desktop system—provides the place to install software and synchronize data.

Web Services, on the other hand, are a general-purpose RPC mechanism that allows a device to access a standard (meaning here the SOAP/XML/HTTP-based standards) Web Service. You will likely use Web Services to call out to third-party services to fetch phone numbers, weather forecasts, travel information, and so on.

For the most part, then, the uses of ActiveSync and Web Services are separate and distinct—use ActiveSync to "phone home" and Web Services

5. See http://www.microsoft.com/smserver/downloads/2003/dmfpbeta.asp.

to "call out." The only real overlap is when you implement Web Services on a PC where a Windows CE device has a partnership. In that case, the decision comes down to whether you want to implement something that is device-driven or desktop-driven. For device-driven operations, implement a Web Service; for desktop-driven operations, use ActiveSync.

ActiveSync Programming Interfaces

ActiveSync provides a set of Win32 functions and COM interfaces to support its various services. This chapter focuses on RAPI and on the Device Connection Manager. Table 14.2 shows these two, along with other ActiveSync function sets available for use.

TABLE 14.2: ActiveSync Application Programming Interfaces

ActiveSync API	Description	Build Files	Runtime Files
RAPI	A set of 78 C-callable functions for accessing the file system, registry, and property databases and for supporting various application setup activities	`rapi.h` `rapi.lib`	`rapi.dll`
File Filter	A COM-based interface for converting whole files as they are copied from a device to the desktop or from the desktop to a device	`replfilt.h`	
Device Connection Manager Notification	A COM-based interface for receiving notifications about when ActiveSync connections start and stop	`dccole.h`	`rapi.dll`
Registry Service Functions	A set of helper functions for reading and writing desktop registry settings in support of ActiveSync	`ceutil.h` `ceutil.lib`	`ceutil.dll`
Database Synchronization	A set of COM-based interfaces called by ActiveSync to keep device-side and desktop-side databases synchronized	`cesync.h`	

Should You Build Managed-Code ActiveSync Applications?

All of the ActiveSync libraries listed in Table 14.2 are unmanaged-code libraries, built with either C-callable exported functions or COM components. That being the case, you might wonder whether you can write ActiveSync applications in managed code and whether you should.

Can you use managed code? Yes, but it is important to remember that you may have device-side code and desktop-side code. For the present, you can only write your desktop-side code as managed code. P/Invoke support lets you call C-callable functions, and COM interop on the desktop supports calling from managed code into a COM object. To access ActiveSync services from managed code, you need a set of P/Invoke wrappers—which is what we have done for you. You can find those wrappers included with the source code available for download from this book's source code Web site. (Or, you can use the P/Invoke Wizard—discussed in detail in Chapter 4—to build your own P/Invoke wrappers.)

While the .NET Compact Framework does not support COM interop, the desktop .NET Framework does have that support. So any desktop-side ActiveSync component that requires COM can be easily created as managed code; but any device-side ActiveSync component that requires COM cannot be written as managed code but instead must be written in native (unmanaged or Win32) code.

The next question is whether you should take this approach. Programmers receive myriad benefits from managed code, which we discussed in Part I of this book. Because of all its benefits, we are partial to managed code. If you are too, the good news is that most ActiveSync features can be accessed in managed code.

A reason not to use managed code is because managed-code software requires the presence of the .NET Framework. Although the desktop .NET Framework is compatible with Windows 98 and later, it was not released until January 2002 and so is not yet widely available. For example, as of this writing only two versions of Microsoft Windows come bundled with the .NET Framework: Windows XP Tablet PC Edition and Windows Server 2003.

To support the installation of the .NET Framework on previous versions of Windows, Microsoft provides a distribution mechanism in the form of a large, downloadable file named `dotnetfx.exe`. This 20MB file installs the .NET Framework, which developers can bundle with their software to be supplied to third-party customers.[6]

RAPI Fundamentals

Windows CE RAPI is a specialized RPC facility. We call it an RPC API because RAPI functions cause remote function calls on connected devices. It is specialized because you can call only a limited subset of device-side functions. Most RAPI functions provide access to a device's object store and device-side file systems. As we described in Chapter 11, the object store is the permanently mounted RAM-based storage area that contains the built-in file system, the system registry, and property databases. This is not the only storage available, however, and RAPI also lets you access whatever installable file system is present to support removable Compact Flash cards, Smart Media cards, disk drives, and so on.

RAPI and .NET Remoting

If you have worked with the desktop .NET Framework and have heard about .NET Remoting, you might be wondering about its relationship to RAPI. Aside from similar names, these two technologies have nothing in common.

The ability to access the object store means that a RAPI program can access any stored data. You can, for example, open a file and copy part of it—or all of it—from the device to the desktop. You could open the system registry and create new keys, or read and write values on existing keys. You have complete access to the property databases in the object store, so

6. Details are available at http://msdn.microsoft.com/library/en-us/dnnetdep/html/redistdeploy.asp.

that you can create a database, delete a database, add or remove database records, and read or write individual property values.

RAPI is a set of functions that are exactly like the Win32 functions used to access files, registry entries, and CE databases. The only difference is that each of the RAPI functions has a slightly different name because of the `Ce` prefix. For example, the Win32 function to open a file is `CreateFile`; its RAPI equivalent is `CeCreateFile`. Once a file is opened, you read a file's contents by calling `CeReadFile` and close the file by calling `CeCloseHandle`. This is different from the approach we took to file access in Chapter 11, where we discussed using `System.IO` classes. And instead of ADO.NET classes, access to property databases is through a set of C-callable functions with names like `CeCreateDatabase` and `CeWriteRecordProps`.

RAPI Names for Property Database Functions

CE property databases were created specifically for Windows CE, and they already have a `Ce` prefix in their names. So device-side database functions have the same name as their RAPI function counterpart. In other words, `CeCreateDatabase` is both a device-side function and a RAPI function.

Most RAPI functions access the object store, but there are also non–object store RAPI functions. Two interesting functions are `CeCreateProcess` and `CeRapiInvoke`. The `CeCreateProcess` function lets you start running a device-side program. The `CeRapiInvoke` function remotely loads and calls a function in a device-side DLL. These functions are very useful, giving you wide latitude to do almost anything on a device. With these two functions, there is almost nothing you cannot do.

For example, you could copy a .NET Compact Framework program onto a Windows CE device and start it running. You could download a Win32 DLL and call a function. You can then keep those files on the target device or remove them—perhaps to save device-side storage space.

Available RAPI Functions

We divide the 78 RAPI functions into eight groups:

- RAPI Support
- Run Program/Load DLL
- File System
- Registry
- CE Property Database
- Object Store Queries
- System Information
- Remote Windowing

Table 14.3 provides details of each group. Although most RAPI functions have an equivalent Win32 function in Windows CE, a few RAPI functions have no Win32 equivalent, such as those used for RAPI management and support. In two cases—`CeFindAllFiles` and `CeFindAllDatabases`—functions were created specifically to boost performance. These two functions access a user-defined subset in a query, allowing for faster queries of available files or databases.

Building .NET ActiveSync Applications

Because ActiveSync applications run on the desktop, when you build them in Visual Studio .NET, you do not create a Smart Device Application. You pick instead any of the various desktop project types. You can build ActiveSync applications either as managed (.NET) applications or as unmanaged (Win32) applications. This book does not cover the Win32 approach because it is covered elsewhere.[7] This chapter focuses instead on building managed-code ActiveSync applications.

7. For example, see Doug Boling's book *Programming Microsoft Windows CE* (Redmond, WA: Microsoft Press, 2001).

TABLE 14.3: Available RAPI Functions

Group 1: RAPI Support	
RAPI Function	**Description**
`CeRapiInit`	Is a blocking initialization function.
`CeRapiInitEx`	Is a nonblocking initialization function that returns a Win32 event handle that gets signaled when a connection is complete.
`CeRapiUninit`	Cleans up for `CeRapiInit` and `CeRapiInitEx`.
`CeRapiGetError`	Queries for RAPI-specific errors.
`CeGetLastError`	Queries for non-RAPI device-side errors (equivalent to `GetLastError`).
`CeRapiFreeBuffer`	Is a free buffer allocated by various functions, including `CeFindAllFiles` and `CeFindAllDatabases`.
Group 2: Run Program/Load DLL	
RAPI Function	**Description**
`CeCreateProcess`	Starts a program running on the Windows CE device.
`CeRapiInvoke`	Calls a named function in a named Win32 DLL on a Windows CE device. Does not support generic RPCs to DLLs because the function called must take a specific set of parameters.
Group 3: File System	
RAPI Function	**Description**
`CeCloseHandle`	Closes a file opened with a call to `CeCreateFile` (or a database opened with `CeOpenDatabaseEx`).
`CeCopyFile`	Copies a file on the device to another location on the device (does not copy between device and desktop system).
`CeCreateDirectory`	Creates a directory in the file system of a device.

continues

TABLE 14.3: Available RAPI Functions (continued)

Group 3: File System	
RAPI Function	**Description**
`CeCreateFile`	Opens a file on the device, optionally creating it at the same time.
`CeDeleteFile`	Deletes a file on the device file system.
`CeFindAllFiles`	Searches for all files in a given directory that match a specific criteria, returning a subset of the data returned by the normal file enumeration functions. This reduction in data causes this function to run faster than the generic file enumeration functions.
`CeFindClose`	Cleans up file enumeration begun with a call to `CeFindFirstFile`.
`CeFindFirstFile`	Starts file enumeration in a given directory for specific search criteria.
`CeFindNextFile`	Continues file enumeration begun with a call to `CeFindFirstFile`.
`CeGetFileAttributes`	Queries the attribute of a file in the device file system.
`CeGetFileSize`	Queries file size.
`CeGetFileTime`	Queries creation, last accessed, and last modified date and time.
`CeGetSpecialFolderPath`	Gets the path name for shell file system folders.
`CeGetTempPath`	Gets the path to the temporary directory.
`CeMoveFile`	Renames an existing file or directory on a device. Files can be moved between different drives; directories can be moved only to a different location on the existing drive.
`CeReadFile`	Reads a number of bytes from a file opened with a call to `CeCreateFile`.
`CeRemoveDirectory`	Deletes an existing empty directory.

Group 3: File System	
RAPI Function	**Description**
`CeSetEndOfFile`	Truncates the file at the current position of the file pointer.
`CeSetFileAttributes`	Modifies the file attribute flags to enable or disable the following bits: archive, hidden, normal, read-only, system, and temporary.
`CeSetFilePointer`	Moves the file pointer in a file opened with `CeCreateFile`.
`CeSetFileTime`	Modifies the directory entry for a file on a device to change the associated created, last accessed, or modified time.
`CeSHCreateShortcut`	Creates a program shortcut on the remote device.
`CeSHGetShortcutTarget`	Queries the path stored in an existing shortcut.
`CeWriteFile`	Writes a number of bytes to a file opened with a call to `CeCreateFile`.

Group 4: Registry	
RAPI Function	**Description**
`CeRegCloseKey`	Closes a registry key opened with a call to either `CeRegOpenKeyEx` or `CeRegCreateKeyEx`.
`CeRegCreateKeyEx`	Creates a new registry key or opens an existing registry key.
`CeRegDeleteKey`	Deletes a named subkey and the associated value in the registry. If the named subkey has subkeys under it, the call fails.
`CeRegDeleteValue`	Deletes one value from the specified registry node.
`CeRegEnumKeyEx`	Enumerates the subkeys of an indicated registry node.
`CeRegEnumValue`	Enumerates the values in an indicated registry node.

continues

TABLE 14.3: Available RAPI Functions (continued)

Group 4: Registry	
RAPI Function	**Description**
`CeRegOpenKeyEx`	Opens a registry node.
`CeRegQueryInfoKey`	Queries details about a given registry node, including number of subkeys and the length of the longest subkey name.
`CeRegQueryValueEx`	Fetches a value from a registry node.
`CeRegSetValueEx`	Writes a value to a registry node.
Group 5: CE Property Database	
RAPI Function	**Description**
`CeCloseHandle`	Closes a database opened with `CeOpenDatabaseEx` (or a file opened with `CeCreateFile`).
`CeCreateDatabase`	Creates a new property database. (Obsolete—use `CeCreateDatabaseEx` instead.)
`CeCreateDatabaseEx`	Creates a new property database with an associated GUID.
`CeDeleteDatabase`	Deletes a database by object ID value.
`CeDeleteDatabaseEx`	Deletes a database by object ID and GUID.
`CeDeleteRecord`	Deletes a database record.
`CeEnumDBVolumes`	Enumerates all mounted property database volumes.
`CeFindAllDatabases`	Returns a subset of the data returned by the general-purpose database enumeration functions. The reduction in requested data causes this to run faster than the general-purpose enumeration functions.
`CeFindFirstDatabase`	Starts enumerating all property databases in the object store.

Group 5: CE Property Database	
RAPI Function	**Description**
`CeFindFirstDatabaseEx`	Starts enumerating all property databases in the system or on the indicated database volume.
`CeFindNextDatabase`	Continues enumeration started with `CeFindFirstDatabase`.
`CeFindNextDatabaseEx`	Continues enumeration started with `CeFindFirstDatabaseEx`.
`CeFlushDBVol`	Forces a save of database changes from program memory to storage.
`CeMountDBVol`	Issues a mount request for a database volume.
`CeOpenDatabase`	Opens a database. (Obsolete—use `CeOpenDatabaseEx` instead.)
`CeOpenDatabaseEx`	Opens a database by name or by GUID.
`CeReadRecordProps`	Reads a database record.
`CeReadRecordPropsEx`	Reads a database record, optionally allocating memory from a provided Win32 heap.
`CeSeekDatabase`	Sets the current database record based on selection criteria.
`CeSetDatabaseInfo`	Modifies various database attributes, including name, type, and sort order.
`CeSetDatabaseInfoEx`	Modifies various database attributes, including name, type, and sort order, as well as the GUID.
`CeUnmountDBVol`	Unmounts a database volume mounted with an earlier call to `CeMountDBVol`.
`CeWriteRecordProps`	Writes a record to the database.

continues

TABLE 14.3: Available RAPI Functions (continued)

Group 6: Object Store Queries RAPI Function	Description
`CeOidGetInfo`	Queries the type of record located within the object store for a given object ID value.
`CeOidGetInfoEx`	Queries the type of record in the object store, or for any mounted database volume, for a given object ID value.
`CeGetStoreInformation`	Queries the total size and free space for the object store.
Group 7: System Information **RAPI Function**	**Description**
`CeCheckPassword`	Compares an entered password to a mobile device password, as set in the Windows CE Control Panel. A password is not passed as a parameter in the normal RAPI startup functions because—when password protection is enabled on a device—ActiveSync automatically prompts for a valid password before allowing the RAPI connection to be established. You would likely check the password only for an extra measure of security before performing an especially sensitive operation.
`CeGetDesktopDeviceCaps`	Queries the graphics capabilities of a remote device (this is equivalent to the `GetDeviceCaps` graphic capability query function).
`CeGetSystemInfo`	Queries the CPU and memory architecture of a remote device.
`CeGetSystemMetrics`	Queries the size of elements on the user interface of the remote system, including the width and height of window borders, icons, scroll bars, etc.
`CeGetSystemPowerStatusEx`	Queries the battery status and whether wall power is available.
`CeGetVersionEx`	Queries Windows CE operating system version information.
`CeGlobalMemoryStatus`	Queries available memory load, amount of physical memory, and available virtual memory.

Group 8: Remote Windowing	
RAPI Function	**Description**
`CeGetClassName`	Queries the window class name for a given window handle.
`CeGetWindow`	Walks the window hierarchy of the remote device.
`CeGetWindowLong`	Queries the state information for an indicated window.
`CeGetWindowText`	Queries the text of an indicated window.

If you plan to call ActiveSync from managed code, you need P/Invoke wrappers to access the Win32 ActiveSync libraries. We built two sets of wrappers—one in C# and the other in Visual Basic—that are included with the source code you can download from the book's source code Web site. We used the P/Invoke Wizard introduced in Chapter 4 and then fine-tuned the output by hand. As we mentioned earlier, you can download the P/Invoke Wizard from The Paul Yao Company Web site.[8]

RAPI Startup and Shutdown

Like other Win32 API function sets, RAPI has startup and shutdown functions. Before calling any other RAPI function, you must call a startup function: either `CeRapiInit` or `CeRapiInitEx`. The difference is that the first function is a blocking function and the second is not.

When startup is a success, your program does its work and then calls the shutdown function, `CeRapiUninit`. If you call a startup function, you must always call the shutdown function. This is true even if the startup fails. When we have run programs that did not follow this guideline, we notice that ActiveSync itself stops running properly until the offending program terminates.

8. Details are available at http://www.paulyao.com/pinvoke.

`CeRapiInit` *versus* `CeRapiInitEx`

At first glance, the `CeRapiInit` function seems the simplest way to establish a RAPI connection. But this is a blocking function, so a call at the wrong time causes a thread to hang, keeping a program in memory when it was supposed to have ended. By contrast, `CeRapiInitEx` is a nonblocking function.

The `CeRapiInitEx` function notifies the caller that a connection has been established through a Win32 event (you can wrap a .NET event object around a Win32 event). This function accepts a pointer to a `RAPIINIT` structure for input, and it returns an `HRESULT` result code. Here are the C# declarations for the `CeRapiInitEx` function and the required `RAPIINIT` structure.

```
[DllImport("rapi.dll", CharSet=CharSet.Unicode)]
public static extern int CeRapiInitEx (ref RAPIINIT pRapiInit);

[StructLayout(LayoutKind.Sequential,Pack=4)]
public struct RAPIINIT
{
   public int cbSize;
   public IntPtr heRapiInit;
   public int hrRapiInit;
};
```

Handling Win32 `HRESULT` Values

Treat Win32 `HRESULT` values as `int` values to stay compatible with the Common Language Specification. Avoid an overflow in C# with the `unchecked` keyword as shown here:

```
int E_FAIL = unchecked((int)0x80004005);
```

To call the `CeRapiInitEx` function, first allocate a `RAPIINIT` structure and set the `cbSize` member to the structure size. If you set the incorrect size, the `CeRapiInitEx` function returns an error (like many other Win32 functions). On return from the function call, the other two structure members hold return values. A Win32 event handle is returned in the location referenced by the second parameter, `heRapiInit`. After that event becomes signaled, `hrRapiInit` holds the initialization result code.

Shutdown with `CeRapiUninit`

After any call to a RAPI initialization function—whether or not a connection was established—you must call the `CeRapiUninit` function. The C# P/Invoke wrapper for this function is shown here.

```
[DllImport("rapi.dll")]
public static extern int CeRapiUninit();
```

Two Approaches to Startup

So far, we have looked at two functions and one structure that provide the first two functions you will need for all RAPI code you write. Now it's time to look at these elements in the context of real working code. We are going to show two different approaches to handling RAPI startup. The first is short and self-contained, suitable for showing all the startup details in one place. The second is a more real-world approach that involves creating a worker thread to handle the startup activity.

Approach 1: Simple, Single-Threaded RAPI Startup. Listing 14.1 shows the simplest possible RAPI startup and shutdown. This program includes all needed P/Invoke declarations for the two required `rapi.dll` functions: `CeRapiInitEx` and `CeRapiUninit`. This program provides a quick starting point for experimenting with other RAPI functions.

LISTING 14.1: `RapiStartup.cs` with Simplest Possible RAPI Startup and Shutdown

```
// RapiStartup.cs - Simple thread-free RAPI startup
// with all P/Invoke declarations included
//
// Code from _.NET Compact Framework Programming with C#_
// and _.NET Compact Framework Programming with Visual Basic .NET_
// Authored by Paul Yao and David Durant.
//

using System;
using System.Threading;
```

continues

continued

```
using System.Windows.Forms;
using System.Runtime.InteropServices;

namespace RapiStartup
{
   public class RapiStartup
   {
      const string m_strAppName = "RapiStartup";

      public RapiStartup()
      {
      }

      // ----------------------------------------------------------
      // rapi.dll Definitions
      // ----------------------------------------------------------
      public struct RAPIINIT
      {
         public int cbSize;
         public IntPtr heRapiInit;
         public int hrRapiInit;
      };

      [DllImport("rapi.dll", CharSet=CharSet.Unicode)]
      public static extern int CeRapiInitEx (ref RAPIINIT p);
      [DllImport("rapi.dll", CharSet=CharSet.Unicode)]
      public static extern int CeRapiUninit ();

      public const int S_OK = 0;

      // ----------------------------------------------------------
      // Main -- Program entry point
      // ----------------------------------------------------------
      public static void Main()
      {
         // Allocate structure for call to CeRapiInitEx.
         RAPIINIT ri = new RAPIINIT();
         ri.cbSize = Marshal.SizeOf(ri);

         // Call the init function.
         int hr = CeRapiInitEx(ref ri);

         // Wrap event handle in the corresponding .NET object.
         ManualResetEvent mrev = new ManualResetEvent(false);
         mrev.Handle = ri.heRapiInit;

         // Wait five seconds, then fail.
         if (mrev.WaitOne(5000, false) && ri.hrRapiInit == S_OK)
         {
```

```
                // Connection is established.
                MessageBox.Show("Connection Established",
                    m_strAppName);
            }
            else
            {
                // On failure, disconnect from RAPI.
                CeRapiUninit();

                MessageBox.Show("Timeout - No Device", m_strAppName);
                return;
            }

            // If we get here, we have established a RAPI connection.

            // ToDo: Put your RAPI calls here...

            // Clean up.
            CeRapiUninit();
        }

    } // class RapiStartup
} // namespace RapiStartup
```

Approach 2: Multithreaded RAPI Startup. Our second method for starting RAPI involves a background thread. At the same time, this sample shows how to connect to the ActiveSync wrapper library. We have two such libraries—a C# version and a Visual Basic version—both of which are named `YaoDurant.Win32.Rapi.dll`. There are at least two ways to use these libraries. You can copy the source-code declarations directly to your source code, or you can call into one of these libraries from your code.

Three pieces are needed to allow an application to access a DLL, no matter what language or API you are using: (1) a piece for the compiler, (2) a piece for the linker, and (3) a piece for the loader. Win32 programmers recognize these pieces as (1) the include (`.h`) file for the compiler, (2) the library (`.lib`) file for the linker, and (3) the DLL itself for the loader. Here is how to provide these three pieces for a .NET DLL.

1. For the compiler (and to help IntelliSense), add a `using` statement to your source file to identify the desired namespace(s):

   ```
   using YaoDurant.Win32;
   ```

2. For the linker, add a reference to the assembly (or DLL file name) from the Visual Studio .NET IDE:
   a. Open the Solution Explorer (select menu items View→Solution Explorer).
   b. Right-click on the `References` entry and select Add Reference....
   c. Click on the Browse... button.
   d. Select the desired library from the list, then click the Open button.
3. For the loader, copy the DLL to the directory of the program that needs to use it. (Visual Studio .NET does this automatically if you add the DLL to the project.)

Once you have completed these steps, you can access the RAPI types using the wrapper class name, `Rapi`. In a Visual Studio .NET editor window, when you type "`Rapi`", IntelliSense shows the types defined within the `Rapi` class.

Listing 14.2 shows `RapiStartupThread.cs`, a source file taken from the `FindPrograms` sample. It performs RAPI initialization on a background worker thread, which is more typical of what a production RAPI program would do.

LISTING 14.2: `RapiStartupThread.cs` with Thread-Based RAPI Startup

```
// Program Name: FindPrograms.exe
//
// File Name: RapiStartupThread.cs - Creates a background thread
// for the purpose of starting RAPI.
//
// Code from _.NET Compact Framework Programming with C#_
// and _.NET Compact Framework Programming with Visual Basic .NET_
// Authored by Paul Yao and David Durant.
//

using System;
using System.Threading;
using System.Windows.Forms;
using System.Runtime.InteropServices;
using System.Diagnostics;
using YaoDurant.Win32;

namespace FindPrograms
{
```

```
// Table of reasons that WorkerThread calls into the
// user interface thread
public enum INVOKE_STARTUP
{
   STARTUP_SUCCESS,
   STARTUP_FAILED,
   STATUS_MESSAGE
}

/// <summary>
/// StartupThread - Wrapper class that spins a thread
/// to initialize RAPI. Calls a delegate to report status.
/// </summary>
public class StartupThread
{
   public string strBuffer;       // Interthread buffer
   public INVOKE_STARTUP itReason;   // Interthread reason

   private Thread m_thrd = null;    // The contained thread
   private Control m_ctlInvokeTarget; // Interthread control
   private EventHandler m_deleCallback; // Interthread delegate
   private bool m_bContinue; // Continue flag

   public bool bThreadContinue // Continue property
   {
      get { return m_bContinue; }
      set { m_bContinue = value; }
   }

   /// <summary>
   /// StartupThread - Constructor
   /// </summary>
   /// <param name="ctl">Owner control</param>
   /// <param name="dele">Delegate to invoke</param>
   public StartupThread(Control ctl, EventHandler dele)
   {
      bThreadContinue = true;
      m_ctlInvokeTarget = ctl;  // Who to call.
      m_deleCallback = dele;    // How to call.
   }

   /// <summary>
   /// Run - Init function for startup thread
   /// </summary>
   /// <returns></returns>
   public bool Run()
   {
      ThreadStart ts = null;
```

continues

continued

```
        ts = new ThreadStart(ThreadMainStartup);
        if (ts == null)
            return false;

        m_thrd = new Thread(ts);
        m_thrd.Start();
        return true;
    }

    /// <summary>
    /// ThreadMainStartup - Start RAPI connection.
    /// </summary>
    private void ThreadMainStartup()
    {
        // Allocate structure for call to CeRapiInitEx.
        Rapi.RAPIINIT ri = new Rapi.RAPIINIT();
        ri.cbSize = Marshal.SizeOf(ri);

        // Call init function.
        int hr = Rapi.CeRapiInitEx(ref ri);

        // Wrap event handle in corresponding .NET object.
        ManualResetEvent mrev = new ManualResetEvent(false);
        mrev.Handle = ri.heRapiInit;

        // Wait five seconds, then fail.
        if (mrev.WaitOne(5000, false) &&
            ri.hrRapiInit == Rapi.S_OK)
        {
            // Notify caller that connection is established.
            itReason = INVOKE_STARTUP.STARTUP_SUCCESS;
            m_ctlInvokeTarget.Invoke(m_deleCallback);
        }
        else
        {
            // On failure, disconnect from RAPI.
            Rapi.CeRapiUninit();

            strBuffer = "Timeout - no device present.";
            itReason = INVOKE_STARTUP.STATUS_MESSAGE;
            m_ctlInvokeTarget.Invoke(m_deleCallback);

            // Notify caller that connection failed.
            itReason = INVOKE_STARTUP.STARTUP_FAILED;
            m_ctlInvokeTarget.Invoke(m_deleCallback);
        }
```

```
            // Trigger that thread has ended.
            m_thrd = null;
        }
    } // class StartupThread
} // namespace FindPrograms
```

The `StartupThread` class provides a wrapper around the startup thread. We put this class into its own file to make it easy for you to reuse. This class uses the `Invoke` function to communicate from the background thread to the user interface thread. This class depends on having a control (or a form) and on that control having a delegate to receive the interthread calls. Our startup wrapper has three methods: a constructor, `Run`, and `ThreadMainStartup`.

The `ThreadMainStartup` method is the thread entry point, and it does the actual work of calling the `CeRapiInitEx` function to initiate the RAPI connection and calling the `CeRapiUninit` function if the attempt to connect fails.

A background thread allows the user interface thread to be available to receive user input. A downside to multithreaded programming is that the two threads need to be carefully crafted to avoid conflicts, which are usually very hard to reproduce because they are often related to timing and thus hard to find. Our approach to this problem is for each thread to run in a separate class and not interact with others, with two exceptions: thread startup code and thread-safe communication code. In this code, there is a one-way communication from the worker thread to the main thread. The communication is handled by the only function in the `Control` class guaranteed to be thread-safe: `Control.Invoke`.

The desktop .NET Framework provides two overloads for the `Invoke` method:

```
public object Invoke(Delegate);
public virtual object Invoke(Delegate, object[]);
```

Each overload accepts a parameter of type `Delegate` (similar to a C function pointer). The second overload, which accepts an array of values to be used as parameters to the called function, is the version most often used in

Why `Control.Invoke` Is Thread-Safe

The `Control.Invoke` method is thread-safe (in both the desktop .NET Framework and the .NET Compact Framework) because it relies on an underlying Win32 feature that is guaranteed thread-safe. That feature is the `SendMessage` function, a Win32 function that has been around since the first version of Windows. This function sends a Win32 message to a window, waiting for the message to be delivered before returning. If the recipient is busy with another message, the `SendMessage` function blocks until the previous message has been handled. Over the years, this function has been the backbone for interthread and interprocess communication in a variety of Windows technologies, including the Dynamic Data Exchange (DDE), OLE, and COM. It is not surprising, then, that this time-tested mechanism is also used by the .NET `Control` class.

the desktop .NET Framework. The .NET Compact Framework, however, supports only the first type of overload, and because this is a .NET Compact Framework book we are going to resist the temptation to do things the desktop .NET Framework way. Here is a call to the `Invoke` method to notify the main thread that a successful RAPI connection has been established.

```
// Notify caller that connection is established.
itReason = INVOKE_STARTUP.STARTUP_SUCCESS;
ctlInvokeTarget.Invoke(deleCallback);
```

The recipient of this function call is a function named `StartupCallback`, a member of the `MainForm` class in our `FindPrograms` sample. We cannot just pass a function pointer like we do in unmanaged C, however. Instead, we pass the .NET equivalent, a delegate of type `EventHandler`. Here is the declaration for the delegate, along with the other declarations needed to support the startup thread.

```
// Startup thread definitions
StartupThread thrdStartup = null;
```

```
private EventHandler deleStartup;
private bool bRapiConnected = false;
```

We initialize the delegate as follows:

```
deleStartup = new EventHandler(this.StartupCallback);
```

and then pass it to the constructor for our startup thread wrapper object:

```
// Create thread to connect to RAPI.
thrdStartup = new StartupThread(this, deleStartup);
if (!thrdStartup.Run())
   thrdStartup = null;
```

After creating the `StartupThread` object, we call the `Run` member to start it. This two-step approach—create the object, then initialize the object—may be familiar to C++ programmers from other object-oriented APIs. A two-step approach works because a constructor cannot easily provide a return value, nor can it report a reason when it fails. A stand-alone initialization function—`Run` in this example—can do both.

Our interthread delegate function, `StartupCallback`, takes two parameters: `sender` and `e`. The parameters have names that suggest they might be useful, but what is suggested by each name does not quite match with what each parameter actually contains. The first, `sender`, identifies the *recipient* of the function call—the control that is receiving the `Invoke` call—and not the sender as the name implies. The second parameter, `e`, is of type `EventArgs`. Because the first parameter gives us no useful information, you might suppose that the second parameter—which seems to want to contain event arguments—would yield a useful hint or two. And while `EventArgs` is the base class for every other event argument class, this type contains no event data. So where does that leave us? With two parameters that are essentially empty.

Because neither parameter is useful, we structure our code so that this function has only one possible caller, the thread wrapper object, `thrdStartup`. The recipient of the call then accesses that caller's public data to receive any parameters needed for the interthread function call and responds accordingly. Because of the way the `Invoke` method works, our background thread is blocked while the main thread runs the `Invoke` target function. In this way, our code is thread-safe.

Listing 14.3 shows the code for the `StartupCallback` function, which receives an interthread call courtesy of the `Invoke` method in the `Controls` class.

LISTING 14.3: `StartupCallback` Accepts `Invoke` Calls from the Startup Thread

```
private void
StartupCallback(object sender, System.EventArgs e)
{
   INVOKE_STARTUP it = this.m_thrdStartup.itReason;
   switch(it)
   {
      case INVOKE_STARTUP.STARTUP_SUCCESS:
         m_bRapiConnected = true;
         EnableUI();
         break;
      case INVOKE_STARTUP.STARTUP_FAILED:
         ResetUI();
         break;
      case INVOKE_STARTUP.STATUS_MESSAGE:
         sbarMain.Text = m_thrdStartup.strBuffer;
         break;
   }
}
```

A key element connecting the main thread to the startup thread is the connection status flag, `m_bRapiConnected`. When the startup thread establishes the RAPI connection, it sends the main thread a `STARTUP_SUCCESS` code, and the main thread sets the connected flag to `true`.

```
m_bRapiConnected = true;
```

This flag reminds us to shut down our RAPI connection at the appropriate time. For example, as shown in Listing 14.4, when the main form closes, we also shut down any running worker threads.

LISTING 14.4: Cleanup of Background Threads and RAPI Connection

```
private void
MainForm_Closed(object sender, System.EventArgs e)
```

```
{
   // If threads are running, trigger shutdown.
   if (this.m_thrdStartup != null)
      this.m_thrdStartup.bThreadContinue = false;
   if (this.m_thrdFindFiles != null)
      this.m_thrdFindFiles.bThreadContinue = false;

   if (m_bRapiConnected)
   {
      Rapi.CeRapiUninit();
      m_bRapiConnected = false;
   }
}
```

Defensive Coding

RAPI is a communications protocol, which means you must code defensively. When a connection has been established, your program must be able to handle lengthy operations—reading or writing data—that may take a long time because either the connection is slow (USB or serial), or the volume of data is large, or both. Also, when communicating between two machines, the connection may get interrupted. For example, ActiveSync is interrupted when a user removes a device from its docking cradle. In addition to interrupted connections, your code must handle the possibility that no connection—meaning no device—is available.

Lengthy operations can be caused by blocking functions, by a slow connection, or simply by the need to move a lot of data. Blocking functions return only when the requested action is finished. For example, the `CeRapiInit` function returns only after a RAPI connection is established, and the function hangs when no device is present. Most RAPI functions, in fact, are blocking (also called *synchronous*) and finish their work before returning. Functions that return a large amount of data might take several seconds or even several minutes to finish.

While these issues require some effort to address, none is entirely daunting. To prevent blocking functions from hanging a program's user interface, we recommend adding threads to your programs. As we discussed in Chapter 5, such programs have a dedicated user interface thread and then one or more worker threads that focus on a single task. Without threads, an application can become unresponsive to a user's input and perhaps make a user worry that the program has hung. Threads—and feedback to the user with progress information—help ease such user concerns.

The final challenge, a disconnected connection, can be a little more difficult to address. For individual function calls, you must use vigilance in checking return values. In addition, you will want to use exception handling (the `try` and `catch` keywords) so that when something fails deep within your code, you can escape the problem by raising an exception and recovering from the failure higher up the call stack. Exception handling simplifies the handling of unexpected failures.

Accessing the Object Store

The majority of RAPI functions involve reading from or writing to the object store. As detailed in Chapter 11, the object store is the RAM-based storage area with three parts: a file system, the registry, and property databases.

The Windows CE file system is very similar to the desktop file system. Both are hierarchical, supporting nested subdirectories (sometimes called *folders*) and long file paths that can be up to 260 characters long. The file system in the object store provides the primary storage area for a Windows CE device. Additional file systems known as *installable file systems* can be added to extend available storage space. Two common installable file systems are Compact Flash memory cards and Secure Digital storage cards. Both are sometimes referred to as *memory cards* because they contain nonvolatile flash memory, but both are used for file storage and not as program memory. You can access both object store files as well as installable file system files by using the RAPI functions.

The registry provides a hierarchy for storing application and system settings. The registry is as important to Windows CE as it is to desktop Windows. The registry contains settings that the operating system uses for a wide range of tasks; examples include device drivers to load and applications to launch at system boot time. Using RAPI functions, you can access any part of the registry of a connected Windows CE device.

The third part of the object store, property databases, provides a memory-efficient way to store and access sparsely populated record information. These databases are used by the built-in PDA applications—the calendar, inbox, task list, and contact list—for their respective storage needs. In general, a property database provides an easy way to store small, relatively static data. As the number of records increases beyond 1,000 records, or as the number of changes increases, the performance of CE property databases drops. The SQL Server CE database meets the needs of large, dynamic databases that need to reside on a Windows CE device. Using RAPI functions, you have full access to any CE property database on a connected device. RAPI does not provide any direct help for SQL Server CE databases, however, and if you needed to remotely update a SQL Server CE database, you would have to implement your own custom solution.

This book has RAPI sample programs for each of the three parts of the object store. Two programs, `FindPrograms` and `FindProgramsFaster`, access the file system. These programs search the device file system for executable programs. You will see how a special RAPI function, `CeFindAllFiles`, helps provide fast directory searches. Our registry sample program, `RegShowStartup`, provides details about the Windows CE system boot process. This program lists the registry entries for programs and DLLs loaded at system boot time. The property database sample program, `ShowDatabases`, provides a list of database volumes and databases that reside on a remotely connected device.

Using RAPI to Access Device Files

When you look at the RAPI file system functions presented earlier in Table 14.3, you see that you can create, delete, and query directories. You can also create and delete files and open, read, and write individual files. With the aid of the RAPI file system functions, your desktop-based programs can access a device file system as if it were a local file system because the RAPI file functions have parameters identical to functions used to access a local file system.

And there are other similarities as well. As mentioned earlier, Windows CE file systems and desktop Windows file systems are both hierarchical and both support long file paths. Files and directories have attributes, so a given file or directory—on either the desktop or a device—could be marked *hidden*, *normal*, *system*, or *read-only*. Such similarities mean you can move entire directory trees from the desktop to a device and back again.

But the two types of file systems are not exactly the same. The desktop shows its MS-DOS (and CP/M[9]) legacy with the use of letters—`C:`, `D:`, and so on—for disk partitions that Windows CE file systems do not support. Instead, a single root directory holds all mounted file systems. For example, when you plug a Compact Flash memory card into the appropriate slot on a device, a directory with a name like `Storage Card` appears in the root directory.

Detecting the Names of Installed File Systems

While you might be tempted to hard-code a name for removable media such as `Storage Card`, there are variations for different Compact Flash and Smart Media storage cards. On the Pocket PC 2002, the Win32 functions `FindFirstFlashCard` and `FindNextFlashCard` enumerate the root directory name for installed file systems. These functions, unfortunately, have no RAPI equivalent.

RAPI functions make it easy, but not fast, to access a device file system. At issue here are limitations in the physical connections that do not involve what ActiveSync is doing or not doing. For example, file I/O through a USB port or a serial port connection is slow when compared with accessing files in a local file system. When designing a solution that moves data with RAPI, you need to think about minimizing the amount of data you move. When something runs too slowly, you need to measure the time taken by various parts of the operation, a process sometimes referred to as *profiling* (i.e., formally measuring the time taken), to help you devise strategies to identify and fix whatever is slowing down your code.

There are two basic ways to profile. The simplest involves the `TickCount` property in the `Environment` class, which returns the milliseconds

9. Old-timers, especially "software archeologists," may remember CP/M—the Control Program for Microcomputers—created by Gary Kildall, founder of Digital Research. It was a predecessor to IBM's PC-DOS and Microsoft's MS-DOS.

since system startup. You can measure time in seconds with code like the following.

```
int cTicks = Environment.TickCount;
// Do something.
int cSeconds = (Environment.TickCount - cTicks + 500) / 1000;
```

You can measure milliseconds by eliminating the division operation in the equation, or you can call a more precise profiling function: `QueryPerformanceCounter`. This Win32 function requires a P/Invoke declaration, and returns the current value for a continually-running counter. A second function, `QueryPerformanceFrequency`, returns the rate of the counter, in units of counts per second.

We wrote two sample programs—`FindPrograms` and `FindProgramsFaster`—to show how to access a device file system. Both programs search for executable files, adding to a `ListBox` control the full path name for programs found. Both sample programs report the search time in the status bar. Figure 14.1 shows `FindPrograms` after searching for all programs in all directories. You can run a program on a device by selecting the program from the list and clicking the `Run` button.

Our two sample programs are identical except in how they access the device file system. `FindPrograms` uses a standard Win32 approach: the

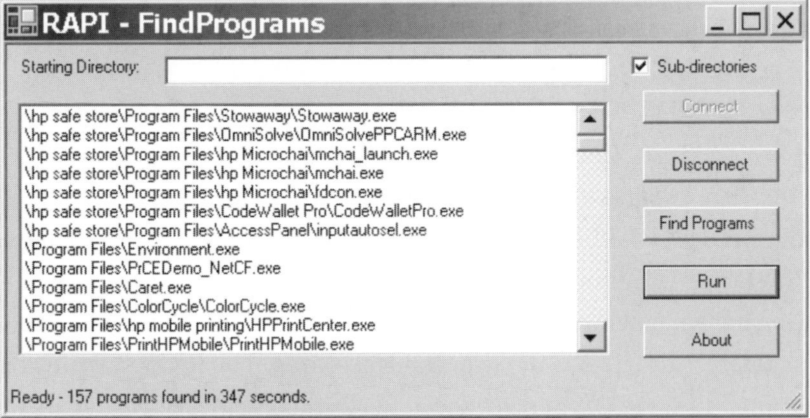

FIGURE 14.1: **`FindPrograms` uses remote file functions to locate executable programs.**

CeFindFirstFile and CeFindNextFile functions. With this approach, it took five minutes to build a complete list of program files from a Pocket PC 2002 (on a Pocket PC connected via USB). As its name suggests, FindProgramsFaster performs a faster search by using another approach to search the file system: the CeFindAllFiles function. This function is faster because it lets you pick a subset of the per-file data that you want to query. By reducing the amount of data that has to be moved from the device to the desktop, you get the results faster.

So how much faster is the CeFindAllFiles function? When connected via USB, the search time was reduced to 15 seconds from 300+ seconds in the original program. We then did the same tests using a 10Mbps network connection, and the search time dropped further still. Our first program did a full search in 6 seconds. The second program again dropped the time, finishing its search in just 2 seconds.

Are You Using Network Debugging in Your CE Development?

It is no surprise that a network connection is faster than a USB connection. Yet when we teach our Windows CE and .NET Compact Framework classes, we find that many developers rely on USB to download and debug on their Windows CE devices. Why? Maybe it is because a USB cradle is provided with most devices. Maybe it is because network connection setup can sometimes prove challenging. Whatever your reason, if your CE device can support a network connection, you owe it to yourself to get connected.

FindPrograms: Using RAPI to Find Files in the Device File System

This program uses RAPI functions to search for executable files and allows a user to start a program running. This program has three source files: MainForm.cs, RapiStartupThread.cs, and RapiFindFilesThread.cs. As usual, MainForm.cs has the user interface code. The RAPI startup code can be found in RapiStartupThread.cs (which appears earlier in this chapter in Listing 14.2).

The third file, `RapiFindFilesThread.cs`, contains all of the code for the actual file system search. As with the RAPI startup we discussed earlier, our RAPI file search is done on a background thread. Results get sent to user interface threads using the thread-safe `Control.Invoke` mechanism. The source code for the `FindFilesThread` class contains the following member functions:

- `FindFilesThread` (class constructor)
- `Run`
- `ThreadMainFindFiles`
- `AddProgramsInDirectory`
- `FetchAndDisplayError`

The constructor makes a local copy of startup data and nothing more, once again leaving the real startup work to an initialization function. In this case, that means the `Run` function.

The `Run` function creates a thread that runs on the `ThreadMainFindFiles` thread entry point. That function, in turn, calls back to the main form with a `FINDFILE_QUERYSTARTPATH` request through the interthread invoke delegate, `deleCallback` (as shown in the following code excerpt), and then calls the `AddProgramsInDirectory` function.

```
itReason = INVOKE_FINDFILES.FINDFILE_QUERYSTARTPATH;
ctlInvokeTarget.Invoke(deleCallback);
string strPath = strBuffer;
AddProgramsInDirectory(strPath);
```

The `AddProgramsInDirectory` function does the actual work of calling RAPI file search functions. This function is recursive, to handle situations when the user clicks the "Sub-directories" checkbox. When checked, the function drills down into other subdirectories in search of more program files. As directories are encountered, they are added to a list—actually an `ArrayList`—and when the search in the current directory is complete, a subdirectory search is started.

The last function, `FetchAndDisplayError`, sends error information to the user interface thread in case of failure.

Listing 14.5 contains the code for the `RapiFindFilesThread.cs` source file, which provides the support for the background thread that actually does the search for a file.

LISTING 14.5: `RapiFindFilesThread.cs` Manages the Background Thread That Searches for a File

```
// Program Name: FindPrograms.exe
//
// File Name: RapiFindFilesThread.cs - Creates a background
// thread to retrieve file names from the device
//
// Code from _.NET Compact Framework Programming with C#_
// and _.NET Compact Framework Programming with Visual Basic .NET_
// Authored by Paul Yao and David Durant.
//

using System;
using System.Threading;
using System.Collections;
using System.Windows.Forms;
using System.Diagnostics;
using YaoDurant.Win32;

namespace FindPrograms
{
   // Reasons our thread invokes user interface thread
   public enum INVOKE_FINDFILES
   {
      FINDFILE_QUERYSTARTPATH,
      FINDFILE_NEWFILE,
      FINDFILE_COMPLETE,
      STATUS_MESSAGE
   }

   /// <summary>
   /// FindFilesThread wraps a thread that supports
   /// RAPI search of device directory.
   /// </summary>
   public class FindFilesThread
   {
      public string strBuffer;        // Interthread buffer
      public INVOKE_FINDFILES itReason;   // Interthread reason

      private Thread m_thrd = null;     // The contained thread
      private Control m_ctlInvokeTarget; // Interthread control
```

```
private EventHandler m_deleCallback; // Interthread delegate
private bool m_bContinue; // Continue flag
private bool m_bIncludeSubDirs = false; // Search subdirs
private int m_cFiles = 0;   // File find counter

public bool bThreadContinue // Continue property
{
   get { return m_bContinue; }
   set { m_bContinue = value; }
}

/// <summary>
/// FindFilesThread - Constructor
/// </summary>
/// <param name="ctl">Owner control</param>
/// <param name="dele">Delegate to invoke</param>
public FindFilesThread(Control ctl, EventHandler dele)
{
   bThreadContinue = true;
   m_ctlInvokeTarget = ctl;  // Who to call
   m_deleCallback = dele;    // How to call
}

/// <summary>
/// Run - Init function for file find thread
/// </summary>
/// <param name="bSubDirs"></param>
/// <returns></returns>
public bool Run(bool bSubDirs)
{
   ThreadStart ts = null;
   ts = new ThreadStart(ThreadMainFindFiles);
   if (ts == null)
      return false;

   m_bIncludeSubDirs = bSubDirs;

   m_thrd = new Thread(ts);
   m_thrd.Start();
   return true;
}

/// <summary>
/// ThreadMainFindFiles - Main thread for file find thread
/// </summary>
private void ThreadMainFindFiles()
{
   int cTicks = Environment.TickCount;
```

continues

continued

```
      itReason = INVOKE_FINDFILES.FINDFILE_QUERYSTARTPATH;
      m_ctlInvokeTarget.Invoke(m_deleCallback);
      string strPath = strBuffer;
      AddProgramsInDirectory(strPath);

      int cSeconds =
         (Environment.TickCount - cTicks + 500) / 1000;
      if (bThreadContinue)
      {
         // Send message for search time.
         strBuffer = "Ready - " + m_cFiles +
            " programs found in " + cSeconds + " seconds.";
         itReason = INVOKE_FINDFILES.STATUS_MESSAGE;
         m_ctlInvokeTarget.Invoke(m_deleCallback);

         // Trigger that search is done.
         itReason = INVOKE_FINDFILES.FINDFILE_COMPLETE;
         m_ctlInvokeTarget.Invoke(m_deleCallback);
      }
   }
   /// <summary>
   /// AddProgramsInDirectory - Recursive function to search
   /// into directory tree.
   /// </summary>
   /// <param name="strDir">Starting directory</param>
   /// <returns></returns>
   private bool AddProgramsInDirectory(string strDir)
   {
      Trace.WriteLine("FindPrograms: " +
         "AddProgramsInDirectory (" + strDir + ")");

      // Update status bar through delegate function.
      strBuffer = "Searching in " + strDir + "...";
      itReason = INVOKE_FINDFILES.STATUS_MESSAGE;
      m_ctlInvokeTarget.Invoke(m_deleCallback);

      // As we add programs, store directory names.
      ArrayList alDirectories = new ArrayList();
      Rapi.CE_FIND_DATA fd = new Rapi.CE_FIND_DATA();

      // Start our search.
      string strSearch = strDir + "*.*";
      IntPtr hff = Rapi.CeFindFirstFile(strSearch, ref fd);
      if ((int)hff == -1)
      {
         FetchAndDisplayError();
```

```
    }
    else
    {
        do
        {
            string strFileName = fd.cFileName;
            int iFlag = (int)
                Rapi.FILE_ATTRIBUTE.FILE_ATTRIBUTE_DIRECTORY;
            if ((fd.dwFileAttributes & iFlag) == iFlag)
            {
                alDirectories.Add(strDir+fd.cFileName);
            }
            else
            {
                if (strFileName.EndsWith(".EXE") ||
                    strFileName.EndsWith(".exe"))
                {
                    m_cFiles++;

                    strBuffer = strDir + fd.cFileName;
                    itReason = INVOKE_FINDFILES.FINDFILE_NEWFILE;
                    m_ctlInvokeTarget.Invoke(m_deleCallback);
                }
            }
        } while (bThreadContinue &&
            Rapi.CeFindNextFile(hff, ref fd) != 0);

        if (bThreadContinue && m_bIncludeSubDirs)
        {
            foreach (string str in alDirectories)
            {
                AddProgramsInDirectory(str + "\\");
            }
        }
    }

    Rapi.CeFindClose(hff);

    return true;
}

/// <summary>
/// FetchAndDisplayError - Displays error in status bar
/// </summary>
public void FetchAndDisplayError()
{
    strBuffer = string.Empty;
```

continues

continued

```
            // Is this a RAPI error?
            int err = Rapi.CeRapiGetError();
            if (err != Rapi.S_OK)
            {
               strBuffer = "RAPI Error (0x" +
                  ((int)err).ToString("x") +")";
            }
            else
            {
               // Check for CE error.
               err = Rapi.CeGetLastError();
               if (err != (int)Rapi.ERROR.ERROR_FILE_NOT_FOUND)
               {
                  strBuffer = "CE Error (code = " +
                     err.ToString("x") + ")";
                }
            }
            if (strBuffer != string.Empty)
            {
               itReason = INVOKE_FINDFILES.STATUS_MESSAGE;
               m_ctlInvokeTarget.Invoke(m_deleCallback);
            }

            // Trigger that thread has ended.
            m_thrd = null;
         }
   } // class FindFilesThread
} // namespace FindPrograms
```

For most purposes, the `CeFindFirstFile` and `CeFindNextFile` functions do a reasonable job of checking whether a given file exists on a device. For searching an entire file system—or even all the files in a directory—a faster approach is needed. That is why RAPI adds a faster search function not otherwise found in the regular Win32 file functions: `CeFindAllFiles`.

`FindProgramsFaster`: *Speeding Up a File Search*

How much faster is the `CeFindAllFiles` function? As we mentioned, a 300-second search done over a USB connection only took 15 seconds, and a

6-second search over a network link got cut to a mere 2 seconds. Obviously, using the `CeFindAllFiles` function is faster than using the `CeFind-FirstFile` and `CeFindNextFile` functions.

Calling the `CeFindAllFiles` function stretches the limits of P/Invoke support and requires us to take some steps not required for simpler functions. The Win32 definition for this function appears here.

```
// Win32 function definition
BOOL CeFindAllFiles(LPCWSTR szPath, DWORD dwFlags,
LPDWORD lpdwFoundCount, LPLPCE_FIND_DATA ppFindDataArray);
```

It takes the following parameters:

- `LPCWSTR szPath`: the path to search
- `DWORD dwFlags`: flags indicating which fields to return
- `LPDWORD lpdwFoundCount`: a pointer to an integer to return the number of items found
- `LPLPCE_FIND_DATA ppFindDataArray`: a pointer to a pointer to an array of `CE_FIND_DATA` structures

From the perspective of the function's work, the important parameters are the first and the last. The first, `szPath`, identifies the directory to search. The last, `ppFindDataArray`, is the address of a pointer variable—what C programmers refer to as a "pointer to a pointer." This function allocates and fills a buffer with an array of found file information and returns a pointer to that buffer in the last parameter.

The `CE_FIND_DATA` structure occupies 300 bytes, which is a lot if you consider that this amount is downloaded for each file with the find first/find next query method. `CeFindAllFiles` speeds up the search by being clever about how it downloads this data. The second parameter, `dwFlags`, lets you pass flags to define a subset of downloaded fields. In addition, a minimum number of characters—and not the 260 defined for the array—are downloaded for the file name. The third parameter, `lpdwFoundCount`, receives the number of files in the array.

Let us take a look, then, at the required P/Invoke declarations for this function, shown here.

```
[DllImport("rapi.dll", CharSet=CharSet.Unicode)]
public static extern int CeFindAllFiles (string szPath,
   FAF dwFlags, ref int lpdwFoundCount,
   ref IntPtr ppFindDataArray);
```

Table 14.4 compares Win32 parameters for the `CeFindAllFiles` function to the comparable .NET parameters. Each parameter to the `CeFindAllFiles` function shows different aspects of P/Invoke.

The first parameter, `szPath`, is a regular C# string, which—because of the `CharSet=CharSet.Unicode` attribute—becomes a pointer to a Unicode string.

The second parameter, `dwFlags`, provides the desired filter and retrieval flags for the search. In our P/Invoke declaration, we put these values within the `FAF` enumeration, which is defined in `YaoDurant.Win32.Rapi` (and which appears in Listing 14.6). We could have defined the second parameter as an integer and then defined a set of integer flag values. But we like using enumerations, which allows IntelliSense to provide a list of possible values from within the code editing window.

LISTING 14.6: Enumeration for File Filter and Retrieval Flags

```
public enum FAF
{
   FAF_ATTRIBUTES = 0x01,
   FAF_CREATION_TIME = 0x02,
   FAF_LASTACCESS_TIME = 0x04,
   FAF_LASTWRITE_TIME = 0x08,
   FAF_SIZE_HIGH = 0x10,
   FAF_SIZE_LOW = 0x20,
   FAF_OID = 0x40,
   FAF_NAME = 0x80,
   FAF_FLAG_COUNT = 8,
   FAF_ATTRIB_CHILDREN = 0x01000,
   FAF_ATTRIB_NO_HIDDEN = 0x02000,
   FAF_FOLDERS_ONLY = 0x04000,
   FAF_NO_HIDDEN_SYS_ROMMODULES = 0x08000,
   FAF_GETTARGET = 0x10000,
}
```

TABLE 14.4: Comparison between Win32 and .NET Parameter Types

Win32 Parameter	.NET Parameter
`LPCWSTR szPath`	`string szPath`
`DWORD dwFlags`	`FAF dwFlags`
`LPDWORD lpdwFoundCount`	`ref int lpdwFoundCount`
`LPLPCE_FIND_DATA ppFindDataArray`	`ref IntPtr ppFindDataArray`

The third parameter, `lpdwFoundCount`, is a pointer to an integer. Passing pointers into Win32 functions is quite common, and the `ref` keyword makes it easy to ask the compiler to generate a pointer when the function call is called.

The fourth parameter, `ppFindDataArray`, is the trickiest: a pointer to a pointer. C# can allocate pointers, but only at a cost: You must declare a function `unsafe` and use the `/unsafe` compiler switch to mark the entire program as unsafe. In some settings, your program would not be allowed to run because of the local security policy. Rather than creating an explicit pointer, we turn to the `Marshal` class for help.

Actually, all of the managed-to-unmanaged code relies on the `Marshal` class. All of the various declarations and attributes we create for Win32 functions are consumed by this class. With this fourth parameter, however, we need to directly call some of the static functions exported by the `Marshal` class.

We define the fourth parameter as `IntPtr`, which is not so much a type as a placeholder for a variety of different things. When calling Win32 functions, this type is used for both handles (e.g., window handles, file handles) and for pointers. Because of the two levels of indirection—we are passing a pointer to a pointer—we use the `ref` keyword for this pointer declaration. With one level of indirection, we would use `IntPtr` without `ref`.

The `ref` keyword is needed both in the function declaration and in the actual function call.

```
// Start our search.
string strSearch = strDir + "*.*";

IntPtr pfdAllFiles = IntPtr.Zero;  // Return pointer.
int cFound = 0;            // Return count of files.

// This call looks for all files in current directory.
Rapi.CeFindAllFiles(strSearch,
    Rapi.FAF.FAF_ATTRIBUTES |
    Rapi.FAF.FAF_NAME,
    ref cFound,
    ref pfdAllFiles);
```

After this call to the `CeFindAllFiles` function, the fourth parameter, `pfdAllFiles`, holds a pointer to an array of `CE_FIND_DATA` values. The third parameter, `cFound`, holds the count of array members. The .NET definition for the `CE_FIND_DATA` structure appears in Listing 14.7.

LISTING 14.7: Return Values Occupying an Array of `CE_FIND_DATA` Structures

```
[StructLayout(LayoutKind.Sequential,Pack=4,
   CharSet=CharSet.Unicode)]
public struct CE_FIND_DATA
{
   public int dwFileAttributes;
   public FILETIME ftCreationTime;
   public FILETIME ftLastAccessTime;
   public FILETIME ftLastWriteTime;
   public int nFileSizeHigh;
   public int nFileSizeLow;
   public int dwOID;
   [ MarshalAs( UnmanagedType.ByValTStr, SizeConst=MAX_PATH)]
   public string cFileName;
};

public const int MAX_PATH = 260;
```

We have a pointer to the data, but because of the strict type checking of C#—and indeed of all .NET languages—we cannot directly access the data referenced by an `IntPtr`. Instead, we need help from the `Marshal` class.

The `Marshal` class resides in the `System.Runtime.InteropServices` namespace and is supported in both the desktop .NET Framework and the .NET Compact Framework. This class provides static functions for moving data between managed memory and unmanaged memory. We call the `Marshal.PtrToStructure` function, defined in the following code, to create a managed object of type `CE_FIND_DATA` from a block of unmanaged memory.

```
public static object PtrToStructure(
   IntPtr ptr, Type structureType );
```

The `PtrToStructure` function accepts an `IntPtr` pointer and the type of the object to create, then allocates and initializes the requested object. This function provides the "secret sauce" needed to create a .NET object from unmanaged memory. Here is how we call the `PtrToStructure` function in the `FindProgramsFaster` sample program.

```
IntPtr pfd = pfdAllFiles;
// . . .
Rapi.CE_FIND_DATA fd = // Output .NET object
   (Rapi.CE_FIND_DATA) // Always cast this
   Marshal.PtrToStructure(  // The function
   pfd,                         // Input Win32 ptr
   typeof(Rapi.CE_FIND_DATA));  // Output type
```

As written, this function reads a single member of the array to provide data on a single file. We read all of the elements in the array by putting the following call into a loop and increment the pointer to access each element of the array as shown here.

```
// Get ready for next loop.
pfd = (IntPtr)((int)pfd + Marshal.SizeOf(fd));
```

The `Marshal.SizeOf` Method

This code shows the `Marshal.SizeOf` method, which is similar to the C/C++ `sizeof` operator.

After looping through all of the array elements, we must free the memory allocated by the `CeFindAllFiles` function. We do not call a `Marshal` class method; instead, we call a RAPI function provided especially for freeing memory allocated by `CeFindAllFiles` (and `CeFindAllDatabases`), the `CeRapiFreeBuffer` function, as shown here.

```
// Free memory returned by CeFindAllFiles.
Rapi.CeRapiFreeBuffer(pfdAllFiles);
```

Listing 14.8 shows these calls in the context of the `FindProgramsFaster` sample program.

LISTING 14.8: The `AddProgramsInDirectory` Function from `FindProgramsFaster`

```
/// <summary>
/// AddProgramsInDirectory - Recursive function to search
/// into directory tree
/// </summary>
/// <param name="strDir">Starting directory</param>
/// <returns></returns>
private bool AddProgramsInDirectory(string strDir)
{
   Trace.WriteLine("FindPrograms: " +
      "AddProgramsInDirectory (" + strDir + ")");

   // Update status bar through delegate function.
   strBuffer = "Searching in " + strDir + "...";
   itReason = INVOKE_FINDFILES.STATUS_MESSAGE;
   m_ctlInvokeTarget.Invoke(m_deleCallback);

   // As we add programs, store directory names.
   ArrayList alDirectories = new ArrayList();

   // Start our search.
   string strSearch = strDir + "*.*";

   IntPtr pfdAllFiles = IntPtr.Zero;  // Return pointer.
   int cFound = 0;           // Return count of files.

   // This call looks for all files in current directory.
   Rapi.CeFindAllFiles(strSearch,
       Rapi.FAF.FAF_ATTRIBUTES |
       Rapi.FAF.FAF_NAME,
       ref cFound,
       ref pfdAllFiles);

   // Loop through all files found.
```

```
    IntPtr pfd = pfdAllFiles;
    while (cFound > 0)
    {
        //
        // Here is the secret sauce. This function uses a
        // Win32 pointer to create a .NET object.
        //
        Rapi.CE_FIND_DATA fd = // Output .NET object
            (Rapi.CE_FIND_DATA) // Always cast this
            Marshal.PtrToStructure(  // The function
                pfd,                           // Input Win32 ptr
                typeof(Rapi.CE_FIND_DATA));  // Output type

        string strFileName = fd.cFileName;
        int iFlag = (int)
            Rapi.FILE_ATTRIBUTE.FILE_ATTRIBUTE_DIRECTORY;
        if ((fd.dwFileAttributes & iFlag) == iFlag)
        {
            alDirectories.Add(strDir+fd.cFileName);
        }
        else
        {
            if (strFileName.EndsWith(".EXE") ||
                strFileName.EndsWith(".exe"))
            {
                m_cFiles++;

                strBuffer = strDir + fd.cFileName;
                itReason = INVOKE_FINDFILES.FINDFILE_NEWFILE;
                m_ctlInvokeTarget.Invoke(m_deleCallback);
            }
        }

        // Get ready for next loop.
        pfd = (IntPtr)((int)pfd + Marshal.SizeOf(fd));
        cFound--;
    }

    // Free memory returned by CeFindAllFiles.
    Rapi.CeRapiFreeBuffer(pfdAllFiles);

    if (bThreadContinue && m_bIncludeSubDirs)
    {
        foreach (string str in alDirectories)
        {
            AddProgramsInDirectory(str + "\\");
        }
    }

    return true;
}
```

Remote Access to Device Registry Entries

A Windows CE object store contains a registry in addition to and outside of the file system. Table 14.3 earlier in this chapter summarizes the ten registry functions found in `rapi.h`. As on desktop Windows, the registry provides a hierarchical structure for storing key name/value pairs. The registry has many uses and many users, including the operating system, device drivers, and applications. The registry serves as a central storehouse for tiny bits of data that might otherwise get lost if put in a file.

If you have not worked with registry functions before, you can get a good idea of the basic layout of the registry with a registry editing tool. One such tool, `regedit.exe`, ships with each 32-bit version of Microsoft Windows. Run this tool by typing its name into the Run dialog box. Another registry tool, the Remote Registry Editor, lets you view the registry of Windows CE devices. This second tool ships with the eMbedded Visual Tools.

Obtaining the eMbedded Visual Tools

The Remote Registry Editor is just one of several very useful tools that Microsoft has created for Windows CE developers but that do not ship with Visual Studio .NET 2003. Other tools include Remote SPY++, Remote Heap Walker, Remote Process Viewer, and Remote Zoomin.

These tools ship with several Microsoft products, including the Windows CE Platform Builder, the eMbedded Visual Tools 3.0, and eMbedded Visual C++ 4.0. If you are building applications for a Pocket PC or Pocket PC 2003, the most useful of these tools is eMbedded Visual Tools 3.0 (which provides both a C/C++ compiler and eMbedded Visual Basic). You can download this tool from the Microsoft Web site. The link sometimes changes, so here is a link that we maintain on our Web site to the Microsoft Pocket PC Download Page: http://www.paulyao.com/resources/links/celinks.asp.

Figure 14.2 shows the Remote Registry Editor viewing some registry contents of a Windows CE device.

The left panel of the Remote Registry Editor shows the hierarchical structure of registry keys. You identify a specific registry key by connecting key names together, separating them from each other with a backslash (\) character just as you do for the file system hierarchy. The status bar of the Remote Registry Editor in Figure 14.2 gives an example—`HKEY_LOCAL_MACHINE\init`. The right panel of the Remote Registry Editor shows all of the values associated with the selected registry key. To access a value in the registry, you open a key (in the left panel) with one set of functions. Then you read and write values (the contents of the right panel) using a second set of functions. When you are done, you must close any key you have opened.

As the Remote Registry Editor shows, the registry holds several hierarchies. You identify the top of each hierarchy using a special "magic number." The C# definitions for these magic numbers are shown here.

```
public static IntPtr HKEY_CLASSES_ROOT   =
   new IntPtr(unchecked((int)0x80000000));
public static IntPtr HKEY_CURRENT_USER   =
   new IntPtr(unchecked((int)0x80000001));
public static IntPtr HKEY_LOCAL_MACHINE =
   new IntPtr(unchecked((int)0x80000002));
public static IntPtr HKEY_USERS          =
   new IntPtr(unchecked((int)0x80000003));
```

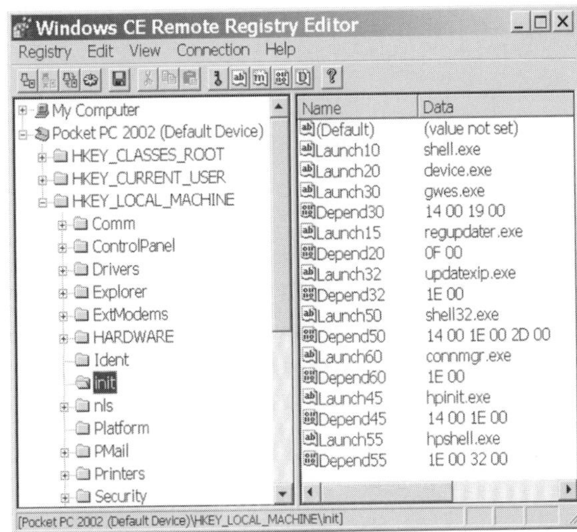

FIGURE 14.2: Remote Registry Editor viewing the contents of a Pocket PC

The unchecked keyword is needed in C# to prevent an overflow exception, which occurs because the initialization values are outside the valid range of values for a signed integer.

Open an existing registry key by calling the CeRegOpenKeyEx RAPI function. The P/Invoke definition for this function is shown here.

```
[DllImport("rapi.dll", CharSet=CharSet.Unicode)]
public static extern
int CeRegOpenKeyEx (IntPtr hKey, string lpszSubKey,
int Reserved1, int Reserved2, ref IntPtr phkResult);
```

Values that can be set to 0 are named Reserved. The CeRegOpenKeyEx function's return value is the last input parameter, phkResult. Here is how to call this function to get the key to the HKEY_LOCAL_MACHINE\init registry node:

```
IntPtr hkeyInit = IntPtr.Zero;

int iResult = Rapi.CeRegOpenKeyEx(Rapi.HKEY_LOCAL_MACHINE, "init",
   0, 0, ref hkeyInit);
```

Another way to open a registry key is to call the CeRegCreateKeyEx function. As the name suggests, this function also creates a key if the named node does not exist.

```
[DllImport("rapi.dll", CharSet=CharSet.Unicode)]
public static extern
int CeRegCreateKeyEx (IntPtr hKey, string lpszSubKey,
   int Reserved, int Reserved2, int Reserved3, int Reserved4,
   int Reserved5, ref IntPtr phkResult,
   ref REGDISP lpdwDisposition);
```

The final parameter, lpdwDisposition, provides a return value with information about whether a key already exists or was created. Our library, YaoDurant.Win32.Rapi.dll, has an enumeration that contains the two possible values for this parameter:

```
public enum REGDISP
{
   REG_CREATED_NEW_KEY = 0x00000001,
```

```
    REG_OPENED_EXISTING_KEY = 0x00000002,
}
```

Once a key has been opened, you can read registry values by calling the `CeRegQueryValueEx` function and write values with the `CeRegSetValueEx` function. We have several definitions for each function to accommodate different types—integer, string, and binary—that can be written to the registry (these definitions are for the most common types). Listing 14.9 shows the P/Invoke wrappers for various overloads that we define to call the `CeRegQueryValueEx` function.

LISTING 14.9: P/Invoke Wrappers for RAPI Registry Query Functions

```
[DllImport("rapi.dll", CharSet=CharSet.Unicode)]
public static extern
int CeRegQueryValueEx (IntPtr hKey, string lpValueName,
   int lpReserved, ref REGTYPE lpType, IntPtr iptrData,
   ref int lpcbData);

[DllImport("rapi.dll", CharSet=CharSet.Unicode)]
public static extern
int CeRegQueryValueEx (IntPtr hKey, string lpValueName,
   int lpReserved, ref REGTYPE lpType, string strData,
   ref int lpcbData);

[DllImport("rapi.dll", CharSet=CharSet.Unicode)]
public static extern
int CeRegQueryValueEx (IntPtr hKey, string lpValueName,
   int lpReserved, ref REGTYPE lpType, ref int piData,
   ref int lpcbData);
```

As before, set parameters with `Reserved` in the name to `0`. The fourth parameter to `CeRegQueryValueEx` is a `REGTYPE` reference, a value from the following enumeration.

```
public enum REGTYPE
{
   REG_NONE = 0,
   REG_SZ = 1,
   REG_EXPAND_SZ = 2,
   REG_BINARY = 3,
   REG_DWORD = 4,
```

continues

continued

```
    REG_DWORD_LITTLE_ENDIAN = 4,
    REG_DWORD_BIG_ENDIAN = 5,
    REG_LINK = 6,
    REG_MULTI_SZ = 7,
    REG_RESOURCE_LIST = 8
}
```

Assuming that you have already opened a registry key—using a function described earlier—here is how to read a string value named `Launch10`.

```
int cbData=32;
Rapi.REGTYPE iType;
string str = new string(new char[cbData]);
Rapi.CeRegQueryValueEx(hkey, "Launch10", 0, ref iType, str,
   ref cbData);
char [] ach = {'\0'};
str = str.Trim(ach);
```

We trim away the extra `null` values to get the string by itself. In addition to returning the value, the `CeRegQueryValueEx` function returns two other pieces of information: the registry key type (`iType`) and the number of bytes in the value (`cbData`).

Set a registry value by calling the `CeRegSetValueEx` function. Here are three overloaded versions of this function in our library.

```
[DllImport("rapi.dll", CharSet=CharSet.Unicode)]
public static extern
int CeRegSetValueEx (IntPtr hKey, string lpValueName,
   int Reserved, REGTYPE dwType, IntPtr lpData, int cbData);

[DllImport("rapi.dll", CharSet=CharSet.Unicode)]
public static extern
int CeRegSetValueEx (IntPtr hKey, string lpValueName,
   int Reserved, REGTYPE dwType, string lpData, int cbData);

[DllImport("rapi.dll", CharSet=CharSet.Unicode)]
public static extern
int CeRegSetValueEx (IntPtr hKey, string lpValueName,
   int Reserved, REGTYPE dwType, ref int lpData, int cbData);
```

The parameters to the `CeRegSetValueEx` function are similar to those passed to the `CeRegQueryValueEx` function. One difference is that there are fewer reference values (the `ref` keyword) because this function does not have to tell us the data type or the size of the input data. Here is how to call this function to write a string value named `Launch90`.

```
string strPath = @"\windows\pword.exe";
int cbData = (strPath.Length + 1) * 2;
Rapi.CeRegSetValueEx(hkeyInit, "Launch90", 0,
   Rapi.REGTYPE.REG_SZ, strPath, cbData);
```

Before shutting down, be sure that your program closes any registry key you opened, using the `CeRegCloseKey` function as defined here.

```
[DllImport("rapi.dll", CharSet=CharSet.Unicode)]
public static extern int CeRegCloseKey (IntPtr hKey);
```

Listing 14.10, which we present at the end of this discussion, shows the registry enumeration code from `RegShowStartup`. This RAPI sample program shows two different enumeration functions: `CeRegEnumKeyEx` enumerates registry keys, and `CeRegEnumValue` enumerates the values in a given key. This sample program lists the startup programs in Windows CE and the startup DLLs. Figure 14.3 shows the startup programs for a Pocket PC as listed by `RegShowStartup`.

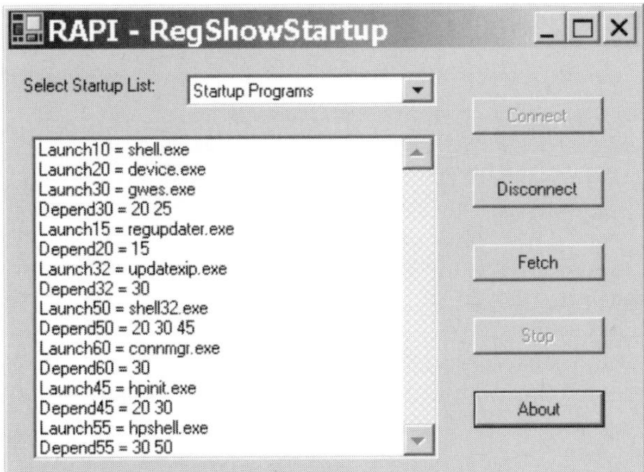

FIGURE 14.3: RegShowStartup with the startup list from a Pocket PC

Just as on desktop Windows, you can set a registry setting in Windows CE to start a program at system boot time. The registry key is `HKEY_LOCAL_MACHINE\init`. There is an important difference between the way Windows CE and desktop Windows use their startup lists. When you turn off the power for a desktop Windows system, the system shuts down completely. Then when the power comes back on, the items in the various startup lists get run.

A Windows CE device goes into a sleep state when the power switch is turned off. When the power is turned on, the system wakes up but does not completely reboot. For the programs in a startup list to run on a Windows CE device, you must do more than just turn the power off and on. You must either warm-boot the device (a reset button is commonly provided) or cold-boot the device by removing and then replacing the batteries.

The startup DLLs in Windows CE are really a special kind of device driver. These *stream interface drivers* are used for a wide range of devices. Such device drivers are outside the scope of this book, but it is worth knowing about them when you want to create an installable device driver. Such drivers must be written as Win32 DLLs.

Listing 14.10 shows the code for `RapiEnumRegistryThread.cs`.

LISTING 14.10: `RapiEnumRegistryThread.cs` from the `RegShowStartup` Program

```
// Program Name: RegShowStartup.exe
//
// File Name: RapiEnumRegistryThread.cs - Creates a thread to
// enumerate both registry keys and registry values
//
// Code from _.NET Compact Framework Programming with C#_
// and _.NET Compact Framework Programming with Visual Basic .NET_
// Authored by Paul Yao and David Durant.
//

using System;
using System.Threading;
using System.Windows.Forms;
using System.Runtime.InteropServices;
using YaoDurant.Win32;

namespace RegShowStartup
{
   // Reasons our thread invokes user interface thread
```

```
public enum INVOKE_ENUMREG
{
   ENUMREG_NEWKEY,
   ENUMREG_NEWVALUE,
   ENUMREG_ENDED,
   STATUS_MESSAGE
}

/// <summary>
/// RapiConnection - Manages ActiveSync RAPI connections
/// </summary>
public class RapiEnumRegistryThread
{
   public string strBuffer;        // Interthread buffer
   public INVOKE_ENUMREG itReason; // Interthread reason

   // Public thread to allow monitoring by UI thread
   public Thread thrd = null;     // The contained thread
   private Control m_ctlInvokeTarget; // Interthread control
   private EventHandler m_deleCallback; // Interthread delegate

   // Private data.
   private bool m_bContinue;      // Continue flag
   private bool m_bKeys;          // Enumerate keys or values
   private IntPtr m_hkeyRoot;     // Root enumeration key
   private string m_strRegNode; // Root enumeration node

   public bool bThreadContinue  // Continue property
   {
      get { return m_bContinue; }
      set { m_bContinue = value; }
   }

   public RapiEnumRegistryThread(
      Control ctl,            // Who to call
      EventHandler dele,      // Notification delegate
      bool bKeys,             // Enum keys or values
      IntPtr hkeyRoot,        // Root of search
      string strRegNode)      // Node to search
   {
      // Make private copies of init data.
      m_ctlInvokeTarget = ctl;
      m_deleCallback = dele;
      m_bKeys = bKeys;
      m_hkeyRoot = hkeyRoot;
      m_strRegNode = strRegNode;

      bThreadContinue = true;
   }
```

continues

continued

```
public bool Run()
{
   ThreadStart ts = null;
   ts = new ThreadStart(ThreadMainEnumReg);
   if (ts == null)
      return false;

   thrd = new Thread(ts);
   thrd.Start();

   return true;
}


/// <summary>
/// ThreadMainEnumReg - Enumerate registry values.
/// </summary>
private void ThreadMainEnumReg()
{
   // Open registry key.
   IntPtr hkeySearchNode = IntPtr.Zero;
   int iResult = Rapi.CeRegOpenKeyEx(
      this.m_hkeyRoot, this.m_strRegNode,
      0, 0, ref hkeySearchNode);
   if (iResult != Rapi.ERROR_SUCCESS && m_bContinue)
   {
      // Send error message.
      itReason = INVOKE_ENUMREG.STATUS_MESSAGE;
      strBuffer = "Error accessing registry key";
      this.m_ctlInvokeTarget.Invoke(m_deleCallback);

      // Trigger end of enumeration.
      itReason = INVOKE_ENUMREG.ENUMREG_ENDED;
      this.m_ctlInvokeTarget.Invoke(m_deleCallback);

      // Trigger that shutdown is complete.
      thrd = null;
      return;
   }

   // Keys or values?
   if (this.m_bKeys)  // Enumerate keys.
   {
      int iIndex = 0;
      while (iResult == Rapi.ERROR_SUCCESS && m_bContinue)
      {
         string strKeyName = new string('\0', 32);
         int cbLength = 32;
         iResult = Rapi.CeRegEnumKeyEx(
```

```
            hkeySearchNode, iIndex++,
            strKeyName, ref cbLength,
            0, 0, 0, 0);
         if (iResult == Rapi.ERROR_SUCCESS && m_bContinue)
         {
            itReason = INVOKE_ENUMREG.ENUMREG_NEWKEY;
            strBuffer = strKeyName;
            this.m_ctlInvokeTarget.Invoke(m_deleCallback);
         }
      } // while
   }
   else               // Enumerate values.
   {
      int iIndex;
      for (iIndex = 0; iResult == Rapi.ERROR_SUCCESS &&
           m_bContinue; iIndex++)
      {
         int cbName = 32;
         string strName = new string('\0', 16);
         Rapi.REGTYPE iType = 0;
         int cbLength = 0;

         // Enumerate key names only (not values).
         iResult = Rapi.CeRegEnumValue(hkeySearchNode,
            iIndex, strName, ref cbName,
            IntPtr.Zero, ref iType, IntPtr.Zero,
            ref cbLength);

         if (iResult == Rapi.ERROR_SUCCESS && m_bContinue)
         {
            if (iType == Rapi.REGTYPE.REG_SZ) // string
            {
               int cbData=32;
               string str = new string(new char[cbData]);
               Rapi.CeRegQueryValueEx(hkeySearchNode,
                   strName, 0, ref iType, str,
                   ref cbData);
               char [] ach = {'\0'};
               strBuffer = strName.Trim(ach) + " = "
                  + str.Trim(ach);
            }
            else if (iType == Rapi.REGTYPE.REG_BINARY)
            {
               // Fetch binary array of short values.
               char [] ach = {'\0'};
               strBuffer = strName.Trim(ach) + " = ";

               // Allocate buffer of short values.
               Int16 sh = 0;
               IntPtr iptr;
```

continues

continued

```
                    int cbSizeOfShort = Marshal.SizeOf(sh);
                    int cbData =  cbSizeOfShort * 5;
                    iptr = Marshal.AllocCoTaskMem(cbData);

                    // Fetch array of short values.
                    Rapi.CeRegQueryValueEx(hkeySearchNode,
                       strName, 0, ref iType, iptr,
                       ref cbData);

                    // Copy array to managed array.
                    int cElements = cbData / cbSizeOfShort;
                    Int16 [] ash = new Int16 [cElements];
                    Marshal.Copy(iptr, ash, 0, cElements);
                    Marshal.FreeCoTaskMem(iptr);

                    // Add values to string for display.
                    for (int i = 0; i < cElements; i++)
                    {
                       strBuffer = strBuffer + ash[i] + " ";
                    }
                 }
                 else
                 {
                    strBuffer = strName + " not expected type";
                 }
                 itReason = INVOKE_ENUMREG.ENUMREG_NEWVALUE;
                 this.m_ctlInvokeTarget.Invoke(m_deleCallback);
              }
           } // for
        } // if

        Rapi.CeRegCloseKey(hkeySearchNode);

        // Trigger end of enumeration.
        itReason = INVOKE_ENUMREG.ENUMREG_ENDED;
        this.m_ctlInvokeTarget.Invoke(m_deleCallback);

        // Trigger that shutdown is complete.
        thrd = null;
     }
  } // class RapiEnumRegistryThread
} // namespace RegShowStartup
```

Remote Access to Device Property Databases

The third kind of entry in the Windows CE object store is the Windows CE property database. This is really a flat-file manager that stores data as records in a memory-efficient way—suitable for small devices with small storage space. Desktop Windows has no comparable support.

Neither the .NET Compact Framework nor the .NET Framework provides any support for accessing Windows CE property databases. Such databases are not the same as SQL Server CE databases or Pocket Access databases; in short, such database files cannot be manipulated using ADO.NET classes. The primary benefits of using property databases are their very small size and their database format in common with non–.NET Compact Framework programs. Access to property databases occurs through a set of Win32 API functions, a subject addressed in existing Windows CE programming books.[10] Another set of database access functions is provided through RAPI, which offers the same level of support for reading and writing database records from a remotely connected PC.

Our sample program, `ShowDatabases`, enumerates the available database volumes as well as the available databases on the connected Windows CE device. Figure 14.4 shows this program with the list of available databases. The code for the database enumeration portion of this program appears in Listing 14.11.

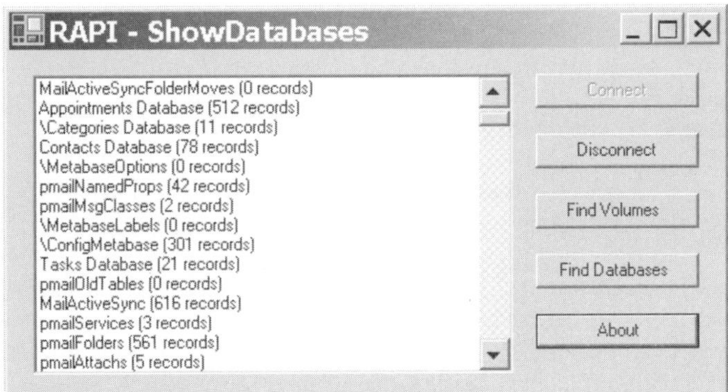

FIGURE 14.4: `ShowDatabases` with names of databases available on a currently connected device

10. For example, Doug Boling covers this topic in his book *Programming Microsoft Windows CE* (Redmond, WA: Microsoft Press, 2001).

LISTING 14.11: RapiEnumDBThread.cs from the ShowDatabases Program

```
// Program Name: ShowDatabases.exe
//
// File Name: RapiEnumDBThread.cs - Creates a background
// thread to names of database volumes and names of databases
//
// Code from _.NET Compact Framework Programming with C#_
// and _.NET Compact Framework Programming with Visual Basic .NET_
// Authored by Paul Yao and David Durant.
//
using System;
using System.Threading;
using System.Collections;
using System.Windows.Forms;
using System.Diagnostics;
using System.Runtime.InteropServices;
using YaoDurant.Win32;

namespace ShowDatabases
{
   // Reasons our thread invokes user interface thread
   public enum INVOKE_ENUMDB
   {
      ENUMDB_NEWVOLUME,
      ENUMDB_NEWDATABASE,
      ENUMDB_COMPLETE,
      STATUS_MESSAGE
   }

   /// <summary>
   /// Summary description for RapiEnumDBThread
   /// </summary>
   public class RapiEnumDBThread
   {
      public string strBuffer;       // Interthread buffer
      public INVOKE_ENUMDB itReason;   // Interthread reason

      private Thread m_thrd = null;    // The contained thread
      private Control m_ctlInvokeTarget; // Interthread control
      private EventHandler m_deleCallback; // Interthread delegate
      private bool m_bContinue; // Continue flag
      private bool m_bVolume;   // Enum volumes or databases?

      public bool bThreadContinue // Continue property
      {
         get { return m_bContinue; }
         set { m_bContinue = value; }
      }
```

```
public RapiEnumDBThread(Control ctl, EventHandler dele,
   bool bVolume)
{
   m_bContinue = true;
   m_ctlInvokeTarget = ctl;  // Who to call
   m_deleCallback = dele;    // How to call
   m_bVolume = bVolume;
}
/// <summary>
/// Run - Init function for enum thread
/// </summary>
/// <param name="bSubDirs"></param>
/// <returns></returns>
public bool Run()
{
   ThreadStart ts = null;
   ts = new ThreadStart(ThreadMainEnumDB);
   if (ts == null)
      return false;

   m_thrd = new Thread(ts);
   m_thrd.Start();
   return true;
}

private void ThreadMainEnumDB()
{
   if (m_bVolume)  // Enumerate volumes.
   {
      Guid guid =
         new Guid("ffffffffffffffffffffffffffffffff");
      int cch = 32;
      string str = new String('\0', cch);
      while (Rapi.CeEnumDBVolumes(ref guid, str, cch) ==
         Rapi.TRUE && m_bContinue)
      {
         strBuffer = str;
         itReason = INVOKE_ENUMDB.ENUMDB_NEWVOLUME;
         m_ctlInvokeTarget.Invoke(m_deleCallback);
      }
   }
   else            // Enumerate databases.
   {
      Int16 cRecords = 0;
      IntPtr pfdbAll = IntPtr.Zero;
      Rapi.CeFindAllDatabases(0,
         Rapi.FAD.FAD_NAME | Rapi.FAD.FAD_NUM_RECORDS,
         ref cRecords,
         ref pfdbAll);
```

continues

continued

```
            IntPtr pfdb = pfdbAll;
            while (cRecords > 0)
            {
               // Set pointer to next record.
               Rapi.CEDB_FIND_DATA dbfd =
                  (Rapi.CEDB_FIND_DATA)
                  Marshal.PtrToStructure(
                     pfdb, typeof(Rapi.CEDB_FIND_DATA));

               // Post name to listbox.
               strBuffer = dbfd.DbInfo.szDbaseName + " (" +
                  dbfd.DbInfo.wNumRecords + " records)";
               itReason = INVOKE_ENUMDB.ENUMDB_NEWDATABASE;
               m_ctlInvokeTarget.Invoke(m_deleCallback);

               // Get ready for next loop.
               pfdb = (IntPtr)((int)pfdb + Marshal.SizeOf(dbfd));
               cRecords--;
            } // while

            // Free memory returned by CeFindAllDatabases.
            Rapi.CeRapiFreeBuffer(pfdbAll);
         } // if

         // Notify main thread that we are done.
         itReason = INVOKE_ENUMDB.ENUMDB_COMPLETE;
         m_ctlInvokeTarget.Invoke(m_deleCallback);

         // Mark thread as done.
         m_thrd = null;
      }

   } // RapiEnumDBThread
} // ShowDatabases
```

Detecting Changes in Device Connection State

ActiveSync provides two ways to let you know that a device has created a connection. We call one method the *auto-start method* and the other the *callback method*. The first is simple but crude, while the second involves more code but is also more elegant. You install both with registry entries in the desktop registry.

The auto-start method relies on registry keys that contain command lines to start programs running. When a connection begins, ActiveSync runs all of the programs in one key. When a connection ends, ActiveSync runs all of the programs in the other key. You could put the same program file in each registry key with a different command-line argument to differentiate when you're connecting from when you're disconnecting.

The callback method uses a callback mechanism—a COM interface—to let you know when the connection state changes. Your program must be running to get this notification. You could rely on the auto-start method to start your program running and then use the callback method to detect specific changes to the connection state.

Let us look at each approach in turn.

The Auto-Start Approach

When ActiveSync establishes a connection to a Windows CE device, it starts all of the programs listed in its `AutoStartOnConnect` registry key. When ActiveSync detects that a connection has been dropped, it starts another set of programs, this time the ones listed in the `AutoStartOnDisconnect` registry key. You can start as many programs as you like, with one registry value entry per program.

An auto-start registry entry is a program command line. Valid command lines include program names, program names with parameters, and data file names with extensions of registered file types. You can test a command line by typing it into the Run dialog box from the Windows Start menu. Examples of valid auto-start registry entries include the following:

- `explorer.exe`
- `"explorer" c:\Temp`
- `"mspaint.exe" MyImage.bmp`
- `MyImage.bmp`

As these examples show, you can pass parameters to the program by putting the program name between quotation marks.

Here is the registry key for start connection command lines: `HKEY_LOCAL_MACHINE\SOFTWARE\Microsoft\Windows CE Services\AutoStartOnConnect`. The registry key for end connection commands is identical except that the final part is `AutoStartOnDisconnect`.

The auto-start approach is easy to set up. A disadvantage is that each event starts a program running, which you have to shut down sooner or later. Another disadvantage is that your auto-start program usually has to let another program know of the start or stop event, which leaves you having to pick an interprocess communication technique. The callback approach, which we discuss next, involves more code but ends up providing a more elegant solution than the auto-start approach.

The Callback Approach

ActiveSync supports a second notification mechanism, an Advise Sink. This COM-oriented approach involves creating an `IDccMan` COM object provided by the RAPI libraries. To get a callback, you must create an object that exposes the `IDccManSink` interface, which gets called when a connection has started or stopped.

ActiveSync uses TCP/IP for its connections. IP networking is so versatile that the IP connection can run on a wide range of physical media, including USB, serial, infrared, and Bluetooth—and, or course, over both wired and wireless networks. For most of the other RAPI operations, the use of TCP/IP is transparent to your application. When you use the callback method for notifications, however, ActiveSync sends you the IP address for the connected device. You can use this IP address to establish a socket connection to a device if you want to establish a direct link to a running program on your device.

Listing 14.12 shows the `RapiConnectDetect.cs` source file, which has the C# declarations needed for the two interfaces used to detect changes to an ActiveSync connection. This source file is part of `FindProgramsOnConnect`, the latest installment in our ongoing saga of running programs on a device from a desktop using RAPI. In this episode, our hero automatically starts a search when a device connection is detected. It uses the faster of the two search methods and so provides a complete list of executable programs whenever a device is connected.

LISTING 14.12: `RapiConnectDetect.cs` for Detecting ActiveSync Connections

```
// Program Name: FindProgramsOnConnect.exe
//
// File Name: RapiConnectDetect.cs - Creates an ActiveSync COM
// object of type IDccMan and an Advise Sink of type IDccManSink
// to detect the start and end of ActiveSync connections
//
// Code from _.NET Compact Framework Programming with C#_
// and _.NET Compact Framework Programming with Visual Basic .NET_
// Authored by Paul Yao and David Durant.
//

using System;
using System.Windows.Forms;
using System.Runtime.InteropServices;

namespace FindPrograms
{
   // Reason we are calling
   public enum INVOKE_CONNECT
   {
      START,
      STOP,
   }

   /// <summary>
   /// Provides notifications of ActiveSync connection
   /// </summary>
   public class RapiConnectDetect : IDccManSink
   {
      public INVOKE_CONNECT itReason;   // Interthread reason

      private EventHandler m_deleCallback; // Callback delegate
      private Control m_ctlTarget; // Target for Invoke calls

      private IDccMan m_pDccMan = null;  // RAPI-provided object
      private bool m_Connected = false;   // Connection state
      private int m_iAdviseSinkContext = 0; // Advise Sink context

      [DllImport("Ole32.dll"), PreserveSig]
      private static extern int
         CoCreateInstance(
         [In] ref Guid clsid,
         [MarshalAs(UnmanagedType.Interface)]
         object punkOuter,
         [MarshalAs(UnmanagedType.I4)] int context,
```

continues

continued

```
        [In] ref Guid iid,
        [In, Out, MarshalAs(UnmanagedType.LPArray)]
        IDccMan[] pDccMan);

    public const int CLSCTX_INPROC_SERVER = 1;

    /// <summary>
    /// RapiConnectDetect -- class constructor
    /// </summary>
    /// <param name="dele"></param>
    public RapiConnectDetect(Control ctl, EventHandler dele)
    {
        m_deleCallback = dele; // Callback for notifications
        m_ctlTarget = ctl;     // Control to notify
    }

    public bool Init()
    {
        System.Guid IID_IDccMan = new
            System.Guid("A7B88841-A812-11CF-8011-00A0C90A8F78");
        System.Guid CLSID_DccMan = new
            System.Guid("499C0C20-A766-11CF-8011-00A0C90A8F78");

        IDccMan [] pTempArray = new IDccMan[1];
        int iErr = CoCreateInstance(ref CLSID_DccMan, null,
            CLSCTX_INPROC_SERVER, ref IID_IDccMan, pTempArray);

        if (pTempArray[0] == null)
            return false;

        m_pDccMan = pTempArray[0];
        return true;
    }

    /// <summary>
    /// Enable - Toggle Advise Sink operation
    /// </summary>
    /// <param name="bEnable"></param>
    public void Enable(bool bEnable)
    {
        if(bEnable && m_iAdviseSinkContext == 0)
        {
            IDccManSink idcc = (IDccManSink)this;
            m_pDccMan.Advise(idcc, ref m_iAdviseSinkContext);
        }

        if (!bEnable && m_iAdviseSinkContext != 0)
```

```
    {
        m_pDccMan.Unadvise(m_iAdviseSinkContext);
        m_iAdviseSinkContext = 0;
    }
}

//
// IDccManSink interface functions
//

public int OnLogAnswered()  { return 0; } // Line detected
public int OnLogActive()    { return 0; } // Line active

/// <summary>
/// OnLogIpAddr - First event when it makes sense to
/// try to do any real work with target device
/// </summary>
/// <param name="dwIpAddr"></param>
/// <returns></returns>
public int OnLogIpAddr(int dwIpAddr) // Link established.
{
    if (!m_Connected) // Notify only if not connected.
    {
        this.itReason = INVOKE_CONNECT.START;
        this.m_ctlTarget.Invoke(this.m_deleCallback);
        m_Connected = true;
    }
    return 0;
}


/// <summary>
/// OnLogDisconnection - Connection ended.
/// </summary>
/// <returns></returns>
public int OnLogDisconnection()
{
    if (m_Connected) // Notify only if connected.
    {
        this.itReason = INVOKE_CONNECT.STOP;
        this.m_ctlTarget.Invoke(this.m_deleCallback);
        m_Connected = false;
    }

    return 0;
}

public int OnLogListen()      { return 0; }
public int OnLogTerminated()  { return 0; }
```

continues

continued

```
      public int OnLogInactive()    { return 0; }
      public int OnLogError()  { return 0; }

   } // class RapiConnectDetect



   #region IDccMan Definitions
   /// <summary>
   /// IDccMan - Interface of COM component provided by RAPI
   /// </summary>
   [Guid("a7b88841-a812-11cf-8011-00a0c90a8f78"),
   InterfaceType(ComInterfaceType.InterfaceIsIUnknown)]
   interface IDccMan   // ActiveSync notification interface
   {
      void Advise (IDccManSink pDccSink, ref int pdwContext);
      void Unadvise(int dwContext);
      void ShowCommSettings ();
      void AutoconnectEnable ();
      void AutoconnectDisable ();
      void ConnectNow ();
      void DisconnectNow ();
      void SetIconDataTransferring ();
      void SetIconNoDataTransferring ();
      void SetIconError ();
   }

   /// <summary>
   /// IDccManSink - Interface we implement to grab notifications
   /// </summary>
   [InterfaceType(ComInterfaceType.InterfaceIsIUnknown)]
   interface IDccManSink
   {
      [PreserveSig] int OnLogIpAddr (int dwIpAddr);
      [PreserveSig] int OnLogTerminated ();
      [PreserveSig] int OnLogActive ();
      [PreserveSig] int OnLogInactive ();
      [PreserveSig] int OnLogAnswered ();
      [PreserveSig] int OnLogListen ();
      [PreserveSig] int OnLogDisconnection ();
      [PreserveSig] int OnLogError ();
   }

#endregion

} // namespace FindPrograms
```

One of the most interesting aspects of the connection detection callback mechanism is that we do not create a separate thread for the callback mechanism. Instead, we run on the program's user interface thread. At first glance, this might seem like the wrong approach to take. After all, any work on the user interface thread can cause unwanted delays in the responsiveness of a program's user interface.

But the work of an Advise Sink, generally speaking, can be done very quickly. What is more important, however, is that an Advise Sink is an interprocess communication that relies on the time-tested Win32 message delivery mechanism (the `GetMessage` or `PeekMessage` "message pump" functions). If we did decide to put the callback on a background thread, we would need to tell the .NET Framework to run the message pump. The desktop .NET Framework provides us with some help to do just that, namely, a static method named `DoEvents` in the `System.Windows.Forms.Application` class. A property of that same class, `MessageLoop`, would even let us know whether a message loop already existed in the thread (in which case we would not have to call the `DoEvents` method). Without a message loop on its thread, an Advise Sink would never work. In our example, we rely on the message loop in the program's main thread for this. You can do the same in your production code, or you can create a background thread—if you make sure that there is a message queue and active polling of that queue in whichever thread owns the callback function. Our connection detection callback object gets created in the constructor of our program's main form with the following code.

```
// Create detect connect object.
m_rapicd = new RapiConnectDetect(this, this.m_deleConnect);
m_rapicd.Init();
m_rapicd.Enable(true);
```

Our connection detection mechanism runs on the user interface thread, which means that we get free synchronization with the program's user interface. Yet we filter all calls from the callback to our controls using the thread-safe `Invoke` function. By giving a single point of contact between the two classes, we make our code easier to support (and, we hope, to reuse!), and we also make it easy to put the callback on a background thread if that becomes necessary. This example shows that calls to the `Invoke` function—which are required for interthread calls to controls—are quite flexible. `Invoke` can be used to call between threads (as shown earlier); it can also be used when the caller and the target control are on the same thread. Newcomers to .NET programming often make the mistake of concluding that the `Invoke` function can be used only for interthread calls, but that is not the case.

As with other callback functions, we first need a declaration for a delegate variable, like this one:

```
private EventHandler m_deleConnect;
```

We initialize this value with a pointer to our target function:

```
m_deleConnect = new EventHandler(this.DetectCallback);
```

Listing 14.13 shows our callback function itself.

LISTING 14.13: `DetectCallback` Detects the Starting and Stopping of Connections

```
/// <summary>
/// DetectCallback - Called to notify start and end of
/// ActiveSync connections
/// </summary>
/// <param name="sender"></param>
/// <param name="e"></param>
private void
DetectCallback(object sender, System.EventArgs e)
{
   INVOKE_CONNECT it = this.m_rapicd.itReason;
   switch(it)
   {
      case INVOKE_CONNECT.START:
         this.cmdConnect_Click(this, new EventArgs());
         this.txtStartDir.Text = @"\";
         this.chkSubs.Checked = true;
         this.cmdFind_Click(this, new EventArgs());
         break;
      case INVOKE_CONNECT.STOP:
         this.cmdDisconnect_Click(this, new EventArgs());
         break;
   }
}
```

When a connection is detected, we simulate the actions a user would perform for a manual connection: Click on the Connect button, fill in the search criteria, then click on the Find button. When a disconnect event is received, we once again simulate the user action, which is to click on the Disconnect button.

Loading Programs and DLLs

Most of the discussion in this chapter has been about using RAPI functions to access the various parts of a device's object store. In this section, we look at starting programs running and also at loading DLLs. You can run any type of program, including Win32 programs and .NET Compact Framework programs. When it comes to loading DLLs, you can load only Win32 DLLs. The reason is that RAPI calls into DLLs at exported functions, and .NET Compact Framework libraries cannot export functions.

Of course, you can access programs and DLLs that are already present in the Windows CE file system. The really interesting scenario, however, involves downloading a program or a DLL to a device and starting it up. For that to work for Win32 executables, you must know what CPU is present on the target system. We are going to spend some time looking at how to retrieve device-side information to know what CPU is present before you download a program.

The requirements for running .NET Compact Framework programs are different. You do not need to know what CPU is present because .NET Compact Framework programs are portable between different CPUs. Before you download and run a .NET Compact Framework program, however, you want to be sure that the .NET Compact Framework itself is present on a system. We will show one way to accomplish that.

Running Device-Side Programs

You start a program running by calling the `CeCreateProcess` function. You can call this function by using either of two P/Invoke wrappers, as shown here.

```
[DllImport("rapi.dll", CharSet=CharSet.Unicode)]
public static extern
```

continues

continued

```
int CeCreateProcess (string lpApplicationName,
   string lpCommandLine, int Res1, int Res2, int Res3,
   int dwCreationFlags, int Res4, int Res5, int Res6,
   ref PROCESS_INFORMATION lpProcessInformation);

[DllImport("rapi.dll", CharSet=CharSet.Unicode)]
public static extern
int CeCreateProcess (string lpApplicationName, int Zero,
   int Res1, int Res2, int Res3, int dwCreationFlags, int Res4,
   int Res5, int Res6,
   ref PROCESS_INFORMATION lpProcessInformation);
```

We define two wrappers to give you a choice of providing arguments for the program or not. The first and last parameters for both wrappers are the most important ones—the rest can be set to some form of zero (either `0` or `string.Empty`). The first parameter is the fully qualified path of the program. If a program is not in the `\windows` directory, you must specify the full path because Windows CE does not have a `PATH` environment variable as desktop Windows has.

The last parameter is a pointer to a `PROCESS_INFORMATION` structure, whose P/Invoke definition is as follows.

```
[StructLayout(LayoutKind.Sequential,Pack=4)]
public struct PROCESS_INFORMATION
{
   public IntPtr hProcess;
   public IntPtr hThread;
   public int dwProcessId;
   public int dwThreadId;
};
```

Here is how to run the calculator program, `calc.exe`, using this data structure and the `CeCreateProcess` function.

```
string strProg = @"\windows\calc.exe"
Rapi.PROCESS_INFORMATION pi = new Rapi.PROCESS_INFORMATION();
Rapi.CeCreateProcess(strProg, 0, 0, 0, 0, 0, 0, 0, 0, ref pi);

Rapi.CeCloseHandle(pi.hProcess);
Rapi.CeCloseHandle(pi.hThread);
```

Notice that we close the handles to the create process and thread after starting the program. Closing the handles does not cause the running program to terminate but only releases the connection we have to that program. Doing so allows Windows CE to clean up properly after the process has terminated.

Loading Device-Side DLLs

Call the `CeRapiInvoke` function from your desktop program to load a device-side DLL and call an entry point in that DLL. The two P/Invoke wrappers for this function are shown here.

```
// Block mode - Set ppIRAPIStream to zero.
[DllImport("rapi.dll", CharSet=CharSet.Unicode)]
public static extern int
CeRapiInvoke (string pDllPath, string pFunctionName, int cbInput,
   IntPtr pInput, ref int pcbOutput, ref IntPtr ppOutput,
   int Res1, int dwReserved);

// Stream mode - Set ppIRAPIStream to valid IRAPIStream interface.
[DllImport("rapi.dll", CharSet=CharSet.Unicode)]
public static extern int
CeRapiInvoke (string pDllPath, string pFunctionName, int cbInput,
   IntPtr pInput, int Res1, int Res2,
   ref IRAPIStream ppIRAPIStream, int dwReserved);
```

This function has two overloads because it has two modes: block and stream. You can tell what mode is selected by looking at the next to last parameter (`Res1`), which is `0` for block mode or a valid COM interface pointer for stream mode. The first function overload supports block mode because it lets you set this key parameter to `0`. The second function overload is for stream mode, for which the `ppIRAPIStream` value must be a valid `IRAPIStream` interface pointer.

Reserved Parameters

When using P/Invoke to call into Win32 libraries, you sometimes run into situations when you need to pass a `NULL` pointer to a Win32 function, as in the call to the `CeRapiInvoke` function to request block mode. To keep things simple, we overload the function and set parameter names to `Reserved` (or when there are several reserved parameters, `Res`*N* where *N* = 1, 2, 3, and so on). Set reserved values to `0`.

Whichever of the two modes you select, when you call the CeRapiInvoke function, it loads the requested DLL and calls the function you name. Version 1.0 of the .NET Compact Framework does not let you create a DLL that exports C-callable functions. The target DLL, then, cannot be a managed-code DLL. It must instead be an unmanaged DLL, and the function you call must be a C or C++ function. To build that DLL, use eMbedded Visual C++ (use version 3.0 for Pocket PC, Pocket PC 2002, Pocket PC 2002 Phone Edition, and the Smartphone; use version 4.0 with Service Pack 3 for Pocket PC 2003, Smartphone 2003, and all other platforms built on Windows CE 4.x).

Whether you are an experienced C++ programmer or not, the Win32 declarations for exporting a DLL function contain elements that are specific to Windows programming. Here is how to declare an exported function named InvokeFunction for a device-side DLL so that the function gets accessed using a call to the CeRapiInvoke function in a desktop-side application.

```
// Win32 declaration for device-side DLL function
extern "C" HRESULT __declspec(dllexport)
InvokeFunction( DWORD cbInput, BYTE  *pInput,
   DWORD *pcbOutput, BYTE  **ppOutput,
   IRAPIStream *pIRAPIStream)
```

Even experienced C/C++ programmers (particularly those who are new to Win32 programming) might be puzzled by this function declaration. Here are details on what each part of this function declaration means.

- extern "C": Retain C-style function names. A C++ style function name gets "decorated" to support function overloading; we disable that feature with this declaration.
- HRESULT: This is the function return value, a COM "result code." The .NET approach to handling such values is to treat them as 32-bit integers (a C# int).
- __declspec(dllexport): This function is exported to make it visible outside the DLL. This or a comparable entry in the EXPORTS section of a module definition (.def) file is needed because DLL functions are private (and therefore hidden) by default in Windows.

- `InvokeFunction`: This is the name of our function. You can choose any name you like, and you must pass this same function name in the call to the `CeRapiInvoke` function as the `pFunctionName` parameter.

The five parameters to the device-side function map directly to five of the eight parameters that get passed to the `CeRapiInvoke` function. How these parameters are interpreted depends on whether the call is being made in block mode or in stream mode. The final parameter, `pIRAPIStream`, is `NULL` for block mode and other than `NULL` for stream mode.

In block mode, the first two parameters refer to data being sent to the device: `cbInput` says how many bytes are in the buffer of data pointed to by `pInput`. The next two parameters are used to send data back to the desktop: `pcbOutput` refers to a buffer for how many bytes are being sent back, and `ppOutput` retrieves a pointer to the buffer holding the return data.

In stream mode (i.e., when `pIRAPIStream` is not `null`), `pIRAPIStream` is a valid pointer to an `IRAPIStream` interface. Stream mode provides an open data pipe, driven by the device-based DLL. This interface contains 14 member functions; the most noteworthy are the `Read` and `Write` member functions. With these two functions, the device-side DLL can exchange data with the calling desktop application.

Building a DLL Using eMbedded Visual C++

To build a DLL that you can invoke from the desktop, use eMbedded Visual C++. At present, there are two supported versions of this tool: version 3.0 and version 4.0. In addition, there are several service packs. You must pick one of these based on the version of Windows CE running on your target device, as summarized in Table 14.5. As shown in this table, version 4.0 had a tight linkage between service pack number and operating system version; the one exception is Service Pack 3, which fixes the compatibility issues.

The reason that the compiler version is so important is that support for C++ exceptions was introduced with eMbedded Visual C++ 4.0. A change was made in the Windows CE kernel to provide the support needed for C++ exceptions on some platforms. This is one of the few times that a compiler version and an operating system version are so closely tied together.

TABLE 14.5: Compatibility between Compiler Versions and Windows CE Versions

C/C++ Compiler	Supported Platforms
eMbedded Visual C++ 3.0	Windows CE 3.0–based platforms, including Pocket PC, Pocket PC 2002, Pocket PC Phone Edition, Smartphone 2002
eMbedded Visual C++ 4.0	Windows CE .NET 4.0
eMbedded Visual C++ 4.0 with Service Pack 1	Windows CE .NET 4.1
eMbedded Visual C++ 4.0 with Service Pack 2	Windows CE .NET 4.2 (includes Pocket PC 2003)
eMbedded Visual C++ 4.0 with Service Pack 3	Windows CE .NET 4.0, 4.1, and 4.2

While each device supports a different version of the operating system, the user interface of each is quite similar. Once you have selected the correct version of the compiler (and, of course, installed it if necessary), you are ready to create a Win32 DLL. Here is a summary of the steps to create a DLL.

1. In eMbedded Visual C++, create a new project. Select WCE Dynamic Link Library as the project type. Create a Simple Windows DLL.
2. Add a reference to the RAPI include file, `rapi.h`:

   ```
   #include <rapi.h>
   ```

3. Add a function to the DLL source code, with the same prototype as the example function, named `InvokeFunction`, shown earlier.
4. In the added function, check for stream or block mode.
5. In stream mode, use the provided interface pointer to exchange data with the desktop application.
6. In block mode, read the data sent in the input buffer.
7. For return data, allocate a buffer by calling the `LocalAlloc` function. Write a copy of the return pointer to the caller's `ppOutput` parameter.
8. Set the size of the return data (to `0` if there is no data) in the caller's `pcbOutput` parameter.

For example, Listing 14.14 shows a DLL function that accepts a Unicode string and converts it to uppercase letters before sending it back to the caller. There are, of course, easier ways to convert a string to uppercase. When you get this function to work, you know that your device-side DLL is functioning properly. This function was taken from the `SimpleBlockModeInvoke` sample program (available online with the rest of the book's source code, with the other C++ source projects in the `CPP` directory tree).

LISTING 14.14: UpperCaseInvoke, a Device-Side Win32 Function

```
//----------------------------------------------------------------
// UpperCaseInvoke -- Win32 device-side function
//-------------------------------------------------------------
extern "C" HRESULT __declspec(dllexport)
UpperCaseInvoke( DWORD cbInput, BYTE  *pInput,
   DWORD *pcbOutput, BYTE  **ppOutput,
   IRAPIStream *pIRAPIStream )
{
   // Init output values
   *pcbOutput = 0;
   *ppOutput = (BYTE *)NULL;

   if (cbInput != 0)
   {
      // Check for a valid input parameter.
      if (IsBadReadPtr(pInput, cbInput))
         return E_INVALIDARG;

      // Allocate a buffer.
      BYTE * pData = (BYTE *)LocalAlloc(LPTR, cbInput);
      if (pData == NULL)
         return E_OUTOFMEMORY;

      // Copy bytes.
      memcpy(pData, pInput, cbInput);

      // Make uppercase.
      LPWSTR lpwstr = (LPWSTR)pData;
      wcsupr(lpwstr);

      // Send return data to caller.
      *pcbOutput = cbInput;
      *ppOutput = pData;
   }

   return S_OK;

} // UpperCaseInvoke
```

Calling a DLL Function with `CeRapiInvoke`

The companion program that calls our DLL is named `CallDeviceDll`. Like the other programs in this chapter, `CallDeviceDll` uses our ActiveSync wrapper library, `YaoDurant.Win32.Rapi.dll`, to access the service of `rapi.dll`.

There are two basic challenges to calling the `CeRapiInvoke` function in block mode. One is getting the data formatted to send down to the device; the second is retrieving the data when we get it back from the device. For both of these, we rely on the `IntPtr` type and the members of the `Marshal` class to do the heavy lifting for us.

To create the unmanaged Unicode string that we send to the device, we call the `Marshal.StringToHGlobalUni` function, which accepts a string as input, allocates an object in the local (unmanaged) heap of the current process, and copies the Unicode string to the memory. We get back a pointer to the memory, which is the parameter we pass as input to the `CeRapiInvoke` function. We must allocate from the process heap because the `CeRapiInvoke` function frees the memory after it is done with it.

Local and Global Memory

The Win32 API contains many sets of memory allocation functions. Two sets of functions trace their roots back to the very first version of Windows: the local allocator (`LocalAlloc`) and the global allocator (`GlobalAlloc`). In the original Win16 API, these memory types were very different. The `GlobalAlloc` set of functions was the segment allocator, and the `LocalAlloc` set of functions was the subsegment allocator. Today, the two sets of functions are supported for backward compatibility, and calls to each get sent to the native Win32 heap allocator function, `HeapAlloc`. There is, in short, no difference between the two.

This is important to know because the RAPI documentation describes how you must call `LocalAlloc` with data you send into `CeRapiInit`, and later call `LocalFree` with the buffer you get back from the function. The .NET P/Invoke helper class, `Marshal`, does not provide a `Local-`

Alloc equivalent, although it does support GlobalAlloc. The two, however, are interchangeable, as you can see by studying our sample program.

Listing 14.15 shows the managed-code method from CallDeviceDll that calls the CeRapiInvoke function.

LISTING 14.15: Calling CeRapiInvoke from Managed Code

```
private void
cmdInvoke_Click(object sender, System.EventArgs e)
{
   // Fetch string from textbox.
   string strInput = textInput.Text;

   // Set up input values - count of bytes.
   int cbInput = (strInput.Length + 1) * 2;
   IntPtr ipInput = Marshal.StringToHGlobalUni(strInput);

   // Set up output values.
   IntPtr ipOutput = IntPtr.Zero;
   int cbOutput = 0;

   // Call device-side DLL.
   Rapi.CeRapiInvoke(@"\windows\SimpleBlockModeInvoke.dll",
      "UpperCaseInvoke",
      cbInput,
      ipInput,
      ref cbOutput,
      ref ipOutput,
      0, 0);

   // Calculate output length (count of characters).
   int cchOut = (cbOutput / 2) - 1;

   // Convert return value to a string.
   string strOutput =
      Marshal.PtrToStringUni(ipOutput, cchOut);

   // Free memory allocated by caller
   Marshal.FreeHGlobal(ipOutput);

   // Display resulting string.
   MessageBox.Show(strOutput, "CallDeviceDll");

} // cmdInvoke_Click
```

CONCLUSION

In this chapter, we looked at using RAPI from managed code. When a connection has been established through ActiveSync, RAPI lets a Windows desktop program connect to and control a Windows CE device. In addition to accessing a device's object store, RAPI also lets you start programs running and load Win32 DLLs. RAPI's various features allow desktop-side code to connect to and manage a Windows CE device while the device is in its home port—its docking cradle.

The next chapter begins the final section of this book, which covers the creation of graphical output from a .NET Compact Framework program. Your need for creating graphical output depends on the type of programming you expect to do. Some programmers rely on existing controls to display information to the user, so they have little need for graphical output. Other programmers want to take full control of the visual display provided by their programs and create custom controls, custom graphical output, and hard-copy output. This second group of programmers is going to find helpful hints in the next section, starting with Chapter 15, which provides the basics for creating graphical output in a .NET Compact Framework program.

PART IV
Creating Graphical Output

15 .NET Compact Framework Graphics

This chapter introduces the basics of creating graphical output from .NET Compact Framework programs.

THIS CHAPTER DESCRIBES the support that the .NET Compact Framework provides programs for creating graphical output. As we mention elsewhere in this book, we prefer using .NET Compact Framework classes whenever possible. To accomplish something beyond what the .NET Compact Framework supports, however, we drill through the managed-code layer to the underlying Win32 API substrate. This chapter and the two that follow discuss the .NET Compact Framework's built-in support for creating graphical output; these chapters also touch on limitations of that support and how to supplement that support with the help of GDI functions.

An Introduction to .NET Compact Framework Graphics

In general, programs do not create graphical output by drawing directly to device hardware.[1] A program typically calls a library of graphical output functions. Those drawing functions, in turn, rely on device drivers that

1. But when necessary for performance reasons or to access device-specific features, a program might bypass the intervening software layers and interact with hardware.

provide the device-specific elements needed to create output on a device. Historically, creating output on a graphic device such as a display screen or a printer involves these software layers:

- Drawing program
- Graphic function library
- Graphic device driver (display driver or printer driver)

The core graphics library on desktop Windows is the Graphics Device Interface (GDI, `gdi32.dll`). With the coming of .NET, Microsoft added a second library (GDI+, `gdiplus.dll`[2]) to supplement GDI drawing support. This second library provides a set of enhancements on top of the core GDI drawing functions. While the primary role for GDI+ was to support graphics for the managed-code library, it also provides a nice bonus for native-mode application programmers: the library can be called from unmanaged (native-mode) C++ programs. On the desktop, these two graphic libraries—GDI and GDI+—provide the underpinnings for all of the .NET graphic classes. And so, with .NET Framework programs running on the Windows desktop, the architecture of graphical output involves the following elements:

- Managed-code program
- Shared managed-code library (`System.Drawing.dll`)
- GDI+ native-code library (`gdiplus.dll`)
- GDI native-code library (`gdi32.dll`)
- Graphic device driver (display driver or printer driver)

Windows CE supports a select set of GDI drawing functions. There is no library explicitly named GDI in Windows CE. Instead, the graphical output functions reside in the `coredll.dll` library. These functions are exactly like their desktop counterparts, so even if there is no library named GDI in Windows CE, we refer to these functions as GDI functions.

---

2. GDI+ is a native-mode, unmanaged-code library.

.NET Framework Drawing and Desktop Graphic Device Drivers

With the introduction of the .NET Framework, no changes were required to the graphic device drivers of any version of Microsoft Windows. That is, the device driver model used by both display screens and printer drivers was robust enough to support the .NET drawing classes.

Of the 400 or so functions that exist on desktop versions of GDI, only about 85 are included in Windows CE. Windows CE has none of the drawing functions from the extended desktop graphics library, GDI+. This places some limits on the extent to which Windows CE can support .NET drawing functions.

With just 85 of the graphical functions from the desktop's GDI library and none of the functions from GDI+, you might wonder whether Windows CE has enough graphics support to create interesting graphical output. The answer is a resounding: Yes! While there are not a lot of graphical functions, the ones that are present were hand-picked as the ones that programs tend to use most. For example, there is a good set of text, raster, and vector functions. A program can use fonts to create rich text output, display bitmaps along with other kinds of raster data (like JPEG files), and draw vector objects such as lines and polygons.

For graphical output, .NET Compact Framework programs rely on `System.Drawing.dll`, which is also the name of the graphical output library in the desktop .NET Framework. At 38K, the .NET Compact Framework library is significantly smaller than the 456K of its counterpart on the desktop. While the desktop library supports five namespaces, the .NET Compact Framework version supports one: `System.Drawing` (plus tiny fragments of two other namespaces). The architecture for drawing from a .NET Compact Framework program is as follows:

- Managed-code program
- Managed-code library (`System.Drawing.dll`)
- GDI functions in the native-code library (`coredll.dll`)
- Graphic device driver (display or printer)

From the arrangement of these software layers, a savvy .NET Compact Framework programmer can divine two interesting points: (1) The managed-code library depends on the built-in GDI drawing functions, and managed-code programs can do the same; and (2) as on the desktop, display screens and printers require a dedicated graphic driver to operate.

If Possible, Delegate Graphical Output to a Control

Before you dig into .NET Compact Framework graphics, ask yourself whether you want to create the graphical output yourself or can delegate that work to a control. If a control exists that can create the output you require, you can save yourself a lot of effort by using that control instead of writing the drawing code yourself. For example, the `PictureBox` control displays bitmaps and JPEG images with little effort. Aside from that single control, however, most controls are text-oriented.

Doing your own drawing—and making it look good—takes time and energy. By delegating graphical output to controls, you can concentrate on application-specific work. The built-in controls support a highly interactive, if somewhat text-oriented, user interface.

Sometimes, however, you do your own drawing to give your program a unique look and feel. In that case, you can create rich, graphical output by using classes in the .NET Compact Framework's `System.Drawing` namespace.

Drawing Surfaces

On the Windows desktop, there are four types of drawing surfaces:

1. Display screens
2. Printers
3. Bitmaps
4. Metafiles

When we use the term *drawing surface*, we mean either a physical drawing surface or a logical drawing surface. Two of the four drawing surfaces in the list are physical drawing surfaces, which require dedicated device drivers: display screens and printers. The other two drawing surfaces are logical drawing surfaces: bitmaps and metafiles. These latter two store pictures for eventual output to a device.

Bitmaps and metafiles are similar enough that they share a common base class in the desktop .NET Framework: the `Image`[3] class. Metafiles are not officially supported in Windows CE, however, and so their wrapper, the `Metafile`[4] class, does not exist in the current version of the .NET Compact Framework. Because metafiles might someday be supported in a future version of the .NET Compact Framework, they are worth a brief mention here.

Display Screens

The display screen plays a central role in all GUI environments because it is on the display screen that a user interacts with the various GUI applications. The real stars of the display screen are the windows after which the operating system gets its name. A window acts as a *virtual console*[5] for interacting with a user. The physical console for a desktop PC consists of a display screen, a mouse, and a keyboard. On a Pocket PC, the physical console is made up of a display screen, a stylus and a touch-sensitive screen for pointing, and hardware buttons for input (supported, of course, by the on-screen keyboard).

All graphical output on the display screen is directed to one window or another. Enforcement of window boundaries relies on *clipping*. Clipping is the establishment and enforcement of drawing boundaries; a program can draw inside clipping boundaries but not outside them. The simplest clipping boundaries are a rectangle. The area inside a window where a program may draw is referred to as the window's *client area*.

3. Fully qualified name: `System.Drawing.Image`.
4. Fully qualified name: `System.Drawing.Imaging.Metafile`.
5. A term we first heard from Marlin Eller, a member of the GDI team for Windows 1.x.

Printers

Printers are the best-established and most-connected peripherals in the world of computers. While some industry pundits still rant about the soon-to-arrive paperless office, just the opposite has occurred. Demand for printed output has continued to go up, not down. Perhaps the world of computers—with its flashing LCD displays, volatile RAM, and ever-shrinking silicon—makes a person want something that is more real.

Printing from Windows CE–powered devices is still in its infancy, which is a nice way to say that this part of the operating system is less feature-rich than other portions. Why is that? The official story is that there is not a good enough business case for adding better printing support, meaning that users have not asked for it. The fundamental question, then, is "Why haven't users asked for better printing for Windows CE?" Perhaps it is because users are used to printing from desktop PCs. Or perhaps the problem stems from the lack of printing support in programs bundled with Pocket PCs (like Pocket Word and Pocket Excel). Whatever the cause, we show you several ways to print in Chapter 17 so that you can decide whether the results are worth the effort.

Bitmaps

Bitmaps provide a way to store a picture. Like its desktop counterparts, Windows CE supports device-independent bitmaps (DIBs) as first-class citizens. In-memory bitmaps can be created of any size[6] and treated like any other drawing surface. After a program has drawn to a bitmap, that image can be put on the display screen.

If you look closely, you can see that Windows CE and the .NET Compact Framework support other raster formats. Supported formats include GIF, PNG, and JPEG. When Visual Studio .NET reads files with these formats (which it uses for inclusion in image lists, for example), it converts the raster data to a bitmap. The same occurs when a PNG or JPEG file is read from the object store into a .NET Compact Framework program. Whatever external format is used for raster data, Windows CE prefers bitmaps. In this chapter, we show how to create a bitmap from a variety of sources and

6. The amount of available system memory limits the bitmap size.

how to draw those bitmaps onto the display screen from a .NET Compact Framework program.

Compressed Raster Support on Custom Windows CE Platforms

Pocket PCs support the compressed raster formats, that is, GIF, PNG, and JPEG files. Custom Windows CE platforms must include the image decompression library, named `imgdecmp.dll`, to receive that same support.

Metafiles

A second picture-storing mechanism supported by desktop Windows consists of metafiles. A metafile is a record-and-playback mechanism that stores the details of GDI drawing calls. The 32-bit version of Windows metafiles are known as *Enhanced Metafiles* (EMFs). The following Win32 native metafile functions are exported from `coredll.dll` but are not officially supported in Windows CE, although they might gain official support in some future version of Windows CE:

- `CreateEnhMetaFile`
- `PlayEnhMetaFile`
- `CloseEnhMetaFile`
- `DeleteEnhMetaFile`

Supported Drawing Surfaces

Of these four types of drawing surfaces, three have official support in Windows CE: display screens, printers, and bitmaps. Only two are supported by the .NET Compact Framework: display screens and bitmaps. Support for bitmaps centers around the `Bitmap`[7] class, which we discuss later in this chapter. We start this discussion of graphical output with the drawing surface that is the focus in all GUI systems: the display screen.

---

7. Fully qualified name: `System.Drawing.Bitmap`.

Drawing Function Families

All of the graphical output functions can be organized into one of three drawing function families:

- Text
- Raster
- Vector

Each family has its own set of drawing attributes and its own logic for how its drawing is done. The distinction between these three kinds of output extends from the drawing program into the graphic device drivers. Each family is complex enough for a programmer to spend many years mastering the details and intricacies of each type of drawing. The drawing support is rich enough, however, so that you do not have to be an expert to take advantage of what is offered.

Text Output

For drawing text, the most important issue involves selection of the font because all text drawing requires a font, and the font choice has the greatest impact on the visual display of text. The only other drawing attribute that affects text drawing is color—both the foreground text and the color of the background area. We touch on text briefly in this chapter, but the topic is important enough to warrant a complete chapter, which we provide in Chapter 16.

Raster Output

Raster data involves working with arrays of pixels, sometimes known as bitmaps or image data. Internally, raster data is stored as a DIB. As we discuss in detail later in this chapter, six basic DIB formats are supported in the various versions of Windows: 1, 4, 8, 16, 24, and 32 bits per pixel. Windows CE adds a seventh DIB format to this set: 2 bits per pixel.

Windows CE provides very good support for raster data. You can dynamically create bitmaps, draw on bitmaps, display them for the user to see, and store them on disk. A bitmap, in fact, has the same rights and privileges as the display screen. By this we mean that you use the same set of drawing functions both for the screen and for bitmaps. This means you can use bitmaps to achieve interesting effects by first drawing to a bitmap and subsequently copying that image to the display screen. An important difference from desktop versions of Windows is that Windows CE does not support any type of coordinate transformations, and in particular there is no support for the rotation of bitmaps; the .NET Compact Framework inherits these limitations because it relies on native Win32 API functions for all of its graphics support.

Vector Output

Vector drawing involves drawing geometric figures like ellipses, rectangles, and polygons. There are, in fact, two sets of drawing functions for each type of figure. One set draws the border of geometric figures with a *pen*. The other set of functions fill the interiors of geometric figures using a *brush*. You'll find more details on vector drawing later in this chapter.

.NET Compact Framework Graphics

The .NET Framework has six namespaces that support the various graphical output classes. In the .NET Compact Framework, just one namespace has made the cut: `System.Drawing`. This namespace and its various classes are packaged in the `System.Drawing.dll` assembly. For a detailed comparison between the graphics support in the .NET Framework and in the .NET Compact Framework, see the sidebar titled Comparing Supported Desktop and Smart-Device Drawing.

Comparing Supported Desktop and Smart-Device Drawing

The `System.Drawing` namespace in the .NET Compact Framework holds the primary elements used to draw on a device screen from managed code. The desktop .NET Framework provides five namespaces for creating graphical output, but in the .NET Compact Framework this has been pared back to two: `System.Drawing` and `System.Drawing.Design` (plus some fragments from two other namespaces).

Table 15.1 summarizes the .NET namespaces supported in the desktop .NET Framework, along with details of how these features are supported in the .NET Compact Framework. The `System.Drawing` namespace supports drawing on a device screen. A second namespace, `System.Drawing.Design`, helps when building a custom control. In particular, this namespace contains elements used to support design-time drawing of controls (i.e., drawing controls while they are being laid out inside the Designer). The elements of this namespace reside in the `System.CF.Design.dll` assembly, a different name from the assembly name used for the desktop. The change in the file name makes it clear that this file supports .NET Compact Framework programming.

On the surface, it would be easy to conclude that Microsoft gutted the desktop `System.Drawing.dll` library in creating the .NET Compact Framework edition. For one thing, the desktop version is a whopping 456K, while the compact version is a scant 38K. What's more, the desktop version supports 159 classes, while the compact version has a mere 17 classes. A more specific example of the difference between the desktop .NET Framework and the .NET Compact Framework—from a drawing perspective—is best appreciated by examining the `Graphics` class (a member of the `System.Drawing` namespace). The desktop .NET Framework version of this class supports 244 methods and 18 properties; the .NET Compact Framework version supports only 26 methods and 2 properties. By this accounting, it appears that the prognosis of "gutted" is correct. Yet, as any thinking person knows, looks can be deceiving.

To understand better the difference between the desktop .NET Framework and the .NET Compact Framework, we have to dig deeper into the `Graphics` class. To really see the differences between the desktop and compact versions, we must study the overloaded methods. If we do, we see that the desktop .NET Framework provides many overloaded methods for each drawing call, while the .NET Compact Framework provides far

TABLE 15.1: **Desktop .NET Framework Drawing Namespaces in the .NET Compact Framework**

Namespace	Description	Support in the .NET Compact Framework
`System.Drawing`	Core drawing objects, data structures, and functions	A minimal set that allows for the drawing of text, raster, and vector objects with no built-in coordinate transformation
`System.Drawing.Design`	Support for the Designer and the various graphic editors of Visual Studio .NET	Support provided by a .NET Compact Framework–specific alternative library named `System.CF.Design.dll`
`System.Drawing.Drawing2D`	Support for advanced graphic features including blends, line caps, line joins, paths, coordinate transforms, and regions	Not supported in the .NET Compact Framework (except for the `CombineMode` enumeration)
`System.Drawing.Imaging`	Support for storage of pictures in metafiles and bitmaps; bitmap conversion; and management of metadata in image files	Not supported in the .NET Compact Framework (except for the `ImageAttributes` class)
`System.Drawing.Printing`	Rich support for printing and the user interface for printing	Not supported in the .NET Compact Framework
`System.Drawing.Text`	Font management	Not supported in the .NET Compact Framework

fewer. For example, the desktop .NET Framework provides six different ways to call `DrawString` (the text drawing function), while there is only one in the .NET Compact Framework. And there are 34 versions of `DrawImage` (the function for drawing a bitmap) but only four in the .NET Compact Framework.

We have, in short, fewer ways to draw objects—but in general we can draw most of the same things with the .NET Compact Framework that we can draw on the desktop. This supports a central design goal of Windows CE, which is to be a small, compact operating system. Win32 programmers who have worked in Windows CE will recognize that a similar trimming has been done to define the Windows CE support for the Win32 API. Instead of calling this a "subset," we prefer to take a cue from the music recording industry and use the term "greatest hits." The .NET Compact Framework implementation of the `System.Drawing` namespace is, we believe, the greatest hits of the desktop `System.Drawing` namespace.

In comparing the desktop .NET Framework to the .NET Compact Framework, an interesting pattern emerges that involves floating-point numbers. In the desktop .NET Framework, most of the overloaded methods take floating-point coordinates. For all of the overloaded versions of the `DrawString` methods, you can *only* use floating-point coordinates. In the .NET Compact Framework, few drawing functions have floating-point parameters—most take either `int32` or a `Rectangle` to specify drawing coordinates. A notable exception is the `DrawString` function, which never takes integer coordinates in the desktop .NET Framework; in the .NET Compact Framework, it is the sole drawing method that accepts floating-point values.

It is worth noting that the underlying drawing functions (both in the operating system and at the device driver level) exclusively use integer coordinates. The reason is more an accident of history than anything else. The Win32 API and its supporting operating systems trace their origins back to the late 1980s, when the majority of systems did not have built-in floating-point hardware. Such support is taken for granted today, which is no doubt why the .NET Framework has such rich support for floating-point values.

A fundamental part of any graphics software is the coordinate system used to specify the location of objects drawn on a drawing surface. The desktop .NET Framework supports seven distinct drawing coordinate systems in the `GraphicsUnit` enumeration. Among the supported coordinates systems are `Pixel`, `Inch`, and `Millimeter`. While the .NET Compact Framework supports this same enumeration, it has only one member: `Pixel`. This means that when you draw on a device screen, you are limited to using pixel coordinates. One exception involves fonts, whose height is always specified in `Point` units.

This brings up another difference between the desktop .NET Framework and the .NET Compact Framework: available coordinate transformations. The desktop provides a rich set of coordinate transformations—scrolling, scaling, and rotating—through the `Matrix` class and the 3×3 geometric transform provided in the `System.Drawing.Drawing2D` namespace. The .NET Compact Framework, by contrast, supports no coordinate mapping. That means that, on handheld devices, application software that wants to scale, scroll, or rotate must handle the arithmetic itself because neither the .NET Compact Framework nor the underlying operating system provides any coordinate transformation helpers. What the .NET Compact Framework provides, as far as coordinates go, is actually the same thing that the underlying Windows CE system provides: pixels, more pixels, and only pixels.

While it might be lean, the set of drawing services provided in the .NET Compact Framework is surprisingly complete. That is, almost anything you can draw with the desktop .NET Framework can be drawn with the .NET Compact Framework. The key difference between the two implementations is that the desktop provides a far wider array of tools and helpers for drawing. Programmers of the desktop .NET Framework are likely to have little trouble getting comfortable in the .NET Compact Framework, once they get used to the fact that there are far fewer features. But those same programmers are likely to be a bit frustrated when porting desktop .NET Framework code to the .NET Compact Framework world and are likely to have to rewrite and retrofit quite a few of their applications' drawing elements.

The Role of the `Graphics` *Class*

The most important class for creating graphical output is the `Graphics`[8] class. It is not the only class in the `System.Drawing` namespace, but only the `Graphics` class has drawing methods. This class holds methods like `DrawString` for drawing a string of text, `DrawImage` for displaying a bitmap onto the display screen,[9] and `DrawRectangle` for drawing the outline of a rectangle. Here is a list of the other classes in the `System.Drawing` namespace for the .NET Compact Framework:

- `Bitmap`
- `Brush`
- `Color`
- `Font`
- `FontFamily`
- `Icon`
- `Image`
- `Pen`
- `Region`
- `SolidBrush`
- `SystemColors`

These other classes support objects that aid in the creation of graphical output, but none has any methods that actually cause graphical output to appear anywhere. So while you are going to need these other classes and will use these other classes, they play a secondary role to the primary graphical output class in the .NET Compact Framework: `Graphics`.

8. Fully qualified name: `System.Drawing.Graphics`.
9. `DrawImage` can also be used to draw bitmaps onto other bitmaps.

Drawing Support for Text Output

Table 15.2 summarizes the methods of the `Graphics` class that support text drawing. The `DrawString` method draws text, while the `MeasureString` method calculates the bounding box of a text string. This calculation is needed because graphical output involves putting different types of graphical objects on a sea of pixels. When dealing with a lot of text, it is important to measure the size of each textbox to make sure that the spacing matches the spacing as defined by the font designer. Failure to use proper spacing creates a poor result. In the worst cases, it makes the output of your program unattractive to users. Even if a user does not immediately notice minor spacing problems, the human eye is very finicky about what text it considers acceptable. Poor spacing makes text harder to read because readers must strain their eyes to read the text. Properly spaced text makes readers—and their eyes—happier than poorly spaced text does.

Drawing Support for Raster Output

Table 15.3 summarizes the methods of the `Graphics` class that draw raster data. We define raster graphics as those functions that operate on an array of pixels. Two of the listed functions copy an icon (`DrawIcon`) or a bitmap (`DrawImage`) to a drawing surface. The other two methods fill a rectangular area with the color of an indicated brush. We discuss the details of creating and drawing with bitmaps later in this chapter.

Drawing Support for Vector Output

Table 15.4 summarizes the seven methods in the `Graphics` class that draw vector `Graphics` objects in the .NET Compact Framework. There

TABLE 15.2: `System.Drawing.Graphics` Methods for Text Drawing

Method	Comment
`DrawString`	Draws a single line of text using a specified font and text color.
`MeasureString`	Calculates the width and height of a specific character string using a specific font.

TABLE 15.3: `System.Drawing.Graphics` Methods for Raster Drawing

Method	Comment
`Clear`	Accepts a color value and uses that value to fill the entire surface of a window or the entire surface of a bitmap.
`DrawIcon`	Draws an icon at a specified location. An icon is a raster image created from two rectangular bitmap masks. The `DrawIcon` method draws an icon by applying one of the masks to the drawing surface using a Boolean AND operator, followed by the use of the XOR operator to apply the second mask to the drawing surface. The benefit of icons is that they allow portions of an otherwise rectangular image to display the screen behind the icon. The disadvantage of icons is that they are larger than comparable bitmaps and also slower to draw.
`DrawImage`	Draws a bitmap onto the display screen or draws a bitmap onto the surface of another bitmap.
`FillRegion`	Fills a region with the color specified in a brush. A region is defined as a set of one or more rectangles joined by Boolean operations.

TABLE 15.4: `System.Drawing.Graphics` Methods for Vector Drawing

Method	Comment
`DrawEllipse`	Draws the outline of an ellipse using a pen.
`DrawLine`	Draws a straight line using a pen.
`DrawPolygon`	Draws the outline of a polygon using a pen.
`DrawRectangle`	Draws the outline of a rectangle using a pen.
`FillEllipse`	Fills the interior of an ellipse using a brush.
`FillPolygon`	Fills the interior of a polygon using a brush.
`FillRectangle`	Fills the interior of a rectangle using a brush.

are substantially fewer supported vector methods than in the desktop .NET Framework. The vector methods whose names start with `Draw` draw lines. The vector methods whose names start with `Fill` fill areas.

Drawing on the Display Screen

The various `System.Drawing` classes in the .NET Compact Framework exist for two reasons. The first and most important reason is for output to the display screen. The second reason, which exists to support the first reason, is to enable drawing to bitmaps, which can later be displayed on the display screen.

Taken together, the various classes in the `System.Drawing` namespace support all three families of graphical output: text, raster, and vector. You can draw text onto the display screen using a variety of sizes and styles of fonts. You can draw with raster functions, including functions that draw icons, functions that draw bitmaps, and functions that fill regions[10] or the entire display screen. The third family of graphical functions, vector functions, supports the drawing of lines, polygons, rectangles, and ellipses on the display screen.

Accessing a `Graphics` Object

For a .NET Compact Framework program to draw on the display screen, it must have an instance of the `Graphics` class—meaning, of course, a `Graphics` object. A quick visit to the online documentation in the MSDN Library shows two interesting things about the `Graphics` class. First, this class provides no public constructors. Second, this class cannot be inherited by other classes. Thus you might wonder how to access a `Graphics` object.

Close study of the .NET Compact Framework classes reveals that there are three ways to access a `Graphics` object. Two are for drawing on a display screen, and one is for drawing on a bitmap. Table 15.5 summarizes three methods that are needed to gain access to a `Graphics` object. We

10. A region is a set of rectangles. Regions exist primarily to support clipping but can also be used to define an area into which one can draw.

TABLE 15.5: .NET Compact Framework Methods for Accessing a `Graphics` Object

Namespace	Class	Method	Comment
`System.Drawing`	`Graphics`	`FromImage`	Creates a `Graphics` object for drawing onto a bitmap. When done drawing, clean up the `Graphics` object by calling the `Dispose` method.
	`Graphics`	`Dispose`	Reclaims memory used by `Graphics` objects.
`System.Windows.Forms`	`Control`	`CreateGraphics`	Creates a `Graphics` object for drawing in the client area of a control. As indicated in Table 15.6, only three control classes support this method. When done drawing, clean up the `Graphics` object by calling the `Dispose` method.
	`Control`	`Paint` event handler	Obtains a `Graphics` object to handle a `Paint` event. As indicated in Table 15.6, only five control classes support this event. Do not call the `Dispose` method when done drawing.

include a fourth method in the table, Dispose, because you need to call that method to properly dispose of a Graphics object in some circumstances.

The display screen is a shared resource. A multitasking, multithreaded operating system like Windows CE needs to share the display screen and avoid conflicts between programs. For that reason, Windows CE uses the same mechanism used by Windows on the desktop: Drawing on a display screen is allowed only in a window (i.e., in a form or a control).

To draw on the display screen, a program draws in a control. You get access to a Graphics object for the display screen, then, through controls. Not just any control class can provide this access, however—only the control classes that derive from the Control class can.

One way to get a Graphics object for the display screen involves the Paint event. The Paint event plays a very important role in the design of the Windows CE user interface, a topic we discuss later in this chapter. Access to a Graphics object is provided to a Paint event handler method as a property of its PaintEventArgs parameter. Incidentally, when you get a Paint event, you are allowed to use the Graphics object while responding to the event. You are not allowed to hold onto a reference to the Graphics object because the .NET Compact Framework needs to recycle the contents of that Graphics object for other controls to use.[11]

A second way to get a Graphics object is by calling the CreateGraphics method, a method defined in the Control class (and therefore available to classes derived from the Control class). Using the Graphics object returned by this call, your program can draw inside a control's client area. Although the method name suggests that it is creating a Graphics object, this is not what happens. Instead, like the Graphics object that arrives with the Paint event, the Graphics object that is provided by the CreateGraphics method is loaned to you from a supply created and owned by the Windows CE window manager. Therefore, you are required to return this object when you are done by calling the Graphics object's Dispose method. Failure to make this call results in a program hanging.

11. Ultimately, the window manager reuses the device context contained within the Graphics object.

Calling the Dispose Method for a Graphics Object

There are two ways to get a Graphics object, but you need to call the Dispose method for only one of those ways. You must call the Dispose method for Graphics objects that are returned by the CreateGraphics method. But you do not call Dispose for Graphics objects that are provided as a parameter to the Paint event handler.

The third way to get a Graphics object is by calling the static FromImage method in the Graphics class. On the desktop, the Image class is an abstract class that serves as the base class for the Bitmap and Metafile classes. Because metafiles are not supported in the .NET Compact Framework, the FromImage method can return only a Graphics object for a bitmap. You can use the resulting Graphics object to draw onto a bitmap in the same way that the Graphics object described earlier is used to draw on a display screen. We are going to discuss drawing to bitmaps later in this chapter; for now, we explore the subject of drawing in controls.

As we discussed in Chapter 7, a main theme for .NET Compact Framework controls is that "inherited does not mean supported." Of the 28 available .NET Compact Framework control classes, only 5 support drawing. To help understand what types of drawing are supported, we start by identifying the specific controls that you can draw onto. We then cover the most important control event for drawing, the Paint event. We then discuss how non–Paint event drawing differs from Paint event handling.

Drawing in Controls

In the desktop .NET Framework, a program can draw onto any type of control (including onto forms). This feature is sometimes referred to as *owner-draw support*, a feature first seen in native-code programming for just a few of the Win32 API controls. The implementers of the .NET Framework for the desktop seem to think that this feature is something that every control should support. On the desktop, every control supports the owner-draw feature. In other words, you can get a Graphics object for every type of control[12] and use that object to draw inside the client area of any control. Owner-draw support is widely available because it allows programmers to inherit from existing control classes and change the behavior and appearance of those classes. This support allows the creation of custom control classes from existing control classes.

Things are different in the .NET Compact Framework, for reasons that are directly attributable to the .NET Compact Framework design goals. As we discussed in detail in Chapter 7, the .NET Compact Framework itself was built to be as small as possible and also to allow .NET Compact Framework programs to run with reasonable performance. The result is a set of controls with the following qualities:

- .NET Compact Framework controls rely heavily on the built-in, Win32 API control classes.
- .NET Compact Framework controls do not support every PME inherited from the base `Control`[13] class.

The result is that only a few .NET Compact Framework controls provide owner-draw support. In particular, five control classes support the `Paint` event. Only three control classes support the `CreateGraphics` method. Table 15.6 summarizes the support for drawing in .NET Compact Framework control classes.

As suggested by the column headings in Table 15.6, there are two types of drawing: `Paint` event drawing and `CreateGraphics` method drawing. The clearest way to describe the difference is relative to events because of the unique role played by the `Paint` event and its associated `Paint` event handler method. From this perspective, the two types of drawing are better stated as `Paint` event drawing and drawing for other events. All five

12. All desktop control classes that we tested support the `CreateGraphics` method. However, a few desktop control classes do not support the overriding of the `Paint` event: the `ComboBox`, `HScrollbar`, `ListBox`, `ListView`, `ProgressBar`, `StatusBar`, `TabControl`, `TextBox`, `Toolbar`, `TrackBar`, `TreeView`, and `VScrollBar` classes.

13. Fully qualified name: `System.Windows.Forms.Control`.

TABLE 15.6: Support for Drawing in .NET Compact Framework Control Classes

Class	`Paint` Event	`CreateGraphics` Method
`Control`	Yes	Yes
`DataGrid`	Yes	Yes
`Form`	Yes	Yes
`Panel`	Yes	No
`PictureBox`	Yes	No

controls in Table 15.6 support `Paint` event drawing. We turn our attention now to the subject of the `Paint` event and its role in the Windows CE user interface.

Anywhere, Anytime Control Drawing

An early definition of .NET talked about "anywhere, anytime access to information." Arbitrary boundaries are annoying. It is odd, then, that you cannot draw onto your controls anywhere at any time. But wait—maybe you can?

If you are willing to step outside of the managed-code box, you can draw on any control at any time. The .NET Compact Framework team did a great job of giving us a small-footprint set of libraries with very good performance. That is why owner-draw support is so limited—not because of any belief on the part of the .NET Compact Framework team that you should not be allowed to draw inside controls.

Native-code drawing means using GDI calls, each of which requires you to have a handle to a *device context* (`hdc`). There are two types of device contexts: those used to draw inside windows and those that can draw anywhere on a display screen. To draw in a window, you first must get the window handle (set focus to a control and then call the native `GetFocus` function). Call the native `GetDC` function to retrieve a device context handle, and call the `ReleaseDC` function when you are done.

A second method for accessing a device context is by using this call: `hdc = CreateDC(NULL, NULL, NULL, NULL)`. The device context that is returned provides access to the entire display screen, not just inside windows. Among its other uses, this type of device context is useful for taking screenshots of the display screen, which can be useful for creating documentation. When done with the device context, be sure to clean up after yourself by calling the `DeleteDC` function.

The `hdc` returned by either of these functions—`GetDC` or `CreateDC`—can be used as a parameter to any GDI drawing function. When done drawing, be sure to provide your own manual garbage collection. In other words, be sure to call the `ReleaseDC` or `DeleteDC` functions.

The `Paint` Event

To draw in a window—that is, in a form or in a control—you handle the `Paint`[14] event. This event is sent by the system to notify a window that the contents of the window need to be redrawn. In the parlance of Windows programmers, a window needs to be redrawn when some portion of its client area becomes *invalid*. To fix an invalid window, a control draws everything that it thinks ought to be displayed in the window.

Generating a `Paint` Event

The purpose of the `Paint` event is to centralize all the drawing for a window in one place. Before we look at more of the details of how to handle the `Paint` event, we need to discuss the circumstances under which a

14. This is what Win32 programmers know as a `WM_PAINT` message, which MFC programmers handle by overriding the `CWnd::OnPaint` method.

`Paint` event gets generated. A `Paint` event gets generated when the contents of a window become invalid. (We use the term *window* to mean a form or any control derived from the `Control` class.) But what causes a window to become invalid? There are several causes.

When a window is first created, its contents are invalid. When a form first appears, every control on the form is invalid. A `Paint` event is delivered to each control (which, in some cases, is handled by the native-code control that sits behind the managed-code control).

A window can also become invalid when it gets hidden. Actually, a hidden window is not invalid; it is just hidden. But when it gets uncovered, the window also becomes invalid. At that moment, a `Paint` event is generated by the system so that the window can repair itself.

A window can also become invalid when it gets scrolled. Every scroll operation causes three possible changes to the contents of a window. Some portion of the contents might disappear, which occurs when something scrolls off the screen. Nothing is required for that portion. Another portion might move because it has been scrolled up (or down, left, or right). Here again, nothing is required. The system moves that portion to the correct location. The third portion is the new content that is now visible to be viewed. This third portion must be drawn in response to a `Paint` event.

Finally, a `Paint` event is triggered when something in the logic of your program recognizes that the graphical display of a window does not match the program's internal state. Perhaps a new file was opened, or the user picked an option to zoom in (or out) of a view. Maybe the network went down (or came up), or the search for something ended.

To generate a `Paint` event for any window, a program calls one of the various versions of the `Invalidate` method for any `Control`-derived class. This method lets you request a `Paint` event for a portion of a window or for the entire window and optionally allows you to request that the background be erased prior to the `Paint` event.

This approach to graphical window drawing is not new to the .NET Compact Framework or even to the .NET environment. All GUI systems have a `Paint` event—from the first Apple Macintosh and the earliest versions of desktop Windows up to the current GUI systems shipping today. A window holds some data and displays a view of that data.

In one sense, drawing is simple: A window draws on itself using the data that it holds. And what happens if the data changes? In that case, a window must declare its contents to be invalid, which causes a `Paint` event to be generated. A control requests a `Paint` event by calling the `Invalidate` method. Two basic problems can be observed with the `Paint` event:

1. Failing to request `Paint` events (which causes cold windows with stale contents)
2. Requesting `Paint` events too often (which causes hot window flickers that annoy users)

These are different problems, but both involve calling the `Invalidate` method the wrong number of times. The first problem arises from not invalidating a window enough. The second problem arises from invalidating the window too often. A happy medium is needed: invalidating a window the right number of times and at just the right times.

To draw in response to a `Paint` event, a program adds a `Paint` event handler to a control. You can add a `Paint` event handler to any `Control`-derived class. But the handler is only going to get called for the five control classes listed in Table 15.6. This is just another example of the "inherited does not mean supported" behavior of .NET Compact Framework controls.

Here is an empty `Paint` event handler.

```
private void FormMain_Paint(
object sender, PaintEventArgs e)
{
   Graphics g = e.Graphics;
   // draw
}
```

The second parameter to the `Paint` event handler is an instance of `PaintEventArgs`.[15] A property of this class is a `Graphics` object, which provides the connection that we need to draw in the form. There is more to be said about the `Graphics` object, but first let us look at the case of drawing for events besides the `Paint` event.

Non-`Paint` Event Drawing

A window that contains any graphical output must handle the `Paint` event. Often, the only drawing that a window requires is the drawing for the `Paint` event. This is especially true if the contents of the window are somewhat static. For example, `Label` controls are often used to display text that does not change. For a `Label` control, drawing for the `Paint` event is all that is required. However, windows whose contents must change quickly might need to draw in response to events other than the `Paint` event. A program that displays some type of animation, for example, might draw in response to a `Timer` event. A program that echoes user input might draw in response to keyboard or mouse events.

Figure 15.1 shows the `DrawRectangles` program, a sample program we presented in Chapter 6. This program draws rectangles in the program's main form, using a pair of (x,y) coordinates. One coordinate pair is collected for the `MouseDown` event, and a second coordinate pair is collected for the `MouseUp` event. As the user moves the mouse (or a stylus on a Pocket PC), the program draws a stretchable rubber rectangle as the mouse/stylus is moved from the `MouseDown` point to the `MouseUp` point. The program accumulates rectangles as the user draws them.

The `DrawRectangles` program uses both `Paint` and non-`Paint` event drawing. In response to the `Paint` event, the program draws each of the accumulated rectangles. In response to the `MouseMove` event, the stretchable rectangle is drawn to allow the user to preview the result before committing to a specific location.

---

15. Fully qualified name: `System.Windows.Forms.PaintEventArgs`.

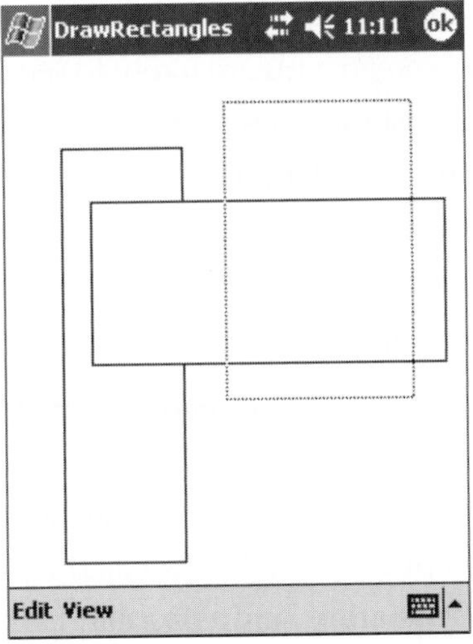

FIGURE 15.1: A stretchable rubber rectangle created in the DrawRectangles program

The basic template for the code used in non–`Paint` event drawing appears here.

```
Graphics g = CreateGraphics();
// Draw
g.Dispose();
```

This follows a programming pattern familiar to some as the *Windows sandwich.*[16] The top and bottom lines of code make up the two pieces of bread—these are always the same. The filling in between the two slices of bread consists of the drawing, which is accomplished with the drawing methods from the `Graphics` class.

Raster Graphics

We define raster graphics as those functions that operate on an array of pixels. The simplest raster operation is to fill a rectangle with a single color.

16. This is what Eric Maffei of *MSDN Magazine* used to refer to as the *Windows Hoagie.*

On a display screen, this is one of the most common operations. If you study any window on any display screen, you are likely to see that the background is a single color, often white or sometimes gray. You can use three methods in the `Graphics` class to fill a rectangular area:

- `Clear`: fills a window with a specified color
- `FillRectangle`: fills a specified rectangle using a brush
- `FillRegion`: fills a specified region using a brush

The `Clear` method accepts a single parameter, a structure of type `Color`.[17] The other two methods accept a `Brush`[18] object as the parameter that identifies the color to use to fill the area. Before we can fill an area with any of these functions, then, we need to know how to define colors and how to create brushes.

Specifying Colors

The most basic type of drawing attribute is color, yet few drawing methods accept colors directly as parameters. Most drawing methods require other drawing attributes that have a built-in color. For example, for filling areas, the color to use for filling the area is the color that is part of a brush. When drawing lines, the line color is the color that is part of a pen. Brushes are also used to specify text color. So even though color parameters are not directly used as parameters to methods, they are indirectly specified through a pen or brush.

There are three ways to specify a color in a .NET Compact Framework program:

- With a system color
- With a named color
- With an RGB value

---

17. Fully qualified name: `System.Drawing.Color`.
18. Fully qualified name: `System.Drawing.Brush`.

System colors are a set of colors used to draw the elements of the user interface. The use of system colors helps create consistency between different programs. For example, a given system might be set up with black text on a white background, or it could be set up with the opposite, white text on a black background. System colors are made available as properties of the `SystemColors`[19] class. Available system colors are listed in Table 15.7 in the System Colors subsection.

Named colors provide access to colors that use human-readable names like `Red`, `Green`, `Blue`, `White`, and `Black`. There are also a large number of colors with less common names like `SeaShell` and `PeachPuff`. Whether or not you like all the names of the colors you encounter, they provide a way to specify colors that is easy to remember. Color names are made available as static properties of the `Color` structure.

When you specify a color using an RGB value, you specify an amount of red, an amount of green, and an amount of blue. Each is defined with a byte, meaning that values can range from `0` to `255`. It is sometimes helpful to remember that RGB is a video-oriented color scheme often used for display screens and televisions. When the energy for all three colors is `0`, the color you see is black; when all the energy for all three colors is at 100% (`255`), the resulting color is white.

System Colors

System colors let you connect your program's graphical output to current system settings. This allows a program to blend in with the current system configuration. On some platforms, users can change system colors from the system control panel (such as on desktop version of Microsoft Windows). Other platforms, like the Pocket PC, do not provide the user with an easy way to modify system color settings. A custom embedded smart device could easily be created with a unique system color scheme—say, to match corporate logo colors or to meet unique environmental requirements such as usage in low-light conditions or in sunlight. For all of these cases, the safest approach to selecting text colors involves using system colors.

---

19. Fully qualified name: `System.Drawing.SystemColors`.

System colors are available as read-only properties in the `SystemColors` class, the contents of which are summarized in Table 15.7. If you study this table, you may notice that several entries have the word `Text` in the name—such as `ControlText` and `WindowText`. There are, after all, many uses of text in the user interface. When specifying the color for drawing text, these system colors provide your best choice.

TABLE 15.7: System Colors in the .NET Compact Framework

Color	Description
`ActiveBorder`	Border color of a window when the window is active
`ActiveCaption`	Color of the background in the caption when a window is active
`ActiveCaptionText`	Color of the text in the caption when a window is active
`AppWorkspace`	Color of the unused area in an MDI[a] application
`Control`	Background color for a three-dimensional control
`ControlDark`	Color of the middle of the shadow for a three-dimensional control
`ControlDarkDark`	Color of the darkest shadow for a three-dimensional control
`ControlLight`	Color of the lightest element in a three-dimensional control
`ControlLightLight`	Color of the lightest edge for a three-dimensional control
`ControlText`	Color for drawing text in controls
`Desktop`	Color of the desktop background
`GrayText`	Color for drawing grayed text (e.g., for disabled controls)
`Highlight`	Background color of highlighted areas for menus, `ListBox` controls, and `TextBox` controls
`HighlightText`	Text color for highlighted text
`HotTrack`	Color of hot-tracked items

a. MDI is not supported on Windows CE or in the .NET Compact Framework.

Color	Description
`InactiveBorder`	Border color of a top-level window when the window is inactive
`InactiveCaption`	Color of the background in the caption when a window is inactive
`InactiveCaptionText`	Color of the text in the caption when a window is inactive
`Info`	Background color of a tool tip
`InfoText`	Text color of a tool tip
`Menu`	Menu background color
`MenuText`	Menu text color
`ScrollBar`	Background color of a scroll bar
`Window`	Background color of a window
`WindowFrame`	Color of a window border
`WindowText`	Color of text in a window

In some cases, there is a pair of system color names: one with and one without the word `Text` in the name (e.g., `Control` and `ControlText`, `Window` and `WindowText`). One color in the pair defines a system color for text, and the other defines the color of the background. For example, when drawing in a form or dialog box, use the `Window` color for the background and `WindowText` for the text color. When you create a custom control, use the `Control` color for the control's background area and `ControlText` for the color of text drawn in a control. In the following code, the background is filled with the default window background color.

```
private void FormMain_Paint(
object sender, PaintEventArgs e)
{
   Graphics g = e.Graphics;
   g.Clear(SystemColors.Window);
}
```

Named Colors

The `System.Drawing.Color` class defines 142 named colors as read-only properties. The names include old favorites like `Red`, `Green`, `Blue`, `Cyan`, `Magenta`, `Yellow`, `Brown`, and `Black`. It also includes some new colors like `AliceBlue`, `AntiqueWhite`, `Aqua`, and `Aquamarine`. With names like `Chocolate`, `Honeydew`, and `PapayaWhip`, you may get hungry just picking a color. The named colors appear in Table 15.8.

The following code draws in the background of a window with the color `PapayaWhip`.

```
private void FormMain_Paint(
object sender, PaintEventArgs e)
{
   Graphics g = e.Graphics;
   g.Clear(Color.PapayaWhip);
}
```

Colors from RGB Values

The third approach that the .NET Compact Framework supports for specifying colors is to specify the three components—red, green, and blue—that make up a color. These three components are packed together into a 32-bit integer with one byte for each. The range for each component is from `0` to `255` (`FF` in hexadecimal). Table 15.9 summarizes color triplet values for common colors.

To create a color from an RGB triplet, use the `Color.FromArgb` method. There are two overloaded versions for this method. We find the following one easier to use.

```
public static Color FromArgb(
   int red,
   int green,
   int blue);
```

When you read the online documentation for this method, you see a reference to a fourth element in a color, the *alpha value*. The .NET Compact Framework does not support this, so you can safely ignore it. (In the desktop .NET Framework, the alpha value defines the transparency of a color, where a value of `0` is entirely transparent and `255` is entirely opaque. In a

TABLE 15.8: Named Colors in the .NET Compact Framework

AliceBlue	DarkGray	Gold	LightSkyBlue	Navy	SandyBrown
AntiqueWhite	DarkGreen	Goldenrod	LightSlateGray	OldLace	SeaGreen
Aqua	DarkKhaki	Gray	LightSteelBlue	Olive	SeaShell
Aquamarine	DarkMagenta	Green	LightYellow	OliveDrab	Sienna
Azure	DarkOliveGreen	GreenYellow	Lime	Orange	Silver
Beige	DarkOrange	Honeydew	LimeGreen	OrangeRed	SkyBlue
Bisque	DarkOrchid	HotPink	Linen	Orchid	SlateBlue
Black	DarkRed	IndianRed	Magenta	PaleGoldenrod	SlateGray
BlanchedAlmond	DarkSalmon	Indigo	Maroon	PaleGreen	Snow
Blue	DarkSeaGreen	Ivory	MediumAquamarine	PaleTurquoise	SpringGreen
BlueViolet	DarkSlateBlue	Khaki	MediumBlue	PaleVioletRed	SteelBlue
Brown	DarkSlateGray	Lavender	MediumOrchid	PapayaWhip	Tan
BurlyWood	DarkTurquoise	LavenderBlush	MediumPurple	PeachPuff	Teal
CadetBlue	DarkViolet	LawnGreen	MediumSeaGreen	Peru	Thistle
Chartreuse	DeepPink	LemonChiffon	MediumSlateBlue	Pink	Tomato
Chocolate	DeepSkyBlue	LightBlue	MediumSpringGreen	Plum	Transparent
Coral	DimGray	LightCoral	MediumTurquoise	PowderBlue	Turquoise
CornflowerBlue	DodgerBlue	LightCyan	MediumVioletRed	Purple	Violet
Cornsilk	Firebrick	LightGoldenrodYellow	MidnightBlue	Red	Wheat
Crimson	FloralWhite	LightGray	MintCream	RosyBrown	White
Cyan	ForestGreen	LightGreen	MistyRose	RoyalBlue	WhiteSmoke
DarkBlue	Fuchsia	LightPink	Moccasin	SaddleBrown	Yellow
DarkCyan	Gainsboro	LightSalmon	NavajoWhite	Salmon	YellowGreen
DarkGoldenrod	GhostWhite	LightSeaGreen			

TABLE 15.9: Color Triplets for Common Colors

Color Name	RGB Triplet (Decimal)	RGB Triplet (Hexadecimal)
Black	`(0, 0, 0)`	`(0, 0, 0)`
White	`(255, 255, 255)`	`(0xFF, 0xFF, 0xFF)`
Red	`(255, 0, 0)`	`(0xFF, 0, 0)`
Green	`(0, 255, 0)`	`(0, 0xFF, 0)`
Blue	`(0, 0, 255)`	`(0, 0, 0xFF)`
Cyan	`(0, 255, 255)`	`(0, 0xFF, 0xFF)`
Magenta	`(255, 0, 255)`	`(0xFF, 0, 0xFF)`
Yellow	`(255, 255, 0)`	`(0xFF, 0xFF, 0)`
Dark Gray	`(68, 68, 68)`	`(0x44, 0x44, 0x44)`
Medium Gray	`(128, 128, 128)`	`(0x80, 0x80, 0x80)`
Light Gray	`(204, 204, 204)`	`(0xCC, 0xCC, 0xCC)`

Knowing Black from White

We give programmers in our training classes the following tip to help remember the correct RGB for black `(0, 0, 0)` and white `(255, 255, 255)`. The RGB color encoding is a light-based scheme, which in a computer CRT is often used to correlate the power to apply to the electron guns in the monitor. Turn the power off, which causes the power to go to zero, and you see black. When the power to the red, green, and blue is turned up all the way, you get white.

In Table 15.9, notice the different shades of gray. By studying the color triplets, you can observe what makes the color gray: equal parts of red, green, and blue.

.NET Compact Framework program, all colors have an alpha value of `255`, which means that all colors are 100% opaque.

The following code draws the window background using a light gray color.

```
private void FormMain_Paint(
object sender, PaintEventArgs e)
{
   Graphics g = e.Graphics;
   g.Clear(Color.FromArgb(204,204,204));
}
```

Creating Brushes

A brush specifies the color and pattern to use for area-filling methods, such as `FillRectangle`. The .NET Compact Framework does not support patterns in brushes, however, so a brush just specifies the color when filling areas. Brushes also specify the color to use when drawing text. The second parameter to the `DrawString` method, for example, is a brush.

The desktop .NET Framework supports five different kinds of brushes, including solid brushes, bitmap brushes, and hatch brushes. Windows CE supports solid brushes and bitmap brushes but not hatch brushes. And in the .NET Compact Framework, things are even simpler: only solid brushes are supported, by the `SolidBrush`[20] class. This class has a single constructor, which takes a single parameter—`Color`. The `SolidBrush` constructor is defined as follows.

```
public SolidBrush(
   Color color);
```

With one constructor, it is natural to assume that there is one way to create a solid brush. But because there are three ways to define a color, there are three ways to create a brush:

- Using the system colors
- Using a named color
- Using an RGB value

20. Fully qualified name: `System.Drawing.SolidBrush`.

The following subsections discuss each of these briefly.

Creating Brushes with System Colors

The following code creates a brush from a system color. This brush is suitable for drawing text within a program's main form or in a dialog box.

```
Brush brText = new SolidBrush(SystemColors.WindowText);
```

The resulting brush provides the same color used by the operating system to draw text. You are not required to select this color, but in doing so you help ensure that your application fits into the color scheme established by the user.

There might be reasons to design your own color scheme. For example, when dealing with financial figures you might display positive numbers in black and display negative numbers in red. Or perhaps when displaying certain types of documents you could highlight keywords in different colors, in the same way that Visual Studio .NET highlights language keywords in blue. To handle these situations, you need to specify the brush color with one of the two other color-defining schemes: using either named colors or RGB colors.

Creating Brushes with Named Colors

Here are examples of creating brushes using named colors.

```
Brush brRed = new SolidBrush(Color.Red);
Brush brPaleGreen = new SolidBrush(Color.PaleGreen);
Brush brLightBlue = new SolidBrush(Color.LightBlue);
```

You might wonder where these color names come from. Some—like `Red`—are, of course, names for common colors. But when you read through the list of names, you see colors like `AliceBlue`, `GhostWhite`, and `WhiteSmoke`. The colors are sometimes called *HTML Color Names* because the more exotic names were first supported as color names in HTML by various browsers. Officially, however, HTML 4.0 includes only 16 color names, not the 140+ names defined in the `Color` structure.

Creating Brushes with RGB Values

To create a brush using an RGB value, call the `FromArgb` method in the `Color` class and pass the return value to the `SolidBrush` constructor. This method accepts three integer parameters, one each for red, green, and blue. Here is how to create three brushes from RGB triplets.

```
Brush brRed = new SolidBrush(Color.FromArgb(255, 0, 0));
Brush brGreen = new SolidBrush(Color.FromArgb(0, 255, 0));
Brush brBlue = new SolidBrush(Color.FromArgb(0, 0, 255));
```

Creating Bitmaps

A bitmap is a two-dimensional array of pixels with a fixed height and a fixed width. Bitmaps have many uses. One is to hold scanned images, such as a company logo. Photographs are stored as bitmaps, commonly in the highly compressed format of JPEG[21] files. Bitmaps can be used to create interesting effects on a display screen, such as smooth scrolling and seamless animation.

Bitmaps are often used to store complex images that a program can easily draw in one or more locations by making a single method call. As useful as this approach can be, it is important to always remember that bitmaps require a lot of room—both in memory and in the file system. If you plan to include any bitmaps with your program, give some thought to the format of those bitmaps. We address this issue later in this chapter.

Bitmaps are sometimes referred to as *off-screen-bitmaps* because of the important role bitmaps have historically played in supporting display screen graphics. The Bitmaps on the Desktop sidebar discusses how bitmaps are used on desktop versions of Windows to support various user interface objects. That same support does not exist in Windows CE because of memory constraints. But bitmaps are still available to Windows CE programs for all of their other uses.

---

21. *JPEG* stands for Joint Photographic Experts Group, the name of the original committee that created the standard. For details on this compression standard, visit http://www.jpeg.org.

Bitmaps on the Desktop

On desktop versions of Windows, bitmaps support the quick appearance and disappearance of menus, dialog boxes, and various other user interface elements. For example, before a menu appears on the screen, a snapshot is taken of the area to be covered by the menu. When the menu disappears, the bitmap is used to redraw the affected part of the screen. This technique helps make the elements of the user interface appear and disappear very quickly. This technique is not employed in Windows CE because of the tight memory restrictions of mobile and embedded systems. But your program could use bitmaps in other ways to support the display of your program's user interface.

In our programming classes, we observe that programmers often get confused when first starting to work with bitmaps. The confusion seems to come from not grasping that bitmaps are inherently off-screen. Or it may arise from an understanding that display screens are supported by memory-mapped video devices and that the memory occupied by a bitmap must somehow be related to the memory used by the display adapter. After creating a bitmap and drawing into a bitmap, some programmers expect that bitmaps are going to appear somewhere on the screen. That does not happen, however, because bitmaps appear on a display screen only when your program explicitly causes them to appear.

Bitmaps: Drawing Surface or Drawing Object?

Bitmaps play two roles in every graphic library built for Microsoft Windows: (1) as drawing surfaces and (2) as drawing objects used to draw onto other surfaces. This is another reason why bitmaps can at first seem confusing for some programmers.

A bitmap is a drawing surface like other drawing surfaces. We say this because a program can obtain a `Graphics` object for a bitmap and then use the methods of that object to draw onto the surface of the bitmap. All of the drawing methods in the `Graphics` object are supported for bitmaps, including text, raster, and vector drawing methods.

The second role played by bitmaps is that of a drawing object. Like other drawing objects, such as pens, brushes, and fonts, a bitmap holds a pattern that can be applied to a drawing surface. Each drawing object has its particular uses, and each produces a different effect, as determined by the various drawing methods. The .NET Compact Framework supports four overloads for the bitmap drawing method, which is named `DrawImage`.

An example might clarify what we mean by each of these two roles. Using a `Graphics` object, a program can draw onto a bitmap by calling drawing methods. One such drawing method is `DrawImage`, which draws a bitmap onto a drawing surface. A program can call the `DrawImage` method to draw one bitmap (the drawing object) onto the surface of another bitmap (the drawing surface).

To push the example one step further, a bitmap can be both the drawing surface and also the drawing object. You could do this by using the `DrawImage` method to draw onto a bitmap while using the bitmap itself as the image source. This may sound like a snake eating its own tail, a seemingly impossible operation. It is possible, however, because it involves copying a rectangular array of pixels from one part of a bitmap to another part. The work required for this type of bitmap handling is well understood and has been part of Windows display drivers for more than a decade. The bitmap drawing code in Windows CE can easily—and correctly—handle cases where, for example, source and destination rectangles overlap. This describes what happens, for example, when a user picks up and moves a window.

The `Bitmap` Class

The .NET Compact Framework supports in-memory bitmaps with the `Bitmap`[22] class. This class is derived from the `Image` class, which is a common base class for the `Bitmap` class and the `Metafile` class. As we mentioned earlier in this chapter, metafiles are not supported in the .NET

---

22. Fully qualified name: `System.Drawing.Bitmap`.

Compact Framework. But because the .NET Compact Framework maintains consistency with the desktop .NET Framework, our bitmap drawing method is called `DrawImage` (instead of, for example, `DrawBitmap`). On the desktop, where metafiles are supported, the `DrawImage` method draws both bitmaps and metafiles.

The dimensions of a bitmap are available through two properties of the `Bitmap` object: `Height` and `Width`. The dimensions are also available through the `Size` property, which provides a convenient package for height and width. These are read-only properties because an image cannot change size once it has been created.

On the desktop, the `Bitmap` class supports 12 constructors, while in the .NET Compact Framework there are only 4 constructors. You can create a bitmap these ways:

- By opening an image file
- By reading an image from a stream
- By starting from an existing bitmap
- By specifying the width and height for an empty bitmap

Table 15.10 maps the constructors to six common sources you might use to create a bitmap.

Creating an Empty Bitmap

One way to create a bitmap is to specify the desired dimensions of the bitmap to the following constructor in the `Bitmap` class.

```
public Bitmap(
   int width,
   int height);
```

This constructor creates a bitmap in program memory with the specified size. This is the quickest and easiest way to create a bitmap, but the empty (i.e., all-black) image means that you must draw into the bitmap before displaying its contents. You might call this a *scratch space* or *double-buffer bitmap* because it provides an off-screen drawing surface for doodling, just like scratch paper. The term *double-buffer* refers to a technique of creating

TABLE 15.10: Sources for Bitmaps and Associated `Bitmap` Class Constructors

Source	Constructor Parameters	Comments
An external image file	`(String)`	Provides the path to the bitmap in the file system
A portion of a file	`(Stream)`	Uses the `FileStream` class to open the file and move the seek position to the first byte of the bitmap
Data in memory	`(Stream)`	Uses the `MemoryStream` class to assemble the bitmap bits as a byte array
A resource	`(Stream)`	Reads bitmap data from a managed resource created as an untyped manifest resource
An existing bitmap	`(Image)`	Copies an existing bitmap
An empty bitmap	`(int,int)`	Specifies the width and height of the empty bitmap

smooth graphic effects by doing complex drawing off-screen and sending the resulting output to the display screen with a single, fast drawing operation. Let's use a bitmap created with this constructor.

After creating the bitmap itself, a program typically obtains a `Graphics` object for the bitmap. As we mentioned earlier in this chapter, we need a `Graphics` object for any type of drawing. We obtain a `Graphics` object for the bitmap by calling the `FromImage` method of the `Bitmap` class. Before drawing anything else in the bitmap, it makes sense to first erase the bitmap's background.

We need to think about cleanup. This is a subject that can often be ignored in managed code, but not when working with resource-intensive objects like bitmaps. So, when done working with a bitmap, your program must use the `Dispose` method to clean up two objects: the bitmap itself and the `Graphics` object. The code in Listing 15.1 shows the whole life cycle of our created bitmap: The code creates a bitmap, erases the bitmap's background, draws the bitmap to the display screen, and then cleans up the two objects that were created.

LISTING 15.1: Dynamic Bitmap Creation

```
private void
CreateAndDraw(int x, int y)
{
   // Create a bitmap and a Graphics object for the bitmap.
   Bitmap bmpNew = new Bitmap(100,100);
   Graphics gbmp = Graphics.FromImage(bmpNew);

   // Clear the bitmap background.
   gbmp.Clear(Color.LightGray);

   // Get a Graphics object for the form.
   Graphics g = CreateGraphics();

   // Copy the bitmap to the window at (x,y) location.
   g.DrawImage(bmpNew, x, y);

   // Clean up when we are done.
   g.Dispose();
   gbmp.Dispose();
   bmpNew.Dispose();
}
```

Creating a Bitmap from an External File

Another way to create a bitmap is by specifying the path to an image file. This is accomplished with a constructor that accepts a single parameter, a string with the path to the candidate file. This second `Bitmap` class constructor is defined as follows.

```
public Bitmap(
   string filename);
```

This method has two important requirements. One is that there must be enough memory to accommodate the bitmap. If there is not, the call fails. A second requirement is that the specified file must have an image in a format that the constructor understands. We have been able to create bitmaps from the following file types:

- Bitmap files (`.bmp`) with 1, 4, 8, or 24 bits per pixel
- JPEG (`.jpg`) files

- GIF (`.gif`) files
- PNG (`.png`) files

Among the unsupported graphic file formats are TIFF (`.tif`) files.

This constructor throws an exception if the file name provided is not a recognized format or if it encounters other problems when attempting to open the file or create the bitmap. For that reason, it makes sense to wrap this constructor in a `try...catch` block. Listing 15.2 provides an example of calling this constructor, with a file name provided by the user in a File Open dialog box.

LISTING 15.2: Creating a Bitmap with a File Name

```
try
{
   bmpNew = new Bitmap(strFileName);
}
catch
{
   MessageBox.Show("Cannot create bitmap from " +
      "File: " + strFileName);
}
```

Creating a Bitmap from a Resource

When a program needs a bitmap for its normal operation, it makes sense to package the bitmap as a resource. Resources are read-only data objects that are bound into a program's executable file[23] at program build time. The benefit of binding a bitmap to an executable file is that it is always available and cannot be accidentally deleted by a user.

Resources have been a part of Windows programming from the very first version of Windows. In a native-mode program, resources are used for bitmaps and icons and also to hold the definitions of dialog boxes and menus. In managed-code programs, resources are still used for bitmaps and icons, although some program elements—including dialog boxes and

23. Resources can be bound into any executable module, meaning any program (`.exe`) or library (`.dll`) file.

menus—are not defined in a resource but instead are defined using code in the `InitializeComponent` method by the Designer.

Where Do Resources Live?

Because memory is scarce on a Windows CE–powered device, it helps to know when and how memory gets used. When a resource gets added to a module, the resource occupies space in the module's file but uses no program memory until the resource is explicitly opened and used. This is true for both native resources and managed resources.

While resources are used in both native code and managed code, native resources can be used only from native mode code, and managed resources can be used only from managed code. The only exception is the program icon for a managed-code program, which is defined as a native icon. In managed code, there are two types of resources: *typed resources* and *untyped resources*.

Typed Resources. We like to use typed resources to hold literal strings, which aid in the localization of programs. To access typed resources, a program creates an instance of a `ResourceManager`[24] class and then makes calls to methods like `GetObject` and `GetString`. We provided an example of using typed resources for literal strings in Chapter 3, in the sample project named `StringResources`.

Typed resources are defined using XML in files that have an extension of `.resx`. In a typed resource, an XML attribute provides type information, as shown in this example.

```
<data name="dlgFileOpen.Location" type="System.Drawing.Point,
 System.CF.Drawing, Version=7.0.5000.0, Culture=neutral,
 PublicKeyToken=b03f5f7f11d50a3a">
     <value>125, 17
     </value>
</data>
```

24. Fully qualified name: `System.Resources.ResourceManager`.

The Designer makes extensive use of typed resources. For each form created in the Designer, there is an associated file used to store a variety of details about the form. The Visual Studio .NET Solution Explorer does not normally display resource files, but you can make them appear by clicking the Show All Files icon.

For example, bitmaps in the image collection of an `ImageList` control on a form are stored as typed resources in the typed resource file of the form that contains the control. The bitmaps themselves are serialized into the XML and are not stored in their original, binary form. While a programmer could convert bitmap files into XML resources, we prefer to avoid this extra step and use untyped resources when we add bitmap resources to a project.

Untyped Resources. Untyped resources are also known as *manifest resources* because they are made available through an assembly's manifest (or table of contents). As the name implies, an untyped resource contains no type information and is made available as a raw stream of bytes. It does have a name, however, created by combining the default project namespace with the file name that contained the original resource data. You must know this name because you use the name to retrieve the resource. If you have trouble figuring out the resource name, the `ildasm.exe` utility can help. Open the program file and then click on the manifest. Listing 15.3 shows three bitmap resource names in a fragment from the manifest for the `ShowBitmap` sample program presented later in this chapter.

LISTING 15.3: Three Bitmap Resource Names from the `ShowBitmap` Manifest

```
.mresource public ShowBitmap.SPADE.BMP
{
}
.mresource public ShowBitmap.CUP.BMP
{
}
.mresource public ShowBitmap.HEART.BMP
{
}
```

Visual Studio .NET creates an untyped resource from an external file when you add the file to a project and assign a build action of Embedded Resource. The default build action for bitmap files, Content, allows the bitmap file to be downloaded with a program, but as a separate file and not as an embedded resource. Figure 15.2 shows the Visual Studio .NET settings to turn the file `CUP.BMP` into an embedded bitmap resource. The name of the resource is `ShowBitmap.CUP.BMP`, which we need to know to access the resource from our code.

You can access an embedded resource by calling a method in the `Assembly` class named `GetManifestResourceStream`.[25] As suggested by the method name, the return value is a `Stream` object; more precisely, you are provided a `MemoryStream`[26] object. You can use all of the elements associated with a `Stream`-derived class (including the ability to query the resource length, which is the same as the resource input file) to seek a location in the stream and to read bytes (the `CanSeek` and `CanRead` properties are both set to `true`). In keeping with the read-only nature of Windows resources, you cannot write to a resource stream[27] (`CanWrite` returns `false`).

The code fragment in Listing 15.4 shows two methods from the `ShowBitmap` sample program. These methods are helper routines to handle the

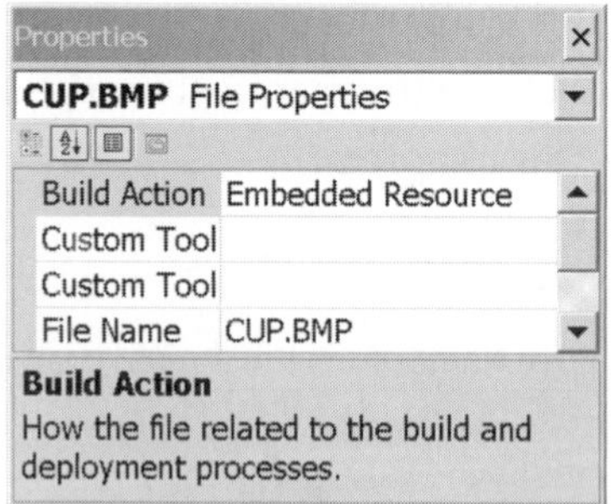

FIGURE 15.2: The settings to turn `CUP.BMP` into an embedded bitmap resource

25. Fully qualified name: `System.Reflection.Assembly.GetManifestResourceStream`.

26. Fully qualified name: `System.IO.MemoryStream`.

27. In contrast to an Apple Macintosh resource fork, which supports both read and write operations.

What Can Go into an Untyped Resource?

This chapter provides an example of putting a bitmap into an untyped resource. But this is not the only type of resource you can create. You can put any custom data into untyped resources, which can then be used to access the data at runtime. When you request an untyped resource, you are provided with a `Stream` object that you can use as you wish. You might, for example, read a resource into an array of bytes and then parse those bytes in whatever way your application needs. Such resources can be any read-only data that your program needs: tax tables, sports scores, or—as we show in the `ShowBitmap` sample program—a set of bitmaps.

A benefit of using custom resources is that we have access to data we need at runtime. But when we are not using that data, it does not occupy scarce program memory. This makes custom resources a useful tool in our toolkit for building memory-wise programs.

initialization and cleanup of resource-based bitmaps. The `LoadBitmap-Resource` method creates a bitmap from a resource; the `DisposeBitmap` method provides the cleanup.

LISTING 15.4: Creating Bitmaps from Untyped Manifest Resources

```
private Bitmap LoadBitmapResource(string strName)
{
   Assembly assembly = Assembly.GetExecutingAssembly();
   string strRes = "ShowBitmap." + strName;
   Stream stream = assembly.GetManifestResourceStream(strRes);
   Bitmap bmp = null;
   try
   {
      bmp = new Bitmap(stream);
   }
   catch { }
   stream.Close();

   return bmp;
}
```

continues

continued

```
private void DisposeBitmap(ref Bitmap bmp)
{
   if (bmp != null)
   {
      bmp.Dispose();
   }
   bmp = null;
}
```

The `LoadBitmapResource` method creates a bitmap by opening a resource stream and uses data read from that stream to create a bitmap. This method gets a reference to the program's assembly by calling a static method in the `Assembly` class named `GetExecutingAssembly`. After creating a bitmap, the stream can be closed. Once a bitmap has been created, it is self-contained and needs no external data. That is why we can close the stream once the `Bitmap` object has been created.

The `DisposeBitmap` method deletes the bitmap to free up its associated memory. It does this by calling the `Dispose` method for a `Bitmap` object. There are only a few situations in which it is mandatory to call the `Dispose` method.[28] Sometimes, however, it is still a good idea—even if it is not, strictly speaking, required. Bitmaps can be large, so we suggest you consider explicitly deleting bitmaps, as we have done in our sample. Among the factors to consider are the size of your bitmaps and the number of bitmaps. We suggest that you explicitly delete bitmaps when you have either many small bitmaps or a few large bitmaps.

We call our two methods using code like the following.

```
private void
mitemResourceCup_Click(object sender, EventArgs e)
{
   DisposeBitmap(ref bmpDraw);
   bmpDraw = LoadBitmapResource("CUP.BMP");
   Invalidate();
}
```

28. The only situation requiring a call to the `Dispose` method is to release a `Graphics` object obtained in a control by calling the `CreateGraphics` method.

After cleaning up the old bitmap, we create a new bitmap and request a `Paint` event by calling the `Invalidate` method. Next, we discuss image file size, and how to save memory by changing the format you use for your images.

Image File Sizes

Bitmaps can occupy a lot of memory, which can create problems in a memory-scarce environment like Windows CE. When placing bitmaps in resources, we recommend that you test different formats and use the smallest one. To provide a starting point, we conducted some tests with three 100 × 100 pixel images stored in different formats. Table 15.11 summarizes our results, which provide the size in bytes for each image file.

Four formats are uncompressed and three are compressed. The first four entries in the table are for DIB files. This well-known format is thoroughly documented in the MSDN Library and is the format that Visual Studio .NET provides for creating bitmap images. Notice that the size of these images is the same for a given number of bits per pixel. This reflects the fact that DIB files are uncompressed.

TABLE 15.11: **Size Comparison for Three 100 x 100 Images in Various Image File Formats**

Format	Bits per Pixel	Size of Single-Color Image (Bytes)	Size of Multicolor Image with Regular Data (Bytes)	Size of Multi-color Image with Irregular Data (Bytes)
Monochrome DIB	1	1,662	1,662	1,662
16-color DIB	4	5,318	5,318	5,318
256-color DIB	8	11,078	11,078	11,078
True-color DIB	24	30,054	30,054	30,054
GIF	8	964	3,102	7,493
PNG	8	999	616	5,973
JPEG	24	823	3,642	5,024

The last three formats are the compressed formats: GIF, PNG, and JPEG. To make sense of these formats, we must discuss the contents of the three images. The single-color image was a solid black rectangle. Each of the three compressed formats easily beat any of the uncompressed formats for the single-color image. The reason is that compressed formats look for a pattern and use that information to store details of the pattern. A single color is a pretty easy pattern to recognize and compress.

The second column, the multicolor image with regular data, shows the results for an image created with a solid background and vertical stripes. We used vertical stripes in an attempt to thwart the compression because run-length encoding of horizontal scan lines is an obvious type of compression. We were surprised (and pleased) to find that PNG compression was able to see through the fog we so carefully created—it created the smallest image in the table.

The third column, the multicolor image with irregular data, shows the sizes for images created with very random data. For this test, we copied text (.NET Compact Framework source code) into an image file. (We never want our work to be called "random," but we wanted an irregular image to push the envelope for the three compression formats.) The result was more like a photograph than any of the other images, which is why JPEG—the compression scheme created for photographs—was able to provide the best compression. It provided the smallest file size with the least loss of information (the monochrome image was smaller, but the image was lost).

To summarize, the two compression schemes that created the smallest image files were PNG (for regular data) and JPEG (for irregular data). One problem is that Visual Studio .NET does not support either of these formats. But Microsoft Paint (`mspaint.exe`) supports both, so we recommend that you make sure your images have been compressed as much as possible prior to embedding your images as resources.

Drawing Bitmaps

The `Graphics` class supports four overloaded versions of the bitmap drawing method, `DrawImage`. These alternatives support the following types of bitmap drawing:

- Drawing the entire bitmap at the original image size
- Drawing part of a bitmap at the original image size
- Drawing part of a bitmap with a change to the image size
- Drawing part of a bitmap with a change to the image size and with transparency

We discuss these four methods in the sections that follow.

Drawing the Entire Bitmap at the Original Image Size

The simplest version of the `DrawImage` method copies an entire bitmap onto a device surface with no change in the image size, as shown here.

```
public void DrawImage(
   Image image,
   int x,
   int y);
```

Listing 15.5 shows an example of calling this method in a `Paint` event handler.

LISTING 15.5: Drawing an Entire Bitmap at the Original Size

```
private void
FormMain_Paint(object sender, PaintEventArgs e)
{
   Graphics g = e.Graphics;
   int x = 10;
   int y = 10;

   g.DrawImage(bmpDraw, x, y);
}
```

Drawing Part of a Bitmap at the Original Image Size

While we sometimes want to draw an entire bitmap, there are also times when we only want to see a portion of a bitmap. The second version of the `DrawImage` method provides the support we need to do just that, as shown on the next page.

```
public void DrawImage(
   Image image,
   int x,
   int y,
   Rectangle srcRect,
   GraphicsUnit srcUnit);
```

This version of the `DrawImage` method has five parameters, while the earlier one has only three. One of the extra parameters is useful, and the second is not so useful. The fourth parameter, `srcRect`, is the useful one, which identifies the rectangular area in the source bitmap that we wish to copy to the destination surface.

The fifth parameter, `srcUnit`, can be set to only one valid value in the .NET Compact Framework: `GraphicsUnit.Pixel`. On the desktop, the presence of this parameter gives the caller the freedom to select a convenient unit of measure for the source rectangle (e.g., inches or millimeters). But the .NET Compact Framework supports only pixel drawing units, which is why this parameter is not so useful in the context of a .NET Compact Framework program. The `srcUnit` parameter is present because of the high level of compatibility between the desktop .NET Framework and the .NET Compact Framework. As such, it represents a small price to pay for the convenience of allowing smart-device code to have binary compatibility with the desktop runtime.

Drawing Part of a Bitmap with a Change to the Image Size

The third overloaded version of the `DrawImage` method allows a portion of a bitmap to be selected for drawing, and that portion can be stretched (or shrunk) to match a specified size on the destination surface. Of course, nothing requires the image to change size: If the width and height of the destination rectangle is the same as the width and height of the source rectangle, no size change occurs. This version of the `DrawImage` method is defined as shown here.

```
public void DrawImage(
   Image image,
   Rectangle destRect,
   Rectangle srcRect,
   GraphicsUnit srcUnit);
```

Drawing Part of a Bitmap with a Change to the Image Size and with Transparency

The final version of the `DrawImage` method adds a new feature to the drawing of bitmaps. It enables transparency while drawing a bitmap. In some ways, this feature breaks our definition of raster graphics. You might recall that we refer to raster graphics as those operations that operate on arrays of pixels. Implicit in this definition is that all operations are rectangular.

The ability to draw a raster operation and touch only a nonrectangular set of pixels on a drawing surface is, therefore, something of a heresy (like having nonrectangular windows on a display screen or a late-night coding session without ordering large quantities of unhealthy food). We hope that readers can accept this change with little loss of sleep. We certainly are happy to break the shackles that have previously limited almost all raster graphics to the boring world of rectangular arrays of pixels. This amazing new feature is available through the following version of the `DrawImage` method.

```
public void DrawImage(
   Image image,
   Rectangle destRect,
   int srcX,
   int srcY,
   int srcWidth,
   int srcHeight,
   GraphicsUnit srcUnit,
   ImageAttributes imageAttr);
```

With its eight parameters, this version of the `DrawImage` method is the most complicated one that the .NET Compact Framework supports. Perhaps it is appropriate that this version matches the other versions in capabilities: It can draw an entire bitmap at its original size, draw a portion of a bitmap at its original size, and draw a portion of a bitmap at a different size.

What makes this version different is the final parameter, a reference to an `ImageAttributes` object. On the desktop, this class supports a variety of color adjustments that can be applied when drawing a bitmap onto a surface. The .NET Compact Framework version is much simpler, with what amounts to a single property: a color key. The color key defines the range of colors that represent transparent portions of an image. In other

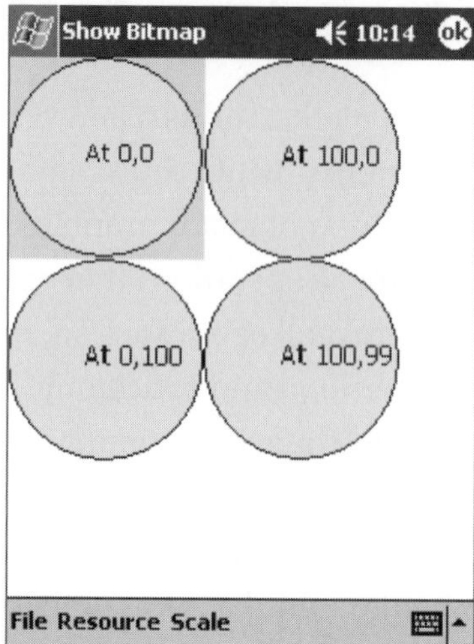

FIGURE 15.3: Four calls to the `DrawImage` method, three with transparency enabled

words, any color that matches the color key is a color that is *not* copied by the call to the `DrawImage` method. The color key settings are controlled through two methods: `SetColorKey` defines the transparency range, and `ClearColorKey` disables the transparency range.

Figure 15.3 shows an example of transparency at work. A 100 × 100 bitmap is first drawn without transparency at the window origin. That same bitmap is then drawn three times, using the version of the `DrawImage` method that supports transparency. The color key is set to light gray, which corresponds to the color outside the ellipse (the interior of the ellipse is set to yellow). Listing 15.6 shows the code, a handler for a `MouseDown` event, which we used to create the example.

LISTING 15.6: Event Handler That Draws a Bitmap with Transparency

```
bool bFirstTime = true;

private void
FormMain_MouseDown(object sender, MouseEventArgs e)
{
   // Get a Graphics object for the form.
   Graphics g = CreateGraphics();
```

```
    // Create a bitmap and a Graphics object for the bitmap.
    Bitmap bmpNew = new Bitmap(100,100);
    Graphics gbmp = Graphics.FromImage(bmpNew);

    // Clear the bitmap background.
    gbmp.Clear(Color.LightGray);

    // Create some drawing objects.
    Pen penBlack = new Pen(Color.Black);
    Brush brBlack = new SolidBrush(Color.Black);
    Brush brYellow = new SolidBrush(Color.Yellow);

    // Draw onto the bitmap.
    gbmp.FillEllipse(brYellow, 0, 0, 98, 98);
    gbmp.DrawEllipse(penBlack, 0, 0, 98, 98);
    gbmp.DrawString("At " + e.X.ToString() + "," + e.Y.ToString(),
       Font, brBlack, 40, 40);

    // Copy the bitmap to the window at the MouseDown location.
    if (bFirstTime)
    {
       // Copy without transparency.
       g.DrawImage(bmpNew, e.X, e.Y);
       bFirstTime = false;
    }
    else
    {
       // Copy the bitmap using transparency.
       Rectangle rectDest = new Rectangle(e.X, e.Y, 100, 100);
       ImageAttributes imgatt = new ImageAttributes();
       imgatt.SetColorKey(Color.LightGray, Color.LightGray);
       g.DrawImage(bmpNew, rectDest, 0, 0, 99, 99,
          GraphicsUnit.Pixel, imgatt);
    }

    // Clean up when we are done.
    g.Dispose();
    gbmp.Dispose();
    bmpNew.Dispose();
}
```

A Sample Program: `ShowBitmap`

Our bitmap drawing sample program shows several features of bitmaps that we have been discussing. This program can open files and create a bitmap. Several formats are supported, including the standard Windows DIB (`.bmp`)

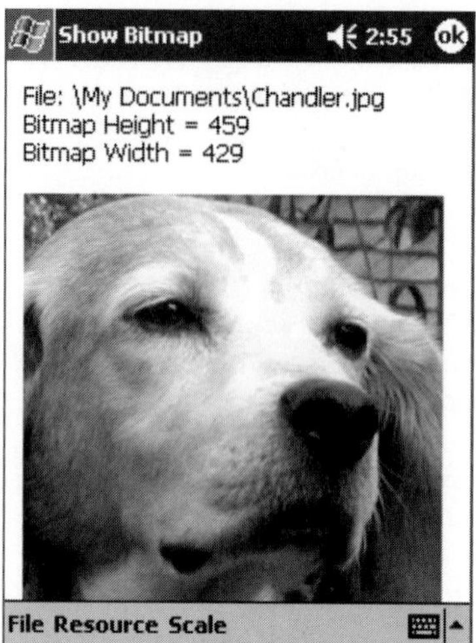

FIGURE 15.4: `ShowBitmap` **displaying a JPEG file scaled to 50%**

files and also a few compressed image file formats such as GIF (`.gif`) files, JPEG (`.jpg`) files, and PNG (`.png`) files. Figure 15.4 shows the `ShowBitmap` program with a JPEG image of Chandler (the office beagle at The Paul Yao Company). This image is drawn scaled to 50%, an effect made possible by selecting the appropriate version of the `DrawImage` method.

Our sample program contains a set of bitmap files that are bound to the program files as embedded resources (see Listing 15.7). As with all types of resources, the resource data does not get loaded into memory until we explicitly load the resource. In this program, we load the resource when the user selects an item on the program's resource menu. Figure 15.5 shows the bitmap resource that was read from a resource identified as `ShowBitmap.CUP.BMP`, drawn at 400% of its original size.

LISTING 15.7: Source Code for `ShowBitmap.cs`

```
using System.Reflection; // Needed for Assembly
using System.IO;         // Needed for Stream
using System.Drawing.Imaging;  // Needed for ImageAttributes
// ...
```

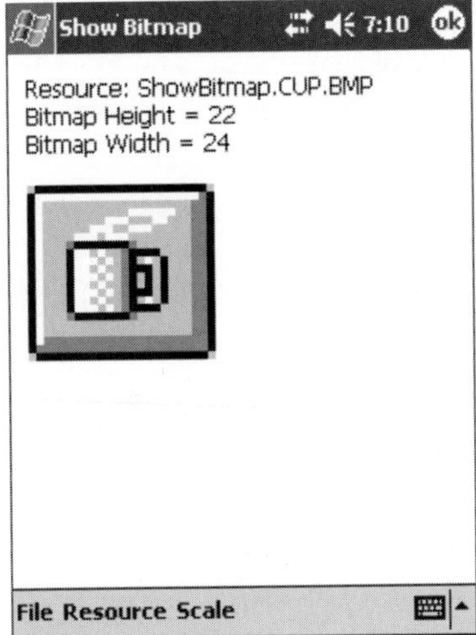

FIGURE 15.5: `ShowBitmap` **displaying a bitmap from a resource**

```
private Bitmap bmpDraw;
bool bFirstTime = true;
bool bResource = false;
string strResName;

// Draw a bitmap using transparency where the MouseDown
// event is received.
private void
FormMain_MouseDown(object sender, MouseEventArgs e)
{
#if false
   CreateAndDraw(e.X, e.Y);
#endif
   // Get a Graphics object for the form.
   Graphics g = CreateGraphics();

   // Create a bitmap and a Graphics object for the bitmap.
   Bitmap bmpNew = new Bitmap(100,100);
   Graphics gbmp = Graphics.FromImage(bmpNew);

   // Clear the bitmap background.
   gbmp.Clear(Color.LightGray);

   // Create some drawing objects.
   Pen penBlack = new Pen(Color.Black);
```

continues

continued

```
    Brush brBlack = new SolidBrush(Color.Black);
    Brush brYellow = new SolidBrush(Color.Yellow);

    // Draw onto the bitmap.
    gbmp.FillEllipse(brYellow, 0, 0, 98, 98);
    gbmp.DrawEllipse(penBlack, 0, 0, 98, 98);
    gbmp.DrawString("At " + e.X.ToString() + "," + e.Y.ToString(),
       Font, brBlack, 40, 40);

    // Copy the bitmap to the window at the MouseDown location.
    if (bFirstTime)
    {
       // Copy without transparency.
       g.DrawImage(bmpNew, e.X, e.Y);
       bFirstTime = false;
    }
    else
    {
       // Copy the bitmap using transparency.
       Rectangle rectDest = new Rectangle(e.X, e.Y, 100, 100);
       ImageAttributes imgatt = new ImageAttributes();
       imgatt.SetColorKey(Color.LightGray, Color.LightGray);
       g.DrawImage(bmpNew, rectDest, 0, 0, 99, 99,
          GraphicsUnit.Pixel, imgatt);
    }

    // Clean up when we are done.
    g.Dispose();
    gbmp.Dispose();
    bmpNew.Dispose();
}

private void FormMain_Paint(object sender, PaintEventArgs e)
{
    Graphics g = e.Graphics;
    float sinX = 10.0F;
    float sinY = 10.0F;
    SizeF szfText = g.MeasureString("X", Font);
    float cyLine = szfText.Height;

    Brush brText = new SolidBrush(SystemColors.WindowText);
    if (bmpDraw != null)
    {
       if (bResource)
       {
          g.DrawString("Resource: " + strResName,
             Font, brText, sinX, sinY);
       }
       else
```

```
    {
       g.DrawString("File: " + dlgFileOpen.FileName,
          Font, brText, sinX, sinY);
    }
    sinY += cyLine;

    g.DrawString("Bitmap Height = " + bmpDraw.Height,
       Font, brText, sinX, sinY);
    sinY += cyLine;

    g.DrawString("Bitmap Width = " + bmpDraw.Width,
       Font, brText, sinX, sinY);
    sinY += cyLine;
    sinY += cyLine;

    if (mitemScale100.Checked)
    {
       g.DrawImage(bmpDraw, (int)sinX, (int)sinY);
    }
    else
    {
       Rectangle rectSrc = new Rectangle(0, 0,
          bmpDraw.Width, bmpDraw.Height);
       int xScaled = 0;
       int yScaled = 0;
       if (mitemScale50.Checked)
       {
          xScaled = bmpDraw.Width / 2;
          yScaled = bmpDraw.Height / 2;
       }
       else if (mitemScale200.Checked)
       {
          xScaled = bmpDraw.Width * 2;
          yScaled = bmpDraw.Height * 2;
       }
       else if (mitemScale400.Checked)
       {
          xScaled = bmpDraw.Width * 4;
          yScaled = bmpDraw.Height * 4;
       }

       Rectangle rectDest = new Rectangle((int)sinX,
          (int)sinY, xScaled, yScaled);
       g.DrawImage(bmpDraw, rectDest, rectSrc,
          GraphicsUnit.Pixel);
    }
}
else
```

continues

continued

```
    {
        g.DrawString("File: None", Font, brText, sinX, sinY);
    }
}

private void
mitemFileOpen_Click(object sender, EventArgs e)
{
    dlgFileOpen.Filter = "Bitmap (*.bmp)|*.bmp|" +
                         "Picture (*.jpg)|*.jpg|" +
                         "PNG Files (*.png)|*.png|" +
                         "TIF Files (*.tif)|*.tif|" +
                         "GIF Files (*.gif)|*.gif |" +
                         "All Files (*.*)|*.*";
    if (dlgFileOpen.ShowDialog() == DialogResult.OK)
    {
        Bitmap bmpNew = null;
        try
        {
            bmpNew = new Bitmap(dlgFileOpen.FileName);
            bResource = false;
        }
        catch
        {
            MessageBox.Show("Cannot create bitmap from " +
                "File: " + dlgFileOpen.FileName);
            return;
        }

        DisposeBitmap (ref bmpDraw);
        bmpDraw = bmpNew;
        Invalidate();
    }
}

private void
mitemScale_Click(object sender, EventArgs e)
{
    // Clear the checkmark on related items.
    mitemScale50.Checked = false;
    mitemScale100.Checked = false;
    mitemScale200.Checked = false;
    mitemScale400.Checked = false;

    // Set the checkmark on selected menu item.
    ((MenuItem)sender).Checked = true;
```

```
    // Request paint to redraw bitmap.
    Invalidate();
}


private void
mitemResourceCup_Click(object sender, EventArgs e)
{
    DisposeBitmap(ref bmpDraw);
    bmpDraw = LoadBitmapResource("CUP.BMP");
    Invalidate();
}

private void
mitemResourceBell_Click(object sender, EventArgs e)
{
    DisposeBitmap(ref bmpDraw);
    bmpDraw = LoadBitmapResource("BELL.BMP");
    Invalidate();
}

private void
mitemResourceSpade_Click(object sender, EventArgs e)
{
    DisposeBitmap(ref bmpDraw);
    bmpDraw = LoadBitmapResource("SPADE.BMP");
    Invalidate();
}

private void
mitemResourceHeart_Click(object sender, EventArgs e)
{
    DisposeBitmap(ref bmpDraw);
    bmpDraw = LoadBitmapResource("HEART.BMP");
    Invalidate();
}

private void
mitemResourceDiamond_Click(object sender, EventArgs e)
{
    DisposeBitmap(ref bmpDraw);
    bmpDraw = LoadBitmapResource("DIAMOND.BMP");
    Invalidate();
}

private void
mitemResourceClub_Click(object sender, EventArgs e)
```

continues

continued

```
{
   DisposeBitmap(ref bmpDraw);
   bmpDraw = LoadBitmapResource("CLUB.BMP");
   Invalidate();
}

private Bitmap LoadBitmapResource(string strName)
{
   Assembly assembly = Assembly.GetExecutingAssembly();
   string strRes = "ShowBitmap." + strName;
   Stream stream = assembly.GetManifestResourceStream(strRes);
   Bitmap bmp = null;
   try
   {
      bmp = new Bitmap(stream);
      strResName = strRes;
      bResource = true;
   }
   catch { }
   stream.Close();

   return bmp;
}

private void DisposeBitmap(ref Bitmap bmp)
{
   if (bmp != null)
   {
      bmp.Dispose();
   }
   bmp = null;
}

// Simplest possible bitmap: Create a bitmap, clear the
// bitmap background, draw the bitmap to the display screen.
private void
CreateAndDraw(int x, int y)
{
   // Create a bitmap and a Graphics object for the bitmap.
   Bitmap bmpNew = new Bitmap(100,100);
   Graphics gbmp = Graphics.FromImage(bmpNew);

   // Clear the bitmap background.
   gbmp.Clear(Color.LightGray);

   // Get a Graphics object for the form.
   Graphics g = CreateGraphics();
```

```
    // Copy the bitmap to the window at (x,y) location.
    g.DrawImage(bmpNew, x, y);

    // Clean up when we are done.
    g.Dispose();
    gbmp.Dispose();
    bmpNew.Dispose();
}
```

Vector Graphics

The available vector drawing methods in the .NET Compact Framework are summarized in Table 15.12 (which appeared earlier in this chapter as Table 15.4 and is repeated here for convenience). As indicated in the table, some shapes are drawn with a pen, a drawing object used for lines. The .NET Compact Framework supports only pens that are 1 pixel wide (unless a programmer drills through to the native GDI drawing support). Other shapes in the table are drawn with a brush. We discussed the three methods for creating brushes earlier in this chapter. We cover the creation of pens in this discussion of vector graphics.

TABLE 15.12: `System.Drawing.Graphics` Methods for Vector Drawing

Method	Comment
`DrawEllipse`	Draws the outline of an ellipse using a pen.
`DrawLine`	Draws a straight line using a pen.
`DrawPolygon`	Draws the outline of a polygon using a pen.
`DrawRectangle`	Draws the outline of a rectangle using a pen.
`FillEllipse`	Fills the interior of an ellipse using a brush.
`FillPolygon`	Fills the interior of a polygon using a brush.
`FillRectangle`	Fills the interior of a rectangle using a brush.

The vector methods with names that start with `Draw` are those that use a pen to draw a line or a set of connected lines. The call to the `DrawRectangle` method, for example, draws the outline of a rectangle without touching the area inside the line. If you pass a blue pen to the `DrawRectangle` method, the result is the outline of a rectangle drawn with a blue line. The .NET Compact Framework supports four line-drawing methods.

Vector methods whose names start with `Fill`, on the other hand, use a brush to fill in the area bounded by the lines. For example, if you pass a red brush to the `FillRectangle` method, the result is a solid red rectangle. There are three such methods in the .NET Compact Framework for drawing ellipses, polygons, and rectangles.

The `Draw` and `Fill` methods complement each other. You could, for example, pass a red brush to the `FillRectangle` method and pass a blue pen to the `DrawRectangle` method using the same coordinates that you used to draw the red, filled rectangle. The result would be a two-colored rectangle, with a blue border and a red interior. This type of two-colored figure is natively available in the Windows API. Yet it seems apparent that few programs need to draw two-colored vector figures. That is, no doubt, a factor that contributed to the design of vector drawing in the .NET Framework and the .NET Compact Framework.

If a programmer is willing to do a bit of work, almost all vector drawing can be accomplished by calling two of these methods: `DrawLine` and `FillPolygon`. Each of the supported method names is of the form <verb><shape>. In the `DrawLine` method, for example, the verb is `Draw` and the shape is `Line`.

Creating Pens

Pens draw lines. The desktop supports a very sophisticated model for pens, including support for scalable geometric pens and nonscalable cosmetic pens. Pens on the desktop support features that allow you to fine-tune how an end of a line appears (rounded or squared) and even how the "elbow" joints are drawn. Pens can be wide or narrow, and even nonsolid pen colors are supported.

Wake up! In the .NET Compact Framework, pens are always 1 pixel wide. Pens provide a quick and simple way to define the color used to draw a line. From the seventeen properties supported for pens on the desktop, one has survived to the .NET Compact Framework: `Color`. And so it should come as no surprise that the one constructor for the `Pen`[29] class has a single parameter, a color as shown here.

```
public Pen(
   Color color);
```

There are three ways to define a pen in a .NET Compact Framework program because there are three ways to specify a color:

1. With a system color
2. With a named color
3. With an RGB value

Earlier in this chapter, we described some of the details about the three ways to pick a color. We showed that each of the color-specifying approaches could be used to create a brush. Now the time has come to show the same thing for pens.

The following code fragment creates three pens. One pen is created using a system color; another pen is created using a named color; and finally, the third pen is created with an RGB value.

```
// Pen from a system color
Pen penCtrl = new Pen(SystemColors.ControlDark);

// Pen from a named color
Pen penRed  = new Pen(Color.Red);

// Pen from an RGB value
Pen penBlue = new Pen(Color.FromArgb(0, 0, 255));
```

A Game: `JaspersDots`

While writing this book, we watched Paul's son, Jasper, playing a paper-and-pencil game with one of his friends. They were having so much fun

29. Fully qualified name: `System.Drawing.Pen`.

that we decided to write a .NET Compact Framework version. The game was Dots, which may be familiar to some readers. In this two-person game, players take turns connecting dots that have been drawn in a grid. A player is awarded a point for drawing the last line that creates a box. We named our version of the game `JaspersDots`, in honor of Paul's son. The playing board for this game is drawn entirely with the following vector graphic methods:

- `FillEllipse`
- `FillRectangle`
- `DrawLine`
- `DrawRectangle`

This program provides extensive use of various `Graphics` objects including colors, pens, and brushes.

Figure 15.6 shows the New Game dialog box. Each player enters a name and picks a color to use for claimed squares. The default board size is 8 × 8, which can be overridden in the New Game dialog box (the maximum board size is 11 × 9).

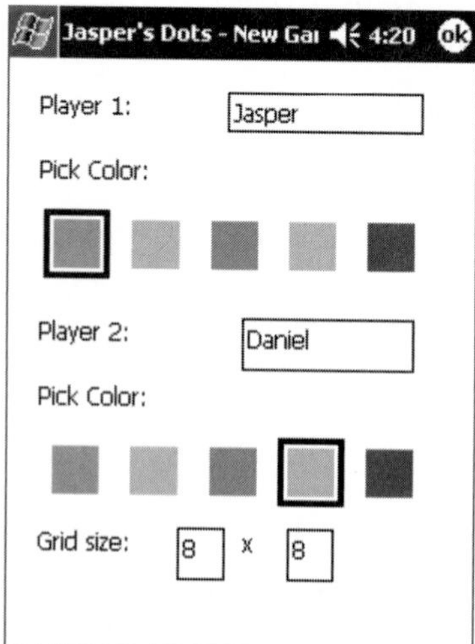

FIGURE 15.6: New Game dialog box for the `JaspersDots` program

The New Game dialog box is a simple dialog box drawn with regular controls, with one small enhancement: This dialog handles a `Paint` event, which draws a selection rectangle around each player's currently selected color. The set of available colors is drawn with `Panel` controls, five for each player. Listing 15.8 shows the source code for the event handlers for responding to the `Click` event for each set of `Panel` controls and to the `Paint` event for the New Game dialog box.

LISTING 15.8: `Paint` and `Click` Event Handlers for the New Game Dialog Box

```
private void
Panel1_Click(object sender, EventArgs e)
{
   if (sender == (object)panel1)
      iColor1 = 0;
   else if (sender == (object)panel2)
      iColor1 = 1;
   else if (sender == (object)panel3)
      iColor1 = 2;
   else if (sender == (object)panel4)
      iColor1 = 3;
   else if (sender == (object)panel5)
      iColor1 = 4;

   // Redraw the window.
   Invalidate();
}

private void
Panel2_Click(object sender, EventArgs e)
{
   if (sender == (object)panelA)
      iColor2 = 0;
   else if (sender == (object)panelB)
      iColor2 = 1;
   else if (sender == (object)panelC)
      iColor2 = 2;
   else if (sender == (object)panelD)
      iColor2 = 3;
   else if (sender == (object)panelE)
      iColor2 = 4;

   // Redraw the window.
   Invalidate();
}
```

continues

continued

```
private void
GameNewDialog_Paint(object sender, PaintEventArgs e)
{
   Panel panel = panel1;

   //
   // Player 1
   //
   // What is the current player 1 panel?
   switch(iColor1)
   {
      case 0:
         panel = panel1;
         break;
      case 1:
         panel = panel2;
         break;
      case 2:
         panel = panel3;
         break;
      case 3:
         panel = panel4;
         break;
      case 4:
         panel = panel5;
         break;
   }
   clr1 = panel.BackColor;

   // Draw a rectangle around the color selected by player 1.
   Pen penBlack = new Pen(Color.Black);
   Rectangle rc = new
      Rectangle(panel.Left - 3,
      panel.Top - 3,
      panel.Width + 5,
      panel.Height + 5);
   e.Graphics.DrawRectangle(penBlack, rc);
   rc.Inflate(1, 1);
   e.Graphics.DrawRectangle(penBlack, rc);
   rc.Inflate(1, 1);
   e.Graphics.DrawRectangle(penBlack, rc);

   //
   // Player 2
   //
   // What is the current player 2 panel?
```

```
    switch(iColor2)
    {
        case 0:
            panel = panelA;
            break;
        case 1:
            panel = panelB;
            break;
        case 2:
            panel = panelC;
            break;
        case 3:
            panel = panelD;
            break;
        case 4:
            panel = panelE;
            break;
    }
    clr2 = panel.BackColor;

    // Draw a rectangle around the color selected by player 2.
    rc = new Rectangle(panel.Left - 3,
        panel.Top - 3,
        panel.Width + 5,
        panel.Height + 5);
    e.Graphics.DrawRectangle(penBlack, rc);
    rc.Inflate(1, 1);
    e.Graphics.DrawRectangle(penBlack, rc);
    rc.Inflate(1, 1);
    e.Graphics.DrawRectangle(penBlack, rc);
}
```

There is a bug in Visual Studio .NET that affects C# programmers. The bug is that supported events for certain controls do not appear in the Designer. You can, however, add an event handler manually. Inside the Visual Studio code editor, you type the control name, the event name, and the += operator, and IntelliSense helps by providing the rest.

In our `JaspersDots` game, we found that the Designer did not support the `Click` event for `Panel` controls. To create `Click` event handlers for the `Panel` controls in the New Game dialog box, we manually typed in event handler names, which were completed for us by IntelliSense. The resulting code appears in Listing 15.9.

LISTING 15.9: Adding Event Handlers Manually

```
// Set up the Click handler for player 1 panels.
// Note: The Designer does not support this
// so we have to do it manually.
panel1.Click += new EventHandler(this.Panel1_Click);
panel2.Click += new System.EventHandler(this.Panel1_Click);
panel3.Click += new System.EventHandler(this.Panel1_Click);
panel4.Click += new System.EventHandler(this.Panel1_Click);
panel5.Click += new System.EventHandler(this.Panel1_Click);

// Set up the Click handler for player 2 panels.
// Note: The Designer does not support this
// so we have to do it manually.
panelA.Click += new EventHandler(this.Panel2_Click);
panelB.Click += new System.EventHandler(this.Panel2_Click);
panelC.Click += new System.EventHandler(this.Panel2_Click);
panelD.Click += new System.EventHandler(this.Panel2_Click);
panelE.Click += new System.EventHandler(this.Panel2_Click);
```

Figure 15.7 shows an example of the `JaspersDots` game in play. Each dot is drawn with a call to the `FillEllipse` method that is drawn in a bounding rectangle that is 4 pixels by 4 pixels. Players draw lines by clicking in the area between dots, and when a hit is detected a line is drawn by

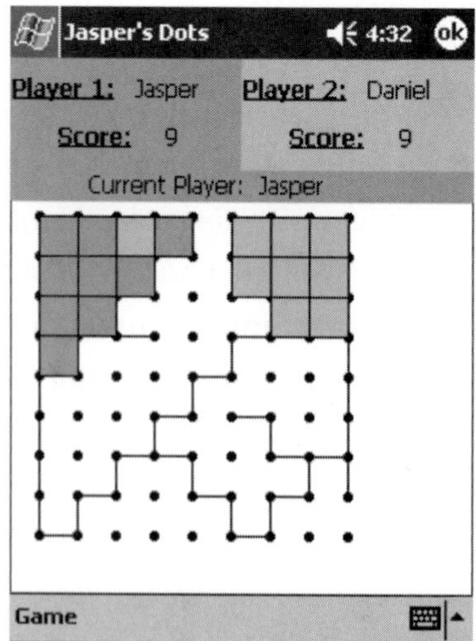

FIGURE 15.7: `JaspersDots` with a game under way

calling the `DrawLine` method. A player's claimed boxes are drawn with calls to the `FillRectangle` method.

The `JaspersDots` program uses a custom control for the game window, our `DotControl` class. Listing 15.10 shows the source code to the `DotControl` class.

LISTING 15.10: The `DotControl` Class

```
public class DotControl : System.Windows.Forms.Control
{
   private FormMain formParent;
   private Brush m_brPlayer1;
   private Brush m_brPlayer2;
   private Squares sq;

   public DotControl(FormMain form)
   {
      formParent = form;

      formParent.Controls.Add(this);
      this.Paint += new
         PaintEventHandler(this.DotControl_Paint);
      this.MouseDown += new
         MouseEventHandler(this.DotControl_MouseDown);
      this.Left = 0;
      this.Top = 64;
      this.Width = 240;
      this.Height = 240;

      sq = new Squares(this);
   }

   public bool SetGridSize(int cxWidth, int cyHeight)
   {
      return sq.SetGridSize(cxWidth, cyHeight);
   }

   public bool SetPlayerColors(Color clr1, Color clr2)
   {
      m_brPlayer1 = new SolidBrush(clr1);
      m_brPlayer2 = new SolidBrush(clr2);

      return sq.SetPlayerBrushes(m_brPlayer1, m_brPlayer2);
   }


   private void
   DotControl_MouseDown(object sender, MouseEventArgs e)
```

continues

continued

```
    {
       // Check result.
       int iResult = sq.HitTest(e.X, e.Y,
          formParent.CurrentPlayer);

       // Click on the available line, no score.
       if(iResult == 1)
       {
          formParent.NextPlayer();
       }

       // Click on the available line, score.
       if (iResult == 2)
       {
          int iScore1 = sq.GetScore(1);
          formParent.DisplayScore(1, iScore1);
          int iScore2 = sq.GetScore(2);
          formParent.DisplayScore(2, iScore2);

          int count = sq.Height * sq.Width;
          if (iScore1 + iScore2 == count)
          {
             string strResult = null;

             if (iScore1 > iScore2)
                strResult = "Player 1 wins! ";
             else if (iScore1 < iScore2)
                strResult = "Player 2 wins! ";
             else
                strResult = "Tie Game! ";

             MessageBox.Show(strResult, "JaspersDots");
          }
       }
    }

    private void
    DotControl_Paint(object sender, PaintEventArgs e)
    {
       // Fill squares which players now own.
       sq.FillSquares(e.Graphics);

       // Draw lines which players have selected.
       sq.DrawLines(e.Graphics);

       // Draw dots in grid.
       sq.DrawDots(e.Graphics);
    }
} // class
```

The DotControl class handles two events: MouseDown and Paint. Most of the work for these events is done by a helper class named Squares. The source code for the Squares class appears in Listing 15.11.

LISTING 15.11: The Squares Class

```
public class Squares
{
   public int Width
   {
      get   { return cxWidth; }
   }
   public int Height
   {
      get   { return cyHeight; }
   }

   private int cxLeft = 15;
   private int cyTop  = 15;
   private int cxWidth;
   private int cyHeight;
   const int cxLine = 20;
   const int cyLine = 20;
   const int cxyDelta = 5;
   private Square [,] m_asq;

   private Control m_ctrlParent;
   private Brush m_brPlayer1;
   private Brush m_brPlayer2;
   private Brush m_brBackground = new _
      SolidBrush(SystemColors.Window);
   private Brush hbrBlack = new SolidBrush(Color.Black);
   private Point ptTest = new Point(0,0);
   Rectangle rc = new Rectangle(0, 0, 0, 0);
   private Size  szDot = new Size(4,4);

   Pen penLine = new Pen(Color.Black);

   public Squares(Control ctrlParent)
   {
      m_ctrlParent = ctrlParent;
   } // Squares()

   public bool SetGridSize(
      int cxNewWidth,     // Width of array.
      int cyNewHeight     // Height of array.
      )
```

continues

continued

```
{
   // Temporary scratch space
   Rectangle rcTemp = new Rectangle(0,0,0,0);
   Point     ptTemp = new Point(0,0);
   Size      szTemp = new Size(0,0);

   // Set up an array to track squares.
   cxWidth = cxNewWidth;
   cyHeight = cyNewHeight;
   m_asq = new Square[cxWidth, cyHeight];
   if (m_asq == null)
      return false;

   int x, y;
   for (x = 0; x < cxWidth; x++)
   {
      for (y = 0; y < cyHeight; y++)
      {
         m_asq[x,y].iOwner = 0; // No owner.
         int xLeft = cxLeft + x * cxLine;
         int yTop = cyTop + y * cyLine;
         int xRight = cxLeft + (x+1) * cxLine;
         int yBottom = cyTop + (y+1) * cyLine;
         int cxTopBottom = cxLine - (2 * cxyDelta);
         int cyTopBottom = cxyDelta * 2;
         int cxLeftRight = cxyDelta * 2;
         int cyLeftRight = cxLine - (2 * cxyDelta);

         // Main rectangle
         ptTemp.X = xLeft + 1;
         ptTemp.Y = yTop + 1;
         szTemp.Width = xRight - xLeft - 1;
         szTemp.Height = yBottom - yTop - 1;
         rcTemp.Location = ptTemp;
         rcTemp.Size = szTemp;
         m_asq[x,y].rcMain = rcTemp;

         // Top hit rectangle
         m_asq[x,y].rcTop =
            new Rectangle(xLeft + cxyDelta,
            yTop - cxyDelta,
            cxTopBottom,
            cyTopBottom);
         m_asq[x,y].bTop = false;

         // Right hit rectangle
         m_asq[x,y].rcRight =
            new Rectangle(xRight - cxyDelta,
            yTop + cxyDelta,
```

```
            cxLeftRight,
            cyLeftRight);
        m_asq[x,y].bRight = false;

        // Bottom hit rectangle
        m_asq[x,y].rcBottom =
            new Rectangle(xLeft + cxyDelta,
            yBottom - cxyDelta,
            cxTopBottom,
            cyTopBottom);
        m_asq[x,y].bBottom = false;

        // Left hit rectangle
        m_asq[x,y].rcLeft =
            new Rectangle(xLeft - cxyDelta,
            yTop + cxyDelta,
            cxLeftRight,
            cyLeftRight);
        m_asq[x,y].bLeft = false;

      } // for y
   } // for x

   return true;
}

public bool
SetPlayerBrushes(
   Brush br1,      // Brush color for player 1
   Brush br2       // Brush color for player 2
   )
{
   m_brPlayer1 = br1;
   m_brPlayer2 = br2;

   return true;
}

//----------------------------------------------------------
public void
FillOneSquare(Graphics g, int x, int y)
{
   Brush brCurrent = m_brBackground;
   if (m_asq[x,y].iOwner == 1)
      brCurrent = m_brPlayer1;
   else if (m_asq[x,y].iOwner == 2)
      brCurrent = m_brPlayer2;
   g.FillRectangle(brCurrent, m_asq[x,y].rcMain);
}
```

continues

continued

```
// FillSquares -- Fill owned squares with a player's color.
//
public void
FillSquares(Graphics g)
{
   int x, y;
   for (x = 0; x < cxWidth; x++)
   {
      for (y = 0; y < cyHeight; y++)
      {
         if (m_asq[x,y].iOwner != 0)
         {
            FillOneSquare(g, x, y);
         }
      }
   }
} // method: FillSquares

//
// DrawOneLineSet
//
public void DrawOneLineSet(Graphics g, int x, int y)
{
   int xLeft = cxLeft + x * cxLine;
   int yTop = cyTop + y * cyLine;
   int xRight = cxLeft + (x+1) * cxLine;
   int yBottom = cyTop + (y+1) * cyLine;

   if (m_asq[x,y].bTop)
      g.DrawLine(penLine, xLeft, yTop, xRight, yTop);
   if (m_asq[x,y].bRight)
      g.DrawLine(penLine, xRight, yTop, xRight, yBottom);
   if (m_asq[x,y].bBottom)
      g.DrawLine(penLine, xRight, yBottom, xLeft, yBottom);
   if (m_asq[x,y].bLeft)
      g.DrawLine(penLine, xLeft, yBottom, xLeft, yTop);
} // DrawOneLineSet()

//
// DrawLines -- Draw lines which have been hit.
//
public void DrawLines(Graphics g)
{
   int x, y;
   for (x = 0; x < cxWidth; x++)
   {
      for (y = 0; y < cyHeight; y++)
```

```
        {
            DrawOneLineSet(g, x, y);
        }
    }
} // DrawLines()

public void DrawDots (Graphics g)
{
    // Draw array of dots.
    int x, y;
    for (x = 0; x <= cxWidth; x++)
    {
        for (y = 0; y <= cyHeight; y++)
        {
            ptTest.X = (cxLeft - 2) + x * cxLine;
            ptTest.Y = (cyTop - 2) + y * cyLine;
            rc.Location = ptTest;
            rc.Size = szDot;
            g.FillEllipse(hbrBlack, rc);
        }
    }
} // DrawDots

public enum Side
{
    None,
    Left,
    Top,
    Right,
    Bottom
}

//
// HitTest - Check whether a point hits a line.
//
// Return values:
// 0 = miss
// 1 = hit a line
// 2 = hit and completed a square.
public int HitTest(int xIn, int yIn, int iPlayer)
{
    int x, y;
    bool bHit1 = false;
    bool bHit2 = false;
    Side sideHit = Side.None;
    for (x = 0; x < cxWidth; x++)
    {
        {         for (y = 0; y < cyHeight; y++)
```

continues

continued

```
      // If already owned, do not check.
      if (m_asq[x,y].iOwner != 0)
         continue;

      // Otherwise check for lines against point.
      if (m_asq[x,y].rcTop.Contains(xIn, yIn))
      {
         // Line already hit?
         if (m_asq[x,y].bTop) // Line already hit?
            return 0;
         // If not, set line as hit.
         sideHit = Side.Top;
         m_asq[x,y].bTop = true;
      }
      else if (m_asq[x,y].rcLeft.Contains(xIn, yIn))
      {
         // Line already hit?
         if (m_asq[x,y].bLeft) // Line already hit?
            return 0;
         // If not, set line as hit.
         sideHit = Side.Left;
         m_asq[x,y].bLeft = true;
      }
      else if (m_asq[x,y].rcRight.Contains(xIn, yIn))
      {
         // Line already hit?
         if (m_asq[x,y].bRight) // Line already hit?
            return 0;
         // If not, set line as hit.
         sideHit = Side.Right;
         m_asq[x,y].bRight = true;
      }
      else if (m_asq[x,y].rcBottom.Contains(xIn, yIn))
      {
         // Line already hit?
         if (m_asq[x,y].bBottom) // Line already hit?
            return 0;
         // If not, set line as hit.
         sideHit = Side.Bottom;
         m_asq[x,y].bBottom = true;
      }

      // No hit in current square -- keep looking.
      if (sideHit == Side.None)
         continue;

      // We hit a side.
      bHit1 = true;
```

```
            // Draw sides.
            Graphics g = m_ctrlParent.CreateGraphics();
            DrawOneLineSet(g, x, y);

            // Check whether square is now complete.
            // We hit a line - check for hitting a square.
            if (m_asq[x,y].bLeft &&
                  m_asq[x,y].bTop &&
                  m_asq[x,y].bRight &&
                  m_asq[x,y].bBottom)
            {
               // Side is complete.
               m_asq[x,y].iOwner = iPlayer;
               bHit2 = true;

               // Fill current square.
               FillOneSquare(g, x, y);
            }

            g.Dispose();

         } // for y
      } // for x

      if (bHit2) return 2;
      else if (bHit1) return 1;
      else return 0;

   } // HitTest

   //
   // GetScore - Get current score for player N.
   //
   public int GetScore (int iPlayer)
   {
      int iScore = 0;
      int x, y;
      for (x = 0; x < cxWidth; x++)
      {
         for (y = 0; y < cyHeight; y++)
         {
            if (m_asq[x,y].iOwner == iPlayer)
               iScore++;
         }
      }
      return iScore;
   } // GetScore

} // class Squares
```

Finally, we define two simple data structures—`Square` and `Players`—to hold details about individual game board squares and details about individual players, respectively. Listing 15.12 shows the code.

LISTING 15.12: The `Square` and `Players` Structures

```
public struct Square
{
   // Coordinate of main rectangle
   public Rectangle rcMain;
   public int iOwner;

   // Hit-rectangles of four edges of main rectangle
   public Rectangle rcTop;
   public bool bTop;
   public Rectangle rcRight;
   public bool bRight;
   public Rectangle rcBottom;
   public bool bBottom;
   public Rectangle rcLeft;
   public bool bLeft;
} // struct Square

public class Players
{
   public string strName1;
   public string strName2;
   public bool bComputerPlaying;
   public System.Drawing.Color clr1;
   public System.Drawing.Color clr2;
}
```

CONCLUSION

Whether or not you believe that good things always come in small packages, it should be clear that some very rich capabilities for creating graphical output have been placed in the very small package of the .NET Compact Framework's `System.Drawing.dll` library. This chapter looked in detail at the four types of drawing surfaces that Windows programmers are used to, two of which are supported in the .NET Compact Framework. This chapter also discussed the three families of drawing functions, which are reasonably well represented by the .NET Compact Framework's capable, though small, feature set.

In this chapter, we explored two of the families in depth: raster and vector drawing functions. In the next chapter, we take an in-depth look at the third family of output—text. This part of the book concludes in Chapter 17 with coverage of an output device that is not officially supported in the .NET Compact Framework, namely, printers. In spite of the lack of managed-code support, we show that there are ways for a .NET Compact Framework program to satisfy the need that users sometimes have for hard copy. We do so by providing something that programmers sometimes need: some sample programs to make it clear how such an unsupported feature can, in fact, be made available.

16
Text and Fonts

This chapter covers controlling the appearance of text by using classes in the `System.Drawing` namespace and also by using P/Invoke to drill through to the underlying Win32 libraries for useful text-drawing features that are otherwise not available in the .NET Compact Framework.

THE FOCUS OF this chapter is on drawing text on the screen of a smart device using the .NET Compact Framework. As we described in Chapter 15, the .NET Compact Framework supports a subset of the graphical output features of the desktop .NET Framework. In general, though, the text-drawing support in the .NET Compact Framework is quite rich. You can do all of the more commonly required text-drawing operations such as selecting different fonts by name, choosing different sizes and styles, and controlling the color of drawn text. Some subtle effects are not available, but this is a small price to pay for the low memory overhead incurred by the .NET Compact Framework.

Drawing Text

A graphical environment provides the programmer with a rich set of tools for creating a wide range of graphical images. Such an environment makes it possible to mingle pictures with text, to display text in a range of font sizes and styles, and to use an array of effects to convey subtle messages to users. In this environment, text itself is treated as a graphical object. Drawing text in a graphical environment is paradoxically more complex than drawing text in a nongraphical environment. In a character-oriented world such as a console program, fixed-pitch fonts[1] are used to place text in orderly rows and columns. In a graphical world, by contrast, both fixed- and variable-pitch fonts float in a sea of pixels. The increase in complexity allows for the free mixing of text and graphics. This freedom comes at a cost, namely, the extra effort required to tame the complexity of graphical text and to use it to enhance a program's graphical output.

Text-Drawing Support in the .NET Compact Framework

A .NET Compact Framework program can draw text using any available font. Using TrueType fonts, that text output can be scaled to any desired size from 8 points up to 72 points and beyond. That text can be drawn in any available color, although most programs are likely to use the default system text color.

By drilling through to the underlying Win32 libraries, a .NET Compact Framework program can do a few more things such as drawing rotated text and accessing ClearType fonts. Table 16.1 summarizes .NET Compact Framework text-drawing features, how to access these features, and this chapter's sample programs, which illustrate each feature. You can find the complete source code to these programs on the book's source-code Web site.

The `DrawString` Method

All .NET Compact Framework text drawing is done with the `DrawString` method, a member of the `Graphics` class that has two available overloaded implementations. (For a detailed discussion of the `Graphics` class, see Chapter 15.) We start our discussion with the simpler of the two overloaded functions, which accepts a pair of (x,y) values for the location where the text is to be drawn. This method does not provide automatic word-wrapping support. So if a string is too long for the available drawing space, the "extra" characters disappear. A second version of the `DrawString` method, which we discuss later in this chapter, does word wrapping for you.

---

1. In a fixed-pitch font, the width of every character in the font is the same.

TABLE 16.1: Text-Drawing Features and Sample Programs

Feature	Comment	Sample Program
Simple text drawing	Call the `DrawString`[a] method to draw text in a control or form.	`SimpleDrawString` shows simplest text drawing, which involves creating a brush (for text color) and using the form's default font.
Simplest font creation	Create a font using the `FontFamily` enumeration to select between a fixed-pitch, serif, or sans serif font without regard to font face name.	`GenericFonts` creates and draws with each of the three generic font families, in a range of styles (regular, bold, italic, strikeout, and underline).
Font enumeration	Font enumeration involves getting a list of available font face names installed in the system. The .NET Compact Framework does not support font enumeration, so we rely on a Win32 DLL that does the font enumeration work for us.	`FontPicker` creates fonts of specific face names (a .NET Compact Framework program). `FontList` enumerates available system fonts (a Win32 DLL).
Text rotation	The .NET Compact Framework does not natively support rotated fonts. For that, we must call the Win32 font creation functions.	`RotateText` uses P/Invoke to call a Win32 font creation program.
ClearType fonts	ClearType is a font technology that aids in reading small text on LCD displays. The .NET Compact Framework does not support this, so we must instead call Win32 font creation functions as illustrated in the `RotateText` sample program.	See `RotateText`, above.
Calculation of graphical text sizes	Optimal positioning of text requires calculating the size of the bounding box of drawn text. This is accomplished using the `MeasureString` method.	`MeasureString` shows how to use results from the `MeasureString` method in drawing.

continues

a. Fully qualified name: `System.Drawing.Graphics`.

Table 16.1: Text-Drawing Features and Sample Programs (continued)

Feature	Comment	Sample Program
Text alignment	By default, text is aligned to the upper-left corner of the textbox. The .NET Compact Framework does not support alternative text alignment settings, so different alignments require manually modifying the (x,y) drawing location.	`TextAlign` shows 12 ways to align text by mixing and matching 4 vertical alignments and 3 horizontal alignments.
Word wrap	The .NET Compact Framework supports two versions of the `DrawString` method, but only one of them supports word wrap. The version that uses a rectangle supports word wrap. In addition to wrapping the text to the indicated rectangle, the text is clipped to that rectangle as well (i.e., text is drawn only within the specified rectangle).	`WordWrap` shows use of the version of the `DrawString` method that supports wrapping and clipping a text string to a specified output rectangle.
Text color	Set the text foreground color by creating a brush. Set the text background color by drawing a colored rectangle before drawing the text.	`TextColor` shows three ways to pick colors: (1) using named colors, (2) using system colors, and (3) with the color picker dialog box (requires P/Invoke).

The simpler version of the `DrawString` method, which takes five parameters, is defined as follows.

```
public void DrawString(
   string str,
   Font font,
   Brush brText,
   float x,
   float y);
```

The first parameter, `str`, identifies the string to draw. While automatic word wrap is not supported, a carriage return or line feed character within the string causes the string to display in multiple lines. (In C#, insert a new line using the `\n` or `\r` character.)

The second parameter, `font`, is the font used for drawing the characters. This could be the default font of a control (the `Font` property) or a font that you dynamically create.

The third parameter, `brText`, identifies the brush that specifies the color of the text foreground pixels; in the world of .NET programming, the background pixels are always left untouched[2] when you draw text.

The fourth and fifth parameters, `x` and `y`, indicate the text-drawing location. This location is the upper-left corner of the rectangle that bounds the text. These coordinate values are single-precision floating-point values, which is different from the integer coordinates used to draw raster and vector graphics.

A Sample Program: `SimpleDrawString`

Our first sample program shows the simplest way to draw in a form. Figure 16.1 shows the program's output. This program uses the form's

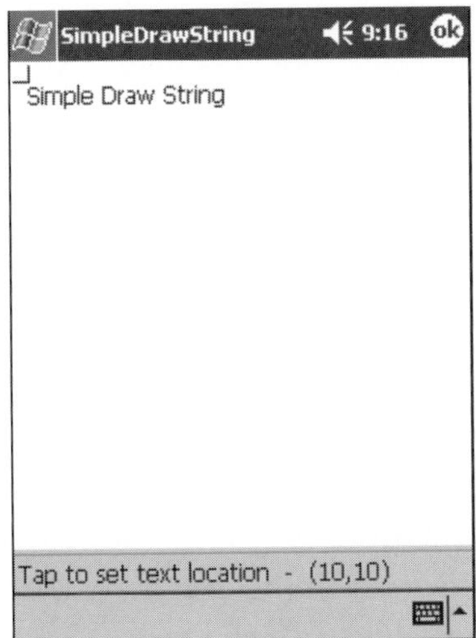

FIGURE 16.1: Output of the `SimpleDrawString` program

2. Win32 programmers may recall that the `Background Color` attribute in a device context allows a text-drawing operation to also affect the background pixels.

default font to draw a character string using the system's default window text color.

As discussed in Chapter 15, the `Paint` event is important to any control that creates graphical output in its client area. Listing 16.1 shows the `Paint` event handler method for our simple text-drawing sample. This method gets called when the program first starts running and then whenever the window's display area needs to be redrawn.

LISTING 16.1: Fragment from `SimpleDrawString.cs` Showing the `Paint` Event Handler

```
private float xDraw = 10;
private float yDraw = 10;

private void
FormMain_Paint(object sender, PaintEventArgs e)
{
   Brush brText = new SolidBrush(SystemColors.WindowText);
   e.Graphics.DrawString("Simple Draw String", Font, brText,
   xDraw, yDraw);

   // Highlight origin.
   int x = (int)xDraw;
   int y = (int)yDraw;
   Pen penBlack = new Pen(Color.Black);
   e.Graphics.DrawLine(penBlack, x, y, x-8, y);
   e.Graphics.DrawLine(penBlack, x, y, x, y-8);

}
```

In our sample program, the text is drawn at (10,10), the coordinates assigned to the `xDraw` and `yDraw` variables. Our program calls the `DrawLine` method to draw two lines—one horizontal and one vertical—that intersect at (10,10). The intersection of those two lines shows the default text alignment, at the upper-left corner of the drawn text. The .NET Compact Framework does not support alternative text alignments.

Alternative alignments allow you to center a string over a column of data or center a text label inside a graphical image. The `TextAlign` sample program, presented later in this chapter, shows some simple techniques for supporting a total of 12 different text alignment points.

Text-Drawing Performance

The `SimpleDrawString` sample program shows one way to pick a font, which is to use the font taken from the `Font` property of a control (in this case, the control is the program's main form). This is an easy way to get a font because the property is always available. The default font can easily be set from the Designer in Visual Studio .NET.

However, there is a tiny performance penalty for drawing text by using this default font. We notice a 10% improvement in drawing speed when we create a font at program startup and use that to draw instead of using the form's `Font` property. For most purposes, the `Font` property provides an easy way to get a font when drawing text. But to squeeze the fastest text drawing from the .NET Compact Framework, we suggest you create a font ahead of time and cache that font for high-volume text drawing.

Font Selection

We now turn our attention to the subject of fonts. Font selection provides the primary way to control the appearance of text. Windows CE supports two basic font technologies: bitmap fonts and TrueType fonts. A given platform can support only one of these two technologies. The decision about which to support is made by the platform creator and cannot be changed by an application program. Some platforms support bitmap fonts to minimize the size of the operating system image. The benefits of supporting TrueType fonts include the ability to draw scalable fonts and the ability to draw rotated text.

What font support is found on Windows mobile devices? The Pocket PC supports TrueType fonts. As we show later, there are three fonts on a typical Pocket PC: Tahoma, Courier New, and Bookdings. The Smartphone supports bitmap fonts. A typical Smartphone has two fonts: an 11-point bold Nina and a 16-point Nina.

The `Font` Property of Controls

The built-in controls use fonts. As shown in Figure 16.2, you select a control's font at design time in the Properties window of the Designer provided as part of Visual Studio .NET. A word of caution is in order because the Designer displays a font picker dialog for whatever fonts are installed on your desktop system. For example, you can select fonts such as Arial and Wingdings. But if you run your program on a device that doesn't have these fonts, you may get results different from what you expect.

Font support in Windows CE—as in desktop Windows—uses a process that is sometimes called *font mapping*. This process takes a request for a font and tries to map that request to a font that is actually present in the system. It works best when the font name or font family is present and when the size you request is available. It fails when either of these conditions is not met; in such situations this feature is sometimes called *font mangling*. The solution is to make sure that you request font names and sizes that are available on the device.

As shown in the `SimpleDrawString` sample program, you can draw in a form or in a control by accessing the `Font` property of the form or control. Here is the line of code that shows this being done:

```
e.Graphics.DrawString("Simple Draw String", Font, brText,
xDraw, yDraw);
```

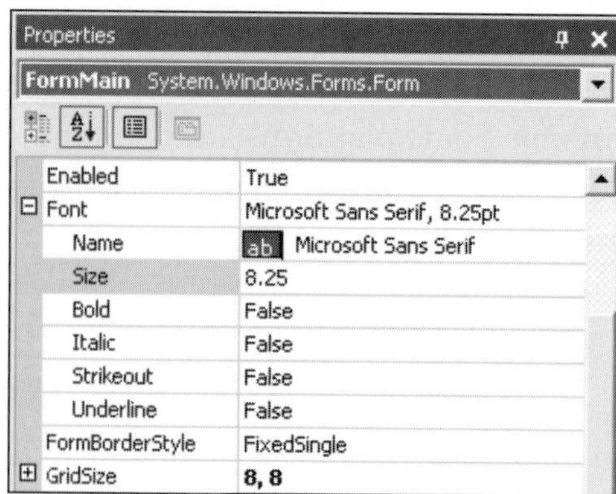

FIGURE 16.2: Selecting a control's font in the Designer

The `Font` property is a read/write property, so you can modify a control's font at runtime using any of the font creation techniques discussed in this chapter.

.NET Compact Framework Controls Do Not Support Ambient Properties

Programmers familiar with the desktop .NET Framework might notice that .NET Compact Framework controls do not support the concept of ambient properties. On the desktop, controls use the ambient properties from the parent control if that property is not specified for the control itself. The following properties of controls in the desktop .NET Framework are ambient properties: `BackColor`, `Cursor`, `Font`, and `ForeColor`.

The built-in .NET Compact Framework controls do not support ambient properties. This means that, for example, if you want to select a new font for a group of controls, you cannot simply change the selected font in the parent for the group of controls. Instead, you must change the font for each and every individual control.

Generic Fonts

There are several ways to get a font, but the easiest is to ask for a generic font because the only other way to ask for a font is by face name—using names like Arial, Times New Roman, and Courier New. And while this doesn't seem that complicated, different systems ship with different available fonts. The three fonts just named, for example, are three fonts you find in all the desktop versions of Windows starting with Windows 95. So if you are writing solely for that environment, you can probably get away with asking for those three fonts by name.

However, on a Windows CE–powered device, the set of available fonts is a bit different. What you find depends on how a specific device was configured. On the Pocket PC 2002, for example, the following fonts are available:

- Bookdings: a special symbol font used by the Pocket PC itself to draw elements of the user interface, such as checkmarks, scroll bar arrows, and other symbols
- Courier New: a fixed-pitch serif font
- Tahoma: a variable-pitch sans serif font

To ask for fonts by name, you must first figure out which specific fonts are installed on a given system. This process is known as *font enumeration*. The .NET Compact Framework does not support font enumeration, so you must use P/Invoke to enumerate fonts in a .NET Compact Framework program. (See the `FontPicker` and `FontList` samples later in this chapter to see how that is done.)

Alternatively, you can request a generic font, as shown here.

```
Font font = new Font(FontFamily.GenericSansSerif, 10,
                     FontStyle.Regular);
```

The `Font` function is one of two constructors for creating fonts (the other uses a face name and a font size). This function takes three parameters and is defined as follows.

```
public Font(
   FontFamily family,
   float emSize,
   FontStyle style);
```

The first parameter, `family`, is a value from the `FontFamily` enumeration,[3] which contains these values:

- `FontFamily.GenericMonospace`: requests a fixed-pitch font (like Courier New)

---

3. We call this an enumeration, but to be accurate this is a class instead of an enumeration because the desktop .NET Framework implementation provides several useful methods.

- `FontFamily.GenericSansSerif`: requests a variable-pitch font without serifs (Arial on the desktop version of Windows and Tahoma on the Pocket PC)
- `FontFamily.GenericSerif`: requests a variable-pitch font with serifs (like Times New Roman on the desktop version of Windows)

The second parameter, `emSize`, is the point size of the desired font. On Windows CE systems such as the Pocket PC that support the TrueType scalable font technology, each font is available in any size you desire. In general, 8 points is considered the smallest readable size on paper and 10 points is commonly the smallest size used on a display screen. And while you can create fonts that are one-half inch (36 points) or a full inch (72 points) tall, such sizes easily overwhelm the available screen space of most Windows CE–powered devices.

The third parameter, `style`, is from the `FontStyle` enumeration that lets you fine-tune the appearance of the requested font. This enumeration provides five different font style modifiers, which you can combine in any combination using the logical OR (`|`) operator:

- `FontStyle.Bold`: requests a bold font
- `FontStyle.Italic`: requests an italicized font
- `FontStyle.Regular`: requests a regular font (the default)
- `FontStyle.Strikeout`: requests a strikeout font
- `FontStyle.Underline`: requests an underlined font

For example, the following code creates three different fonts using three different font families and three different font styles.

```
// Create monospace bold 10-point font.
Font fontMono = new Font(FontFamily.GenericMonospace, 10,
                         FontStyle.Bold);

// Create sans serif italic 10-point font.
Font fontSans = new Font(FontFamily.GenericSansSerif, 10,
                         FontStyle.Italic);

// Create serif italic and underlined 10-point font.
Font fontSerif = new Font(FontFamily.GenericSerif, 10,
                 FontStyle.Italic | FontStyle.Underline);
```

A Sample Program: `GenericFonts`

`GenericFonts` is a sample program that shows the creation of generic fonts in various sizes and styles. Figure 16.3 shows the output of this program for three 10-point fonts. This program lists the name of the actual font selected. If you study the figure, you may notice that both the serif and the sans serif fonts have the same face name, Tahoma.

This does not reflect a bug in our program or even a bug in the .NET Compact Framework. It occurs, instead, because Tahoma—a sans serif font—is the closest available match for either a serif font or a sans serif font on a Pocket PC 2002. This result is an artifact of font mapping, which we discussed earlier in this chapter, and also the limited number of fonts available on the Pocket PC 2002.

Listing 16.2 contains a portion of the code used to create this output. This program creates three fonts based on the type of font rather than the font name. While this approach is somewhat less precise than using the exact font name, it benefits from the fact that it is very simple to ask for a style of font.

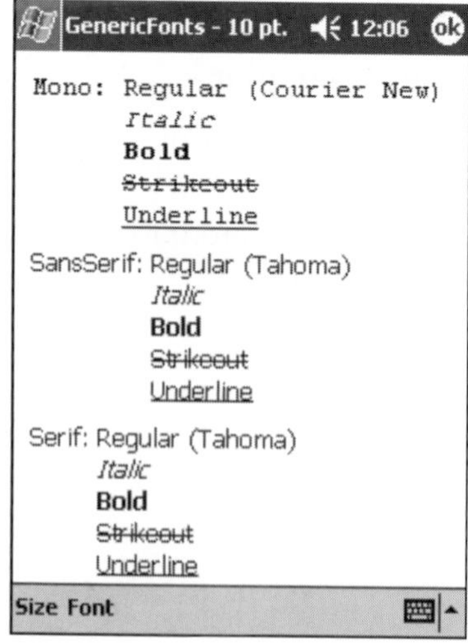

FIGURE 16.3: Output of the `GenericFonts` program for three 10-point fonts

LISTING 16.2: Fragment from GenericFonts.cs

```
private void
DisplaySerifFont(Graphics g, ref float x, ref float y)
{
   // Create a brush for the standard text color.
   Brush brText = new SolidBrush(SystemColors.WindowText);

   // Create a serif regular m_ptSize point font.
   Font font = new Font(FontFamily.GenericSerif, m_ptSize,
      FontStyle.Regular);
   string str = "Serif: ";
   x = 10;
   g.DrawString(str, font, brText, x, y);
   SizeF sizeString = g.MeasureString(str, font);
   x += sizeString.Width;

   // Draw with the serif regular m_ptSize point font.
   str = "Regular (" + font.Name + ")";
   g.DrawString(str, font, brText, x, y);
   sizeString = g.MeasureString(str, font);
   y += sizeString.Height;

   // Create a serif italic m_ptSize point font.
   font = new Font(FontFamily.GenericSerif, m_ptSize,
      FontStyle.Italic);
   str = "Italic";
   g.DrawString(str, font, brText, x, y);
   sizeString = g.MeasureString(str, font);
   y += sizeString.Height;

   // Create a serif bold m_ptSize point font.
   font = new Font(FontFamily.GenericSerif, m_ptSize,
      FontStyle.Bold);
   str = "Bold";
   g.DrawString(str, font, brText, x, y);
   sizeString = g.MeasureString(str, font);
   y += sizeString.Height;

   // Create a serif strikeout m_ptSize point font.
   font = new Font(FontFamily.GenericSerif, m_ptSize,
      FontStyle.Strikeout);
   str = "Strikeout";
   g.DrawString(str, font, brText, x, y);
   sizeString = g.MeasureString(str, font);
   y += sizeString.Height;
```

continues

continued

```
    // Create a serif underline m_ptSize point font.
    font = new Font(FontFamily.GenericSerif, m_ptSize,
       FontStyle.Underline);
    str = "Underline";
    g.DrawString(str, font, brText, x, y);
    sizeString = g.MeasureString(str, font);
    y += sizeString.Height;

    // Add spacing between text blocks.
    y += sizeString.Height / 2;
}

private void
FormMain_Paint(object sender,
System.Windows.Forms.PaintEventArgs e)
{
   Graphics g = e.Graphics;
   float x = 10;
   float y = 10;

   //
   //  GenericMonospace Font Styles
   //
   if (mitemFontMono.Checked)
   {
      DisplayMonoFont(g, ref x, ref y);
   }

   //
   //  GenericSansSerif Font Styles
   //
   if (mitemFontSans.Checked)
   {
      DisplaySansSerifFont(g, ref x, ref y);
   }

   //
   //  GenericSerif Font Styles
   //
   if (mitemFontSerif.Checked)
   {
      DisplaySerifFont(g, ref x, ref y);
   }
}
```

The drawing in our program is controlled by the `Paint` event handler method, `FormMain_Paint`. Based on the style of font that a user wishes to see, any (or all) of the three drawing methods may be called: `DisplayMonoFont`, `DisplaySansSerifFont`, or `DisplaySerifFont`. Our listing includes the source for the last of these methods because it provides a representative example of what you find in the other two.

The basic pattern to drawing text, as shown in the accompanying listing, is as follows:

- Create a brush with a color of `SystemColors.WindowText`.
- Create a font.
- Draw text by calling the `DrawString` method.
- Query the size of the text by calling the `MeasureString` method, and update the drawing coordinates to make them ready to draw the next string.

The only item not discussed previously is the call to the `MeasureString` method, which provides the height and width (in pixels) of a text string drawn on a device using a given font. Its use is helpful for drawing multiple lines of text.

We are going to return to the `MeasureString` method and discuss it in detail later in this chapter, when we present our sample program named, appropriately enough, `MeasureString`. For now, we are going to look at a more precise way to create a font: by asking for the precise font we want by name.

Creating Named Fonts

Font selection by font family is easy, but it is not very precise. For example, we might ask for a serif font, but we do not know which serif font we are going to get. For applications with simple output needs, this may be adequate. When you want more precise control of your program's graphical output, however, you need to rely on creating named fonts. For this to succeed, you must know the name of the font you wish to create. On a Pocket PC, that means you have a choice of the following TrueType fonts:

- Bookdings
- Courier New
- Tahoma

Armed with this information, here is a constructor to create a font.

```
public Font(
   string familyName,
   float emSize,
   FontStyle style);
```

The `NamedFonts` sample program creates three fonts by name and displays one line of text for each font. The code for the `Paint` event handler appears in Listing 16.3.

LISTING 16.3: The `Paint` Event Handler from `NamedFonts.cs`

```
private void
FormMain_Paint(object sender, PaintEventArgs e)
{
   Graphics g = e.Graphics;
   float x = 10;
   float y = 10;

   Font font1 = new Font("Tahoma", 14, FontStyle.Regular);
   Font font2 = new Font("Courier New", 10, FontStyle.Regular);
   Font font3 = new Font("Bookdings", 12, FontStyle.Regular);

   Brush brText = new SolidBrush(SystemColors.WindowText);

   g.DrawString("14 Point Tahoma", font1, brText, x, y);
   SizeF sizeX = g.MeasureString("X", font1);
   y += sizeX.Height;

   g.DrawString("10 Point Courier New", font2, brText, x, y);
   sizeX = g.MeasureString("X", font2);
   y += sizeX.Height;

   g.DrawString("12 Point Bookdings", font3, brText, x, y);
}
```

Figure 16.4 shows the output of the `NamedFonts` sample. The three fonts are the ones found on a Pocket PC. Two of the fonts create reasonable output, but the output of the third font (the font named Bookdings) does not seem quite right. The call to the `DrawString` method in Listing 16.3 for that font received the string `"12 Point Bookdings"`, but that is not what Figure 16.4 displays.

The output seems wrong because the Bookdings font does not contain regular text characters (or *glyphs* in the language of font specialists). This font is used to draw various elements of the Pocket PC user interface and is similar to the Webdings and Wingdings fonts, which ship with Windows XP.

The Bookdings font is used by Microsoft Reader, a program for viewing online books that ships with the Pocket PC 2002. The program can also play audiobooks, such as those featured at the Web site http://www.audible.com. Bookdings contains a number of graphical images, which you can use inside your .NET Compact Framework programs.

Figure 16.5 shows one way you could use the images from the Bookdings font in push buttons. Using a font in this way provides the benefit that the characters in a TrueType font can be scaled across a broad range of sizes and still appear pleasing to the eye; bitmaps and bitmap fonts do not provide

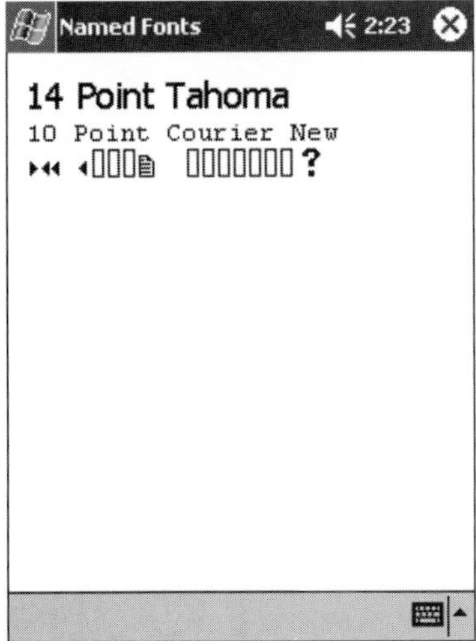

FIGURE 16.4: Output of the `NamedFonts` program showing text for three Pocket PC fonts

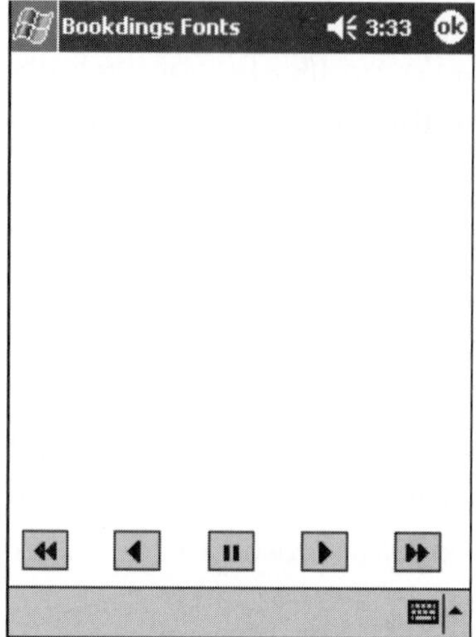

FIGURE 16.5: Bookdings images used for buttons

the same visual appeal when scaled to different sizes. (The sample program that drew the figure is named `BookDings` and is available online with the rest of the source code for this book.)

The Visual Studio .NET Designer does not let you request a font that it cannot create, so you must create a font at runtime and connect that font to the related controls. Listing 16.4 shows this being done during the loading of a form.

LISTING 16.4: Setting the Font to Bookdings at Runtime for Button Controls

```
private void FormMain_Load(object sender, System.EventArgs e)
{
   Font fontBookDings = new Font("BookDings", 14, FontStyle.Bold);

   // [ << ] button
   cmdRewind.Font = fontBookDings;
   cmdRewind.Text = "2";

   // [ <  ] button
   cmdBack.Font = fontBookDings;
   cmdBack.Text = "3";

   // [ || ] button
```

```
    cmdPause.Font = fontBookDings;
    cmdPause.Text = "0";

    // [ >  ] button
    cmdNext.Font = fontBookDings;
    cmdNext.Text = "4";

    // [ >> ] button
    cmdForward.Font = fontBookDings;
    cmdForward.Text = "7";
}
```

Enumerating Fonts

To successfully create a named font, the desired font must be present. The .NET Compact Framework does not provide a way to get a list of available fonts like the desktop .NET Framework does,[4] so we rely instead on the Win32 approach, known as font enumeration. We can enumerate fonts by calling the `EnumFontFamilies` function. There is a complication, however, which requires more work to call this function from a .NET Compact Framework program. This function requires a callback function—essentially a pointer to a function—which is then called for each available font family. While the desktop .NET Framework supports callback functions, the .NET Compact Framework does not.

Instead, we must put the actual font enumeration code within a Win32 DLL and then call the DLL from our .NET Compact Framework program. To illustrate this, we present two samples. The first, `FontPicker`, is a .NET Compact Framework program that lets the user pick an available font by face name, size, and style. To help reuse this code, we put the salient parts of the font collection in a separate class: `YaoDurant.Drawing.FontCollection`. The second sample, `FontList`, is a Win32 DLL that does the actual work of enumerating the fonts and returning the font face names in a manner that is compatible with the .NET Compact Framework.

4. In the desktop .NET Framework, the `Families` property of the `FontFamily` class does the trick.

FIGURE 16.6: Output of the `FontPicker` program with a sample of an available font

A Sample Program: `FontPicker`

Figure 16.6 shows the `FontPicker` sample program, with its three `ComboBox` controls for specifying the desired face name from available fonts, the desired size, and the font style. A `TextBox` control displays a sample of the resulting font.

Listing 16.5 shows the `FontCollection` class, which provides the managed-code portion of the font enumeration process.

LISTING 16.5: The `FontCollection` Class

```
// YaoDurant.Drawing.FontCollection.cs - Font enumeration
// wrapper class for fontlist.dll
//
// Code from _.NET Compact Framework Programming with C#_
// and _.NET Compact Framework Programming with Visual Basic .NET_
// Authored by Paul Yao and David Durant.
//

using System;
using System.Collections;
using System.Runtime.InteropServices;
```

```
namespace YaoDurant.Drawing
{
   /// <summary>
   /// Summary description for YaoDurant
   /// </summary>
   public class FontCollection
   {
      // Constructor
      public FontCollection()
      {
         IntPtr hFontList = FontList_Create();
         int count = FontList_GetCount(hFontList);
         int i;
         string strFace;
         IntPtr ip;
         for (i = 0; i < count; i++)
         {
            ip = FontList_GetFace(hFontList, i);
            strFace = Marshal.PtrToStringUni(ip);
            m_alFaceNames.Add(strFace);
         }

         FontList_Destroy(hFontList);
      }

      public void Dispose()
      {
         m_alFaceNames.Clear();
      }

      // P/Invoke declarations for fontlist.dll
      [DllImport("fontlist.dll")]
      public static extern IntPtr FontList_Create ();

      [DllImport("fontlist.dll")]
      public static extern
      int FontList_GetCount (IntPtr hFontList);

      [DllImport("fontlist.dll")]
      public static extern
      IntPtr FontList_GetFace (IntPtr hFontList, int iFace);

      [DllImport("fontlist.dll")]
      public static extern
      int FontList_Destroy (IntPtr hFontList);

      // Count of available face names
      public int Count
```

continues

continued

```
      {
         get { return m_alFaceNames.Count; }
      }

      private ArrayList m_alFaceNames = new ArrayList();

      public string this [int index]
      {
         get
         {
            if (index < 0 || index >= m_alFaceNames.Count)
               return string.Empty;
            else
               return (string)m_alFaceNames[index];
         }
      }

   } // class
} // namespace
```

A Sample Library: `FontList`, a Win32 Font Enumeration DLL

We prefer managed code. We call unmanaged (Win32) code only to access features that aren't directly available in managed code. Most of the time, only a few P/Invoke declarations are needed to connect our managed code to unmanaged functions. Sometimes, though, we must create an intermediary unmanaged-code library to serve as a bridge between some managed code and a set of unmanaged functions.

In the .NET Compact Framework, managed code cannot call unmanaged functions that involve callback functions.[5] The term *callback function* means that the caller passes a function pointer to the target function. In such cases, the target function uses the function pointer to call back to the caller. Managed code does, in fact, support callback functions. A managed callback function is called a *delegate*. But the .NET Compact Framework

5. By contrast, callback functions from unmanaged to managed code are fully supported in the desktop .NET Framework. For an example, see the excellent discussion by Dino Esposito, "Cutting Edge: Window Hooks in the .NET Framework" in the October 2002 edition of *MSDN Magazine*. The article is available at http://msdn.microsoft.com/msdnmag/issues/02/10/cuttingedge/.

supports only managed-code-to-managed-code delegates; callback functions from unmanaged code back into managed code are not supported.

To solve this problem for font enumeration, we present the `FontList` sample. `FontList` is a DLL that enumerates available fonts and puts that set of fonts into a linked list. The caller creates, queries, and cleans up the font list through these exported functions:

- `FontList_Create`: creates the linked list of fonts
- `FontList_GetCount`: returns the number of fonts in the list
- `FontList_GetFace`: gets the face name of a font at index N
- `FontList_Destroy`: frees all allocated font list memory

The complete source code for `FontList.cpp` appears in Listing 16.6.

LISTING 16.6: `FontList.cpp`: C++/Win32 Font Enumeration Helper

```
// FontList.cpp : Win32 Font enumeration helper functions
//
// Code from _.NET Compact Framework Programming with C#_
// and _.NET Compact Framework Programming with Visual Basic .NET_
// Authored by Paul Yao and David Durant.
//

#include "stdafx.h"
#include "fontlist.h"

BOOL APIENTRY
DllMain( HANDLE hModule,
         DWORD  ul_reason_for_call,
         LPVOID lpReserved)
{
    return TRUE;
}
extern "C"
{

typedef struct __FACENAME
{
   WCHAR FaceName[LF_FACESIZE];
   struct __FACENAME * pNext;
} FACENAME, *LPFACENAME;
```

continues

continued

```
typedef struct __HEADER
{
   int signature;
   int count;
   struct __FACENAME * pFirst;
   struct __FACENAME * pLast;
} HEADER, *LPHEADER;


#define HEADER_SIGNATURE 0xf0f0

//-----------------------------------------------------------------
//-----------------------------------------------------------------

int CALLBACK FontEnumProc(
    const ENUMLOGFONT FAR *lpelf,
    const TEXTMETRIC FAR *lpntm,
    int FontType,
    LPARAM lParam)
{
   LPHEADER pfl = (LPHEADER)lParam;

   // Allocate a block to hold face name information.
   LPFACENAME pfnNext = (LPFACENAME)malloc(sizeof(FACENAME));
   if (pfnNext == NULL)
      return FALSE;

   wcscpy(pfnNext->FaceName, lpelf->elfLogFont.lfFaceName);
   pfnNext->pNext = NULL;

   // First time called -- link to the header block.
   if (pfl->pFirst == NULL)
   {
       pfl->pFirst = pfnNext;
   }
   else // Link to the previous block.
   {
       LPFACENAME pfn = pfl->pLast;
       pfn->pNext = pfnNext;
   }

   // Current block becomes the end of the list.
   pfl->pLast = pfnNext;

   pfl->count++; // Increment the face name count.

   return TRUE;
}
```

```
//---------------------------------------------------------------
//---------------------------------------------------------------
HANDLE __cdecl FontList_Create(void)
{
   LPHEADER pfl = (LPHEADER)malloc(sizeof(HEADER));
   if (pfl == NULL)
      return NULL;

   // Init font list.
   pfl->count = 0;
   pfl->pFirst = NULL;
   pfl->pLast = NULL;
   pfl->signature = HEADER_SIGNATURE; 0xf0f0;

   HDC hdc = GetDC(NULL);
   EnumFontFamilies(hdc, NULL, (FONTENUMPROC)FontEnumProc,
   (LPARAM)pfl);
   ReleaseDC(NULL, hdc);

   return (HANDLE)pfl;
}

//---------------------------------------------------------------
//---------------------------------------------------------------
int __cdecl  FontList_GetCount(HANDLE hFontList)
{
   LPHEADER pfl = (LPHEADER)hFontList;
   if (pfl->signature != HEADER_SIGNATURE)
      return -1;

   return pfl->count;
}

//---------------------------------------------------------------
//---------------------------------------------------------------
LPTSTR __cdecl   FontList_GetFace(HANDLE  hFontList, int iFace)
{
   LPHEADER pfl = (LPHEADER)hFontList;
   if (pfl->signature != HEADER_SIGNATURE ||
       pfl->count <= iFace)
      return NULL;

   LPFACENAME pfn = pfl->pFirst;
   if (iFace != 0)
   {
      iFace--;
      for (int i = 0; i <= iFace; i++)
      {
```

continues

continued

```
            pfn = pfn->pNext;
        }
    }

    return pfn->FaceName;
}

//-----------------------------------------------------------------
//-----------------------------------------------------------------
BOOL __cdecl   FontList_Destroy(HANDLE hFontList)
{
    LPHEADER pfl = (LPHEADER)hFontList;
    if (pfl->signature == HEADER_SIGNATURE)
        return NULL;

    LPFACENAME pfnNext;   LPFACENAME pfnFirst = pfl->pFirst;

    int cItems = pfl->count;
    for (int i = 0; i < cItems; i++)
    {
        pfnNext = pfnFirst->pNext;
        free(pfnFirst);
        pfnFirst = pfnNext;
    }

    free(pfl);

    return TRUE;
}


}
```

The actual font enumeration function is `EnumFontFamilies`, which we call in the `FontList_Create` function. The callback function is `FontEnumProc`, which creates a structure of type `HEADER` that points to the start and end of the linked list. Each font face name is stored in a `FACENAME` structure. Our callback function stores only the font face name, which is all we need to access the fonts. But the font enumeration function gets far more details about each of the fonts, as represented by the `ENUMLOGFONT` and `TEXTMETRIC` data structures. You can extend the set of details that are stored by adding additional elements to the `FACENAME` structure.

As mentioned, `FontList` creates a list of font names. A program can take the list of fonts and display them for the user to pick, which we demonstrated earlier in the `FontPicker` sample program. Or a font name can be used to create a font and attach that font to a control. We do this in the `BookDings` sample program, which uses the graphical images from a TrueType font to create push buttons that display nontext images. A third use of font names is to create Win32 fonts directly, which is useful for accessing features such as drawing rotated text—which we demonstrate in the `RotateText` sample program later in this chapter—or to create ClearType fonts.

Building C++ Projects

You cannot use Visual Studio .NET 2003 to build unmanaged C++ projects for Windows CE, even though this tool can be used to build unmanaged C++ projects for desktop versions of Microsoft Windows. Instead, you need to use one of two special embedded compilers. For Windows CE 3.0 (including Pocket PC and Pocket PC 2002), you must use eMbedded Visual C++ 3.0. For Windows CE .NET 4.0 and later, which includes the Pocket PC 2003 and the Smartphone 2003, you must use eMbedded Visual C++ 4.x. Both tools are available for download from the Microsoft Web site.[6]

Native-Code Fonts

You can access most font features by creating fonts in managed code. There are a few cases, however, when you must go to unmanaged code—meaning P/Invoke-based native calls—to create fonts. The downside to creating fonts in unmanaged code is that such fonts can be used only through additional calls to unmanaged code. For example, these fonts cannot be used with managed-code drawing functions; nor can they be connected to .NET

6. These tools can be found by browsing to http://www.pocketpc.com and then clicking on the Developer link and the Download link.

Compact Framework controls. The following font features are available only when using fonts created in unmanaged code.

- **Rotate text**: As illustrated by the `RotateText` sample program, you can create TrueType fonts that are rotated at any angle.
- **ClearType fonts**: Microsoft developed the ClearType font technology to improve the readability of text on LCD screens.
- **Vertical fitting**: This feature allows you to select fonts based on the character cell height instead of traditional em height. This is useful for getting the largest text that can be squeezed within a space, such as the largest readable text that can be drawn in a spreadsheet cell. The em height is the size of uppercase letters and does not allow for the extra space needed for text to look good when horizontally challenged.
- **Horizontal fitting**: This feature allows you to create fonts based on the desired average character width instead of height.
- **Alternative character set**: With this feature, you can create fonts for an alternative character set from the default character set. For example, to select a font with a Russian or Greek character set on a U.S. English device, the font must be available on the device, and you must explicitly request the character set.

Creating Fonts in Unmanaged Code

To create a font in unmanaged code, you populate a `LOGFONT` structure and call the `CreateFontIndirect` function. The function returns a font handle, which you pass to other unmanaged functions. `LOGFONT`, the "logical font" structure, has 14 members—5 integers, 8 byte-size flags, and 1 character array for the font face name. The last member, the character array, causes a complication because of limitations in how P/Invoke works.

The .NET Compact Framework supports passing strings to unmanaged code. But the passing of strings within structures is not supported. Or, to be more precise, the marshaling of strings within a structure is not *automatically* supported. Instead, to create the `LOGFONT` structure that we need, we have to *manually* assemble the data structure. This is simpler than it sounds because of a set of helper functions found in the `Marshal` class.[7]

Listing 16.7 shows the creation of fonts in unmanaged code. This code was taken from the `RotateText` sample program.

LISTING 16.7: Fragment Showing Font Creation in Unmanaged Code

```
//
// Helpful GDI support functions
//
[DllImport("coredll.dll")]
public static extern IntPtr GetDC (IntPtr hWnd);
[DllImport("coredll.dll")]
public static extern int ReleaseDC (IntPtr hWnd, IntPtr hDC);
[DllImport("coredll.dll")]
public static extern int GetDeviceCaps (IntPtr hdc, int iIndex);
[DllImport("coredll.dll")]
public static extern IntPtr CreateFontIndirect (IntPtr lplf);

// The logical font structure -- minus the face name
public struct LOGFONT
{
   public int  lfHeight;
   public int  lfWidth;
   public int  lfEscapement;
   public int  lfOrientation;
   public int  lfWeight;
   public byte lfItalic;
   public byte lfUnderline;
   public byte lfStrikeOut;
   public byte lfCharSet;
   public byte lfOutPrecision;
   public byte lfClipPrecision;
   public byte lfQuality;
   public byte lfPitchAndFamily;
   //         public TCHAR [] lfFaceName;
};

public const int LF_FACESIZE = 32;
public const int LOGPIXELSY = 90;

//
// Memory allocation functions and definitions
```

continues

7. Fully qualified name: `System.Runtime.InteropServices.Marshal`.

continued

```
//
[DllImport("coredll.dll", CharSet=CharSet.Unicode)]
public static extern IntPtr LocalAlloc (int uFlags, int uBytes);
[DllImport("coredll.dll", CharSet=CharSet.Unicode)]
public static extern IntPtr LocalFree (IntPtr hMem);
public const int LPTR = 0x0040;

//---------------------------------------------------------
//---------------------------------------------------------
public static IntPtr
Create(
   string strFace,
   int iSize,
   int degrees)
{
   // Calculate the font height based on this ratio:
   //
   //    Height in Pixels       Desired Point Size
   //   -------------------  =  ------------------
   //    Device Resolution              72
   //
   // (72 points = approx. 1 inch)
   //
   // Which results in the following formula:
   //
   // Height = (Desired_Pt * Device_Res) / 72
   //
   IntPtr hdc = GetDC(IntPtr.Zero);
   int cyDevice_Res = GetDeviceCaps(hdc, LOGPIXELSY);
   ReleaseDC(IntPtr.Zero, hdc);

   // Calculate the font height.
   float flHeight = ((float)iSize * (float)cyDevice_Res) / 72.0F;
   int iHeight = (int)(flHeight + 0.5);

   // Set the height negative to request 'em height' (versus
   // 'character cell height' for positive size).
   iHeight = iHeight * (-1);

   // Allocate the managed-code logfont structure.
   LOGFONT logfont = new LOGFONT();
   logfont.lfHeight = iHeight;
   logfont.lfWidth = 0;
   logfont.lfEscapement = degrees * 10;
   logfont.lfOrientation = 0;
   logfont.lfWeight = 0;
   logfont.lfItalic = 0;
```

```
    logfont.lfUnderline= 0;
    logfont.lfStrikeOut= 0;
    logfont.lfCharSet = 0;
    logfont.lfOutPrecision = 0;
    logfont.lfClipPrecision = 0;
    logfont.lfQuality = 0;
    logfont.lfPitchAndFamily = 0;

    // Allocate the unmanaged-code logfont structure.
    int cbLogFont = Marshal.SizeOf(logfont);
    int cbMem =  cbLogFont + LF_FACESIZE;
    IntPtr iptrLogFont = LocalAlloc(LPTR, cbMem);

    if (iptrLogFont == IntPtr.Zero)
       return IntPtr.Zero;

    // Copy the managed structure to the unmanaged buffer.
    Marshal.StructureToPtr(logfont, iptrLogFont, false);

    // Set the pointer to the end of the structure.
    IntPtr ipFaceDest = (IntPtr)((int)iptrLogFont + cbLogFont);

    // Copy the string to a character array.
    char [] achFace = strFace.ToCharArray();
    int cch = strFace.Length;

    // Copy the face name to the unmanaged buffer.
    Marshal.Copy(achFace, 0, ipFaceDest, cch);

    return CreateFontIndirect(iptrLogFont);
}
```

The Memory Allocation That Never Fails

Within Listing 16.7, there is a line of code that looks like it is allocating memory, but it is not. We are referring to this line of code:

```
LOGFONT logfont = new LOGFONT();
```

It looks like memory allocation because of the presence of the `new` keyword. But no memory allocation takes place because the `LOGFONT` structure is a value type and not a reference type. As a local variable, this structure is allocated on the stack.

Why is this important? It is important because a casual glance at this code might convince an experienced programmer that we left out some important error checking. If this statement did require an allocation of an object from the heap, it is possible that the call could fail. To write truly robust code, we would need to add some simple error checking like the following:

```
if (logfont == null);
   return false;
```

That would be the correct code to write if `LOGFONT` were a reference type (that is, defined as a class). But `LOGFONT` is a value type, a structure, and so the compiler flags a fatal error message when you attempt this type of comparison.

The implications of this are broader than might appear at first, especially in the context of types that have been defined and widely used. For such types, if you change a value type to a reference type, you must go back and add error-checking code to guard against failure in object allocation. And with a widely used reference type that is changed to a value type, you risk breaking code that does the required error checking because it is not allowed—and is not necessary—for value types.

Drawing with Fonts in Unmanaged Code

A font created in unmanaged code can be used only by making other calls to unmanaged code.[8] A created font is not connected to any device or drawing surface. To establish that connection, we call the `SelectObject` function. Once that is done, we can make drawing calls to unmanaged text-drawing functions such as `ExtTextOut` and `DrawText`. You can see an example of this in the handling of the `Paint` event in the upcoming `RotateText` sample program.

---

8. Experienced .NET Framework programmers are often surprised that .NET Compact Framework objects do not expose the handles of underlying Win32 objects as is done in the desktop .NET Framework.

Cleanup

A key benefit enjoyed by all .NET programmers is automatic garbage collection. The runtime cleans up memory as needed for .NET Compact Framework programmers, for ASP.NET programmers, and also for Windows Forms programmers. Automatic garbage collection addresses a long-standing problem that Win32 programmers have previously had to handle manually.

In unmanaged code, we must manually dispose of GDI objects with the `DeleteObject` function. One requirement must be satisfied for graphical objects to be properly disposed of: The object cannot be connected to any device. For example, if a font is connected to the display screen, the call to delete the object fails. The reason is that the underlying data structure—the device context — must always point to valid objects.

The basic pattern for all GDI drawing objects is the same. Whether you are dealing with fonts, pens, brushes, bitmaps, or regions, the basic structure of the Win32 calls follows this sequence.

1. Create the drawing object by calling the `CreateFontIndirect`, `CreatePen`, `CreateSolidBrush`, `CreateBitmap`, or `CreateRectRgn` functions. The return value is an object handle.
2. Select the object into the device context by calling the `SelectObject` function. Save the return value because it is the "old" font, pen, brush, bitmap, or region.
3. Draw by calling various drawing functions.
4. Select the "old" object into the device context by calling the `SelectObject` function again.
5. Delete the drawing object created in step 1 by calling the `DeleteObject` function.

A Sample Program: `RotateText`

The `RotateText` sample program creates fonts by making calls to unmanaged code. The sample program has several styles of output, as illustrated in Figures 16.7 and 16.8. As shown in Figure 16.7, the program can draw a single line of text rotated at 45 degrees (or at any angle, as selected by the user). A second style of output, which we call a "fan blade," appears in Figure 16.8.

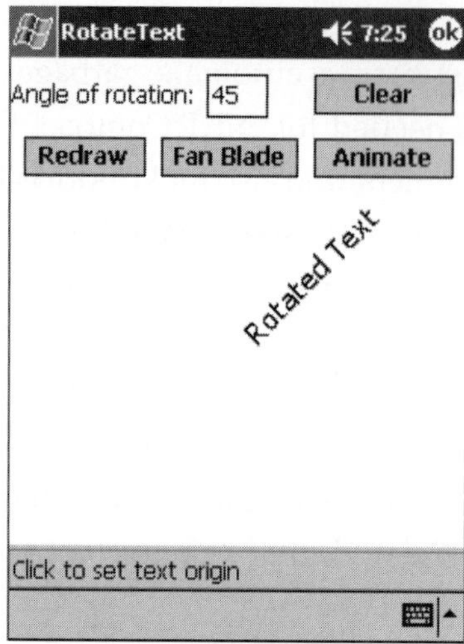

FIGURE 16.7: A line of text rotated by 45 degrees in the `RotateText` program

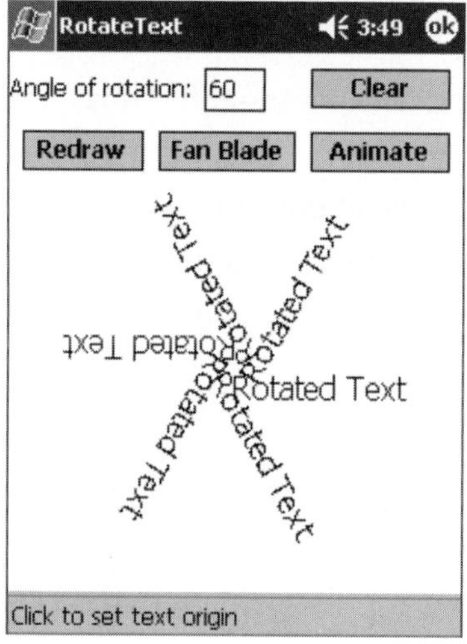

FIGURE 16.8: "fan blade" created by the `RotateText` program

This effect was created by drawing the same line of text several times using a different drawing angle each time the line of text is drawn.

We should mention that font rotation requires the presence of the TrueType font engine (and, of course, one or more available TrueType fonts). On devices like the Pocket PC that support TrueType fonts, this program displays correctly. Windows CE supports one of two font-rendering technologies on a given platform: either the TrueType fonts or bitmapped fonts, depending on what the platform creator decides to include in the operating system image.

As of this writing, the .NET Compact Framework (version 1.0) supports the Smartphone 2003. Because the Smartphone has bitmapped fonts—that is, fonts that cannot be rotated—when the `RotateText` program is run on such a device, only nonrotated text gets drawn.

Listing 16.7, presented earlier, shows the details of the font creation function. Listing 16.8 shows a fragment taken from the `RotateText` program, including the `Paint` event handler and other core pieces used to draw the rotated text.

LISTING 16.8: Fragment from `RotateText` with the Elements to Support Rotated Text

```
private int m_xText;
private int m_yText;
private int m_degRotate = 0;

public int degRotate
{
   get
   {
      string strRotate = textAngle.Text;
      m_degRotate = 0;
      try { m_degRotate = int.Parse(strRotate); }
      catch {}
      return m_degRotate;
   }
}


private void
FormMain_Paint(object sender, PaintEventArgs e)
{
   // Fetch a Win32 device context (DC).
   IntPtr hdc = DC.GetDC(this);

   // Create a Win32 font.
   IntPtr hfont = YaoDurant.Drawing.Font.Create(
      "Tahoma", 12, m_degRotate);

   // Select font into the DC.
   IntPtr hfontOld = DC.SelectObject(hdc, hfont);
```

continues

continued

```
    // Draw using the Win32 text-drawing function.
    YaoDurant.Drawing.DC.ExtTextOut(hdc, m_xText, m_yText,
       0, IntPtr.Zero, "Rotated Text", 12, IntPtr.Zero);

    // Disconnect font from DC -- *Critical* because....
    DC.SelectObject(hdc, hfontOld);

    // ... clean up of Win32 font object requires font to
    // be disconnected from any and all DCs.
    DC.DeleteObject(hfont);

    // Disconnect from the Win32 DC.
    DC.ReleaseDC(this, hdc);
}

private void
FormMain_MouseDown(object sender, MouseEventArgs e)
{
    m_xText = e.X;
    m_yText = e.Y;
    Invalidate();
}

private void
cmdRedraw_Click(object sender, System.EventArgs e)
{
    m_degRotate = degRotate;
    Invalidate();
}

private void cmdFanBlade_Click(object sender, EventArgs e)
{
    int cIncrement = degRotate;
    if (cIncrement == 0)
       cIncrement = 45;

    IntPtr hdc = YaoDurant.Drawing.DC.GetDC(this);

    for (int i = 0; i < 360; i += cIncrement)
    {
       IntPtr hfont = YaoDurant.Drawing.Font.Create(
          "Tahoma", 12, i);
       IntPtr hfontOld =
          YaoDurant.Drawing.DC.SelectObject(hdc, hfont);
       DC.ExtTextOut(hdc, m_xText, m_yText, 0, IntPtr.Zero,
          "Rotated Text", 12, IntPtr.Zero);
       DC.SelectObject(hdc, hfontOld);
       DC.DeleteObject(hfont);
    }
```

```
    YaoDurant.Drawing.DC.ReleaseDC(this, hdc);

}

private void cmdClear_Click(object sender, EventArgs e)
{
    Graphics g = this.CreateGraphics();
    g.Clear(SystemColors.Window);
}

private void cmdAnimate_Click(object sender, EventArgs e)
{
    // Use degrees as the rotational increment.
    int cIncrement = degRotate;
    if (cIncrement == 0)
        cIncrement = 45;

    for (int i = 0; i < 360; i += cIncrement)
    {
        m_degRotate = i;
        Invalidate();
        Update();
    }

    m_degRotate = 0;
    Invalidate();
    Update();
}
```

Placing Text

In a graphical world, text is treated as a graphical object. This has some nice benefits. You can freely mix text and graphical images together. You can also use several fonts together to create a richer style of output. The drawback to this added power is that some effort is required to coordinate the placement of the various graphical objects in the available drawing area. By contrast, a console-style application can send its text to an output window, where automatic word wrapping and automatic scrolling take the worry out of creating text output. In a graphical environment, you—the programmer—must measure the space that text occupies. The reward for this effort is total control in text placement.

Even if you are drawing only text, with no other kind of graphical object, you still have some work to do. For example, drawing multiple lines of text requires you to calculate the height of each line of text so that you can position each line the correct distance from the previous line. For this and other text-measuring tasks, the .NET Compact Framework provides the `MeasureString` method, which resides in the `Graphics` class.[9] We discuss this next.

Text Size and the `MeasureString` Method

Most people have looked at text their entire lives. Yet using text to read and write is not the same as managing the display of graphical text. If you look closely at individual characters, for example, the letter *G*, you see a very complicated piece of artwork that a font designer spent many hours perfecting. To efficiently deal with text without getting lost in each glyph,[10] graphic programmers simplify a text string.

We handle graphical text in terms of an imaginary bounding box that surrounds the text string. To place graphical text, we organize the placement of the bounding box within the drawing area, relative to other text and nontext graphical objects. This simplification is the basis of all efforts to measure the size of text in a graphics system.

The `MeasureString` method returns the width and height of a text string by providing a `SizeF` structure. The `F` at the end of the structure name indicates that the structure contains floating-point values (a Hungarian-like suffix). For our purposes, `SizeF` has two interesting properties.

```
public float Width {get; set;}
public float Height {get; set;}
```

The `MeasureString` method returns the height and width for a specified string drawn with a given font. To calculate the bounding box, we spec-

9. Fully qualified name: `System.Drawing.Graphics`.

10. A *glyph* is the graphical image of a character. Display and printer driver writers, among others, use this term to make sure that the output—the mapping from the character in a font on a specific device—looks correct. Two images of the letter *A*—one drawn with 10-point Arial and the other with 12-point Arial—represent two glyphs but the same character code.

ify both the character string and the font to be used in drawing the string. Here is the definition of the `MeasureString` method.

```
public SizeF MeasureString(
   string text,
   Font font);
```

A Sample Program: `MeasureString`

The `MeasureString` method is simple, so the accompanying sample program is also simple. The greatest challenge is that the bounding box size is always provided as floating-point values. You must create conversion logic if your text-drawing code interacts with other code that uses integer coordinates. Among other things, this includes mouse input coordinates and the coordinates for drawing vector or raster graphics.

To make our sample more interesting, we add font selection logic from the `FontPicker` sample that appeared earlier in this chapter. A textbox allows the user to type in some text. As shown in Figure 16.9, the sample draws white text on a black background to highlight the size and placement of the bounding box. We also went a little crazy with some line drawing to illustrate the relationship between the reported height and width

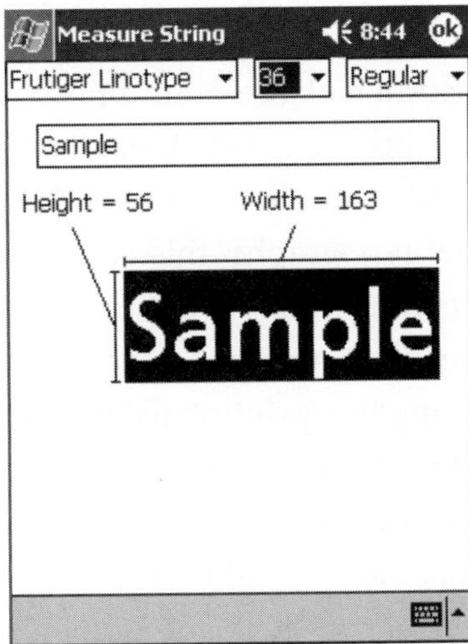

FIGURE 16.9: Output produced by the `MeasureString` program

and the resulting text. Listing 16.9 provides a fragment of the code in the `Paint` event handler for measuring and drawing the string.

LISTING 16.9: Fragment Showing the Call to the `MeasureString` Method

```
string str = textSample.Text;
Brush brFore = new SolidBrush(SystemColors.Window);
Brush brBack = new SolidBrush(SystemColors.WindowText);
float sinX = 240 / 4;
float sinY = 320 / 3;

SizeF szf = e.Graphics.MeasureString(str, Font);

// Draw a rectangle in the text background.
int xRect = (int)sinX;
int yRect = (int)sinY;
int cxRect = (int)szf.Width;
int cyRect = (int)szf.Height;
Rectangle rc;
rc = new Rectangle(xRect, yRect,cxRect,cyRect);

e.Graphics.FillRectangle(brBack, rc);

// Draw the string.
e.Graphics.DrawString(str, Font, brFore, sinX, sinY);
```

The bounding box for the text is visible in Figure 16.9. When we specify the location for the text, the drawing coordinate in the `DrawString` method corresponds with the upper-left corner of the bounding box. Our next sample program, `TextAlign`, shows how to get 11 other alignments.

You might notice that the top of the bounding box contains a blank horizontal area. In the world of digital typography, this is referred to as the *internal leading*. The term *leading* comes from typesetting as done in the predigital era when cubes holding character images had to be individually placed to form lines of text. Using this printing technology, a typesetter placed a long, thin piece of metal—known as the *leading*—between the rows of letters to provide the interline spacing. In the world of digital fonts, leading is split into two parts: the internal leading and the external leading. The names reflect whether or not the leading is included in the reported height.

The interline spacing that the `MeasureString` method reports works reasonably well in most cases, especially given the small screen size of a typical device like a Pocket PC that runs .NET Compact Framework programs.[11] Programmers who work in depth with digital font technology may notice that absolute precision in text placement requires an additional element, the *external leading* value. For many TrueType fonts at smaller sizes, the external leading is zero and so can often be ignored.

Text Alignment

The .NET Compact Framework supports two overloads to the `DrawString` method. One overload positions the text with an (x,y) coordinate pair. We use this overload in all the samples presented up to this point. The second overload positions the text within a rectangle, and it performs word wrapping of the text and clipping to the rectangle. We consider this overload later in this chapter. For the purposes of this discussion, we consider the simpler of the two functions—that is, the function that involves a coordinate pair.

When text is drawn with the coordinate-pair version of the `DrawString` method, the text is drawn below and to the right of the point. In other words, the default text alignment is to the top and left of the textbox. For example, in Figure 16.10, the text coordinate is the intersection of the vertical and horizontal lines.

This approach has been part of every version of Windows since Microsoft Windows 1.01 shipped in 1985. It is likely an outgrowth of the fact that the default origin of a drawing surface is the upper-left corner, which no doubt results from the convention in European languages of reading and writing from left to right and from top to bottom.[12]

Whatever the origin, the default alignment is not always the most convenient. This alignment does not help when you try to center some text

---

11. To help address this need, we provide the P/invoke declarations for the `GetTextMetrics` function and the `TEXTMETRIC` structure in the `RotateText` and `TextAlign` sample programs.

12. Not every language follows this convention. Some languages are read from right to left.

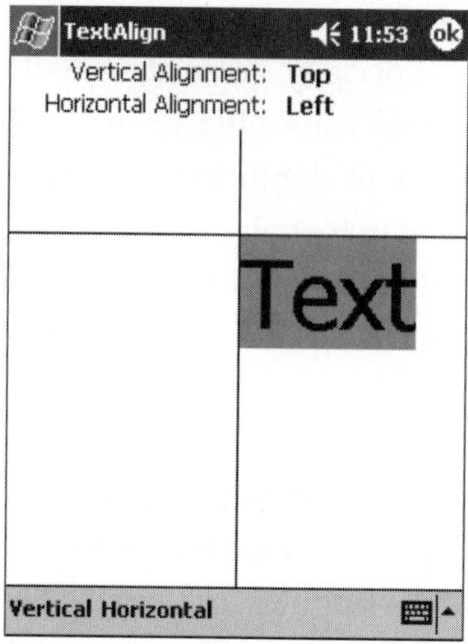

FIGURE 16.10: The default text alignment: top and left

within an object (e.g., a rectangle or a window). Nor does this default alignment help center text over a column of numbers.

The .NET Compact Framework does not provide automatic text alignment. For other alignments, you calculate an offset from the desired point to the upper-left corner of the textbox.

A Sample Program: `TextAlign`

The `TextAlign` sample program supports a total of 12 different alignments. This number is the result of supporting 4 vertical alignments (top, middle, baseline, and bottom) and 3 horizontal alignments (left, center, and right). Of the 12 alignments, 9 position the text relative to the text bounding box, so these 9 alignments are available with the results returned by the `MeasureString` method.

Three text alignment settings cannot be calculated by calling the `MeasureString` method, namely, baseline-left, baseline-center, and baseline-right. Figure 16.11 shows baseline-left alignment. As before, the reference point for positioning the text is the point where the two axes cross. To create the desired alignment, the program calculates x and y values as offsets from the reference point to the upper-left corner of the textbox. This offset

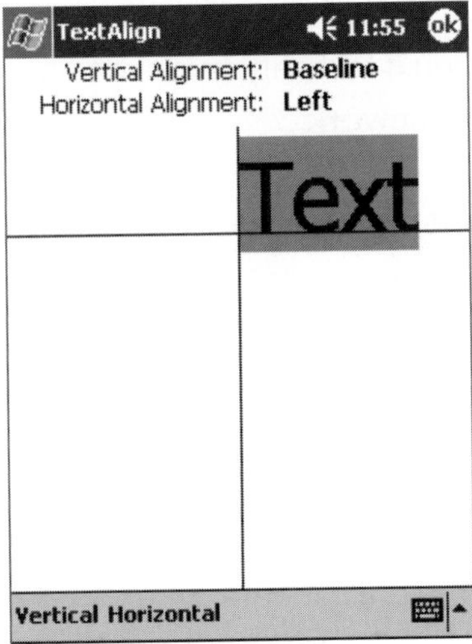

FIGURE 16.11: One of 12 possible text alignments

gets added (or subtracted) to the x- and y-coordinates passed in the call to the `DrawString` method.

In Figure 16.11, the letters in the word "Text" are sitting on the x-axis. To position text in this way, we modify the y value in the text-drawing call by a distance known as the *ascent*. This value is not available through the .NET Compact Framework. Instead, as shown in the sample program, we call the Win32 `GetTextMetrics` function to get this (and other) font metric values. Supporting the three baseline alignments requires more work than the other alignments do.

All of the standard .NET Compact Framework controls support a single font, as specified by the `Font` property. To get rich text in a .NET Compact Framework program, you have two choices: Build a custom control with rich text support, or create a `RichInk` control, an unmanaged control available on the Pocket PC through P/Invoke calls.

If you built your own custom control, you could use the baseline text alignment to allow text drawn from different fonts to appear together correctly. This is the type of text alignment used by all word processors (including, on a Pocket PC, Pocket Word).

Listing 16.10 shows the code for the `TextAlign` sample program, which shows how to support additional text alignment options for programs written for the .NET Compact Framework.

LISTING 16.10: `TextAlign` Program Showing How to Support 12 Text Alignment Settings

```
private int m_cxAdjust = 0;
private int m_cyAdjust = 0;
private string strDisplay = "Text";

public enum Alignment
{
   V_TOP,
   V_MIDDLE,
   V_BASELINE,
   V_BOTTOM,
   H_LEFT,
   H_CENTER,
   H_RIGHT
}

//
// Handlers for menu item selections
//
private void mitemVerticalTop_Click(object sender,
System.EventArgs e)
{
   SetVerticalAlignment(Alignment.V_TOP);
}

private void mitemVerticalMiddle_Click(object sender,
System.EventArgs e)
{
   SetVerticalAlignment(Alignment.V_MIDDLE);
}

private void mitemVerticalBaseline_Click(object sender,
System.EventArgs e)
{
   SetVerticalAlignment(Alignment.V_BASELINE);
}

private void mitemVerticalBottom_Click(object sender,
System.EventArgs e)
{
   SetVerticalAlignment(Alignment.V_BOTTOM);
}
```

```
private void mitemHorizontalLeft_Click(object sender,
System.EventArgs e)
{
   SetHorizontalAlignment(Alignment.H_LEFT);
}

private void mitemHorizontalCenter_Click(object sender,
System.EventArgs e)
{
   SetHorizontalAlignment(Alignment.H_CENTER);
}

private void mitemHorizontalRight_Click(object sender,
System.EventArgs e)
{
   SetHorizontalAlignment(Alignment.H_RIGHT);
}

//
// Calculate offset for vertical alignment.
//
private void SetVerticalAlignment(Alignment align)
{
   // Remove checkmarks from all menu items.
   mitemVerticalTop.Checked = false;
   mitemVerticalMiddle.Checked = false;
   mitemVerticalBaseline.Checked = false;
   mitemVerticalBottom.Checked = false;

   // Calculate the size of the string bounding box.
   Graphics g = CreateGraphics();
   SizeF size = g.MeasureString(strDisplay, Font);
   g.Dispose();

   // Update based on the selected alignment.
   switch (align)
   {
      case Alignment.V_TOP:
         mitemVerticalTop.Checked = true;
         m_cyAdjust = 0;
         lblVert.Text = "Top";
         break;
      case Alignment.V_MIDDLE:
         mitemVerticalMiddle.Checked = true;
         m_cyAdjust = (int)(size.Height / 2);
         lblVert.Text = "Middle";
         break;
```

continues

continued

```
        case Alignment.V_BASELINE:
            mitemVerticalBaseline.Checked = true;
            m_cyAdjust = GetFontBaseline(Font.Name,
                (int)Font.Size);
            lblVert.Text = "Baseline";
            break;
        case Alignment.V_BOTTOM:
            mitemVerticalBottom.Checked = true;
            m_cyAdjust = (int)size.Height;
            lblVert.Text = "Bottom";
            break;
    }
    // Redraw
    Invalidate();
} // SetVerticalAlignment

//
// Calculate the offset for horizontal alignment.
//
public void SetHorizontalAlignment(Alignment align)
{
    // Remove checkmarks from all menu items.
    mitemHorizontalLeft.Checked = false;
    mitemHorizontalCenter.Checked = false;
    mitemHorizontalRight.Checked = false;

    // Calculate the size of the string bounding box.
    Graphics g = CreateGraphics();
    SizeF size = g.MeasureString(strDisplay, Font);
    g.Dispose();

    // Update based on the selected alignment.
    switch(align)
    {
        case Alignment.H_LEFT:
            mitemHorizontalLeft.Checked = true;
            m_cxAdjust = 0;
            lblHorz.Text = "Left";
            break;
        case Alignment.H_CENTER:
            mitemHorizontalCenter.Checked = true;
            m_cxAdjust = (int)(size.Width / 2);
            lblHorz.Text = "Center";
            break;
        case Alignment.H_RIGHT:
            mitemHorizontalRight.Checked = true;
            m_cxAdjust = (int)size.Width;
```

```
         lblHorz.Text = "Right";
         break;
   }
   // Redraw
   Invalidate();
} // SetHorizontalAlignment

//
// Calculate the font baseline for baseline alignment.
//
private int GetFontBaseline(string strFont, int cptHeight)
{
   int cyReturn;

   // Fetch a Win32 DC.
   IntPtr hdc = YaoDurant.Drawing.DC.GetDC(this);

   // Create a Win32 font.
   IntPtr hfont = YaoDurant.Drawing.Font.Create(
      strFont, cptHeight, 0);
   // Select font into DC.

   IntPtr hfontOld = DC.SelectObject(hdc, hfont);

   // Allocate the font metric structure.
   YaoDurant.Drawing.Font.TEXTMETRIC tm =
      new YaoDurant.Drawing.Font.TEXTMETRIC();

   // Fetch font metrics.
   YaoDurant.Drawing.Font.GetTextMetrics(hdc, ref tm);

   // Fetch the return value.
   cyReturn = tm.tmAscent;

   // Disconnect font from DC -- *Critical* because ...
   DC.SelectObject(hdc, hfontOld);

   // ... clean up of Win32 font object requires font to
   // be disconnected from any and all DCs.
   DC.DeleteObject(hfont);

   // Disconnect from Win32 DC.
   YaoDurant.Drawing.DC.ReleaseDC(this, hdc);

   return cyReturn;
} // GetFontBaseline

//
```

continues

continued

```
// Handler for the Paint event
//
private void FormMain_Paint(object sender,
System.Windows.Forms.PaintEventArgs e)
{
   Graphics g = e.Graphics;

   int x = this.Width / 2;
   int y = this.Height / 3;

   // Adjust values to accommodate alignment request.
   float sinTextX = (float)(x - m_cxAdjust);
   float sinTextY = (float)(y - m_cyAdjust);

   // Calculate the size of the string bounding box.
   SizeF size = g.MeasureString(strDisplay, Font);
   int cxWidth  = (int)size.Width;
   int cyHeight = (int)size.Height;

   // Draw the text bounding box.
   Brush hbrFill = new SolidBrush(Color.Gray);
   Rectangle rc = new Rectangle((int)sinTextX,
                                (int)sinTextY,
                                cxWidth,
                                cyHeight);
   g.FillRectangle(hbrFill, rc);

   // Draw the string.
   Brush brText = new SolidBrush(SystemColors.WindowText);
   g.DrawString(strDisplay, Font, brText, sinTextX, sinTextY);

   // Draw reference cross-hairs.
   Pen penBlack = new Pen(SystemColors.WindowText);
   g.DrawLine(penBlack, x, 0, x, this.Height);
   g.DrawLine(penBlack, 0, y, this.Width, y);
} // FormMain_Paint
```

Word Wrap

A word processor automatically inserts new lines when the length of a line of text exceeds the available space. This feature, known as *word wrap*, is taken for granted by end users of word processing programs. (Even Notepad supports word wrap.) To the user, word wrap is easy because it is automatic. A programmer who tries to create this feature has a different view, especially when word wrap involves matching the expected printed output to what a user sees on the screen ("WYSIWYG"). Among .NET Compact Framework controls, the `TextBox` control supports word wrap when two properties are set to `true` (namely, `Multiline` and `WordWrap`).

One of the overloaded versions of the `DrawString` method supports word wrap. That version is defined as follows.

```
public void DrawString(
   string s,
   Font font,
   Brush brush,
   RectangleF layoutRectangle);
```

Up to this point in this chapter, we used only the other version of the `DrawString` method, which takes an (x,y) coordinate pair for the text location. This word-wrap version of the `DrawString` method takes a rectangle to specify the text location. When we specify the rectangle, we are doing more than just defining the location for the text because the rectangle also defines the *word-wrap rectangle* and the *clip rectangle* for the text.

The word-wrap rectangle defines a bounding box for the function to use in applying automatic word wrapping to a string. In addition to the automatic word wrapping, you can force a new line by inserting a carriage return or line feed character into a string. (In C#, insert a new line using the `\n` or `\r` character.)

The rectangle also serves a second role as the clip rectangle. In graphics programming, clipping involves a boundary that marks the edge of the allowable drawing area. Clipping was invented at the Palo Alto Research Center (PARC) to support windowed output. A clipping boundary is like a fence around a yard that keeps a dog within its owner's yard; such a fence defines the boundary of a dog's allowable space just as a clipping boundary defines the boundary of the allowable drawing area.

In the case of the `DrawString` method, this means that the drawn text is limited to the boundaries specified by the rectangle. Any text that does not fit within the boundaries of the rectangle is clipped—meaning that the user does not see it drawn at all.

A Sample Program: WordWrap

The `WordWrap` sample program, shown in Figure 16.12, draws a long text string. We need to clarify one point about the figure: For the purposes of this illustration, we added code to draw a rectangle that corresponds to the location of the rectangle that we pass to the `DrawString` method. The `DrawString` method itself did not draw the rectangle in the figure.

The first half of the long string in our sample contains explicit new line characters to show how these are handled. Unlike what happens in other programming APIs,[13] the .NET Compact Framework supports new line characters. The second half of the string contains no new line characters, to allow the built-in word-wrap support of the `DrawString` method to operate. The whole string does not fit into the rectangle, and only the top portion of the last line displayed is visible.

We have a bit of fun with this sample, which allows the user to move the text rectangle with a click-and-drag operation. We use a stretch rectangle (also called a rubber rectangle) to give the user feedback about where the

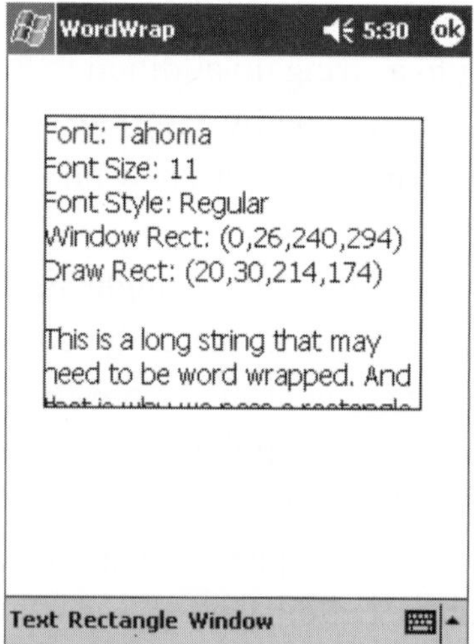

FIGURE 16.12: Text drawn with the word-wrapping version of `DrawString`

13. *API* stands for Application Programming Interface; we are referring here to Win32 and MFC, which do not support new line characters in graphical output.

rectangle is to be placed (for details on this code, see the `DrawRectangles` sample program in Chapter 6).

Listing 16.11 shows the `Paint` event handler from the `WordWrap` sample program's code.

LISTING 16.11: The `Paint` Event Handler from the `WordWrap` Program

```
private RectangleF rcDraw = new RectangleF(16, 16, 208, 160);
private StretchRectangle stretch = new StretchRectangle();

private void
FormMain_Paint(object sender,
System.Windows.Forms.PaintEventArgs e)
{
   string str = "Font: " + Font.Name + "\n" +
      "Font Size: " + Font.Size.ToString() + "\n" +
      "Font Style: " + Font.Style.ToString() + "\n" +
      "Window Rect: (" +
         Bounds.X.ToString() + "," +
         Bounds.Y.ToString() + "," +
         Bounds.Right.ToString() + "," +
         Bounds.Bottom.ToString() + ")\n" +
      "Draw Rect: (" +
         rcDraw.X.ToString() + "," +
         rcDraw.Y.ToString() + "," +
         rcDraw.Right.ToString() + "," +
         rcDraw.Bottom.ToString() + ")\n\n" +
      "This is a long string " +
      "that may need to be word wrapped. " +
      " And that is why we pass a rectangle " +
      "in the call to DrawString. ";

   // Set the text color.
   Brush brText;
   if (mitemTextDefault.Checked)
      brText = new SolidBrush(SystemColors.WindowText);
   else if (mitemTextRed.Checked)
      brText = new SolidBrush(Color.Red);
   else
      brText = new SolidBrush(Color.Blue);

   // Set the background color.
   Brush brRect;
   if (mitemRectangleDefault.Checked)
      brRect = new SolidBrush(SystemColors.Window);
   else if (mitemRectangleAqua.Checked)
```

continues

continued

```
        brRect = new SolidBrush(Color.Aqua);
    else
        brRect = new SolidBrush(Color.Yellow);

    // Create an integer rectangle (for vector calls).
    Rectangle rc = Rectangle.Round(rcDraw);

    // Fetch the background color.
    Color clrClear;
    if (mitemWindowBlack.Checked)
        clrClear = Color.Black;
    else if (mitemWindowGreen.Checked)
        clrClear = Color.Green;
    else
        clrClear = SystemColors.Window;

    // Erase the background.
    e.Graphics.Clear(clrClear);

    // Draw the background rectangle.
    e.Graphics.FillRectangle(brRect, rc);

    // Draw the text.
    e.Graphics.DrawString(str, this.Font, brText, rcDraw);

    if (mitemRectangleBorder.Checked)
    {
        e.Graphics.DrawRectangle(new Pen(Color.Black), rc);
    }
} // FormMain_Paint
```

Text Color

Brushes describe color. When you draw text, you use a brush to specify a color for drawing the text. Both raster and vector drawing also involve brushes: In raster drawing, brushes are used for filling rectangular areas, and in vector drawing brushes are used for filling shapes. The focus of this chapter is on drawing text, but you use the same method to create brushes whatever kind of drawing you are doing.

Foreground and Background Text Colors

Both of the supported overloads for the text-drawing method, `DrawString`, accept one brush as a parameter. This determines the foreground color for the text, the color used to draw each of the foreground elements of text—the lines and crossbar in the *H*, the round surface in the letter *O*.

The background color is the color used to draw the nonforeground pixels in the `TextBox` control. The .NET frameworks do not support the idea of text background color, by which we mean that the various versions of the `DrawString` method do not support drawing in the background pixels. However, you can change the text background color by drawing with a vector-drawing method (such as `FillRectangle`) to fill the text bounding box prior to drawing text.

Why Not Use the `ForeColor` Property for Text Color?

The sample programs in this chapter use explicit colors for drawing text instead of using the `ForeColor` property. We chose explicit colors to focus the discussion on drawing and the members of the `System.Drawing` namespace. Also, a minor complication when drawing in a form is that the Visual Studio .NET Designer does not display foreground color as a property supported by the form. (On the other hand, the background color property, `BackColor`, does show up in the Properties window.)

When building a custom control, however, you likely will use the `ForeColor` property to draw and also make that property appear in the Designer-side view of your control.

A Sample Program: `TextColor`

We close this chapter with a sample program that uses all three methods for setting the text foreground and text background colors. The `TextColor` program provides menu selections to set colors using system color constants, named colors, and RGB values. These are the three methods that the .NET Compact Framework supports for defining colors.

Whatever method you choose to set a color, the result is the same: an RGB triplet. As shown in Figure 16.13, the sample program shows the red,

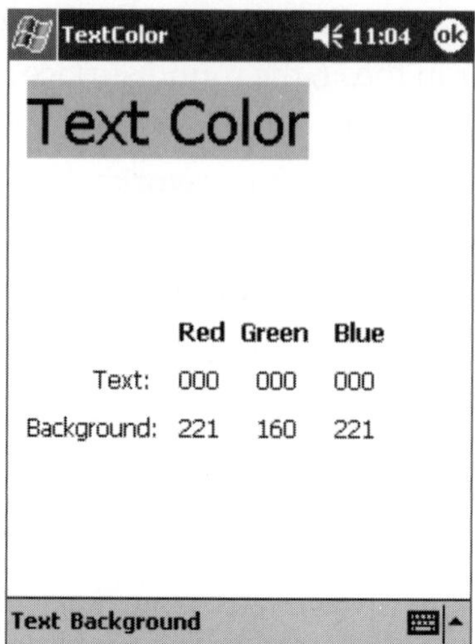

FIGURE 16.13: `TextColor` **program displaying text foreground and background color values**

green, and blue components of the selected text foreground color and text background color. Listing 16.12 shows the `Paint` event handler from the sample program.

LISTING 16.12: Color Extracting and the `Paint` Event Handler for the `TextColor` Program

```
// Private data
Color m_clrBack = SystemColors.Window;
Color m_clrText = SystemColors.WindowText;

private void
   FormMain_Paint(object sender, PaintEventArgs e)
{
   Graphics g = e.Graphics;

   // The string to draw
   string strDraw = "Text Color";

   // String location -- in floating point
   float sinX = 10F;
   float sinY = 10F;

   // Location as integers
   int x = (int)sinX;
   int y = (int)sinY;
```

```
    // Draw the background if needed.
    if (m_clrBack != SystemColors.Window)
    {
        // Calculate the size of the string bounding box.
        SizeF size = g.MeasureString(strDraw, Font);
        int cx = (int)size.Width;
        int cy = (int)size.Height;

        // Draw the text bounding box.
        Rectangle rc = new Rectangle(x, y, cx, cy);

        Brush brBack = new SolidBrush(m_clrBack);
        g.FillRectangle(brBack, rc);
    }

    Brush brText = new SolidBrush(m_clrText);
    g.DrawString(strDraw, Font, brText, sinX, sinY);
} // FormMain_Paint

private void DisplayRGBComponents()
{
    byte byt = m_clrText.R;
    lblTextR.Text = byt.ToString("000");
    byt = m_clrText.G;
    lblTextG.Text = byt.ToString("000");
    byt = m_clrText.B;
    lblTextB.Text = byt.ToString("000");

    byt = m_clrBack.R;
    lblBackR.Text = byt.ToString("000");
    byt = m_clrBack.G;
    lblBackG.Text = byt.ToString("000");
    byt = m_clrBack.B;
    lblBackB.Text = byt.ToString("000");
} // DisplayRGBComponents

private void SetTextColor(Color clr)
{
    m_clrText = clr;
    Invalidate();
    DisplayRGBComponents();
}

private void SetBackColor(Color clr)
{
    m_clrBack = clr;
    Invalidate();
    DisplayRGBComponents();
}
```

continues

continued

```
private void
mitemTextControlText_Click(object sender, EventArgs e)
{
   SetTextColor(SystemColors.ControlText);
}

private void
mitemTextGrayText_Click(object sender, EventArgs e)
{
   SetTextColor(SystemColors.GrayText);
}
```

The standard way to select colors on the desktop is with a color picker dialog box. The .NET Compact Framework does not support a color picker dialog box, but the underlying Windows CE libraries do. Figure 16.14 shows the color picker dialog box as it appears on a Pocket PC. Listing 16.13 shows the code for our `ChooseColorDlg` class. The code that creates and displays the dialog box appears in Listing 16.14.

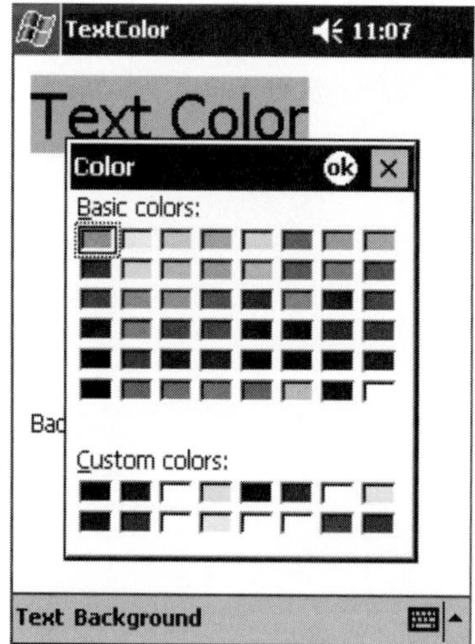

FIGURE 16.14: `TextColor` **program displaying the color picker dialog box**

LISTING 16.13: The `ChooseColorDlg` Class That Wraps the Color Picker Dialog Box

```
// YaoDurant.Drawing.ChooseColor.cs - Wrapper for calling Win32
// color picker common dialog box
//
// Code from _.NET Compact Framework Programming with C#_
// and _.NET Compact Framework Programming with Visual Basic .NET_
// Authored by 2004 Paul Yao and David Durant.
//

using System;
using System.Drawing;
using System.Windows.Forms;
using System.Runtime.InteropServices;

namespace YaoDurant.Drawing
{
   /// <summary>
   /// Summary description for YaoDurant
   /// </summary>
   public class ChooseColorDlg
   {
      public ChooseColorDlg()
      {
      }

      // Private data -- the Win32 CHOOSECOLOR structure
      private CHOOSECOLOR m_cc;

      // Class initialization function
      public bool Init(Control ctrlParent)
      {
         // Allocate the array for initial colors.
         int cbColorData = 16 * 4;
         IntPtr ipColors = LocalAlloc(LMEM_FIXED, cbColorData);
         if (ipColors == IntPtr.Zero)
            return false;

         m_cc = new CHOOSECOLOR();
         m_cc.lStructSize = Marshal.SizeOf(m_cc);
         m_cc.hwndOwner = GetHwndFromControl(ctrlParent);
         m_cc.hInstance = IntPtr.Zero;
         m_cc.rgbResult = 0;
         m_cc.lpCustColors = ipColors;
         m_cc.Flags = CC_RGBINIT;
         m_cc.lCustData = 0;
         m_cc.lpfnHook = IntPtr.Zero;
         m_cc.lpTemplateName = IntPtr.Zero;
```

continues

continued

```
      return true;
   }

   public bool ShowDialog(ref Color clrValue)
   {
      int iRet = 0;
      byte Red = clrValue.R;
      byte Green = clrValue.G;
      byte Blue = clrValue.B;

      m_cc.rgbResult = (Blue << 16) + (Green << 8) + Red;

      iRet = ChooseColor(ref m_cc);
      if (iRet != 0)
      {
         Red   = (byte)(m_cc.rgbResult & 0xff);
         Green = (byte)((m_cc.rgbResult & 0xff00) >> 8);
         Blue  = (byte)((m_cc.rgbResult & 0xff0000) >> 16);
         clrValue = Color.FromArgb(Red, Green, Blue);
         return true;
      }
      else
         return false;
   }

   //
   // Memory allocation functions and values
   //
   public const int LMEM_FIXED = 0x0000;
   [DllImport("coredll.dll")]
   public static extern
   IntPtr LocalAlloc (int uFlags, int uBytes);
   [DllImport("coredll.dll")]
   public static extern IntPtr LocalFree (IntPtr hMem);

   public static int INVALID_HANDLE_VALUE = -1;

   //
   // Color dialog function & values.
   //
   [DllImport("commdlg.dll")]
   public static extern int ChooseColor (ref CHOOSECOLOR lpcc);
   public struct CHOOSECOLOR
   {
      public int lStructSize;
      public IntPtr hwndOwner;
```

```
         public IntPtr hInstance;
         public int rgbResult;
         public IntPtr lpCustColors;
         public int Flags;
         public int lCustData;
         public IntPtr lpfnHook;
         public IntPtr lpTemplateName;
      };
      public const int CC_RGBINIT = 0x00000001;
      public const int CC_FULLOPEN = 0x00000002;
      public const int CC_PREVENTFULLOPEN = 0x00000004;
      public const int CC_ENABLEHOOK = 0x00000010;
      public const int CC_ENABLETEMPLATE = 0x00000020;
      public const int CC_ENABLETEMPLATEHANDLE = 0x00000040;
      public const int CC_SOLIDCOLOR = 0x00000080;
      public const int CC_ANYCOLOR = 0x00000100;

      //
      // Focus functions
      //
      [DllImport("coredll.dll")]
      public static extern IntPtr GetFocus ();
      [DllImport("coredll.dll")]
      public static extern IntPtr SetFocus (IntPtr hWnd);

      public IntPtr GetHwndFromControl(Control ctrl)
      {
         IntPtr hwndControl;

         // Check whether the control has focus.
         if (ctrl.Focused)
         {
            hwndControl = GetFocus();
         }
         else
         {
            IntPtr ipFocus = GetFocus();
            ctrl.Focus();
            hwndControl = GetFocus();
            SetFocus(ipFocus);
         }

         return hwndControl;
      }

   } // class
} // namespace
```

LISTING 16.14: Creating and Summoning the Color Picker Dialog Box

```
//
// Display the color picker dialog box -- foreground color.
//
private void
mitemTextSetColor_Click(object sender, EventArgs e)
{
   ChooseColorDlg ccdlg = new ChooseColorDlg();
   ccdlg.Init(this);
   if (ccdlg.ShowDialog(ref m_clrText))
   {
      Invalidate();
      DisplayRGBComponents();
   }
}

//
// Display the color picker dialog box -- background color.
//
private void
mitemBackgroundSetColor_Click(object sender, EventArgs e)
{
   ChooseColorDlg ccdlg = new ChooseColorDlg();
   ccdlg.Init(this);
   if (ccdlg.ShowDialog(ref m_clrBack))
   {
      Invalidate();
      DisplayRGBComponents();
   }
}
```

CONCLUSION

You now have the complete story on all the different ways to draw text in the .NET Compact Framework. This chapter discussed the two overloaded versions of the `DrawString` method, both of which accept a font and a brush as parameters. The font specifies the shape and size of text to be drawn; the brush determines the color. Brushes are useful for drawing text, as the examples in this chapter show.

In the next chapter, we step a bit out of bounds to address a subject that is important to some programmers: creating hard-copy output. We say we are stepping out of bounds because the .NET Compact Framework itself has no support for printing. But that does not mean it is not important for some types of applications. To help you assess some of the available choices, in the next chapter we present four different ways to print.

17
Printing

This chapter describes a model for printing called the printing pipeline *and presents four approaches to printing from a .NET Compact Framework program.*

A DECADES-OLD BELIEF is that paper output will eventually be eliminated through the use of computers. Sometimes referred to as the *paperless office*, the idea returns whenever a new use of computers gains widespread acceptance. In the 1980s, the impetus was the rise of personal computers with word processing software. In the 1990s, the widespread use of e-mail and of the World Wide Web triggered predictions about the demise of paper output. We believe the elimination of paper output will never happen because we see the opposite taking place: Instead of reducing it, computer use increases the need for paper output.[1]

Whether or not some future paperless office ever becomes a reality, the focus of this chapter is on helping you create printed output today on a Pocket PC or other Windows CE–powered smart device. In so doing, we wish to dispel two myths about printing and the Pocket PC.

One myth suggests that users of Pocket PCs and other mobile devices do not want to print. However, we have spoken to countless developers and technical support people who tell us that their users do want to print.

1. This issue is explored in *The Myth of the Paperless Office* by Abigail Sellen and Richard Harper (Cambridge, MA: MIT Press, 2001).

But the obstacles to getting printing to work have defeated all but the most determined power users. Most give up or rely on other means for creating hard copy.

A second myth follows on the heels of the first: that a Pocket PC cannot create printed output. Several factors seem to contribute to this myth. First, none of the built-in Pocket PC applications support printing, including Pocket Word and Pocket Excel. Second, a Pocket PC has nothing that looks like a printer port: no Centronics parallel port, no serial port, and no USB port. Many Pocket PCs have a USB synchronization cradle and so might seem to allow a USB connection to a printer. But the provided USB cable is used to connect to a computer—the flat end of a USB cable—and a square, printer-compatible connector is not typically available. With this evidence, it is easy to see why some people have concluded that Pocket PCs cannot print.

Can Pocket PCs support printing? The answer is an emphatic yes! To support this claim, this chapter demonstrates not just one but four different ways to print from a Pocket PC or other .NET Compact Framework–enabled Windows CE device:

- Printing by sending output directly to a printer
- Printing with GDI rendering to built-in device drivers
- Printing with GDI rendering to device drivers provided with the HP Mobile Printing Toolkit[2]
- Printing with PrinterCE, a product of FieldSoftware[3] that has a built-in graphics API and built-in printer device drivers

Users of mobile devices who are willing to try these techniques find that printing from a Pocket PC or mobile phone is a delightful experience, putting users back in control of their own data.

---

2. The HP Mobile Printing Toolkit is an add-on library for Pocket PCs. For details, visit http://www.hpdevelopersolutions.com/mobile/.

3. FieldSoftware provides add-on libraries for Pocket PC and other Windows CE–powered devices. For details, visit http://www.fieldsoftware.com.

The Printing Pipeline

To set the stage for this coverage of printing from a .NET Compact Framework program, we start with a discussion of the *printing pipeline*. The printing pipeline is a model for printing that applies equally well to enterprise printing on dedicated print servers and to printing from mobile and embedded client devices. There are five elements of the printing pipeline.

1. A *printing program* creates the request to print.
2. A *graphics subsystem* converts drawing commands into a printer-specific page description language (PDL).
3. A *print job* is a stream of bytes containing details of what is to be printed.
4. An *I/O channel* carries the print job from the printing program to the printer.
5. A *printer* converts the print job to a physical form (ink[4] on paper[5]).

A printing program starts the printing process by connecting to a graphics subsystem and submitting a set of drawing calls. These calls are converted by the graphics subsystem into a print job. The print job is ultimately just a stream of bytes that gets carried through an I/O channel to a printer. A printer responds to the byte stream by creating whatever output it is capable of.

The sequence just described follows the chronology of printing. However, we are going to address the printing pipeline in the reverse order, starting at the printer end of the pipeline because the capabilities and features of the printer drive the choices available at each earlier stage in the printing pipeline.

---

4. By "ink" we mean anything commonly used in printers to make marks on paper (or other media), including toner, dye, wax, and heat on thermal-sensitive paper.
5. While paper is the most common print media, some students in our printer driver workshops create some other interesting output as well, including engravings on metal or wood. Some "printed" output creates no paper output but instead reformats some data; the best-known example is output as Adobe Acrobat (`*.pdf`) files.

Printer

A printer receives a print stream and responds by putting ink on paper. In a sense, the printer is the ultimate embedded device. We say this because many printers have fast, capable CPUs that run sophisticated software,[6] just like a PC or other computer, and yet few people think of printers as computers.[7] Printers as a device category long ago achieved a status that the Pocket PC is today striving to achieve. Namely, a printer is considered to be an appliance.

We say that printers have achieved the status of appliances because of how easy they are to set up. Printers work without requiring users to think about *how* they work. A user can normally take a new printer out of a box, plug it in, and start printing. On Windows desktop systems, local printer support for plug and play means that the correct printer driver gets installed with little user intervention. On good days, printers are reliable, dependable, consistent, and therefore invisible. Printers have done well because they have far more good days than bad.

One reason that printers are easier to use than desktop (or mobile) computers is that they operate in batch mode. When new features are added to computer software programs, the user interface almost inevitably gets more complicated. This statement is as true for application programs as it is for the operating system itself. On the other hand, many new features added to printers produce tangible results—faster output, improved text quality, richer grayscale support, high-quality printing of photographs—without adding complexity. Like a faithful dog, a printer waits patiently for its master to throw it something to chew on; the printer responds by chewing up the print stream and using it to create the hard-copy output.

Page Description Languages (PDLs)

Some printers support proprietary PDLs whose syntaxes are known only to the printer manufacturer. For some PDLs, the syntaxes have been made

6. The control software embedded in a printer's ROM is referred to as its *firmware*.

7. When Apple Computer shipped the Apple LaserWriter in 1985, some people said it was the most powerful computer that Apple had ever made (owing perhaps to its fast CPU).

publicly available. Two of the better-known public PDLs in use in printers from a wide range of manufacturers include the following:

- Printer Control Language (PCL) from HP
- Postscript from Adobe Systems

To help you understand these PDLs, we'll provide some background information here.

PCL. HP's PCL has evolved over many years. This printer language began as an effort to standardize the control codes for text-only printers. Subsequent versions added support for font cartridges and rich text. Raster graphic support was added next, followed by vector graphics support. Throughout the evolution, the company focused on building a simple instruction set that could be implemented cheaply in a printer's firmware, thus keeping the cost of printer hardware to a minimum. PCL printers have evolved with an eye toward providing good results with a maximum of efficiency.

PCL is a language in the sense that there are command sequences and rules for how those command sequences (and their arguments) are to be used. PCL commands start with an `Escape` character (hex byte `0x1B` or decimal `27`). Some PCL commands define the desired printer configuration, such as the printing resolution, paper size, and drawing coordinates to use. Other PCL commands set the current font or define fonts and glyphs[8] being downloaded to a printer. Any text not within the bounds of an escape sequence is considered text to be printed. PCL supports three text commands that do not require a leading `Escape` character: carriage return, line feed, and form feed.

Unlike C# and Visual Basic .NET, PCL is not a procedural language. PCL does not support conditional execution, branching, or looping. A stream of PCL does not contain variables that can be defined, named, or

8. A *glyph* is the graphical representation of a character. For example, the 12-point Tahoma *A* and the 14-point Tahoma *A* are two separate glyphs for the same character.

referenced. So PCL does not have the same type of code and data that programmers associate with programming languages. Instead, PCL is a *display-list language* because a print job consists of a list of items to be displayed (or printed). A PCL printer has software that interprets the stream of PCL data and uses that data to create the printed output.

Postscript. Postscript was created at Adobe Systems, whose two founders, Charles Geschke and John Warnock, had been researchers at the Palo Alto Research Center (PARC). They left PARC because they did not agree with the plans that Xerox had for the future of Interpress, a proprietary printer language invented at PARC.[9]

The Postscript language[10] contains a set of drawing primitives, just like PCL. There are commands to set the state of the printer, to define the coordinate system, and to draw text, raster, and vector objects. Postscript has a number of features that are not present in PCL, including the ability to perform complex coordinate transformations such as rotating graphical objects. (With a PCL printer, two-dimensional coordinate transformation—rotation, scaling, and scrolling—must be handled prior to sending a print job to a printer.)

Postscript has elements of modern programming languages that PCL does not. For example, Postscript supports procedures, loops, and conditional execution. Data values can be stored in named variables or in arrays. Postscript provides a rich programming environment, which is one reason that a Postscript printer often requires more resources (a faster CPU and more memory) than a PCL printer.

Postscript is an interesting PDL for several reasons. One is that Postscript was created by a company that does not manufacture or sell printers. Instead, Adobe Systems licenses its software to printer manufacturers. There are other Postscript interpreters besides the ones from Adobe Systems. For example, there exists an open source version of Postscript known

---

9. As described by Henry Chesbrough in *Open Innovation* (Boston, MA: Harvard Business School Press, 2003).

10. For a brief introduction to Postscript, written by Peter Weingartner, visit this URL: http://www.cs.indiana.edu/docproject/programming/postscript/postscript.html.

as Ghostscript. But as the creator of Postscript, Adobe Systems has taken the lead in the development and support of that language.

This chapter focuses on printers and printing, and there are many printers that use Postscript as a PDL. But nothing in Postscript makes it work only with printers. For example, some computers have used Postscript to create graphical output on a display screen—a use that is sometimes called *Display Postscript*.

I/O Channel

Continuing to move backward along the printing pipeline, let's now discuss the I/O channel, which acts like a logical data pipe that starts at the printing program and ends at the printer. The job of the I/O channel is to transport a stream of bytes, without knowing what is contained in those bytes. An I/O channel might be as simple as a cable from a Pocket PC to a printer. Or it could be so complex that it travels from a Pocket PC on one side of the world to a printer on the other side of the world via the Internet. Both are possible; users pick the path that best accomplishes what they are trying to achieve.

To someone writing a printing program, the most important element of the I/O channel is a printer port. On the printer end of the I/O channel, a printer might have one of the following ports:

- Serial port
- Parallel (Centronics) port
- Infrared port
- USB port
- Ethernet wired network
- Wi-Fi (802.11b) wireless network
- Bluetooth wireless network

Microsoft considers serial ports and parallel ports to be outdated technology and recommends USB ports as a better alternative. As a result, many PC vendors are shipping computers without either serial or parallel ports.

Printer vendors have accepted this view of suitable I/O support, and the last few years have seen an increase in the number of USB-only printers targeting the market for smaller, personal printers. All Windows CE devices have an infrared port, and many laptops do as well. Only a few printers have the required infrared printer port, however, so most PC users are not familiar with support for infrared printing. It is, however, more common for users of small devices.

Most medium-sized to large printers ship with a network (i.e., wired Ethernet) connection. Few printers of any size support the relatively new wireless network protocols (i.e., Wi-Fi and Bluetooth). However, we have noticed several aftermarket products that either connect a printer to a Wi-Fi network or add Bluetooth wireless connectivity to a printer.

On the smart-device side of the printing pipeline, a Windows CE–powered smart device can certainly have a serial port, a parallel port, or both. In keeping with the theme established earlier in this book, we are going to focus our attention on the Pocket PC because it represents a well-defined platform. In spite of this focus, we expect this discussion to apply to all Windows CE–powered smart devices.

To establish an I/O channel from a Pocket PC to a printer, you start by exploring available hardware. Because expandability is limited, a built-in choice is preferable to one that requires an add-on card. A Pocket PC does not have the large number of "empty slots" for expansion cards that desktop PCs do. But most Pocket PCs can add one (and sometimes two) I/O cards, which might be a PC card, a Compact Flash card, or a Smart Digital I/O card. If printing is really important, it might be worth dedicating the single expansion slot to that purpose.

For the sake of completeness, we start with the infrared port. Every Pocket PC is equipped with one, so many readers are likely to start here as well. One potential problem is that few printers created for the PC market are equipped with infrared ports. External adapters to add support for infrared—a.k.a. "infrared dongles"—exist but are difficult to find. For example, the clerk in a local computer store gave us a funny look when asked about an infrared dongle. In all fairness, we have heard accounts of success with the use of infrared dongles to support printing; the trick is to a find a printer that has a built-in infrared port.

Another choice, available with every Pocket PC, is to use the ActiveSync synchronization cable to connect to a printer. We have had success creating printed output from a Pocket PC by using a serial synchronization cable attached to the serial port of a printer. One downside to this approach is that serial ports are an endangered species on desktop printers, so in the long term this might not be a viable solution. However, if you have mobile devices that are so equipped and available printers that have a serial port, this could provide a reasonable solution. One reason that serial ports are so widespread is that the hardware for them is so inexpensive[11] and quite reliable.

Most Pocket PCs ship with a USB synchronization cable (or as part of a docking cradle). Given the success of USB printers, this seems like the ideal solution. But it is not, because not all USB devices are created equal. Serial ports are simple devices, with two simple electrical channels. USB cables are also simple, but the USB specification[12] supports 128 channels through a fairly involved protocol. To support a printer, the USB port on a Pocket PC must provide Host Adapter support. Few Pocket PCs support this feature, however.[13]

Some of the higher-end Pocket PCs have built-in support for wireless networking. Pocket PCs generally support one of two standard wireless network standards: Wi-Fi or Bluetooth. Wi-Fi cards allow a Pocket PC to connect to a wireless access point on an Ethernet network. In some cases, a Wi-Fi device can be configured for peer-to-peer (AdHoc) mode.

Bluetooth cards allow a Pocket PC to connect to other Bluetooth-enabled devices. The Bluetooth standard comes from the mobile phone industry and was created with low power consumption in mind. We were able to create a connection from our Pocket PC to a printer equipped with a parallel port by using a printer dongle created by AnyCom.[14]

---

11. Our thanks to Steve Maillet at Entelechy Consulting (http://www.entelechyconsulting.com) for this insight.
12. For details, visit http://www.usb.org.
13. Our thanks to Tim Field at FieldSoftware for pointing out that some Casio and Toshiba products provide Host Adapter support.
14. For product information, visit http://www.anycom.com.

Wi-Fi Development Connections

We have used a pair of Wi-Fi cards to establish an AdHoc mode connection between a Pocket PC and a laptop equipped with Visual Studio .NET 2003. It worked very well for fast download and lightning-fast debugging (no waiting when stepping through code!). It is not quite a fully wireless solution, however, because the Wi-Fi card drains the battery so quickly that we felt compelled to plug the charger into the Pocket PC. Still, it was hard to beat the downloading and debugging speeds.

When a Pocket PC does not have built-in support for the desired I/O channel, we look for an add-on card. To get an idea of available add-on cards, we suggest a visit to an online retailer like Mobile Planet,[15] which specializes in gear for mobile users. On a casual visit to that Web site, we found I/O adapters for serial, USB, wired Ethernet, Wi-Fi, and Bluetooth in all the standard form factors—as PC cards, Compact Flash cards, and Smart Digital I/O cards.

Print Job

The third element in our printing pipeline is the print job, which we define in very generic terms: The print job consists of the data to be printed. We use the term to include all the different forms that the data might take, starting with the data inside the printing program and including work done on that data by a graphical library and associated device drivers. The end result is a stream of bytes that are sent over an I/O channel to a printer.

What we mean by *print job* is broader than what is traditionally meant by this term. To most people, a print job refers to a single file in a print queue that waits to be sent to the printer. We use a broader meaning because of the cost—in time and memory—of transforming data from one form to another. Choosing an optimal approach involves understanding trade-offs between the different approaches. One way to compare the dif-

15. See http://www.mobileplanet.com.

ferent approaches is to benchmark the time each approach takes. Understanding that there are transformations to a print job as it travels from a printing program to a printer can help you understand the differences in benchmark times. Later in this chapter, we present the results of some simple timing tests we performed on our sample printing programs.

Graphics Subsystem

One element in creating graphical output is the API and its supporting libraries and device drivers. A .NET Compact Framework programmer has access to two separate graphical programming interfaces: the native GDI drawing functions available in `coredll.dll` and the managed `System.Drawing` classes in the `system.drawing.dll` library. The managed library supports drawing on the display screen, but not for the printed page. Sending output to the printer from a .NET Compact Framework program requires the use of P/Invoke functions to call native GDI drawing calls (or the use of a third-party library).

Later in this chapter, we provide four sample printing programs. Two programs (`PrintGDI` and `PrintHPMobile`) use the native GDI drawing calls to create printed output. One program (`PrintField`) uses a third-party graphics library to create printed output. The remaining program (`PrintDirect`) does not use a graphics library but sends output directly to a printer using file and socket I/O functions.

Application programmers do not need to know about (and usually do not want to know about) the many details involved in rendering graphical output. A programmer makes a drawing call, the drawing appears—end of story. But when dealing with printed output from Windows CE systems, you do need to know about a key architectural detail. It involves a trade-off made in the printer device driver interface.

In Chapter 1, we discussed that the highest-priority design goal was that Windows CE be small. The Windows CE graphical subsystem was inspired by and derived from the graphical subsystem of the 32-bit Windows operating systems (e.g., Windows NT, Windows 2000, Windows XP). The graphical device driver interface was optimized for the most important graphical device, the display screen. Because display devices are largely raster devices, the graphical device driver interface is devoted entirely to raster output functions. This is important in considering printed output because—just like on desktop Windows—display drivers and printer drivers share a common device driver interface.

As currently implemented, Windows CE treats all printer drivers as raster devices. To draw text to a graphical device, a raster call is made to deliver the raster image of a character to a device. When a program draws a vector object such as a circle or a rectangle to a graphical device, the system responds by drawing that object to a raster buffer. This approach makes display drivers very small and somewhat easy to write. It also means that all data sent to a printer is first converted to raster graphics.

The benefit of this approach is that it makes printer drivers small and simple as well. The trade-off here is that the output of printer drivers is all raster graphics, which can make the size of print jobs larger than they might otherwise be. This, in turn, can make printing slow. How much slower? In one set of benchmarks, presented later in this chapter, printing to a network printer took about twice as long when using the Windows CE printer driver compared to printing directly to a printer. We expect the difference to be even greater when printing through other, slower ports because the bottleneck for printing is normally the I/O channel.

There are alternatives, such as sending a stream of raw, binary output directly to a printer—an approach that we refer to as *direct printing*. This approach has the advantage that it provides you, the programmer, with total control over the output. The downside is that, except for the simplest output, the direct printing approach may take more work than other approaches and can make your program dependent on one specific printer family or printer model. Except in the case of vertical-market or vendor-specific software, we expect that few programmers are going to take this approach.

Another alternative is to use third-party graphic libraries and printing subsystems. There are some third-party applications that support end-user printing under Windows CE, as any decent Web search engine can show. But there are not a lot of programmer tools that provide this support. One that we have heard a lot about is a library called PrinterCE from FieldSoftware. We use PrinterCE for a sample program in this chapter.

FieldSoftware provides two printing libraries, one to support native-code development (PrinterCE SDK) and another for managed-code development (PrinterCE.NetCF SDK). Our focus is on the managed-code library. Both libraries provide a proprietary graphical API and also a set of built-in printer device drivers. Because it provides an alternative print path to what is natively available with a Windows CE printer driver, PrinterCE can be a bit more efficient. As shown in our benchmark tests, that translates into faster printing times than more traditional printing models provide.

Printing Program

A printing program collects and organizes some set of data. Such programs normally do other things in addition to printing. For example, a program that prints might also allow a user to enter and edit data, monitor the operation of some piece of machinery and record its status, store the data collected, or display the data on the screen. The printing portion must work in a way that does not interfere with the program's other tasks.

The task of printing often gets delegated to a dedicated worker thread. By separating the task from a program's main user interface thread, printing can be accomplished in the background while other work takes place. When this is done, safeguards are needed to prevent the actions of the printing threads from adversely affecting the actions of other threads and vice versa. For example, a conflict exists when one thread deletes the contents of a buffer while another thread is reading that same buffer as input to printing.

Why Don't the Sample Printing Programs Use Background Threads?

A background thread is helpful when printing, and this technique is commonly employed by production programs. However, we do not use background threads in the sample programs in this chapter because we want to keep the samples as simple as possible.

If a program does not support printing, getting printed output requires extraordinary measures. With that support, all that is needed is a mouse click (or, in the case of a Pocket PC, a stylus tap). We do not mean to suggest that creating printed output is at all simple for the programmer. In fact, the opposite is more likely to be the case. Anyone who has struggled to create a good-looking on-screen view of a program knows how much time and energy goes into that effort. The same effort—and sometimes more—is required to get usable and attractive printed output. So put that effort into a project only when your users really want it or when you are sure they will get value from the output.

Programming for Printed Output

It seems safe to say that any program that accepts input from a user ought to be able to print that data. So we are surprised by the lack of printing support from two standard Pocket PC applications: Pocket Word and Pocket Excel. This omission is, no doubt, an element of the myth that a Pocket PC cannot print. But of course there are methods for printing Pocket Word and Pocket Excel files. One is by sending those files through ActiveSync to their desktop counterparts and printing from a desktop Windows system. Another is to use an add-on program to enable printing from the Pocket PC itself. A casual visit to the Handango[16] Web site reveals five programs that enable printing of Pocket Word and Pocket Excel programs (and other vendors offer some options too).

Not all programs need to print. But any program that interacts with users is probably going to be more useful if it can print. As a simple example, consider a calculator program like the one bundled with the Pocket PC or the one bundled with Windows XP. Neither can print. You might argue that such programs do not need a printing feature. Their job, after all, is combining numbers and displaying a result; no hard copy is required.

Is there any use in creating hard copy from a calculator? A visit to an office supply store reveals that many calculators produce output on rolled papers. Cash registers in even the smallest retail store are nothing but glorified calculators that produce printed output. Anyone who spends time

16. See http://www.handango.com.

adding up lists of numbers probably could get some use from being able to print those lists. Hard copy helps when you're creating an expense report for reimbursement, reconciling a check register, or organizing receipts for a tax return. Sometimes a spreadsheet is overkill, and for those cases, printout from a calculator can be handy. Perhaps the Pocket PC needs a more capable calculator![17]

Overview of Printing Sample Programs

The four sample programs[18] in this chapter demonstrate four different approaches to printing, as summarized in Table 17.1. We do not claim that this is an exhaustive list; other third-party libraries may exist that support the creation of printed output from a Windows CE program. Intermec, for example, has a printing control that allows a .NET Compact Framework program to print to an Intermec printer. However, these sample programs do provide some idea of the range of choices available for producing hard-copy output from a Pocket PC or other Windows CE–powered smart device.

TABLE 17.1: The Four Sample Printing Programs Featured in This Chapter

Sample Program	Description
`PrintDirect`	Uses a `FileStream` object for direct printing to a local printer connected to a hardware port, or a remote printer that can be reached with either an IP address or a universal naming convention (UNC) network address
`PrintGDI`	Creates output by using a Windows CE printer driver and calls to GDI drawing functions supported by Windows CE
`PrintHPMobile`	Creates output by using the HP Mobile Printing printer driver and calls to GDI drawing functions supported by Windows CE
`PrintField`	Creates output by using PrinterCE, a library from FieldSoftware (http://www.fieldsoftware.com)

17. Windows XP has a similar need.

18. As in previous chapters, all of the source code for this chapter's sample programs is available for download from the following URL: http://www.paulyao.com/cfbook/code.

Each of the sample programs in this chapter uses a common starting point: a program for editing text files. The first version of this program was the sample named `DialogBoxes`, which appeared in Chapter 9 in our discussion of dialog boxes. Then in Chapter 11, we enhanced the program by adding file I/O support and also use of the system registry to save and restore program settings; for that chapter, we renamed the program to `Storage`. We provide four different ways to finish this program in this chapter with the addition of four different approaches to printing.

The first sample program listed in Table 17.1, `PrintDirect`, creates a print job by sending a print stream directly to a printer. With nothing between the printing program and the printer, this is the fastest way to create printed output. But there are trade-offs. This approach works only with printers that can accept and print text-only output, which includes printers that support HP's page description language, PCL. Output must be text, and you can print with only a single font (whatever default font is supported by the printer).

The last three choices on the list support a richer type of printed output. These programs support printing both raster and vector graphics as well as printing text with different fonts. Each of these approaches involves doing some of the work on the Pocket PC and some on the printer itself. In contrast, for the direct printing case, very little work is actually done on the Pocket PC because we send raw, unprocessed text to the printer.

For the cases that don't involve direct printing, a printer device driver is involved. Two of the choices involve a standard Windows CE printer device driver (the Windows CE printer driver and the HP Mobile Printing printer driver). The use of the PrinterCE library involves a proprietary printer driver technology that FieldSoftware created and owns.

Table 17.2 summarizes the details of how our printing pipeline model applies to each of our four sample programs.

Timing Tests for the Sample Printing Programs

Table 17.3 summarizes our timing results for printing a short text file (162 lines) onto a networked printer. We tested the *click-to-clunk time*, a term commonly used for benchmarking printers. Print job timing starts with a *click*, which means the last user action needed to request the print job has

TABLE 17.2: **Mapping the Sample Printing Programs to the Printing Pipeline Model**

Element	`PrintDirect`	`PrintGDI`	`PrintHPMobile`	`PrintField`
Printing program	Native or managed	Native or managed	Native or managed	Native or managed
Graphics subsystem	None	• Graphic API provided by GDI functions in `coredll.dll` • Rendering done by Windows CE printer drivers (such as `pcl.dll`)	• Graphic API provided by GDI functions in `coredll.dll` • Rendering done by Windows CE printer drivers (such as `pcl.dll`)	• Graphic API provided by PrinterCE functions in `PrinterCE.NetCF.dll` • Rendering done by a built-in printer driver model
Print job	Application-generated byte stream	Printer driver–generated byte stream	Printer driver–generated byte stream	FieldSoftware printer driver–generated byte stream
I/O channel	Provided by program	Provided by port monitor	Provided by port monitor	Provided with proprietary support in `PrCE_NetCF.dll`
Printer	PCL and compatible printers	PCL laser, PCL inkjet, and other printers with Windows CE–compatible printers	A select set of HP, Epson, and Canon printers	A wide range of vendors, including Brother, Canon, Epson, HP, Seiko, Extech, O'Neil, Zebra, Citizen, IPX, and SiPix

TABLE 17.3: Printing Times for the Sample Printing Programs

Program	Comments	Time (Seconds)	Job Size (Bytes)
`PrintDirect`	Sent text to a printer using a `FileStream` object	19.7	5430
`PrintField`	Sent text to a printer using Field-Software's PrinterCE .NET Compact Framework library	25.1	132,295
`PrintGDI`	Sent text to a printer using GDI drawing calls and the built-in PCL printer driver	36.2	159,046
`PrintHPMobile`	Sent text to a printer using GDI drawing calls and printer driver support provided by HP Mobile Printing	50.2	334,508

started. Timing ends when the last page of a print job exits the printer, which is the *clunk*.

For each of the tests, we printed the same text file, a source file from this chapter's direct printing sample program.[19] We printed to a networked PCL-compatible laser printer from a networked Pocket PC. We printed each print job three times and averaged the times for the results shown in Table 17.3. We determined the print job size from a pop-up window that reported at the end of every print job, courtesy of Pocket PC Networking.

In setting up our tests, we checked to make sure that the output from each of the test cases produced similar output. In particular, we wanted the output from each program to match the output from every other program. This required two changes, both involving the selection and handling of fonts.

We set the font for each case to 12-point Courier New, a standard Windows CE fixed-pitch font. We chose this font to make the output from each program appear identical to the output obtained by direct printing (the one case in which we did not have control of font selection).

19. The specific file we used was `PrintJob_Direct.cs`.

A second change we made was to hard-code the line height for the program that printed with the PrinterCE library. As we detail later in this chapter, PrinterCE reports a different text height from that reported by GDI. This allowed the output from each program to be identical, again increasing our confidence in the validity of our timing tests.

Our Results

One conclusion seems obvious: Smaller print jobs printed faster. The best printing times were for the direct printing sample program (`PrintDirect`). The primary disadvantage of this approach, of course, is that it is a text-only approach to printing. We had no control over font selection because the sample sent raw text with no font commands. Our output used the default font for the printer, which was 12-point Courier. As suggested by the fastest printing time and smallest print job size, the chief value of the direct printing times are that they suggest a lower limit for possible printing time.

The printing times for the PrinterCE sample program (`PrintField`) were the second best. We attribute the faster times to the superior printer driver architecture. In our discussion of the graphics subsystem earlier in this chapter, we mentioned that the Windows CE printer driver model forces all output to be rasterized. Until Microsoft improves the architecture of Windows CE printer drivers, custom solutions—like that provided by FieldSoftware—are going to have the edge with smaller print jobs and faster printing times.

The GDI sample program (`PrintGDI`) and the HP Mobile Printing sample program (`PrintHPMobile`) were created from the same base program. Both use the same native GDI drawing calls—and the underlying printer device driver model—to create output. They differ in how they select a printer and create a device context. These two programs were the slowest among the four. While we were able to get somewhat faster printing when we selected draft mode, the text appeared light gray and was harder to read than the text output by the other two programs.

We created this timing test to provide a basis for comparing four printing methods. This is a very limited test, however, because we printed only text to keep the test simple. Many applications have some requirement for vector drawing (lines on forms) as well as raster graphics (pictures, scanned images, and so on). If you need to decide which library to use and you wish to use printing time as a basis for comparison, we suggest that you create your own test programs to reflect the mix of text, raster, and vector graphics you want to print. Our test also involved a single I/O channel, which is the fastest I/O channel available. We expect slower results from other I/O channels. We recommend including that variable in any tests you conduct so you have a more accurate idea of the expected performance when printing from your Pocket PC programs.

Pocket PC Printing Support

The Pocket PC supports a Print dialog box as one of the common dialog boxes in the system's `commdlg.dll` library. The Print dialog box displays a list of available printer drivers and a set of printer ports, as shown in Figure 17.1. This dialog box looks like the Print dialog boxes you encounter on desktop Windows systems, but do not let its looks deceive you. The desktop Print dialog box displays the results of a dynamic discovery process for available printers and printer ports.

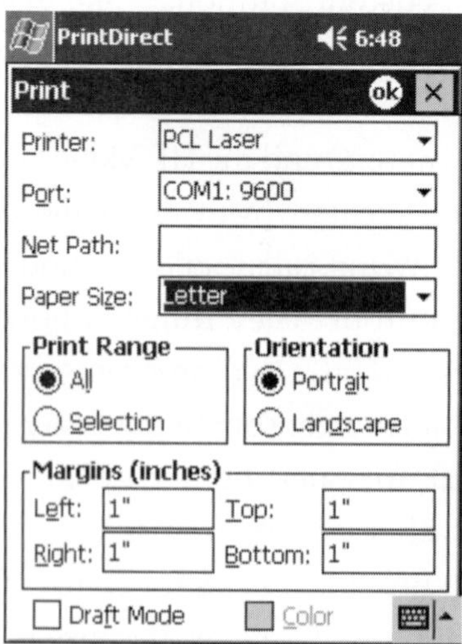

FIGURE 17.1: The Print dialog box on a Pocket PC

On a Pocket PC, the Print dialog box displays available printer drivers and the printer ports as defined in the registry. These settings are statically read from the registry, not dynamically queried as on the desktop. Available printer drivers appear under the `HKEY_LOCAL_MACHINE\Printers` key. Available printer ports appear under the `HKEY_LOCAL_MACHINE\Printers\Ports` key.

The reliance on static registry settings can result in a confusing situation because choices that appear in the Print dialog box might not be available. One example is the `LPT1:` port. This appears as a standard printer port even when no driver actually supports this port. We know that this port does not exist—even though it appears in the Print dialog box—because the port name does not appear in the active drivers list, which is dynamically updated in the following registry key: `HKEY_LOCAL_MACHINE\Drivers\Active`.

While the .NET Compact Framework libraries support the creation of graphical output, the various `System.Drawing` classes support drawing only on the display screen. The drawing classes do not support printers. For this reason, a .NET Compact Framework program must call native GDI drawing functions or a third-party graphics library for printed output that is more graphical than simple single-font text.

The Print Dialog Box

Two of our sample programs use the Print dialog box support built into the Pocket PC and two do not.[20] The built-in Pocket PC Print dialog box is a common dialog box that is part of the Win32 API. The coding for each common dialog box follows this pattern: Fill a data structure, then call a function. Unfortunately, the .NET Compact Framework supports only two common dialog boxes: File Open and File Save (which we discussed in Chapter 9). To get access to the Print dialog box, we must resort to some P/Invoke code to access the Print dialog box function (`PageSetupDlgW`) found in the Windows CE `commdlg.dll` library. Listing 17.1 contains the declarations for the

20. Two libraries, the `PrintField` library and the HP Mobile Printing library, have built-in Print dialog boxes.

PrintSetupDlg class, which we create to wrap the elements needed to summon the Print dialog box.

Printing Support on the Desktop .NET Framework

The desktop .NET Framework has a set of printing classes provided in the System.Drawing.Printing namespace. None of these classes are available in the .NET Compact Framework. A word on those classes is nonetheless worthwhile because today's .NET Compact Framework programmers are tomorrow's desktop .NET programmers.

The desktop .NET Framework supports printing in the form of two separate Print dialog boxes and support for print preview. The various printing classes support printer-specific features, such as paper size, paper type, input bins, and print margins.

There are no printer-specific drawing classes. Instead, output to a printer relies on the same drawing methods defined in the Graphics[21] class. In other words, the same set of drawing functions used to draw on the display screen are also used to draw on the printed page.

LISTING 17.1: Print Dialog Box Declarations in the PrintSetupDlg Class

```
// YaoDurant.Drawing.PrintSetupDlg.cs - Generic Print
// dialog box.
//
// Code from _.NET Compact Framework Programming with C#_
// and _.NET Compact Framework Programming with Visual Basic .NET_
// Authored by Paul Yao and David Durant.
//

using System;
using System.Runtime.InteropServices;
using YaoDurant.Win32;

namespace YaoDurant.Drawing
```

21. Fully qualified name: System.Drawing.Graphics.

```
{
   /// <summary>
   /// Summary description for YaoDurant
   /// </summary>
   public class PrintSetupDlg
   {
      //-----------------------------------------------------
      // Declarations for native printing dialog boxes
      //-----------------------------------------------------
      [DllImport("commdlg.dll", CharSet=CharSet.Unicode)]
      public static extern
      int PageSetupDlgW (ref PAGESETUPDLGSTRUCT lppsd);
      [DllImport("commdlg.dll", CharSet=CharSet.Unicode)]
      public static extern int CommDlgExtendedError ();

      //-----------------------------------------------------
      // Clean up memory allocated by the call to PageSetupDlgW.
      //-----------------------------------------------------
      public static
      void Close (ref PAGESETUPDLGSTRUCT lppsd)
      {
         if (lppsd.hDevMode != IntPtr.Zero)
            NativeHeap.LocalFree(lppsd.hDevMode);
         if (lppsd.hDevNames != IntPtr.Zero)
            NativeHeap.LocalFree(lppsd.hDevNames);
      }

      //-----------------------------------------------------
      // Allocate and initialize PAGESETUPDLGSTRUCT structure.
      //-----------------------------------------------------
      public static
      void InitDlgStruct(
         ref PAGESETUPDLGSTRUCT psd,
         IntPtr hwndParent)
      {
         psd.lStructSize = Marshal.SizeOf(psd);
         psd.Flags = 0;
         psd.hwndOwner = hwndParent;
      }

      //-----------------------------------------------------
      // Display the dialog box.
      //-----------------------------------------------------
      public static
      int ShowDialog(ref PAGESETUPDLGSTRUCT psd)
      {
         return PageSetupDlgW( ref psd);
      }
```

continues

continued

```
    //-----------------------------------------------------------
    // Fetch the error string.
    //-----------------------------------------------------------
    public static
    string GetErrorString()
    {
       // User clicked cancel [x] button -or- we have an error.
       int ierrDlg = CommDlgExtendedError();
       if (ierrDlg == 0)
          return "Ok";

       string strReason = string.Empty;

       if (ierrDlg >= (int)PDERR.PRINTERCODES &&
          ierrDlg <= (int)PDERR.DEFAULTDIFFERENT)
       {
          PDERR pderr = (PDERR)ierrDlg;
          strReason = "PDERR_" + pderr.ToString();
       }
       else
       {
          strReason = "0x" + ierrDlg.ToString("x");
       }

       return strReason;
    }


    //-----------------------------------------------------------
    public static
    string QueryOutputPort(ref PAGESETUPDLGSTRUCT lppsd)
    {
       // Create a managed structure for DEVNAMES.
       DEVNAMES dn = new DEVNAMES();
       Marshal.PtrToStructure(lppsd.hDevNames, dn);

       // Get the base address of the native structure.
       int iBase = (int)lppsd.hDevNames;

       // Get the pointer to the output port.
       IntPtr iptrOutput = (IntPtr)(iBase + dn.wOutputOffset);
       string strOutput = Marshal.PtrToStringUni(iptrOutput);

       return strOutput;
    }

 } // class
```

```
//--------------------------------------------------------
//--------------------------------------------------------
public struct PAGESETUPDLGSTRUCT
{
   public int lStructSize;
   public IntPtr hwndOwner;
   public IntPtr hDevMode;  // Return value
   public IntPtr hDevNames; // Return value
   public int Flags;
   public System.Drawing.Point ptPaperSize;
   public System.Drawing.Rectangle rtMinMargin;
   public System.Drawing.Rectangle rtMargin;
   public IntPtr hInstance;
   public int lCustData;
   public IntPtr lpfnPageSetupHook;
   public IntPtr lpfnPagePaintHook;
   public IntPtr reserved; // string lpPageSetupTemplateName;
   public IntPtr hPageSetupTemplate;
};

/* Size of a device name string */
// #define CCHDEVICENAME 32

/* Size of a form name string */
// #define CCHFORMNAME 32

public struct CHARNAME32
{
   public char ch00, ch01, ch02, ch03, ch04;
   public char ch05, ch06, ch07, ch08, ch09;
   public char ch10, ch11, ch12, ch13, ch14;
   public char ch15, ch16, ch17, ch18, ch19;
   public char ch20, ch21, ch22, ch23, ch24;
   public char ch25, ch26, ch27, ch28, ch29;
   public char ch30, ch31;
}

public class DEVNAMES
{
   public short wDriverOffset;
   public short wDeviceOffset;
   public short wOutputOffset;
   public short wDefault;
};

public enum PSD
{
   MINMARGINS = 0x00000001,
   MARGINS = 0x00000002,
```

continues

continued

```
        INTHOUSANDTHSOFINCHES = 0x00000004,
        INHUNDREDTHSOFMILLIMETERS = 0x00000008,
        DISABLEMARGINS = 0x00000010,
        DISABLEPRINTER = 0x00000020,
        DISABLEORIENTATION = 0x00000100,
        RETURNDEFAULT = 0x00000400,
        DISABLEPAPER = 0x00000200,
        ENABLEPAGESETUPHOOK = 0x00002000,
        ENABLEPAGESETUPTEMPLATE = 0x00008000,
        ENABLEPAGESETUPTEMPLATEHANDLE = 0x00020000
    } // enum

    public enum PDERR
    {
        PRINTERCODES = 0x1000,
        SETUPFAILURE = 0x1001,
        PARSEFAILURE = 0x1002,
        RETDEFFAILURE = 0x1003,
        LOADDRVFAILURE = 0x1004,
        GETDEVMODEFAIL = 0x1005,
        INITFAILURE = 0x1006,
        NODEVICES = 0x1007,
        NODEFAULTPRN = 0x1008,
        DNDMMISMATCH = 0x1009,
        CREATEICFAILURE = 0x100A,
        PRINTERNOTFOUND = 0x100B,
        DEFAULTDIFFERENT = 0x100C,
    } // enum

} // namespace
```

Listing 17.2 shows the basic template of how to call the Print dialog box. As with other dialog boxes, we create them when we need them, use them, and then delete them. Doing so helps keep our program's memory footprint small, and (by not creating the dialog box when the program starts to run) it helps minimize the startup time for the program.

LISTING 17.2: Basic Pattern for Calling the Print Dialog Box

```
// Init Print dialog box data.
PAGESETUPDLGSTRUCT psd;
psd = new PAGESETUPDLGSTRUCT();
PrintSetupDlg.InitDlgStruct(ref psd, hwndForm);
```

```
try
{
   // Display the Print dialog box.
   int iErr = PrintSetupDlg.ShowDialog(ref psd);
   if (iErr != 0)
   {
      // Printing
   }
   else
   {
      // Error handling
   }
}
finally
{
   // Clean up resources associated with the Print dialog.
   PrintSetupDlg.Close(ref psd);
}
```

You can use this Print dialog box with any of the four printing approaches that we discuss in this chapter. Both of the third-party libraries (i.e., the HP approach and the FieldSoftware approach) include their own Print dialog boxes. We expect most programmers are going to use the library-specific print dialogs because they provide access to library-specific features. Let's take a look, then, at the four approaches to printing from a .NET Compact Framework program, starting with direct printing.

Direct Printing

One choice for printing involves sending output directly from a printing program to a printer. By sending output directly to a printer, a program takes on two printing pipeline roles: as the printing program and as the graphics subsystem. In the latter role, the program does the work that might otherwise be done by GDI drawing calls and a printer device driver.

The benefit of direct printing is speed and total control. As we described earlier in this chapter, the Windows CE printing model rasterizes all graphical output on the Windows CE device itself. This means that all printed output first gets converted into one or more bitmaps, and the bitmaps themselves get sent to a printer. This works very well for low-cost "dumb" printers. But this printing architecture does not provide any way to take advantage of the work a printer might be able to do. All of the hard work of printing, in other words, is done on the Windows CE end of the printing pipeline, with no higher-level work offloaded to the printer.

A simple way to understand this architecture is to think about what this means. All printed pages are converted into bitmaps. Consider, for example, a letter-size piece of paper printing at 300 dots per inch on a monochrome printer. A page-sized bitmap (with one-inch margins) requires 640K. This is a lot of bytes for a single page of output, especially considering that the same page might have less than 1K of text. By sending output directly to a printer, a program can add printer-specific control codes to help cut down on the size of the print job, which, in turn, helps speed up printing.

In the good old days of MS-DOS programming, direct printing was the only available way to print. In those days, application programs typically shipped with a set of device drivers to control the printer, the display screen, and other hardware. The need for program-specific device drivers was largely eliminated on desktop versions of Windows because of the built-in device drivers that the operating system supports.

Some Windows CE–compatible printer drivers exist, but nowhere near the thousands that are available for desktop Windows. For that reason, and because of the limited storage space on a Windows CE–powered device, it might make sense for a Pocket PC programmer to take the direct approach to printing, just as MS-DOS programmers did.

Direct printing works best when printing in a controlled environment where you know exactly what types of printers are going to be available to your program. For example, direct printing might work well for programs that are part of a single-vendor, turnkey solution. When a printer and a Pocket PC are bundled and sold together as a unit, it might make sense to write programs that support a single printer or a single family of printers.

Our direct printing sample program, `PrintDirect`, provides a minimal direct printing example. It sends text and a few control codes. But if a program is going to be bundled with a special-purpose printer, there is no reason to stop there. For dedicated programs, you no doubt are going to want to use any and all features of the printer to your best advantage.

When creating output for a single printer (or a single class of printers), you can have fun by experimenting with different control codes, printer commands, paper orientations, and so on. Once you have tamed the printer, the next step is to master all the various I/O channels. For example, once your printer is working well with a wired network connection, you might want to explore establishing a serial connection, an infrared connection, or a Bluetooth connection.

There are drawbacks to direct printing. The first is that you are limiting the printers your program can use. Any graphical commands included in your program will be specific to one printer or to one family of printers. If you try to add support for many printers, you might find yourself spending most of your time writing printer-specific code and less time adding features to your program.

If you are creating programs that must work with many different printers that use different PDLs, direct printing probably will not work for you. You might even have problems when the printers use the same PDL but come from different vendors or when you use different generations of printers from the same vendor (there are often variations in how a PDL is implemented on different printers). If any of these describe the printers that might be available to the users of your programs, direct printing is probably not for you.

Another alternative exists. Direct printing can provide a supplement for printers that lack a Windows CE–compatible printer driver. For example, a program could use GDI rendering when printer drivers exist and direct printing for printer models that lack a compatible printer driver. This approach allows more complete coverage for a broader range of printers than a GDI-only approach. The trade-off in this case is that your program would need to have some amount of duplicate code: one set of routines for GDI-based printing and a second set for direct printing.

Direct Printing to a PCL Printer

A characteristic of the PCL language is that the first version, PCL 1, was created for text-only printers. Subsequent versions of PCL maintain backward compatibility with the first version. This is useful to know because a program can create text-only output by sending a stream of text to a PCL printer. The output is limited to text, but sometimes that is all you need. The `PrintDirect` sample program takes advantage of this fact.

Our sample program sends the simplest possible PCL—text with the three text control codes. Not surprisingly, we get only text for output, and the text appears in the default font for the printer. For some HP printers, the default font is 12-point Courier. Other vendors may use a different default font. In some cases, a user can set a printer's default font from the printer's control panel. Table 17.4 shows the command codes supported by all PCL printers.

It would be a simple matter to add more PCL commands to create richer types of output. We could, for example, request a different font. Other PCL commands could be used to draw lines, such as might appear on an order form. A little more work would be needed to send raster data to a printer, but that certainly is possible. To understand the limits of the kind of output you can create, you would need to study the available commands on whatever printer you were targeting.

Our sample program demonstrates direct printing to a PCL printer, but direct printing is not limited to just PCL printers. You can send output directly to any printer that supports any PDL. The only requirement is that you know what specific control codes are supported by the printers available to your users.

TABLE 17.4: Text Command Codes for All PCL Printers

Command	Action	Decimal/ Hexadecimal	C# Literal String	Visual Basic .NET Constant
Carriage return	Moves the print head to the start of the line	13/D	`"\r"`	`vbCr`
Line feed	Advances the paper one line	10/A	`"\n"`	`vbLf`
Form feed	Ejects the page from the printer	12/C	`"\f"`	`vbFormFeed`

`PrintDirect` does not produce any output on Postscript printers because—unlike a PCL printer—a Postscript printer cannot accept a print job that consists of only the text to be displayed. With just a little knowledge of Postscript, it would not take a lot of effort to modify the sample to be compatible with Postscript. In part, this is simple because the interpreter inside a Postscript printer accepts command input as text. We would simply need to add a header that tells the interpreter that what we are sending is indeed a valid sequence of Postscript commands, then embed each text string in the proper command, and finally add support for ejecting each page when it is done. If you are interested in Postscript, you might like to try this.

A Sample Program: `PrintDirect`

Like the other sample programs in this chapter, `PrintDirect` is built on the text editor created in Chapters 9 (`DialogBoxes`) and 11 (`Storage`). When a user selects the File→Print... menu item, the event handler from `PrintDirect.cs`, shown in Listing 17.3, gets executed. It displays the standard Print dialog box shown earlier in Figure 17.1.

Listing 17.3: Handling the File→Print... Menu Selection (from `PrintDirect.cs`)

```
IntPtr hwndForm;
private void mitemFilePrint_Click(object sender, EventArgs e)
{
   // Init the Print dialog box data.
   PAGESETUPDLGSTRUCT psd;
   psd = new PAGESETUPDLGSTRUCT();
   PrintSetupDlg.InitDlgStruct(ref psd, hwndForm);

   try
   {
      // Display the Print dialog box.
      int iErr = PrintSetupDlg.ShowDialog(ref psd);
      if (iErr != 0)
      {
         // Fetch the port name from printer setup data.
         string strPort;
         strPort = PrintSetupDlg.QueryOutputPort(ref psd);
```

continues

continued

```
            // Check whether the port is an IP address.
            if (PrintJob_Socket.IsIPAddress(strPort))
            {
               PrintJob_Socket.PrintText(textInput, strPort);
            }
            else
            {
               // Send the text to the selected port.
               PrintJob_Direct.PrintText(textInput, strPort);
            }
         }
         else
         {
            string strErr = PrintSetupDlg.GetErrorString();
            if (strErr != "Ok")
            {
               MessageBox.Show(strErr, "PrintDirect");
            }
         }
      }
      catch
      {
         MessageBox.Show("Error printing. ", "PrintDirect");
      }
      finally
      {
         // Clean up resources associated with the Print dialog.
         PrintSetupDlg.Close(ref psd);
      }
   }
```

The Print dialog box collects several pieces of information from a user, but our program is interested in only one thing: the port name.

A port name takes several forms. Here are the port names as they appear in the default settings:

- `COM1: 57600`
- `COM1: 9600`
- `IRDA`
- `LPT1:`
- `Network`

When a user selects either of the two choices for the `COM1:` serial port, the string that gets returned with the port name includes the expected baud rate for the port. We strip this out in our code, and we have no special handling for establishing the baud rate.

When the user selects a network printer, the returned port name is the string that the user types in the textbox labeled "Net Path." This can be a network path in the form of `\\<server>\<printer>`, as in `\\YaoDurant-Svr\Laser1`. The `PrintDirect` program treats a UNC printer name and a local port name the same way: It creates a `FileStream`[22] object using the network name or port name as the path. This is demonstrated in Listing 17.4.

LISTING 17.4: Direct Printing to a Port (from `PrintJob_Direct.cs`)

```
private const byte CR = 0x0a;
private const byte LF = 0x0d;
private const byte FF = 0x0c;

//---------------------------------------------------------
//---------------------------------------------------------
public static void PrintText(TextBox textIn, string strPort)
{
   // Open the printer port.
   System.IO.FileStream fs;
   fs = new System.IO.FileStream(strPort, FileMode.Create);
   if (fs == null)
   {
      throw (new ApplicationException("Cannot open port. "));
   }

   try
   {
      // Split the input data into separate lines of text.
      char [] achNewLine = new char[] { '\n' };
      String [] astrSplit;
      astrSplit = textIn.Text.Split(achNewLine);

      // Calculate the longest string in the document.
      int cchMax = 0;
      int cstr = astrSplit.Length;
      for (int i = 0; i < cstr; i++)
      {
```

continues

22. Fully qualified name: `System.IO.FileStream`.

continued

```
            if (astrSplit[i].Length > cchMax)
                cchMax = astrSplit[i].Length;
        }

        // Allocate the conversion buffer.
        byte[] byteData = new Byte[cchMax];
        char[] chData = new Char[cchMax];
        System.Text.Encoder d;
        d = System.Text.Encoding.UTF8.GetEncoder();

        // Loop through the list of strings.
        for (int i = 0; i < cstr; i++)
        {
            int cch = astrSplit[i].Length;
            if (cch > 0)
            {
                chData = astrSplit[i].ToCharArray();

                // Convert the Unicode string to UTF-8 encoding.
                d.GetBytes(chData, 0, cch, byteData, 0, true);

                // Output the bytes to the printer.
                fs.Write(byteData, 0, cch);
            }

            // Put a carriage return at the line end.
            byte[] byteCrLf = new byte[] { CR };
            fs.Write(byteCrLf, 0, 1);
        }

        // Put a form feed at the end of the document.
        byte[] byteFF = new byte[] { FF };
        fs.Write(byteFF, 0, 1);
    }
    finally
    {
        // Close the file stream.
        fs.Close();
    }
}
```

The `PrintDirect` program also supports connecting to network printers identified by an IP address. To do so, however, it must take a different approach to creating the output. The reason is that IP port connections cannot be accomplished using the `FileStream` class. (What you get instead are files whose names consist of the IP address.) To connect to a printer by IP address, you must instead use the `Socket`[23] class as demonstrated in Listing 17.5.

LISTING 17.5: Direct Printing to an IP Printer (from `PrintJob_Socket.cs`)

```
public class PrintJob_Socket
{
   private const byte CR = 0x0a;
   private const byte LF = 0x0d;
   private const byte FF = 0x0c;

   //-------------------------------------------------------------
   //-------------------------------------------------------------
   public static void PrintText(TextBox textIn, string strPort)
   {
      // Split the input data into separate lines of text.
      char [] achNewLine = new char[] { '\n' };
      String [] astrSplit;
      astrSplit = textIn.Text.Split(achNewLine);

      // Calculate the longest string in the document.
      int cchMax = 0;
      int cstr = astrSplit.Length;
      for (int i = 0; i < cstr; i++)
      {
         if (astrSplit[i].Length > cchMax)
            cchMax = astrSplit[i].Length;
      }

      // Allocate the conversion buffer.
      byte[] byteData = new Byte[cchMax];
      char[] chData = new Char[cchMax];
      System.Text.Encoder d;
      d = System.Text.Encoding.UTF8.GetEncoder();

      Socket s = null;

      try
      {
         // Connect to the printer.
         s = new Socket(AddressFamily.InterNetwork,
            SocketType.Stream, ProtocolType.IP);
         IPAddress addr = IPAddress.Parse(strPort);
         IPEndPoint ipep = new IPEndPoint(addr, 9100);
         s.Connect(ipep);
```

continues

23. Fully qualified name: `System.Net.Sockets.Socket`.

continued

```
            // Loop through the list of strings.
            for (int i = 0; i < cstr; i++)
            {
               int cch = astrSplit[i].Length;
               if (cch > 0)
               {
                  chData = astrSplit[i].ToCharArray();

                  // Convert the Unicode string to UTF-8 encoding.
                  d.GetBytes(chData, 0, cch, byteData, 0, true);

                  // Output the bytes to the printer.
                  s.Send(byteData,0, cch,SocketFlags.None);
               }

               // Put a carriage return at the line end.
               byte[] byteCrLf = new byte[] { CR };
               s.Send(byteCrLf,0, 1,SocketFlags.None);
            }

            // Put a form feed at the end of the document.
            byte[] byteFF = new byte[] { FF };
            s.Send(byteFF,0, 1,SocketFlags.None);
         }
         finally
         {
            s.Close();
         }
      }

      //-----------------------------------------------------------
      public static bool IsIPAddress(string strIn)
      {
         bool bRetVal = true;
         try
         {
            IPAddress.Parse(strIn);
         }
         catch
         {
            bRetVal = false;
         }

         return bRetVal;
      }

   } // class
```

One complication for our program is that all strings in a .NET Compact Framework program are Unicode strings. But a PCL printer does not understand Unicode, so we must convert each string into an array of 8-bit characters, which are then sent to the printer. We accomplish this Unicode-to-ASCII conversion with an encoder from the `System.Text` namespace.

Getting the Right Version of `fontlist.dll`

All of the sample programs in this chapter use a native DLL, `fontlist.dll`. The role of that library is to create a list of available fonts. When you build and download the printer programs to the emulator, make sure to include the Intel x86 emulator version of the font library. When building and downloading for Pocket PCs, make sure to include the StrongARM version of the font library.

Rendering with GDI

A more traditional approach for creating hard-copy output—more traditional for Windows programmers, that is—involves calling the built-in Windows CE drawing functions. We refer to these as *GDI functions* because their origin can be traced to the various GDI libraries as implemented on 16-bit (`gdi.exe`) and 32-bit (`gdi32.dll`) versions of Windows on the desktop. Windows CE does not have a stand-alone GDI library. Instead, GDI functions under Windows CE reside in `coredll.dll`. You need to know this library name to specify it for the `DllImport` declaration required for each of these functions you wish to call.

GDI Design Notes

The GDI drawing functions provide a kind of device-independent language for creating graphical output. We must be careful to define what we mean when we use the term *device-independent*. Some people interpret the term to mean that GDI functions can read your mind and figure out how to do the "right thing" on any graphic device. But that is not what *device-independent* means.

The device-independent support built into GDI does not mean that you can write drawing code without any knowledge of the device you are drawing onto. That is an impossible ideal that cannot be achieved with a general-purpose graphics library. Graphical output can be very rich, but the challenge is that getting the output to display correctly requires the programmer to make choices that a graphics library cannot make on its own. The challenge is all the greater because human beings are a very fussy species. In the best possible cases, an imperfection in a program's graphical output only creates a distraction. In the worst cases, an imperfection may cause loss of information. Reasonable graphical output requires a great deal of care and precision. What looks good on a low-resolution display screen might look bad on a high-resolution printer.

To get good results, programmers adopt a drawing model that might better be called *device-aware* graphics programming. Before drawing, a program must determine the capabilities of a graphic device. A program determines the capabilities of a device by calling various GDI query functions. Before we look at any GDI functions, we must first discuss GDI's drawing model.

Device-Independent Logical Drawing Model

A central principle of the original GDI development team[24] was that "our functions never fail." This sounds like a bold promise. The statement is true because of a common logical drawing model that applies to all devices that GDI supports. The drawing model is based around a set of logical drawing objects. These objects include fonts, pens, brushes, palettes, colors, and drawing coordinates. Text is drawn using logical fonts, lines are drawn using logical pens, areas are filled using logical brushes, and colors are expressed as logical (RGB) colors.

GDI drawing objects are defined in a manner that is independent of any particular device. Programs create a set of drawing objects that correspond to the desired output. GDI maps the logical objects to the closest physical representation that a device can support.

---

24. We are referring here to the team that worked in the early 1980s on the GDI library that shipped with Windows 1.01.

Logical Drawing Coordinates: Desktop Windows and Windows CE

On the desktop, GDI provides rich support for drawing coordinates. A program can draw using a variety of units, including pixels, inches, millimeters, and points. Under Windows CE, GDI is not that flexible; the only available drawing units are pixels, both on the display screen and on a printer. There is, in short, a 1:1 mapping between logical drawing coordinates and physical pixels.

Another issue related to drawing coordinates is the location of the origin, the (0,0) coordinate. Just as the drawing origin in a window is located at the upper-left corner of the window's client area, the origin on a printed page is located in the upper-left corner of the paper.

If a program wants to draw a red line on a black-and-white device, GDI does not fail the call. Instead, it draws a line using the closest color. The result is either a black line, a white line, or a gray line because those are the colors available on a black-and-white device. The exact requested color is not available, but GDI does what it can. The basic idea in all of this can be summed up as follows: *The wrong mark is better than no mark at all.*

As another example, consider the case when a program requests that the string "Hello Windows" be drawn in 18-point Helvetica. GDI attempts to match that request as closely as possible. In some cases, when the requested font is available in the requested size for the targeted device, GDI provides an exact match.

But when the exact font and/or size is not available, GDI responds by selecting a font. Perhaps the closest match is 12-point Courier because that is the only font available for the target device. Again, the following principle is at work: *It is better to use the wrong font than to display nothing at all.*

Is this a reasonable thing to do? Yes, it is. By providing the closest match, GDI allows for the case when what is drawn is good enough. At the same time, when the output is not good enough, a user—whether a programmer tweaking code or an end user clicking on program options—can use the feedback to further refine the drawing request.

Consider an alternative in which GDI failed the drawing requests when an exact match is not available. One result is that programmers would need to work harder to get everything exactly right for all drawing on all devices. In many cases, that level of effort would make it not worthwhile to create any output. Worse, however, is that when bugs did happen, the only evidence would be the lack of something appearing. In a worst-case scenario, with nothing appearing on the screen (or on the printed page), it might be difficult for a user to determine the cause. A printer might have run out of ink or toner; the wrong printer driver might be installed; an I/O channel might be failing. When nothing appears, in other words, it increases the number of places that a user must look to identify the failure. In contrast, when the "wrong" graphic appears, a user can rule out other potential problems and focus instead on refining the input to produce output that is closer to what is wanted.

Device-Independent Programming Interface

Another valid meaning of *device-independent* is provided through a common programming interface that can be used on all supported device types. GDI provides a single set of functions for printers and display screens, and this set of functions also is used to draw onto memory bitmaps. (GDI treats bitmaps as drawing surfaces with all the rights and privileges of other drawing surfaces like display screens and printers.)

Windows CE Support for GDI Functions

Because a single set of GDI drawing functions is used for all devices, GDI programmers call the `ExtTextOut` function to draw text on the display screen as well as onto a printed page. GDI programmers call the `Polyline` function to connect an arbitrary set of points on any GDI-compatible drawing surface. And the `StretchDIBits` function is the function to call when you want to draw the contents of a device-independent bitmap onto any GDI-compatible device.

GDI Query Functions

To get the most control over the appearance of graphical output, the savvy GDI programmer operates with as much knowledge of a target device as possible. This is achieved with a set of GDI query functions that allows a program to understand a specific graphical device before starting to draw. Table 17.5 summarizes some aspects of printers that play a role in creating printed output and the associated GDI query functions.

For example, how large is the available drawing surface? A program must know the size of a drawing surface in order to place its output where a user can see it. As we mentioned earlier, GDI is very forgiving. In the context of drawing surface size, this means that GDI does not generate an error message or fail a drawing call when a program draws outside the visible range for a device. It might seem that GDI is too permissive, but this freedom allows a program to create interesting and useful effects. For example, a program might zoom in to display the details of a large image. When this is done, a program might intentionally draw some things that appear only partially on the printed page or do not appear at all. This can work because GDI does not require that every drawing call create visible output.

TABLE 17.5: Graphic Device Attributes and Associated GDI Query Functions

Attribute	GDI Function
Drawing area	`GetDeviceCaps(hdc, HORZRES)` `GetDeviceCaps(hdc, VERTRES)`
Choice of monochrome or color	`GetDeviceCaps(hdc, NUMCOLORS)`
Offset for the nonprintable area	`GetDeviceCaps(hdc, PHYSICALOFFSETX)` `GetDeviceCaps(hdc, PHYSICALOFFSETY)`
Physical paper size	`GetDeviceCaps(hdc, PHYSICALWIDTH)` `GetDeviceCaps(hdc, PHYSICALHEIGHT)`
Printer resolution	`GetDeviceCaps(hdc, LOGPIXELSY)`
Supported fonts	`GetDeviceCaps(hdc, NUMFONTS)` `EnumFonts(...)` and `EnumFontFamilies(...)`

Drawing to a printed page is complicated by the fact that few printers draw on the entire surface of a piece of paper. Printers normally must leave a tiny margin around the edges of a page, which might be anywhere from one-tenth to one-quarter of an inch. This area, known as the *offset for the nonprintable area*, defines the offset in pixels for the logical origin (0,0) of a device, which is rarely the same as the physical origin (upper-left corner) of the physical page.

When attempting to draw with any amount of precision, a program must take the nonprintable area into account. It must be factored into the calculations when creating, for example, a document with a one-inch margin. Failure to adjust for the nonprintable area can cause variation between how output from different printers appears.

GDI Printing and Drawing Functions

Once a program has surveyed the layout of the target printer, the next step to create printed output is to create a connection to the printer. In GDI, this is done with a data structure called a *device context*. This data structure is created and maintained by the GDI support functions. GDI does not provide a pointer to this structure to printing programs, but it does provide a handle. The handle returned by the call to the `CreateDC`[25] function is then used in every GDI function call that accesses a device. Once a device context is created, a program controls the printing process by using the various printing functions listed in Table 17.6. At the end of printing, a program cleans up by call the `DeleteDC` function.

Boundaries in print jobs are marked with two sets of Win32 API functions. The `StartDoc` and `EndDoc` function pair marks the hard boundaries of a print job. Without those calls, there is no print job. Inside the print job, page boundaries are marked with pairs of calls to `StartPage` and `EndPage`.

25. The `CreateDC` function has a `W` suffix, so that the name of the actual function you call is `CreateDCW`. This suffix indicates that the function accepts "wide" (Unicode) strings, like most Win32 API functions under Windows CE.

TABLE 17.6: GDI Printing Functions

Function	Description
CreateDCW	Creates a connection to a printer. The return value is a handle to a device context (hdc), which serves as the first parameter to all GDI drawing calls.
DeleteDC	Destroys the device context created by calling CreateDCW. Failure to do this causes memory leaks.
StartDocW	Marks the beginning of a print job.
EndDoc	Marks the end of a print job.
StartPage	Marks the start of a printed page.
EndPage	Marks the end of a printed page.
AbortDoc	Terminates a print job.
SetAbortProc	Defines a callback function to support terminating a print job.

Between the page boundary calls, a program creates output by calling the various GDI drawing functions. We summarize these functions in Table 17.7. Even though the Win32 API on Windows CE has fewer functions than the Win32 API on desktop Windows, the Windows CE team did

TABLE 17.7: GDI Drawing Functions in Windows CE, by Drawing Family

Text	Raster	Vector
DrawTextW ExtTextOut GetCharABCWidths GetCharWidth32 GetTextExtentExPointW	BitBlt GetPixel GradientFill MaskBlt PatBlt SetDIBitsToDevice SetPixel StretchBlt StretchDIBits TransparentImage	DrawEdge DrawFocusRect DrawFrameControl Ellipse FillRect FillRgn LineTo MoveToEx Polygon Polyline Rectangle RoundRect

a very good job of selecting a very useful set of functions to implement in Windows CE. A close look at the set of drawing functions shows that most of the more commonly used text, raster, and vector functions are supported under Windows CE.

GDI Drawing Attributes

The GDI drawing functions are important because without them you cannot draw. But the drawing functions by themselves are only half of the story of what GDI can do. The other half consists of the functions that control the actual appearance of graphical output. In a sense, then, the GDI drawing attributes—and the functions that control these attributes—are the real power behind the throne. The supported GDI drawing attribute functions are summarized in Tables 17.8, 17.9, and 17.10.

For example, the `ExtTextOut` function draws a line of text. It is, then, a useful and important function. However, there are several drawing attributes that control how that text is drawn. First among these is the font. The selected font determines the size, shape, and rotation of the displayed text. (For details on rotating TrueType fonts, see Chapter 16.)

In addition to the font, other drawing attributes affect the appearance of text. Text alignment, for example, allows a program to override the default relationship between a text-drawing coordinate and the resulting text (the

TABLE 17.8: GDI Query and Drawing Attribute Functions

Query Functions	Drawing Attribute Functions
`GetDeviceCaps`	`GetBkColor`
`GetNearestColor`	`GetBkMode`
`GetSysColor`	`GetCurrentPositionEx`
`GetSystemMetrics`	`GetDIBColorTable`
	`GetTextAlign`
	`GetTextColor`
	`SetBkColor`
	`SetBkMode`
	`SetROP2`
	`SetTextAlign`
	`SetTextColor`
	`SetViewportOrgEx`

TABLE 17.9: GDI Drawing Object Functions

Generic Object Functions	Pen Functions	Brush Functions	Font Functions
DeleteObject GetCurrent-Object GetObject-Type GetObject GetStock-Object SelectObject	CreatePen CreatePen-Indirect	CreateDIB-PatternBrushPt CreatePattern-Brush CreateSolid-Brush GetSysColor-Brush SetBrushOrgEx	AddFontResource CreateFont-Indirect EnumFontFamilies EnumFonts GetTextFace GetTextMetrics RemoveFont-Resource

TABLE 17.10: GDI Bitmap, Palette, and Region Functions

Bitmap Functions	Palette Functions	Region Functions
CreateBitmap CreateBitmapFromPointer CreateCompatibleBitmap CreateCompatibleDC CreateDIBSection SetBitmapBits SetDIBColorTable	CreatePalette GetNearestPalette-Index GetPaletteEntries GetSystemPalette-Entries SelectPalette SetPaletteEntries	CreateRectRgn CreateRectRgn-Indirect SelectClipRgn

default alignment is top-left). Text color and background color (along with background mode) determine the color used for the text and also for the bounding box around the text.

A Sample Program: `PrintGDI`

Like the rest of the sample programs in this chapter, we built the `PrintGDI` sample on the text editor sample that started in Chapter 9 (`DialogBoxes`) and further evolved in Chapter 11 (`Storage`). Each of the earlier programs used a `TextBox` control to display and edit text. With the `PrintGDI` sample program, we add the ability to print that text.

Listing 17.6 shows the event handler that gets called when a user selects the Print item on the File menu in the `PrintGDI` sample program.

LISTING 17.6: The File→Print Handler for GDI Printing

```
IntPtr hwndForm;
private void
mitemFilePrint_Click(object sender, EventArgs e)
{
   // Display the dialog box to select printer and port.
   PAGESETUPDLGSTRUCT psd;
   psd = new PAGESETUPDLGSTRUCT();
   PrintSetupDlg.InitDlgStruct(ref psd, hwndForm);
   int iErr = PrintSetupDlg.ShowDialog(ref psd);
   if (iErr == 0)
   {
      // Either error ...
      string strErr = PrintSetupDlg.GetErrorString();
      if (strErr != "Ok")
      {
         MessageBox.Show(strErr, "PrintGdi");
      }
      // ... or user clicked <Cancel>.
      return;
   }

   IntPtr hdcPrinter = IntPtr.Zero;
   IntPtr hfont = IntPtr.Zero;
   IntPtr hfontOld = IntPtr.Zero;
   try
   {
      // Connect to the printer by creating a device context.
      hdcPrinter = Printing.CreatePrinterDC(ref psd);
      if (hdcPrinter != IntPtr.Zero)
      {
         // Select the font.
         hfont = GdiFont.Create(textInput.Font.Name,
            (int)textInput.Font.Size, 0, hdcPrinter);
         hfontOld = GdiGraphics.SelectObject(hdcPrinter, hfont);

         // Print.
         PrintJob_Gdi.PrintText(textInput, hdcPrinter);
      }
      else
      {
         throw new System.Exception();
      }
   }
```

```
    catch
    {
       MessageBox.Show("Error connecting to printer. ",
          "PrintGdi");
    }
    finally
    {
       // Clean up.
       GdiGraphics.SelectObject(hdcPrinter, hfontOld);
       GdiGraphics.DeleteObject(hfont);
       Printing.DeleteDC(hdcPrinter);

       // Clean up resources associated with the Print dialog.
       PrintSetupDlg.Close(ref psd);
    }
 }

 private void FormMain_GotFocus(object sender, EventArgs e)
 {
    hwndForm = WinFocus.GetFocus();
 }
```

The event handler does five things to enable printing. First, it summons the Print dialog box, which allows the user to select a printer and a printer port. Using the information about the printer and the port, the program next creates a device context and receives back a handle to a device context (`hdcPrinter`). This native handle gets used as the first parameter to all GDI drawing calls, so clearly it has an important role. The handler then creates a font to match the font that the user selects for the textbox. The actual printing is done by calling the `PrintText` method in the `PrintJob_Gdi` class. When the printing is done, the event handler cleans up all the native objects that were created. This cleanup is important because native Win32 API objects do not have the automatic garbage collection support that managed objects do, so we must perform manual garbage collection on them. (See Chapter 3 for details on the different types of garbage collection.)

The printing method, `PrintJob_Gdi.PrintText`, appears in Listing 17.7. Like all the other text printing methods we discuss in this chapter, this method receives a reference to the `TextBox` control that holds the text. It parses the texts into individual lines for printing. The assumption is that the text already has line breaks and does not require us to provide any form of word wrapping.

Listing 17.7: Printing with GDI's Help (from `PrintJob_GDI.cs`)

```
public class PrintJob_Gdi
{
   //-----------------------------------------------------------
   public static void PrintText(TextBox textIn, IntPtr hdc)
   {
      // Split the input data into separate lines of text.
      char [] achNewLine = new char[] { '\n'};
      String [] astrSplit;
      astrSplit = textIn.Text.Split(achNewLine);

      // Calculate the longest string in the document.
      int cchMax = 0;
      int cstr = astrSplit.Length;
      for (int i = 0; i < cstr; i++)
      {
         if (astrSplit[i].Length > cchMax)
            cchMax = astrSplit[i].Length;
      }

      // Allocate the conversion buffers.
      byte[] byteData = new Byte[cchMax];
      char[] chData = new Char[cchMax];
      System.Text.Encoder d;
      d = System.Text.Encoding.UTF8.GetEncoder();

      // Get the device resolution.
      int cxyInch =
         GdiGraphics.GetDeviceCaps(hdc, CAPS.LOGPIXELSY);
      // In draft mode, the PCL driver returns the wrong value.
      if (cxyInch == 0)
      {
         cxyInch = 150;
      }

      // Calculate the page size.
      int cxPhysPage =
         GdiGraphics.GetDeviceCaps(hdc, CAPS.PHYSICALWIDTH);
      int cyPhysPage =
         GdiGraphics.GetDeviceCaps(hdc, CAPS.PHYSICALHEIGHT);
      int cxOff =
         GdiGraphics.GetDeviceCaps(hdc, CAPS.PHYSICALOFFSETX);
      int cyOff =
         GdiGraphics.GetDeviceCaps(hdc, CAPS.PHYSICALOFFSETY);

      // Calculate the line height.
      TEXTMETRIC tm = new TEXTMETRIC();
      GdiFont.GetTextMetrics(hdc, ref tm);
      int cyLineHeight = tm.tmHeight + tm.tmExternalLeading;
```

```
// Init the text-drawing coordinates.
int xText = cxyInch - cxOff;
int yText = cxyInch - cyOff;

// Calculate the page boundaries.
int yFirst = yText;
int yLast  = cyPhysPage - cxyInch;

// Notify GDI of document and page start.
DOCINFO di = new DOCINFO();
di.cbSize = Marshal.SizeOf(di);
Printing.StartDoc(hdc, ref di);
Printing.StartPage(hdc);

try
{
   // Set iEnd -- trim extra carriage return from text.
   int iEnd = 0;
   int cchString = astrSplit[0].Length;
   char ch = astrSplit[0][cchString-1];
   if (ch == '\r') iEnd = -1;

   // Loop through the list of strings.
   for (int i = 0; i < cstr; i++)
   {
      cchString = astrSplit[i].Length;
      if (cchString > 0)
      {
         // Draw the line of text.
         GdiGraphics.ExtTextOut(hdc, xText, yText, 0,
            IntPtr.Zero, astrSplit[i], cchString + iEnd,
            IntPtr.Zero);
      }

      // Advance to the next line.
      yText += cyLineHeight;

      // Skip to the next page (if not at document end).
      if (yText >= yLast && (i+1) < cstr)
      {
         Printing.EndPage(hdc);
         Printing.StartPage(hdc);
         yText = yFirst;
      }
   }
}
finally
{
```

continues

continued

```
            // End of page and end of document.
            Printing.EndPage(hdc);
            Printing.EndDoc(hdc);
        }

    } // PrintText()

} // class
```

HP Mobile Printing

HP is one of the world's biggest computer companies, second in size only to IBM. HP makes many different Windows CE–powered devices, including a line of Pocket PCs sold under the iPaq brand name. HP as a company, in short, has invested a lot of effort and achieved much success in creating smart devices that use the Windows CE operating system and the .NET Compact Framework.

HP has also had success in manufacturing and selling printers. Its leadership in printing has provided HP a leading market share in both inkjet and laser printers. The HP printer product line covers a wide gamut, from small personal printers up to large department printers and wide-format printers.

Given the success that HP has had with Pocket PCs and printers, it makes sense that HP has created tools to bridge the gap between Pocket PCs and printers. These tools are part of a larger effort to connect HP printers to a wide range of mobile devices, as summarized in Table 17.11. Some are beyond the scope of this book, but we include them in the table because we expect some readers will find them interesting.

HP Mobile Printing for Pocket PC

As shown in Table 17.11, HP provides Pocket PC users an add-on known as HP Mobile Printing for Pocket PC. Available as a free download from the HP Web site, this add-on supports every Pocket PC, from HP or any other manufacturer. When installed, the add-on puts the following two programs into the program list of a Pocket PC:

1. HP Mobile Printing
2. Print Manager

TABLE 17.11: **HP Mobile Printing Support**

Item	Description
HP Mobile Printing for Pocket PC[a]	Add-on for Pocket PC. Adds printing support of various standard Pocket PC file formats, including Pocket Word, Pocket Excel, text files, and other formats. Adds printer driver support for HP printers and a "select set of non-HP printers."
HP Mobile Printing Software Development Kit (SDK) for Pocket PC[b]	Add-on for eMbedded Visual C++, which allows a program to connect to the printers installed with HP Mobile Printing for Pocket PC.
HP Mobile Printing SDK with Microsoft Visual Studio .NET Support[b]	Add-on for Visual Studio .NET that provides managed-code support for calling the HP Mobile Printing for Pocket PC libraries from .NET Compact Framework programs.
HP Mobile Printing for Notebook Computers[a]	Add-on for notebook computers running Windows 2000 and Windows XP to help with discovery of printers for traveling workers. Supports printing to a new generation of Postscript printers from HP.

a. Mobile printing solutions are available at http://www.hp.com/mobile.

b. Developer kits are available at http://www.hpdevelopersolutions.com/mobile.

The first program, HP Mobile Printing, supports printing to network, infrared, and Bluetooth printers. To start printing, a user must configure a printer. This involves defining the printer port and a printer's manufacturer and model.

Once a printer has been defined, a user can submit files to be printed. These programs support a batch-mode style of printing, which involves naming files to be printed. The entire file is then printed. This same approach can be taken from any printing program, using functions defined in the Mobile Printing SDKs. Among the supported file types that can be printed are the following:

- Pocket Word documents (`*.psw`, `*.rtf`)
- Notes documents (`*.pwi`)
- Pocket Outlook files (e-mail, calendar, task list, and contact list)

- Plain text files (`*.txt`)
- Image files: bitmap files (`*.bmp`), picture files (`*.jpg`), and portable network graphics files (`*.png`) provided by built-in ClearVue Image support
- Desktop files formats: Adobe Acrobat (`*.pdf`), Microsoft PowerPoint (`*.ppt`, `*.pps`), and Microsoft Word (`*.doc`)[26]

The second program, the Print Manager, does the actual work of taking the file, rendering it for a target printer, and sending the print job to that printer. This program also tracks print jobs and allows you to configure various aspects of printing.

In addition to these two programs, the HP Mobile Printing for Pocket PC add-on adds a Print menu to the various parts of Pocket Outlook: the calendar, contact list, task list, and e-mail manager.

When the HP Mobile Printing support is installed, a set of printer drivers are copied. But these drivers do not get added to the list of drivers that appears in the regular Print dialog box. To access these drivers, your Pocket PC programs must call special functions in the Mobile Printing API library, `mprint.dll`. Providing programmers with access to that library is the role of HP's Mobile Printing SDKs.

HP Mobile Printing Software Development Kits

HP provides two versions of SDKs that allow application programmers to access the printer support provided by the HP Mobile Printing for Pocket PC add-on. These SDKs are available for download to programmers who are members of the HP Printing and Digital Imaging Solution Provider Program. You can sign up for the free program on the HP Web site and download the two SDKs. The names of the two SDKs are as follows:

1. HP Mobile Printing SDK for Pocket PC
2. HP Mobile Printing SDK with Microsoft Visual Studio .NET Support

---

26. This requires purchase of Westtek ClearVue viewers. For details, see http://www.westtek.com.

An Opinion: Some Shortcomings of HP Mobile Printing

We have some concerns about how HP Mobile Printing operates. In configuring a printer, the printer setup screens start by asking a user to "Choose a Kind of Printer," and the program displays three choices: Bluetooth, IR, and Network. These are not printer types, however, but types of I/O channels. This is more than a semantic argument because once a printer has been configured this way, there is no way to change the channel—or printer port, to use the more common term. This is perhaps a minor complaint because a typical user probably uses only one I/O channel. For software developers or test engineers, however, this is going to cause a bit of extra work because each new I/O channel requires another printer, at least when printing with the HP Mobile Printing libraries.

A second concern, which also relates to the I/O channel, is that the HP mobile approach is network-centric. Whether wired or wireless, the assumption is that a mobile user is not going to connect via a serial port. For example, there is no way to define a printer as connected by the `COM1:` printer port. Nor is there any way to print to a file, an approach that is arguably somewhat arcane and not typical of what end users need or want. But, again, an important group of end users are the software engineers and test engineers who may need to use arcane methods—like printing to a file—to help figure out why two apparently similar test cases produce results that are different in unexpected ways.

The following subsections briefly discuss each of these SDKs.

HP Mobile Printing SDK

One SDK is for programmers using eMbedded Visual C++ to build native (unmanaged) Pocket PC programs with the Win32 API. The HP Mobile Printing SDK provides the elements that C++ programmers are used to: an include file (`mprint.h`), a link library file (`mprint.lib`), some documentation, and cabinet files for the HP Mobile Printing files.

The SDK supports the following types of printing:

- Batch printing from a file
- Batch printing from a memory-resident buffer
- Printing with GDI rendering functions

To print a file, a program calls the `mPrint::PrintJob` function with the name of the file. The file must be a supported file type. Printing from a memory-resident buffer is done by calling another version of the `mPrint::PrintJob` function that accepts a pointer to a buffer for its input.

The HP Mobile Printing SDK relies on the built-in GDI drawing calls for a graphic API. The library provides two C++ functions: `mPrintRender::CreatePrinterContext` and `mPrintRender::DeletePrinterContext`. These two functions replace GDI's `CreateDC` and `DeleteDC` functions. For experienced GDI programmers, this makes the Mobile Printing libraries easy to use. For example, we found it very easy to convert our GDI drawing sample program, `PrintGDI`, to use the Mobile Printing libraries as demonstrated in our `PrintHPMobile` sample program. That, in fact, was most of the work we had to do, and it took only a few minutes.

The job was not quite done, however, because we also had to remove the call to the built-in Windows CE Print dialog box. We did not need to display a Print dialog box because the HP Mobile Printing SDK's `CreatePrinterContext` function displays its own Print dialog box, as shown in Figure 17.2.

HP Mobile Printing SDK with Microsoft Visual Studio .NET Support

A second version of the HP Mobile Printing SDK supports .NET Compact Framework programs. This SDK provides the elements of the native printing SDK, but packaged in a way that is compatible with managed code. This is required because the HP Mobile Printing library, `mprint.dll`, was built from a set of C++ classes, which are difficult to call directly from managed code.[27]

---

27. They are difficult to call because the P/Invoke declarations require ordinals and not function names and because nonstatic C++ functions require a valid `this` pointer to an object instance.

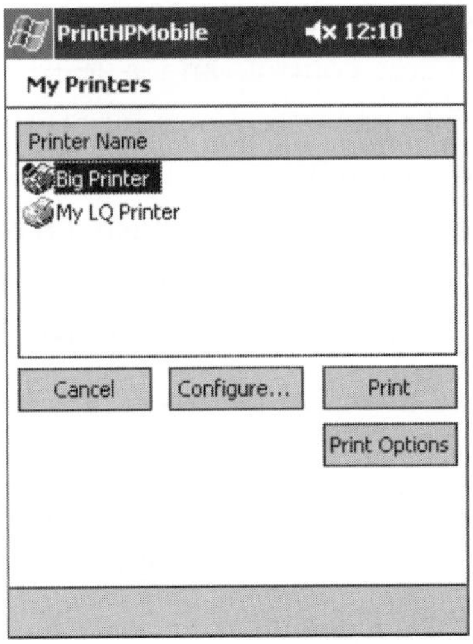

FIGURE 17.2: The HP Mobile Printing dialog box

A second native library, `mPrintWrapper.dll`, provides a set of wrapper functions that can be accessed using a set of P/Invoke declarations. This library also provides wrappers around some native GDI drawing calls. For example, it's a pretty good guess that the function named `NativeExtTextOut` does little more than call the `ExtTextOut` function. While this sample library is useful as a demonstration, we prefer creating our own P/Invoke wrappers that directly call the drawing calls in the Windows CE system library, `coredll.dll`.

Aside from a set of managed-code wrappers around the native Mobile Printing functions, the managed-code SDK does not add any other managed-code libraries. There are not, for example, any managed classes or compatibility with the standard `System.Drawing` classes and drawing support.

The managed-code SDK does add a few items to Visual Studio .NET 2003, however. For example, a new project template is added to the New Project Wizard. The template name is Print Enabled Smart Device Application. We tested version 2.0 of the SDK, dated October 2003, which only includes templates for C# programs and not for Visual Basic .NET programs.

This SDK also adds a set of custom controls to the Visual Studio .NET control Toolbox. The three controls provide another way to add printing to a .NET Compact Framework program. There is a MobilePrintComponent control, a MobilePrintButton control, and a MobilePrintMenuItem control. These controls seem to generate a nice bit of support code for C#, but they do not generate any Visual Basic .NET code. One slight problem is that the custom controls are available when a Visual Basic project is open, but you cannot use them in a Visual Basic program because they create only C# code—even when you are working with a Visual Basic project.

A Sample Program: PrintHPMobile

We built the PrintHPMobile sample program by modifying the PrintGDI sample. This approach worked well because both printing approaches use the same set of GDI functions for drawing. For the new program, we replaced the call to GDI's CreateDC function with a call to the HP Mobile Printing SDK's CreatePrinterContext function. Because the new function displayed a Print dialog box, we were able to eliminate a bit of code in the process. Calling the PrintSetupDlg function was redundant, so we removed that function call. We also replaced the call to GDI's DeleteDC function with the comparable function in the HP Mobile Printing SDK: DeletePrinterContext. Listing 17.8 shows the details of the event handler for when users select Print from the File menu. Other than the changes just described, the remainder of the program is identical to the program from which it was derived.

LISTING 17.8: The File→Print Handler for HP Mobile Printing

```
private void
mitemFilePrint_Click(object sender, EventArgs e)
{
   IntPtr hdcPrinter = IntPtr.Zero;
   IntPtr hfont = IntPtr.Zero;
   IntPtr hfontOld = IntPtr.Zero;
   try
   {
      // Connect to the printer by creating a device context.
      hdcPrinter =
         mPrint.mPrintRenderWrapper.CreatePrinterContext();
      if (hdcPrinter != IntPtr.Zero)
      {
         // Select the font.
```

```
            hfont = GdiFont.Create(tboxInput.Font.Name,
               (int)tboxInput.Font.Size, 0, hdcPrinter);
            hfontOld = GdiGraphics.SelectObject(hdcPrinter, hfont);

            // Print.
            PrintJob_Gdi.PrintText(tboxInput, hdcPrinter);
         }
         else
         {
            throw new System.Exception();
         }
      }
      catch
      {
         MessageBox.Show("Error connecting to printer. ",
            "PrintHPMobile");
      }
      finally
      {
         // Clean up.
         GdiGraphics.SelectObject(hdcPrinter, hfontOld);
         GdiGraphics.DeleteObject(hfont);
         mPrint.mPrintRenderWrapper.DeletePrinterContext(hdcPrinter);
      }
   }
```

Rendering with PrinterCE

The fourth approach to printing that we present in this chapter uses another third-party add-on, FieldSoftware's PrinterCE library. There are two versions of this library, one for native application development using eMbedded Visual C++ and a second for managed-code (i.e., .NET Compact Framework) development. We focus on the .NET Compact Framework development support.

At first glance, the PrinterCE library seems just like the HP Mobile Printing library. Both are third-party add-ons that support printing. Each introduces its own Print dialog box (the PrinterCE Print dialog box appears in Figure 17.3). But that is where the similarity ends. A deeper look reveals just how different the two approaches are.

The key difference is that the HP tools supplement the Windows CE model. A printing program built for the HP libraries summons the HP

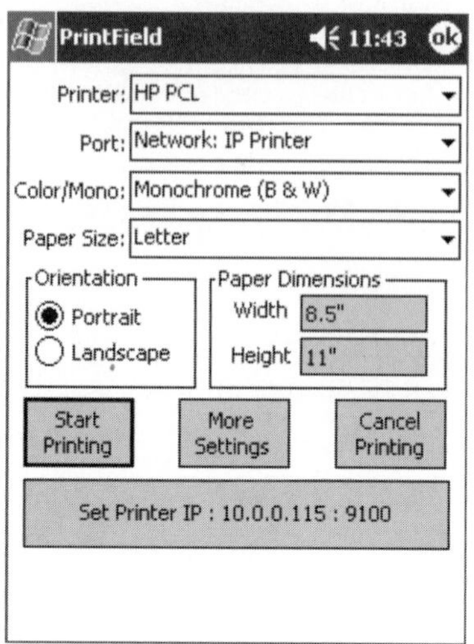

FIGURE 17.3: The PrinterCE Print dialog box

Print dialog box but then uses regular Windows CE drawing calls, with output sent to traditional Windows CE printer drivers. The HP approach supplements the I/O support provided by Windows CE with its own I/O library and does not use the built-in Windows CE port monitor.

While the HP tools supplement what Windows CE provides, the FieldSoftware tools replace the Windows CE model. A printing program built with the FieldSoftware tools calls a managed graphics library that provides drawing calls that are unlike GDI drawing calls and also unlike .NET Compact Framework drawing calls. They are, instead, a set of functions focused on the tasks that programmers need to print. These graphic functions are not as extensive as the GDI functions, but they were created with an eye toward printed output, not to the display screen.[28]

Printer output is rendered by proprietary printer driver support that is part of the PrinterCE libraries. This support does not use the Windows CE printer driver model, which must rasterize all printer output to a bitmap.

---

28. A focus on printer output is refreshing in light of the display-screen-centric philosophy that seems implicit in every version of Microsoft Windows on both desktop and embedded versions.

We suspect this contributed to the faster printing we observed with the PrinterCE sample program (as described earlier in this chapter).

Finally, PrinterCE has solid support for various I/O channels. This includes the well-known and well-established I/O channels such as direct printing to an IP address and printing to a network printer identified by a standard URL. PrinterCE also supports printing to a serial (`COM1:`) port, which the HP Mobile Printing approach does not. PrinterCE also has print-to-file support. This might not seem remarkable, but it is. Windows CE itself does not support printing to files, a technique that is useful for software engineers and test engineers to capture and compare different printing cases. PrinterCE also supports a relatively recent I/O channel, Bluetooth.

The Bluetooth wireless network protocol started life as a proposal for low-power wireless connections from mobile phones to other smart devices. With a power requirement that is less than 20% of comparable Wi-Fi network adapters, Bluetooth is kinder to battery-powered mobile devices than other wireless protocols. Because this standard is still in the formative stage, extra effort is required to work correctly with the range of new Bluetooth products now available. PrinterCE has built-in support for Bluetooth adapter cards that reside, for example, in the adapter slot of a Pocket PC. PrinterCE also supports Bluetooth printer dongles, like the one from AnyCom that plugs into a printer's Centronics port and instantly turns a printer into a Bluetooth printer.

Another important aspect of the PrinterCE library is that it supports a broader range of printers than are built into Windows CE, which supports only PCL laser and PCL inkjet printers. PrinterCE also supports a wider range of printers than the HP Mobile Printing libraries, which support only HP printers.

The PrinterCE Library

The .NET Compact Framework version of the PrinterCE library defines a new printing programming interface. We summarize the elements of that library here to help provide a sense of what is available. This is not intended as a replacement for the documentation from FieldSoftware, however, which is available from the company's Web site.

The PrinterCE managed-code library, `PrinterCE.NetCF.dll`, has six public classes, as reported by `ildasm.exe`:

- `AsciiCE`
- `BarcodeCE`
- `PrinterCE`
- `PrinterCEException`
- `PrinterCE_Base`
- `PrinterCE_DLL`

Our focus is on the `PrinterCE` class, which is the main class for printing with the graphical API that our sample program uses. A printing program creates an instance of this class and creates output using the methods and properties of this class. Tables 17.12 through 17.16 summarize elements of the `PrinterCE` class. In these tables we use categories similar to the ones

TABLE 17.12: Graphic Device Attributes and Associated PrinterCE Query Properties

Attribute	PrinterCE Property
Drawing area	Available through `PrPgWidth`; read-only property. Available through `PrPgHeight`; read-only property.
Choice of monochrome or color	Available through `IsColor`; read-only property.
Offset for nonprintable area	Available through `SetupPrSettings_All`; included in drawing area and paper margin values.
Physical paper size	Available through `SetupPrSettings_All`.
Printer resolution	Available through `PrinterResolution`; read-only property in `ScaleMode` units.
Supported fonts	Not available through PrinterCE properties. A program must instead query supported fonts using GDI functions `EnumFonts` and `EnumFontFamilies`.

TABLE 17.13: PrinterCE Printing Functions

Function	Description
`PrinterCE` constructors	Create a `PrinterCE` object, which is needed for a printer connection
`ShutDown`	Frees resources allocated for a `PrinterCE` object
`SelectPrinter`	Displays the Print dialog box and marks the start of a print job
`EndDoc`	Marks the end of a print job
`NewPage`	Marks the end of a printed page (and implicitly the start of a new page)
`KillDoc`	Terminates a print job

TABLE 17.14: PrinterCE Drawing Functions, by Drawing Family

Text	Raster	Vector
`DrawText`	`DrawPicture`	`DrawCircle`
`DrawTextFlow`	`DrawPoint`	`DrawEllipse`
		`DrawLine`
		`DrawRect`
		`DrawRoundedRect`

TABLE 17.15: PrinterCE Coordinate Attributes

Drawing Coordinates
`ConvertCoord`
`ScaleMode`
`PrinterResolution`
`Rotation`

TABLE 17.16: PrinterCE Drawing Attributes

Page Attributes	Text Attributes	Raster Attributes	Vector Attributes
PgIndentLeft	FontBold	GetPictureDims	DrawStyle
PgIndentTop	FontBoldVal		DrawWidth
PrBottomMargin	FontItalic		FillColor
PrLeftMargin	FontName		FillStyle
PrOrientation	FontSize		
PrPaperSelection	FontStrikethru		
PrPgHeight	FontUnderline		
PrPgWidth	ForeColor		
PrPrintQuality	GetStringHeight		
PrRightMargin	GetStringWidth		
PrTopMargin	TextX		
	TextY		

we used in the summary of the GDI programming interface in Tables 17.7 through 17.10 earlier in this chapter. There was a limit in how far we could go with this approach, owing to the different architecture of the two graphic libraries.

In writing the PrinterCE sample program, we focused on the text-drawing support. We encountered two differences from the managed-code graphics that a .NET Compact Framework program uses to draw on the display screen. The first difference is that there are two ways to set the font height. As described in the Two Ways to Set Font Sizes sidebar, we multiply the point size by –1 to get the same size that the .NET Compact Framework uses.

The second difference is that the library reports the font size as the text cell height. There are two ways to set the font size, but the text cell height is not adjusted to take this difference into account. This means that in some cases, the reported height of a text cell is too short.[29] This problem appears

29. We define "too short" as compared to the height reported by GDI and as produced when printing using the same font from Microsoft Word and the default settings.

only when multiple lines of text are drawn, as our sample program does. It does not matter whether you draw the text or you ask the library to do it for you—both produce identical results. We discuss this difference in detail in the Differences in Reported Text Height sidebar.

Two Ways to Set Font Sizes

PrinterCE supports two methods to select font height. Positive height values result in the use of one method, and negative height values result in the use of the other method. Figure 17.4 shows the results from requesting a positive 72-point font and a negative 72-point font. The I beam between the two pairs of characters illustrates the relative actual height of 72 points.

The outermost rectangle around each character pair shows the textbox, the amount of space defined by the font creator for properly displaying the text. The hatched rectangle at the top of each character pair illustrates the *internal leading*, a term that refers to the physical space that separates lines of text included in the textbox.

The difference between the two font selection methods is this: whether or not to include the internal leading—the hatched area—in the requested height. Using a positive height (shown on the left side of Figure 17.4) results in a font with a height that includes the internal leading. Using

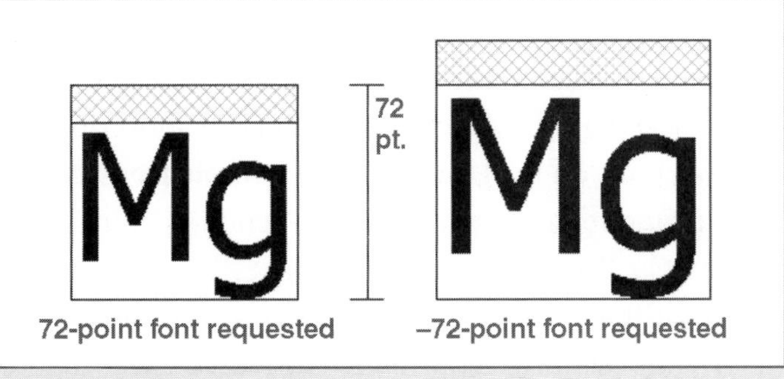

FIGURE 17.4: Two methods for selecting font size, as supported by PrinterCE and GDI

a negative height (shown on the right side of Figure 17.4) results in a font with a height that excludes the internal leading. Why have two methods?

The positive (character cell) height approach is useful when you know the amount of space you want to draw into and you want a font that fills that space without appearing crowded. We call this the "spreadsheet font-sizing method" because it works well with a grid of data cells; you have a cell to draw into without crossing the top or bottom boundary of the box.

The negative (em) height approach is useful for selecting text size based strictly on the height of the upper- and lowercase letters. This method ignores the space between lines of text because it is the height of the letters themselves that is of interest. This latter approach describes how word processors work, so we call this the "word processor font-sizing method."

Both the PrinterCE library and GDI drawing calls provide the choice of these two font-sizing techniques. The .NET Compact Framework, on the other hand, only uses the word processor font-sizing method; a program specifies a positive height value to the .NET Compact Framework controls. Unseen by you, when the controls call the underlying GDI drawing calls, they request a font using a negative height value. Our `PrintField` sample program uses the negative point size method to request font sizes so that its output conforms with the output created by the other sample programs presented in this chapter.

A Sample Program: `PrintField`

Like the other three sample programs in this chapter, the `PrintField` sample program was built on the file I/O sample program (`Storage`) from Chapter 11, which itself was built on the `DialogBoxes` sample from Chapter 9. As such, this sample program opens a text file and sends a paginated file to the printer. Unfortunately, this means that the `PrintField` program does not demonstrate any of the graphical drawing support provided by the PrinterCE library. If your printing requirements involve more than basic text, you will want to experiment with how well—and how quickly—the PrinterCE library can draw raster and vector graphics. FieldSoftware provides a free demo program that you can download from the company's Web site.[30]

Differences in Reported Text Height

When using the em height (negative value) method for selecting font height, the text height reported by PrinterCE is different from the size reported by GDI.[31] This was an issue during our timing tests because this caused the output produced by the PrinterCE program to differ significantly from the output of the other programs. To reproduce our timing tests, as noted in the code, hard-code the line height (`cyLineHeight`) to 46 pixels. Otherwise, PrinterCE reports a line height of 42 pixels, which reduces the overall text length.

Listing 17.9 shows the event handler for our sample program's File→Print menu item. In this code, we create a `PrinterCE` object, set the font as selected by the user in the program's dialog box for font selection, and display a Print dialog box with a call to the `SelectPrinter` function.

LISTING 17.9: The File→Print Handler for PrinterCE Printing

```
using FieldSoftware.PrinterCE_NetCF;
// ...

private void mitemFilePrint_Click(object sender, EventArgs e)
{
   PrinterCE prce = null;
   try
   {
      // Create the PrinterCE object needed for printing.
      prce = new PrinterCE("LICENSE KEY");
```

continues

30. For the demo program's source code, visit http://www.fieldsoftware.com/PrinterCE_NetCF_download.htm.

31. The difference with em height spacing is that internal leading is excluded. With cell height spacing, external leading is excluded from text height calculations.

continued

```
         // Select the font.
         prce.FontName = tboxInput.Font.Name;
         prce.FontSize = (int)( tboxInput.Font.Size * (-1));

         // Connect to the printer.
         prce.SelectPrinter(true);

         // Print.
         PrintJob_Field.PrintText(tboxInput, prce);
      }
      catch (PrinterCEException )
      {
         MessageBox.Show("PrinterCE Exception","Exception");
      }
      finally
      {
         if (prce!=null)
         {
            // Disconnect from the printer.
            prce.ShutDown();
         }
         prce=null;
      }
   }
```

Listing 17.10 shows the code we wrote to cycle through the text in the program's main text editing window. If you compare this source file with the other print job files in this chapter, you'll see that the basic structure of printing is the same, no matter the approach taken. (We kept the elements as similar as possible to aid you in comparing these sample programs.)

LISTING 17.10: Printing with the FieldSoftware Library (from `PrintJob_Field.cs`)

```
public class PrintJob_Field
{
   //-----------------------------------------------------
   //-----------------------------------------------------
   public static void PrintText(TextBox textIn, PrinterCE prce)
   {
      // Define the drawing coordinates.
      // Units are pixels.
      prce.ScaleMode = PrinterCE.MEASUREMENT_UNITS.PIXELS;

      // Get the device resolution.
      double cxyInch = prce.PrinterResolution;
```

```
// Set margins to 1 inch.
prce.PrLeftMargin = cxyInch;
prce.PrTopMargin = cxyInch;
prce.PrRightMargin = cxyInch;
prce.PrBottomMargin = cxyInch;

// Calculate the page size.
double cxPhysPage = prce.PrPgWidth;
double cyPhysPage = prce.PrPgHeight;

// Calculate the line height.
// For timing tests, hard-code this value to
// 46 for line height for 10-point Courier New.
double cyLineHeight = prce.GetStringHeight;

// Init the text-drawing coordinates.
double xText = 0;
double yText = 0;

// Calculate the page boundaries.
double yFirst = yText;
double yLast  = cyPhysPage;

// Split the input data into separate lines of text.
char [] achNewLine = new char[] { '\n'};
String [] astrSplit;
astrSplit = textIn.Text.Split(achNewLine);

// Check for the longest string in the document.
int i;
int cchMax = 0;
int cstr = astrSplit.Length;
for (i = 0; i < cstr; i++)
{
   if (astrSplit[i].Length > cchMax)
      cchMax = astrSplit[i].Length;
}

// Set iEnd -- trim extra carriage return from text.
int iEnd = 0;
int cchString = astrSplit[0].Length;
char ch = astrSplit[0][cchString-1];
if (ch == '\r') iEnd = -1;

// Loop on available strings.
for (i = 0; i < cstr; i++)
{
   cchString = astrSplit[i].Length;
   if (cchString > 0)
```

continues

continued

```
            {
               // Draw the line of text.
               prce.DrawText(astrSplit[i], xText, yText,
                  cchString + iEnd);
            }

            // Advance to the next line.
            yText += cyLineHeight;

            // Skip to the next page (if not at end of document).
            if (yText >= yLast && (i+1) < cstr)
            {
               prce.NewPage();
               yText = yFirst;
            }
         }

         // End of page and end of document.
         prce.EndDoc();

      } // PrintText()

   } // class
```

CONCLUSION

Do your users want hard-copy output from your .NET Compact Framework programs? If so, they are not alone. Many users want to print from mobile smart devices. In this chapter, we showed four approaches to satisfying your users in their requests for printing. Each has its merits, and you may find that a blended approach is the best one to take.

Direct printing gives you total control but may require you to write code that involves low-level printer commands. GDI printing works but requires extra effort with some I/O channels (e.g., Bluetooth). The HP Mobile Printing SDK makes printing very easy, especially if your program creates output in one of its standard, built-in formats (e.g., text, Pocket Word, Pocket Excel). Finally, PrinterCE from FieldSoftware provides an example of a third-party library that combines a fast rendering model with extensive I/O support.

Great software—like any great innovation—comes from the hard work of people pushing the boundaries of what was previously thought possible. The motivation to make that effort comes from knowing that your customers want something you can provide. We wrote this book to help you push through those boundaries to write great software. As we bring this book to a close, we wish you the best in your software development efforts, and we look forward to touching base with you in person at one of our classes or at an industry conference, or online via newsgroups, online chats, and e-mail.

PART V
Appendixes

A

Hungarian Notation for .NET Programs

Version 1.3
March 15, 2004
By Paul Yao and David Durant

TIME IS A software developer's most precious resource. For that reason, anything that can help you save time—at any phase of the project—while maintaining or increasing productivity is a good thing. When we started to work on this book,[1] we began by collaborating on a set of guidelines to minimize the differences between our coding styles. As the project moved forward, we refined and updated various elements of this file.

We offer this set to you as a starting point for your own coding guidelines. To get an editable copy of this file in Microsoft Word format, e-mail info@paulyao.com. Be sure to ask for the Hungarian Notation for .NET Programs file.

We expect to continue updating the various elements of this file and maintaining it on our Web site (http://www.paulyao.com/cfbook), and we welcome your comments and suggestions. We particularly welcome any additions for types not included in this document; if you develop extensions to the set described here, please send them to us! We will

1. This appendix first appeared on the book review Web site for the following two titles by Paul Yao and David Durant: *.NET Compact Framework Programming with C#* and *.NET Compact Framework Programming with Visual Basic .NET* (Boston, MA: Addison-Wesley, 2004).

update the document and post it to our Web site (with, of course, credit given to contributors).

Goals and Objectives

Our primary goal in creating this set of Hungarian names is to increase efficiency and productivity, for both the developer writing the code and—most importantly—all future developers who need to read, update, maintain, and debug code. Toward that end, we created these guidelines that would meet the following goals:

1. Make it easy to create variable names.
2. Make it easy to write code that is consistent from one developer to another.
3. Enhance code readability by attaching type-specific tags to names so that a variable makes sense on its own, without the need to search for its definition.
4. Create names for program elements—classes, properties, methods, events, fields—that help distinguish program-specific names from names that come from the .NET Compact Framework.
5. Work equally well in both C# and Visual Basic .NET.
6. Work equally well in .NET Compact Framework code as well as desktop .NET Framework code.

Guidelines

We created these guidelines for a coding project that exclusively uses Microsoft's .NET technology: the C# and Visual Basic .NET languages. Thus these recommendations apply specifically to .NET projects. These guidelines were created with the following principles in mind.

- *Use Hungarian notation.* This style of naming is officially out of favor, but we have always liked it. In addition, Hungarian notation seems to sneak back through the back door of the official documentation, in sample code, and in some of the code automatically generated by the various wizards. For that reason, we decided to throw open the front door and embrace a style that has served us well in the past.

- *Create case-insensitive names.* C# is case-sensitive, but Visual Basic .NET is not. For that reason, we avoided any convention that relied on distinguishing uppercase from lowercase names. The exceptions to this rule are the names for constants and for members of enumerations, which we decided to make all uppercase.
- *Use default names when possible.* The Visual Studio .NET Forms Designer suggests names, some of which can be left alone but others are likely to change. For example, the Designer gives label controls names such as `label1`, `label2`, `label3`, and so on. In many cases, programmers have no interest in changing these. As much as possible, the naming scheme described here works with the default names provided by the Designer.
- *Include elements in the .NET Compact Framework.* The focus of this book is the .NET Compact Framework, so we attempt to make this as complete as possible for the classes that are in the .NET Compact Framework, especially the more commonly used classes. Programmers targeting the .NET Framework may still find this list useful, but many .NET Framework types are not defined here. You are welcome, however, to use this as a starting point for your own guidelines.
- *Avoid terse abbreviations for prefixes and variable names.* Instead, in general we chose to make prefixes and variable names more meaningful. While terse names are easier to type, they are somewhat harder to remember. For example, the prefix for `TextBox` is `tbox` rather than the shorter but less understandable `txt`.
- *Use terse abbreviations for commonly used types.* There is a bit of a judgment call for this guideline because our commonly used types might differ from yours. For strings (`str`), integer loop indices (`i`), and events (`e`), it seems that shorter is better; these abbreviations become easy to remember because they are used so often.
- *Use longer abbreviations (or no abbreviation) for less commonly used types.* Again, this involves a judgment call. Operating system threads (`thread`)

are arguably common objects that everyone needs and uses, but the creation and management of those threads in code is done by a relatively small amount of code. The savings to be gained by some arbitrary abbreviation—such as `thrd`, `thd`, or `thred`—would not offset the clarity of just using the longer `thread`. (In other words, we avoid abbreviating for the sake of abbreviating for less common types.)

- *Do not try to make every single instance in all code exactly consistent with a standard.* The goal is to increase your productivity, which does not occur if you rework all your old code to match some change in your standard. For that reason, there are inconsistencies with this set of definitions and what you find in this printed book and in the online code. So be it. Consistency within a single program is far more important than consistency across different programs. (For example, with the `TextBox` control prefix, we waffled between using `txt` and `text`, finally settling on `tbox`—and this could even change again.)

.NET Naming Guidelines

The Microsoft .NET documentation provides some guidelines for .NET naming. Of particular interest is a section titled "Design Guidelines for Class Library Developers."[2] This strict set of rules helps ensure that new class libraries—custom controls, SQL data adapters, and so on—are easily understood by programmers who are already familiar with .NET conventions.

Rather than provide the copious detail of those design guidelines, we have summarized the key points in Table A.1. This book follows most of these guidelines for classes that we expect to be public; for our private code, we use more Hungarian notation than these guidelines allow. These guidelines can help you write public class library code that is generally more readable and maintainable by you and more usable and understandable by those programmers who use your class library.

---

2. See details at http://msdn.microsoft.com/library/en-us/cpgenref/html/cpconnamingguidelines.asp.

TABLE A.1: **Microsoft Guidelines for .NET Naming**

Type	Convention	Examples
Containing Elements		

Namespaces	Combine the following elements for namespace names in public libraries:
	Company name
	Technology name
	Feature
	Design
		Examples:
		`Microsoft.WindowsCE.Forms`
		`YaoDurant.Drawing`
		`YaoDurant.Win32`

Classes	Use nouns or noun phrases for class names.
	For derived classes, create compound names for classes by appending the base class name at the end of the new class name.
		Examples of nouns as class names:
		`Form`
		`TextBox`
		Examples of derived class names:
		`MainForm`
		`DateTextBox`

Contained Elements		

Attributes	Use the `Attribute` suffix for custom attribute classes.	Examples:
		`HelpFileAttribute`
		`AuthorAttribute`

Enumerations	Do not use `Enum` in the name of an enumeration.	Examples:
		`CombineMode`
		`FontStyle`
		`GraphicsUnit`
		`Keys`
		`DayOfWeek`
		`FileShare`

Event argument classes	Use the `EventArgs` suffix for event argument classes.	Examples:
		`RowUpdatedEventArgs`
		`KeyEventArgs`
		`MouseEventArgs`

continues

TABLE A.1: Microsoft Guidelines for .NET Naming (continued)

Type	Convention	Examples
Contained Elements		

Event handlers	Use the `EventHandler` suffix for event handlers.	Examples:
		`TreeViewEventHandler`
		`KeyEventHandler`

Event-handling methods	Name protected methods as `OnXXX`, where `XXX` is the event name.	Examples:
		`OnParentChanged`
		`OnRowUpdated`
		`OnKeyDown`
		`OnMouseMove`

Event names	Use verbs for event names.	Examples:
		`ParentChanged`
		`EnabledChanged`
		`GotFocus`
		`LostFocus`

Exceptions	Use the `Exception` suffix for exception names.	Examples:
		`ArithmeticException`
		`DivideByZeroException`
		`IndexOutOfRangeException`

Interfaces	Use the I prefix for interface names.
	Use nouns, noun phrases, or adjectives that describe behavior for the rest of the name.
		Examples:
		`ICollection`
		`IComparer`
		`IDictionary`
		`IEnumerable`
		`IEnumerator`
		`IList`

Methods	Use verbs or verb phrases for method names.	Examples:
		`Activate`
		`Close`
		`Invoke`
		`ShowDialog`

Method parameters	Use descriptive parameter names.
	Do not use Hungarian notation.
	Use type-based parameter names sparingly.
		Examples:
		`bool disposing`
		`object sender`

Type	Convention	Examples
Contained Elements		

Properties	Use nouns or noun phrases for property names.
	Do not use Hungarian notation.
		Examples:
		`BackColor`
		`Font`
		`Text`
		`Width`

Static fields	Use nouns, noun phrases, or noun abbreviations for static field names.
	Use Hungarian notation.
		Examples:
		`Empty`
		`NotDefinedValue`

Hungarian notation has fallen out of favor at Microsoft, so the official word in the .NET community is to avoid Hungarian. Some .NET programmers—ourselves included—continue to use this style; others do not. Feelings run deep on this issue. In a Web log entry for November 14, 2003,[3] a reader of a Web-based copy of this book, Paul Gielens, asked for feedback from .NET programmers about whether they use .NET naming or not. The majority admitted to using Hungarian notation at least some of the time.

You will encounter programmers who advise against using Hungarian. Others advise using it for private names but sticking to the Microsoft guidelines for public symbols. Others only use the notation for user interface controls. You decide: Pick what works for you and your development team, always keeping in mind that the purpose of this notation is to save you time and energy. Where it accomplishes that end, use the notation; where it does not, don't use the notation.

3. The Web log entry, titled "What? Hungarian naming for .NET," can be found at this URL: http://weblogs.asp.net/pgielens/archive/2003/11/14/37566.aspx.

Hungarian Notation

Hungarian notation—often referred to as *Hungarian naming*—refers to a style of creating meaningful variable names. An MSDN Technical Article gives the following explanation for how this approach got its name:

> It came to be known as "Hungarian notation" because the prefixes make the variable names look a bit as though they're written in some non-English language and because Simonyi is originally from Hungary.
>
> —Note from Dr. Gui, November 1999

Rather than repeat all the details that are so well described in that technical article, we refer you to a reprint of Charles Simonyi's original white paper on this naming convention if you wish to learn more.[4]

Hungarian notation is not a standard. In other words, you will not find an ISO standards committee (or, for that matter, an ANSI, IEEE, or ECMA committee) that dictates which prefixes you can and cannot use. While there are many lists of suggested prefixes, including this appendix, none claim to be the definitive one that supersedes all others.

Hungarian notation is, instead, a *style*. Lists (like this one) that call themselves "standards" (or, in our case, "guidelines") are starting points for project-specific data types because, with few exceptions, every programming project has its own unique set of types. You'll get the greatest benefits from Hungarian notation on projects where everyone agrees to use the same set of types. It provides a common language so that any team member can look at any code—whether that individual wrote it or it was written by someone else—and read it, understand it, and modify it with a minimum of extra effort.

We have a friend who used to work at Microsoft. He states that the disciplined use of Hungarian notation—and a project-specific set of types and

---

4. See http://msdn.microsoft.com/library/en-us/dnvsgen/html/hunganotat.asp.

associated Hungarian prefixes—allowed him to transfer to the Excel team during a crunch period and be productive very quickly.

Our Use of Hungarian Notation

We use Hungarian notation throughout this book for data types. We do so because we find it makes our code more readable and therefore more understandable.

The use of Hungarian notation also provides another important benefit: It allows you to quickly find names in an IntelliSense list. IntelliSense is a feature of the Visual Studio .NET text-editing windows. Just about every time you type a dot operator, IntelliSense pops up with possible choices for the next part of an operation.

For example, suppose you are writing some code and need to know the name of a string variable that is a data member of the class you are writing. The old-fashioned way to find the variable name would be to do a search or to scroll to the top of your source file (or wherever you normally put such things). When you get there, you might find a list of string names defined like this:

```
string strFirstName;
string strLastName;
string strAddress;
string strCity;
string strState;
string strPostalCode;
```

Another alternative is to ask IntelliSense to help you. By typing "`this.str`" in the text-editing window, you give IntelliSense enough details to help you remember the specific name you were looking for. Figure A.1 shows the IntelliSense window displaying the available data members that start with a `str` prefix.

The `m_` Prefix for Private Data

A variation to the Hungarian style that we adopt in this book is the use of an additional prefix, `m_`, for private class data members. This helps us instantly distinguish public data from private data. It is particularly helpful in

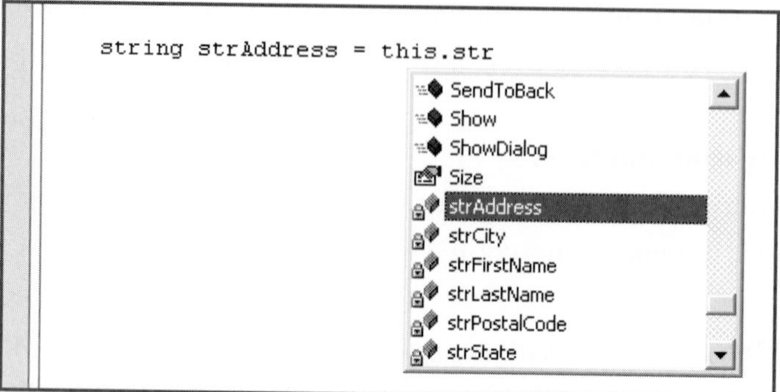

FIGURE A.1: Hungarian notation helps IntelliSense remind you of variable names.

allowing a public property and an associated private data member to have essentially the same name—the only difference being that the private data member has the `m_` prefix. Here is an example.

```
private bool m_bThreadContinue; // Continue flag

public bool bThreadContinue // Continue property
{
   get { return m_bThreadContinue; }
   set { m_bThreadContinue = value; }
}
```

The programmer writing code that calls into this class always uses the public `bThreadContinue` property, which gets translated into the private `m_bThreadContinue` field that is visible only within our class.

The Designer creates some private data members for you—one for each control created in a form. We do not use the `m_` prefix for such private data members because the extra effort would not be worth the potential benefit.

While we were assembling this set of guidelines, the `m_` prefix prompted the most discussion. We both found it useful but wanted to make sure it would be reasonable for .NET Compact Framework code. We found it widely used in pre-.NET technologies, including C++ projects (for the MFC class library and the ATL template library), Visual Basic projects, and Active Server Pages.

What convinced us of its applicability to the .NET Compact Framework was its use in various .NET-based technologies, including Rotor, the shared source code implementation of the Common Language Infrastructure (CLI). We also found that the .NET Compact Framework itself uses `m_` for all of its private fields, none of which are documented but which become visible with a tool like `ildasm.exe`.

Hungarian Prefixes for CTS Value Types

The common type system (CTS) defines a set of types that all languages must support to be compatible with .NET. The CTS, which we discussed in detail in Chapter 3, is part of a specification known as the Common Language Specification (CLS). C# supports types outside this specification, most of which are unsigned types. In the .NET documentation, these are marked as "not CLS-compliant." To enhance code portability, we only use CLS-compliant types, and so Table A.2 only includes CLS-compliant types.

TABLE A.2: Hungarian Prefixes for Standard Value Types

.NET Class	C# Alias	Visual Basic .NET Alias	Size (Bytes)	Prefix
`System.Boolean`	`bool`	`Boolean`	1	`b`
`System.Char`	`char`	`Char`	2	`ch`
`System.DateTime`	N/A	`Date`	8	`date`
`System.Decimal`	`decimal`	`Decimal`	16	`dec`
Integer Types				
`System.Byte`	`byte`	`Byte`	1	`byt`
`System.Int16`	`short`	`Short`	2	`sh`
`System.Int32`	`Int`	`Integer`	4	`i`
`System.Int64`	`long`	`Long`	8	`l`

continues

TABLE A.2: Hungarian Prefixes for Standard Value Types (continued)

.NET Class	C# Alias	Visual Basic .NET Alias	Size (Bytes)	Prefix
Platform-Specific Pointer or Handle Type				
`System.IntPtr`	N/A		4	`iptr`[a]
Floating-Point Types				
`System.Single`	`float`	`Single`	4	`sin`
`System.Double`	`double`	`Double`	8	`dbl`
Other Type				
`System.Guid`	N/A		16	`guid`

a. In general, we do not use this prefix for `IntPtr`. Instead, we use the prefix for the type being represented by the `IntPtr` variable. For example, a Win32 window handle will have a prefix of `hwnd` instead of `iptr`. This accomplishes the goal of making our code more readable and reduces the coding errors that arise from misusing variables.

Tables A.3 through A.14 list our recommendations for Hungarian prefixes for various .NET Compact Framework types. Because .NET Compact Framework namespaces, classes, and other types have the same names as their .NET Framework counterparts, this set of Hungarian prefixes can also work for .NET Framework projects.

TABLE A.3: Hungarian Prefixes for Usage and `System` Classes

Class or Usage Type	Prefix	Examples
Integer used as a count of bytes	`cb`	`cbReturnBuffer`, `cbLength`
Integer used as a count of characters	`cch`	`cchMaxName`, `cchSearchBuffer`

Class or Usage Type	Prefix	Examples
Integer used as an index for a loop	i	iItem, iFont, iFile

Array of any type	a (used prior to type-specific type)	int [] ai = new int[10]; // Array of integers
		ai[0] = 1;
		ai[1] = 2;
		string [] astrName; // Array of strings
		char [] achPassword; // Array of characters
		Button [] acmdWizard; // Array of buttons
		Control [] actrlSearch; // Array of controls

Delegate	dele	deleFileFound, deleAddItem
EventArgs	e	e (the standard event argument for all event handlers)
Exception	ex	ex (the standard exception argument for all exception types)
Object	obj	objDebugInput, objItem, objCollectionStart
String	str	strPath, strFileName, str

TABLE A.4: Hungarian Prefixes for System.Text Classes

Class	Prefix	Examples
Decoder	decode	decodeFileBuffer, decodeHTML
Encoder	encode	encodeDisplayBuffer, encodeConvert
StringBuilder	strbld	strbldInputBuffer, strbldErrorLog

TABLE A.5: Hungarian Prefixes for `System.Collection` Classes

Class	Prefix	Examples

ArrayList	al<type>	ArrayList ali = new ArrayList(); // Integer ArrayList
		ali.Add(1);
		ali.Add(2);

BitArray	bitarr	bitarrDisplayFlags, bitarrCollectionType
HashTable	hash	hashFileNames, hashLeftover
Queue	queue	queueSendRequest, queueWaitingList
Stack	stack	stackFunctionCall, stackUndoCommands

TABLE A.6: Hungarian Prefix for `Microsoft.Win32` Class (Desktop .NET Framework Only)

Class	Prefix	Examples
RegistryKey	regkey	regkeyRoot, regkeySoftware, regkeyVer10

TABLE A.7: Hungarian Prefixes for `System.Windows.Forms` Classes

Class	Prefix	Examples
Button (used for command buttons)	cmd	cmdOk (OK button) cmdReset (button to reset a form)
CheckBox	chk	chkWordWrap, chkToolbar, chkCloseWhenDone
ComboBox	combo	comboStates, comboTaxSettings
ContextMenu	cmenu	cmenuMain, cmenuOptions
Control	ctrl	ctrlParent
DataGrid	dgrid	//a "data-bound grid" dgridPhoneList

Class	Prefix	Examples
DomainUpDown	dupdown	dupdownState dupdownCountry
Form	frm	frmMain (main form) frm (temporary variable)
Form used as a dialog box	dlg	dlgFileOpen dlgFileSave
HScrollBar	hscroll	hscrollLines, hscrollElevation
ImageList	ilist	ilistFile, ilistEdit
Label	label	label1 (default label name) labelStatus
ListBox	lbox	lboxFileNames
ListView	lview	lviewVisitors, lviewSymptoms
MainMenu	menu	menuMain, menuNew
MenuItem	mitem	mitemFileOpen, mitemEditCopy
NumericUpDown	nupdown	nupdownMaxItems, nupdownPassengers
Panel	panel	panelColorScroll, panelDiscountGroup
PictureBox	pbox	pboxPreview, pboxThumbnail
ProgressBar	pbar	pbarDownload, pbarRecalc
RadioButton	opt	optRed, optGreen, optBlue (opt stands for "option button")
StatusBar	status	statusMain, statusHelpWindow
TabControl	tab	tabFileDialog, tabOptionsDialog
TabPage	tpage	tpageOptions, tpageFormat
TextBox	tbox	tboxName, tboxFirst, tboxPassword

continues

TABLE A.7: Hungarian Prefixes for `System.Windows.Forms` Classes (continued)

Class	Prefix	Examples
`Timer`	`timer`	`timerPowerSave`
`ToolBar`	`tbar`	`tbarFile`, `tbarOptions`
`ToolBarButton`	`tbb`	`tbbFileOpen`, `tbbEditCopy`
`TrackBar`	`trbar`	`trbarItems`
`TreeView`	`tview`	`tvwDirectory`, `tvwOrgChart`
`VScrollBar`	`vscroll`	`vscrollRed`, `vscrollGreen`, `vscrollBlue`

TABLE A.8: Hungarian Prefixes for `Microsoft.WindowsCE.Forms` Classes (.NET Compact Framework Only)

Class	Prefix	Examples
`InputPanel`	`sip`	`sipMain` (sip stands for "Software Input Panel")
`Message`	`msg`	`msgIn`
`MessageWindow`	`msgwnd`	`msgwndTextBox`, `msgwndSearchDone`

TABLE A.9: Hungarian Prefixes for `System.Drawing` Classes

Class	Prefix	Examples
`Bitmap`	`bmp`	`bmpThumb`, `bmpNext`
`Brush`	`br`	`brRed`, `brGreen`, `brYellow`
`Color`	`color`	`colorBlack`, `colorActiveWindow`
`Font`	`font`	`fontCurrent`, `fontArial`
`Graphics`	`g`	`G` (standard for Graphics objects)
`Icon`	`icon`	`iconHelp`, `iconQuestion`, `iconMain`

Class	Prefix	Examples
ImageAttributes	imgatt	imgattWhiteColorKey, imgattRedColorKey
Pen	pen	penRed, penBlack
Point	pt	ptStart, ptEnd
PointF	ptf	ptfName, ptfString
Rectangle	rect	rectStory
RectangleF	rectf	rectfPreview
Region	reg	regScroll
Size	sz	szBackground
SizeF	szf	szfStringSize

TABLE A.10: Hungarian Prefixes for System.Data Classes

Class	Prefix	Examples
ConstraintException	ex	ex
DataColumn	dcol	dcolName dcolProduct
DataColumnChangeEventArgs	e	e
DataException	ex	ex
DataRelation	drel	drelCustomerOrder drelStudentSchedule
DataRow	drow	drowFirst drowNext
DataRowChangeEventArgs	e	e
DataSet	dset	dsetCustomer dsetBugReport

continues

TABLE A.10: Hungarian Prefixes for `System.Data` Classes (continued)

Class	Prefix	Examples
DataTable	dtab	dtabOrder dtabAddress
DataView	dview	dviewCurrentOrder dviewProduct
DBConcurrencyException	ex	ex
DeletedRowInaccessibleException	ex	ex
DuplicateNameException	ex	ex
EvaluateException	ex	ex
FillErrorEventArgs	e	e
ForeignKeyConstraint	fkey	fkeyCustomerOrder fkeyCustomerProducts
InRowChangingEventException	ex	ex
InvalidConstraintException	ex	ex
InvalidExpressionException	ex	ex
MissingPrimaryKeyException	ex	ex
NoNullAllowedException	ex	ex
ReadOnlyException	ex	ex
RowNotInTableException	ex	ex
StateChangeEventArgs	e	e
SyntaxErrorException	ex	ex
VersionNotFoundException	ex	ex

TABLE A.11: Hungarian Prefixes for `System.Data.SqlServerCe` Classes

Class	Prefix	Examples
SqlCeCommand	cmnd	cmndAddOrderItems cmndSelectNextItem
SqlCeCommandBuilder	cbld	cbldUpdate
SqlCeConnection	conn	connInternalServer connMain
SqlCeDataAdapter	dapt	daptNewOrders daptProductList
SqlCeDataReader	drdr	drdrResult
SqlCeEngine	db	db
SqlCeError	err	errLastCommand
SqlCeException	ex	ex

TABLE A.12: Hungarian Prefixes for `System.IO` Classes

Class	Prefix	Examples
BinaryReader	bread	breadPasswordInfo
BinaryWriter	bwrite	bwritePasswordInfo
EndOfStreamException	ex	ex
ErrorEventArgs	e	e
FileInfo	finfo	finfoNew finfoNext
FileStream	fs	fsInput fsOutput fsDebugLog

continues

TABLE A.12: Hungarian Prefixes for `System.IO` Classes (continued)

Class	Prefix	Examples
`IOException`	`ex`	`ex`
`MemoryStream`	`ms`	`msBitmap` `msString`
`StreamReader`	`sread`	`sreadInput`
`StreamWriter`	`swrite`	`swriteOutput`
`StringReader`	`stringread`	`stringreadInput`
`StringWriter`	`stringwrite`	`stringwriteOutput`

TABLE A.13: Hungarian Prefixes for `System.Threading` Classes

Class	Prefix	Examples
`AutoResetEvent`	`autoevent`	`autoeventStartLogging`
`ManualResetEvent`	`manevent`	`maneventAutoSave`
`Mutex`	`mutex`	`mutexInputBuffer` `mutexCheckRealtimeThread`

`Thread`	`thread`	`threadMain`
		`threadNetworkListener`
		`threadCommPortReadWrite`
		`threadPrint`

`Timer`	`timer`	`timerStart`

TABLE A.14: Hungarian Prefixes for System.Xml Classes

Class	Prefix
NameTable	ntable
XmlAttribute	xattr
XmlAttributeCollection	xattcoll
XmlCDataSection	xcdatasec
XmlCharacterData	xchardata
XmlComment	xcom
XmlDeclaration	xdecl
XmlDocument	xdoc
XmlDocumentFragment	xdfrg
XmlElement	xel
XmlEntityReference	xeref
XmlImplementation	ximp
XmlNamedNodeMap	xnnm
XmlNamespaceManager	xnsmanager
XmlNodeChangedEventArgs	e
XmlNodeReader	xnreader
XmlParserContext	xcontext
XmlProcessingInstruction	xpi
XmlQualifiedName	xqname
XmlResolver	xresolver

continues

TABLE A.14: Hungarian Prefixes for `System.Xml` Classes (continued)

Class	Prefix
XmlSignificantWhitespace	xsigwhite
XmlText	xtext
XmlTextReader	xtr
XmlTextWriter	xtw
XmlUrlResolver	xuresolver
XmlWhitespace	xwhite

B

Supported PMEs for .NET Compact Framework Controls

THIS APPENDIX SUMMARIZES the support for the PMEs that .NET Compact Framework controls provide for elements inherited from the base `Control` class.

To help the first version of the .NET Compact Framework achieve an ambitious size goal, the .NET Compact Framework code controls rely on the native, unmanaged controls to do a lot of the required work. But there is a cost associated with crossing the boundary from native code to managed code, and—in support of the performance goal—not all of the inherited PMEs of the .NET Compact Framework controls are supported.

What Is a PME?

The set of properties, methods, and events for a .NET class is sometimes referred to as the *PMEs,* and we use that term throughout this appendix (and the book).

The utility used to detect support for PMEs, `ControlPME`, is described in Chapter 9 and is available for download from the book's portal,[1] which is hosted on The Paul Yao Company Web site.

1. Visit the book's Web site at http://www.paulyao.com/cfbook/code.

Table B.1 summarizes the PMEs supported in all controls that derive from the `System.Windows.Forms.Control` base class. Tables B.2 through B.23 summarize the supported PMEs for the .NET Compact Framework controls. For the purpose of this test, we used Service Pack 2 of the .NET Compact Framework. The Service Pack 2 binaries report a version number of `1.0.3316.0`; this complicated version number indicates the value of four properties, namely the `Major`, `Minor`, `Build`, and `Revision` properties of the `Environment.Version` class. (In Service Pack 1, the reported version number was `1.0.3111.0`, which indicates that there were 205 system builds between the two service packs.)

This appendix includes information about the following control classes:

- `Button`
- `CheckBox`
- `ComboBox`
- `DataGrid`
- `DomainUpDown`
- `HScrollBar`
- `Label`
- `ListBox`
- `ListView`
- `NumericUpDown`
- `Panel`
- `PictureBox`
- `ProgressBar`
- `RadioButton`
- `StatusBar`
- `TabControl`
- `TabPage`
- `TextBox`
- `ToolBar`

- `TrackBar`
- `TreeView`
- `VScrollBar`

PMEs Associated with Data Binding

We were unable to test the PMEs associated with data binding, so we have omitted them from the tables. This includes the following:

- Properties: `BindingContext`, `DataBindings`
- Event: `BindingContextChanged`

TABLE B.1: Inherited PMEs Supported by All `Control`-Derived Control Classes

Properties	Methods	Events
Bottom	Dispose	Disposed
Bounds	Equals	EnabledChanged
Capture	GetHashCode	GotFocus
ClientRectangle	GetType	KeyDown[a]
ClientSize	PointToClient	KeyPress[a]
ContextMenu	PointToScreen	KeyUp[a]
Controls	RectangleToClient	LostFocus
Font	RectangleToScreen	ParentChanged
Height	Refresh	Validated
Left	SendToBack	Validating
Location	ToString	
Parent		
Right		
Size		
Top		
Visible		
Width		

a. Supported for all controls in Service Pack 2; only partially supported for original release and for Service Pack 1.

TABLE B.2: Inherited PMEs Supported by the Button Class

Properties	Supported?	Methods	Supported?	Events	Supported?
BackColor	Yes	BringToFront	Yes	Click	Yes
Enabled	Yes	CreateGraphics	No	EnabledChanged	Yes
Focused	Yes	Focus	Yes	GotFocus	Yes
ForeColor	Yes	Hide	Yes	KeyDown	Yes
Text	Yes	Invalidate	Yes	KeyPress	Yes
TopLevelControl	Yes	Invoke	Yes	KeyUp	Yes
Visible	Yes	PointToClient	Yes	LostFocus	Yes
		PointToScreen	Yes	MouseDown	No
		RectangleToClient	Yes	MouseMove	No
		RectangleToScreen	Yes	MouseUp	No
		Refresh	Yes	Paint	No
		SendToBack	Yes	ParentChanged	Yes
		Show	Yes	Resize	No
		Update	Yes	TextChanged	Yes
				Validated	Yes
				Validating	Yes

TABLE B.3: Inherited PMEs Supported by the CheckBox Class

Properties	Supported?	Methods	Supported?	Events	Supported?
BackColor	Yes	BringToFront	Yes	Click	Yes
Enabled	Yes	CreateGraphics	No	EnabledChanged	Yes
Focused	Yes	Focus	Yes	GotFocus	Yes
ForeColor	Yes	Hide	Yes	KeyDown	Yes
Text	Yes	Invalidate	Yes	KeyPress	Yes
TopLevelControl	Yes	Invoke	Yes	KeyUp	Yes
Visible	Yes	PointToClient	Yes	LostFocus	Yes
		PointToScreen	Yes	MouseDown	No
		RectangleToClient	Yes	MouseMove	No
		RectangleToScreen	Yes	MouseUp	No
		Refresh	Yes	Paint	No
		SendToBack	Yes	ParentChanged	Yes
		Show	Yes	Resize	No
		Update	Yes	TextChanged	Yes
				Validated	Yes
				Validating	Yes

TABLE B.4: Inherited PMEs Supported by the ComboBox Class

Properties	Supported?	Methods	Supported?	Events	Supported?
BackColor	Yes	BringToFront	Yes	Click	No
Enabled	Yes	CreateGraphics	No	EnabledChanged	Yes
Focused	Yes	Focus	Yes	GotFocus	Yes
ForeColor	Yes	Hide	Yes	KeyDown	Yes
Text	No	Invalidate	Yes	KeyPress	Yes
TopLevelControl	Yes	Invoke	Yes	KeyUp	Yes
Visible	Yes	PointToClient	Yes	LostFocus	Yes
		PointToScreen	Yes	MouseDown	No
		RectangleToClient	Yes	MouseMove	No
		RectangleToScreen	Yes	MouseUp	No
		Refresh	Yes	Paint	No
		SendToBack	Yes	ParentChanged	Yes
		Show	Yes	Resize	No
		Update	Yes	TextChanged	No
				Validated	Yes
				Validating	Yes

TABLE B.5: Inherited PMEs Supported by the DataGrid Class

Properties	Supported?	Methods	Supported?	Events	Supported?
BackColor	No	BringToFront	Yes	Click	Yes
Enabled	Yes	CreateGraphics	Yes	EnabledChanged	Yes
Focused	Yes	Focus	Yes	GotFocus	Yes
ForeColor	No	Hide	Yes	KeyDown	Yes
Text	No	Invalidate	Yes	KeyPress	Yes
TopLevelControl	Yes	Invoke	Yes	KeyUp	Yes
Visible	Yes	PointToClient	Yes	LostFocus	Yes
		PointToScreen	Yes	MouseDown	Yes
		RectangleToClient	Yes	MouseMove	Yes
		RectangleToScreen	Yes	MouseUp	Yes
		Refresh	Yes	Paint	Yes
		SendToBack	Yes	ParentChanged	Yes
		Show	Yes	Resize	Yes
		Update	Yes	TextChanged	Yes
				Validated	Yes
				Validating	Yes

TABLE B.6: Inherited PMEs Supported by the `DomainUpDown` Class

Properties	Supported?	Methods	Supported?	Events	Supported?
BackColor	No	BringToFront	Yes	Click	No
Enabled	Yes	CreateGraphics	No	EnabledChanged	Yes
Focused	Yes	Focus	Yes	GotFocus	Yes
ForeColor	Yes	Hide	Yes	KeyDown	Yes
Text	Yes	Invalidate	Yes	KeyPress	Yes
TopLevelControl	Yes	Invoke	Yes	KeyUp	Yes
Visible	Yes	PointToClient	Yes	LostFocus	Yes
		PointToScreen	Yes	MouseDown	No
		RectangleToClient	Yes	MouseMove	No
		RectangleToScreen	Yes	MouseUp	No
		Refresh	Yes	Paint	No
		SendToBack	Yes	ParentChanged	Yes
		Show	Yes	Resize	No
		Update	Yes	TextChanged	Yes
				Validated	Yes
				Validating	Yes

TABLE B.7: Inherited PMEs Supported by the `HScrollBar` Class

Properties	Supported?	Methods	Supported?	Events	Supported?
`BackColor`	No	`BringToFront`	Yes	`Click`	No
`Enabled`	Yes	`CreateGraphics`	No	`EnabledChanged`	Yes
`Focused`	Yes	`Focus`	Yes	`GotFocus`	Yes
`ForeColor`	No	`Hide`	Yes	`KeyDown`	Yes
`Text`	No	`Invalidate`	Yes	`KeyPress`	Yes
`TopLevelControl`	Yes	`Invoke`	Yes	`KeyUp`	Yes
`Visible`	Yes	`PointToClient`	Yes	`LostFocus`	Yes
		`PointToScreen`	Yes	`MouseDown`	No
		`RectangleToClient`	Yes	`MouseMove`	No
		`RectangleToScreen`	Yes	`MouseUp`	No
		`Refresh`	Yes	`Paint`	No
		`SendToBack`	Yes	`ParentChanged`	Yes
		`Show`	Yes	`Resize`	No
		`Update`	Yes	`TextChanged`	Yes
				`Validated`	Yes
				`Validating`	Yes

TABLE B.8: Inherited PMEs Supported by the `Label` Class

Properties	Supported?	Methods	Supported?	Events	Supported?
`BackColor`	Yes	`BringToFront`	Yes	`Click`	No
`Enabled`	Yes	`CreateGraphics`	No	`EnabledChanged`	Yes
`Focused`	Yes	`Focus`	Yes	`GotFocus`	Yes
`ForeColor`	Yes	`Hide`	Yes	`KeyDown`	Yes
`Text`	Yes	`Invalidate`	Yes	`KeyPress`	Yes
`TopLevelControl`	Yes	`Invoke`	Yes	`KeyUp`	Yes
`Visible`	Yes	`PointToClient`	Yes	`LostFocus`	Yes
		`PointToScreen`	Yes	`MouseDown`	No
		`RectangleToClient`	Yes	`MouseMove`	No
		`RectangleToScreen`	Yes	`MouseUp`	No
		`Refresh`	Yes	`Paint`	No
		`SendToBack`	Yes	`ParentChanged`	Yes
		`Show`	Yes	`Resize`	No
		`Update`	Yes	`TextChanged`	Yes
				`Validated`	Yes
				`Validating`	Yes

TABLE B.9: Inherited PMEs Supported by the `ListBox` Class

Properties	Supported?	Methods	Supported?	Events	Supported?
`BackColor`	Yes	`BringToFront`	Yes	`Click`	No
`Enabled`	Yes	`CreateGraphics`	No	`EnabledChanged`	Yes
`Focused`	Yes	`Focus`	Yes	`GotFocus`	Yes
`ForeColor`	Yes	`Hide`	Yes	`KeyDown`	Yes
`Text`	No	`Invalidate`	Yes	`KeyPress`	Yes
`TopLevelControl`	Yes	`Invoke`	Yes	`KeyUp`	Yes
`Visible`	Yes	`PointToClient`	Yes	`LostFocus`	Yes
		`PointToScreen`	Yes	`MouseDown`	No
		`RectangleToClient`	Yes	`MouseMove`	No
		`RectangleToScreen`	Yes	`MouseUp`	No
		`Refresh`	Yes	`Paint`	No
		`SendToBack`	Yes	`ParentChanged`	Yes
		`Show`	Yes	`Resize`	No
		`Update`	Yes	`TextChanged`	No
				`Validated`	Yes
				`Validating`	Yes

TABLE B.10: Inherited PMEs Supported by the `ListView` Class

Properties	Supported?	Methods	Supported?	Events	Supported?
`BackColor`	Yes	`BringToFront`	Yes	`Click`	No
`Enabled`	Yes	`CreateGraphics`	No	`EnabledChanged`	Yes
`Focused`	Yes	`Focus`	Yes	`GotFocus`	Yes
`ForeColor`	Yes	`Hide`	Yes	`KeyDown`	Yes
`Text`	No	`Invalidate`	Yes	`KeyPress`	Yes
`TopLevelControl`	Yes	`Invoke`	Yes	`KeyUp`	Yes
`Visible`	Yes	`PointToClient`	Yes	`LostFocus`	Yes
		`PointToScreen`	Yes	`MouseDown`	No
		`RectangleToClient`	Yes	`MouseMove`	No
		`RectangleToScreen`	Yes	`MouseUp`	No
		`Refresh`	Yes	`Paint`	No
		`SendToBack`	Yes	`ParentChanged`	Yes
		`Show`	Yes	`Resize`	No
		`Update`	Yes	`TextChanged`	Yes
				`Validated`	Yes
				`Validating`	Yes

Table B.11: Inherited PMEs Supported by the `NumericUpDown` Class

Properties	Supported?	Methods	Supported?	Events	Supported?
BackColor	No	BringToFront	Yes	Click	No
Enabled	Yes	CreateGraphics	No	EnabledChanged	Yes
Focused	Yes	Focus	Yes	GotFocus	Yes
ForeColor	Yes	Hide	Yes	KeyDown	Yes
Text	Yes	Invalidate	Yes	KeyPress	Yes
TopLevelControl	Yes	Invoke	Yes	KeyUp	Yes
Visible	Yes	PointToClient	Yes	LostFocus	Yes
		PointToScreen	Yes	MouseDown	No
		RectangleToClient	Yes	MouseMove	No
		RectangleToScreen	Yes	MouseUp	No
		Refresh	Yes	Paint	No
		SendToBack	Yes	ParentChanged	Yes
		Show	Yes	Resize	No
		Update	Yes	TextChanged	Yes
				Validated	Yes
				Validating	Yes

TABLE B.12: Inherited PMEs Supported by the `Panel` Class

Properties	Supported?	Methods	Supported?	Events	Supported?
BackColor	Yes	BringToFront	Yes	Click	Yes
Enabled	Yes	CreateGraphics	No	EnabledChanged	Yes
Focused	Yes	Focus	Yes	GotFocus	Yes
ForeColor	No	Hide	Yes	KeyDown	Yes
Text	No	Invalidate	Yes	KeyPress	Yes
TopLevelControl	Yes	Invoke	Yes	KeyUp	Yes
Visible	Yes	PointToClient	Yes	LostFocus	Yes
		PointToScreen	Yes	MouseDown	Yes
		RectangleToClient	Yes	MouseMove	Yes
		RectangleToScreen	Yes	MouseUp	Yes
		Refresh	Yes	Paint	Yes
		SendToBack	Yes	ParentChanged	Yes
		Show	Yes	Resize	Yes
		Update	Yes	TextChanged	Yes
				Validated	Yes
				Validating	Yes

TABLE B.13: Inherited PMEs Supported by the `PictureBox` Class

Properties	Supported?	Methods	Supported?	Events	Supported?
BackColor	Yes	BringToFront	Yes	Click	Yes
Enabled	Yes	CreateGraphics	No	EnabledChanged	Yes
Focused	Yes	Focus	Yes	GotFocus	Yes
ForeColor	No	Hide	Yes	KeyDown	Yes
Text	No	Invalidate	Yes	KeyPress	Yes
TopLevelControl	Yes	Invoke	Yes	KeyUp	Yes
Visible	Yes	PointToClient	Yes	LostFocus	Yes
		PointToScreen	Yes	MouseDown	Yes
		RectangleToClient	Yes	MouseMove	Yes
		RectangleToScreen	Yes	MouseUp	Yes
		Refresh	Yes	Paint	Yes
		SendToBack	Yes	ParentChanged	Yes
		Show	Yes	Resize	Yes
		Update	Yes	TextChanged	Yes
				Validated	Yes
				Validating	Yes

TABLE B.14: Inherited PMEs Supported by the `ProgressBar` Class

Properties	Supported?	Methods	Supported?	Events	Supported?
`BackColor`	No	`BringToFront`	Yes	`Click`	No
`Enabled`	Yes	`CreateGraphics`	No	`EnabledChanged`	Yes
`Focused`	Yes	`Focus`	Yes	`GotFocus`	Yes
`ForeColor`	No	`Hide`	Yes	`KeyDown`	Yes
`Text`	No	`Invalidate`	Yes	`KeyPress`	Yes
`TopLevelControl`	Yes	`Invoke`	Yes	`KeyUp`	Yes
`Visible`	Yes	`PointToClient`	Yes	`LostFocus`	Yes
		`PointToScreen`	Yes	`MouseDown`	No
		`RectangleToClient`	Yes	`MouseMove`	No
		`RectangleToScreen`	Yes	`MouseUp`	No
		`Refresh`	Yes	`Paint`	No
		`SendToBack`	Yes	`ParentChanged`	Yes
		`Show`	Yes	`Resize`	No
		`Update`	Yes	`TextChanged`	Yes
				`Validated`	Yes
				`Validating`	Yes

TABLE B.15: Inherited PMEs Supported by the RadioButton Class

Properties	Supported?	Methods	Supported?	Events	Supported?
BackColor	Yes	BringToFront	Yes	Click	Yes
Enabled	Yes	CreateGraphics	No	EnabledChanged	Yes
Focused	Yes	Focus	Yes	GotFocus	Yes
ForeColor	Yes	Hide	Yes	KeyDown	Yes
Text	Yes	Invalidate	Yes	KeyPress	Yes
TopLevelControl	Yes	Invoke	Yes	KeyUp	Yes
Visible	Yes	PointToClient	Yes	LostFocus	Yes
		PointToScreen	Yes	MouseDown	No
		RectangleToClient	Yes	MouseMove	No
		RectangleToScreen	Yes	MouseUp	No
		Refresh	Yes	Paint	No
		SendToBack	Yes	ParentChanged	Yes
		Show	Yes	Resize	No
		Update	Yes	TextChanged	Yes
				Validated	Yes
				Validating	Yes

TABLE B.16: Inherited PMEs Supported by the StatusBar Class

Properties	Supported?	Methods	Supported?	Events	Supported?
BackColor	No	BringToFront	Yes	Click	No
Enabled	Yes	CreateGraphics	No	EnabledChanged	Yes
Focused	Yes	Focus	Yes	GotFocus	Yes
ForeColor	No	Hide	Yes	KeyDown	Yes
Text	Yes	Invalidate	Yes	KeyPress	Yes
TopLevelControl	Yes	Invoke	Yes	KeyUp	Yes
Visible	Yes	PointToClient	Yes	LostFocus	Yes
		PointToScreen	Yes	MouseDown	No
		RectangleToClient	Yes	MouseMove	No
		RectangleToScreen	Yes	MouseUp	No
		Refresh	Yes	Paint	No
		SendToBack	Yes	ParentChanged	Yes
		Show	Yes	Resize	No
		Update	Yes	TextChanged	Yes
				Validated	Yes
				Validating	Yes

TABLE B.17: Inherited PMEs Supported by the `TabControl` Class

Properties	Supported?	Methods	Supported?	Events	Supported?
BackColor	No	BringToFront	Yes	Click	No
Enabled	Yes	CreateGraphics	No	EnabledChanged	Yes
Focused	Yes	Focus	Yes	GotFocus	Yes
ForeColor	No	Hide	Yes	KeyDown	Yes
Text	No	Invalidate	Yes	KeyPress	Yes
TopLevelControl	Yes	Invoke	Yes	KeyUp	Yes
Visible	Yes	PointToClient	Yes	LostFocus	Yes
		PointToScreen	Yes	MouseDown	No
		RectangleToClient	Yes	MouseMove	No
		RectangleToScreen	Yes	MouseUp	No
		Refresh	Yes	Paint	No
		SendToBack	Yes	ParentChanged	Yes
		Show	Yes	Resize	No
		Update	Yes	TextChanged	Yes
				Validated	Yes
				Validating	Yes

TABLE B.18: Inherited PMEs Supported by the TabPage Class

Properties	Supported?	Methods	Supported?	Events	Supported?
BackColor	No	BringToFront	Yes	Click	Yes
Enabled	Yes	CreateGraphics	No	EnabledChanged	Yes
Focused	Yes	Focus	Yes	GotFocus	Yes
ForeColor	No	Hide	Yes	KeyDown	Yes
Text	Yes	Invalidate	Yes	KeyPress	Yes
TopLevelControl	Yes	Invoke	Yes	KeyUp	Yes
Visible	Yes	PointToClient	Yes	LostFocus	Yes
		PointToScreen	Yes	MouseDown	Yes
		RectangleToClient	Yes	MouseMove	Yes
		RectangleToScreen	Yes	MouseUp	Yes
		Refresh	Yes	Paint	Yes
		SendToBack	Yes	ParentChanged	Yes
		Show	Yes	Resize	No
		Update	Yes	TextChanged	No
				Validated	Yes
				Validating	Yes

TABLE B.19: Inherited PMEs Supported by the `TextBox` Class

Properties	Supported?	Methods	Supported?	Events	Supported?
`BackColor`	Yes	`BringToFront`	Yes	`Click`	No
`Enabled`	Yes	`CreateGraphics`	No	`EnabledChanged`	Yes
`Focused`	Yes	`Focus`	Yes	`GotFocus`	Yes
`ForeColor`	Yes	`Hide`	Yes	`KeyDown`	Yes
`Text`	Yes	`Invalidate`	Yes	`KeyPress`	Yes
`TopLevelControl`	Yes	`Invoke`	Yes	`KeyUp`	Yes
`Visible`	Yes	`PointToClient`	Yes	`LostFocus`	Yes
		`PointToScreen`	Yes	`MouseDown`	No
		`RectangleToClient`	Yes	`MouseMove`	No
		`RectangleToScreen`	Yes	`MouseUp`	No
		`Refresh`	Yes	`Paint`	No
		`SendToBack`	Yes	`ParentChanged`	Yes
		`Show`	Yes	`Resize`	No
		`Update`	Yes	`TextChanged`	Yes
				`Validated`	Yes
				`Validating`	Yes

TABLE B.20: Inherited PMEs Supported by the `ToolBar` Class

Properties	Supported?	Methods	Supported?	Events	Supported?
BackColor	No	BringToFront	Yes	Click	No
Enabled	Yes	CreateGraphics	No	EnabledChanged	Yes
Focused	No	Focus	Yes	GotFocus	No
ForeColor	No	Hide	Yes	KeyDown	No
Text	No	Invalidate	Yes	KeyPress	No
TopLevelControl	Yes	Invoke	Yes	KeyUp	No
Visible	No	PointToClient	Yes	LostFocus	No
		PointToScreen	Yes	MouseDown	No
		RectangleToClient	Yes	MouseMove	No
		RectangleToScreen	Yes	MouseUp	No
		Refresh	Yes	Paint	No
		SendToBack	Yes	ParentChanged	Yes
		Show	Yes	Resize	No
		Update	Yes	TextChanged	Yes
				Validated	No
				Validating	No

TABLE B.21: Inherited PMEs Supported by the `TrackBar` Class

Properties	Supported?	Methods	Supported?	Events	Supported?
`BackColor`	Yes	`BringToFront`	Yes	`Click`	No
`Enabled`	Yes	`CreateGraphics`	No	`EnabledChanged`	Yes
`Focused`	Yes	`Focus`	Yes	`GotFocus`	Yes
`ForeColor`	No	`Hide`	Yes	`KeyDown`	Yes
`Text`	No	`Invalidate`	Yes	`KeyPress`	Yes
`TopLevelControl`	Yes	`Invoke`	Yes	`KeyUp`	Yes
`Visible`	Yes	`PointToClient`	Yes	`LostFocus`	Yes
		`PointToScreen`	Yes	`MouseDown`	No
		`RectangleToClient`	Yes	`MouseMove`	No
		`RectangleToScreen`	Yes	`MouseUp`	No
		`Refresh`	Yes	`Paint`	No
		`SendToBack`	Yes	`ParentChanged`	Yes
		`Show`	Yes	`Resize`	No
		`Update`	Yes	`TextChanged`	Yes
				`Validated`	Yes
				`Validating`	Yes

TABLE B.22: Inherited PMEs Supported by the `TreeView` Class

Properties	Supported?	Methods	Supported?	Events	Supported?
`BackColor`	No	`BringToFront`	Yes	`Click`	No
`Enabled`	Yes	`CreateGraphics`	No	`EnabledChanged`	Yes
`Focused`	Yes	`Focus`	Yes	`GotFocus`	Yes
`ForeColor`	Yes	`Hide`	Yes	`KeyDown`	Yes
`Text`	No	`Invalidate`	Yes	`KeyPress`	Yes
`TopLevelControl`	Yes	`Invoke`	Yes	`KeyUp`	Yes
`Visible`	Yes	`PointToClient`	Yes	`LostFocus`	Yes
		`PointToScreen`	Yes	`MouseDown`	No
		`RectangleToClient`	Yes	`MouseMove`	No
		`RectangleToScreen`	Yes	`MouseUp`	No
		`Refresh`	Yes	`Paint`	No
		`SendToBack`	Yes	`ParentChanged`	Yes
		`Show`	Yes	`Resize`	No
		`Update`	Yes	`TextChanged`	Yes
				`Validated`	Yes
				`Validating`	Yes

TABLE B.23: Inherited PMEs Supported by the VScrollBar Class

Properties	Supported?	Methods	Supported?	Events	Supported?
BackColor	No	BringToFront	Yes	Click	No
Enabled	Yes	CreateGraphics	No	EnabledChanged	Yes
Focused	Yes	Focus	Yes	GotFocus	Yes
ForeColor	No	Hide	Yes	KeyDown	Yes
Text	Yes	Invalidate	Yes	KeyPress	Yes
TopLevelControl	Yes	Invoke	Yes	KeyUp	Yes
Visible	Yes	PointToClient	Yes	LostFocus	Yes
		PointToScreen	Yes	MouseDown	No
		RectangleToClient	Yes	MouseMove	No
		RectangleToScreen	Yes	MouseUp	No
		Refresh	Yes	Paint	No
		SendToBack	Yes	ParentChanged	Yes
		Show	Yes	Resize	No
		Update	Yes	TextChanged	Yes
				Validated	Yes
				Validating	Yes

C

Data Synchronization Wizards[1]

MERGE REPLICATION AND RDA require the presence of a virtual directory on the Web server machine. The Virtual Directory Creation Wizard is used to create this directory. Merge Replication also requires that one or more publications be defined on the SQL Server machine. The Create Publication Wizard is used to define these publications. This appendix shows the screens displayed by the wizards and the selections we made to set up Merge Replication. Comments about the screens (and in some cases about the selections we made) appear below the figures. When used in this appendix, the term *data synchronization* includes both Merge Replication and RDA.

The Virtual Directory Creation Wizard

Figures C.1 through C.5 show the steps that must be followed when creating a virtual directory for use by an RDA application or a Merge Replication application. You can initiate the Virtual Directory Creation Wizard from the Start menu by selecting Programs→Microsoft SQL Server CE 2.0→Configure Connectivity Support in IIS.

1. Some material in this appendix first appeared in an article which we wrote, "SQL Server CE: New Version Lets You Store and Update Data on Handheld Devices," published in *MSDN Magazine*, 16(6), June 2001. Reprinted with permission of *MSDN Magazine*.

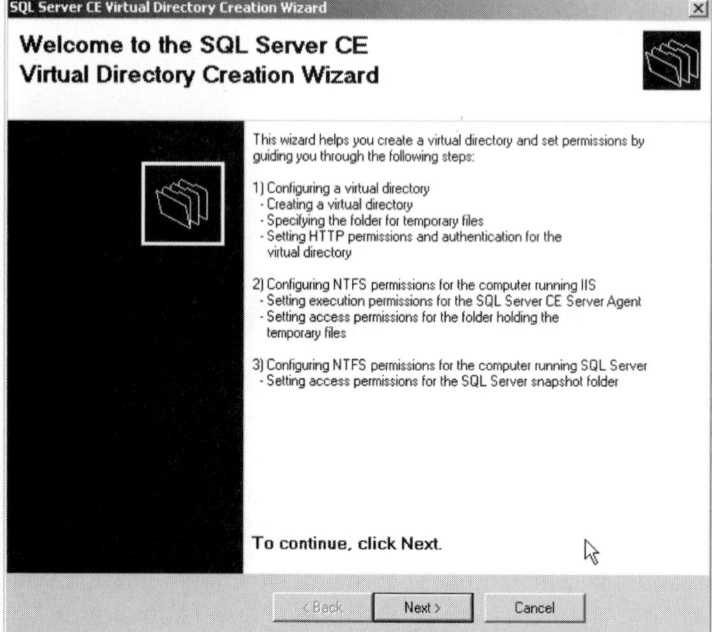

FIGURE C.1: The Virtual Directory Creation Wizard, Screen 1. The Welcome screen lists the steps the wizard guides you through.

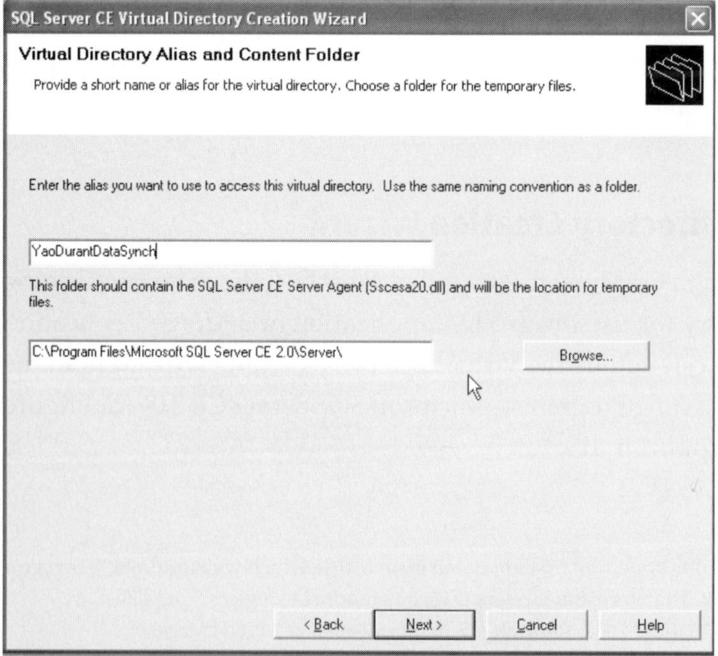

FIGURE C.2: The Virtual Directory Creation Wizard, Screen 2. Enter the name and location of the Web site that will be used for data synchronization.

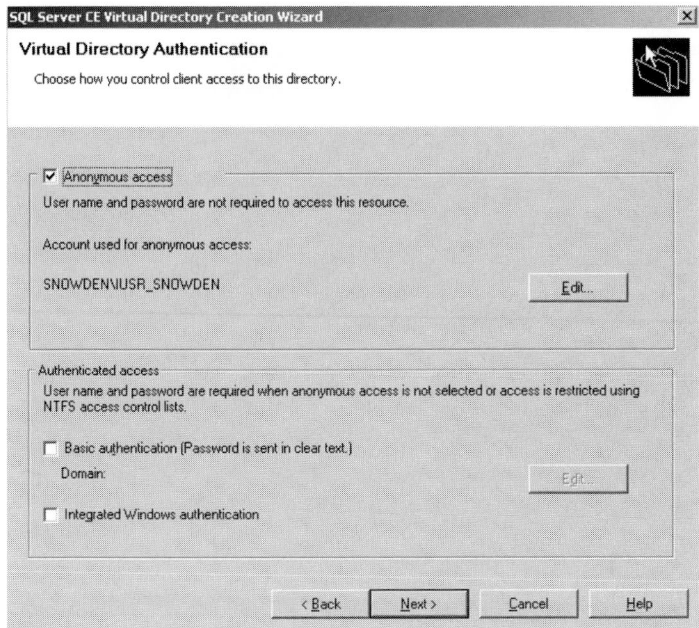

FIGURE C.3: The Virtual Directory Creation Wizard, Screen 3. Choose whether to authenticate users when they attempt to initiate data synchronization, and if so, choose the method to use.

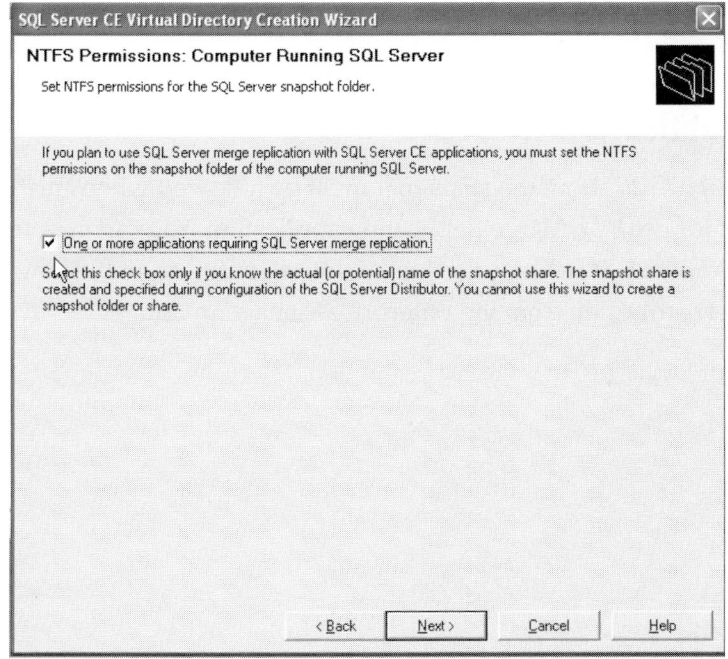

FIGURE C.4: The Virtual Directory Creation Wizard, Screen 4. Select the checkbox on this screen if your application requires Merge Replication. In our example in Chapter 13, we used Merge Replication as well as RDA, so we selected the checkbox on this screen.

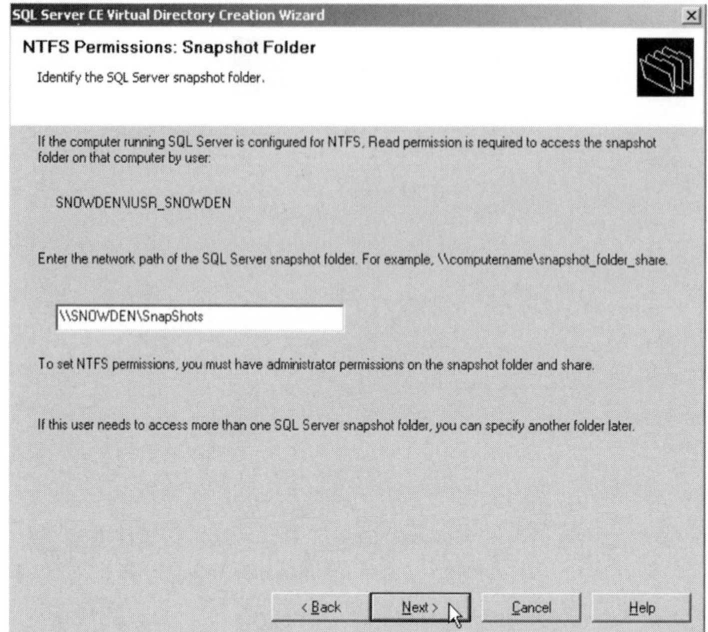

FIGURE C.5: The Virtual Directory Creation Wizard, Screen 5. Enter the location where Merge Replication will place snapshots of data and some database schema information. The user requesting data synchronization must have read permission on this directory.

The Create Publication Wizard

Figures C.6 through C.26 show the steps that must be followed when creating a publication for use by a Merge Replication application. You can initiate the Create Publication Wizard by selecting Action→Configure Publishing, Subscribers, and Distribution from the Enterprise Manager menu.

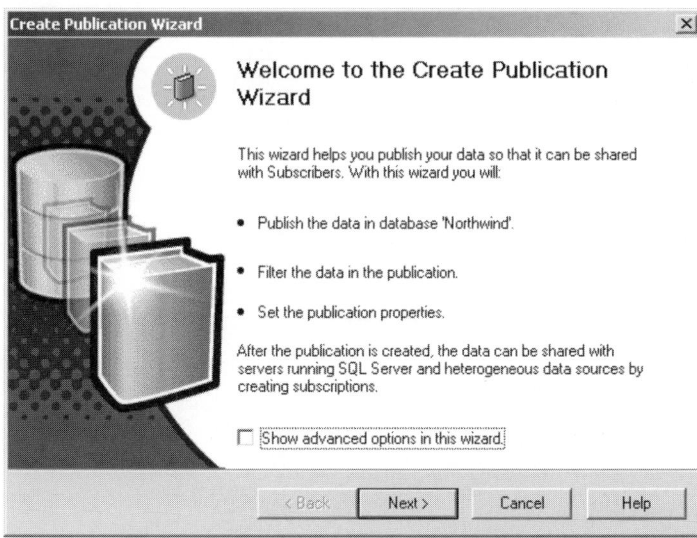

FIGURE C.6: Create Publication Wizard, Screen 1. The Welcome screen lists what the wizard will help you do. The checkbox near the bottom of the screen lets you choose whether to show advanced options in the wizard.

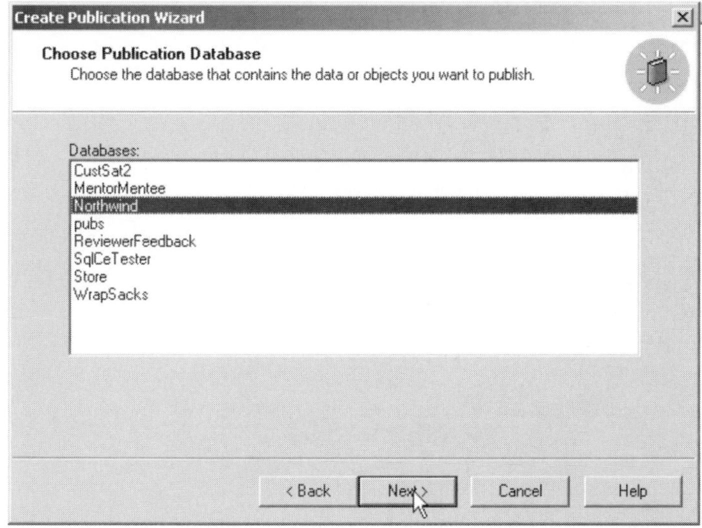

FIGURE C.7: Create Publication Wizard, Screen 2. Choose the appropriate publication for your program. For our example in Chapter 13, we chose the Northwind database.

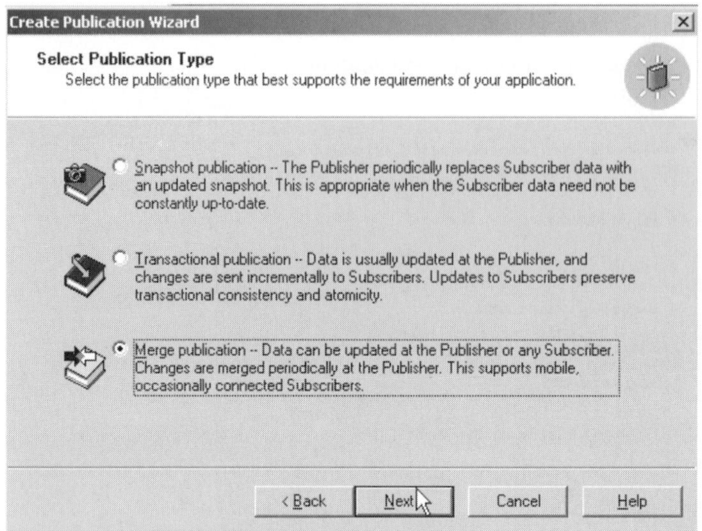

FIGURE C.8: Create Publication Wizard, Screen 3. Choose the publication type. "Merge publication" is the most common choice for mobile applications.

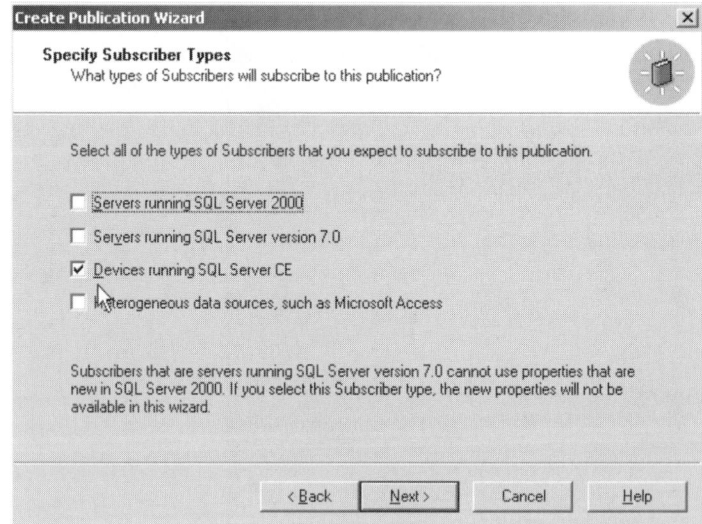

FIGURE C.9: Create Publication Wizard, Screen 4. Select as many types of subscribers as you anticipate will access your publication. Always include SQL Server CE, as shown in this figure.

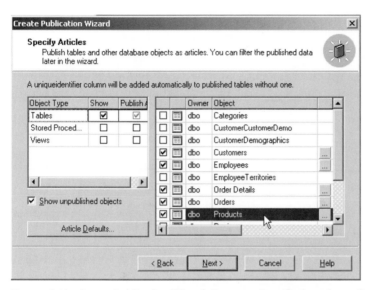

FIGURE C.10: Create Publication Wizard, Screen 5. Specify the subset of tables to be replicated. Note that stored procedures and views cannot be replicated to SQL Server CE.

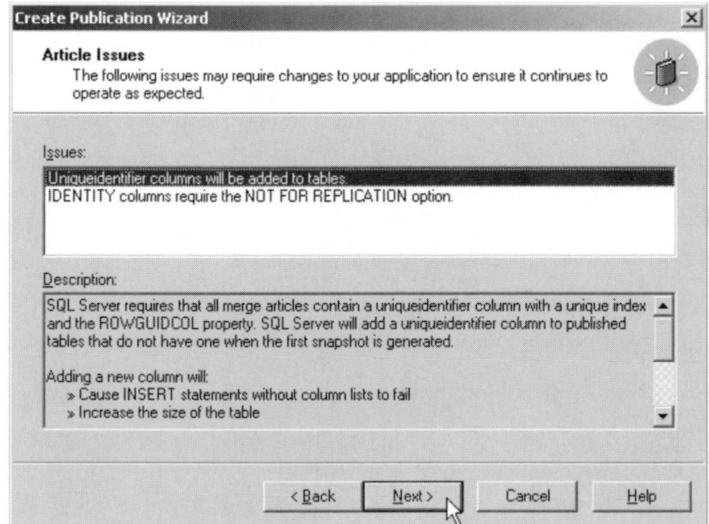

FIGURE C.11: Create Publication Wizard, Screen 6. This screen informs you of issues that may require changes to your application. In our example in Chapter 13, this screen told us that columns would be added to the publication tables and that we needed to modify some `IDENTITY` properties.

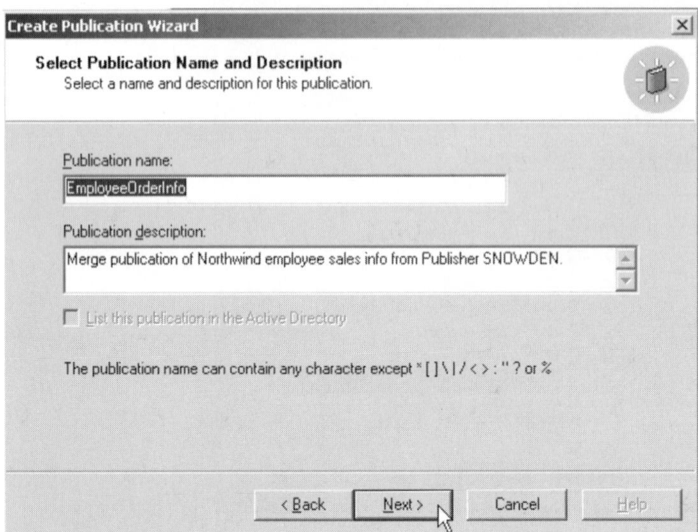

FIGURE C.12: Create Publication Wizard, Screen 7. Enter a name and description for your publication. Make the name as meaningful as possible. It will be referenced by administrative tools and by your application code.

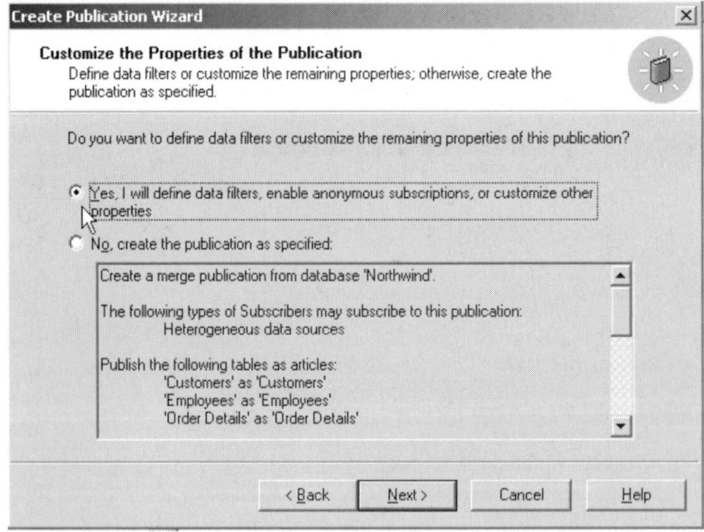

FIGURE C.13: Create Publication Wizard, Screen 8. On this screen, you must select "Yes." Mobile applications require anonymous subscriptions. Also, you will probably want to specify some filtering.

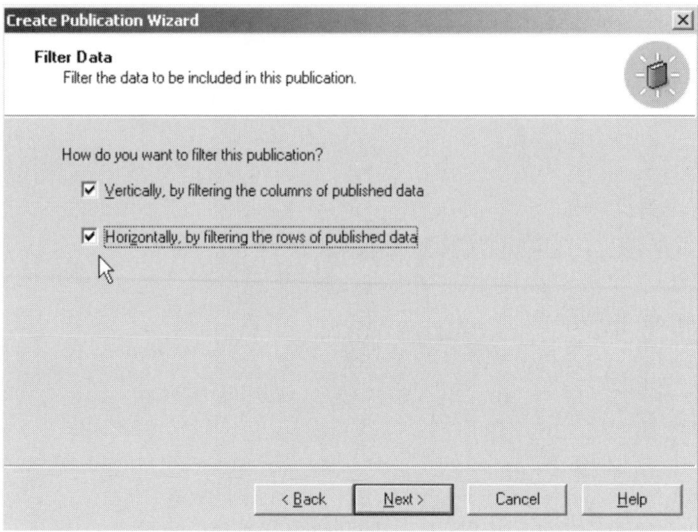

FIGURE C.14: Create Publication Wizard, Screen 9. Choose how you want to filter the data included in your publication.

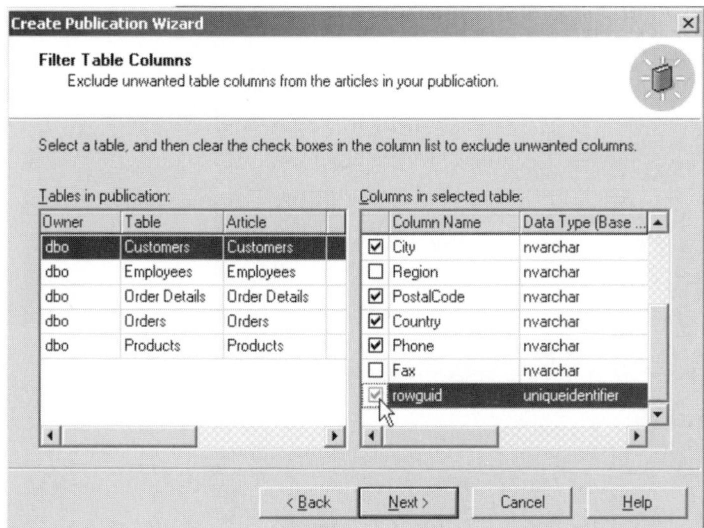

FIGURE C.15: Create Publication Wizard, Screen 10. For each table, specify the desired columns. The rowguid column cannot be unselected. The primary key columns are optional but desirable. Merge Replication will use the rowguid column to identify rows, not the primary key column(s).

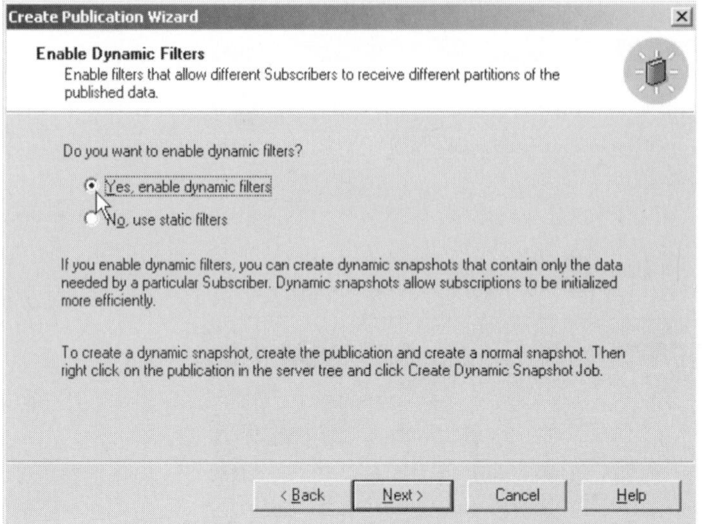

FIGURE C.16: Create Publication Wizard, Screen 11. Dynamic filters allow you to filter data based on who is subscribing to that data. It is essential for our sample application's "synchronize all orders for the current user" publication.

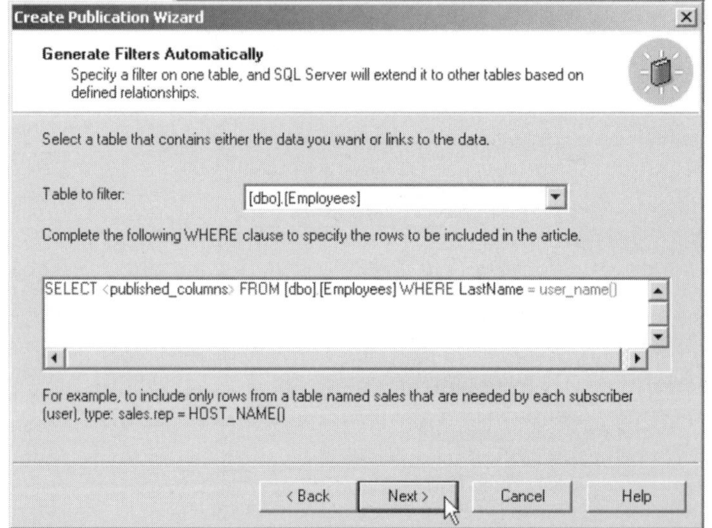

FIGURE C.17: Create Publication Wizard, Screen 12. Add your criteria to the `SELECT` statement after the word `WHERE`. Our example shown in the figure specifies the current user, that is, the user executing the subscription.

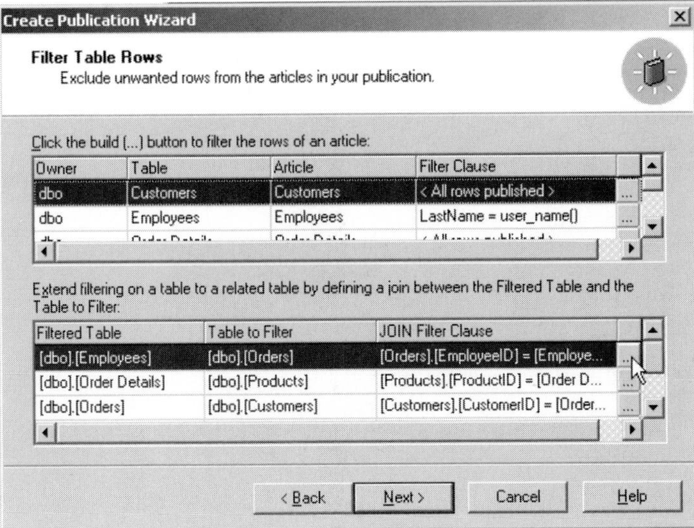

FIGURE C.18: Create Publication Wizard, Screen 13. The row for `LastName = user_name()` appears in the upper list because we added it in the previous screen (see Figure C.17). All join logic in the lower list was written by the wizard, which uses the foreign key definitions to do so.

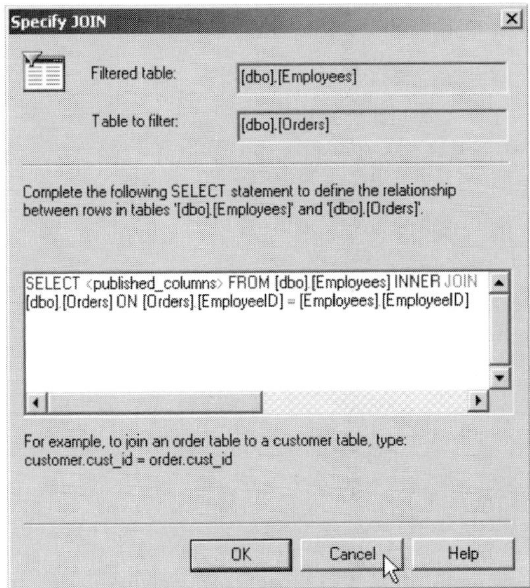

FIGURE C.19: Create Publication Wizard, Screen 14. The default wording for the `SELECT` statement, shown here, is generated by the wizard, again based on the foreign key definitions.

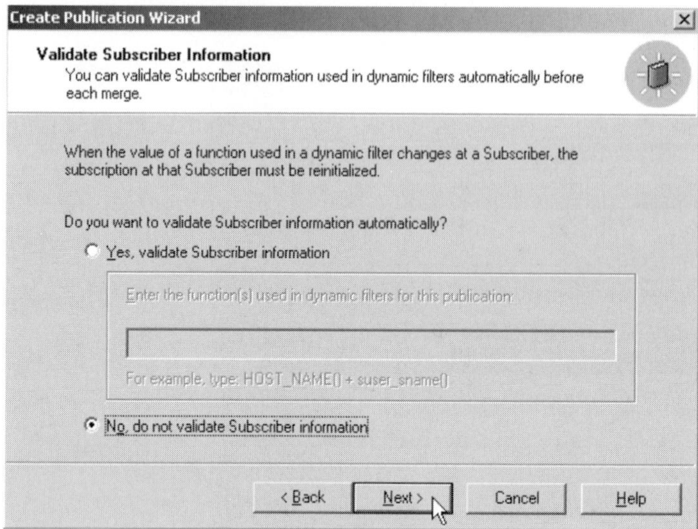

FIGURE C.20: Create Publication Wizard, Screen 15. Choose whether to validate subscriber information automatically. In our example, we selected "No" here because an employee's user name will not change over time. Otherwise, we would select "Yes."

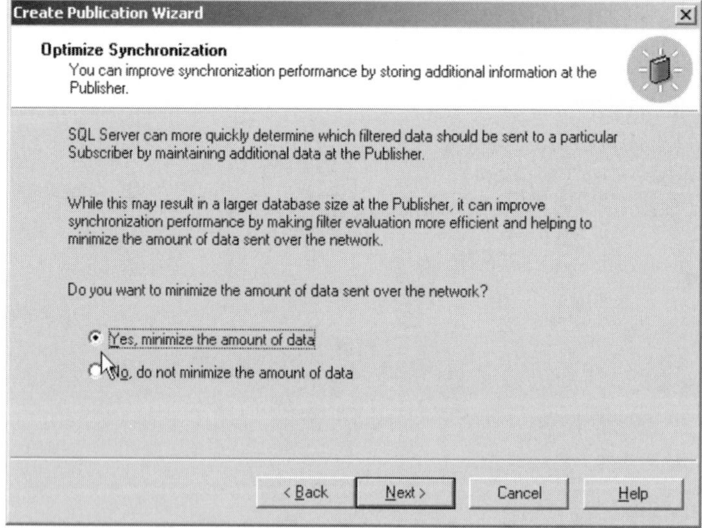

FIGURE C.21: Create Publication Wizard, Screen 16. Most .NET Compact Framework applications synchronize in a world of limited bandwidth and processor speed. Choose "Yes" to make the server do more work so that the device will do less work.

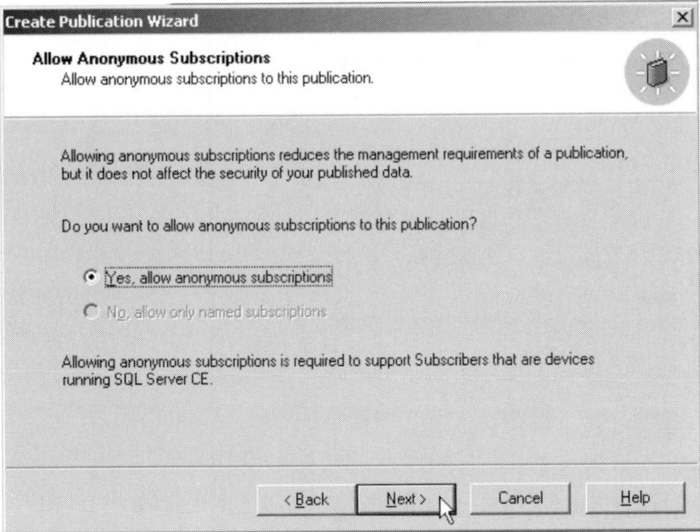

FIGURE C.22: Create Publication Wizard, Screen 17. For our example, there is no other choice but to allow anonymous subscriptions. The "No" choice was disabled because we selected "Devices running SQL Server CE" in screen 4 (see Figure C.9).

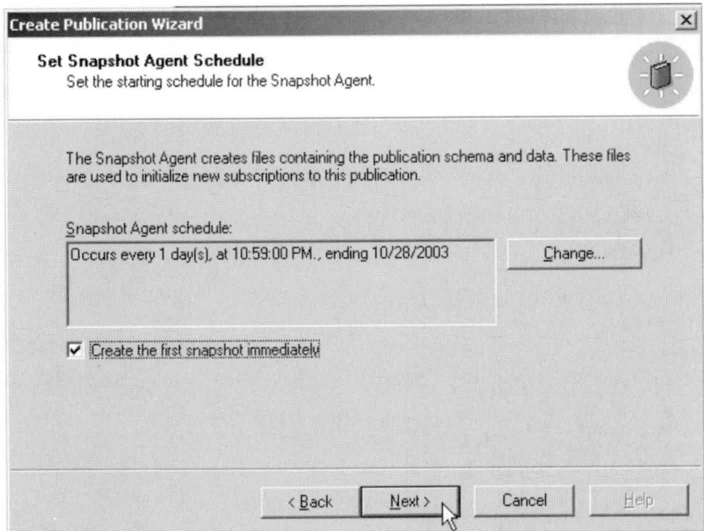

FIGURE C.23: Create Publication Wizard, Screen 18. Set the schedule for the Snapshot Agent. A snapshot is a complete resynchronization of all the data in a subscription, not merely the data that has changed since the previous synchronization. It is usually done less frequently than a modified-data-only synchronization. Typically, a modified-data-only synchronization might be done every night, while a snapshot would be done once a week or less.

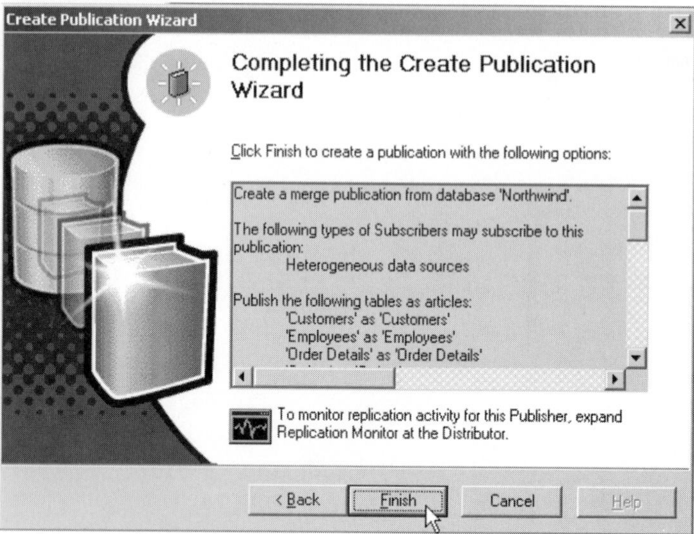

FIGURE C.24: Create Publication Wizard, Screen 19. This screen presents the last chance to review your choices before creating the publication. Click the Back button if you want to make any changes.

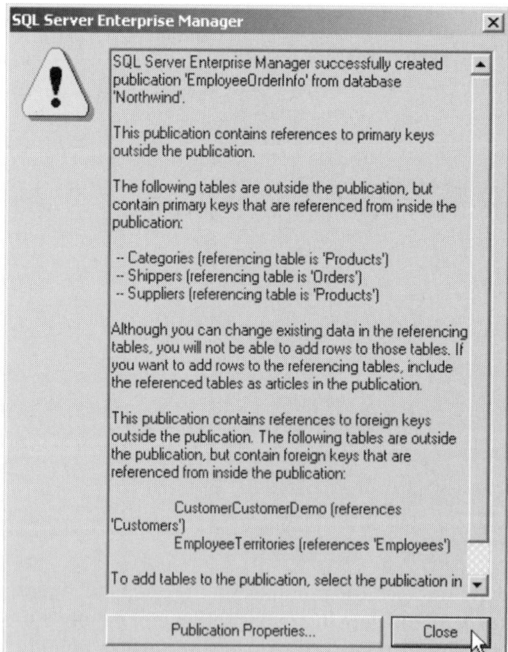

FIGURE C.25: Create Publication Wizard, Screen 20. Some warnings about the impact of your choices are presented in this screen. It is not as complete as the information provided in Table 13.4 earlier in the book, but it is based on the same reasoning.

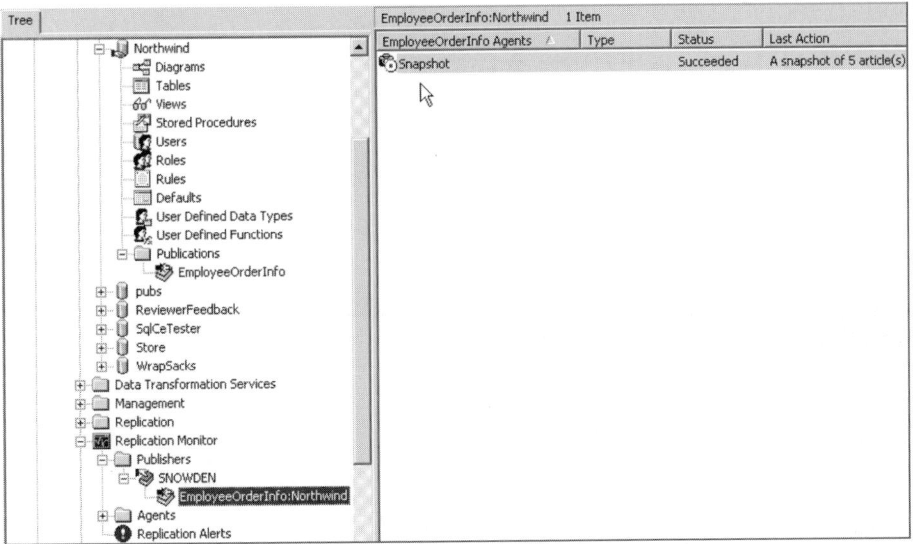

FIGURE C.26: Create Publication Wizard, Screen 21. The publication information is displayed in Enterprise Manager's Tree window. Double-clicking on the Snapshot line on the right-hand side of the screen displays the execution history.

D

Windows API Allocation and Cleanup Functions

WHEN DOING .NET Compact Framework programming, we prefer to write managed code. There are times, however, when you want to do something—or must do something—that cannot be done with managed code alone. At such times, you call through to the underlying Windows API using the P/Invoke support built into the .NET Compact Framework (see Chapter 4).

The Windows API is an object-based programming interface, which is to say that objects are allocated and handles are issued for each object. In managed code, when you create managed objects, the cleanup of memory for those objects is handled for you automatically. This is often referred to as *garbage collection*, although we prefer calling this *automatic garbage collection* to highlight the fact that sometimes *manual garbage collection* is needed.

Manual garbage collection is needed for most Windows API objects that are allocated; but which objects need to be freed up, and how do you do it? Our answer is provided in this appendix. In particular, Table D.1 shows the functions that create Windows API objects and the functions that clean up the objects, and it also indicates whether or not cleanup is required. If nothing else, this table should help programmers appreciate the complexities that the managed classes handle for them. There are more than forty types of objects in this table and more than twice that number of functions for allocating these objects. Many objects have two or more allocation functions. There are, for example, eight different functions for creating bitmaps.

TABLE D.1: Windows API Objects and Object Support Functions

Object	Comment	Win32 Allocation Function	Win32 Cleanup Function	Cleanup Required?
Accelerators	Keyboard accelerators.	CreateAcceleratorTable	DestroyAcceleratorTable	Yes
		LoadAccelerators	DestroyAcceleratorTable	Yes
Atoms	String table.	GlobalAddAtom	GlobalFreeAtom	Yes
Bitmap: new with no initialization	Device-dependent bitmap (DDB).	CreateBitmap	DeleteObject	Yes
		CreateCompatibleBitmap	DeleteObject	Yes
Bitmap: in-memory DIB, with no initialization	Device-independent bitmap (DIB).	CreateDIBSection	DeleteObject	Yes
Bitmap: from resource	DDB.	LoadBitmap	DeleteObject	Yes
Bitmap: from a file	DDB.	LoadImage	DeleteObject	Yes
		SHLoadDIBitmap	DeleteObject	Yes
Bitmap: from a GIF	DDB.	SHLoadImageFile	DeleteObject	Yes
		SHLoadImageResource	DeleteObject	Yes
Brush	Used for filling areas.	CreateDIBPatternBrushPt	DeleteObject	Yes
		CreatePatternBrush	DeleteObject	Yes
		CreateSolidBrush	DeleteObject	Yes
Caret	Keyboard pointer.	CreateCaret	DestroyCaret	Yes
Clipboard	Used for user-driven data sharing.	OpenClipboard	CloseClipboard	Yes
Critical section	Synchronization object for use in a single process.	InitializeCriticalSection	DeleteCriticalSection	Yes

Object	Comment	Win32 Allocation Function	Win32 Cleanup Function	Cleanup Required?
Cursor	Mouse pointer.	`CreateCursor`	`DestroyCursor`	Yes
		`LoadCursor`	`DestroyCursor`	Yes
Database	Windows CE–property database.	`CeCreateDatabaseEx`	`CloseHandle`	Yes
		`CeCreateDatabaseEx` (RAPI version)	`CeCloseHandle` (RAPI version)	Yes
		`CeOpenDatabaseEx`	`CloseHandle`	Yes
		`CeOpenDatabaseEx` (RAPI version)	`CeCloseHandle` (RAPI version)	Yes
Database enumerator	Enumerates Windows CE property databases.	`CeFindFirstDatabase`	CloseHandle	Yes
		`CeFindFirstDatabase` (RAPI version)	`CeCloseHandle` (RAPI version)	Yes
		`CeFindAllDatabases` (RAPI version)	`CeRapiFreeBuffer` (RAPI version)	Yes
Device context	Connects graphic devices, including the display screen, printers, bitmaps, and metafiles.	`CreateDC`	`DeleteDC`	Yes
		`CreateCompatibleDC`	`DeleteDC`	Yes
		`GetDC`	`ReleaseDC`	Yes
		`BeginPaint`	`EndPaint`	Yes

continues

TABLE D.1: Windows API Objects and Object Support Functions (continued)

Object	Comment	Win32 Allocation Function	Win32 Cleanup Function	Cleanup Required?
Dialog box	Modeless and modal dialog boxes.	`CreateDialog`	`DestroyWindow`	Yes
		`CreateDialogIndirect`	`DestroyWindow`	Yes
		`CreateDialogIndirectParam`	`DestroyWindow`	Yes
		`CreateDialogParam`	`DestroyWindow`	Yes
		`DialogBox`	`EndDialog`	Yes
		`DialogBoxIndirect`	`EndDialog`	Yes
		`DialogBoxIndirectParam`	`EndDialog`	Yes
		`DialogBoxParam`	`EndDialog`	Yes
Event	Win32 synchronization object.	`CreateEvent`	`CloseHandle`	Yes
File (and device)	Connection to file in file system, to installable stream-interface drivers, and to devices (`COM1:` port).	`CreateFile`	`CloseHandle`	Yes
		`CeCreateFile` (RAPI version)	`CeCloseHandle` (RAPI version)	Yes
File enumerator	Enumerates files and directories.	`FindFirstFile`	`FindClose`	Yes
		`CeFindFirstFile` (RAPI version)	`CeFindClose` (RAPI version)	Yes
		`CeFindAllFiles` (RAPI version)	`CeRapiFreeBuffer` (RAPI version)	Yes
File-mapping object	Maps the contents of a file to memory; also supports sharing memory between processes.	`CreateFileForMapping`	`CloseHandle`	Yes
		`CreateFileMapping`	`CloseHandle`	Yes

Object	Comment	Win32 Allocation Function	Win32 Cleanup Function	Cleanup Required?
Font	Used to draw text.	`CreateFontIndirect` `AddFontResource`	`DeleteObject` `RemoveFontResource`	Yes Yes
FTP file handle	Connection to a remote file for reading or writing.	`FtpOpenFile`	`InternetCloseHandle`	Yes
GDI stock object	Built-in set of fonts, pens, and brushes.	`GetStockObject`	N/A	No
Hook	A mechanism for intercepting message traffic (present but not documented in Windows CE).	`SetWindowsHookEx`	`UnhookWindowsHookEx`	Yes
HTTP connection	Creates a connection to a server using the HTTP protocol.	`HttpOpenRequest`	`InternetCloseHandle`	Yes
Icon	Created from two bitmap masks, an AND mask and an XOR mask.	`CreateIcon` `LoadIcon`	`DestroyIcon` `DestroyIcon`	Yes Yes
Library	Also called dynamic link library (DLL). DLLs provide the foundation for both native and managed programming interfaces.	`LoadLibrary` `LoadLibraryEx`	`FreeLibrary` `FreeLibrary`	Yes Yes

continues

TABLE D.1: Windows API Objects and Object Support Functions (continued)

Object	Comment	Win32 Allocation Function	Win32 Cleanup Function	Cleanup Required?
Memory: component	Functions support allocations shared between COM/ActiveX components.	CoTaskMemAlloc CoTaskMemRealloc	CoTaskMemFree CoTaskMemFree	Yes Yes
Memory: heap	A Windows CE process can contain one or more heaps.	LocalAlloc malloc	LocalFree free	Yes Yes
Memory: page[a]	Functions allocate pages; are the foundation for all other allocators.	VirtualAlloc MapViewOfFile	VirtualFree UnmapViewOfFile	Yes Yes
Menu	Two types of menus: program and pop-up menus.	CreateMenu CreatePopupMenu LoadMenu	DestroyMenu DestroyMenu DestroyMenu	No No No
Metafile	A mechanism to record and play back GDI drawing calls (present but not documented in Windows CE).	CreateEnhMetaFile	DeleteEnhMetaFile	Yes
Mutex	A type of Win32 synchronization object.	CreateMutex	CloseHandle	Yes
Palette	Color table for use with bitmaps and for updating the set of colors displayed by a device.	CreatePalette	DeleteObject	Yes

a. Windows CE was built for paged virtual memory systems.

Object	Comment	Win32 Allocation Function	Win32 Cleanup Function	Cleanup Required?
Pen	Used for drawing lines.	`CreatePen` `CreatePenIndirect`	`DeleteObject` `DeleteObject`	Yes Yes
Process	Operating system process—maximum of 32 in Windows CE. Closing a process handle does not terminate the process.	`CreateProcess` `CeCreateProcess` (RAPI version)	`CloseHandle` `CeCloseHandle` (RAPI version)	Yes
RAPI connection	Links a desktop program to a Windows CE smart device.	`CeRapiInit` `CeRapiIniEx`	`CeRapiUninit` `CeRapiUninit`	Yes Yes
Region	Defines the clipping areas for graphical output.	`CreateRectRgn` `CreateRectRgnIndirect`	`DeleteObject` `DeleteObject`	Yes Yes
Registry key	Needed to access the registry (see Chapter 11).	`RegOpenKeyEx` `RegCreateKeyEx`	`RegCloseKey`	Yes
Resource	A read-only data object mapped to a program's address space; these functions access native resources, not managed resources.	`FindResource` `LoadResource`	N/A N/A	No No
Semaphore	A type of Win32 synchronization object.	`CreateSemaphore`	`CloseHandle`	Yes

continues

Table D.1: Windows API Objects and Object Support Functions (continued)

Object	Comment	Win32 Allocation Function	Win32 Cleanup Function	Cleanup Required?
Socket	Part of a network API.	`socket`	`closesocket`	Yes
String resource	Native string tables support localization and delayed loading of string data.	`LoadString`	N/A	No
Thread	The unit of scheduling in the operating system; after starting a thread, must close handle to allow object cleanup.	`CreateThread`	`CloseHandle`	Yes
Timer	Low-resolution timer oriented to the user interface.	`SetTimer`	`KillTimer`	No
Window	Visible user interface object, dialog box, dialog box control, and so on.	`CreateWindow` `CreateWindowEx`	`DestroyWindow` `DestroyWindow`	Yes Yes

Glossary

The world of technology has always been filled with new terms and new acronyms. We are not immune to using—and sometimes overusing—them, so we provide this glossary to help you sort out the terms and perhaps learn some new ones. Some of the terms used to define an entry are themselves included as glossary entries, so if you don't know what something means, try looking it up here.

.NET COMPACT FRAMEWORK: A set of native-code and managed-code libraries that bring the benefits of managed-code programs to the world of Windows CE–powered smart devices, including the Pocket PC, Pocket PC 2002, and Windows Mobile–enabled devices such as the Pocket PC 2003 and the Smartphone 2003. A high level of compatibility between the .NET Compact Framework and the desktop .NET Framework allows .NET Compact Framework assemblies to run on desktop versions of Windows when the .NET Framework version 1.1 is installed.

.NET FRAMEWORK: A set of libraries created for desktop-based versions of Microsoft Windows to provide the runtime support for the creation of .NET managed-code applications. Among the types of programs supported are Windows Forms applications, Web Forms applications, and Web Services. The .NET Framework is supported on all versions of Microsoft Windows, starting with Windows 98.

ACTIVE SERVER PAGES (ASP): Microsoft's first generation of services for creating Web pages. ASP predates the .NET-compatible, managed-code solutions of ASP.NET. (See also *ASP.NET* and *ASP.NET Mobile Controls*.)

ACTIVESYNC: A set of services that supports the interaction between desktop versions of Windows and Windows CE–powered smart devices. Automatic synchronization is available through the creation of ActiveSync providers. Also available with ActiveSync are the Remote API (RAPI) functions. RAPI functions run on the desktop and provide access to data stored on Windows CE–powered smart devices. (For details, see Chapter 14.)

ADO.NET: Defines a set of .NET-compatible classes for creating in-memory databases. The .NET Compact Framework provides a rich subset of the ADO.NET features provided in the .NET Framework.

ADVISE SINK: A term for a COM interface that receives notification of events, in use with various COM components. For example, the ActiveSync Remote API library uses an Advise Sink to notify a desktop program about changes in the state of the connection to a Windows CE–powered device. (For details, see Chapter 14.)

ALLOCATED OBJECT MAP: A table kept by the runtime memory manager to keep track of objects that have been allocated. The garbage collector uses this map to help determine which objects are unreachable and therefore subject to cleanup.

ALPHA VALUE: A portion of a `Color` structure that describes the relative opacity or transparency of a color in .NET graphics. Alpha values are present in the .NET Compact Framework, but there is only one valid value: an alpha value of 255 (fully opaque).

API: See *Application Programming Interface.*

APPLICATION DOMAIN: Defines the memory owned by a particular program in the .NET runtime. An application domain runs within an operating system process. As on the desktop with the .NET Framework, on devices the .NET Compact Framework supports the creation of multiple application domains inside a single operating system process. Windows CE can create no more than 32 processes; application domains provide one mechanism by which this limitation is effectively removed for .NET Compact Framework programmers.

APPLICATION PROGRAMMING INTERFACE (API): Describes a set of services provided by an operating system, or a system-level library, to support the creation of application software. The Windows API, also known as Win32, provides one set of APIs that are available in Windows. The .NET Framework provides another API for the creation of managed-code software on desktop versions of Windows. A subset of that API is what defines the .NET Compact Framework, an API that supports the creation of managed-code software on Windows CE–powered smart devices such as the Pocket PC and Smartphone.

ASP: See *Active Server Pages*.

ASP.NET: Microsoft's Web server technology that supports the use of managed code to build interactive Web applications.

ASP.NET MOBILE CONTROLS: A set of controls for ASP.NET Web servers to support small-screen devices. Supported markup languages include HTML 3.2, which is used by the Pocket Internet Explorer on the Pocket PC. Other supported markup languages include WAP/WML (used on mobile phones), Compact HTML (cHTML), and XHTML.

ASSEMBLY: Defines the unit of packaging in .NET. On the desktop, an assembly consists of one or more modules (`.exe` and/or `.dll` files) that are connected through an assembly manifest. The .NET Compact Framework does not support multimodule assemblies, so a .NET Compact Framework assembly is identical to a Windows API module—both refer to a `.exe` or `.dll` file that can contain some combination of code and/or data.

ATTRIBUTE: Defines a qualifier that can be applied to individual language elements in a .NET program. For example, the `DllImport` attribute is used in function declarations for calling functions in unmanaged-code libraries.

AUTOMATIC GARBAGE COLLECTION: See *garbage collection*.

AUTOMATIC PARAMETER MARSHALING: Built-in support for parameter passing for calls from managed code to unmanaged code.

BINARY PORTABILITY: Describes support for running a program in multiple environments. .NET Compact Framework programs have binary portability to desktop versions of Windows running version 1.1 of the .NET Framework. Windows API (Win32) programs, by contrast, do not have binary portability between desktop versions of Windows and Windows CE–powered devices such as the Pocket PC and Smartphone. (See also *source-code portability*.)

BLITTABLE TYPE: In the context of calling unmanaged functions using P/Invoke, a blittable type is a data type that has the same representation in managed data as in unmanaged data. Included among blittable types are integer types, data structures, and data structures nested within other data structures. Arrays of integers, data structures, and data structures nested within other data structures are also blittable types. Non-blittable types include objects and objects nested within structures.

BOXING: The conversion of value types to reference types for the purpose of treating them like objects. (See also *unboxing*.)

BRUSH: A graphical object used to fill an area.

BY-REFERENCE PARAMETER: See *pass by reference*.

BY-VALUE PARAMETER: See *pass by value*.

`Capture`: The property of the `Control` (or derived) class that describes whether a window is capturing all input from the mouse (or stylus, or other pointing device). See Chapter 6.

CARET: A user interface object that echoes the current keyboard input location (called a *cursor* in other environments). The caret is the only user interface object with built-in support for blinking at a rate set by the Windows API `SetCaretBlinkTime` function. See Chapter 6.

CIL: See *Common Intermediate Language*.

CLI: See *Common Language Infrastructure*.

CLIENT AREA: The portion of a window (a control or form) for receiving input and for displaying output. See *non-client area*.

CLIPPING: The establishment and enforcement of drawing boundaries when creating graphical output.

CLR: See *Common Language Runtime*.

CLS: See *Common Language Specification*.

COMMON DIALOG BOXES: A set of dialog boxes for a common set of services that programs often need. The common dialog box library, `commdlg.dll`, is a native-code (unmanaged-code) library. Of the eight dialog boxes supported on the desktop, only four are supported in Windows CE: File Open, File Save, Print, and Color Picker.

COMMON INTERMEDIATE LANGUAGE (CIL): A byte-code, machine-level instruction set that provides binary portability for .NET-compatible programs between different CPU architectures. CIL instructions are converted to native machine instructions, per method, on a just-in-time basis through a process known as JITting. CIL is also known as Microsoft Intermediate Language (MSIL), sometimes shortened to just IL. CIL has been submitted to Ecma International[1] as an industry standard.

COMMON LANGUAGE INFRASTRUCTURE (CLI): Refers to the base-level set of services and standards that Microsoft submitted as an Ecma International standard. CLI

1. See http://www.ecma-international.org.

does not include the high-level framework classes (Windows Forms, Web Forms, and Web Services). But it does include the Common Language Specification and the common type system.

COMMON LANGUAGE RUNTIME (CLR): The base set of services needed to support the loading, execution, and management of .NET-compatible programs.

COMMON LANGUAGE SPECIFICATION (CLS): A set of rules for language compilers to promote language interoperability when building .NET-compatible software.

COMMON TYPE SYSTEM (CTS): The core set of data types that must be supported by any .NET-compatible language compiler or development tool.

CTS: See *common type system*.

CURSOR: A user interface object that echoes the current mouse location. Only one cursor is supported on Pocket PCs and Smartphones: the wait cursor.

DATA PROVIDER: An ADO.NET programming concept that describes the set of classes that must be implemented to support persistent storage for ADO.NET classes. The .NET Compact Framework ships with data providers for SQL Server CE and for SQL Server 2000, which support the ability to move data between the database engine and ADO.NET objects.

DELEGATE: A managed-code function pointer.

DEVICE CONTEXT: The data structure for Graphics Device Interface functions to hold state information used to create graphical output; programs do not have direct access to a device context, but instead refer to a device context by using a handle (managed programs typically store handles as type `IntPtr`).

DEVICE-INDEPENDENT BITMAP (DIB): A standard format for raster data. All DIB formats are single-plane. The supported formats include 1, 4, 8, 16, 24, and 32 bits per pixel. In addition, Windows CE adds support for a 2-bit-per-pixel format.

DIB: See *Device-independent bitmap*.

DLL: See *dynamic link library.*

DLL HELL: A general term for a deployment scenario that .NET fixes. In DLL hell, problems arise when two programs need different versions of the same DLL name, and differences between each version create incompatibilities for one of the programs.

DYNAMIC LINK LIBRARY (DLL): A loadable executable module for holding code and data intended to be shared by two or more programs. Both native and managed libraries are supported. A software developer can view the contents of a native DLL using a tool such as `depends.exe`; and the contents of a managed DLL can be viewed using a tool such as `ildasm.exe`.

EMBEDDED VISUAL BASIC: A tool from Microsoft for creating Windows CE programs using the Basic language. This tool is now obsolete; the Pocket PC 2003 is the last Windows CE device that will be able to run eMbedded Visual Basic programs.

EMBEDDED VISUAL C++: A tool from Microsoft that allows for the creation of native programs and dynamic link libraries that run under Windows CE.

EMBEDDED VISUAL TOOLS: The name of a product for Windows CE 3.0 software development that includes eMbedded Visual C++, version 3.0, and eMbedded Visual Basic, version 3.0.

EMULATOR: A program that runs a .NET Compact Framework program in a window on a computer running a desktop version of Microsoft Windows. Windows CE emulators run x86 machine instructions, but otherwise they provide an execution environment that closely mimics that found on a smart device such as a Pocket PC or a Smartphone.

ENHANCED METAFILE: Provides a mechanism for storing a graphic image as a set of calls to Graphics Device Interface drawing and attribute functions.

EXECUTE IN PLACE (XIP) REGION: An area of ROM that contains uncompressed program and library modules that are executed directly in ROM without requiring RAM for code storage.

FILE ALLOCATION TABLE (FAT) FILE SYSTEM : A format developed by Microsoft for storing data on storage media such as floppy diskettes, hard drives, and flash memory cards. FAT file system support has been included in every Microsoft operating system, starting with the first version of MS-DOS. Every version of Microsoft Windows, including Windows CE, supports the FAT file system.

FIELD: A data member of an object or class.

FOCUS: Refers to the form or control that is to receive keyboard input. Only controls derived from the `Control`[2] class can get the focus.

FONT: A collection of graphical images, or glyphs, used to draw text. Fonts typically have a user-friendly name and are measured by the height of characters using the point unit of measure.

2. Fully qualified name: `System.Windows.Forms.Control`.

GAC: See *global assembly cache.*

GARBAGE COLLECTION: The cleanup of allocated objects when they are no longer needed. The common language runtime performs automatic garbage collection for managed data. (For details, see Chapter 3.)

GARBAGE COLLECTOR POOLS: The portion of memory from which object instances are loaded. In .NET programs, automatic garbage collection is provided for unreachable objects.

GDI: See *Graphics Device Interface.*

GLOBAL ASSEMBLY CACHE (GAC): Refers to a set of shared libraries (in the .NET Compact Framework) that are expected to be called from many different programs. The addition of a library to the GAC allows a single copy on a smart device to be shared by different programs. For example, all of the libraries in the .NET Compact Framework itself are added to the GAC when installed on a Windows CE–powered smart device.

GLYPH: Refers to the graphical representation of individual text characters. A font is said to consist of a collection of glyphs. A glyph is not the same as a character because a 10-point Arial *a* is not the same as a 10-point Times New Roman *a*, even though the character rendered is the same.

GRABBING EVENTS: A technique to overcome some of the limitations on .NET Compact Framework controls that we presented in Chapter 9.

GRAPHICS DEVICE INTERFACE: The common name for the set of drawing functions defined in the Windows API. On the desktop, these functions reside in `gdi32.dll`; on smart devices, these same functions reside in `coredll.dll`.

HUNGARIAN NOTATION: A style of naming program variables with a prefix to suggest the variable's type or how it is intended to be used. (For details, see Appendix A.)

IL: See *Common Intermediate Language.*

`ildasm.exe`: Intermediate Language Disassembler, a tool provided by Microsoft for displaying the contents of .NET-compatible modules.

INPUT METHOD: An input window inside the Software Input Panel that receives keyboard data.

INSTALLABLE FILE SYSTEM: Allows access to types of storage media—whether in flash memory, rotating media, or floppy diskette—that are not in the object store. Windows CE .NET 4.1 supports a maximum of 255 installable file systems (previous versions of Windows CE supported a maximum of 10).

JIT: Abbreviation for "just-in-time."

JIT COMPILATION: Refers to the process of converting CIL instructions to native instructions. On both the desktop and on smart devices, JIT compilation is performed on a per-method basis when a specific method is called for the first time. Compiled methods are cached in RAM to minimize the performance impact of subsequent calls.

JITTED CODE POOL: Describes the memory occupied by native code that has been generated by the JIT compiler. This memory is subject to garbage collection, as we describe in Chapter 3.

JITTING: See *JIT compilation*.

JPEG FILE: A raster image file that has been compressed using the Joint Photographic Experts Group[3] (JPEG) standard. The current JPEG standards support lossy compression, which means that repeated compression and decompression may cause loss of information. This format works best when a raster image contains a photograph.

MANAGED CODE: Refers to .NET-compatible code that is compiled to CIL/MSIL, verified at runtime for type safety, and converted to native code by a JIT compiler. In the .NET Compact Framework, managed code implies managed data, which refers to the tracking and automatic cleanup of objects. (For details, see Chapter 3.) On the desktop, some managed code can access unmanaged data; for example, the Managed Extensions for C++ extend support for the C++ language so that managed code can access both managed data and unmanaged data.

MANUAL MEMORY MANAGEMENT: Memory cleanup performed by explicit calls made in application code. Windows (Win32) API programs require manual memory management. Manual memory management is required in .NET Compact Framework programs in only a few cases (such as with the `Graphics` object returned by the `CreateGraphics` method for .NET Compact Framework controls).

MANUAL PARAMETER MARSHALING: A process required because of limitations in the built-in support for parameter passing for calls from managed code to unmanaged code. (For details, see Chapter 4.)

MARSHALING: The movement of data across a boundary, usually to support a function call that would normally be prevented by that boundary. Some data gets sent in (meaning across the boundary), including parameters being sent to the target func-

3. See http://www.jpeg.org.

tion. Other data gets received back out, including return values and parameters designed to provide output information. The term originates in COM programming, where marshaling enables the crossing of both process boundaries and network boundaries. COM function calls that cross a process boundary are sent to a local server. Distributed COM (or DCOM) function calls cross network boundaries and are sent to remote servers. In a .NET Compact Framework program, marshaling is most often used in discussions of Platform Invoke for the calling of unmanaged code from managed code.

MEMORY LEAK: Refers to memory that has been allocated but not properly deallocated. Programmer error often leads to memory leaks in unmanaged code. Managed code provides for automatic memory deallocation of unreachable allocated objects, which dramatically reduces the incidence of memory leaks.

MERGE REPLICATION: A service provided by SQL Server 2000 databases that incorporates a publish-and-subscribe model for creating SQL Server CE databases and managing the synchronization of the device-side databases with the server-side databases.

METADATA: Descriptive information contained in every .NET-compatible assembly. The metadata defines the type information in a given assembly, including the classes, structures, and enumerations. Metadata also provides details about every method in an assembly and is used to provide verification and safety tests (e.g., for such things as array overruns) on managed code. A large percentage of every .NET assembly consists of metadata (to see this, start the `ildasm.exe` program using the hidden `/adv` switch).

METHOD: A code member of an object or class.

MICROSOFT MOBILE INTERNET TOOLKIT: A product from Microsoft that has been renamed to ASP.NET Mobile Controls. See *ASP.NET Mobile Controls*.

MODULE: The generic term for a portable executable (PE) file. The two most common types are program (`.exe`) modules and library (`.dll`) modules.

MSIL: See *Common Intermediate Language*.

NAME DECORATING: Refers to changes made to C++ function names in support of overloaded methods. Name decorating can interfere with P/Invoke calls from managed-code to native-code library functions, because a decorated function name contains characters that are not valid as a C# function name (then it is referred to as *name mangling*).

NAME MANGLING: See *name decorating*.

NAMESPACE: A feature of many .NET-compatible languages for grouping type information. For example, .NET Compact Framework drawing types reside in the `System.Drawing` namespace.

NATIVE CODE: Refers to code that does not use the .NET runtime to allocate and manage memory. For example, programs written for the Windows API and built using eMbedded Visual C++ run as unmanaged code. Managed code can call unmanaged code using Platform Invoke. (For details, see Chapter 4.)

NATIVE IMAGE CACHE: The set of native code that has been JITted from IL and that is available to execute. Unlike the desktop .NET runtime, the .NET Compact Framework does not store a native image cache on disk. (`ngen.exe`, a tool that adds a managed module to the native image cache on the desktop, does not exist for the .NET Compact Framework.) However, JITted IL methods are kept in RAM in the JITted code pool. When system memory is low, the JITted code pool is subject to garbage collection; to minimize performance impact, however, the JITted code pool is flushed only as a last resort.

NON-CLIENT AREA: The area of a window owned and operated by the operating system and used to receive input for system commands and to display output in the form of window state. Included in the non-client area of a window are the borders, caption bar, and other system-provided ornaments such as the minimize box and Ok button (on a Pocket PC).

NONDETERMINISTIC GARBAGE COLLECTION: A type of memory cleanup in which there is a delay between when an object becomes a candidate for garbage collection and when the memory it occupies is actually reclaimed. This describes the type of memory cleanup supported by the various .NET runtimes. By contrast is deterministic cleanup, which means that cleanup is done immediately. This describes the type of cleanup that occurs with ActiveX/COM components.

OAL: See *OEM Adaptation Layer.*

OBJECT LINKING AND EMBEDDING (OLE): The earliest type of application that served as the launching point for the Component Object Model (COM), version 2.0.

OBJECT STORE: A RAM-resident area for persistent data storage used by Windows CE. The object store can hold three categories of items: a file system, the system registry, and property databases. (For details, see Chapter 11.)

OEM ADAPTATION LAYER (OAL): A low-level component in a Windows CE platform that provides core services to the Windows CE kernel.

OLE: See *Object Linking and Embedding*.

OWNER-DRAW SUPPORT: A feature of some native controls that allows a program to supply its own drawing code to create a custom look and feel for that control.

PAGE DESCRIPTION LANGUAGE: The set of command codes and rules by which those codes are used to control the actions of a printer.

PASS BY REFERENCE: Refers to one of two parameter passing techniques. Pass by reference passes a pointer to a parameter and not the parameter itself. Pass by reference is primarily used with value types as a way to generate a pointer to some blittable data. Pass by reference can be used with reference types but is much less common.

PASS BY VALUE: Refers to one of two parameter passing techniques. When used with value types, a copy of datum is passed to the called function; the called function cannot modify the original value. When used with reference types, a pointer to the reference object is passed; the called function can modify the contents of the original object.

PASS THROUGH SUPPORT: A feature of ActiveSync that allows a device in a docking cradle to access TCP/IP network services through the intervention of the ActiveSync libraries.

PDL: See *page description language*.

PE FILE: See *portable executable file*.

PEN: A graphical object used to draw a line.

P/INVOKE: See *Platform Invoke*.

P/INVOKE WIZARD: A tool from The Paul Yao Company that generates C# and Visual Basic .NET declarations for calling the exported functions of unmanaged-code libraries.

PLATFORM: Refers to a unique combination of hardware and software. Examples of some platforms include Pocket PC 2003 and Smartphone 2003.

PLATFORM BUILDER: A tool provided by Microsoft for creating a custom Windows CE operating system image.

PLATFORM INVOKE: A feature of the .NET runtime that allows native, unmanaged libraries to be called from managed code. (For details, see Chapter 4.)

PMEs: See *properties, methods, and events*.

PNG: Portable Network Graphics, a file format.

POCKET PC: The brand name of a Windows CE–powered personal digital assistant that was designed by Microsoft and licensed to various OEM manufacturers.

POINT: A unit of measure for fonts. Historically, printers in England and the United States used a point size equal to 1/72.27 inch. In desktop digital font usage, driven largely by the success of Adobe and its Postscript PDL, a value of 72 points per inch is typically used, for the performance gain from the use of integer arithmetic.

PORTABILITY: Refers to the ease with which a program that was written for one environment (operating system, runtime library, CPU) can also be run in another environment. (See also *source-code portability* and *binary portability.*)

PORTABLE EXECUTABLE FILE: The file format used for both native and managed-code programs and DLLs. Also known as a *PE file* because these two letters appear as the signature in the file header.

PROCESS: In Windows CE, a process is the unit of ownership. When a process terminates, all resources that were in use by the process are cleaned up.

PROPERTIES, METHODS, AND EVENTS (PMEs): The core of the .NET programming interface for any object consists of the public properties, public methods, and public events that allow the object to be instantiated and used. The subject of PMEs comes up in this book in the context of .NET Compact Framework controls.

PROPERTY DATABASE: Refers to a Windows CE–specific data storage mechanism that provides for the reading and writing of record-oriented data. The .NET Compact Framework itself does not support accessing Windows CE property databases. (For details, see Chapter 11.)

RAPI: See *Remote API.*

RDA: See *Remote Data Access.*

REACHABLE DATA: Objects that can be accessed from a live variable, either directly or indirectly. If unpinned, such data can be moved by the garbage collector; however, the garbage collector does not reclaim the memory allocated by reachable data.

REFERENCE TYPE: Those types that are created from classes (in the .NET type system) and that therefore are full participants in the benefits of object-oriented programming.

REFLECTION: Refers to a set of services provided in the `System.Reflection` namespace. These services provide programmatic access to the metadata information of a .NET assembly.

REGISTRY: Refers to the hierarchical storage provided in both Microsoft Windows CE and on desktop versions of Microsoft Windows. The registry is used by the operating system, by device drivers, and by applications to store user preferences and system settings. It is not supported by the .NET Compact Framework. (For details, see Chapter 11.)

REMOTE API (RAPI): The set of services provided by ActiveSync for accessing the object store in a Windows CE–powered smart device from a desktop system. (For details, see Chapter 14.)

REMOTE DATA ACCESS: A mechanism used to automate the movement of data between SQL Server CE databases and SQL Server 7 and SQL Server 2000 databases. (For details, see Chapter 13.)

REMOTE SPY++: A Microsoft tool for capturing the window layout and observing message traffic on a Windows CE–powered device. This tool must be run from a desktop development system.

REMOTE TOOLS: A set of tools provided by Microsoft that provides detailed information about programs running on Windows CE–powered devices. These tools must be run from a desktop development system.

REMOTE ZOOMIN: A Microsoft tool for capturing a bitmap image of the display screen of a Windows CE–powered device. This tool must be run from a desktop development system.

RESOURCES: Read-only data objects that are bound to executable files. There are managed resources, which are accessible from managed code, and unmanaged resources, for use from unmanaged code. .NET Compact Framework programs—just like desktop .NET Framework programs—use unmanaged icons for the application icon.

SAFE CODE: See *managed code*.

SDK: See *Software Development Kit*.

SIMPLE OBJECT ACCESS PROTOCOL (SOAP): The rules of the road for interactions between Web Service clients and Web Service servers.

SIP: See *Software Input Panel*.

SOAP: See *Simple Object Access Protocol*.

SOFTWARE DEVELOPMENT KIT (SDK): Provides a set of include files, libraries, and help files in eMbedded Visual C++ that support the development of native code for a specific Windows CE platform. Platform Builder supports the creation of custom, platform-specific SDKs.

SOFTWARE INPUT PANEL (SIP): Refers to an on-screen area used to enter character data on a Windows CE–powered system. Each different type of input window is referred to as an *input method*. Among available input methods are an on-screen keyboard and various recognizers for interpreting handwritten input. (On a Tablet PC, the term *TIP*—for Tablet Input Panel—is used instead of SIP.)

SOURCE-CODE PORTABILITY: The ability of the source code written for one environment to be rebuilt to run in a different environment. Source-code portability has always been a key feature of the Windows (Win32) API.

STACK: A temporary data area that holds parameters passed between functions, data that is local to a function, and the return addresses for function calls.

STREAM INTERFACE DRIVERS: Native DLLs that support a stream-oriented I/O model in Windows CE. Stream interface drivers are used to support installable file systems, including Compact Flash and Smart Digital I/O (SDIO) flash memory drives. Stream interface drivers also support a broad range of system services, including the Windows CE Web Server, Microsoft Message Queue, Universal Plug and Play, and the Audio Compression Manager.

STRONG NAME: An attribute of a .NET assembly that can be used to verify that the integrity of modules has not been breached. Strong names also provide version control; for example, by default a program can run only with a version of a shared library that the program has been built for.

SUBCLASSING: A Windows (Win32) API technique for trapping the messages sent to a specific window. By controlling the flow of messages, the behavior and appearance of a window can be altered. We discussed this technique in Chapter 9 and provided an example in the `TextBoxClipboard` sample program.

TODAY SCREEN: The screen that shows the day's appointments on a Pocket PC. The Today screen can be customized through the creation of native COM libraries.

THREAD: The unit of scheduling in a Microsoft Windows CE process. Every process has at least one thread; programs can create additional threads to allow large tasks to be performed in the background and also to manage asynchronous hardware devices. In order for the garbage collector to run, all managed-code threads must be stopped.

THUNK: A tiny piece of placeholder code. Managed-code thunks are created as placeholders for methods that have not been loaded into memory. Thunks were first introduced in Real Mode Windows 1.x, which used a wide range of thunks. A new set of thunks (flat thunks and universal thunks) was introduced for protected-mode Windows 3.0 and another set for Windows NT.

UNBOXING: The process of recreating a value type that has been boxed as an object. (See also *boxing*.)

UNMANAGED CODE: See *native code*.

UNMANAGED THREAD: A thread executing unmanaged code in a .NET Compact Framework program. Unmanaged threads can continue running when the garbage collector is cleaning memory, but such threads are blocked if they return to unmanaged code during garbage collector cleanup.

UNREACHABLE OBJECT: An object that is not referenced, either directly or indirectly, by any variable. In a .NET program, unreachable objects are subject to garbage collection and finalization.

UNSAFE CODE: See *native code*.

VALUE TYPE: Those types that are not created from classes (in the .NET type system). Value types are stored as a streamable set of bits and so are often called blittable types. Such types reside on the stack when defined as local variables and on the heap when defined as a field in an object.

VERIFIABLE CODE: See *managed code*.

VISUAL STUDIO .NET: A tool provided by Microsoft that provides an integrated development environment for writing code and building and debugging programs. The first version of the .NET Compact Framework requires Visual Studio .NET 2003.

XIP REGION: See *eXecute In Place region*.

XML WEB SERVICES: See *Web Services*.

WEB SERVICES: A set of standards (originally known as XML Web services) for creating client/server software based on a set of industry standards including the SOAP protocol. Web Services support several types of interactions, including remote function calls (or remote procedure calls, RPCs) and document distribution. As of this writing, Web Services are still evolving as a mechanism to support distributed computing.

WIN32 API: The Windows 32-bit API, the programming interface that provides the primary services on Windows CE–powered devices.

WIN32 CODE: See *native code*.

WINDOWS API: See *Win32 API.*

WINDOWS CE : An operating system written from scratch by Microsoft to support the creation of mobile and embedded smart devices built on 32-bit microprocessors. Unlike desktop versions of Windows, Windows CE is a highly configurable operating system that can be built for a wide range of CPUs and widely varying I/O support. See also *Platform Builder.*

WINDOWS MOBILE: The branding created by Microsoft in the summer of 2003 for two smart mobile devices powered by Windows CE: Pocket PC 2003 and Smartphone 2003.

WINDOWS SANDWICH: A programming pattern that describes a three-phase approach to using native objects: allocate, use, and free. The object allocation and object freeing are represented by the bounding bread slices; the object use represents the sandwich filling.

WORKING SET: The memory that has been allocated and is currently in use.

Z-ORDER: Refers to an imaginary z-axis that comes straight out of the screen and complements the x-axis and y-axis used to address pixels on the screen itself.

Index

D

Q

R

U

V

W

X

Z

Microsoft .NET Development Series

0321154894

0321113594

0321180593

0201734117

0321160770

0321154916

0321228391

0201760401

0201760398

0321169514

For more information go to
www.awprofessional.com/msdotnetseries/

0321228960

0321154932

0201734958

0321116208

0321125193

0201770180

0201745682

0321174038

0321174046